East Africa

Mary Fitzpatrick
Tim Bewer, Matthew D Firestone

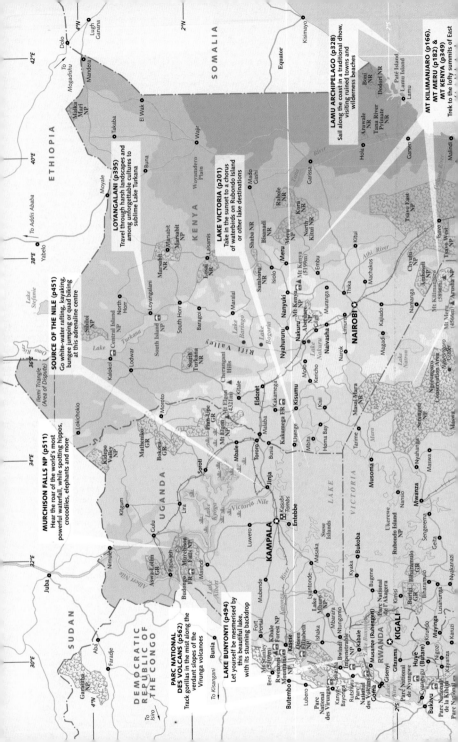

MURCHISON FALLS NP (p511)
Hear the roar of the world's most powerful waterfall, while spotting hippos, crocodiles, elephants and more

SOURCE OF THE NILE (p451)
Go white-water rafting, kayaking, bungee jumping or quad biking at this adrenaline centre

LOYANGALANI (p395)
Travel through harsh landscapes and among unforgettable cultures to sublime Lake Turkana

LAKE VICTORIA (p201)
Take in the sunset to a chorus of waterbirds on Rubondo Island or other lake destinations

LAMU ARCHIPELAGO (p328)
Sail along the coast in a traditional dhow, visiting ruined towns and wilderness beaches

MT KILIMANJARO (p166), MT MERU (p182) & MT KENYA (p349)
Trek to the lofty summits of East

PARC NATIONAL DES VOLCANS (p562)
Track gorillas in the mist along the verdant slopes of the Virunga volcanoes

LAKE BUNYONYI (p494)
Let yourself be mesmerised by this beautiful lake, with its stunning backdrop

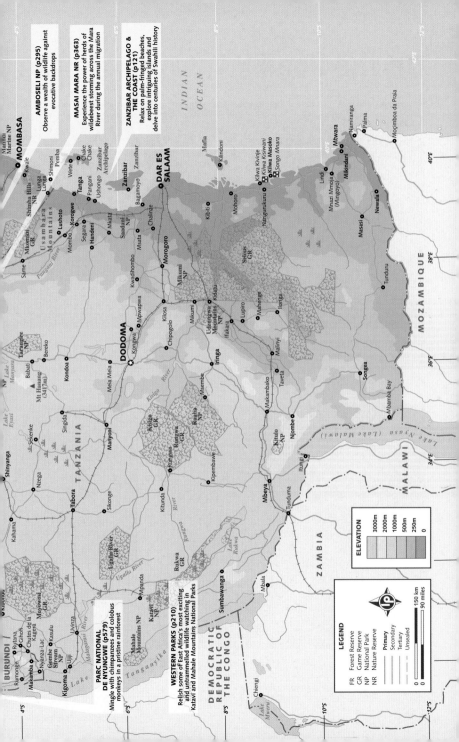

AMBOSELI NP (p295)
Observe a wealth of wildlife against evocative backdrops

MASAI MARA NR (p363)
Experience the power of herds of wildebeest storming across the Mara River during the annual migration

ZANZIBAR ARCHIPELAGO & THE COAST (p121)
Relax on palm-fringed beaches, explore intriguing islands and delve into centuries of Swahili history

PARC NATIONAL DE NYUNGWE (p579)
Mingle with chimpanzees and colobus monkeys in a pristine rainforest

WESTERN PARKS (p210)
Relish some of East Africa's most exciting and untrammelled wildlife watching in Katavi and Mahale Mountains National Parks

INDIAN OCEAN

TANZANIA

MOZAMBIQUE

MALAWI

ZAMBIA

DEMOCRATIC REPUBLIC OF THE CONGO

BURUNDI

LEGEND

FR Forest Reserve
GR Game Reserve
NP National Park
NR Nature Reserve

Primary
Secondary
Tertiary
Unsealed

ELEVATION

3000m
2000m
1000m
500m
250m
0

0   150 km
0   90 miles

On the Road

MARY FITZPATRICK Coordinating Author
Tanzania's coast is magical, with its excellent beaches, ancient ruins and the mystique of its long history. This shot was taken on Pemba (p142). Just behind me, the vines open up onto an almost pristine white-sand cove that was irresistibly inviting for a swim.

MATTHEW D FIRESTONE This shot was taken while tracking eastern mountain gorillas in Parc National des Volcans (p562) in Rwanda. While I'm trying to look calm and composed for the camera, I'm actually trembling in the knees and sweating bullets. Silverbacks are a lot larger than they look in the photos…

TIM BEWER Uganda has so much more than just mountain gorillas, but coming face to face with these gentle giants here in Mgahinga Gorilla National Park (p499) is an experience that is hard to top. It was absolutely worth the five hours of trekking and two hours of rain.

For author biographies see p644.

East Africa Highlights

In a region encompassing the Equator, the drama of the Rift Valley, countless archetypal African scenes, quintessential wildlife panoramas and exuberant local residents, East African highlights are tough to narrow down. Myriad attractions include safaris, gorillas in the mist and snow on the equator; colourful tribal cultures, beaches and coral reefs; vast lakes and savannah that stretches towards the horizon; and wildlife. Here are some of our favourite sights and attractions; you'll soon have some East African highlights of your own.

ADRIAN BAILEY

BWINDI IMPENETRABLE NATIONAL PARK

Uganda's Bwindi Impenetrable Forest (p488) has been so named for good reason! The arduous trek was worth it, however, to have a close encounter with a family of mountain gorillas. We were given strict instructions to stay 7m away from the gorillas, but they must have missed the briefing, running wherever they wanted among the trekkers. It took our breath away when one suddenly got up and ran right at us, missing us by centimetres!

Laura Clapham & Chris McPherson, Travellers

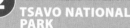

CHRISTER FREDRIKSSON

GORILLA TRACKING

Gorilla tracking (p76) is one of the world's greatest animal adventures. But, unlike swimming with sharks or some other adrenaline-fuelled encounter, the magic of visiting gorillas comes from the fact that these gentle giants patiently let you into their world.

**Tim Bewer,
Lonely Planet Author**

MARK D

3

TSAVO NATIONAL PARK
2

While I'd heard about Kenya's famed 'Man-eaters of Tsavo' (p302), I had seen enough lions on safari to not be scared by a few overgrown cats. Of course, my attitude quickly changed after we got a flat tyre in lion country. It's one thing to stare down the king of the jungle inside a 4WD, but it's quite another to see one prowling around in the distance at eye-level.

Matthew D Firestone, Lonely Planet Author

MARK DAF

4

MIKUMI NATIONAL PARK

Camping for three nights in Mikumi National Park (p224) in Tanzania allowed us to have many close encounters of the wildlife kind. Elephants frequently wandered in between our tents; a buffalo came by to say hi; and during one incredible evening a pride of lions passed through, although we didn't discover this until we saw their newly laid tracks the following morning, just 3m from our tent.

Becky Rangecroft, Lonely Planet Staff

LAKE TANGANYIKA

Life on the Tanzanian shoreline of Lake Tanganyika (p220) is kilometres and worlds away from Dar es Salaam and the rest of the country. The mountains of the Congo rise up like purple shadows across the lake, while the sun glows orange as it slides out of view. As night falls, the lanterns of dozens of tiny fishing boats flicker over the water. Village life centres around the seasons and the weekly runs of the MV *Liemba* up and down the lake – the only lifeline many inhabitants have with the rest of the world.

Mary Fitzpatrick, Lonely Planet Author

5

MNEMBA ATOLL

One memorable day we took a boat trip and went snorkelling in the crystal-clear waters around the Mnemba Atoll, a protected reef off the east coast of Zanzibar, Tanzania. We submerged ourselves in the beautiful world of brilliantly coloured fish, but we were careful not to step on Mnemba Island (p142). Only hotel guests are permitted to use the beaches on the private island and rates start from over $1000 per night.

Becky Rangecroft, Lonely Planet Staff

6

7

SERENGETI NATIONAL PARK

On Christmas day in the Serengeti (p186), our Tanzanian guide smiles, the 4WD rounds a bend and then we're looking at a dozen hippos wallowing in one of the dry season's last water holes. It stank, the water was putrid, and the crocodiles had long since moved ashore – but the sight was a Christmas memory I'll keep forever.

Simon Tillema, Lonely Planet Staff

JUDY BELLAH

NAIROBI

Kenya's Nairobi is vilified as one of the most dangerous cities in the world, so you get a bizarre sense of satisfaction after spending a month living there without so much as having your wallet lifted. Ignore the hype and check it out – Nairobi really is one of the continent's great capitals, and there is so much more to do here than you'd imagine.

**Matthew D Firestone,
Lonely Planet Author**

PETER ADAMS PHOTOGRAPHY LTD/A

9

8

PRIMATES IN RWANDA

No matter how many gorillas you may have seen at the zoo, nothing can prepare you for the experience of tracking (p79) the largest primates through equatorial rainforest in Rwanda. Silverbacks are a lot larger than you think, especially when staring you down in the open jungle. Fortunately, they're passive – and vegetarian!

**Matthew D Firestone,
Lonely Planet Author**

MARK DAF

10

WHITE-WATER RAFTING ON THE NILE

When you first see the roiling rapids you'll wonder just how people manage to make it through East Africa's wildest ride in one piece (p454), but you'll know right away that you have to try it too.

Tim Bewer, Lonely Planet Author

Contents

Regional Map Contents

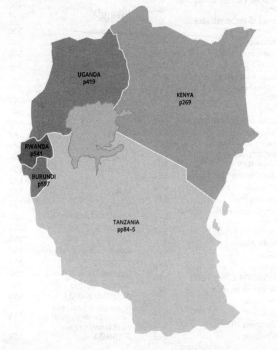

UGANDA
p419

KENYA
p269

RWANDA
p541

BURUNDI
p597

TANZANIA
pp84–5

Destination East Africa

East Africa's allure is legendary. It has a string of charming old Swahili towns, some of Africa's most evocative safari destinations and the world's last remaining mountain gorillas. Wildebeest pound over the savannah in the Serengeti-Masai Mara ecosystem, rhinos stand in the shade in Ngorongoro Crater and chimpanzees brush past visitors in western Tanzania's Gombe Stream and Mahale Mountains parks. Dotting the coast are moss-covered ruins and the magical archipelagos of Lamu and Zanzibar, while inland, verdant landscapes rise into rolling hills and stunning mountain panoramas. Red-garbed Maasai warriors rub shoulders with semi-nomadic Hadzabe hunters and the bead-bedecked Turkana – all part of a vibrant kaleidoscope of cultures where over 300 tribal groups live within close proximity in an area roughly a quarter of the size of Australia.

Yet, it is only too recently that East Africa's powerhouse, Kenya, erupted in post-election ethnic violence, shaking the region's upwards-oriented image and sending visitor numbers plummeting. Northern Uganda, although increasingly stable, continues to be plagued by conflict. Parts of Burundi are still shadowed by scattered rebel elements, and the eastern Democratic Republic of Congo (DRC; formerly Zaire) is as shaky as ever. HIV/AIDS – although slowly declining in many areas – continues to ravage the younger generation, and has left over two million children orphans, while malaria claims the lives of countless East Africans daily.

What is the real picture? Is East Africa moving up and on, its allure still intact? Or is it mired down in conflict, corruption and poverty? After spending a combined total of six months visiting all its corners, our vote is resoundingly with the first scenario. Not only is East Africa on the upswing, but its pull on travellers is as addictive as ever.

The topography alone is a huge draw: there are few other places where it's possible within a radius of about 1200km to go from lazing on white sands and snorkelling in turquoise seas to wandering down cobbled alleyways past donkey-drawn carts or shivering on the snow-dusted upper slopes of Mt Kenya or Mt Kilimanjaro. Flamingo-studded lakes and acacia-dotted plains mix with rolling hills and lush rainforest, while elephants, lions, zebras and more treat visitors to ever-changing glimpses of nature's magnificent rhythms.

Urban life has its appeal and energy as well. Overflowing *matatus* (minibuses) careen wildly along crowded city streets, young and not-so-young wait in line at crowded internet cafes, overflow crowds pack churches on Sunday mornings and mosques at midday on a Friday and sidewalk vendors hawk everything from fresh pineapples to mobile phones. Massive billboards tout the virtues of condoms and abstinence, tree-planting campaigns and anti-plastic bag legislation put the region firmly in the running with the rest of the world to go green, and each day East Africans shake their collective head about the deplorable antics of some of their politicians.

Yet, in the end, East Africa's legendary allure – the quality that makes the region so memorable for visitors – is East Africans themselves, with their exuberance, energy and unique way of looking at life, with their warmth and hospitality, their spirit and their cultural diversity

If all this appeals, plan your East Africa travels early, and allow as much time there as possible – there's so much to see and do. Our bet is that no matter how much time you spend in the region, you'll wish it had been more.

FAST FACTS

Area: 1,816,753 sq km

Highest Point: Mt Kilimanjaro's Uhuru Peak (5896m)

Lowest Point: Floor of Lake Tanganyika (358m below sea level)

Famous for: Serengeti-Masai Mara wildebeest migration; wildlife & safaris; Africa's highest mountain; gorillas and chimpanzees; traditional cultures; islands; dhows

Languages: Swahili, English, French and many other African languages

Getting Started

Hotel and restaurant selection in East Africa varies considerably throughout the region, with tourist areas and major towns offering a variety of options for all budgets. In off-the-beaten-track places, choice is considerably more limited. Midrange and top-end travellers can travel comfortably. If you're travelling on a shoestring, things get more rugged. Expect to stay in basic guesthouses, and to put in time bumping over rough roads on crowded buses. The rewards: experiencing more fully the pulse of East Africa, and seeing how most locals live. Throughout the region, costs range from high for upscale safari lodges (especially in Tanzania, which is generally East Africa's most expensive destination) to modest for living local style.

Regardless of budget, there is a wide range of activities available, from mountain trekking, wildlife safaris and chimpanzee tracking to exploring coastal ruins, relaxing on palm-fringed beaches and hiking.

For more information, see Climate (p606) and the Climate sections in the country Directories.

It's quite easy to set your itinerary as you go, but especially for organised safaris and treks you'll get better quality and prices by doing some advance planning. When charting your route, one of the most important things to keep in mind is East Africa's size – avoid the temptation to try to take everything in on one visit. While major destinations are connected by reasonably good air connections and reliable (albeit often rather gruelling) bus routes, it takes plenty of time to cover the long distances. It's much better, more satisfying and more culturally and environmentally friendly to focus on one or two areas, and save other attractions for another time.

WHEN TO GO

East Africa can be rewardingly visited at any time of year, with the main tourist seasons (and peak-season hotel prices) during the warmer months of mid-December through January, and the cool, drier months from late June to August. Climate varies considerably, and in general shouldn't be a major determinant of when to schedule a visit. That said, there are a few considerations to keep in mind. During the March through May seasonal rains, expect fewer tourists, decreased accommodation prices, scenic green landscapes and

---

DON'T LEAVE HOME WITHOUT...

You can buy almost anything you'll need in major cities except specialist trekking and sporting equipment, and certain toiletries such as contact lens solution. However choice is generally limited and prices are high. Some things to bring from home:

- binoculars and a field guide for wildlife watching and birding
- torch (flashlight)
- passport
- mosquito repellent and net (p631)
- zoom lens for wildlife shots; a spare battery and extra storage chip for digital shots
- sleeping bag and waterproof gear for trekking
- sturdy water bottle
- travel insurance, including medical evacuation (p609)
- wind- and waterproof jacket, especially for highland areas
- yellow fever vaccination certificate (p632)

CUTTING COSTS

Some tips if you're trying to cut costs:

- Travel in the low season.
- Always ask about children's discounts.
- Travel in a group (four is ideal) for organised treks and safaris.
- Keep your schedule flexible to take advantage of last minute deals.
- Carry a tent, and camp when possible.
- Focus on easily accessed parks and reserves to minimise transportation costs.
- Use public transport.
- Eat local food.
- Stock up on food and drink in major towns to avoid expensive hotel fare and pricey shops in tourist areas and national parks.
- Offer to pay in cash – sometimes this may result in a discount.

---

muddy or sometimes impassable secondary roads in affected areas (although main routes usually remain open). Hiking isn't recommended during the long rains, and some coastal hotels may close for a month or two.

For wildlife watching, very generally speaking, animals can be more easily spotted during the dry season, when vegetation is less dense, when getting around within the parks is often easier and when, in some ecosystems, the animals tend to congregate around the limited remaining water sources. However, there are many exceptions to this – Tanzania's southeastern Serengeti, with its massive concentrations of wildebeest in the wetter months from February to April, is a classic example. Birding is also generally prime in wetter months throughout the region. Check out the individual national park entries for more information on tailoring your trip to optimise wildlife watching.

COSTS & MONEY

Travel in East Africa is considerably more expensive than in Asia, India or South America, and you'll need to work to stick to a shoestring budget. That said, it's quite possible to get by on limited funds, and in so doing you'll be able to immerse yourself more fully into local life. At the other end of the spectrum, the region has an array of expensive lodges and hotels, with all the corresponding comforts. Tanzania is generally the most expensive country in the region for travel, especially around the northern circuit parks, and Uganda the cheapest. Accommodation in Rwanda and Burundi tends to be expensive, thanks in part to the large international presence in these countries.

At the budget level, plan on spending from US$25 to US$40 per day, staying at budget guesthouses, eating mostly local food, travelling with local transport and excluding safaris and other organised activities. For midrange hotels, western-style meals and more travel comfort, a realistic budget begins at around US$60 per person per day excluding 'extras' such as park entrance fees, visa fees, the price of vehicle rentals or safaris, plus any airfares. Top-end luxury lodge travel costs from US$150 to US$500 or more per person per day, with prices at the upper end of this spectrum usually for all-inclusive safari packages.

ATM machines are relatively widespread in Kenya, Tanzania and Uganda. In Rwanda and Burundi, you'll need to rely on cash and (in capital cities only) travellers cheques or cash advances on credit cards. In rural areas throughout the region, cash is the only realistic option. For more, see p610 and the country chapters.

HOW MUCH?

Midrange safari US$150–US$250/person/day

Safari Lager US$1

Plate of *ugali* US$1

National Park Entry Fees US$15–US$100/person/day

Short Taxi Ride US$2.50

TRAVELLING RESPONSIBLY

Tourism is big business in East Africa, especially in Tanzania and Kenya, and making environmentally- and culturally-sensitive choices can have a significant impact. Following are a few guidelines. For tips on etiquette, see p36. For more on deforestation and other environmental problems, see p54. Community and environmentally friendly entities in this book are listed in the Greendex on p662.

ResponsibleTravel.com (www.responsibletravel.com) has a good selection of East African itineraries.

- Support local enterprise, buy locally whenever possible, and buy souvenirs directly from those who make them.
- Choose safari and trekking operators that treat local communities as equal partners, and that are committed to protecting local eco systems.
- For cultural attractions, try to pay fees directly to the locals involved, rather than to tour company guides or other middlemen.
- Always ask permission before photographing people.
- Avoid indiscriminate gift giving. Donations to recognised projects are more sustainable, less demeaning of and injurious to local cultural values and have a better chance of reaching those who need them most.
- Don't buy items made from ivory, skin, shells etc.
- Save natural resources, especially water and wood, and don't take hot showers if water is heated by firewood. To wash yourself or your clothing, fill a container with water and carry it elsewhere.
- Respect local culture and customs.
- Don't litter! On treks, in parks or when camping, carry out all your litter, and leave trails, parks and campsites cleaner than you found them.
- Try to maximise your 'real' time with locals: take advantage of cultural tourism programs where they are available, and choose itineraries that are well-integrated with the communities in the areas where you will be travelling.
- A major danger in parks, especially in Kenya, is land degradation resulting from too many vehicles crisscrossing the countryside. Keep to the tracks when on safari.

FAVOURITE FESTIVALS

The best festivals and events are often the unannounced ones, such as a small-town wedding, a rite of passage celebration, or local market day. Larger-scale happenings include:

- The Serengeti–Masai Mara wildebeest migration (p186) – one of Earth's greatest natural spectacles.
- Ziff/Festival of the Dhow Countries (p255) – taking place in Zanzibar around July, and part of the Festival of the Dhow Countries, this is one of East Africa's major cultural gatherings.
- Sauti za Busara Swahili Music Festival (p255) – a celebration of all things Swahili, held around February in Zanzibar, and featuring artists from throughout East Africa.
- Maulid – (p332) – marking the birthday of the Prophet Mohammed, and best experienced in Lamu in Kenya
- Eid al-Fitr (p609) – the end of Ramadan fasting, and especially colourful in Zanzibar and elsewhere along the coast.
- Kenya Music Festival (p288) – Kenya's major music and cultural festival, held in Nairobi and other venues, currently in August
- Lamu Cultural Festival (p332) – In Lamu Old Town; dates vary

TOP **PICKS**

ECO-LODGES

Relax for a day or few at these lovely lodges and camps, and know your money is supporting the local community and environment.

- Chole Mjini (p241)
- Chumbe Island Eco-Bungalows (p142)
- Basecamp Masai Mara (p367)
- Virunga Lodge (p562)
- Sabyinyo Silverback Lodge (p572)
- Clouds Lodge (p491)
- Boomu Women's Group (p514)

CULTURAL EXPERIENCES

East Africa's allure lies just as much in its people and cultures as in its wildlife. Here are some ways to get introduced to local life.

- celebrate Maulid on Lamu (p332)
- share a plate of *ugali* (East African staple made from cassava or maize flour) and sauce with locals (p40)
- listen to church singing
- watch traditional dancing
- sail on a dhow
- travel with local transport

MUST-SEE MOVIES

East Africa's stunning panoramas and turbulent human history have featured in many films. Among the highlights:

- *War/Dance* (2007) – An anguished but beautiful glimpse into northeastern Uganda
- *Kibera Kid* (2006) – Life in Kibera, Nairobi's largest slum
- *Hotel Rwanda* (2004) – A real-life story from the Rwandan genocide
- *Africa – The Serengeti* (1994) – Classic footage of the annual wildebeest migration
- *The Last King of Scotland* (2006) – The film version of a best-selling novel set during the Idi Amin era

TRAVEL LITERATURE

Three classics, all of which provide atmospheric introductions to the region, are Peter Matthiessen's *The Tree Where Man Was Born,* which offers a timeless portrayal of life on the East African plains; Ernest Hemingway's *The Snows of Kilimanjaro,* which deals with some of the larger questions of life in an East African setting; and Karen Blixen's *Out of Africa,* a nostalgic perspective on life in colonial-era Kenya. Elspeth Huxley's *The Flame trees of Thika* is another East African classic, filled with snippets that help convey the region's magic.

More recent titles include *The Shadow of Kilimanjaro – On Foot Across East Africa* by Rick Ridgeway, a close-up look at East Africa from a hiker-conservationist's perspective and *The Worlds of a Maasai Warrior – an Autobiography* by Tepilit Ole Saitoti, a fascinating glimpse into Maasai life and culture. If you're travelling with children, look for the similar but easier to read *Facing the Lion – Growing Up Maasai on the African Savanna* by Joseph Lemasolai Lekuton. *I Laugh So I Won't Cry – Kenya's Women Tell the Stories of Their Lives* by Helena Halperin is on the academic side, but readable and full of insights into local life.

Photojourney books focusing on the region include *Africa Adorned* by Angela Fisher and *Africa's Great Rift Valley* by Nigel Pavitt.

INTERNET RESOURCES

Afrol.com (www.afrol.com) News and current affairs.

ArtMatters (www.artmatters.info) Focuses on Kenyan arts, but also has many regional cultural links.

East Africa Living Encyclopedia (www.africa.upenn.edu/NEH/neh.html) Part of the University of Pennsylvania's African Studies Center, with country information and lots of links.

Integrated Regional Information Network (www.irinnews.org) Regional news and humanitarian issues.

Kamusi Project (www.kamusiproject.org) An internet 'Living Swahili Dictionary' and an East Africa focused discussion forum

Lonely Planet (www.lonelyplanet.com) Travel tips, the Thorn Tree forum, and helpful links to other sites.

Pambazuka (www.pambazuka.org) Articles on regional social and humanitarian issues.

The For Tourists page on www.tourismconcern .org.uk is full of tips and info for responsible travel.

Itineraries
CLASSIC ROUTES

WILDLIFE & BEACHES

Two to Three Weeks / Serengeti–Masai Mara to the Coast

This combination mixes wildlife watching with beaches and the Swahili coast. It's possible to squeeze in the essentials in seven to 10 pressed days, but doubling this allows you to explore at a more leisurely pace.

After arriving at Tanzania's Kilimanjaro airport and **Arusha** (p170), head to **Serengeti National Park** (p186) and **Ngorongoro Crater** (p192), or alternatively **Tarangire** (p185) and **Lake Manyara** (p183) national parks. Then, travel eastwards to the **Zanzibar Archipelago** (p121) for diving, snorkelling and relaxing, plus taking in the charm and historical attractions of Zanzibar island's old **Stone Town** (p125). Fly out of Zanzibar or **Dar es Salaam** (p92).

A Kenya variant starts in **Nairobi** (p279), from where you can head to **Masai Mara National Reserve** (p363) or **Amboseli National Park** (p295), continuing then via **Mombasa** (p305) to the ruins at **Gede** (p322) and on to Lamu (p328).

With extra time, take in more en route – hiking in Tanzania's Usambara Mountains around **Lushoto** (p155), trekking on **Mt Kilimanjaro** (p166) or, in Kenya, and with a bit more detouring, visiting the otherworldly **Lake Turkana** (p394).

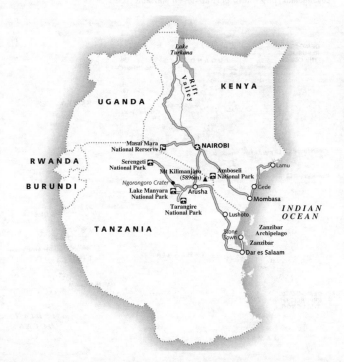

Travel from acacia-studded savannahs and stampeding wildebeest to the romance and magic of the Swahili coast. The itinerary can be easily trimmed or extended, depending on the time at hand. The distance: about 850km, although detours can considerably lengthen this.

OVERLANDERS' CLASSIC Two to three Months / Dar es Salaam to Nairobi

This itinerary is recommended if you want to expand on the popular safari-island circuit described on p19 and experience East Africa in more depth. Unless you have plenty of time, you should focus on one or two segments, rather than doing the whole route.

Starting from **Dar es Salaam** (p92), head up the coast to **Tanga** (p152), detouring en route to **Saadani National Park** (p149), **Pangani** (p151) and possibly the **Zanzibar Archipelago** (p121), before continuing to the **Usambara mountains** (p154), **Moshi** (p159), **Arusha** (p170) and the northern safari circuit. Allow enough time here to visit at least one or two of the parks and the **Ngorongoro Crater** (p192) before continuing northwest to **Mwanza** (p201), **Lake Victoria** (p201) and **Rubondo Island National Park** (p206). Once in this part of Tanzania, it's relatively straightforward to continue on into Rwanda. **Kigali** (p548) merits at least several days, as does the stellar **Parc National des Volcans** (p562) and the **Nyungwe Forest** (p579). The route then continues northwards into Uganda, where there's lovely **Lake Bunyonyi** (p494), and the beautiful **Murchison Falls National Park** (p511) with its wildlife and waterfalls. **Kampala** (p427) and the adrenalin chargers of **Jinja** (p451) and **Bujagali Falls** (p456) are ideal spots to re-energise before continuing eastwards into Kenya.

Once in Kenya, the **Kakamega Forest Reserve** (p376) is well worth a stop, as are **Masai Mara National Reserve** (p363), **Amboseli National Park** (p295) and enchanting **Lamu** (p328), **Mombasa** (p305) and other destinations on the **Kenyan coast** (p303) before turning inland again and finishing up in **Nairobi** (p279). Security situation permitting, also consider a detour northwards for a **Lake Turkana** (p394) safari, including stops at **Maralal** (p392), **South Horr** (p394), **Loyangalani** (p395) and perhaps even **Marsabit** (p391).

This classic overland itinerary gets in all the essentials, but much more as well – optimal if you're seeking to feel East Africa's pulse. Travel as rough or luxuriously as you wish – the main requirement for covering the 3500km-plus route is time.

ROADS LESS TRAVELLED

OFF-BEAT EAST AFRICA   Three Months / Kampala to Nairobi

If you've been to East Africa before and are now keen to delve in more deeply, try all or part of this journey. After arriving in **Kampala** (p427), begin with gorilla tracking in **Bwindi Impenetrable National Park** (p488) or white-water rafting at the **source of the Nile** (p451) close to **Jinja** (p451). Adventurous travellers could also visit the lovely **Kidepo Valley National Park** (p469), security situation permitting.

Journey into Rwanda, where essential stops should include **Kigali** (p548), **Parc National des Volcans** (p562), **Gisenyi** (p572) and **Parc National de Nyungwe** (p579). Security situation permitting, continue on into Burundi, with a few days in **Bujumbura** (p598) to get acquainted with the country. The next stop is Tanzania, where both **Gombe Stream National Park** (p215) and **Kigoma** (p213) merit several days. From Kigoma, board the MV *Liemba* (p262) and cruise down Lake Tanganyika to **Mahale Mountains National Park** (p216), or **Kipili** (see boxed text, p220). Make your way to **Katavi National Park** (p219), and then to **Tabora** (p210) and on via train to **Dodoma** (p195). Here, there's the option of heading north to the **Kolo-Kondoa rock art sites** (p199) and onwards to **Arusha** (p170), or south to **Iringa** (p226) and then via **Makambako** (p231) to **Njombe** (p237), **Songea** (p238), **Tunduru** (p239) and over to **Mikindani** (p249), **Mtwara** (p247) and the coast. Travel up the coast via **Kilwa Kisiwani** (p246) and **Mafia Island** (p239) to **Dar es Salaam** (p92) and your flight home. Or, continue north via **Saadani National Park** (p149) and the beaches south of **Pangani** (p151) over the border to **Mombasa** (p305) and other destinations in Kenya before flying out of **Nairobi** (p279).

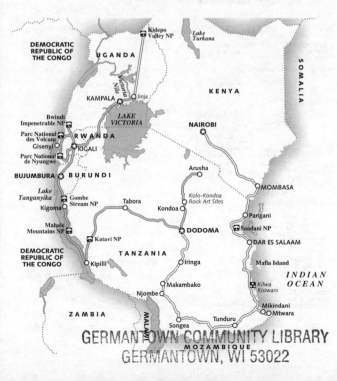

The safari circuits and Zanzibar are wonderful, but those just scratch the surface. If you were hooked on an earlier visit and are back for more, try all or part of this 4000km-plus trail to immerse yourself in East Africa well away from the crowds.

BEST OF THE WEST   Two months / Kigali to Kampala

East Africa's western edge is very much off beat, but fascinating to explore. **Kigali** (p548) is a good first stop, with a lush, mountainous setting, lively nightlife and upbeat vibe. In addition to taking in the city's vibe and beauty, also allow time to visit the **Kigali Memorial Centre** (p552), the sobering genocide memorial. Next, head southwest via **Huye (Butare)** (p576) to **Parc National de Nyungwe** (p579), with its chimpanzees and other primates, and then via **Cyangugu** (p583) to the scenic inland beaches on Lake Kivu around **Kibuye** (p584) and **Gisenyi** (p572). From here, it's just a short hop on to **Musanze (Ruhengeri)** (p559) and the mountain gorillas of **Parc National des Volcans** (p562), and then back to Kigali.

In Burundi, **Bujumbura** (p598) makes an agreeable introduction to the country, and merits a several-day detour, security situation permitting.

Moving on from either Rwanda or Burundi into Tanzania, **Kigoma** (p213) is the first town of note, from where you can make a detour to **Gombe Stream National Park** (p215) to observe the chimpanzees. Then take the MV *Liemba* steamer south to **Mahale Mountains National Park** (p216) or, alternatively, to **Kipili** (see boxed text, p220) for a few days relaxing and exploring the lakeshore. From Kipili, you can make your way to **Katavi National Park** (p219) and then via **Tabora** (p210) northwards to **Mwanza** (p201) and **Bukoba** (p207), from where you could continue on to **Kampala** (p427), **Murchison Falls** (p511), **Queen Elizabeth** (p484) or **Kibale Forest** (p475) national parks, or (security situation permitting) through Karamojaland to **Kidepo Valley National Park** (p469) before finishing up again in Kampala.

Another option: head from Kipili to **Sumbawanga** (p221) and then up the Tanzam highway to **Dar es Salaam** (p92) and the coast.

Travelling around East Africa's western edge is guaranteed to be rough, remote and the adventure of a lifetime. Even if you don't have time for all of this approximately 2000km route, try to get in a section or two.

TAILORED TRIPS

THE SWAHILI COAST

East Africa's Swahili heritage fuses African, Arabian, Indian, Asian and European influences, and exploring brings you on a journey through the continents and the centuries.

Zanzibar (p122) and **Pemba** (p142) are worth as much time as you can spare, although to immerse yourself in things Swahili, you'll need to get away from the resorts and into the villages. Across the Zanzibar Channel is **Dar es Salaam** (p92), where modern-day urbanity is only a thin veneer over long Swahili roots. From here, it's an easy detour to **Bagamoyo** (p147) or **Pangani** (p151), both once major coastal ports. Alternatively, continue south to the ruins at **Kilwa Kisiwani** (p246) – silent witnesses to the days when this part of the coast was the centre of far-flung trading networks. Further south are pretty, palm-fringed **Lindi** (p247), and tiny **Mikindani** (p249), a charming Swahili village. If there's time remaining, follow old trade caravan routes inland to **Tabora** (p210), and to **Ujiji** (p215), with its Swahili-style houses and flourishing tradition of dhow building.

In Kenya, the narrow streets of **Lamu** (p328) are an ideal place to start, followed by visits to **Pate Island** (p334) and nearby islands. **Mombasa** (p305), with its fascinating old town, the mystery-shrouded ruins at **Gede** (p322) and the equally intriguing **Mnarani ruins** (p319) at Kilifi are other essential stops.

WORLD HERITAGE SITES

To sample East Africa's wildlife, culture and history, consider a trip focused on Unesco World Heritage sites. In Tanzania, these range from the heights of **Mt Kilimanjaro** (p166) to the plains of the **Serengeti** (p186) and the expanses of the **Ngorongoro Conservation Area** (p190), and from the **Kolo-Kondoa Rock Art Sites** (p199) to the vast **Selous Game Reserve** (p242). On the coast, the ruins at **Kilwa Kisiwani** (p246) and **Songo Mnara** (p246) carry you back into the centuries, while the winding, cobbled alleyways of Zanzibar's **Stone Town** (p125) draw you deeper into history with every turn.

In Kenya, divide your time between magical **Lamu** (p328), with its preserved Swahili lifestyle and time-warp atmosphere; the **Sacred Mijikenda Kaya Forests** (see boxed text, p318); the glacier-clad summit and forested slopes of **Mt Kenya National Park** (p349); and the remote Lake Turkana national parks in the far north – consisting of **South Island National Park** (p395), **Central Island National Park** (p399), and **Sibiloi National Park** (p396), with its wealth of ancient archaeological finds.

In Uganda Unesco sites include the rugged heights of **Rwenzori Mountains National Park** (p481), the misty **Bwindi Impenetrable National Park** (p488) and the mystery-shrouded **Kasubi tombs** (p431) in Kampala, which are at the spiritual heart of traditional Uganda.

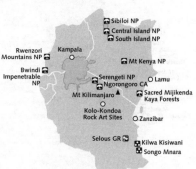

ACTIVE TRAVEL

There's plenty to do in East Africa if you're not keen on spending your visit cooped up in a bus or minibus. The region's mountains are an obvious draw – trek to the top of Africa in **Mt Kilimanjaro National Park** (p166); enjoy sunrise while making your way up **Mt Meru** (p182) or the snowy peak of **Mt Kenya** (p349); or watch the mists roll back from the summit of Mt Stanley in Uganda's **Rwenzori Mountains National Park** (p481). For trekking that's almost as rewarding as in the Rwenzoris, but easier and at only a fraction of the price, try Uganda's **Mt Elgon National Park** (p462), but check on security first.

An alternative to mountain trekking areas is the easy, rolling terrain around Tanzania's **Lushoto** (p155) – walking country, where it's possible to

hike for days along winding paths past picturesque villages. The **crater lakes** (p473) area near Uganda's Fort Portal also offers village-to-village walking. More rugged is Tanzania's **Ngorongoro Conservation Area** (p190), with its range of volcanoes and calderas, stunning, varied topography and often challenging hiking.

Other active pursuits include white-water rafting, kayaking or mountain biking at the **source of the Nile** (p451) near Jinja; diving around the **Zanzibar Archipelago** (p121), **Malindi** (p324) or **Watamu** (p320) in Tanzania; rock-climbing at Kenya's **Hell's Gate National Park** (p337); or walking and cycling near Tanzania's **Lake Manyara National Park** (p183).

EAST AFRICAN WILDLIFE

East Africa is home to an unparalleled collection of national parks and reserves. An undisputed highlight is the magnificent **Serengeti-Masai Mara** (p186 and p363) ecosystem, famed for the annual wildebeest migration. Nearby are Tanzania's wildlife-packed **Ngorongoro Crater** (p192) and **Tarangire National Park** (p185), with its baobabs and elephants. Serene **Ruaha National Park** (p229) has evocative topography and a wealth of animals, while **Katavi National Park** (p219), in Tanzania's far west, is one of the region's last great frontier areas. For observing chimpanzees at close range, make your way to **Mahale Mountains** (p216) or **Gombe Stream** (p215) National Parks.

In Kenya, don't miss the lush **Kakamega Forest Reserve** (p376), which is known for its birds; **Amboseli National Park** (p295), with elephants, giraffes and other wildlife in a lovely setting framed by Mt Kilimanjaro in the background; **Lake Nakuru National Park** (p340), with birds, rhinos and hippos; and **Tsavo National Park** (see boxed text, p299), with its sweeping plains and the 'Big Five'. In Rwanda, the star attraction is **Parc National des Volcans** (p562), with its gorillas, while Uganda's offerings include **Kibale Forest National Park** (p475), with its chimpanzees; thundering falls and wildlife at **Murchison Falls National Park** (p511); **Queen Elizabeth National Park** (p484), with its tree-climbing lions and hiking; remote and beautiful **Kidepo Valley National Park** (p469); and the gorillas at **Bwindi Impenetrable National Park** (p488).

History

THE DAWN OF MANKIND

East Africa has one of the longest documented human histories of any region in the world. Ancient hominid (human-like) skulls and footprints, some over three million years old, have been found at various sites in the region, including at Olduvai Gorge in Tanzania and Lake Turkana in Kenya. Although similarly ancient traces have also been found elsewhere on the continent, the East African section of the Great Rift Valley is popularly considered the 'cradle of humanity'.

By about one million years ago, these early ancestors had come to resemble modern humans, and had spread well beyond East Africa, including as far as Europe and Asia. Roughly 100,000 years ago, and possibly earlier, *homo sapiens* – modern man – had arrived on the scene.

See www.pbs.org/wgbh /evolution/humans /humankind/d.html for an overview of human evolution in East Africa.

The earliest evidence of modern-day East Africans dates to around 10,000 years ago, when much of the region was home to Khoisan-speaking hunter-gatherer communities. On the western fringes of East Africa, including parts of the area that is now Rwanda and Burundi, there were also small populations of various so-called Pygmy groups.

THE GREAT MIGRATIONS

Beginning between 3000 and 5000 years ago, a series of migrations began that were to indelibly shape the face of East Africa. Cushitic- and Nilotic-speaking peoples from the north and Bantu-speakers from the west converged on the Khoisan and other peoples already in the area, creating over the centuries the rich tribal mosaic that is East Africa today.

The first to arrive were Cushitic-speaking farmers and cattle herders who made their way to the region from present-day Ethiopia, and settled both inland and along the coast. They moved mostly in small family groups, and brought with them traditions that are still practiced by their descendents, including the Iraqw around Tanzania's Lake Manyara and the Gabbra and Rendille in northern Kenya.

Zamani – A Survey of East African History, edited by renowned Kenyan historian BA Ogot with JA Kieran, is a classic introduction to the region's pre-colonial and colonial history from an African perspective.

The next major influx began around 1000 BC when Bantu-speaking peoples from West Africa's Niger Delta area began moving eastwards, arriving in East Africa around the 1st century BC. Thanks to their advanced agricultural skills and knowledge of ironworking and steel production – which gave them a great advantage in cultivating land and establishing settlements – these Bantu-speakers were able to absorb many of the Cushitic- and Khoisan-speakers who were already in the region, as well as the Pygmy populations

TIMELINE

c 3.5 million BC	c 100 BC	c 750 – 1200 AD
Fossils found at Kenya's Lake Turkana and at Laetoli, Tanzania show that hominid (human-like) creatures were wandering around the East African plains over three million years ago.	The first Bantu-speakers arrive in the region, part of a series of great population migrations that shaped the face of East Africa as it is today.	Islam reaches East Africa and Swahili civilisation is born. Settlements are established at Lamu, Gede, Kilwa and elsewhere along the coast.

around the Great Lakes. Soon, they became East Africa's most populous ethnolinguistic family – a status which they continue to hold today.

A final wave of migration began somewhat later when smaller groups of Nilotic peoples began to arrive in East Africa from what is now southern Sudan. This influx continued through to the 18th century, with the main movements taking place in the 15th and 16th centuries. Most of these Nilotic peoples – whose descendants include the present-day Maasai and Turkana – were pastoralists, and many settled in the less fertile areas of southern Kenya and northern Tanzania where their large herds would have sufficient grazing space.

Africa – A Biography of the Continent by John Reader is a sweeping journey through Africa from its earliest days, including some fascinating text on East Africa.

Today, the population diversity resulting from these migrations is one of the most fascinating aspects of travel in East Africa.

MONSOON WINDS

As these migrations were taking place in the interior, coastal areas were being shaped by far different influences. Azania, as the East African coast was known to the ancient Greeks, was an important trading post as early as 400 BC, and had likely been inhabited even before then by small groups of Cushitic peoples, and by Bantu-speakers. The *Periplus of the Erythraean Sea*, a navigator's guide written in the 1st century AD, mentions Rhapta as the southernmost trading port. Although its location remains a mystery, it is believed to have been somewhere along the Kenyan or Tanzanian coast, possibly on the mainland opposite Manda or Paté Islands (north of Lamu), or further south near the Pangani or Rufiji estuaries.

'…Two days' sail beyond, there lies the…last market-town of the continent of Azania, which is called Rhapta…in which there is ivory in great quantity, and tortoise-shell…' (*Periplus of the Erythraean Sea*)

Trade seems to have grown steadily throughout the early part of the first millennium. Permanent settlements were established as traders, first from the Mediterranean and later from Arabia and Persia, came ashore on the winds of the monsoon and began to intermix with the indigenous peoples, gradually

---

SWAHILI

The word 'Swahili' ('of the coast', from the Arabic word *sāhil*) refers both to the Swahili language, as well as to the Islamic culture of the peoples inhabiting the East African coast from Mogadishu (Somalia) in the north down to Mozambique in the south. Both language and culture are a rich mixture of Bantu, Arabic, Persian and Asian influences.

Although Swahili culture began to develop in the early part of the first millennium AD, it was not until the 18th century, with the ascendancy of the Omani Arabs on Zanzibar, that it came into its own. Swahili's role as a *lingua franca* was solidified as it spread throughout East and Central Africa along the great trade caravan routes. European missionaries and explorers soon adopted the language as their main means of communicating with locals. In the second half of the 19th century, missionaries, notably the German Johan Ludwig Krapf, also began applying the Roman alphabet. Prior to this, Swahili had been written exclusively in Arabic script.

15th Century	1850–1870	1890
The king of Malindi sends the Chinese emperor a giraffe. Vasco da Gama arrives in East Africa on his way en route to the Orient, stopping at Mombasa and Malindi before continuing on to India.	Zanzibar's slave market becomes the largest in East Africa. According to some estimates, from 10,000 to 50,000 slaves were passing through its market each year.	Britain and Germany establish 'spheres of influence' for themselves. Zanzibar becomes a British 'protectorate'. Following WWI, the formerly German area of Rwanda-Urundi (later to become Rwanda and Burundi) comes under Belgian control.

giving rise to Swahili language and culture. The traders from Arabia also brought Islam, which by the 11th century had become entrenched.

Between the 13th and 15th centuries these coastal settlements – including those at Shanga (on Paté Island), Gede, Lamu and Mombasa (all in present-day Kenya) and on the Zanzibar Archipelago and at Kilwa Kisiwani (both in Tanzania) – flourished, with trade in ivory, gold and other goods extending as far away as India and China.

EXPEDITIONING EUROPEANS

The first European to reach East Africa was the intrepid Portuguese explorer, Vasco da Gama, who arrived in 1498, en route to the Orient. Within three decades, the Portuguese had disrupted the old trading networks and subdued the entire coast, building forts at various places, including Kilwa and Mombasa. Portuguese control lasted until the early 18th century, when they were displaced by Arabs from Oman.

As the Omani Arabs solidified their foothold, they began to turn their sights westwards, developing powerful trade routes that stretched inland as far as Lake Tanganyika and Central Africa. Commerce grew at such a pace that in the 1840s, the Sultan of Oman moved his capital from Muscat to Zanzibar Island.

The slave trade also grew rapidly during this period, driven in part by demand from European plantation holders on the Indian Ocean islands of Réunion and Mauritius. Soon slave traders, including the notorious Tippu Tip, had established stations at Tabora (Tanzania) and other inland towns. By the mid-19th century, the Zanzibar Archipelago had become the largest slave entrepôt along the East African coast, with nearly 50,000 slaves, abducted from as far away as Lake Tanganyika, passing through Zanzibar's market each year.

COLONIAL CONTROL

In addition to reports of the horrors of the still-ongoing regional slave trade, tales of the attractions of East Africa also made their way back to Europe, and Western interests were piqued. In 1890, Germany and Great Britain signed an agreement defining 'spheres of influence' for themselves, which formally established a British protectorate over the Zanzibar Archipelago. Most of what is now mainland Tanzania, as well as Rwanda and Burundi, came under German control as German East Africa (later Tanganyika), while the British took Kenya and Uganda.

The 19th century was also the era of various European explorers, including Gustav Fischer (a German whose party was virtually annihilated by the Maasai at Hell's Gate on Lake Naivasha in 1882), Joseph Thomson (a Scot who reached Lake Victoria via the Rift Valley lakes and the Aberdare Highlands in 1883), and Count Teleki von Szek (an Austrian who explored the Lake Turkana region and Mt Kenya in 1887). Anglican bishop James

Chinese porcelain fragments have been discovered at Gede and elsewhere along the East African coast – testaments to old trade routes between Africa and the Orient.

Portuguese influence is still seen in East Africa's architecture, customs and language. The Swahili *gereza* (jail), from Portuguese *igreja* (church) dates to the days when Portuguese forts contained both in the same compound.

1952	1961–1963	1980s
The Mau Mau rebellion begins in Kenya as a protest against colonial land-grabbing in Kikuyu lands. By the time it was suppressed, thousands of Kikuyus had been killed, with thousands more put into detention camps.	Following a period of intensifying discontent with colonial rule, the countries of East Africa gain independence.	Kenya's Mungiki sect – responsible for a series of brutal murders in 2008 – emerges, inspired in part by the Mau Mau rebellion of 1952.

THE SLAVE TRADE

Slavery has been practised in Africa throughout recorded history, but its greatest expansion in East Africa came with the rise of Islam, which prohibits the enslavement of Muslims. Demands of European plantation holders on the islands of Réunion and Mauritius were another major catalyst, particularly during the second half of the 18th century.

At the outset, slaves were taken from coastal regions and shipped to Arabia, Persia and the Indian Ocean islands. Kilwa Kisiwani, off the southern Tanzanian coast, was one of the major export gateways. As demand increased, traders made their way further inland, so that during the 18th and 19th centuries, slaves were being brought from as far away as Malawi and the Congo. By the 19th century, with the rise of the Omani Arabs, Zanzibar Island had eclipsed Kilwa Kisiwani as East Africa's major slave-trading depot. According to some estimates, by the 1860s from 10,000 to as many as 50,000 slaves were passing through Zanzibar's market each year. Overall, close to 600,000 slaves were sold through Zanzibar between 1830 and 1873, when a treaty with Britain paved the way for the trade's ultimate halt in the region in the early 20th century.

As well as the human horrors, the slave trade caused major social upheavals on the mainland. In the sparsely populated and politically decentralised south of present-day Tanzania, it fanned up inter-clan warfare as ruthless entrepreneurs raided neighbouring tribes for slaves. In other areas, the slave trade promoted increased social stratification and altered settlement patterns. Some tribes, for example, began to build fortified settlements encircled by trenches, while others concentrated their populations in towns as self-defence. Another fundamental societal change was the gradual shift in the nature of chieftaincy from religiously based to a position resting on military power or wealth – both among the 'gains' of trade in slaves and commodities.

The slave trade also served as an impetus for European missionary activity in East Africa, prompting establishment of the first mission stations and missionary penetration of the interior. One of the most tireless campaigners against the horrors of slavery was Scottish missionary-explorer David Livingstone (1813–74), whose efforts, combined with the attention attracted by his funeral, were an important influence mobilising British initiatives to halt human trafficking in the region.

Hannington set out in 1885 to establish a diocese in Uganda, but was killed when he reached the Nile. Other explorers included Burton and Speke, who were sent to Lake Tanganyika in 1858 by the Royal Geographical Society, and the famous Henry Morton Stanley and David Livingstone.

The World of the Swahili by John Middleton is a fine introduction to East Africa's Swahili culture.

By the turn of the 20th century, Europeans had firmly established a presence in East Africa. Both the British and German colonial administrations were busy building railways and roads to open their colonies to commerce, establishing hospitals and schools, and encouraging the influx of Christian missionaries. Kenya's fertile and climatically favourable highlands proved eminently suitable for European farmers to colonise. In Tanganyika, by contrast, large areas were unable to support agriculture and were plagued by the tsetse fly, which made cattle grazing and dairy farming impossible.

1984	1994	1996
Kenya reports its first AIDS case. Within a decade, an estimated 800,000 people were infected with HIV.	The presidents of Rwanda and Burundi are killed when their plane was shot down during landing, unleashing the Rwandan genocide.	Femrite – the Ugandan Women Writers Association – is launched with the goal of giving women writers a platform from which to contribute to national development/and write

INDEPENDENCE

As the European presence in Africa solidified, discontent with colonial rule grew and nationalist demands for independence became more insistent. In the 1950s and early 1960s, the various nationalist movements coalesced and gained force across East Africa, culminating in the granting of independence to Tanzania (1961), Uganda, Rwanda and Burundi (all in 1962), and Kenya (1963). Independence and post-independence trajectories varied from country to country. In Kenya, the path leading to independence was violent and protracted, with some of the underlying issues reflected in the country's current political difficulties; in Tanzania and Uganda the immediate pre-independence years were relatively peaceful, while in Rwanda and Burundi, long-existing tribal rivalries were a major issue – the effects of which are still being felt today.

In Kenya, the European influx increased rapidly during the first half of the 20th century, so that by the 1950s there were about 80,000 settlers in the country. Much of the land that was expropriated for their farms came from the homelands of the Kikuyu people. The Kikuyu responded by forming an opposition political association in 1920, and by instigating the Mau Mau rebellion in the 1950s, which marked a major turning point in Kenyan politics.

In Tanganyika, the unpopular German administration continued until the end of WWI, when the League of Nations mandated the area to the British, and Rwanda and Burundi to the Belgians. British rule was equally unpopular, with the Brits neglecting development of Tanganyika in favour of the more lucrative and fertile options available in Kenya and Uganda. Political consciousness soon began to coalesce in the form of farmers' unions and cooperatives through which popular demands were expressed. By the mid-20th century, there were over 400 such cooperatives, which soon joined to form the Tanganyika Africa Association (TAA), a lobbying group for the nationalist cause based in Dar es Salaam.

In Uganda, the British tended to favour the recruitment of the powerful Buganda people for the civil service. Members of other tribes, unable to acquire responsible jobs in the colonial administration or to make inroads into the Buganda-dominated commercial sector, were forced to seek other ways of joining the mainstream. The Acholi and Lango, for example, chose the army and became the tribal majority in the military. As resentment grew, the seeds were planted for the intertribal conflicts that were to tear Uganda apart following independence.

In Rwanda and Burundi, the period of colonial rule was characterised by increasing power and privilege of the Tutsi. The Belgians administrators found it convenient to rule indirectly through Tutsi chiefs and their princes, and the Tutsi had a monopoly on the missionary-run educational system. As a result, long-existing tensions between the Tutsi and Hutu were exacerbated, igniting the spark that was later to explode in the 1994 Rwanda genocide.

For more about the independence movements, and the history of each country since independence, see the country chapters.

Hotel Rwanda (2004) tells the real-life story of a Rwandan Hutu who sheltered hundreds of refugees in his four-star hotel during the outbreak of the Rwandan genocide.

Fanning the flames under Kenya's political cauldron are the Mungiki – for an overview, see http://news.bbc.co.uk/2/hi/africa/6685393.stm

1996	1998	2004
The Mwalimu Nyerere Foundation is established to continue Nyerere's ideals of promoting peace and unity in East Africa and beyond.	Terrorist attacks hit US embassies in Nairobi and Dar es Salaam.	Uganda's aggressive anti-AIDS campaign begins to show results, with adult prevalence rates down to about 6% from about 18% a decade earlier.

EAST AFRICA TODAY

In East Africa today, all these threads of the region's history are still very much in evidence – from Olduvai Gorge, with its fascinating fossil finds, to the winding lanes and ornate lintels of old Swahili settlements such as Lamu and Zanzibar, to bustling coastal dhow ports, Portuguese-era garrisons and the colonial-era architecture lining Dar es Salaam's waterfront. Interspersed with all this is East Africa's more modern face – high-rise office blocks, elegant luxury lodges and western-style resorts. And, tying it all together are the rich tribal heritages that are the region's lifeblood.

Reconciling all of these influences – traditional and modern, foreign and local – has long been a major undercurrent in East African life and politics. As the region approaches its 50-year mark of post colonial-era government, observers local and foreign are increasingly taking stock. Peace has gained a foothold in Rwanda, and is coalescing, albeit slowly, in Burundi. Tourism is more than holding its own as one of the fastest-growing regional industries, especially in Tanzania, where it is gradually helping the country establish a firmer economic base. The regional cultural scene also continues as vibrant as ever. In contrast to this is the still fragile situation in northern Uganda and the shadowy spectre of Kenya's still simmering post-election troubles (see p268 for more), which gave rise to a sense of deep frustration with the current state of affairs among large sectors of the populace. Although Kenya is no longer in the headlines as it was in early 2008, and is safe for travel, the long and complex roots of the problem persist. They encompass everything from long-standing tribal enmities, shortages of land and entrenched corruption at the highest levels to a widening gap between rich and poor and still-uneven access to education outside Nairobi, and reflect many of the challenges facing the region as a whole.

2006	Dec 2007-Jan 2008	2008
Tropical Fish – Stories Out of Entebbe, a collection of short stories by Ugandan Doreen Baingana, wins a Commonwealth Writers Prize	Kenya is wracked by post-election violence as hundreds are killed and thousands displaced from their homes in the Rift Valley and Central areas.	Kilimanjaro's snows are predicted to disappear entirely by 2020. Climate change is also linked to an increase in malaria and other vector-borne diseases.

Culture

DAILY LIFE

It's a wild place, the East African bush, and hospitality counts because it has to. You never know if you'll soon be the one on the asking end – whether for a cup of water, a meal or a roof over your head for the night – and strangers are accordingly welcomed as family. In a region where a 10km walk to the nearest water source, the nearest medical clinic or the nearest primary school is commonplace, time takes on an altogether different dimension. Daily rhythms are determined by the sun and the seasons, and arriving is the most important thing, not when or how. *Nitafika* – I will arrive. *Safiri salama* – travel in peace. *Umefika* – you have arrived; *karibu* – welcome. Additional words are not necessary.

No monthly social security cheques arrive in the mail, and community life is essential – for support in times of sickness and age, as well as in ensuring a proper upbringing for the young. Mourning is a community affair, as is celebrating. It would be unheard of not to attend the funeral of your mother's second cousin once removed, just as it would be equally unheard of to miss celebrating the wedding of your father's stepbrother's neighbour. Proper jobs are scarce, and if you're one of the lucky few to have found one, it's expected that you'll share your good fortune with the extended family. Throughout East African society, 'I' and 'me' are very much out, while 'our' and 'we' are in.

Emphasis in all aspects of daily life is on the necessary. If you do attend that funeral, forget bringing flowers – a bag of rice, or money, would be a more appropriate way of showing your solidarity with the bereaved. At all levels of society, invisible social hierarchies lend life a sense of order. Age groups play a central role among many tribes, and the elderly and those in positions of authority are respected. Men rule the roost in the working world and, at least symbolically, in the family as well. Although women arguably form the backbone of the economy throughout the region – with most juggling child-rearing plus work on the family farm or in an office – they are frequently marginalised when it comes to education and politics. Some positive contrasts to this are found in Kenya, which is notable for its abundance of nongovernmental organisations, many headed by women, and Uganda, where women play prominent roles in educational and literary circles.

With the exception of Tanzania, where local chieftaincies were abolished following independence, tribal identity and tribal structures are strong – sometimes with disastrous consequences, as seen in the Rwandan genocide and in recent events in Kenya. Otherwise, clashes between traditional and modern lifestyles are generally fairly low profile.

For tips on how travellers can behave responsibly in the East African cultural context, see boxed text, p36.

ECONOMY

East Africa's economy is a mixed picture. On the one hand, inflation is at low to moderate levels, economies are growing, and tourism is a major and increasingly important money earner. Yet, all of the five countries covered in this book are ranked in the bottom third globally on the UN Human Development Index, which measures the overall achievements of a country according to factors such as income, life expectancy and education standards. And annual per-capita income levels are just a fraction of what they are in most Western countries.

In coastal areas, the hands and feet of brides and married women are often adorned with henna painting – intricate designs made with a paste from leaves of the henna plant.

Left to Tell: Discovering God Amidst the Rwandan Holocaust by Immaculée Ilibagiza is a moving account of the Rwandan genocide by a young Tutsi woman.

These figures are tempered by the extensive informal economy that exists throughout the region, as well as by wide variations between rural and urban areas. There are also significant income disparities, with Kenya, for example – one of the world's poorest countries – also registering one of the largest gaps between rich and poor.

Yet in human terms, the statistics mean that daily life is a struggle for most East Africans. Life expectancy averages around 45 years for the region as a whole, and an average East African has between a 30% and 50% statistical probability at birth of not surviving to age 40. Reliable banking services and savings accounts remain inaccessible for most people, especially rural dwellers, and it's a common scenario for those few students who make it through secondary school to be faced with only meagre job prospects upon graduation.

While all this can be rather discouraging, it's worth keeping in mind that East Africa is not an area of cohesion or sweeping generalities, whether the topic be economic development or politics. It's only relatively recently that the region has been packaged into the neatly bordered national entities that we take for granted today, and just 200 years ago the main forces were relatively small, community-based tribal groupings. This means that as a traveller, the most encouraging aspects of the East African economic picture that you're likely to see are those at the village or community level – a sustainable microlending scheme, for example, or a profitable women's cooperative. While successes at this level are no excuse for neglecting the bigger picture, they at least help to put some of the statistics into a more balanced perspective and serve as proof that the efforts of one or several individuals can make a difference.

Kibera Kid (2006) is a short film showing life in Kibera, Nairobi's largest slum. It was filmed on location, with local actors.

Hot Sun ('Jua Kali') Foundation (www.kiberakid .com) – an outgrowth of the short fiction film *Kibera Kid* – is working to train slum youth to tell their stories as a path of social and community transformation.

GOVERNMENT & POLITICS

East Africa has made headlines in recent years – for the wrong reasons, with the Kenyan post-election events (see p271), and – more positively – with slow but steady steps towards reactivation of a modified version of the old East African Community customs union. Until 1977 Kenya, Uganda and Tanzania were members of the East African Community (EAC), an economic union that linked the currencies of the three countries and provided for freedom of

---

AIDS IN EAST AFRICA

Together with malaria, AIDS is now the leading cause of death in sub-Saharan Africa, and East Africa is no exception. In Uganda alone, there are almost one million AIDS orphans under 17 years of age. The figures elsewhere in the region are just as sobering. Women are particularly hard hit. In Burundi, for example, where an estimated 9% of urban dwellers (versus a countrywide average of about 6%) are HIV positive, urban infection rates in women are more than double those for men.

On the positive side, East African governments now discuss the situation openly, and you'll notice AIDS-related billboards in Dar es Salaam, Nairobi, Kampala and elsewhere in the region. Ugandan President Yoweri Museveni has often been cited for his outspokenness and leadership in combating the scourge, and thanks to vigorous public awareness campaigns and other government efforts Uganda's AIDS rates have dropped over the past decade. Yet, at the grassroots level in many areas of the region, the stigma remains and, especially away from urban centres, real discussion remains limited. AIDS-related deaths are often kept quiet, with 'tuberculosis' used euphemistically as a socially acceptable catch-all diagnosis. And many of the AIDS clinics and counselling centres that exist still operate anonymously; if a sign were hung out, many victims wouldn't enter for fear of recognition. In one study in Kenya, over half of the women surveyed who had acquired HIV hadn't told their partners because they feared being beaten or abandoned.

GETTING REAL *Mary Fitzpatrick*

Hassani, a 30-something, long-time taxi driver friend from Dar es Salaam, was putting things in perspective for me one day. He'd love to travel – he heard about opportunities in Japan for manual labourers that were relatively well paid, and was thinking about pursuing this. But, what about your wife and young son, I asked, would they go with you? And, assuming you could sort out the logistics of visas and the like, Japan is a difficult society to break into linguistically and culturally – wouldn't you be lonely, or miss life here in East Africa. Yes, yes, he replied, all good points. I'd miss things here, and for sure would miss my family, who would stay back. But I've now been working as a driver for about eight years, and have been able to save up about US$2000 during this time. As I see it, my options are to use that to buy my own car – with US$2000, I could make a decent down payment – or use it to go elsewhere and try to improve my earnings. What I really want to do is finish secondary school – I never had the chance – but that's not a realistic option for me now.

As he spoke, I was making my own calculations. Hassani was incredibly hard-working and responsible, yet over all this time, this – an amount he was proud of – was the most he had been able to save. It's what many travellers pay for just a round-trip air ticket to East Africa, let alone what is then paid to climb Kilimanjaro or go on safari. The commission he (like many local taxi drivers) needed to pay weekly to the owner of his taxi, high fuel prices and the needs of daily living eat up the rest. His house, in Dar es Salaam's far-from-luxurious Temeke neighbourhood, was adequate and warm with hospitality, but very simple. And his young son, his pride and his hope for the future, would soon be needing school fees.

It made me think of the many others I know in Dar es Salaam, Nairobi and elsewhere in the region – seeking the chance to do university studies abroad (something that is almost taken for granted by so many in the West) or simply looking for a job with a decent salary. I began to appreciate more the sense of frustration that so many youths here experience at the end of their schooling – all dressed up, but nowhere to go. What a contrast with gap-year students whose future, or at least future schooling, seems assured.

movement and shared telecommunications and postal facilities. Following the EAC's break-up and a decade of regional disputes, in 1996 the presidents of Tanzania, Kenya and Uganda established the Tripartite Commission for East African Cooperation, which laid the groundwork for re-establishing the old economic and customs union in 2000. It is this new **East African Community** (www.eac.int) that today serves as the main intragovernmental organisation in the region. A common passport was adopted in 1997, and in early 2005 a customs union came into effect with the ultimate goal of duty-free trade between the three countries. Currently on the agenda are consolidation of the customs union, and establishment of a common market by 2012.

MULTICULTURALISM

Almost since the dawn of humankind, outsiders have been arriving in East Africa and have been assimilated into its seething, simmering and endlessly fascinating cultural melting pot. From the Bantu-, Nilotic- and Cushitic-speaking groups that made their way to the region during the early migrations (see p25), to Arab and Asian traders, to colonial-era Europeans, a long stream of migrants have left their footprints. Today the region's modern face reflects this rich fusion of influences, with 300-plus tribal groups, as well as small but economically significant pockets of Asians, Arabs and Europeans – most well-integrated linguistically – all rubbing shoulders. For more on some of the major groups, see Tribal Cultures (p44) later in this chapter.

While national identities have become entrenched over the past half-century of independence, tribal loyalties also remain strong in many areas. The highest-profile conflicts resulting from intertribal clashes have been

The Constant Gardener Trust (www.theconstant gardenertrust.org) was set up by the cast and crew of *The Constant Gardener* – a 2005 film set in Kenya's Loiyangalani and the Kibera slum of Nairobi – to improve education in these areas.

THE GENDER GAP

The good news on the East African educational scene is that at the primary school level, the 'gender gap' (the difference between the percentage of boys versus the percentage of girls enrolled in school) is gradually lessening, and in some cases has been completely eliminated. In Tanzania and Kenya, for example, initial primary school enrolment is roughly evenly divided between boys and girls. In Uganda, which has the highest level of overall primary school enrolment in the region, the gender gap is about 9%, in favour of boys, but less than it was a decade ago. However, the rest of the picture is less rosy. In Tanzania, only 5% of girls obtain a secondary level education, while in Uganda and Kenya the figures are 9% and 22%, respectively.

Comparatively low initial enrolment rates and high drop-out rates among girls at the secondary level are due in part to cultural attitudes, with traditional preferences for sons diminishing the value of girls' education. Early marriage and early pregnancies are another factor. In Uganda – which has the dubious distinction of having the highest rate of adolescent pregnancy in sub-Saharan Africa – 43% of girls are either pregnant or have given birth by age 17, and 70% by age 19. HIV/AIDS is also a major contributor. As the number of AIDS orphans in the region rises, girls are required to stay home to take care of ill family members or younger siblings. Among East Africa's nomadic and pastoralist communities, such as those in parts of northeastern Kenya, the demands of a migratory lifestyle often cause families to remove girls from school. Sexual harassment both in and out of school also leads to non-attendance and dropping out.

Several countries in the region have signed on to a continent-wide African Girl's Education Initiative, although there has been little measurable progress thus far. A few countries, including Kenya, have also adopted re-entry policies for school-aged girls who give birth, although these remain largely ineffectual. There are a handful of private girls' schools around the region that have registered some impressive gains, and steady progress is also being made at the grassroots level in increasing awareness of the value of education for all children, including girls. However, especially in rural areas, attitudes are slow to change and there's still a long way to go.

in Rwanda – where longstanding tensions exploded in 1994, leading to a brutal genocide, which still scars the nation; in Burundi, where intertribal conflicts culminated in a long civil war; and, most recently, in Kenya, where the 2007 presidential elections were marred by interethnic violence. At the other end of the spectrum is Tanzania, which has earned a name for itself for its remarkably harmonious society, and its success in forging tolerance and unity out of diversity.

Although intrareligious (primarily Christian-Muslim) frictions exist, they are at a generally low level, and not a major factor in contemporary East African politics.

SPORT

Football (soccer) dominates sporting headlines throughout the region, and matches always draw large and enthusiastic crowds. Kenya's national team, the Harambee Stars, regularly participates in pan-African competitions and World Cup qualifiers, and there are also occasional appearances by Uganda's Kobs and Rwanda's Amavubi (Wasps). A new national stadium in Dar es Salaam, a new coach and enthusiastic backing from the president are giving Tanzania's Taifa Stars an improved profile.

More low-key than football at home, but surpassing it on the international sports stage, is running, where Kenya dominates in long-distance competitions throughout the world.

The 3000km **East African Safari Rally** (www.eastafricansafarirally.com) – which has been held annually since 1953 – passes through Kenya, Uganda and Tanzania along public roadways, and attracts an international collection of drivers with their vintage (pre-1971) automobiles. Just as rugged, if not more so, is the

Get a glimpse into coastal East Africa's cultures at www.pbs.org/wonders /fr_e2.htm.

Tour d'Afrique (www.tourdafrique.com) bicycle race that passes through East Africa (Kenya and Tanzania) en route between Cairo and Cape Town.

Also likely to get increasing regional press coverage in the near future is Kenya's bid to host the 2016 Olympic Games, although recent political events overshadow chances of success.

RELIGION

The vibrant spirituality that pervades the African continent fills East Africa as well. The major religions are Christianity and Islam, with Islam especially prevalent in coastal areas. There are also a sizeable number of adherents of traditional religions, as well as small communities of Hindus, Sikhs and Jains.

Christianity

The first Christian missionaries reached East Africa in the mid-19th century. Since then the region has been the site of extensive missionary activity, and today most of the major denominations are represented, including Lutherans, Catholics, Seventh Day Adventists, Baptists and others. In many areas, mission stations have been the major, and in some cases the only, channels for development assistance. This is particularly so with health care and education, with missions still sometimes providing the only schools and medical facilities in remote areas.

We Wish to Inform You That Tomorrow We Will be Killed With Our Families: Stories from Rwanda by Philip Gourevitch is another compelling account of the Rwandan genocide and its aftermath, as told by survivors.

In addition to the main denominations, there is also an increasing number of home-grown African sects, especially in Kenya. Factors that are often cited for their growth include cultural resurgence, an ongoing struggle against neo-colonialism and the alienation felt by many jobseekers who migrate to urban centres far from their homes.

Church services throughout East Africa are invariably highly colourful and packed to overflowing. Even if you can't understand the language, it's worth going to listen to the unaccompanied choral singing, which East Africans do with such beauty and precision.

Islam

Islam was founded in the early 7th century by the Prophet Mohammed. By the time of his death, the new religion had begun to spread throughout the Arabian peninsula, from where it was then carried in all directions over the subsequent centuries, including along the East African coast, where it is today flourishing, although – in typical East African fashion – in a considerably less dogmatic form than in other parts of the world.

BAO

It's not exactly sport, but *bao* (also known as *kombe*, *mweso* and by various other names) is one of East Africa's favourite pastimes. It's played throughout the region, and is especially popular on the Zanzibar Archipelago and elsewhere along the coast, where you'll see men in their *kanzu* (white robe-like outer garment worn by men – often for prayer – on the Zanzibar Archipelago and in other Swahili areas) and *kofia* (a cap, usually of embroidered white linen, worn by men on the Zanzibar Archipelago and in other Swahili areas) huddled around a board watching two opponents play. The rules vary somewhat from place to place, but the game always involves trying to capture the pebbles or seeds of your opponent, which are set out on a board with rows of small hollows. Anything can substitute for a board – from finely carved wood to a flattened area of sand on the beach, and playing well is something of a patiently acquired art form. For more on the intricacies of *bao*, see the comprehensive www.gamecabinet.com/rules/Bao.html or www.driedger.ca/mankala/Man-1.html.

The five pillars of Islam that guide Muslims in their daily lives:

Haj (pilgrimage) It is the duty of every Muslim who is fit and can afford it to make the pilgrimage to Mecca at least once.

Sala (prayer, sometimes written *salat*) This is the obligation of prayer, done five times daily when muezzins call the faithful to pray, facing Mecca and ideally in a mosque.

Sawm (fasting) Ramadan commemorates the revelation of the Qur'an to Mohammed, and is the month when Muslims fast from dawn to dusk.

Shahada (the profession of faith) 'There is no God but Allah, and Mohammed is his Prophet' is the fundamental tenet of Islam.

Zakat (alms) Giving to the poor is an essential part of Islamic social teaching.

Most East African Muslims are Sunnis, with a small minority of Shiites, primarily among the Asian community. The most influential of the various Shiite sects represented are the Ismailis, followers of the Aga Khan.

Traditional Religions

Erupting volcanoes, snow-covered peaks, torrential rains, scorching drought – for most East Africans, how else could any of these be explained other than with reference to a deity or the spirits? The natural and spiritual worlds are part of the same continuum in East Africa, and mountain peaks, lakes, forests, certain trees – these and many more natural features – are viewed as dwellings of the supreme being or of the ancestors.

Most local traditional beliefs acknowledge the existence of a supreme deity. Many also hold that communication with this deity is possible through the intercession of the ancestors. The ancestors are thus accordingly honoured, and viewed as playing a strong role in protecting the tribe and family – maintaining

Former Kenyan president Jomo Kenyatta once argued that FGM was such an integral part of initiation rites and Kikuyu identity that its abolition would destroy the tribal system.

RESPONSIBLE TRAVEL – CONDUCT IN EAST AFRICA

East Africa comfortably mixes a generally conservative outlook on life with a great deal of tolerance and openness towards foreigners, and meeting locals is one of the highlights of regional travel. Following are a few tips to smooth the way.

- While most East Africans are likely to be too polite to tell you so directly, they'll be privately shaking their head about travellers doing things like not wearing enough clothing or sporting tatty clothes. Especially along the Muslim coast, cover up the shoulders and legs, and avoid plunging necklines, skin-tight fits and the like.

- Pleasantries count. Even if you're just asking for directions, take time to greet the other person. Handshake etiquette is also worth learning, and best picked up by observation. In many areas, East Africans often continue holding hands for several minutes after meeting, or even throughout an entire conversation.

- Don't eat or pass things with the left hand.

- Respect authority; losing your patience or undermining an official's authority will get you nowhere, while deference and a good-natured demeanour will see you through most situations.

- Avoid criticising the government of your host country, and avoid offending locals with public nudity, open anger and public displays of affection (between people of the same or opposite sex).

- When visiting a rural area, seek out the chief or local elders to announce your presence, and ask permission before setting up a tent or wandering through a village – it will rarely be refused.

- Receive gifts with both hands, or with the right hand while touching the left hand to your right elbow. Giving a gift? Don't be surprised if the appreciation isn't expressed verbally.

FEMALE GENITAL MUTILATION

Female genital mutilation (FGM) – often euphemistically referred to as 'female circumcision' – is the partial or total removal of the female external genitalia. In Kenya, an estimated one-third of women – most in the northeast, near Somalia – have undergone FGM. In Tanzania, the figures are estimated at between 10% and 18%, while in Uganda, it's about 5%.

Female genital mutilation is usually carried out for reasons of cultural or gender identity, and is entrenched in tribal life in some areas. Longstanding traditional beliefs about hygiene, aesthetics and health also play a role in the continuance of FGM. Yet among the very real risks of the procedure are infection, shock and haemorrhage, as well as lifelong complications and pain with menstruation, urination, intercourse and childbirth. For women who have had infibulation – in which all or part of the external genitalia are removed, and the vaginal opening then narrowed and stitched together – unassisted childbirth is impossible, and many women and children die as a consequence.

Since the mid-1990s there have been major efforts to reduce the incidence of the practice, with slow but real progress.

In both Kenya and Tanzania, FGM has been declared illegal, although the number of prosecutions are small and the practice continues in many areas. Particularly in Kenya, several nongovernmental women's organisations have taken a leading role in bringing FGM to the forefront of media discussion. There is also a growing movement towards alternative rites that offer the chance to maintain traditions while minimising the health complications, such as *ntanira na mugambo* (circumcision through words).

In Uganda, FGM has been condemned by the government, and while it is not yet officially illegal, womens' groups have recently renewed their demands to the high court that it be declared so. The main area where the practice continues is the northeast, where support is waning and where local community leaders have declared that they want to eradicate it completely within the next decade.

proper relations is essential for general well-being. However, among the Maasai, the Kikuyu and several other tribes, there is no tradition of ancestor worship, with the supreme deity (known as Ngai or Enkai) the sole focus of devotion.

Traditional medicine in East Africa is closely intertwined with traditional religion, with practitioners using divining implements, prayers, chanting and dance to facilitate communication with the spirit world.

ARTS
Architecture

East Africa is an architectural treasure trove, with its colonial-era buildings and religious architecture, including both churches and mosques. The real highlights, however, are the old town areas of Zanzibar and Lamu (both Unesco World Heritage Sites) and of Mombasa – all of which display mesmerising combinations of Indian, Arabic, European and African characteristics in their buildings and street layouts.

In Lamu, Pate and elsewhere along the coast, Swahili architecture predominates. At the simplest level, Swahili dwellings are plain rectangular mud and thatch constructions, set in clusters and divided by small, sandy paths. More elaborate stone houses are traditionally constructed of coral and wood along a north–south axis, with flat roofs and a small open courtyard in the centre, which serves as the main source of light.

The various quarters or neighbourhoods in Swahili towns are symbolically united by a central mosque, usually referred to as the *msikiti wa Ijumaa* (Friday mosque). In a sharp break with Islamic architectural custom elsewhere, traditional Swahili mosques don't have minarets; the muezzin gives the call to prayer from inside the mosque, generally with the help of a loudspeaker.

Cinema

East Africa's long languishing and traditionally under-funded film industry received a major boost with the opening of the Zanzibar International Film Festival (ZIFF, p255), which has been held annually on Zanzibar island since 1998, and continues to be one of the region's premier cultural events. The festival serves as a venue for artists from the Indian Ocean basin and beyond, and has had several local prize winners, including *Maangamizi – The Ancient One*, shot in Tanzania and co-directed by Tanzanian Martin M'hando. M'hando is also known for his film, *Mama Tumaini* (Women of Hope). Other regional winners have included *Makaburi Yatasema* (Only the Stones are Talking), about AIDS and directed by Chande Omar Omar, and *Fimbo ya Baba* (Father's Stick), a 2006 Chande Omar Omar production focusing on AIDS. In 2005 Tanzania's Beatrix Mugishawe won acclaim (and two prizes) for *Tumaini*, which focuses on AIDS orphans.

> The ZIFF website (www .ziff.or.tz) is a good jumping off point into the world of East African cinema.

Rwandan Eric Kabera is known worldwide for his *Keepers of Memory, 100 Days* (produced together with Nick Hughes), and *Through My Eyes*, all documenting the Rwandan genocide and its aftermath, and also ZIFF award winners.

Another notable East African cinematographer is Tanzanian Flora M'mbugu-Schelling, who won acclaim for *These Hands*, a short but powerful documentary focusing on the life of Mozambican women refugees working by crushing rocks in a quarry near Dar es Salaam.

For more on films from the region, see the country chapters.

Literature

East Africa's first known Swahili manuscript is an epic poem dating from 1728 and written in Arabic script. However, it wasn't until the second half of the 20th century – once Swahili had become established as a regional language – that Swahili prose began to develop. One of the best known authors from this period was Tanzanian Shaaban Robert; see p87.

> Although Swahili prose got a relatively late start, Swahili oral poetry traditions have long roots. Check out www.humnet .ucla.edu/humnet/aflang /swahili/SwahiliPoetry /index.htm for more.

In more recent years there has been a flowering of English-language titles by East African writers, including *Weep Not, Child* and *Detained: A Prison Writer's Diary*, both by Kenyan Ngugi wa Thiong'o; *Song of Lawino* by Ugandan Okot p'Bitek; *Abyssinian Chronicles* by Ugandan Moses Isegawa; and *Desertion* by Zanzibari Abdulrazak Gurnah. See the country chapters for more on these and other authors.

There is also a rich but often overlooked body of English-language literature by East African women, particularly in Uganda, where women writers have organised as **Femrite** (www.femriteug.org), the Ugandan Women Writers' Association. Some names to watch out for include Mary Karooro Okurut, whose *A Woman's Voice: An Anthology of Short Stories by Ugandan Women* provides a good overview, and the internationally recognised Kenyan writer Grace Ogot, known in particular for *The Promised Land*.

Music & Dance

The single greatest influence on the modern East African music scene has been the Congolese bands that began playing in Dar es Salaam and Nairobi in the early 1960s, and which brought the styles of rumba and soukous into the East African context. Among the best known is Orchestre Super Matimila, which was propelled to fame by the renowned Congolese-born and Dar es Salaam-based Remmy Ongala ('Dr Remmy'). Many of his songs (most are in Swahili) are commentaries on contemporary themes such as AIDS, poverty and hunger, and – while he's less active these days due to failing health – Ongala has been a major force over the past decades in popularising music from the region beyond Africa's borders. Another of the Congolese bands is Samba Mapangala's Orchestra Virunga. Mapangala, a Congolese vocalist, first gained a footing in Uganda in the mid-1970s with a group known as Les Kinois before moving to Nairobi and forming Orchestra Virunga.

As Swahili lyrics replaced the original vocals, a distinct East African rumba style was born. Its proponents include Simba Wanyika (together with offshoot Les Wanyika), which had its roots in Tanzania, but gained fame in the nightclubs of Nairobi.

In the 1970s Kenyan benga music rose to prominence on the regional music scene. It originated among the Luo of western Kenya and is characterised by its clear electric guitar licks and bounding bass rhythms. Its ethnic roots were maintained, however, with the guitar taking the place of the traditional *nyatiti* (folk lyre), and the bass guitar replacing the drum, which originally was played by the *nyatiti* player with a toe ring. One of the best-known proponents of benga has been DO Misiani, whose group Shirati Jazz has been popular since the 1960s.

In Zanzibar and along the coast, the music scene has long been dominated by *taarab*, which has experienced a major resurgence in recent years, and which gets airplay in other parts of the region as well. For more, see boxed text, p135.

Throughout East Africa, dance plays a vital role in community life, although masked dance is not as common in most parts of the region as it is in West Africa. A wide variety of drums and rhythms are used depending on the occasion, with many dances serving as expressions of thanks and praise, or as a means of communicating with the ancestors or telling a story. East Africa's most famous dance group is the globally acclaimed Les Tambourinaires du Burundi.

For more about *taarab* music, visit the Dhow Countries Music Academy website (www.zanzibar music.org).

Textiles & Handicrafts

Women throughout East Africa wear brightly coloured lengths of printed cotton cloth, typically with Swahili sayings printed along the edge and known as *kanga* in Kenya, Tanzania and parts of Uganda. Many of the sayings are social commentary or messages – often indirectly worded, or containing puns and double meanings – that are communicated by the woman wearing the *kanga*, generally to other women. Others are simply a local form of advertising, such as those bearing the logo of political parties.

In coastal areas, you'll also see the *kikoi*, which is made of a thicker textured cotton, usually featuring striped or plaid patterns, and traditionally worn by men. Also common are batik-print cottons depicting everyday scenes, animal motifs or geometrical patterns.

A guide to *kanga* sayings: www.glcom.com/has san/kanga.html.

Jewellery, especially beaded jewellery, is particularly beautiful among the Maasai and the Turkana. It is used in ceremonies as well as in everyday life, and often indicates the wearer's wealth and marital status.

Basketry and woven items – all of which have highly functional roles in local society – also make lovely souvenirs.

Visual Arts

PAINTING

In comparison with woodcarving (see below), painting has a fairly low profile in East Africa. One of the more popular styles is Tanzania's Tingatinga painting (p89).

SCULPTURE & WOODCARVING

East Africa is renowned for its exceptional figurative art, especially that of Tanzania's Makonde, who are acclaimed throughout the region for their skill at bringing blocks of hard African blackwood (*Dalbergia melanoxylon* or, in Swahili, *mpingo*) to life in often highly fanciful depictions. Among the most common carvings are those with *ujamaa* motifs, and those known as *shetani,* which embody images from the spirit world. *Ujamaa* carvings are designed as a totem pole or 'tree of life' containing interlaced human and animal figures around a common ancestor. Each generation is connected to those that preceded it, and gives support to those that follow. Tree of life carvings often reach several metres in height, and are almost always made from a single piece of wood. *Shetani* carvings are much more abstract, and even grotesque, with the emphasis on challenging viewers to new interpretations while giving the carver's imagination free reign.

For more on one of East Africa's up-and-coming musicians, see www.myspace.com/mauricekirya.

FOOD & DRINK

It would be easy to come away from East Africa thinking that the region subsists on rice or *ugali* (one of the main staples) and sauce. But if you hunt around, there are some treats to be discovered. In general, the best cuisine is found along the coast, where savoury seafood dishes cooked with coconut milk, coriander and other spices are a speciality. Inland, watch for grilled meat kebabs and tilapia (Nile perch). Otherwise, meals tend to centre around a staple with beans or sauce, but lively local atmosphere and hospitality compensate for the frequently bland offerings.

Staples & Specialities

Vendors hawk grilled maize, or deep-fried yams seasoned with a squeeze of lemon juice and a dash of chilli powder. Sticks of *pweza* (octopus) sizzle over the coals. Women squat near large, piping-hot pots of super-sweet *uji* (millet porridge). Other streetside favourites include *sambusas* (deep-fried pastry triangles stuffed with spiced mince meat – but be sure they haven't been sitting around too long), *maandazi* (semi-sweet doughnut-like products) and *chipsi mayai* – a puffy omelette with chips mixed in. *Nyama choma* (seasoned barbecued meat) is found throughout the region, but is especially popular in Kenya. Whether for the taste or simply the ambience, the street-food scene is one of the highlights of travelling in East Africa, as well as a mainstay of the local cuisine scene.

For dozens of links on art in Africa, including East Africa, check Columbia University's Art and Archaeology of Africa page (www.columbia.edu/cu/lweb/indiv/africa/cuvl/AfArt.html) or the similar www.library.stanford.edu/africa/art.html.

For sit-down meals, one of the most common staples is *ugali* – a thick, filling dough-like mass made from maize or cassava flour, or both, and known as *posho* in Uganda. Especially around Lake Victoria, the staple is just as likely to be *matoke* (cooked plantains), while along the coast, women shred coconuts with a *mbuzi* (literally, a 'goat' – a wooden stool with a protruding neck with a sharp metal edge) and prepare rice with coconut milk. Whatever the staple, it's always accompanied by a sauce, usually with a piece of meat floating around in it.

Three meals a day is the norm, with the main meal eaten at midday and breakfast frequently nothing more than tea or instant coffee and packaged white bread. In out-of-the way areas, many places are closed in the evening and street food is often the only option.

Drinks

Tap water is best avoided. Also be wary of ice and fruit juices that may have been diluted with unpurified water. Bottled water is widely available, except in remote areas, where it's worth carrying a filter or purification tablets.

Sodas (soft drinks) – especially Coca Cola and Fanta – are found almost everywhere, even where bottled water isn't. Freshly squeezed juices, especially pineapple, sugar cane and orange, are a treat, although check first to see whether they have been mixed with unsafe water. Local milkshakes are also worth hunting for – fresh juice, chilled milk and syrup. Also refreshing, and never a worry hygienically, is the juice of the *dafu* (green) coconut. Western-style supermarkets sell imported fruit juices.

Although East Africa exports high-quality coffee and tea, what's usually available locally is far inferior, and instant coffee is the norm. Both tea and coffee are generally drunk with lots of milk and sugar. On the coast, sip a smooth spiced tea (chai masala) or sample a coffee sold by vendors strolling the streets carrying a freshly brewed pot in one hand, cups and spoons in the other.

Among the most common beers are the locally brewed Tusker, Primus and Kilimanjaro, and South Africa's Castle Lager, which is also produced locally. Especially in Kenya, many locals prefer their beer warm, so getting a cold beer can be a task.

Kenya and Tanzania have small and very fledgling wine industries, although neither will be putting wine importers out of business anytime soon.

Locally produced home brews are widely available – fermented mixtures made with bananas or millet and sugar. However, avoid anything distilled – in addition to being illegal, it's also often lethal.

Where to Eat & Drink

For dining local style, take a seat in a small local eatery, known as *hoteli* in Swahili-speaking areas, and watch life pass by. The day's menu – rarely costing more than US$1 – is usually written on a chalkboard. Rivalling *hoteli* for local atmosphere are the bustling night markets found in many areas, where vendors set up grills along the roadside and sell *nyama choma* and other street food.

For Western-style meals, stick to cities or main towns, where there's usually an array of restaurants, most moderately priced compared with their European counterparts. Every capital city has at least one Chinese restaurant. In many parts of East Africa, especially along the coast, around Lake Victoria and in Uganda, there's usually also a selection of Indian cuisine – found both at inexpensive eateries serving Indian snacks, as well as in pricier restaurants. Supermarkets in main towns sell imported products, such as canned meat, fish and cheese.

These Hands and *From Sun Up* – both directed by Flora M'mbugu-Schelling – give insights into the lives of women in East Africa.

Vegetarians & Vegans

While there isn't much in East Africa that is specifically billed as 'vegetarian', there are many veggie options, and you can find cooked rice and beans almost everywhere. The main challenges will be keeping some variety and balance in your diet and getting enough protein, especially if you don't eat eggs or seafood. In larger towns, Indian restaurants are the best places to try for vegetarian meals. Elsewhere, try asking Indian shop owners if they have any suggestions; many will also be able to help you find fresh yoghurt. Peanuts and cashews are widely available, and fresh fruits and vegetables are abundant in most areas. If you eat seafood, you'll have no problems along the coast or near any of the lakes, and even in inland areas good fish is often available from rivers and streams. Most tour operators are willing to cater to special dietary requests, such as vegetarian, kosher or halal, with advance notice.

For an overview of the East African music scene: http://members.aol .com/dpaterson/eamusic .htm

Eating with Children

Dining out with children is no problem. Hotel restaurants occasionally have high chairs, and while special children's meals aren't common, it's easy enough to find items that are suitable for young diners. Avoid curries and

---

DINING EAST AFRICAN STYLE

If you're invited to join in a meal, the first step is hand washing. Your hostess will bring around a bowl and water jug; hold your hands over the bowl while she pours water over them. Sometimes soap is provided, and a towel for drying off.

At the centre of the meal will be *ugali* (a staple made from maize or cassava flour, or both) or a similar staple, which is normally taken with the right hand from a communal pot, rolled into a small ball with the fingers, dipped into some sort of sauce and eaten. Eating with your hand is a bit of an art and may seem awkward at first, but after a few tries it will start to feel more natural. It's worth persevering. Note that food is never handled or eaten with the left hand, and in some areas it is even considered impolite to give someone something with the left hand.

The underlying element in all meal invitations is solidarity between the hosts and the guests, and the various customs, such as eating out of a communal dish, are simply expressions of this. If you receive an invitation to eat but aren't hungry, it's OK to explain that you have just eaten. However, still share a few bites of the meal in order to demonstrate your solidarity with the hosts, and to express your appreciation.

At the end of the meal, don't be worried if you can't finish what is on your plate, as this shows your hosts that you have been satisfied. However, try to avoid being the one who takes the last handful from the communal bowl, as this may leave your hosts thinking that they haven't provided enough.

Except for fruit, desserts are rarely served; meals conclude with another round of hand washing. Thank your hostess by saying *chakula kizuri* or *chakula kitamu*.

---

other spicy dishes, uncooked, unpeeled fruits and vegetables, meat from street vendors (as it's sometimes undercooked) and unpurified water. Supermarkets stock child-size boxes of fresh juice, and fresh fruits (tangerines, bananas and more) are widely available. Also see p605.

Habits & Customs

Meals connected with any sort of social occasion are usually drawn-out affairs for which the women of the household will have spent several days preparing. Typical East African style is to eat with the (right) hand from communal dishes in the centre of the table. There will always be somewhere to wash your hands – either a basin and pitcher of water that are passed around, or a sink in the corner of the room. Although food is shared, it's not customary to share drinks, and children generally eat their meals separately.

Street snacks and meals-on-the-run are common. European-style restaurant dining – while readily available in major cities – is not an entrenched part of local culture. Much more common are large gatherings at home, or perhaps at a rented hall, to celebrate special occasions, with the meal as the focal point.

Throughout East Africa, lunch is served between about noon and 2.30pm, and dinner from about 6.30pm or 7pm to 10pm, The smaller the town, the earlier its dining establishments are likely to close; after about 7pm in rural areas it can be difficult to find anything other than street food. During Ramadan, many restaurants in coastal areas close completely during daylight fasting hours.

Eat Your Words

The following Swahili words and phrases will help in Kenya, Tanzania and some parts of Uganda. For pronunciation guidelines, see p636. Also see Lonely Planet's *Swahili* and *French* phrasebooks.

Although cash is becoming an increasingly common replacement, cattle are still a coveted bride price in many parts of East Africa.

USEFUL PHRASES

I'm vegetarian.	*Nakula mboga tu.* (I just eat vegetables.)
I don't eat meat.	*Mimi sili nyama.*
Is there a restaurant near here?	*Je, kuna hoteli ya chakula hapo jirani?*
Do you serve food here?	*Mnauza chakula hapa?*
I'd like ...	*Ninataka/Ninaomba ...*
Without hot pepper, please.	*Bila pilipili, tafadhali.*
Please bring me the bill.	*Nipe bili/risiti tafadhali.*

MENU DECODER

biryani – casserole of spices and rice with meat or seafood
maandazi – semi-sweet, flat doughnuts
matoke – cooked plantains
mchuzi – sauce, sometimes with bits of beef and very well-cooked vegetables
mishikaki – kebab
ndizi – banana
nyama choma – roasted meat
pilau – spiced rice cooked in broth with seafood or meat and vegetables
supu – soup usually somewhat greasy, and served with a piece of beef, pork or meat fat in it
ugali – thick, porridge-like maize- or cassava-based staple, available almost everywhere, and known as *posho* in Uganda
wali na kuku/samaki/nyama/maharagwe – cooked white rice with chicken/fish/meat/beans

ENGLISH–SWAHILI GLOSSARY

Basics

cold	*baridi*
cup	*kikombe*
fork	*uma*
hot	*ya moto*
knife	*kisu*
napkin	*kitambaa cha mikono*
plate	*sahani*
spoon	*kijiko*
sweet	*tamu*

Staples

beans	*maharagwe*
bread	*mkate*
chips	*chipsi*
plantains	*ndizi ya kupika* or (when cooked and mashed) *matoke*
potatoes	*viazi*
rice (cooked)	*wali*

Other dishes & condiments

eggs (boiled)	*mayai (ya kuchemsha)*
salt	*chumvi*
sugar	*sukari*
yoghurt	*mgando, mtindi, maziwalala,* maziwa ganda

Meat & Seafood

beef	*nyama ya ng'ombe*
chicken	*kuku*
crab	*kaa*
fish	*samaki*
goat	*nyama mbuzi*
pork	*nyama ya nguruwe*
octopus	*pweza* (usually served grilled, at street markets)

Fruits & Vegetables

banana	*ndizi*
coconut (green)	*dafu*
coconut (ripe)	*nazi*
fruit	*matunda*
mango	*embe*
onions	*vitunguu*
orange	*chungwa*
papaya	*papai*
pineapple	*nanasi*
spinach (boiled)	*sukuma wiki*
tomatoes	*nyana*
vegetables	*mboga*

Drinks

beer (cold)	*bia (baridi)*
orange juice	*jusi ya machungwa*
soda	*soda*
water (boiled/drinking/mineral)	*maji (yaliyochemshwa/kwenye chupa/ya madini)*

TRIBAL CULTURES

East Africa has a rich mosaic of tribal cultures, with over 300 different groups packed into an area roughly a quarter the size of Australia. The vitality of their traditions is expressed in everything from splendid ceremonial attire to pulsating dance rhythms, refined artistry and highly organised community structures, and experiencing these is likely to be among the highlights of your travels. Following are short profiles of several groups.

AKAMBA

The Akamba – at home in the area east of Nairobi towards Tsavo National Park – are relative newcomers to East Africa, having first migrated here from the south about 200 years ago in search of food. Because their own low-altitude land was poor, they were forced to barter to obtain food stocks from the neighbouring Maasai and Kikuyu. Soon, they acquired a reputation as savvy traders, with business dealings extending from the coast as far inland as Lake Victoria and north to Lake Turkana. Renowned for their martial prowess, many Akamba were drafted into Britain's WWI army, and today are still well represented among Kenyan defence and law enforcement brigades.

Turkana: Kenya's Nomads of the Jade Sea by Nigel Pavitt is a photo-documentation of one of East Africa's most colourful tribes.

In the 1930s, during the height of the colonial-era, the British administration settled large numbers of white farmers in traditional Akamba lands and tried to limit the number of cattle the Akamba could own by confiscating them. In protest, the Akamba formed the Ukamba Members Association, which marched en masse to Nairobi and squatted peacefully at Kariokor Market until their cattle were returned. Large numbers of Akamba were subsequently dispossessed to make way for Tsavo National Park.

All Akamba go through initiation rites at about the age of 12, and have the same age set groups common to many of the region's peoples (see boxed text, opposite). Young parents are known as 'junior elders' (*mwanake* for men, *mwiitu* for women) and are responsible for the maintenance and upkeep of the village. They later become 'medium elders' (*nthele*), and then 'full elders' (*atumia ma kivalo*), with responsibility for death ceremonies and administering the law. The last stage of a person's life is that of 'senior elder' (*atumia ma kisuka*), with responsibility for holy places.

AGE SETS

Age-based groups – in which all youths of the same age belong to an age set, and pass through the various stages of life and their associated rituals together – continue to play an important role in tribal life throughout much of East Africa. Each group has its own leader and community responsibilities, and definition of the age sets is often highly refined. Among the Sukuma, for example, who live in the area south of Lake Victoria, each age-based group traditionally had its own system for counting from one to 10, with the system understood by others within the group, but not by members of any other group. Among the Maasai, who have one of the most highly stratified age group systems in the region, males are organised into age sets and further into subsets, with inter-set rivalries and relationships one of the defining features of daily life.

BAGANDA

Uganda's largest tribal group, the Baganda comprise almost 20% of the population, and are the source of the country's name ('Land of the Baganda'; their kingdom is known as Buganda). Although today the Baganda are spread throughout the country, their traditional lands are in the areas north and northwest of Lake Victoria, including Kampala. Thanks to significant missionary activity most Baganda are Christian, although animist traditions persist.

The Baganda, together with the neighbouring Haya, have a historical reputation as one of East Africa's most highly organised tribes. Their traditional political system was based around the absolute power of the *kabaka* (king), who ruled through district chiefs. This system reached its zenith during the 19th century, when the Baganda came to dominate various neighbouring groups, including the Nilotic Iteso (who now comprise about 8% of Uganda's population). Baganda influence was solidified during the colonial era, with the British favouring their recruitment to the civil service. During the chaotic Obote/Amin years of the late 1960s and early 1970s, the Bagandan monarchy was abolished, to be restored in 1993, although with no political power.

EL-MOLO

The Cushitic-speaking El-Molo are one of East Africa's smallest tribes, numbering less than 4000. Historically the El-Molo were one of the region's more distinct groups, but in recent times they have been forced to adapt or relinquish many of their old customs in order to survive, and intermarriage with members of other tribes is now common.

The El-Molo – whose ancestral home is on two small islands in the middle of Kenya's Lake Turkana – traditionally subsisted on fish, supplemented by the occasional crocodile, turtle, hippopotamus or bird. Over the years an ill-balanced diet and the effects of too much fluoride began to take their toll. The El-Molo became increasingly susceptible to disease and, thus weakened, to attacks from stronger tribes. Their numbers plummeted.

Today, while the El-Molo have temporarily stabilised their population, they face an uncertain future. While some continue to eke out a living from the lake, others have turned to cattle herding or work in the tourism industry. Commercial fishing supplements their traditional subsistence and larger, more permanent settlements in Loyangalani, on Lake Turkana's southeastern shores, have replaced the El-Molo's traditional dome-shaped island homes.

HAYA

The Haya, who live west of Lake Victoria around Bukoba, have both Bantu and Nilotic roots, and are one of the largest tribes in Tanzania. The Haya also have an exceptionally rich history, and in the pre-colonial era boasted one of the most highly developed early societies on the continent.

At the heart of traditional Haya society were eight different states or kingdoms, each headed by a powerful and often despotic *mukama* who ruled in part by divine right. Order was maintained through a system of appointed chiefs and officials, assisted by an age group-based army. With the rise of European influence in the region, this era of Haya history came to an end. The various groups began to splinter, and many chiefs were replaced by persons considered more malleable and sympathetic to colonial interests.

Resentment of these propped-up leaders was strong, spurring the Haya to regroup and form the Bukoba Bahaya Union in 1924. This association was initially directed towards local political reform but soon developed into the more influential and broad-based African Association. Together with similar groups established elsewhere in Tanzania it constituted one of the country's earliest political movements and was an important force in the drive towards independence.

Today the Haya are renowned dancers and singers, and count East African pop stars Saida Karoli and Maua among their numbers.

KALENJIN

The Kalenjin people are one of the largest groups in Kenya and – together with the Kikuyu, Luo, Luyha and Kamba – account for about 70% of the country's population. Although often viewed as a single ethnic entity, the term 'Kalenjin' was actually coined in the 1950s to refer to a loose collection of several different Nilotic groups, including the Kipsigis, Nandi, Marakwet, Pokot and Tugen (Former Kenyan president Daniel arap Moi's people). These groups speak different dialects of the same language (Nandi), but otherwise have distinct traditions and lifestyles. Thanks to the influence of arap Moi, the Kalenjin have amassed considerable political power in Kenya. They are also known for their female herbalist doctors, and for their many world-class runners.

> Swahili is spoken in more countries and by more people than any other language in sub-Saharan Africa.

The traditional homeland of the various Kalenjin peoples is along the western edge of the central Rift Valley area, including Kericho, Eldoret, Kitale, Baringo and the land surrounding Mt Elgon. Originally pastoralists, Kalenjin today are known primarily as farmers. An exception to this are the cattle-loving Kipsigi, whose cattle rustling continues to cause friction between them and neighbouring tribes.

The Nandi, who are the second largest of the Kalenjin communities, and comprise about one-third of all Kalenjin, settled in the Nandi Hills between the 16th and 17th centuries, where they prospered after learning agricultural techniques from the Luo and Luyha. They had a formidable military reputation and, in the late 19th century, managed to delay construction of the Uganda railway for more than a decade until Koitalel, their chief, was killed.

As with many tribes, the Kalenjin have age set groups into which a man is initiated after circumcision. Administration of the law is carried out at the *kok,* an informal court led by the clan's elders.

KARAMOJONG

The marginalised Karamojong – at home in Karamoja, in northeastern Uganda – are one of East Africa's most insulated, beleaguered and colourful tribes. As with the Samburu, Maasai and other Nilotic pastoralist peoples, life for the Karamojong centres around cattle, who are kept at night in the centre of the family living compound and grazed by day on the surrounding plains. Cattle are the main measure of wealth, ownership is a mark of adulthood, and cattle raiding and warfare are central parts of the culture. When cattle are grazed in dry-season camps away from the family homestead, the Karamojong warriors tending them live on blood from live cattle, milk and sometimes meat. In times of scarcity, protection of the herd is considered so important that milk is reserved for calves and children.

Long the subject of often heavy-handed government pressure to abandon their pastoralist lifestyle, the Karamojong's plight has been exacerbated by periodic famines, and by the loss of traditional dry-season grazing areas with the formation of Kidepo National Park in the 1960s. While current Ugandan president Yoweri Museveni has permitted the Karamojong to keep arms to protect themselves against raids from other groups, including the Turkana in neighbouring Kenya, government expeditions targeted at halting cattle raiding continue. These, combined with easy access to weapons from neighbouring Sudan and a breakdown of law and order, have made the Karamoja area off-limits to outsiders in recent years.

KIKUYU

The Kikuyu, who comprise about 20% of Kenya's population and are the country's largest tribal group, have their heartland surrounding Mt Kenya. They are Bantu peoples who are believed to have migrated into the area from the east and northeast from around the 16th century onwards, and to have undergone several periods of intermarriage and splintering. According to the rich oral traditions of the Kikuyu, there are nine original clans (*mwaki*), all of which trace their origins back to male and female progenitors known as Kikuyu and Mumbi. The administration of these clans, each of which is made up of many family groups (*nyumba*), was originally overseen by a council of elders, with great significance placed on the roles of the witch doctor, medicine man and blacksmith.

Initiation rites consist of ritual circumcision for boys and clitoridectomy for girls, though the latter is becoming less common. The practice of clitoridectomy was a source of particular conflict between the Kikuyu and Western missionaries during the late 19th and early 20th centuries. The issue eventually became linked with the independence struggle, and the establishment of independent Kikuyu schools.

The Kikuyu god, Ngai, is believed to reside on Mt Kenya, and many Kikuyu homes are still oriented to face the sacred peak.

The Kikuyu are also known for the opposition association they formed in the 1920s to protest European seizure of large areas of their lands, and for their subsequent instigation of the Mau Mau rebellion in the 1950s. Due to the influence of Jomo Kenyatta, Kenya's first president, the Kikuyu today are disproportionately represented in government – President Mwai Kibaki is a Kikuyu – and business. This has proved to be a source of ongoing friction with other groups, and a persistent stumbling block on Kenya's path to national integration.

LUO

The tribe of US president Barack Obama's father, the Luo live on the northeastern shores of Lake Victoria. The Luo people began their migration to the area from Sudan around the 15th century. Although their numbers are relatively small in Tanzania, in Kenya they comprise about 12% of the population and are the country's third largest group.

During the independence struggle, many of Kenya's leading politicians and trade unionists were Luo, including Tom Mboya (assassinated in 1969) and the former vice-president Jaramogi Oginga Odinga, and they continue to form the backbone of the Kenyan political opposition. Kenya's current prime minister, Raila Odinga, is also a Luo.

The Luo have also had a decisive influence on the East African musical scene. They are notable in particular for their contribution to the highly popular *benga* style, which has since been adopted by musicians from many other tribes.

The Luo were originally cattle herders, but the devastating effects of rinderpest in the 1890s forced them to adopt fishing and subsistence agriculture, which continue to be the main sources of livelihood of most Luo today. Luo family groups consist of the man, his wife or wives, and their sons and daughters-in-law. The family unit is part of a larger grouping of families or *dhoot* (clan), several of which in turn make up *ogandi* (a group of geographically related people), each led by a *ruoth* (chief). Traditional Luo living compounds, which you'll still see when travelling around Lake Victoria, are enclosed by fences, and include separate huts for the man and for each wife and son. The Luo view age, wealth and respect as converging, with the result that elders control family resources and represent the family to the outside world.

> Instead of circumcision, the Luo traditionally extracted four to six teeth at initiation.

MAASAI

Although comprising less than 5% of the population in Kenya and Tanzania, it is the Maasai, more than any other tribe, who have become for many the quintessential symbol of 'tribal' East Africa. With a reputation (often exaggerated) as fierce warriors, and a proud demeanour, they have insisted on maintaining their ethnic identity and traditional lifestyle, often in the face of great government opposition. Today the life of the Maasai continues to be inextricably bound with that of their large herds of cattle, which they graze along the Tanzania–Kenya border.

The Maasai are Nilotic people who first migrated to the region from Sudan about 1000 years ago. They eventually came to dominate a large area of what is now central Kenya until, in the late 19th century, their numbers were decimated by famine and disease, and their cattle herds routed by rinderpest.

During the colonial era in Kenya, it was largely Maasai land that was taken for European colonisation through two controversial treaties. The creation of Serengeti National Park in Tanzania and the continuing colonial annexation of Maasai territory put much of the remaining traditional grazing lands of the Maasai off-limits. During subsequent years, as populations of both the Maasai and their cattle increased, pressure for land became intense and conflict with the authorities was constant. Government-sponsored resettlement programs have met with only limited success, as Maasai traditions scorn agriculture and land ownership.

One consequence of this competition for land is that many Maasai ceremonial traditions can no longer be fulfilled. Part of the ceremony where a man becomes a *moran* (warrior) involves a group of young men around the age of 14 going out and building a small livestock camp after their circumcision ceremony. They then live alone there for up to eight years before returning to the village to marry. Today, while the tradition and will survive, land is often unavailable.

The Maasai have vibrant artistic traditions that are most vividly seen in the striking body decoration and beaded ornaments worn by both men and women. Women in particular are famous for their magnificent beaded plate-like necklaces, while men typically wear the red-checked *shuka* (blanket) and carry a distinctive balled club.

While tourism provides an income to an increasing number of Maasai, the benefits are not widespread. In recent years many Maasai have moved to the cities or coastal resorts, becoming guards for restaurants and hotels.

The Samburu people who live directly north of Mt Kenya are closely related to the Maasai linguistically and culturally.

MAKONDE

Although they have their home in one of the most isolated areas of East Africa, the Makonde have gained fame throughout the region and beyond for their beautiful and highly refined ebony woodcarvings.

The tribe has its origins in northern Mozambique, where many Makonde still live, although in recent years a subtle split has begun to develop between the group's Tanzanian and Mozambican branches. Today most Tanzanian Makonde live in southeastern Tanzania on the Makonde plateau, although many members of the carving community have since migrated to Dar es Salaam.

Like many of their southern Tanzanian neighbours, the Makonde are matrilineal. Although customs are gradually changing, children and inheritances normally belong to the woman, and it's still common for husbands to move to the villages of their wives after marriage. Makonde settlements are widely scattered – possibly a remnant of the days when the Makonde sought to evade slave raids – and there is no tradition of a unified political system. Despite this, a healthy sense of tribal identity has managed to survive. Makonde villages are typically governed by a hereditary chief and a council of elders. The Makonde traditionally practised body scarring, and many elders still sport facial markings and (for women) wooden lip plugs.

Because of their remote location, the Makonde have succeeded in remaining largely insulated from colonial and postcolonial influences. They are known in particular for their steady resistance to Islam. Today most Makonde still adhere to traditional religions, with the complex spirit world given its fullest expression in their carvings.

PARE

The Bantu-speaking Pare people inhabit the Pare mountains in northeastern Tanzania, where they migrated several centuries ago from the Taita Hills area of southern Kenya.

The Pare are one of Tanzania's most educated groups, and despite their small numbers, have been highly influential in shaping the country's recent history. In the 1940s they formed the Wapare Union, which played an important role in Tanzania's drive for independence.

The Pare are also known for their rich oral traditions, and for their elaborate rituals centring on the dead. Near most villages are sacred areas in which skulls of tribal chiefs are kept. When people die, they are believed to inhabit a netherworld between the land of the living and the spirit world. If they are allowed to remain in this state, ill fate will befall their descendants. As a result, rituals allowing the deceased to pass into the world of the ancestors hold great significance. Traditional Pare beliefs also hold that when an adult male dies, others in his lineage will die as well until the cause of his death has been found and 'appeased'. Many of the possible reasons for death have to do with disturbances in moral relations within the lineage or in the village, or with sorcery.

Among the patrilineal Pare, a deceased male's ghost influences all male descendants for as long as the ghost's name is remembered.

SUKUMA & NYAMWEZI

The Sukuma, who live in the southern Lake Victoria region, comprise almost 15% of Tanzania's total population, although it is only relatively recently that they have come to view themselves as a single entity. Bantu speakers, they are closely related to the Nyamwezi, Tanzania's second largest tribal group around Tabora.

The Sukuma are renowned for their sophisticated drumming, and for their skilled and energetic dancing, especially for their hyena, snake and porcupine dances. Among the focal points of tribal life are lively meetings between the two competing dance societies, the Bagika and the Bagulu.

EAST AFRICA'S FOREST DWELLERS

East African society is full of contrasts, but nowhere is the clash between traditional and Western ways of life more apparent than among the region's hunter-gatherer and forest-dwelling peoples. These include the Twa, who live primarily in the western forests of Rwanda and Burundi, where they comprise less than 1% of the overall population, and the Hadzabe, whose traditional lands are in north-central Tanzania around Lake Eyasi. Typically, these communities are among the most marginalised in East African society, lacking political influence and discriminated against by more prominent groups.

For the Twa, the Hadzabe and other communities, loss of land and forest means loss of the only resource base that they have. Over the past decades the rise of commercial logging, the ongoing clearing of forests in favour of agricultural land, and the establishment of parks and conservation areas have combined to dramatically decrease the forest resources and wildlife on which these people depend for their existence. Additional pressures come from hunting and poaching, and from nomadic pastoralists – many of whom in turn have been evicted from their own traditional areas – seeking grazing lands for their cattle. The Hadzabe say that the once plentiful wildlife in their traditional hunting areas is now gone, and that many days they return empty-handed from their daily search for meat. Others lament the fact that once-prized skills such as animal tracking and knowledge of local plants are being relegated to irrelevance.

Although some Hadzabe have turned to tourism and craft making for subsistence, the benefits of this are sporadic and limited in scope. Some now only hunt for benefit of the increasing numbers of tourists who come to their lands, and a few have given up their traditional lifestyle completely. In Rwanda, the Twa have begun mobilising to gain increased political influence and greater access to health care and education. However, throughout the region, it's likely to be at least several decades before these people are given a real voice, and the chance to define their own role in today's East African society.

The Sukuma are also known for their highly structured form of village organisation in which each settlement is subdivided into chiefdoms ruled by a *ntemi* (chief) in collaboration with a council of elders. Divisions of land and labour are made by village committees consisting of similarly aged members from each family in the village. These age-based groups perform numerous roles, ranging from assisting with the building of new houses to farming and other community-oriented work. As a result of this system – which gives most families at least a representational role in many village activities – Sukuma often view houses and land as communal property.

SWAHILI

East Africa's coast is home to the Swahili (People of the Coast) – descendants of Bantu-Arab traders who share a common language and traditions. Although they are generally not regarded as a single tribal group, the Swahili have for centuries had their own distinct societal structures, and consider themselves to be a single civilisation.

Swahili culture first began to take on a defined form around the 11th century, with the rise of Islam. Today almost all Swahili are adherents of Islam, although it's generally a more liberal version than that practised in the Middle East. Thanks to this Islamic identity, the Swahili have traditionally considered themselves as historically and morally distinct from peoples in the interior, and with links eastwards towards the rest of the Muslim world.

Swahili festivals follow the Islamic calendar. The year begins with Eid al-Fitr, a celebration of feasting and almsgiving to mark the end of Ramadan fasting. The old Persian new year's purification ritual of Nauroz or Mwaka was also traditionally celebrated, with the parading of a bull counter clockwise through town followed by its slaughter and several days of exuberant dancing and feasting. In many areas, Nauroz has now become merged with Eid al-Fitr and is no longer celebrated. The festival of *maulidi* (marking the birth of the Prophet) is another major Swahili festival, marked by decorated mosques and colourful street processions.

TURKANA

The Turkana, one of East Africa's most colourful tribes, are a Nilotic people who live in the harsh desert country of northwestern Kenya where they migrated from southern Sudan and northeastern Uganda. Although the Turkana only emerged as a distinct tribal group during the early to mid-19th century, they are notable today for their strong sense of tribal identification. The Turkana are closely related linguistically and culturally to Uganda's Karamojong people.

Like the Samburu and the Maasai (with whom they are also linguistically linked), the Turkana are primarily cattle herders, although in recent years increasing numbers have turned to fishing and subsistence farming. Some also earn a livelihood through basket weaving and producing other crafts for the tourism industry. Personal relationships based on the exchange of cattle, and built up by each herd owner during the course of a lifetime, are of critical importance in Turkana society and function as a social security net during times of need.

Turkana men were traditionally tattooed on the shoulder and upper arm for killing an enemy – the right shoulder for killing a man, the left for a woman.

The Turkana are famous for their striking appearance and traditional garb. Turkana men cover part of their hair with mud, which is then painted blue and decorated with ostrich and other feathers. Despite the intense heat of the Turkana lands, the main garment is a woollen blanket, often with garish checks. Turkana accessories include a stool carved out of a single piece of wood, a wooden fighting staff and a wrist knife. Tattooing is another hallmark of Turkana life. Witch doctors and prophets are held in high regard, and scars on the lower stomach are usually a sign of a witch doctor's attempt to cast out an undesirable spirit.

In addition to personal adornment, other important forms of artistic expression include finely crafted carvings and refined a cappella singing. Ceremonies play a less significant role among the Turkana than among many of their neighbours, and they do not practice circumcision or clitoridectomy.

Environment

THE LAND

Straddling the equator, edged to the east by the Indian Ocean and to the west by a chain of Rift Valley lakes, East Africa is as diverse geographically and environmentally as it is culturally.

Along the coast are coral reefs, white-sand beaches, river deltas teeming with life, littoral forest and – most famously – the Lamu and Zanzibar Archipelagos. This low-lying coastal belt stretches inland for between 15km and 65km before starting to rise, steeply at times, to a vast central plateau averaging between 1000m and 2000m above sea level and extending westwards beyond Rwanda and Burundi. The plateau is punctuated by escarpments, ravines, mountain ranges and lakes, and spliced by the East African rift system, which – in addition to accounting for most of the region's lakes – also gives rise to its highest mountains: glacier-capped Mt Kilimanjaro (5896m) and Mt Kenya (5199m). The Rwenzori Mountains on the Uganda–Democratic Republic of the Congo (DRC; formerly Zaire) border are also a result of rift-system geology, formed where uplift occurred between parallel geological fault lines. Other major mountain ranges include the Eastern Arc chain (in southern Kenya and northeastern Tanzania) and the Aberdare Range (Kenya).

Rimming East Africa's central plateau to the northeast, and extending from central Kenya to the borders of Somalia and Ethiopia, is a vast, trackless area of bushland, scrub and desert, where rainfall is sparse and the land is suitable only for cattle grazing.

> Eastern Arc Mountains Information Source (www.easternarc.org) is an information clearinghouse for the many environmental projects being undertaken in the Eastern Arc range in Kenya and Tanzania.

The Great Rift Valley

Part of the East African rift system, the Great Rift Valley is one of the continent's most outstanding natural features. The rift system – a massive geological fault slicing its way almost 6500km across the African continent, from the Dead Sea in the north to Beira (Mozambique) in the south – was formed more than 30 million years ago when the tectonic plates that comprise the African and Eurasian landmasses collided and then diverged again. As the plates moved apart, massive tablets of the earth's crust collapsed between them, resulting over the millennia in the escarpments, ravines, flatlands and lakes that mark much of East Africa today.

> Since they were first measured in the early 20th century, Kilimanjaro's glaciers have lost over 80% of their ice.

The rift system is especially famous for its calderas and volcanoes (including Mt Kilimanjaro, Mt Meru and the calderas of the Crater Highlands) and for its lakes. Some of these lakes – including Lakes Tanganyika and Nyasa – are very deep, with floors plunging well below sea level, although their surfaces may be several hundred metres above sea level.

The East African section of the Rift Valley consists of two branches formed where the main rift system divides north of Kenya's Lake Turkana. The western branch, or Western Rift Valley, makes its way past Lake Albert in Uganda through Rwanda and Burundi down to Lake Tanganyika, after which it meanders southeast to Lake Nyasa. Seismic and volcanic disturbances still occur throughout the western branch. The eastern branch, known as the Eastern or Gregory Rift, runs south from Lake Turkana past Lake Natron and Lake Manyara in Tanzania before joining again with the Western Rift in northern Malawi. The lakes of the Eastern Rift are smaller and shallower than those in the western branch, with some of them just waterless salt beds.

> Gorillas in the Mist by Dian Fossey offers an intriguing look at the complexities of halting poaching while recounting the author's life among Rwanda's mountain gorillas.

Places where the escarpments of the Rift Valley are particularly impressive include Kenya's Rift Valley Province (p334), the Nkuruman Escarpment east of Kenya's Masai Mara National Reserve (p363), and the terrain around Ngorongoro Conservation Area (p190) and Lake Manyara National Park (p183) in Tanzania.

WILDLIFE

East Africa's primeval natural splendour and untamed rawness are among the region's major drawcards for visitors, and are at the centre of local and international conservation efforts.

Animals

The wildlife that most visitors come to see ranges from the 'Big Five' (lions, buffaloes, elephants, leopards and rhinos) to lesser profile animals such as zebras, hippos, giraffes, wildebeests, antelopes and more, plus major populations of primates. All these are not only impressive to watch, but also are essential linchpins in a beautifully complex natural web where each species has its own niche. The longer you are able to spend on safari in East Africa, and the longer you are able to stay and explore a particular area, the better and more deeply you will be able to glimpse into the natural drama taking place around you. For more on safaris, see p60.

In addition to the large animals, which are present in such high concentration and diversity, other players include over 60,000 insect species, several dozen types of reptiles and amphibians, many snake species and abundant marine life, both in the Indian Ocean, and inland. Lake Tanganyika and Lake Nyasa are notable for having among the highest fish diversities of any lakes in the world, with an exceptionally large number of colourful cichlid species. Completing the picture are close to 1500 different types of birds, including many rare birds, such as the elusive shoebill stork. Uganda alone – which many ornithologists consider to be one of the continent's premier bird-watching destinations – hosts over 1000 bird species within its 236,000 sq km. For a survey of the region's major wildlife species, see p105. See p75 for more on mountain gorillas.

In Battle for the Elephants, *Iain and Oria Douglas-Hamilton describe with harsh clarity the ongoing political battles over elephants and the ivory trade in Africa.*

ENDANGERED SPECIES

Black rhinos have gained one of the highest profiles among East Africa's endangered species, with their horns coveted for use in traditional medicines in Asia and for dagger handles in Yemen. Thanks to major conservation efforts, black rhino numbers are again on the rise, although there are still very few in the wild. Rhino sanctuaries and breeding areas include those in Mkomazi Game Reserve (p159), Tsavo West National Park (p297) and Lake Nakuru National Park (p340). Otherwise, Tanzania's Ngorongoro Crater (p192) is one of the best places for trying to spot one.

*The grey-faced sengi (*Rhynochocyon udzungwensis*) – a newly-discovered species of elephant shrew – is at home in Tanzania's Udzungwa Mountains.*

DON'T FEED THE ELEPHANTS

One of East Africa's major attractions is the chance to get 'up close and personal' with the wildlife. Remember, however, that the region's animals are not tame and their actions are often unpredictable. In addition to environmental considerations, security is an important issue. Heed the warnings of guides and rangers when on safari and in safari camps and lodges, and seek the advice of knowledgeable locals before venturing off on your own. Never get between a mother and her calves or cubs, and if you want good photos, invest in a telephoto lens instead of approaching an animal at close range. Be particularly aware of the dangers posed by crocodiles and hippos – a quick dip in an isolated waterhole or a beckoning river can have greater consequences than you bargained for. Never leave children unattended, even for a moment, at camps in wildlife areas.

Other species fighting for survival include mountain gorillas (see p75); wild dogs (most likely spotted in Tanzania's Selous Game Reserve, p242); hawksbill, green, olive ridley and leatherback turtles; dugongs; red colobus monkeys (best seen in Zanzibar's Jozani Forest, p141); and Pemba flying fox bats.

Rare or endangered bird species include Uganda's shoebill stork; Uluguru bush shrikes; Usambara weavers; Amani sunbirds; and roseate terns.

Plants

As is the case with the region's animals, East Africa's plant life is intricately interwoven into the larger natural backdrop. Local botanical environments range from cool, dark patches of moist, tropical forest to the dusty, acacia-studded bushlands and thickets so typical of the East African savannah. While much of the region's original forest cover has been cleared for agriculture, small but significant areas remain. The rainforests of southwestern Uganda and in bordering areas of Rwanda are the most extensive. There are also small but highly biodiverse areas of tropical rainforest in northeastern Tanzania. Montane forests exist throughout the highlands of Kenya and in western Uganda, and high-altitude heather and moorlands are found above the tree line in these areas. Along the coast are stands of coconut palms and extensive mangrove forests, while inland are various species of acacia, including the distinctive flat-topped acacia trees that are among the first impressions of East Africa for many visitors, as well as the baobab – with root-like branches that make it look as if it were standing on its head.

NATIONAL PARKS

East Africa has one of the world's most impressive collections of national parks, all of which are worth as much time as you are able to spare.

Parks (the term is used loosely here to refer to national parks, wildlife reserves and conservation areas) notable for their high concentrations and diversity of wildlife include Serengeti National Park (p186) and Ngorongoro Conservation Area (p190) in Tanzania, and Masai Mara National Reserve (p363) and Amboseli National Park (p295) in Kenya. Other parks are famous for a particular type of animal, such as Parc National des Volcans (p566) in Rwanda and Bwindi Impenetrable National Park (p488) in Uganda (both set aside for the protection of the endangered mountain gorillas), and Gombe Stream National Park (p215) and Mahale Mountains National Park (p216) in Tanzania and Kibale Forest National Park (p475) in Uganda – all of which have chimpanzees as their focal point.

Trekking and hiking parks include Kenya's Mt Kenya National Park (p349), Mt Elgon National Park (Kenya and Uganda, p462), and Tanzania's Kilimanjaro (p166), Arusha (p179), Udzungwa Mountains (p225) and Kitulo (p235) National Parks and the Ngorongoro Conservation Area (p190).

Marine national parks include Malindi (p325) and Watamu (p320) Marine National Parks in Kenya, and Mafia Island (p239) and Mnazi Bay-Ruvuma Estuary Marine Park (p250) in Tanzania. Major parks are summarised in the table on pp55-6. For more information on these, and on others not listed here, see the country chapters.

ENVIRONMENTAL ISSUES

Despite the abundance of national parks and other protected areas, East Africa suffers from several major environmental scourges. One of the most notorious is poaching, which occurs throughout the region. In one sense, it's not difficult to see why: 1kg of ivory is worth about US$300 wholesale, and rhino horn is valued at US$2000 per kilogram. This amounts to as much

Mangroves play an essential role in coastal ecosystems by controlling erosion, enriching surrounding waters with nutrients and providing local communities with insect-resistant wood.

For an overview of conservation projects and themes throughout the continent, including in East Africa, see www .africanconservation.com.

The Green Belt Movement by Wangari Maathai chronicles East Africa's first female Nobel Peace Prize winner as she launches a highly successful grass-roots initiative.

PARK ETIQUETTE

Whichever of East Africa's parks you visit, help conserve the environment by following these guidelines:

- Only camp in official sites.
- Drive only on established tracks.
- Don't honk your car horn.
- Don't drive within park borders outside the officially permitted hours.
- Don't litter, and be especially careful about discarding burning cigarette butts and matches.
- Don't pick flowers or remove or destroy any vegetation.
- Keep within the speed limits (in most parks, between 30km/h and 50km/h).

as US$30,000 for a single horn, or about 100 times what the average East African earns in a year. Poaching is also difficult to control due to resource and personnel shortages and the vastness and inaccessibility of many areas. Entrenched interests are also a major contributing factor, with everyone from the poachers themselves (often local villagers struggling to earn some money) to ivory dealers, embassies and government officials at the highest levels trying to get a piece of the pie.

In 1990, following a vigorous campaign by conservation groups, the Convention on International Trade in Endangered Species (Cites) implemented a ban on ivory import and export. Although this worldwide ban was subsequently downgraded in some areas to permit limited trade in ivory, it allowed dwindling elephant populations in East and southern Africa to make marked recoveries. Whether these gains will be lasting remains to be seen. The now partially reopened ivory trade seems to have resulted in an increase in poaching across the continent, although this connection is disputed by those who note that funds from legal ivory sales can be used towards conservation.

Just as worrisome as poaching is deforestation, with East Africa's forest areas today representing only a fraction of the region's original forest cover. On the Zanzibar Archipelago, for example, only about 5% of the dense tropical forest that once blanketed the islands still remains. In sections of the long Eastern Arc mountain chain, which sweeps from southern Kenya down towards central Tanzania, forest depletion has caused such serious erosion that entire villages have had to be shifted to lower areas. In densely populated Rwanda and Burundi, many previously forested areas have been completely cleared to make way for agriculture.

Deforestation brings with it soil erosion, shrinking water catchment and cultivable areas, and decreased availability of traditional building materials, foodstuffs and medicines. It also means that many birds and animals lose their habitats, and that local human populations risk losing their lifeblood. While the creation of forest reserves, especially in Kenya and Tanzania, has been a start in addressing the problem, tree-felling prohibitions are often not enforced.

Unregulated tourism and development also pose serious threats to East Africa's ecosystems. In northern and eastern Zanzibar, for example, new hotels are being built at a rapid rate, without sufficient provision for waste disposal and maintenance of environmental equilibrium. Inappropriate visitor use is another aspect of the issue: the tyre tracks criss-crossing off-road areas of Kenya's Masai Mara, the litter found along some popular trekking routes on Mt Kilimanjaro, and the often rampant use of firewood by visitors and tour operators alike are prime examples.

Work has begun on the controversial Bujugali Falls dam in Uganda, threatening the falls, and possibly also Lake Victoria.

Excellent conservation work is being done throughout East Africa. For an example, see www.southernhigh landstz.org.

EAST AFRICA'S TOP PARKS & RESERVES

Park	Features
Kenya	
Aberdare NP	dramatic highlands, waterfalls & rainforest; elephants, black rhinos, bongo antelopes, black leopards
Amboseli NP	dry plains & scrub forest; elephants, buffaloes, lions, antelopes
Arabuko Sokoke FR	coastal forest; Sokoke scops owls, Clarke's weavers, elephant shrews, butterflies, elephants
Hell's Gate NP	dramatic rocky outcrops & gorges; lammergeyers, eland, giraffes, lions
Kakamega FR	virgin tropical rainforest; red-tailed monkeys, flying squirrels, 330 bird species
Lake Bogoria NR	scenic soda lake; flamingos, greater kudu, leopards
Lake Nakuru NP	hilly grassland & alkaline lakeland; flamingos, black rhinos, lions, warthogs, birds
Malindi MNP & Watamu MNP	clear waters & coral reefs; tropical fish, turtles
Masai Mara NR	savannah & grassland; Big Five, antelopes, cheetahs, hyenas
Meru NP	rainforest, swamplands & grasslands; white rhinos, elephants, lions, cheetahs, lesser kudu
Mt Elgon NP	extinct volcano & rainforest; elephants
Mt Kenya NP	rainforest, moorland, glacial mountain & mountain flora; elephants, buffaloes
Nairobi NP	open plains with urban backdrop; black rhinos, birdlife, rare antelopes
Saiwa Swamp NP	swamplands & riverine forest; sitatunga antelopes, crown cranes, otters, colobus monkeys
Samburu, Buffalo Springs & Shaba NRs	semi-arid open savannah; elephants, leopards, crocodiles
Shimba Hills NR	densely forested hills; elephants, sable antelopes, leopards
Tsavo NP	sweeping plains & ancient volcanic cones; Big Five
Rwanda	
PN de l'Akagera	woodlands, wetlands & mountains; buffaloes, zebras, hippos, crocodiles
PN des Volcans	towering volcanoes; mountain gorillas
PN de Nyungwe	dense tropical forest & waterfalls; chimpanzees, Angolan colobus monkeys
Tanzania	
Arusha NP	Mt Meru, lakes & crater; zebras, giraffes, elephants
Gombe Stream NP	Lake Tanganyika & forest; chimpanzees
Katavi NP	floodplains, lakes & woodland; buffaloes, hippos
Lake Manyara NP	Lake Manyara; hippos, waterbirds, elephants
Mahale Mountains NP	Mahale Mountains, Lake Tanganyika; chimpanzees
Mikumi NP	Mkata floodplains; lions, giraffes, elephants
Mt Kilimanjaro NP	Mt Kilimanjaro
Ngorongoro CA	Ngorongoro Crater, Crater Highlands; black rhinos, lions, elephants, zebras, flamingos
Ruaha NP	Ruaha River; elephants, hippos, giraffes
Rubondo Island NP	Lake Victoria; birdlife, sitatungas, hippos, crocodiles
Saadani NP	Wami River & beach; birds, hippos, crocodiles
Selous GR	Rufiji River, lakes & woodland; elephants, hippos, wild dogs, black rhinos, birds
Serengeti NP	plains & grasslands, Grumeti & Mara Rivers; wildebeests, zebras, lions, cheetahs, giraffes
Tarangire NP	Tarangire River, woodland, baobabs; elephants, zebras, wildebeests, birds
Uganda	
Bwindi Impenetrable NP	primeval tropical forest; mountain gorillas
Kibale Forest NP	lush forest; highest density of primates in Africa
Kidepo Valley NP	mountain-fringed savannah landscapes; cheetahs, elephants, ostriches
Lake Mburo NP	savannah & lakes; zebra, impalas, eland, topi
Mgahinga Gorilla NP	volcanoes; mountain gorillas
Mt Elgon NP	extinct volcano; duikers, buffalos, lammergeyer vultures
Murchison Falls NP	thundering falls & the Victoria Nile; elephants, hippos, crocodiles, shoebill storks
Queen Elizabeth NP	lakes, gorges & savannah; hippos, birds, chimpanzees
Rwenzori Mountains NP	Africa's highest mountain range; blue monkeys, chimpanzees, hyraxes

Key

CA – Conservation Area	FR – Forest Reserve	GR – Game Reserve	MNP – Marine National Park

Activities	Best Time to Visit	Page
trekking, fishing, gliding	year-round	p346
wildlife drives	Jun-Oct	p295
bird tours, nature trails, cycling	year-round	p322
cycling, walking	year-round	p337
walking, bird-watching	year-round	p376
bird-watching, walking, visiting hot springs	year-round	p342
wildlife drives	year-round	p340
diving, snorkelling	Oct-Mar	p325 & p320
wildlife drives, ballooning	wildebeest migration, Jul-Oct	p363
wildlife drives, fishing	year-round	p359
trekking, fishing	Dec-Feb	p382
trekking, climbing	Jan-Feb, Aug-Sep	p349
wildlife drives, walking	year-round	p286
walking, bird-watching	year-round	p381
wildlife drives	year-round	p388
walking, forest tours	year-round	p313
wildlife drives, rock climbing, walking	year-round	p297
wildlife drives	May-Sep	p585
gorilla tracking, volcano climbing	May-Sep	p562
chimp tracking	May-Sep	p579
trekking, wildlife drives	year-round	p179
chimp tracking	year-round	p215
wildlife drives & walking safaris	Jun-Oct	p219
wildlife drives, walking & cycling in nearby areas	Jun-Feb	p183
chimp tracking	year-round	p216
wildlife drives, short walks	year-round	p224
trekking	year-round	p166
wildlife drives, trekking	Jun-Feb	p190
wildlife drives, short walks	Jul-Oct	p229
short walks, boating, fishing	Jun-Nov	p206
boating, wildlife drives, beach walks	Jun-Feb	p149
boat, walking & wildlife drives	Jun-Oct, Jan-Feb	p242
wildlife drives, balloon safaris, walking in border areas	year-round	p186
wildlife drives, limited walking	Jun-Oct	p185
gorilla tracking, bird-watching	May-Sep	p488
chimp tracking, forest elephant viewing	May-Aug	p475
wildlife drives & walking safaris; bird-watching	year-round	p469
boat trips, walking	year-round	p502
gorilla tracking, visiting pygmy villages, bird-watching	Jun-Sep	p499
trekking	Dec-Feb & Jun-Aug	p462
launch trip, wildlife drives	year-round	p511
launch trip, chimp tracking	year-round	p484
trekking	Jun-Aug	p481

NP – National Park   NR – National Reserve   PN – Parc National

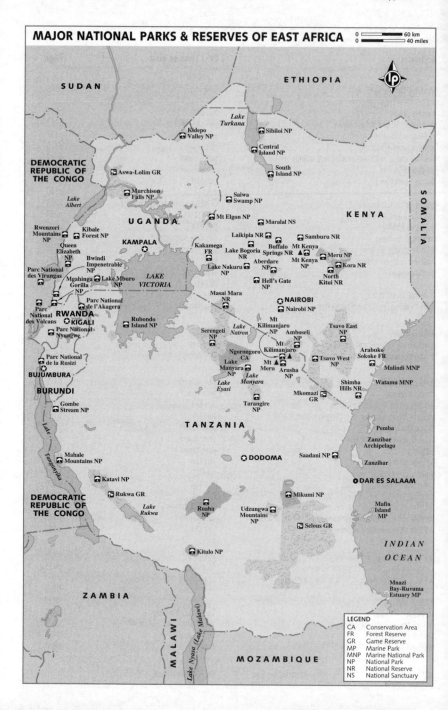

MAJOR NATIONAL PARKS & RESERVES OF EAST AFRICA

| 0 | | 60 km |
| 0 | | 40 miles |

SUDAN

ETHIOPIA

DEMOCRATIC REPUBLIC OF THE CONGO

Lake Turkana

Kidepo Valley NP

Sibiloi NP

Central Island NP

South Island NP

Aswa-Lolim GR

Lake Albert

Murchison Falls NP

Saiwa Swamp NP

UGANDA

Mt Elgon NP

Maralal NS

KENYA

S O M A L I A

Rwenzori Mountains NP

Kibale Forest NP

Laikipia NR

Samburu NR

Kakamega FR

Buffalo Springs NR

Mt Kenya

Queen Elizabeth NP

KAMPALA

Lake Bogoria NR

Meru NP

Parc National des Virunga

Bwindi Impenetrable NP

Lake Nakuru NP

Aberdare NP

Mt Kenya

Kora NR

Mgahinga Gorilla NP

Lake Mburo NP

LAKE VICTORIA

Hell's Gate NP

North Kitui NR

RWANDA

Parc National de l'Akagera

Masai Mara NR

NAIROBI

Parc National des Volcans

KIGALI

Rubondo Island NP

Nairobi NP

Parc National Nyungwe

Lake Natron

Mt Kilimanjaro NP

Amboseli NP

Tsavo East NP

Parc National de la Rusizi

Serengeti NP

Ngorongoro CA

Mt Kilimanjaro

Arabuko Sokoke FR

BUJUMBURA

Lake Manyara NP

Mt Meru

Arusha NP

Tsavo West NP

Malindi MNP

BURUNDI

Lake Eyasi

Lake Manyara

Watamu MNP

Gombe Stream NP

Shimba Hills NR

Tarangire NP

Mkomazi GR

Lake Tanganyika

TANZANIA

Pemba

Zanzibar Archipelago

Mahale Mountains NP

DODOMA

Saadani NP

Zanzibar

DEMOCRATIC REPUBLIC OF THE CONGO

Katavi NP

Rukwa GR

Lake Rukwa

Ruaha NP

Udzungwa Mountains NP

Mikumi NP

DAR ES SALAAM

Mafia Island MP

Selous GR

INDIAN OCEAN

Kitulo NP

ZAMBIA

Mnazi Bay-Ruvuma Estuary MP

M A L A W I

Lake Nyasa (Lake Malawi)

MOZAMBIQUE

LEGEND
CA	Conservation Area
FR	Forest Reserve
GR	Game Reserve
MP	Marine Park
MNP	Marine National Park
NP	National Park
NR	National Reserve
NS	National Sanctuary

PARK HOPPING ON A BUDGET

Visiting East Africa's parks can be a challenge if you're on a budget. Park fees, transport and accommodation costs, and the costs of getting around once you're in the park quickly add up. To save, consider:

- Visiting parks with lower entry fees.

- Fees at many parks in the region cover a 24-hour period. For maximum value for money, enter at about noon to take advantage of good evening and morning wildlife-watching hours before leaving (or having to pay again at noon the next day).

- Camping is possible in or near most parks, and can save considerably on costs compared with staying in a lodge or luxury tented camp. However, check camping prices in advance, as some park sites are expensive, especially in Tanzania, where public ('ordinary') camp sites cost US$30 per person per night.

- Parks located near a convenient access town are usually a good bet, as there will be public transport, or transport organised with a tour operator will be relatively inexpensive. Parks where you can take public transport to the gate, and then get around on your own steam – eg by hiking or organising a walking safari – will be the cheapest.

The Solutions?

For years, the conservation 'establishment' regarded human populations as a negative factor in environmental protection, and local inhabitants were often excluded from national parks or other protected areas because it was assumed that they damaged natural resources. A classic example is that of the Maasai, who were forced from parts of their traditional grazing lands around Serengeti National Park for the sake of conservation and tourism.

Fortunately, the tide is slowly turning, and it's now recognised that steps taken in the name of conservation will ultimately backfire if not done with the cooperation and involvement of local communities. Community-based conservation has become a critical concept as tour operators, funding organisations and others recognise that East Africa's protected areas are unlikely to succeed in the long term unless local people can obtain real benefits. If there are tangible benefits for local inhabitants – benefits such as increased local income from visitors to wilderness areas – then natural environments have a much better chance of evading destruction.

Much of this new awareness is taking place at the grassroots level, with a sprouting of activities such as Kenya's Green Belt Movement (www.green beltmovement.org) and community-level erosion control projects. It also helps when visitors become more aware of the issues; see p16 for some tips on what you can do.

Plastic bags pollute, provide malarial mosquitoes a breeding ground and harm soil, plant and animal life. Thin plastic bags are now officially banned in Rwanda, Zanzibar and much of the rest of East Africa, with varying degrees of enforcement.

Safaris

Wildlife watching tops East Africa's list of attractions, and little wonder. There are enough elephants wandering around the region to populate a large city, plus equally impressive numbers of zebras, wildebeest, giraffe, lions and more. The region's array of parks is stellar and diverse, ranging from dense mountain forests to the flat, acacia-studded plains of the famed Serengeti–Masai Mara ecosystem. Throughout, the sheer number and variety of animals combined with the evocative topography ensure that wildlife watching is always rewarding. Yet, an East African safari can also be expensive.

This chapter provides an overview of factors to consider when planning a safari; many apply in equal measure to organised treks. At the budget end, reliability is a major factor, as there's often only a fine line between operators running no-frills but good-value safaris, and those that are either dishonest or have cut things so close that problems are bound to arise. At the higher end of the price spectrum, ambience, safari style and the operator's overall focus are important considerations.

PLANNING A SAFARI
Booking

Booking (and paying for) a safari before arriving in East Africa is common, and is also advisable if you'll be travelling in popular areas during peak seasons, when lodges tend to fill up completely months in advance, or if your schedule is tight or inflexible. Only pre-book with operators that you have thoroughly checked out, and take particular care at the budget end of the spectrum. Confirm that the operator you're considering is registered with the relevant national regulatory body (see p70) and get as much feedback as possible from other travellers.

Booking a safari after arriving in East Africa can save you money, and gives you more flexibility. However, allow at least a day to shop around, don't rush into any deals, and steer clear of any attempts at intimidation by touts or dodgy operators to get you to pay immediately or risk losing your place in a departing vehicle.

For a preview of East Africa's major parks, check out www.tanzaniaparks.com (Tanzania); www.kws.org (Kenya) and www.uwa.or.ug/parks.html (Uganda).

Safari companies who have their own hotels will almost certainly accommodate you there. In some cases, this is a plus. Arusha-based Roy Safari's new and lovely African Tulip hotel (p175) – where it's a real pleasure to sleep – is a good example. It also can save you some money, as rooms are almost always discounted if you're doing a safari with the company. However, in other cases, where hotel quality is poor, it can be a distinct minus, so it's worth checking this out in advance.

Costs

There are essentially two types of organised safaris – those where you camp, and those where you stay in lodges or luxury tented camps. Camping safaris cater to shoestring travellers and to those who are pre-

---

POLE POLE (SLOWLY, SLOWLY)

Wherever you plan to take your safari, don't be tempted to try to fit too much into the itinerary. Distances in East Africa are long, and moving too quickly from park to park is likely to leave you tired, unsatisfied, and feeling that you haven't even scratched the surface. Try, instead, to plan a stay at just one or two parks – exploring in depth what each has to offer, and taking advantage of nearby cultural and walking opportunities.

SAFARI Q & A

Q. When is the best time of year to go?

A. This depends completely on which park(s) you'll be visiting, and what your interests are (eg bird-watching, catching the wildebeest migration). During the rains, some parks are inaccessible, while others are at their prime. In general, the cooler, dry season, when foliage is also less dense and water sources scarcer, is considered optimal for wildlife watching, but this varies tremendously, so get as much park-specific information as you can in advance.

Q. Which country/location is best?

A. Again, this depends on your interests and, in part, also on your budget. Each has its own unique appeal. For chimpanzees, western Tanzania. For mountain gorillas, Rwanda and Uganda. For the Big Five, Tanzania and Kenya.

Q. How fit do I need to be?

A. For a standard vehicle safari, the main consideration would be just being able to withstand bouncing around on bumpy roads. For cycling or multi-day walking safaris, a basic degree of fitness would be helpful.

Q. Where will we sleep?

A. Either in a tent or budget guesthouse (for camping safaris), or in a hotel or tented camp. Tented camps run the range from simple to super-luxurious.

Q. How much will it cost?

A. This depends on what you want to get out of the experience. Basic budget safaris, where you'll be sharing your vehicle with others and camping, cost anywhere from US$80 to US$130 per person, per day. For a top-tier upmarket safari with quality guiding and optimally-situated accommodation, prices will be from US$250 per person per day and up.

Q. Is it best to book/pay before leaving home?

A. If your time in the region is limited, or if you'll be travelling to popular areas during the high season, then yes. If cutting costs and maintaining maximum flexibility are priorities, then it can often work out better to book once in East Africa.

Q. How can I be sure I'm getting a good deal?

A. Do as much research as you can before leaving home on the operators and parks you're considering, including talking with other travellers who have gone on safari with the same operator.

---

pared to put up with a little discomfort and who don't mind helping to pitch the tents and set up camp. Safaris based in lodges or tented camps cost more, with the price usually directly proportional to the quality of the accommodation and staff, and the amount of individualised attention you'll get.

When comparing prices, see what's included. Relevant items here are park entrance fees; camping fees and accommodation costs; transport and fuel; number of meals per day; tent rental; and wildlife drives or walks. Drinks (whether alcoholic or not) are usually excluded, and budget camping safari prices usually exclude sleeping bag rental (from US$5 per day to US$15 per trip). For group safaris, find out how many people will be sharing the vehicle with you (our prices in this section are based on a group size of four), and how many people per tent or room. Prices quoted in this chapter are based on the cost per person for shared occupancy during the high season. If quotes are for accommodation-only, you'll need to pay extra to go out from the lodge and actually look for wildlife. Costs for this vary considerably, ranging from about US$25 per person for a walk to US$200 per vehicle per day for a wildlife drive.

There isn't necessarily a relationship between the price paid and the likelihood of the local community benefiting from your visit. Find out as much as you can about an operators' social and cultural commitment

Jane Goodall's classic, *In the Shadow of Man*, is essential and fascinating reading for anyone planning to go chimpanzee tracking in East Africa.

TIPPING

Assuming service has been satisfactory, tipping is an important part of the East African safari experience (especially to the driver/guides, cooks and others whose livelihoods depend on tips), and this will always be in addition to the overall safari price quoted by the operator. Many operators have tipping guidelines. Depending on where you are, for camping safaris this averages about US$10 per day per group for the driver-guide/cook, more for upscale safaris, large groups or an especially good job. Another way to calculate things is to give an additional day's wage for every five days worked, with a similar proportion for a shorter trip, and a higher than average tip for exceptional service. Wages in East Africa are low, and it's never a mistake to err on the side of generosity while tipping those who have worked to make your safari experience memorable. Whenever possible, give your tips directly to the staff you want to thank.

before booking, and check out our Greendex (p662), which highlights operators and establishments with positive community links.

Kenya is the cheapest place in the region for safaris and Tanzania the most expensive. In Uganda, most companies rely heavily on pricier lodge and hotel accommodation, and even where camping is involved, it's usually the luxury tented variety.

BUDGET

The goal of keeping costs to a minimum on budget safaris is achieved by camping or staying in basic guesthouses; by working with comparatively large group sizes to minimise per-head transport costs; and, by keeping to a no-frills set up with basic meals and a minimal number of staff. In some areas the camping grounds may be outside park boundaries to save on park entry fees and high park camping fees – though this means you'll lose time during prime morning and evening wildlife viewing hours shuttling to and from the park. For most safaris at the budget level, as well as for many in the midrange, there are also kilometre limits placed on how far the vehicle drives each day – meaning your driver may be unwilling or unable to follow certain lengthier routes – though operators seldom publicise this.

The bare minimum for a budget camping safari in Kenya/Tanzania is about US$80/100 per person per day, although most reliable operators charge closer to US$110/130. Be wary of anyone offering you prices much below this, as there are bound to be problems. Genuine budget camping safaris are few and far between in Uganda, although a few companies offer reasonably priced three-day trips to Murchison Falls and Queen Elizabeth National Parks for about US$70 to US$100 per person per day, camping or sleeping in dorms.

MIDRANGE

Most midrange safaris use lodges, where you can expect to have a comfortable room and to eat in a restaurant. In general, you can expect reliability and reasonably good value in this category. A disadvantage is that the safaris may have a packaged-tour atmosphere, although this can be minimised by carefully selecting a safari company and accommodation, and giving attention to who and with how many other people you travel. In both Kenya and Tanzania, expect to pay from about US$150 to US$250 per person per day for a midrange lodge safari. Particularly in Tanzania, good deals are available at some of the lodges during low season, so be sure to always ask.

Lonely Planet's *Watching Wildlife East Africa* is full of tips on spotting wildlife, maps of East Africa's parks and background information on animal behaviour and ecology.

In Uganda, plan on anywhere from US$100 to US$150 per person per day. However, it's worth noting that most of Uganda's parks don't have midrange accommodation, but rather a choice between simple *bandas* (thatch-roofed huts) or dorms and luxury-priced lodges. For some parks, you can stay at midrange places outside the park.

TOP END
Private lodges, luxury tented camps and sometimes private fly camps are used in top-end safaris, all with the aim of providing guests with as authentic and personal a bush experience as possible while not forego-ing the comforts. For the price you pay (from US$250 up to US$800 or more per person per day), expect a full range of amenities, as well as top-quality guiding, a high level of personalised attention and an intimate atmosphere.

When to Go
Getting around is easier in the dry season (July to October), and in many parks this is when animals are easier to find around waterholes and rivers. Foliage is also less dense, making it easier to spot wildlife. However, as the dry season corresponds in part with the high travel season, lodges and camps get crowded and accommodation prices are at a premium.

In addition to the Big Five (elephant, lion, leopard, buffalo and rhino), there's also a Little Five (elephant shrew, ant lion, leopard tortoise, buffalo weaver and rhino beetle).

Apart from these general considerations, the ideal time to make a safari very much depends on which parks and reserves you want to visit and your particular interests. For example, the wet season is the best time for bird-watching in many areas, although some lowland parks may be completely inaccessible during the rains. Wildlife concentrations also vary markedly, depending on the season. See the country chapters for more information. If you're timing your safari around specific events, such as the wildebeest migration in the Serengeti–Masai Mara ecosystem (p363), remember that there are no guarantees, as seasons vary from year to year and are difficult to predict in advance.

WHAT TO BRING

- binoculars
- field guides
- a good-quality sleeping bag (for camping safaris)
- mosquito repellent
- rain gear and waterproofs for wet-season camping safaris
- sunglasses
- camera (plus batteries and film/extra memory chips)
- extra contact lens solution and your prescription glasses (the dust can be irritating)
- mosquito net (top-end lodges and tented camps usually have nets, but you'll often need one for budget guesthouses)

Additional items for walking safaris include lightweight, long-sleeved/-legged clothing in subdued colours, a head covering and sturdy, comfortable shoes.

For budget safaris, bring extra food and snacks and a roll of toilet paper. In and near the parks, there's usually little available; if you're on a tight budget, stock up on bottled water and supplies beforehand.

TYPES OF SAFARI
Organised Vehicle Safaris

Four to six days is often ideal. At least one full day will normally be taken up with travel, and after six you may well feel like a rest. Packing too much distance or too many parks into a short period means you'll likely feel as if you've spent your whole time in transit.

Minivans are the most common safari transport throughout Kenya and northern Tanzania, but if you have a choice, go for a good Land Rover–style 4WD instead – preferably one with a pop-up style roof (versus a simple hatch that flips open or comes off) as it affords some shade. Minivans accommodate too many people for a good experience, the rooftop opening is usually only large enough for a few passengers to use at once, and at least some passengers will get stuck in middle seats with poor views.

Whatever the vehicle, avoid crowding. Most price quotes are based on groups of three to four passengers, which is about the maximum for comfort for most vehicles. Some companies put five or six passengers in a standard 4WD, but the minimal savings don't compensate for the extra discomfort.

SAFARI STYLE

While price can be a major determining factor in safari planning, there are other considerations that are just as important:

- **Ambience** Will you be staying in or near the park? (Staying well outside means you'll miss the good early morning and evening wildlife-viewing hours.) Are the surroundings atmospheric? Will you be in a large lodge or an intimate private camp?

- **Equipment** Mediocre vehicles and equipment can significantly detract from the overall experience, and in remote areas, lack of quality equipment or vehicles and appropriate back-up arrangements can be a safety risk.

- **Access and activities** If you don't relish the idea of hours on bumpy roads, consider parks and lodges where you can fly in. To get out of the vehicle and into the bush, target areas offering walking and boat safaris.

- **Guides** A good driver/guide can make or break your safari. Staff at reputable companies are usually knowledgeable and competent. With operators trying to cut corners, chances are that staff are unfairly paid and are not likely to be knowledgeable or motivated.

- **Community commitment** Look for operators that do more than just give lip-service to 'eco-tourism' principles, and that have a genuine, long-standing commitment to the communities where they work. In addition to being more culturally responsible, they'll also be able to give you a more authentic and enjoyable experience.

- **Setting the agenda** Some drivers feel that they have to whisk you from one good 'sighting' to the next. If you prefer to stay in one place for a while to experience the environment and see what comes by, discuss this with your driver. Going off in wild pursuit of the Big Five means you'll miss the more subtle aspects of your surroundings.

- **Extracurriculars** In some areas, it's common for drivers to stop at souvenir shops en route. While this gives the driver an often much-needed break from the wheel, most shops pay drivers commissions to bring clients, which means you may find yourself spending more time souvenir shopping than you'd bargained for. If you're not interested, discuss this with your driver at the outset, ideally while still at the operator's offices.

- **Less is more** If you'll be teaming up with others to make a group, find out how many people will be in your vehicle, and try to meet your travelling companions before setting off.

- **Special interests** If bird-watching or other special interests are important, arrange a private safari with a specialised operator.

Other Safaris

There is an increasing number of options for walking, cycling and other more energetic pursuits, sometimes on their own, and sometimes in combination with a vehicle safari. At all parks, any out-of-vehicle activities in areas with large wildlife needs to be accompanied by an armed ranger.

WALKING, HIKING & CYCLING SAFARIS

At many national parks, you can arrange walks of two to three hours in the early morning or late afternoon, with the focus on watching animals rather than covering distance. Following the walk, you'll return to the main camp or lodge or alternatively to a fly camp.

Multi-day or point-to-point walks are available in some areas, as are combination walking-hiking-cycling itineraries with side trips by vehicle into the parks to see wildlife. Popular areas include, in Kenya, Mt Kenya National Park (p349), Mt Elgon National Park (p382), the Cherangani Hills and around the Rift Valley (p334) lakes. In Tanzania, places where you can walk in 'big game' areas include Selous Game Reserve (p242), and Ruaha (p229), Mikumi (p224), Katavi (p219) and Arusha (p179) national parks, and in wildlife areas bordering Tarangire National Park (p185). Cycling activities in the area around Lake Manyara park are popular, and there are several parks – notably Kilimanjaro (p166), Udzungwa Mountains (p225) and Kitulo (p235) national parks – that can only be explored on foot. You'll also be exclusively on foot in both Gombe Stream National Park (p215) and Mahale Mountains National Park (p216) parks, tracking chimpanzees. Uganda also offers some fine opportunities – everything from tracking gorillas and chimpanzees to bird-watching walks in Bwindi Impenetrable (p488) and Kibale Forest (p475) national parks, to wildlife walks in Queen Elizabeth (p484), Kidepo Valley (p469) and Lake Mburo (p502) national parks, to climbing Mt Elgon (p462) or trekking in the Rwenzoris (p481).

> Check out www.eawild life.org for an overview of conservation efforts in East Africa.

BOAT & CANOE SAFARIS

Like walking safaris, boat safaris are an excellent way to experience the East African wilderness, and offer a welcome break from dusty, bumpy roads. Good destinations include along the Rufiji River in Tanzania's Selous Game Reserve (p242), with boat safaris of two to three hours' duration; and in Uganda, Queen Elizabeth National Park (p484), or the launch trip (p511) up the Victoria Nile to the base of Murchison Falls.

CAMEL SAFARIS

Most camel safaris take place in Kenya's Samburu (p388) and Turkana tribal, with Maralal (p392) a logical base. Although you may see wildlife along the way, the main attractions are the journey itself, the chance to immerse yourself in nomadic life and to mingle with the indigenous people. You can either ride the camels or walk alongside them. Most travelling is done in the cooler parts of the day, and a campsite is established around noon. Most operators provide camping equipment or offer it for retail. There are also camel safaris in Maasai areas near Arusha National Park – see www.mkurucamelsafari.com.

> Tsetse flies can be unwelcome safari companions in some areas. To minimise the nuisance, wear thick, long-sleeved shirts and trousers in khaki or other drab shades, and avoid bright, contrasting and very dark clothing.

BALLOON SAFARIS

The main places for balloon safaris are Kenya's Masai Mara National Reserve, and Serengeti National Park (p186) and Selous Game Reserve (p242), in Tanzania. Everything depends on wind and weather conditions, spotting animals can't be guaranteed and flight time is generally limited to a maximum of one hour. However the captains try to stay between 500m and 1000m above ground, which means that if animals are there you'll be able to see them. Most balloon safaris are followed by a champagne breakfast in the bush.

HORSEBACK RIDING SAFARIS

Horseback riding in big game areas is possible in the West Kilimanjaro area of Tanzania. See p252.

DO-IT-YOURSELF SAFARIS

It's quite possible to visit most of East Africa's parks with your own vehicle, without going through a safari operator, though it's less commonly done than in some southern African safari destinations. Although unless you're already based in the region or familiar with it, experienced at driving in the bush and self-sufficient as far as repairs and mechanical issues go, the modest (if any) cost savings are generally offset by the comparative ease of having someone else handle the logistics for you.

For most areas, you'll need a 4WD. In addition to park admission fees, there's often a daily vehicle fee and, in some areas, a guide fee as well. You'll need to carry extra petrol, as it's not available in most parks, as well as spares. Carrying a tent is also recommended.

> The 3 Peaks 3 Weeks Challenge (www.3peaks3weeks .org) involved 10 women trekking Kili, Meru and Mt Kenya to raise money and awareness for education, HIV/AIDS and environmental issues in Africa.

OPERATORS

A good operator is the single most important variable for your safari, and it's worth spending time thoroughly researching those you're considering. Those listed in this chapter are recommended at the time of writing, although the lists are not exclusive. If you plan on organising your safari through your hotel or lodge, confirm in advance that they will have a vehicle and guide available for wildlife drives.

TANZANIA

ITINERARIES
Northern Circuit

Arusha National Park (p179) is a good bet for a day trip, while Tarangire National Park (p185) and Lake Manyara National Park (p183) are each easily accessed as overnight trips from Arusha, although all these parks deserve more time to do them justice. For a half-week itinerary, try any of the northern parks alone (although for the Serengeti, it's worth flying at least one way, since it's a full day's drive from Arusha), or Ngorongoro Crater (p192) together with either Lake Manyara or Tarangire. With a week, you'll have just enough time for the classic combination of Lake Manyara, Tarangire, Ngorongoro and Serengeti (p186), but it's better to focus on just two or three of these. Many operators offer a standard three-day tour of Lake Manyara, Tarangire and Ngorongoro (or a four- to five-day version including the Serengeti). However, distances to Ngorongoro and the Serengeti are long, and the trip is likely to leave you feeling that you've spent too much time rushing from park to park and not enough time settling in and experiencing the actual environments. If you're serious about a safari in the north, especially if you want to visit Serengeti National Park, allow a minimum of five days from Arusha.

In addition to these more conventional vehicle safari itineraries, there are countless other possibilities combining wildlife viewing with visits to or activities in other areas. For example, a vehicle safari in the Ngorongoro Crater could be combined with trekking elsewhere in the Ngorongoro Conservation Area (p190), relaxing and walking based from one of the lodges around Karatu (p193), or a hiking-biking itinerary around Lake Manyara and up the escarpment in the Silela forest area. Another option is combining a Serengeti safari with travel around Lake Victoria (p201) and a visit to Rubondo Island National Park (p206). There are various cultural activities and cycling is possible in the area around Lake Manyara. Alternatively, combine a visit to the park with an excursion up towards Lake Natron (p194). West Kilimanjaro (p169) is another destination for walking, horseback riding and cultural interaction.

Southern Circuit

Mikumi National Park (p224) and Saadani National Park (p149) are both good destinations if you have only one or (better) two nights. With a bit more time, Mikumi makes a good safari-hiking combination with Udzungwa Mountains National Park (p225), or as a stop in a longer itinerary into the southern highlands. Saadani has the attraction of the beach, and can be combined with Zanzibar (p122) or elsewhere along the coast. With three to four days, try Selous Game Reserve (where you can do a boat safari on the Rufiji River, see p242), or Ruaha National Park (p229) if you fly. With a bit longer, you could combine Ruaha and Selous or Ruaha and Katavi (in the west). The Ruaha–Katavi combination in particular is increasingly popular given the availability of flights between the two parks, as well as a long but eminently doable overland connection. For adventurous overlanders or monied fly-in travellers, it's straightforward to combine Katavi with Lake Tanganyika (p220) – both Mahale Mountains National Park (p216), as well as other lakeshore points. An expanded flight network linking the southern and western parks with the coast has also opened up the possibility for some longer itineraries combining time on the coast or islands with safaris in Selous, Ruaha, Mahale and/or Katavi. Selous plus Mafia Island (p239) or Zanzibar is a recommended safari-beach combination.

Western Parks

Katavi (p219), Mahale Mountains (p216) and Gombe Stream (p215) national parks can all be visited via public transport (combining train, bus and ferry), but you will need time and a taste for adventure. Most upmarket itineraries use flights. For Katavi alone, plan on a minimum of three days in the park. With more time, the park is easily and enjoyably combined with time on Lake Tanganyika (p220) around Kipili. For a six- to seven-day itinerary, Katavi and Mahale make a fine combination; unless you arrange a private charter, flight schedules require three days in one park and four in the other. Ruaha–Katavi and Ruaha–Katavi–Mahale are straightforward combinations, although at least nine or 10 days should be allotted for the latter. Another rewarding option is Katavi together with Lake Tanganyika around Kipili, and then Mahale Mountains park, but you'll need to do a bit of juggling around with boat and/or flight schedules for this. For Gombe Stream alone, budget two to three days, plus a day or two in Kigoma on each end.

> ResponsibleTravel.com (www.responsibletravel.com) is a good place to start planning a culturally and environmentally responsible safari.

Rubondo Island National Park (p206) sits on its own in Lake Victoria and is well worth a detour. There is a rugged bus route linking Kigoma on Lake Tanganyika with the Lake Victoria area. However, the best connections to Rubondo are from Bukoba (p207) and Mwanza (p201), and it is more straightforward to combine the park with the Serengeti (p186) or a northern circuit–Lake Victoria itinerary.

Other Areas

Mkomazi Game Reserve (p159) is an intriguing, off-beat stop on any itinerary linking Dar es Salaam and the coast around Pangani with Arusha and the northern circuit. It also makes a rewarding stand-alone bush experience in combination with coastal destinations or with hiking in the Usambara

Mountains (p154). Kitulo National Park can easily be worked in to itineraries in the Mbeya-Tukuyu area. In the southeast, Mnazi Bay-Ruvuma Estuary Marine Park (p250) is best done as a stand-alone excursion from either Mtwara (p247) or Mikindani (p249), while diving in Mafia Island Marine Park (p239) is easily incorporated into a stay on Mafia island. The Mafia–Selous combination is easy to arrange (though it will involve a flight or two). Mafia–Zanzibar is another possibility.

OPERATORS
Arusha

Africa Travel Resource (ATR; ☎ UK 01306-880770; www.africatravelresource.com) A web-based safari broker that matches your safari ideas with an operator, and helps you plan and book customised itineraries. Their website contains extensive background information on Tanzania, the safari circuits and lodges, and their quotes are generally extremely detailed about the areas to be visited. Mid- to upper midrange.

Dorobo Safaris (☎ 027-250 9685, tel/fax 027-254 8336; dorobo@habari.co.tz) Culturally oriented treks in and around the Ngorongoro Conservation Area, and wilderness walks in the areas bordering Ruaha and Serengeti national parks. All work is done in partnership with local communities, with the emphasis on exploring remote areas in a way that benefits these communities and the environment. Midrange.

Duma Explorer (☎ 0787-079127; www.dumaexplorer.com; Njiro Hill) Northern Tanzania safaris, Kilimanjaro and Meru treks, northern Tanzania cultural tours and safari-coast combinations. Budget to midrange.

George Mavroudis Safaris (☎ 027-254 8840; www.gmsafaris.com) An upmarket operator, highly respected in industry circles and specialising in exclusive, customised safaris in the northern circuit done in vintage style. They also run a wonderful, classic bush camp in Mkomazi Game Reserve, and a getaway on Lukuba Island in Lake Victoria – the latter a fine combination with a Serengeti safari. Top end.

CHOOSING AN OPERATOR

Competition among safari companies is fierce and corners are often cut, especially at the budget level. Some companies enter wildlife parks through side entrances to avoid park fees, while others use glorified *matatu* or *dalla-dalla* (minibus or pick-up) drivers as guides, offer sub-standard food and poorly maintained vehicles, or underpay and otherwise poorly treat their staff. There are also many high quality companies who have excellent track records. Companies recommended in this chapter enjoyed a good reputation at the time of research, as do many others that couldn't be listed due to space considerations. However, we can't emphasise enough the need to check on the current situation with all of the listed companies and any others you may hear about. Following are some things to keep in mind when looking for an operator:

- Do some legwork (the internet is a good start) before coming to East Africa. Get personal recommendations, and once in the region, talk with as many people as you can who have recently returned from a safari or trek with the company you're considering.

- Be sceptical of price quotes that sound too good to be true, and don't rush into any deals, no matter how good they sound.

- Don't fall for it if a tout tries to convince you that a safari or trek is leaving 'tomorrow' and that you can be the final person in the group. Take the time to shop around at reliable outfits to get a feel for what's on offer, and if others have supposedly registered, ask to speak with them.

- In Tanzania and Kenya, check with TATO or KATO, and in Uganda with the Uganda Tourist Board, to find out whether the operator you're considering is licensed. See p70 for contact details.

Hoopoe Safaris (Map pp172-3; ☎ 027-250 7011; www.hoopoe.com; India St) A long-standing, highly regarded operator offering fine-value luxury camping and lodge safaris in the northern circuit with an emphasis on individualised itineraries and service. Hoopoe has its own tented camps in Lake Manyara and West Kilimanjaro areas, mobile camps in the Serengeti, and in other parts of the northern circuit, where they have formed partnerships with the surrounding communities. Combination itineraries with Kenya, Uganda, Rwanda and Sudan are also possible. Several years ago, distinguished as Best Eco-Tourism Operator in the World by *Condé Nast Traveler*. Upper midrange.

IntoAfrica (☎ UK 44-114-255 5610; www.intoafrica.co.uk) A small operator specialising in fair-traded cultural safaris and treks in northern Tanzania. It directly supports local communities in the areas where it works, consistently garners positive reviews from travellers and is an ideal choice if your interest is more in gaining insight into local life and culture, than in experiencing the luxury lodge atmosphere. One popular itinerary is a seven-day wildlife-cultural safari in Maasai areas. Midrange.

Kahembe's Trekking & Cultural Safaris (☎ 027-253 1088, 0784-397477; www.kahembe culturalsafaris.com) Mt Hanang treks and no-frills cultural safaris around Babati. They can also can be booked through Responsible Travel (p67). Budget.

Africa – The Serengeti (1994) features the annual wildebeest migration, showcasing magnificent footage of the cycle of life on the Serengeti plains.

Maasai Wanderings (☎ 0755-984925; www.maasaiwanderings.com) Northern Tanzania safaris and treks, including safaris for families and seniors, plus Zanzibar packages; profits are channelled into various community projects. Midrange.

Nature Beauties (Map pp172-3; ☎ 027-254 8224, 0732-971859; www.naturebeauties.com; Old Moshi Rd) A low-key outfit offering Kilimanjaro treks and northern circuit safaris, and Tanzania–Kenya combination itineraries. Budget.

Nature Discovery (☎ 0732-971859; www.naturediscovery.com) Individualised, environmentally responsible northern-circuit safaris, and treks on Kilimanjaro, Meru and in the Crater Highlands. Midrange.

Roy Safaris (Map pp172-3; ☎ 027-250 2115; www.roysafaris.com; Serengeti Rd) A highly-regarded family-run company offering budget and semiluxury camping safaris in the northern

■ Don't give money to anyone who doesn't work out of an office, and don't arrange any safari deals at the bus stand or with touts who follow you to your hotel room. Also be wary of sham operators trading under the same names as companies listed in this or other guidebooks. Don't let business cards fool you; they're easy to print up and are no proof of legitimacy.

■ Go with a company that has its own vehicles and equipment. If you have any doubts, don't pay a deposit until you've seen the vehicle that you'll be using. (Also be aware that it's not unknown for an operator to show you one vehicle, but then on the actual departure day, arrive in an inferior one.)

■ Especially at the budget level, there's a lot of client swapping between companies whose vehicles are full and those that aren't. You could easily find yourself on safari with a company that isn't the one you booked with; reputable companies will inform you if they're going to do this. Although getting swapped into another company's safari isn't necessarily a bad thing, be sure that the safari you booked and paid for is what you get, and try to meet the people you'll be travelling with before setting off.

■ Unless you speak the local language, be sure your driver can speak English.

■ Go through the itinerary in detail and confirm what is expected/planned for each stage of the trip. Be sure that the number of wildlife drives per day and all other specifics appear in the written contract, as well as the starting and ending dates and approximate times. Normally, major problems such as complete vehicle breakdown are compensated for by adding additional time onto your safari. If this isn't possible (for example, if you have an onward flight), reliable operators may compensate you for a portion of the time lost. However don't expect a refund for 'minor' problems such as punctured tyres or lesser breakdowns. Also note that park fees are non-refundable.

KATO & TATO

The **Kenyan Association of Tour Operators** (KATO; www.katokenya.org) and the **Tanzanian Association of Tour Operators** (TATO; www.tatotz.org) serve as local regulatory bodies. Reputable safari companies in Kenya and Tanzania will be registered members. While they're not always the most powerful of entities, going on safari with one of their members (both have member lists on their websites) will give you at least some recourse to appeal in case of conflict or problems. They're also good sources of information on whether a company is reputable or not, and it's well worth checking in with them before finalising your plans.

Uganda's equivalent – the **Association of Uganda Tour Operators** (AUTO; ☎ 041-4542599; www.auto.or.ug) – has absolutely no policing power, but does screen perspective new members to confirm they are at least competent.

Other good sources of information on tour operators are the **Tanzania Tourist Board Tourist Information Centre** (☎ 027-250 3842/3; ttb-info@habari.co.tz; Boma Rd, Arusha); the **Uganda Tourist Board** (www.visituganda.com) and the **Kenya Professional Safari Guides Association** (www.safariguides.org).

---

circuit, as well as competitively-priced luxury lodge safaris, and Kilimanjaro and Meru treks. Known for its high-quality vehicles and value for money. All budgets.

Safari Makers (☎ 027-254 4446; www.safarimakers.com) No-frills northern circuit camping and lodge safaris and treks at surprisingly reasonable prices; some safaris and treks also incorporate Cultural Tourism Program tours. Budget.

Summits Africa (www.summits-africa.com) Upmarket adventure safaris, including treks in the Ngorongoro Conservation Area and to Lake Natron, West Kilimanjaro walking safaris, multi-night bike safaris and combination bike-safari trips, plus custom-tailored mountain trekking and trekking-safari combinations. Upper midrange and top end.

Sunny Safaris (Map pp172-3; ☎ 027-250 8184, 027-250 7145; www.sunnysafaris.com; Colonel Middleton Rd) No-frills camping and lodge safaris, as well as Kilimanjaro and Meru treks and day walks in the area around Arusha. Budget.

Tropical Trails (off Map pp172-3; ☎ 027-250 0358, 027-250 5578; www.tropicaltrails.com; Masai Camp, Old Moshi Rd) Treks and walking safaris on Kilimanjaro, Meru, in the Crater Highlands and in the Monduli Mountains, as well as northern circuit camping and lodge safaris, and cultural tours around Arusha. Kosher treks, photographic camping safaris and other special interest tours can be arranged, and a portion of the company's profits goes towards supporting education projects in Maasai schools. Midrange.

Moshi

The following Moshi-based companies focus on Kilimanjaro treks.

Key's Hotel (off Map p163; ☎ 027-275 2250; www.keys-hotel-tours.com; Uru Rd) Standard Kilimanjaro packages. Midrange.

Moshi Expeditions & Mountaineering (Map p163; ☎ 027-275 4234; www.memtours.com; Kaunda St) Kilimanjaro treks. Budget to midrange.

Shah Tours (Map p163; ☎ 027-275 2370, 027-275 2998; www.kilimanjaro-shah.com; Sekou Toure Rd) A long-established operator offering Kilimanjaro and Meru treks, as well as treks in the Ngorongoro highlands. Midrange.

Zara Tanzania Adventures (Map p163; www.zara.co.tz) Another longstanding operator with Kilimanjaro and Meru treks. Budget to midrange.

Marangu

Almost all Marangu hotels organise Kilimanjaro treks; see p165. Also worth noting is Marangu Hotel's 'hard way' option that's one of the cheapest deals available for a reliable trek. For US$350 plus park fees for a six-day Marangu climb, the hotel will take care of hut reservations and provide a guide with porter, while you provide all food and equipment.

Bernhard Grzimek's 1959 film, The Serengeti Shall Not Die, was one of the most influential wildlife films ever made, drawing world attention not just to the Serengeti but to conservation throughout the continent.

Dar es Salaam

The following agencies can help you book southern-circuit safaris, or combination itineraries involving Mikumi, Ruaha and Katavi National Parks, Selous Game Reserve, and Zanzibar and Mafia islands.

Afriroots (☎ 0732-926350; www.afriroots.co.tz) Backpacker-oriented village-based biking, hiking and other tours around Dar es Salaam, in the Uluguru, Usambara and Udzungwa mountains and in the southern highlands, plus itineraries to the Selous Game Reserve and other areas. Budget.

Authentic Tanzania (☎ 022-276 2093; www.authentictanzania.com) A flexible, knowledgeable operator offering a variety of good-value itineraries throughout the south and along the coast, as well as to Katavi. Set departure destinations from Dar es Salaam include Udzungwa Mountains, Mikumi, Selous, Kilwa and Ruaha, and customised itineraries are also available. They're also recommended if you're interested in an adventurous Katavi road trip, taking in Ruaha and other stops enroute. Midrange.

Coastal Travels (Map p96; ☎ 022-211 7959, 022-211 7960; safari@coastal.cc; Upanga Rd) A long-established and recommended outfit with its own fleet of planes, and safari camps and lodges in Ruaha park, the Selous and on Mafia island. It has frequent 'last-minute' flight-and-accommodation deals, and is a good contact for putting together itineraries taking in different parts of the country, or combining safaris with non-safari touring. Offerings include competitively priced Ruaha packages, day trips to Zanzibar and Selous-Mafia combinations. Midrange.

Foxes African Safaris (☎ UK 01452-862288, Tanzania 0744-237422; www.tanzaniasafaris.info) A long-standing family-run company with lodges and camps in Mikumi, Ruaha and Katavi National Parks, on the coast near Bagamoyo and in the Southern Highlands. It's a good choice for personalised combination itineraries to these destinations using plane and road. Midrange to top end.

Hippotours & Safaris (Map p96; ☎ 022-212 8662/3; www.hippotours.com; Nyumba ya Sanaa, Ohio St) Itineraries in the south and west and along the coast, including Selous Game Reserve and Mafia Island. Midrange to top end.

Tent with a View (☎ 022-211 0507, 0741-323318; www.saadani.com) This reliable group runs lodges in Selous Game Reserve and Saadani National Park, and organises midrange and upmarket combination itineraries involving these and other areas, including honeymoon packages. Upper midrange.

Kilimanjaro: To the Roof of Africa (2002) is a gripping preview of what is to come if you're contemplating climbing the mountain, and a good armchair adventure if you're not.

Mwanza

For Mwanza-based safari operators, see p203.

Elsewhere in Tanzania

In Mbeya, **Gazelle Safaris** (Map p232; ☎ 025-250 2482, 0713-069179; www.gazellesafaris.com; Jacaranda Rd) organises transport, guides and vehicle rental for destinations around Mbeya and elsewhere in the southern circuit.

KENYA

ITINERARIES

Whether you take a camping safari or a lodge safari, there's a plethora of options available ranging from two days to 15 days and, in some cases, up to six weeks.

Most shorter itineraries of half a week or less concentrate on Masai Mara National Reserve (p363) and Lake Nakuru National Park (p340), while short Amboseli (p295) and Tsavo (p297) national parks safaris are also common. You'll need a little more time to head north to the other popular parks of Samburu and Buffalo Springs national reserves (p388), while a week will give you time to tag on visits to lakes Nakuru, Bogoria (p342) and Baringo (p342) to either a Masai Mara, Amboseli or northern parks itinerary. With a week and a half you could take in two or more of the Rift Valley lakes plus Masai Mara, Amboseli and Tsavo, or Samburu and Buffalo Springs, Meru (p359), Lake Nakuru and Masai Mara. Most of the safari companies cover the standard routes, but some also specialise in different routes designed to take you off the beaten track. Meru, Mt Elgon (p382), Saiwa Swamp (p381) and the Aberdare (p346) national parks are all possible. Also popular are itineraries combining wildlife safaris with visits to Lake Turkana – for example, visiting either or both of Samburu and Buffalo Springs and either Meru National Park or Shaba National Reserve (p388) and then heading up to Marsabit National Park (p391) before crossing the Chalbi Desert to Lake Turkana.

In the high season, many companies have daily or every second day departures to the most popular national parks – Amboseli, Masai Mara and Tsavo. To the less frequented parks, such as Samburu and Buffalo Springs, Shaba and Meru, they generally leave only once or twice per week. In addition, most companies will leave for any of the most popular national parks at any time so long as you have a minimum number of people wanting to go – usually four. If you are on your own you may have to wait around for a while to be put together with a larger group, which means it makes sense to book ahead or get a group together yourself rather than just turning up and expecting to leave the next morning.

> About 8000 elephants roam Tsavo's expanses – one-third of Kenya's overall total, but a huge drop from the 40,000-plus elephants at home here before poaching took its toll.

OPERATORS

Basecamp Explorer (off Map pp282-3; ☎ 020-577490; www.basecampexplorer.com; Ole Odume Rd, Hurlingham, Nairobi) An excellent Scandinavian-owned ecotourism operator offering comprehensive camping itineraries in Samburu, Lake Nakuru and the Masai Mara, with walking at Mt Kenya, Lake Bogoria and Lake Baringo. The firm also has its own luxury site in the Masai Mara and runs plenty of high-end conservation-based safaris, including trips to Lamu, Tanzania, Mt Kenya and Kilimanjaro.

Bike Treks (off Map p289; ☎ 020-446371; www.biketreks.co.ke; Kabete Gardens, Westlands, Nairobi) This company offers just about every possible combination of walking and cycling safaris that range from quick three-day jaunts to full on expeditions. A minimum of three people guarantees departure, and trips can easily be combined with more traditional safari options.

Bushbuck Adventures (off Map pp282-3; ☎ 020-7121505; www.bushbuckadventures.com; Peponi Rd, Westlands, Nairobi) Bushbuck is a small company specialising in personalised safaris. It has a private, semi-permanent camp in the northwest corner of the Masai Mara. As a result, it's relatively expensive, though company profits are put into conservation projects. The company is also strong on walking safaris throughout the country.

Eastern & Southern Safaris (Map pp284-5; ☎ 020-242828; www.essafari.co.ke; Finance House, Loita St, Nairobi) A classy and reliable outfit aiming at the midrange and upper end of the market, with standards to match. Classic Kenyan trips as well as safaris in Tanzania and Uganda are available. Departures are guaranteed with just two people for some itineraries.

Gametrackers (Map pp284-5; ☎ 020-338927; www.gametrackersafaris.com; Nginyo Towers, cnr Koinange & Moktar Daddah Sts, Nairobi) Long established and very reliable, this company offers a full range of camping and lodge safaris around Kenya, including routes in the remote Lake Turkana, short excursions to Nairobi National Park, walking treks in Aberdare National Park, Mt Kenya treks and numerous long-haul trips to Tanzania, Uganda and further afield.

IntoAfrica (☎ 0114-2555610; www.intoafrica.co.uk; 40 Huntingdon Cres, Sheffield, S11 8AX, UK) One of the most highly praised safari companies in East Africa, IntoAfrica specialises in 'fair-traded' trips providing insights into African life and directly supporting local communities. The company's commendable safaris explore cultures *and* offer wildlife viewing, and offers accommodation in a good mix of hotels, bush camps and permanent tented camps. Trips leave on scheduled dates, though if you're a small group, you can pay a bit more and begin the trip when you want.

Let's Go Travel (Map pp284-5; ☎ 020-340331; www.lets-go-travel.net; Caxton House, Standard St, Nairobi) This popular travel agent runs its own safaris and excursions, and also sells on an amazing range of trips from other companies, covering Tanzania, Uganda, Ethiopia and even the Seychelles, as well as plenty of specialist and remote options in Kenya itself. Prices are on the high side for camping, but the scope justifies the expense, and it's also a good port of call for unusual lodge safaris and car hire. Note however that we have received mixed reports from travellers, so it might be worth checking around before you part with your cash.

Ontdek Kenya (☎ 061-2030326; www.ontdekkenya.com; PO Box 2352, Nyeri) This small operator has been recommended by several readers for its unique tailor-made trips. In addition to the usual safari outings, Ontdek really pulls out the specialty cards by offering walking trips catered specifically to women, vegetarians and bird-watchers.

Origins Safaris (Map pp284-5; ☎ 020-312137; www.originsafaris.info) Origins also offers a superb range of exclusive cultural safaris around the country, including such rare sights as Samburu circumcision ceremonies and tribal initiation rites in southern Ethiopia. Midrange to top end.

Safari Seekers (www.safari-seekerskenya.net) Nairobi (Map pp284-5; ☎ 020-652317; Jubilee Insurance Exchange Bldg, Kaunda St); Mombasa (Map p308; ☎ 041-220122; Diamond Trust Arcade, Moi Ave) This budget company, which has been operating for a number of years now, has its own permanent campsites in Amboseli, Samburu and Masai Mara, and runs camping and lodge safaris in Kenya, Tanzania and Uganda. Departures are at least once a week, or any time with at least four people. Safari Seekers also offers fly-in safaris to Amboseli and Masai Mara with accommodation at luxury lodges or tented camps. Budget.

Safe Ride Tours & Safaris (Map pp284-5; ☎ 020-253129; www.saferidesafaris.com; Avenue House, Kenyatta Ave, Nairobi) A relatively new budget operator consistently recommended by readers for its camping excursions. Safe Ride can also arrange minor conveniences such as airport transfers, car rentals and flight tickets to East African destinations as far flung as Zanzibar. Budget.

Sana Highlands Trekking Expeditions (Map pp284-5; ☎ 020-227820; www.sanatrekking kenya.com; Contrust House, Moi Ave, Nairobi) A big budget player that has had a good reputation in the past for walking safaris and trekking trips to some of Kenya's more remote parks. They also offer the usual camping and lodge itineraries.

Somak Travel (www.somak-nairobi.com) Nairobi (Map p287; ☎ 020-535508; Somak House, Mombasa Rd); Mombasa (☎ 041-487349; Somak House, Nyerere Ave) A Kenyan-based operator with more than 30 years of experience on the safari circuit, Somak is a home-grown favourite. They offer the usual in Kenyan classics as well as a few interesting Tanzanian options. Midrange.

Southern Cross Safaris (www.southerncrosssafaris.com) Nairobi (Map p292; ☎ 020-884712; Symbion House, Karen Rd); Mombasa (Map p307; ☎ 041-475074; Kanstan Centre, Nyali Bridge, Malindi Rd); Malindi (Map p326; ☎ 042-30547; Malindi Complex, Lamu Rd) An extremely professional Kenyan-specialist company, Southern Cross is a good choice for individually designed safaris. You can choose from their suggested tours, or design one that meets your specific needs. Midrange to top end.

The Wildlife Conservation Society's Africa page (www.wcs.org/interna tional/Africa) has links detailing conservation projects in wildlife and wilderness areas.

UGANDA

ITINERARIES

Uganda is a compact country and most safaris last about a week to 10 days. Virtually all trips focus on the southwest, usually combining a gorilla visit in Uganda or neighbouring Rwanda (depending on where the companies can get permits) with big game watching in Queen Elizabeth National Park (p484) and Murchison Falls National Park (p511) and chimp visits in Kibale Forest National Park (p475). Few itineraries include Kidepo Valley National Park (p469) in the far northeast, but if you have the time, it's definitely worth it.

Keep in mind that midrange safaris require a bit of flexibility because in many parks the only accommodation choices fall squarely in the budget or top-end classes.

OPERATORS

Bird Uganda Safaris (☎ 0777-912938; www.birduganda.com; Kampala) Run by Herbert Byaruhanga, one of Uganda's pioneering bird-watchers, who leads most of the trips himself but also gets local guides at all of the sites to ensure top spotting. Bird-watching is the bread and butter, of course, but gorilla tracking and other wildlife encounters can be added to the mix. Herbert offers excellent value and has earned a multitude of rave reviews. Midrange to top end.

Classic Africa Safaris Entebbe (☎ 0414-320121; www.classicuganda.com; 77 Erica Magala Rd) USA (☎ 304-876-1315) One of the best luxury companies in Uganda, Classic offers excellent service both in trip planning and in the parks. Top end.

Gorilla Tours Kampala (☎ 0772-370263; www.gorillatours.com) Netherlands (☎ 50-5732424) Gorillas are the specialty, but they have itineraries covering all the major parks of southwest Uganda. The trips offer very good value, and they manage some of the country's best midrange hotels including Travellers Rest Hotel (p498) in Kisoro and Kalebas Camp on Lake Bunyonyi. All budgets.

Uganda's Murchison Falls park is one of the few places in the world for spotting the rare shoebill stork.

Great Lakes Safaris (Map pp428-9 ☎ 0414-267153; www.safari-uganda.com; Suzie House, Gaba Rd, Kampala) One of the better all-round safari companies in Uganda, they offer a wide variety of safaris at prices for every pocket. Besides the usual wildlife trips, Great Lakes offers cultural encounters, and they will customise a blend of both experiences in any proportion that you wish. All budgets.

Magic Safaris (Map pp428-9; ☎ 0414-342926; www.magic-safaris.com; 3 Parliament Av, Raja Chambers, Kampala) We must admit that some of the office staff aren't up to snuff, but Magic gets rave reviews where it matters most, on the road. Besides offering standard lodge safaris, the company sets its self apart with its luxury camping safaris (at midrange prices) which give you that much more time out in nature. Many of these are scheduled trips, but private safaris are available too. Midrange to top end.

Matoke Tours Kampala (Map pp428-9; ☎ 0782-374667; www.travel-uganda.net; 8 Bukoto St); Netherlands (☎ 31-736123364) The Matoke team focuses on the underserved midrange bracket. Besides excellent and enthusiastic service, they also stand out as one of the few quality companies who will take you to Kidepo Valley National Park overland. All budgets.

RWANDA

ITINERARIES

The few organised safaris that include Rwanda are generally short – most less than a week – yet expensive due to the lack of competition. All concentrate on trips to Parc National des Volcans. See opposite for details on gorilla excursions.

OPERATORS

Amahoro Tours Rwanda (Map p560; ☎ 8687448; www.amahoro-tours.com; Market St, Musanze) A small, locally-run operator that gets rave reviews from readers, Amahoro can help you arrange permits as well as cultural activities and homestays in the surrounding area.

Bizidanny Tours & Safaris (Map p550; ☎ 55102004; www.bizidanny.com; Rue Commerciale, Kigali) This small start-up operator runs individually customized tours throughout the country, and can help you organise tracking permits.

The Kingdon Field Guide to African Mammals by Jonathan Kingdon makes a fine safari companion, with a wealth of information on East African wildlife. Field Guide to the Birds of East Africa by Terry Stevenson & John Fanshawe is similar for bird-watching.

Highland Gorilla Tour & Travel (Map p560; ☎ 8414488; www.shyirsdiocese.or.rw; Ave du 5 Juillet, Musanze) Another small but reliable operator, this agency is run by the local diocese.

Kiboko Tours & Travel (Map p550; ☎ 501741; www.kibokotravels.org.rw; Rue de la Paix, Kigali) Another small operator that is a good starting point for securing permits and organising trips and treks throughout the country.

Thousand Hills (Map p550; ☎ 501151; www.thousandhills.rw; office at the Hotel des Mille Colines, Kigali) One of the more well-established tour operators, Thousand Hills is an excellent choice if you want to increase your likelihood of getting your hands on a gorilla permit. Top end.

Volcanoes Safaris (Map p550; ☎ 502452; www.volcanoessafaris.com; office at the Hotel des Mille Colines, Kigali) Probably the most professional operator in Rwanda, Volcanoes Safaris runs customised trips ranging from budget-friendly transfers to exclusive fly-ins, and own the exclusive Virunga Lodge (see p562) in Parc National Des Volcans. Top end.

Mountain Gorillas

Coming face to face with mountain gorillas is one of life's great experiences. No bars, no windows, you're a humble guest in their domain. Nothing quite prepares you for the moment when you come upon a gorilla family in the wild; the first glimpse of black as a juvenile jumps off a nearby branch, a toddler clings to its mother's back and a giant silverback rises to size you up.

There are thought to be around 710 mountain gorillas (Gorilla beringei beringei) left in the world, all in a small area of East Africa straddling the borders of Uganda, Rwanda and the Democratic Republic of the Congo (DRC; formerly Zaire).

Relations between humans and gorillas have not always been fraternal. For centuries gorillas were considered fearsome and aggressive (with portrayals such as King Kong hardly helping their image) and it was only last century that we finally learned they are gentle and vegetarian. Chimpanzees are far more aggressive than relatively docile gorillas.

The first non-African to encounter a mountain gorilla was Oscar von Beringei, in 1902. He shot two on the slopes of Mt Sabyinyo and the 'new' subspecies was named after him. Hunting gorillas was a popular pastime until one hunter, Carl Akeley, decided that something must be done to preserve the population of these magnificent creatures. In 1925 he persuaded the Belgian government to create Africa's first protected area, Albert National Park, which is now Parc National des Virungas (p538) in DRC. Sadly, over the years agriculture and administrative division have reduced the size of this protected area, and poaching has further reduced the number of gorillas.

The first scientific study of the mountain gorillas in the Virunga volcanoes area was undertaken by George Schaller in 1959. His work was continued by Dian Fossey (see p564) from 1967 and her story has been made into the film Gorillas in the Mist. Fossey's confrontational, uncompromising stance on poaching probably led to her murder in 1985.

Gorilla: Struggle for Survival in the Virungas (1996) is co-authored by George Schaller, the primatologist who pioneered the study of mountain gorillas in the Virungas. It details efforts undertaken to protect the species.

GORILLA TOURISM

German adventurer Walter Baumgärtel was one of the first people to recognise that tourism could provide a reason for locals to support preservation of the forests, which would thus ensure the survival of mountain gorillas. He bought the Travellers Rest Hotel (p498) in Kisoro, Uganda, in 1955 and people soon came to try to track the great apes. By the late 1960s, gorilla tracking had become quite popular.

Gorilla tourism today stands at a crossroads. All three countries where the remaining mountain gorillas live have a history of instability that makes it hard for international conservation organisations to operate with any certainty. Several organisations promote sustainable agricultural and tourism practices and encourage the active participation of local communities in conservation, and this has played a large part in ensuring the gorillas' survival during turbulent times. However, many of the residents of local communities around these protected areas remain bitter; they're aware of the vast sums of money flowing in from visitors, and that very little of it reaches them.

In 1978 Bill Weber and Amy Vedder began studying mountain gorillas with Dian Fossey in Rwanda. *In the Kingdom of Gorillas: Fragile Species in a Dangerous Land* tells their story.

THE GORILLAS

Gorillas are the largest of the great apes and share 97% of their biological make-up with human beings. Gorillas used to inhabit a swathe of land that cut right across central Africa, but the ice age diminished the forests and divided them into three groups: the western lowland gorilla, the eastern

---

GORILLA TRACKING Q&A

Q. When is the best time of year to go?
A. Any time you can. The experience will be incredible no matter when you go, but there are advantages to different times of the year. It's generally easier to track gorillas in the rainy seasons (April to May and September to November) because they hang out at lower altitudes. You may also get better photos in the rainy season, assuming it isn't raining at the moment when you're with the gorillas, because they love to sunbathe after getting wet.

The busiest times on the mountains are December to February and July to August. Scoring permits takes more effort during these months, but that won't matter if a tour company is handling things for you.

Q. How fit do I need to be?
A. If getting a beer from the fridge qualifies as exercise in your life, forget about tracking. With the combination of mud, steep hills and altitude, it's usually hard work; but you also don't need to be an athlete to make it, just determined. True, the gorillas sometimes wander near the visitor centres and might be found in less than 30 minutes, but this isn't very common. You're usually looking at two to four hours, and some trackers have wandered across the mountains for an entire day.

Q. Where will I sleep?
A. Wherever you want. The parks are fairly remote, but the steady stream of visitors means there's plenty of accommodation to suit all styles and budgets.

Q. What should I bring?
A. For the most part you don't need anything special beyond the usual outdoor essentials such as sunscreen, insect repellent, and food and water (enough for the whole day, just in case). Good boots are important. Some people like rubber boots because they keep the mud and fire ants at bay, but they have no ankle support. Plan for rain no matter what month you're tracking (you'll be in a rainforest afterall), and it's also often chilly in the morning, so you might want a warm top.

The International Gorilla Conservation Project (IGCP; www.mountain gorillas.org), a unique partnership between the African Wildlife Foundation (AWF), Fauna & Flora International (FFI) and World Wide Fund for Nature (WWF), seeks to protect the gorillas' habitat by improving the lives of the people who live around it.

Baby gorillas weigh just 2.2kg when born.

lowland gorilla and the mountain gorilla. Mountain gorillas are now found only in two small populations in the forests of Bwindi Impenetrable National Park (about 330 individuals) in Uganda and on the slopes of the Virunga volcanoes (around 380), encompassing Uganda's Mgahinga Gorilla National Park (p499), Rwanda's Parc National des Volcans (p562) and DRC's Parc National de Virungas (p538).

Mountain gorillas are distinguished from their lowland relatives by longer hair, broader chests and wider jaws. Some experts even go so far as to suggest that the Bwindi gorillas are a distinct subspecies from the Virunga gorillas. The most obvious thing that sets the gorillas in Bwindi apart from those of the Virungas is that they are less shaggy, most likely due to the lower altitude.

Daily Life

Gorillas spend 30% of their day feeding, 30% moving and foraging, and the remainder resting. They spend most of their time on the ground, moving around on all fours, but stand up to reach for food. Gorillas are vegetarians and their diet consists mainly of bamboo shoots, giant thistles and wild celery, all of which contain water and allow the gorillas to survive without drinking for long periods of time. Insects are sometimes a source of protein. A silverback can eat his way through more than 30kg of bamboo a day.

A group's dominant silverback dictates movements for the day, and at night each gorilla makes its own nest. Gorillas usually travel about 1km a day, unless they have met another group in which case they may move further.

You may have to trudge through thorns and stinging nettle, so trousers and long-sleeve shirts with some degree of heft may save you some irritation. For the same reason, garden gloves can come in handy.

Finally, don't forget to bring your passport with you on tracking day; you'll need it during registration.

Q. How much will it cost?

A. Due to simple economics (for most of the year demand far outstrips supply) gorilla tracking permits in Uganda and Rwanda now cost US$500. Tracking, when possible, costs US$400 in the Democratic Republic of the Congo (DRC; formerly Zaire), but as you have to pay to get across the border and hire a guide to get you to the park, in the end it usually also works out to US$500.

The price includes park entry, guides and armed escorts, while porters are available for a little extra. These people will expect (and we think, deserve) a small tip.

Q. Is it best to book before leaving home?

A. Though the number of habituated gorilla groups has grown in recent years, it can still be difficult to get tracking permits in the high season, especially for Bwindi Impenetrable National Park, so definitely book ahead here if you're planning to visit December to February or July to August. The rest of the year, if your travel plans mean you have a very small window of opportunity, then you still should make a reservation as far in advance as possible to be safe, but the more flexibility you have, the less urgency there is.

To make a phone booking for Rwanda, you need to pay a deposit by bank transfer, while in Uganda you'll need to provide all the money up front. If you can't get a permit on your own, you'll need to go through a tour operator, which is often a good idea anyway: in Uganda because the operators can get permits up to two years in advance as opposed to just three months for individuals, and in Rwanda (where everyone gets access to permits two years in advance) because it is a major hassle to do it yourself.

Families

Gorillas generally live in family groups of varying sizes, usually including one to two older silverback males, younger blackback males, females and infants. Most groups contain between 10 and 15 gorillas but they can exceed 40.

There are strong bonds between individuals and status is usually linked to age. Silverbacks are at the top of the hierarchy, then females with infants or ties to the silverbacks, then blackbacks and other females.

Most gorillas leave the group when they reach maturity, which helps prevent interbreeding among such a small population.

Conflict

Gorillas are relatively placid primates and serious confrontations are rare, although violence can flare if there's a challenge for supremacy between silverbacks. Conflicts are mostly kept to shows of strength and vocal disputes.

Conflict between groups is also uncommon, as gorillas aren't territorial; though if two groups meet, there's usually lots of display and bravado on the part of silverbacks, including mock charges. Often the whole group joins in and it's at this point that young adult females may choose to switch allegiance.

If gorillas do fight, injuries can be very serious as these animals have long canine teeth and silverbacks pack a punch estimated at eight times stronger than a heavyweight boxer. If a dominant male is driven from a group by another silverback, it's likely the new leader will kill all the young infants to establish his mating rights.

Dian Fossey spent most of her adult life fighting to protect the mountain gorillas and the Dian Fossey Gorilla Fund International (www .gorillafund.org) continues her work through antipoaching measures, habitat protection, monitoring, research, education and supporting local communities.

Communication

Gorillas communicate in a variety of ways, including facial expressions, gestures and around two dozen vocalisations. Adult males use barks and roars during confrontations or to coordinate the movement of their groups to a different area. Postures and gestures form an important element of intimidation and it's possible for a clash to be diffused by a display of teeth-baring, stiff-legging and charging.

Friendly communication is an important part of group bonding and includes grunts of pleasure. Upon finding food, gorillas will grunt or bark to alert other members of the group. Grooming, however, isn't as common as among other primates.

For a better understanding of how intelligent gorillas are, take a look at www.koko.org, dedicated to Koko the gorilla who has a working vocabulary of 100 signs.

Biology

Gorillas are the largest primates in the world and mountain gorillas are the largest of the three gorilla species; adult male mountain gorillas weigh as much as 200kg (440lb). Females are about half this size.

Males reach maturity between eight and 15 years, their backs turning silver as they enter their teens, while females enter adulthood at the earlier age of eight. Conception is possible for about three days each month, and once a female has conceived for the first time, she spends most of her life pregnant or nursing.

The duration of a gorilla pregnancy is about 8½ months. Newborn infants are highly dependent on adults, and a young infant will rarely leave its mother's arms during its first six months. In its second year, a young gorilla begins to interact with other members of the group and starts to feed itself. Infant gorillas and silverbacks often form a bond, and it's not uncommon for a silverback to adopt an infant if its mother dies. This distinguishes gorillas from other primates, where child-rearing duties are left to females. From about three years, young gorillas become quite independent, and build their own nests.

No mountain gorillas have ever been successfully reared in captivity, contributing to the precarious nature of their existence.

WHERE TO TRACK THE GORILLAS

For many visitors to East Africa, a gorilla visit is the single largest expenditure they'll make in the region. It's worth putting some thought into where to visit these incredible creatures since each place has its pros and cons.

The main options are Bwindi Impenetrable National Park (p488) in Uganda and Parc National des Volcans (p562) in Rwanda. Because the gorillas in Uganda's Mgahinga Gorilla National Park (p499) sometimes slip over the border, reservations here are taken no more than two weeks in advance. This makes it ideal for travellers who don't want to fix a date until the last minute. At the time of research, the Rushegura group in Bwindi had gone on holiday to DRC, and when it returns the park may institute a similar short-notice reservation system for this group. Check for details on the ground.

ILLEGAL GORILLA VISITS

We hear occasional reports of people approaching visitors to offer illegal gorilla visits. Sometimes they deliver on the promise but usually they just disappear with your money.

Illegal gorilla visits can increase the animals' stress levels, which in turn reduces immunity to disease. The threat of increased stress levels should not be underestimated, considering four out of 10 gorillas die before adulthood. Although seeing gorillas may be the highlight of your trip, the only way illegal visits can be stopped is if visitors play by the rules.

Visiting gorillas in DRC is an on-again, off-again proposition due to the country's unsteady security situation. It was off-again when we were last there, and we fear it's going to stay this way for some time, which may spell an ominous future for that country's gorillas.

When you add all the money spent on hotels, food, transport and the like – not to mention the tracking permits – gorilla tourism nets Uganda, Rwanda and DRC an estimated US$20 million annually.

Bwindi Impenetrable National Park, Uganda

Since the middle of the 1990s up until recently, Bwindi was the number one place to track mountain gorillas, both because of the intrigue behind the amazing jungle here and the perceived dangers of travel in Rwanda. Even now, with Parc National des Volcans drawing crowds again, Bwindi Impenetrable National Park remains a beguiling destination.

As the name suggests, this is a dense forest with steep slopes, so tracking can be hard work, especially at the Nkuringo and Ruhija sectors, and visibility isn't as good as it is in the bamboo forest and open field where the Virunga gorillas tend to hang out. On the other hand, Bwindi's gorillas are more likely to be seen swinging from the trees. Getting here by public transport is possible, but quite a hassle. See p488 for more information.

ARRANGING PERMITS

Even though the number of tracking permits has increased to 48 per day, it can still be difficult to get them. There are three mountain gorilla groups that can be visited from the Buhoma sector of the park, two (the Nsongi group has begun on a trial basis) from the dramatic Nkuringo sector and one in the remote east at Ruhija. Permits, which cost US$500, must be booked at the **Uganda Wildlife Authority** (UWA; ☎ 0414-355000; www.uwa.or.ug; 🕑 8am-5pm Mon-Fri, 9am-1pm Sat) headquarters in Kampala or through a Ugandan tour operator (see p73 and p430).

For more on mountain gorillas in Uganda, see the Uganda Wildlife Authority website at www.uwa.or.ug.

Mgahinga Gorilla National Park, Uganda

Mgahinga encompasses Uganda's share of the Virunga volcanoes, which sit squarely on the tri-nation border. This park is popular with independent travellers because reservations aren't possible more than two weeks in advance, due to the only habituated gorilla group's tendency to duck over the border into Rwanda or DRC. Of course, the down side of this is that it means they can't always be tracked. It often takes longer to find the gorillas here than in Bwindi, but the walking is usually much easier, unless the gorillas are hanging out really high up on the mountain.

There's no public transport to Mgahinga, but it's just 14km from Kisoro, so not too expensive to reach by special-hire and you can usually find people to share the price. See p499 for more information.

ARRANGING PERMITS

Reservations for the eight places available daily are taken only at the **Mgahinga Gorilla National Park Office** (☎ 0486-430098; Main St; 🕑 8am-5pm) in Kisoro. The US$500 fee is paid at the park headquarters on the morning of your tracking.

The *National Geographic* article 'Who Murdered the Virunga Gorillas' (http://ngm.nationalgeographic.com/geopedia/Virunga_Gorillas) tells the disturbing tale of the 2007 murders of at least seven mountain gorillas in Parc National des Virungas, and clearly lays out just how precarious the existence of these amazing creatures is.

Parc National des Volcans, Rwanda

Many people feel Volcans is the best place to see mountain gorillas. Part of the appeal is that this is where Dian Fossey was based and where the film about her work was made. Also, the towering volcanoes form a breathtaking backdrop. Tracking here is usually easier that in Bwindi because the mountains offer a more gradual climb, and the visibility is often better too. Another appealing benefit of Volcans over Bwindi is that visitors here are

RULES FOR GORILLA TRACKING

When meeting the mountain dwellers of East Africa, all visitors must observe several rules:

■ Anyone with an illness cannot track the gorillas. Shared biology means shared illness. In Rwanda you'll get a full refund if you cancel because of illness and produce a doctor's note, while Uganda gives you back half.

■ Eating and smoking near the gorillas is prohibited.

■ If you have to cough or sneeze, cover your mouth and turn your head.

■ Flash photography is banned; turn off the autoflash or you'll be mighty unpopular with both rangers and gorillas.

■ Speak quietly and don't point at the gorillas or make sudden movements; they may see these as threats.

■ Leave nothing in the park; you shouldn't even spit.

■ Keep a few metres back from the gorillas and follow your guide's directions promptly and precisely about where to walk.

■ Hard as it seems to stand still when faced by 200kg of charging silverback, never, ever run away...crouch down until he cools off.

■ Children under 15 years of age aren't allowed to visit the gorillas.

assigned gorilla groups on tracking day, not when reservations are made, so those who aren't in such good shape will get one of the groups requiring the least amount of walking.

The park is about 13km from Musanze (Ruhengeri; p559) in northwestern Rwanda, and though there's no public transport available, it's easy to arrange rides with other visitors. See p562 for more information.

For more on mountain gorillas in Rwanda, see the Office Rwandais du Tourisme et des Parcs Nationaux (ORTPN) website at www.rwandatourism.com.

ARRANGING PERMITS

There are seven habituated gorilla groups meaning 56 tracking permits (US$500) are available each day, and even though you may have to wait more than a week during the peak seasons of July to August, and December to January, it's still easier to snag a permit here than in Bwindi.

You can book a permit with the **Office Rwandaise du Tourisme et des Parcs Nationaux** (ORTPN; ☎ 576514; www.rwandatourism.com; 1 Blvd de la Revolution; ⊙ 7am-5pm Mon-Fri, 7am-noon Sat & Sun) in Kigali, but it is so disorganised it's easier to go to a tour operator (see p74, p552 and p560).

Parc National des Virungas, DRC

Due to a serious flare up of the rebel activity that has been happening off and on for decades, tracking in DRC ceased in mid-2008. When it's again both possible and safe (not always the same thing) to visit, this is the easiest place to pick up permits on short notice since tour operators and most tourists stay far away. There are two places here to track mountain gorillas: Bukima (with four habituated families), 40km north of Goma, and Djomba (with one family), 8km from the Ugandan border by Kisoro. Both are in stunning locations and lie at the end of very rough roads.

For more on mountain gorillas in Democratic Republic of the Congo, see http://gorilla.cd.

We don't predict a rapid turnaround of the security situation, but we hope we're wrong. Ask around at Hotel Virunga (p498) in Kisoro, Backpackers Hostel (p435) in Kampala, Lake Kivu Serena Hotel (p575) in Gisenyi or Thousand Hills (p552) in Kigali for the latest advice. And keep in mind that potential guides in Gisenyi and Kisoro are *not* reliable sources of safety advice. See p534 for more details on the park.

Tanzania

Let Tanzania get its grip on you and you won't be able to shake loose. There's a magic to this country, an alluring equanimity and simplicity, a natural magnificence that all only begin to take hold slowly. But, once they do, they never let go.

Along the coast, thick vines force their way between the stones of centuries-old ruins, voices of Arabic traders and Indian merchants echo through the centuries in the sultry air, a full moon shines on tiny dhow ports as the straining groan of timber signals that it's time to set sail. The fleeting coolness and pastel skies of Indian Ocean dawn give way to a burning equatorial sun. Brightly clad women walk along the white sand, buckets balanced on their heads and babies on their backs.

Inland, the stillness is broken by the sound of elephants crushing the underbrush, by the pounding hoof beats of thousands of wildebeest on vast plains. Solitary acacia trees dot the savannahs. Rhythmic drumbeats sound into the night, Kilimanjaro awakens as porters and trekkers pack their tents and continue their trek towards the snowy summit. Maasai herders pull their red-plaid *shukas* (blankets) more tightly around them to ward off a morning chill. Market vendors set up their stalls for a day's trading.

This is the land of Zanzibar, Kilimanjaro, Serengeti and Ngorongoro. Of cloves and coffee, spices and tea. It's the land of the Maasai, the Makonde and over 100 other tribes, the land of *umoja* (oneness) and *ujamaa* (familyhood).

Step in, let yourself be seduced. Stay as long as you can. And don't be surprised if you can't wait to return for more.

FAST FACTS

- **Area** 943,000 sq km
- **Birthplace of** Humankind
- **Capital** Dodoma (legislative), Dar es Salaam (economic)
- **Country Code** ☎ 255
- **Famous for** Serengeti; Mt Kilimanjaro; Zanzibar; Julius Nyerere; cloves; chimpanzees
- **Languages** Swahili, English
- **Money** Tanzanian Shilling (TSh); US$1 = TSh1327; €1 = TSh1821
- **Population** 37.6 million

HIGHLIGHTS

- **Mt Kilimanjaro and Mt Meru** (p166) Tanzania's highest mountains rise splendidly over the surrounding landscapes – scale them, or hike on their lower slopes

- **Northern Circuit** (p159) Stand in awe as nature's age-old rhythms play themselves out on the Serengeti plains, on Ngorongoro crater's floor and amid Tarangire's ancient baobabs

- **Zanzibar Archipelago** (p121) Learn the ways of traditional fishermen, watch an Indian Ocean moonrise and lose yourself in Zanzibar's old Stone Town

- **Western Parks** (p210) Appreciate East Africa's splendid wilderness, with vast herds of animals dotting the plains and chimpanzee hoots echoing up forested mountainsides

- **Southern Circuit** (p239 & p221) Discover Swahili culture along the coast, let grunting hippos lull you to sleep in Selous Game Reserve or Ruaha National Park, and explore the southern highlands countryside

CLIMATE & WHEN TO GO

Tanzania has a tropical climate year-round, although there are significant regional variations. The coast is warmer and humid, with the climate determined in large part by the monsoon winds. These bring rains in two major periods – the long rains (*masika*) from mid-March to May, and the short rains (*mvuli*) from November through December and sometimes into January. During the long rains it rains heavily almost every day, although seldom for the whole day, and the air gets unpleasantly sticky.

Tanzania's central plateau is arid and somewhat cooler. In the mountainous areas of the northeast and southwest, temperatures may drop below 15°C at night during June and July, and it can rain at any time of year. Countrywide, the coolest months are from June to October, and the warmest from December to March.

The best time to visit is from mid-June through October when the rains have finished and the air is coolest. However, this is also when hotels and park lodges are full and airfares most expensive. From March through May, you can often save substantially on accommodation costs, have things to yourself, and enjoy landscapes that are green and full of life. The disadvantages: secondary roads are often very muddy or impassable and hotels in coastal areas and some of the southern parks close.

HISTORY

Tanzania's history begins with the dawn of humankind. Hominid (humanlike) footprints unearthed near Olduvai Gorge (p194), together with archaeological finds from Kenya and Ethiopia, show that our earliest ancestors were likely to be roaming the Tanzanian plains over three million years ago. For more on these and subsequent millennia, and an overview of colonial-era developments, see p25.

The Independence Struggle

The 1905 Maji Maji rebellion (see boxed text, p238) contains the earliest seeds of Tanzanian independence. During the following decades the nationalist movement in Tanganyika – as mainland Tanzania was then known – solidified. Farmers' cooperatives began to play an increasingly important political role, as did an up-and-coming group known as the Tanganyika Africa Association (TAA). Soon the TAA came to dominate Tanganyika's political scene, serving as the main channel for grass-roots resentment against colonial policies.

In 1953 the TAA elected an eloquent young teacher named Julius Nyerere as its president. He quickly transformed the group into an effective political organisation. A new internal

---

HOW MUCH?

- **Midrange safari** From US$200 per person per day
- **Plate of ugali** TSh500
- **Serengeti National Park entry** US$50 per person per entry
- **Papaya** TSh200
- **Short taxi ride** TSh2000

LONELY PLANET INDEX

- **Litre of petrol** TSh1900
- **Litre of bottled water** TSh500
- **Safari Lager** TSh1000
- **Souvenir T-shirt** TSh12,000
- **Street snack (mishikaki)** TSh200

constitution was introduced on 7 July 1954 (now celebrated as Saba Saba Day) and the TAA became the Tanganyika African National Union (TANU), with the rallying cry of 'uhuru na umoja' (freedom and unity).

Independence was the main item on TANU's agenda. In 1958 and 1959 TANU-supported candidates decisively won general legislative elections, and in 1959 Britain – which at the time held the reins in Tanganyika as governing 'caretaker' – agreed to the establishment of internal self-government. On 9 December 1961 Tanganyika became independent and on 9 December 1962 it was established as a republic, with Nyerere as president.

On the Zanzibar Archipelago, which had been a British protectorate since 1890, the main push for independence came from the radical Afro-Shirazi Party (ASP). Opposing the ASP were two minority parties, the Zanzibar & Pemba People's Party (ZPPP) and the sultanate-oriented Zanzibar Nationalist Party (ZNP), both favoured by the British. As a result, at Zanzibari independence in December 1963, it was the two minority parties that formed the first government.

This government did not last long. Within a month a Ugandan immigrant named John Okello initiated a violent revolution against the ruling ZPPP-ZNP coalition, leading to the toppling of the government and the sultan, and the massacre or expulsion of most of the islands' Arab population. The sultan was replaced by an entity known as the Zanzibar Revolutionary Council, which was comprised of ASP members and headed by Abeid Karume.

On 26 April 1964 Nyerere signed an act of union with Karume, creating the United Republic of Tanganyika (renamed the United Republic of Tanzania the following October).

Formation of the union, which was resented by many Zanzibaris from the outset, was motivated in part by the then-prevailing spirit of pan-Africanism, and in part as a cold war response to the ASP's socialist program.

Karume's government lasted until 1972, when he was assassinated by four gunmen, and succeeded by Aboud Jumbe. Shortly thereafter, in an effort to subdue the ongoing unrest resulting from the merger of the islands with the mainland, Nyerere authorised formation of a one-party state and combined TANU and the ASP into a new party known as Chama Cha Mapinduzi (CCM; Party of the Revolution). This merger, which was ratified in a new union constitution on 27 April 1977, marked the beginning of the CCM's dominance of Tanzanian politics, which endures to this day.

The Great Socialist Experiment

Nyerere took the helm of a country that was economically floundering and politically fragile, its stability plagued in particular by the mainland's lack of control over the Zanzibar Archipelago. Education had also been neglected, and at independence there were only a handful of university graduates in the entire country.

This inauspicious beginning eventually led to the Arusha Declaration of 1967, which committed Tanzania to a policy of socialism and self-reliance. The policy's cornerstone was the ujamaa (familyhood) village – an agricultural collective run along traditional African lines, with an emphasis on self-reliance. Basic goods and tools were to be held in common and shared among members, while each individual was obligated to work on the land.

In the early days of the ujamaa system, progressive farmers were encouraged to expand in the hope that other peasants would follow their example. This approach proved unrealistic, and was abandoned in favour of direct state control. Between 1973 and 1978, 85% of Tanzania's rural population was resettled, often forcibly, into over 7000 planned villages in an effort to modernise the agricultural sector and improve access to social services. Yet this approach was also unsuccessful, and resentment towards compulsory resettlement was widespread.

Tanzania's experiment in socialism was acclaimed in the days following independence, and is credited with unifying the country and expanding education and health care. Economically, however, it was a failure. Per capita income plummeted, agricultural production stagnated and industry limped along at less than 50% of capacity. The decline was precipitated by a combination of factors, including steeply rising oil prices, the 1977 break-up of the East African Community (an economic and customs union between Tanzania, Kenya and Uganda), and sharp drops in the value of coffee and sisal exports.

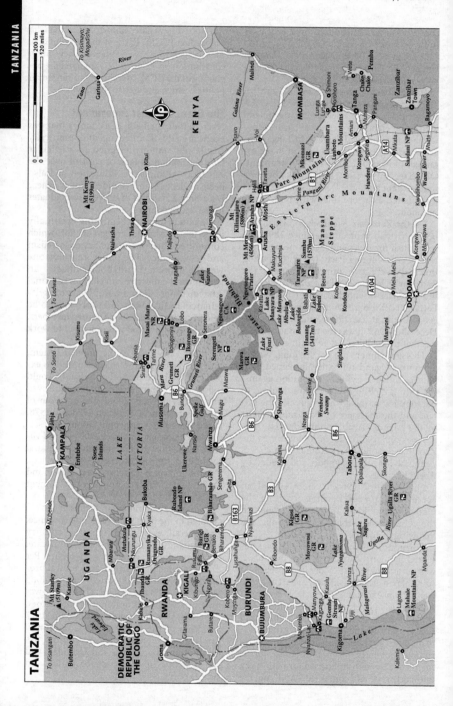

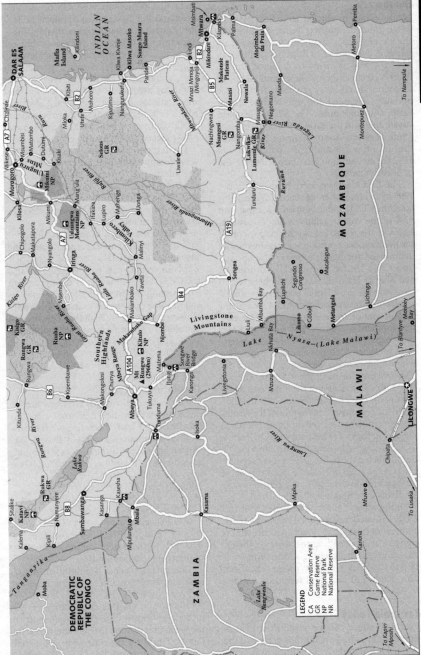

Democracy

Nyerere was re-elected to a fifth term in 1980, amid continuing dissatisfaction with the socialist experiment. In 1985 he resigned, handing over power to Zanzibari Ali Hassan Mwinyi. Mwinyi tried to distance himself from Nyerere and his policies, and instituted an economic recovery program. Yet the pace of change remained slow, and Mwinyi's presidency was unpopular. The fall of European communism in the early 1990s, and pressure from Western donor nations, accelerated the move towards multiparty politics, and in 1992 the constitution was amended to legalise opposition parties.

The first elections were held in October 1995 in an atmosphere of chaos. On the mainland, the CCM, under Benjamin Mkapa, won 62% of the vote in relatively smooth balloting. On the Zanzibar Archipelago, voting for the Zanzibari presidency was universally denounced for its dishonesty. The opposition Civic United Front (CUF) candidate, Seif Shariff Hamad, was widely believed to have won the presidential seat despite official results marginally favouring CCM incumbent Salmin Amour. In the ensuing uproar, foreign development assistance was suspended and most expatriates working on the islands left.

In October 2000 the elections proceeded without incident on the mainland, with a decisive victory for incumbent Mkapa and the CCM. On Zanzibar the balloting was again highly controversial. In January 2001 the CUF called for demonstrations to protest the results. The government declared the demonstrations illegal, but they were held anyway. On Pemba, a CUF stronghold where demonstrators greatly outnumbered the police, government security units responded with force, resulting in at least several dozen deaths and causing many Pembans to temporarily flee the island.

In the wake of the violence, the CCM and CUF initiated renewed attempts to reach agreement through dialogue. An accord was signed aimed at ending the strife on the archipelago and negotiating a long-term solution to the crisis. However, progress has been only modest at best, and tensions continue to simmer.

Tanzania Today

One of the effects that the introduction of multiparty politics had on Tanzanian life was the unmasking of underlying political, economic and religious frictions, especially between the mainland and the Zanzibar Archipelago. Yet – the Zanzibar situation notwithstanding – Tanzania as a whole remains reasonably well integrated, with comparatively high levels of religious and ethnic tolerance, particularly on the mainland. Tanzanians have earned a name for themselves in the region for their moderation and balance, and most observers consider it highly unlikely that the country would disintegrate into the tribal conflicts that have plagued some of its neighbours.

On the political front, President Mkapa was constitutionally prevented from seeking another term in the 2005 presidential elections, which were won in a landslide by CCM's Jakaya Kikwete, the charismatic former Foreign Minister. The next elections are scheduled for late 2010.

Perhaps more significant is the future of multiparty politics in Tanzania. If anything, this seems to have taken several steps backwards in recent years with entrenchment of the CCM and splintering of the opposition. Progressing beyond this situation may result in some growing pains in the short term. However, chances are high that Tanzania will continue to move forward, maintaining the stable and moderate outlook that has characterised its development since independence.

THE CULTURE
The National Psyche

Tanzania is notable for its relatively harmonious and understated demeanour. In contrast to Kenya and other neighbours, tribal rivalries are almost nonexistent. It's rare for a Tanzanian to identify themselves at the outset according to tribe; primary identification is always as a Tanzanian, and the *ujamaa* ideals of Julius Nyerere still permeate society. Religious frictions are minimal, with Christians and Muslims living side by side in a relatively easy coexistence. Although political differences flare up, especially on the Zanzibar Archipelago, they rarely come to the forefront in interpersonal dealings.

Tanzanians place a premium on politeness and courtesy. Greetings are essential, and you'll probably be given a gentle reminder should you forget this and launch straight into a question without first enquiring as to the wellbeing of your listener and his or her family. Children are trained to greet their elders with a respectful *shikamoo* (literally, 'I hold your feet'), often accompanied in rural areas by a slight curtsey, and strangers are frequently addressed as *dada* (sister); *mama*, in the case of an older woman; *kaka* (brother); or *ndugu* (relative or comrade).

Daily Life

When visiting a Tanzanian home, first call out *'hodi'*, then wait for the inevitable *'karibu'* (welcome). Apart from some impressive, Western-style houses in posh residential areas of Dar es Salaam, home for most Tanzanians is of cinderblock or mudbrick, with roofing of corrugated tin or thatch, a latrine outside and water drawn from a nearby pump or river. Mealtimes typically centre around a pot of *ugali* (the stiff and doughy maize- and/or cassava-based national dish) or a similar staple served with sauce, and rural rhythms dominate, with women and children spending much of their day working a small *shamba* (farm plot).

Family life is central, although it's sometimes hard to know where the family ends and the community begins. Doors are always open, helping out others in the *jamaa* (clan, community) is assumed and celebrations involve everyone. Child-raising is the expected occupation for women, and breadwinning for men. Village administrators (known as *shehe* on Zanzibar) make important decisions in consultation with other senior community members. Tribal structures, however, range from weak to nonexistent – a legacy of Nyerere's abolishment of local chieftaincies following independence.

While Tanzania's 6.5% adult HIV/AIDS infection rate has prompted a spate of billboards and public awareness campaigns, real public discussion remains limited, and AIDS deaths are still often explained away as tuberculosis, or with silence.

Population

Tanzania is home to about 120 tribal groups, although most tribes are very small, with almost 100 of them combined accounting for only one-third of the total population.

The vast majority of Tanzanians are of Bantu origin, with the largest groups including the Sukuma (who live around Mwanza and southern Lake Victoria), the Makonde (southeastern Tanzania), the Haya (around Bukoba) and the Chagga (around Mt Kilimanjaro). The Maasai and several smaller northern groups are of Nilo-Hamitic or Nilotic origin. The Iraqw, around Karatu and northwest of Lake Manyara, are Cushitic, as are the tiny northern-central tribes of Gorowa and Burungi, while the Sandawe and, more distantly, the Hadzabe (around Lake Eyasi), belong to the Khoisan ethnolinguistic family.

About 3% of Tanzania's total population, or about one million people, live on the Zanzibar Archipelago, with about one-third of these on Pemba. Members of the archipelago's non-African population consider themselves descendants of immigrants from Shiraz in Persia (Iran). Filling out Tanzania's melting pot are small but economically significant Asian (primarily from the Indian subcontinent) and Arabic populations, concentrated in major cities and along the coast, and a small European community.

City dwellers constitute about 37% of the population, with the urban growth rate increasing at a rate of about 6% per year. Average population density is 40 people per sq km, although this varies radically from one area to the next.

RELIGION

About 35% to 40% of Tanzanians are Muslim and between 40% and 45% are Christian. The remainder follow traditional religions. There are also small communities of Hindus, Sikhs and Ismailis. Muslims are traditionally found along the coast and in the inland towns that line the old caravan routes.

The population of the Zanzibar Archipelago is almost exclusively Sunni Muslim, with tiny Christian and Hindu communities.

ARTS
Literature

Tanzania's literary scene is dominated by poet and writer Shaaban Robert (1909–62), who spearheaded development of a modern Swahili prose style. Among his works are the autobiographical *Maisha yangu* (My Life), and several collections of folk tales.

Zanzibari Muhammed Said Abdulla, who gained fame with his *Mzimu wa watu wa kale* (Graveyard of the Ancestors), is considered the founder of Swahili popular literature.

A widely acclaimed contemporary writer is Zanzibari Abdulrazak Gurnah. His novel *Paradise*, which is set in East Africa during WWI, made the shortlist for the UK's Booker Prize in 1994, while *Desertion* was

LOCAL VOICES *As Related to Mary Fitzpatrick*

Neema – mother of three, Temeke area, Dar es Salaam

'My husband works in business, travels for two to three weeks, then returns home for a few days', began the ever-friendly Neema with a smile. 'His business is connected with the cashew industry, so off season it's difficult for him to find enough earnings. I work, too, usually until about 8pm. We have three young children, one still a baby, the other two in primary school. Schools in our area of Dar es Salaam are overfilled, there's no real instruction going on. When my husband and I are home, we help our children with tutoring, so they can advance in school, but it's difficult. Malaria? My children always have malaria. We sleep under nets, but they get it anyway.'

Massawe – watch and mobile phone repairman, Dar es Salaam

'I grew up here in Dar es Salaam, went to an English-medium primary school and then to technical college', said Massawe, a mobile phone and watch *fundi* (skilled technician) *par excellence* who was eager to talk to while away the long afternoon on the street. He spends his days seated in the shade on busy Samora Ave, amid a constant stream of cars and pedestrians, his services in high demand from the nearby shops. We interrupted him to ask about a shady looking character loitering nearby. 'Him? No, no need to worry – I know all the thieves here on this stretch, there are many, but he's not one of them. Now, back to my story: after finishing at the technical college, I was able to set up my stand here on Samora Ave. I know it's not much, but it's hard to find work here, so I am grateful that I have something. At night I roll the stand into that alley there, it has a locking gate. I'd love to have my own shop inside one day, a real place to work, but that's expensive. I've tried to negotiate with shop owners for space inside one of their places, but they don't want us street *fundi* there. They're worried we'd take business from them, and they would be upset if they saw that we get more clients than they do. But, for now this is OK, at least it is work. I'm not married yet, and no children – I'm still young, 23. My 19-year old friend, he just had a baby with his girlfriend, but that's too young for me.'

Frank – park bookkeeper, southern Tanzania

'You see', began Frank, a clean-cut, well-dressed bookkeeper working for the national park service, 'most rangers in the area where I work don't have more than a 7th-grade education. Park ranger work is considered a good job for that level of schooling, but it can be a difficult life. Family members usually can't accompany the ranger to his post, and the living situation is isolated. On off days, when staff can go to town, one woman may be shared by five men. HIV/AIDS is a big issue – bigger here than in Dar es Salaam, where I went to school.'

shortlisted for the Commonwealth Writers' Prize in 2006.

Other contemporary Tanzanian authors of English-language works include Peter Palangyo (*Dying in the Sun*), William Kamera (known for his poetry and for *Tales of the Wairaqw of Tanzania*) and May Balisidya (*Shida – Hardships*), one of the few first-generation women writers of Swahili literature.

Music & Dance

Traditional musical instruments include the *kayamba* (shaker), *mbira* (a thumb piano with metal strips of varying lengths), *marimba* (xylophone) and *ngoma* (drums). The same word (*ngoma*) is used for both dance and drumming, illustrating the intimate relationship between the two, and many dances can only be performed to the beat of a particular type of drum.

The single greatest influence on Tanzania's modern music scene has been the Congolese bands that began playing in Dar es Salaam in the early 1960s, and that brought the styles of rumba and soukous (*lingala* music) into the East African context. Among the best known is Orchestre Super Matimila, which was propelled to fame by Democratic Republic of the Congo (DRC; formerly Zaire)–born and Dar es Salaam-based Remmy Ongala. For more, see p38.

Masked dancing is mainly practiced in the southeast, where it is used in the initiation ceremonies of the Makonde (famous for their *mapiko* masks) and the Makua. These were highlighted for the first time in 2008 with the **Makuya Traditional Performing & Cultural Arts Festival** (http://makuyafestival.blogspot .com), focusing on the traditional dances of the Makonde, the Makua and the Yao. Leading names in the country's contemporary dance scene are Aloyce Makonde and his Mionzi Dance Theatre.

Painting

Tanzania's best-known school of painting is Tingatinga, which takes its name from the self-taught artist Edward Saidi Tingatinga, who began this style in the 1960s. Tingatinga paintings are traditionally composed in a square format, and feature brightly coloured animal motifs set against a monochrome background.

Mawazo Gallery & Art Café and Wasanii Art Gallery (both p100) are good first stops for getting acquainted with the contemporary Tanzanian art scene. Also try Dar es Salaam's cultural centres and Nyumba ya Sanaa (p100), with occasional exhibitions by contemporary Tanzanian artists.

Cinema

Tanzania's tiny indigenous film industry holds its own with those of other countries in the region; see p38. In addition to the Tanzanian-produced titles mentioned earlier in that section, films shot at least in part in Tanzania include the 1951 classic *The African Queen*, starring Katharine Hepburn and Humphrey Bogart; and *Mogambo* (1953), with Clark Gable, Ava Gardner and Grace Kelly.

Bongoland (2003), the first film of up-and-coming Tanzanian director Josiah Kabira, focuses on the realities of life for immigrants to the USA from the fictionalised Bongoland (Tanzania). Kabira followed this with *Tusamehe* (2005), focusing on the impact of AIDS on a family who has emigrated

from Tanzania (Bongoland in the film) to the USA. Not locally directed (although the codirector is transplanted Zanzibari Yusuf Mahmoud), but with great entreé into local life, is *As Old As My Tongue*, a documentary about Zanzibari music legend Bi Kidude.

Sculpture & Woodcarving

Tanzania's Makonde are renowned for their highly stylised ebony woodcarvings; see p39. Major centres of Makonde carving are in the southeast on the Makonde Plateau and in Dar es Salaam.

A good introduction into carving, and the full range of other Tanzanian arts and crafts, is **Makutano** (www.makutanotz.com), with a twice-yearly fair in Dar es Salaam.

ENVIRONMENT
The Land

At over 943,000 sq km, Tanzania is almost four times the size of the UK, and East Africa's largest country. It's bordered to the east by the Indian Ocean, and to the west by the deep lakes of the Western Rift Valley. Much of the mainland consists of a central highland plateau, averaging between 900m and 1800m in altitude, and nestled between the eastern and western branches of the geological fault known as the Great Rift Valley. In the northwest is the enormous, shallow Lake Victoria basin. Tanzania's mountain ranges are grouped into a sharply rising northeastern section (the Eastern Arc), and an open, rolling central and southern section (the Southern Highlands or Southern Arc). But not only mountains: there is also a range of volcanoes, part of the Crater Highlands, that rises from the side of the Great Rift Valley in northern Tanzania.

The largest river is the Rufiji, which drains the Southern Highlands region. Other major waterways include the Ruvu, the Wami, the Pangani and the Ruvuma (forming the border with Mozambique).

Wildlife
ANIMALS

Tanzania's more than four million wild animals encompass representatives of 430 species and subspecies, including all the 'classic' African animals mentioned under Wildlife on p53. Tanzania's elephant population is one of the largest on the continent. The country is also notable for its large cats, especially

---

AFRICA'S MELTING POT

Tanzania is the only African country with indigenous inhabitants from all of the continent's main ethnolinguistic families (Bantu, Nilo-Hamitic, Cushitic, Khoisan). They live in closest proximity around Lakes Eyasi and Babati, in north-central Tanzania.

lions, which are routinely seen in Serengeti National Park and Ngorongoro Crater, and for its large herds of wildebeests, buffalos and zebras.

There are over 1000 species of birds, including various types of kingfisher, hornbills (around Amani), bee-eaters (along the Rufiji and Wami Rivers), fish eagles (Lake Victoria) and flamingos (Lake Magadi in the Ngorongoro Crater, Lake Manyara and Lake Natron, among other places). Species unique to Tanzania include the Udzungwa forest partridge, the Pemba green pigeon and the Usambara weaver.

PLANTS

Botanically speaking, few places on the continent surpass Tanzania's Eastern Arc range, where small patches of tropical rainforest provide home to a rich assortment of plants. Many of these, such as the Usambara or African violet (*Saintpaulia*) and *Impatiens*, are found wild nowhere else in the world. South and west of the Eastern Arc range are impressive stands of baobab. Kitulo National Park – one of the continent's few parks with flowers as a focal point – is home to over 50 orchid species.

Away from the mountain ranges, much of the country is covered by *miombo* or 'moist' woodland, where the main vegetation is various types of *Brachystegia* tree. Savannah, bushland and thickets cover much of the central plateau, while grasslands cover the Serengeti plains and other areas lacking good drainage.

National Parks & Reserves

Tanzania currently has 14 mainland national parks (with two more – Mkomazi Game Reserve and Saa Nane Game Reserve – on the way), 14 wildlife reserves, the Ngorongoro Conservation Area (NCA), two marine parks and several protected marine reserves.

Development and tourism long focused almost exclusively on the so-called northern circuit: Serengeti, Lake Manyara, Tarangire, Arusha and Kilimanjaro National Parks and the NCA. As a result, all of these places are easily accessible, well equipped with facilities and heavily visited. In addition to the natural beauty, the northern circuit's main attractions are the high concentrations, diversity and accessibility of its wildlife.

The 'southern circuit' – Ruaha, Mikumi and Udzungwa Mountains National Parks and the Selous Game Reserve – has been receiving increased attention in recent years, although it still doesn't see close to the number of visitors that the north does. Most areas tend to have more of a wilderness feel and the wildlife is just as impressive, although it's often spread over larger areas.

In western Tanzania are Mahale Mountains and Gombe Stream National Parks, where the main drawcards are the chimpanzees, and Katavi National Park, with its large herds of wildlife. Rubondo Island National Park in Lake Victoria is of particular interest to bird-watchers. Saadani National Park, north of Dar es Salaam, is the only terrestrial park along the coast.

For an overview of the major parks and reserves, see table, p57.

NATIONAL PARKS

All parks are managed by the **Tanzania National Parks Authority** (Tanapa; www.tanzaniaparks.com). For the northern parks, an electronic payment system is being introduced. Currently, any visitor arriving with a tour or safari operator must pay with either Visa or MasterCard (depending on the park). Independent visitors can pay in cash, in theory, although at the gate, electronic payment is often required instead. Our advice is to travel with Visa, MasterCard and enough cash to cover park fees until the system is sorted out. For the southern and western parks, entry fees are currently payable only in hard currency, preferably US dollars cash, though this is also scheduled to change in the near future to an electronic system, as in the northern parks. Travellers cheques are no longer accepted in any parks.

For information on park entry, guides and other fees, see the park listings.

WILDLIFE RESERVES

Wildlife reserves are administered by the **Wildlife Division of the Ministry of Natural Resources & Tourism** (☎ 022-286 6064, 022-286 6376; scp@africaonline.co.tz; cnr Nyerere & Changombe Rds, Dar es Salaam). Fees should be paid in US dollars cash. The main ones of interest to visitors are Selous and the soon-to-be-a-national-park Mkomazi. Large areas of most others have been leased as hunting concessions.

MARINE PARKS & RESERVES

The Ministry of Natural Resources & Tourism's **Marine Parks & Reserves Unit** (Map p96; ☎ 022-215 0420, 022-215 0621; www.marineparktz .com; Olympio St, Upanga, Dar es Salaam) oversees marine parks and reserves. These include Mafia Island Marine Park, Mnazi Bay-Ruvuma Estuary Marine Park, Maziwe Island Marine Reserve and the Dar es Salaam Marine Reserves (Mbudya, Bongoyo, Pangavini and Fungu Yasini islands).

NGORONGORO CONSERVATION AREA

The Ngorongoro Conservation Area (p190) was established as a multiple use area to protect both wildlife and the pastoralist lifestyle of the Maasai, who had lost other large areas of their traditional territory with the formation of Serengeti National Park. It is administered by the **Ngorongoro Conservation Area Authority** (www.ngorongor ocrater.org).

Environmental Issues

Although Tanzania has one of the highest proportions of protected land of any African country (about 39% is protected in some form, including several Unesco World Heritage sites), limited resources hamper conservation efforts, and erosion, soil degradation, desertification, deforestation and corruption all combine to whittle away at the natural wealth. According to some estimates, Tanzania loses 3500 sq km of forest land annually as a result of agricultural and commercial clearing, and about 95% of the tropical high forest that once covered Zanzibar and Pemba are now gone. In the national parks, poaching and inappropriate visitor use threaten wildlife and ecosystems. Dynamite fishing has also been a serious threat in the marine parks, although significant progress has been made in halting this practice.

However, on the positive side, great strides have been made in recent years to involve communities directly in conservation, and local communities are now stakeholders in numerous lodges and other tourist developments.

The main local contact on environmental issues is the **Wildlife Conservation Society of Tanzania** (www.wcstonline.org; Garden Ave, Dar es Salaam). For more on what you can do to help, see p16.

FOOD & DRINK

Tanzania's unofficial national dish is *ugali*. For more on this and other local cuisine, see p40. Another favourite is *mishikaki* (marinated meat kebabs). Some Tanzanians start their day with *uji*, a thin, sweet porridge made from bean, millet or other flour. Watch for ladies stirring bubbling pots of it on the street corners in the early morning. *Vitambua* – rice cakes vaguely resembling tiny, thick pancakes – are another morning treat. On Zanzibar, look for *mkate wa kumimina*, a bread made from a batter similar to that used for making *vitambua*, and for the thick, soft, pancake-like bread called *mkate wa ufuta* (sesame bread).

In major towns there's a good selection of places to eat, ranging from local food stalls to Western-style restaurants. In smaller towns you're likely to just find *hoteli* (small, informal restaurants) and *mama lishe* (informal food stalls where the resident 'mama' does the 'home' cooking) serving chicken, beef or fish with rice, chips, *ugali* or another staple. The main meal is at noon; in rural areas many places are closed in the evening, with street food often the only option.

Bottled water and soft drinks are widely available; tap water should be avoided. Tanzania's beer selection includes the local Safari and Kilimanjaro labels, plus Castle Lager and various Kenyan and German beers. Finding a beer is usually no problem, but – as elsewhere in the region – finding one cold can be a challenge.

GREAT CUPS OF COFFEE

Despite Tanzania's many coffee plantations, it can be difficult to find a cup of the real stuff. Here are our picks for some of the best local brews; let us know if you find others.

- Stone Town Café, Zanzibar Town (p134)
- Msumbi Coffee House, Dar es Salaam (p99)
- Rumaliza Coffee & Grill, Zanzibar Town (p134)
- Utengule Country Hotel, Mbeya (p232)
- Zanzibar Coffee House, Zanzibar Town (p134)
- Coffee Shop, Moshi (p162)
- Tanzania Coffee Lounge, Moshi (p162)

TANZANIA

DAR ES SALAAM

☎ 022 / pop approx 3 million

The first things you notice are the air – thick, humid, sultry – and the ever-present traffic. It's only as you settle in that the city – Tanzania's largest by far – begins to unfold. Narrow, winding streets are lined with Indian trading houses and and massive container ships anchor in the harbour. Colonial-era buildings overlook Kivukoni Front – the paint on their wooden shutters and narrow balconies peeling in the salty air. Overflow crowds spill out onto the pavement in front of mosques during Friday midday prayer. Densely populated suburbs sprawl for kilometres, with compact, corrugated-roofed houses lining their winding, sandy lanes and bustling night markets doing business to the light of dozens of small kerosene lanterns. On the Msasani Peninsula, with its large foreign population, clipped lawns fringed by magenta bougainvillea flowers lead to stately ambassadorial residences and several chic shopping centres.

While it's easy enough to bypass 'Dar' completely, the city merits a visit as Tanzania's political and economic hub. It's also an agreeable place to break your travels, with an array of services and well-stocked shops, nearby beaches and Zanzibar island just a short ferry ride away.

HISTORY

Until the mid-19th century, what is now Dar es Salaam was just a humble fishing village, one of many along the East African coast. In the 1860s Sultan Sayyid Majid of Zanzibar decided to develop the area's inland harbour into a port and trading centre, and named the site Dar es Salaam (Haven of Peace). No sooner had development of the harbour begun, than the sultan died and the town sunk again into anonymity, overshadowed by Bagamoyo, an important dhow port to the north. It wasn't until the 1880s that Dar es Salaam assumed new significance, first as a station for Christian missionaries making their way from Zanzibar to the interior, and then as a seat for the German colonial government, which viewed Dar es Salaam's protected harbour as a better alternative for steamships than the dhow port in Bagamoyo. In 1891 the colonial administration was officially moved from Bagamoyo to Dar es Salaam. Since then the city has remained Tanzania's undisputed political and economic capital, although the legislature was transferred to Dodoma in 1973.

ORIENTATION

The city centre runs along Samora Ave from the clock tower to the Askari monument, with banks, foreign-exchange bureaus, vendors and shops. Northwest of Samora Ave, around India and Jamhuri Sts, is the Asian quarter, with narrow streets lined with Indian merchants and traders. West of Mnazi Mmoja Park are the rougher but colourful neighbourhoods of Kariakoo and Ilala.

On the other side of town, northeast of the Askari monument, are shady, tree-lined streets with the National Museum, Botanical Gardens and State House. Proceeding north from here along the coast, you first reach the upper-middle class section of Upanga and then, after crossing Selander Bridge, the fast-developing diplomatic and upmarket residential areas of Oyster Bay and Msasani.

Maps

The Tanzania Tourist Board Information Centre (p95) has free photocopied city maps, and there are many city maps on sale in hotel bookshops. The city's official tourist map – *Dar es Salaam City Map & Guide* (1:20,000) – is available from the **Surveys & Mapping Division Map Sales Office** (Map p96; cnr Kivukoni Front & Luthuli St; ☉ 8am-2pm Mon-Fri), but it's dated, large and unwieldy.

INFORMATION

Bookshops

A Novel Idea (☎ 022-260 1088) Msasani Slipway (Map p94; Msasani Slipway, Msasani Peninsula); Sea Cliff Village (Map p94; Sea Cliff Village, Toure Dr, Msasani Peninsula); Steers (Map p96; cnr Ohio St & Samora Ave) Classics, modern fiction, travel guides, Africa titles, maps and more.

Cultural Centres

Alliance Française (Map p94; ☎ 022-213 1406/2; afdar@africaonline.co.tz; Ali Hassan Mwinyi Rd)
British Council (Map p96; ☎ 022-211 6574/5/6; info@ britishcouncil.or.tz; cnr Ohio St & Samora Ave)
Nyumba ya Sanaa (Mwalimu Julius K Nyerere Cultural Centre; Map p96; Ohio St)
Russian Cultural Centre (Map p94; ☎ 022-213 6578; cnr Ufukoni & Ocean Rds)

Emergency

Central police station (Map p96; ☎ 022-211 5507; Sokoine Dr) Near the Central Line Railway Station.

First Air Responder (Map p94; ☎ 022-276 0087, 0754-777100, 0754-777073; www.knightsupport.com; Ali Hassan Mwinyi Rd) Emergency transport and ambulance for members.

Flying Doctors/Amref (Map p96; ☎ Nairobi emergency 254-020-315454/5, 254-020-600090; www.amref.org; Ali Hassan Mwinyi Rd) Emergency evacuations for members; see p609.

IST Clinic (Map p94; ☎ 022-260 1307/0784-783393, 24hr emergency line 0754-783393; www.istclinic.com; Ruvu Rd; ☺ 8am-6pm Mon-Fri, 8am-noon Sat) Western-run clinic with a doctor always on call; located just off Chole Rd.

Oyster Bay police station (Map p94; ☎ 022-266 7332; Toure Dr) North of Coco Beach.

Traffic police headquarters (Map p96; ☎ 022-211 1747; Sokoine Dr) Near the Central Line Railway Station.

Immigration Office

Wizara ya mambo ya ndani (Immigration Office; Map p96; ☎ 022-211 8640/3; www.tanzania.go.tz/immigrationf.html; cnr Ghana Ave & Ohio St; ☺ 8am-noon Mon-Fri for visa applications, until 2pm for visa collection)

Internet Access

CSS Internet Café (Map p94; 1st fl, Sea Cliff Village, Toure Dr, Msasani Peninsula; per hr TSh5000; ☺ 7am-9pm Mon-Fri, 9am-6pm Sat, 2-6pm Sun)

Post Office Internet Café (Map p96; Maktaba St; per hr TSh1200; ☺ 8am-7pm Mon-Fri, 9am-2pm Sat)

Printout@Slipway (Map p94; 2nd fl, Msasani Slipway, Msasani Peninsula; per hr TSh2000; ☺ 7.30am-8pm Mon-Fri, 8am-7pm Sat & Sun)

Royal Palm Business Centre (Map p96; Mövenpick Royal Palm Hotel, Ohio St; per 10min TSh1000; ☺ 7am-8pm Mon-Fri, 8.30am-4pm Sat, 9am-1pm Sun)

Southern Sun Business Centre (Map p96; Southern Sun hotel, Garden Ave; per hr TSh6000; ☺ 7am-10pm)

YMCA Internet Café (Map p96; Upanga Rd; per hr TSh1000; ☺ 8am-7.30pm Mon-Fri, 8am-2pm Sat)

Media

Advertising Dar Free weekly with restaurant, club and event listings; widely available around town in restaurants and shops.

Dar es Salaam Guide Free monthly with restaurant and club listings etc; available from hotels, travel agencies and the Tanzania Tourist Board Information Centre.

Medical Services

IST Clinic (Map p94; ☎ 022-260 1307/8, 0784-783393, 24hr emergency line 0754-783393; istclinic@istclinic.com;

Ruvu Rd; ☺ 8am-6pm Mon-Fri, 8am-noon Sat) See listing under Emergency (left); located just off Chole Rd.

Premier Care Clinic (Map p94; ☎ 022-266 8385, 022-266 8320; www.premiercareclinic.com; Ali Hassan Mwinyi Rd) Tanzanian-French run clinic next to Big Bite restaurant.

Money

Forex bureaus give the fastest service and best exchange rates. Most are in the city centre on or near Samora Ave (all open standard business hours), or try the following:

Galaxy Forex Bureau (International Arrivals Area, Airport; ☺ 6am-11pm) Cash and travellers cheques; to the right when exiting customs.

Mövenpick Royal Palm Forex Bureau (Map p96; Mövenpick Royal Palm Hotel, Ohio St; ☺ 8am-8pm Mon-Sat, 10am-1pm Sun & public holidays) Cash and travellers cheques (receipts required).

National Bank of Commerce (NBC; Map p96; cnr Azikiwe St & Sokoine Dr) Cash and travellers cheques, and has an ATM (Visa).

Sea Cliff Forex Bureau (Map p94; Sea Cliff Village, Toure Dr, Msasani Peninsula; ☺ 11am-7pm) Cash only.

ATMS

Barclays Bank Mövenpick Royal Palm Hotel (Map p96; opposite Mövenpick Royal Palm Hotel, Ohio St); Msasani Slipway (Map p94; Msasani Slipway, Msasani Peninsula) Visa and MasterCard.

Kilimanjaro Kempinski (Map p96; Kilimanjaro Kempinski hotel, Kivukoni Front) Visa, MasterCard, Cirrus, Maestro.

NBC Bank (Map p96; cnr Azikiwe St & Sokoine Dr) ATMs at all branches, including this main branch.

Stanbic Bank (Map p96; Sukari House, cnr Ohio St & Sokoine Dr) Visa, MasterCard, Cirrus, Maestro.

Standard Chartered Bank JM Mall (Map p96; Harbour View Towers, cnr Samora Ave & Mission St); NIC Life House (Map p96; cnr Ohio St & Sokoine Dr); Shoppers' Plaza (Map p94); Southern Sun hotel (Map p96, Garden Ave); Visa.

Post

Main Post Office (Map p96; Maktaba St; ☺ 8am-5pm Mon-Fri, 9am-noon Sat)

Telephone

For buying or repairing mobile phones, try **Midcom** (Map p94; Ali Hassan Mwinyi Rd), opposite the Selander Bridge police station, or **Sapna Electronics** (Map p96; Samora Ave), between Askari Monument and Mkwepu St.

The **Telecom Office** (Map p96; cnr Bridge St & Samora Ave; ☺ 7.30am-6pm Mon-Fri, 9am-3pm Sat)

TANZANIA

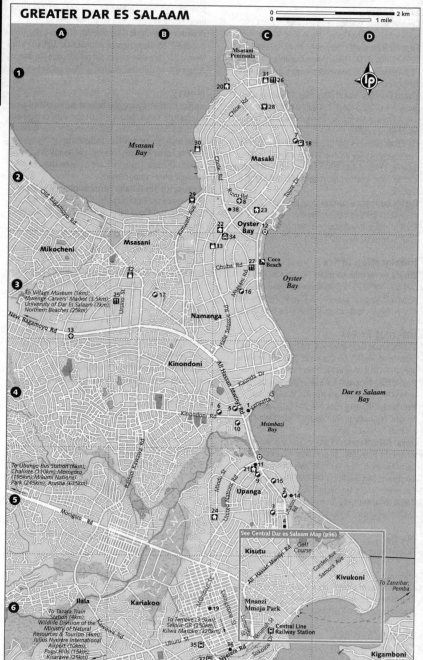

GREATER DAR ES SALAAM

0 _____ 2 km
0 _____ 1 mile

Msasani Penisula

Msasani Bay

Chole Rd

Masaki

Old Bagamoyo Rd

Mikocheni

Msasani

Kimwei Ave

Chole Rd

Ruvu Rd

Toure Dr

Oyster Bay

Ghuba Rd

Coco Beach

Oyster Bay

Haile Selassie Rd

Msasani Rd

Namanga

To Village Museum (1km);
Mwenge Carvers' Market (3.5km);
University of Dar Es Salaam (7km);
Northern Beaches (25km)

Uhindu St

New Bagamoyo Rd

Kinondoni

Ali Hassan Mwinyi Rd

Kunduchi Dr

Kinondoni Rd

Kenyatta Dr

Msimbazi Bay

Dar es Salaam Bay

To Ubungo Bus Station (6km);
Chalinze (110km); Morogoro
(195km); Mikumi National
Park (245km); Arusha (635km)

Rashidi Kawawa Rd

Morogoro Rd

Upanga

United Nations Rd

Asindu St

Upanga Rd

See Central Dar es Salaam Map (p96)

Kisutu

Golf Course

Garden Ave

Samora Ave

Kivukoni

To Zanzibar;
Pemba

Ilala

To Tazara Train
Station (4km);
Wildlife Division of the
Ministry of Natural
Resources & Tourism (4km);
Julius Nyerere International
Airport (10km);
Pugu Hills (15km);
Kisarawe (25km)

Kawawa Rd

Kariakoo

Bibi Titi Mohamed St

Mnanzi Mmoja Park

To Temeke (3.5km);
Selous GR (250km);
Kilwa Masoko (320km)

Uhuru St

Nyerere Rd

Mkwepu St

Sokoine

Central Line
Railway Station

Kigamboni

behind the Extelecoms House sells phone cards for TSh1000 that you can top up and use at any TTCL (landline) phone for international calls. Starter packs and top-up cards for Vodacom, Tigo and other mobile phone operators are sold in shops all around the city.

Tourist Information
Tanzania Tourist Board Information Centre (Map p96; ☎ 022-212 0373, 022-213 1555; www.tanzania touristboard.com; Samora Ave; ⏰ 8am-4pm Mon-Fri, 8.30am-12.30pm Sat) Just west of Zanaki St, with free tourist maps, brochures and city information.

Travel Agencies
For safari and trekking operator listings, see p68.
Afri-Roots (www.afriroots.co.tz) Budget cycling, hiking and camping in and around Dar es Salaam.
Coastal Travels (Map p96; ☎ 022-211 7959/60; www.coastal.cc; Upanga Rd) For flights around the country; especially recommended for travel to Zanzibar, and to northern and southern safari circuit destinations. Also offers city tours, day trips to Zanzibar and Mikumi National Park excursions.
Kearsley Travel (www.kearsleys.com) Sea Cliff Village (Map p94; ☎ 022-260 0467; Sea Cliff Village, Toure Dr, Msasani Peninsula); Southern Sun hotel (Map p96; ☎ 022-213 1652/3; Garden Ave)

DANGERS & ANNOYANCES
Dar es Salaam is considered to be safer than some other big cities in the region, notably Nairobi, though it also has its share of muggings and thefts, and urban-area precautions should be taken. Be alert and watch out for pick-pocketing, particularly at crowded markets and bus and train stations, and for bag snatching through vehicle windows. Stay aware of your surroundings, minimise carrying conspicuous bags or cameras, try not to look like a tourist, and if possible, leave your valuables in a reliable hotel safe. At night take a taxi – from a taxi rank at an established hotel – rather than taking a *dalla-dalla* (minibus) or walking, and avoid walking alone along the path paralleling Ocean Rd, along the seaside Toure Dr on the Msasani Peninsula and on Coco Beach (which is only safe on weekend afternoons, when it's packed with people).

SIGHTS & ACTIVITIES
National Museum
The **National Museum** (Map p96; ☎ 022-211 7508; www.houseofculture.or.tz; Shaaban Robert St; adult/student US$5/2; ⏰ 9.30am-6pm) houses the famous fossil discoveries of *Zinjanthropus* (nutcracker man) from Olduvai Gorge, although the display is currently closed for renovations. There are

TANZANIA

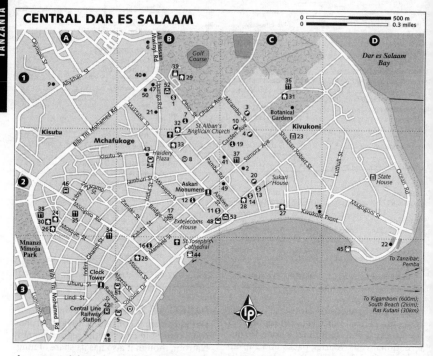

CENTRAL DAR ES SALAAM

also scattered displays on other topics, ranging from the Shirazi civilisation of Kilwa to the Zanzibar slave trade and the German and British colonial periods. There's also a collection of vintage automobiles, including the Rolls Royce used first by the British colonial government and later by Julius Nyerere. It's located near the Botanical Gardens, between Samora Ave and Sokoine Dr.

Village Museum

The centrepiece of the open-air **Village Museum** (☎ 022-270 0437; www.museum.or.tz; cnr New Bagamoyo Rd & Makaburi St; adult/student US$5/2; �9.30am-6pm) is a collection of authentically constructed dwellings illustrating traditional life in various parts of Tanzania. There are traditional music and dance performances some afternoons.

The museum is 10km north of the city centre – catch a Mwenge *dalla-dalla* from New Posta transport stand (30 minutes).

Swimming

There's a large, lovely **swimming pool** (Map p94; adult/child TSh10,000/5000; �),7am-6pm) at Golden Tulip Hotel on Toure Dr just south of Sea

Cliff Village – one of the few hotel pools in the city open to walk-in guests.

Markets

Dar es Salaam's **fish market** (Map p96; Ocean Rd), near Kivukoni Front, is fairly calm as urban markets go, and makes a good introduction. For more excitement, get a reliable taxi driver or Tanzanian friend to take you to the sprawling **Kariakoo Market** (Map p94; cnr Msimbazi & Mkunguni Sts), Tanzania's largest; don't bring valuables, and watch out for pickpockets. For Western-style shopping, see p100.

DAR ES SALAAM FOR CHILDREN

Diversions include the **beaches** and **water parks** north of the city (see p103); the supervised **play area** at Sea Cliff Village (Map p94), where you can leave your child with a nanny while you shop; **Msasani Slipway** (Map p94), with ice-cream cones, movies and a small playground; and, the **swimming pool** at Golden Tulip Hotel (see left). There are **children's reading corners** at the A Novel Idea bookshop branches at Msasani Peninsula and Sea Cliff Village (see Bookshops, p92).

INFORMATION
- A Novel Idea.....(see 37)
- Barclays Bank.....1 B1
- British Council.....2 C2
- British High Commission.....3 C1
- Canadian High Commission.....4 C2
- Central Police Station.....5 B3
- Dutch Embassy.....(see 3)
- Flying Doctors & AMREF.....6 B1
- German Embassy.....(see 3)
- Immigration Office.....7 B1
- Kearsley Travel.....(see 31)
- Kilimanjaro Kempinski ATM.....(see 27)
- Main Post Office.....8 B2
- Malawian High Commission.....(see 20)
- Marine Parks & Reserves Unit.....9 A1
- Mozambique High Commission.....10 C1
- Mövenpick Royal Palm Forex Bureau.....(see 29)
- NBC Bank.....11 B2
- Nyumba ya Sanaa.....(see 39)
- Post Office Internet Café.....(see 8)
- Royal Palm Business Centre.....(see 29)
- Sapna Electronics.....12 B2
- Southern Sun Business Centre.....(see 31)
- Stanbic Bank ATM.....13 C2
- Standard Chartered Bank.....(see 31)
- Standard Chartered Bank.....14 C2
- Standard Chartered Bank ATM.....(see 25)
- Surveys & Mapping Division Map Sales Office.....15 C2
- Tanzania Tourist Board Information Centre.....16 B3
- Telecom Office.....17 B2
- Traffic Police Headquarters.....18 A3
- Wildlife Conservation Society of Tanzania.....19 C2
- YMCA Internet Café.....(see 32)
- Zambian High Commission.....20 C2

SIGHTS & ACTIVITIES
- Coastal Travels.....21 B1
- Fish Market.....22 D3
- National Museum.....23 C2

SLEEPING
- Econolodge.....24 A2
- Harbour View Suites.....25 B3
- Jambo Inn.....26 A2
- Kilimanjaro Kempinski.....27 C2
- Luther House Centre Hostel.....28 C2
- Mövenpick Royal Palm Hotel.....29 B1
- Safari Inn.....30 A2
- Southern Sun.....31 C1
- YMCA.....32 B2
- YWCA.....33 B2

EATING
- Al Basha.....34 A2
- Baraza.....(see 31)
- Chef's Pride.....35 A2
- City Supermarket.....(see 25)
- Debonairs Pizza.....(see 37)
- Holiday Out.....36 C1
- Kibo Bar.....(see 29)
- Kilimanjaro Kempinski.....(see 27)
- Oriental.....(see 27)
- Steers.....37 C2
- Tausi.....38 A2
- YMCA.....(see 32)

DRINKING
- Level 8.....(see 27)

ENTERTAINMENT
- Mwalimu Julius K Nyerere Cultural Centre.....(see 39)

SHOPPING
- JM Mall.....(see 25)
- Mawazo Gallery & Art Café.....(see 32)
- Nyumba ya Sanaa.....39 B1

TRANSPORT
- Air India.....40 B1
- Air Tanzania.....41 C2
- Avis.....(see 1)
- Avis.....(see 27)
- British Airways.....(see 29)
- Coastal Aviation.....(see 21)
- Dalla-Dallas to Temeke.....42 A3
- Dar Express Booking Office.....(see 46)
- Emirates Airlines.....43 B2
- Ethiopian Airlines.....(see 1)
- Ferries to Zanzibar Archipelago.....44 B3
- Ferry to Kigamboni & Southern Beaches.....45 D3
- Kenya Airways.....(see 47)
- Kisutu Area Bus Stand.....46 A2
- KLM.....47 B1
- Linhas Aéreas de Moçambique.....(see 25)
- New Posta Transport Stand.....(see 8)
- Old Posta Transport Stand.....48 B2
- Precision Air.....49 C2
- Royal Coach Booking Office.....(see 46)
- South African Airways.....50 B1
- Stesheni Transport Stand.....51 B3
- Swiss International Airlines.....(see 28)
- Taxi Stand.....52 B1
- Taxi Stand.....53 C2
- Zambian Airways.....54 B2

SLEEPING

If you're relying on public transport, it's cheaper and more convenient to stay in the city centre, which is where most budget lodging is anyway. If you don't mind paying for taxis, or travelling the distance from the airport (about 20km), the hotels on Msasani Peninsula are a break from the urban scene.

The closest places for camping are at Pugu Hills (p104), and at the beaches north and south of town (p102).

City Centre

BUDGET

In the busy, central area around the main post office:

YWCA (Map p96; ☎ 0713-622707; ywca.tanzania@africaonline.co.tz; Maktaba St; d TSh25,000, s/d with shared bathroom TSh10,000/15,000) Centrally located just up from the post office (although the entrance is around the corner on a tiny side street), with faded, noisy rooms with mosquito net, fan and sink, and clean-ish shared bathrooms. Men and women are accepted. The attached restaurant serves inexpensive local-style meals (although there's no dinner on Saturday and Sunday).

YMCA (Map p96; ☎ 022-213 5457; Upanga Rd; s/d with shared bathroom US$10/13) Around the corner from the YWCA, cleaner and quieter with a nice inner courtyard. The no-frills rooms are good value and well kept, with mosquito net, and there's a canteen serving inexpensive, filling meals. Men and women are accepted.

Luther House Centre Hostel (Map p96; ☎ 022-212 6247, 022-212 0734; luther@simbanet.net; Sokoine Dr; s/tw/d US$30/35/40;) Just back from the waterfront about two blocks southeast of the post office. The small-ish and now faded rooms have fan, mosquito net and air-con, and breakfast is available (at extra charge) at the restaurant downstairs.

In the busy Kisutu area is another clutch of budget places, all within walking distance of Royal Coach and other Kisutu area bus booking offices.

Safari Inn (Map p96; ☎ 022-213 8101; www.darsafari inn.com; s/d US$10/20, d with air-con US$25; ✶ ☐) A popular travellers haunt in Kisutu, on the western edge of the city centre. Rooms have fan and hot water but no mosquito net, although they are sprayed each evening.

Jambo Inn (Map p96; ☎ 022-211 4293; jamboinn hotel@yahoo.com; Libya St; s/d US$20/25) Around the corner from Safari Inn, and also popular, with a mix of twin and double-bedded rooms with fan, flyscreens in the windows and erratic hot-water supplies. It has a good, cheap restaurant with Indian dishes, plus burgers and other standards.

Econolodge (Map p96; ☎ 022-211 6048/9; econolodge@ raha.com; s/d/tr US$18/24/30, s/d/tr with air-con US$30/35/40; ✶) Clean, good, no-frills rooms hidden away in an unaesthetically appealing high-rise near the Kisutu bus stand booking offices and around the corner from Safari Inn and Jambo Inn. Continental breakfast is included; otherwise there's no food.

MIDRANGE & TOP END

our pick **Harbour View Suites** (Map p96; ☎ 022-212 4040; www.harbourview-suites.com; Harbour View Towers, cnr Samora Ave & Mission St; s/d from US$150/170; ✶ ☐) Well-equipped, centrally located business travellers' studio apartments with views over the city or the harbour, in-room wi-fi connections and a business centre – good value. Some rooms have mosquito nets, and all have modern furnishings and a kitchenette. Breakfast costs US$7. A pool, fitness centre, restaurant and additional rooms are being built. Underneath is JM Mall shopping centre, with an ATM, supermarket and forex bureau.

Southern Sun (Map p96; ☎ 022-213 7575; www .southernsuntz.com; Garden Ave; s/d from US$254/274; ✶ ☐) This place – formerly Holiday Inn – is solid value, with modern rooms and the standard amenities, including TV, telephone and a business centre that's open until 10pm. It's on a quiet, leafy side street near the National Museum and next to Standard Chartered Bank.

Kilimanjaro Kempinski (Map p96; ☎ 022-213 1111; www.kempinski-daressalaam.com; Kivukoni Front; r from US$250; ✶ ☐ ☲) This once-classic waterfront hotel has been completely refurbished by the Kempinski chain. The ultramodern rooms are arguably the best in the city – especially those with views over the harbour – with sleek, modern bathrooms and attractive décor. The lobby is rather lacking in character, but the Level 8

rooftop bar is an ideal spot to appreciate the city's port and harbour setting.

Other recommendations:

Mövenpick Royal Palm (Map p96; ☎ 022-211 2416; www.moevenpick-daressalaam.com; Ohio St; r from US$235; ✶ ☐ ☲) Spacious, recently refurbished rooms, a large, beautiful pool, lush gardens and a central location.

Msasani Peninsula & Upanga

Q Bar & Guest House (Map p94; ☎ 022-260 2150, 0754-282474; www.qbardar.com; cnr Haile Selassie & Msasani Rds; dm US$12, s/d with shared bathroom US$35/45, with private bathroom US$45/55, executive s/d from US$50/65; ✶) Spotless rooms – the executive rooms on the upper floors are huge – all with satellite TV, minifridge and bathroom, plus a four-bed backpackers' dorm room and a standard double, both sharing bathrooms. Laundry service is included in room prices, and breakfast is included with all rooms except the dorm. Food is served downstairs, and there's also a bar with live music on Friday evenings.

Swiss Garden Hotel (Map p94; ☎ 022-215 3219; www.swisshostel.net; Mindu St; s/d incl breakfast from US$70/90; ✶ ☐) A cosy B&B in a quiet, leafy neighbourhood, with small, spotless rooms with internet connections and helpful hosts. Breakfast is included; other meals can be arranged. It's in Upanga, just off United Nations Rd.

Palm Beach Hotel (Map p94; ☎ 022-212 2931, 022-213 0985; www.pbhtz.com; Ali Hassan Mwinyi Rd; s/d/tr US$85/100/110; ✶ ☐) This Dar es Salaam institution was completely renovated several years ago – look for the bright blue Art Deco architecture – with spartan but spacious rooms, with TV, wi-fi and a restaurant.

Coral Beach (Map p94; ☎ 022-260 1928, 0784-783858; www.coralbeach-tz.com; s/d from US$160/180, family r US$205; ✶ ☐ ☲) A quiet, often overlooked boutique hotel catering to business travellers, with large and comfortable rooms – though many don't have views – in a secluded location near the northern end of Msasani Peninsula. The family rooms have two large beds, and there's a restaurant.

Other recommendations:

Msasani Slipway Apartments (Map p94; ☎ 022-260 0893; slipway@coastal.cc; Msasani Slipway; r/apt US$70/90; ✶ ☐ ☲) Furnished apartments at the Msasani Slipway (reception is next to Barclays Bank). All have a hotplate and refrigerator, and some have bay views.

Sea Cliff Court Apartments (Map p94; ☎ 022-260 1967; www.seacliffcourt.com; s studio/1-bedroom

apt/2-bedroom apt from US$170/190/240; ☒ ▣ ☒)
Modern, new serviced apartments for short- or long-term
rental. Discounted monthly rates available.

EATING
City Centre

Most restaurants in the city centre are closed
on Sunday.

BUDGET

our pick **Holiday Out** (Map p96; Garden Ave; meals about
TSh2500; ☖ 7.30am-4pm Mon-Fri) Great-value local
food. There's no signboard, and no official
name, but locals have dubbed it Holiday
Out, thanks to its location diagonally opposite the former Holiday Inn hotel (now
Southern Sun). Go to the cashier, request
the meal you'd like, pay and you'll be given
a small coupon that you then take to the back
'kitchen' area where you'll be given a portion of steaming *nyama pilau* (meat and seasoned rice), *wali na kuku* (rice and chicken)
or whatever else you may fancy. It's all very
sanitary, and for dessert there are bowls of
freshly cut fruit salad, avocadoes and cucum-
bers for just TSh1000.

YMCA (Map p96; ☎ 022-213 5457; Upanga Rd; meals
about TSh2500; ☖ lunch & dinner) More filling, inexpensive local food, operating on the same
coupon system as Holiday Out.

Chef's Pride (Map p96; Chagga St; meals from TSh2500;
☖ lunch & dinner, closed during Ramadan) A long-standing, popular local eatery within easy walking
distance of the Kisutu area budget hotels. The
large menu features standard fare, plus pizzas,
Indian and veg dishes.

Al Basha (Map p96; ☎ 022-212 6888, 0787-909000;
Indira Gandhi Rd; snacks from TSh1500, meals TSh6000;
☖ breakfast, lunch & dinner) A no-frills eatery with
hummus and other Lebanese dishes, plus
burgers and subs. It's just off Morogoro Rd,
and a few blocks northwest of Samora Ave.

Other recommendations:

Steers (Map p96; cnr Samora Ave & Ohio St; meals from
TSh2000; ☖ 8am-11pm) Burgers and fast food. Also in
the same complex is Wheatfields.

Debonairs Pizza (Map p96; cnr Samora Ave & Ohio St;
pizzas from TSh5500) In the same complex as Steers.

City Supermarket (Map p96; JM Mall, Harbour View
Towers, cnr Samora Ave & Mission St) For self-catering.

MIDRANGE & TOP END

Tausi (Map p96; ☎ 022-211 4126; www.peacock-hotel
.co.tz; Bibi Titi Mohamed Rd; meals from TSh8500; ☖ lunch &
dinner) This restaurant at Peacock Hotel has a
mix of local and Western fare, and a welcome
local touch.

Kibo Bar (Map p96; ☎ 022-211 2416; Mövenpick Royal
Palm hotel, Ohio St; meals TSh10,000-15,000; ☖ lunch-
11.30pm) Design-your-own pasta, sandwich,
omelette and salad stations at lunchtime on
weekdays, and pub fare at all hours.

Baraza (Map p96; ☎ 022-213 7575; Southern Sun hotel,
Garden Ave; meals from TSh10,000; ☖ breakfast, lunch & dinner) Á la carte dining featuring seafood grills
and Swahili cuisine.

Oriental (Map p96; ☎ 022-213 1111; www.kempinski
-daressalaam.com; Kilimanjaro Kempinski hotel, Kivukoni
Front; meals from US$20; ☖ lunch & dinner Tue-Sun)
Considered by some connoisseurs to be the
best restaurant in town, with excellent sushi
and Asian fusion cuisine, and an ambience
that's as optimal for business lunches as it is
for a romantic evening out.

Msasani Peninsula

Eateries at the **Msasani Slipway** (Map p94;
☎ 022-260 0893; Msasani Slipway; ☖ all day) include **Fairy Delights Ice Cream Shop** (cones from
TSh2500); **Melela Bustani** (breads from TSh1000) for
sustainably produced bakery and gourmet
cheese and sausage products; and the **Terrace
Restaurant** (meals TSh8500-30,000; ☖ dinner Mon-Fri,
lunch & dinner Sat), with a selection of Italian and
seafood dishes.

Addis in Dar (Map p94; ☎ 0713-266299; 35 Ursino
St; meals from TSh8000; ☖ lunch & dinner Mon-Sat)
Ethiopian dishes and a range of vegetarian
selections, all in a lovely ambience with in-
door and outdoor seating. It's signposted off
Mgombani St.

Sweet Eazy Restaurant & Lounge (Map p94; ☎ 0755-
754074; Oyster Bay Shopping Centre, Toure Dr; meals from
TSh10,000) Tasty Thai and seafood specialities,
and live music Thursdays.

Karambezi Restaurant (Map p94; ☎ 022-260 0380;
Toure Dr; meals from TSh10,000) Appetising seafood
and grills overlooking the sea at the (currently closed) Sea Cliff Hotel at the tip of
Msasani Peninsula.

Sea Cliff Village (Map p94; Toure Dr, Msasani Peninsula)
A small and frequently changing selection
of eateries, including Épi d'Or bakery, a
pizzeria, an Indian restaurant and Msumbi
Coffee House.

For self-catering:

Village Supermarket (Map p94; Sea Cliff Village,
Toure Dr, Msasani Peninsula) Pricey but wide selection of
Western foods and imported products.

Shoprite (Map p94; Msasani Slipway)

TANZANIA

DRINKING

Slipway Pub (Map p94; ☎ 022-260 0893; Msasani Slipway, Msasani Peninsula; ◷ noon–11pm) A cosy British pub near the water, with drinks and meals, and sports TV.

Garden Bistro (Map p94; ☎ 022-260 0800; Haile Selassie Rd) Relaxed restaurant-nightclub with a *sheesha* (water pipe) lounge, sports bar, happy hours Sunday through Thursday and live music at weekends. Meals available from TSh5000.

Q-Bar (Map p94; ☎ 022-260 2150; cnr Haile Selassie & Msasani Rds) Happy hours (5pm to 7pm Monday to Friday), live music on Fridays and big-screen sports TV.

Level 8 (Map p96; 8th fl, Kilimanjaro Kempinski hotel, Kivukoni Front) A rooftop bar with views over the harbour, lounge seating and live music some evenings.

O'Willie's Irish Whiskey Tavern (Map p94; www .owillies.com; Peninsula Seaview Hotel, Chui Bay Rd) A classic Irish pub, and popular with the expat crowd, with live music (check its website for the program), pub food, pizzas and seafood grills.

Coco Beach (Map p94; Toure Dr) An amenable seaside setting for sipping an inexpensive beer while watching the local scene. Weekends only.

ENTERTAINMENT

Mwalimu Julius K Nyerere Cultural Centre (Map p96; Nyumba ya Sanaa, Ohio St) Traditional dance performances are held at 7pm on Fridays, and its bulletin board posts notices about traditional dance events around town.

Village Museum (☎ 022-270 0437; www.museum.or.tz; cnr New Bagamoyo Rd & Makaburi St) *Ngoma* (drumming and dancing) performances are held from 4pm to 6pm on Saturday and Sunday, plus occasional special afternoon programs highlighting the dances of individual tribes.

For what's on in town, check the listings magazines and the bulletin board at Nyumba ya Sanaa.

SHOPPING

Shopping venues include **Msasani Slipway Weekend Craft Market** (Map p94; Msasani Slipway, Msasani Peninsula; ◷ Sat & Sun), with a wide range of textiles, carvings and more; **Nyumba ya Sanaa** (Map p96; Ohio St; ◷ daily), a local artists cooperative with a small selection of textiles and crafts; **Mawazo Gallery & Art Café** (Map p96; ☎ 0784-782770; Upanga Rd; ◷ 10am-5.30pm Mon-Fri, 10am-2pm

Sat), with high-quality paintings, woodcarvings and crafts; **Wasanii Art Gallery** (Map p94; Msasani Slipway, Msasani Peninsula; ◷ 1-8pm Mon-Fri, to 6pm Sat), with paintings; and **Tingatinga Centre** (Map p94; Morogoro Stores, Haile Selassie Rd, Oyster Bay; ◷ 8.30am-5pm), where you can also watch the Tingatinga artists at work.

On the edge of town is **Mwenge Carvers' Market** (Sam Nujoma Rd; ◷ 8am-6pm), opposite the Village Museum and just off New Bagamoyo Rd. It's packed with vendors, and you can watch carvers at work. Take the Mwenge *dalla-dalla* from New Posta transport stand to the end, from where it's five minutes on foot down the small street to the left.

Also watch for the excellent twice-yearly **Makutano Arts & Crafts Fair** (www.makutanotz.com), showcasing (and selling) work of Tanzanian artists. For more markets, see p96.

For Western-style shopping, there are the shops at **Msasani Slipway** (Map p94) and **Sea Cliff Village** (Map p94; both on Msasani Peninsula). **Shoppers' Plaza** (Map p94), in the Namanga area, and **JM Mall** (Map p96; Samora Ave), in the city centre, also have supermarkets.

GETTING THERE & AWAY
Air

Julius Nyerere International Airport is Tanzania's domestic and international hub. Most regularly scheduled domestic flights and all international flights depart from Terminal Two (the 'new' terminal, and the first one you reach coming from town), while many flights on small planes and most charters depart from Terminal One (the 'old' terminal, about 700m further down the road.

Airline offices in Dar es Salaam include the following. Note **Air Uganda** (www.air-uganda .com) doesn't yet have its own booking office; book through travel agents, or with Air Tanzania (with whom it has a codeshare on some flights).

Air India (Map p96; ☎ 022-215 2642; cnr Ali Hassan Mwinyi & Bibi Titi Mohamed Rds)

Air Tanzania City Centre (Map p96; ☎ 022-211-7500, 022-284 4239; Ohio St); Airport (Terminal 2, Airport; ◷ 4am-9pm)

British Airways (Map p96; ☎ 022-211 3820, 022-284 4082; Mövenpick Royal Palm hotel, Ohio St)

Coastal Aviation (Map p96; ☎ 022-211 7959/60, 022-284 3293; aviation@coastal.cc; Upanga Rd) Also at Terminal One, Airport.

Emirates Airlines (Map p96; ☎ 022-211 6100; Haidery Plaza, cnr Kisutu & India Sts)

Ethiopian Airlines (Map p96; ☎ 022-211 7063; Ohio St) Opposite Mövenpick Royal Palm hotel.

Kenya Airways (Map p96; ☎ 022-211 9376/7; Upanga Rd)

KLM (Map p96; ☎ 022-213 9790/1; Upanga Rd) Located with Kenya Airways.

Linhas Aéreas de Moçambique (Map p96; ☎ 022-213 4600; 1st fl, JM Mall, Harbour View Towers, cnr Samora Ave & Mission St) At Fast-Track Travel (www.fasttracktanzania.com).

Precision Air City Centre (Map p96; ☎ 022-216 8000, 022-284 3547, 0787-888407; cnr Samora Ave & Pamba Rd); Airport (Terminal 2, Airport; ☼ 5am-10pm)

South African Airways (SAA; Map p96; ☎ 022-211 7044; Raha Towers, cnr Bibi Titi Mohamed & Ali Hassan Mwinyi Rds)

Swiss International Airlines (Map p96; ☎ 022-211 8870; Luther House, Sokoine Dr)

Tropical Air (☎ 024-223 2511; tropic@zanzinet.com; Terminal 1, Airport)

Zambian Airways (Map p96; ☎ 022-212 8885/6; Ground fl, Haidery Plaza, cnr Kisutu & India Sts)

ZanAir (☎ 022-284 3297; Terminal 1, Airport)

Boat

The main passenger routes are between Dar es Salaam, Zanzibar and Pemba.

TO/FROM ZANZIBAR & PEMBA

There are several 'fast' ferry trips (on *Sea Star*, *Sea Express* or *Seabus*) daily between Dar es Salaam and Zanzibar, departing at 7am, 10am, 1pm and 4pm. All take 1½ hours and cost US$35/40 regular/VIP (VIP gets you a seat in the air-con hold). There are also several slow ferries. The main one is *Flying Horse*, which departs daily at 12.30pm (US$25 one way, 3½ to four hours). *Sea Gull* and *Aziza* each depart several times weekly at about the same time (US$25, 3½ to four hours). Departures from Zanzibar are daily at 7am (*Sea Star*), 11am (*Seabus*), 1pm (*Seabus*), 4pm (*Sea Express*) and 10pm (*Flying Horse*, arriving before dawn the next day).

Only buy your tickets at the ticket windows – all on Kivukoni Front opposite St Joseph's Cathedral – and don't fall for touts at the harbour trying to collect extra fees for 'doctors' certificates', departure taxes and the like. The only fee is the ticket price (which includes the US$5 port tax). Also, avoid touts who want to take you into town – or to anywhere other than the real ticket offices – to buy 'cheaper' ferry tickets, or

who offer to purchase ferry tickets for you at less expensive resident rates. Unless you have a resident permit, there's no such thing as a discounted ticket, and you'll just get caught later.

For ferry connections to Pemba, see p144.

Bus

Except as noted following, all buses depart from and arrive at the main bus station at Ubungo, about 8km west of town on Morogoro Rd. It's a sprawling place with the usual assortment of bus station hustle and touts. Keep an eye on your luggage and your wallet and try to avoid arriving at night. *Dalla-dallas* to Ubungo leave from New Posta and Old Posta local transport stands (Map p96), as well as from various other spots in town. Taxis from the city centre cost from about TSh10,000. If you're coming into Dar es Salaam on Scandinavian Express, Dar Express and Royal Coach bus lines, you can sometimes stay on the bus past Ubungo until the bus line's town office – which is worth doing as it will be less chaotic and you'll have a cheaper taxi fare to your hotel. Except for Scandinavian Express buses (which you can also ticket and board at its terminal), it doesn't work out leaving the city, since departures are directly from Ubungo.

Buses to Kilwa Masoko, Mtwara and other points south leave from Ubungo, but it's better to catch them at the Sudan Market area of Temeke, located about 5km southwest of the city centre, off Nelson Mandela Rd, where all the southern lines also have ticket offices.

Major bus lines serving Dar es Salaam include the following:

Dar Express (Map p96; Libya St, Kisutu) Daily buses to Arusha (TSh20,000 to TSh25,000) depart at 6am, 7am, 8am, 9am and 10am from Ubungo. The Libya St office no longer sells tickets – it's just for handling packages and freight – but some Dar Express buses arriving into the city continue here after Ubungo.

Royal Coach (Map p96; ☎ 022-212 4073; Libya St, Kisutu) Daily departures to Arusha (TSh22,000) at 9am from Ubungo. Tickets can be purchased at Ubungo, or at the Libya St office.

Scandinavian Express (Map p94; ☎ 022-218 4833/4; cnr Msimbazi St & Nyerere Rd) Has its own terminal for arrivals and departures (which is also where you book tickets), though all Scandinavian Express buses also pass by Ubungo. There's at least one bus daily to Iringa (TSh17,000) and Mbeya (TSh26,000), another via Iringa to Njombe and Songea (about TSh30,000), two daily to Dodoma (TSh12,000 to TSh15,000) and two daily to Arusha (TSh20,000 to TSh25,0000), but many routes were slated to be cut, so check with Scandinavian for an update.

Train

For information about the Tazara line between Dar es Salaam, Mbeya and Kapiri Mposhi (Zambia), see p266. The **Tazara train station** (☎ 022-286 5187, 0713-225292; www.tazara.co.tz; cnr Nyerere & Nelson Mandela Rds; ☺ ticket office 7.30am-12.30pm & 2-4.30pm Mon-Fri, 9am-12.30pm Sat) is about 6km southwest of the city centre (TSh8000 in a taxi). *Dalla-dallas* to the train station leave from either New Posta or Old Posta transport stands, and are marked Vigunguti, U/Ndege or Buguruni.

For more on Central Line trains between Dodoma, Kigoma and Mwanza (the Dar to Dodoma section is closed), see p266. **Tanzanian Railways Corporation (Central Line) station** (Map p96; ☎ 022-211 7833; www.trctz.com; cnr Railway St & Sokoine Dr) is in the city centre southwest of the Zanzibar ferry terminal, on the opposite side of the road.

GETTING AROUND
To/From the Airport

Julius Nyerere International Airport is about 12km from the city centre. *Dalla-dallas* (marked U/Ndege) go to the airport from New Posta transport stand. In traffic the trip can take over an hour, and there's generally no room for luggage. Taxis from the airport to central Dar es Salaam cost from TSh15,000 (TSh25,000 to Msasani Peninsula).

Car & Motorcycle

Also see p265. Recommended rental agencies:

Avis (www.avisworld.com) Kivukoni Front (Map p96; Kilimanjaro Kempinski, Kivukoni Front); Ohio St (Map p96; ☎ 022-211 5381, 022-212 1061/2; Skylink Travel & Tours, Ohio St & Ali Hassan Mwinyi Rd) The branch at Skylink Travel & Tours is opposite Mövenpick Royal Palm hotel.

Green Car Rentals (Map p94; ☎ 022-218 2022, 022-218 2107; www.greencars.co.tz; Nyerere Rd) Well recommended, with competitive rates. It's near MD Motors in the Gerezani area.

Travel Mate (Map p94; ☎ 022-260 0573; www.travel mate.co.tz; Chole Rd) Located near the Slipway turn-off.

Public Transport

Dalla-dallas (minibuses) are invariably packed to overflowing, and difficult to board with luggage. First and last stops are shown in the front window, but routes vary, so confirm that the driver is going to your destination. Terminals include the following:

New Posta transport stand (Map p96; Maktaba St) At the main post office.

Old Posta transport stand (Map p96; Sokoine Dr) Down from the Azania Front Lutheran Church.

Stesheni transport stand (Map p96; Algeria St) Off Samora Ave near the Central Line Railway Station; *dalla-dallas* to Temeke bus stand also leave from here; ask for 'Temeke *mwisho*'.

Taxi

Short rides within the city centre cost TSh2000. Fares from the city centre to Msasani Peninsula start at TSh8000 (TSh10,000 to Sea Cliff Village).

Taxi ranks include those opposite the Mövenpick Royal Palm hotel (Map p96), on the corner of Azikiwe St and Sokoine Dr (Map p96; opposite the Azania Front Lutheran Church) and on the Msasani Peninsula on the corner of Msasani and Haile Selassie Rds (Map p94).

For airport pick-ups and travel in and outside of the city, contact **Jumanne Mastoka** (☎ 0784-339735; mjumanne@yahoo.com), based opposite the Mövenpick Royal Palm hotel.

AROUND DAR ES SALAAM

SOUTHERN BEACHES

The coastline south of Dar es Salaam gets more attractive, tropical and rural the further south you go, and makes a convenient getaway. The budget places begin south of Kigamboni, which is across the water from Kivukoni Front and reached in a few minutes by ferry. Further down (about 25km from the ferry) are a few upmarket resorts.

Kigamboni
☎ 022

The beach south of Kigamboni ('South Beach') is the closest spot to Dar es Salaam for camping. It's also an easy day trip from the city, and fills up at weekends.

SLEEPING & EATING

Kipepeo Beach & Village (☎ 0754-276178; www
.kipepeovillage.com; camping US$5, s/d/tr beach banda
US$15/25/35, s/d/tr cottage US$55/75/105) Situated
about 8km south of the ferry dock, with
raised cottages lined up about 300m back
from the beach and a beachside restaurant-bar. There's also a shadeless camping
area and an unappealing compound with
makeshift *bandas* (thatched-roof hut) with
nets but no windows. It's a bit of a hike to
the nearest bathroom. At weekends there's
a TSh3000 day use fee, redeemable at the
restaurant-bar.

Sunrise Beach Resort (☎ 022-282 0222; www
.sunrisebeachresort.co.tz; camping US$5, 2-person 'safari'
tent US$12, s/d standard US$30/36, s/d sea view US$60/80,
s/d executive US$80/95) Straightforward 'stand-
ard' and 'sea view' rooms (although not all
of these look out onto the sea) are crowded
together on a long stretch of beach located
just up from Kipepeo. Behind are rather
dowdy air-con 'executive' rooms in two-
storey brick rondavels, and on the sand
is a row of clean canvas tents with mattresses. There's a per person day use fee of
TSh5000 at weekends, partially redeemable
at the restaurant.

Also recommended:

South Beach Resort (☎ 022-282-0666; www.south
beachresort-tz.com; s/d/tr US$90/100/120; 🏊) New
rooms overlooking a terraced courtyard fronting the sea.

GETTING THERE & AWAY

The Kigamboni ferry (per person/vehicle
TSh100/800, five minutes) runs throughout
the day between the eastern end of Kivukoni
Front and Kigamboni village, from where
dalla-dallas head south throughout the day.
Taxis from Kigamboni charge from about
TSh5000 to the resorts.

Ras Kutani

This cape about 30km south of Dar es
Salaam boasts secluded tropical surroundings, fishing and beach walking. There's
no diving. Nesting sea turtles favour this
section of coast, and both resorts listed
here are involved in local conservation
projects. Both can also arrange snorkelling
and horse-riding.

The exclusive **Ras Kutani** (www.raskutani.com;
per person all-inclusive US$305, ste per person full board
US$390; ☿ Jun–mid Mar; 🏊), set between the
sea and a small lagoon, has nine spacious

bungalows with beach-facing verandas, plus
four more upmarket suites, each with its
own plunge pool.

Just south and around the bend is the
peaceful **Amani Beach Hotel** (☎ 0754-410033; www
.amanibeach.com; s/d full board US$270/480; 🎮 🖥 🏊),
with 10 spacious cottages set on a low cliff
directly above the beach, backed by flowering gardens, plus a beachside pool and
delicious cuisine.

NORTHERN BEACHES
☎ 022

The beaches about 25km north of central
Dar es Salaam and east of New Bagamoyo
Rd are lined with resorts and are popular
weekend getaways. While they lack the exotic
ambience of Zanzibar's beaches, they make
a relaxing break from the city. They're close
enough that you can visit for the day, or use
them as a base if you want to avoid Dar es
Salaam entirely.

Activities

Diving, including courses, can be arranged at
Sea Breeze Marine (www.seabreezemarine.org) next to
White Sands Hotel.

There are several water parks, with pools,
water slides and more, including **Kunduchi
Wet 'n' Wild** (☎ 022-265 0326, 022-265 0332; wetnwild@
raha.com; adult/child TSh4950/4500; ☿ 9am-6pm, Tue
women only), next to Kunduchi Beach Hotel
& Resort.

Sleeping & Eating

All hotels charge an entry fee for day visitors at weekends and holidays (TSh3000 to
TSh5000 per person).

Silver Sands Beach Hotel (☎ 022-265 0428, 0754-
850001; www.silversands.netfirms.com; camping person/
vehicle TSh4000/2000, s/d standard TSh30,000/32,000, s/d
deluxe TSh45,000/46,000; 🏊) Past its prime, but
nevertheless a respectable budget choice. The
camping facilities have hot water (usually) and
reasonable security, and there are basic but
adequate rooms set around a grassy square
just in from the beach, all with nets. Meals
cost from TSh4500.

White Sands Hotel (☎ 022-264 7620/1; www
.hotelwhitesands.com; s/d US$130/150, deluxe apt from
US$160; 🎮 🖥 🏊) This large, hectic and often
full beachside place has well-kept rooms
in two-storey rondavels, plus self-catering
apartments, a gym and a business centre.
Room prices include free entry to the nearby

Water World water park. There's a night-club available on most weekend evenings, and a weekend lunchtime buffet (per person (Tsh16,000).

Kunduchi Beach Hotel & Resort (☎ 022-265 0050; www.kunduchiresort.com; s/d from US$144/168; ✷ ☐ ⚲) A recently refurbished hotel situated on the best stretch of beach, with no jetties to mar the view, this place also offers lovely beach-facing rooms, green grounds, a generally quiet ambience and a mediocre restaurant.

Getting There & Away

White Sands is reached via a signposted turn-off from the Bagamoyo road. About 3km further north along the Bagamoyo road is the signposted turn-off for Kunduchi Beach and Silver Sands Beach.

To get here, take a *dalla-dalla* from the New Posta transport stand in Dar es Salaam to Mwenge. From Mwenge to White Sands Hotel, take a 'Tegeta' *dalla-dalla* to Africana Junction, from where you'll need to take one of either a bicycle taxi (TSh500), *majaji* (auto rickshaw; TSh1000) or taxi (TSh2500) for the remaining couple of kilometres. It is also possible to get a direct *dalla-dalla* from Kariakoo straight to Tegeta. For Kunduchi Beach and Silver Sands, stay on the Tegeta *dalla-dalla* until Mtongani (near the Kunduchi junction), where you'll need to take a taxi the remaining distance (TSh3000 to Silver Sands). Be sure not to walk, as there have been several muggings along this stretch of road.

Taxis from Dar es Salaam cost from TSh15,000 one way (about TSh30,000 from the airport).

PUGU HILLS

The lightly wooded Pugu Hills area, which begins about 15km southwest of Dar es Salaam and extends past Kisarawe, makes a relaxing break from the city.

Pugu Hills (☎ 0754-565498, 0754-394875; www .puguhills.com; admission TSh2000, camping US$7, d banda US$70-90), a recommended, laid-back place on a hillside bordering a forest reserve, has four spacious, *bandas* with private bathroom, a camping area, a restaurant and nearby hiking paths. Large groups and overland trucks cannot be accommodated. Call or SMS in advance, whether for overnight or day visits.

Getting There & Away

Dalla-dallas going to Kisarawe leave from Msimbazi St in Kariakoo, and from Nyerere Rd just near the airport turn-off. For Pugu Hills, ask the *dalla-dalla* driver to drop you at the old Agip station (located about 7km past the airport). Continue straight along the unsealed Kisarawe road for about 200m, right through to the end of a tiny group of shops on your left, where there's a dirt path leading up to Pugu Hills (about 15 minutes further on foot); ask around for Bwana Kiki's place. If you're going by vehicle, from the old Agip station follow the sealed road to the left, continue about 1.2km, then turn right at an unmarked dirt path running past a chicken warehouse (the turn-off is about 50m before the railroad tracks). Continue 2km uphill along a rough road that will take you to Pugu Hills.

OFFSHORE ISLANDS

The islands of Bongoyo, Mbudya, Pangavini and Fungu Yasini, all located just off the coast of Dar es Salaam, were gazetted in 1975 to form part of the **Dar es Salaam Marine Reserve system** (adult/child TSh6000/4000, usually included in the price of excursions & collected before departure). Bongoyo and Mbudya are the main destinations for travellers.

Bongoyo, about 7km north of Dar es Salaam, has a white-sand beach, clear snorkelling waters and non-tide-dependent swimming. Shade, plus simple meals and drinks, are available, and there's snorkelling equipment for rent. A boat goes to Bongoyo daily from Mashua Waterfront Bar & Grill at Msasani Slipway, Msasani Peninsula, departing at 9.30am, 11.30am, 1.30pm and 3.30pm, and returning at 10.30am, 12.30pm, 2.30pm and 5pm (TSh16,000 return, including marine reserve entry fees; minimum four people).

Mbudya, situated directly offshore from Kunduchi Beach Hotel & Resort, has several beaches, snorkelling and **camping** (per person with own tent or under open-sided banda TSh20,000, per person incl tent rental TSh30,000). The island is best reached from the beach hotels located to the north of Dar es Salaam, all of which organise excursions (about TSh10,000 per person, minimum two people, including entry fees).

(Continued on page 121)

WILDLIFE & HABITAT David Lukas

Think of East Africa and the word 'safari' comes to mind – but travel west from the big wildlife parks of Tanzania and Kenya and you cross through a world of gorgeous lakes and rivers before ascending into a mystical realm of snowy, cloud-draped peaks that straddle Africa's continental divide. Many parts of the verdant western region remain relatively unknown and are seldom visited, providing welcome respite from overbooked safaris and lodges to the east. But no matter where you travel, East Africa – home to an outstanding abundance and diversity of wildlife – is sure to amaze.

①

Cats

In terms of behaviour, the six common cats of East Africa are little more than souped-up housecats; it's just that some weigh half as much as a horse and others jet along as fast as a speeding car. With their excellent vision and keen hearing, cats are superb hunters. If you stumble across a big cat making its kill, you won't easily forget the energy and ferocity of these life-and-death struggles.

① Leopard

Weight 30-60kg (female), 40-90kg (male); length 170-300cm More common than you might realise, the leopard relies on expert camouflage to stay hidden. During the day you might see one reclining in a tree only after it twitches its tail, but at night there is no mistaking the bone-chilling groans which sound like wood being sawn at high volume. Leopards are highly agile and climb well, spending more time in trees than other big cats – they hoist their kills into trees to eat without fear.

② Serval

Weight 6-18kg; length 90-130cm Twice as large as a housecat, with towering legs and very large ears, the beautifully spotted serval is adapted for walking in tall grass and making prodigious leaps to catch rodents and birds. More diurnal than most cats, it may be seen tossing food in the air and playing with it.

③ Cheetah

Weight 40-60kg; length 200-220cm More greyhound than cat, the cheetah is a world-class sprinter. Although it reaches 112km/h, the cheetah runs out of steam after 300m and must cool down for 30 minutes before hunting again. This speed comes at another cost – the cheetah is so well adapted for running that it lacks the strength and teeth to defend its food or cubs from attack by other large predators.

④ Lion

Weight 120-150kg (female), 150-225kg (male); length 210-275cm (female), 240-350cm (male) Those lions sprawled out lazily in the shade are Africa's most feared predators. Equipped with teeth that tear effortlessly through bone and tendon, they can take down an animal as large as a bull giraffe. Each group of adults (a pride) is based around generations of females that do all the hunting; swaggering males fight among themselves and eat what the females catch.

⑤ Caracal

Weight 8-19kg; length 80-120cm The caracal is a gorgeous tawny cat with extremely long, pointy ears. This African version of the northern lynx has jacked-up hind legs like a feline dragster. These beanpole kickers enable this slender cat to make vertical leaps of 3m and swat birds out of the air.

⑥ Wildcat

Weight 3-6.5kg; length 65-100cm If you see what looks like a tabby wandering along open plains or forest edges, you're likely to be seeing a wildcat, the direct ancestor of our domesticated housecats. Occurring wherever there are abundant mice and rats, the wildcat is readily found on the outskirts of villages. It can be best identified by its unmarked rufous ears and longish legs.

Primates

East Africa is the evolutionary cradle of primate diversity, giving rise to more than 30 species of monkeys, apes and prosimians (the 'primitive' ancestors of modern primates). Somewhere along the way, one branch of the family tree apparently tottered onto the path that gave rise to humans – a controversial hypothesis supported by Leakey's famous excavations at Olduvai Gorge. No matter what you believe, it is possible to see hints of human society in the complex social lives of East Africa's many primates.

❶ Olive Baboon

Weight 11-30kg (female), 22-50kg (male); length 95-180cm Although the formidable olive baboon has 5cm-long fangs and can kill a leopard, its best defence may consist of running up trees and showering intruders with liquid excrement. Either way, you won't want to alarm this animal. Intelligent and opportunistic, troops of these greenish baboons are becoming increasingly abundant throughout western East Africa.

❷ Mountain Gorilla

Weight 70-115kg (female), 160-210kg (male); length 140-185cm It is not a stretch of the imagination to say that gorilla-viewing has become the top tourism draw in Uganda and Rwanda, so expect some effort or expense getting a coveted slot on a gorilla tour. Seem like a hassle? Just wait until you're face-to-face with a massive silverback male on his home turf and nothing else will matter!

❸ Vervet Monkey

Weight 4-8kg; length 90-140cm If any monkey epitomises East Africa, it would be the widespread and adaptable vervet monkey. Each troop of vervets comprises females who defend a home range passed down from generation to generation, and males who fight each other for bragging rights and access to females. If you think their appearance too drab, check out the extraordinary blue and scarlet colours of their sexual organs when aroused.

❹ Black-and-White Colobus

Weight 10-23kg; length 115-165cm Also known as the guereza, the black-and-white colobus is one of East Africa's most popular primates due to the flowing white bonnets of hair arrayed across its black body. Like all colobus, this agile primate has a hook-shaped hand so it can swing through the trees with the greatest of ease. When two troops run into each other expect to see a real show.

❺ Chimpanzee

Weight 25-40kg; length 60-90cm Travelling to the forests of western East Africa may be off the beaten path, but it's hard to deny the allure of these uncannily humanlike primates. It won't take a brain surgeon to perceive the deep intelligence and emotion lurking behind such eerily familiar deep-set eyes. Researchers at Gombe Stream and Mahale Mountains National Parks are making startling discoveries about chimp behaviour – you deserve to see for yourself.

1

Cud-chewing Mammals

Africa is arguably most famous for its astounding variety of ungulates –
hoofed mammals that include everything from buffaloes to giraffes and
rhinos. Many of these animals live in herds to protect themselves from the
continent's formidable predators, with herds numbering in the millions. Ungulates that ruminate (chew their cud) and have horns are called bovines.
Among this family, antelopes are particularly numerous, with about 40 amazingly different species in East Africa alone.

4

① Wildebeest
Weight 140-290kg; length 230-340cm Few animals evoke the spirit of the African plain like the wildebeest. Over a million gather on the Serengeti alone, where they form vast, constantly moving herds accompanied by a host of predators and wide-eyed tourists.

② Thomson's Gazelle
Weight 15-35kg; length 95-150cm Lanky and exceptionally alert, Thomson's gazelle is one of several long-legged antelopes built for speed. The 400,000 on the Serengeti Plains migrate in great herds along with zebras and wildebeest. Look for their attractive black flank stripes.

③ Gerenuk
Weight 30-50kg; length 160-200cm The gerenuk is one of the strangest creatures you'll ever see – a tall slender gazelle with a giraffelike neck. Adapted for life among semiarid brush, the gerenuk stands on its hind legs to reach 2m-high branches.

④ African Buffalo
Weight 250-850kg; length 220-420cm Imagine a cow on steroids then add a particularly fearsome set of curling horns and you get the gigantic African buffalo. Thank goodness they're usually docile – an angry or injured buffalo is an extremely dangerous animal.

⑤ Greater Kudu
Weight 120-315kg; length 215-300cm The oxen-sized greater kudu is a study in elegance. One of the tallest antelopes, it relies on white pinstripes to conceal it in brushy thickets. The very long spiralling horns of the male are used in ritualised combat.

⑥ Hartebeest
Weight 120-220kg; length 190-285cm Yes, the long stretched face of the hartebeest looks odd, but it is an adaptation that helps this short-necked antelope reach down to graze. Commonly seen on open plains, the hartebeest is easily recognised by its set of backward-twisted horns.

⑦ Bush Duiker
Weight 12-25kg; length 80-130cm When you're a tiny antelope on every predator's menu, you need clever ways to protect yourself. The bush duiker lives in dense thickets and marks out escape routes with scent glands on its face.

⑧ Waterbuck
Weight 160-300kg; length 210-275cm If you're going to see any antelope on safari, it's likely to be the big, shaggy, and, some say, smelly waterbuck. Dependent on waterside vegetation, waterbuck numbers fluctuate dramatically between wet and dry years.

⑨ Uganda Kob
Weight 60-120kg; length 170-200cm Kobs, medium-sized golden antelopes, gather in great numbers on the floodplains of Uganda. The presence of so many females rouses males to heights of sexual excitement, fighting and strutting to show off their curved horns.

Hoofed Mammals

A full stable of Africa's megacharismatic animals can be found in this group of ungulates. Other than the giraffe, these ungulates are not ruminants and can be seen over a much broader range of habitats than bovines. They have been at home in Africa for millions of years and are among the most successful mammals to have ever wandered the continent. Without human intervention, Africa would be ruled by elephants, zebras, hippos and warthogs.

① Black Rhinoceros

Weight 700-1400kg; length 350-450cm Pity the black rhinoceros for having a horn that is worth more than gold. Once widespread and abundant south of the Sahara, the rhino has been poached to the brink of extinction. Unfortunately, females may only give birth every five years.

② African Elephant

Weight 2200-3500kg (female), 4000-6300kg (male); height 2.4-3.4m (female), 3-4m (male) No one, not even a human or lion, stands around to argue when a towering bull elephant rumbles out of the brush. Commonly referred to as 'the king of beasts', elephant society is actually ruled by a lineage of elder females.

③ Warthog

Weight 45-75kg (female), 60-150kg (male); length 140-200cm Despite their fearsome appearance and sinister tusks, only the big males are safe from lions, cheetahs and hyenas. To protect themselves when attacked, most warthogs run for burrows, and back in while slashing wildly with their tusks.

④ Giraffe

Weight 450-1200kg (female), 1800-2000kg (male); height 3.5-5.2m The 5m-tall giraffe does such a good job with upward activity – reaching up to grab high branches and towering above the competition – that stretching down to get a simple drink of water is difficult. Though they stroll along casually, they can outrun any predator.

⑤ Rock Hyrax

Weight 1.8-5.5kg; length 40-60cm It doesn't seem like it, but those funny tailless squirrels you see lounging around on rocks are an ancient cousin to the elephant. You won't see some of the features that rock hyraxes share with their larger kin, but look for tusks when one yawns.

⑥ Plains Zebra

Weight 175-320kg; length 260-300cm My oh my, those plains zebras sure have wicked stripes. Although each animal is as distinctly marked as a fingerprint, scientists still aren't sure what function these patterns serve. Do they help zebras recognise each other?

⑦ Hippopotamus

Weight 510-3200kg; length 320-400cm The hippopotamus is one strange creature. Designed like a floating beanbag with tiny legs, the 3000kg hippo spends its time in or very near water chowing down on aquatic plants. Placid? No way! Hippos have tremendous ferocity and strength when provoked.

Carnivores

It is a sign of Africa's ecological richness that the continent supports a remarkable variety of predators. In addition to six common cats, East Africa's other two dozen carnivores range from slinky mongooses to social hunting dogs. All are linked in having 'carnassial' or slicing teeth, but visitors may be more interested in witnessing the superb hunting prowess of these highly efficient hunters. When it comes to predators expect the unexpected and you'll return home with a lifetime of memories!

❶ Spotted Hyena
Weight 40-90kg; length 125-215cm The spotted hyena is one of East Africa's most unusual animals. Living in packs ruled by females that grow penislike sexual organs, these savage fighters use their bone-crushing jaws to disembowel terrified prey on the run or to do battle with lions. The sight of maniacally giggling hyenas at a kill, piling on top of each other in their eagerness to devour hide, bone and internal organs, is unsettling.

❷ Golden Jackal
Weight 6-15kg; length 85-130cm It barks and yelps like a dog and looks like a skinny mutt, but the golden jackal is one of Africa's scrappiest critters. Despite its diminutive form, the jackal fearlessly stakes a claim at the dining table of the African plain. If not through sheer ferocity and bluff, then through tact and trickery, a jackal manages to fill its belly while holding hungry vultures and hyenas at bay. Golden jackals are often the most numerous carnivores in open savannah.

❸ Banded Mongoose
Weight 1.5-2kg; length 45-75cm East Africa's eight species of mongoose may be difficult to separate, but the commonly observed banded mongoose is easily recognised by its finely barred pattern and social nature. Bounding across the savannah on their morning foraging excursions, family groups are a delightful sight when they stand up on their hind legs for a better view. Not particularly speedy, they find delicious snacks in toads, scorpions and slugs.

❹ Hunting Dog
Weight 20-35kg; length 100-150cm Fabulously and uniquely patterned so that individuals recognise each other, hunting dogs run in packs of 20 to 60 to ruthlessly chase down antelopes and other animals. Organised in complex hierarchies maintained by rules of conduct, these highly social canids are incredibly efficient hunters. At the same time, disease and persecution have pushed them into near extinction and they now rank as one of Africa's foremost must-see animals.

❺ Ratel
Weight 7-16kg; length 75-100cm Don't be misled by the small size and skunklike appearance of the ratel – it may be the fiercest of all African animals. Some Africans say they would rather face a lion than a ratel, and even lions relinquish their kill when a ratel shows up. Also known as 'honey badger', the ratel finds its favourite food by following honey guides, birds that lead the badger to bee hives.

Birds of Prey

East Africa has nearly 100 species of hawks, eagles, vultures and owls. More than 40 species may be spotted at a single park, making these some of the best places in the world to see an incredible variety of birds of prey. Look for them perching on trees, soaring high overhead or gathered around a carcass, though the scolding cries of small birds harassing one of these feared hunters may be your first clue to their presence.

① African Fish Eagle

Length 75cm Given its name, it's not surprising that you'll see the African fish eagle hunting for fish around water. With a wingspan over 2m, this replica of the American bald eagle presents an imposing appearance but is most familiar for its loud, ringing vocalisations that have become known as 'the voice of Africa'.

② Secretary Bird

Length 100cm In a country full of bizarre birds, the secretary bird literally stands head and shoulders above the masses. With the body of an eagle and the legs of a crane, the secretary bird stands 1.3m tall and walks up to 20km a day in search of vipers, cobras and other snakes, which it kills with lightning speed and agility. This idiosyncratic, grey-bodied raptor is commonly seen striding across the savannah.

③ White-backed Vulture

Length 80cm All eight of East Africa's vultures can be seen mingling with lions, hyenas and jackals around carcasses. Through sheer numbers, they compete for scraps of flesh and bone. It's not a pretty sight when they take over a carcass that no other scavenger wants, but it's the way nature works. The white-backed vulture, with its fuzzy neck and head and white back, is the most common vulture.

④ Bateleur

Length 60cm The bateleur is an attractive serpent-eagle with a funny name. French for 'tightrope-walker', the name refers to its distinctive low-flying aerial acrobatics. In flight, look for this eagle's white wings and odd tailless appearance; close up look for the bold colour pattern and scarlet face.

⑤ Augur Buzzard

Length 55cm Perhaps the most common raptor in the region, the augur buzzard occupies a wide range of wild and cultivated habitats. Virtually identical to the red-tailed hawk of the Americas, this buzzard is sometimes called the African red-tailed hawk. One of its most successful hunting strategies is to float motionlessly in the air by riding the wind, then swoop down quickly to catch unwary critters.

①

Other Birds

Bird-watchers from far and wide travel to East Africa in search of the region's 1400 species of birds – an astounding number by any measure – including birds of every shape and in every colour imaginable. No matter where you travel in the country you will be enchanted and amazed by an ever-changing avian kaleidoscope.

4

① Lilac-breasted Roller
Length 40cm Nearly everyone on safari gets to know the gorgeously coloured lilac-breasted roller. Related to the kingfishers, the roller get its name from the tendency to 'roll' side to side in flight as a way of showing off its iridescent blues, purples and greens.

② Saddle-billed Stork
Length 150cm Not only is the saddle-billed stork the most stunning of the eight stork species, it is also one of the more remarkably coloured of any bird. As if its 2.7m wingspan wasn't impressive enough, check out its brilliant red kneecaps and bill.

③ Grey-crowned Crane
Length 100cm Uganda's national bird is extremely elegant. Topped with a frilly yellow bonnet, this blue-grey crane dances wildly and shows off its red throat pouch during the breeding season.

④ Lesser Flamingo
Length 100cm Coloured deep rose-pink and gathering by the hundreds of thousands on shimmering salt lakes, the lesser flamingo creates one of the most dramatic wildlife spectacles found in Africa, especially when they all fly at once or perform synchronised courtship displays.

⑤ Shoebill
Length 124cm The reclusive shoebill is one of the most highly sought-after birds in East Africa, where it lurks in undisturbed swamps. Looking somewhat like a stout-bodied stork with an ugly old clog stuck on its face, the shoebill baffles scientists because it has no clear relative in the bird world.

⑥ Ostrich
Length 200-270cm If you think the ostrich looks prehistoric, you aren't far off. Standing 2.7m and weighing upwards of 130kg, these ancient flightless birds escape predators by running away at 70km/h or lying flat on the ground to resemble a pile of dirt.

⑦ Speckled Mousebird
Length 35cm Not every bird in East Africa is the biggest, best or most colourful. The highly gregarious speckled mousebird is none of those things, but it does attract attention due to its comical habit of hanging from branches and wires while resting or sleeping.

⑧ Red-billed Oxpecker
Length 18cm The odd little red-billed oxpecker is a starling that sits on the backs of large mammals, eating 100 ticks a day. Any benefit to the animal is cancelled out, as the oxpecker keeps old wounds open to drink blood and pus.

⑨ Superb Starling
Length 18cm The starling is a stellar example of the many birds in East Africa that slap together bright colours and call it a day. With black face, yellow eyes and metallic blue-green upperparts contrasting sharply with its red-orange belly, it seems like an exotic discovery, but is actually surprisingly abundant.

Habitats

Nearly all wildlife in East Africa occupies a specific type of habitat, and you will hear rangers and fellow travellers refer to these habitats repeatedly as if they were secret code words. Your wildlife-viewing experience will be greatly enhanced if you learn how to recognise these habitats and the animals you might expect to find in each one.

❶ Savannah

Savannah is *the* classic East African landscape – broad rolling grasslands shaped by fire and grazing animals, and dotted with lone acacia trees. The openness of this landscape makes it a perfect home for large herds of grazing animals, in addition to fast-sprinting predators like cheetahs.

❷ Woodland

Tanzania is the only place in East Africa where you'll find dry woodlands, locally known as *miombo*. This important habitat provides homes for many birds, small mammals and insects. Here the trees' continuous canopy cover offers shelter from predators and harsh sunlight. Where fingers of woodland mingle with savanah, animals like leopards and antelopes find shade and places to rest during the day.

❸ Semiarid Desert

Parts of Kenya and Tanzania see so little rainfall that shrubs and hardy grasses, rather than trees, are the dominant vegetation. Lack of water limits larger animals such as zebras, gazelles and antelopes to waterholes, but when it rains this habitat explodes with plant and animal life.

(Continued from page 104)

ZANZIBAR ARCHIPELAGO

Zanzibar's allure is legendary. One of East Africa's great trading centres, the archipelago has been for centuries a crossroads of culture, a melting pot of influences where Africa, India and Arabia meet, a complete change of pace from the mainland, a place where life's rhythms are set by the monsoon winds and the cycles of the moon.

While Zanzibar gets most of the attention, the archipelago is also made up of Pemba to the north, plus numerous smaller islands and islets. Each of the main islands has its own distinct character. Zanzibar's major attraction is Stone Town, with its whitewashed, coral-rag houses, quaint shops, bazaars, mosques, courtyards and squares. Another draw card is its spectacular sea, edged by fine, white-sand beaches. Although many places have become very developed, there are still some quiet spots left.

Verdant Pemba, in contrast, is hilly, densely vegetated and seldom visited. Voodoo flourishes amid its hilly terrain, winding creeks lace the shoreline, and the mangrove-lined coast opens occasionally onto hidden, pristine coves and bays the colour of emerald.

History

The archipelago's history stretches back at least to the start of the first millennium, when Bantu-speaking peoples from the mainland first travelled across the Zanzibar and Pemba channels. The islands were likely to have been visited at an even earlier date by traders and sailors from Arabia. From around the 8th century Shirazi traders from Persia also began to make their way to East Africa, where they established settlements on Pemba and probably also at Zanzibar's Unguja Ukuu.

Between the 12th and 15th centuries the archipelago came into its own, as trade links with Arabia and the Persian Gulf blossomed. Zanzibar became a powerful city-state, supplying slaves, gold, ivory and wood to places as distant as India and Asia, while importing spices, glassware and textiles. Along with the trade from the east came Islam and the Arabic architecture that still characterises the archipelago today.

The arrival of the Portuguese in the early 16th century temporarily interrupted this golden age, as Zanzibar and then Pemba fell under Portuguese control. Yet Portuguese dominance didn't last long. It was challenged first by the British and then by Omani Arabs. By the early 19th century Oman had gained the upper hand on Zanzibar, and trade on the island again flourished, centred on slaves, ivory and cloves. Caravans set out for the interior, and trade reached such a point that in the 1840s the Sultan of Oman relocated his court here from the Persian Gulf.

From the mid-19th century, with increasing European interest in East Africa and the end of the slave trade, Omani rule over Zanzibar began to weaken, and in 1862 the sultanate was formally partitioned. Zanzibar became independent from Oman, with Omani sultans ruling under a British protectorate. This arrangement lasted until Zanzibari independence on 10 December 1963. In January 1964 the sultans were overthrown in a bloody revolution instigated by the ASP, which then assumed power. On 12 April 1964 Abeid Karume, president of the ASP, signed a declaration of unity with Tanganyika (mainland Tanzania) and the union, fragile from the outset, became known as the United Republic of Tanzania.

Karume was assassinated in 1972, and Aboud Jumbe assumed the presidency of Zanzibar until resigning in 1984. A succession of leaders followed, culminating in 2000 with the controversial election of Aman Abeid Karume, son of the first president.

Today the archipelago's two major parties are CCM and the opposition CUF, which has its stronghold on Pemba. Tensions between the two peaked in the disputed 1995 national elections (see p86), and have been simmering ever since. While efforts at dialogue between the CCM and CUF have restored a fragile

---

UNGUJA VS ZANZIBAR

Unguja is the Swahili name for Zanzibar, and is often used locally to distinguish the island from the Zanzibar Archipelago (which also includes Pemba), as well as from Zanzibar Town. In this book, for ease of recognition, we've used Zanzibar.

TANZANIA

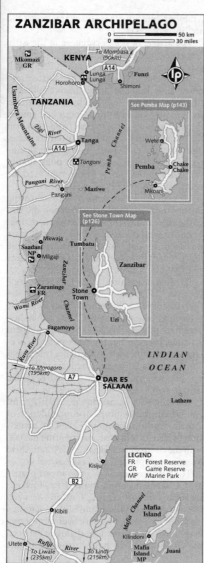

ZANZIBAR ARCHIPELAGO

0 — 50 km
0 — 30 miles

LEGEND
FR   Forest Reserve
GR   Game Reserve
MP   Marine Park

Zanzibar Town and along the beaches, and there have been several recent violent robberies on east-coast beaches.

Avoid isolated areas, especially isolated stretches of beach, and keep your valuables out of view. If you go out at night in Zanzibar Town, take a taxi or walk in a group. Also avoid walking alone in Stone Town during the pre-dawn hours. It's generally best to leave valuables in your hotel safe, preferably sealed or locked.

If you've hired a bicycle or motorcycle, avoid isolated stretches of road, and don't stop if you're flagged down in isolated areas.

Given the ongoing history of political tensions on Zanzibar and Pemba, it's a good idea to check your government's travel advisory site (see boxed text, p609), especially if you plan on travelling to the archipelago in late 2010, when elections are scheduled.

ZANZIBAR
☎ 024

Whether you're arriving for the first time or the fiftieth, Zanzibar never seems to loose its touch of the exotic. After two wind-buffeted and salt-sprayed hours on the ferry (or 20 smooth minutes in a plane), the waters calm and turn turquoise as Stone Town's skyline slides into view. The spires of St Joseph's Cathedral, Forodhani Gardens, the Old Fort, a jumble of rooftops and then the harbour itself – an earthy, timeless mix of grime, touts, dockyard workers and ships. And then, after negotiating passport controls and taxis, you're there, walking through cobbled alleyways, past women clad in *bui-bui* (black cover-all worn by some Islamic women outside the home), small shops smelling of spices, children playing ball, elderly men dressed in *kanzu* (white robe-like outer garment worn by men – often for prayer) and *kofia* (a cap, usually of embroidered white linen, worn by men) playing *bao* (a popular board game) and chatting. Ancient Persia mixes with the old Omani sultanate and India's Goan coast. Mainland life seems far away as island rhythms take over and (once again) you're hooked.

Most visitors arrive at Zanzibar Town, the island's hub. At its heart is the old Stone Town, with its labyrinthine alleyways and architecture. Within easy reach of here is a fine collection of powdery white beaches fringed by coconut palms and sun-baked villages and lapped by the turquoise sea.

calm, this has been broken several times, and little progress has been made at resolving the underlying issues.

Dangers & Annoyances

While Zanzibar remains a relatively safe place, incidents of robberies, muggings and the like occur with some frequency, especially in

Getting There & Around

There are daily flights linking Zanzibar and Pemba with Dar es Salaam, Tanga, Arusha and the northern safari circuit airstrips and Selous Game Reserve. Ferries link Zanzibar with Dar es Salaam daily, and with Pemba several times weekly. Once on Zanzibar, taxi and motorbike hire is quite affordable, and networks of cheap and crowded *dalla-dallas* or faster and pricier private minibuses cover the island.

A Tanzanian visa is required to visit Zanzibar; there are no separate visa requirements for the archipelago, but you may be required to complete separate arrival forms.

Orientation

Zanzibar Town, on the western side of the island, is the heart of the archipelago. The best-known section by far is the old Stone Town, surrounded on three sides by the sea and bordered to the east by Creek Rd. Directly east is the bustling but less atmospheric section of Ng'ambo. Except as noted, all listings in this section are in Stone Town.

MAPS

The widely available **MaCo** (www.gtmaps.com) map has a detailed map of Stone Town on one side and Zanzibar island on the other.

Information

BOOKSHOPS

Gallery Bookshop (Map p126; ☎ 024-223 2721; 48 Gizenga St; ☺ 9am-6pm Mon-Sat, 9am-2pm Sun) Travel guides, Africa titles, historical reprint editions, maps and more.

CONSULATES

Mozambique (Map p126; ☎ 024-223 0049; Mapinduzi Rd)
Oman (Map p126; ☎ 024-223 0066/0700; Vuga Rd)

INTERNET ACCESS

Shangani Post Office Internet Café (Map p126; Kenyatta Rd; per hr TSh2000; ☺ 8am-9pm Mon-Fri, 8.30am-7pm Sat & Sun)

MEDIA

Recommended in Zanzibar Free quarterly listings magazine with cultural events, transport schedules, tide tables etc.
Swahili Coast (www.swahilicoast.com) Free publication, with hotel and restaurant listings, cultural articles and more.

MEDICAL SERVICES

Shamshuddin Pharmacy (Map p126; ☎ 024-231262, 024-223 3814; Market St; ☺ 9am-8.30pm Mon-Thu & Sat, 9am-noon & 3-8.30pm Fri, 9am-1.30pm Sun) Just behind (west of) the Darajani market.

PAPASI

In Zanzibar Town you'll undoubtedly come into contact with street touts, known in Swahili as *papasi* (ticks). They are not registered guides, although they may carry (false) identification cards, and while a few can be helpful, others can be aggressive and irritating.

If you do decide to use the services of a tout (and they're hard to avoid if you're arriving at the ferry dock for the first time and don't know your way around), tell them where you want to go or what you're looking for, and your price range. You shouldn't have to pay anything additional, as many hotels pay commissions. If they tell you your hotel of choice no longer exists or is full, take it with a grain of salt, as it could well be that they just want to take you somewhere where they know they'll get a better commission.

Another strategy is to make your way out of the port arrivals area and head straight for a taxi. This will cost you more, and taxi drivers look for hotel commissions as well, but most are legitimate, and once you are 'spoken for', hassles from touts usually diminish.

Most *papasi* are hoping that your stay on the island will mean ongoing work for them as your guide, so if you do use one to help you find a hotel, they'll invariably be outside waiting for you later. If you're not interested in this, explain so (politely) once you've arrived at your hotel. If you want a guide, it's better to arrange one with your hotel or a travel agency. If you're being hassled, a polite but firm approach usually works best – yelling or showing irritation just makes things worse. Another thing to remember is that you have a better chance of getting a discount on your hotel room if you arrive alone, since the hotel can then give you the discount that would have been paid to the touts as commission.

When arranging tours and excursions, never make payments on the street – be sure you're paying at a legitimate office, and get a receipt.

TANZANIA

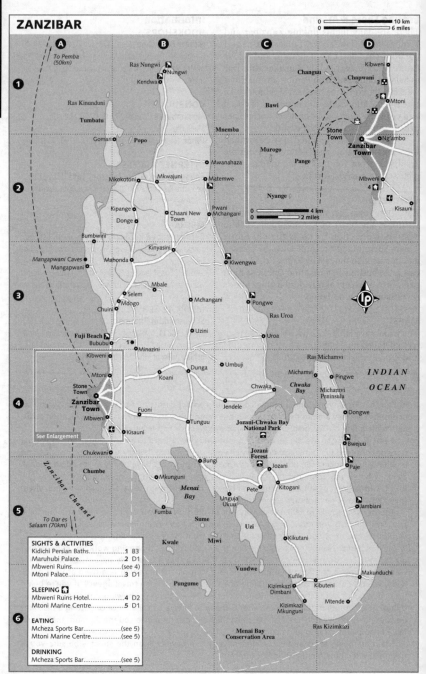

ZANZIBAR

0 ——— 10 km
0 ——— 6 miles

To Pemba
(50km)

A · **B** · **C** · **D**

Ras Nungwi
Nungwi
Kendwa

Ras Kinunduni

Tumbatu

Mnemba

Gomani · Popo

Mwanahaza

Mkokotoni · Mkwajuni
Matemwe

Kipange
Donge · Chaani New Town · Pwani Mchangani

Bumbwini

Kinyasini

Mangapwani Caves · Mahonda
Mangapwani · Kiwengwa

Mbale

Selem
Mdogo · Mchangani · Pongwe
Chuini
Ras Uroa

Fuji Beach
Bububu · Uzini · Uroa
Minazini

Kibweni · Dunga · Umbuji
Mtoni · Koani

Stone Town · Chwaka · Chwaka Bay · Michamvi · Pingwe
Zanzibar Town · Michamvi Peninsula
Mbweni · Fuoni · Jendele · Dongwe

See Enlargement · Kisauni · Tunguu

Chukwani · Bungi · Jozani-Chwaka Bay National Park
Bwejuu

Chumbe · Jozani Forest · Paje
Jozani

Mkunguni · Pete
Menai Bay · Kitogani

Fumba · Unguja Ukuu · Jambiani

Sume

Kwale · Miwi · Uzi

To Dar es Salaam (70km)

Vundwe · Kikutani

Pungume

Kufile · Makunduchi
Kizimkazi Dimbani · Kibuteni
Kizimkazi Mkunguni · Mtende

Ras Kizimkazi

Menai Bay Conservation Area

INDIAN OCEAN

Zanzibar Channel

Enlargement (inset):

Changuu · Kibweni
Chapwani · 3
Bawi · 5 · Mtoni
2
Stone Town
Murogo · Pange
Zanzibar Town · Ng'ambo

Nyange · Mbweni
4
Kisauni

0 ——— 4 km
0 ——— 2 miles

MONEY

There are many forex bureaus – most open until about 8pm Monday to Saturday, and often also on Sunday – where you can change cash and sometimes travellers cheques with a minimum of hassle. Rates vary, so it pays to shop around; rates in Stone Town are better than elsewhere on the island. Officially, accommodation on Zanzibar must be paid for in US dollars, and prices are quoted in dollars, but especially at the budget places, it's almost never a problem to pay the equivalent in shillings.

Barclays Bank (Map p126; Kenyatta Rd) ATM (Visa, MasterCard, Cirrus, Maestro). Next to Mazsons Hotel.

Maka T-Shirt Shop (Map p126; Kenyatta Rd) Changes travellers cheques and cash.

NBC Bank (Map p126; Shangani St) Changes cash and has an ATM (Visa only). There's also an MBC ATM near the Tourist Information Office.

Speed Cash/TanPay (Map p126; Kenyatta Rd) ATM (Visa, MasterCard, Cirrus, Maestro). Diagonally opposite Mazsons Hotel.

Costs

While Zanzibar doesn't need to be expensive, you'll need to work a bit to keep to a budget. Plan on at least US$15 per night for accommodation, and from TSh10,000 per day for food, plus extra for transport, excursions and diving or snorkelling. During the low season or for extended stays, you'll often be able to negotiate discounts, although even at the cheapest places it won't go much below US$10/20 per single/double. Many midrange and top-end hotels charge peak-season supplements during August and the Christmas to New Year holiday period.

Prices are higher away from Stone Town, and at the beach budget hotels it can be difficult to find an inexpensive meal. If you're on a tight budget, consider stocking up on food in Stone Town. Many hotels and restaurants close from March to May.

POST & TELEPHONE

Shangani post office (Map p126; Kenyatta Rd; 8am-4.30pm Mon-Fri, 8am-12.30pm Sat) Operator-assisted calls from TSh1300 per minute.

TOURIST INFORMATION

Zanzibar Tourist Corporation (ZTC) Tourist Information Office (Map p126; 0777-482356; Creek Rd; 8am-5pm) Just down from Darajani market, with tourist information, ferry bookings and standard tours at reasonable prices.

TRAVEL AGENCIES & TOUR OPERATORS

All the following can help with island excursions, and plane and ferry tickets. Only make bookings and payments inside the offices, and not with anyone outside claiming to be staff.

Eco + Culture Tours (Map p126; 024-223 0366; www.ecoculture-zanzibar.org; Hurumzi St) Opposite 236 Hurumzi hotel; culturally friendly tours and excursions

Gallery Tours & Safaris (024-223 2088; www.gallerytours.net) Top of the line tours and excursions; it also arranges Zanzibar weddings and honeymoon itineraries.

Madeira Tours & Safaris (Map p126; 024-223 0406; madeira@zanlink.com; just off Kenyatta Rd) All price ranges.

Sama Tours (Map p126; 024-223 3543; www.sama tours.com; Hurumzi St) Reasonably priced budget tours.

Tabasam (Map p126; 024-223 0322; www.tabasam zanzibar.com; Kenyatta Rd) Opposite Stone Town Café; midrange and upmarket tours

Tropical Tours (Map p126; 024-223 3695, 0777-413454; http://tropicaltours.villa69.org; Kenyatta Rd) Budget tours.

Zan Tours (Map p126; 024-223 3042, 024-223 3116; www.zantours.com; Malawi Rd) A wide range of upmarket tours.

Sights

If Zanzibar Town is the archipelago's heart, Stone Town is its soul, with a magical jumble of cobbled alleyways where it's easy to spend days wandering around and getting lost – although you can't get lost for long because, sooner or later, you'll end up on either the seafront or on Creek Rd. Nevertheless, each twist and turn of the narrow streets brings something new, be it a school full of children chanting verses from the Quran, a beautiful old mansion with overhanging verandas, a coffee vendor with his long-spouted pot fastened over coals, clacking cups to attract custom, or a group of women in *bui-bui* sharing a joke and local gossip. Along the way, watch the island's rich cultural melange come to life: Arabic-style houses with their recessed inner courtyards rub shoulders with Indian-influenced buildings boasting ornate balconies and latticework, and bustling oriental bazaars alternate with lively street-side vending stalls.

While the best part of Stone Town is simply letting it unfold before you, it's worth putting in an effort to see its major features.

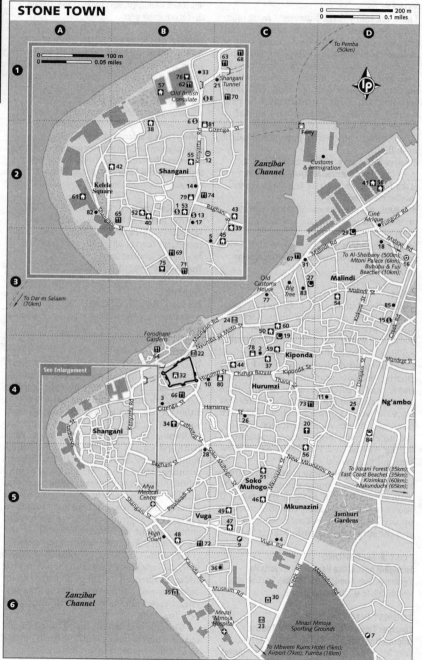

BEIT EL-AJAIB (HOUSE OF WONDERS)

Beit el-Ajaib – home to the **Zanzibar National Museum of History & Culture** (Map p126; www.zan zibarheritage.go.tz; Mizingani Rd; adult/child US$3/1; ☺ 9am-6pm) – was built in 1883 by Sultan Barghash (r 1870–88) as a ceremonial palace. In 1896 it was the target of a British naval bombardment. After it was rebuilt, Sultan Hamoud (r 1902–11) used the upper floor as a residential palace until his death. Inside are exhibits on the dhow culture of the Indian Ocean, Swahili civilisation and 19th-century Zanzibar, plus smaller displays on *kangas* (printed cotton wraparound, incorporating a Swahili proverb, worn by women) and the history of Stone Town. There's also a life-sized *mtepe* (a traditional Swahili sailing vessel made without nails, the planks held together only with coconut fibres and wooden pegs).

BEIT EL-SAHEL (PALACE MUSEUM)

Just north of the Beit el-Ajaib is **Beit el-Sahel** (Map p126; www.zanzibarheritage.go.tz; Mizingani Rd; adult/child US$3/1; ☺ 9am-6pm), which served as the sultan's residence until 1964 when the dynasty was overthrown. Now it's a museum devoted to the era of the Zanzibar sultanate.

The ground floor has details of the formative period of the sultanate from 1828 to 1870. There is also memorabilia of Princess Salme, a Zanzibari princess who eloped with a German to Europe, and later wrote an autobiography. The exhibits on the 2nd floor are on the period of affluence from 1870 to 1896, during which modern amenities such as piped water and electricity were introduced to Zanzibar under Sultan Barghash. The 3rd floor consists of the modest living quarters of the last sultan, Khalifa bin Haroub (r 1911–60), and his two wives.

DRESSING FOR SUCCESS

At its heart, away from all the tourist developments, Zanzibar is a conservative, Muslim society. You'll gain more respect and have fewer hassles by respecting local customs, especially regarding dress, as many locals take offence at scantily clad Westerners. For women this means no sleeveless tops, and preferably pants, skirts or at least knee-length shorts away from the beach. For men it means shirts around town, and pants or knee-length shorts. During Ramadan respect local sensibilities by not eating or drinking in public places.

OLD FORT

Just south of the Beit el-Ajaib is the **Old Fort** (Map p126), a massive, bastioned structure originally built around 1700 on the site of a Portuguese chapel by Omani Arabs as a defence against the Portuguese. It now houses the Zanzibar Cultural Centre. Inside is an open-air theatre for music and dance performances, and a restaurant.

ANGLICAN CATHEDRAL & OLD SLAVE MARKET

Built in the 1870s by the Universities' Mission to Central Africa (UMCA), the **Anglican cathedral** (Map p126; off Creek Rd, Mkunazini; admission TSh3500; ☑ 8am-6pm Mon-Sat, noon-6pm Sun) was the first Anglican cathedral in East Africa. Built on the site of the old slave market alongside Creek Rd, nothing remains of the slave market today other than some holding cells under St Monica's Hostel next door. Services are still held at the cathedral; the entrance is next to St Monica's Hostel.

ST JOSEPH'S CATHEDRAL

The spires of **St Joseph's Roman Catholic cathedral** (Map p126; Cathedral St) are one of the first sights travellers see when arriving at Zanzibar by ferry. To reach the church, follow Kenyatta Rd to Gizenga St, then take the first right to the back gate, which is usually open, even when the front entrance is closed. The cathedral, which was designed by French architect Beranger, celebrated its centenary in 1998, and is still in active use.

MOSQUES

The oldest of Stone Town's mosques is **Msikiti wa Balnara** (Malindi Minaret Mosque; Map p126), originally built in 1831, enlarged in 1841

and extended again by Seyyid Ali bin Said in 1890. Others include the **Aga Khan Mosque** (Map p126) and the impressive **Ijumaa Mosque** (Map p126). It's not possible to enter many of the mosques, as they're all in active use, although exceptions may be made if you are appropriately dressed.

HAMAMNI PERSIAN BATHS

Built by Sultan Barghash in the late 19th century, these **baths** (Map p126; Hamamni St; admission TSh500), which are no longer functioning, were the first public baths on Zanzibar. Ask the caretaker across the alley to unlock the gate.

BEIT EL-AMANI (PEACE MEMORIAL MUSEUM) & NATURAL HISTORY ANNEX

The larger of the two buildings that make up **Beit el-Amani** (Map p126; cnr Kaunda & Creek Rds) previously contained a history of the island from its early days until independence, and is currently closed for renovations. The **Natural History Annex** (admission TSh1000; ☑ 8am-3.30pm), housed in a smaller building across the road, has recently reopened with a photo display focusing on Zanzibar's flora and fauna by wildlife photographer Dick Persson.

OLD DISPENSARY

Near the port, the **Old Dispensary** (Map p126; Mizingani Rd) was built at the turn of the 20th century by a wealthy Indian merchant. It was renovated by the Aga Khan Charitable Trust, and is currently closed for further renovations.

DARAJANI MARKET

You'll find everything from fruits and vegetables to spices and auto spares in the dark, narrow passageways of chaotic **Darajani market** (Map p126). It's just off Creek Rd, and at its best in the morning, before the heat and the crowds, and when everything is still fresh.

VICTORIA HALL & GARDENS

Diagonally across from Mnazi Mmoja hospital on Kaunda Rd, **Victoria Hall** (Map p126) housed the legislative council during the British era. Today it's closed to the public, as is the **State House** (Map p126), opposite.

RUINS

There are a number of historical sites around Zanzibar Town, many of which are included in spice tours (see p130).

Mbweni

Around 5km south of Zanzibar Town, **Mbweni** (Map p124) was the site of a 19th-century UMCA mission station that was used as a settlement for freed slaves. In addition to the small and still functioning St John's Anglican church, dating to the 1880s, you can see the ruins of the UMCA's St Mary's School for Girls in the grounds of the Mbweni Ruins Hotel.

Maruhubi Palace

The once-imposing **Maruhubi Palace** (Map p124), about 4km north of Zanzibar Town, was built by Sultan Barghash in 1882 to house his large harem. In 1899 it was destroyed by fire, although the remaining ruins hint at its previous scale. The ruins are just west of the Bububu road.

Mtoni Palace

The ruins of **Mtoni Palace** (Map p124), built by Sultan Seyyid Said as his residence in the early 19th century, are just northeast of Maruhubi. In its heyday the palace was a beautiful building with a balconied exterior and an observation turret and a mosque, although nothing remains today other than a few walls. You can get an idea of how it once must have looked by reading Emily Said-Reute's *Memoirs of an Arabian Princess*. There's also excellent background information on www.mtoni.com/palace ruins.html, including details about the Mtoni Palace conservation project. A guide can be arranged at the ruins, or you can book a Princess Salme tour through Mtoni Marine Centre (p133). Continue north past the Maruhubi Palace turn-off for about 2km, from where the ruins are signposted to the west.

Kidichi Persian Baths

Northeast of Zanzibar Town, the **Kidichi Persian Baths** (Map p124) are another construction of Sultan Seyyid, built in 1850 for his Persian wife at the island's highest point. They're rather unremarkable now, but with a bit of imagination, you can see the Sultan's lavishly garbed coterie disrobing to test the waters. Take a *dalla-dalla* 502 to the Bububu junction, from where it's about a 3km walk east down an unpaved road. The baths are also included in the Princess Salme tour (see Mtoni Palace, above).

Activities

TRADITIONAL SPA

There are several traditional spas in Stone Town, where you can treat yourself to Zanzibari beauty rituals. One of the best is **Mrembo** (www.mtoni.com/mrembo) Mtoni Marine Centre (Map p124); Stone Town (Map p126), with branches at Mtoni Marine Centre (p133) and in Stone Town signposted past St Joseph's Cathedral, with a traditional 'singo' flower scrub and more, enjoyed with *taarab* (Zanzibari music) music in the background.

DHOW CRUISES & ISLAND TOURS

Enjoy the Stone Town skyline from the water on a sunset cruise. Prices start at about US$35 per person with a minimum of two people. Contacts include **One Ocean/The Zanzibar Dive Centre** (Map p126; ☎ 024-223 8374; www.zanzibarone ocean.com; off Shangani St) and **The Original Dhow Safaris** (www.dhowsafaris.net).

All the listings under Travel Agencies & Tour Operators (p125), plus the Zanzibar Tourist Corporation (ZTC) Tourist Information Office (p125), can arrange day excursions to the offshore islands near Stone Town. Another option is **Safari Blue** (www.safariblue.net), which organises day dhow excursions around Menai Bay. The excursions, which leave from Fumba, include a seafood and fruit lunch, plus snorkelling equipment, and time relaxing on a sandbank. Before booking it's worth checking weather conditions, as some months – notably April/May and July/August – can get quite windy or rainy.

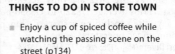

THINGS TO DO IN STONE TOWN

- Enjoy a cup of spiced coffee while watching the passing scene on the street (p134)
- Watch sunset from Forodhani Gardens (p134)
- Walk through Darajani market in the morning, when everything is still fresh (opposite)
- Visit the old slave market (opposite)
- Buy a *kanga* or *kikoi* (p134)
- Take a Princess Salme tour (left)
- Go diving or snorkelling (p130)
- Indulge yourself with a traditional beauty treatment (above)

FREDDIE MERCURY

Queen lead vocalist Freddie Mercury was born Faroukh Bulsara in 1946 in Stone Town to Parsee parents. He lived on the island until he was about eight years old, when he was sent to India for boarding school. His family left Zanzibar in the wake of the 1964 revolution, never to return. There's no agreement as to which house or houses Freddie and his family actually occupied, and several make the claim. For anyone wanting to make a pilgrimage, two places to start are the **Zanzibar Gallery** (Map p126; cnr Kenyatta Rd & Gizenga St), with a gold plaque on the outside memorialising Mercury, and **Mercury's** (Map p126; ☎ 024-223 3076; Mizingani Rd; ☽ 10am-midnight) restaurant, which doesn't claim that he lived there, but capitalises on his name. Freddie Mercury died on 24 November 1991 in London of complications from AIDS.

SPICE TOURS

While spices no longer dominate Zanzibar's economy as they once did, plantations still dot the centre of the island. It's possible to visit them – learning about what cloves, vanilla and other spices look like in the wild – on 'spice tours'. These half-day excursions take in some plantations, as well as ruins and other sights of historical interest.

All of the listings under Travel Agencies & Tour Operators (p125) organise spice tours, which take about five hours and range in price from about US$12 to US$15 per person for a group tour, and about US$25 per person for a private tour. Many include lunch, and some include a swim stop at Mangapwani beach (see p137).

Diving & Snorkelling

For more on diving, see boxed text, opposite. Snorkelling equipment hire costs US$5 to US$15; when you're selecting it, pay particular attention to getting a good mask. Most snorkelling sites are only accessible by boat. Trips average US$20 to US$50 per half day, often including a snack or lunch. Recommended operators:

Bahari Divers (Map p126; ☎ 0777-415011, 0784-254786; www.zanzibar-diving.com; Shangani St) A small, friendly and professional outfit that primarily organises dives around the islands offshore from Stone Town. It offers a range of PADI certification courses, and caters to families (including rental of children's masks and fins). Its office is near NBC bank, with a branch planned soon for Nungwi.

One Ocean/The Zanzibar Dive Centre (Map p126; ☎ 024-223 8374; www.zanzibaroneocean.com; off Shangani St) A PADI five-star centre and one of the best dive operators on the islands. It has various branches along the east coast, and organise dives there, as well as around Stone Town, for divers of all levels. The main office is just down from the Shangani tunnel and NBC bank.

Festivals & Events

Muslim holidays are celebrated on Zanzibar; see p609. For other festivals, see p255.

Sleeping
BUDGET

In and around the Mkunazini area, on the eastern edge of town near the Anglican cathedral:

Flamingo Guest House (Map p126; ☎ 024-223 2850; flamingoguesthouse@hotmail.com; Mkunazini St; s/d with private bathroom US$15/30, with shared bathroom US$12/24) No frills but cheap and fine, with straightforward rooms – all with nets and fans – around a courtyard, a common TV and a rooftop sitting-breakfast area.

Haven Guest House (Map p126; ☎ 024-223 5677/8; s/d US$13/25) A backpacker-friendly place with clean, no-frills rooms, a travellers' bulletin board, free coffee and tea, and a small kitchenette for self-catering. It's just south of Mkunazini, between Soko Muhogo St and Vuga Rd.

Jambo Guest House (Map p126; ☎ 024-223 3779; jamboguest@hotmail.com; s/d/tr with shared bathroom US$20/30/45; ☒) Just around the corner from Flamingo Guest House, and also popular with backpackers, Jambo has free tea and coffee, clean rooms, including some with air-con, decent breakfasts and an internet café opposite.

St Monica's Hostel (Map p126; ☎ 024-223 0773; monicaszanzibar@hotmail.com; s/d US$30/40, s/d/tr with shared bathroom US$20/25/30) An old, rambling place next to the Anglican cathedral, with spacious rooms, including some with a small veranda.

Near the southern edge of Stone Town, around Vuga Rd:

Florida Guest House (Map p126; ☎ 0777-421421; floridaznz@yahoo.com; Vuga Rd; s/d/tr US$25/40/60; ☒) Small, clean rooms with hot water and mini-fridge (check out a few as they're all different). It's next to Culture Musical Club.

Garden Lodge (Map p126; ☎ 024-223 3298; Kaunda Rd; s/d/tr US$30/40/60) A quiet location – diagonally opposite the High Court – and clean, decent rooms, especially the upstairs ones, which are bright and spacious, with hot water, nets and ceiling fans. There's a rooftop breakfast terrace.

On the northern side of town, and about a five-minute walk from the port, is another clutch of lodges:

Bandari Lodge (Map p126; ☎ 024-223 7969; bandarilodge@hotmail.com; s/d/tw/tr US$15/25/30/35) Clean rooms with high ceilings, nets and fan, plus a common kitchen and a fridge. Turn left as you exit the port – it's just a two-minute walk ahead on the right-hand side.

Warere Town House (Map p126; ☎ 024-223 3835; s/d/tr US$20/35/45) Reasonable-value rooms – some with small balconies and all with hot water – plus a rooftop terrace. It's just minutes from the port (staff will come meet you), and behind Bandari Lodge.

Another five minutes' walk from the port, in and around the Kiponda area, roughly between the Old Fort and Malindi:

Pyramid Hotel (Map p126; ☎ 024-223 3000; pyramidhotel@yahoo.com; s/d/tr with private bathroom US$20/30/45, d with shared bathroom US$25) Notable for its very steep staircase, Pyramid has a mix of rooms, most with private bathrooms and hot water, some with small balconies and all with Zanzibari beds, nets and fans. Look at a few as standards vary. There's a rooftop terrace.

Hotel Kiponda (Map p126; ☎ 024-223 3052; www.kiponda.com; Nyumba ya Moto St; s/d/tr US$25/45/60) This hotel is slightly pricier than others in this category, but rooms are spotless and good value and the location – tucked away in a small lane near the waterfront – is convenient. Most

---

DIVING THE ZANZIBAR ARCHIPELAGO

The Zanzibar Archipelago's turquoise waters are just as amazing below the surface as they are from above, with hard and soft corals and many sea creatures. Diving is possible year-round, although conditions vary dramatically. Late March until mid-June is generally the least favourable time because of erratic weather patterns and frequent storms, although good days are possible, especially in March when water temperatures are warmer. July or August through to February/March tend to be the best months overall, although again, conditions vary and wind is an important factor. On both Zanzibar and Pemba, the calmest time is generally from around September to November during the lull between the annual monsoons.

Water temperatures range from lows of about 22°C in July and August to highs of about 29°C in February and March, with the average about 26°C. Throughout, 3mm wetsuits are standard; 4mm suits are recommended for some areas during the July to September winter months, and 2mm suits are fine from around December to March or April.

Costs, Courses & Planning

Costs are somewhat cheaper on Zanzibar than on Pemba. Expect to pay from US$350 for a four-day Professional Association of Dive Instructors (PADI) open-water course, about US$50/80 for a single-/double-dive package and from about US$60 for a night dive. Most places discount about 10% if you have your own equipment, and for groups. In addition to open-water certification, many operators also offer other courses, including Advanced Open Water, Medic First Aid, Rescue Diver and speciality courses, including underwater photography and navigation.

As for deciding where to dive: generally speaking, Zanzibar is known for the corals and shipwrecks offshore from Stone Town, and for fairly reliable visibility, high fish diversity, and the chance to see pelagics to the north and northeast. While some sites are challenging, there are also many easily accessed beginner sites.

Unlike Zanzibar, which is a continental island, Pemba is an oceanic island located in a deep channel with a steeply dropping shelf. Diving here tends to be more challenging, with an emphasis on wall and drift dives, though there are some sheltered areas for beginners, especially around Misali Island.

Dive Operators & Safety

For more on safety, see boxed text, p603.

rooms have their own bathroom, and there's a rooftop restaurant.

In and around the Shangani area, at the western tip of Stone Town:

Karibu Zanzibar (Map p126; r US$50) A small place with spartan rooms, with fan and air-con, nets and TV. It's in a small alley opposite Al-Johari hotel, and a couple of blocks in from Zanzibar Serena Inn.

MIDRANGE

Clove Hotel (Map p126; ☎ 0777-484567; www.zanzibar hotel.nl; Hurumzi St, Hurumzi; s/d/f from US$40/60/85) Spartan but pleasant rooms (check out a few) with nets and fans in a quiet location. The family rooms have small balconies with views down onto the small square below, and there's a rooftop terrace.

Abuso Inn (Map p126; ☎ 024-223 5886; inafaa@hotmail .com; Shangani St, Shangani; s/d/tr US$50/65/75) A family-run place, with no-frills but spotless and mostly spacious rooms with large windows, wooden floors, hot water and fan or air-con. Some rooms have glimpses of the water.

Shangani Hotel (Map p126; ☎ 024-223 3688, 024-223 6363; www.shanganihotel.com; Kenyatta Rd, Shangani; s/d/tr US$55/75/85) An unpretentious place opposite Shangani post office, with cluttered but reasonable rooms, most with TV, fridge and fan, plus a restaurant.

Stone Town B&B (Map p126; ☎ 0773-861313; bar aka@zanlink.com; Kenyatta Rd, Shangani; s/d incl breakfast US$70/80; ✲) Above Stone Town Café, with four (more on the way) simple, spotless rooms – all with hot-water bathrooms and cable TV, and a good, healthy breakfast.

Mazsons Hotel (Map p126; ☎ 024-223 3694; www .mazsonshotel.net; Kenyatta Rd, Shangani; s/d from US$70/90; ✲) The long-standing Mazsons has impressively restored lobby woodwork and a convenient location, which go some way to compensating for its rooms – modern and comfortable, though rather soulless. There's also a restaurant.

Chavda Hotel (Map p126; ☎ 024-223 2115; chavda hotel@zanlink.com; Baghani St, Shangani; s/d from US$90/110; ✲) Chavda is a quiet, reliable hotel, with some period décor and a range of bland, carpeted rooms with TV, telephone and minibar. The rooftop bar and restaurant are open during the high season only.

Zanzibar Coffee House Hotel (Map p126; ☎ 024-223 9319; www.riftvalley-zanzibar.com; Hurumzi; s/d with private bathroom from US$75/95,with shared bathroom US$60/75, s/d upstairs US$115/145, family ste US$145) A boutique-style hotel above the eponymous coffee house, with eight good-value rooms, most spacious, some with private bathroom, and all decorated with Zanzibari beds and décor. There's a great rooftop breakfast (both the rooftop area and the breakfast). It's no frills, but in a comfortable, atmospheric sort of way, and gets good reviews.

TOP END

Dhow Palace (Map p126; ☎ 024-223 3012; dhowpalace@ zanlink.com; Shangani; s/d US$75/100; ☽ Jun-Mar; ✲) A classic place with old Zanzibari décor, a fountain in the tastefully restored lobby and comfortable, well-appointed rooms. It's just off Kenyatta Rd, and under the same management as Tembo House Hotel.

Ahlan Palace Hotel (Map p126; ☎ 024-223 1435; www.ahlanpalace.com; Shangani; s/d US$80/110; ✲) A welcoming, down-to-earth place with simply furnished but clean, comfortable and atmospheric rooms. It's centrally located diagonally opposite Chavda Hotel.

Tembo House Hotel (Map p126; ☎ 024-223 3005; www.tembohotel.com; Shangani St, Shangani; s/d US$95/110; ✲ ▯ ✲) This attractively restored building has a prime waterfront location, including a small patch of beach (no swimming), efficient management and good-value rooms – some with sea views, many with Zanzibari beds – in new and old wings. Most have a TV and fridge, and there's a small pool, a restaurant (no alcohol) and a great buffet breakfast on the seaside terrace.

Zanzibar Palace Hotel (Map p126; ☎ 024-223 2230; www.zanzibarpalacehotel.com; Kiponda; s US$95-110, d US$95-225, ste US$285; ✲) Rooms all have Zanzibari beds and period design, some have separate sitting areas, some have small balconies, most have large raised or sunken-style bathtubs, and most have air-con. No credit cards accepted.

Al-Johari (Map p126; ☎ 024-223 6779; www.al-jo hari.com; Shangani; r incl breakfast US$140-350; ✲ ▯) Ultramodern rooms with wi-fi and a few Zanzibari touches, an air-con, glassed-in restaurant upstairs and a breezy rooftop bar with views. A full buffet breakfast is served, and children under 12 years old stay for free. Take the small road off Kenyatta Rd in front of Mazsons Hotel and follow it down a few hundred metres towards the CC Africa office; Al-Johari is just to the left.

236 Hurumzi (Map p126; ☎ 0777-423266; www .236hurumzi.com; Hurumzi St, Hurumzi; r US$185-225, apt US$90) Formerly Emerson & Green, this Zanzibar institution is in two adjacent historic buildings that have been completely restored along the lines of an *Arabian Nights* fantasy, and are full of character. Each room is unique – one has its own private rooftop teahouse – and all are decadently decorated to give you an idea of what Zanzibar must have been like in its heyday. On the rooftop is the **Towertop Restaurant** (meals US$25-30), with reservations essential. It's several winding blocks east of the Old Fort.

Beyt al-Chai (Map p126; ☎ 0777-444111; www.blue bayzanzibar.com/beyt_el_chai; Kelele Sq, Shangani; s US$125-275, d US$155-330; ☷ Jun-Apr) This converted tea house is an atmospheric choice, with just six rooms, each individually designed, and all with period décor. For a splurge, try one of the top-floor Sultan suites, with views to the sea in the distance, and raised Jacuzzi-style baths. Downstairs is a restaurant.

Zanzibar Serena Inn (Map p126; ☎ 024-223 2306, 024-223 3587; www.serenahotels.com; Shangani; s/d from US$325/475; ☷ ▢ ☷) The Zanzibar Serena, in the refurbished Extelecoms House, has a beautiful waterside setting, rooms with all the amenities, and a business centre, although we've had some complaints about lackadaisical staff and service.

Outside Stone Town are a few more options that make agreeable bases if you want proximity to the town with quieter surroundings.

Mtoni Marine Centre (Map p124; ☎ 024-225 0140; www.mtoni.com; Bububu Rd; club s/d US$70/90, palm court s/d US$110/140; ☷ ▢ ☷) A long-standing family-friendly establishment, with spacious 'club rooms' and more luxurious 'palm court' rooms with private balconies. There's a small beach, large gardens, a popular waterside bar and a restaurant. It's on the beach (swimming at high tide) about 3km north of town along the Bububu road. The hotel is affiliated with Coastal Travels (p95), and it has package deals from Dar es Salaam.

Mbweni Ruins Hotel (Map p124; ☎ 024-223 5478; www.mbweni.com; s/d US$120/200; ☷ ▢ ☷) Mbweni is a genteel establishment with well-appointed rooms in large, lushly vegetated gardens about 5km from town, and several kilometres off the airport road. There's also a restaurant, the Mangrove Bar, and a private jetty for dhow transfers to and from Stone Town or elsewhere can be arranged. The property was formerly the site of the UMCA mission school for the children of freed slaves.

Eating

During the low season and Ramadan many restaurants close or operate reduced hours.

RESTAURANTS

Luis Yoghurt Parlour (Map p126; Gizenga St; meals from TSh6000; ☷ 10.30am-2pm & 6-8pm Mon-Sat) This old favourite serves delicious and spicy home-cooked Goan cuisine, plus lassis, yoghurt and milkshakes.

Radha Food House (Map p126; ☎ 024-223 4808; thalis TSh10,000) A small place tucked away on a side street just before the Shangani tunnel. The menu – strictly vegetarian – features thalis, lassis, homemade yoghurt and other dishes from the subcontinent.

Archipelago Café-Restaurant (Map p126; ☎ 024-223 5668; Shangani St; mains from TSh5000-11,000; ☷ lunch & dinner) A fine, breezy location on a 1st-floor terrace overlooking the water opposite NBC bank in Shangani, and a menu featuring such delicacies as vegetable coconut curry, chicken pilau and homemade cakes. There's no bar, but you can bring your own alcohol.

Pagoda Chinese Restaurant (Map p126; ☎ 024-223 1758; off Shangani St; meals from TSh8000; ☷ lunch & dinner) Tasty Chinese food near the Africa House Hotel.

Mcheza Sports Bar (Map p124; Bububu rd; meals from TSh12,000; ☷ lunch & dinner) Next to the Mtoni Marine Centre is this beachside bar, with pub food, seafood, South African steaks, a pizza oven and live music on Saturday evenings during high season.

Sambusa Two Tables Restaurant (Map p126; ☎ 024-223 1979; off Kaunda Rd; meals TSh15,000; ☷ dinner) For sampling authentic Zanzibari dishes it's hard to beat this small, family-run restaurant, where the proprietors bring out course after course of local delicacies. Advance reservations are required; up to 15 guests can be accommodated.

Mercury's (Map p126; ☎ 024-223 3076; Mizingani Rd; meals TSh8000-16,000; ☷ 10am-midnight) A popular waterside hang-out, with seafood grills, pasta dishes and pizzas, a well-stocked bar and a sundowners terrace.

Monsoon Restaurant (Map p126; ☎ 0777-410410; Mizingani Rd; meals from TSh9000; ☷ lunch & dinner) Traditional-style dining on floor cushions, and well-prepared Swahili and Western cuisine served to a backdrop of live *taarab* music on Wednesday and Saturday evenings. It's at the southwestern edge of Forodhani Gardens.

La Fenice (Map p126; ☎ 0777-411868; Shangani St; meals from TSh10,000; ☺ lunch & dinner) A breezy little patch of Italy on the waterfront, with tasty Italian cuisine and outdoor tables where you can enjoy your pasta while gazing out at the turquoise sea.

Mtoni Marine Centre (Map p124; ☎ 024-225 0117; mtonirestaurant@zanzibar.cc; Bububu rd; meals TSh10,000-TSh27,000; ☺ dinner) A well-regarded restaurant with a range of seafood and meat grills, and waterside barbecues several times weekly, with a backdrop of *taarab* or other music.

CAFÉS

Buni Café (Map p126; Shangani St; snacks & light meals from TSh3000; ☺ 8.30am-6.30pm) Just before the Shangani tunnel, with a similar menu to Stone Town Café (though no all-day breakfasts), and a porch for watching the passing scene.

Zanzibar Coffee House Café (Map p126; ☎ 024-223 9319; coffeehouse@zanlink.com; Hurumzi; snacks from TSh3000) A cosy place below the Zanzibar Coffee House Hotel, with a large coffee menu, plus milkshakes, fruit smoothies and cakes.

Rumaliza Coffee & Grill (Map p126; Kenyatta Rd; snacks & light meals TSh3000-7000) Milkshakes, smoothies, sandwiches, coffees and more.

Stone Town Café (Map p126; Kenyatta Rd; breakfast TSh5000, meals TSh4000-8000; ☺ 8am-8pm Mon-Sat) All-day breakfasts, milkshakes, cakes, salads, quiche, vegie wraps and good coffee.

QUICK EATS

Al-Sheibany (☎ 024-223 9560; off Malawi Rd; meals from TSh2000; ☺ 10am-3pm) A local favourite on a small side street off Malawi Rd and just east of Creek Rd (in from the Sealand container sign) serving delicious pilau, biryani and more, to eat there or take away.

Forodhani Gardens (Map p126; Mizingani Rd; meals from TSh2500; ☺ dinner) These waterside gardens come alive at sundown, when dozens of vendors serve grilled fish and meat, Zanzibari pizza (rolled-up, omelette-filled chapati), sesame bread and more, eaten while sitting on benches or on the lawn. The gardens are along the seafront opposite the Old Fort, and were closed for rehabilitation when this book was researched.

SELF-CATERING

Shamshuddin's Cash & Carry (Map p126) Just behind Darajani market.

Drinking & Entertainment

Dharma Lounge (Map p126; Vuga Rd; ☺ 7.30pm-late; ✗) Zanzibar's first and only cocktail lounge, with big cushions for relaxing, a well-stocked bar and music. It's next to the Culture Musical Club.

Africa House Hotel (Map p126; www.theafricahouse-zanzibar.com; off Shangani St) Terrace-level sundowners overlooking the water.

Mcheza Sports Bar (Map p124; ☎ 024-225 0117; mtonirestaurant@zanzibar.cc; Bububu rd) A happening sports bar.

Livingstone Beach Restaurant (Map p126; off Shangani St) Waterside drinks and (slow) meals

Mercury's (Map p126; ☎ 024-223 3076; Mizingani Rd) Sundowners and evening beach bonfires, plus live music Wednesday, Friday, Saturday and Sunday nights.

Al-Johari (Map p126; ☎ 024-223 6779; www.al-johari .com; Shangani) Half-price happy-hour drinks in the rooftop bar.

TRADITIONAL MUSIC & DANCE

On Tuesday and Friday evenings from 7pm to 10pm there are *ngoma* and *taarab* performances at the Old Fort (Map p126; see p128).

A recommended contact for anything related to traditional music and dance, including performances and lessons, is the **Dhow Countries Music Academy** (Map p126; www.zanzibar music.org; Top fl, Old Customs House, Mizingani Rd), next to the Palace Museum and diagonally opposite Mercury's restaurant.

Shopping

Stone Town has wonderfully atmospheric craft shopping. A good place to start is Gizenga St, which is lined with small shops and craft dealers.

Zanzibar Gallery (Map p126; ☎ 024-223 2721; gallery@ swahilicoast.com; cnr Kenyatta Rd & Gizenga St; ☺ 9am-6.30pm Mon-Sat, 9am-1pm Sun) A large collection of souvenirs, textiles, woodcarvings, antiques and more.

Memories of Zanzibar (Map p126; Kenyatta Rd) For jewellery, textiles and curios.

Moto Handicrafts (Map p126; www.solarafrica .net/moto; Hurumzi St) Sells baskets, mats and other woven products made by local womens' cooperatives using environmentally sustainable technologies.

Doreen Mashika (Map p126; www.doreenmashika .com; 268 Hurumzi St) Jewellery, plus super-stylish handbags, shoes and other accessories will be sold at this soon-to-open shop.

TAARAB MUSIC

Taarab is the archipelago's most famous musical export, combining African, Arabic and Indian influences. Originally introduced from Arabia, *taarab*-style music was played in Zanzibar as early as the 1820s. However, it wasn't until the 1900s, when Sultan Seyyid Hamoud bin Muhammed encouraged formation of the first *taarab* clubs, that it became more formalised. The performances themselves are quite an event, and audience participation is key. There is also always a singer involved, with themes centring around love, and many puns and double meanings intertwined.

Famous *taarab* singers include Siti Binti Saad, who was the first *taarab* singer on the archipelago, and Bi Kidude, the first lady of *taarab* music, who helped popularise *taarab* clubs. Today most Zanzibaris distinguish between 'old *taarab*', which is played by an orchestra using primarily traditional instruments, and 'modern *taarab*', which expands *taarab*'s traditional base with keyboards, guitars and synthesised sound.

For an introduction, stop by the **Zanzibar Serena Inn** (Map p126; ☎ 024-223 2306, 024-223 3587; www.serenahotels.com; Shangani), where a group called the Twinkling Stars plays from about 6pm to 7.30pm on Tuesday and Friday. For something livelier, head to the **Culture Musical Club** (Map p126; Vuga Rd), with rehearsals from about 7.30pm to 9.30pm Monday to Friday. An excellent time to see *taarab* performances is during the **Festival of the Dhow Countries** (p255) in July.

Getting There & Away

AIR

There are daily flights connecting Zanzibar with Dar es Salaam (US$65), Arusha (about US$170 to US$220), Pemba (US$90), Selous Game Reserve and the northern parks on Coastal Aviation and ZanAir. Coastal Aviation also goes daily to/from Tanga via Pemba (US$100), and has day excursion packages from Dar es Salaam to Stone Town for about US$120, including return flights, lunch and airport transfers. Tropical Air is another contact, with daily flights between Zanzibar, Dar es Salaam, Mafia and sometimes Saadani. Air Tanzania and Precision Air fly daily between Zanzibar and Dar es Salaam, with connections to Kilimanjaro, Arusha and (on Precision Air) Nairobi (Kenya). Precision Air, in partnership with Kenya Airways, also has a direct flight between Zanzibar and Nairobi. Note that the Nairobi–Zanzibar flight is routinely overbooked, and passengers are frequently bumped (especially if they've been booked through Precision Air). Reconfirm your seat, and arrive early at the airport.

Airline offices in Zanzibar Town include the following:

Air Tanzania (Map p126; ☎ 023-223 0213; airtanzania@zanlink.com; Shangani St) Next to Abuso Inn.

Coastal Aviation (Map p126; ☎ 024-223 3489, 024-223 3112; www.coastal.cc; Kelele Sq) Next to Zanzibar Serena Inn, and at the airport.

Kenya Airways (Map p126; ☎ 024-223 4520/1; www.kenya-airways.com; Mizingani Rd) Just southeast of the Big Tree.

Precision Air (Map p126; ☎ 024-223 4520/1; www.precisionairtz.com; Mizingani Rd) Located with Kenya Airways.

Tropical Air (Map p126; ☎ 0777-431431, 024-223 2511; tropic@zanzinet.com; Creek Rd) Just down from the Zanzibar Tourist Corporation (ZTC) Tourist Information Office.

ZanAir (Map p126; ☎ 024-223 3670/2993, 0777-421300; www.zanair.com) Off Malawi Rd, opposite Ciné Afrique.

BOAT

For ferry connections between Zanzibar and Dar es Salaam, see p101. For ferry connections between Zanzibar and Pemba, see p144. At the time of writing tickets for most Dar es Salaam ferries were being sold several hundred metres southwest of the port on Malindi Rd, while for most Pemba ferries, the offices are still at the port. Ask your hotel, or book through any of the listings under Travel Agencies & Tour Operators (p125) or through the ZTC Tourist Information Office (p125). If you leave Zanzibar on the *Flying Horse* night ferry, take care with your valuables, especially when the boat docks in Dar es Salaam in the early morning hours.

Dhows link Zanzibar with Dar es Salaam, Tanga, Bagamoyo and Mombasa (Kenya). Foreigners are not permitted on dhows between Dar es Salaam and Zanzibar. For other routes, the best place to ask is at the beach behind Tembo House Hotel. Allow anywhere from 10 to 48 hours or more to/from the mainland. If you do want to do this journey, it's better to do it from the mainland to Zanzibar with one of the private hotel dhows leaving from around Pangani (see p152). See also boxed text, p622.

Getting Around

TO/FROM THE AIRPORT

The airport is about 7km southeast of Zanzibar Town (TSh10,000 to TSh15,000 in a taxi). Bus 505 also does this route (TSh700, 30 minutes), departing from the corner opposite Mnazi Mmoja hospital (Map p126). From the airport, departures are from the *dalla-dalla* stand at the start of the road into town. Ask to be dropped at the Mnazi Mmoja hospital, from where you can walk to central guesthouses and hotels.

CAR & MOTORCYCLE

It's easy to arrange car, moped or motorcycle rental and prices are reasonable, although breakdowns are fairly common, as are moped accidents. Considering how small the island is, it's often more straightforward and not that much more expensive to work out a good deal with a taxi driver.

You'll need either an International Driving Permit (together with your home licence), a licence from Kenya, Uganda or South Africa, or a Zanzibar driving permit – there are police checkpoints along the roads where you'll be asked to show one or the other. Zanzibar permits can be obtained on the spot at the **traffic police office** (Map p126; cnr Malawi & Creek Rds). If you rent through a tour company, it will sort out the paperwork.

Daily rental rates average from about US$35 for a moped or motorcycle and from US$55 for a Suzuki 4WD, with better deals for longer-term rentals. You can rent through any of the tour companies, through **Asko Tours & Travel** (Map p126; ☎ 024-223 0712; Kenyatta Rd), next to Shangani post office, which also organises island excursions, or by asking around in front of the market, near the bus station. If you're not mechanically minded, bring someone along who can check that the motorbike or vehicle you're renting is in reasonable condition, and take a test drive. Full payment is usually required at the time of delivery, but don't pay any advance deposits.

DALLA-DALLAS

Open-sided *dalla-dallas* piled with people and produce link all major towns on the island, leaving from the transport stand (Map p126) on Creek Rd opposite Darajani market. For all the main beaches, there are several vehicles daily, with the first ones departing from about 6am and the last ones back to Stone Town departing by about 3pm or 4pm. None of the routes cost more than about TSh1500, and all take plenty of time (eg about three hours from Zanzibar Town to Jambiani). Major routes include the following:

Route No	Destination
101	Mkokotoni
116	Nungwi
117	Kiwengwa
118	Matemwe
206	Chwaka
214	Uroa
308	Unguja Ukuu
309	Jambiani
310	Makunduchi
324	Bwejuu
326	Kizimkazi
502	Bububu
505	Airport (marked 'U/Ndege')

PRIVATE MINIBUS

Private minibuses run daily to the north- and east-coast beaches, although stiff competition and lots of hassles with touts mean that a splurge on a taxi isn't a bad idea. Book through any travel agency the day before you want to travel, and the minibuses will pick you up at your hotel in Stone Town between 8am and 9am. Travel takes 1½ to two hours to any of the destinations, and costs from a negotiable TSh6000 per person. Don't pay for the return trip in advance. Most drivers only go to hotels where they'll get a commission, and will go to every length to talk you out of other places, including telling you that the hotel is closed/full/burned down etc.

TAXI

Taxis don't have meters, so agree on a price with the driver before getting into the car. Town trips cost from TSh2000.

AROUND ZANZIBAR

Beaches

Zanzibar has superb beaches, with the best along the island's east coast and to the north. Although some have become overcrowded and built-up, all offer a wonderful respite from bumping along dusty roads on the mainland. The east-coast beaches are protected by coral reefs offshore and have fine, white coral sand. Depending on the season, they may also have lots of seaweed (most abundant from December to February).

Everyone has a favourite, and which beach to choose is a matter of preference. For meeting other travellers, enjoying some nightlife and staying at relatively inexpensive accommodation, the best choices are central and west Nungwi in the far north (although for a beach, you'll need to go around the corner to Kendwa), followed by Paje on the east coast. Bwejuu and Jambiani on the east coast are also popular – and among the finest stretches of palm-fringed sand you'll find anywhere – but everything is more spread out and somewhat quieter than in the north. For an even calmer atmosphere, try Matemwe or Pongwe. Except for Kendwa, where you can take a dip at any time, swimming at all of the beaches is tide dependent.

BUBUBU (FUJI BEACH)

This modest stretch of sand, 10km north of town in Bububu, is the closest place to Zanzibar Town for swimming. It's accessed via the dirt track heading west, just north of the Bububu police station.

Bububu Beach Guest House (☎ 024-225 0110; www .bububu-zanzibar.com; s/d from US$15/25) is a budget haunt with airy no-frills rooms near the beach, and meals with advance notice. It's at the end of the dirt track heading west from the Bububu police station.

Hakuna Matata Beach Lodge (☎ 0777-454892; www.hakuna-matata-beach-lodge.com; s US$130-165, d US$160-210; ❄ ▢ ▨), an amenable place built among the old Chuini Palace ruins and overlooking a small cove, has stone and thatch bungalows, gardens, a restaurant and a spa. It's about 12km north of Stone Town.

MANGAPWANI

The small and unremarkable beach at Mangapwani is notable mainly for its nearby caves, and is frequently included as a stop on spice tours. The caves are located about 20km north of Zanzibar Town along the coast. They consist of a large **natural cave** with a freshwater pool, supposedly used in connection with the slave trade, and – north of here – the sobering **slave cave**, a dank, dark cell that was used as a holding pen to hide slaves after the legal trade was abolished in the late 19th century.

Follow the main road north past Bububu to Chuini, from where you head left down a dirt road for about 8km towards Mangapwani village. Continue towards the sea until you see a small sign for the slave cave.

Dalla-dallas run between Stone Town and Mangapwani village.

NUNGWI

This large village, nestled among the palm groves at Zanzibar's northernmost tip, is a dhow-building centre, and one of the island's major tourist destinations – despite now lacking any sort of substantial beach during much of the year, thanks to shifting tidal patterns and development-induced erosion. It's also where traditional and modern knock against each other with full force. Fishermen sit in the shade repairing their nets while the morning's catch dries on neat wooden racks nearby. Yet take a few steps back from the waterfront to enter into another world, with blaring music, an internet café, a rather motley collection of guesthouses packed in against each other and a party vibe. For some travellers it's the only place to be on the island (and it's one of the few places you can swim without needing to wait for the tides to come in); others will probably want to give it a wide miss. If partying isn't your scene, head to east Nungwi, where there are some lovely, quiet patches of sand.

There's an internet café and forex bureau at Amaan Bungalows.

Diving

Locally based operators:

East Africa Diving & Water Sport (www.diving-zanzi bar.com) Next to Jambo Brothers Beach Bungalows.

Ras Nungwi Beach Hotel (☎ 024-223 3767; www.rasnungwi.com) A PADI five-star centre at Ras Nungwi Beach Hotel.

Sleeping & Eating – Budget

Central Nungwi – with the main cluster of guesthouses and all the activity, but no beach to speak of – is on the western edge of the peninsula, and just west of the main square of Nungwi village. Past the lighthouse in east Nungwi, everything gets much quieter, with a handful of good hotels spread along a low cliff overlooking the water and a beach at low tide.

Nungwi Guest House (☎ 0777-494899, 0784-234980; http://nungwiguesthouse.tripod.com; Nungwi village; d/tr US$25/30) In the village centre and a good budget option, with simple, clean rooms with private bathroom, set around a small garden courtyard, all with nets and fans and meals on request.

Jambo Brothers Beach Bungalows (jambobunga lows@yahoo.com; central Nungwi; s/d with shared bathroom US$20/30) This low-key place on the sand has been spruced up a bit, though rooms are still quite basic and a bit tatty. Meals can be arranged with advance notice.

Union Beach Bungalows (central Nungwi; s/d with shared bathroom US$20/30) Next to Jambo Brothers Beach Bungalows and a step up, although nothing special, with small, two-room cottages near the beach.

Amaan Bungalows (☎ 024-224 0024/6; www .amaanbungalows.com; central Nungwi; tw from US$60, with sea view US$120; ✷ ▣) This large place is at the centre of the action. Accommodation ranges from small garden-view rooms with fans to spacious sea-view rooms with air-con and small balconies. All have hot water, and there's a waterside restaurant-bar, internet access and moped rental. No credit cards accepted.

Flame Tree Cottages (☎ 024-224 0100; www.flame treecottages.com; east-central Nungwi; s/d US$95/120; ✷) Simply furnished cottages in a small fenced-in garden just in from the beach. All have fan and air-con, and some have a small kitchenette (US$10 extra) and minifridge. Meals can be arranged.

Smiles Beach Hotel (☎ 024-224 0472; www.smiles beachhotel.com; east-central Nungwi; s/d US$75/100; ✷) Clean, well-maintained rooms in two-storey tile-roofed cottages overlooking a manicured lawn and a small patch of beach. All have small sea-facing balconies, and it's quieter than at some of the other central hotels.

Mnarani Beach Cottages (☎ 024-224 0494; www .lighthousezanzibar.com; east Nungwi; s/d US$78/120, d/q family cottage US$140/249, deluxe d US$170, honeymoon ste US$190, all rates incl half board; ▣ ▣) This small owner-managed place is on a low rise overlooking the sea just after the lighthouse, and warmly recommended. There are small, spotless cottages, some with sea views, plus a few larger beachfront family cottages with minifridge and a loft, as well as a honeymoon suite and deluxe rooms in the 'Zanzibar House', which also has a rooftop bar with superb views over Nungwi. There's also a beachside restaurant and hammocks and swings for lounging.

Ras Nungwi Beach Hotel (☎ 024-223 3767; www.ras nungwi.com; east Nungwi; per person half board without/with sea view from US$195/240; ❤ Jun-Mar) An attractive, upmarket place with sea-view chalets on a hillside overlooking the sea plus 'garden-view'

rooms in the main lodge. The hotel organises fishing and water sports, and there's a dive centre.

KENDWA

Southwest of Nungwi is Kendwa, a long, wide stretch of sand known for its laid-back atmosphere and its full-moon parties. Apart from the full-moon parties, when it's loud until the wee hours, the beach is lovely and tranquil, swimmable at all hours, and without Nungwi's crush of activity and accommodation.

Scuba Do (www.scuba-do-zanzibar.com), at Sunset Bungalows, is a PADI five-star Gold Palm, with courses and certification.

Sleeping & Eating

Kendwa Rocks (☎ 0777-415475; www.kendwarocks .com; s/d banda with shared bathroom US$15/30, s/d wooden banda from US$50/65, s/d stone bungalows from US$55/78) A Kendwa classic, with straightforward wooden bungalows on the sand, cooler stone and thatch versions nearby, including some with air-con, simple *bandas* sharing bathroom up on the small cliff away from the water, and the biggest full-moon parties.

Sunset Bungalows (☎ 0777-414647, 0777-413818; www.sunsetkendwa.com; s/d US$40/55, s/d with air-con from US$65/75, s/d deluxe beachfront with air-con US$75/95; ✷) Straightforward, good rooms and cottages on a small cliff overlooking the beach, plus better, cheerily decorated ones lined up in facing rows on the sand, including a few 'deluxe bungalows' closer to the water. There's a resident dive operator, and a beachside restaurant-bar with evening bonfires.

Kendwa Beach Resort (☎ 0777-492552; www .kendwabeachresort.com; d US$70-120) A large place towards the southern end of Kendwa with a waterside restaurant and various rooms, ranging from small 'hill-view' rooms, set well back from the water on a hill, to larger, 'ocean bungalows' closer to the beach.

Getting There & Away

You can walk to Kendwa from Nungwi at low tide in about 25 to 30 minutes, but take care as there have been some muggings. Alternatively, inexpensive boats go from near Amaan Bungalows depending on demand. Via public transport from Stone Town, have *dalla-dalla* 116 (Nungwi) drop you at the sign for Kendwa Rocks (a few kilometres south of Nungwi), from where it's about a 2km walk to the beach.

MATEMWE

The long, idyllic beach at Matemwe has some of the finest sand on Zanzibar. It's also the base for diving and snorkelling around Mnemba, just offshore. As you head south along the coast, the sands of Matemwe slide almost imperceptibly into those of Pwani Mchangani, a large fishing village that acts as a buffer before the string of Italian resorts further south at Kiwengwa.

For diving and snorkelling, contact **One Ocean/The Zanzibar Dive Centre** (☎ 0777-473128; oneoceanmatemwe@zanlink.com), based at Matemwe Beach Village.

Sleeping & Eating

Mohammed's Restaurant & Bungalows (☎ 0777-431881; r per person US$15) The only truly budget option, with four basic bungalows, each with two large beds, just back from the beach, and grilled fish meals on order.

Nyota Beach Bungalows (☎ 0777-484303; www .nyotabeachbungalows.com; d with garden/sea view US$65/80) Straightforward bungalows set amid the palms and papaya trees just back from the beach, and a restaurant.

Zanzibar Retreat Hotel (☎ 0773-079344; www.zan zibarretreat.com; s/d US$135/145; 🛏 🖳 🖳) A well-located place on the beach with seven small but well-appointed rooms with wi-fi and beautiful common areas – all with polished hardwood floors, and including an upstairs bar overlooking the beach. There's also satellite TV.

Matemwe Beach Village (☎ 0777-417250, 0777-437200; www.matemwebeach.com, www.matemwebeach .net; s/d/ste/honeymoon ste half board US$120/170/250/400;

🖳 🖳) This recommended and good-value beachfront place has a wonderful setting, spacious, airy bungalows with small verandas set around vegetated beachside gardens and a large but cosy chill-out lounge with throw pillows. For a splurge, try one of the two-storey shamba suites or – for complete pampering – the beachfront honeymoon suite with its own plunge pool, outdoor bathroom and chef. In Stone Town, bookings can also be made through One Ocean/The Zanzibar Dive Centre (p130).

Matemwe Bungalows (www.asilialodges.com; ste per person full board about US$280; 🌙 mid-Jun–Easter; 🖳 🖳) About 2km north of Matemwe Beach Village, Matemwe has a dozen spacious seaside bungalow suites, all with their own verandas and hammocks, and a pampered, upmarket ambience.

Getting There & Away

Matemwe village is about 25km southeast of Nungwi, and reached via a road branching east off the main road by Mkwajuni. *Dalla-dallas* to/from Stone Town go daily between about 6am and 4pm. Early in the day, they continue as far as the fish market at the northern end of the beach. Otherwise, the start/terminus of the route is at the main Matemwe junction.

KIWENGWA

Kiwengwa village is spread out along a fine, wide beach, much of which is occupied by large, Italian-run resort hotels, although there are some quiet stretches to the north and south.

Shooting Star Lodge (☎ 0777-414166; www.shooting starlodge.com; s/d garden lodge US$125/195, s/d sea-view cottages US$160/280; 🖳) is classy and intimate. It's recommended, both for its location on a small cliff overlooking an excellent stretch of beach – well away from the larger resort developments further north and south – and for its top-notch cuisine and lovely décor. Rooms range from simpler and smaller garden-view 'lodge rooms' to spacious sea-view cottages. There's a salt-water infinity pool and a beachside bar.

PONGWE

This quiet arc of beach, about 5km south of Kiwengwa, is dotted with palm trees and backed by dense vegetation, and is about as close to the quintessential tropical paradise as you can get. The nearby village is very tiny, and there are no shops.

NGALAWA BURNING IN MATEMWE

'Mama, all things shall be explained to you according to the ways of Allah', the elderly fisherman began in melodic Swahili, when I asked him why, on many mornings, Matemwe's fishermen light fires inside their *ngalawas* (outrigger sailing boats). 'The boats must be seaworthy, to go beyond the reef to the high seas,' he continued, gesturing across the turquoise shallows to where the surf was crashing about 1km beyond. 'And so, in the course of things, the wood gets waterlogged. Once each week or two, if the boat has spent much time on the sea, we light the fires to help dry out the wood, and keep algae and other growth away.'

Santa Maria Coral Park (www.santamaria-zanzibar .com; s/d/tr US$30/60/90) is a laid-back budget beach haunt with simple *makuti* (thatch) *bandas* or stone-and-thatch bungalows. There's a no-frills restaurant, and a beachside bar with evening bonfires.

The unassuming **Pongwe Beach Hotel** (☎ 0784-336181; www.pongwe.com; s/d from US$95/160) has 10 bungalows (including one honeymoon bungalow), nestled among the palms on a wonderful arc of beach. All are sea facing and spacious, and the cuisine is very good. It's justifiably popular and often fully booked.

PAJE

This wide, white beach is at the junction where the coastal road north to Bwejuu and south to Jambiani joins with the road from Zanzibar Town. It's quite built-up, with a dense cluster of mostly unremarkable places all within a few minutes' walk of each other, and somewhat of a party atmosphere, although it's quieter than Nungwi. For diving, there's the **Paje Dive Centre** (☎ 024-224 0191; www.pajedivecentre.com), on the beach at Arabian Nights hotel.

Sleeping & Eating

Paradise Beach Bungalows (☎ 024-223 1387; www .geocities.jp/paradisebeachbungalows; s/d from $45/55) A long-standing Japanese-run place on the beach with adequate rooms, each with two large beds, and a restaurant.

Paje by Night (☎ 0777-460710; www.pajebynight .net; s/d from US$70/80, d jungle bungalow US$95) This chilled place, known for its bar and its vibe, has a mix of standard and more spacious king rooms, plus several double-storey four-person thatched jungle suites. There's a good restaurant with a pizza oven.

Dhow Inn (☎ 0773-215929; www.dhowinn.com; s/d US$87/101) A small place set just back from the beach in the centre of Paje with a handful of nice rooms, with fans, nets and wi-fi, and a good restaurant.

Hakuna Majiwe (☎ 0777-454505; www.hakuna majiwe.net; s/d US$180/235; 🏊) Nicely decorated cottages with shady porches and Zanzibari beds, and décor that's a fusion of mostly Zanzibar with a touch of Italy. It's at the southernmost end of Paje.

BWEJUU

The large, somnolent village of Bwejuu lies about 3km north of Paje on a long, languid, palm-shaded beach. It's very spread out and quieter than Paje, with nothing much more to do other than listen to the breezes rustling the palm trees.

Sleeping & Eating

Robinson's Place (☎ 0777-413479; www.robinsonsplace .net; per person US$20-35) A cosy Robinson Crusoe–style getaway with a small collection of rooms amid the palms directly on the beach. The two-storey Robinson House has an upstairs tree-house double room. Some rooms have their own bathroom, and the shared bathroom is spotless. There's no electricity.

Bahari Beach Village (www.bahari-beach-village .com; d bungalow US$40) A refreshingly local beachfront place with simple, nice bungalows, with private bathroom and meals available, on a lovely, palm-shaded stretch of sand. It's at the far northern end of Bwejuu, about 2.5km past the end of the *dalla-dalla* route. Just keep heading up the track until you see the sign.

Evergreen Bungalows Bwejuu (☎ 024-224 0273; www.evergreen-bungalows.com; d palmgrove bungalow back from beach US$70, d beach bungalow with hot water US$70-80) Pricey but spiffy and spotless two-storey bungalows, plus several single-storey cottages back from the beach, a restaurant and various activities, including an on-site dive operator, all in a good beachside location north of Bwejuu village.

MICHAMVI PENINSULA

Beginning about 4km north of Bwejuu, the land begins to taper off into the narrow Michamvi Peninsula, with nontidal swimming in Chwaka Bay on its western side.

Breezes Beach Club & Spa (☎ 0774-440883; www .breezes-zanzibar.com; per person half board from US$170; 🏊 💻 🏊 🛜) is a large place with lovely garden-view rooms, plus deluxe rooms and suites closer to the sea, diving, a gym and plenty of other activities to balance out time on the beach.

JAMBIANI

Jambiani is a long village on a stunning stretch of coastline. The village itself – a sunbaked and somnolent collection of thatch and coral-rag houses – is stretched out over more than a kilometre. The sea is an ethereal shade of turquoise and is usually dotted with *ngalawa* (outrigger canoes) moored just offshore. It's quieter than Paje and Nungwi, and has accommodation in all price ranges.

Sleeping & Eating

Oasis Beach Inn (☎ 0777-858720; oasisbeachinn45@
yahoo.co.uk; s/d with private bathroom US$35/50, with shared
bathroom US$25/35) A straightforward beachside
place with no-frills rooms, friendly staff and
meals on order.

Dhow Beach Village (☎ 0777-417763; www.dhow
beachvillage.com; s/d/tw with private bathroom US$35/50/55,
s/d with shared bathroom US$20/30) A vibey place with
a restaurant, a handful of straightforward
rooms with private bathroom, and three
simpler, noisier rooms with fan and shared
bathroom, plus beach volleyball and full-
moon parties.

Red Monkey Bungalows (☎ 024-224 0207, 024-223
5361; standard@zitec.org; s/d US$50/90) At Jambiani's
far southern end, with clean, agreeable sea-
facing bungalows that have gone somewhat
upmarket in recent times, a beachside garden
and a lovely stretch of sand.

Casa Del Mar Hotel Jambiani (☎ 024-224 0401,
0777-455446, www.casa-delmar-zanzibar.com; d downstairs/
upstairs US$65/85) Two double-storey blocks of six
pleasant rooms each – the upper-storey rooms
have lofts – set around a small, well-vegetated
garden in a small, enclosed beach area. There's
also a restaurant.

Blue Oyster Hotel (☎ 024-224 0163; www.zanzibar.de;
s/d US$63/69, with sea view US$78/85, with shared bathroom
US$40/4) This German-run place on the beach
at the northern end of Jambiani has pleasant,
spotless and good-value rooms and a breezy
terrace restaurant.

Jambiani Guest House (www.zanzibar-guesthouse
.com; per house US$155, per d rm US$50) A large whitewashed thatched-roofed self-catering house
on the beach, with five rooms with nets, and
a cook available on request.

KIZIMKAZI

This small village actually consists of two adjoining settlements: Kizimkazi Dimbani to the
north and Kizimkazi Mkunguni to the south.
It's known mainly for the dolphins that favour
the nearby waters. Dolphin trips can be organised through Kizimkazi-based hotels, tour
operators in Stone Town or through hotels at
Paje and Jambiani for about US$15 to US$25
per person. While the dolphins are beautiful,
the tours – especially those organised out of
Stone Town – are often quite unpleasant, due
to the hunt-and-chase tactics used by many
of the tour boats, and they can't be recommended. If you do go out, the best time is
early morning when the water is calmer and

the sun not as hot. Late afternoon is also good,
although winds may be stronger (and if it's
too windy, it's difficult to get in and out of
the boats to snorkel).

Kizimkazi is also the site of an early 12th-
century Shirazi **mosque**, although much of
what is left today is from later restorations.
Inside, in the mihrab, are inscribed Quranic
verses dating to 1107 – among the oldest
known examples of Swahili writing. It's in
Kizimkazi Dimbani, just north of the main
beach area.

For diving and snorkelling, contact **One
Ocean/The Zanzibar Dive Centre** (☎ 0773-573411;
www.ungujaresort.com/activities.htm), based at
Unguja Resort.

Sleeping & Eating

Kizimkazi Coral Reef Village (Kizimkazi Mkunguni; s/d
US$40/50) Six rooms with private bathroom,
fan and nets set somewhat back from the sea,
and meals.

Karamba (☎ 0773-166406; www.karambaresort
.com; Kizimkazi Dimbani; s/d from US$100/136; ☾ mid
Jun–mid April) A dozen whitewashed cottages
on a small cliff overlooking the sea, some
with open-roof showers. There's also a restaurant serving a mix of dishes – vegetarian,
Mediterranean, sushi, sashimi and milkshakes
included – and a beachside chill-out bar with
throw pillows.

Unguja Resort (☎ 0774-477477; www.ungujaresort
.com; per person half board US$200; ☒) Ten spacious
two-storey villas with a beautiful open architectural design set amid reasonably mature
gardens dotted with baobab trees. Very relaxing if you can afford it.

Getting There & Away

Bus 326 runs direct to Kizimkazi. Alternatively, take bus 310 (Makunduchi) as far as
Kufile junction, where you'll need to get out
and wait for another vehicle heading towards
Kizimkazi, or walk (about 5km). Approaching
from Stone Town go right at Kufile junction (ie towards Kizimkazi) and then right
again at the next fork to Kizimkazi Dimbani.
Kizimkazi Mkunguni is to the left at this last
fork.

Jozani Forest

Jozani – now protected as part of the **Jozani-
Chwaka Bay National Park** (adult/child incl guide US$8/4;
☾ 7.30am-5.30pm) – is the largest area of mature forest left on Zanzibar, and is known in

particular for its population of the rare red colobus monkey. There's a short nature trail and a tiny café.

When observing the monkeys, park staff recommend approaching no closer than 3m – both for your safety and that of the animals. In addition to the risk of being bitten by the monkeys, there's concern that if the monkeys were to catch a human illness it could spread and rapidly wipe out the already threatened population.

Jozani is about 35km southeast of Zanzibar Town off the road to Paje, and best reached via bus 309 or 310, by chartered taxi, or with an organised tour from Zanzibar Town (often in combination with dolphin tours to Kizimkazi). The best times to see red colobus monkeys are in the early morning and late evening.

Menai Bay, Unguja Ukuu & Fumba

Menai Bay, fringed by the sleepy villages of Fumba to the west and Unguja Ukuu to the east, is home to an impressive assortment of corals, fish and mangrove forests, some idyllic sandbanks and deserted islets, and a sea-turtle breeding area. Since 1997 it's been protected as part of the **Menai Bay Conservation Area** (admission US$3). Unguja Ukuu is notable as the site of what is believed to be the earliest settlement on Zanzibar, dating to at least the 8th century, although there is little remaining today from this era.

Fumba Beach Lodge (☎ 0777-860540; www.fumba beachlodge.com; s/d full board from US$230/400), approximately 20km south of Zanzibar Town on the western side of Menai Bay, has about two dozen cottage-style rooms set in large grounds, plus a small spa built around a baobab tree (including a great Jacuzzi up in the tree) and a resident dive operator. It's also the base for Safari Blue (see p129). The beach is quiet and lovely, although speckled with coral rock and not quite as 'picture perfect' as those on the east coast.

Offshore Islands

CHANGUU

Changuu ('Prison Island'), about 5km northwest of Zanzibar Town, was originally used to detain 'recalcitrant' slaves and later as a quarantine station. Today it's known for its large family of giant tortoises, believed to have been brought from Aldabra in the Seychelles around the turn of the 20th century. There's

a small beach and a nearby snorkelling reef, plus the former house of the British governor General Lloyd Matthews. The island is now privately owned, and open only to guests of **Changuu Private Island Paradise** (www.privateislands -zanzibar.com; per person half board & airport transfers US$190-230; ☒), although snorkelling and visits to the tortoises and the (pricey) restaurant are still permitted. Day excursions from Stone Town cost from about US$25 per person, including the US$4 entry fee to the island.

MNEMBA

Tiny Mnemba, just offshore from Matemwe, is the ultimate tropical paradise for those who have the money to enjoy it. Access to the island is restricted to guests of the exclusive **Mnemba Island Lodge** (www.andbeyond.com; per person all-inclusive US$1250), but the surrounding, stunning, coral reef – one of Zanzibar's best diving and snorkelling sites – can be visited by anyone.

CHUMBE

This uninhabited island, 12km south of Zanzibar Town, has a shallow-water coral reef along its western shore that is in close to pristine condition and abounding with fish. In 1994 the reef was gazetted as Zanzibar's first marine sanctuary. It's now run as Chumbe Island Coral Park, a private, nonprofit nature reserve, and has gained widespread acclaim for its ecolodge and local environmental education programs.

Chumbe can be visited as a day trip (per person US$80), although staying overnight in one of the seven **ourpick** **Chumbe Eco-Bungalows** (☎ 024-223 1040; www.chumbeisland.com; s/d all-inclusive US$300/500) is highly recommended. Each bungalow has its own rainwater collection system and solar power, and a loft sleeping area opening to the stars. Advance bookings for all visits are essential.

PEMBA
☎ 024

About 50km north of Zanzibar across the deep waters of the Pemba Channel lies hilly, verdant Pemba – the archipelago's 'other' island, seldom visited and long overshadowed by Zanzibar, its larger, more visible and more politically powerful neighbour to the south.

Unlike flat, sandy Zanzibar, Pemba's terrain is hilly, fertile and heavily vegetated. Dense mangrove swamps line its coast, opening only

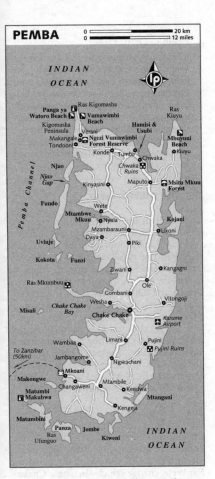

PEMBA

0 ——————— 20 km
0 ——————— 12 miles

INDIAN
OCEAN

Ras Kigomasha
Panga ya
Watoro Beach
Kigomasha
Peninsula
Makangale
Tondooni
Vumawimbi
Beach
Ngezi Vumawimbi
Forest Reserve
Konde
Tumbe
Chwaka
Ras
Kiuyu
Hamisi &
Usubi
Mbuyuni
Beach
Kiuyu
Njao
Njao
Gap
Chwaka
Ruins
Maputo
Msitu Mkuu
Forest
Fundo
Kinyasini
Wete
Mtambwe
Mkuu
Nyala
Verani
Mzambarauni
Daya
Piki
Kojani
Likoni
Uvinje
Kokota
Funzi
Ziwani
Ole
Kangagni
Ras Mkumbuu
Gombani
Wesha
Vitongoji
Misali
Chake Chake
Bay
Chake Chake
Karume
Airport
Wambaa
Limani
Pujini
Pujini Ruins
To Zanzibar
(50km)
Jambangome
Ngwachani
Makongwe
Mkoani
Matumbi
Makubwa
Changaweni
Mtambile
Kendwa
Mtangani
Kengeja
Matumbini
Panza
Ras
Ufunguo
Jombe
Kiweni
INDIAN
OCEAN

Pemba
Channel

occasionally onto stunning white-sand coves, while inland, a patchwork of neat farm plots covers the hillsides. In the days of the Arab traders it was even referred to as al Khuthera ('the Green Island'). Throughout much of the period when the sultans of Zanzibar held sway over the East African coast, it was Pemba, with its extensive clove plantations and agricultural base, that provided the economic foundation for the archipelago's dominance.

Pemba has also been long renowned for its voodoo and traditional healers, and people still make their way here from elsewhere in East Africa seeking cures or to learn the skills of the trade.

Thanks to the mangroves lining much of the coast, Pemba is not a beach destination.

However, there are a few lovely stretches of sand and some idyllic offshore islets, and the surrounding waters offer rewarding diving.

Tourism on Pemba is still in its infancy, and infrastructure is for the most part fairly basic. Much of the island is relatively 'undiscovered' and you'll still have things more or less to yourself, which is a big part of Pemba's charm. The main requirement for travelling around independently is time, as there's little transport off main routes.

History

Pemba is geologically much older than Zanzibar and is believed to have been settled at an earlier date, although little is known about its original inhabitants. The Shirazi presence on Pemba is believed to date from at least the 9th or 10th century.

The Portuguese attacked Pemba in the early 16th century and sought to subjugate its inhabitants by ravaging towns and demanding tributes. By the late 17th century the Busaidi family of Omani Arabs had taken over the island and driven away the remaining Portuguese. In 1890 Pemba, together with Zanzibar, became a British protectorate.

Following the Zanzibar revolution in 1964, President Karume closed Pemba to foreigners in an effort to contain strong antigovernment sentiment. The island remained closed until the 1980s, although the situation continued to be strained. Tensions peaked during the 1995 elections, and relations deteriorated thereafter, with Pembans feeling increasingly marginalised and frustrated. In January 2001 tensions again peaked, resulting in at least several dozen deaths and causing many people to flee the island. Now, most have long since returned, and daily life is back to normal.

Orientation

Chake Chake, on the island's central west coast, is Pemba's main town. The only other towns of any size are Wete to the north, and Mkoani in the south, where the ferries arrive.

MAPS

The Bureau of Lands & Environment just outside Chake Chake in Machomane sells a map (1:100,000). Head north from the town centre for 1km and take the first right; the bureau is 100m down in a two-storey white building.

Information

There's no accommodation outside main towns except for a few resorts. Away from hotels and guesthouses, the main eating venues are Pemba's night markets – found in all the major towns, but best in Chake Chake. Other than hotel bars and local brew there's little alcohol available on the island.

Most businesses operate from 8am to 4pm, and almost everywhere shuts down for prayers from about 4pm or 4.30pm, and at midday on Friday.

There is a Chinese-run government hospital in Mkoani, but it's better to get yourself to the mainland or to Nairobi (Kenya).

Getting There & Around

Mkoani is Pemba's main ferry port, with sporadic connections also from the mainland to Wete. The only airport is near Chake Chake. Getting around Pemba is easy but slow using the plodding local bus network. To reach destinations off the main routes, you'll either have to walk, rely on sporadic pick-ups or negotiate an additional fee with the bus driver. There are no regular taxis, but there are plenty of pick-up trucks that you can charter – best arranged in Chake Chake.

Mkoani

Although it is Pemba's major port, Mkoani has managed to fight off all attempts at development and remains a very small and boring town. However, its good budget guesthouse goes a long way to redeeming it, and it makes a convenient base for exploring southern Pemba.

The immigration officer usually meets all boat arrivals. Otherwise, if you're coming from anywhere other than Zanzibar, you'll need to go to the immigration office and get stamped in. It's 500m up the main road from the port in a small brown building with a flag.

SLEEPING & EATING

Jondeni Guest House (☎ 024-245 6042; jondeniguest@ hotmail.com; dm/s/d US$10/20/30, s/d with hot water US$25/35, s/d with shared bathroom US$15/25) This recommended backpackers' guesthouse has simple but spotless rooms with nets and meals (TSh7000). Ally, the manager, has heaps of information on Pemba, and can help arrange excursions. Head left when exiting the port, and walk about 700m up to the top of the hill.

PEMBA FLYING FOX

In addition to being known for its voodoo, Pemba is also known for its 'flying fox' – a large and critically endangered species that isn't found anywhere else in the world. You can see these (and support local community initiatives) at the **Kidike Roost Site** (admission per person US$3) in Ole, about 10km northeast of Chake Chake, just off the *dalla-dalla* 334 route, where local villagers have set up a small visitors centre.

GETTING THERE & AWAY
Boat

The small-ish and uncomfortable (especially on rough seas, when it bounces around like a cork) *Sea Express* does the Pemba (Mkoani)– Zanzibar–Dar es Salaam route on Monday, Thursday and Saturday, departing from Dar es Salaam at 7am, Zanzibar at 9.30am and Pemba at 12.30pm (US$45/60 in economy class between Pemba and Zanzibar/Dar es Salaam, including port tax).

There are slow ferries (currently *Serengeti* and *Maendeleo*) departing from Zanzibar at 10pm on Monday, Tuesday, Thursday, Friday and Saturday, arriving in Pemba at about 6am. Departures from Mkoani are at 12.30pm, reaching Zanzibar about 4pm (US$25).

Bus

Bus 603 runs throughout the day between Mkoani and Chake Chake (TSh1200, two hours). The bus station is about 200m east of the port, up the hill and just off the main road. For Wete, change vehicles in Chake Chake.

Kiweni

Kiweni, marked as Shamiani or Shamiani Island on some maps, is a remote backwater area just off Pemba's southeastern coast, where little seems to have changed for decades. With its undisturbed stretches of sand and quiet waterways, it's also one of the island's more scenic and alluring corners, as well as home to five of Pemba's six endemic bird species and a nesting ground for some sea-turtle colonies.

At the moment there's nowhere to stay. However, **Pemba Lodge** (www.pembalodge.com), under the same management as Mnarani Beach Cottages in Nungwi (p138), is planned to open soon. Southwest of Kiweni, in southernmost Pemba near Panza island, is the **Manta**

Boathouse (www.themantaboathouse.com; s/d full board US$138/219) – a moored hydrofoil with simple rooms and a dive operator.

Wambaa

The main reason to come to Wambaa – south of Chake Chake on the coast – is to luxuriate at **Fundu Lagoon Resort** (☎ 0774-438668; www.fundulagoon.com; s/d full board from US$475/670; ☻ mid-Jun–mid-Apr).

Chake Chake

Set on a ridge overlooking Chake Chake Bay, Chake Chake is Pemba's main town. Although it has been occupied for centuries, there is little architectural evidence of its past other than the ruins of an 18th-century **fort** near the hospital and some ruins at nearby Ras Mkumbuu. About 6km east of town are some tiny, baobab-dotted **beaches** near Vitongoji.

INFORMATION

There's a Speed Cash ATM (Visa only) at the old People's Bank of Zanzibar building on the main road. This is currently the only place on the island to access cash, so carry some extra in case it's out of service.

Adult Computer Centre (Main Rd; per hr TSh1500; ☻ 8am-8pm) Opposite the telecom building, with internet access and telephone facilities.

Baacha Travel & Tours (☎ 0777-423429, 0787-423429; samhamx@yahoo.com; Main Rd) Near ZanAir; ferry ticket bookings and excursions.

Pemba Island Reasonable Tours & Safaris (☎ 024-245 2023, 0777-435266; Main Rd) At Evergreen Hotel; ferry ticket bookings and excursions.

SLEEPING & EATING

Annex of Pemba Island Hotel (☎ 024-245 2215; s/d/tw with shared bathroom US$10/20/30) Related to Pemba Island Hotel, this place has basic and noisy but clean rooms in a multistorey building about 100m down the road to the market.

Pemba Island Hotel (☎ 024-245 2215; Wesha Rd; s/d/tw US$35/45/55; ☻) Small, clean rooms with nets, TV, minifridge and hot water, and a rooftop restaurant (meals from TSh3000). It's about 100m downhill from the main junction.

Pemba Clove Inn (☎ 024-245 2794/5; pembacloveinn@ zanzinet.com; Wesha Rd; s/d from US$50/70) Adjoining the Social Security Administration buildings,

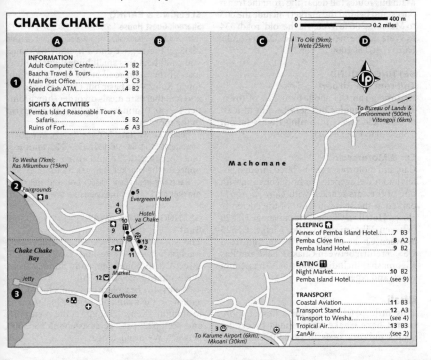

CHAKE CHAKE

0   400 m
0   0.2 miles

To Ole (9km);
Wete (25km)

INFORMATION
Adult Computer Centre.................1 B2
Baacha Travel & Tours..................2 B3
Main Post Office............................3 C3
Speed Cash ATM...........................4 B2

SIGHTS & ACTIVITIES
Pemba Island Reasonable Tours &
    Safaris.....................................5 B2
Ruins of Fort.................................6 A3

To Bureau of Lands &
Environment (500m);
Vitongoji (6km)

To Wesha (7km);
Ras Mkumbuu (15km)

Machomane

Fairgrounds

5
Evergreen Hotel

Hoteli
ya Chake

Chake Chake
Bay

Jetty

Market

Courthouse

SLEEPING
Annex of Pemba Island Hotel........7 B3
Pemba Clove Inn...........................8 A2
Pemba Island Hotel........................9 B2

EATING
Night Market................................10 B2
Pemba Island Hotel...................(see 9)

TRANSPORT
Coastal Aviation...........................11 B3
Transport Stand............................12 A3
Transport to Wesha..................(see 4)
Tropical Air.................................13 B3
ZanAir.......................................(see 2)

To Karume Airport (6km);
Mkoani (30km)

TANZANIA

about 700m down from the main junction, rooms here are short on ambience, but clean, spacious and well equipped.

Chake Chake's **night market** – spread out along the roadway around Hoteli ya Chake – has grilled *pweza* (octopus), *maandazi* (doughnuts) and other local delicacies at rock-bottom prices.

GETTING THERE & AWAY
Air

There are flights daily with **ZanAir** (☎ 024-245 2990, 0777-431143; Main Rd), **Coastal Aviation** (☎ 024-245 2162, 0777-418343; Main Rd) and (in the high season) **Tropical Air** (☎ 0777-859996, 0777-431431; tropic@zanzinet.com; Main Rd) between Chake Chake and Zanzibar (US$90), with connections to Dar es Salaam (US$110). Coastal also flies daily between Pemba and Tanga (US$70).

Boat

See p144 for ferry schedules between Zanzibar and Mkoani (from where you'll need to take a *dalla-dalla* to Chake Chake).

Bus

Main bus routes (all departing from the transport stand behind the market) include the 603 to Mkoani; 306 to Wete via the 'old' road; 334 to Wete via the 'new' road; and 335 to Konde. Fares cost TSh1000 to TSh2000.

GETTING AROUND
To/From the Airport

Karume airport is about 6km east of town. There's no regular bus service, but at least one vehicle meets incoming flights (about TSh8000 to Chake Chake's centre).

Car & Motorcycle

Cars and motorbikes can be hired through hotels and travel agencies, or by negotiating with one of the cars marked with *Gari ya Abiria* parked at the stand in front of the currently closed Hoteli ya Chake. Prices average US$20 between Mkoani and Chake Chake; US$25 between Chake Chake and Wete; and from US$35 return between Chake Chake and Ras Kigomasha, including stops at Vumawimbi beach and Ngezi.

Misali

This little patch of paradise lies offshore from Chake Chake, surrounded by crystal waters and coral reefs. In 1998 the island and surrounding coral reef were gazetted as the **Misali Island Marine Conservation Area** (adult/student US$5/3). Camping is not permitted; guides can be arranged at the visitors centre on the beach where the boats dock.

To reach the island take bus 305 to Wesha, from in front of the old People's Bank of Zanzibar building. Once in Wesha, you can negotiate with local boat owners to take you over to Misali (about TSh35,000 per person return). There's no food or drink on the island. It's only slightly more expensive to arrange Misali excursions through hotels or travel agencies in Chake Chake, through Sharook Guest House (below) in Wete, or through Jondeni Guest House (p144) in Mkoani.

Wete

This lively port and market town makes an agreeable base from which to explore northern Pemba. Sharook Guest House (see below) is the best place in town for arranging excursions and booking ferry tickets; there's internet access at the Umati office just down the road.

SLEEPING & EATING

Sharook Guest House (☎ 024-245 4386, 0777-431012; sharookguest@yahoo.com; r with shared/private bathroom US$15/20) For service and a friendly welcome, you can't beat this small budget guesthouse, just off the main road at the western end of town. Rooms are basic but clean, all with net and fan, there are meals on order (lunch/dinner TSh4000) and free breakfast if you arrive in the morning.

Pemba Crown Hotel (☎ 024-245 4191; www.pembacrown.com; Main Rd; s/d US$25/35; 🗶) Spotless, nice rooms with fan and air-con diagonally opposite the market. There's no food.

Ramsally (meals from TSh500) Located near the market and serves inexpensive food.

GETTING THERE & AWAY
Boat

The workhorse ship *New Spice Islander* sails weekly between Wete and Tanga (US$25, three to five hours, currently Sunday from Wete and Monday from Tanga).

Wete is the best place on Pemba to look for a dhow to the mainland – either to Tanga, or to Shimoni (Kenya). Inquire at the Wete port, and see p622; passage costs about TSh5000 between Wete and Tanga.

Bus

The 'old' road connects Wete with Chake Chake via Ziwani. East of here, the 'new' road connects Wete with Chake Chake via Ole. The main bus routes are 306 (Wete to Chake Chake via the 'old' road), 334 (Wete to Chake Chake via the 'new' road) and 324 (Wete to Konde).

Ngezi

The small, dense forest at Ngezi is part of the much larger natural forest that once covered wide swathes of Pemba. Today it's part of the **Ngezi Vumawimbi Forest Reserve** (admission TSh4000; 🕙 8am-4pm), with a short nature trail. Ngezi is along the main road between Konde and Tondooni. Take the bus to Konde, from where it's a 3km to 4km walk. Bus drivers may be willing to drop you at the information centre for an additional TSh2000 or so. Better: combine Ngezi with a visit to Vumawimbi beach (see below).

Kigomasha Peninsula

The Kigomasha Peninsula is rimmed by the beautiful, palm- and forest-fringed **Vumawimbi beach** on its eastern side. On the peninsula's northwestern tip are **Panga ya Watoro beach**, and the superbly situated **Manta Resort** (www .themantaresort.com; s/d all-inclusive from US$211/364, full board in 'divers village' US$168/277), on an escarpment with views over the open ocean. It has several types of rooms, plus a spa, a restaurant and a PADI five-star dive operator. The same management also runs the Manta Boathouse (p145) in southern Pemba.

To the peninsula's southwest near Tondooni is the low-key **Verani Beach Hotel** (☎ 0777-414408; www.veranibeach.com; camping with own/hotel's tent US$5/10, s/d bungalow US$35/50), which is still in process. For now, it has two no-frills stone-and-thatch bungalows, plus a few tents. Meals can be arranged.

Kervan Saray Beach Lodge (☎ 0773-176737, satellite +88-21652-012134; www.kervansaraybeach.com; dm about US$45, bungalow per person about US$130) – a diver-oriented place – is situated on the beach near Makangale village, about 5km south of the Manta Resort. There's a six-bed divers' bunk dorm, stone-and-thatch bungalows with private bathroom, a restaurant (lunch/dinner about US$15/30), and sunset cruises, kayaking trips and other excursions. Pick-ups can be arranged from Chake Chake or Mkoani, or you can take a dalla-dalla to Konde, from where pick-ups cost about US$25.

Other than hiring a vehicle in Chake Chake, the best way to get to all of these places is on bicycle from Konde. Alternatively, try to negotiate a lift with one of the Konde bus drivers, although you'll then need to make arrangements for your return.

NORTHEASTERN TANZANIA

Northeastern Tanzania is located between Tanzania's most popular attractions – the northern safari circuit and the Zanzibar Archipelago – but it's still quite low-key as far as tourism is concerned. It's a rewarding area to explore if you're looking for something more off-the-beaten-track than the standard tourist loop but don't have time to venture further afield. Among the region's highlights are its old coastal settlements, its long, quiet beaches and its picturesque mountain villages. Most places are easily accessed from both Dar es Salaam and Arusha, and it's quite possible to combine coastal attractions – Saadani National Park and the beaches north or south of Pangani – with inland mountain areas such as Amani and the western Usambaras within a reasonable time frame and budget.

BAGAMOYO
☎ 023

Bagamoyo was once one of the most important dhow ports along the East African coast and was the terminus of the trade caravan route linking Lake Tanganyika with the sea. Later it served as a way station for missionaries travelling from Zanzibar to the interior, and many of the European explorers, including Burton, Stanley and Livingstone, began and ended their trips here. From 1887 to 1891 Bagamoyo was the capital of German East Africa, and in 1888 it was the site of the first major uprising against the colonial government. In 1891 the capital was transferred to Dar es Salaam, sending Bagamoyo into decline. While most buildings are now in an advanced stage of decay, Bagamoyo's long history, sleepy charm and nearby beaches make it an agreeable day or weekend excursion from Dar es Salaam.

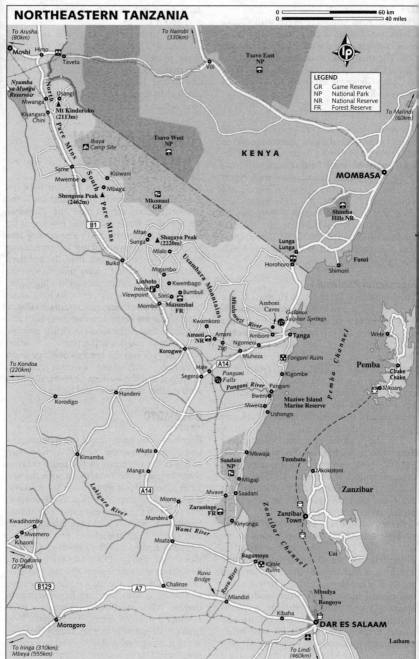

NORTHEASTERN TANZANIA

| 0 | 60 km |
| 0 | 40 miles |

LEGEND

GR	Game Reserve
NP	National Park
NR	National Reserve
FR	Forest Reserve

To Arusha (80km)

To Nairobi (330km)

Moshi
Himo
Taveta

Tsavo East NP

Voi

Nyumba ya Mungu Reservoir

Usangi
Mwanga
Kisangara Chini

Mt Kindoroko (2113m)

Ibaya Camp Site

Tsavo West NP

KENYA

To Malindi (60km)

MOMBASA

North Pare Mtns

Same
Mwembe
Kisiwani
Mbaga

Shengena Peak (2462m)

Mkomazi GR

Shimba Hills NR

South Pare Mtns

B1

Mtae
Sunga
Shagayu Peak (2220m)
Mlalo

Buiko

Migambo

Lushoto
Irente Viewpoint
Soni
Bumbuli
Mombo
Mazumbai FR
Kwamkoro

Lunga Lunga

Horohoro

Funzi
Shimoni

Usambara Mountains

Amboni Caves
Galanos Sulphur Springs

Amani NR
Amani
Zigi
Ngomeni
Amboni
Tanga

Wete

Korogwe

Muheza

Tongoni Ruins

Pemba Channel

Pemba

Chake Chake

Mkoani

To Kondoa (220km)

Hale
Segera
Pangani Falls
Pangani River
Pangani

Kigombe

A14

Bweni
Mwera
Ushongo

Maziwe Island Marine Reserve

Korodigo
Handeni

Kimamba

Mkata
Manga

Saadani NP
Mkwaja
Mligaji
Saadani

Tumbatu
Mkokotoni

Zanzibar

A14

Miono
Mandera

Zaraninge FR

Mvave

Kinyonga

Zanzibar Channel

Zanzibar Town

Uzi

Kwadihombo
Mvomero
Kibaoni

Msata

Wami River

To Dodoma (275km)

B129
A7

Chalinze

Ruvu Bridge

Bagamoyo
Kaole Ruins

Mbudya
Bongoyo

Lukigura River

Ruvu River

Mlandizi

Kibaha

DAR ES SALAAM

Morogoro

To Iringa (310km); Mbeya (555km)

To Lindi (460km)

Latham

Lukigura River
Mkulumuzi River

Information

Bagamoyo Tourism Institute (internet per hr TSh2000; 8.30am-5pm Mon-Fri, 8.30am-2pm Sat) Internet access, plus help with local guides and excursions, including to Kaole ruins.

National Microfinance Bank (NMB) At town entrance; changes cash only.

Sights & Activities

With its crumbling German-era colonial buildings and narrow streets dotted with Zanzibar-style carved doors, **central Bagamoyo** is worth a leisurely stroll, especially the area along Ocean Rd. Nearby on the beach is the lively **fish market**.

About 2km north of town and reached via a mango-shaded avenue is **Holy Ghost Catholic Mission**, with an excellent **museum** (023-244 0010; adult/student TSh1500/500, camera/video TSh1000/5000; 10am-5pm). Nearby is the chapel where Livingstone's body was laid before being taken to Zanzibar Town en route to Westminster Abbey.

About 500m south of Bagamoyo along the road to Dar es Salaam is **Chuo cha Sanaa** (College of Arts; 023-244 0149, 023-244 0032; www.college-of-arts .org), a renowned theatre and arts college.

Located further south along the beach are the **Kaole ruins** (adult/student TSh1500/500; 8am-4pm Mon-Fri, 8am-5pm Sat & Sun), including the remains of a 13th-century mosque and some graves, some dating back to the 15th century. Head south along the beach for about 5km past Kaole village into the mangrove swamps. Where the beach apparently ends, go a few hundred metres inland and look for the stone pillars. There's an easier, slightly longer route along the road running past Chuo cha Sanaa. Both, and especially the beach route, have a reputation for muggings, so it's best to walk in a group and with a guide, and not carry valuables. If you want to walk with an English-speaking guide, arrange this in advance at either the tourist institute or with your hotel.

Sleeping & Eating

Kizota Guest House (r with shared bathroom TSh5000) No-frills rooms in a local-style guesthouse along the road leading from the main junction to the beach places, and about a 10-minute walk from the dalla-dalla stand. Hot-water buckets available on request.

Travellers Lodge (023-244 0077; www.travellers -lodge.com; camping with shower TSh6000, s/d garden cottage US$51/73, beach cottage US$65/87;) The best-value on offer of the beach places, this well-situated lodge has clean, pleasant cottages scattered around expansive grounds, including some on the beach, some with two large beds and all with mosquito nets. There's also a restaurant and a children's play area. It's located on the road running parallel to the beach, just south of the entrance to the Catholic mission.

Bagamoyo Beach Resort (023-244 0083; bbr@ baganet.com; banda per person with shared bathroom US$15, s/d/tr US$50/64/81;) Fine and friendly at a seaside location just north of Travellers Lodge, with rooms in two blocks (ask for the one closer to the water), a few no-frills bandas on the beach with just a bed and net, and a restaurant.

Getting There & Away

Bagamoyo is about 70km north of Dar es Salaam along good tarmac. Dalla-dallas run throughout the day from Mwenge (north of Dar es Salaam along New Bagamoyo Rd, and accessed via dalla-dalla from New Posta transport stand) to Bagamoyo (TSh1800, two hours), dropping you about 700m from the town centre.

SAADANI NATIONAL PARK

About 70km up the coast from Bagamoyo is tiny Saadani National Park, a 1000-sq-km patch of coastal wilderness. It's a good choice for a one- or two-night excursion from Dar es Salaam if you don't have time to explore further afield. The main activities are boat trips along the Wami River, wildlife drives and walks along the lovely, mostly deserted beach.

While terrestrial wildlife viewing can't compare with that in the better-known national parks, animal numbers are slowly but surely increasing, and it's likely you'll see hippos and crocs in the Wami River, plus giraffes, perhaps elephants and a plethora of birds. The birding is wonderful.

Information

Entry to **Saadani** (www.saadanipark.org) costs US$20/5 per day per adult/child and guides cost US$10 per day. There's a US$20 per person per day fee for river usage if you'll be doing a boat safari. The park stays open year-round, but access during the March to May long rains is difficult.

TANZANIA

Sleeping

There are several park **camp sites** (camping adult/child US$30/5), for which you'll need to be completely self-sufficient. There's also the **Tanapa resthouse** (r adult/child US$30/10) near Saadani village, which has cooking facilities and bedding, but otherwise you'll need to bring all you'll need.

Kisampa (☎ 0753-005442; www.sanctuary-tz.com; per person all-inclusive from US$220) Set in a private nature reserve bordering the park and well away from the beach is this community-oriented place, with 'stargazer' tents and bungalows and a range of walks and excursions. Village fees paid by each guest go to the local community to support health and other initiatives, and there are many chances to get acquainted with local life.

Saadani Safari Lodge (☎ 022-277 3294; www .saadanilodge.com; s/d full board plus 1 activity per day US$285/480; 🐾) The only lodge within the park, and a fine base, with nine cottages on the beach, an open restaurant and a sundowner deck. Activities include boat safaris on the Wami River, vehicle safaris, walks and snorkelling excursions to a nearby sandbank. No children under six years old.

Tent With A View Safari Lodge (☎ 022-211 0507, 0713-323318; www.saadani.com; s/d full board US$275/390, all-inclusive US$385/590) A lovely place, with raised treehouse-style *bandas* tucked away among the coconut groves. It's just outside the park's northern boundary on a beautiful stretch of deserted, driftwood-strewn beach. Excursions include walking and vehicle safaris in the park and walks to a nearby green turtle nesting site. Park entry fees are payable only for days you enter the park. No children under six years old. The same management runs a lodge in Selous Game Reserve, and offers combination itineraries.

Getting There & Away
AIR

There are airstrips for charter flights near all the camps/lodges. Contact them, or any of the charter companies listed on p263 to see if a charter is going with extra seats for sale. One-way fares average about US$200/300 from Zanzibar/Dar es Salaam for a three-passenger plane. Tropical Air has frequent scheduled flights between Saadani and Zanzibar (about US$60), and Regional Air has daily connections, assuming sufficient demand, between Saadani, Dar es Salaam, Pangani and Zanzibar.

BOAT

Local fishing boats sail regularly between Saadani and Zanzibar (from behind Tembo Hotel), but the journey is known for being rough and few travellers do it. Better to arrange a boat charter with one of the lodges in Saadani, or with the lodges further up the coast north and south of Pangani.

ROAD

All the lodges provide road transport to/from Dar es Salaam for about US$250 per vehicle (one way). Allow 4½ to five hours for the journey.

From Dar es Salaam, the route is via Chalinze on the Morogoro road, and then north to Mandera village (about 50km north of Chalinze on the Arusha highway). At Mandera bear east along a reasonable dirt road (4WD) for about 60km to Saadani. Once at the main park gate (Mvave Gate), there's a signposted turn-off to Kisampa (about 30km south along a road through the Zaraninge forest). Saadani village and Saadani Safari Lodge (about 1km north of the village) are about 17km straight on. For Tent With A View Safari Lodge, continue north from the village turn-off for about 25km. Via public transport, there's a daily bus from Dar es Salaam's Ubungo bus station to Saadani village (TSh6500, five to six hours), departing from Dar es Salaam at 1pm and Saadani at 6am.

Coming from Pangani, take the ferry across the Pangani River, then continue south along a rough (4WD) road to Mkwaja to the reserve's northern gate at Mligaji. Transfers can be arranged with the lodges from about US$150 per vehicle each way (1½ to two hours). There's also a daily bus between Tanga and Mkwaja (TSh6000, five hours), on the park's northern edge, from where you could arrange to be collected by the lodges. However, it's prone to frequent breakdowns and the whims of the Pangani River ferry. Departures from Tanga are around 11am, and from Mkwaja around 5am.

If you've arrived in the park via public transport, there is no vehicle hire in the park for a safari, unless you've arranged something in advance with one of the lodges.

Until the ferry over the Wami River is repaired, there's no direct road access to Saadani from Bagamoyo, although you can arrange boat pick-ups with some of the lodges.

PANGANI
☎ 027

About 55km south of Tanga is the small and dilapidated Swahili outpost of Pangani. It rose from obscure beginnings as just one of many coastal dhow ports to become a terminus of the caravan route from Lake Tanganyika, a major export point for slaves and ivory, and one of the largest ports between Bagamoyo and Mombasa. By the end of the 19th century, focus had shifted to Tanga and Dar es Salaam, and Pangani again faded into anonymity.

The most interesting area of town is near the river, where there are some carved doorways, buildings from the German colonial era and old houses of Indian traders. About 10km offshore is **Maziwe Island Marine Reserve** (admission TSh1000), a small sand island where you can snorkel. The island can only be visited at low tide, and there's no food or drink. All the hotels organise Maziwe excursions and town tours, as does the **Pangani Cultural Tourism Programme office** (⏰ 8am-5pm Mon-Fri, 8am-noon Sat) on the riverfront. The closest banks are in Tanga. Use caution when walking along the beaches close to town.

Sleeping & Eating
Most visitors stay at one of the beaches running north or south of town.

TOWN CENTRE
Stopover Bar & Guest House (☎ 0784-498458; d with private bathroom TSh7000) Simple doubles with nets and fan, and meals. It's by the beach – turn right after the petrol station at the northern end of town.

NORTH OF PANGANI
Tinga Tinga Lodge (☎ 027-264 6611, 0784-403553; www.tingatingalodge.com; camping US$5, s/d/tr US$75/110/150) Spacious, twin-bedded bungalows set slightly inland, and just north of the main junction. Five minutes' walk away is a restaurant-bar gazebo overlooking the water, with swimming possible just below. Walking tours and sunset cruises can be organised.

Peponi Holiday Resort (☎ 0784-202962, 0713-540139; www.peponiresort.com; camping US$4, s & d banda US$50/50, extra adult beds in family banda US$20; 🛱) This recommended place is set in expansive bougainvillea-dotted grounds on a long, good beach about 19km north of Pangani. Accommodation ranges from simple dou-

ble *bandas* to larger five-person chalets and a shady camp site (bring all supplies with you) with clean ablution blocks. A restaurant, a nearby reef for snorkelling and mangrove stands rich with birdlife to the north complete the picture. The resort has its own motorised dhow and a curio shop. Discounted family and backpacker rates are available. Take any bus running along the Pangani–Tanga coastal route and ask the driver to drop you near Kigombe village at the Peponi turn-off (about TSh1000 from Pangani, TSh1500 from Tanga), from where it's a short walk. Taxis from Tanga cost from TSh20,000.

Capricorn Beach Cottages (☎ 0784-632529; www.capricornbeachcottages.com; s/d US$70/104; 🖥) A classy but low-key self-catering place on the beach just south of Peponi with three spacious and spotless self-catering cottages in large, lush grounds dotted with baobab trees. There's a beachside grill area, and the hosts go out of their way to be sure you're not lacking for anything. Homemade bread, fresh seafood, cheese and other gourmet essentials are sold at a small deli on the premises.

SOUTH OF PANGANI
Around 15km south of Pangani around Ushongo is a long, palm-fringed beach. Swimming isn't tide dependent, and apart from the area in the immediate vicinity of Ushongo village, it's clean (though seaweed prone at some times of year) and often empty. Diving and snorkelling, including trips to Maziwe island, plus kayaking, windsurfing and short *ngalawa* (outrigger canoe) sails, can be arranged with the lodges, or through **Kasa Divers** (www.kasadivers.com), next to Emayani Beach Lodge.

Beach Crab Resort (☎ 0784-543700; www.thebeachcrab.com; camping US$4, s/d safari tent with shared bathroom from US$15/24, s/d banda with private bathroom US$70/96) A backpacker-friendly place at the southern end of the beach with camping (including tents for rent) and permanent tents just in from the beach, plus self-contained *bandas* on a hill behind. There's also a beachside-bar-restaurant, diving and windsurfing.

Emayani Beach Lodge (☎ 027-264 0755; www.emayanilodge.com; s/d half board US$105/160) At the northern end of Ushongo, and about 3km north of Beach Crab Resort, with a row of very simple *makuti* bungalows on the sand, and a restaurant.

Tulia Beach Lodge (☎ 027-264 0680; www.tulia beachlodge.com; r per person half board US$50) Formerly Coco Beach Resort, this place, south of Emayani, has had a complete facelift. It offers small, clean block-style rooms set a bit back from the beach, and meals.

our pick **The Tides** (☎ 027-264 0844, 0713-325812; www.thetideslodge.com; s/d half board US$178/262, family cottage half board US$467; 🖳) This lovely and unpretentious place mixes a prime seaside location with spacious beachside bungalows and excellent cuisine, all to good effect. There are also two four-person family cottages set away from the main lodge area and a beachside bar and restaurant area. Excursions include dhows to Maziwe island, Zanzibar or along the Pangani River, and inshore and offshore fishing. It's an ideal honeymooners' destination.

Getting There & Away

AIR

Regional Air has daily flights connecting Pangani (Mashado or Kwajoni airstrips) with Arusha (one way/return US$234/337), Zanzibar (one way US$85) and Saadani.

BOAT

Dhows sail regularly between Pangani and Mkokotoni, on the northwestern coast of Zanzibar. Better: several of the lodges near Pangani arrange dhow charters to Zanzibar's Stone Town from about US$150. Check with Peponi Holiday Resort, The Tides and Emayani Beach Lodge.

ROAD

About four buses daily run between the Pangani ferry and Tanga via the rehabilitated coastal road (TSh2500, 1½ hours), with the first departure from Pangani at about 6.30am, so you can connect with a Tanga–Arusha bus, and the last leaving Tanga at about 4pm. It's also possible to reach Pangani from Muheza, from where there are connections to Tanga or Korogwe, but the road is worse and connections sporadic.

For Ushongo and the beaches south of Pangani, all the hotels there do pick-ups from both Pangani and Tanga. There's also a daily bus from Tanga to Mkwaja village (at the northern edge of Saadani National Park) that passes Mwera village (6km from Ushongo) daily at about 7am going north, and at about 3.30pm going south. It's then easy to arrange a pick-up from Mwera with the lodges. *Dalla-dallas* also sporadically do the stretch from Bweni (the first village after the Pangani ferry) to Mwera.

The vehicle ferry over the Pangani River runs in theory between 6.30am and 6.30pm daily (TSh100/4000 per person/vehicle), and there are small passenger boats (large enough to take a motorcycle) throughout the day (TSh200).

TANGA
☎ 027

One of Tanzania's major industrial towns until the collapse of the sisal market, and still an important seaport, Tanga today has a sleepy, semicolonial atmosphere. There's little reason to make a special detour to visit, although it makes a convenient stop en route to and from Mombasa. The most interesting areas are around Jamhuri Park, with an old German-built **clock tower**, and the park and cemetery surrounding the **Askari monument** at the end of Sokoine St. Just offshore is **Toten Island**.

Tanga Yacht Club (day admission TSh2000) has a small swimming beach, showers and a recommended restaurant-bar area overlooking the water.

Information

CRDB Bank (Tower St) ATM (accepts Visa).

Kaributanga.com (Sokoine St; per hr TSh1000; ⊙ 9am-8pm Mon-Thu, 9am-noon & 2-7pm Fri, 9am-2pm & 4-7pm Sat & Sun) Internet access.

NBC Bank (cnr Bank & Sokoine Sts) Just west of the market; changes cash and travellers cheques; ATM (Visa only).

Tayodea Tourist Information Centre (☎ 027-264 4350; www.tayodea.org; cnr Independence Ave & Usambara St; ⊙ 8.30am-5pm) Information and English-speaking guides for local excursions.

Sleeping & Eating

Inn by the Sea (☎ 027-264 4614; Hospital Rd; r TSh25,000; ⊠) A prime waterside setting on the southwestern edge of Ras Kazone, but quite basic rooms, although they're fair enough value for the price.

Mbuyukenda Hostel (☎ 027-264 0094; tumaini@elct -ned.org; Ras Kazone; s/d TSh10,000/15,000; ⊠) An old mission station with clean, pleasant rooms divided among several houses set around a large garden, and inexpensive meals.

Ocean Breeze Hotel (cnr Tower & Sokoine Sts; r with fan/air-con TSh10,000/20,000; ⊠) Faded and no-frills

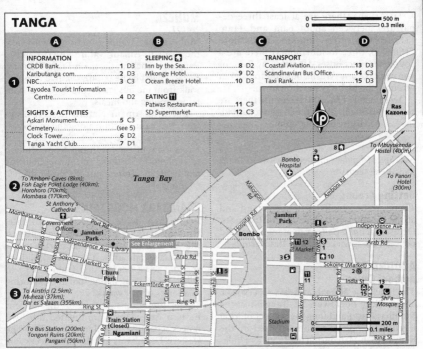

TANGA

INFORMATION	
CRDB Bank	1 D3
Kaributanga com	2 D3
NBC	3 C3
Tayodea Tourist Information Centre	4 D2

SIGHTS & ACTIVITIES	
Askari Monument	5 C3
Cemetery	(see 5)
Clock Tower	6 D2
Tanga Yacht Club	7 D1

SLEEPING	
Inn by the Sea	8 D2
Mkonge Hotel	9 D2
Ocean Breeze Hotel	10 D3

EATING	
Patwas Restaurant	11 C3
SD Supermarket	12 C3

TRANSPORT	
Coastal Aviation	13 D3
Scandinavian Bus Office	14 C3
Taxi Rank	15 D3

but adequate rooms, all with private bathroom and many with nets. It's just east of the market.

Panori Hotel (☎ 027-264 6044; panori@africaonline .co.tz; Ras Kazone; s/d in new wing TSh31,000/42,000, in old wing TSh22,000/29,000; ❉) If you don't mind the location, set in a residential area about 3km from the town centre (no public transport), this long-standing place is a decent midrange choice, with clean, adequate rooms in the new wing, all with nets, fan and TV, and an outdoor restaurant. To get here, take Hospital Rd east to Ras Kazone and follow the signposts.

Mkonge Hotel (☎ 027-264 3440; mkongehotel@ kaributanga.com; Hospital Rd; s/d from US$60/75; ❉) An imposing waterside place with pleasant rooms – ask for a sea view – and a restaurant.

Fish Eagle Point Lodge (info@outposttanzania.com; s/d full board from US$120/170) Outpost Lodge (p175) in Arusha is soon to open this option, about an hour's drive north of Tanga on the coast. Check Outpost's website for an update.

Patwas Restaurant (Mkwakwani Rd; meals from TSh1500; ☼ 8am-8pm Mon-Sat) An unassuming, friendly place just south of the market,

with fresh juices and lassis, and good-value local-style meals.

SD Supermarket (Bank St) For self-caterers; behind the market.

Getting There & Away

AIR

There are daily flights on **Coastal Aviation** (☎ 027-264 6060, 0713-566485; off India St) between Tanga, Dar es Salaam, Zanzibar and Pemba (one way between Tanga and Pemba/Dar es Salaam US$70/130). Its office is near the mobile phone tower and the Shi'a mosque. The airstrip is about 3km west of town along the Korogwe road.

BUS

To/from Dar es Salaam, **Scandinavian Express** (☎ 027-264 4337) departs daily at 7.30am in each direction (TSh12,000, 5½ hours) from its office on Ring St, between the stadium and the train station and near the corner of Makwakwani St. Raha Leo also has several buses daily on this route between about 7am and 3pm, departing Tanga from the bus station.

To Arusha, there are at least three departures between about 6am and 11am (TSh15,000, seven hours). To Lushoto (TSh5000, three to four hours) there are a couple of direct buses departing by 7am, or you can take any Arusha bus and transfer at Mombo, the highway junction town.

To Pangani (TSh2500, 1½ hours) there are several buses daily along the coastal road, with the last departure at about 4pm.

BOAT

New Spice Islander sails weekly between Tanga and Wete; see p146.

Getting Around

There are taxi ranks at the bus stand and at the junction of Usambara and India Sts. Occasional *dalla-dallas* run along Ocean Rd between the town centre and Ras Kazone.

AROUND TANGA
Amboni Caves

The limestone **Amboni Caves** (admission TSh3000), about 8km northwest of Tanga off the Mombasa road and long the subject of local legend, are said to have been used by the Kenyan Mau Mau during the 1950s as a hideout from the British. Bring along a torch, and wear closed shoes to avoid needing to pick bat droppings off your feet afterwards.

Hire a taxi, or take a *dalla-dalla* towards Amboni village and get out at the turn-off for the caves, which is near the forestry office. From here, it's about 2.5km on foot to Kiomoni village, from where the caves stretch west along the Mkulumuzi River. Guides can be arranged locally or at the tourist information centre in Tanga.

Tongoni Ruins

About 20km south of Tanga along the coastal road are the time-ravaged **Tongoni ruins** (admission TSh1000), dating from the 14th or 15th century, when Tongoni was a major coastal trading port. They include the crumbling remains of a mosque and about 20 overgrown Shirazi pillar-style tombs – the largest collection of such tombs on the East African coast.

Take any vehicle heading towards Pangani along the coastal road and get out at the turn-off (look for a rusty signboard). The ruins *(magofu)* are about 1km further east on foot, on the far edge of the village. Taxis from Tanga charge from about TSh15,000 return.

MUHEZA
☎ 027

Muheza is a scrappy junction town where the roads to Amani Nature Reserve and to Pangani branch off the main Tanga highway. **Elephant Guest House** (r TSh12,000), five minutes' walk from the bus stand, has basic self-contained rooms and meals.

Buses to Amani Nature Reserve leave from the main junction along the road leading up towards the market. There are direct buses daily in the mornings from Muheza to Lushoto (TSh3000), and throughout the day between Muheza and Tanga (TSh1500, 45 minutes).

USAMBARA MOUNTAINS

With their wide vistas, cool climate, winding paths and picturesque villages, the Usambaras are one of northeastern Tanzania's highlights. It's easily possible to spend a week here hiking from village to village, or relaxing in one spot and exploring as a series of day walks.

The mountains – part of the ancient Eastern Arc chain – are divided into two ranges separated by a 4km-wide valley. The western Usambaras are the most accessible and developed. Both ranges are densely populated, with the main tribes the Sambaa, the Kilindi, the Zigua and the Mbugu.

While the climate is comfortable year-round, paths get very muddy during the rains.

Amani Nature Reserve

Amani is west of Tanga in the heart of the eastern Usambara mountains. It's a peaceful, lushly vegetated patch of montane forest humming with the sounds of rushing water, chirping insects and singing birds. For getting around, there's a network of short (one to three hours), easy walks along shady forest paths that can be done with or without a guide.

INFORMATION

At Zigi, there is an **information centre** (8am-5pm) at the old Station Master's House focusing on local plants and traditional medicines. The main office for the **reserve** (/fax 027-264 0313; adult/child US$30/5, per Tanzania-registered/foreign vehicle TSh5000/US$30) is at Amani. The exorbitant entry fee and guide fees (adult/child per day US$20/10) can be paid here, or at Zigi.

Trails are detailed in the booklet, *A Guide to Trails and Drive Routes in Amani Nature Reserve*, on sale at the reserve office.

SLEEPING & EATING

It's possible to **camp** (per person US$5) at both Zigi and Amani with your own tent.

The **Amani Conservation Centre** (☎ 027-264 0313; anr@twiga.com) runs two guesthouses, the **Amani Conservation Centre Rest House** (r with shared bathroom TSh10,000) at Amani and the **Zigi Rest House** (r TSh10,000) at Zigi. Both have warm water for bathing and filtered water for drinking. Meals (breakfast/lunch/dinner TSh1500/3000/3000) are available at both, though bring fruit and snacks as a supplement.

GETTING THERE & AWAY

Amani is 32km northwest of Muheza. There is at least one truck daily between Muheza and Amani (TSh2500, two hours), continuing on to Kwamkoro, 9km beyond Amani. Departures from Muheza are between about 1pm and 2pm. Going in the other direction, transport usually passes Amani from about 6am, stopping near the Amani Conservation Centre office.

In the dry season you can make it in a 2WD as far as Zigi (25km from Muheza), after which you'll need a 4WD. Allow 1½ to two hours between Muheza and Amani, less in a good car with high clearance. Walking from Zigi up to Amani along one of the trails takes about 2½ to three hours.

Lushoto
☎ 027

Lushoto is a leafy highland town nestled in a fertile valley at about 1200m, and surrounded by pines and eucalyptus mixed with banana plants and other tropical foliage. It's the centre of the western Usambaras and makes a fine base for hikes into the surrounding hills.

During the German era, Lushoto (or Wilhelmstal, as it was then known) was a favoured vacation spot for colonial administrators, and was even slated at one point to become the colonial capital.

INFORMATION

Friends of Lushoto (☎ 027-264 0132) Just down the small road running next to the bank. Arranges guides and hikes.

Mount Usambara Communication Centre Internet Café (Main Rd; per hr TSh2000; ☉ 7.30am-8pm Mon-Sun) Diagonally opposite NMB bank.

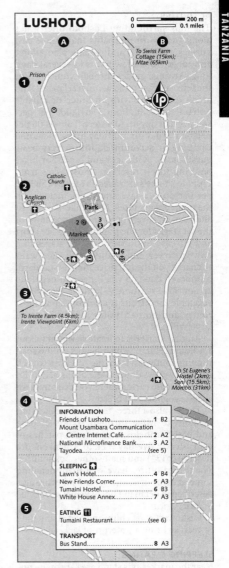

LUSHOTO

0 _____ 200 m
0 _____ 0.1 miles

To Swiss Farm Cottage (15km); Mtae (65km)

Prison

Catholic Church

Anglican Church

Park

Market

To Irente Farm (4.5km); Irente Viewpoint (6km)

To St Eugene's Hostel (2km); Soni (15.5km); Mombo (31km)

INFORMATION
Friends of Lushoto..............................1 B2
Mount Usambara Communication
   Centre Internet Café..................2 A2
National Microfinance Bank..............3 A2
Tayodea.....................................(see 5)

SLEEPING
Lawn's Hotel.................................4 B4
New Friends Corner.........................5 A3
Tumaini Hostel...............................6 B3
White House Annex..........................7 A3

EATING
Tumaini Restaurant.......................(see 6)

TRANSPORT
Bus Stand....................................8 A3

NMB Bank (Main Rd; ☉ 8am-3pm Mon-Fri) Changes cash and travellers cheques (minimum US$40 commission for travellers cheques). There's no ATM for international cards.

Tayodea (☎ 0784-861969; youthall2000@ yahoo.com) On the small hill behind the bus stand, and next to New Friends Corner guest house. Arranges guides and hikes.

ACTIVITIES

The hills surrounding Lushoto offer walks along well-worn footpaths that weave past villages, cornfields and banana plantations, and range from a few hours to several days' long. Arrange guides through your hotel or the tourist offices, and avoid freelancers who aren't associated with an office or reliable hotel. Rates cost about TSh10,000 per person per half day up to a steep TSh60,000 per person per day on multiday hikes, including camping or accommodation in very basic guesthouses, guide fees and food. For hikes entering forest reserves (most hikes from Lushoto), there's also a reserve fee of TSh5000 per person per day, sometimes included in the quoted daily rates. Note that if you're fit and keen on covering some distance, most of the set stages for the popular hikes are short and it's easy to do two or three stages in a day. However, most guides will then want to charge you the full price for the 'standard' number of days, so you'll need to negotiate an amicable solution. A limited selection of vegetables and fruits is available along most routes and bottled water is sold in some larger villages.

An easy starter is to **Irente viewpoint** (about 1½ hours return), which begins on the road running southwest from the Anglican church and offers views down to the plains below. En route is Irente Farm, where you can buy fresh cheese, yoghurt and bread.

There's also a three- to four-day hike from Lushoto to Mtae through stands of pine and past cornfields, villages and patches of wild asters, a five-day walk to Amani Nature Reserve (p154) and many other possibilities. The tourist offices have wall maps detailing some of the routes, and several hikes are also described in detail in Lonely Planet's *Trekking in East Africa*.

Lushoto can get chilly and wet at any time of year, so bring a waterproof jacket.

SLEEPING & EATING

Near the market-bus stand area are many no-frills guesthouses, all with serviceable, undistinguished rooms and hot-water buckets on request. They include the following two options. For both, head left when exiting the bus park and cross the small footbridge. New Friends Corner is straight ahead, next to the Tayodea office. White House Annex is left and up the hill.

White House Annex (d with shared bathroom TSh10,000, s/d TSh9000/15,000) Cramped and noisy but arguably the best of the bunch, with hot water, and meals on order.

New Friends Corner (s with shared bathroom TSh4500, d TSh6000) Basic and noisy, but decent value rooms.

There are also several considerably quieter and nicer choices in and around town.

Tumaini Hostel (☎ 027-264 0094; tumaini@elct-ned.org; Main Rd; s/d US$10/17, ste US$25) Soulless but spotless twin-bed rooms with nets and hot-water showers in a two-storey compound overlooking small gardens. It's in the town centre near the Telecom building and just behind **Tumaini Restaurant** (☎ 027-264 0027; Main Rd; meals from TSh1200; ⏰ breakfast, lunch & dinner), which has banana milkshakes, plus the usual assortment of standard fare, all well prepared.

Lawn's Hotel (☎ 027-264 0005, 0784-420252; www.lawnshotel.com; camping with hot shower US$6, s/d US$40/45; 🖥) Vine-covered buildings surrounded by extensive gardens, spacious, musty rooms, a fireplace and a bar-restaurant. It's also one of the better bets for camping (on the surrounding lawns). It's at the entrance to town and signposted – follow the unpaved road up and around to the main entrance.

St Eugene's Hostel (Montessori Centre; ☎ 027-264 0055, 0784-523710; steugenes_hostel@yahoo.com; s/tw/tr US$25/45/54) A quiet place with spotless rooms, all with hot showers and balconies with views over the hills. It's run by an order of sisters and profits go to support their work with local children. Meals are available, and homemade cheese and jam are sold on the premises. It's along the main road about 3km before Lushoto, on the left coming from Soni.

Irente Farm (☎ 027-264 0000, 0784-502935, 0784-674046; murless@elct.org; camping TSh3000, r with shared bathroom TSh6000, d with private bathroom TSh20,000-40,000, 6-bed house TSh100,000) A working farm about a 4.5km walk from town just off the road to Irente Viewpoint, with camp sites, several tiny rooms sharing cold-water ablutions, and converted farm buildings that can be rented as rooms or as self-catering apartments with kitchen (bring your own food). Delicious homemade cheese, bread and muesli are sold on the premises.

Swiss Farm Cottage (☎ 027-264 0155; 0784-469292; swiss-farm-mkuzi@bluewin.ch) This long-standing place has new owners, and once up-and-running promises to be well worth checking out. It has a six-person and a two-person cottage with some more planned, good meals and (soon) a shop selling fresh farm produce. It's in the hills about 15km north of Lushoto – follow the road leading uphill on the northeast edge of town.

GETTING THERE & AWAY

There are *dalla-dallas* throughout the day between Lushoto and Mombo (TSh2000, one hour), the junction town on the main highway.

Daily direct buses travel between Lushoto and Tanga (Sashui and Tashrif lines; TSh6000, four hours, 7am and 9am), Dar es Salaam (Mbaruku and Shambalai lines; TSh9500, six to seven hours, 6am, 8am, 9am and noon) and Arusha (Fasaha and Chakito lines; TSh10,000, six hours, 6.30am and 7am), all of which stop for a while in Mombo to collect more passengers. If you're going from Lushoto to either Dar es Salaam, Moshi or Arusha, it often works out just as fast to take a *dalla-dalla* or taxi (about TSh25,000) to Mombo and then get one of the larger express buses to Dar es Salaam. The place to wait is at New Liverpool Hotel, on the main highway about 1km west of the Mombo junction, where all the Dar es Salaam–Arusha buses stop for a rest break. Buses from Dar es Salaam begin arriving at the New Liverpool Hotel from about 10am.

Soni

☎ 027

Tiny Soni, about halfway along the Mombo–Lushoto road, lacks Lushoto's infrastructure, but makes a good change of pace if you'll be staying a while in the Usambaras. Walks include a two- to three-day hike to the Mazumbai Forest Reserve and Bumbuli town (per person per day TSh50,000) and a short stroll (three to five hours return) to pine-clad **Sakharani**, a Benedictine mission that sells locally produced wine. Guides can be arranged at Maweni Farm, or in Lushoto.

Soni Falls Resort (☎ 0784-384603, 0784-510523; d or tr TSh28,000, f TSh48,000) is a restored colonial-era house on a hill about 100m from the main junction. It has three enormous rooms – all with hard-wood flooring and lots of windows. There are no meals.

Maweni Farm (☎ 027-264 0426/7; www.maweni .com/lodge; s/d safari tent half board US$69/93, s/d with

shared bathroom & half board US$44/67, ste half board US$93/114) is an atmospheric old farmhouse set in lush grounds about 3km from the main junction (from where it's signposted). There are spacious rooms, some in the main house and some in a separate block, plus four safari-style tents with private bathroom and meals.

Soni is about 12km below Lushoto along the Mombo road, with frequent *dalla-dallas* from both towns (TSh800 from Lushoto, TSh1000 from Mombo).

Mombo

☎ 027

Mombo is the scruffy junction town at the foot of the Usambaras Mountains where the road to Lushoto branches off the main Dar es Salaam–Arusha highway. There's no recommendable accommodation, though you should have no trouble getting a *dalla-dalla* up to Soni or Lushoto to sleep.

PARE MOUNTAINS

The Pare Mountains, northwest of the Usambaras, are also part of the Eastern Arc chain, and like the Usambaras they are divided into two ranges: north and south. The best way to explore is to spend a night at Mwanga (for the north Pares) or Same (for the south Pares) to get organised, and then head up to either Usangi or Mbaga, from where you can access the best hikes.

Lodging and food in the Pare Mountains are for the most part very basic. With the exception of Hill-Top Tona Lodge in Mbaga, most accommodation is with villagers, or camping.

The best places to arrange guides are through Hill-Top Tona Lodge in Mbaga or at local guesthouses in Usangi. Elephant Motel in Same can also put you in touch with guides. For organised hikes, expect to pay from about TSh20,000 per person per day, including guide, camping fees and meals. There is a TSh5000 per visit forest fee for any walks that go into forest reserves, including walks to Shengena Peak. This is payable at the Catchment office in Same, or through your guide. For any hikes done with guides, the stages are generally quite short – two or three can usually be easily combined for anyone who's reasonably fit – although your guide will still expect you to pay for the same number of days.

Same

☎ 027

Same (*sah*-may) – the main town in the South Pares – has essentially no tourist infrastructure, and is more suitable as a starting point for excursions into the Pares than as a base. The Catchment office (for paying forest reserve fees) is at the end of town, on the main road past the market.

NMB bank (go left out of the bus stand, up one block, then left again) changes cash.

Amani Lutheran Centre (☎ 027-275 8107; s/d TSh7000/10,000) has simple, clean rooms around a quiet compound, and meals on order. It's along the main road, just south of the market, and about five minutes' walk from the bus stand.

Elephant Motel (☎ 027-275 8193; www.elephant motel.com; camping US$5, s/tw/tr US$20/25/30), on the main highway about 1km southeast of town, has faded but reasonable rooms and a cavernous restaurant serving decent meals.

GETTING THERE & AWAY

Most buses on the Dar es Salaam–Arusha highway stop at Same on request. Otherwise, minibuses travel daily between Same, Dar es Salaam and Moshi, leaving Same in the morning. There is a direct bus between Arusha and Same, departing from Arusha at around 8am (TSh5000, 2½ hours).

Mbaga

☎ 027

Mbaga, about 30km southeast of Same near Mkomazi Game Reserve, offers hikes to the surrounding hills and villages, and to the top of 2462m Shengena Peak (two or three days' walk), the highest in the Pare Mountains.

Hill-Top Tona Lodge (☎ 0754-852010; tona_lodge@ hotmail.com; camping TSh7000, r per person with shared bathroom US$12) is a former mission house and a good base, with views, simple cottages, meals (TSh3000) and guides for hiking.

GETTING THERE & AWAY

There are one or two vehicles daily around midday between Same and Mbaga, departing from Same between about 11am and 2pm (TSh3500, two to three hours, 40km). If you're coming from Moshi, this means that you'll need to get a bus by 8am in order to get to Mbaga on the same day. Coming from Dar es Salaam, you'll probably need to overnight in Same. Hiring a vehicle up to Mbaga costs

about TSh40,000 one way; ask at Elephant Motel or one of the other Same guesthouses to help you arrange this. From Mbaga back to Same, transport departs by 6am or earlier. It's also possible to catch one of the several daily *dalla-dallas* running from Same to Kisiwani and then walk about 5km uphill to Mbaga.

For self-drivers, there is an alternative route via Mwembe, which can be reached by following the Dar es Salaam–Arusha highway 5km south to the dirt road leading off to the left.

Mwanga

☎ 027

This district capital sprawls across the plains at the foot of the Pares about 50km north of Same on the Dar es Salaam–Arusha highway. The main reason to come here is to change vehicles to get to Usangi, the jumping-off point for the northern Pares.

Anjela Inn (☎ 027-275 8381; d TSh10,000, in newer annex TSh15,000) has clean, albeit noisy doubles with nets in the main building, and similar but larger and quieter rooms in a house next door, plus meals. It's about 10 minutes' walk from the highway and bus stand – follow the main road in towards the 'new' market, turn left down a wide, tree-lined lane at the clutch of signboards and then keep straight on.

Usangi

☎ 027

Pretty Usangi, lying in a valley ringed by mountains about 25km east of Mwanga, is the centre of the northern Pares and a possible base for exploring the region.

The main point of interest in town as far as hiking is concerned is **Lomwe Secondary School**, where you can arrange guides. There's a camping ground here with water, and the school serves as a **hostel** (camping & dm per person TSh5000) when classes are not in session. Alternatively, try **Usangi Guesthouse** (r with shared bathroom TSh4000), near the mosque, with basic rooms and food.

It's possible to arrange a day hike through Kindoroko Forest Reserve (which begins about 7km south of Usangi village) to the top of Mt Kindoroko – at 2113m, the highest peak in the North Pares – returning again in the late afternoon to sleep in Usangi village.

GETTING THERE & AWAY

Several *dalla-dallas* run daily along the unpaved but decent road between Mwanga and Usangi (TSh2500, 1½ hours), from around

10am. Hiring a taxi costs about TSh30,000. From Arusha and Moshi there is a direct bus to Usangi, departing in the morning (four hours from Arusha). Ask the driver to drop you at Lomwe Secondary School.

MKOMAZI GAME RESERVE

The wild and undeveloped Mkomazi Game Reserve (Mkomazi-Umba Game Reserve) – soon to be gazetted as Mkomazi National Park – spreads along the Kenyan border in the shadow of the Pare Mountains, its dry savannah lands contrasting sharply with the moist forests of the Pares. The reserve, which is contiguous with Kenya's Tsavo West National Park, is known for its black rhinos, which were introduced into the area from South Africa for breeding, and which are part of a pioneering and little-publicised conservation success story. There are currently nine rhinos (up from zero since 1989, when Tony Fitzjohn – the force behind conservation work in Mkomazi – started his work there). All are within a heavily protected 45 sq km enclosure and not viewable as part of general tourism. In addition to the rhinos, there are wild dogs (also reintroduced and, as part of a special endangered species program, also not viewable as part of general tourism). Animals that you're more likely to spot include oryx, eland, dik-dik, the rarely seen gerenuk, kudu, Coke's hartebeest and an array of birds. The main reasons for coming to Mkomazi – apart from enjoying Babu's Camp (see right) – are to appreciate the alluring wilderness area and evocative nyika bush landscapes studded with baobab and thorn acacia and broken by low, rocky hills.

Information

Reserve admission costs US$20 per day and camping costs US$20/5 per adult/child, though these fees will change once Mkomazi's national park status is formalised. The main entrance to the reserve is at Zange Gate, about 5km east of Same, which is also the location of **reserve headquarters** (☎ 027-275 8249; ⊙ 9am-4pm), and the place to arrange an armed ranger for bush walks (US$20). Self-drivers need 4WD for a visit.

Sleeping

There is a basic **camp site** (camping adult/child US$20/5) at Ibaya, about 15km from Zange Gate. Bring everything with you.

Babu's Camp (☎ 027-254 8840; www.babuscamp .com; s/d full board US$248/440) This classic safari-style camp has five tents set amid baobabs and thorn acacias in the northern part of reserve looking towards the Gulela Hills. The cuisine is delicious and the ambience and evocative surrounding landscapes evoke images of quintessential East Africa. Wildlife drives and walks can be arranged, as can night drives.

Getting There & Away

Regional Air has flights (assuming sufficient demand) connecting Mkomazi with Arusha, Zanzibar, Pangani and Saadani.

Dalla-dallas between Same and Mbaga will drop you at Zange Gate, from where you can arrange guides and begin a walking safari. Babu's Camp provides transfers for its guests.

NORTHERN TANZANIA

With snow-capped Mt Kilimanjaro, the wildlife-packed Ngorongoro Crater, the Serengeti plains and superb wildlife watching, northern Tanzania draws more visitors than anywhere else in the country, and embodies what is for many quintessential Africa.

Exploring the region is relatively easy. The tourist infrastructure is good, with a wide range of accommodation and dining options in major towns. There's also direct air access from Europe and elsewhere in East Africa via Kilimanjaro International Airport (KIA), which is becoming an increasingly important hub. The main caveat is price – the north is Tanzania's most costly region, especially if you do an organised safari. If you don't mind roughing things a bit, there are some inexpensive alternatives, including an array of Cultural Tourism Programs (see boxed text, p180).

MOSHI

☎ 027

Moshi is home of the Chagga people and centre of one of Tanzania's major coffee-growing regions. Most visitors use the town as a starting point for climbing Mt Kilimanjaro, although it's a pleasant place in its own right to relax for a couple of days. It also tends to be less expensive than nearby Arusha.

TANZANIA

NORTHERN TANZANIA

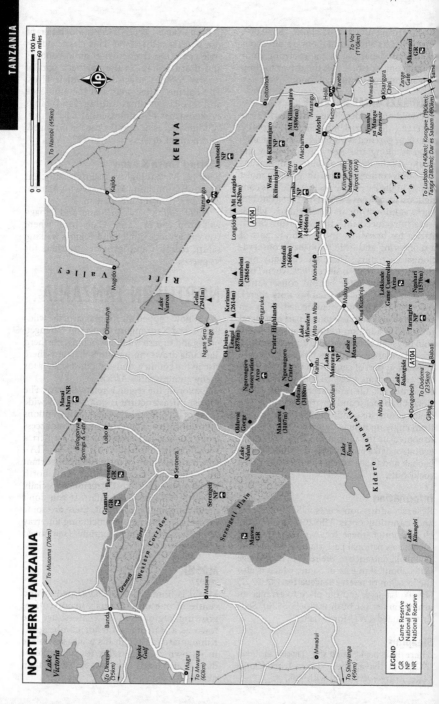

100 km
60 miles

KENYA

Rift Valley

Eastern Arc Mountains

Crater Highlands

Ngorongoro Conservation Area

Serengeti Plain

Western Corridor

Kidero Mountains

Lake Victoria

Speke Gulf

LEGEND

GR	Game Reserve
NP	National Park
NR	National Reserve

Information

For trekking operators, see p70.

EasyCom (Ground fl, Kahawa House, Clock Tower roundabout; per hr TSh1500; ☺ 7.30am-8.30pm) Tnternet access and cheap internet dialling.

Executive Bureau de Change (Boma Rd; ☺ 8.30am-6pm Mon-Fri, 9am-5pm Sat) Changes cash and travellers cheques.

Exim Bank (Boma Rd) ATM accepts Visa, MasterCard, Maestro and Cirrus.

Fahari Cyber Café (Hill St; per hr TSh1000; ☺ 8.30am-8pm Mon-Sat) Next to the Coffee Shop.

Immigration office (Boma Rd; ☺ 7.30am-3.30pm Mon-Fri) Visa extensions handled while you wait.

Kilimanjaro Christian Medical Centre (☎ 027-275 4377/8; Sokoine Rd) About 3km northwest of town off Kilimanjaro Rd.

NBC Bank (Clock Tower roundabout) Cash and travellers cheques; ATM accepts Visa.

Stanbic Bank (Boma Rd) ATM accepts Visa, MasterCard, Maestro and Cirrus.

Standard Chartered Bank (Rindi Lane) ATM accepts Visa.

TTCL (cnr Boma & Mawenzi Rds) Telephone cards; located near the clock tower.

Sights & Activities

Central Moshi is full of activity and atmosphere, and makes an interesting walk, especially the area around the market and Mawenzi Rd, which has a vaguely Asian flavour, with a **Hindu temple**, several mosques and many Indian traders.

There's a 25m **pool** (adult/child TSh3000/1500; ☺ 9am-6pm Mon-Sat, 9am-4.30pm Sun) at the YMCA (right).

The area outside Moshi is lushly vegetated and beautiful, and Machame and other towns above Moshi on Kilimanjaro's lower slopes are linked by easy-to-follow footpaths. Any of the listings on p70, plus Kilemakyaro Lodge (p162) and Protea Hotel Aishi Machame (p164) can help you organise guides.

Sleeping

BUDGET

Honey Badger Kilimanjaro View Guesthouse & Campsite (☎ 027-275 4608; www.hbcc-campsites.com; camping US$5, r per person US$25) Camping on a large lawn, plus basic rooms in a converted house, or in a separate dorm block. Meals cost US$5. Cultural activities can be arranged at extra cost. It's 6km from town off Marangu Rd.

Kilimanjaro Backpackers Hotel (☎ 027-275 5159; www.kilimanjarobackpackers.com; Mawenzi Rd; s/tw with shared bathroom US$4/8) Formerly Da Costa Hotel, this place has tiny, clean rooms with fan, as well as a bar and a restaurant

YMCA (☎ 027-275 1754; Taifa Rd; s/d with shared bathroom US$10/13; ☒) Spartan, noisy rooms, some with views over Kilimanjaro, and a swimming pool. It's north of the clock tower on the roundabout between Kibo and Taifa Rds.

A&A Hill St Accommodation (☎ 027-275 3455, 0754-299469; sajjad_omar@hotmail.com; Hill St; s/d/tr TSh15,000/20,000/30,000) Clean, quiet rooms with fan, just one block from the bus stand, with an internet café and inexpensive restaurant below. There's no breakfast.

Buffalo Hotel (☎ 027-275 0270; New St; r with shared bathroom TSh12,000, s/d with private bathroom TSh20,000/25,000, d with air-con TSh30,000; ☒) Straightforward rooms with fan and mosquito net, and a restaurant. The entrance is on a small street off Mawenzi Rd.

Zebra Hotel (☎ 027-275 0611; New St; s/d/tr US$30/35/45) A high-rise next to Buffalo Hotel, with clean rooms with hot water, and a restaurant.

Kindoroko Hotel (☎ 027-275 4054; www.kindoroko hotel.com; Mawenzi Rd; s/d US$15/30, d/tr with shared bathroom US$15/45; ☒) A busy place and an easy walk from the bus stand, with small but clean rooms, a rooftop bar, a forex bureau and a restaurant.

Horombo Lodge (☎ 027-275 0134; horombohotel@ yahoo.com; Old Moshi Rd; s/d US$25/35) Diagonally opposite Precision Air, with sterile rooms with fan, and a restaurant.

MIDRANGE & TOP END

Lutheran Uhuru Hostel (☎ 027-275 4512, 0753-037216; www.uhuruhotel.org; Sekou Toure Rd; s/d US$40/50, in newer wing US$45/55, in annexe with shared bathroom US$30/40; ☒) Spotless good-value rooms, some with balconies, in leafy, expansive grounds, and a good restaurant. In a nearby annexe are budget rooms with shared facilities and kitchen. Rooms are wheelchair accessible. It's 3km northwest of the town centre on the Arusha road (TSh2000 in a taxi).

Kilimanjaro Crane Hotel (☎ 027-275 1114; www .kilimanjarocranehotels.com; Kaunda St; s/d US$40/50; ☒ ☒ ☒) This reliable place has good-value rooms with fans, nets, TV and large beds backing onto a small garden. Downstairs is a restaurant and upstairs is a rooftop terrace-bar. It's on a small side street running parallel to and just east of Old Moshi Rd.

Parkview Inn (☎ 027-275 0711; www.pvim.com; Aga Khan Rd; s/d US$45/55; ☒ ☒ ☒) A small centrally located business travellers' hotel with modern rooms with internet access, a restaurant and a pool. It's signposted just off the Arusha road.

Key's Hotel (☎ 027-275 2250; www.keys-hotel-tours .com; Uru Rd; s/d US$55/65, air-con extra US$20; 🕾 🖳) Key's, about 1.5km northeast of the clock tower on a quiet side street, has been popular with travellers for years. Accommodation is in spacious, high-ceilinged rooms in the main building, or in small, dark rondavels out the back for the same price, and there's a restaurant and a bar.

Keys Mbokomu (s/d US$55/65, air-con extra US$20; 🕾) If Key's Hotel is full, try their partner hotel, 4km from town off Marangu Rd.

Bristol Cottages (☎ 027-275 5083; www.bristol cottages.com; Rindi Lane; s/d/tr cottage US$60/72/90, s/d from US$45/60; 🕾) Spotless, modern attached cottages – some with air-con and others with fan – in quiet grounds adjoining Standard Chartered Bank. There are also newer rooms in a two-storey block, and a small restaurant.

AMEG Lodge (☎ 027-275 0175; www.ameglodge.com; s/d from US$69/99; 🕾 🖳) Spacious rooms in detached cottages – all with TV, small porches and fans – set around a grassy compound, plus a small gym and a restaurant. It's signposted off Lema Rd in Shanty Town.

Kilemakyaro Lodge (☎ 027-275 4925; www.kiliman jarosafari.com; s/d/tr US$75/125/185) Rooms here – in stone rondavels with TV and private bathroom – are fine though undistinguished, but the open hilltop setting, with views to Kilimanjaro in the distance, compensates. It's about 7km from the town centre off the Kibosho road.

Impala Kilimanjaro Hotel (☎ 027-275 3443/4; Lema Rd; s/d US$80/100; 🕾) Well-appointed rooms in prim, tranquil grounds, and a restaurant. It's about 4km northwest of the clock tower roundabout in Shanty Town, and under the same management as Impala Hotel in Arusha.

Eating & Drinking

Coffee Shop (☎ 027-275 2707; Hill St; snacks & meals from TSh1000; 🕑 8am-5pm Mon, 8am-8pm Tue-Fri, 8am-6pm Sat) A laid-back vibe, garden seating, good coffee, and an assortment of homemade breads, cakes, yoghurt, breakfast and light meals. Proceeds go to a church project.

Tanzania Coffee Lounge (☎ 027-275 1006; Chagga St; snacks and light meals from Tsh2000; 🕑 8am-7pm Mon-Sat, noon-4pm Sun; 🖳) Milkshakes, bagels, great coffees and cappuccino, waffles and an internet connection.

Hill Street Food Snacks & Take Away (Hill St; meals about Tsh2000) Cheap plates of local fast food below A&A Hill Street Accommodation.

Salzburger Café (☎ 027-275 0681; Kenyatta St; meals TSh3500-5000; 🕑 8am-11pm) The Alps meet Africa at this classic place, which comes complete with waitresses sporting faux-leopard skin vests, Austrian *Kneipe* (bar) décor on the walls and a selection of good, cheap dishes.

Indotaliano Restaurant (☎ 027-275 2195; New St; meals about TSh4000; 🕑 10am-11pm) The Indo portion of the menu – a range of standards, including some veg dishes – at this small, dark sidewalk restaurant is better than the Italian part (mediocre pizzas). It's opposite Buffalo Hotel.

El Rancho (☎ 027-275 5115; meals from TSh4000; 🕑 closed Mon) Tasty Indian food, including veg dishes, in a garden setting. It's about 3km northwest of the town centre off Lema Rd (no public transport).

For self-catering, try **Aleem's Grocery** (Boma Rd) or **Abbas Ally's Hot Bread Shop** (Boma Rd), opposite.

Shopping

Some places to try for crafts:

Our Heritage (Hill St) Carvings, beadwork and other crafts; next to the Coffee Shop.

Shah Industries (☎ 027-275 2414; shahind@ kilinet.co.tz) Leatherwork and other crafts, many made by disabled people. It's south of town over the railway tracks.

Tahea Kili Crafts (www.taheakili.org; Hill St) Opposite the Coffee Shop, with batiks, basketry and woodcarvings; a portion of profits goes to a local women's group.

Getting There & Away

AIR

Kilimanjaro International Airport (KIA) is 50km west of the town centre off the main highway. There's also the small Moshi airport about 3km southwest of town along the extension of Market St, which handles occasional charters.

From KIA, there are daily flights to Dar es Salaam (TSh168,500), Zanzibar (from TSh185,000) and Entebbe on **Air Tanzania** (☎ 027-275 5205; Rengua Rd), near the clock tower. **Precision Air** (☎ 027-275 3495; Old Moshi Rd) has daily flights connecting KIA with Dar es Salaam, Mwanza (via Shinyanga, from about TSh250,000 to Mwanza) and Nairobi (US$250).

MOSHI

0 — 400 m
0 — 0.2 miles

INFORMATION
EasyCom.......................**1** C3
Executive Bureau de Change.**2** C3
Exim Bank.......................**3** C3
Fahari Cyber Café.............(see 15)
Immigration Office.............**4** C3
Kilimanjaro Porter Assistance
  Project Office.................(see 19)
NBC Bank.......................**5** D3
Stanbic Bank....................**6** C3
Standard Chartered Bank....**7** C4
TTCL..............................**8** C4

SIGHTS & ACTIVITIES
Hindu Temple...................**9** C5
KNCU Building & Kahawa
  Shamba Booking Office....**10** D3
Moshi Expeditions &
  Mountaineering..............**11** D4
Mosque..........................**12** C4

Shah Tours.......................**13** A2
YMCA Pool......................(see 23)
Zara Tanzania Adventures...**14** C3

SLEEPING
A&A Hill St Accommodation.**15** C5
Bristol Cottages.................**16** C4
Buffalo Hotel.....................**17** C5
Horombo Lodge................**18** D3
Kilimanjaro Backpackers
  Hotel............................**19** B5
Kilimanjaro Crane Hotel......**20** D3
Kindoroko Hotel................**21** C5
Parkview Inn.....................**22** B4
YMCA..............................**23** D2
Zebra Hotel......................**24** C5

To Key's Hotel
(400m)

To Kilimanjaro Christian
Medical Centre (3km);
Kilemakyaro Lodge (7km);
Kibosho (12km)

To Keys Mbokomu (4km);
Honey Badger Kilimanjaro
View Guesthouse &
Campsite (5km);
Marangu (40km);
Dar es Salaam (555km)

To Hostel
Hoff (50m)

Catholic
Cathedral

To Lutheran Uhuru Hostel (700m);
Impala Kilimanjaro Hotel (1.5km);
AMEG Lodge (1.5km);
El Rancho (2km)

To Umbwe (14km);
Machame (26km);
Kilimanjaro International
Airport (45km);
Arusha (80km)

Kiusa

Market

To Moshi
Airport (3km)

EATING
Abbas Ally's Hot Bread
  Shop.............................**25** C3
Aleem's Grocery...............**26** C3
Coffee Shop.....................**27** C5
Hill Street Food Snacks &
  Take Away.....................(see 15)
Indotaliano Restaurant.......**28** C5
Salzburger Café................**29** B5
Tanzania Coffee Lounge....**30** B5

SHOPPING
Our Heritage....................**31** C5
Shah Industries.................**32** C6
Tahea Kili Crafts...............**33** C5

TRANSPORT
Air Tanzania....................**34** C3
Akamba Bus Office...........(see 17)
Central Bus Station...........**35** C4
Dalla-Dalla Stand.............**36** C4
Dar Express Bus Office......**37** B3
Impala Shuttle..................**38** C3
Precision Air....................**39** D3
Riverside Shuttle..............**40** C3
Royal Coach Bus Office.....**41** C4
Scandinavian Express Bus
  Office...........................**42** B4
Taxi Stand......................**43** C4
Taxi Stand......................**44** C3

Train Station
(Closed)

Clock
Tower

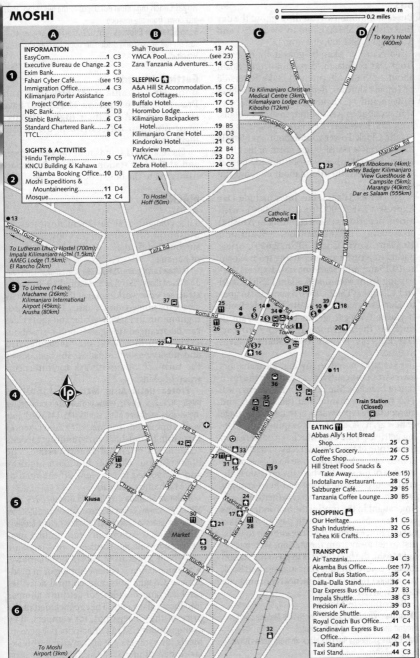

BUS

Buses and minibuses run throughout the day to Arusha (TSh1800, one to 1½ hours) and Marangu (TSh1200, one hour).

To Nairobi, Akamba goes daily en route from Dar es Salaam, departing from Moshi about 1.30pm. Alternatively, take Riverside or Impala shuttles, departing from Moshi at 6.30am and 11.30am, though you'll need to wait an hour in Arusha in transit; for details, see p259. **Riverside** (1st fl, THB Bldg, Boma Rd) is just off the Clock Tower roundabout, and **Impala** (☎ 027-275 3444; Kibo Rd) is just north of the clock tower. Several other Nairobi-bound shuttles also leave from the roundabout at about the same time.

To Dar es Salaam, bus lines include Dar Express (TSh20,000 to TSh25,000), with Moshi departures (all originating in Arusha) at 6.30am, 7.15am, 8.30am, 9.30am and 10.30am; Royal Coach (TSh22,000), originating in Arusha and departing from Moshi at 10.15am; and Scandinavian Express, departing from Moshi at 9.30am (TSh20,000) and 12.30pm (TSh25,000). Akamba also goes to Dar es Salaam, en route from Nairobi. If you're trying to get to Dar es Salaam in time for the afternoon ferry to Zanzibar, Dar Express' 6.30am bus usually arrives in time.

Except as noted following, all transport leaves from the central bus station in the town centre between Market St and Mawenzi Rd. The station is chaotic and full of touts and disreputable types wanting to take advantage of new arrivals, and it can be quite intimidating getting off the bus (which is a good reason to take one of the lines that let you disembark at their offices). To minimise hassles, look for the area of the station where the taxis are gathered before disembarking and head straight over and hire a driver there, rather than getting caught in the fray by the bus door. Unless you know Moshi, it's worth paying for a taxi to your hotel, even if it's close enough to walk, just to get away from the station. When leaving Moshi, the best thing is to go to the station the day before without your luggage and book your ticket then, so that the next morning you can just arrive and board.

Bus offices in Moshi:

Akamba (☎ 027-275 3908; cnr New & Makinga Sts) Around the corner from Buffalo Hotel.

Dar Express (Boma Rd) One block up from Abbas Ally's Hot Bread Shop.

Royal Coach (Aga Khan Rd) Opposite the bus stand, and just down from the mosque.

Scandinavian Express (☎ 027-275 1387; Selous St) Just off Hill St, past and diagonally opposite Mawenzi Hospital.

Getting Around

Both Air Tanzania (currently free) and Precision Air (per person TSh10,000) have shuttles to KIA for their flights, departing from their offices two hours before flight time.

There are taxi stands near the clock tower and at the bus station. *Dalla-dallas* depart from next to the bus station.

MACHAME
☎ 027

This village lies about 25km northwest of Moshi on Mt Kilimanjaro's lower slopes, surrounded by dense vegetation and stands of banana.

Makoa Farm (☎ 0754-312896; www.makoa-farm.com; d full board about US$270) is a restored 1930s farmstead set on a working farm that is primarily a base for horse-riding safaris. There's a two-night minimum stay; walking and short rides can be arranged (for guests only). It's about 17km from Moshi, off the Machame road and unsignposted. Most Moshi taxis know the turn-off; otherwise ask for directions when booking.

Protea Hotel Aishi Machame (☎ 027-275 6948, 027-275 6941; www.proteahotels.com/protea -hotel-aishi-machame.html; s/d US$115/145; ☒) has well-appointed rooms with dark-wood furnishings and lush surrounding gardens reminiscent of an old country estate. The hotel is about 6km off the main highway and signposted to the right off the road to the Machame trailhead.

Kahawa Shamba (☎ 027-275 0464, 027-275 2785, 0784-517995; www.kahawashamba.co.tz; camping US$6; per person full board in Chagga hut including cultural activities US$103/166) is a community-run venture near Lyamungo village, southeast of Machame and about 27km from Moshi near Umbwe. Accommodation is either camping or in modernised Chagga huts, and cultural activities can be arranged – ideal for getting a glimpse into local Chagga life. They're included in the price of the Chagga hut; for campers, they average about US$15 per activity per person. Meals for campers are also available (breakfast/lunch/dinner US$4/6/6). Book at least two weeks in advance, either via email, or at Kahawa Shamba's Moshi booking office in the KNCU building just off the clock tower roundabout. From Moshi, take a *dalla-dalla* to Kibosho-Umbwe (TSh800, 45 minutes), from where you'll need to walk 20 to 30 minutes to Lyamungo-Kibera area and Kahawa Shamba. Staff can also help you arrange taxi or minibus transfer, and tents and sleeping bags are available for rent.

MARANGU
☎ 027

This small town on the slopes of Mt Kilimanjaro is about 40km northeast of Moshi, and a convenient overnight stop for Marangu route trekkers. It's also a pleasant place in its own right, with an agreeable highland atmosphere, cool, leafy surroundings and walks and cultural activities possibilities on the mountain's lower slopes.

There's an internet connection at **Marangu Computer Centre** (per hr TSh2000; ☉ 8am-6pm) behind the post office.

Sights & Activities
Most Marangu hotels organise Kilimanjaro treks and can provide English-speaking guides (about US$15 per day) to visit nearby waterfalls, local blacksmiths' workshops and other cultural attractions. Banana Jungle Lodge and Kilimanjaro Mountain Resort have authentic models of traditional Chagga houses, and at Kilimanjaro Mountain Resort there's also the **Chagga Live Museum** (admission US$2; ☉ 10am-5pm), illustrating traditional Chagga life.

It's possible to do a **day hike** in Mt Kilimanjaro National Park from Marangu Gate as far as Mandara Hut (about two hours up, one hour down; US$60 per person for park fees, plus US$10 per guide, arranged at the park gate).

Sleeping & Eating
Coffee Tree Campsite (☎ 0754-691433; www.coffeetree campsite.com; camping US$8, rondavel per person US$12, chalet per person US$15) Expansive, well-maintained grounds, hot-water showers, tents for hire (TSh10,000 per day), plus several four- to six-person rondavels and chalets. It's about 700m east of the main road, and signposted near Nakara Hotel.

Babylon Lodge (☎ 027-275 6355; www.babylon lodge.com; camping US$5, s/d US$30/50) A budget hotel at heart, masquerading behind midrange prices, Babylon has a row of small, clean twin- and double-bed rooms clustered around a tiny lawn. It's about 700m east of the main junction.

Banana Jungle Lodge (☎ 027-275 6565, 0754-270947; www.yellowpages.co.tz/jungle/index.htm; camping student/nonstudent US$5/10, s/d/tr US$50/60/75) A large family homestead with bungalow-style rooms or modernised Chagga huts set on the expansive grounds of the owners' house. It's not luxurious, although all the basics are there, but it's a refreshingly genuine place to learn about Chagga life and culture. Meals are available for US$4 to US$6. It's located about 5km east of Marangu in Mamba, off the road leading to the Rongai Route trailhead. Head right (east) at Marangu's main junction, go 2km to the Mamba Lutheran church, turn left at the signboard and then follow the signboards further for about another 2.5km.

Kibo Hotel (☎ 027-275 1308; www.kibohotel.com; camping US$5, s/d US$45/69) The Kibo, well over 100 years old, is where Hans Meyer stayed overnight before starting his famous first ascent of Kilimanjaro. It's now well past its prime, but atmospheric and rooms – albeit rustic – are quite spacious, and there's a restaurant. It's about 1.5km west of the main junction.

Kilimanjaro Mountain Resort (☎ 027-275 8950; camping US$12, s/d from US$50/90) This stately building is surrounded by gardens and forest 3km west of the main junction, with spacious, well-appointed rooms – some with enormous beds – a restaurant (lunch/dinner US$12/15) and the adjoining Chagga Live Museum.

Marangu Hotel (☎ 027-275 6594; www.maranguhotel .com; camping with hot showers US$5, s/d half board US$85/120; ☙) This long-standing place is the first hotel you reach coming from Moshi, with a clipped British ambience, rooms set around expansive grounds and a camp site. Room discounts are available if you join one of the hotel's fully equipped climbs.

Getting There & Away
Minibuses run throughout the day between Marangu and Moshi (TSh1200). In Marangu they'll drop you at the main junction from where there are sporadic pick-ups to the park gate (TSh500), 5km further. For the Holili border, you'll need to change at Himo junction.

TANZANIA

TREKKING ON MT KILIMANJARO

At 5896m, Mt Kilimanjaro is the highest peak in Africa and one of the continent's most magnificent sights. From cultivated farmlands on the lower levels, the mountain rises through lush rainforest, alpine meadows and a barren lunar landscape to the twin summits of Kibo and Mawenzi.

A trek up 'Kili' lures hundreds of trekkers each year, and is even more attractive because, with the right preparation, you can walk all the way to the summit without the need of ropes or technical climbing experience. Yet the climb is a serious (as well as expensive) undertaking, and only worth doing with the right preparation. For more details about

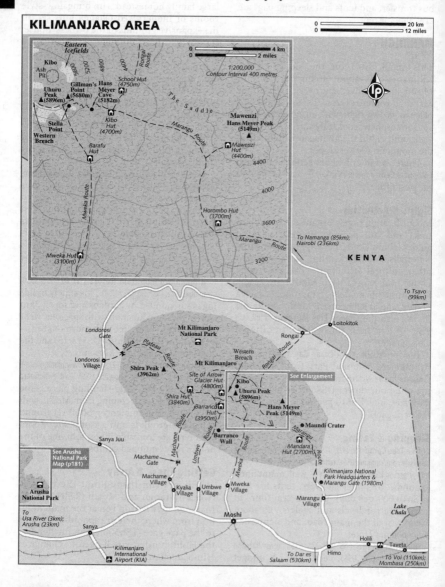

KILIMANJARO AREA

trekking on the mountain, check out Lonely Planet's *Trekking in East Africa*.

Information

Entry fees to **Mt Kilimanjaro National Park** (☎ 027-275 6605, 027-275 6602; kinapa@iwayafrica.com), which encompasses the mountain, are US$60/10 per adult/child, and are calculated per day, not per 24-hour period. Huts (Marangu Route) cost US$50 per person per night, as does camping on all routes, and there is a US$20 rescue fee per person per trip for treks on the mountain. Kilimanjaro can only be climbed with a licensed guide. Unless you are a Tanzania resident and well versed in the logistics of Kili climbs, the only realistic way to organise things is through a tour company. For operator listings, see p68.

Park fees are generally included in price quotes, and paid on your behalf by the trekking operator, but you'll need to confirm this before making any bookings. Guide and porter fees (but not tips) are handled directly by the trekking companies. Park authority offices are at the main **park gate** (🕑 8am-6pm) in Marangu.

Weather conditions on the mountain are frequently very cold and wet, no matter what the time of year it is, so waterproof your gear and bring a full range of waterproof cold-weather clothing and equipment. While you can hire sleeping bags and some cold-weather gear at the Marangu gate, quality and availability can't be counted on.

ROUTES

There are at least 10 trekking routes that begin on the lower slopes, but only three continue to the summit. Of these, the **Marangu Route** is the 'easiest' and the most popular, though Machame Route (see following) is getting closer in popularity. A trek on this route is typically sold as a five-day, four-night return package, although at least one extra night is highly recommended to help acclimatisation, especially if you've just flown in to Tanzania or just arrived from the lowlands. Lonely Planet's *Trekking in East Africa* has detailed descriptions of the standard stages of this and other main routes, as does *Kilimanjaro – The Trekking Guide to Africa's Highest Mountain* by Henry Stedman.

Other routes on Kili usually take six days (which cost more, but helps acclimatisation) and pass through a wider range of scenic areas than the Marangu Route, although trekkers must use tents. The **Machame Route** has a gradual ascent, including a spectacular day contouring the southern slopes before approaching the summit via the top section of the Mweka Route. The **Umbwe Route** is much steeper, with a more direct way to the summit – very enjoyable if you can resist the temptation to gain altitude too quickly. Unfortunately, some trekking companies now push attractively priced five-day four-night options on the Umbwe Route in an effort to attract business. Although the route is direct, the top, very steep section up the Western Breach is often covered in ice or snow, which makes it impassable or extremely dangerous. Many trekkers who attempt it without proper acclimatisation are forced to turn back. An indication of its seriousness is that until fairly recently, the Western Breach was considered a technical mountaineering route. It has only gained in popularity recently because of intense competition for business and crowding on other routes. The bottom line is that you should only consider this route if you are experienced and properly equipped, and travelling with a reputable operator. Reliable operators will suggest an extra night for acclimatisation.

Another thing to watch out for is operators who try to sell a 'short' version of the Machame Route, which ascends the Machame Route for the first few stages, but then switches near the top to the final section of the Umbwe Route and summits via the Western Breach. This version is a day shorter (and thus less expensive) than the standard Machame Route, but the same considerations outlined in the preceding paragraph apply here, and you should only consider this combination if you are experienced, acclimatised and properly equipped.

The **Rongai Route**, which has also become increasingly popular in recent years, starts near the Kenyan border and goes up the northern side of the mountain. It's possible to do this in five days, but it's better done in six. The attractive **Shira Plateau Route** (also called the Londorosi Route) is somewhat longer than the others, but good for acclimatisation if you start trekking from Londorosi Gate (rather than driving all the way to the Shira Track road head, higher up along the route), or if you take an extra day at Shira Hut.

Trekkers on the Machame and Umbwe routes descend via the Marangu Route or the **Mweka Route**, which is for descent only. Some Marangu treks also descend on the Mweka Route.

COSTS

No-frills five-day/four-night treks up the Marangu Route start at about US$900, including park fees, and no-frills budget treks of six to seven days on the Machame Route start at around US$1000, although it's highly recommended to budget at least one additional night for the ascent. Better-quality six-day trips on the Marangu and Machame routes start at about US$1200. The Umbwe Route is often sold by budget operators for about the same price as Marangu, and billed as a quick and comparatively inexpensive way to reach the top. Don't fall for this – the route should only be done by experienced trekkers, and should have an extra acclimatisation day built in. For more information, see Routes (p167). Prices start at about US$800 on the Rongai Route, and about US$1200 for a seven-day trek on the Shira Plateau Route. As the starting points for these latter routes, particularly Rongai, are further from Moshi than those for the other routes, transport costs can be significant, so clarify whether they are included in the price.

Whatever you pay for your trek, remember that at least US$525 of this goes to park fees for a five-day Marangu Route climb, and more for longer treks (US$750 for a seven-day Machame Route climb). The rest of the money

covers food, tents (if required), guides, porters and transport to and from the start of the trek. Most of the better companies provide dining tents, decent to good cuisine and various other extras to make the experience more enjoyable (as well as to maximise your chances of getting to the top). If you choose a really cheap trip, you risk having inadequate meals, mediocre guides, few comforts, and problems with hut bookings and park fees. Also remember that an environmentally responsible trek usually costs more. Bringing a stove and fuel, for example, requires additional porters because of the greater weight. (It's not permitted to use firewood on the mountain.)

GUIDES & PORTERS

Guides, and at least one porter (for the guide), are obligatory and are provided by your trekking company. You can carry your own gear on the Marangu Route, although porters are generally used, but one or two porters per trekker are essential on all other routes.

All guides must be registered with the national park authorities. If in doubt, check that your guide's permit is up to date. On Kili, the guide's job is to show you the way and that's it. Only the best guides, working for reputable companies, will be able to tell you about wildlife, flowers or other features on the mountain.

Porters will carry bags weighing up to 15kg (not including their own food and clothing, which they strap to the outside of your bag), and your bags will be weighed before you set off.

SERIOUS BUSINESS

Whatever route you choose, remember that climbing Kilimanjaro is a serious undertaking. While many hundreds of trekkers reach Uhuru Peak without major difficulty, many more don't make it because they ascend too quickly and suffer from altitude sickness. And every year a few trekkers die on the mountain. Come prepared with appropriate footwear and clothing, and most importantly, allow yourself enough time. If you're interested in reaching the top, seriously consider adding at least one extra day onto the 'standard' climb itinerary, no matter which route you do. Although paying an additional US$150 or so per extra day may seem like a lot when you're planning your trip, it will seem a relatively insignificant saving later on if you've gone to the expense and effort to start a trek and then need to come down without having reached the top. And don't feel badly about insisting on an extra day with the trekking companies: standard medical advice is to increase sleeping altitude by only 300m per day once above 3000m – which is about one-third of the daily altitude gains above 3000m on the standard Kilimanjaro climb routes offered by most operators. Another perspective on it all: Uhuru Peak is several hundred metres higher than Everest Base Camp in the Nepal Himalaya, which trekkers often take at least two weeks to reach from Kathmandu.

FAIR PLAY

Kilimanjaro guides and porters have a reputation for being aggressive and demanding when it comes to tips, and higher tips are expected here than elsewhere in the region. Yet there's another side, too, with porter abuse and exploitation becoming a serious concern.

Most of the porters who work on Kilimanjaro are local residents who work freelance, usually with no guarantees of a salary beyond the present job. The work is hard, rates are low and it's safe to say that even the best-paid porters earn only a pittance in comparison with the salaries of many of the trekkers whose bags they are carrying. Due to stiff job competition, it's common for porters to agree to back-to-back treks without sufficient rest in between. It's also common for porters to work without proper shoes or equipment, and without adequate protection at night from the mountain's often cold and wet conditions. Equally concerning are cases where unscrupulous guides – interested in keeping an extra porter's salary for themselves – bribe the rangers who weigh porters' loads, so that the porter is faced with the choice of carrying an overly heavy load or not getting the job at all.

Porters depend on tourism on the mountain for their livelihood, but as a trekker you can help ensure that they aren't exploited and that working conditions are fair. When selecting a trekking operator, tell them this is a concern. Be aware of what goes on around you during your trek, and if you see exploitative treatment, tell the tour operator when you get back. Also get in touch with the UK-based **Tourism Concern** (www.tourismconcern.org.uk), which has mounted a worldwide campaign to improve conditions for porters. Another contact is the **International Mountain Explorers Connection** (IMEC; www.mountainexplorers.org), which started the **Kilimanjaro Porter Assistance Project** (KPAP; www.kiliporters.org; Kilimanjaro Backpackers Hotel, Mawenzi Rd, Moshi), a nonprofit group that arranges informal English-language training opportunities for porters and lobbies local tour operators to establish a code of conduct on porter pay and conditions. IMEC has porter treatment guidelines at www.hec.org/club/properporter.htm£guidelines. Both KPAP and Tourism Concern keep lists of trek operators who promote fair treatment of their staff.

The guides and porters provided by some of the cheaper trekking outfits leave a lot to be desired. If you're a hardy traveller, you might not worry about basic meals and substandard tents, but you might be more concerned about incompetent guides or dishonest porters. Stories abound about guides who leave the last hut deliberately late on the summit day, to avoid going all the way to the top. The best way to avoid scenarios like this is by going with a reputable company, familiarising yourself with all aspects of the route and – should problems arise – being polite but firm with your guide.

Porter treatment is another serious concern, with trekking companies at all budget levels. For more on some of these issues, see the boxed text above.

Most guides and porters receive only minimal wages from the trekking companies and depend on tips as their major source of income. As a guideline, plan on tipping about 10% of the total amount you've paid for the trek, divided up among the guides and porters. For the Marangu Route, tips are commonly from US$50 to US$60 for the guide, and from US$20 each for the porters. Plan on more for the longer routes, or if the guide and porters have been particularly good.

WEST KILIMANJARO

The West Kilimanjaro area – encompassing the Maasai lands running north of Sanya Juu village up to the Kenyan border and Amboseli National Park and around to Loitokitok – gained attention in recent times when eight local villages were granted permission to form the Enduimet Wildlife Management Area, one of just a handful of such community-managed wildlife areas in the country. For visitors, West Kilimanjaro is of interest for its savannah bushlands and its wildlife. This includes, most notably, its elephants, lying as it does along an elephant corridor linking Amboseli with Mt Kilimanjaro National Park. Other draws include the possibility of arranging visits to Maasai *bomas* (fortified living compounds; in colonial times, an administrative office), walks and other cultural activities. West Kilimanjaro also offers easy access to the western routes for mountain treks.

Hoopoe Safaris has a long-standing partnership with the local Maasai, and runs the excellent **Hemingway's Camp** (www.hemingways -camp.com; s/d full board & wildlife drives US$810/1020), an intimate place with just seven tents and a superb wilderness ambience, plus the chance for wildlife walks and drives and Maasai cultural activities.

ARUSHA
☎ 027

There are two faces to Arusha. One is impossible to miss – long lines of taxis and safari vehicles inching their way down single-spur Old Moshi Rd towards the Clock Tower roundabout during rush hour, the insistent buzzing of touts along Boma Rd, *sister, serengetisafarig oingtomorrow, justoneplaceleft, paynowandit-canbe yours, wantabatik? goodprice,* the low-rise jumble of 1950s-style Indian shops lining Sokoine Rd, the newspaper vendors trying to guess your nationality, *dutch? here, yesterday' spapergoodprice? heraldtribune, justUS$5, no, thenUS$3, howaboutUS$2.50,* and the brightly clad sidewalk mamas sitting in front of neatly stacked piles of mangos, papayas, bananas and oranges. Then, there's the town's more hidden face. The thick cloud mists that envelop the surrounding countryside on winter mornings, clearing to reveal the stately, perfectly shaped cone of Mt Meru rising over the landscape, the rich, moist, black soil that seems to sprout banana, coffee bushes and corn overnight, the narrow paths disappearing off the sides of the Moshi–Nairobi highway into dense forests of towering banana plants, the green-ness of everything, broken by splashes of orange from flowering tulip trees, neighbourhoods of aluminum-roofed houses joined by winding, muddy lanes, and churches packed with overflow crowds on Sundays and resounding with singing.

If records were kept, Arusha – perennially cool, at 1300m in altitude – would get top honours for being the town most visited by Tanzania travellers. Most are just passing through, en route to Serengeti National Park and the rest of the northern safari circuit, or organising a Kilimanjaro trek, but Arusha also makes an optimal stocking-up and chilling-out point.

Orientation
The small Naura River valley winds through town, with bus stations, the market and many budget hotels to the west, and upmarket hotels, the post office, immigration, government buildings, safari companies, airline offices, craft shops and the Arusha International Conference Centre (AICC) building to the east. The heart of Arusha, and about a 10- to 15-minute walk from the central bus station, is the Clock Tower roundabout, marked by a profusion of signs giving the distances to Cape Town, Cairo and other points along the Great North Rd. The Clock Tower is also where Arusha's two main roads meet – Sokoine Rd (which slides westwards into the Dodoma road) and Old Moshi Rd to the east.

MAPS
A good map of Arusha, widely available around town, is put out by **MaCo** (www.gtmaps .com). There are small, free photocopied town maps at the Tourist Information Centre.

Information
IMMIGRATION OFFICE
Immigration office (Simeon Rd; ☽ 7.30am-3.30pm Mon-Fri) Near the Makongoro Rd junction; visa extensions are usually processed while you wait.

INTERNET ACCESS
Cybernet Café (India St; per hr TSh1500; ☽ 9.30am-5pm Mon-Fri, 9.30am-1pm Sat)
Internet Café (Boma Rd; per hr TSh1000; ☽ 24hr) Located at the New Safari Hotel.
Internet Café (Sokoine Rd; per hr TSh1500; ☽ 7am-6.30pm Mon-Sat, 8.30am-2.30pm Sun) Located at Patisserie; also has wi-fi.

MEDICAL SERVICES & EMERGENCIES
Arusha Medical Centre (☎ 027-250 8020; Haile Selassie Rd, Plot 54; ☽ 24hr) Off Old Moshi Rd; lab tests and a doctor on call 24 hours.
Moona's Pharmacy (☎ 027-250 9800, 0713-510590; Sokoine Rd; ☽ 8.45am-5.30pm Mon-Fri, 8.45am-2pm Sat) Well-stocked pharmacy, west of NBC bank.

MONEY
In addition to the forex bureaus at Impala Hotel and other large hotels (most open on Sundays and until late on weekdays), there are many forex bureaus clustered around the northern end of Boma Rd, and along Joel Maeda St, near the Clock Tower. The best place to change travellers cheques is the Impala Hotel forex bureau.
Barclays Bank (Sopa Lodges Bldg, Serengeti Rd) ATM (Visa and MasterCard).

Exim Bank (cnr Sokoine & Goliondoi Rds) ATM (Visa, MasterCard, Cirrus and Maestro).

NBC Bank (Sokoine Rd) ATM (Visa); also changes travellers cheques.

Stanbic Bank (Sokoine Rd) ATM (Visa, MasterCard, Cirrus and Maestro).

Standard Chartered Bank (Goliondoi Rd) ATM (Visa).

POST
Main post office (Boma Rd)
Meru post office (Sokoine Rd)

TELEPHONE
TTCL (Boma Rd; ☺ 9am-4.30pm Mon-Fri, 9am-noon Sat) Sells phone cards for domestic and international calls using TTCL phones.

TOURIST INFORMATION
The travellers' bulletin board at the Tourist Information Centre is a good spot to find safari mates.

Ngorongoro Conservation Area Authority (NCAA) Information Office (☎ 027-254 4625; www.ngorongoro-crater-africa.org; Boma Rd; ☺ 8am-1pm & 2-5pm Mon-Fri, 8am-1pm Sat) Booklets on Ngorongoro and a relief map of the Ngorongoro Conservation Area.

Tanzania National Parks Headquarters (Tanapa; ☎ 027-250 3471/4082/8216; www.tanzaniaparks.com; Dodoma road) About 5km west of town.

Tanzania Tourist Board (TTB) Tourist Information Centre (☎ 027-250 3842/3; ttb-info@habari.co.tz; Boma Rd; ☺ 8am-4pm Mon-Fri, 8.30am-1pm Sat) Just up from the post office and the Clock Tower roundabout, with helpful staff, information on Arusha, the nearby parks and other attractions, and booking help for Cultural Tourism Programme tours (see p179 and boxed text, p180). Also has a 'blacklist' of tour operators and a list of registered tour companies.

TRAVEL AGENCIES
For listings of Arusha-based safari and trekking operators – most of which can also arrange itineraries elsewhere in the country – see p68.

Coastal Aviation (☎ 027-250 0087; arusha@coastal .cc; Boma Rd) Northern and southern circuit itineraries, Zanzibar and flight charters.

Rickshaw Travels (☎ 027-250 6655; www.rickshawtz .com; Sokoine Rd) Domestic and international flight bookings.

Dangers & Annoyances
Arusha is the worst place in Tanzania for street touts and slick tour operators who prey on the gullibility of newly arrived travellers by offering them safaris and treks at ridiculously low prices. Their main haunts include the central bus station, Boma and Goliondoi Rds, and near the budget hotels at the northern and western ends of town. Ensure that any tour company you sign up with is properly registered; get recommendations from other travellers and check the current 'blacklist' at the TTB Tourist Information Centre on Boma Rd. Also see boxed text, p68.

At night, take a taxi if you go out. It's not safe to walk after dusk, especially over the bridge on Old Moshi Rd near the Clock Tower. Even during the daytime, try to avoid carrying a bag, camera or anything that could tempt a thief.

Sights & Activities
The **Arusha Declaration Museum** (☎ 027-250 7800; www.museum.or.tz; Makongoro Rd; adult/student US$5/2; ☺ 9am-5.30pm) near the Uhuru monument has a display on postcolonial Tanzanian history, while the **Natural History Museum** (☎ 027-250 7540; www.museum.or.tz; Boma Rd; adult/student US$5/2; ☺ 9am-5.30pm Mon-Fri, 9.30am-5.30pm Sat & Sun), in the old German *boma*, has a few fossils and old photos. Other diversions include the colourful **market**, which is a good place to buy the tire-tread sandals worn by many Maasai as protection against thorns in the bush, and the many **cultural tourism programs** (see boxed text, p180) in the surrounding countryside.

It's still possible to observe the proceedings of the **UN International Criminal Tribunal for Rwanda** at the AICC building on Simeon Rd, which take place Monday to Thursday; admission is free but you'll need your passport.

Sleeping
BUDGET
Camping
Masai Camp (☎ 027-250 0358, 0754-829514; http://ma saicamp.tripod.com; camping US$5, banda per person with shared bathroom US$10, s/d with shared bathroom US$15/25; 💻) A long-time favourite, popular with overlanders, on the noisy side and an institution on the Arusha party scene, with expansive grounds, hot showers, pool tables, satellite TV, and a restaurant with pizzas, burgers and other meals until late, and a happening bar, especially on weekends. Tents and sleeping bags can be hired, and there are a few no-frills rooms. It's 3km southeast of the town centre off Old Moshi Rd (TSh2500 in a taxi), and also the base for Tropical Trails (see p68).

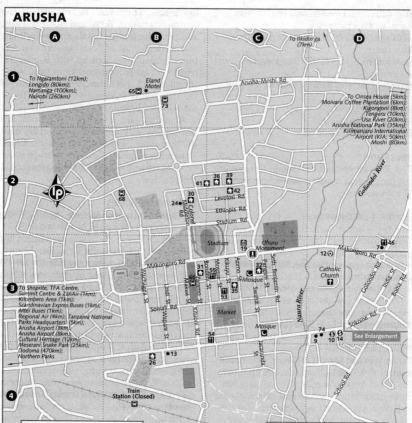

ARUSHA

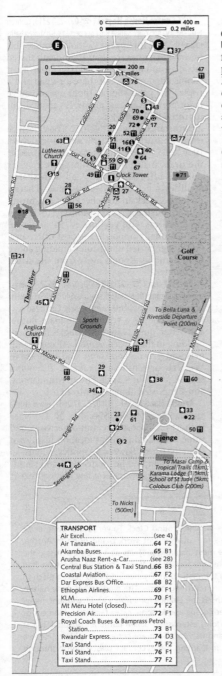

Meserani Snake Park (☎ 027-253 8282; www.mes eranisnakepark.com; camping incl admission to snake park US$10) An overlander-oriented place with good facilities, including hot showers, a vehicle repair shop and emergency rooms if you're ill. Meals are available for US$6. Short walks and camel rides in the surrounding Maasai area can be organised, and there's a snake park and a small Maasai cultural museum. It's 25km west of Arusha, just off the Dodoma road.

Guesthouses & Hotels – Colonel Middleton Rd Area

In the small dusty streets just east of Colonel Middleton Rd and north of the stadium (a 10-minute walk from the central bus station) is a clutch of cheap places offering no-frills rooms – most twin-bedded with nets and shared bathrooms (hot water available on request), and most without food. The area isn't great, but many travellers stay here because it's reasonably close to the bus station, and prices are among the lowest in town. While some of the accommodations are decent value, others let flycatchers onto their premises and should be avoided. Watch out for smooth talkers wanting to sell you safaris or trying to steer you to a hotel other than the one you've picked out.

Levolosi Guest House (s/d with shared bathroom TSh7000/10,000) Diagonally opposite the main Monjes Guesthouse building, with undistinguished although adequate rooms around an enclosed cement courtyard.

Kitundu Guesthouse (s/d with shared bathroom TSh7000/12,000, d TSh15,000) A decent, reliable choice, with clean, no-frills rooms, including a few with private bathroom.

Monjes Guesthouse (s with shared bathroom TSh10,000, d TSh15,000) This friendly establishment is among the better ones of the bunch, with clean, no-frills rooms with hot water. It's split between a main building and an annexe diagonally opposite.

Golden Rose (☎ 027-250 7959; Colonel Middleton Rd; s/d TSh30,000/45,000) Functional twin and double-bedded rooms – all with private bathroom and hot-water showers – in a convenient central location.

Guesthouses & Hotels – Market Area

These places are all in the busy central market area in the western part of town, marginally closer to the central bus station than the Colonel Middleton Rd area hotels, and generally a few steps up in both price and quality.

Kilimanjaro Villa Guest House (☎ 027-250 8109; Azimo St; s/d with shared bathroom TSh10,000/15,000) Well past its prime, with tatty but acceptable rooms and warm-ish water in the shared bathrooms. It's on a small side street a few blocks east of the central bus station. There's no food.

Arusha Backpackers (☎ 027-250 4474; www.arushabackpackers.co.tz; Sokoine Rd; s/d/q US$8/14/24; 🖳) Cheap, tidy rooms and clean shared facilities. However, most of the doubles have only interior windows, and a few have no windows at all. Several rooms have fans. There's also a two-bunk quad. It's managed by Kindoroko Hotel in Moshi.

Hotel Fort de Moines (☎ 027-250 7406, 027-254 8523; s/d US$25/30) The incongruously named Fort de Moines is a few steps up from the others in this category in both price and standard, with bland straightforward rooms with fans but no nets. It's good value if you're looking for a 'proper' hotel at budget prices.

Hotel 7-11 (☎ 027-250 1261; Zaramo St; s/d/tw US$25/30/35) Directly opposite the central bus station (look for the white multistorey building), with clean, albeit noisy rooms. The street outside is chaotic enough that it's only worth considering if you have an early morning departure.

Arusha Centre Inn (☎ 027-250 0421; s/d US$25/37) Next door to Hotel Fort de Moines, and nicer, with spotless rooms that are good value for the price, a restaurant and a location within easy walking distance of the central bus station.

Guesthouses & Hotels – Clock Tower Roundabout & Beyond

All of the following places are in the green and leafy and overall quieter eastern part of town. There are also budget rooms at L'Oasis Lodge (see opposite).

VTC Centre House Hostel (☎ 027-250 2313; cathcenterhouse@yahoo.com; Kanisa Rd; r per person with shared bathroom TSh10,000) Run by the Catholic diocese, this no-frills place has spacious rooms with shared facilities, and meals (TSh3000) on order. Most rooms are doubles, but there's a quad and a triple. The gates shut at 10pm unless you've made previous arrangements. It's about 300m in from Old Moshi Rd.

Lutheran Centre (☎ 027-250 8856/7; lutherancentre@yahoo.com; Boma Rd; s/tw with shared bathroom TSh20,000/35,000, tw with private bathroom TSh45,000) If the drab, institutional atmosphere doesn't put you off, rooms here – all with shared facilities – are quite decent value. There's no food. Check-in and check-out are during regular business hours Monday to Friday only, unless you've booked in advance. It's diagonally opposite the post office in a poorly signposted multistorey building above Café Bamboo. Rooms away from the street are quieter.

Everest Inn (☎ 027-250 8419, 0784-255277; everesttzus@yahoo.com; Old Moshi Rd; s/d/tr US$40/50/65) Clean, homey rooms behind the Everest Chinese restaurant. There's a triple in the main house, and better, quiet twins and doubles in a small building in the garden behind. All come with nets and private bathroom, and a choice of Western or Chinese breakfast. It's 500m southeast of the Clock Tower roundabout, and signposted along Old Moshi Rd.

Arusha Naaz Hotel (☎ 027-257 2087; www.arushanaaz.net; Sokoine Rd; s/d/tr US$45/60/75; 🗷 🖳) Naaz is short on atmosphere, but otherwise good value, with a convenient location just down from the Clock Tower and spotless rooms, all with TV, fan and hot water. Size and standards vary, so check out a few. Downstairs is

---

PLASTER HOUSE

Well away from the long line of safari vehicles inching around Clock Tower roundabout, away from the touts and cafés on Boma Rd, there's lots of excellent work being done in Arusha, though it rarely makes the spotlight. One of the most inspiring projects we've come across is the **Plaster House** (www.plasterhouse.org), a long-term care facility for Maasai children who have had major orthopaedic surgery or surgery following traumatic burn injuries, and who need a place to recover and get essential physical therapy before returning home. The work being done here is life changing in the best sense of the word: without the chance for surgery and treatment, many of these children would remain severely disabled for life and in some cases face abandonment or worse. The Plaster House is affiliated with the long-established Selian Lutheran Hospital, but is dependent on donations to continue and expand its work. Staff are currently unable to receive independent visitors, but if you are interested in learning more, contact plaster house through the email on their website.

a restaurant with inexpensive breakfasts, a good-value daily except Sunday lunch buffet, and a car-rental office.

Outpost Lodge (☎ 027-254 8405; www.outposttanzania.com; Serengeti Rd; 6-bed dm US$25, s/d/tr US$48/66/78; 🖥 🕿) The Outpost, in a leafy residential area 500m off Old Moshi Rd and about 1km southeast of the Clock Tower roundabout, has a few dorm-style rooms in an old two-storey house, plus small and pleasant detached garden bungalows scattered around the lawns. All have nets and TV, and there's a restaurant and a tiny gym.

MIDRANGE

Le Jacaranda (☎ 027-254 4624; www.chez.com/jacaranda; s/d/tr US$45/50/70) Spacious, pleasantly faded rooms in a large house set in pretty gardens, and a restaurant (meals from TSh7000). It's on a quiet side street about 100m north of Old Moshi Rd at the eastern end of town.

L'Oasis Lodge & Restaurant (☎ 027-250 7089; www.loasislodge.com; s/d/tr US$79/97/127, backpackers r per person with shared bathroom US$20; 🖥 🕿) A mix of African-style rondavels and stilt houses set around large gardens, plus a dozen clean, twin-bedded backpacker rooms sharing hot-water bathrooms. There's also a good restaurant, a sports bar and a tree-house dining-drinking area. Accommodation prices include full breakfast, and there are discounts for Peace Corps, VSOs and other volunteers for the nonbackpacker rooms. An amenable overall combination, and a good place to get introduced to Arusha. It's 2km northwest of the Clock Tower, about 1km off the Moshi–Nairobi road and signposted diagonally opposite the old Mt Meru Hotel.

Impala Hotel (☎ 027-250 8448/51, 027-250 2362; www.impalahotel.com; cnr Moshi & Old Moshi Rds; s/d US$80/100; 🍴 🖥 🕿) This is a long-standing, reliable and centrally located place, with a forex bureau, several restaurants and a small garden area. The showers are hot, breakfasts good, staff efficient and credit cards are accepted.

New Safari Hotel (☎ 027-250 3261; www.thenewsafarihotel.com; Boma Rd; s/d/tr US$85/105/135; 🍴 🖥) Good-value rooms catering to business travellers in a centrally located high-rise, plus a restaurant, secure parking and 24-hour internet access.

Karama Lodge (☎ 0754-475188; www.karama-lodge.com; s/d US$100/135; 🖥) Karama, on a forested hillside in the Suye Hill area just south of town, has about two dozen rustic and very lovely stilt bungalows with verandas and

views to both Kilimanjaro and Meru on clear days. There are short walking trails, a good restaurant, which also caters to vegetarians, and (soon) a spa. Follow Old Moshi Rd south about 2km from the edge of town to the signpost; turn left and continue 1.5km further.

Moivaro Coffee Plantation (☎ 027-255 3242/3; www.moivaro.com; s/d US$110/150; 🖥 🕿) Set amid the coffee plantations outside of Arusha, with cottages, each with its own fireplace, set in extensive gardens. It's 5km east of town along the road to Moshi, then about 2km off the highway along a signposted, unpaved road. Day rooms are also available.

TOP END

Kibo Palace Hotel (☎ 027-254 4472; www.kibopalacehotel.com; Old Moshi Rd; s/d from US$145/165; 🖥 🕿) The new Kibo Palace has lovely, well-appointed rooms, a restaurant, and a pool in small, green grounds.

African Tulip (☎ 027-254 3004/5; www.theafricantulip.com; Serengeti Rd; s/d US$135/170, ste from US$290; 🍴 🖥 🕿) Classy, good-value and impeccably appointed rooms – all with wi-fi, cable TV and minifridge, and some with their own terrace – and lovely carved-wood décor in the common areas. It's conveniently located on a green, quiet side street off Old Moshi Rd. Downstairs is a good restaurant and a genteel bar, and surrounding is a small, well-tended garden. The hotel is run by Roy Safaris, and favourably priced safari-accommodation packages are offered.

Onsea House (www.onseahouse.com; s/d US$145/175; 🕿) A small place self-described with some accuracy as the 'best luxury bed and breakfast in Arusha'. Each room has its own theme, there's a bar, an excellent restaurant and gardens. Very tranquil and very classy. The turn-off is signposted along the Moshi road about 4km from town, from where it's another 1km or so further.

Kigongoni (☎ 027-255 3087; www.kigongoni.net; s/d US$165/230; 🕿) Kigongoni has a tranquil hilltop perch about 8km outside Arusha, spacious cottages with porches and large bathtubs, and a cosy common area with fireplaces and reading nooks, plus a restaurant. Birding and village walks are possible in the surrounding area, and a portion of the lodge's profits go to support a nearby clinic for mentally disabled children. Follow the Moshi road east for 8km to the signposted turn-off, from where it's another 1km.

Arusha Hotel (☎ 027-250 7777/8870; www.thearusha hotel.com; Clock Tower roundabout; r from US$200; 💻 💷) The Arusha Hotel (formerly the New Arusha Hotel) has been completely renovated and is a recommended centrally located choice in this category. Rooms are of a high standard, there's a restaurant with a daily lunch buffet (TSh15,000) and attractive gardens behind.

Eating

Geekay's Take-Away (India St; meals from TSh1000; ⏰ 7.30am-6pm Mon-Sat) For local flavour try this place, with inexpensive plates of rice, *ugali* and sauce.

Arusha Naaz Hotel (☎ 027-257 2087; www.arusha naaz.net; Sokoine Rd; lunch buffet US$5; ⏰ lunch Mon-Sat) There's a great-value lunch buffet at this hotel, with mostly Indian and Tanzanian cuisine.

Old Rock Restaurant (Mosque St; meals TSh2000-5000) Near the main market, clean and no-frills, with burgers and local-style meals.

Big Y Bar & Grill (☎ 0787-778395; big-y@habari.com; meals TSh2000-5000; ⏰ 10am-midnight) Known especially for its *nyama choma* (barbecued meat), this is a good stop for local vibes and ambience. Also on the menu are other local favourites, such as *nyama na ndizi* (green banana and meat stew), *kuku nazi na wali* (coconut chicken and rice) and *ngombe masala* (marinated beef). There's sports TV and a bar area, or quieter seating upstairs. It's reached from the Moshi–Arusha road via an unsignposted turn-off opposite the old Mt Meru hotel, from where it's about 1.5km further.

Watamu Swahili Restaurant (☎ 0752-022677; watamu@gmail.com; Multichoice Bldg, Moshi Rd; meals TSh3500-6000; ⏰ breakfast, lunch & dinner) Small and spotless, with inexpensive Tanzanian cuisine and both indoor and outdoor seating.

Sazan (Old Moshi Rd; meals TSh5000-6000) A tiny place, directly on the roadside adjoining a used-car lot, with inexpensive Japanese fast food–style meals.

Khan's Barbecue (Mosque St; mixed grill from TSh6000; ⏰ from 6.30pm) This Arusha institution – 'Chicken on the Bonnet' – is an auto-spares shop by day and a popular barbecue by night, with a heaping spread of grilled, skewered meat and salads. Look for the Zubeda Auto Spares sign.

Jambo's Makuti Bar & Restaurant (Boma Rd; meals from TSh6000; ⏰ to 10pm) European café vibes in a Tanzanian setting. There's an à la carte menu with a mix of Tanzanian and local dishes, and a plate of the day for about TSh5500.

Jambo's Coffee House (Boma Rd; snacks from Tsh1500) Next door to Jambo's Makuti Bar & Restaurant, this place has cakes, snacks and good coffee.

Via Via (meals TSh5000-8000; ⏰ 9.30am-10pm Fri-Wed, until midnight Thu, closed Sun) Set in quiet gardens behind the Natural History Museum, this laid-back place is a popular meeting spot, with salads, sandwiches, fresh bread, cakes, yoghurt and light meals (a mixture of local and European fare), plus a bar and live music on Thursdays from 9pm.

Blue Heron (50 Haile Selassie Rd; light meals about TSh6000; ⏰ 8.30am-5pm Mon-Fri, 8.30am-4pm Sat) Pasta dishes, sandwiches, ice cream and other light meals, plus crafts for sale. It's in a private house overlooking green lawns, and a break from the bustle of town.

Arusha Masai Café (☎ 0755-765640; info@warm heartart.com; Simeon Rd; meals from TSh6500) Pasta dishes and excellent pizzas. It's opposite the AICC building.

Everest Inn (☎ 027-250 8419; everesttzus@yahoo .com; Old Moshi Rd; meals from TSh7000; ⏰ breakfast, lunch & dinner) Tasty Chinese food served in an outdoor garden, or indoors in an old, atmospheric house.

Dragon Pearl (☎ 027-254 4107; Old Moshi Rd; meals TSh7000-TSh10,000; ⏰ lunch & dinner) Delicious Chinese food, with a garden setting, fast service and an attentive host. It's around the corner from Impala Hotel.

Impala Hotel (☎ 027-250 8448/51; www.impala hotel.com; cnr Moshi & Old Moshi Rds; meals from TSh7000) There are several eateries here, with the open-air Indian restaurant the best of the bunch, with tandoori and veg choices and more.

Lounge (☎ 027-250 7089; L'Oasis Lodge & Restaurant; meals from TSh8000; ⏰ from 10am until late) Homemade tagliatelle, gourmet wraps, crispy salads, meat and seafood grills, pizzas and 'Kilimanjaro nachos'. Everything is freshly made and served in generously large portions against a backdrop of lounge seating and music. It's at L'Oasis Lodge on the northern edge of town.

Pepe's (Kanisa Rd; pizza from TSh6000, mains TSh8000-15,000; ⏰ lunch & dinner) Outdoor garden seating or indoors under a large, covered pavilion, serving well-prepared Italian and continental food, and (evenings) Indian cuisine. It's 500m off Old Moshi Rd and signposted.

For inexpensive burgers, pizza, sandwiches and other Western-style fast food try the **Patisserie** (Sokoine Rd; snacks & meals from TSh1500;

7.30am-6.30pm Mon-Sat, 8.30am-2pm Sun), which also has soup, light meals and an internet café; **McMoody's** (Sokoine Rd; meals from Tsh2000; 11am-10pm Tue-Sun), with mostly burgers; and a branch of the South African chain, **Steers** (Joel Maeda St; meals from Tsh2500).

On the edge of town adjoining Shoprite is the TFA Centre, with gelato and gourmet coffee shops, and the recommended **Vama Restaurant** (0784-326325; vamarestaurant@yahoo .co.uk; TFA Centre, Dodoma road; meals from TSh9000), with delicious north Indian cuisine.

For self-caterers:

Shoprite (TFA Centre, Dodoma road; 9am-7pm Mon-Fri, 8am-5pm Sat, 9am-1pm Sun) About 2km west of the town centre.

Clocktower Supermarket (Clock Tower roundabout)

Drinking & Entertainment

Via Via (Boma Rd) A good spot for a drink and also for finding out about upcoming music and traditional dance events; it's in the grounds of the Natural History Museum.

Greek Club (cnr Old Moshi & Serengeti Rds; closed Mon & Thu) A popular expat hang-out, especially on weekend evenings; it has free movies on Sunday afternoons, good pizza and a lively sports bar.

Nick's (Njiro Hill Rd, Njiro; from 6pm) Popular with locals and expats, with drinks, a great crowd and good *nyama choma*.

Colobus Club (Old Moshi Rd; admission TSh5000; 9pm-dawn Fri & Sat) Arusha's loudest and brashest nightclub.

Shopping

The small alley just off Joel Maeda St is lined with vendors selling woodcarvings, batiks, Maasai jewellery and other crafts. Quality is generally good, but hard bargaining is required.

Other places to try include the following:

Craft Shop (027-254 8565; Goliondoi Rd) Near Joel Maeda St, with mostly carvings.

Cultural Heritage (Dodoma Rd) Large and unmissable, 12km west of town. Quality and selection are good, although middlemen get a fairly large cut of the (high) purchase prices.

Aminata Boutique (Sokoine Rd) Located in the covered entry passage to Arusha Naaz Hotel and selling textiles.

Shanga Shangaa (www.shanga.org) A cooperative for disabled artists, marketing its lovely beaded necklaces at various spots around town, including the craft shop at Blue Heron (opposite).

Colourful local-produce markets include the **Ngaramtoni market** (Nairobi road), on Thursday and Sunday, 12km north of town, which draws Maasai from miles around; and the **Tengeru market** (Moshi road), 10km east of town, on Saturday, with a smaller market on Wednesday.

Getting There & Away
AIR

There are daily flights to Dar es Salaam and Zanzibar (ZanAir, Coastal Aviation, Precision Air and Air Tanzania), Nairobi (Kenya; Precision Air), Seronera and other airstrips in Serengeti National Park (Coastal Aviation, Air Excel, Regional Air); Mwanza (Precision Air, via Shinyanga), and Lake Manyara and Tarangire National Parks (Coastal Aviation, Air Excel, Regional Air). Some flights use Kilimanjaro International Airport (KIA), about halfway between Moshi and Arusha off the main highway, while others leave from Arusha airport, 8km west of town along the Dodoma road; verify the departure point when buying your ticket. International airlines flying into KIA include KLM and Ethiopian Air, and it's rumoured that British Airways may soon start this route as well. Some sample prices: Arusha–Dar es Salamm (from TSh185,000), Arusha–Mwanza (TSh250,000 to TSh300,000), Arusha–Seronera (US$175) and Kilimanjaro–Kigali (US$210).

Airline offices in Arusha include the following:

Air Excel (027-254 8429, 027-250 1597; reservations@ airexcelonline.com; 2nd fl, Subzali (Exim Bank) Bldg, Goliondoi Rd) Diagonally opposite Standard Chartered Bank.

Air Tanzania (027-250 3201, 027-250 3203; www .airtanzania.com; Boma Rd)

Coastal Aviation (027-250 0087; 0754-317808; arusha@coastal.cc; Boma Rd)

Ethiopian Airlines (027-250 6167, 027-250 4231; www.ethiopianairlines.com; Boma Rd)

KLM (027-250 8062/3; reservations.arusha@klm.com; Boma Rd)

Precision Air (027-250 2818/2836; www.precision airtz.com; Boma Rd; 8am-5pm Mon-Fri, 8am-2pm Sat & Sun) Also handles Kenya Airways bookings.

Regional Air (027-250 4477, 027-250 4164; www .regionaltanzania.com; Nairobi road)

Rwandair Express (0732-978558; www.rwandair.com; Sokoine Rd) Just up from Moona's Pharmacy.

ZanAir (027-254 8877; www.zanair.com; Ground fl, Summit Centre, Dodoma road)

BUS

Arusha's central bus station is near the market, although several of the major lines – Dar Express, Royal Coach, Scandinavian Express and Akamba – have their own booking offices and departure points (details following). It's worth taking these lines just to avoid the fray at the central bus station, which is chaotic and a popular haunt for flycatchers and touts; watch your luggage, and don't negotiate any safari deals at the station. If you're arriving for the first time, head straight for a taxi or duck into the lobby of Hotel 7-11, directly across the street, to get your bearings.

If you're arriving at the central bus station (and unless you're staying in the central budget-hotel area, in which case it makes sense to stay on the bus), you can avoid the bus station altogether by asking the driver to drop you off in front of the (currently closed) Mt Meru Hotel. All buses coming from Dar es Salaam and Moshi pass by here. There are taxis just opposite, and the scene, while still the usual rough and tumble, is considerably less hectic than at the central bus station. Fares from here to central hotels shouldn't be more than about TSh3000. When leaving Arusha, the best thing to do is book your ticket the day before, so that in the morning when you arrive with your luggage you can get straight on your bus and avoid dealing with the touts. For pre-dawn buses, take a taxi to the central bus station and ask the driver to drop you directly at your bus. Despite what you may hear, there are no luggage fees (unless you have an extraordinarily large pack).

Dar es Salaam

The main bus lines to/from Dar es Salaam (about nine hours) include the following. All depart from and arrive at their own offices.

Dar Express (Wachagga St) Located several blocks north of Meru post office and Arusha Backpackers, on the left. Tickets cost TSh20,000 to TSh25,000; buses depart from Arusha at 5.15am and 6am sharp and, with luck, arrive in Dar es Salaam in time to catch the 4.15pm ferry to Zanzibar. If you're trying to do this, don't get off at Ubungo bus station in Dar es Salaam, but stay on the bus until it terminates at its offices in the city centre near Kisutu, from where it's about 10 minutes in a taxi to the ferry docks. If the bus is running behind schedule from Arusha, it's occasionally faster to get off at Ubungo and get a taxi from there straight to the ferry dock, but only marginally so, and the taxi from Ubungo will cost you several times as much. Other departures from Arusha are at 7am, 8am, 9am and 9.30am.

Royal Coach (cnr Nairobi & Colonel Middleton Rds) Tickets cost TSh22,000; departures at 9am from Bamprass petrol station on the Nairobi road in Mianzini.

Scandinavian Express (small side street branching off Sokoine Rd opposite Shoprite/TFA Centre) Tickets cost TSh20,000/25,000 (ordinary/luxury), with ordinary and luxury departures at 8.30am and a second luxury bus at 11.30am.

Moshi

Buses and minibuses run throughout the day between Arusha and Moshi (about TSh2000, one hour). It's pricier but safer and more comfortable to take one of the Arusha–Nairobi (Kenya) shuttles (p259; per resident/nonresident TSh5000/US$10 between Moshi and Arusha).

Nairobi (Kenya)

For information on this route see p259. Akamba buses to Nairobi en route from Dar es Salaam depart Arusha at about 2.30pm from next to Eland Motel in Mianzini, along the Nairobi road.

Babati, Kolo, Kondoa & Dodoma

Mtei line buses run three to four times daily between Arusha and Babati (TSh6000, four hours). Departures are between 6am and 2pm from the Mtei booking office next to the Scandinavian Express booking office in the Kilombero area near Shoprite. The 6am bus continues on to Kondoa (TSh12,000, seven hours). Otherwise, for Kondoa and Dodoma (about 12 hours) you'll need to change vehicles at Babati, as most transport to Dodoma uses the longer tarmac route via Chalinze. This generally involves an overnight in Babati, as most southward transport from Babati departs early in the morning.

Musoma & Mwanza

Most lines, including Mohammed Trans, now use the route via Singida and Shinyanga along a long but vastly improved road (TSh45,000, 12 to 13 hours). It's also possible to go via Nairobi (Kenya) and Musoma (TSh47,000 plus US$20 for a Kenyan transit visa, 20 hours) on Akamba, departing from Arusha at about 3.30pm.

Lushoto

Fasaha and Chikito line buses depart daily from the Central Bus Station at about 6.30am (TSh10,000, six hours). However, it often works out just as fast (although more expensively) to take an express bus heading for Dar es Salaam as far as Mombo, and then get local transport from there to Lushoto.

Tanga

Tashriff and Ngoryka line buses depart daily from Arusha's Central Bus Station for Tanga by about 8.30am (TSh15,000 seven hours).

Getting Around

TO/FROM KILIMANJARO INTERNATIONAL AIRPORT

Air Tanzania and Precision Air have shuttles to KIA for their passengers, departing from their offices about two hours before the scheduled flight departure (free for Air Tanzania; TSh10,000 for Precision Air).

The standard price for taxis from town to KIA is US$50, though it should be possible to bargain this down a bit.

TO/FROM ARUSHA AIRPORT

Any *dalla-dalla* heading out along the Dodoma road can drop you at the junction, from where you'll have to walk about 1.5km to the airstrip. Taxis from town charge from TSh10,000.

CAR & MOTORCYCLE

For a selection of 2WD and 4WD vehicles, **Arusha Naaz Rent-a-Car** (☎ 027-250 2087; www.arusha naaz.net) is a reliable outfit based at Arusha Naaz Hotel. Self-drive rentals can sometimes be arranged for Arusha town rentals only. Rates (US$80 to US$120 per day for 4WD) include 120 free kilometres per day.

TAXI

There are taxi stands around the central bus station, opposite the old Mt Meru Hotel, at Arusha Hotel and New Safari Hotel, and at the eastern end of Makongoro Rd. Town rides cost from TSh2000.

AROUND ARUSHA
Cultural Tourism Programs

The following is just a sampling of the various cultural tourism programs on offer in the area around Arusha; for more details and for bookings, go to the Tanzania Tourist Board (TTB) Tourist Information Centre (p171) in Arusha, and see boxed text, p180.

Ng'iresi A village about 7km northeast of Arusha on the slopes of Mt Meru where you can visit local irrigation projects and Maasai homes, plus do some walking and visit a local farm.

Longido Hike to the top of Mt Longido (2629m, eight to 10 hours return from the main road), and visit a Maasai cattle market at this village, about 80km north of Arusha.

Ilkidin'ga Walks (ranging from half-day strolls to a three-day 'cultural hike') and the chance to experience the traditional culture of the Arusha people around Ilkidin'ga, 7km north of Arusha.

Mkuru Camel safaris in Maasai areas from Mkuru village, near Arusha National Park. Also see www.mkurucamelsafari.com.

Mulala About 30km northeast of Arusha, and implemented completely by women. The program involves visits to a local womens' cooperative and some short walks.

Usa River

This tiny, nondescript village, on the Arusha–Moshi road about 20km east of Arusha, is of interest for its proximity to Arusha National Park, and for the handful of atmospheric, upmarket lodges based in the lushly vegetated surrounding area. All are signposted from the main road.

Rivertrees Country Inn (☎ 027-255 3894; www .rivertrees.com; s/d from US$145/175; 🖳) has a genteel old-world ambience and excellent cuisine served family-style around a large wooden dining table. Accommodation is in the main building – a renovated colonial-era farmhouse – or in garden rooms, or two private 'river cottages' with fireplaces and one with wheelchair access.

The nearby **Ngare Sero Mountain Lodge** (☎ 027-255 3638; www.ngare-sero-lodge.com; per person full board garden cottage/main house US$150/200) is another lovely lodge – once a colonial-era farming estate – set in lush, flowering gardens. Accommodation is in small, attached garden cottages or in more expansive suites in the atmospheric main house. There are also two family-style cottages, and fishing, walking, canoeing, cultural tours and yoga can be arranged.

ARUSHA NATIONAL PARK
☎ 027

Although it's one of Tanzania's smallest parks, Arusha National Park is one of its most beautiful and topographically varied. Its main features are Ngurdoto Crater, the Momela Lakes and Mt Meru. The park has a variety of vegetation zones supporting many animal species, and wildlife viewing is usually quite rewarding, though on a smaller scale than in the other northern parks. You'll probably see zebras, giraffes, elephants, klipspringers

TANZANIA

and buffaloes. There are no lions, however, and no rhinos due to poaching. On the more positive side, there are no tsetse flies, and no malaria-carrying mosquitoes.

The **Momela Lakes** are particularly good for bird-watching. Like many in the Rift Valley, they are shallow and alkaline and attract a wide variety of wader birds. The lakes are fed by underground streams; due to their varying mineral content, each lake supports a different type of algal growth, which gives them different colours. Birdlife also varies quite distinctly from one lake to another, even where they are only separated by a narrow strip of land.

While you can see much of the park in a day, it's better to allow at least a night or two to appreciate the wildlife and do a walking safari.

Information

Entry fees are US$35/10 per adult/child, and can only be paid at the gate with a Visa card. There is a US$20 rescue fee per person per trip for treks on Mt Meru. Guides cost US$15 per day (US$20 for walking), and the huts on Mt Meru cost US$20.

The main park entrance is at Ngongongare Gate, about 10km from the main road, while **park headquarters** (☎ 027-255 3995, 0732-971303; ⏰ 6.30am-6.30pm) – the main contact for making camp site or resthouse reservations and for arranging guides and porters to climb Mt Meru – are about 14km further in near Momela Gate. There is another entrance at

Ngurdoto Gate, on the southeastern edge of the park. All gates are open from 6am to 6pm. Walking is permitted on the Mt Meru side of the park, and there is also a walking trail along part of the Ngurdoto Crater rim (though it's not permitted to descend either on foot or in a vehicle to the crater floor). **Green Footprint Adventures** (www.greenfootprint.co.tz) does canoe safaris on the Momela Lakes.

The best map of the park is the MaCo *Arusha National Park* map, widely available in Arusha.

There's nowhere in the park to buy food or petrol.

Sleeping & Eating

The park has four **public camp sites** (camping adult/child US$30/5) – three near Momela Gate (including one with a shower), and one near Ngurdoto Gate.

Momella Wildlife Lodge (☎ 027-250 6423/6; www.lions-safari-intl.com/momella.html; s/d/tr half board US$70/93/115) This long-standing establishment, 1.5km off the road from Momela Gate, has small, serviceable cottages set around modest gardens, and a vehicle for rent for visiting the park.

Meru View Lodge (☎ 0784-419232; www.meru-view-lodge.de; s/d US$90/130; 🖳 🖭) An unassuming, good-value place with a mix of large and small cottages (all priced the same) set in pleasant grounds on the main park road. A vehicle safari costs from US$90 per day, including park fees.

SEEING ANOTHER SIDE OF TANZANIA: CULTURAL TOURISM PROGRAMS

Numerous villages outside Arusha have organised 'cultural tourism programs' that offer an alternative to the safari scene and an opportunity to experience local culture. They range in length from a few hours to a few days, and usually centre around light hikes and cultural activities.

Although some have now deviated from their initial founding purpose of serving as income generators for community projects – often revolving instead these days around the enterprising individuals who run them – they nevertheless offer a fine chance to get to know Tanzania at the local level. Most have various 'modules' available, from half a day to several nights, and fees are generally reasonable, starting from TSh20,000/30,000 per person for a half-/full-day program with lunch (less for two or more people). Payments should be made on site; always ask for a receipt. For overnight tours, camping or home stays can be arranged, though expect conditions to be very basic and rustic.

All tours in the Arusha area can be booked through the Tanzania Tourist Board (TTB) Tourist Information Centre (p171) in Arusha, which can also tell you the best transport connections. Tours elsewhere should be arranged directly with the local coordinator, although the Arusha TTB may also be able to help. Book a day in advance for the more distant ones; for Ng'iresi and other programs close to town, guides usually wait at the TTB office on stand-by each morning. Check with the TTB to ensure the one you go with is authorised.

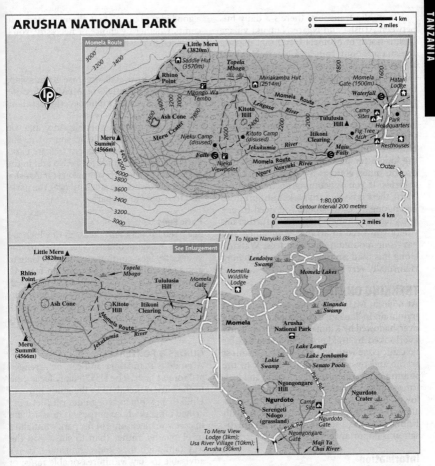

ARUSHA NATIONAL PARK

Hatari Lodge (☎ 027-255 3456/7; www.hatarilodge .com; r per person full board US$280) Upmarket and atmospheric – the property was originally owned by Hardy Kruger, of *Hatari!* film fame – with 'modern retro' room décor, a prime location on large lawns frequented by giraffes, and views of Meru and Kilimanjaro on clear days. Rooms are spacious, with large windows, and there's a fireplace and top-notch cuisine. It's on the edge of the park, about 2km north of Momela Gate.

Getting There & Away

Arusha National Park gate is 35km from Arusha. Take the main road between Arusha and Moshi until you reach the signboard, where you turn left. From here, it's about 10km to Ngongongare Gate, where you pay your fees. This is also where the road divides, with both forks joining up again at Momela Gate.

Transport from Arusha can be arranged with all of the lodges (about US$100 per vehicle for a drop, and about double this for an all-inclusive one-day safari). If you arrive at the park without your own vehicle, most of the lodges can arrange wildlife-viewing drives for guests from about US$70 per day, transport only. If you arrive with your own vehicle and want to climb Mt Meru, you can leave it at Momela Gate (where you will have to pay standard park fees) or, less expensively, at Momella Wildlife Lodge. Once in the park, there's a good series of gravel roads and tracks leading to all the main features and viewing points.

Via public transport, there's a daily bus between Arusha and Ngare Nanyuki village (10km north of Momela Gate) that departs Arusha at about 1pm and Ngare Nanyuki at 7am, and can drop you at the park gate (TSh2000, 1½ hours). Otherwise, you could take any bus between Arusha and Moshi, and get off at Usa River village, 1km east of the park junction. From Usa River there are sporadic pick-ups that run most days through the park en route to Ngare Nanyuki. However, unless you've arranged with one of the lodges for pick-up, these options won't do you much good as the park doesn't rent vehicles. If you're planning on trekking Mt Meru, there is no onward park transport from Ngongongare Gate, where you need to pay entry fees, to Momela Gate, 14km further on, where you need to arrange your guide and pay your mountain-climbing fees. Walking along this road isn't permitted, and hitching is normally very slow.

TREKKING ON MT MERU

At 4566m, Mt Meru is the second-highest mountain in Tanzania. Although completely overshadowed by Kilimanjaro and frequently overlooked by trekkers, it is a spectacular volcanic cone with one of East Africa's most scenic and rewarding climbs. A trek to the summit takes you through grassland and lush forest on the mountain's lower slopes, followed by a dramatic and exhilarating walk along the knife edge of the crater rim. As with Kilimanjaro, it's a serious trek and acclimatisation is important.

Information

The Momela route is the only route up Meru. It starts at Momela Gate on the eastern side of the mountain and goes to the summit along the northern arm of the horseshoe crater. The route can be done comfortably in four days and three nights (recommended), although trekkers sometimes do it in three days by combining Stages 3 and 4. It is detailed in Lonely Planet's *Trekking in East Africa*.

There are two large bunkhouses (Miriakamba and Saddle Huts), conveniently spaced for a three- or four-day trek. At Saddle Hut there's also a newly constructed bunkhouse block with individual four-bed rooms. However, all the bunkhouses operate on a first-come, first-served basis, and during the high season often fill up. For this reason, it's a good idea to carry a tent, though even if you camp, whether by choice or necessity, you'll still need to pay hut fees.

COSTS

Most companies that organise Kilimanjaro treks also organise treks on Mt Meru. See p68 for listings. Rates for a four-day trip cost about US$450 to US$650.

Organised treks are not obligatory, and you can do things quite easily on your own. The main costs for an independent trek are park-entrance, hut and guide fees. Also add in the costs of food (which you should get in Arusha, as there's nowhere to stock up near the park) and transport to the park.

Park Fees

See p180 for park entry fees, all of which are payable at Ngongongare Gate. After paying your entry fees, continue to Momela Gate to arrange a guide and pay mountain fees. All this can take a couple of hours, so it's worth getting an early start or making arrangements the afternoon before. If you enter the park at Ngurdoto Gate, you can pay your entry fees there.

GUIDES & PORTERS

A guide is mandatory and can be arranged at Momela Gate. The US$20 daily fee is paid to the park rather than to the guide himself. Unlike on Kilimanjaro, guides on Meru are armed rangers whose purpose is to assist you in case you meet some of the park's buffaloes or elephants, rather than to show you the way (although they know the route), so it's advisable to stay within reasonable range of your guide.

Porters, whose services are optional, are also available at Momela Gate for US$5 per porter per day, though most trekkers go up with only a guide. The fee is paid at the gate and given to the porters after the trip. You also have to pay park-entrance (TSh1500) and hut fees for porters (TSh800 per night). Porters will carry packs weighing up to 15kg, not including their own food and clothing.

Guides on Mt Meru receive a fixed monthly salary for their work as rangers, and get no additional payment from the park for guiding. In fact, without tips a guide has little extra incentive to take you to the summit, so it's worth calculating tips as part of your fixed costs. Make it clear to the guide that you'll tip, but that payment is conditional on him guiding you at an appropriate pace to the summit. We've heard all-too-frequent reports of poorly motivated guides rushing their clients on the early stages of the climb, with the result that the trekkers themselves are forced to bail out before reaching the top. As a guideline, for a good guide who has gone with you to the summit, plan on from about TSh15,000 per day per group. Porter tips for a standard trek average about TSh7000 per porter.

Momela Route

STAGE 1: MOMELA GATE TO MIRIAKAMBA HUT

(10km, 4-5hr, 1000m ascent)

There's a choice of two routes from Momela Gate. The more interesting one is a track going through the forest towards the crater floor and then steeply up to Miriakamba Hut (2514m), although to use this route you'll need to start your trek before 10am. The second, shorter option climbs gradually through the grassland to Miriakamba, and makes a good descent route. Some guides prefer to go up and down the shorter route, and it may require some persuading to take the forest route.

STAGE 2: MIRIAKAMBA HUT TO SADDLE HUT

(4km, 2-3hr, 1050m ascent)

From Miriakamba the path climbs steeply up through pleasant glades between the trees to reach Topela Mbogo (Buffalo Swamp) and Mgongo Wa Tembo (Elephant Ridge), from where there are good views into the crater and up to the cliffs below the summit. It continues through some open grassy clearings and over several stream beds (usually dry) to Saddle Hut (3570m). There are side trips from Saddle Hut to Little Meru (3820m) and to Rhino Point, both of which offer impressive views of Meru's Ash Cone.

STAGE 3: SADDLE HUT TO MERU SUMMIT & DESCENT

(5km, 4-5hr, 1000m ascent; 5km, 2-3hr, 1000m descent)

This stage, along a very narrow ridge between the outer slopes of the mountain and the sheer cliffs of the inner crater, is one of the most dramatic and exhilarating sections of trekking anywhere in East Africa. During the rainy season, ice and snow can occur on this section of the route, so take care.

From Saddle Hut, the path goes across a flat area, then steeply up through bushes before giving way to bare rock and ash. Rhino Point is marked by a cairn and a pile of bones. From Rhino Point the path drops slightly then rises again to climb steeply around the edge of the rim over ash scree and bare rock patches. Continue for three to four hours to reach Meru summit.

If the sunrise is your main interest but you're not keen on attempting this section in the dark, the views at dawn are just as impressive from Rhino Point, about an hour from Saddle Hut.

STAGE 4: SADDLE HUT TO MOMELA GATE

(9km, 3-5½hr, 2000m descent)

From Saddle Hut, retrace the Stage 2 route to Miriakamba (1½ to 2½ hours). From Miriakamba, you can either return through the forest (2½ to three hours), or take a shorter route down the ridge directly to Momela Gate (1½ to 2½ hours).

LAKE MANYARA NATIONAL PARK

☎ 027

Among the attractions of the often underrated Lake Manyara National Park are its birdlife, its elusive tree-climbing lions, its abundance of hippos and its setting beneath the dramatic western escarpment of the Rift Valley.

Information

Entry fees are US$35/10 per adult/child. The park gate and **park headquarters** (☎ 027-253 9112/45; manyara@tanapa.org, manyarapark@africaonline .co.tz) are at the northern tip of the park near Mto Wa Mbu village, where there is also a helpful tourist information office and a visitors centre. MaCo and Harms-ic put out park maps, available at the park gate, together with a bird checklist.

Hoopoe Safaris (p68) offers upmarket cycling and cycling-safari combination trips in the Lake Manyara area. **Green Footprint Adventures** (www.greenfootprint.co.tz; Lake Manyara Serena Lodge) organises village walks, mountain biking and forest hikes around Lake Manyara, all upmarket, plus night drives in the park. Budget cultural walks and cycling outside the park can be organised through the Mto Wa Mbu Cultural Tourism Programme office (p184).

Walking safaris of about three to four hours are possible in the southern part of Manyara near the Marang forest (US$20 per person, plus US$20 ranger fee per group). Bookings should be made through park headquarters.

Sleeping

There are two **public camp sites** (camping adult/child US$30/5) and three **special camp sites** (camping adult/child US$50/10), plus about 10 double **bandas** (adult/child US$20/10) with private bathroom, hot water, bedding and a cooking area. Basic foodstuffs are available in Mto Wa Mbu village, 3km east of the park gate on the Arusha road. For saving money, it's cheaper to stay in Mto Wa Mbu village.

Ol Mesera Tented Camp (☎ 0784-428332; www.ol -mesera.com; s/d US$60/120, student & backpacker discounts available) A small place, with straightforward tented *bandas*, cultural walks in the surrounding Maasai area, and excursions to Lake Manyara and Ngorongoro Crater. It's in Selela village, 14km north of Mto wa Mbu and signposted off the Engaruka road. Public transport towards Engaruka will drop you at the turn-off, from where it's a 1.5km walk.

Kirurumu Luxury Tented Camp (☎ 027-250 7011, 027-250 7541; www.kirurumu.com; s/d full board US$238/386) The highly regarded Kirurumu has spacious, impeccably appointed tents plus stone luxury chalets in a very natural setting, completely surrounded by bush and with views to Lake Manyara in the distance. Maasai-guided ethno-botanical walks, hikes to the edge of the escarpment and fly-camping can be organised. It's on the escarpment about 12km from the park gate and 6km from the main road.

Lake Manyara Serena Lodge (☎ 027-253 9160/1; www.serenahotels.com; s/d full board US$375/550; 🏊) A large complex on the escarpment overlooking the Rift Valley, with two-storey conical thatched bungalows, buffet-style dining and wonderful views from its pool-bar area. It's about 2km from the main road and signposted.

Other recommendations:

Lake Manyara Wildlife Lodge (☎ 027-254 4595/4795; www.hotelsandlodges-tanzania.com; r per person full board US$380; 🏊) Formerly the government hotel, this place has a prime location on the edge of the escarpment, which goes quite a way to compensating for its merely adequate rooms and cuisine.

Lake Manyara Tree Lodge (www.andbeyond.com; per person all-inclusive US$855; 🌙 Jun-Mar; 🏊) An exclusive lodge, with 10 stilted tree houses with private decks and views, set in a mahogany forest at the southern end of the park.

Mto Wa Mbu
☎ 027

Mto Wa Mbu (River of Mosquitoes) is a small village with a hard edge and a large number of aggressive touts, although it's somewhat redeemed by its lively market and its profusion of palms, baobabs and acacia trees framed by the backdrop of the Rift Valley escarpment. It's just north of Lake Manyara, and makes a convenient base for visiting the park.

There are cultural walks in the surrounding area, organised through the **Cultural Tourism Programme office** (☎ 027-253 9303; www.mtowambu culturaltourism.org) at the Red Banana Café on the main road, opposite the post office. Rates average about TSh22,000 to TSh33,000 per person per day (less if you're in a group); bike rental can also be arranged.

SLEEPING & EATING

Sayari Lodge (d with shared bathroom TSh5000) Local budget guesthouse, behind the market, with no-frills rooms named after the planets (*sayari* means planet in Swahili).

New Continental Luxury Lodge (s/d TSh15,000/20,000) A block from Sayari Lodge and also a budget option. Its rooms, with private bathroom, mosquito net, fan and hot water, are all named after the continents.

Twiga Campsite & Lodge (camping US$5, old d/tr with shared bathroom US$30/45, new d/tr US$60/63; 🏊) A popular place set in a large compound along the main road, with cooking facilities, restaurant, ablution blocks with hot and cold water, and newer rooms in attached blocks. Car hire to visit Lake Manyara and Ngorongoro Conservation Area costs US$140 per day, including petrol and driver.

Jambo Lodge & Campsite (☎ 027-253 9170; www .njake.com; camping US$7, camping with tent & bedding rental US$25, s/d US$70/95; 🏊) Signposted along the main road about 200m east of Twiga, this place has a shaded and well-maintained grassy camping area, plus a dozen or so rooms with private bathroom in double-storey chalet blocks, and helpful staff. Car hire can be arranged from US$130 per day.

Marowiwi Green House (☎ 027-253 9273; marowiwi@ yahoo.com; s/d/tr US$30/60/90) On the north side of the road, and just before the park gate, with no-frills but clean and quiet rooms in a dark green house. It's just after the Lutheran hospital and signposted. Meals can be arranged.

Lake Manyara Tented Camp (☎ 027-255 3242; www .moivaro.com; s/d full board US$140/187) The main attraction of this place is its setting, in a grove of fever trees echoing with bird calls. There are 13 small tents set around large, grassy grounds and a camp site with hot water and a mess tent. It's 2km south of the main road.

Getting There & Away

AIR
Coastal Aviation, Air Excel and Regional Air offer scheduled daily, or near-daily, services between Arusha and Lake Manyara (one way US$75). The airstrip is at the northwestern edge of the park.

BUS
There are several buses daily to Arusha (TSh4500) and Karatu (TSh1200), and at least one bus daily direct to Dar es Salaam (TSh32,000). Departures are from the transport stand along the main road in the town centre near Red Banana Café.

CAR & MOTORCYCLE
The only road access into the park is from Arusha via Makuyuni and Mto Wa Mbu (where petrol is available). There's no vehicle hire at the park, although vehicles can be rented with Jambo and Twiga Campsites and some of the other listings in Mto wa Mbu. Quoted prices usually include Manyara and Ngorongoro Crater, but you should be able to negotiate something better if you will only be visiting Lake Manyara, as much less driving is involved.

TARANGIRE NATIONAL PARK
☎ 027
Baobab-studded Tarangire stretches southeast of Lake Manyara around the Tarangire River. Like nearby Lake Manyara National Park, it's often assigned no more than a day visit as part of a larger northern-circuit safari, although it's well worth longer exploration. Tarangire is a classic dry-season destination, particularly between August and October, when it has one of the highest concentrations of wildlife of any of the country's parks.

Tarangire is part of an extended ecosystem through which animals freely roam, and it's possible to do walks and night drives in the border areas.

Information
Entry fees are US$35/10 per adult/child. The entry gate and park headquarters are at the northwestern tip of the park, together with a visitors' centre. Within the park, walking accompanied by rangers is only permitted in the Silale area near Oliver's Camp. Otherwise, most of the camps and lodges located outside the park boundaries offer walking and night drives.

MaCo/GT Maps puts out a Tarangire map, available in Arusha and at the park gate.

Sleeping
There is a **public camp site** (camping adult/child US$30/5) near park headquarters and about 12 **special camp sites** (camping adult/child US$50/10) all in the upper-eastern and upper-western areas, near Matete, Burungi and Kitibong. For all, you'll need to be self-sufficient.

Tarangire Safari Lodge (☎ 027-254 4752; www .tarangiresafarilodge.com; s/d from US$89/128; 🏊) A large lodge, notable for its prime location on a bluff overlooking the Tarangire River, about 10km inside the park gate. Accommodation is in closely spaced tents or thatched bungalows.

Tarangire River Camp (☎ 022-213 0501; www .mbalimbali.com; s/d full board US$210/320) An 18-tent camp set amid baobabs near the seasonal Minjingu River, and accessed via a signposted turn-off 3km before the park gate. Views – including of elephant and other wildlife in season – are impressive, and cultural walks can be arranged in the surrounding Maasai areas.

Kikoti (☎ 027-250 8790; www.africanconservancy company.com; s/d full board plus bush walks US$270/450) On a rise just east of the park boundaries, this 18-tent camp offers spacious tents, good cuisine, and the chance for nature walks and night drives.

Tarangire Treetops Lodge (☎ 027-250 0630; www.elewana.com; per person all-inclusive US$630; 🏊) Pampered and upmarket, with 20 spacious suites set on low stilts or built tree house–style around the baobabs. It's just outside Tarangire's northeastern border, with walking safaris and night drives.

Other recommendations:

Tarangire Sopa Lodge (☎ 027-250 0630/39; www .sopalodges.com; s/d full board US$320/550) Comfortable rooms in a mediocre location about 30km from the gate.

Tarangire Swala (☎ 027-250 9816; www.sanctu arylodges.com; per person all-inclusive US$530/800) A premiere-class nine-tent camp, nestled in a grove of acacia trees and overlooking the Gurusi wetlands in the south western part of the park.

THE MAASAI

In the beginning was Ngai, the creator. The heavens and earth were one, and there was grass on the earth in abundance and countless heads of cattle. But then heaven and earth split. Ngai was above in the heavens. It was the Maasai whom Ngai entrusted with care for the cattle, and in turn also for the earth, that its face not be scarred with shovels, that it continue to provide nourishment for Ngai's cattle.

In this legend is rooted the traditional lifestyle of the Maasai that endures to this day. Maasai culture centres around the cattle, which are considered sacred, and which provide many of their needs. This includes milk, blood and meat for their diet, and hides and skins for clothing – although sheep and goats also play an important dietary role, especially during the dry season.

The colour and rich traditional life of the Maasai have attracted considerable tourist attention, especially in recent years. In an effort to cope, specially designated cultural villages have been established where you can see Maasai dancing, photograph as much as you want and buy crafts, albeit for a steep US$50 or higher fee per vehicle. It is generally a rather disappointing and contrived experience. For more authentic encounters with the Maasai, visit Maasai areas within the framework of a Cultural Tourism Programme, take advantage of the chance for guided walks (many camps offer these), or arrange a longer stay or hike at Loliondo, West Kilimanjaro and other areas where partnerships with the Maasai have been established.

Getting There & Around

AIR

Coastal Aviation, Air Excel and Regional Air stop at Tarangire on their flights between Arusha and Lake Manyara (per seat US$100). The airstrip is in the northern section of the park near Tarangire Safari Lodge.

CAR & MOTORCYCLE

There's no vehicle hire at the park. The closest petrol is in Makuyuni, 32km from the park gate.

Tarangire is reached via the Makuyuni road from Arusha. At Kwa Kuchinja village, there's a signposted turn-off to the park gate, which is 7km further down a good dirt access road.

SERENGETI NATIONAL PARK

Siringit – endless plains – is how the Serengeti is known to the Maasai, the area's original guardians. These undulating, almost treeless expanses, dotted with granite kopjes, are traversed by tens of thousands of hoofed animals constantly on the move in search of fresh grassland. Drive through in a day, and the vastness will impress. Stay for longer, and the magnificence and raw power of nature's rhythms will begin to work their magic and take an inescapable hold.

Serengeti, which covers 14,763 sq km and is contiguous with Masai Mara National Reserve in Kenya, is easily Tanzania's most famous national park. Among its most famous residents are the wildebeest, of which there are over one million, and their annual migration is the Serengeti's biggest drawcard.

During the rainy season between December and May the wildebeest are widely scattered over the southern section of the Serengeti and the Ngorongoro Conservation Area (NCA). As these areas have few large rivers and streams, they dry out quickly when the rains cease. The wildebeest concentrate on the few remaining green areas, forming large herds that migrate north and west in search of food. From about July to October, they are on vacation in the Masai Mara, before they again start moving south in anticipation of the rains. One of the most spectacular sights of this eons-old cycle takes place around February, when over 8000 wildebeest calves are born per day, although about 40% of these will die before they are four months old.

In addition to the wildebeest, the Serengeti is also famous for its lions, as well as cheetahs, zebras (of which there are about 200,000) and giraffes. You're also likely to see Thomson's and Grant's gazelles, elands, impalas, klipspringers and warthogs, as well as diverse birdlife.

The Serengeti offers unparalleled safari opportunities, and the beauty and synchrony of nature can be appreciated here as in few other places. If you're able to visit, it's a chance not to be missed. Try to set aside as much time as possible to explore the park's varied zones.

TANZANIA

Information

Entry fees are US$50/10 per adult/child. Bookings for camp sites, resthouses and the hostel should be made through the **Tourism Warden** (☎ 028-262 1515; www.tanzaniaparks.com). Park headquarters are at Fort Ikoma, just outside the park, while the tourism division is at Seronera. There's an excellent Visitors Information Centre at Seronera.

Wildlife concentrations are greatest between about December and June, although the Serengeti can be visited rewardingly at any time of year. If you're primarily interested in the wildebeest, the best base from about December to April is at one of the camps near Seronera or in the southeastern part of the park. The crossing of the Grumeti River, which

runs through the park's Western Corridor, usually takes place sometime between May and July, although the actual viewing window can be quite short. In particularly dry years, the herds tend to move northwards sooner, avoiding or only skirting the Western Corridor. The northern Serengeti, around Lobo and Klein's Gate, is a good base during the dry season, particularly between August and October.

Almost all shorter safaris, and those done as part of a quick northern circuit loop, use Seronera as a base, although other sections of the park are just as rewarding, if not more so. In the low season you will see few other vehicles outside of Seronera, although even in the high season the park is large enough that it doesn't feel overrun.

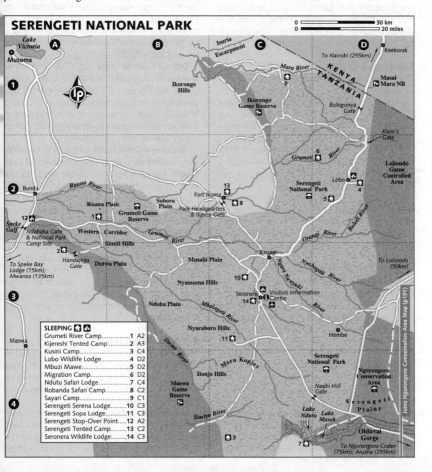

SERENGETI NATIONAL PARK

0 — 30 km
0 — 20 miles

SLEEPING

Grumeti River Camp	1 A2
Kijereshi Tented Camp	2 A3
Kusini Camp	3 C4
Lobo Wildlife Lodge	4 D2
Mbuzi Mawe	5 D2
Migration Camp	6 D2
Ndutu Safari Lodge	7 C4
Robanda Safari Camp	8 C2
Sayari Camp	9 C1
Serengeti Serena Lodge	10 C3
Serengeti Sopa Lodge	11 C3
Serengeti Stop-Over Point	12 A2
Serengeti Tented Camp	13 C2
Seronera Wildlife Lodge	14 C3

Joins Ngorongoro Conservation Area Map (p191)

Activities

Balloon trips – about an hour floating over the plains at dawn, followed by a champagne breakfast in the bush – are offered by **Serengeti Balloon Safaris** (☎ 027-250 8578, 027-254 8967; www .balloonsafaris.com; per person US$479). Book directly, or through any of the central Serengeti lodges.

Short (two-to three-hour) walks outside the park and Maasai cultural activities can be arranged through lodges based in border areas or through any of the central Serengeti lodges. Balloon safaris are also now offered over western Serengeti from the main western Serengeti lodges.

The main 'activity' is finding the animals. There is a wealth of information available about the best times for seeing the wildebeest. One of our favourite sites for tracking them down, as well as for appreciating the Serengeti's wildlife throughout the year is www.go-safari.com – follow the links through to Serengeti.

Sleeping & Eating

There are about nine **public camp sites** (camping adult/child US$30/5) in the Serengeti, including six around Seronera, one at Lobo, one at Kirawira in the Western Corridor and one near Ndabaka Gate in the far west along the Mwanza–Musoma road. There are at least two dozen **special camp sites** (camping adult/child US$50/10), which should be booked well in advance. A 30% nonrefundable deposit is required one month before your arrival date.

There are also several resthouses at Seronera with running water, blankets and cooking facilities. You'll need to bring your own food, although there's a small shop at Seronera selling soft drinks, water and a few basics.

LODGES & TENTED CAMPS
Central & Southern Serengeti

Central Serengeti is the most visited area of the park, and readily accessed from both Arusha and from Mwanza via the Western Corridor. The main lodge area is at Seronera. Southeast of here near the Ngorongoro Conservation Area (NCA) boundary and Lake Ndutu is a prime base for wildlife watching during the December to April wet season, when it's full of wildebeests. The southwest, in addition to being well placed for the wildebeest during the wet season, is also notable for its lion and leopard sightings, especially around the Moru Kopjes area, which has a substantial resident wildlife population year-round.

Ndutu Safari Lodge (☎ 027-250 6702/2829; www .ndutu.com; s/d full board US$249/385) This place is in a lovely setting just outside the southeastern Serengeti in the far western part of NCA. It's well placed for wildlife viewing, especially for observing the enormous herds of wildebeests during the wet season, and walking safaris are possible in the surrounding NCA. In addition to NCA fees, you'll need to pay Serengeti fees any time that you cross into the park. Accommodation is in unpretentious but comfortable cottages with private bathroom, and the atmosphere is relaxed and rustic.

Serengeti Sopa Lodge (☎ 027-250 0630/39; www .sopalodges.com; s/d full board US$320/550; 🐾) Rather ponderous and architecturally unappealing, but the rooms are spacious – with small sitting rooms, two double beds and views. It's about 20km south of Seronera as the bird flies, on the edge of the Nyaroboro Hills, and well located for wildlife watching.

Serengeti Serena Lodge (☎ 027-250 4153/8; www .serenahotels.com; s/d full board US$375/550; 🐾) About 20km northwest of Seronera airstrip, this place is not as favourably located as Seronera Wildlife Lodge but is otherwise a good choice, with accommodation in well-appointed two-storey Maasai-style bungalows.

Seronera Wildlife Lodge (☎ 027-254 4595/4795; www.hotelsandlodges-tanzania.com; r per person full board US$400) A prime location in the heart of the Serengeti, well situated for wildlife drives, modest but pleasant rooms and a lively end-of-the-day safari atmosphere at the evening buffet.

Kusini Camp (☎ 027-250 9816; www.sanctuarylodges .com; per person all-inclusive from US$530/800) Laid-back luxury in a prime wet-season setting amid rocky outcrops in the remote southwestern Serengeti, with 12 well-spaced and well-appointed tents. Somewhat unusually for camps of this standard, there are no age restrictions on children.

Northern Serengeti

The hillier and more heavily vegetated northern Serengeti receives relatively few visitors, but makes a fine base between August and October, when the migration passes through.

Lobo Wildlife Lodge (☎ 027-254 4595/4795; www .hotelsandlodges-tanzania.com; r per person full board US$440) Well located and similar in standard to the Seronera Wildlife Lodge. If your budget is limited, it's the best value in this part of the park.

Migration Camp (☎ 027-250 0630; www.elewana .com; per person all-inclusive US$630; ☒) A luxurious camp, recently completely rebuilt, with an intimate bush atmosphere and 20 spacious tents with views over the Grumeti River in a good wildlife-viewing area.

Other recommendations:

Mbuzi Mawe (☎ 027-250 4158, 028-262 2040/2; www .serenahotels.com; s/d full board US$375/550) A 16-tent camp – each with two double beds and views – and an excellent location about 45km north of Seronera.

Sayari Camp (www.asilialodges.com; per person full board plus wildlife drives about US$650; ☒ Jun-Apr) This 16-bed previously mobile camp is now permanently based on the south side of the Mara River – well placed for the migration from about July to November.

Western Serengeti

Apart from the park camp sites, the western Serengeti is the only area that has options for budget travellers (all outside the park). In addition to seasonal proximity to the migration (which generally passes through the area from around May/June), it offers the forest-fringed Grumeti River and relatively reliable year-round wildlife watching.

Serengeti Stop-Over Point (☎ 028-262 2273; www .serengetistopover.com; camping US$10, s/d US$30/60) On the Mwanza–Musoma road about 1km from Ndabaka Gate, with camping with hot showers and a cooking area, plus 10 simple rondavels, and a restaurant-bar. Cultural excursions can be arranged and safari vehicle hire is sometimes possible (with advance notice only). Buses along the Mwanza–Musoma road can drop you at the entrance.

Kijereshi Tented Camp (☎ 028-262 1231; www.ki jereshiserengeti.com; camping US$15, s/d tented r half board US$85/125, d bungalow half board US$150; ☒) Just outside park boundaries, 18km east of the Mwanza–Musoma road and about 2km from the Serengeti's Handajega Gate. It's a popular base for overlanders, with functional tented accommodation (you can also pitch your own), plus some rooms, a restaurant and cooking facilities.

Serengeti Tented Camp (☎ 027-255 3242; www .moivaro.com; s/d full board US$160/213) A small camp 3km from Ikoma Gate and just outside the park boundary, with 12 no-frills tents with private bathrooms and hot water, plus the chance for night drives and guided walks in the border area.

Other recommendations:

Robanda Safari Camp (☎ 0754-282251; www .robanda-safari-camp.com; s/d full board US$145/200) A new, small semipermanent camp near Robanda village just outside Ikoma Gate with domed tents with private bathroom and a restaurant. It's all rather spartan but nevertheless a good option between camping safaris and something more luxurious. There's no vehicle hire at the moment, although it is planned for the near future, which means you could arrive here by public transport and do a safari.

Speke Bay Lodge (☎ 028-262 1236; www.speke bay.com; s/d tents with shared bathroom & full board US$81/138, s/d bungalows full board US$144/210) On Lake Victoria about 15km southwest of Ndabaka Gate and 125km north of Mwanza, and a good choice if you want to combine the Serengeti with Lake Victoria. There are simple tents with shared facilities, and spotless, if rather soulless, four-person bungalows with private bathroom. The lodge can help you organise boat, fishing or birding excursions on the lake, and mountain biking. There's no vehicle hire.

Grumeti River Camp (www.andbeyond.com; per person all-inclusive US$855; ☒) An exclusive 20-bed camp in a prime migration location.

MOBILE CAMPS

There are many semipermanent, mostly up-market camps that move seasonally with the wildlife, with the goal of always being optimally positioned for the migration. Try to include at least one in your Serengeti itinerary. In addition to the following listings, Hoopoe Safaris (p68) is also a recommended contact for mobile camp itineraries.

Serengeti Safari Camp (www.nomad-tanzania.com; per person s/d all-inclusive US$590/930) A highly exclusive mobile camp that follows the wildebeest migration, with top-notch guides.

Olakira Camp (www.asilialodges.com; per person all-inclusive US$450) A six-tent camp based in the Ndutu area with the wildebeest from December until March, and in central Serengeti from June to November.

Simiyu Camp (www.africawilderness.com; s/d full board US$575/860) In the southern Serengeti from December to March, in the Seronera area from May to August and in the north from September to November.

Getting There & Around
AIR

Coastal Aviation, Air Excel and Regional Air fly daily between Arusha and various Serengeti airstrips, including Seronera (one way US$175) and Grumeti (US$200). Coastal Aviation's flight continues to Mwanza.

CAR & MOTORCYCLE

Most travellers visit the Serengeti with an organised safari or in their own vehicle. For budget travellers the only other option to try to get a glimpse of the animals is to take a bus travelling between Arusha and Mwanza or Musoma via the Western Corridor route – check with Coast bus line at the Arusha or Mwanza bus stations – although you won't be able to stop to observe the wildlife, and will be careening too fast for most of the journey to enjoy the passing scene. You'll also need to pay park fees and, if you disembark at Seronera, you'll have the problem of getting onward transport, as hitching is not permitted in the park.

Access from Arusha is via **Naabi Hill Gate** (☉6am-6pm) at the southeastern edge of the park. From here, it's 75km further to Seronera. **Ndabaka Gate** (☉6am-4pm) is about 140km northeast of Mwanza along the Mwanza–Musoma road, and gives you direct access to the Western Corridor. Ikoma Gate is also accessed from the Mwanza–Musoma road, from a track running east from Bunda. Bologonya Gate, 5km from the Kenyan border, is the route to/from Kenya's Masai Mara National Reserve, but the border is open only to East African residents or citizens. There are other entry points at Handajega Gate (Western Corridor) and in the north at Klein's Gate. Driving is not permitted in the park after 7pm.

Petrol points en route from Arusha include Makuyuni, Mto Wa Mbu and Karatu. Petrol is sometimes available at Ngorongoro Crater (Park Village) and at the Seronera Wildlife Lodge, although it's expensive. It's not available anywhere else in the park. Coming from the west, the most reliable petrol points are Mwanza and Musoma.

NGORONGORO CONSERVATION AREA

☎ 027

The Ngorongoro Crater is just one part of a much larger area of interrelated ecosystems consisting of the beautiful Crater Highlands together with vast stretches of plains, bush and woodland. The entire Ngorongoro Conservation Area (NCA) covers about 8300 sq km and encompasses Olduvai (Oldupai) Gorge, the alkaline Lakes Ndutu and Masek (although Ndutu is actually just over the border in the Serengeti), and a long string of volcanoes and collapsed volcanoes (often referred to as calderas), most of which are inactive. Just outside the NCA's eastern boundary is the archaeologically important Engaruka, and to the south is Lake Eyasi. To the northeast of the NCA on the Kenyan border is the alkaline Lake Natron.

Information

The NCA is under the jurisdiction of the Ngorongoro Conservation Area Authority (NCAA), which has its **headquarters** (☎ 027-253 7006, 027-253 9108, 027-253 7019; www.ngorongorocrater .org) at Park Village at Ngorongoro Crater.

Entry fees – payable for all activities within the NCA – are US$50/10 per adult/child per 24-hour period. Guides, including for walking safaris, cost US$20 per day per group. There is a vehicle fee of US$40/TSh10,000 per foreign/Tanzanian-registered vehicle per entry and an additional, steep crater-service fee of US$200 per vehicle per entry to drive down into Ngorongoro Crater.

The two official entry points to the NCA are **Lodoare Gate** (☎ 027-253 7031; ☉ 6am-6pm), just south of Ngorongoro Crater, and **Naabi Hill Gate** (☎ 027-253 7030; ☉ 6am-6pm), on the border with Serengeti National Park.

Both MaCo and Harms-ic put out maps of the NCA, available at the NCAA Information Office (p171) in Arusha and at Lodoare Gate.

Crater Highlands

The ruggedly beautiful Crater Highlands consist of an elevated range of volcanoes and collapsed volcanoes that rises up from the side of the Great Rift Valley and runs along the eastern edge of the NCA. The peaks include Oldeani (3216m), Makarot (3107m), Olmoti (3100m), Loolmalasin (3648m), Empakaai (3262m, also spelled Embagai), the still-active Ol Doinyo Lengai (2878m, 'Mountain of God' in Maasai) and Ngorongoro (2200m).The main residents of the area are the Maasai, who have grazed cattle here for hundreds of years.

TREKKING IN THE CRATER HIGHLANDS

The highlands are best explored on foot, although because of the logistics involved, trekking here is expensive. Treks range from

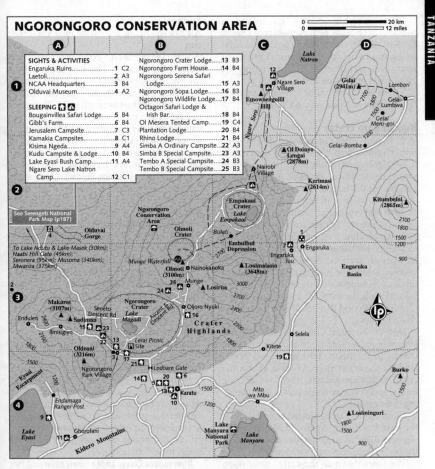

NGORONGORO CONSERVATION AREA

0 ___ 20 km
0 ___ 12 miles

SIGHTS & ACTIVITIES
Engaruka Ruins.....................1 C2
Laetoli.................................2 A3
NCAA Headquarters.............3 B4
Olduvai Museum..................4 A2

SLEEPING
Bougainvillea Safari Lodge.......5 B4
Gibb's Farm........................6 B4
Jerusalem Campsite.............7 C3
Kamakia Campsites..............8 C1
Kisima Ngeda......................9 A4
Kudu Campsite & Lodge.......10 B4
Lake Eyasi Bush Camp..........11 A4
Ngare Sero Lake Natron
Camp..............................12 C1

Ngorongoro Crater Lodge.....13 B3
Ngorongoro Farm House.......14 B4
Ngorongoro Serena Safari
Lodge..............................15 A3
Ngorongoro Sopa Lodge......16 B3
Ngorongoro Wildlife Lodge...17 B4
Octagon Safari Lodge &
Irish Bar...........................18 B4
Ol Mesera Tented Camp.......19 C4
Plantation Lodge.................20 B4
Rhino Lodge.......................21 B4
Simba A Ordinary Campsite...22 A3
Simba B Special Campsite.....23 A3
Tembo A Special Campsite....24 B3
Tembo B Special Campsite....25 B3

short day jaunts to excursions of up to two weeks or more. For all routes, you'll need to be accompanied by a guide, and for multiday hikes you will need donkeys or vehicle support to carry water and supplies.

Various Arusha-based companies do treks to Empakaai and to Ol Doinyo Lengai (just outside the NCA boundaries), but for most trekking in this region you'll need to contact a specialist operator. These include Summits Africa (p70), **Dorobo Safaris** (dorobo@habari.co.tz) and **Amazing Tanzania** (www.amazingtanzania.com). Expect to pay from about US$200 per person per day in a group of four, including NCA entry fees.

Alternatively, you can arrange your trek through the NCAA. However, this requires

at least one month's notice, and usually winds up costing about the same as going through a tour company. You'll need to provide all camping equipment and supplies yourself, including water; you'll also need to rent a vehicle (essential for accessing all treks) and arrange for someone to drive the car to the end of the trek to collect you, as most routes are not circuits. The NCAA will take care of arranging the camp sites, guides and donkeys.

A popular multiday trek starts just north of Ngorongoro Crater and crosses the highlands to finish at Ngare Sero village near Lake Natron. This normally takes four days, but can be cut to three by starting at Nainokanoka.

For something shorter, try hiking at Makarot or Oldeani, or at Empakaai or Olmoti Craters. All of these can easily be done in a day or less from a base at Ngorongoro Crater, and apart from transport costs, involve only the NCA entry and guide fees.

There are no camps or lodges apart from the facilities at Ngorongoro Crater.

Ngorongoro Crater

With its blue-green vistas, close-range viewing opportunities and high wildlife concentrations, Ngorongoro is one of East Africa's most visited destinations. At about 20km wide it's also one of the largest calderas in the world. Within its walls is an astounding variety of animals and vegetation, including grasslands, swamps, forests, saltpans, a freshwater lake and rich birdlife. You are likely to see lions, elephants, buffaloes and many of the plains herbivores, such as wildebeest, Thomson's gazelles, zebras and reedbucks, as well as hundreds of flamingos wading in the shallows of Lake Magadi, the soda lake at the crater's base. Chances are good that you'll also see a black rhino or two.

Despite the crater's steepness, there's considerable movement of animals in and out, thanks to the permanent water and grassland on the crater floor. Wildlife shares the crater with local Maasai, who have grazing rights, and you may come across them tending their cattle.

Ngorongoro can be visited at any time of the year, but during April and May it can be wet and difficult to negotiate, and access to the crater floor may be restricted.

The gates down to the crater floor open at 7am, and close (for descent) at 4pm; all vehicles must be out of the crater area before 6pm.

It can get very cold and raw on the crater rim, so bring a jacket and come prepared, especially if you're camping.

SLEEPING

Camping

There are many **special camp sites** (camping adult/child US$50/10), but the only **public camp site** (camping adult/child US$30/10) is Simba A, with basic but generally clean facilities (latrines and cold showers) and views over the crater if you're lucky enough to be there when there is no cloud cover. It's along the road from Lodoare Gate.

Lodges

All the following are on or near the crater rim.

Rhino Lodge (☎ 0762-359055; www.ngorongoro.cc; s/d full board US$125/220) The first lodge within the NCA when coming from Arusha. It was opened together with the local community and is targeted just as much at the Tanzanian market as at foreign tourists, and offers fine value, especially considering its location just about 500m back from the crater rim (though no views of the crater). It's possible to reach the lodge by public bus from Arusha (see Getting There & Away, below). Once at the lodge, vehicle hire can be arranged (for about the same price as in Karatu), as can walks with Maasai guides in the NCA.

Ngorongoro Wildlife Lodge (☎ 027-254 4595/4795, direct 027-253 7058, 027-253 7073; www.hotelsandlodges -tanzania.com; r per person full board US$420) The former government hotel, with a prime setting on the southern crater rim and reasonable rooms.

Ngorongoro Sopa Lodge (☎ 027-250 0630/39; www .sopalodges.com; s/d full board US$320/550) On the eastern crater rim near a crater descent/ascent road, with spacious, well-appointed rooms, each with two double beds.

Ngorongoro Serena Safari Lodge (☎ 027-250 4153/8; www.serenahotels.com; s/d full board US$375/550) Well located on the southwestern crater rim near the main descent route, with typically Serena standards, although during the high season its popularity, especially with groups, can detract somewhat from the ambience. Green Footprint Adventures (www.greenfootprint.co.tz) organises short hikes from the lodge, including to Olmoti.

Ngorongoro Crater Lodge (www.andbeyond.com; per person all-inclusive US$1115) An exclusive place, and the most interesting of the rim lodges in terms of design, with an eclectic collection of styles and décor. Prices include your own butler.

GETTING THERE & AWAY

There are several buses daily between Arusha and Karatu (about TSh6000, three hours), departing from Arusha's central bus station, with at least one daily (look for Ditto KK and Kulinge lines – both departing about 10am) continuing on to Lodoare Gate (about four hours) and NCAA park village. Coast line between Arusha and Mwanza via the Serengeti also stops at Lodoare Gate, departing from Arusha by 5am.

GETTING AROUND

Vehicle hire and guides can be arranged at Lodoare Gate. Car hire – which is done informally with private cars belonging to staff, as the NCAA no longer hires vehicles – costs about US$130 per day plus crater and NCA fees. It's more reliable, and about the same price, to hire vehicles in Karatu or through Rhino Lodge inside the NCA for about the same price. Fill up in Karatu.

The main route in is the Seneto descent road, which enters the crater on its western side, just west of Lake Magadi. To come out, use the Lerai ascent road, which starts near the Lerai picnic site to the south of Lake Magadi and leads to the rim near Ngorongoro Crater Lodge. There is a third access route on the northeastern edge of the crater near the Ngorongoro Sopa Lodge, which can be used for ascents and descents. Only 4WDs are allowed down into the crater. All roads into the crater have been recently graded, though all are steep, so be sure your vehicle can handle the conditions.

Karatu

☎ 027

This scruffy town 20km southeast of Lodoare Gate is surrounded by some beautiful countryside. Many camping safaris out of Arusha use Karatu as an overnight stop to economise on entry fees for the crater, but it's also worth considering the town as a base in itself if you're interested in walking in the nearby hills.

There is a post office, and an NBC bank branch that exchanges cash and travellers cheques and has an ATM. Several hotels have internet access, and there's an internet café at Ngorongoro Safari Resort.

Most of the accommodation we've listed can organise vehicle hire for visits to Ngorongoro Crater from about US$130 per day plus NCA and crater fees.

SLEEPING & EATING
Budget & Midrange

ELCT Karatu Lutheran Hostel (☎ 027-253 4230; s/d/tr TSh22,000/30,000/40,000) Simple, clean rooms with hot water, and meals (TSh6000). It's on the main road at the western end of town.

Ngorongoro Camp & Lodge (☎ 027-253 4287; camping US$7, s/d US$79/128; 🖳) Crowded camping with hot showers, a covered dining area and some overpriced rooms. It's on the main road in the town centre. Car hire to Ngorongoro costs US$150 plus entry and crater fees.

Kudu Campsite & Lodge (☎ 027-253 4055; www.kuducamp.com; camping US$10, s/d/tr bungalow US$105/110/132, d/tr rondavel from US$132/176; 🖳) At Karatu's western end and signposted south of the main road, with quiet gardens, a large lawn to pitch your tent, hot-water showers, clean bungalows and a bar-restaurant (meals US$5 to US$8). Vehicle hire can be arranged.

Bougainvillea Safari Lodge (☎ 027-253 4083; www.bougainvillealodge.net; s/d/tr US$70/125/150) Just off the main road west of Karatu, with two dozen spacious attached stone bungalows – all with fireplaces and small verandas – plus a restaurant. Cultural activities can be arranged.

Octagon Safari Lodge & Irish Bar (☎ 027-253 4525; www.octagonlodge.com; per person half board US$120) Cosy, comfortable rooms set amid lush gardens, as well as a restaurant and an Irish bar. Cultural walks can be arranged, as can Ngorongoro safaris.

Top End

Plantation Lodge (☎ 027-253 4364/5, 027-253 4405; www.plantation-lodge.com; s/d full board from US$193/295; 🖾) A genteel place with spacious cottages set in expansive grounds and a cosy, highland ambience. It's about 2km north of the main road.

Ngorongoro Farm House (☎ 027-250 4093, 0784-207727; www.africawilderness.com; s/d half board US$198/276; 🖾) An atmospheric place set in the grounds of a 500-acre coffee plantation about 5km from Lodoare Gate. The rooms are spacious and the suites have large bathtubs. There's a terrace dining area, a pool backed by flame trees and views towards Oldeani, and walks in the area.

Gibb's Farm (☎ 027-253 4397; www.gibbsfarm.net; s/d half board in standard r US$225/314, in new farm cottages US$493/702; ☒ mid-May–mid-Apr) A long-standing place with a highland ambience, views over the nearby coffee plantations, walking and impeccably appointed cottages set around the gardens. There's also a spa, and an in-house safari operator. It's about 5km north of the main road and signposted.

GETTING THERE & AWAY

For transport details, see the Ngorongoro Crater Getting There & Away section (opposite). The bus stand in Karatu is at the western end of town, behind the Total petrol station.

Olduvai Gorge

Olduvai (Oldupai) Gorge is a canyon about 50km long and up to 90m deep running to the northwest of Ngorongoro Crater. Thanks to its unique geological history, in which layer upon layer of volcanic deposits were laid down in orderly sequence over a period of almost two million years, it provides remarkable documentation of ancient life.

The most famous of Olduvai's fossils is the 1.8-million-year-old ape-like skull known as *Australopithecus boisei*, which was discovered by Mary Leakey in 1959 and which gave rise to a heated debate about human evolution. The skull is also often referred to as *Zinjanthropus*, which means 'nutcracker man', referring to its large molars. In 1972 hominid (humanlike) footprints estimated to be 3.7 million years old were discovered at Laetoli, about 45km south of Olduvai Gorge. Other lesser-known but significant fossils excavated from the upper layers of Olduvai provide some of the oldest evidence of *Homo sapiens* in the area.

The small **Olduvai museum** (☎ 027-253 7037; www.ngorongorocrater.org/oldupai.html; adult/ child TSh3000/1500; ☻ 9am-5pm) documents the Olduvai fossil finds. The site is about 5km off the road to Serengeti. Guides to the gorge can be arranged at the museum (guide fee included in museum entry fee, but tips appreciated).

Engaruka

Engaruka, on the eastern edge of the NCA, is a small village known for its ruins of a complex and mysterious irrigation system with terraced stone housing sites estimated to be at least 500 years old. There's speculation about the origin of the ruins; some say they were built by ancestors of the Iraqw (Mbulu) people who live in the area today, while others suggest that the site was built by the Sonjo, a Bantu-speaking people.

There's a cultural tourism program of sorts here, which offers tours of the ruins and cultural tours. Arrange things through the Arusha TTB Tourist Information Centre, or at Jerusalem Campsite in Engaruka.

There are several camp sites, including one in Engaruka village, and the shaded **Jerusalem Campsite** (camping TSh10,000), about 5km west of the main road in the Engaruka Juu area.

Engaruka is about 60km north of Mto Wa Mbu. There's a daily bus to/from Arusha via Mto wa Mbu (about TSh7000, four to five hours from Arusha, and about TSh3500 from Mto wa Mbu), departing from Arusha by about 10am. Shortly before reaching Engaruka, you'll need to pay a TSh6000 per person village fee. Departures from Engaruka are by about 6am.

Lake Natron

This lake – in a desolate area on the Kenyan border – is known for the huge flocks of flamingos that gather here at the end of the rainy season. It's also the main base for climbing Ol Doinyo Lengai, 25km south.

Kamakia Campsites (camping TSh10,000) – there are actually two camp sites, one near the waterfall and one near the village – are good budget bets, though facilities are quite basic. Meals are available, as are guides for walks and mountain climbs.

Ngare Sero Lake Natron Camp (☎ 027-255 3638; www.ngare-sero-lodge.com; s/d full board plus village & conservation fees US$185/300) has eight tents set near a small stream, and meals are available. Guides are available for walks and mountain climbs, and there are discounted rates for multinight stays.

OL DOINYO LENGAI

Ol Doinyo Lengai (2878m) – 'Mountain of God' to the Maasai – is an almost perfect volcanic cone with steep sides rising to a small flat-topped peak. It's the youngest volcano in the Crater Highlands, and still active. There were major eruptions in 1966 and 1993, with the most recent eruptions and major activity in late 2007 and early 2008. At the peak, you can clearly see hot steam vents and growing ash cones in the still-active north crater. A trek from the base village of Ngare Sero is possible in one long day. In addition to the traditional ascent route along the mountain's northwest flank, there's now a new route from the southeast. Although interest in scaling Ol Doinyo Lengai has exploded in recent years, the north crater poses significant danger to trekkers who approach too closely. Read the safety overview at www.mtsu.edu/~fbelton/safety .html, and for more on the mountain, see www.mtsu.edu/~fbelton/lengai.html.

GETTING THERE & AWAY

Lake Natron is accessed via Ngare Sero village, about 60km north of Engaruka. There's no public transport north of Engaruka, but vehicle hire can be arranged in Engaruka through Jerusalem Campsite (from about US$120), or in Arusha. Ngare Sero Lake Natron Camp provides transfers for its guests. There's a US$15 per person district council fee to enter the area, payable at the entrance to Ngare Sero. For upmarket bike safaris to the lake, contact Summits Africa (p70). Once at Natron, the rough road continues northwest to Loliondo and into the Serengeti.

Lake Eyasi

This starkly beautiful lake is in a hot, dry area that is home to the Hadzabe (also known as Hadzapi or Tindiga) people, who continue to follow hunting-and-gathering traditions. The main village is Ghorofani, at the lake's northeastern end.

English-speaking guides to visit Hadzabe communities can be arranged at Lake Eyasi Bush Camp for TSh40,000 per person (TSh50,000 including camping at its camp site) and at Kisima Ngeda.

Lake Eyasi Bush Camp (Momoya's Camp; camping TSh6000, camping plus Hadzabe visit TSh50,000) is a no-frills place with minimal facilities, meals with notice and tents sometimes available for rent. The well-signposted office is at the main Ghorofani junction.

Kisima Ngeda (☎ 027-253 4128, 027-254 8715; www.kisimangeda.com; camping US$5, s/d luxury tented bungalow half board US$220/340) has a sublime setting on the lakeshore with doum palms in the background and six tented bungalows along the lake. The same management also runs three budget camp sites – the only camping on the lakeshore, all with toilet and shower and hot water on request. It's about 7km from Ghorofani and signposted.

GETTING THERE & AWAY

Public transport goes several times daily between Karatu and Ghorofani (TSh5000, two rough hours), from where you'll need to walk to the camp sites or pay extra to have the driver drop you off. Transport in Karatu leaves late morning from the Land Rover stand behind the petrol station at the western end of town. Returning, transport leaves from the main Ghorofani junction at about 3am or 4am, although it's often possible to find something else later in the day.

CENTRAL TANZANIA

Central Tanzania has several intriguing attractions for hardy travellers looking to experience the country well off the beaten path. These include the Kolo-Kondoa rock art sites; Mt Hanang; and Dodoma, the country's legislative capital. To the northwest are Singida, with its lakes, and the diamond mines around Shinyanga. The region's main attraction, though, is the window it offers on areas little touched by visitors. If you're prepared to rough things with transport and accommodation, you'll undoubtedly have a memorable time here.

DODOMA

☎ 026 / pop 150,000

Arid Dodoma sits in not-so-splendid isolation in the geographic centre of the country, at a height of about 1100m. Since 1973 the town has been Tanzania's official capital and headquarters of the ruling CCM party, although Dar es Salaam remains the unrivalled economic and political centre of the country.

Dodoma is a logical springboard to the Kolo-Kondoa rock art sites (p199), 180km north. Otherwise, there's little reason to visit. With its grandiose street layout and imposing architecture of many church and government buildings – all sharply contrasting with the slow-paced reality of daily life – it's easy to get the feeling that the town is dressed in clothes that are several sizes too big.

Photography is prohibited in most areas.

Orientation

From the bus stand, the main (Dar es Salaam) road heads west into the city centre where it meets Kuu St at a large roundabout. Just south of here are the railway tracks. To the north, a warren of small avenues runs off Kuu St into the busiest part of the city, with the market and many shops. Further north is the airfield, and to the north and east are several residential areas and a few hotels.

TANZANIA

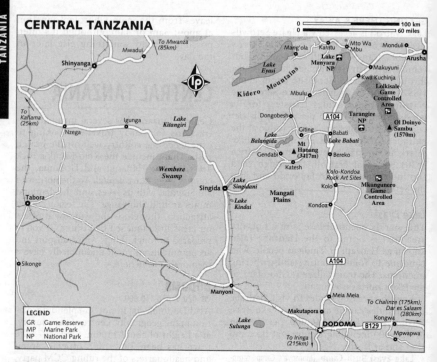

Information

CRDB Bank (Kuu St) ATM (Visa only).

Mission Aviation Fellowship (☎ 026-235 2810/6; Dodoma Airfield) Evacuation assistance in medical emergencies.

NBC Bank (Kuu St) Changes cash, and has an ATM (Visa only).

Main post office (Railway St) Just west of the train station.

RAL Internet Café (Kuu St; per hr TSh1000; ⏰ 8am-9pm Mon-Sat) Just north of the main roundabout.

TanPay/Speed Cash (Dar es Salaam road) ATM (Visa only); opposite the Jamatini *dalla-dalla* stand.

Sights & Activities

The **Museum of Geosciences** (Nyumba ya Mayonyesho ya Madini; adult/child TSh500/100; ⏰ 8am-3.30pm Mon-Fri), behind New Dodoma Hotel, contains rock samples and geological information on the entire country.

There's a small **swimming pool** (admission TSh3000; ⏰ 10am-10pm) at Climax Club, about 2.5km west of the city centre, and a cleaner **swimming pool** (nonguests TSh3500; Railway St) at New Dodoma Hotel.

The **Parliament** (Bunge) is housed in a striking new building on the eastern edge of town just off the Dar es Salaam road, although it was temporarily closed to the public when this book was researched. If access resumes, you'll need to bring your passport along. Photography both inside and out is prohibited.

Sleeping

Hotels fill up whenever parliament is in session, so don't be surprised if you need to try several before finding a room.

BUDGET

Yarabi Salama (r with shared bathroom TSh5000) The cheapest recommendable option near the bus stand, with very basic twin-bedded rooms with mosquito nets. It's about a 10-minute walk west of the bus stand and two blocks east of Kuu St, and often full.

Christian Council of Tanzania (CCT; s/tw/ste TSh6000/10,000/12,000) A central location (at the main roundabout next to the Anglican church, and an easy walk from the bus stand), no-frills rooms with nets, and buckets of hot water for bathing on request. Breakfast costs extra.

Dodoma Blue Guest House (☎ 026-232 2085; Mpwapwa Rd; r with shared bathroom TSh8000, s TSh12,000) Clean rooms with fan – most either with twin beds or with one larger bed. There's no food. It's about 1.2km north of the main roundabout off Kuu St, and about a 20-minute walk from the bus stand.

MIDRANGE
National Vocational Training Centre (VETA; ☎ 026-232 2181; s with shared bathroom TSh8500, s/d TSh13,000/17,000) Simple, clean rooms, professional staff and a slow restaurant (meals from TSh400). It's set in pleasant grounds about 2km east of the city centre off the Dar es Salaam road, and is frequently full.

Cana Lodge (☎ 026-232 1199; Ninth St; s/d from TSh15,000/22,000, ste TSh25,000) Small, spotless rooms, plus an inexpensive restaurant and an internet café next door.

New Dodoma Hotel (Dodoma Rock Hotel; ☎ 026-232 1641; reservation_newdodomahotel@yahoo.com; Railway St; s/d with air-con TSh65,000/80,000, ste from Tsh80,000; ❄ 🖥 ☎) The former Railway Hotel, and Dodoma's most upmarket option, with a large inner courtyard, solid-value rooms – the suites face the main street and are noisier than the standard rooms – and a good Chinese restaurant (meals from TSh5000).

Eating
Aladdin's Cave (snacks TSh500-1500; ☺ 9.30am-1pm Mon, 9.30am-1pm & 3.30-8.30pm Tue-Sun) Great milkshakes, soft-serve ice cream, yoghurt, apples and other snacks. It's one block east of Kuu St, north of the Ismaili mosque.

Swahili Restaurant (meals from TSh1500; ☺ lunch & dinner) A local-style place serving Indian snacks and standard fare, including a few vegetarian dishes. It's near the main roundabout and one block north of the Dar es Salaam road.

Food Junction (Tembo Ave; meals from TSh1000; ☺ 8.30am-3.30pm & 6.45-10pm Mon-Sat) Inexpensive chicken and rice, and Indian snacks. It's near the main roundabout, two blocks west of Kuu St.

Yashna's Minimarket (Kuu St) For self-catering; it's behind the petrol station near the main roundabout.

Getting There & Away
AIR
Coastal Aviation flies daily between Dodoma and Arusha (US$220), and occasionally has seats on charters to/from Dar es Salaam (US$390). The airfield is about 2km north of the main roundabout.

BUS
Going to/from Dar es Salaam, Scandinavian Express has daily departures in each direction at 9.30am (ordinary; TSh12,000, six hours) and 11.15am (luxury; TSh15,000) from its bus station situated about 1km east of town along the Dar es Salaam road. Otherwise, there are daily buses from the bus stand, with the last departure at about 11am.

To Iringa, there's a daily bus via Makatapora; for details, see p228. Going via Chalinze (Urafiki and Shabiby lines) costs about TSh20,000.

To Kondoa (TSh8000) and Kolo (TSh12,000), Kings Cross and Satellite Coach lines depart daily at 6am, 10am and 12pm from the bus stand. Book at the bus stand, or at New Victory Hotel off Kuu St, at the northern edge of Mwalimu JK Nyerere Park and diagonally opposite the CCM building.

To Singida, there are daily direct buses (TSh16,500, five to six hours), many of which come from Dar es Salaam and are full by the time they reach Dodoma (about noon). On Tuesday, Thursday and Saturday, buses originating in Dodoma depart at 8.30am for Singida.

To Arusha, there are several lines (including Shabiby and Urafiki) going via Chalinze from about TSh20,000. Otherwise, you'll need to go in stages via Kondoa and Babati.

The *dalla-dalla* stand, known as Jamatini, is on the Dar es Salaam road just east of the Ismaili mosque.

TRAIN
Dodoma lies on the Central Line to Kigoma and Mwanza (it's currently the start and end of both routes, until service between Dodoma and Dar es Salaam resumes), and there's also a spur line between Dodoma and Singida; see p266.

TANZANIA

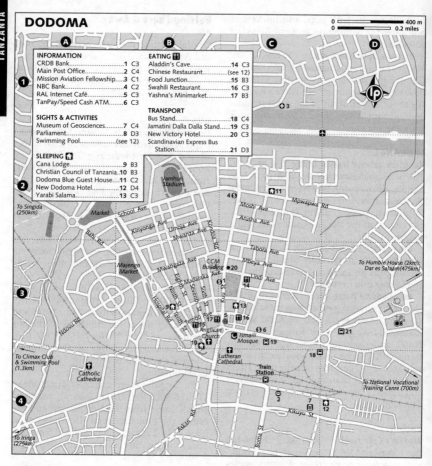

DODOMA

0 — 400 m
0 — 0.2 miles

INFORMATION
CRDB Bank.........................1 C3
Main Post Office................2 C4
Mission Aviation Fellowship...3 C1
NBC Bank...........................4 C2
RAL Internet Café...............5 C3
TanPay/Speed Cash ATM......6 C3

SIGHTS & ACTIVITIES
Museum of Geosciences........7 C4
Parliament..........................8 D3
Swimming Pool.............(see 12)

SLEEPING 🛏
Cana Lodge.........................9 B3
Christian Council of Tanzania..10 B3
Dodoma Blue Guest House...11 C2
New Dodoma Hotel..............12 D4
Yarabi Salama....................13 C3

EATING 🍴
Aladdin's Cave...................14 C3
Chinese Restaurant.........(see 12)
Food Junction...................15 B3
Swahili Restaurant.............16 C3
Yashna's Minimarket..........17 B3

TRANSPORT
Bus Stand.........................18 C4
Jamatini Dalla Dalla Stand.....19 C3
New Victory Hotel...............20 C3
Scandinavian Express Bus
   Station...........................21 D3

To Singida
(250km)

Jamhuri Stadium

Market

School Ave

Bahi Rd

Kinyonga Ave

Umoja Ave

Mwanza Ave

Kondoa Rd

Moshi Ave

Mpwapwa Rd

Arusha Ave

Majengo Market

Mwangaza Ave

Madaraka Ave

Eighth St

Ninth St

Seventh St

Sixth St

CCM Building

Tabora Ave

Mbeya Ave

Lindi Ave

To Humble House (2km);
Dar es Salaam (475km)

Ndovu Rd

Hospital Rd

Tenth St

Tembo Ave

Anglican Church

Ismaili Mosque

Lutheran Cathedral

Train Station

To Climax Club
& Swimming Pool
(1.3km)

Catholic Cathedral

To National Vocational
Training Centre (700m)

Askari Rd

Boma St

Kikuyu St

To Iringa
(275km)

BABATI
☎ 027

Babati, on the edge of the Rift Valley about 175km southwest of Arusha, is the jumping-off point for Mt Hanang climbs, and for travel to Singida, Mwanza and Lake Victoria along the southern loop via Ngeza and Shinyanga.

There are internet connections at **Rainbow Internet Café** (per hr TSh2000; ⏱ 8am-7pm Mon-Sat) behind Motel PaaPaa, and at **Huddinge** (per hr TSh2000; ⏱ 9am-6pm Mon-Sat), at the southern end of town. The **NMB Bank** (Main road) changes major currencies, cash only.

The Cultural Tourism Program office, next to Kahembe's Guest House, organises Hanang climbs and trips with local fishermen on the lake.

Sleeping & Eating
Motel Paa Paa (☎ 027-253 1111; r with shared/private bathroom TSh3000/5000) No-frills rooms near the bus stand and market.

Maitsa Executive Guest House (r with shared/private bathroom TSh4000/6000, with private bathroom & TV TSh8000) Simple, clean rooms, each with one large bed and net; there's no food. It's a five-minute walk from the bus stand, just up from Kahembe's Guest House.

Kahembe's Guest House (☎ 027-253 1088, 0784-397477; kahembeculture@hotmail.com; s/d US$15/25) Just across the large field in front of the bus stand, this place offers twin- and double-bedded rooms (the singles with one large-ish double bed), hot-water showers and full breakfast.

TANZANIA

Abida Best Bites (meals from TSh2000; ☺ breakfast, lunch & dinner) On the side street turning off the Dodoma road next to Dodoma Transport Hotel, with curries, chips, *ugali* and even a few vegetarian offerings.

Getting There & away

Mtei line buses run between Arusha and Babati, departing between 6am and 1pm (TSh6000, 3½ to four hours, three daily). The 6am bus continues to Kondoa (TSh5000, about three hours from Babati to Kondoa). The last bus from Babati to Arusha departs at 4pm.

MT HANANG

The volcanic Mt Hanang (3417m) rises steeply above the surrounding plains about 180km southwest of Arusha. It's Tanzania's fourth-highest mountain, with a satisfying trek to the summit. The surrounding area is home to a colourful array of ethnic groups, including the seminomadic Barabaig.

The most popular route to the top is the Jorodom Route, which begins in the town of **Katesh** on Hanang's southern side, and can be done in one long day (with an additional day necessary for making arrangements). You'll need to go with a guide, best arranged through Kahembe's Trekking & Cultural Safaris (p68) in Babati. It costs US$130 per person for a two-day Hanang climb from Arusha, excluding bus transport costs. Don't go with any of the freelance guides who hang around Katesh and Babati saying they're with Kahembe's or the local municipality. There have been several instances of travellers who have organised things on their own being taken part way up the mountain and then relieved of their valuables.

For all trekking on the mountain you'll need to pay a US$30 forest reserve fee per person per trip, plus a TSh2500 village fee per person per trip for climbs on the Jorodom Route (both included in Kahembe's price). Water supplies up high are unreliable; carry at least 4L.

Colt (☎ 027-253 0030; s/d TSh8000/10,000), just past the Katesh market, has straightforward rooms with hot water on request. **Tip Top** (r TSh11,000), near the bus stand, has cold water only. For meals, try Kabwogi's, near the Lutheran church.

Katesh is also known for its large **mnada** (market auction) held on the 9th and 10th,

and on the 27th of each month, when Maasai, Barabaig, Iraqw and others converge at the base of the mountain to trade their wares. It's about a 10-minute walk from town past the bank.

Mtei buses from Arusha and Babati pass through Katesh on their way to Singida, with the last Arusha departure at 9am. Otherwise, you'll need to spend a night in Babati and catch a bus to Katesh the next morning.

KOLO-KONDOA ROCK ART SITES

Kondoa district, especially around tiny Kolo village, lies at the centre of a major collection of ancient rock paintings. Little is known about the paintings' artists or their ages. While some date back more than 3000 years, others are probably not more than several hundred years old. One theory maintains they were made by the Sandawe, who are distantly related linguistically to South Africa's San. Others posit that the more recent paintings were made by Bantu-speaking peoples who moved into the area at a later date.

To visit, you'll need to arrange a permit (TSh2000) and a guide with the Department of Antiquities on the main road in Kolo. There are between 150 and over 300 sites, of which only a portion have been officially documented. The closest sites – Kolo B1, B2 and B3, which also are among the most interesting – are spread out in the hills rising up near the seasonal Kolo (Hembe) River about 9km from Kolo. It's possible to cover most of this distance with a 4WD, except for the final rocky climb up to the sites.

It's possible to hire a vehicle in Kondoa, though prices are elevated. The Kolo B1-3 sites can be reached with some effort with 2WD with clearance during the dry season.

Despite its recently elevated status as a Unesco World Heritage Site, visitors are not exactly flocking to the rock art sites. Dodoma and Arusha are the logical jumping-off points for independent travellers, but for anything organised, it can be difficult to find an Arusha-based safari operator willing to sort things out for you. For upmarket tours, try **East African Safari & Touring Company** (www.eastafricansafari.info). Budget-level visits can be arranged with Kahembe's Trekking & Cultural Safaris (p68) or through the Arusha TTB Tourist Information Centre (ask for the Kondoa-Rangi Cultural Tourism Programme).

There's a basic **camp site** (camping TSh2000) near the Kolo (Hembe) River bed about 4km from Kolo. Otherwise, the closest overnight base is Kondoa, 20km south.

Kolo is 100km south of Babati and 275km southwest of Arusha. There are several buses daily from Babati to Kolo and on to Kondoa (TSh5000), and at least one direct bus daily between Arusha and Kondoa via Kolo, leaving Arusha at 6am (TSh12,000, six hours). Kolo can also be reached from Dodoma, 180km to the south.

KONDOA
☎ 026

This district capital – centre of the Irangi people and a former stop along the old caravan route between the interior and the coast – is of interest as a springboard to visit the Kolo-Kondoa rock art sites. There's no internet connection, and no ATM; the local branch of NMB bank changes US dollars and euros cash. The town itself is about 3km off the Babati–Dodoma road.

New Planet (☎ 026-236 0357; s/d with shared bathroom TSh8000/10,000, s/d TSh10,000/12,000), three-minutes' walk from the bus stand, has clean rooms with nets, fan and TV, hot-water buckets on request and meals. Down the street, and under the same management, is **New Pluto Guest House** (r with shared bathroom TSh4000), with tiny, no-frills rooms.

Kings Cross, Satellite and Machame Inv bus lines run daily between Kondoa and Dodoma, departing from Kondoa at 6am, 8am, 10am and 12.30pm (TSh7000, four to six hours). From Kondoa to Kolo (TSh3000, one hour), and on to Babati, departures are at 6am, 11am and 1pm. Hiring a taxi to the Kolo rock art sites (sites B1-3) will cost from TSh30,000, and can be arranged through New Planet.

SHINYANGA
☎ 028

Large, sprawling Shinyanga lies near the centre of an important mineral mining area, and has boomed in recent years with the increase in local diamond and gold mining.

NBC Bank (Mwanza Rd), along the main tarmac road just south of Shinyanga Motel, has an ATM. There's an **internet café** (Mwanza Rd; per hr TSh1000; ☽ 8am-6pm Mon-Fri, 9am-1pm Sat) next to the post office, just north of Shinyanga Motel. The main tarmac road runs along the east-

ern edge of town, with the market, bus stand and guesthouse areas spreading westwards from here.

Sleeping & Eating
Makoa Hotel (r downstairs/upstairs TSh15,000/20,000) Small, spotless rooms with nets, and a restaurant. It's diagonally opposite and one block in from the bus stand, and signposted near the Mohammed Trans office.

Shinyanga Motel (☎ 028-276 2458, 028-276 2369; r TSh25,000, with air-con from TSh30,000; ✗) Opposite the train station, this multistorey, orange building has simple, clean and large twin-bedded rooms with nets, window screens, fan and hot water, and food on order.

Getting There & Away
Mohammed Trans goes daily to Tabora (TSh8000, six hours, departing by 7am; book in advance) and to Mwanza (TSh4000, three hours, several departures between 6am and 8.30am). Departures are from its office, on a side street opposite the bus stand.

There are daily buses to Kahama (four hours), from where you can get onward transport to Kigoma, or to the Rwanda and Burundi borders via Nyankanazi junction.

NZEGA
☎ 026

This junction town is where the roads to Kahama (for the Rwanda and Burundi borders) and Singida branch off from the Mwanza–Tabora road.

Forest Guest House (☎ 026-269 2555; r TSh10,000-12,000, ste TSh25,000) has clean self-contained rooms. It's about 1km from the bus stand, just off the old (unpaved) Kahama road and signposted. For light meals, try **Garden Café** (snacks from TSh250), near the market.

SINGIDA
☎ 026

Singida – with its huge granite boulders, two lakes and waterbirds – makes a possible stopover if you're travelling between Lake Victoria and central Tanzania. There's an **internet café** (per hr TSh2000) just north of the market, and an NBC bank with ATM (Visa card only) near the post office.

Stanley Hotel (☎ 026-250 2351; s/d with shared bathroom TSh7000/9500, d TSh16,000), near the bus stand, has small, decent rooms with TV and bathroom, and a restaurant.

J-Four (Legho) Motel (☎ 026-250 2526; r TSh17,000) Quieter than the Stanley, with a small garden, a restaurant, and rooms with nets and bathrooms. It's on the northwestern edge of town, about 10 minutes on foot from the bus stand.

Getting There & Away

Buses go daily to/from Arusha (eight hours) via Katesh and Babati. The road to Nzega, Shinyanga and on to Mwanza (seven hours) is also traversed by daily buses. To Dodoma (TSh16,500, five to six hours), buses run daily, or you can take the train. There's one direct bus daily to/from Dar es Salaam via Dodoma, departing in both directions by 6am (12 hours).

LAKE VICTORIA

Lake Victoria is Africa's largest lake and the second-largest freshwater lake in the world. While the Tanzanian part of this enormous patch of blue sees only a trickle of tourists, the region is well worth ex-

ploring for anyone interested in seeing Tanzania off the beaten track, or in linking travels between Uganda, Kenya and Tanzania. Highlights include Rubondo Island National Park, Bukoba and the surrounding Kagera region, and the Bujora Cultural Centre near Mwanza. Lake Victoria also makes a convenient gateway to the western Serengeti.

Many lakeshore areas are infested with bilharzia and swimming from the coastline isn't recommended.

MWANZA
☎ 028

Mwanza is Tanzania's second-largest city, a major port and the economic centre of the lake region. The surrounding area – marked by hills strewn with enormous boulders – is home to the Sukuma, the country's -largest tribe.

Despite its size, Mwanza has managed to retain a low-key ambience and a bit of a village feel. The city makes a convenient starting/finishing point for a Serengeti safari, though don't expect many budget deals.

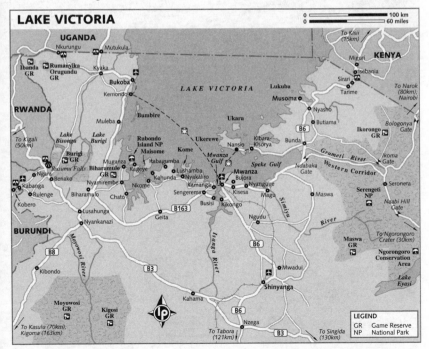

TANZANIA

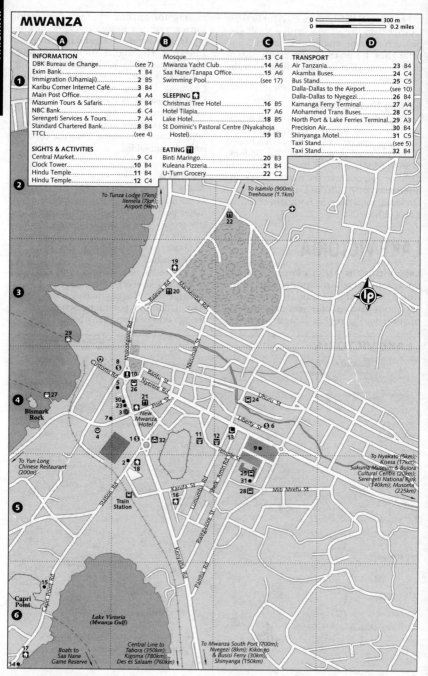

MWANZA

0 — 300 m
0 — 0.2 miles

INFORMATION
DBK Bureau de Change................(see 7)
Exim Bank...**1** B4
Immigration (Uhamiaji)...................**2** B5
Karibu Corner Internet Café..........**3** B4
Main Post Office..............................**4** A4
Masumin Tours & Safaris................**5** B4
NBC Bank...**6** C4
Serengeti Services & Tours............**7** A4
Standard Chartered Bank...............**8** B4
TTCL..(see 4)

SIGHTS & ACTIVITIES
Central Market..................................**9** C4
Clock Tower....................................**10** B4
Hindu Temple.................................**11** B4
Hindu Temple.................................**12** C4

Mosque...**13** C4
Mwanza Yacht Club.......................**14** A6
Saa Nane/Tanapa Office................**15** A6
Swimming Pool..............................(see 17)

SLEEPING
Christmas Tree Hotel.....................**16** B5
Hotel Tilapia....................................**17** A6
Lake Hotel.......................................**18** B5
St Dominic's Pastoral Centre (Nyakahoja
  Hostel)..**19** B3

EATING
Binti Maringo..................................**20** B3
Kuleana Pizzeria.............................**21** B4
U-Turn Grocery...............................**22** C2

TRANSPORT
Air Tanzania....................................**23** B4
Akamba Buses.................................**24** C4
Bus Stand..**25** C5
Dalla-Dallas to the Airport...........(see 10)
Dalla-Dallas to Nyegezi.................**26** B4
Kamanga Ferry Terminal................**27** A4
Mohammed Trans Buses................**28** C5
North Port & Lake Ferries Terminal...**29** A3
Precision Air....................................**30** B4
Shinyanga Motel.............................**31** C5
Taxi Stand.......................................(see 5)
Taxi Stand..**32** B4

Orientation

To the west, and a short walk from the Clock Tower, are the passenger-ferry docks and several banks and shops. East of the Clock Tower area are more shops, guesthouses and mosques; further east are the market and bus stand. Located in the southwestern corner of town, about a 10-minute walk from the Clock Tower, is the train station. Just beyond here is Capri Point, a small peninsula with lake views and an upmarket hotel.

Information

DBK Bureau de Change (Post St) At Serengeti Services & Tours; the easiest place to change cash and travellers cheques.

Exim Bank (Kenyatta Rd) ATM (MasterCard only).

Immigration (Uhamiaji; Station Rd) Just up from and diagonally opposite the train station.

Karibu Corner Internet Café (cnr Post St & Kenyatta Rd; per hr TSh1000; ☺ 8am-8.30pm Mon-Fri, 8am-7pm Sat, 9am-7pm Sun) Internet access and internet dialling.

Main post office (Post St; ☺ 8am-5pm Mon-Fri, 9am-noon Sat)

NBC Bank (Liberty St) ATM (Visa only); also changes travellers cheques.

Standard Chartered Bank (Makongoro Rd) ATM (Visa only); near the Clock Tower.

TRAVEL AGENCIES

For a two-day, one-night return trip to Seronera in Serengeti National Park, transport only, expect to pay from about US$400 per vehicle (four to six persons), including petrol and a driver.

Masumin Tours & Safaris (☎ 028-254 1127, 028-250 0233, 028-250 0192, 028-250 3295; www.masumintours .com; Kenyatta Rd)

Serengeti Services & Tours (☎ 028-250 0061, 028-250 0754; www.serengetiservices.com; Post St)

Sights & Activities

Central Mwanza has an Oriental feel due to its many **mosques** and **Hindu temples**, especially in the area around Temple St. To the southeast is the chaotic **central market**. The towering stack of boulders balanced just offshore from Yun Long Chinese Restaurant is **Bismarck Rock**, a major local landmark.

Hotel Tilapia has a **swimming pool** (adult/child TSh8000/3500).

SAA NANE GAME RESERVE

The **Saa Nane Game Reserve** (adult/child TSh800/400), on a tiny island off Capri Point, is slated – in somewhat of a credibility stretch – to become Tanzania's newest national park (at which point entry fees will increase). Its former collection of suffering animals has been removed and rehabilitation work is underway. It makes a pleasant getaway from town, with a few short walkways and lookout points. A boat departs every two hours in each direction between 9am and 5pm at weekends from the pier opposite the **Saa Nane/Tanapa office** (☎ 028-254 1819; Capri Point; ☺ 8am-5pm Mon-Fri), about 200m north of Hotel Tilapia (per person return TSh800, 20 minutes). On weekdays, you'll need to charter a park boat (return per boat TSh10,000, eight passengers maximum). At the Saa Nane/Tanapa office is a small natural history museum. The Saa Nane office is a good place for booking accommodation and transport arrangements to/from Rubondo Island National Park.

Sleeping

BUDGET

It's sometimes possible to arrange camping on the grounds of the Mwanza Yacht Club, next to Hotel Tilapia. Otherwise, the closest places for camping are Bujora Cultural Centre (p205), or near the Serengeti's Ndabaka Gate.

St Dominic's Pastoral Centre (Nyakahoja Hostel) (☎ 028-250 0830; off Balewa Rd; s/d with shared bathroom in old wing TSh10,000/15,000, with private bathroom TSh18,000/25,000) A centrally located church-run hostel offering spartan rooms with shared cold-water bathroom, plus nicer, newer ones with private bathroom with hot water, and a canteen (breakfast TSh1000, lunch/dinner TSh2000). It's five minutes' walk north of the clock tower roundabout.

Christmas Tree Hotel (☎ 028-250 2001; off Karuta St; r TSh15,000) Clean, serviceable rooms with a small double bed plus hot water and TV. Some have nets, and there's a restaurant. The hotel is just off Karuta St. There's also an entrance from Kenyatta Rd.

Lake Hotel (☎ 028-250 0658; Ground fl, Station Rd; s/d TSh15,000/20,000, upstairs d TSh30,000) This hotel is ageing and tatty, but its shortcomings are easy to overlook if you've just disembarked from a 24-hour-plus haul on the Central Line train. Upstairs rooms – with trickling hot-water shower, fan and nets – are better, and management lets three people sleep in a double room for no additional charge.

Treehouse (☎ 028-254 1160; treehouse@streetwise -africa.org; s with shared bathroom US$35, s/d from US$45/55, 5-person family banda US$65; ☐) A B&B-style place with a range of clean rooms plus lake views in the distance. Earnings support the affiliated Streetwise Africa charity. It's about 2km northeast of town in Isamilo, and TSh2000 in a taxi. Discounts are offered for volunteers.

MIDRANGE & TOP END

Tunza Lodge (☎ 028-256 2215, 0767-788180; www.tunza lodge.com; s/tw/d TSh45,000/50,000/60,000) Small cottages scattered over expansive, lakeside grounds, a waterside bar and restaurant, and beach volleyball at weekends. It's about 8km from the town centre and 2km from the airport: from town, follow the airport road to the Ilemela *dalla-dalla* station, turn left and continue down a dirt road about 2.5km to the lake, staying left at the forks. Public transport goes as far as Ilemela, from where it's a 20-minute walk.

Hotel Tilapia (☎ 028-250 0517, 028-250 0617; www .hoteltilapia.com; Capri Point; r incl breakfast US$90-130; 🛇 ☐ 🐾) The Tilapia – overlooking the water on the eastern side of Capri Point – is the hotel of choice for many business travellers, and is frequently fully booked. There's a lakeside bar and sundowners deck, a tiny business centre, a restaurant offering pizzas, Indian and continental fare, and a choice of either somewhat dowdy standard rooms or spiffier, more spacious bungalow-style suites. A good buffet breakfast is served. Credit cards are accepted (5% surcharge).

Eating

Kuleana Pizzeria (☎ 028-256 0566; Post St; meals TSh2500; 🛇 7am-9pm) Simple good meals – pizzas, omelettes, sandwiches, fruit and fresh-squeezed juices – and a mix of locals and expats. It's just down from New Mwanza Hotel.

Binti Maringo (Balewa Rd; meals TSh3000-TSh7000; 🛇 9am-10pm Mon-Sat) Open-air seating and well-prepared local food, including a Saturday breakfast buffet, plus textiles and crafts for sale and clothes tailoring. Profits support a training program for street children. It's next to the Kuleana Centre for Children's Rights, just off Makongoro Rd.

Yun Long Chinese Restaurant (meals TSh6000-12,000; 🛇 lunch & dinner) Chinese food overlooking Bismarck Rock and the lake. Turn left one block west of the post office and continue along the dirt road paralleling the water for about 500m.

U-Turn Grocery (Balewa Rd; 🛇 8am-8pm Mon-Fri, 8am-2pm & 6-8pm Sat, 10am-2pm Sun) For self-catering.

Getting There & Away

AIR

There are daily flights to/from Dar es Salaam (TSh208,000) and to (but not from) Kilimanjaro International Airport (KIA; TSh170,000) on **Air Tanzania** (☎ 028-250 1059, 028-250 0046; Kenyatta Rd). **Precision Air** (☎ 028-250 0819, 028-256 0027; pwmwz@africaonline.co.tz; Kenyatta Rd) also flies daily between Mwanza, KIA (continuing on to Nairobi, Kenya) and Dar es Salaam, and several times weekly to Shinyanga and Musoma.

Coastal Aviation (☎ 028-256 0441; mwanza@coastal .cc; Airport) flies daily between Mwanza and Arusha (one way US$260) via the Serengeti, and between Mwanza and Geita.

Auric Air (☎ 028-256 1286, 028-256 0524; www.auricair .com) has two flights daily between Mwanza and Bukoba (one way TSh120,000). In Mwanza, book through Masumin Tours & Safaris. Auric Air also does charters to Rubondo Island, as does **RenAir** (☎ 028-256 2069, 028-256 1158; www.renair .com; Airport) and Coastal Aviation.

BOAT

For ferries between Mwanza and Bukoba, see p264.

Ferries to Bukoba and Ukerewe depart Mwanza's North Port, near the clock tower. For information on the ferries crossing the Mwanza Gulf, see p206. The Kamanga ferry departs Mwanza from its own port just south of North Port. Cargo boats to Port Bell (Uganda) and Kenya depart Mwanza South Port, about 1.5km southeast of the town centre.

A fast catamaran to Bukoba and Ukerewe was planned to start service imminently; ask around in Mwanza.

BUS

The main departure point for southern destinations is Nyegezi bus stand, about 10km south of the town centre along the Shinyanga road. Buses for Musoma, Nairobi (Kenya) and other points north depart from Nyakato, about 6km north of town along the Musoma road (TSh300 in a *dalla-dalla* and about TSh5000 in a taxi).

Akamba buses depart the **Akamba office** (☎ 028-250 0272), just north of the small footbridge near Majukano Hotel and between

Liberty and Uhuru Sts. Mohammed Trans buses depart from the **Mohammed Trans office** (just off Miti Mrefu St) diagonally up from the bus stand.

To Musoma, Mohammed Trans and other lines go several times daily between 6am and 2pm (TSh6000, three hours), with some continuing to the Kenyan border.

To Tabora (TSh15,000, seven hours), Mohammed Trans goes daily via Shinyanga, departing in each direction at 6am and 1pm. Mohammed Trans also runs almost hourly buses to Shinyanga (TSh5000, three hours).

To Bukoba and points west of Mwanza around Lake Victoria, it's best to do the trip in stages via Biharamulo (although if your destination is Bukoba itself, it's better to take the ferry or fly). Heading west from Mwanza, there are daily buses direct to Geita and Biharamulo (TSh10,000, six to seven hours). It's usually just as 'fast' to cross the Mwanza Gulf on the first Kamanga ferry, and then get onward transport to Geita and Biharamulo from the other side. Once in Biharamulo, there are onward connections to Bukoba, and to Lusahunga (TSh2000). From Lusahunga, you can continue to Benako and Ngara for the Rwanda and Burundi borders. There's also a direct bus between Mwanza and Benako departing by about 7am in each direction (TSh22,000). For more on getting to Rwanda and Burundi, see p261 and p258.

Akamba goes daily to Arusha/Moshi (TSh47,000) and Dar es Salaam (TSh71,000 plus US$20 for a Kenyan transit visa, about 30 hours) via Nairobi (TSh28,000 plus visa costs, about 15 hours), but you'll need to change buses in Nairobi. A generally better option is Mohammed Trans, which does the route via Singida (TSh45,000, about 12 hours to Arusha). It's also possible to go to Arusha via the Serengeti on Coast line, but in addition to the fare (TSh30,000, 14 hours) you'll need to pay entry fees for both Serengeti (US$50) and Ngorongoro Conservation Area (US$50), and the bus goes too fast for any serious wildlife watching. Departures are currently at 5am on Tuesday and Friday from Arusha, and at 6am on Monday and Thursday from Mwanza.

To Kigoma (TSh25,000, 15 to 17 hours), there are two buses daily, going via Biharamulo and Lusahunga, and departing from Mwanza at 4.30am. The no-frills Shinyanga Motel next to the Mwanza's bus stand is a local favourite and a convenient overnight spot for passengers departing on this route.

To Nkome (for Rubondo Island), go to the Kamanga ferry terminal and look for Nyahunge or Msukuma bus lines, both of which go to Nkome, departing from Mwanza at about 10am (TSh5000, four to five hours). Alternatively, go first to Geita, from where there are two vehicles daily to Nkome (TSh3000 from Geita to Nkome). Returning from Nkome to Mwanza, there's a daily departure at 5.30am; otherwise you'll need to go via Geita.

TRAIN
Mwanza is the terminus of a branch of the Central Line. See p266.

Getting Around
TO/FROM THE AIRPORT
Mwanza's airport is 10km north of the town centre (TSh8000 in a taxi). *Dalla-dallas* leave from near the clock tower.

BUS & TAXI
Dalla-dallas for destinations along the Musoma road, including Kisesa and Igoma (for Bujora Cultural Centre) depart from the Bugando Hill stand, southeast of the market, while those running along the airport road depart from near the clock tower. *Dalla-dallas* to Nyegezi bus stand depart from Nyerere Rd.

There are taxi stands at the intersection of Station and Kenyatta Rds, and on Kenyatta Rd, in front of Masumin Tours & Safaris. One of the drivers at this latter stand told us it was called *standi ya wazee* – the old men's taxi rank – because the drivers here are all 'old and honest'...

AROUND MWANZA
Bujora Cultural Centre (Sukuma Museum)
The **Sukuma Museum & Bujora Cultural Centre** (www.sukumamuseum.org; admission TSh8000; ⏱ 8am-6pm Mon-Fri, 10am-6pm Sat & Sun) makes a worthwhile day trip from Mwanza, with traditional Sukuma dwellings, the house of a traditional healer and the royal drum pavilion, built in the shape of the stool used by Sukuma kings. The church in the centre of the grounds was built in 1969 by David Fumbuka Clement, the Quebecois missionary priest who founded the museum.

There's **camping** (camping TSh5000) on the grounds of the cultural centre; meals can be arranged.

Bujora is about 20km east of Mwanza off the Musoma road. Take a *dalla-dalla* to Igoma, from where you can get a pick-up to Kisesa. Once in Kisesa, walk a short way along the main road until you see the sign for Bujora Primary School (Shule ya Msingi Bujora). Turn left and follow the dirt road for 2km to 3km to the cultural centre.

Ukerewe

☎ 028

Ukerewe is known for its traditional healers and birdlife, and makes a possible stop en route between Mwanza and the Serengeti.

Kazoba Guesthouse (r TSh6500), in the centre of Nansio – Ukerewe's only major town – has no-frills rooms and bucket baths. **Monarch Beach Resort** (☎ 028-256 0879; www.monarchhotel mwanza.com; s/d TSh25,000/32,000) – a few minutes' walk from the ferry on the Nansio lakeshore – is Ukerewe's only proper hotel, with self-contained rooms (though no running water) and meals.

GETTING THERE & AWAY

The MV *Butiama* and MV *Clarius* sail on alternate days between Mwanza's North Port and Nansio, departing from Mwanza at 9am and 2pm, and from Nansio at 8am and 1.30pm (2nd/3rd class TSh6500/4600 plus US$5 port tax, two hours).

It's also possible to reach Nansio from Bunda, about 30km north of the Serengeti's Ndabaka Gate on the Mwanza–Musoma road. Take any vehicle between Mwanza and Musoma to Bunda, from where you can get transport to Kibara-Kisorya (TSh4000). It's then a short boat ride (TSh500, 30 minutes) to Rugezi village on Ukerewe. This route is usually operated by a vehicle ferry running every two to three hours between about 8am and 5pm. Leave Bunda by about 3pm at the latest to catch the last ferry to Ukerewe.

Once on Ukerewe, a few vehicles meet boat arrivals, and there are *dalla-dallas* between Nansio and Rugezi for catching the boat over to Kibara-Kisorya. Otherwise, the only options are walking or cycling.

MWANZA TO BUKOBA

Travelling by road from Mwanza westwards along the southern part of Lake Victoria entails crossing the Mwanza Gulf. There are two ferries. The northernmost (Kamanga) ferry docks just south of the passenger ferry terminal at Mwanza's North Port, departing from Mwanza at 7.30am, 8.30am, 10.30am, 12.30am, 2.30pm (except Sunday), 4.30pm and 6pm (passenger/vehicle TSh800/6500, 30 minutes). Departures from Kamanga are roughly every two hours from 8am until 6.30pm, except there's no 2pm ferry on Sunday. If you are continuing from Kamanga to Geita, see if the Geita bus is in the vehicle queue lined up to board the ferry, and buy your bus ticket before crossing to avoid the rush on the other side. Otherwise, the only option is the *dalla-dallas* waiting on the other side. The more southerly Busisi ferry operates daily from 7am to 9pm (passenger/vehicle TSh500/5000). The boat is new, and in reasonably good nick these days, although as it's often used by trucks, the wait can be long. Its eastern terminus is at Kikongo, 30km south of Mwanza.

Once across the Mwanza Gulf, the main towns of interest en route to Bukoba are the gold-mining hub of Geita, and Biharamulo, from where there's onward transport to Lusahunga, with connections to Nzega, Kigoma, and the Burundi and Rwanda borders. East of Biharamulo, along the Geita road, is the turn-off to reach Nyamirembe and then Muganza village – a jumping-off point for Rubondo Island National Park.

North of Biharamulo, there are some beautiful lake vistas from the hills.

RUBONDO ISLAND NATIONAL PARK

Rubondo Island is one of Tanzania's least visited parks, alluring for its tranquillity, sublime scenery and birding. The park consists of Rubondo, plus about a dozen smaller islands, including 'Bird Island'. You're likely to see hippos, crocodiles, elephants (introduced several decades ago) and sitatungas – a type of antelope seen better in Rubondo than almost anywhere else in East Africa. Rubondo's chimpanzees are not habituated, and even with concerted effort, the chances of spotting them are low.

Information

Park entry fees are US$20/5 per adult/child. The park is open year-round, with the easiest time to visit from June to early November. The rainy season is prime for appreciating Rubondo's orchids, other wildflowers and butterflies.

Book park *bandas* in advance through Mwanza's **Saa Nane/Tanapa office** (☎ 028-254

1819; Capri Point; ⏰ 8am-5pm Mon-Fri) or with **park headquarters** (☎ 028-252 0720; sitatunga@tanapa.org). These are at Kageye on Rubondo's eastern side, with a warden's office (same contacts) near Nkome village on the mainland.

Sleeping

The park runs a **public camp site** (camping adult/child US$30/5) and some lovely double **bandas** (per person US$20) on the lakeshore near park headquarters. The *bandas* have electricity, nets and warm-water showers, and there's a large communal kitchen. A wonderful, tranquil set-up. There's a tiny shop about 1km away from the *bandas* in the staff quarters selling soft drink, beer and mineral water, but otherwise, bring all food and drink with you.

   Rubondo Island Camp (☎ 027-250 8790; www .africanconservancycompany.com; s/d full board plus airstrip transfers US$265/400; 🏊) is in a serene lakeshore setting several coves south of the park *bandas*, with large safari-style tents at the edge of the forest.

Getting There & Away
AIR

Charter flights from Mwanza cost about US$1400 return for a five-seater plane. See p204 for charter companies.

BOAT

There are two main ways to reach Rubondo by boat. The first is from Bukoba: take public transport to Muganza, from where it's about 25 minutes by boat to Rubondo Island and another 20 minutes by park vehicle to drive across the island to Kageye and the park *bandas*. Arrange in advance for the park boat to come and collect you – best done through Mwanza's Saa Nane/Tanapa office (p203), or through Kiroyera Tours (right) in Bukoba. The boat plus vehicle transfer to Kageye costs US$95 return per boat. In Muganza itself, you'll need to make your way from the bus stand down to the port area and wait there to be collected. There's a range of basics at the market if you need to stock up.

   The second way is to travel from Mwanza to Nkome by chartered vehicle (about US$400 return) or by bus, and then from there by boat to Rubondo. Nkome to Kageye per boat costs US$185 return and takes about one to 1½ hours. Expect quite choppy water once away from the mainland. Bookings should be made as per the Muganza route. If you take public transport to Nkome, you'll need to walk from the bus stand about 3km to the park warden's office outside town, which is the boat pick-up/ drop-off point. Bottled water and food basics are available at Nkome's market. Returning to Mwanza via this route, you'll need to overnight in Nkome, as transport from Nkome to Mwanza departs early. There are several basic local guesthouses, and with your own tent and food, it's possible to camp in the lakeside grounds of the Nkome ranger post.

BUKOBA
☎ 028

Bukoba, home of the Haya people, is Tanzania's second-largest port on Lake Victoria, and an agreeable and convenient stop if you're combining travels in Tanzania and Uganda.

   The **Kagera Museum** (☎ 028-222 0203; kmuseum@ kiroyeratours.com; Nyamukazi area; admission US$2, guided tour per group TSh2500; ⏰ 9.30am-6pm) houses a display of wildlife photographs and local tribal items. Traditional dancing and drumming performances can be organised (from about US$50 per group). The museum is on the far side of Bukoba's airstrip. Kiroyera Tours can help with directions and a guide.

Information

Bukoba Cyber Centre (cnr Jamhuri & Kashozi Rds; per hr TSh1000; ⏰ 8.30am-7pm Mon-Sat)
CRDB Bank (cnr Jamhuri & Kashozi Rds) ATM (Visa); diagonally opposite Bukoba Cyber Centre.
Global Travel Services (☎ 028-222 0009; Jamhuri Rd) Flight bookings; just up from New Rose Café.
Kiroyera Tours (☎ 028-222 0203; www.kiroyeratours .com; Sokoine St) An excellent place, opposite the market, and an essential stop for information on nearby attractions, cultural and historical excursions in and around Bukoba, and bus and ferry ticket bookings.
NBC Bank (Jamhuri Rd) ATM (Visa); also changes cash.
Post Office & Post Office Internet Café (cnr Barongo & Mosque Sts; per hr TSh1200; ⏰ 8am-6pm Mon-Fri, 9am-noon Sat)

Sleeping & Eating

Kiroyera Campsite (www.kiroyeratours.com/campsite .htm; vehicle per day TSh2500, camping with own/rental tent TSh4000/6000, tw banda per person TSh12,000) A great backpackers' spot on the lakeshore, with shady beachside camping, showers and three *msonge* – traditional Haya huts with electricity and shared bathroom – plus local-style meals (breakfast per person TSh4000, meals TSh6000 to TSh7000) and a bar.

TANZANIA

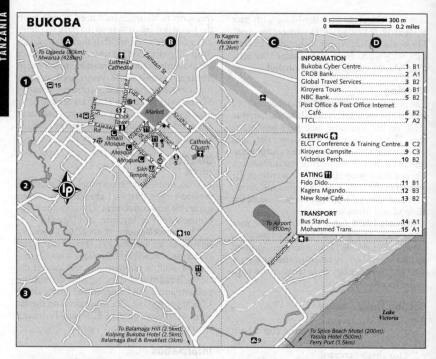

BUKOBA

INFORMATION	
Bukoba Cyber Centre..................1	B1
CRDB Bank..................................2	A1
Global Travel Services.................3	B2
Kiroyera Tours............................4	B1
NBC Bank...................................5	B2
Post Office & Post Office Internet	
Café.......................................6	B2
TTCL...7	A2

SLEEPING	
ELCT Conference & Training Centre..8	C2
Kiroyera Campsite.......................9	C3
Victorius Perch.........................10	B2

EATING	
Fido Dido.................................11	B1
Kagera Mgando.........................12	B3
New Rose Café...........................13	B2

TRANSPORT	
Bus Stand................................14	A1
Mohammed Trans......................15	A1

Spice Beach Motel (☎ 028-222 0124; s/d TSh10,000/15,000; ✗) A small guesthouse on the water near the port, with one single room sharing facilities, and several small doubles with private bathroom, TV and a restaurant.

ELCT Conference & Training Centre (☎ 028-222 3121; www.elctbukobahotel.com; Aerodrome Rd; s/d with shared bathroom US$12/14, r with private bathroom US$30; ✗ 🖳) Clean, comfortable rooms – some with lake views – and large grounds along the airport road bordering the lake. Breakfast costs extra.

Yassila Hotel (☎ 028-222 0251; d with shared bathroom TSh10,000, s/d TSh20,000/30,000; ✗) Near Spice Beach Motel and the port, with self-contained rooms (ask for one upstairs) with net, fan and hot water, and some with lake views, plus a restaurant.

Kolping Bukoba Hotel (☎ 028-222 0199, 0784-350003; s/d TSh30,000/40,000) On Balamaga Hill, about 3km from town (TSh5000 in a taxi), with spotless, breezy, good-value rooms – ask for one that's lake facing – a restaurant and wide views over the lake.

Balamaga Bed & Breakfast (☎ 0787-757289; www .balamagabb.com; s/d from TSh34,000/54,000; 🖳) In

the Balamaga Hill area above the port, just past Kolping Bukoba hotel, is this private house with four spacious rooms (two with private bathroom), lovely gardens, cable TV and meals.

Victorius Perch (☎ 028-222 0115; d/tw/ste TSh45,000/50,000/80,000; ✗ 🖳) A new local business travellers' hotel in the town centre, with small, well-appointed rooms with TV, hot water and a restaurant.

New Rose Café (Jamhuri Rd) Inexpensive meals and snacks.

For self-catering try **Fido Dido** (cnr Sokoine & Jamhuri Rds). **Kagera Mgando** (Uganda road) sells fresh yoghurt.

Getting There & Away

AIR

There are two flights daily to/from Mwanza (TSh120,000) on **Auric Air** (☎ 028-256 1286, 028-256 0524; www.auricair.com). Book through Kiroyera Tours or Global Travel Services.

BOAT

For the MV *Victoria* ferry between Bukoba and Mwanza, see p264.

BUS

All the bus companies and their ticket offices are based at or near the bus stand at the western end of town. Mohammed Trans has its own office in the Kanoni area: continue from the bus stand northwest along the Uganda road – it's about 500m further, just after the small bridge, and to the right of the Uganda road. Kiroyera Tours also helps with bus ticket bookings.

Several lines, including Mohammed Trans, go daily to Biharamulo (TSh8500) and on to Lusahunga (TSh10,000), from where you can catch onward transport to Ngara or Benako and the Burundi and Rwanda borders.

To Kigoma (TSh27,000, 15 to 17 hours), Adventure and Visram lines go twice weekly, departing at 5.30am in each direction. It's also possible (but longer and slightly more expensive) to do the trip in stages, changing at Muleba, Nyakanazi, Kibondo and Kasulu.

To Mwanza, Mohammed Trans departs Bukoba at 6am (TSh30,000, 10 hours), changing buses inconveniently at Nzega. Otherwise, make your way in stages via Biharamulo and Geita, but it's better to take the ferry or fly.

To Dar es Salaam, Mohammed Trans (TSh60,000) goes daily via Biharamulo, Kahama, Nzega, Singida and Dodoma, departing from Mwanza at 6am, arriving in Dodoma about 9pm, where it sleeps, departing from Dodoma by 5am the next day and reaching Dar es Salaam by about 11am. Falcon does this same Dar es Salaam route several times weekly (TSh59,000).

To Muganza (for Rubondo Island; TSh7000, four to five hours), there's one direct vehicle daily except Sunday. Otherwise, get any vehicle going to Muleba (about halfway), from where you can get onward transport.

To Tabora (TSh35,000), Mohammed Trans departs daily at 6am to Nzega (about eight hours), where you'll need to change vehicles to Tabora (four to five hours from Nzega).

MUSOMA

☎ 028

The small fishing port of Musoma, on a peninsula surrounded by low hills dotted with large boulders and favoured by waterbirds, is capital of the Mara region and an agreeable stopping point en route between Mwanza and Kenya.

There are ATMs (both Visa only) at the NBC (four blocks south of the main street) and CRDB banks – one block north of the main street. NBC also changes cash. For internet try **Musoma Communications Centre** (per hr TSh1000; 🕙 8.30am-7.30pm), about two blocks east of CRDB bank on a side street opposite Precision Air, and at **Kokos Internet Café** (per hr TSh1000; 🕙 8am-7pm) about one block west of CRDB bank.

Musoma hosts a large army base outside town in Makoko; photography in this area is prohibited.

Sights

The **Nyerere Museum** (☎ 028-262 1338; www.museum.or.tz/nyerere; adult/student US$5/2; 🕙 9.30am-6pm), about 45km southeast of Musoma in Butiama, contains memorabilia from Tanzania's early post-independence days, Nyerere's personal effects and a large collection of photographs. Nearby are the Nyerere family home and the graves of Nyerere and his parents.

Take a minibus to Nyasho, from where you can get transport to Butiama. Taxis charge about TSh20,000 return.

Sleeping & Eating

Stigma Hotel (☎ 028-262 0088; s/d TSh10,000/12,000) A quiet, central place, with clean rooms with private bathroom. It's on the same street as NBC bank, about two to three blocks further down.

New Tembo Beach Hotel (☎ 028-262 2887; camping TSh5000, r TSh15,000) An amenable choice, with simple, clean rooms – the ones upstairs have a loft bed, those downstairs are all on one level and have a fan – on the lakeshore. There's also camping, a restaurant and sunset views. It's about 500m from the town centre; take the road out of town past CRDB bank and follow the signs.

Hotel Matvilla (☎ 028-262 2445; s/d TSh20,000/30,000; 🕸) Directly opposite Musoma Communications Centre Internet Café in the town centre, this place caters to local business travellers with small, dark-ish but clean rooms and a restaurant.

Hotel Orange Tree (☎ 028-262 0021; Kawawa St; meals from TSh3000; 🕙 lunch & dinner) has tasty grilled fish and rice. **Rama Dishes** (meals from TSh1200), a local eatery around the corner from NBC bank, is good for plantains or chicken and chips.

For self-catering, try **Flebs Traders** (Main St), or **Kotra's Supermarket** (Mwanza Rd), about 2.5km from the town centre.

Getting There & Away

AIR

The airfield is about 1km west of the market. Precision Air flies three times weekly from Dar es Salaam en route to Mwanza and Shinyanga. The local Precision Air booking agent is **Global Travel** (☎ 028-262 2707, 0713-264294) opposite Musoma Communications Centre.

BOAT

Local boats to lakeside villages and Lukuba island depart from the Mwigobero section of town near Afrilux Hotel.

BUS

Buses and minibuses go to/from Mwanza between 6am and 2pm (TSh6000, four hours), including Mohammed Trans (Mwanza/Shinyanga TSh6000/12,000, departures at 6am, 9am and 1.30pm). Minibuses go throughout the day to Sirari on the Kenyan border, where you can change to Kenyan transport. To Arusha, Kimotco line goes several times weekly via the Serengeti (TSh35,000 plus entry fees for Serengeti and Ngorongoro Conservation Area). Otherwise, Akamba goes via Nairobi, Kenya.

Dalla-dallas run between the town centre and the Makoko section of Musoma from the *dalla-dalla* stand along the road between town and the airfield.

LUKUBA ISLAND

Known locally as Rukuba – 'place of lightning' in the local Kwaya language – Lukuba is about 12km offshore northwest of Musoma. It consists of two main islands, plus smaller islets.

The lovely and recommended **Lukuba Island Lodge** (☎ 027-254 8840, 027-250 3094; www .lukubaisland.com; s/d full board US$287/520; 🕿) is the only accommodation, with five spacious stone-and-thatch bungalows on the lakeshore, a pretty beach, walking, birding and boating. An excellent getaway. Rates include speedboat transfers from Musoma, guided walks or local boat trips around the island, fly or traditional fishing, and community concession fees.

There's a public boat between Musoma's Mwigobero port and the main village on the largest of the islands, departing three times daily in each direction, at 7am, 11am and 1pm (TSh1500, 1½ to two hours).

WESTERN TANZANIA

Head west, and adventure is guaranteed. Whether you rattle your way slowly across vast, trackless expanses on the ageing Central Line train or gather on the tarmac in the early morning greyness at Arusha airport for a charter flight, adventure is the common denominator in this rough, remote frontier land. And it is this adventure potential together with chimpanzees and opportunities for wildlife watching in a singularly untrammelled setting that is drawing an increasing number of travellers.

Western Tanzania's highlights include three national parks and Lake Tanganyika – fringed by isolated fishing villages and almost as unknown today as two centuries ago when the first foreign explorers arrived.

Unless you're flying in and staying at one of the west's handful of upmarket camps and lodges, expect few tourist facilities and rugged travel, with train, boat and truck often the only options.

TABORA

☎ 026

Tabora – with mango- and flame tree-lined avenues – was once a major trading centre along the old caravan route connecting Lake Tanganyika with Bagamoyo and the sea. Known in its early days as Kazeh, it was the domain of famed Nyamwezi king Mirambo, and headquarters of infamous slave trader Tippu Tib, and a string of European explorers passed through its portals. After the Central Line railway was constructed, Tabora became the largest town in German East Africa.

Information

CRDB Bank (Jamhuri St) ATM (Visa).

NBC Bank (Market St) Changes cash and travellers cheques; ATM (Visa).

Tabora On-Line (Lumumba St; per hr TSh1000; 🕒 8am-5.30pm) Next to the library and opposite the Mohammed Trans office.

Sights

About 6km southwest of town in Kwihara is **Livingstone's tembe** (admission TSh2000; 🕒 8am-5pm), where he stayed in 1872 after being found by Stanley in Ujiji. Today it houses a diary and other Livingstone memorabilia. Take any

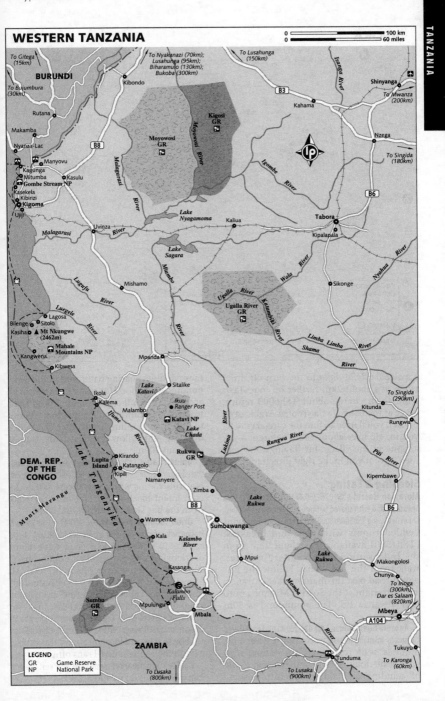

WESTERN TANZANIA

0 — 100 km
0 — 60 miles

BURUNDI

To Gitega (15km)

To Nyakanazi (70km); Lusahunga (95km); Biharamulo (130km); Bukoba (300km)

To Lusahunga (150km)

To Bujumbura (30km)

Kibondo

B3

Shinyanga

Rutana

Kahama

To Mwanza (200km)

Makamba

Nyanza-Lac

Nzega

Manyovu

B8

Kigosi GR

Moyowosi GR

To Singida (180km)

Kagunga

Mitumba

Kasulu

Gombe Stream NP

B6

Kasekela

Kibirizi

Kigoma

Ujiji

Uvinza

Malagarasi River

Lake Nyagamoma

Kaliua

Tabora

Kipalapala

Lake Sagara

Igombe River

Igurubi River

Mishamo

Lugufu River

Mlumbo

Wala River

Sikonge

Luegele

Lagosa

Sitolo

Ugalla River GR

Blienge

Kasiha

▲ Mt Nkungwe (2462m)

Mahale Mountains NP

Kalambili River

Limba Limba River

Kangwena

Shama River

River

Kibwesa

Mpanda

Sitalike

To Singida (290km)

Ikola

Lake Katavi

Ikuu Ranger Post

Kalema

Katavi NP

Kitunda

Malambo

Lake Chada

Rungwa

DEM. REP. OF THE CONGO

Lupita Island

Kirando

Rukwa GR

Lukima River

Rungwa River

Rungwa

Katangolo

Kipili

Namanyere

Zimba

Lake Tanganyika

Piti River

Kipembawe

Wampembe

Lake Rukwa

B6

Monts Marangu

Kala

Ijume River

Kalambo River

Sumbawanga

Mpui

Lake Rukwa

Makongolosi

Kasanga

Chunya

To Iringa (300km); Dar es Salaam (820km)

Sumbu GR

Kalambo Falls

Mpulungu

Mbala

Momba River

Mbeya

A104

ZAMBIA

Tukuyu

To Karonga (60km)

Tunduma

To Lusaka (800km)

To Lusaka (900km)

LEGEND
GR Game Reserve
NP National Park

TABORA

0 — 200 m
0 — 0.1 miles

INFORMATION

CRDB Bank..............................1 B2
NBC Bank..............................2 B1
Tabora On-Line......................3 B1

SLEEPING 🏠

Aposele Guest House.............4 D2
Moravian Hostel....................5 A1
Orion Tabora Hotel................6 C2

EATING 🍴

Kaidee's Supermarket............7 B2
Mayor's Restaurant & Ice Cream
Parlour...............................8 B1

TRANSPORT

Bus & Taxi Stand...................9 B2
Mohammed Trans..................10 B1
Precision Air..........................11 B1
Taxi Stand..............................12 B2

Kipalapala *dalla-dalla* to the turn-off, from where it's about 2km further on foot. Taxis from town charge about TSh6000 return. Once at the *tembe* (a flat-roofed Arabic-style house), you'll need to find the caretaker to let you in. He lives about 500m before it – ask anyone in the village for 'Livingstone' and they'll point you in the right direction.

Sleeping & Eating

Moravian Hostel (☎ 026-260 4710, 0787-401613; Old Mwanza Rd; d with shared bathroom in old wing TSh3000, s/d in new wing TSh5000/8000) Spartan, quiet twin-bedded rooms with nets, and breakfast (TSh1500) available. It's about 2km from the train station, and about 10 minutes' walk from the bus stand. Follow the un-paved road past the main market entrance, and turn right at the Soko la Mitumba onto Old Mwanza Rd. The compound is 50m further on.

Aposele Guest House (☎ 026-260 4510; d with shared bathroom in main section/annexe TSh4000/6000) Five minutes' walk from the train station, with very basic doubles in an annexe with a mix of 'standing' and 'sitting' toilets, plus some

more doubles sharing bathroom in the main building next door. Hot-water buckets can be arranged. From the train station, head right towards the railway police building. Ignore the right turn immediately after the police building and follow the next path straight for about 200m.

Golden Eagle (☎ 026-260 4623; Jamhuri St; r with shared/private bathroom TSh6000/15,000, with TV TSh25,000) No-frills rooms with clean sheets, fan and a convenient location just five minutes' walk from the bus stand towards NBC bank.

Orion Tabora Hotel (☎ 026-260 4369; cnr Boma & Station Rds; s/d TSh60,000/72,000, ste d from TSh60,000/72,000) Spacious, good-value rooms overlooking large gardens in the atmospheric and nicely restored former Railway Hotel. All have TV and nets, there's a good restaurant (meals from TSh5000) and staff are usually around for pre-dawn train arrivals.

Mayor's Hotel & Ice Cream Parlour (Lumumba St; snacks from TSh500, meals TSh1500; ☺ breakfast, lunch & dinner) For snacks and local meals, try this eatery, next to the Mohammed Trans office.

Kaidee's Supermarket (Jamhuri St) For self-catering; next Wadudu's Auto Spares.

Getting There & Away

AIR
Flights with **Precision Air** (☎ 026-260 4818; Market St) stop at Tabora daily en route from Dar es Salaam to Kigoma. The airport is 5km south of town.

BUS
The bus stand is along the extension of Market St, past NBC bank.

Mohammed Trans (Lumumba St) goes to/from Mwanza, departing from Tabora daily at 6am and 10am (TSh15,000, 7½ hours) from its office, opposite the library. If you're heading east, you can disembark at Nzega and then catch a bus to Singida, though this often means sleeping in Nzega.

To Mpanda (TSh16,000), NBS line goes twice weekly in the dry season.

To the Rwanda border, Mohammed Trans goes daily to Kahama (via Shinyanga, where you'll need to change buses). From Kahama, there's onward transport to Benako and the border.

To Kigoma, there's no regular public transport except the train. The track between Tabora and Mbeya is serviced by three to four buses weekly during the dry season.

TRAIN
Tabora is the Central Line junction for trains north to Mwanza, west to Kigoma and south to Mpanda; see p266. Trains from Mpanda reach Tabora about 3am, trains from Kigoma and Mwanza arrive by about 5am, and trains from Dar es Salaam reach Tabora by about 9pm. Travelling between Kigoma and Mwanza, you will need to spend the day in Tabora, and reconfirm your onward reservation.

Getting Around
There are taxi stands near the bus stamd, and at the corner of Jamhuri Rd and Nyamwezi St. Taxis meet all train arrivals (TSh2000 to the town centre). If arriving in the middle of the night, ask the driver to wait until you're sure that there's someone around at your hotel to let you in.

KIGOMA
☎ 028
This scrappy but agreeable town sprawls along the lakeshore in a green and tropical waterside setting with views to the DRC mountains in the distance. It's the major Tanzanian port on Lake Tanganyika, the end of the line if you've slogged across the country on the Central Line train, and a jumping-off point for visits to Gombe Stream National Park and for boat travel to Mahale Mountains National Park.

Information
There are consulates for **Burundi** (☎ 028-280 2865; Kakolwa Ave; ☉ 10am-3pm Mon-Fri) and the **Democratic Republic of the Congo** (Kaya Rd; ☉ 8.30am-4pm Mon-Fri). See p254 for visa details.

An immigration officer is posted at the ferry port on Wednesday for travellers departing for Zambia on the MV *Liemba*. The immigration office is on the main road towards Ujiji.

Baby Come & Call (Lumumba St; per hr TSh2000; ☉ 8am-7pm Mon-Sat) Just up from the train station.

CRDB Bank (Train Station Roundabout) ATM (Visa only).

Heri Hospital Mission-run hospital about two hours' drive from Kigoma near the Burundi border.

Mbali Mbali (☎ 028-280 4437; www.mbalimbali.com) For boat rentals and visits to Gombe Stream and Mahale Mountains National Parks; located at Kigoma Hilltop Hotel.

Mission Aviation Fellowship (MAF; ☎ 028-280 4940) May be able to help with emergency medical evacuations.

NBC Bank (Lumumba St) Changes cash; ATM (Visa only).

TCCIA (Chamber of Commerce) Internet Café (Lumumba St; per hr TSh2000; ☉ 8.30am-7pm Mon-Sat, 10am-1pm Sun)

Sights & Activities
Kigoma's **market** abounds with the pineapples for which the town is famous, as well as other produce, and is worth a stroll. Nearby, at the base of Lumumba St, is the German-built **train station**.

For relaxing or swimming, head to **Jakobsen's (Mwamahunga) Beach** (admission TSh4000), which is actually two small coves reached via steps down a vegetated section of hillside about 5km southwest of town. There are a few *bandas* for shade, the water is bilharzia-free and the setting – especially during the week when nobody is around – is idyllic. There's no food or drink. Head west from town past Kigoma Hilltop Hotel, keeping right at the small fork until the signpost, from where it's about 3km further uphill and signposted. Via public transport, catch a Katonga *dalla-dalla* from the *dalla-dalla* stand at the roundabout near the train station and ask the driver to drop you at the turn-off, from where it's 30 to 40 minutes' further on foot.

TANZANIA

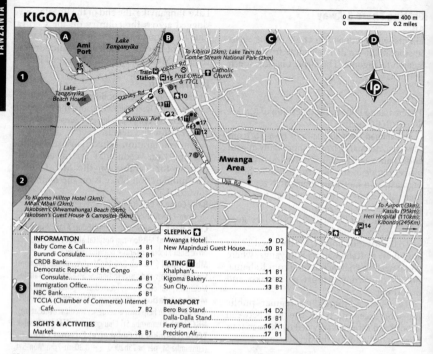

KIGOMA

INFORMATION	
Baby Come & Call.........................**1** B1	
Burundi Consulate........................**2** B1	
CRDB Bank....................................**3** B1	
Democratic Republic of the Congo	
Consulate................................**4** B1	
Immigration Office......................**5** C2	
NBC Bank......................................**6** B1	
TCCIA (Chamber of Commerce) Internet	
Café...**7** B2	

SIGHTS & ACTIVITIES	
Market...**8** B1	

SLEEPING	
Mwanga Hotel.............................**9** D2	
New Mapinduzi Guest House........**10** B1	

EATING	
Khalphan's..................................**11** B1	
Kigoma Bakery.............................**12** B2	
Sun City......................................**13** B1	

TRANSPORT	
Bero Bus Stand............................**14** D2	
Dalla-Dalla Stand.........................**15** B1	
Ferry Port....................................**16** A1	
Precision Air................................**17** B1	

Sleeping

New Mapinduzi Guest House (☎ 028-280 4978; Lumumba St; s/d with shared bathroom TSh5000/7000, with private bathroom TSh8000/10,000) In a tiny alley just opposite the large white and yellow National Housing Corporation building, and within five minutes' walk of the train station and *dalla-dalla* stand. Rooms are no-frills but clean, with net and no fan, and the location is convenient. There's no food.

Jakobsen's Guest House (www.kigomabeach.com; per family per night TSh40,000, per additional adult TSh15,000, electricity per hr TSh3500) This private guesthouse is located well out of town on an escarpment above Jakobsen's Beach. It's generally rented out in its entirety – three double beds and seven twins divided among several rooms, plus two kitchens and two bathrooms – though space permitting, individual rooms are available as well. The quiet, cliff-top perch is lovely. Five minutes' walk down the hillside and just up from the beach are two shaded, grassy **camp sites** (camping adult TSh6000, tent rental per night TSh10,000), with ablutions, a grill, lanterns and water supply. For both camping and the guesthouse, bring your own food from town.

Kigoma Hilltop Hotel (☎ 028-280 4437; kht@ raha.com; www.mbalimbali.com; s/d from US$60/80; ❁ ▣ ▣) Situated on a prime setting on an escarpment overlooking the lake, this place offers small, slightly faded cottages including minifridge, TV and air-con, and a restaurant. The same management also runs camps in Mahale Mountains, Gombe Stream and Katavi National Parks and can organise safaris.

Also recommended:

Mwanga Hotel (r TSh6000; Ujiji Rd) In the Mwanga area – about 3km southeast of the train station, but within about 500m of the Bero bus stand, and useful if you have an early bus. Coming from town, it's about 400m before the Kibondo/Kasulu junction, with no-frills rooms and hot-water buckets on request.

Eating

Sun City (Lumumba St; meals TSh1500-TSh3000) Has inexpensive meals, including a chicken or fish biryani special on Sundays and fresh juices.

For self-catering, try **Khalphan's** (just off Lumumba St), opposite Precision Air, and **Kigoma Bakery** (Lumumba St), which also sells fresh juices and – sometimes – ice cream.

Getting There & Away

AIR

Just around the corner from NBC bank, **Precision Air** (☎ 028-280 4720) flies daily between Kigoma and Dar es Salaam (about TSh350,000), stopping in Tabora en route from Dar to Kigoma.

The airport is about 5km southeast of the town centre.

BOAT

Ferries

For information on the MV *Liemba* between Kigoma and Mpulungu (Zambia) via Lagosa (for Mahale Mountains National Park) and Kipili, see p262. The MV *Liemba* departs from the ferry port area, just south of the Lake Tanganyika Beach House.

Cargo ferries to Burundi and the DRC – many of which also take passengers – depart from the Ami port, reached by following the dirt lane down to the left of the train station. Watch for the sign 'To Kigoma Port, Managed by APO'.

Lake Taxis

Lake taxis are small, wooden motorised boats, piled high with people and produce, that connect villages along the lakeshore as far north as the Burundi border, including a stop at Gombe Stream National Park. They are inexpensive, but offer no shade or other creature comforts, and are invariably loaded to capacity plus. The lake taxis don't stop at Kigoma itself, but at Kibirizi village, a rough-and-tumble fishing village about 2.5km north of Kigoma. To get there, follow the road uphill past the post office, turn left at the top and continue straight for about 2km (TSh3000 in a taxi).

BUS

Roads from Kigoma in all directions are rough, although they are improving. All long-distance buses depart from Bero bus stand on the small road turning left off Ujiji Rd just before Bero petrol station. Buy your tickets there, or at one of the booking offices signposted along the main road in the Mwanga area.

To Mwanza, buses depart Kigoma three times weekly at 5am (TSh25,000, 15 hours, 17 hours on a bad day), with most going via Lusahunga, Biharamulo and the Busisi ferry crossing.

To Bukoba (TSh27,000, 15 hours), there are two to three direct buses weekly departing at 5am, though it's often just as fast to take a Mwanza-bound bus as far as Biharamulo and get onward transport there. Although significantly longer in distance, it can sometimes be just as fast – especially if you're driving – to travel to Mwanza via Nyakanazi junction, Kahama and Shinyanga, as the stretch from Nyakanazi to Mwanza is tarmac the whole way, and there's no need to wait for the ferry near Mwanza.

The road from Kigoma to Mpanda via Uvinza is in various stages of repair, with Sanas line running two to three buses weekly (TSh20,000).

TRAIN

For information on the ageing Central Line train from Dodoma, Tabora or Mwanza, see p266.

Getting Around

Dalla-dallas from the town centre to Bero bus stand, Mwanga and Ujiji run throughout the day, departing from the *dalla-dalla* stand just uphill from the train station. Taxis between the town centre and Bero bus stand charge about TSh2000.

UJIJI

Tiny Ujiji, one of Africa's oldest market villages, earned its place in history as the spot where explorer-journalist Henry Morton Stanley uttered his famously casual 'Dr Livingstone, I presume?' The site where Stanley's encounter with Livingstone allegedly occurred is commemorated by a plaque set in a walled compound near a small garden. Nearby are two mango trees, said to have been grafted from the original tree that shaded the two men during their encounter. An information centre, including a restaurant and hostel rooms, is under construction. The site is about 300m off the main road coming from Kigoma and signposted – just ask for Livingstone and the *dalla-dalla* driver will ensure you get off at the right place.

Ujiji is about 8km south of Kigoma and connected throughout the day by *dalla-dallas*.

GOMBE STREAM NATIONAL PARK
☎ 028

With an area of only 52 sq km, Gombe Stream is Tanzania's smallest national park. It is also the site of the longest-running study of any wild animal population in the world and, for those interested in primates, a fascinating place.

The Gombe Stream area was gazetted as a wildlife reserve in 1943. In 1960 British researcher Jane Goodall arrived to begin a study of wild chimpanzees, and in 1968 Gombe was declared a national park. Goodall's study is now in its fifth decade.

Gombe's approximately 150 chimps are well habituated and sightings are almost guaranteed. Other animals you may see include colobus and vervet monkeys, bushbucks, aggressive baboons and bush pigs.

Information

Gombe Stream is open year-round. Entry fees are US$100/20 per adult/child per 24 hours. They technically apply from when you land on the beach at Kasekela – the base for research and tourism – but in practice, park officials tend to interpret the guidelines generously, and only charge you for the time you spend in the forest – which means that for a two-night stay (necessary, assuming you arrive/depart via lake taxi) and one day of chimp tracking, you're likely to be charged only for one 24-hour entry. Guides cost US$20 per group per day. Children aged under seven are not permitted in the park.

There's a park office in Kibirizi (near Kigoma), at the far end of the beach, and about a 10-minute walk from the footbridge at the entrance to the village. It's unsignposted, but anyone should be able to point out the way. Make accommodation bookings here or directly through **park headquarters** (☎ 028-280 2586; gonapachimps@yahoo.com) if you want to stay in the park hostel.

While it's generally easier finding the chimpanzees in Gombe Stream than in Mahale Mountains National Park, it can still be difficult, sweaty work. For photos, bring high-speed film or appropriate equipment for use in the forest; flashes aren't permitted.

Sleeping & Eating

The park resthouse is being rebuilt and will have a restaurant (scheduled to open soon). Meanwhile, there are basic rooms in the park **hostel** (per person US$20) at Kasekela, on the beach near the centre of the park. Camping is not permitted. There are no cooking facilities, but there is a small shop at park headquarters selling soft drink and and it's sometimes possible to arrange inexpensive local meals with staff.

Otherwise, unless you're staying at the luxury tented camp, or have confirmed in Kigoma that the restaurant is open, bring whatever food and drink you will need from Kigoma.

Gombe Forest Lodge (☎ 028-280 4437; www.mbalimbali.com; per person all-inclusive US$445) On the beach at Mitumba in the northern part of the park, this is Gombe's only upmarket camp, with tents with private bathroom and a shady location. It's affiliated with Kigoma Hilltop Hotel in Kigoma.

Getting There & Away

Gombe Stream is about 20km north of Kigoma on the shores of Lake Tanganyika. The only way to reach the park is by boat – either charter or lake taxi. At least one lake taxi to the park departs Kibirizi (see p215) between about noon and 2pm (TSh2500, three to 3½ hours). Returning, they pass by Gombe (Kasekela) at about 7am (which means you'll need to spend two nights at the park if travelling by public transport). There are no boats in either direction on Sunday.

Alternatively, you can arrange with local fishermen to charter a boat. Expect to pay from about TSh80,000 to TSh100,000 return. You may have to pay an advance for petrol (which should not be more than one-third of the total price), but don't pay the full amount until you have arrived back in Kigoma. It's common practice for local boat owners to try to convince you that there are no lake taxis, in an effort to get business.

Faster boats taking about two hours can be organised through Kigoma Hilltop Hotel (p214; US$655 return per boat, plus a US$50 per night stopover fee from the second night onwards).

MAHALE MOUNTAINS NATIONAL PARK

Lushly vegetated mountains echoing with bird and chimpanzee calls cascade down to small coves and the clear waters of Lake Tanganyika in Mahale Mountains – Tanzania's most isolated national park. Like Gombe Stream to the north, Mahale is primarily a chimpanzee sanctuary, although its larger area makes viewing more challenging, with steep, sweaty treks of several hours the norm. In addition to the chimpanzees, Mahale also hosts populations of warthogs, baboons and bushbucks (all frequently seen), as well as the less visible roan antelopes, buffaloes, zebras and leopards.

Information

Entry fees are US$80/30 per adult/child, and concession fees (applicable to those staying at a luxury camp) are US$30 per person; children under seven years of age aren't permitted in the park. Park *bandas* can be booked directly through **park headquarters** (sokwe@mahale .org; www.mahalepark.org), or – with more difficulty – through Kigoma Hilltop Hotel (p214) in Kigoma. Guide fees are US$20 per group (up to six people) per trek. Chimpanzee permits are expected to be introduced in the near future – most likely limiting visitors to one trek per stay, in which case the above fees will change.

Whether arriving by boat or air, all visitors need to go first to park headquarters at Bilenge, in the park's northwestern corner and about 30 to 45 minutes by boat south of the airstrip. All fees are paid here – for entry, guides and park *bandas*. About 10km south of Bilenge is Kasiha (site of the park *bandas*), followed to the south by the Sinsiba and Kangwena beach areas, each with an upmarket camp.

Climbs of Mt Nkungwe (2462m) – Mahale's highest peak – must be organised through park headquarters and accompanied by an armed ranger. There are several routes, but the usual arrangement is two days up and one day down, camping midway and again near the peak. The climb requires a reasonable degree of fitness, and willingness to scramble and hack your way through the bush on the partly overgrown trails.

Mahale is open year-round, although during the rains the mountain slopes get very muddy and the private camps close. There are no roads; walking (and boating, along the shoreline) are the only ways to get around. At any time of year be prepared for strenuous trekking up steep, often densely vegetated slopes to find the chimpanzees, sometimes through dense brush away from established footpaths. Bring high-speed film or appropriate equipment for use in the forest; flashes aren't permitted.

Following an outbreak of human influenza virus among Mahale's chimpanzees in 2006, park officials currently require all visitors to wear surgical-style masks while chimpanzee trekking, and not to approach closer than within 10m of the chimps. Each group's viewing time is also limited – currently to one hour per day, and maximum group size is six. No eating or drinking is permitted within sight of the chimps.

Sleeping & Eating

Park Bandas (per person US$30) The only budget option are the five basic but quite decent, twin-bedded park *bandas* set about 200m in from the lakeshore at the edge of the forest in Kasiha. All have private bathrooms with cold-water showers, flush toilets and electricity, and there's a communal, well-equipped kitchen. While the *bandas* lack the lake views of the upmarket camps, their position at the edge of the forest means the night sounds are wonderful. Apart from a small selection of drinks sold at park headquarters, there's nothing available in or near the park, so bring all food and drink with you.

Kungwe Beach Lodge (☎ 027-254 7007; www .mbalimbali.com; per person all-inclusive US$465; ☉ May-Feb) A lovely place in a beautiful setting on the beach at Sinsiba, with a handful of spacious double tents and a large dining area-lounge with wooden decks overlooking the water. Both the cuisine and the guides are top-notch, and the camp offers good value for money.

Other recommendations:

Mahale Camp (www.nomad-tanzania.com; per person all-inclusive from US$750; ☉ mid-May–mid-March) An exclusive camp nestled beneath the mountains on Kangwena beach that mixes old-style safari ambience with nouveau bush chic. Book through upmarket travel agencies or safari operators.

Flycatcher Camp (www.flycat.com; ☉ Feb, Jul-Oct) A handful of simple tents directly on the beach several coves north of Kungwe Beach Lodge. For Flycatcher Safari guests only.

Getting There & Away

AIR

Twice-weekly scheduled charters are available with **Zantas Air** (www.zantasair.com) between Arusha and Mahale via Katavi on Mondays and Thursdays (about US$1500 return). **Safari Airlink** (www.safariaviation.info) offers a similarly priced service between Ruaha and Mahale via Katavi on the same days. The airstrip is just north of the park boundary at Sitolo – about 40 minutes by boat from park headquarters, and a bit over an hour from the camps. If you've booked in advance with the camps, a boat will be waiting to meet your flight. Otherwise, you'll need to make arrangements in advance for a boat pick-up with park headquarters (per boat US$50). Unless you charter your own plane, the twice-weekly rotations of the scheduled charters mean that fly-in guests will need to plan on a minimum stay of three or four days in the park.

BOAT

The MV *Liemba* stops at Lagosa (also called Mugambo), to the north of the park (1st/2nd/economy class US$25/20/15, about 10 hours from Kigoma) on its run between Kigoma and Mpumalanga (Zambia). From Lagosa, it's possible to continue with small local boats to park headquarters, about two hours further south, but not recommended, due to the dubious safety of the local boats and the fact that the *Liemba* reaches Lagosa at about 2am or 3am on Thursday morning. It's better to email park headquarters in advance and arrange a pick-up – the boat will then be waiting for you when you disembark from the *Liemba*. The park boat costs US$50 per boat one way from Lagosa to Bilenge, although if the park is sending a boat up anyway, this may be waived or discounted. From Bilenge to the park *bandas* costs US$50 return, although this is sometimes negotiable if a boat is going anyway. Coming from Mpulungu (Zambia) the *Liemba* passes Lagosa sometime between late Saturday night and early Sunday morning at around 3am or 4am.

The other option is to charter a boat through Kigoma Hilltop Hotel (p214; return per boat US$4125, plus US$50 per night stopover charge from the second night onwards, about four hours) or park headquarters (one way for the park speed boat for up to eight people US$1400, about four hours).

MPANDA

☎ 025

Mpanda, a sprawling district capital with tidy dirt roads and several bustling markets, is of interest mainly as a starting point for visits to Katavi National Park, and as an access point for travel to/from Lake Tanganyika.

New Super City Hotel (☎ 025-282 0459; r TSh10,000) has clean, no-frills rooms, each with one small double bed, bathroom, net and fan, and a restaurant. Buses to Katavi and Sumbawanga depart from out the front. It's about 1.5km from the town centre on the first roundabout you reach when coming from Sumbawanga.

Ask for 'Super City Ghorofani'. From the train station (TSh2000 in a taxi), wind your way out following the wide dirt path to the train station roundabout. Turn right and continue about 2km, watching for the pastel-pink, blue, mustard and ochre building with small gazebos at the front.

Highway Guesthouse (☎ 025-282 0001; s/d TSh8000/10,000) has small, clean rooms with private bathroom, nets and fan. There's neither food nor hot water. It's diagonally opposite Super City on the other side of the roundabout and just off the road,

At **Baraka Guest House** (☎ 025-282 0485; r with shared/private bathroom TSh10,000/15,000) all rooms have one large bed, net, TV, fan and hot water. It's on the road running down from the market.

For inexpensive meals, try Tanganyika Café, near the small Buzogwe market and opposite the still-under-construction Moravian church.

Getting There & Away

BUS

To Sumbawanga (TSh15,000, seven hours) Sumry buses depart Mpanda at around 8am daily from New Super City Hotel. The Sumry office is in the town centre near the Buzogwe market. To continue to Mbeya, you'll need to overnight in Sumbawanga. For Sitalike and Katavi National Park (TSh2000, 45 minutes), get on a Sumbawanga bus and have them drop you off. Alternatively, several smaller vehicles daily run to/from Sitalike, departing from Mpanda from in front of Marangu Hotel & Bar in the town centre near the market. The road as far as Sitalike (40km) has been recently graded and is in good shape.

To Tabora, NBS line buses go Tuesday and Saturday during the dry season (TSh16,000), starting from its office opposite the half-built Moravian church in the town centre.

To Kigoma, train is the better option, but Sanas bus line is also a possibility, departing from Mpanda on Tuesday, Thursday and Saturday (TSh20,000). Its office is behind the half-built Moravian church.

To Kalema on Lake Tanganyika (TSh7000, three hours), a bus departs daily from the train station roundabout at 9am, with an extra vehicle going to meet MV *Liemba* ferry arrivals. Departures from Kalema are in the mornings.

TRAIN

A Central Line spur connects Mpanda with Tabora via Kaliua; see p266. To reach Kigoma or Mwanza from Mpanda, you'll need to spend at least a day in Tabora.

KATAVI NATIONAL PARK

Wild Katavi, 40km southwest of Mpanda, is Tanzania's third-largest national park. At its heart is the vast Katisunga flood plain, especially around Ikuu area. In the shoulder and dry seasons, when the plain echoes with bird calls and fills with vast herds of animals drawn by the remaining pools of water, it evokes comparisons with how earth must have looked at the beginning before the arrival of humans. Katavi makes a superb wilderness destination, and is well worth the effort to get here.

Information

Entry fees are US$20/5 per adult/child. There's also a US$40 per person per day conservation fee payable by all those staying at camps/lodges inside the park boundaries. Guide fees are US$20 per day per group.

Katavi is best visited during the dry season, between June and November/December, with the peak wildlife-watching months from August to October. For booking park *bandas*, contact **park headquarters** (☎ 025-282 0213; www .katavipark.org, katavinp@yahoo.com, katavi.tanapa@gmail .com). Its office – for paying entry fees and arranging guides and vehicle hire – is just off the main road, about 1.5km south of Sitalike, on the park's northern edge. Park fees can also be paid at Ikuu 2 ranger post near Ikuu airstrip – convenient if you're driving and want to access the Ikuu area direct from Sumbawanga and other points south.

Katavi's tsetse flies are definitely a factor to consider when contemplating doing a wildlife drive in an open or nonair-conditioned vehicle. If you arrive with public transport, vehicle hire can be arranged through the park for US$200 per day, including 100km, plus US$2 per kilometre thereafter.

Walking safaris are permitted with an armed ranger.

Sleeping & Eating

There are **public camp sites** (camping adult/child US$30/5) near Lake Chada; at Ikuu ranger post, near Lake Katavi and about 2km from park headquarters. Also near park headquarters are nice double-bedded **park bandas** (per person US$30) with private bathroom, generator-supplied electricity and hot-water showers. There are no cooking facilities, but meals can be arranged at the nearby park resthouse with advance notice. In Sitalike village just outside the park gate, there are a few other budget places and inside the park are several upmarket camps.

Riverside Campsite (☎ 0784-754740; camping US$8, r per person TSh30,000) Straightforward, no-frills rooms and a pleasant camping area with a cooking banda about 300m back from the river and an easy walk from the bus stand. The owner is the best contact in Sitalike for arranging vehicle hire into the park, from about US$250 per day.

Katavi Hippo Garden Hotel (☎ 025-282 0393; camping US$5, r per person US$30) This place is operating at half-mast following the death of the owner, but is still worth a look, with a row of clean, no-frills rooms along the river in front of Riverside Campsite, and meals on order. With a day's advance notice staff make homemade bread – ideal for a park picnic.

Katavi Wildlife Camp (☎ 0754-237422; www.tan zaniasafaris.info; s/d full board plus wildlife drives US$475/750) This comfortable, rustic camp in a prime setting near Ikuu ranger post offers good overall value and arguably the best-positioned of the camps, with spacious tents with private bathroom overlooking the floodplains. It's owned by Foxes African Safaris (p71), which also runs camps in Ruaha and Mikumi.

Other recommendations:

Flycatcher Safaris Camp (www.flycat.com) Another excellent setting, in Ikuu area about 1km from Katavi Wildlife Camp, with very simple seasonal tents overlooking the flood plains. For Flycatcher safari guests only.

Katuma Tented Camp (☎ 022-213 0501; www.mbali mbali.com; per person all-inclusive US$430; ☺ May-Feb) Six spacious tents on low stilts, well-located on the edge of the flood plain in a prime wildlife-viewing area.

Getting There & Away

AIR

Zantas Air flies Arusha–Katavi–Mahale–Arusha on Monday and Thursday (Arusha–Katavi one way US$625). Safari Airlink flies Ruaha–Katavi–Mahale–Ruaha on the same days (Ruaha–Katavi US$450), meaning that fly-in visitors need to plan on a three- or four-day stay in the park. There are airstrips at Sitalike and at Ikuu ranger post. Note that if you're flying in, but not staying with the private camps (all of which provide airstrip

LAKE TANGANYIKA

Lake Tanganyika is the world's longest (670km) and second-deepest (over 1400m) fresh-water lake, and makes an excellent adventure destination for anyone travelling in western Tanzania. The best way to get a feel for local life is to set off on the MV *Liemba,* which calls in at a string of small ports as it makes its way down the shoreline. There are few docking jetties, so at each place where the *Liemba* pulls in, it's met by dozens of small boats racing out to the ferry, with boat owners and food vendors all jostling for custom from the passengers. At night the whole scene is lit up by the glow of dozens of tiny kerosene lamps, waving precariously in the wind and waves.

Besides Kigoma (the largest town on the Tanzanian lakeshore), Ujiji (one of the oldest lakeshore settlements) and Lagosa village (for Mahale Mountains National Park), ports of note include Kalema and Kipili. Kalema, which is also reachable by road from Mpanda, was the site of an old Catholic mission station, parts of which were originally a Belgian fort before being handed over to the White Fathers in 1889. Kipili is the site of an old Benedictine mission – now visitable but overgrown – in a hilltop perch with wide views over Kipili bay. For accommodation, there's the small **St Bernard's Monastery & Guest House** (r TSh7000), with basic rooms, on the edge of town.

About 2km further along the lakeshore is the highly recommended **Lake Shore Lodge & Campsite** (☎ 0763-993166, 0752-540792; www.laketanganyikaadventuresafaris.com; camping US$12, s/d banda US$45/70, d/q chalet US$315/585; 🖳). It has camping with spotless ablutions, good-value double *bandas* with views over the lake and four-person chalets, all with a lovely, open 'African Zen' design, and all directly on the lakeshore. There's a lakeside honeymoon chalet with private Zen garden, private beach and loft lounge. Sunset on the beach in front of the lodge, with the Democratic Republic of the Congo (DRC; formerly Zaire) mountains in the distance, is magical. Meals (breakfast/lunch/dinner US$7/10/15) are made with ingredients from the owners' organic farm, and there's kayaking on the lake, quad biking down the escarpment from Katavi National Park, diving (if you're PADI-certified), and much more. The lodge makes a great combination with Katavi National Park, and with advance notice, staff can organise combination itineraries with Katavi and Mahale Mountains National Parks (including a vehicle for a Katavi safari).

About 3km offshore from Kipili on Lupita island is the exclusive **Lupita Island Resort & Spa** (www.firelightexpeditions.com; s/d all-inclusive US$1100/1725).

In addition to the *Liemba* connection, Kipili is also straightforward to reach overland. There are buses daily except Sunday from Sumbawanga via Nyamanyere to Kirando (north of Kipili on the lake), that will drop you at Katangolo village. Katangolo is just 8km from Lake Shore Lodge & Campsite – with advance notice staff will come and collect you.

pick-ups), you'll need to arrange an airstrip pick-up with park headquarters; walking without a ranger isn't permitted.

BUS & CAR

Buses between Mpanda and Sumbawanga stop in Sitalike, from where you can walk – downhill along the main road and over the bridge – about 2km to park headquarters, or about 500m to Riverside Campsite. Car hire can be organised at either place. For driving, the closest petrol stations are in Mpanda and Sumbawanga. The Mpanda–Sumbawanga road passes through the park, but park fees are only payable if you leave this main road (which you'll need to do to get to the best wildlife-viewing areas).

When considering driving yourself around the park (or negotiating vehicle hire), it's worth keeping in mind that there's no need to drive far in Katavi. Once in Ikuu area, it's quite possible to find a strategic spot and just sit, letting the buffalo herds, crocodiles, hippos, zebras and more parade by. That said, if you have several days in the park, it's easy to rack up the kilometres exploring its different areas.

Katavi is a logical combination with Mahale Mountains National Park for fly-in visitors, and is also easily combined with travels on Lake Tanganyika for overlanders. The main routes to this location are via Mpanda and Kalema, or via Namanyere and Kipili.

SUMBAWANGA
☎ 025

The peppy capital of the Rukwa region is set on the fertile Ufipa Plateau at about 1800m altitude, and makes a useful stopping point for travel between Zambia or Mbeya and Katavi. East of Sumbawanga, below the escarpment, is the vast, shallow Lake Rukwa. There's an ATM (Visa only) at the NBC bank on the main road.

The three hotels of choice are **Moravian Conference Centre** (☎ 025-280 2853/4; Nyerere Rd; s/d standard TSh7000/14,000, executive TSh12,000/20,000), in a quiet compound along the road to the Regional Block area; **Mbizi Forest Hotel** (☎ 025-280 2746; s/d TSh15,000/20,000), in an amenable setting about 3km from town off Nyerere Rd and signposted; and **Forestway Country Club** (☎ 028-280 2800, 028-280 2412; Nyerere Rd; r TSh20,000), about 2km from town along Nyerere Rd in the Regional Block area, past the Moravian Conference Centre (TSh2000 in a taxi from the bus stand). All have clean, rooms with private bathroom with hot water, and a restaurant.

Getting There & Away

Sumry has two buses daily to/from Mbeya via Tunduma, departing in each direction between 5.30am and 7am (TSh15,000, seven hours). To Mpanda, Sumry departs Sumbawanga daily by 10am or earlier, and during the dry season again at about 2pm (TSh15,000, six to seven hours), though the later bus reaches Mpanda at night and isn't recommended because it gets in too late. It's better to spend a night in Sumbawanga and continue the next day. To Zimba (for Lake Rukwa), there's a daily pick-up leaving from near the market; returning, the last vehicle usually leaves by about 4.30pm. To Kasanga (for catching the MV *Liemba* or visiting Kalambo Falls), there are several vehicles weekly in the dry season (TSh7500, five to six hours).

KASANGA & KALAMBO FALLS

The 250m Kalambo Falls, on the Zambian border, is the second-highest single-drop waterfall in Africa. Stone Age archaeological finds have been made in the surrounding area. From Kasanga, you'll need to look for a lift towards the falls, and then walk for about four hours in each direction.

There's a **guesthouse** (r with shared bathroom TSh2000) in the Muzei section of Kasanga, about 4km from the ferry dock, where you can also arrange a guide. One reader also wrote to recommend the Bismarck Guest House, before Muezi, with twin-bedded huts and a garden.

Vehicles go between Sumbawanga and Kasanga in the dry season (TSh7500, five to six hours), and a bus meets the MV *Liemba* arrivals. These are anywhere between midnight and 6am, although the boat often remains at the dock until dawn. You're allowed to stay on board, but the boat pulls out without much warning so ask staff to wake you in time to disembark.

THE SOUTHERN HIGHLANDS

Officially, the Southern Highlands begin at Makambako Gap, about halfway between Iringa and Mbeya, and extend southwards into Malawi. In this book the term is used to designate the entire region along the mountainous chain running between Morogoro in the east and Lake Nyasa and the Zambian and Malawi borders in the west. It's a scenic area, with wide, rolling panoramas, a temperate climate and a profusion of wildflowers on the hillsides during the rains.

MOROGORO
☎ 023

Bustling Morogoro would otherwise be a fairly scruffy town were it not for its verdant setting at the foot of the Uluguru Mountains. While there's no real reason to come here, it's an agreeable place, with some easily arranged hiking, beginning just outside town.

Information

Chilunga Cultural Tourism (☎ 0754-477582, 0713-663993; www.chinacotz.org; YWCA Compound, Rwegasore Rd) Organises hikes in the Uluguru mountains and village visits. Prices average from about TSh20,000 per day for a guide, plus village and administration fees.

Daus Internet Café (off Lumumba St; per hr TSh1000; ⏰ 8am-10pm Sun-Fri, 7-10pm Sat) Around the corner from Pira's Supermarket.

Exim Bank (Lumumba St) Opposite Pira's Supermarket; ATM (Mastercard, Visa, Cirrus and Maestro).

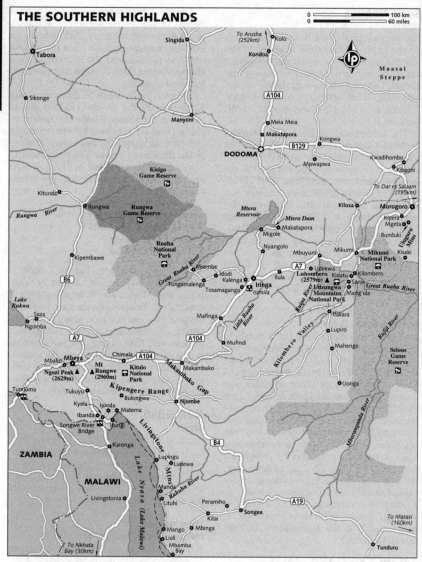

THE SOUTHERN HIGHLANDS

Immigration Office Signposted about 200m south of the main road, though visa extensions generally must be done in Dar es Salaam.

NBC Bank (Old Dar es Salaam Rd) Changes cash; ATM (Visa).

Sleeping & Eating

Princess Lodge (☎ 0754-319159; Mahenge St; r with shared bathroom TSh7000) Clean, small no-frills

rooms, all with double bed, fan and net, and an inexpensive restaurant downstairs. It's one block in from the main road in the town centre.

Mt Uluguru Hotel (☎ 023-260 3489; s/d TSh15,000/20,000, d with air-con TSh30,000; ☒) A nondescript multistorey hotel worth a look for its central location. Rooms are reasonable (ask for one with a view), and there's an inexpensive restaurant and a large outdoor bar. It's south of the main road, off Mahenge St.

Hotel Oasis (☎ 023-261 4178, 0754-377602; hotel oasistz@morogoro.net; Station St; s/d/tr incl breakfast US$35/40/50; ✷ ▣) Faded but good-value rooms – all with fan, air-con, TV and minifridge – plus grassy grounds and a popular restaurant serving good Indian cuisine, plus Chinese and continental dishes. A breakfast buffet is served.

New Acropol Hotel (☎ 023-261-3403, 0754-309410; www.newacropolhotel.biz; Old Dar es Salaam Rd; s/d from TSh45,000/55,000, ste TSh80,000; ✷ ▣) This B&B-style hotel has spacious rooms with TV, fridge and large double bed, and there's a popular restaurant, tasty local coffee, a pub and a porch overlooking the small gardens. It's about 300m east of the centre on Old Dar es Salaam Rd.

Mbuyuni Farm Retreat (☎ 023-260 1220; kim@ kimango.com; per person US$80, half board US$100, 4-person self-catering cottage US$120; ▣) Two (soon to be three) spacious self-catering cottages in the lovely private gardens of a farm just outside Morogoro overlooking the Uluguru mountains. The cottages can be rented on a catered or self-catering basis. It's about 12km east of Morogoro – turn left (north) off the main highway at the end of Kingolwira village onto a lane lined with mango trees and continue over a small bridge to the farm. Via public transport, ask for a drop at Kingolwira, where you can hire a lift on

a bicycle or motorbike the remaining 3km to the farm.

Pira's Supermarket (Lumumba Rd) For self-catering; located just north of the main road.

Getting There & Away

The main bus station is about 3km north of town on the main Dar es Salaam road, about 300m east of Msamvu roundabout (TSh2500/TSh200 in a taxi/dalla-dalla). It's chaotic, with no real order to things – you'll need to ask where to find buses to your destination. The Scandinavian Express office is on the other side of the roundabout in its own compound.

Scandinavian Express buses go daily to Dodoma, Mikumi, Iringa, Mbeya and Dar es Salaam, but none originate in Morogoro, so you will need to book in advance at its office. Smaller buses to Dar es Salaam leave throughout the day, from 5.45am until about 4pm (TSh3500, 3½ hours). Buses from Dar es Salaam going towards Mikumi and Iringa begin passing through Morogoro about 9am.

To Arusha, several direct buses daily do the route (nine hours), including Shabiby, originating in Dodoma.

To Tanga, there is a direct bus daily (five hours), departing by 8am.

The main dalla-dalla stand is in front of the market, where there is also a taxi rank. There's another dalla-dalla stop and taxi rank further east along Old Dar es Salaam Rd before the post office.

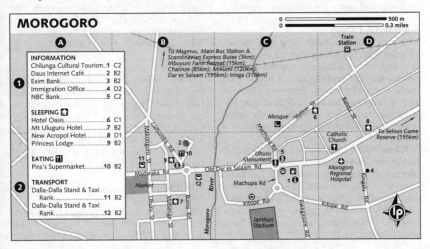

MOROGORO

0 — 500 m
0 — 0.3 miles

INFORMATION
Chilunga Cultural Tourism..1 C2
Daus Internet Café............2 B2
Exim Bank........................3 B2
Immigration Office...........4 D2
NBC Bank.........................5 C2

SLEEPING 🛏
Hotel Oasis......................6 C1
Mt Uluguru Hotel.............7 B2
New Acropol Hotel..........8 D1
Princess Lodge................9 B2

EATING 🍴
Pira's Supermarket.........10 B2

TRANSPORT
Dalla-Dalla Stand & Taxi
  Rank.............................11 B2
Dalla-Dalla Stand & Taxi
  Rank.............................12 B2

To Msamvu, Main Bus Station &
Scandinavian Express Buses (3km);
Mbuyuni Farm Retreat (15km);
Chalinze (85km); Mikumi (120km);
Dar es Salaam (195km); Iringa (310km)

Train Station

Mosque

Catholic Church

To Selous Game Reserve (155km)

Uhuru Monument

Morogoro Regional Hospital

Madaraka Rd

Market

Old Dar es Salaam Rd

Machupa Rd

Kitope Rd

Kitope Rd

Jamhuri Stadium

MIKUMI NATIONAL PARK
☎ 023

Lovely Mikumi – part of the vast Selous eco-system – is Tanzania's fourth-largest national park. It's also the most accessible from Dar es Salaam, and, with almost guaranteed sightings of wildlife, makes an ideal safari destination for anyone without much time to spare.

To the south, Mikumi is contiguous with Selous Game Reserve, although there's currently no all-weather road linking the two (most operators go via Morogoro), and only minimal track development. More feasible is a combination of Mikumi with Udzungwa National Park, which is about a two-hour drive south.

Information
Entry fees are US$20/5 per adult/child, and there's a US$30 per person per day concession fee payable by all those staying at camps/lodges inside the park boundaries.

Mikumi is best visited in the dry season. During the December to May wet season, some areas become inaccessible and the animals are more widely scattered. For booking camp sites and park *bandas,* contact the **senior park warden** (☎ 023-262 0487). Foxes African Safaris, which runs two lodges in the park, has safari vehicles for its guests (US$120 per half day). Otherwise, there is no vehicle hire. Two-hour guided walking safaris can be arranged at the park entrance, but these are currently being done mainly in the more heavily vegetated area of the park just south of the main highway, and may leave you disappointed.

Sleeping & Eating
The park has four **public camp sites** (camping adult/child US$30/5), for which you'll need to be self-sufficient, and there is a **special camp site** (camping adult/child US$50/10) near Choga Wale in the north of the park. There are also new and spotless **park bandas** (s/d US$50/60) just behind the park office complex, with clean, communal hot-water bathrooms, nets and a shared kitchen.

Mikumi Wildlife Camp (Kikoboga; ☎ 022-260 0352/4; obh@bol.co.tz; s/d full board US$173/302; 🖳) Kikoboga, about 500m northeast of the park entrance, has stone cottages spread along a grassy field frequented by grazing zebras and gazelles. Given its proximity to the highway, it's not a wilderness experience, but the animals don't seem to mind, and you're likely to see plenty

from your front porch. Wildlife drives cost US$130/200 per vehicle per half/full day.

Vuma Hills Tented Camp (☎ 0754-237422; www.tanzaniasafaris.info; s/d full board plus wildlife drives US$335/510; 🖳) This camp is set on a rise about 7km south of the main road, with views over the plains in the distance. The 16 tented cottages with private bathroom each have a double and a single bed, and the mood is relaxed and the cuisine is good. A recommended family choice. The turn-off is diagonally opposite the park entrance.

Foxes Safari Camp (☎ 0754-237422; www.tanzaniasafaris.info; s/d full board plus wildlife drives US$335/510; 🖳) Under the same management as Vuma Hills Tented Camp, and with good access to the wildlife-viewing circuits around Chamgore and Mwanambogo dam in Mikumi's north-eastern section. It's 6km off the tarmac road, and accessed via a signposted turn-off about 29km northeast of the park entrance.

Also see Sleeping options in Mikumi town (opposite), 23km west.

Getting There & Around
BUS
Although getting to Mikumi's entrance is easy via public transport (take any of the buses running along the Morogoro–Iringa highway and ask the driver to drop you off), there is no vehicle hire at the park (although Foxes African Safaris has vehicles for guests of its two camps).

Budget options for visiting the park include one of the frequent special deals offered by Dar es Salaam–based tour operators (see p95). Alternatively, take the bus to Mikumi town and organise transport to the park through Genesis Motel or Tan-Swiss Hotel (see opposite).

CAR
The park entrance is about a four-hour drive from Dar es Salaam; speed limits on the section of main highway inside the park during the day/night are 70km/50km per hour. A limited network of roads in Mikumi's northern section are accessible with a 2WD during most of the year; the south is strictly 4WD, except the road to Vuma Tented Camp.

MIKUMI
☎ 023

Mikumi is the last of the lowland towns along the Dar es Salaam–Mbeya highway before it starts its climb through the Ruaha River gorge up into the hills and mountains of the Southern Highlands. It's of interest primarily as a starting point for visits to Mikumi or Udzungwa Mountains National Parks.

Sleeping & Eating

Kilimanjaro Village Inn (☎ 023-262 0429; bill_wil lynm2003@yahoo.co.uk; Main Hwy; s/d with shared bathroom TSh3000/4000, with private bathroom TSh6000/8000) No-frills rooms with nets and most with fan, and inexpensive meals. It's about 1km east of the Ifakara junction and just west of the railway tracks.

Genesis Motel (☎ 023-262 0461; www.genesismotel .com; Main Hwy; camping US$5, r per person US$20, half board US$35) A mix of newer (better) and older rooms, plus a restaurant and an attached snake park. It's about 2.5km east of the Ifakara junction. For campers, there are hot-water showers and a kitchen. A vehicle is sometimes available for hire for visits to Mikumi and Udzungwa Mountains National Parks.

Tan-Swiss Hotel & Restaurant (☎ 0755-191827, 0784-246322; zillern@vtxmail.ch; Main Hwy; camping TSh3000, d/tr with private bathroom TSh45,000/60,000) Spotless rooms with nets, fans, small porches and wooden floors, and a restaurant-bar. Staff can help you organise visits to Mikumi and Udzungwa Mountains National Parks.

Getting There & Away

Minibuses heading towards Udzungwa Mountains National Park (TSh7000, two hours) and on to Ifakara leave throughout the day from the Ifakara junction just south of the main highway. The Dar es Salaam–Ifakara bus passes the junction at about noon.

Going west, Scandinavian Express and other bus lines from Dar es Salaam begin passing Mikumi en route to Iringa, Mbeya and Songea, beginning about 9.30am and stopping along the main highway just east of the Ifakara junction. Few buses originate in Mikumi, so you'll need to stand on the roadside and wait until one comes by with space. Smaller buses from Mikumi to Iringa go throughout the day from the bus stand at the Ifakara junction (three to four hours), from about 9am. There is also a direct bus from Kilombero to Iringa, passing Mikumi about 5.30am. Going east, buses to Dar es Salaam start to pass Mikumi from about 8.30am.

If you're staying at Genesis or Tan-Swiss, staff will help you arrange that the bus stops in front of the hotel, so you don't need to go to the junction.

UDZUNGWA MOUNTAINS NATIONAL PARK
☎ 023

Towering steeply over the Kilombero Plains about 350km southwest of Dar es Salaam are the wild, lushly forested slopes of the Udzungwa Mountains, portions of which are protected as part of Udzungwa Mountains National Park. In addition to an abundance of unique plants, the park is home to 10 primate species – more than in any of Tanzania's other parks – and makes an intriguing off-beat destination for anyone botanically inclined or interested in hiking away from the crowds.

There are no roads in Udzungwa; instead there are about eight major and several lesser hiking trails winding through various sections of the park. The most popular route is a short (three to five hours) but steep circuit from Sanje village through the forest to **Sanje Falls**, where swimming and camping are possible. More satisfying is the two-night, three-day hike up to **Mwanihana Peak** (2080m), the park's second-highest point. There are also several trails in the baobab-studded northwestern corner of the park around Mbatwa Ranger Post, and a multi-day trail from Udekwa up to Luhombero Peak (2579m).

Information

Entry fees are US$20/5 per adult/child. The park is best visited between June and October. For all hikes, you'll need to be accompanied by a guide (US$10 per day, or US$15 for an armed ranger, necessary for longer hikes). Porter fees are TSh10,000 per porter per day. For overnight hikes, allow an extra day at Mang'ula to organise things, and time to get from park headquarters to the trailheads.

The main entrance gate and **park headquarters** (☎ 023-262 0224; www.udzungwa.org) are in Mang'ula, 60km south of Mikumi town along the Ifakara road. There are also entry posts at Msosa, about 10km off the main highway just south of Mbuyuni, and at Udekwa village, on the western side of the park, and accessed via a turn-off from the main highway at Ilula (from where it's 60km further). Both are useful if you are coming from Iringa, although they are not always staffed. If you want to enter the park from either of these entry posts, contact park headquarters in advance.

TANZANIA

There's a tiny market in Mang'ula near the train station, and another small one in town to the north of the train station, both with limited selections. Stock up on major items in Dar es Salaam or Morogoro.

Sleeping

There are three **public camp sites** (camping adult/child US$30/5) near park headquarters, though visitors rarely stay at them as they have only the most basic facilities, versus the better and cheaper camping at Udzungwa Mountain View Hotel. There are also several camp sites along the longer trails, and a **camp site** (camping US$5) near Msosa gate on the park's western side that's affiliated with Riverside Campsite in Iringa (contact Riverside Campsite for bookings; opposite).

Udzungwa Mountain View Hotel (☎ 023-262 0218; camping US$5, r per person US$30) Under the same management as Genesis Motel in Mikumi, with no-frills rooms in a forested setting and a restaurant (set menu TSh7500). It's about 500m south of the park entrance, along the main road.

Getting There & Away

BUS

Minibuses and pick-ups run daily between Mikumi town (from the *dalla-dalla* stand on the Ifakara road just south of the main highway) and Kilombero, where you'll need to wait for onward transport towards Mang'ula. However, it's faster to wait for one of the larger direct buses coming from either Dar es Salaam or Morogoro to Ifakara and Mahenge via Mang'ula. These depart both Morogoro and Dar es Salaam between 6.30am and 10am, and pass Mikumi any time from about 8.30am to 2pm. Going in the other direction, there are several departures each morning from Ifakara, passing Mang'ula between about 7am and noon; park staff can help you with the connections. The fare between Mang'ula and Mikumi (two hours) is TSh4500.

From Iringa to Kilombero (about TSh10,000), there are one or two buses daily in each direction, departing by around noon from Iringa and between 5am and 7am from Kilombero.

Allow plenty of time to get from the park gate (where you pay your entry fee) to Sanje village, 10km to the north, which is the trailhead for a few of the hikes. There

are sporadic minibuses between Mang'ula and Sanje, and with luck you may be able to arrange a lift on a park vehicle (US$10). Walking, the route is along the main road. Entering the park from the west, you can take any bus along the main highway and ask to be dropped at Mbuyuni (sometimes called locally Ruaha Mbuyuni), from where you can either hire a taxi or walk 10km further to Msosa. Iringa-based tour operators can help organise excursions into the western part of the park, including drops at Msosa gate, although this will be expensive.

TRAIN

Tazara ordinary trains stop at Mang'ula. The train station is about a 30-minute walk from park headquarters. Express trains stop only at Ifakara, about 50km further south.

It's also easy to combine the Udzungwas with Selous Game Reserve by train, doing the Selous first, then getting your lodge to drop you at Kisaki train station, from where you can take the train on to Mang'ula. Scheduled departures from Kisaki are currently at 2pm Monday and at 8pm on Tuesday and Friday, although be prepared for delays.

IRINGA

☎ 026

Iringa – perched at a cool 1600m on a cliff-side overlooking the valley of the Little Ruaha River – was initially built up by the Germans at the turn of the 20th century as a bastion against the local Hehe people. Today, with its bluff-top setting, jacaranda-lined streets and highland feel, it makes an agreeable stop along the Dar es Salaam–Mbeya highway.

Information

CRDB Bank (Uhuru Ave) ATM (Visa only).

Iringa Info (☎ 026-270 1988; riversidecampsitetz@ hotmail.com; Uhuru Ave; ☻ 9am-5pm Mon-Fri, 9am-3pm Sat) A good place to organise Ruaha safaris, as well as reliable car hire and excursions. It's opposite Hasty Tasty Too.

Myomboni Pharmacy (☎ 026-270 2277, 026-270 2617; ☻ 7.30am-7.30pm) Just downhill from the Aga Khan Health Centre.

NBC Bank (Uhuru Ave) Opposite the Catholic Cathedral at the western end of town. Changes cash and has an ATM (Visa only).

Post Office (☻ 8am-4.30pm Mon-Fri, 9am-noon Sat) Just off Uhuru Ave.

Skynet (Uhuru Ave; per hr TSh1000; ☻ 8am-8pm Mon-Fri, 8.30am-3pm Sat & Sun) Internet access; also good for

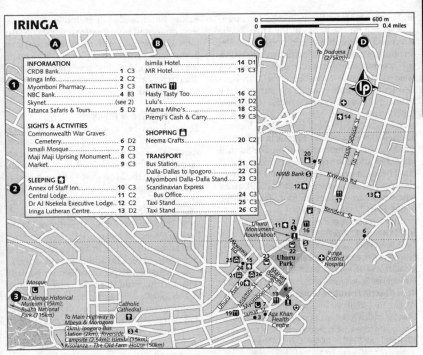

IRINGA

INFORMATION	
CRDB Bank	**1** C3
Iringa Info	**2** C2
Myomboni Pharmacy	**3** C3
NBC Bank	**4** B3
Skynet	(see 2)
Tatanca Safaris & Tours	**5** D2

SIGHTS & ACTIVITIES	
Commonwealth War Graves	
Cemetery	**6** D2
Ismaili Mosque	**7** C3
Maji Maji Uprising Monument	**8** C3
Market	**9** C3

SLEEPING	
Annex of Staff Inn	**10** C3
Central Lodge	**11** C2
Dr AJ Nsekela Executive Lodge	**12** C2
Iringa Lutheran Centre	**13** D2

Isimila Hotel	**14** D1
MR Hotel	**15** C3

EATING	
Hasty Tasty Too	**16** C2
Lulu's	**17** D2
Mama Miho's	**18** C3
Premji's Cash & Carry	**19** C3

SHOPPING	
Neema Crafts	**20** C2

TRANSPORT	
Bus Station	**21** C3
Dalla-Dallas to Ipogoro	**22** C3
Myomboni Dalla-Dalla Stand	**23** C3
Scandinavian Express	
Bus Office	**24** C3
Taxi Stand	**25** C3
Taxi Stand	**26** C3

uploading digital photos and other services. Located next to Iringa Info.

Tatanca Safaris & Tours (☎ 026-270 0601, 0787-338335; tatancatours@iringanet.com; Uhuru Ave) An efficient operator offering Ruaha safaris, as well as excursions elsewhere in the country. It's around the corner from Neema Crafts.

Telecom Shop (☼ 8am-7.30pm) diagonally opposite TTCL (look for the yellow sign); calls cost Tsh2000 per minute to anywhere.

TTCL Next to the post office; sells phone cards.

Sights & Activities

Iringa's colourful **market** – with fruits, vegetables, locally made Iringa baskets and much, much more – is well worth a stroll. Placed nearby, in front of the police station, is a **monument** to the Africans who fell during the Maji Maji uprising between 1905 and 1907. West along this same street is Iringa's main trading area, dominated by the German-built **Ismaili Mosque** with its distinctive clock tower.

Southeast of town is a **Commonwealth War Graves Cemetery**, with graves of the fallen from both world wars.

Sleeping

Iringa Lutheran Centre (☎ 026-270 2489; Kawawa Rd; tr/q dm per bed TSh2500, s/d with shared bathroom TSh3000/4000) Reasonably clean dorm-style rooms with nets, and hot-water buckets on request. There's no food. It's on the north-eastern edge of town, about 700m southeast of Neema Crafts and the main road.

Annex of Staff Inn (☎ 026-270 1344, 026-270 0165; Uhuru Ave; r TSh10,000-25,000) Small and crowded but reliable, with clean, no-frills rooms with hot water, nets and some with TV, plus a restaurant with inexpensive meals. It's along the main road, about five minutes' walk from the bus station.

Central Lodge (☎ 0786-126888; Uhuru Ave; d TSh15,000-20,000, tr TSh30,000) Simple, quiet rooms with private bathrooms in a convenient central location around a small garden. The front garden-facing rooms are spacious; smaller rooms are in the row behind. It's behind Iringa Info – look for the signpost.

Riverside Campsite (☎ 0755-033024, 0787-111663; www.riversidecampsite-tanzania.com; camping US$6, tented/stone banda per person US$15/20, day visitor TSh1500) Riverside Campsite, 13km northeast of Iringa and signposted from the main road, has a tranquil setting on the banks of the Little Ruaha River and is a recommended stop for families and budget travellers (50% children's discounts for accommodation and meals). There's a shaded riverside camping area, twin-bedded tented *bandas*, a rustic six-person stone banda, hot-water showers, meals (breakfast/lunch/dinner US$5/8/10), and a small shop with basics. Good overall value. Tents, bicycles and vehicles are available to hire, including for Ruaha safaris. There are also on-site Swahili language and culture courses. Take a *dalla-dalla* heading towards Ilula and ask the driver to drop you at the turn-off (TSh1000), from where it's 2km further on foot. Taxis charge about TSh12,000 from town.

Other recommendations:

Isimila Hotel (☎ 026-270 1194; Uhuru Ave; s/d TSh15,000/19,000; 🖳) Very no-frills and faded but fairly priced rooms, with nets and private bathrooms with sporadic hot water, and a restaurant. It's past the Bankers' Academy (see following listing) at the northern end of town.

Dr AJ Nsekela Executive Lodge (Bankers' Academy; ☎ 026-270 2407; Uhuru Ave; s/d TSh12,000/14,000) Clean but soulless rooms and an institutional ambience, with no food served. It's at the northern end of town.

MR Hotel (☎ 026-270 2006, 026-270 2779; www .mrhotel.co.tz; Mkwawa Rd; s/d/ste US$30/35/40; 🐾 🖳) A multistorey local business travellers' hotel in a convenient but noisy location next to the bus station, with faded and not always clean rooms (no nets) and a restaurant (meals TSh4000).

Eating

Hasty Tasty Too (☎ 026-270 2061; Uhuru Ave; snacks & meals from TSh500; 🕑 7.30am-8pm Mon-Sat, 10am-2pm Sun) Good breakfasts, yoghurt, shakes and reasonably priced main dishes, attracting a mix of local and expat clientele. Staff will pack picnic sandwiches to go, and can arrange food for Ruaha camping safaris.

Lulu's (☎ 027-270 2122; meals TSh3500-8000; 🕑 8.30am-3pm & 6.30-9pm Mon-Sat) A quiet place with mostly Chinese and Asian dishes, plus soft-serve ice cream. It's one block southeast of the main road, just off Kawawa Rd.

For self-catering try **Mama Miho's** (Jamat St), opposite the police and fire stations, or the pricier **Premji's Cash & Carry** (Jamat St).

Shopping

Neema Crafts (Kawawa Rd; 🕑 9am-5.30pm Mon-Fri, 9am-4.30pm Sat) A vocational training centre for Iringa's young deaf and disabled people,

selling hand-made paper and cards, jewellery, quilts and homemade cookies. Upstairs is the Gallery Café, with local coffee and teas, homemade cookies and pies and ice cream. It's off Uhuru Ave, just past NMB bank, on the corner, although scheduled to relocate, so ask around.

Getting There & Away

To catch any bus not originating in Iringa, you'll need to go to the Ipogoro bus station, about 3km southeast of town below the escarpment (about TSh2500 in a taxi from town), where the Morogoro–Mbeya highway bypasses Iringa. This is also where you'll get dropped off if you're arriving on a bus continuing towards Morogoro or Mbeya. *Dalla-dallas* to Ipogoro leave from the edge of Uhuru Park in town. All buses originating in Iringa start at the bus station in town, and stop also at Ipogoro to pick up additional passengers.

Scandinavian Express and Sumry go daily between Iringa and Dar es Salaam (TSh17,000 to TSh20,000, 7½ hours); book in advance – Scandinavian Express' office is opposite the bus station in town, Sumry's is at the bus station.

To Mbeya, Chaula Trans and several other lines depart daily by 8am (TSh13,000, four to five hours). Otherwise, you can book a seat on the Scandinavian Express bus from Dar es Salaam that passes Iringa (Ipogoro) about 1pm, or just show up at the bus station and take your chances that there will be space.

To Njombe (TSh8500, 3½ hours) and Songea (TSh15,000, eight hours), Super Feo departs at 6am from the bus station in town, with a second bus to Njombe only departing at 10am. Alternatively, you can wait for the Scandinavian Express bus from Dar es Salaam (best booked in advance).

To Dodoma, Kings Cross – an old relic of a vehicle stuffed with chickens, baskets and produce – and Urafiki depart on alternate days at 8am (TSh12,000, nine to 10 hours), going via Nyangolo and Makatapora. Otherwise, all transport is via Morogoro.

Getting Around

The main *dalla-dalla* stand ('Myomboni') is just down from the market and near the bus station. *Dalla-dallas* also stop along the edge of Uhuru Park, and some also leave from the town bus stand. Taxi ranks are along the small road between the bus station and the market, in front of MR Hotel, and at the Ipogoro bus station.

AROUND IRINGA
Isimila Stone-Age Site

About 20km from Iringa, off the Mbeya road, is **Isimila** (admission TSh3000; ☺ 8am-5.30pm), an area of small canyons and eroded sandstone pillars where in the late 1950s archaeologists unearthed Stone Age tools estimated to be between 60,000 and 100,000 years old. The main pillar area is accessed via a walk down into a steep valley, for which you'll need a guide (small tip expected).

Via public transport, take an Ifunda *dalla-dalla* from the bus station and ask the driver to drop you at the Isimila junction, from where it's a 20-minute walk to the site. Alternatively, you can catch a 'Njia Panda ya Tosa' *dalla-dalla* from the Myomboni *dalla-dalla* stand, and ask the driver to take you all the way in to Isimila. The charge is about TSh1000 per person, but most drivers are only willing to do this if there are enough people wanting to go. Taxis charge from about TSh10,000 for the return trip.

Kalenga

The former Hehe capital of Kalenga is 15km from Iringa on the road to Ruaha National Park. It was here that Chief Mkwawa – one of German colonialism's most vociferous resistors – had his administration until Kalenga fell to the Germans in the 1890s, and it was here that he committed suicide rather than succumb to the German forces.

The small **Kalenga Historical Museum** (admission TSh2000) contains Mkwawa's skull and a few other relics. It's just off the park road and signposted.

RUAHA NATIONAL PARK

Ruaha National Park, together with neighbouring Rungwa and Kisigo Game Reserves and several smaller conservation areas, forms the core of a wild and extended ecosystem covering about 40,000 sq km and providing home to one of Tanzania's largest elephant populations. In addition to the elephants, the park hosts herds of buffaloes, as well as greater and lesser kudus, Grant's gazelles, wild dogs, ostriches, cheetahs, roan and sable antelopes, and more than 400 different types of birds. Bird life is especially prolific along the Great Ruaha River, which winds through the eastern side of the park, as are hippos and crocodiles. Also running through the park are several 'sand' rivers, most of which dry up during the dry season, when they are used by wildlife as corridors to reach areas where water remains.

Information

Entry fees are US$20/5 per adult/child. There's also a US$30 per person per day conservation fee payable by all those staying at camps/lodges inside the park boundaries. There are two official entry points to the park, one at the main gate about 8km inside the park boundary on its eastern side, and the other at Msembe airstrip, about 6km northeast of the main gate, where visitors arriving by plane can pay their entry fees. Park headquarters are at Msembe.

The park can be visited at any time of year, although wildlife spotting is considerably easier from June to November, with August through October the peak months.

Sleeping
INSIDE THE PARK

There are two **public camp sites** (per adult/child US$30/5) about 9km northwest of park headquarters, both with pit toilets only (no water). There are also about five **special camp sites** (per adult/child US$50/10). Near the river and close to park headquarters are several rather basic **park bandas** (per person US$20). Water is available for showers and the park sells soft drinks and a few basics, but otherwise you'll need your own supplies. All park accommodation should be booked through Iringa Info (p226) or directly with park headquarters.

Ruaha River Lodge (☎ 0754-237422; www.tanzania safaris.info; s/d full board with wildlife drives US$375/590) This unpretentious 28-room lodge about 15km inside the gate was the first in the park. It's also the largest, and – in a prime setting – is the only place on the river. Discounted drive-in accommodation rates are offered.

Mwagusi Safari Camp (☎ UK 44-20-8846 9363; tropicafrica.uk@virgin.net; s/d all-inclusive from US$530/940; ☺ Jun-Mar) This 16-bed tented camp is well-situated on the Mwagusi Sand River about 20km inside the park gate, and known for its rustic, personalised atmosphere and top-notch guiding. Bush walks can be arranged.

Mdonya Old River Camp (☎ 022-245 2005; www .adventurecamps.co.tz; s/d all-inclusive US$345/580; ☺ Jun-Mar) The rustic, relaxed Mdonya Old River Camp, about 1½ hours drive from Msembe, has eight tents set in the shade on the bank of the Mdonya Sand River. It's run by Coastal

Travels in Dar es Salaam (p71), and if you take advantage of Coastal's 'last minute' and other specials, it offers fine value for a Ruaha safari.

OUTSIDE THE PARK
There are several places just outside the park boundaries along the Tungamalenga village road; take the left fork at the junction when coming from Iringa.

Chogela Camp (camping US$5) Spacious shaded camping grounds, a large cooking-dining area and hot-water showers. Come with your own transport, food and drink, and bring your own tent or hire one through Riverside Campsite in Iringa.

Tungamalenga Camp (☎ 026-278 2196, 0754-983519; www.ruahatungacamp.com; camping US$10, r per person with breakfast/full board US$20/40; meals TSh7000). In Tungamalenga village, about 35km from the park gate and close to the Tungamalenga bus stand, with a small garden for camping, small, clean en suite rooms and a restaurant. Cultural tours in the area can be arranged.

Tandala Tented Camp (www.tandalatentedcamp .com; per person full board US$120; ☺ Jun-Mar) About 12km from the park gate and shortly before the Tungamalenga road rejoins the main park access road, with raised tents scattered around shaded grounds and an amenable bush ambience. (Elephants and other animals are frequent visitors.) Vehicle hire to Ruaha and guided walks in park border areas can be arranged.

Getting There & Away
AIR
There are airstrips at Msembe and Jongomero.

Coastal Aviation flies from Dar es Salaam to Ruaha via Selous Game Reserve (US$330 from Dar es Salaam, US$270 from Selous Game Reserve), and between Ruaha and Arusha (US$330). Foxes African Safaris (p71) has a plane based in Ruaha for flights to Katavi (US$450), Dar es Salaam (US$300), Selous (US$270), Mikumi and other destinations on request.

BUS
Upendo and Shanila lines alternate on the daily run between Iringa and Tungamalenga village, departing Iringa at 1pm and Tungamalenga (from the village bus stand, just before Tungamalenga Camp) at 5am

(TSh3000, five to six hours). However, there is no onward transport to the park from Tungamalenga, other than rental vehicles arranged in advance through the camps along the Tungamalenga road, and there is no vehicle hire once at Ruaha.

A good contact for independent travellers is Iringa Info (p226), which offers day safaris for US$225 per vehicle per day plus park fees and overnight safaris for US$200 per day, and may also be able to help you put a group together. Tatanca Tours in Iringa also arranges Ruaha safaris that are pricey for day trips (US$300), but work out at roughly the same price for multi-night stays in the park (US$100 for each additional day).

CAR & MOTORCYCLE
Ruaha is 115km from Iringa along an un-sealed road. About 58km before the park, the road forks; both sides go to Ruaha, and the distance is about the same each way. To access Tungamalenga and accommodation outside the park, take the left fork. The right fork ('never-ending road') is maintained by the park and is generally in marginally better condition.

The closest petrol station to Ruaha is in Iringa.

IRINGA TO MAKAMBAKO
From Iringa, the Tanzam highway gradu-ally winds its way up, past dense stands of pine, before reaching the junction town of Makambako.

our pick Kisolanza – The Old Farm House (www .kisolanza.com; camping with hot showers US$4, tw in stables US$22, tw chalet US$25, d/f cottage US$45/55, luxury cottage per person half board US$75) About 50km south-west of Iringa and just off the highway, this 1930s farm homestead fringed by stands of pine and rolling hill country comes highly rec-ommended, both for its accommodation and for its cuisine. There are camp sites for over-landers and for private vehicles; twin-bed-ded dorm rooms ('stables') sharing bathroom; wooden two-person chalets; cosy camp site cottages with private bathroom; two large, luxury cottages surrounded by gardens; a bar; a restaurant (breakfast/dinner US$7/12); and a farm shop. The entire set-up is lovely, and the cuisine is excellent. Buses will drop you at the Kisolanza turn-off, from where it's about a 1.5km walk in to the lodge. Advance bookings are advisable.

About 45km further along the highway is **Mafinga**, the turn-off point to reach the forested highlands around **Mufindi**. The family-run **Mufindi Highlands Lodge** (☎ 0754-237422; www.tanzaniasafaris.info; s/d full board US$200/280) – set amid the hills and tea plantations around Mufindi – is another recommended place for anyone looking for cool highland air and the chance to hike or recharge. The lodge is about 45km in from Mafinga; pick-ups can be arranged (no public transport).

MAKAMBAKO
☎ 026

This dry, windy highland town is the junction where the road from Songea and Njombe meets the Dar es Salaam–Mbeya highway, and a stop on the Tazara railway line. There's an **internet café** (per hr TSh1500) adjoining Midtown Lodge.

Midtown Lodge (r TSh7000-10,000) has clean rooms with private bathroom, and a restaurant. It's about 1½ blocks in from both the Mbeya and Songea roads, and signposted from both.

Jay Jay Highlands Hotel (☎ 026-273 0475, 0784-310177; s/d TSh15,000/20,000) has small, clean and somewhat over-furnished rooms and a restaurant serving good-value meals. It's about 1km south of the main junction along the Njombe road.

The bus stand is about 1.5km south of the main junction along the Njombe road. The first bus to Mbeya (about TSh6000, three hours) leaves at 6am, with another bus at 7am. Otherwise, you can wait at the main junction for passing transport. The first buses (all smaller minibuses, or 'Coastals'/*thelathinis*) to Njombe (TSh2000) and Songea (TSh9000) depart at about 6.30am, and there's a larger bus departing at 6.30am for Iringa and Dar es Salaam.

MBEYA
☎ 025

Mbeya lies in a gap between the verdant Mbeya Range to the north and the Poroto Mountains to the southeast. The town is on the scruffy side, but it's a good place for stocking up, and a transit point en route to/from Zambia and Malawi. The surrounding area is lush, mountainous and highly scenic, and the climate is pleasantly cool year-round.

Information
CRDB Bank (Karume Ave) ATM (Visa).
Gazelle Safaris (☎ 025-250 2482, 0713-069179; www .gazellesafaris.com; Jacaranda Rd) Vehicle hire and guides for excursions around Mbeya, including to Kitulo National Park. There's an internet café in its office.
Nane Information Centre Internet Café (per hr TSh1000; Market Sq; ☼ 8am-6.30pm Mon-Sat)
NBC Bank (cnr Karume & Kaunda Aves) Changes cash; ATM (Visa).
Sisi Kwa Sisi (Station Rd) Near the rhino statue between the market and the bus station, this sometimes-on-sometimes-off place can be useful for arranging guides to local attractions.
Stanbic Bank (Karume Ave) ATM (Visa, MasterCard, Maestro, Cirrus); just up from CRDB bank.

Dangers & Annoyances
Mbeya attracts many transients, particularly in the area around the bus station. Watch your luggage, don't change money with anyone, only buy bus tickets in the bus company offices and avoid walking alone through the small valley behind the station. Be wary of anyone presenting themselves as a tourist guide, and don't make tourist arrangements with anyone outside of an office.

Sleeping
Warsame Guest House (Sisimba St; s/d with shared bathroom TSh4000/6000) One of Mbeya's cheapest options, with no-frills rooms (no nets), grubby shared facilities and a central location just northwest of the market.

New Millennium Inn (☎ 025-250 0599; Mbalizi Rd; s with shared bathroom TSh6000, with private bathroom TSh7000-10,000) Directly opposite the bus station, and convenient if you have an early bus. Rooms are small, noisy and reasonably clean; there's no food. The more expensive rooms have beds big enough for two, but there's no same-gender sharing.

Nkwenzulu Hotel Number 1 (☎ 025-250 2225; Mbalizi Rd; s/d TSh15,000/20,000) Next to New Millennium Inn and of similar standard, this hotel is not to be confused with the grubbier Nkwenzulu Hotel Number 3, which is at the base of the small hill and is the closest place to get a meal.

Karibuni Centre (☎ 025-250 3035, 025-250 4178; mec@maf.or.tz; camping TSh4000, d/tr TSh20,000/25,000) This mission-run place has straightforward rooms and camping in a small enclosed compound, plus a restaurant (no lunch and dinner on Sundays). It's 3km southwest of

TANZANIA

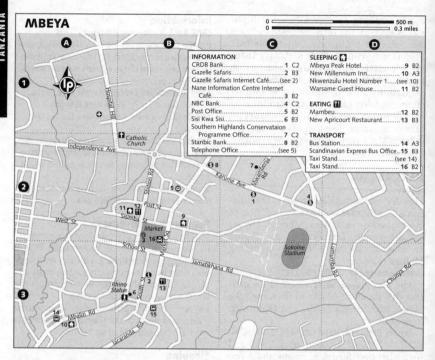

MBEYA

0		500 m
0		0.3 miles

INFORMATION
CRDB Bank...............................**1** C2
Gazelle Safaris..........................**2** B3
Gazelle Safaris Internet Café......(see 2)
Nane Information Centre Internet
   Café..**3** B2
NBC Bank..................................**4** C2
Post Office................................**5** B2
Sisi Kwa Sisi.............................**6** B3
Southern Highlands Conservataion
   Programme Office.................**7** C2
Stanbic Bank............................**8** B2
Telephone Office.................(see 5)

SLEEPING
Mbeya Peak Hotel......................**9** B2
New Millennium Inn..................**10** A3
Nkwenzulu Hotel Number 1.....(see 10)
Warsame Guest House..............**11** B2

EATING
Mambeu..................................**12** B2
New Apricourt Restaurant.........**13** B3

TRANSPORT
Bus Station.............................**14** A3
Scandinavian Express Bus Office..**15** B3
Taxi Stand.............................(see 14)
Taxi Stand..............................**16** B3

the town centre, and about 10 minutes' walk from the *dalla-dalla* stop for transport into town. Watch for the signpost along the north side of the main highway and about 500m west of the first junction coming from Dar es Salaam. From the turn-off, head through what looks like an empty lot for about 300m to the gate.

Mbeya Peak Hotel (☎ 025-250 3473; Acacia St; s/d/ste TSh17,500/20,000/50,000) A central setting, a restaurant (meals from TSh4000) and decent rooms, some with views over the hills. It's on a small side street about 300m east of the market.

Utengule Country Hotel (☎ 025-256 0100, 0753-020901; www.riftvalley-zanzibar.com; camping per site US$10, s/tw/ste/family r from US$55/80/135/140, cottage per person US$30; ⊠) This lodge is set in expansive grounds on a working coffee plantation in the hills about 20km west of Mbeya. There's camping, standard rooms and two-storey king-size suites with an upper balcony. Guides and pricey car hire can be arranged. Take the Tunduma road west from Mbeya for about 12km to Mbalizi, where there's a signposted turn-off to the right. Follow this road for 8.5km, keeping left at the first fork.

The lodge is signposted to the right. Via public transport, take any Tunduma-bound *dalla-dalla* to Mbalizi, from where sporadic pick-ups en route to Chunya will take you within about 2km of the lodge. Free pick-ups from Mbeya are offered if you're staying more than one night.

Eating

Mambeu (cnr Sisimba St & Market Sq; meals TSh1000) A local staple, with inexpensive *ugali*, chips and chicken.

New Apricourt Restaurant (Jacaranda Rd; meals from Tsh2000) Inexpensive meals, just opposite Gazelle Safaris and just up from Scandinavian Express.

Utengule Country Hotel (☎ 025-256 0100; meals about TSh12,500) A daily set menu or á la carte, and a bar. On Sunday afternoons there's a pizza and barbecue lunch on the lawn. Speciality coffees (including to take home) are a feature.

For self-catering, try the small shops around the market area, most of which have reasonable selections of boxed juices, tinned cheese and the like.

Getting There & Away

BUS

There are daily departures with **Scandinavian Express** (Jacaranda St) to Dar es Salaam at 7am (TSh30,000, 12 hours), going via Iringa and Morogoro. Departures are from its office, just down from Gazelle Safaris. Sumry also goes daily to Dar es Salaam at 6.30am.

To Njombe (four hours) and Songea (TSh15,000, eight hours), Super Feo departs daily at 6am, sometimes with a later departure as well.

To Tukuyu (TSh1500), Kyela (TSh3000) and the Malawi border, there are two or three smaller Coastal/*thelathini* minibuses daily. For more on connections between Mbeya and Malawi, see p260. It's also possible to get to the Malawi border via *dalla-dallas* that run throughout the day, but you'll need to change vehicles in Tukuyu. For Itungi port, you'll need to change vehicles in Kyela.

To Tunduma, on the Zambian border, there are daily minibuses (about TSh2500, two hours).

To Sumbawanga, the best bet is Sumry, which goes daily at 6am and 8am (TSh15,000, seven hours). For Mpanda, you'll need to change vehicles in Sumbawanga. Plan on spending the night there, since most vehicles to Mpanda depart Sumbawanga in the morning. Sometimes in the dry season it's possible to get a direct connection without overnighting in Sumbawanga, but this has you arriving quite late in Mpanda.

To Tabora, there are a few vehicles weekly during the dry season, going via Rungwa. Some – which you can pick up at Mbalizi junction – take the western route via Saza and Makongolosi, while others – catch them along the main Tanzam highway just east of central Mbeya – go via Chunya.

TRAIN

Tickets for all classes should be booked at least several days in advance at the **Tazara train station** (8am-noon & 2-5pm Mon-Fri, 10am-1pm Sat). See p266 for schedules and fares between Mbeya and Dar es Salaam, and p261 for information about connections with Zambia.

Getting Around

Taxis park at the bus station and near the market. The Tazara train station is 4km out of town on the Tanzania–Zambia highway (TSh4000 in a taxi). *Dalla-dallas* from the road in front of Nkwenzulu Hotel Number 1 and directly opposite the bus station, run to the train station and to Mbalizi, but the ones to the train station are often too full if you have luggage.

AROUND MBEYA

Mbeya Peak

Mbeya Peak (2826m), the highest peak in the Mbeya range, can be climbed as a day hike from Mbeya. The most common route goes from Mbalizi junction, 12km west of town on the Tunduma road. Take a *dalla-dalla* to Mbalizi, get out at the sign for Utengule Country Hotel, head right and follow the dirt road for 900m to a sign for St Mary's Seminary. Turn right and follow the road up past the seminary to Lunji Farm, and then on to the peak (about four to five hours return). The peak should only be climbed with a guide, which you can arrange at Sisi Kwa Sisi or Gazelle Safaris in Mbeya (see p231).

Lake Rukwa

Alkaline Lake Rukwa is notable for its many waterbirds and its crocodiles. As the lake has no outlet, its water level varies significantly between the wet and dry seasons. The main approaches are from Sumbawanga (see p221), or from Mbeya via Chunya and Saza to Ngomba, on the lakeshore (4WD). There are no facilities.

TUKUYU

☎ 025

This small town is set amid a beautiful area of hills and orchards north of Lake Nyasa. There are many hikes and natural attractions nearby, but only basic tourist infrastructure (though this is slowly changing).

The NBC bank in the centre of town changes cash and has an ATM (Visa only), and you can get online at **Syaka Internet Café** (per hr TSh1000), diagonally opposite the bank.

Rungwe Tea & Tours (www.rungweteatours.com), next to the post office, can help you organise guides for hikes and excursions. Prices start at about TSh15,000 per day.

Hiking

There are many hikes in the area around Tukuyu. For all, guides can be arranged with Rungwe Tea & Tours or Bongo Camping (p234).

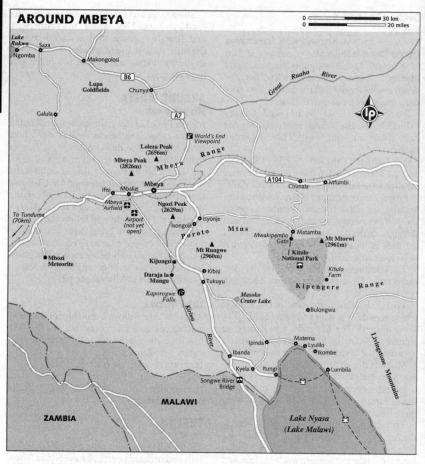

AROUND MBEYA

One possibility is the 2960m **Mt Rungwe**, to the east of the main road between Tukuyu and Mbeya. There are several routes, including one starting from near Rungwe Secondary School, signposted off the Mbeya road about 15km north of Tukuyu. Allow about 10 hours.

Further north and about 7km west of the main road is the volcanic **Ngozi Peak** (2629m), which has an impressive crater lake that is the subject of local legends. Take any *dalla-dalla* travelling between Mbeya and Tukuyu and ask to be dropped at the (signposted) turn-off. Once at the turn-off, you'll be approached by local guides if you haven't already come with one; the going rate is about TSh3000. It's also possible to go about half the distance from the main road to Ngozi by vehicle and then walk the remainder

of the way. Once at the base, it's another steep hour or so on foot up to the crater rim.

Sleeping & Eating

Bongo Camping (☎ 0784-823610; www.bongocamping .com; camping TSh5000) This community-integrated place has camping with showers and toilets, cooking facilities for campers, secure parking and tents for rent. It's at Kibisi village just off the main road – coming from Mbeya, it's signposted to the left shortly before reaching Tukuyu.

DM Motel (☎ 025-255 2332; r with private bathroom TSh10,000) Clean rooms with a large bed (no same-gender sharing permitted) and meals on request. It's just off the main road at the turn-off into Tukuyu town, and signposted.

Landmark Hotel (☎ 025-255 2400, 022-245 0510; landmahotel@yahoo.co.uk; camping per site TSh8000, s/d/tw from TSh20,000/25,000/30,000) Modern rooms, all with TV and hot water, small grounds where you can pitch a tent and a restaurant. It's the large multistorey building at the main junction just up from NBC bank.

Ima's Kitchen (Main Rd; meals from TSh1000) Just downhill from NBC bank, with inexpensive meals and snacks.

Getting There & Away

Minibuses run several times daily between Tukuyu and both Mbeya (TSh1500, one to 1½ hours) and Kyela (TSh1500, one hour).

Two roads connect Tukuyu with the northern end of Lake Nyasa. The main tarmac road heads southwest and splits at Ibanda, with the western fork going to Songwe River Bridge and into Malawi, and the eastern fork to Kyela and Itungi port. A secondary dirt road heads southeast from Tukuyu to Ipinda and then east towards Matema.

KITULO NATIONAL PARK

Tanzania's newest national park protects the flower-clad Kitulo Plateau, together with sections of the former Livingstone Forest Reserve, which runs south from the plateau paralleling the Lake Nyasa shoreline. The area – much of which lies between 2600m and 3000m in the highlands northeast of Tukuyu – is beautiful and inviting for hiking. The highest point is Mt Mtorwi (2961m), southern Tanzania's highest peak. The park reaches its prime during the rainy season from about December until April, when it explodes in a profusion of colour, with orchids and many more flowers carpeting its grassy expanses.

Information

Park infrastructure is still rudimentary. Entry fees should be paid at Tanapa's temporary **park headquarters** (adult/child US$20/5) at Matamba village, where guides can also be arranged, although with a GPS it's no problem to hike on your own. You'll need to be self-sufficient with food and water (there are plenty of sources within the park area). The best source of route descriptions is Liz de Leyser's *A Guide to the Southern Highlands of Tanzania*. The **WCS/Southern Highlands Conservation Programme office** (www.southernhighlandstz.org; off Lumumba Rd) in Mbeya sells copies.

Sleeping & Eating

There's camping inside the park, but sites are still being established, so you'll need to enquire at park headquarters. Otherwise, there are several inexpensive guesthouses in Matamba village.

Fema (r per person TSh5000) No-frills, clean rooms sharing bathroom in a large house behind the Tanapa office (across the field), hot water (usually) and meals (breakfast/lunch/dinner about TSh2500/4000/4000).

Zebra Park Guest House (s with shared/private bathroom TSh2000/3000) One block in from the main road, and signposted just beyond the turn-off for Edeni Guest House, with clean, no-frills rooms and bucket baths.

Green Garden Restaurant (meals TSh1000) For meals, try this place, at the junction of the roads from Mfumbi and Chimala, and near the Tanapa office.

Getting There & Away

The easiest access to Kitulo is via Mfumbi village, about 90km east of Mbeya along the main highway, from where a small, unpaved all-weather road winds its way 32km up to Matamba village and the park's temporary base. From Matamba, it's about an hour further via 4WD with high clearance (or about two hours on foot) along a rough road up onto the plateau itself.

It's also possible to reach Kitulo via the signposted park turn-off 2km west of Chimala town, about 80km east of Mbeya along the main highway. From here, a rocky (4WD essential) but beautiful road winds its way 9km up the escarpment via a series of 50-plus hairpin turns, offering wide vistas over the Usangi plains below. Once on top, it's a further 12km or so to Matamba.

Public transport to Kitulo goes via Mfumbi village, from where one or two pick-ups daily go as far as Matamba (TSh3500, one hour) from Mfumbi's *'standi ya uwanje'*.

In Mbeya, Gazelle Safaris (see p231) and Utengule Country Hotel (p232) can both help organise transport to the park.

LAKE NYASA

Lake Nyasa (Lake Malawi) is Africa's third-largest lake after Lake Victoria and Lake Tanganyika, and hosts close to one-third of the earth's known cichlid (freshwater fish) species. The Livingstone Mountains to the east form a stunning backdrop. Few roads reach the towns along the lake's eastern shore, and for hiking you'll need to be self-sufficient (including with water filter and GPS). Places of interest around the Tanzanian side of the lake include the following (from north to south).

Kyela
☎ 025

There's no reason to linger in this scruffy, nondescript transit town unless your boat arrives late at Itungi and you need somewhere to spend the night. Photography is prohibited in most areas.

There's **internet access** (per hr TSh1000; ♈ 7am-9pm) in the container shop at the entrance to Matema Beach Hotel. There are no ATMs; try hotel proprietors or shop owners for changing money.

Pattaya Hotel (☎ 025-254 0015; s/d from TSh7000/15,000) has rooms with either one or two large beds, nets and private bathrooms. It's in the town centre, on the road of the old Scandinavian Express bus office. One block north is **Steak Inn Restaurant** (meals TSh1500), with inexpensive meals (though no steaks).

Matema Beach Hotel (☎ 025-254 0158, 0786-565117; matemabeach2002@yahoo.com; Tukuyu Rd; s/d from TSh12,000/20,000; ⌘) is an incongruous place about 500m before town with rooms trying to be midrange, and a restaurant.

GETTING THERE & AWAY

Minibuses go several times daily from Kyela to Tukuyu (TSh1500) and Mbeya (TSh3000) from the minibus stand about two blocks north of Pattaya Hotel. Pick-ups run daily between Kyela and Itungi port (TSh300), in rough coordination with boat arrivals and departures.

Itungi

Itungi, about 11km southeast of Kyela, is the main port for the Tanzanian Lake Nyasa ferry service. There is no accommodation, and taking photos isn't allowed. Pick-ups run sporadically to and from Kyela (TSh300) in rough coordination with ferry schedules (see p264).

Matema
☎ 025

This quiet lakeside settlement is the only spot on northern Lake Nyasa that has any sort of tourist infrastructure, and with its beachside setting backed by lush mountains it makes

an ideal spot to relax for a few days. There's nowhere to change money, so bring enough shillings with you.

SLEEPING & EATING

Matema Lake Shore Resort (☎ 025-250 4178, 0754-487267; mec@maf.or.tz; camping with shower TSh3000, d with shared bathroom TSh10,000, 3-, 4- & 5-bed r TSh20,000-45,000) On the beach about 300m past the Lutheran Guest House, with two chalets with private bathroom, each accommodating up to five people, plus two smaller cottages with private bathroom and a grill. Simple meals can be arranged. Book through Karibuni Centre in Mbeya.

Lutheran Guest House (☎ 0787-275164; d/q with shared bathroom TSh15,000/25,000) Rooms at this beachside place are rather dilapidated these days, although the local ambience and cuisine are amenable. Check in first with the **Lutheran mission** (☎ 025-255 2597/8) in Tukuyu, downhill from the NBC bank, to see if space is available.

GETTING THERE & AWAY
Boat

The MV *Iringa* (p264) stops at Matema on its way from Itungi port down the eastern lakeshore. Note that the MV *Songea* (p262) doesn't stop here, which means you'll going to head back to Itungi port if you're going to Malawi.

Bus

From Tukuyu, pick-ups to Ipinda leave around 8am most mornings from the roundabout by the NBC bank (TSh1500, two hours). Although drivers sometimes say they are going all the way to Matema, generally they go only as far as Ipinda. About 20km out of Tukuyu en route to Ipinda is the scenic **Masoko Crater Lake**, into which fleeing Germans allegedly dumped a small fortune of gold pieces and coins during WWI. From Ipinda, pick-ups run sporadically to Matema (TSh1500, 35km), departing around 2pm, which means you'll need to wait around in Ipinda for a while. Departures from Matema back to Ipinda are in the morning. Chances are better on weekends for finding a lift between Matema and Ipinda with a private vehicle. If you get stuck in Ipinda, there are several basic guesthouses.

There's also at least one pick-up daily from Kyela to Ipinda (TSh1500), a few of which then continue on to Matema. From Kyela, it's also fairly easy to hire a vehicle to drop you off.

Car & Motorcycle

If you are heading to Matema in your own vehicle, the usual route from Tukuyu is via Ipinda (not via Kyela). During the dry season, and with a 4WD, it's also possible to take the main road from Tukuyu to Kyela, and then head east along a signposted, bad road to Ipinda and on to Matema. The Lutheran Mission in Tukuyu can sometimes arrange transport between Tukuyu and Matema from about US$70 per vehicle one way (about US$120 return, including waiting time).

Mbamba Bay

Mbamba Bay is the southernmost Tanzanian port on Lake Nyasa. With its low-key ambience and attractive beach fringed by palm, banana and mango trees, it makes a good spot to spend a day or few waiting for the ferry.

Nyasa View (d with shared bathroom TSh8000) has no-frills rooms with meals on request, and lake views. To get here, continue straight through town after the bridge, towards the beach.

Several readers have also recommended **St Bernadetta Sister's Guest House** (s/d about TSh10,000/20,000), also with lake views and meals.

GETTING THERE & AWAY

There's one direct vehicle daily from Songea, but otherwise you will need to change vehicles at Mbinga. See the Songea Getting There & Away section (p238).

For ferry connections between Mbamba Bay and Itungi port, see p264. For ferry connections with Nkhata Bay, see p262.

From Mbamba Bay northbound, there are occasional 4WDs to Liuli mission station. Between Liuli and Lituhi there is no public transport and little traffic, and from Lituhi northwards there is no road along the lake, only a footpath.

Entering or leaving Tanzania via Mbamba Bay, you will need to stop at the immigration post/police station near the boat landing to take care of passport formalities.

NJOMBE
☎ 026

Njombe would be unmemorable but for its highly scenic setting on the eastern edge of the Kipengere mountain range at almost 2000m, surrounded by rolling hills. There's no tourist infrastructure, so any hiking will need to be under your own steam and with a GPS. For route suggestions, look for *A Guide to the Southern Highlands of Tanzania* (see p235).

There's an internet connection at **Altek Computing Centre** (per hr TSh1000; ☺ 8am-8pm), behind the TFA building along the main road. There are no ATMs.

Sleeping & Eating

Chani Motel (☎ 026-278 2357, 0784-324644; s/d TSh8500/10,500) Modest but clean and good-value rooms with hot running water, as well as small gardens and a restaurant with what are arguably Njombe's best meals (TSh2000 to TSh4000). It's signposted at the northern end of town, and about 600m off (west of) the main road.

Mwambasa Lodge (☎ 026-278 2301; Main Rd; r TSh10,000-12,000) Clean budget rooms with private bathroom and hot water, small double beds and continental breakfast. It's about 500m north of and diagonally opposite the bus stand.

Mexons Cliff Hotel (☎ 026-278 2282, 0787-282725; s/d/ste TSh20,000/25,000/35,000) Njombe's newest hotel has a prime setting on the escarpment overlooking the surrounding countryside, although most of the rooms are rather small and somewhat cramped, with windows looking out on the back parking lot (parking is available). There's also a restaurant. It's at the northern end of town and signposted just off the main road.

Duka la Maziwa (Cefa Njombe Milk Factory; ☎ 026-278 2851; ☺ noon-6pm Mon, 8.30am-1pm & 3-6pm Tue-Fri, 8.30am-6pm Sat) Fresh milk and yoghurt and excellent cheeses. It's two blocks off the main road – turn in by the TFA building.

Getting There & Away

The bus stand is on the west side of the main road, and about 600m south of the water tank.

Super Feo line goes daily to Songea (TSh9000, four hours), Makambako (TSh2000, one hour) and Mbeya (TSh8500, four hours), with the first departures at 6.30am.

For hikers, there are daily pick-ups to both Bulongwa (departing from Njombe at about 10am) and Ludewa (departing by 8am), from where you can walk down to Matema and Lupingu, respectively, both on the Lake Nyasa shoreline.

THE MAJI MAJI REBELLION

The Maji Maji rebellion was the strongest local revolt against the colonial government in German East Africa. It began about the turn of the 20th century when colonial administrators set about establishing enormous cotton plantations in southern Tanzania. Workers were recruited as forced labour and required to work under miserable conditions. Soon, anger at this harsh treatment and long-simmering resentment of the colonial government combined to ignite a powerful rebellion. The first outbreak was in 1905 in the area around Kilwa, on the coast. Soon all of southern Tanzania was involved, from Kilwa and Lindi in the southeast to Songea in the southwest. Thousands died, both on the battlefield and due to the famine precipitated by the Germans' 'scorched-earth' tactics, in which fields and grain silos were set on fire. Fatalities were exacerbated by a belief among the Africans that enemy bullets would turn to water before killing them, and that their warriors would therefore not be harmed – hence the name Maji Maji (*maji* means water in Swahili). By 1907, when the rebellion was finally suppressed, close to 100,000 people had lost their lives and large areas of the south were left devastated.

The uprising resulted in the temporary liberalisation of colonial rule. More significantly, it promoted development of a national identity among many tribal groups and intensified anticolonial sentiment, kindling the movement towards independence.

SONGEA

☎ 025

This bustling regional capital will look like a major metropolis if you've just come from Tunduru or Mbamba Bay. The main tribal group is the Ngoni, and the town takes its name from one of their greatest chiefs, who was killed following the Maji Maji rebellion and is buried about 1km from town near the small **Maji Maji museum** (admission free but donation appreciated; ☽ 8am-4pm Mon-Fri).

NBC bank, behind the market, changes cash, and both NBC and CRDB banks (at the beginning of the Njombe road) have ATMs (Visa only). There's internet access at **Valongo Computer Centre** (per hr TSh1000; ☽ 7.30am-9pm) on a side street opposite the main market entrance. The Immigration Office (for getting your passport stamped if you are travelling to/from Mozambique) is at the beginning of the Tunduru Rd, about 400m up from and opposite Angoni Arms hotel.

Sleeping & Eating

Anglican Church Hostel (☎ 026-260 0693; s/d with shared bathroom TSh2000/2500, with private bathroom TSh3000/3500) No-frills rooms with mosquito nets set around a small courtyard. Head uphill from the bus stand, past the market to the Tanesco building. Go left and wind your way back about 400m to the Anglican church compound. It's also signposted from the Njombe road.

Don Bosco Hostel (q with shared bathroom per bed TSh3000, s TSh5000) A church-run hostel with reasonably clean, no-frills rooms and a central location. It's two blocks off the main road, diagonally behind the Catholic church and a five-minute walk from the bus stand.

White House Inn (☎ 025-260 0892; r TSh15,000) Small, clean rooms and a good restaurant (meals from TSh1500), and decent value if you have your own transport. It's about 2.5km north of the town centre in the Bomba Mbili neighbourhood, about 200m off the Njombe road.

Seed Farm Villa (☎ 025-260 2500, 0752-842086; seedfarmvilla@yahoo.co.uk; s/d from TSh40,000/46,000) Eight spacious rooms with TV and nets, meals on order and garden surroundings away from the town centre in the Seed Farm area. Take the Tundumu Rd out of town for 2.5km to the signposted turn-off, from where it's 200m further. Sometimes camping can be arranged in the grounds.

Agape Cafe (Main Rd; snacks & meals from TSh1000) Pastries and inexpensive meals just uphill from the Catholic church.

Getting There & Away

To Dar es Salaam, Scandinavian Express bus line has currently suspended its routes. In the meanwhile, the best bets are Sumry line, followed by Super Feo, both of which go daily, departing by about 6am (TSh35,000, 12 to 13 hours).

To Mbeya, Super Feo departs daily at 6am in each direction (TSh15,000, eight hours) via Njombe (four hours). There are also departures to Njombe at 9.30am and 3pm.

For Mbamba Bay, there's one direct vehicle departing daily at 7am (about TSh8000, six to eight hours). Otherwise, you'll need to get transport to Mbinga (four hours) and from there on to Mbamba Bay. During the wet season, when the trip often needs to be done with 4WDs, prices rise.

Transport to Mozambique departs from the Majengo C area, southwest of the bus stand and about 600m in from the main road – ask locals to point out the way through the back streets, and see p260 for more details.

TUNDURU

Tunduru is in the centre of a gemstone-mining region, and the overnight point for travel between Songea and Masasi. The better guesthouses are at the western end of town. There are plenty to chose from, all around the same standard.

There's at least one bus daily between Tunduru and Masasi, departing by 6am (TSh10,000, five hours). To/from Songea, 4WDs go daily (about TSh17,000, seven to eight hours, departing from Tunduru between 3am and 7am and Songea by 6am), and there's a bus in the dry season. If you are staying at a guesthouse near the 4WD 'station', you can arrange for the driver to come and wake you before departure. There is little en route, so bring food and water with you.

SOUTHEASTERN TANZANIA

Remote and untrammelled, southeastern Tanzania is a destination for the adventurous, or for anyone looking for an immersion into traditional coastal life. Wild animals roam the interior, a handful of old Swahili trading towns dot the shoreline and cultural links often seem stronger going south towards Mozambique rather than northwards towards the rest of Tanzania.

Attractions include Selous Game Reserve, the ruins on Kilwa Kisiwani, the Swahili trading towns of Mikindani and Kilwa Kivinje, and lovely Mafia island, with its slow pace, low-key resorts and diving.

A full range of amenities are available on Mafia and in Selous Game Reserve. Otherwise, to really explore Tanzania's southeast, allow plenty of time and be ready to rough things, especially on road journeys.

MAFIA ISLAND
☎ 023

Mafia island lies off the coast, sandwiched between the Rufiji River delta and the high seas. Among its draws are its lack of hustle and bustle, a fascinating history, and the chance to dive and snorkel in the surrounding waters, part of which have been gazetted as a national marine park. Mafia is also notable as a breeding ground for green and hawksbill turtles, which have nesting sites along the eastern shores of Mafia and on the nearby islands of Juani and Jibondo. Between about November and February, Mafia island is noted for its whale sharks, which are best seen offshore near Kilindoni.

There's an **internet café** (Kilindoni; per hr TSh2000) at New Lizu hotel. **NMB Bank** (Airport road) changes cash (US dollars, euros and pounds). There are no ATMs.

Sights & Activities

Chole island (per person US$5) has 19th-century **ruins**. At Kua on nearby **Juani** island there are also ruins, including the remains of several mosques dating from a Shirazi settlement during the 18th and 19th centuries.

On Mafia itself, there are **beaches** at the Chole Bay lodges, and some nearby sandbanks, but one of the longest is on the western side of the island running roughly southwestwards from Ras Mbisi.

At **Ras Mkumbi**, Mafia's windswept northernmost point, there's a lighthouse dating to 1892, as well as Kanga beach and a forest that's home to monkeys, blue duikers and many birds.

Mafia Island Marine Park (www.marineparktz.com; adult/child per day US$10/5) encompasses the entire southern and eastern part of the archipelago, including Chole Bay, Juani and Jibondo. Entry fees must be paid by everyone who enters the park area, whether you dive or not. They are collected at a barrier gate on the main road about 1km before Utende, and can be paid in any major currency. Save your receipt, as it's checked again when you leave.

Recommended dive operators – both also arrange certification courses, snorkelling and island excursions:

Big Blu (☎ 0784-918069; www.bigblumafia.org; Chole Bay) On the beach just north of Mafia Island Lodge.

Mafia Island Lodge Watersports Centre (☎ 022-260 1530; www.mafialodge.com; Mafia Island Lodge, Chole Bay)

TANZANIA

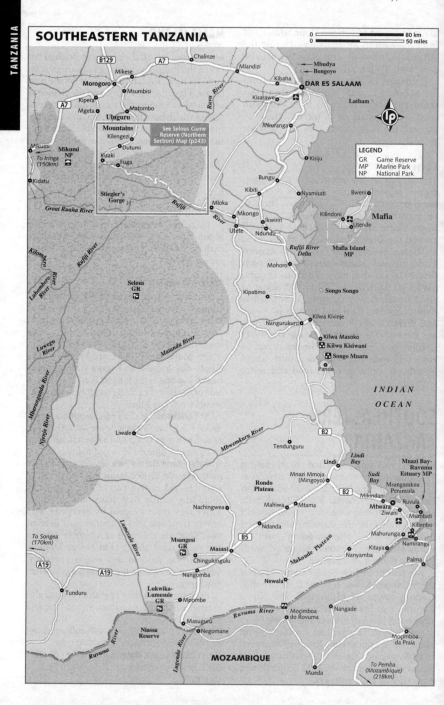

SOUTHEASTERN TANZANIA

0 — 80 km
0 — 50 miles

LEGEND
GR   Game Reserve
MP   Marine Park
NP   National Park

Sleeping & Eating

For all Chole Bay accommodation, you'll need to pay marine park entry fees, whether you go diving or not. Except as noted, it's not included in accommodation rates.

BUDGET

Whale Shark Lodge (Sunset Camp; ☎ 023-201 0201, 0755-696067; carpho2003@yahoo.co.uk; Kilindoni; camping US$7, banda per person with shared bathroom & breakfast US$20) A backpacker-friendly place on a cliff overlooking the sea on the edge of Kilindoni. There are simple, clean twin-bedded *bandas* with nets and fans, and communal ablutions and meals on order. It's behind the hospital, and TSh2000 in a taxi from the harbour.

New Lizu Hotel (☎ 023-201 0180, 023-240 2683, 0754-273722; Kilindoni; s/d TSh6000/10,000; 🖳) Clean, spartan rooms with basic bathrooms, nets and fan, good cheap food and a central location at Kilindoni's main junction, less than a 10-minute walk from both the airfield and the harbour.

MIDRANGE & TOP END

Big Blu (☎ 0784-918069; www.bigblumafia.org; Chole Bay; r per person US$44) Simple, clean rooms just in from the beach next to Mafia Island Lodge, all with nets and hot-water showers, and meals available (breakfast/lunch/dinner US$4/10/12). It's mainly a divers' base, but others can be accommodated on a space-available basis.

Mafia Island Lodge (☎ 022-260 1530; www.mafia lodge.com; Chole Bay; s/d standard US$110/184, s/d club US$135/227; ❄ 🖳) A solid midrange place directly opposite Chole island with a mix of renovated ('club') and standard rooms on a hillside about 50m up from a good beach. There's a restaurant, excursions, a watersports centre, beach volleyball and a beachside bar.

Ras Mbisi Lodge (☎ 0754-663739; www.mafiaislandtz .com; per person full board US$140; 🍹) A lovely setting on Mafia's western coast, nine tented *bandas* nestled amid the coconut palms overlooking a wonderful, long, usually deserted beach, a restaurant and a sundowner bar. Excursions include dhow trips to Ras Kisimani and nearby islands, and whale shark outings. It's a fine, good-value off-the-beaten-track alternative. Rates include transfers from Kilindoni.

Kinasi Lodge (☎ 022-284 2525; www.mafiaisland.com; Chole Bay; s/d garden view full board US$207/398, sea view full board US$265/455; 🍹 Jun-Mar; 🖳 🍹) A beautiful place with 14 stone-and-thatch cottages

on a long, manicured hillside sloping down to Chole Bay, Moroccan-influenced décor, a lounge with satellite TV, a dive centre and a spa.

Pole Pole Bungalow Resort (☎ 022-260 1530; www .polepole.com; Chole Bay; s/d full board US$315/485; 🍹 Jun-Mar; 🖳) An understated but classy place set amid the tropical vegetation on a long hillside overlooking Chole Bay. It can be visually underwhelming at first glance, but its quiet style, impeccable service, cuisine and the simple elegance of its bungalows make it a fantastic getaway. A range of excursions is offered, and there's a resident masseuse. Rates include airport transfers.

Chole Mjini (☎ 0787-712427; 2chole@bushmail.net; s/d full board with marine park & village fees US$320/480; 🍹 Jul–mid Mar) This eclectic place on Chole island has six imaginatively designed tree houses (a couple of which are actually lower stilt houses), each with views over the bay, the mangroves or the Chole ruins. There's no electricity, and the bathrooms are at ground level. Excursions and diving can be arranged, as can day or overnight dhow excursions. Chole Mjini grew out of the owners' commitment to the local community,

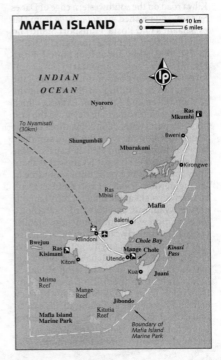

MAFIA ISLAND

which is still the heart of the undertaking, and a portion of earnings is channelled back into health and education projects on the island. No children under two permitted.

Getting There & Away

AIR

Coastal Aviation and Tropical Air fly daily between Dar es Salaam and Mafia (US$110), and Coastal also flies daily between Mafia and Kilwa Masoko (US$110, minimum two passengers), both routes with connections on to Zanzibar, Selous Game Reserve and Arusha. Kinasi Lodge has its own charter aircraft for its guests, with seats open on a space-available basis to other passengers. All the Chole Bay hotels arrange airfield transfers for their guests; except as noted, it's not included in room rates (about US$10 to US$30 per person).

BOAT

The best (albeit adventurous and not without its risks) boat connection to/from the mainland is at Nyamisati, along the coast south of Dar es Salaam. Get a south-bound *dalla-dalla* from Mbagala or Rangi Tatu (both along the Kilwa road on the southwestern edge of Dar es Salaam, and reached via *dalla-dalla* from Dar es Salaam's Old Posta Transport Stand) no later than about 11am to Nyamisati (TSh4000 to TSh5000, allow about four hours). From Nyamisati, a very rudimentary (ie no comforts whatsoever) but motorised boat – the boat varies depending on the day, but the MV *Junubeen* and *Kilindoni Express,* which currently sail on alternate days, are the best bets – departs daily (TSh7000, three to four hours) to Kilindoni. Departures are anywhere between 4pm and 1am, with the usual routine being to board the boat at Nyamisati at about 4pm and then sleep on it until sometime in the night, when it will set sail. Tourists aren't an everyday sight at the rather scruffy harbour area in Nyamisati, and it's worth exercising a bit of caution with your belongings. Smaller boats also regularly capsize on this route, so don't disembark on anything that you have doubts about. Once at Mafia's harbour, to get to the centre of Kilindoni and the guesthouses, head straight up the hill for about 300m. Departures from Kilindoni are daily between 6am and 7am. Once at Nyamisati, it's easy to find *dalla-dallas* north to Mbagala and central Dar es Salaam. On Mafia, purchase boat tickets the afternoon before at the harbour.

Getting Around

Dalla-dallas connect Kilindoni with Utende (TSh2500, 45 minutes) and Bweni (TSh2500, four to five hours), with at least one vehicle daily in each direction. On the Kilindoni–Utende route, vehicles depart Kilindoni at about 1pm and Utende at about 7am, with sporadic vehicles later in the day – the last departure from Utende is about 4.30pm. Departures from Kilindoni to Bweni are at about 1pm, and from Bweni at about 7am. In Kilindoni, the *dalla-dalla* stop is along the road leading down to the port.

You can hire pick-ups in Kilindoni to take you around the island. Bargain hard, and expect to pay at least TSh15,000 return between Kilindoni and Utende.

Local boats to Chole island sail throughout the day from the beach in front of Mafia Island Lodge (TSh100). Boats also leave from here to Juani, and from Chole it's possible to walk to Juani at low tide.

SELOUS GAME RESERVE

With an area of approximately 45,000 sq km, the Selous is one of Africa's largest wildlife reserves, although only the northernmost section is open for tourism. It provides shelter for large numbers of elephants, as well as populations of buffaloes, wild dogs, hippos and crocodiles, a rich variety of birdlife and some of Tanzania's last remaining black rhinos.

Although overall wildlife density is lower in the Selous than in some of the northern-circuit parks, visitor numbers are also lower. It's generally possible to see plenty of wildlife, usually without undue congestion. Another advantage is that you can explore the reserve by boat – along the Rufiji River, which is at the heart of the Selous – or on foot. Boat safaris down the Rufiji or in adjoining lakes are offered by most of the camps and lodges. Most also organise walking safaris, usually three-hour hikes near the camps, or further afield with the night spent at a fly camp.

Information

Entry fees are US$50/30 per adult/child. There's also a US$15 per person per day conservation fee payable by all those staying at camps inside the reserve boundaries. The vehicle fee is US$30 per vehicle per day, guide fees are US$10 to US$20 per group per day and fees for a wildlife guard (required for camping areas) are US$20 per day.

The best times to visit the Selous are from June to October, and again in January and February. Many areas are inaccessible between March and May, and some camps close. The Mtemere and Matambwe entry gates are open from 6am to 6pm daily.

Sleeping

BUDGET & MIDRANGE

There are **public camp sites** (camping adult/child US$20/5) at Beho Beho Bridge, 12km southeast of Matambwe, and at Lake Tagalala, midway between Mtemere and Matambwe. **Special camp sites** (camping adult/child US$50/10) can be arranged with the Wildlife Division (p90) or at the reserve gates.

Mloka Best (s/d TSh5000/6500) A no-frills place in Mloka village, just east of Mtemere Gate, and a potential budget option if you have your own transport to get around inside the reserve.

Selous River Camp (www.selousrivercamp.com; camping US$10, mud hut per person US$35) A few tents for rent plus a 'mud hut' bungalow with private bathroom, and a vehicle available for wildlife-viewing drives.

Ndovu (☎ 0754-782378; camping/tent per person US$10/35) Camping, plus several no-frills permanent tents sharing bath, and boat safaris. Bring all your own food.

Selous Mbega Camp (☎ 022-265 0250; www.selous-mbega-camp.com; camping US$10, s/d 'backpackers' special for those arriving by public bus, with excursions extra, US$85/120, full board US$135/190) Eight no-frills tents set back from the riverbank, and a small camping ground (for which you'll need to be self-sufficient with food). Boat safaris and wildlife drives can be arranged. It's about 500m outside the eastern boundary of the Selous near Mtemere Gate and about 3km from Mloka village.

Also recommended:

Jimbiza Lodge (☎ 022-261 8057; www.jimbizalodges.com; camping US$15, tented banda per person full board US$150) In a reasonably good location on the river on the edge of Mloka village and before reaching Selous Mbega Camp, with camping and permanent tents, plus a vehicle available to rent for wildlife drives.

TOP END

Sable Mountain Lodge (☎ 022-211 0507; www.selouslodge.com; s/d full board from US$200/290, all-inclusive from US$330/550; 🏊) Friendly and relaxed,

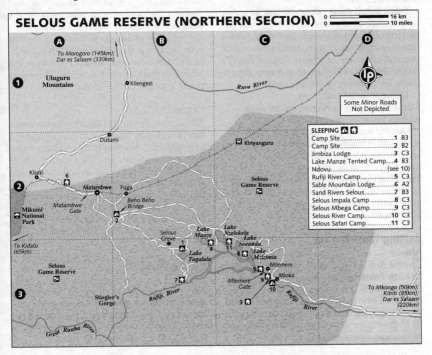

SELOUS GAME RESERVE (NORTHERN SECTION)

0 —— 16 km
0 —— 10 miles

SLEEPING 🅰 🏠
Camp Site.....................................1 B3
Camp Site.....................................2 B2
Jimbiza Lodge.............................3 C3
Lake Manze Tented Camp....4 B3
Ndovu...................................(see 10)
Rufiji River Camp........................5 C3
Sable Mountain Lodge.........6 A2
Sand Rivers Selous...................7 B3
Selous Impala Camp.................8 C3
Selous Mbega Camp.................9 C3
Selous River Camp...............10 C3
Selous Safari Camp.............11 C3

To Morogoro (145km);
Dar es Salaam (330km)

Uluguru Mountains

Kilengezi

Ruvu River

Some Minor Roads Not Depicted

Dutumi

Kinyanguru

Kisaki

Matambwe   Fuga

Selous Game Reserve

Mikumi National Park

Matambwe Gate

Beho Beho Bridge

To Kidatu (65km)

Selous Grave

Lake Manze

Lake Nzelekela

Lake Siwanda

Lake Mzizima

Mtemere

Selous Game Reserve

Lake Tagalala

Mtemere Gate

Mloka

Stiegler's Gorge

Rufiji River

Rufiji River

To Mkongo (50km);
Kibiti (85km);
Dar es Salaam (220km)

Great Ruaha River

Sable Mountain is about halfway between Matambwe Gate and Kisaki village on the northwestern boundary of the reserve, with cosy stone cottages or more upmarket tented *bandas*. In addition to walking safaris and wildlife drives, the lodge offers a combined wildlife drive and boat safari on Lake Tagalala, and night drives outside the reserve. Free pick-ups and drop-offs are provided to the Kisaki train station (watch for fly-rail specials) and staff are helpful if you're travelling independently.

Lake Manze Tented Camp (☎ 022-245 2005; www .adventurecamps.co.tz; s/d all-inclusive US$345/580; ☼ Jun-Mar) Run by the same management as Selous Impala Camp, this 12-tent place is more rustic than its sister camp, but pleasant and well situated along an arm of Lake Manze.

Rufiji River Camp (☎ 0754-237422; www.rufijiriver camp.com; s/d full board plus wildlife drives US$375/590; 🐾) A long-standing and unpretentious camp with a fine location on a wide bend in the Rufiji River about 1km inside Mtemere Gate. The 20 tents with private bathroom all have river views. It's run by Foxtreks, which also has camps and lodges elsewhere in the southern circuit.

Selous Impala Camp (☎ 022-245 2005; www.adven turecamps.co.tz; s/d all-inclusive US$515/890; ☼ Jun-Mar; 🐾) Impala is one of the smallest of the Selous camps, with just eight tents, and is solid value if you take advantage of some of Coastal Travel's favourably priced flight-and-accommodation deals. Fly camping can be arranged.

Other recommendations:

Selous Safari Camp (www.selous.com; per person full board plus airstrip transfers & activities US$625; ☼ Jun–mid Mar; 🐾) On a side arm of the Rufiji River in a particularly beautiful and lush setting overlooking Lake Nzelekela, with 12 spacious tents and the chance for fly-camping and walking safaris.

Sand Rivers Selous (www.sand-rivers-selous.com; s/d all-inclusive US$870/1450; 🐾) One of the most exclusive options, with excellent guiding. On the Rufiji River south of Lake Tagalala.

Getting There & Away

AIR

Coastal Aviation and ZanAir have daily flights linking Selous Game Reserve with Dar es Salaam (one way US$150), Zanzibar (US$180) and (via Dar) to Arusha, with connections to other northern circuit airstrips. Coastal also flies between the Selous and Mafia, and between Selous and Ruaha National Park (US$270).

BUS

Akida journeys daily between Dar es Salaam's Temeke bus stand (departing from the Sudan Market area) and Mloka village, located about 10km east of Mtemere Gate (TSh10,000, seven to nine rough hours). Departures in both directions are at 5am. From Mloka, you'll need to arrange a pick-up with one of the camps in advance, as there is no hitching in the Selous, and no vehicles for hire in Mloka itself.

Coming from Morogoro, there's a daily bus ('Madaganya') to Kisaki village departing from Morogoro at about 10am (TSh11,000, seven hours). From Kisaki, you'll need to arrange a pick-up with one of the camps in advance.

CAR & MOTORCYCLE

There's no vehicle hire at the reserve, and motorcycles aren't permitted.

There are two road options. The first is from Dar es Salaam to Mkongo via Kibiti and then on to Mtemere (250km, about seven to eight hours). Alternatively, you can go from Dar es Salaam to Kisaki via Morogoro and then on to Matambwe on a scenic road and recently much improved road through the Uluguru Mountains (350km, five hours).

From Dar es Salaam to Mtemere, the last petrol station is at Kibiti (about 100km northeast of Mtemere gate), and coming from the other direction, it's at Morogoro. There's no petrol available in the Selous.

TRAIN

All Tazara trains stop at Kisaki, which is about five to six hours from Dar es Salaam and the first stop for the express train. Ordinary trains stop at Kinyanguru and Fuga stations (both of which are closer to the central camps) and at Matambwe (near Matambwe Gate). All the lodges will do pick-ups (arranged in advance). It works best to take the train from Dar es Salaam to the Selous Game Reserve, as in the reverse direction there are often long delays.

KILWA MASOKO

☎ 023

Sleepy Kilwa Masoko (Kilwa of the Market), about halfway between Dar es Salaam and Mtwara, is the springboard for visiting the ruins of the 15th-century Arab settlements at Kilwa Kisiwani and Songo Mnara.

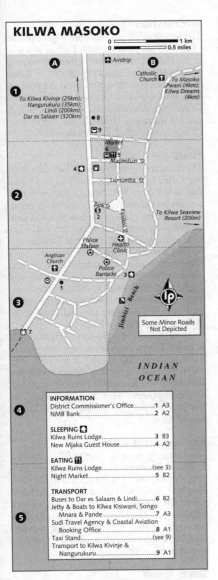

KILWA MASOKO

Sleeping & Eating

New Mjaka Guest House (☎ 023-201 3071; Main Rd; s with shared bathroom TSh3000, s/d banda with private bathroom TSh10,000/20,000) Basic rooms with fans and nets in the main building sharing facilities and somewhat nicer *bandas* with private bathroom next door. There's no food.

Kilwa Dreams (☎ 0784-585330; www.kilwadreams .com; Masoko Pwani; camping US$10, d/f bungalow US$60/80) A handful of bright blue, spartan bungalows with nets, cold water and no electricity on the lovely beach at Masoko Pwani, and a beachside bar-restaurant with meals from about TSh10,000.

Kilwa Seaview Resort (☎ 022-265 0250; www.kilwa .net; Jimbizi Beach; camping US$5, s/d/tr/q US$60/70/80/90, per person full board US$15 extra; 🖳) Straightforward A-frame cottages perched along a small escarpment at the eastern end of Jimbizi beach and a restaurant. The beach is about a five-minute walk away. Driving, the access turn-off is signposted from the main road. By foot, the quickest way to get here from the bus stand is to head south along the main road (towards the port), then turn left near the police station, making your way past the police barracks and health clinic down the hill by Kilwa Ruins to Jimbizi Beach. Pick-ups can be arranged from the bus stand. Airport transfers per vehicle cost TSh5000.

Kilwa Ruins Lodge (☎ 023-240 2397; www.kilwaruins lodge.com; Jimbizi Beach; per person full board US$120-175; 🖳 🖳) An upmarket angling camp in the centre of Jimbizi beach, with a popular waterside bar-restaurant and various levels of chalets, all spotless and well equipped. There's a full array of fishing equipment and excursions. Book in advance if you plan on visiting during the late October peak fishing season.

The night market, between the main street and the market, has inexpensive fish and other street snacks most evenings from dusk onwards.

Getting There & Away

There are daily flights with **Coastal Aviation** (Main Rd) between Dar es Salaam and Kilwa (one way US$130) and between Kilwa and Mafia (US$110, minimum two passengers). Book through its Dar es Salaam office (p95), or in Kilwa through **Sudi Travel Agency** (☎ 023-201 3004; Main Rd), north of the petrol station. The airstrip is about 2km north of town along the main road.

INFORMATION
District Commissioner's Office............1 A3
NMB Bank.....................................2 A2

SLEEPING 🏠
Kilwa Ruins Lodge..........................3 B3
New Mjaka Guest House....................4 A2

EATING 🍽
Kilwa Ruins Lodge........................(see 3)
Night Market.................................5 B2

TRANSPORT
Buses to Dar es Salaam & Lindi..........6 B2
Jetty & Boats to Kilwa Kisiwani, Songo
Mnara & Pande............................7 A3
Sudi Travel Agency & Coastal Aviation
Booking Office............................8 A1
Taxi Stand..................................(see 9)
Transport to Kilwa Kivinje &
Nangurukuru................................9 A1

The **NMB Bank** (Main Rd) changes cash. There's no internet connection or ATM.

On the eastern edge of town is **Jimbizi Beach**, an attractive, baobab-studded arc of sand. Better is the long, idyllic palm-fringed beach at **Masoko Pwani**, about 5km northeast of town, and best reached by bicycle or taxi (one way TSh5000).

To Kilwa Kivinje (TSh1800, 45 minutes), pick-ups depart daily from the transport stand on the main road just north of the market. To Dar es Salaam, there is at least one bus daily (stopping also in Kilwa Kivinje), departing in each direction at about 5am (TSh9000, six hours) from the market; book a day in advance. Departures in Dar es Salaam are from the Temeke bus stand (Sudan Market area). To Lindi, there's at least one direct bus daily (TSh8000, four hours) departing from the market, and continuing on to Mtwara; book a day in advance.

AROUND KILWA MASOKO
Kilwa Kisiwani

Kilwa Kisiwani ('Kilwa on the Island', historically known simply as Kilwa) was once East Africa's most important trading settlement – the seat of sultans and the centre of a vast trading network linking the gold fields of Zimbabwe with the Orient. Today the ruins of the settlement (some of which have been rehabilitated), together with the ruins of nearby Songo Mnara, are considered to be one of the most significant groups of Swahili buildings on the East African coast, and have been declared a Unesco World Heritage Site.

HISTORY

Although the coast near Kilwa Kisiwani has been inhabited for several thousand years, evidence of early settlements in the area dates back only to around the 9th century. In the early 13th century trade links developed with Sofala, 1500km to the south in present-day Mozambique. Ultimately, Kilwa came to control Sofala and dominate its lucrative gold trade, and it soon became the most powerful trade centre along the East African coast.

In the late 15th century Kilwa's fortunes began to turn. Sofala freed itself from the island's dominance, and in the early 16th century Kilwa came under the control of the Portuguese. It wasn't until 200 years later that Kilwa regained its independence and became a significant centre again – this time as a centre for the shipment of slaves to the islands of Mauritius, Réunion and Comoros. In the 1780s Kilwa came under the control of the sultan of Oman. By the mid-19th century the island town had completely declined and the local administration was relocated to Kilwa Kivinje.

INFORMATION

To visit the ruins, you will need to get a permit (TSh1500 per person), issued while you wait at the **District Commissioner's Office** (Halmashauri ya Wilaya ya Kilwa; ⏰ 7.30am-3.30pm Mon-Fri) in Kilwa Masoko, diagonally across from the post office. Ask for Ofisi ya Utamaduni (Antiquities Office). Guides (required to visit the island) can be arranged through the Antiquities Office, or through Kilwa Seaview Hotel.

RUINS

The ruins are in two groups. When approaching Kilwa Kisiwani, the first building you'll find is the Arab **fort**, built in the early 19th century by Omani Arabs. To the southwest of the fort are the ruins of the now restored **Great Mosque**, some sections of which date to the late 13th century. Behind the Great Mosque is a smaller **mosque**, which dates from the early 15th century and is considered to be the best preserved of the buildings at Kilwa Kisiwani. To the west of the small mosque are the crumbling remains of the **Makutani**, a large walled enclosure in the centre of which lived some of the sultans of Kilwa Kisiwani.

About 1.5km from the fort along the coast is **Husuni Kubwa**, once a massive complex of buildings covering about 0.8 hectares and, together with the nearby **Husuni Ndogo**, the oldest of Kilwa Kisiwani's ruins, though now very overgrown. To get here, walk along the beach at low tide, or take the slightly longer inland route.

GETTING THERE & AWAY

Local boats go from the port at Kilwa Masoko to Kilwa Kisiwani whenever there are passengers (one way TSh200). Chartering your own boat costs TSh1000 each way (TSh10,000 return for a boat with motor). There's also a TSh300 port fee, payable at the small office just right of the entry gate. Kilwa Seaview Hotel arranges excursions for US$20 per person, minimum two people.

Songo Mnara

Songo Mnara, about 8km south of Kilwa Kisiwani, contains ruins at its northern end that are believed to date from the 14th and 15th centuries, and are considered in many respects to be more significant than those at Kilwa, although they're less visually impressive. The Kilwa Kisiwani permit includes the ruins at Songo Mnara.

You can charter a boat from the District Commissioner's Office in Kilwa Masoko or from Kilwa Seaview Hotel (from about US$80 per motorised dhow, maximum five people).

Kilwa Kivinje

Kilwa Kivinje (Kilwa of the Casuarina Trees) owes its existence to Omani Arabs from Kilwa Kisiwani who set up a base here in the early 19th century following the fall of the Kilwa sultanate. By the mid-19th century the settlement had become the hub of the regional slave-trading network, and by the late 19th century, a German administrative centre. Today it's a crumbling, moss-covered and atmospheric relic of the past.

Kilwa Kivinje can easily be visited as a half-day or day trip from Kilwa Masoko. For overnight stays, head to **Ukaya House** (☎ 022-261 8057; info@jimbizalodges.com; s/d TSh35,000/70,000), with spacious rooms with private bathroom in a restored colonial-era house two streets back from the waterfront.

Pick-ups travel several times daily to/from Kilwa Masoko, and the bus between Dar es Salaam and Kilwa Masoko also stops at Kilwa Kivinje.

LINDI
☎ 023

Lindi was once part of the sultan of Zanzibar's domain, a terminus of the slave caravan route from Lake Nyasa, the regional colonial capital and the main town in southeastern Tanzania. Today Lindi is a lively, pleasant place with a bustling dhow port, a smattering of carved doorways and crumbling ruins lining the dusty streets, and a Hindu temple and Indian merchants serving as reminders of once-prosperous trade routes to the east.

Information

Brigita Dispensary (☎ 023-220 2679; Makonde St) Just up and around the corner from Gift Guest House, and the best place for medical emergencies.

Malaga Internet Café (Uhuru St; per hr TSh2000; ☼ 9am-6pm) Located near Precision Air.

NBC Bank (Lumumba St) Changes cash and has an ATM.

Sleeping & Eating

Adela Guest House ('Adela II'; ☎ 023-220 2310; Ghana St; r TSh10,000) Not to be confused with the eponymous Adela Guest House I several blocks closer to the town centre, this place has clean

rooms, with net, fan, TV and bathroom, and a restaurant. It's inside a walled compound – look for the large, unmarked grey metal gate.

Malaika (☎ 023-220 2880; Market St; s/d TSh10,000/12,000, ste TSh15,000) One block east of the market, with clean, no-frills rooms with net and fan, and meals on order.

Lindi Oceanic Hotel (Waterfront road) This hotel was being built on the waterfront just down from the harbour, and should soon be open with Lindi's best rooms.

Himo-One (Jamhuri St; meals TSh3000) and **Muna's** (Amani St; meals TSh2000), a few blocks up from the harbour, both have local meals. The cheapest and best street food is at the bus stand, where there's a row of stalls dishing up grilled chicken and chips each evening, plus a few stools to sit and watch the passing scene.

Getting There & Away

There are currently no scheduled flights to Lindi.

All buses depart from the **main bus & taxi stand** (Uhuru St). Minibuses to Mtwara depart daily between about 5.30am and 11am. Otherwise, there are minibuses throughout the day to Mingoyo junction (Mnazi Mmoja; TSh2000), where you can wait for the Masasi–Mtwara bus.

To Masasi, there are two or three direct buses daily, departing between about 5am and noon. Alternatively, go to Mingoyo, and wait for onward transport there. The latest Mtwara–Masasi bus passes Mingoyo at about 2pm.

To Dar es Salaam, there are direct buses daily, departing from Lindi at about 5am (about TSh18,000, eight to 10 hours).

To Kilwa Masoko, there's a direct bus leaving Lindi daily at around 5am (TSh8000, four hours).

MTWARA
☎ 023

Mtwara, southeastern Tanzania's major settlement, is a sprawling, friendly town on Mtwara Bay, and a convenient staging point on the overland journey to/from Mozambique.

Mtwara was first developed after WWII by the British as part of their East African Groundnut Scheme, a project aimed at alleviating the postwar shortage of plant oils through the implementation of large-scale groundnut (peanut) production. Following

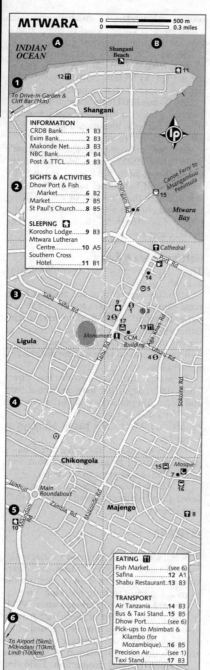

MTWARA

0   500 m
0   0.3 miles

INDIAN OCEAN

Shangani Beach

To Drive-In Garden & Cliff Bar (1km)

Shangani

INFORMATION
CRDB Bank...............1   B3
Exim Bank................2   B3
Makonde Net............3   B3
NBC Bank.................4   B4
Post & TTCL.............5   B3

SIGHTS & ACTIVITIES
Dhow Port & Fish
   Market................6   B2
Market.....................7   B5
St Paul's Church.....8   B5

SLEEPING
Korosho Lodge........9   B3
Mtwara Lutheran
   Centre..............10   A5
Southern Cross
   Hotel.................11   B1

Canoe Ferry to Msangamkuu Peninsula

Mtwara Bay

Cathedral

Ligula

Monument

CCM Building

Chikongola

Mosque

Majengo

To Airport (5km);
Mikindani (10km);
Lindi (100km)

Main Roundabout

EATING
Fish Market............(see 6)
Safina 12   A1
Shabu Restaurant..13   B3

TRANSPORT
Air Tanzania..........14   B3
Bus & Taxi Stand...15   B5
Dhow Port............(see 6)
Pick-ups to Msimbati &
   Kilambo (for
   Mozambique)....16   B5
Precision Air..........(see 1)
Taxi Stand............17   B3

the failure of the scheme, Mtwara's port continued to serve as a regional export channel, while development of the town came to a standstill.

Orientation

Mtwara is loosely centred around a business and banking area to the northwest, near Uhuru and Aga Khan Rds, and the market and bus stand about 1.5km away to the southeast, bordered by the lively neighbourhoods of Majengo and Chikongola. About 30 to 40 minutes on foot from the bus stand is the Shangani quarter, with a small beach.

Information

CRDB Bank (Tanu Rd) ATM (Visa).

Exim Bank (Tanu Rd) ATM (MasterCard and Cirrus).

Makonde Net (per hr TSh1000; ☾ 8.30am-6pm Mon-Sat, 9am-2pm Sun) Just off Aga Khan Rd in the town centre.

Main Post Office (Tanu Rd)

NBC Bank (Uhuru Rd) Changes cash and travellers cheques, and has an ATM (Visa).

Post Office & TTCL (Tanu Rd; ☾ 8am-12.45pm & 1.30-4.30pm Mon-Fri, 9am-12.30pm Sat)

Sights & Activities

The **market** has a small traditional-medicine section next to the main building. The Msangamkuu **dhow port** and adjoining **fish market** are particularly colourful in the early morning and late afternoon. **Shangani beach** is popular for swimming on weekends (high tide only). For some impressive artwork, look inside **St Paul's church** in the Majengo area of town, south of the market.

Sleeping & Eating

Drive-In Garden & Cliff Bar (☎ 023-233 3911, 023-233 3146; Shangani; camping TSh5000, r per person TSh10,000) Shady, secure camping, meals with advance notice and several simple, clean rooms in a six-bed house that also has a refrigerator and small cooker. Go left at the main Shangani junction and follow the road paralleling the beach for about 1.25km to the small signpost on your left. If you have trouble finding it, ask at Safina 'container shop' at the main Shangani junction, just after the Shangani Dispensary.

Mtwara Lutheran Centre (☎ 023-233 3294; Mikindani Rd; dm TSh3000, d with shared bathroom TSh6000, s/d TSh12,000/15,000) No-frills rooms with nets; the rooms vary, so check a few. It's on the southern edge of town, just off the main roundabout along the road heading to Mikindani.

Arriving by bus, ask the driver to drop you at the roundabout.

Korosho Lodge (☎ 023-233 4093; Tanu Rd; r with fan/air-con TSh25,000/30,000, ste TSh35,000; ✖) Spartan rooms with cold water, and a restaurant. It's diagonally opposite the taxi stand.

Southern Cross Hotel (Msemo; ☎ 023-233 3206, 0713-506047; www.msemo.com; Shangani; s/d US$35/55) Spotless rooms, all with fan, TV and a sea-facing window, plus a waterside restaurant and Shangani beach nearby. Profits from the hotel are to be channelled into primary healthcare services in the Mtwara region.

The fish market at the Msangamkuu boat dock is good for street food. **Shabu Restaurant** (Aga Khan Rd; meals TSh20m000; ✖ 8am-10pm Mon-Sat, 8am-1pm Sun) in the town centre has local fare and snacks.

For self-caterers: there are several useful shops along Uhuru Rd, including the first one on the left after passing the taxi stand. **Safina** ('Container Shop'; Shangani; ✖ 8am-79pm) has a good selection, including frozen meat and sausages and cold drinks.

Getting There & Away
AIR
There are daily flights between Mtwara and Dar es Salaam (one way TSh150,000) on **Air Tanzania** (☎ 023-233 3147; Bodi ya Korosho Bldg, Tanu Rd; ✖ closed during flight arrivals & departures) and **Precision Air** (☎ 023-233 4116; Tanu Rd), next to CRDB bank, which also sometimes stops in Lindi.

BUS
All long-distance buses depart between about 5am and 8am from the bus stand just off Sokoine Rd near the market.

To Masasi, there are roughly hourly departures between about 6am and 2pm (TSh6000, five to six hours); once in Masasi you'll need to change vehicles for Tunduru and Songea.

To Lindi (three hours), there are several direct minibuses daily, departing in both directions in the morning. Otherwise, take any Masasi bus to Mingoyo junction, and wait for onward transport from there. There is also a post bus, departing from Mtwara at around noon daily, except Tuesday.

There's at least one direct bus daily to Kilwa Masoko (five hours), departing between 5am and 6am in each direction.

Direct buses to Newala (about TSh6000, six to eight hours) use the southern route via Nanyamba. Departures from Mtwara are

between 6am and 8am daily, except during the wet season when services are more sporadic. It's also possible to reach Newala via Masasi, although this often entails an overnight stay in Masasi.

To Dar es Salaam, there are daily buses (about TSh20,000, 10 to 12 hours, sometimes longer), departing in each direction by about 6am. Lines to watch for include Wifi and Sollo's. Book in advance; in Dar es Salaam, departures are from Ubungo, or – better – from Temeke's Sudan Market area, where all the southbound bus lines also have booking offices.

To Mozambique, there are several pickups daily to the Tanzanian immigration post at Kilambo (about TSh5000), departing from Mtwara between about 8am and 11am. Departures are from the eastern side of the market near the mosque, in front of the yellow Aaliyah Trading Company building. For information on crossing the Ruvuma River, see p260. The best places for updated information on the vehicle ferry are The Old Boma and Ten Degrees South Lodge, both in Mikindani (see below). Note that Mozambican visas are not issued at this border, and there is no Mozambique consulate in Mtwara (the closest one is in Dar es Salaam). Long-distance buses depart from the bus stand just off Sokoine Rd near the market; most departures are in the morning.

Getting Around
Taxis to or from the airport (6km southeast of the main roundabout) cost from TSh6000. There are taxi and tuk-tuk (majaji) ranks at the bus stand and near the corner of Uhuru and Tanu Rds. A few dalla-dallas run along Tanu Rd to and from the bus stand.

MIKINDANI
☎ 023
This tiny Swahili town has a long history, coconut groves and a picturesque bay. It's easily visited as a day trip from Mtwara, and makes an amenable base in its own right.

The town gained prominence early on as a dhow port and a terminus for trade caravans travelling from Lake Nyasa. In the 19th century Mikindani served as headquarters of the German colonial government and several buildings from the era remain, including the boma, built in 1895.

The closest banking facilities are in Mtwara. There's internet access at the Old Boma.

Ten Degrees South Lodge (☎ 0784-855833; www .eco2.com; r with shared/private bathroom US$10/60) is a budget travellers' base, with no-frills rooms – all with large beds and nets – plus some nice ones with private bathroom and balcony, and a restaurant-bar. **ECO2** (www.eco2.com) is based here.

Old Boma at Mikindani (☎ 023-333875; www.mi kindani.com; r US$110-180; 🖳 🖳) has been beautifully restored, with spacious, high-ceilinged double room, flowering gardens and a restaurant. Climb the tower for views over town.

Getting There & Away

Mikindani is 10km from Mtwara along a sealed road. Minibuses run between the two towns throughout the day. Taxis charge from about TSh8000.

MNAZI BAY-RUVUMA ESTUARY MARINE PARK

Tanzania's newest marine park encompasses a sliver of coastline extending from Msangamkuu peninsula (just north and east of Mtwara) in the north to the Mozambique border in the south. The heart of the conservation area is **Msimbati Peninsula**, together with the bordering Mnazi Bay. Most visitors head straight to the tiny settlement of **Ruvula**, which is about 7km beyond Msimbati village along a sandy track (or along the beach at low tide). It has a fine stretch of sand, although its magic has been considerably tarnished by rigs set up nearby in connection with exploitation of offshore gas fields in Mnazi Bay.

Entry fees are US$10/5 per adult/child per day, collected at the park gate at the entrance to Msimbati village. Diving can be arranged with **ECO2** (www.eco2.com) in Mikindani.

Ruvula Sea Safari (☎ 0784-367439; www.ruvula .net; day visitors TSh5000, camping US$12, s/d banda full board US$80/140), on the beach in Ruvula, has simple, overpriced *bandas* near the sea and grilled fish meals. If you're camping, stock up in Mtwara.

There is at least one pick-up daily in each direction between Mtwara and Msimbati (TSh2000, two hours), departing from Mtwara by or before about 11am from the eastern side of the market near the mosque. Departures from Msimbati are at around 5.30am from the police post near the park gate.

Driving from Mtwara, take the main road from the roundabout south for 4km to the village of Mangamba, branch left at the signpost onto the Mahurunga road and continue for about 18km to Madimba. At Madimba, turn left again and continue for 20km to Msimbati.

There is no public transport between Msimbati and Ruvula. You can arrange a lift on a motorbike (about TSh5000) with one of the locals, or walk along the beach at low tide (over one hour). Taxis from Mtwara to Ruvula Sea Safari charge from TSh50,000 return.

MAKONDE PLATEAU & AROUND

The remote Makonde Plateau, much of which lies between 700m and 900m above sea level, is home to the Makonde people, famed throughout East Africa for their carvings, although unless you're based here for a while and get out into the villages, you'll have better chances of finding carvings at Mwenge Carvers' Market in Dar es Salaam.

Newala

☎ 023

Dusty, bustling Newala is the major settlement on the plateau, with views over the Ruvuma Valley and an old German fort (now the police station). **Country Lodge Bed & Breakfast** ('Sollo's'; ☎ 023-241 0355; s/d TSh22,000/30,000) – about 600m from the town centre along the Masasi road – has rooms with nets and private bathroom, and a restaurant.

Buses run daily from Newala to Mtwara and to Masasi (about TSh4000, three hours).

Masasi

☎ 023

Masasi, a bustling district centre off the edge of the Makonde Plateau, is a transport hub for travel west towards Tunduru and north to Nachingwea and Liwale.

Better guesthouses include **Holiday Guest House** (r TSh7000), at the western end of town near the petrol station, and **Sayari Hotel** (☎ 023-251 0095; r TSh11,000), at the eastern end of town near the post office.

Sayari Hotel also has meals, as does **Mummy's** (meals TSh2000), behind the bus stand and near the district council building.

GETTING THERE & AWAY

The bus stand is at the far western end of town on the Tunduru road. Coming from Mtwara, ask the driver to drop you at your hotel or at the petrol station to avoid the walk back to town. Buses leave for Mtwara (TSh6000, five hours) approximately hourly between 6am and 2pm.

Land Rovers and (in the dry season) buses go to Tunduru daily (six hours, 200km), departing from Masasi before dawn.

TANZANIA DIRECTORY

This section covers Tanzania-specific information. For regional information, see p602.

ACCOMMODATION

In July and August, and again around the Christmas and New Year holidays, many hotels levy an additional 'peak-season' charge on top of high-season rates. During the March through May low season you can often get discounts of up to 50% on room prices. A residents' permit also entitles you to some discounts.

Many lodges and luxury camps around the parks quote all-inclusive prices, which means accommodation and full board plus excursions, such as wildlife drives, short guided walks or boat safaris. Park entry fees and airport transfers are also sometimes included.

Camping
NATIONAL PARKS

There are camp sites in and around most national parks. While camping near the parks can save you some money, camping in the parks themselves will cost at least US$30 per person per night. 'Public' or 'ordinary' camp sites have basic facilities; generally pit toilets and sometimes a water source. 'Special' camp sites are more remote, with no facilities at all; the idea is that the area remain as close to pristine as possible. Unlike public camp sites, which can be booked on the spot, special camp sites must be booked in advance, and you'll often have them to yourself. For most national park camp sites, you'll need to bring everything in with you, including drinking water. Most parks also have simple huts or *bandas*, and several have resthouses. Both the *bandas* and resthouses have communal cooking facilities.

ELSEWHERE

There are camp sites in or near most major towns, and it's a good idea to carry a tent if you're planning to travel in off-the-beaten-track areas. Camping away from established sites is not advisable. In rural areas, seek permission first from the village head or elders before pitching your tent. Camping is not permitted on Zanzibar.

Hostels, Guesthouses & Budget Hotels

In Tanzanian Swahili, *hotel* (or *hoteli*) refers to food and drink, rather than accommodation. The better term if you're looking for somewhere to sleep is *nyumba ya kulala wageni* – or, less formally, *pa kulala*. Water can be a problem during the dry season, and many of the cheapest places won't have running or hot water, though all will arrange a bucket if you ask.

Hotels, Lodges & Luxury Camps

En suite rooms (ie with private bathroom) are widely referred to as 'self-contained' or 'self-container' rooms. There's a rapidly increasing selection of midrange and top-end accommodation in major towns, as well as beautiful luxury lodges on the safari circuits and along the coast.

ACTIVITIES
Beachcombing & Island Hopping

Highlights include the Zanzibar Archipelago (p121); Mafia island (p239); the southeastern coast, including the ruins at Kilwa Kisiwani (p246); and the mainland coast from Saadani National Park (p149) up to Pangani and Tanga (p152).

Inland highlights include the Lake Nyasa shoreline (p235), the Lake Tanganyika shoreline (p216) and Rubondo Island National Park (p206).

PRACTICALITIES

- Tanzania uses the metric system for weights and measures.

- Access electricity (220-250V AC, 50Hz) with British-style three-square-pin or two-round-pin plug adaptors.

- English-language newspapers include: *Guardian* and *Daily News* (dailies); and *Business Times*, *Financial Times* and *East African* (weeklies).

- English-language radio stations include: Radio Tanzania (government aligned); Radio One; Radio Free Africa; BBC World Service; and Deutsche Welle.

Bird-Watching

Top birding spots include national parks, Lake Victoria and the eastern Usambara mountains. Useful websites include the Tanzania Bird Atlas (www.tanzaniabirdatlas.com), the Tanzania Hotspots page on www.camac donald.com/birding/africatanzania.htm and http://birds.i ntanzania.com.

Boating

Local dhow trips are easily arranged along the coast, but are generally best booked for short sails – eg a sunset or afternoon sail – rather than longer journeys. Many coastal hotels arrange charters, often with their own dhows, including The Tides (p152), Peponi Holiday Resort (p151), Ten Degrees South Lodge (p250), Old Boma at Mikindani (p250), Fundu Lagoon Resort (p145) and any of the Chole Bay lodges on Mafia island (p241). See p129 for Zanzibar listings. Another contact is Tanzania Yacht Charters (www.tanzania yachts.com).

Chimpanzee Tracking

Gombe Stream National Park (p215) and Mahale Mountains National Park (p216) have both hosted international research teams for decades, and are the places to go if you're interested in observing chimpanzees at close range.

Cycling & Mountain Biking

For general information, see p621. For Tanzania contacts, see p263.

Diving & Snorkelling

Zanzibar is the main hub for snorkelling activities, followed by Mafia and the southeast around Msimbati and Mtwara. Highlights include extensive coral reef systems and colourful marine life, and a generally favourable mix of conditions, although in many areas, dives involve at least a 30-minute boat ride to the sites. For more information, see boxed text p131. Mnemba Atoll (p142) is a snorkelling highlight.

Fishing

Contacts for arranging deep-sea fishing charters include Ras Mbisi Lodge on Mafia (p241), Pemba and Zanzibar, Kilwa Ruins Lodge (p245), KJT Investments Tanzania (www.fishing-tanza nia.com) in Kilwa and on Mafia, and Jodari Fishing Club (www.jodarifishingclub.com) in Kizimkazi.

Contacts on Lake Victoria include Lukuba Island Lodge (p210) and Wag Hill Lodge (www .wagh ill.com).

Hiking & Trekking

Hiking areas in Tanzania include the Usambara and Pare Mountains, Udzungwa Mountains National Park, the Uluguru Mountains, the lower slopes of Mt Kilimanjaro around Marangu and Machame, and the Crater Highlands. Other possibilities include Mt Hanang and the southern highlands around Tukuyu and Kitulo National Park. Except in the western Usambaras around Lushoto (where there's an informal guide organisation and a network of guesthouses) and in the Crater Highlands (where most hiking is organised through operators), you'll need to organise things yourself. In most areas it's required or recommended to go with a guide, which, apart from adding to the cost, can feel constraining if you're used to just setting off on your own. When formalising your arrangements, be sure you and the guide agree on how much territory will be covered each day, as local expectations about suitable daily sections on standard routes are often unsatisfyingly short if you're an experienced hiker.

The main trekking destinations are Mt Kilimanjaro (p166) and Mt Meru (p182). All trekking requires local guides and (usually) porters. Be aware of the dangers of Acute Mountain Sickness (AMS; p633).

Horse-riding

Contacts for arranging riding safaris in the West Kilimanjaro and Lake Natron areas include Equestrian Safaris (www.safaririding.com) and Makoa Farm (p164).

Wildlife Watching

This is one of Tanzania's top attractions. See p66 and the Wildlife & Habitat special section (p105).

BOOKS

Lonely Planet's *Tanzania* covers the country in more depth.

Tanzania – Portrait of a Nation by Paul Joynson-Hicks and *Tanzania – African Eden* by Graham Mercer and Javed Jafferji both give alluring photographic introductions to the country, while *Serengeti – Natural Order on the African Plain,* by Mitsuaki Iwago, documents the rhythms of nature on the Serengeti plains.

An Ice-Cream War by William Boyd gives a snapshot of present-day Tanzania during WWI.

Memoirs of an Arabian Princess by Emily Said-Ruete is the very readable autobiography of a Zanzibari princess who elopes with a German to Europe in the days of the sultans.

In *The Gunny Sack*, Tanzanian-bred MG Vassanji explores Tanzania's rich ethnic mix through several generations of an immigrant Indian family.

Sand Rivers by Peter Matthiessen takes you on safari into the heart of Selous Game Reserve.

Through a Window by Jane Goodall offers a vivid portrayal of the author's research and life with the chimpanzees of Gombe Stream National Park.

BUSINESS HOURS

Most forex bureaus remain open until 5pm Monday through Friday, and until noon on Saturday. Shops and offices often close for one to two hours between noon and 2pm, and – especially in coastal areas – on Friday afternoons for mosque services.

CHILDREN

All Tanzanian parks and reserves are free for children under five years of age, and entry and camping fees are discounted for those under 16 years of age. Hotel accommodation is usually discounted for those under 12 and free for those under two years old; extra children's beds added to double rooms usually cost about US$10 to US$20. You'll need to specifically request children's discounts on entry fees and accommodation rates, especially when booking through tour operators.

Most upscale hotels have pools or grassy areas where children can play, although good playgrounds are a rarity. Mosquito nets for the family are best brought from home. Many wildlife lodges have restrictions on accommodating children under 12 years old.

Child-friendly destinations include anywhere along the coast, the area around Lushoto (for children old enough to enjoy walking) and the water amusement parks north of Dar es Salaam (p103).

COURSES
Language

Schools (many of which can arrange home stays) include the following. Another contact is Riverside Campsite (p227) in Iringa.

ELCT Language & Orientation School (www.stud yswahili.com; Lutheran Junior Seminary, Morogoro)

Institute of Swahili & Foreign Languages (Map p126; ☎ 024-223 0724, 223 3337; takiluki@zanlink.com; PO Box 882, Zanzibar, attn: Department of Swahili for Foreigners; Vuga Rd, Stone Town) Also see www.glcom .com/hassan/takiluki.html.

KIU Ltd (☎ 022-285 1509; www.swahilicourses.com) At various locations in Dar es Salaam, plus branches in Iringa and Zanzibar.

Makoko Language School (☎ 028-264 2518; swahili musoma@juasun.net) In Makoko neighbourhood, on the outskirts of Musoma; also see www.stgertrude.org/frben /makoko/makoko.htm.

MS Training Centre for Development Cooperation (☎ 027-255 3837/8; www.mstcdc.or.tz) About 15km outside Arusha, near Usa River.

University of Dar es Salaam (☎ 022-241 0757; www.udsm.ac.tz/kiswahilicourses.html)

CUSTOMS

Exporting seashells, coral, ivory and turtle shell is illegal. You can export up to TSh2000 without declaration. There's no limit on importation of foreign currency; amounts over US$10,000 must be declared.

DANGERS & ANNOYANCES

Tanzania is in general a safe, hassle-free country, and can be a relief if you've recently been somewhere like Nairobi, Kenya. That said, you do need to keep your wits about you and take the usual precautions. In particular, avoid isolated areas, especially isolated stretches of beach, and in cities and tourist areas take a taxi at night.

Especially in Arusha, Moshi and Zanzibar, touts and flycatchers can be extremely aggressive, particularly around bus stations and budget tourist hotels. Do everything you can to minimise the impression that you're a newly arrived tourist. Duck into a shop if you need to get your bearings, and don't walk around more than necessary with your luggage. While looking for a room, leave your bag with a friend or hotel rather than walking around town with it. Buy your bus tickets a day in advance (without your luggage), and when arriving in a new city, take a taxi from the bus station to your hotel. Be very wary of anyone who approaches you on the street, at the bus station or in your hotel offering safari deals, and never pay any money for a safari or trek in advance until you've thoroughly checked out the company. Also be wary of anyone who tries to sell you a yellow-fever vaccination card.

In western Tanzania there are occasional outbreaks of banditry near the Burundi border; get an update from your embassy first. See also p607.

EMBASSIES & CONSULATES
Tanzanian Embassies & Consulates

Australia Sydney (☎ 03-9667 0243; www.tanzaniaconsul.com; Level 2, 222 La Trobe St, Melbourne, VIC 3000); Perth (☎ 08-9221 0033; legal@murcia.com.au; 3rd fl, MPH Bldg, 23 Barrack St, Perth WA 6000)

Burundi (tzrepbj@sina.com; 4 United Nations Rd, Plot 382, Bujumbura)

Canada (☎ 0613-232 1500; tzottawa@synapse.net; 50 Range Rd, Ottawa, Ontario KIN 8J4)

France (☎ 01-53 70 63 66; www.amb-tanzanie.fr; 13 Ave Raymond Poincaré, 75116 Paris)

Germany (☎ 030-303 0800; www.tanzania-gov.de; Eschenallee 11, 14050 Berlin-Charlottenburg)

Italy (☎ 06-334 85801; www.tanzania-gov.it; Viale Cortina d'Ampezzo 185, Rome)

Japan (☎ 03-3425 4531; www.tanzaniaembassy.or.jp; 4-21-9, Kamiyoga, Chome Setagaya-Ku, Tokyo 158-0098)

Kenya (☎ 020-311948; Reinsurance Plaza, 9th fl, btwn Tarifa Rd & Aga Khan Walk, Nairobi)

Malawi (☎ 01-775038, 01-770148; Plaza House, Capital City, Lilongwe 3)

Mozambique (☎ 21-490110; Ujamaa House, 852 Ave Mártires de Machava, Maputo)

The Netherlands (☎ 0180-312 644; Parallelweg Zuid 215, 2914 LE Nieuwerkerk aan den Ijssel)

Rwanda (☎ 756567; tanzarep@rwandatell.rwandal.com; 15 Ave Paul VI, Kigali)

South Africa (☎ 012-342 4371; www.tanzania.org.za; 822 George Ave, Arcadia 0007, Pretoria)

Uganda (☎ 0414-256272; tzrepkla@imul.com; 6 Kagera Rd, Kampala)

UK (☎ 0207-569 1470; www.tanzania-online.gov.uk; 3 Stratford Place, London W1C 1AS)

USA Washington (☎ 1-202-939 6125; www.tanzaniaembassy-us.org; 2139 R St, NW, Washington DC 20008); New York Consulate (☎ 1-212-972 9160; 201 East 42nd St, Ste 1700, New York, NY 10017)

Zambia (☎ 01-227698; tzreplsk@zamnet.zm; Ujamaa House, 5200 United Nations Ave, Lusaka)

Embassies & Consulates in Tanzania

All of the following are in Dar es Salaam, and are open from 8.30am to at least noon. Visa applications should be made in the morning. Australians can contact the Canadian embassy (www.embass y.gov.au).

Belgium (Map p94; ☎ 022-211 2688; daressalaam@diplobel.org; 5 Ocean Rd, Upanga)

Burundi (Map p94; ☎ 022-212 7008; Lugalo St, Upanga; ☼ 8am-3.30pm) Just up from the Italian embassy, opposite the army compound. Three-month single-entry visas cost US$50 plus two photos, and are issued in 24 hours. The consulate in Kigoma (p213) issues one-month single-entry visas for US$40 plus two photos within 24 hours.

Canada (Map p96; ☎ 022-216 3300; www.dfait-maeci.gc.ca/tanzania; Umoja House, cnr Mirambo St & Garden Ave)

Democratic Republic of the Congo (Map p94; 435 Maliki Rd, Upanga; ☼ 10am-1pm & 2-3.30pm) Three-month single-entry visas cost US$150 plus two photos and a letter of invitation from someone in the DRC. Allow plenty of time for issuing. The consulate in Kigoma (p213) is much easier, issuing single-entry visas for US$50 (US$30 for Tanzania residents) plus two photos within two days or less.

France (Map p94; ☎ 022-219 8800; www.ambafrance-tz.org; Ali Hassan Mwinyi Rd)

Germany (Map p96; ☎ 022-211 7409 to 7415; www.daressalam.diplo.de/en/Startseite.html; Umoja House, cnr Mirambo St & Garden Ave)

India (Map p94; ☎ 022-266 9040; www.hcindiatz.org; 82 Kinondoni Rd)

Ireland (Map p94; ☎ 022-260 2355/6; iremb@raha.com; Toure Dr) Opposite Golden Tulip Hotel.

Italy (Map p94; ☎ 022-211 5935; www.ambdaressalaam.esteri.it; 316 Lugalo Rd, Upanga)

Kenya (Map p94; ☎ 022-266 8285; www.kenyahighcomtz.org; 127 Mafinga St, Kinondoni)

Malawi (Map p96; ☎ 022-213 6951; 1st fl, Zambia House, cnr Ohio St & Sokoine Dr; ☼ 8am-3pm) Many nationalities, including USA, UK and various European countries, do not require visas.

Mozambique (Map p96; ☎ 022-211 6502; 25 Garden Ave; ☼ 8.30am-3pm) One-month single-entry visas cost US$40 (US$55 for express service) plus two photos and are issued within three days.

Netherlands (Map p96; ☎ 022-211 0000; www.netherlands-embassy.go.tz; Umoja House, cnr Mirambo St & Garden Ave)

Rwanda (Map p94; ☎ 022-211 5889, 022-213 0119; 32 Ali Hassan Mwinyi Rd, Upanga; ☼ 8am-noon & 2-4pm) Three-month single-entry visas cost US$60 plus two photos, and are issued within 48 hours. Citizens of the USA, Germany, South Africa, Canada and various other countries do not require visas.

Uganda (Map p94; ☎ 022-266 7009; 25 Msasani Rd, ☼ 8.30am-3pm) Three-month single-entry visas cost US$30 plus two photos and are issued the same day. Located near Oyster Bay Primary School.

JK (Map p96; ☎ 022-211 0101; www.britishhighcom mission.gov.uk/tanzania; Umoja House, cnr Mirambo St & Garden Ave)

USA (Map p94; ☎ 022-266 8001; http://usembassy state.gov/tanzania; Old Bagamoyo & Kawawa Rds)

Zambia (Map p96; ☎ 022-212 5529; Ground fl, Zambia House, cnr Ohio St & Sokoine Dr; ⏲ 9am-2pm Mon, Wed & Fri for visa applications, 2-3.30pm Tue, Thu & Mon for pick-up) One-month single-entry visas cost TSh25,000 to TSh125,000 depending on nationality plus two photos, and are issued the next day.

Mozambique (Map p126; ☎ 024-223 0049; Mapinduzi Rd)

Oman (Map p126; ☎ 024-223 0066/0700; Vuga Rd)

FESTIVALS & EVENTS

Sauti za Busara (www.busaramusic.org) A three-day music and dance festival centred around all things Swahili, traditional and modern, held in February on Zanzibar.

Kilimanjaro Marathon (www.kilimanjaromarathon .com) In the foothills near Moshi; February/March.

Festival of the Dhow Countries (www.ziff.or.tz) A two-week extravaganza of dance, music, film and literature from Tanzania and other Indian Ocean countries, with the Zanzibar International Film Festival as its centrepiece; early July.

Mwaka Kogwa A four-day festival in late July to mark Nairuzim (the Shirazi New Year); festivities are best in Makunduchi on Zanzibar.

Charity Goat Races (www.goatraces.com) A take-off on Kampala's goat races (p434), these are held annually in Dar es Salaam to benefit local charities; August.

HOLIDAYS

New Year's Day 1 January
Zanzibar Revolution Day 12 January
Easter March/April – Good Friday, Holy Saturday and Easter Monday
Union Day 26 April
Labour Day 1 May
Saba Saba (Peasants' Day) 7 July
Nane Nane (Farmers' Day) 8 August
Independence Day 9 December
Christmas 25 December
Boxing Day 26 December

Islamic holidays are also celebrated as public holidays; see p609.

INTERNET RESOURCES

Eco-Tanzania (www.ecotz.com) Tanzania's ecoportal; check out especially the link to Carbon Tanzania.

Tanzania National Parks (www.tanzaniaparks.com) Tanapa's official website.

Tanzania Natural Resources Forum (www.tnrf.org) Natural-resource management, community-based tourism and more.

Tanzania On-Line (www.tzonline.org) An intro to all things official, with links to the government site (www .tanzania.go.tz) and more.

Tanzania Page (www.sas.upenn.edu/African_Studies /Country_Specific/Tanzania.html) Heaps of links.

Tanzania Tourist Board (www.tanzaniatouristboard .com) The TTB's official site.

MAPS

Recommended country maps include those published by Nelles (1:1,500,000) and Harmsic, both available in Tanzania. Harms-ic also publishes maps for Lake Manyara National Park, the Ngorongoro Conservation Area and Zanzibar.

An excellent series of colourful maps, hand drawn by Giovanni Tombazzi and marketed under the name **MaCo** (www.gtmaps.com), covers Zanzibar, Arusha and the northern parks. They're widely available in bookshops in Dar es Salaam, Arusha and Zanzibar Town.

MONEY

Tanzania's currency is the Tanzanian shilling (TSh). There are bills of TSh10,000, 5000, 1000 and 500, and coins of TSh200, 100, 50, 20, 10, five and one shilling(s). For exchange rates, see Fast Facts, p81. For information on costs, see p15.

Travel in Tanzania is expensive, especially if you're doing an organised safari. While travelling on a modest or even a shoestring budget is possible, it takes some work, and you'll need to rough things. Whatever your budget, there are few real deals – comforts abound, but you'll need to pay. For tips on cutting costs, see boxed text, p15.

The best currency to bring is US dollars in a mixture of large and small denominations, plus a Visa card for withdrawing money from ATMs and some travellers cheques as an emergency standby (although these are changeable in major cities only). Euros are fine in major cities, but elsewhere can be problematic to change. Credit cards are frequently not accepted, including by many upmarket hotels, and if accepted, it's often only with a minimum 5% commission.

There's a 20% value-added tax (VAT), usually included in quoted prices.

ATMs

ATMs are widespread in major towns, with Standard Chartered, Barclays, NBC, Stanbic, CRDB and TanPay/SpeedCash the major operators. All allow you to withdraw shillings to a maximum of TSh300,000 to TSh400,000 per transaction. Visa is by far the most useful card for ATM cash withdrawals (and still the only one possible in many towns – NBC and CRDB machines take only Visa). However, Barclays and Stanbic ATMs also accept MasterCard and cards tied in with the Cirrus/Maestro network, and there are a few ATMS that only work with MasterCard. All ATMs are open 24 hours, although they are frequently temporarily out of service or out of cash, so don't rely on them as your only source of funds. Withdrawals are often rejected for rather arbitrary reasons (no matter what reason the ATM gives), and it's always worth trying again.

Cash

Cash can be changed by travellers with a minimum of hassle at banks and foreign exchange (forex) bureaus in larger towns. Forex bureaus are quicker, less bureaucratic and offer higher rates, although smaller towns don't have them. The most useful bank for changing money is NBC, with branches throughout the country. Old-style US bills are not accepted anywhere, and US$50 and US$100 bills get better rates of exchange than smaller denominations. Euros, British pounds and other major currencies are accepted in major towns. Avoid changing money on the street at all costs – problems range from counterfeit bills to counting scams and worse.

To reconvert Tanzanian shillings to hard currency at the end of your trip, save at least some of your exchange receipts, though they are seldom checked. The easiest places to reconvert currency are at the airports in Dar es Salaam and Kilimanjaro.

In theory, it's required for foreigners to pay for accommodation, park fees, organised tours, upscale hotels and the Zanzibar ferries in US dollars, but in practice, you'll find shillings are accepted almost everywhere at the going rate.

Credit Cards

Some top-end hotels and tour operators accept credit cards – most with a 5% to 10% commission – though many (most) don't, so always confirm in advance that you can pay with a card. Otherwise, credit cards (primarily Visa) are useful for withdrawing money at ATMs.

Tipping

On treks and safaris, it's common practice to tip drivers, guides, porters and other staff if the service has been good. For guidelines on amounts see boxed text, p62 (for safaris), and p168 and p182 (for treks).

Travellers Cheques

Travellers cheques can be cashed in Dar es Salaam, Arusha, Zanzibar and Mwanza, but not at all or only with difficulty or very high commissions elsewhere. Exchange rates are slightly lower than for cash, and most hotels and safari operators won't accept them as direct payment. Almost all banks and forex bureaus that accept travellers cheques require you to show the *original purchase receipt* before exchanging the cheques, in addition to your passport. Most banks (but not forex bureaus) charge commissions ranging from 0.5% of the transaction amount (at NBC) to more than US$40 per transaction (Standard Chartered) for exchanging travellers cheques.

TELEPHONE

There are very few public phones, and Tanzania Telecom (TTCL) no longer provides call-and-pay service. Instead, it sells dialling cards for TSh1000, which you can then top up at any TTCL office and use (together with the accompanying PIN number) at any land line (TTCL) phone for domestic and international calls. Budget about US$2 per minute for international calls. Local calls are cheap – about TSh100 per minute. Domestic long-distance rates vary depending on distance, but average about TSh1000 for the first three minutes plus TSh500 per minute thereafter. Calls to mobile phones cost about TSh500 per minute.

Mobile Phones

The mobile phone network covers major towns and many outlying areas, although especially in the south, west and centre, coverage gets spotty. Mobile phone numbers are six digits, preceded by 07XX; major companies include Celtel, Vodacom, Tigo and (on Zanzibar) Zantel. All sell prepaid starter packages for about US$2, and top-up cards are on sale at shops throughout the country. Watch for frequent specials, such as SIM card giveaways. Dialling internationally from the mobile phone network is generally significantly cheaper than using TTCL. The cheapest is internet dialling, though this can be hard to find.

To reach a mobile phone number from outside Tanzania, dial the country code, then the mobile phone code without the initial 0 and then the six-digit number. Within Tanzania, keep the initial 0 and don't use any other area code.

Phone Codes

The country code is ☎ 255. To make an international call, dial ☎ 000, followed by the country code, local area code (without the initial '0') and telephone number. Land-line area codes (included with all numbers in this chapter) must be used whenever you dial long distance or from a mobile phone.

TOURIST INFORMATION

The **Tanzania Tourist Board** (TTB; www.tanzaniatouristboard.com) has offices in Dar es Salaam (p95) and Arusha (p171). In the UK, the TTB is represented by the **Tanzania Trade Centre** (www.tanzatrade.co.uk).

VACCINATION CERTIFICATES

It's not required to carry a certificate of yellow-fever vaccination unless you're arriving from an infected area (which includes Kenya, although arrivals aren't always checked). However, it's a requirement in some neighbouring countries, including Rwanda. It is also requested by some officials anyway, and is a good idea to carry. For more, see p632.

VISAS

Almost everyone needs a visa, which costs US$20 to US$50, depending on nationality, for a single-entry visa valid for up to three months. It's best to get the visa in advance (and necessary if you want a multiple-entry visa), although single-entry visas are currently readily issued at Dar es Salaam and Kilimanjaro airports, and at most land border crossings (all nationalities US$50, US dollars cash only or the Tanzanian shilling equivalent).

One month is the normal visa validity, and three months the maximum. For extensions within the three-month limit, there are immigration offices in all major towns; the process is free and straightforward. Extensions after three months are difficult – you'll usually need to leave the country and apply for a new visa.

VOLUNTEERING

See p614 for general information. Tanzania-specific contacts include **Trade Aid** (www.tradeaiduk.org/volunteer.html); **School of St Jude** (www.schoolofstjude.co.tz); **Livingstone Tanzania Trust** (www.livingstonetanzaniatrust.com); and **Hostel Hoff** (www.hostelhoff.com). For ways to help out closer to home, see www.books4tanzania.org.uk, **Friends of Tanzania** (www.fotanzania.org) and www.adventureskope.com/plasterhouse.

TRANSPORT IN TANZANIA

GETTING THERE & AWAY

For information on getting to East Africa from outside the region, see p616.

Entering Tanzania

Visas are available at all major points of entry, and must be paid for in US dollars cash. You'll need proof of yellow-fever vaccination only if you're coming from a yellow fever–infected area (including Kenya), though it often isn't checked.

Passport

There are no entry restrictions for any nationalities.

Air

Tanzania's air hub is **Julius Nyerere International Airport** (DAR; ☎ 022-284 2461, 022-284 2402; www.tanzaniairports.com) in Dar es Salaam. **Kilimanjaro International Airport** (JRO; ☎ 027-255 4252, 027-255 4707; www.kilimanjaroairport.co.tz), midway between Arusha and Moshi, handles many international flights and is the best option if you'll be concentrating on Arusha and the northern safari circuit. It shouldn't be confused with the smaller **Arusha Airport** (code ARK), about 8km west of Arusha, which handles some domestic flights. There are international flights to/from **Zanzibar International Airport** (code ZNZ). **Mwanza Airport** (code MWZ) and **Mtwara Airport** (code MYW) handle some regional flights.

Air Tanzania (TC; ☎ 022-211 8411, 022-284 4239; www.airtanzania.com; hub Julius Nyerere International Airport) is the national airline, with a limited but generally reliable network. Regional destinations are Moroni (Comoros), Entebbe (Uganda) and Johannesburg (South Africa).

DEPARTURE TAX

The departure tax for regional and international flights (US$30) is included in the ticket price for mainland departures, but is levied separately at the airport on Zanzibar (payable in either US dollars or Tanzanian shillings).

Other regional and international carriers include the following (with useful flights between Tanzania and elsewhere in East Africa highlighted). All airlines service Dar es Salaam, except as noted.

Air India (AI; ☎ 022-215 2642; www.airindia.com; hub Mumbai)

Air Kenya (REG; ☎ 027-250 2541; www.airkenya.com; hub Nairobi) Affiliated with Regional Air in Arusha; flies Nairobi to Kilimanjaro, among other routes.

Air Uganda (U7; www.air-uganda.com; hub Entebbe) Entebbe to Kilimanjaro, Dar es Salaam and Zanzibar; bookings at Air Tanzania office or through travel agents.

British Airways (BA; ☎ 022-211 3820; www.britishair ways.com; hub Heathrow Airport, London)

Emirates Airlines (EK; ☎ 022-211 6100; www.emir ates.com; hub Dubai International Airport)

Ethiopian Airlines (ET; ☎ 022-211 7063; www.ethio pianairlines.com; hub Addis Ababa) Also serves Kilimanjaro and Zanzibar international airports.

Kenya Airways (KQ; ☎ 022-211 9376/7; www.kenya -airways.com; hub Jomo Kenyatta International Airport, Nairobi) Nairobi and Mombasa to Dar es Salaam and Zanzibar in partnership with Precision Air.

KLM (KL; ☎ 022-213 9790/1; www.klm.com; hub Schiphol Airport, Amsterdam) Also serves Kilimanjaro International Airport.

Linhas Aéreas de Moçambique (TM; ☎ 022-213 4600; www.lam.co.mz; hub Mavalane International Airport, Maputo)

Precision Air (PW; ☎ 022-216 8000; www.precision airtz.com; hub Dar es Salaam) In partnership with Kenya Airways; connections between Nairobi, Mombasa, Entebbe and various cities in Tanzania.

Rwandair Express (WB; ☎ 0732-978558; www .rwandair.com; hub Kigali) Kigali to Kilimanjaro International Airport, plus other routes within East Africa

South African Airways (SA; ☎ 022-211 7044; www.flysaa.com; hub OR Tambo International Airport, Johannesburg)

Swiss International Airlines (LX; ☎ 022-211 8870; www.swiss.com; hub Kloten Airport, Zurich)

Zambian Airways (Q3; ☎ 022-212 8885/6; www .zambianairways.com; hub Lusaka International Airport)

Land

BUS

Buses cross the borders between Tanzania and Kenya, Uganda, Malawi and Zambia. Apart from sometimes lengthy waits at the border for passport checks, there are usually no hassles. At the border, you'll need to disembark on each side to take care of visa formalities, then reboard your bus and continue. Visa fees are not included in bus-ticket prices for trans-border routes.

CAR & MOTORCYCLE

Arriving via car or motorcycle, you'll need the vehicle's registration papers and your license (p265), plus a temporary import permit (TSh20,000 for one month, purchased at the border), third-party insurance (TSh50,000 for one year – purchased at the border or in the nearest large town) and a one-time fuel levy (TSh5000). You'll also need a *carnet de passage en douane*; see p623.

Tanzania hire companies don't permit their vehicles to cross international borders.

For road rules, see p623. Most border posts don't have petrol stations or repair shops – you'll need to wait until the nearest large town.

TO/FROM BURUNDI

There are crossings at Kobero Bridge between Ngara and Muyinga (Burundi); at Manyovu, north of Kigoma, and at Kagunga (south of Nyanza-Lac).

For Kobero Bridge: the trip is done in stages via Nyakanazi and Lusahunga (from where there's regular transport north towards Biharamulo and Lake Victoria and southeast via Kahama towards Nzega and Shinyanga). From Mwanza, the trip is best done in stages via Biharamulo and Lusahunga, or alternatively, along the longer but paved route via Shinyanga and Kahama. The road from Nzega to the Burundi border via Ngara is in good condition.

For the Manyovu crossing *dalla-dallas* leave Kigoma from behind Bero petrol station (about TSh5000, three hours). Once through the Tanzanian side of the border, you can sometimes find cars going to Bujumbura (about TSh5000, three to four hours). Otherwise, take one of the many waiting vehicles across the border and on to Makamba (about 70km from Manyovu and the Burundian immigration post, and from there get another vehicle on to Bujumbura.

For the route via Kagunga and Nyanza-Lac, see p262.

TO/FROM KENYA

The main route is the sealed road between Arusha and Nairobi via the Namanga border post (open 24 hours). There are also border crossings at Horohoro, north of Tanga; at Holili, east of Moshi; at Bologonya in the northern Serengeti; and at Sirari, northeast of Musoma. With the exception of the Serengeti–Masai Mara crossing (Bologonya), there is public transport across all Tanzania–Kenya border posts.

Kisii

Buses and minibuses depart between about 6am and 2pm from Mwanza towards the Sirari/Isebania border post (three hours). From here, there's one direct bus daily to Kisumu (TSh8000, four hours). Otherwise, take a *matatu* (minibus) to Kisii, and from there get transport to Kisumu or Nairobi. Akamba bus line passes Sirari and Kisii en route between Mwanza and Nairobi (TSh28,000, 15 hours between Mwanza and Nairobi), with some buses continuing to Arusha and Dar es Salaam.

Masai Mara

There's no public transport between the northern Serengeti and Kenya's Masai Mara Game Reserve, and only East African residents and citizens can cross here. If you're a resident and are exiting Tanzania here, take care of immigration formalities in Seronera. Entering Tanzania from Masai Mara, park fees should be paid at the Lobo ranger post.

BORDER HASSLES

At the Namanga border post watch out for touts – often claiming they work for the bus company – who tell you that it's necessary to change money, pay a fee or come over to 'another building' to arrange the necessary payments to enter Tanzania/Kenya. Apart from your visa, there are no border fees, payments or exchange requirements for crossing, and the rates being offered for forex are substandard.

Mombasa

Scandinavian Express and other bus lines between Tanga and Mombasa depart daily in the morning in each direction (TSh8000, four to five hours).

The road is well sealed between Dar es Salaam and Tanga, in poor condition between Tanga and the border at Horohoro, and in good condition from the border to Mombasa. There's nowhere official to change money at the border. Touts here charge extortionate rates, and it's difficult to get rid of Kenyan shillings once in Tanga, so plan accordingly.

Nairobi

Akamba and Scandinavian Express lines go daily between Dar es Salaam and Nairobi via Arusha (TSh40,000, 14 hours from Dar, TSh18,000 from Arusha, departing from Dar at 6am and Arusha at 4pm). Scandinavian Express continues on to Kampala. Akamba also has a daily bus between Mwanza and Nairobi (TSh28,000, 15 hours), departing from Mwanza at about 2pm and departing Nairobi at about 10pm.

Between Arusha and Nairobi, there are several buses daily (TSh15,000, six hours) in each direction departing between 6.30am and 8am. Departures in Arusha are from the bus station; in Nairobi most leave from Accra Rd. It's more comfortable to take one of the daily shuttle buses, departing daily at 8am and 2pm in each direction (five hours). Following are the main bus companies – both of which also have one bus daily to/from Moshi:

Impala Arusha (☎ 027-250 7197, 027-250 8448/51; Impala Hotel, cnr Moshi & Old Moshi Rds, Arusha); Nairobi (☎ 020-273 0953; Silver Springs Hotel)

Riverside Arusha (☎ 027-250 2639, 027-250 3916; riverside_shuttle@hotmail.com; Booking office Sokoine Rd, departure point Bella Luna, Moshi Rd); Nairobi (☎ 020-229618, 020-241032; Pan African Insurance House, 3rd fl, Room 1, Kenyatta Ave, departure point Parkside Hotel, Monrovia St)

Both charge about US$25 one way between Nairobi and Arusha, and with a little prodding, it's easy enough to get the residents' price (TSh20,000). In Arusha, departure and drop-off points are at Bella Luna. In Nairobi, the departure point is Parkside Hotel – from where several other Arusha-bound shuttles also depart – and from Jomo Kenyatta International Airport, if you've made an advance booking (they'll meet your flight). Drop offs are at centrally located hotels and at Jomo

Kenyatta International Airport. Confirm the drop-off point when booking, and insist on being dropped off as agreed.

Voi

Dalla-dallas go daily between Moshi and the border town of Holili via Himo junction (TSh1500, one hour). At the **border** (🕑 6am-8pm), hire a *piki-piki* (motorbike; TSh500) or bicycle to cross 3km of no-man's land before arriving at the Kenyan immigration post at Taveta. From Taveta, sporadic minibuses go to Voi along a rough road (KSh300), where you can then find onward transport to Nairobi and Mombasa. If you're arriving/departing with a foreign-registered vehicle, the necessary paperwork is only done from 8am to 1pm and 2pm to 5pm daily.

TO/FROM MALAWI

The only crossing is at **Songwe River bridge** (🕑 7am-7pm Tanzanian time, 6am-6pm Malawi time), southeast of Mbeya.

Buses go several times weekly between Dar es Salaam and Lilongwe (27 hours), though they are overcrowded (even if you have a ticket, it's often not possible to board midroute in Mbeya), often delayed and not recommended. Better is to travel from Dar es Salaam to Mbeya via bus or train, and then continue in stages from there. (There is no direct transport, despite what you may be told at Mbeya bus station.) To do this, take one of the daily minibuses or 'Coastals'/*thelathinis* connecting both Mbeya (TSh3000, two hours) and Kyela with the border. In Mbeya, look for buses going to Kyela (these detour to the border) and verify that your vehicle is really going all the way to the border, as some say that they are stop at Tukuyu (40km north) or at Ibanda (7km before the border). Asking several passengers (rather than the minibus company touts) should get you the straight answer. Your chances of getting a direct vehicle are better in the larger Coastals/*thelathinis*, which depart Mbeya two or three times daily and usually go where they say they're going. The buses stop at the transport stand, about a seven-minute walk from the actual border, so there's no real need for the bicycle taxis that will approach you.

Once across the Tanzanian side, there's a 500m walk to the Malawian side, and minibuses to Karonga. There's also one bus daily between the border and Mzuzu, departing from the border by midafternoon and arriving by evening.

Coming from Malawi, the best option is to take a minibus from the border to Mbeya, and then get an express bus from there towards Dar es Salaam. This entails overnighting in Mbeya, as buses to Dar es Salaam depart Mbeya between 6am and 7am.

TO/FROM MOZAMBIQUE

The main crossing is at Kilambo (south of Mtwara). Travelling by boat, there are immigration officials at Msimbati (Tanzania) and at Palma and Moçimboa da Praia (Mozambique). You can also cross south of Songea. Mozambique visas are not issued anywhere along the Tanzania border, so arrange one in advance.

Pick-ups depart Mtwara daily between 6am and 9am to the Kilambo border post (about TSh5000, one hour) and on to the Ruvuma, which is crossed via dugout canoe (TSh2000, 10 minutes to over an hour, depending on water levels, and dangerous during heavy rains) or ferry. On the Mozambique side (Namiranga, also known as Namoto), there are usually two pick-ups daily to the Mozambique border post (4km further) and on to Moçimboa da Praia (US$12, four hours), with the last one departing by about noon. The Ruvuma crossing is notorious for pickpockets. Watch your belongings, especially when getting into and out of the boats, and keep up with the crowd when walking to/from the river bank.

Further west, Land Rovers or trucks depart daily from Songea's Majengo C area by about noon, reaching the Ruvuma in the evening (TSh11,000, six hours plus). Try to get a seat in the cab rather than with the cargo load. Cross the river via dugout canoe (TSh2000) and spend a night on the river banks before continuing the next morning to Lichinga (TSh25,000, eight to 10 hours) via Segundo Congresso (where you'll need to change vehicles) to Macalogue. There's no accommodation on the Tanzanian side of the border, nor any official immigration post (take care of formalities in Songea). On the Mozambique side there are basic rooms near the Immigration post, a short walk from the river. The whole journey is rugged and hardcore. It's best to pay in stages, rather than paying the entire TSh36,000 Songea to Lichinga fare in Songea, as is sometimes requested.

Car & Motorcycle

There is currently no vehicle ferry in operation at Kilambo (the previous one having sunk). Get an update first at the Old Boma at Mikindani (p250) or Ten Degrees South Lodge (p250), both in Mikindani, or at **Russell's Place** (Cashew Camp; ☎ in Mozambique 82-686 2730; www .pembamagic.com) in Mozambique.

The Unity Bridge over the Ruvuma at Negomano (well southwest of Kilambo, near the confluence of the Lugenda River) is scheduled to be completed during the lifetime of this book.

TO/FROM RWANDA

The main crossing is at Rusumu Falls, southwest of Bukoba.

Daily minibuses go from Kigali to Rusumu (Rwanda; US$6, three hours), where you'll need to walk across the Kagera river bridge. Once across, there are vehicles to the tiny town (and former refugee camp) of Benako (marked as Kasulo on some maps; TSh2500, 25 minutes), about 20km southeast. Daily buses go from Benako to Mwanza (TSh22,000, eight hours), departing by about 7am (which means you'll need to overnight in Benako), though it's often just as fast to go in stages via Kahama and Shinyanga along the tarmac road (eight hours between Benako and Kahama). There are also daily connections from Benako to Nyakanazi junction, where you can try squeezing into a bus on to Kibondo, Kasulu and Kigoma (TSh5000 and two hours from Benako to Nyakanazi, plus TSh10,000 and about seven hours from there to Kigoma).

TO/FROM UGANDA

The main post is located at Mutukula, northwest of Bukoba (although you actually get stamped in and out of Tanzania at Kyaka, about 30km south of the Mutukula border), with good tarmac access routes on both sides. There's another crossing further west at Nkurungu, but the road is bad and sparsely travelled.

Dolphin (also called Gateway) and Ariazi Tours lines go daily between Bukoba and Kampala, departing from Bukoba at 7am (TSh13,000, six hours). Departures from Kampala are at 10.30am for Ariazi and 11am for Dolphin. Tawfiq/Falcon goes twice weekly along this route, continuing on to Nairobi (TSh30,000) and Dar es Salaam (TSh75,000, 30 hours between Kampala and Dar es Salaam), though if you're headed to Nairobi, it's better to sleep in Kampala and continue the next

day. A better connection to Dar es Salaam is on Scandinavian Express, which does the route to/from Kampala four times weekly via Nairobi (TSh85,000, about 30 hours). Akamba also does the route (TSh85,000 to TSh95,000 depending on the bus).

It's also possible to travel the stretch between Bukoba and Kampala in stages via Mutukula and Masaka; see p504.

From Mwanza, Akamba goes Wednesday, Friday and Sunday to/from Kampala (TSh31,000, 19 hours), departing from Mwanza at 2pm.

TO/FROM ZAMBIA

The main border crossing is at **Tunduma** (⏰ 7.30am-6pm Tanzania time, 6.30am-5pm Zambia time), southwest of Mbeya. There's also a crossing at Kasesha, between Sumbawanga and Mbala (Zambia).

At the time of research, there was no direct bus service to Lusaka from either Dar es Salaam or Mbeya, although there's talk of it resuming. (If this happens, plan on about TSh75,000 and 30 hours from Dar es Salaam). Meanwhile, minibuses ply between Mbeya and Tunduma (TSh3000, two hours), where you walk across the border for Zambian transport to Lusaka (about US$20, 18 hours). Be prepared for more than the normal share of touts and chaos.

For the Kasesya crossing, there are pickups from Sumbawanga to the border, where you'll need to change to Zambian transport. If driving from Zambia into Tanzania, note that vehicle insurance isn't available at the Kasesya border, but must be purchased 120km further on in Sumbawanga.

Train

The Tanzania–Zambia (Tazara) line links Dar es Salaam with Kapiri Mposhi in Zambia (1st/2nd/economy class TSh55,000/40,000/33,000, about 40 hours) twice weekly via Mbeya and Tunduma. Departures from Dar es Salaam are at 3.50pm Tuesday and 3pm Friday, and from Kapiri Mposhi at about 3pm on the same days. Departures from Mbeya to Zambia are at 2.30pm Wednesday and Saturday. Students with ID get a 50% discount. From Kapiri Mposhi to Lusaka, you'll need to continue by bus.

Sea & Lake

There's a US$5 port tax for all boats and ferries from Tanzanian ports.

TANZANIA

TO/FROM BURUNDI

Passenger ferry service between Kigoma and Bujumbura is suspended. However, it's possible to take a lake taxi from Kibirizi (just north of Kigoma) or from Gombe Stream National Park to Kagunga (the Tanzanian border post). Once there, look for passage in one of the frequent small cargo boats going on to Nyanza-Lac, from where there is regular transport on to Bujumbura.

It's also sometimes possible to arrange passage on one of the regular cargo ferries between Kigoma's Ami port and Bujumbura; ask at the port for the Alnorak office.

TO/FROM DEMOCRATIC REPUBLIC OF THE CONGO

Cargo boats go two to three times weekly from Kigoma's Ami port, departing Kigoma about 5pm and reaching Kalemie (DRC) before dawn (deck class only US$20, seven hours). Check with the Congolese embassy in Kigoma about sailing days and times. Bring food and drink with you, and something to spread on the deck for sleeping.

TO/FROM KENYA

Dhow

Dhows sail sporadically between Pemba, Tanga and Shimoni (Kenya), but the journey can be long, rough and risky and is not recommended.

Ferry

There's no passenger ferry service on Lake Victoria between Tanzania and Kenya.

TO/FROM MALAWI

The MV *Songea* sails between Mbamba Bay and Nkhata Bay (Malawi), in theory departing Mbamba Bay on Friday morning and Nkhata Bay on Friday evening (1st/economy class US$10/4, four to five hours). The schedule is highly variable and sometimes cancelled.

TO/FROM MOZAMBIQUE

Dhow

Dhows between Mozambique and Tanzania (12 to 30 or more hours) are best arranged at Msimbati and Moçimboa da Praia (Mozambique).

Ferry

The official route between southwestern Tanzania and Mozambique is via Malawi on the MV *Songea* between Mbamba Bay and Nkhata Bay, and then from Nkhata Bay on to Likoma island (Malawi), Cóbuè and Metangula (both in Mozambique) on the MV *Ilala*. (The small boats that sail along the eastern shore of Lake Nyasa between Tanzania and Mozambique are risky and not recommended.)

See the preceding Malawi section (left) for schedule information for the MV *Songea*. The MV *Ilala* departs Monkey Bay (Malawi) at 10am Friday, arriving in Metangula (Mozambique) at 6am Saturday, reaching Cóbuè (Mozambique) around noon, Likoma island (Malawi) at 1.30pm and Nkhata Bay (Malawi) at 1am Sunday morning. Southbound, departures are at 8pm Monday from Nkhata Bay and at 6.30am Tuesday from Likoma island, reaching Cóbuè at 7am and Metangula at noon. The schedule changes frequently; get an update from **Malawi Lake Services** (☎ in Malawi 01-587311; ilala@malawi.net). Fares are about US$40/20 for 1st-class cabin/economy between Nkhata Bay and Cóbuè. There's an immigration officer at Mbamba Bay, Mozambique immigration posts in Metangula and Cóbuè, and immigration officers on Likoma island and in Nkhata Bay for Malawi. You can get a Mozambique visa at Cóbuè, but not at Metangula.

TO/FROM UGANDA

There's no passenger-ferry service, but it's possible – albeit rough and officially not permitted – to arrange passage between Mwanza's South Port and Kampala's Port Bell on the cargo ships that sail several times weekly on varying schedules. Departures are generally in the evening, and you'll need to first check in at the immigration office at South Port to have your passport stamped. The journey takes about 17 hours; expect to pay about US$20, plus TSh5000 port tax, and bring some water and food along for the journey. Crew members are sometimes willing to rent out their cabins for a negotiable extra fee.

TO/FROM ZAMBIA

The venerable MV *Liemba*, which has been plying the waters of Lake Tanganyika for the better part of a century, connects Kigoma with Mpulungu in Zambia weekly (1st/2nd/economy class US$60/45/40, US dollars cash only, at least 40 hours). Stops en route include Lagosa (for Mahale Mountains National

Park), Kalema (southwest of Mpanda), Kipili and Kasanga (southwest of Sumbawanga). Departures from Kigoma are on Wednesday at 4pm, reaching Mpulungu Friday morning. Departures from Mpulungu are Friday afternoon about 2pm, arriving back in Kigoma on Sunday afternoon. Food is available, but bring some supplements and drinking water. First class is relatively comfortable, with two reasonably clean bunks, a window and a fan. Second-class cabins (four bunks) and economy-class seating are poorly ventilated and uncomfortable – it's better to find deck space than pay for economy-class seating. Keep watch over your luggage, and book early for a cabin – Monday morning is your best bet.

There are docks at Kigoma and Kasanga, but at many smaller stops you'll need to disembark in the middle of the lake, exiting from a door in the side of the boat into small boats that take you to shore. It can be rather nerve-wracking at night, if the lake is rough or you have a heavy pack.

Tours

For tour operators covering Tanzania and elsewhere in East Africa, see p624. For safari and trekking operators, see p68.

GETTING AROUND
Air

The national airline, **Air Tanzania** (www.air tanzania.com) Arusha (☎ 027-250 3201/3); Dar es Salaam (Map p96; ☎ 022-211 8411, 022-284 4293); Zanzibar (☎ 024-223 0213) has flights connecting Dar es Salaam with Mwanza, Mtwara and Kilimanjaro. Other airlines flying domestically, all of which also do charters, include the following:

Air Excel (☎ 027-254 8429, 027-250 1597; reserva tion@airexcelonline.com) Arusha, Serengeti, Lake Manyara, Dar es Salaam and Zanzibar.
Coastal Aviation (☎ 022-284 3293, 022-211 7959; www.coastal.cc) Recommended, with flights to many parks and major towns, including Arusha, Dar es Salaam, Dodoma, Geita, Kilwa Masoko, Lake Manyara National Park, Mafia, Mwanza, Pemba, Ruaha National Park, Selous Game Reserve, Serengeti National Park, Tanga, Tarangire National Park and Zanzibar.
Precision Air (☎ 022-216 8000; www.precisionairtz .com) Most major towns, including Dar es Salaam, Kigoma, Kilimanjaro, Lindi, Mtwara, Mwanza, Shinyanga, Tabora and Zanzibar.
Regional Air Services (☎ 027-250 4477, 027-250 2541; www.regionaltanzania.com) Arusha, Dar es Salaam,

---

DEPARTURE TAX

Airport departure tax for domestic flights is TSh5000. It's sometimes included in the ticket price on the mainland. On Zanzibar, it's payable separately at the airport.

Kilimanjaro, Lake Manyara National Park, Mkomazi, Ndutu, Pangani, Saadani, Serengeti National Park and Zanzibar.
Safari Airlink (☎ 0773-723274; www.safariaviation .info) Dar es Salaam, Katavi National Park, Mahale Mountains National Park, Mufindi, Ruaha National Park and Zanzibar.
Tropical Air (☎ 0777-431431, 024-223 2511; tropic@ zanzinet.com) Dar es Salaam, Zanzibar, Pemba and Mafia.
ZanAir (☎ 024-223 3670/8; www.zanair.com) Arusha, Dar es Salaam, Lake Manyara National Park, Mafia, Pangani, Pemba, Selous Game Reserve, Serengeti National Park, Tarangire National Park and Zanzibar.
Zantas Air (☎ 022-213 0553; www.mbalimbali.com) Twice-weekly scheduled charter between Arusha, Katavi and Mahale Mountains National Parks.

Bicycle

See p621 for general information.

International Bicycle Fund (www.ibike.org /bikeafrica) organises cycling tours in the Usambaras, and between Zanzibar and Moshi. Other contacts include AfriRoots (p95), Hoopoe Safaris (p69) and Summits Africa (p70). Also try **Tanzanian Bike Safaris** (www.tanzania biking.com).

Boat
DHOW

Main routes include those connecting Zanzibar and Pemba with Tanga, Pangani, Bagamoyo and Shimoni (Kenya), and those connecting Kilwa Kivinje, Lindi, Mikindani and Mtwara with other coastal towns. Foreigners are officially prohibited on non-motorised dhows, and on any dhows between Zanzibar and Dar es Salaam; captains are subject to fines if they're caught. See also boxed text, p622, and p252.

FERRY

Ferries operate on Lake Victoria, Lake Tanganyika and Lake Nyasa, and between Dar es Salaam, Zanzibar and Pemba. There's a US$5 port tax per trip on all routes. For details of ferries between Dar es Salaam, Zanzibar and Pemba, see the relevant Getting There & Away sections.

Lake Nyasa

In theory, the MV *Songea* departs Itungi port about noon on Thursday and makes its way down the coast via Lupingu, Manda, Lundu, Mango and Liuli (but not Matema) to Mbamba Bay (1st/economy class TSh12,500/7500, 18 to 24 hours) and Nkhata Bay (Malawi) before returning.

The smaller MV *Iringa* services lakeside villages between Itungi and Manda, departing Itungi by about noon on Monday and stopping at Matema and several other ports before turning back again on Tuesday. Schedules for both boats are highly unreliable and change frequently.

Lake Tanganyika

For the MV *Liemba* schedule between Kigoma and Mpulungu (Zambia), see p262. See p262 for boat connections between Kigoma and Bujumbura (Burundi).

Lake Victoria

The MV *Victoria* departs Mwanza for Bukoba at 9pm on Tuesday, Thursday and Sunday (1st class/2nd-class sleeping/2nd-class sitting/3rd class TSh30,500/20,500/17,000/15,500 plus port tax, nine hours). Departures from Bukoba are at 9pm Monday, Wednesday and Friday. First class has two-bed cabins, and 2nd-class sleeping has six-bed cabins. Second-class sitting isn't comfortable, so if you can't get a spot in 1st class or 2nd-class sleeping (both fill quickly), the best bet is to buy a 3rd-class ticket. With luck, you may then be able to find a comfortable spot in the 1st-class lounge. Food is available on board.

For information on connections to/from Ukerewe island, see p206.

Bus

Both 'express' and 'ordinary' buses run on major long-distance routes. Express buses make fewer stops, are less crowded than ordinary buses and depart on schedule. Some have air-con and toilets, and the nicest ones are called 'luxury' buses. On secondary routes, the only option is ordinary buses, which are often packed to overflowing, make many stops and run to a less rigorous schedule.

For popular routes, book your seat at least one day in advance. You can sometimes get a place by arriving at the bus station an hour prior to departure. Each bus line has its own booking office, usually at or near the bus station.

Most express buses have a compartment underneath for luggage. Otherwise, stow your pack under your seat or in the front of the bus, where there's usually space near the driver.

Prices are basically fixed, although overcharging isn't unheard of. Most bus stations are chaotic, and at the ones in tourist areas you'll be incessantly hounded by touts. Buy your tickets inside the office, and not from the touts, and don't believe anyone who tries to tell you there's a luggage fee.

For short stretches along main routes, express buses will drop you off, though you'll often be required to pay the full fare to the next major destination.

Major lines along the Dar es Salaam–Arusha route include Dar Express, Royal Coach and Scandinavian Express. Scandinavian Express is also considered one of the better lines for destinations between Dar es Salaam and Mbeya, and from Dar es Salaam to Njombe and Songea, although its fleet is ageing and service is often very mediocre these days. You'll generally need to pay for its luxury buses to enjoy a reasonably comfortable ride.

MINIBUS & SHARED TAXI

For shorter trips away from the main routes, the choice is often between 30-seater buses ('Coastals' or *thelathini*) and *dalla-dallas*. Both options come complete with chickens on the roof, bags of produce wedged under the seats and no leg room. Shared taxis are relatively rare, except in northern Tanzania near Arusha. Like ordinary buses, minibuses and shared taxis leave when full; they're probably the least safe of the various transport options.

Car & Motorcycle

If you're familiar with driving in East Africa and have a group to split the costs, touring mainland Tanzania by car poses no particular problems, although most hire companies require you to take a driver along. However, it's more common to focus on one part of the country and then arrange local transport through a tour or safari operator. On Zanzibar, it's easy and economical to hire a car or motorcycle for touring, and self-drive is permitted. For information about bringing your own vehicle, see p623.

If you visit national parks with your own vehicle, there is a daily vehicle fee per foreign-/Tanzanian-registered car of US$40/TSh10,000.

PERILS OF THE ROAD

Road accidents are probably your biggest safety risk while travelling in Tanzania, with speeding buses among the worst offenders. Road conditions are poor and driving standards leave much to be desired. Overtaking blind is a problem, as are high speeds. Your bus driver may in fact be at the wheel of an ageing vehicle with a cracked windshield and marginal brakes on a winding, potholed road. However, he'll invariably be driving as if he were piloting a sleek racing machine coming down the straight – nerve-wracking to say the least. Many vehicles have painted slogans such as *Mungu Atubariki* ('God Bless Us') or 'In God we Trust' in the hope that a bit of extra help from above will see them safely through the day's runs.

To maximise your chances of uneventful travels, stick with more reputable companies (ask locally to find out the current best ones) and when possible go with a full-sized bus rather than a minibus or 30-seater bus.

Buses aren't permitted to drive at night, and the last departure is generally timed so that the bus should reach its destination by evening. For cross-border routes, departures are usually timed so that night driving will be done once outside Tanzania.

DRIVING LICENCE
On the mainland you'll need your home driving licence or (preferable) an International Driving Permit together with your home licence. On Zanzibar you'll need an International Driving Permit plus your home licence, or a permit from Zanzibar (p136), Kenya, Uganda or South Africa.

FUEL & SPARE PARTS
Petrol costs about TSh1900 per litre (TSh2000 for diesel). Filling and repair stations are found in all major towns, but are scarce elsewhere, so fill up at every opportunity and carry a range of spares. In remote areas and in national parks, it's essential to carry jerry cans with extra fuel.

HIRE
In Dar es Salaam, daily rates for 2WD start at US$55, excluding fuel, plus US$20 to US$40 for insurance plus tax (20%). Daily rates for 4WD cost US$80 to US$200 plus insurance (US$30 to US$40 per day), tax, fuel and driver (US$15 to US$35 per day). Outside the city, most companies require 4WD. Also, most don't permit self-drive outside of Dar es Salaam, and none offer unlimited kilometres. Per-kilometre charges cost US$0.50 to US$2. Clarify what the company's policy is in the event of a breakdown.

Elsewhere, you can rent 4WDs in Arusha, Karatu, Mwanza, Mbeya, Zanzibar Town and other centres through travel agencies, tour operators, hotels and businessmen. Except on Zanzibar, most come with driver. Rates average US$80 to US$200 per day plus fuel, less on Zanzibar.

See city and town listings for rental agencies.

ROAD CONDITIONS & HAZARDS
About 25% of Tanzania's road network is sealed, with roadworks underway at an impressive pace. Major arteries include the roads from Dar es Salaam to Arusha via Chalinze, and from Dar es Salaam to Mbeya via Iringa. Secondary roads range from good to impassable, depending on the season. For most trips outside major towns you'll need 4WD with high clearance.

Hazards include vehicles overtaking on blind curves, pedestrians and animals on the road, and children running into the road.

ROAD RULES
In theory, driving is on the left, and traffic already in roundabouts has the right of way. Unless otherwise posted, the speed limit is 80km/h; on major routes, police have radar. Tanzania has a seatbelt law for drivers and front-seat passengers. The official traffic-fine penalty is TSh20,000.

Motorcycles aren't permitted in national parks, except for the section of the Dar es Salaam to Mbeya highway passing through Mikumi National Park, and on the Sumbawanga–Mpanda road via Katavi National Park. Also see p623.

Hitching
Hitching is generally slow going and is prohibited inside national parks. However, in remote areas hitching a lift with truck drivers may be your only transport option, for which you'll need to pay. See also p624.

Local Transport

DALLA-DALLA

Local routes are serviced by *dalla-dallas* and, in rural areas, pick-up trucks or old Land Rovers. Prices are fixed, costing about TSh300 to TSh600. The vehicles make many stops and are crowded. Accidents are frequent, particularly in minibuses. Many are caused when the drivers race each other to a station in order to collect new passengers. Destinations are posted in the front window, or called out by the driver's assistant, who also collects fares.

TAXI

Taxis, which have white plates on the mainland and a *gari la abiria* ('passenger vehicle') sign on Zanzibar, can be hired in all major towns. None have meters, so agree on the fare with the driver before getting in. The standard rate for short town trips is about TSh2000. In major centres, many drivers have an 'official' price list, although rates shown on it – often calculated on the basis of TSh1000 per 1km – are generally significantly higher than what is normally paid. If you're unsure of the price, ask locals what it should be and then use this as a base for negotiations. Especially at night, only take taxis from hotels or established taxi ranks.

Tours

For safari and trekking operators, see p68. For local tour operators, see town and city listings.

Train

Tanzania has two rail lines: **Tazara** (☎ 022-286 5137, 022-286 0340/4, 0713-225292; www.tazara .co.tz; cnr Nyerere & Nelson Mandela Rds, Dar es Salaam), linking Dar es Salaam with Kapiri Mposhi in Zambia via Mbeya, and the Tanzanian Railway Corporation's **Central Line** (Map p96; ☎ 022-211 7833; www.trctz.com; cnr Railway St & Sokoine Dr, Dar es Salaam), linking Dodoma with Kigoma and Mwanza via Tabora. (Service between Dodoma and Dar es Salaam is suspended.) Central Line branches link Tabora with Mpanda, and Dodoma with Singida.

Tazara is more comfortable and efficient, but on both lines, breakdowns and long delays – up to 12 hours or more – are common. If you want to try the train, consider shorter stretches (eg from Dar es Salaam into the Selous Game Reserve, or between Tabora and Kigoma).

CLASSES

There are three classes: 1st class (two- or four-bed compartments); 2nd-class sleeping (six-bed compartments); and economy class (benches, usually very crowded). Some trains also have a '2nd-class sitting section', with one seat per person. Men and women can only travel together in the sleeping sections by booking the entire compartment.

At night, secure your window with a stick, and don't leave your luggage unattended, even for a moment.

RESERVATIONS

Tickets for 1st and 2nd class should be reserved several days in advance; occasionally you'll be able to get a seat on the day of travel. Economy-class tickets can be bought on the spot.

SCHEDULES & COSTS

Both lines are undergoing renovations and management changes, so expect schedule and price changes.

Tazara

Tazara runs three trains weekly: two 'express' trains between Dar es Salaam and Kapiri Mposhi in Zambia via Mbeya; and an 'ordinary' train between Dar es Salaam and Mbeya.

For express train information see p261. Ordinary trains depart Dar es Salaam at 9am Monday, reaching Mbeya about 10am the next day (1st/2nd/economy class TSh20,700/14,500/12,000, 24 hours); departures from Mbeya are at 1.30pm Tuesday.

Central Line

Trains depart Dodoma four evenings weekly for both Kigoma and Mwanza (splitting at Tabora). Both journeys cost about TSh40,000/28,000/13,000 in 1st/2nd-sitting/economy class and take about 24 hours, though it's often much longer. Trains from Mwanza and Kigoma eastwards depart in the mornings. Travelling between Mwanza and Kigoma, you'll need to overnight in Tabora.

Trains between Tabora and Mpanda (1st/2nd-sitting/economy class about TSh20,000/15,000/7000, about 14 hours) run three times weekly, departing Tabora in the evening and Mpanda around noon.

Trains depart Dodoma for Singida (TSh5000, about seven hours) three times weekly, departing in each direction in the morning, economy class only.

Kenya

Few destinations the world over can evoke such powerful and visceral images as Kenya, one of East Africa's premier safari destinations. Indeed, the acacia-dotted savannahs of Kenya are inhabited by classic African animals, from towering elephants and prancing gazelles to prides of lions and stalking leopards. The country also plays host to the annual wildebeest migration, which is the largest single movement of herd animals on the entire planet.

However, what makes Kenya truly stand out as a traveller's destination is the vast palette of landscapes that comprise this visually stunning country. While the flaunted image of the savannahs of the Masai Mara National Reserve is perhaps the single key selling point for Kenya's tourist industry, intrepid travellers can also explore the barren expanses of the Rift Valley, the glacial ridges of Mt Kenya and the beaches of the Swahili Coast. This rich diversity of quintessential African environments presents opportunities for hiking, trekking, diving, sailing and so much more.

But, to simply focus on Kenya's wildlife and nature is to ignore the people that make this country so dynamic. Kenya is a thriving multicultural country that presents a wide cross-section of everything that is classic and contemporary Africa. Everyday life brings together traditional tribes and urban families, ancient customs and modern sensibilities. While internal political life is at times tumultuous, it seems that Kenyans retain an innate self-confidence, a belief that things are improving, and a desire to see their homeland take a prominent place on the world stage.

FAST FACTS

- **Area** 583,000 sq km
- **Birthplace of** Louis and Richard Leakey; Paul Tergat; Dennis Oliech
- **Capital** Nairobi
- **Country code** ☎ 254
- **Famous for** the Maasai Mara; meat eating (nyoma choma); marathon runners
- **Languages** Kiswahili, English, tribal languages
- **Money** Kenya Shilling (KSh); US$1 = KSh79; €1 = KSh118
- **Population** 37.9 million

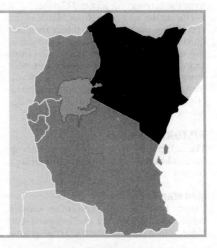

HIGHLIGHTS

- **Masai Mara National Reserve** (p363) Expansive savannah, unmatched wildlife and the world's most fascinating traffic jam – the annual wildebeest migration.
- **Mt Kenya** (p349) Tremendous treks and jagged peaks await on this sacred mountain, Kenya's tallest and Africa's second tallest.
- **Lamu Archipelago** (p328) The ultimate Swahili cultural-immersion experience that makes Tanzania's Zanzibar blush with envy.
- **Amboseli National Park** (p295) Elephants and Kilimanjaro, two big bulks combined in Kenya's most famous picture-postcard views.
- **Loyangalani** (p395) Home to harsh conditions, unforgettable tribes and the sublime Lake Turkana, the jade jewel at the end of a long quest.

HOW MUCH?

- **Local matatu (minibus transport) ride** KSh30
- **Plate of stew/biryani/pilau** KSh150
- **Large juice** KSh75
- **Pair of kangas** KSh350
- **Taxi around town** KSh400

LONELY PLANET INDEX

- **1L of petrol** KSh100
- **1L of bottled water** KSh60
- **Bottle of Tusker** KSh100
- **Souvenir T-shirt** KSh1200
- **Street snack (sambusa)** KSh20

CLIMATE & WHEN TO GO

There are a number of factors to take into account when considering what time of year to visit Kenya. The main tourist season is January and February, when the weather is generally considered to be the best – hot and dry, with high concentrations of wildlife. However, the parks can get crowded and rates for accommodation go through the roof. Avoid the Christmas and Easter holiday periods unless you want to pay a fortune. From June to October the annual wildebeest migration takes place, with thousands of animals streaming into the Masai Mara National Reserve from the Serengeti in July and October.

During the long rains (from March to the end of May, the low season) things are much quieter, and you can get some good deals; this is also true during the short rains from October to December. The rains generally don't affect your ability to get around but you may get rained on, especially in the Central Highlands and western Kenya. For more details see p606 and p403.

HISTORY

The early history of Kenya, from prehistory up until independence, is covered in the History chapter (p25).

Mau Mau Rebellion

Despite plenty of overt pressure on Kenya's colonial authorities, the real independence movement was underground. Tribal groups of Kikuyu, Maasai and Luo took secret oaths, which bound participants to kill Europeans and their African collaborators. The most famous of these movements was Mau Mau, formed in 1952 by disenchanted Kikuyu people, which aimed to drive the white settlers from Kenya forever.

The first blow was struck early with the killing of a white farmer's entire herd of cattle, followed a few weeks later by the massacre of 21 Kikuyu loyal to the colonial government. The Mau Mau rebellion had started.

Within a month, Jomo Kenyatta and several other Kenyan African Movement (KAU) leaders were jailed on spurious evidence, charged with 'masterminding' the plot. The various Mau Mau sects came together under the umbrella of the Kenya Land Freedom Army, led by Dedan Kimathi, and staged frequent attacks against white farms and government outposts. By the time the rebels were defeated in 1956, the death toll stood at more than 13,500 Africans (guerrillas, civilians and troops) and just more than 100 Europeans.

Upon his release in 1959 Kenyatta resumed his campaign for independence. Soon even white Kenyans began to feel the winds of change, and in 1960 the British government officially announced their plan to transfer power to a democratically elected African government. Independence was scheduled for December 1963, accompanied by grants and loans of US$100 million to enable the Kenyan assembly to buy out European farmers in the highlands and restore the land to the tribes.

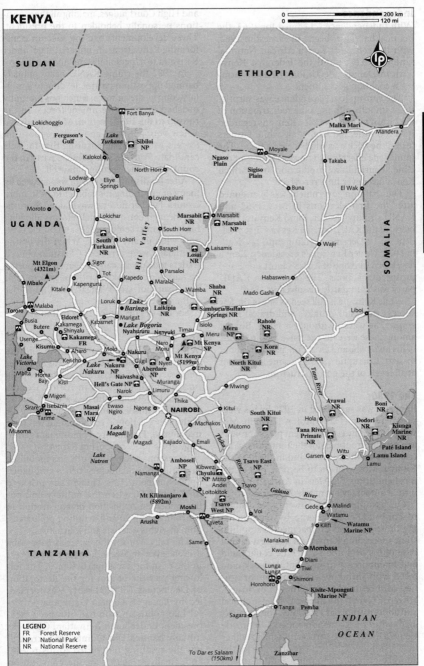

KENYA

Independence

With independence scheduled for 1963, the political handover began in earnest in 1962, with the centralist Kenya African National Union (KANU) and the federalist Kenya African Democratic Union (KADU) forming a coalition government.

The run-up to independence was surprisingly smooth, although the redistribution of land wasn't a great success; Kenyans regarded it as too little, too late, while white farmers feared the trickle would become a flood. The immediate effect was to cause a significant decline in agricultural production, from which Kenya has never fully recovered.

The coalition government was abandoned after the first elections in May 1963 and KANU's Kikuyu leader, Jomo Kenyatta (formerly of the KAU), became Kenya's first president on 12 December, ruling until his death in 1978. Under Kenyatta's presidency, Kenya developed into one of Africa's most stable and prosperous nations. The opposition KADU party was voluntarily dissolved in 1964.

While Kenyatta is still seen as one of the few success stories of Britain's withdrawal from empire, he wasn't without his faults. Biggest among these were his excessive bias in favour of his own tribe and escalating paranoia about dissent. Corruption soon became a problem at all levels of the power structure.

The 1980s

Kenyatta was succeeded in 1978 by his vice-president, Daniel arap Moi. A Kalenjin, Moi was regarded by establishment power brokers as a suitable frontman for their interests, as his tribe was relatively small and in thrall to the Kikuyu. Moi went on to become one of the most enduring 'Big Men' in Africa, ruling in virtual autocracy for nearly 25 years.

On assumption of power, Moi sought to consolidate his regime by marginalising those who had campaigned to stop him from succeeding Kenyatta. Lacking a capital base of his own upon which he could build and maintain a patron-client network, and faced with shrinking economic opportunities, Moi resorted to a politics of exclusion. He reconfigured the financial, legal, political and administrative institutions. For instance, a constitutional amendment in 1982 made Kenya a de jure one-party state, while another in 1986 removed the security of tenure for the attorney-general, comptroller, auditor general and High Court judges, making all these positions personally beholden to the president. These developments had the effect of transforming Kenya from an 'imperial state' under Kenyatta to a 'personal state' under Moi.

In 1982 the ruling KANU party publicly banned opposition parties, leading to a military coup by the air force, which was promptly quashed by pro-government forces. In the run-up to the 1987 election, Moi introduced a new voting system and jailed opposition leaders without trial, ensuring that the sole candidate from the sole political party in the country won the election – himself.

After his disputed win, Moi was accused by many of expanding his cabinet to fit in more cronies. Furthermore he was blamed for rushing through constitutional reforms allowing him to dismiss senior judges and public servants without any redress. When dissenting politicians were arrested, Christian church leaders took up the call for change, supported by another outspoken critic of government nepotism Professor Wangari Maathai, leader of the Green Belt Movement.

Sooner or later, something had to give.

The 1990s

With the collapse of communism and the break-up of the Soviet Union, it was no longer necessary for Western powers to prop up noncommunist regimes in Africa. Donors who had previously turned a blind eye to civil-rights misdemeanours began calling for multiparty elections if economic aid was to be maintained. The multiparty movement gained huge grass-roots support in Kenya.

In response, KANU Youth was mobilised to disrupt pro-democracy rallies and harass opposition politicians. Things came to a head on 7 July 1990 when the military and police raided an opposition demonstration in Nairobi, killing 20 and arresting politicians, human-rights activists and journalists.

The rally, known thereafter as Saba Saba ('seven seven' in Swahili), was a pivotal event in the push for a multiparty Kenya. The following year the Forum for the Restoration of Democracy (FORD) party was formed, led by Jamagori Oginga Odinga, a powerful Luo politician who had also been vice-president under Jomo Kenyatta. FORD was initially banned and Odinga was arrested, but the resulting outcry led to his release and, finally, a change in the constitution that allowed opposition parties to register for the first time.

Faced with a foreign debt of nearly US$9 billion and blanket suspension of foreign aid, Moi was pressured into holding multiparty elections in early 1992, but independent observers reported a litany of electoral inconsistencies. To make matters worse, about 2000 people were killed during ethnic clashes in the Rift Valley, widely believed to have been triggered by KANU agitation. Nonetheless, Moi was overwhelmingly re-elected.

Following the elections, the KANU bowed to some Western demands for economic reforms, but agitation and harassment of opposition politicians continued unabated. The 1997 election, too, was accompanied by violence and rioting, particularly during the Saba Saba anniversary rally. Again persons unknown stirred up ethnic violence, this time on the coast. European and North American tour companies cancelled their bookings and around 60,000 Kenyans lost their jobs. Moi was able to set himself up as peacemaker, calming the warring factions and gaining 50.4% of the seats for KANU, compared with the 49.6% won by the divided opposition parties.

The scene was set for a confrontational parliament, but in a trademark Moi manoeuvre, the KANU immediately entered into a cooperative arrangement with the two biggest opposition parties, the Democratic Party (DP) and the National Development Party (NDP). Other seats were taken by FORD-Kenya and its various splinter groups.

While all this was going on, Kenya was lashed first by torrential El Niño rains and then by a desperate drought that continued right up to 2000, causing terrible hardship in rural areas.

Preoccupied with internal problems, Kenya was quite unprepared for the events of 7 August 1998. Early in the morning massive blasts, believed to have been masterminded by Al Qaeda, simultaneously ripped apart the American embassies in Nairobi and Dar es Salaam in Tanzania, killing more than 200 people. The effect on Kenyan tourism, and the economy as a whole, was devastating.

The New Millenium
In June 2001 the KANU entered into a formal coalition government with the NDP and DP, creating a formidable power base. However,

with Moi's presidency due to end in 2002, many feared that Moi would alter the constitution again. This time, though, he announced his intention to retire – on a very generous benefits package – with elections to be held in December 2002.

Moi put his weight firmly behind Uhuru Kenyatta, the son of Jomo Kenyatta, as his successor. Meanwhile, 12 opposition parties – including the DP, FORD-Kenya, FORD-Asili, the National Party of Kenya and Saba Saba–Asili – and several religious groups united under the umbrella of the National Alliance Party of Kenya (NAK), later known as the National Rainbow Coalition (Narc). Presidential candidate Mwai Kibaki was the former head of the Democratic party.

Although initially dogged by infighting, within weeks the opposition transformed itself into a dynamic and unified political party. When the election came on 27 December 2002 it was peaceful and fair and the result was dramatic – a landslide two-thirds majority for Mwai Kibaki and Narc. Despite being injured in a car accident while campaigning, Kibaki was inaugurated as Kenya's third president on 30 December 2002. However, his biggest electoral test was still yet to come.

Kenya Today
On 27 December 2007, Kenya held presidential, parliamentary and local elections. While the parliamentary and local government elections were largely credible, the presidential elections were marred by serious irregularities, as reported by neutral observers. Nonetheless, the Electoral Commission declared Mwai Kibaki the winner, triggering a wave of violence across the country, stemming from discontent and frustration at perceived tribal precedence.

The Rift Valley, Western Highlands, Nyanza Province and Mombasa – areas afflicted by years of political machination, previous election violence and large-scale displacement – exploded in ugly ethnic confrontations. The violence left more than 1000 people dead and more than 600,000 people homeless.

Fearing the stability of the most stable lynch pin of East Africa, UN Secretary Kofi Annan and a panel of eminent african persons flew to Kenya to mediate talks. After protracted negotiations a power-sharing agreement was signed on 28 February 2008 between President Kibaki and Raila Odinga, the leader of the ODM (Orange Democratic Movement) opposition.

KENYA

CAN KENYA BOUNCE BACK FROM ITS POST-ELECTION CLASHES? *Kennedy O Opalo*

Before December 2007, Kenya was world famous for being an oasis of peace in the volatile East African region. With Somalia, southern Sudan and northern Uganda up in flames, Kenya served as a safe haven for refugees fleeing from violence back home. But that is not all that Kenya was famous for. With its unique blend of tourist attractions, including beautiful tropical beaches, a vast array of wildlife and diverse geographical features, Kenya remained a favoured destination for tourists from all over the world.

But all this was to be put on the line after a disputed presidential election on 27th December 2007. The election was a close call, and was marred by various misdeeds on the part of the two leading parties. In the end, the Electoral Commission proclaimed the president the winner, sparking riots from opposition supporters who were convinced that their man, the then opposition leader, had won the election. The riots soon degenerated into all-out violence that very nearly plunged the country into civil war. The images on TV screens across the world were both shocking and disappointing. Kenyans turned on each other with machetes and all manner of crude weapons.

Unfortunately, the news reporting of the violence did not get the entire picture. Both the local and international media erroneously labelled the clashes as tribal. While it is true that most of the fighting was along tribal lines, the real causes were economic and political. Economic causes included perceived historical injustices in the distribution of land in the Rift Valley province (where casualties were highest) and the unequal distribution of government resources.

The political causes were obvious – supporters of the opposition fought against supporters of the government. Most of those killed for political reasons died from bullet wounds as police forcefully quelled protests over the disputed election in cities and major towns all across country. Most analysts agree that the violence was not inherently tribal. After all, Kenyans had coexisted

The coalition provided for the establishment of a prime ministerial position (to be filled by Raila Odinga) as well as a division of cabinet posts according to the parties representation in parliament. Key to the negotiations was the amendment of the constitution stating that the prime minister can only be sacked by parliament and not by the president.

Sworn in on 17 April 2008, the fragile coalition government has now started the complex task of long-term reform. If it is to succeed in any measure observers have noted that it will have to address the key issues of constitutional reform (a new constitution is now slated for April 2009), land tenure reform, judicial reform and, more importantly, the poverty and inequality that plagues the country. Personal politics must be institutionalised and an effective system of checks and balances put in place to curb corruption and injustice. Local economists also estimate that Kenya needs to achieve growth of at least 12% if the country is to achieve any trickle-down effect; although election violence has caused an estimated US$1 billion loss in the tourism industry alone.

The challenge is huge. Inflation is on the rise, fuel and food price rises are cutting deep, while the manufacturing sector was forced to cut back operations by 70% due to insecurity.

But the main key to success will be the relationship between Kibaki and Odinga. Can they really transition Kenya safely into a new era of political maturity and maximise the huge potential of this vibrant and vital country?

THE CULTURE
The National Psyche

It's fair to say that there is not a great sense of national consciousness in Kenya. Many residents of Kenya are more aware of their tribal affiliation than of being a 'Kenyan'; this is one of the more fascinating aspects of Kenyan life, but the lack of national cohesion undoubtedly holds the country back.

This focus on tribe, however, is generally accompanied by an admirable live-and-let-live attitude, such that only on rare occasions do tribal animosities or rivalries spill over into violence. In fact, Kenyans generally approach life with great exuberance. Be it on a crowded *matatu* (minibus), in a buzzing marketplace, or enjoying a drink in a bar, you cannot fail to notice that Kenyans are quick to laugh and are never reluctant to offer a smile.

This willingness to participate in life as it happens is perhaps a reflection of a casual approach to time. You will be doing well to press a Kenyan into rushing anything.

peacefully for more than four decades in one state. However, the disputed election did serve as an opportunity for people to seek redress over various injustices they had endured since Kenya got its independence in 1963, such as land distribution and exclusion from government.

Luckily for the people of Kenya, the international community cared enough to not let them descend into the mess that many an African country has found itself in over the last few decades. A concerted effort on the part of the UN, the US and the EU ensured that the president and the opposition reached an agreement, resulting in the formation of a unity government. Since then, the situation in the country has returned to normal, although a section of those displaced by the violence are yet to return home.

The brief hiatus had enormous human and material costs for the Kenyan economy. About 1500 people died, and hundreds of thousands were displaced from their homes. Government estimates put the economic cost at KSh60 billion. Tourism, a mainstay of the Kenyan economy, was particularly affected. With the sector contributing about 12% of GDP and 9% of wage employment, the decline in visits due to the violence was devastating.

Fortunately, the new unity government has tried to woo back tourists. The charismatic tourism minister, Najib Balala, has spearheaded an effort to rebrand Kenya as a safe tourist destination – most recently with a swanky commercial on CNN, the first ever of its kind about Kenya. To the ministry's credit, tourists have been trickling back, and the country's wounds seems to be healing.

This should not come as a surprise. Kenya's wildlife, beautiful beaches, geographical features and cultural diversity remain attractive to tourists from all over the globe. From the annual wildebeest migration in Masai Mara National Reserve to the picture-perfect beaches of the Swahili coast, Kenya remains one of Africa's most alluring tourist destinations.

Kennedy O Opalo is a Kenyan who is studying at Yale University in New Haven, Connecticut., USA

Education is of primary concern to Kenyans. Literacy rates are around 85% and are considerably higher than in any of the country's neighbours. Although education isn't compulsory, the motivation to learn is huge, particularly now that it's free, and you'll see children in school uniform everywhere in Kenya, even in the most impoverished rural communities.

Despite their often exuberant and casual approach, Kenyans are generally quite conservative, and are particularly concerned with modesty in dress. T-shirts and shorts are almost unheard of, though foreign men may *just* be able to pull it off. Shirts are an obsession for Kenyan men and almost everyone wears one, often with a sweater or blazer.

As Kenya undergoes a slow process of modernisation, tradition and modernity are locked in an almighty struggle, often resulting in the marginalisation of some elements of society. This is particularly the case as urbanisation happens apace. Kenya has its fair share of poverty, alienation and urban overcrowding, but even in the dustiest shanty towns life is lived to the full.

Daily Life

Tribe may be important in Kenya, but family is paramount. Particularly as the pace and demands of modern life grow, the role of the extended family has become even more important. It is not unusual to encounter Kenyan children who are living with aunts, uncles or grandparents in a regional town while their parents are working a desk job in Nairobi or working at a resort in Watamu. Nonetheless, filial bonds remain strong, and the separation that brings about such circumstances in the first place is without exception a result of a parent's desire to further opportunities for their family and their children.

The strength of the family in Kenya is mirrored in the community. Life is generally played out in the streets and communal places. There is no such thing as daycare for young Kenyans; you will inevitably encounter the archetypical African scene where a range of children of different ages, usually with at least one older sister with a younger sibling on her hip, congregate and observe the hustle and bustle of daily life. This happens across Kenya, from coastal communities to villages in the Central Highlands to the shanty towns in Nairobi. And even as urbanisation happens and traditional community structures are fractured, street life remains lively. In any town of any size the afternoon rush hour is always a spectacle: it seems that all the world is afoot as Kenyans head home past street stalls and wandering pedlars and the dust rises gently into the coppery African twilight.

For all this, as Kenya gains a foothold in the 21st century it is grappling with increasing poverty. Once classed a middle-income country, Kenya has fallen to be a low-income country, with the standard of living dropping drastically from 2002 to 2005.

Population

Kenya's population in 2008 was estimated at 37.9 million. The population growth rate, currently at around 2.75%, has slowed in the last few years due to the prevalence of HIV/AIDS, which affects 7% to 8% of adults according to the UN (with life expectancy at 56 years). However, this still represents a significant population growth rate and one that brings with it worrying concerns.

Multiculturalism

Kenya's population is made up almost entirely of Africans, with small but influential minorities of Asians (about 80,000), Arabs (about 30,000) and Europeans (about 30,000).

AFRICANS

Kenya is home to more than 70 tribal groups. The majority of Kenya's Africans fall into two major language groups: the Bantu and the Nilotic. The Bantu people arrived in East Africa in waves from West Africa after 500 BC, and include the Kikuyu, Meru, Gusii, Embu, Akamba and Luyha, as well as the Mijikenda, who preceded the Swahili in many parts of the coast.

Nilotic speakers migrated into the area from the Nile Valley some time later. This group includes the Maasai, Turkana, Samburu, Pokot, Luo and Kalenjin, which, together with the Bantu speakers, account for more than 90% of Kenya's African population. The Kikuyu and the Luo are by far the most populous groups, and between them hold practically all the positions of power and influence in the country.

A third language grouping, and in fact the first migrants into the country, are the Cushitic speakers. They occupy the northeast of the country, and include such tribes as the El-Molo, Somali, Rendille and Galla.

On the coast, Swahili is the name given to the local people who, although they have various tribal ancestries, have intermarried with Arab settlers over the centuries and now have a predominantly Arabic culture.

ASIANS

India's connections with East Africa go back to the days of the spice trade, but the first permanent settlers from the Indian subcontinent were indentured workers, brought here from Gujarat and the Punjab by the British to build the Uganda Railway. After the railway was finished, the British allowed many workers to stay and start up businesses, and hundreds of *duka* (small shops) were set up across the country.

Asian numbers were augmented after WWII and the Indian community came to control large sectors of the East African economy. However, few gave their active support to the black nationalist movements in the run-up to independence. This earned the distrust of the African community, who felt the Indians were simply there to exploit African labour.

Although Kenya escaped the anti-Asian pogroms that plagued Uganda during the rule of Idi Amin, thousands of shops owned by Asians were confiscated and Asians were forbidden to trade in rural areas. Kenya has learned from the lessons of the economic collapse in Uganda and today the Asian community continues to be a driving force in the economy, dominating the retail, construction and manufacturing industries.

SPORT

Soccer is a big deal in Kenya. People are nuts about it, and even those who don't follow a local team will probably claim to support Arsenal or Manchester United. In the Kenyan Premiership, Harambee Stars, AFC Leopards and Mathare United vie for top slot, often drawing big crowds. The action is fast, furious and passionate, sometimes spilling onto the terraces. Tickets cost KSh300 to KSh600 and it's quite an experience.

Kenyan long-distance runners, such as Paul Tergat, are among the best in the world, although much of their competitive running takes place outside the country. Even trials and national events in Kenya sometimes fail to attract these stars, despite being flagged in the press well in advance.

The annual **East African Safari Rally** (www.eastafricansafarirally.com) is a rugged 3000km rally that passes through Kenya, Uganda and Tanzania along public roadways, attracting an international collection of drivers with their vintage (pre-1971) automobiles.

RELIGION

It's probably true to say that most Kenyans outside the coastal and eastern provinces are Christians of one sort or another, while most of those on the coast and in the eastern part of the country are Muslim. Muslims make up some 30% of the population. In the more remote tribal areas you'll find a mixture of Muslims, Christians and those who follow their ancestral tribal beliefs, though the latter are definitely a minority.

ARTS
Music

Although there is an indigenous Kenyan music scene, the overriding African musical influence here, as in the rest of East Africa, is Congolese *lingala* (dance music, also known as soukous). Kenyan bands produced some of the most popular songs in Africa in the 1960s, including Fadhili William's famous *Malaika* (Angel), and *Jambo Bwana*, Kenya's unofficial anthem, by the hugely influential Them Mushrooms.

Benga is the contemporary dance music of Kenya, characterised by electric guitar licks and bounding bass rhythms. It originated among the Luo people and became popular in the 1950s. Since then it has spread throughout the country, and been taken up by Akamba and Kikuyu musicians. Well-known exponents include DO Misiani and his group Shirati Jazz, who have been around since the 1960s. You should also look out for Globestyle, Victoria Kings and Ambira Boys.

Contemporary Kikuyu music often borrows from benga. Stars include Sam Chege, Francis Rugwati and Daniel 'Councillor' Kamau, popular in the 1970s and still going strong. Joseph Kamaru, the popular musician and notorious nightclub owner of the late 1960s, converted to Christianity in 1993 and now dominates the gospel-music scene.

Popular bands today are heavily influenced by benga, soukous and Western music, with lyrics often in Swahili. These include bands such as Them Mushrooms (now reinvented as Uyoya) and Safari Sound. For upbeat dance tunes, Nameless, Ogopa DJs and Deux Vultures are recommended acts.

The biggest thing in Kenya right now is American-influenced hip hop, which has spawned both an avid listening public and an active subculture, particularly in Nairobi. Look out for local stars, such as Necessary Noize, Nonini, Emmanuel Jal, the Homeboyz DJs and the Nairobi Yetu collective.

Literature

Two of Kenya's best authors are Ngugi wa Thiong'o and Meja Mwangi. Thiong'o is uncompromisingly radical, and his harrowing criticism of the Kenyan establishment landed him in jail for a year (described in his *Detained – A Prison Writer's Diary*), lost him his job at Nairobi University and forced him into exile. Meja Mwangi sticks more to social issues and urban dislocation but has a brilliant sense of humour that threads its way right through his books, including his latest, *The Mzungu Boy*.

Kenya's latest rising star is Binyavanga Wainaina, currently a writer for the South African *Sunday Times* newspaper, who won the Caine Prize for African Writing in July 2002. The award-winning short story *Discovering Home* is about a young Kenyan working in Cape Town who returns to his parents' village for a year.

Another interesting writer is Marjorie Oludhe Magoye, whose *The Present Moment* follows the life stories of a group of elderly women in a Christian refuge. For more writing by women in Africa try *Unwinding Threads*, a collection of short stories by many authors from all over the continent.

ENVIRONMENT
The Land

Kenya straddles the equator and covers an area of some 583,000 sq km, including around 13,600 sq km of Lake Victoria. It is bordered to the north by the arid bushlands of Ethiopia and Sudan, to the east by the Indian Ocean and the deserts of Somalia, to the west by Uganda and Lake Victoria, and to the south by Tanzania.

Kenya is dominated by the Rift Valley, a vast range of valleys that follows a 5000km-long crack in the earth's crust. Within the Rift are numerous 'swells' (raised escarpments) and 'troughs' (deep valleys, often containing lakes), and there are some huge volcanoes, including Mt Kenya, Mt Elgon and Mt Kilimanjaro (across the border in Tanzania).

The Rift Valley divides the flat plains of the coast from the hills along the lakeshore. Nairobi, the capital, sits in the Central Highlands, which are on the eastern edge of

NATIONAL PARK ENTRY FEES

Admission to parks in Kenya is gradually being converted to a 'smartcard' system, for payment of entry and camping fees. The cards must be charged with credit in advance and can only be topped up at certain locations. Any credit left on the card once you finish your trip cannot be refunded.

At the time of writing the smartcard system was in use at Nairobi, Lake Nakuru, Aberdare, Amboseli, Tsavo East and Tsavo West National Parks. The other parks still work on a cash system. You can purchase and charge smartcards at the Kenya Wildlife Service (KWS) headquarters in Nairobi and Mombasa, at the main gates of the participating parks and at the Malindi Marine National Park office.

There are four categories of parks in Kenya. These are as follows:

Category	Park
A	Aberdare, Amboseli, Lake Nakuru, Meru, Tsavo East, Tsavo West & Nairobi
B	Shimba Hills, Arabuko Sokoke, Ndere Island, Tana Primate, Kakamega & all other park & reserves
C	All marine parks & reserves
D	Nairobi Safari Walk, Animal Orphanage & Impala Sanctuary

The Masai Mara, Samburu, Buffalo Springs and Shaba National Reserves have the same entry fees as category A national parks; entry to Mt Kenya National Park is US$20/10 per adult/child.

Entry and camping fees to the parks per person per day are as follows:

Category	Nonresident adult/child (US$)	Resident adult/child (KSh)	Camping nonresident (US$)/resident (KSh)
A	40/20	1000/500	10/300
B	20/10	500/250	5/150
C	10/5	300/150	5/150
D	10/5	300/150	5/150

The land-based parks and reserves charge KSh300 for vehicles with fewer than six seats and KSh800 for vehicles seating six to 12. In addition to the public camping areas, special campsites cost US$25 per adult nonresident, plus a KSh7500 weekly reservation fee. Guides are available in most parks for US$30/KSh2500 nonresidents/residents per day.

All fees cover visitors for a 24-hour period, but you cannot leave and re-enter without paying twice. There are rumours that park fees will rise again shortly – the exact fee is not known, but expected to be in the region of US$60 for category A parks.

Be aware that at some non-smartcard parks and reserves (not always KWS run) ticket guards may ask if you require a receipt. If not they take your money (often with a discount) and then pocket the cash. Note that many unscrupulous drivers and safari guides are wise to this and just split your fee with the park guides without you being any the wiser.

the Rift Valley. Kenya can roughly be divided into four zones: the coastal plains; the Rift Valley and Central Highlands; the lakeshore; and the wastelands of northern Kenya.

The main rivers in Kenya are the Athi/Galana River, which empties into the Indian Ocean near Malindi, and the Tana River, which runs the course midway between Malindi and Lamu. Aside from Lake Victoria, Kenya has numerous small volcanic lakes and mighty Lake Turkana, which straddles the Ethiopian border.

Within volcanic craters, and on the Rift Valley floor, are several soda lakes, rich in sodium bicarbonate, created by the filtering of water through mineral-rich volcanic rock and subsequent evaporation.

Wildlife
ANIMALS

There's such a dazzling array of animals in Kenya that viewing them in the national parks is one of the main reasons for visiting. The 'Big Five' – lion, buffalo, elephant, leopard and rhino – and a huge variety of other animals can be seen in at least two of the major parks. Some of the most interesting animals are described in the Wildlife Guide (p105), or in much more detail in Lonely Planet's *Watching Wildlife East Africa*.

The birdlife here is equally varied, and includes such interesting species as the ostrich, vulture and marabou stork. Around bodies of water you may see flamingos, cranes, storks and pelicans, while the forests are home to hornbills and rare species, such as the sunbird and touraco. There are also dozens of species of weaver bird, which make the distinctive baglike nests seen hanging from acacia trees.

Endangered Species

Many of Kenya's major predators and herbivores have become endangered because of the continuous destruction of their natural habitat and merciless poaching for ivory, skins, horn and bush meat.

The black rhino is probably Kenya's most endangered species, due to poaching for its horn. Faced with relentless poaching by heavily armed gangs in the 1980s, the wild rhino population plummeted from 20,000 in 1969 to just 458 today. **Rhino Ark** (☎ 020-604246; www .rhinoark.org) raises funds to create rhino sanctuaries in the parks, complete with electric fencing and guards, and donations are always appreciated. There are currently sanctuaries in Tsavo and Lake Nakuru National Parks, while Aberdare National Park is in the process of being fenced.

While the elephant is not technically endangered, it is still the target of poachers, and a large number are killed every year, especially in the area around Tsavo East National Park. Current numbers are estimated at 35,000.

PLANTS

Kenya's flora is notably diverse because of the country's wide range of physiographic regions. The vast plains of the south are characterised by distinctive flat-topped acacia trees, interspersed with the equally recognisable baobab trees and savage whistling thorn bushes, which made early exploration of the continent such a tortuous process.

The savannah grassland of the Masai Mara National Reserve supports a huge variety of animal life. The grass grows quickly after the rains, providing food for a huge range of herbivores

and insects, which in turn feeds a variety of predators. Trampling and grazing by herbivores promotes the growth of grasses, rather than broadleaf plants, which are more vulnerable to damage from grazing, drought and fire.

On the slopes of Mt Elgon and Mt Kenya the flora changes with altitude. Thick evergreen temperate forest grows between 1000m and 2000m, giving way to a belt of bamboo forest up to about 3000m. Above this height is mountain moorland, characterised by the amazing groundsel tree and giant lobelias. In the semidesert plains of the north and northeast the vegetation cover is thorny bush, which can seem to go on forever. In the northern coastal areas mangroves are prolific and there are still a few small pockets of coastal rainforest.

National Parks & Reserves

Around 10% of Kenya's land area is protected by law, and the national parks and reserves here rate among the best in Africa. Despite the ravages of human land exploitation and poaching, there is still an incredible variety of birds and mammals in the parks, and going on safari is an integral part of the Kenyan experience.

More popular parks, such as the Masai Mara National Reserve and Amboseli National Park, can become heavily overcrowded in the high season (January to February). Fortunately, the smaller and more remote parks, such as Saiwa Swamp National Park, see only a handful of visitors at any time of the year. A number of marine national parks have also been established, providing excellent diving and snorkelling.

Although all the parks provide the opportunity to get 'up close and personal' with wildlife, remember that these are wild animals and their actions can be unpredictable. Heed the warnings of guides and rangers while on safari, and seek local advice before venturing off alone into the wilds.

Environmental Issues

DEFORESTATION

More than half of Africa's forests have been destroyed over the last century, and forest destruction continues on a large scale in Kenya – less than 3% of the country's original forest cover remains. Land grabbing, illegal logging, charcoal burning and agricultural encroachment all take their toll. However, millions of

KENYA

JIKO

One innovative idea to minimise firewood use is the *jiko* stove, based on a Thai design and modified to suit the Kenyan way of cooking. Easy and cheap to manufacture, the *jiko* consists of an hourglass-shaped metal casing and a ceramic insulator that delivers 25% to 40% of the heat from the fire to the pot, much more than open fires. After some uncertainty, Kenyans have embraced the *jiko* with enthusiasm and hundreds of open-air workshops now provide stoves for nearly a million households.

Kenyans still rely on wood and charcoal for cooking fuel, so travellers will almost certainly contribute to this deforestation whether they like it or not. To try to minimise the damage, stay at an ecolodge, or donate money to a charity that is involved in reforestation.

The degazetting of protected forests is another contentious issue, sparking widespread protests and preservation campaigns. On the flip side, locals in forest areas can find themselves homeless if the government does enforce protection orders.

Despite these problems, some large areas of protected forest remain. The Mt Kenya, Mt Elgon and Aberdare National Parks, Kakamega Forest Reserve and Arabuko Sokoke Forest are all tremendous places to visit, packed with thousands of species of fauna and flora.

KENYA WILDLIFE SERVICE (KWS)

With a total ban on hunting imposed in 1977, the Kenya Wildlife Service (KWS) was free to concentrate solely on conserving Kenya's wildlife. This came just in time, as the 1970s and '80s were marred by a shocking amount of poaching linked to the drought in Somalia, which drove hordes of poachers across the border into Kenya. A staggering number of Kenya's rhinos and elephants were slaughtered, and many KWS officers worked in league with poachers until famous palaeontologist Dr Richard Leakey cleaned up the organisation in the 1980s and '90s. A core part of his policy was allowing KWS rangers to shoot poachers on sight, which seems to have dramatically reduced the problem.

However, there have been several new raids on elephants and rhinos since 2001. As a result, there is now open talk of abandoning some of the more remote parks and concentrating resources where they can achieve the best results and on the park, that receive most visitors. At the same time community conservation projects are being encouraged, and many community-owned ranches are now being opened up as private wildlife reserves, with the backing of the KWS and international donors.

PRIVATE CONSERVATION

It has been claimed that more than 75% of Kenya's wildlife lies outside the national parks and reserves, and an increasing number of important wildlife conservation areas now exist on private land. Private wildlife reserves often have the resources to work intensively on specific conservation issues and it is no accident that some of the largest concentrations of rhinos are within these areas. Supporting these projects is a great way for visitors to contribute to Kenyan communities and assist wildlife preservation.

The **Laikipia Wildlife Forum** (☎ 062-31600; www .laikipia.org) is an umbrella organisation representing many lodges and conservation areas in Laikipia, the large slab of ranch land northwest of Mt Kenya. Ranches in this area are particularly active in wildlife conservation, and the forum is a good source of up-to-date information. Other private wildlife ranches and conservation areas can be found around Tsavo and Amboseli National Parks.

TOURISM

The tourist industry is a cause of serious environmental problems, most notably heavy use of firewood by tourist lodges and erosion caused by safari minibuses, which cut across and between trails and follow wildlife into the bush, creating virtual dustbowls in parks such as Amboseli, Samburu and Masai Mara.

The KWS now insists that every new lodge and camp must be designed in an ecofriendly manner. As a result, there are growing numbers of ecolodges in Kenya, which keep their impact on the environment to a minimum through recycling, use of renewable energy resources, and strict controls on dumping of refuse and the types of fuel that are used.

As a visitor, the best way to help combat these problems is to be very selective about who you do business with. While you may end up paying more for an ecofriendly trip, in the long term you'll be investing in the preservation of Kenya's delicate environment.

FOOD & DRINK

The food in Kenya is essentially the same as you'll find in the rest of this region. *Nyama choma* is the one local speciality; this is technically barbecued meat, but bears little resemblance to any Western understanding of the term. You buy the meat (usually goat) by the kilogram, it's cooked over a charcoal pit and served in bite-sized pieces with a vegetable side dish. Sometimes it's surprisingly good, but often you'll require a large supply of toothpicks.

Despite the fact that Kenya grows some of the finest tea and coffee in the world, getting a decent cup of either can be difficult. Chai (tea) is drunk in large quantities, but the tea, milk and sugar are usually boiled together and stewed for ages, coming out milky and horrendously sweet. For tea without milk ask for *chai kavu*. Coffee is also sweet and milky, with a bare minimum of instant granules. In Nairobi there are a handful of excellent coffee houses, and you can usually get a good filter coffee at any of the big hotels. With all the Italian tourists, you can get a decent cappuccino pretty much anywhere on the coast.

Soft drinks, such as Coke, Sprite and Fanta, are available everywhere under the generic term of sodas. The nation's favourite juice is passionfruit; pineapple, orange and mango juices also feature on most menus.

The local beers are Tusker, White Cap and Pilsner (all manufactured by Kenya Breweries), sold in 500mL bottles. Guinness is also available, but tastes nothing like the real thing. Beers are cheapest from supermarkets (KSh45 for 500mL); bars charge KSh100 to KSh200. Other bottled drinks include Hardy's cider, Redd's and Kingfisher (fruity alcopops), and the ubiquitous Smirnoff Ice.

Kenya has a fledgling wine industry and the Lake Naivasha Colombard wines are said to be quite good, unlike local papaya wine, which tastes foul and smells worse. You can get cheap imported wine by the glass for around KSh150 in Nairobi restaurants. In the big supermarkets you'll pay anything from KSh500 to KSh1500 for a bottle of South African wine.

Although it is strictly illegal to brew or distil liquor, this still goes on. *Pombe* is the local beer, usually a fermented brew made with bananas or millet and sugar. It shouldn't do you any harm.

NAIROBI & AROUND

☎ 020 / pop three million

Nairobi has a reputation as the most dangerous city in Africa, beating stiff competition from Johannesburg and Lagos. Carjacking, robbery and violence are daily occurrences, and the social ills behind them are unlikely to disappear in the near future. The city has garnered the unfortunate nickname of 'Nairobbery', and most first-timers are keen on holing up in their hotel rooms and counting down the minutes until their safari departure. While the crime statistics are unsettling, it's easy enough to sidestep the worst dangers here, and although you might not believe us at first glance, Nairobi is actually an extremely dynamic and cosmopolitan city full of tourist attractions.

The central business district has more going for it than any other Kenyan conurbation: there's a comprehensive range of shops, the *matatus* are the funkiest around, most safari companies are based here, the cultural scene is thriving, the nightlife is unbridled and it's virtually the only place in the country where you can get a truly varied diet. Even café culture has reached the downtown area, adding a soupçon of sophistication to the supposed urban badlands. Even if the inner city does terrify you, a quick *matatu* ride can whisk

---

LETHAL BREW

Kenya has a long tradition of producing its own bootleg liquor, but you should steer well clear of *chang'a*. In mid-2005, 48 people died near Machakos after drinking a bad batch of the stuff; a further 84 were hospitalised and apparently treated with vodka! Such incidents are not uncommon. Sorghum Baridi, from Central Province, contains so much methyl alcohol that the bottles are actually cold to the touch! Perhaps the most dangerous *chang'a* comes from Kisii, and is fermented with marijuana twigs, cactus mash, battery alkaline and formalin. Needless to say these brews can be lethal and we don't recommend that you partake.

KENYA

KENYA

you into the secluded suburbs for that much-needed rural escape.

HISTORY

As you might guess from all the tower blocks, Nairobi is a modern creation and almost everything here has been built in the last 100 years. Until the 1890s the whole area was just an isolated swamp, but as the rails of the East Africa Railway fell into place, a depot was established on the edge of a small stream known to the Maasai as *uaso nairobi* (cold water). Nairobi quickly developed into the administrative nerve centre of the Uganda Railway, and in 1901 the capital of the British Protectorate was moved here from Mombasa.

Even when the first permanent buildings were constructed, Nairobi remained a real frontier town, with rhinos and lions freely roaming the streets, and lines of iron-roofed bungalows stretching across the plain. However, once the railway was up and running, wealth began to flow into the city. The colonial government built some grand hotels to accommodate the first tourists to Kenya – big game hunters, lured by the attraction of shooting the country's naively tame wildlife. Sadly almost all of the colonial-era buildings were replaced by bland modern office buildings following *uhuru* (independence) in 1963.

ORIENTATION

The compact city centre is bounded by Uhuru Hwy, Haile Selassie Ave, Tom Mboya St and University Way. Northeast of the centre, on the eastern side of Tom Mboya St, is the rougher River Rd area where most of the bus offices are found.

Various suburbs surround the downtown area. Southwest of the centre, beyond Uhuru and Central Parks, are Nairobi Hill, Milimani and Hurlingham, with several hostels, campsites and hotels. Further out are Wilson Airport, Nairobi National Park and the expat enclaves of Langata and Karen. The country's main airport, Jomo Kenyatta International Airport, is southeast of the centre.

North of the centre are the expat-dominated suburbs of Westlands and Parklands, home to large European and Indian communities. The suburbs further out, such as Kibera, Kayole and Githurai, are mainly poverty-stricken slums with terrible reputations for violent crime.

INFORMATION

Bookshops

Book Villa (Map pp284-5; ☎ 020-337890; Standard St)
Bookpoint (Map pp284-5; ☎ 020-211156; Moi Ave)
Bookstop (☎ 020-714547; Yaya Centre, Hurlingham)

Cultural Centres

Alliance Française (Map pp284-5; ☎ 020-340054; www.ambafrance-ke.org; cnr Monrovia & Loita Sts; ☼ 8.30am-6.30pm Mon-Fri, to 5pm Sat)
British Council (Map pp282-3; ☎ 020-334855; www .britishcouncil.org/kenya; Upper Hill Rd; ☼ 9.30am-5.30pm Mon-Fri, 9.30am-1pm Sat)
Goethe Institut (Map pp284-5; ☎ 020-224640; www .goethe.de/nairobi; Maendeleo House, cnr Monrovia & Loita Sts; ☼ 10am-12.30pm Thu-Tue, 2-5pm Mon-Fri)
Japan Information & Culture Centre (Map pp284-5; ☎ 020-340520; www.ke.emb-japan.go.jp; ICEA Bldg, Kenyatta Ave; ☼ 8.30am-5pm Mon-Fri)
Nairobi Cultural Institute (Map pp282-3; ☎ 020-569205; Ngong Rd; ☼ 8:30am-5pm Mon-Fri)

Emergency

AAR Health Services (Map pp282-3; ☎ 020-271737; Fourth Ngong Ave)
Aga Khan Hospital (Map pp282-3; ☎ 020-3662000; Third Parklands Ave; ☼ 24hr)
Emergency services (☎ 999) Fire, police and ambulance. Don't rely on their prompt arrival.
Flying Doctors Service (☎ 020-602495, emergency 020-315454; www.amref.org) Part of the African Medical and Research Foundation (AMREF).
Police (☎ 240000) For less urgent police business.

Internet Access

There are literally hundreds of internet cafés in central Nairobi, most of them tucked away in anonymous office buildings. Connection speed is usually pretty good and rates are around KSh2 per minute.
AGX (Map pp284-5; Barclays Plaza, Loita St; ☼ 8am-8pm Mon-Sat)
Avant Garde e-centre (Map pp284-5; Fedha Towers, Kaunda St; ☼ 7.30am-9pm Mon-Sat, 11am-6pm Sun)
EasySurf (Map p289; ☎ 020-3745418; Sarit Centre, Parklands Rd, Westlands; per min KSh4; ☼ 9am-8pm Mon-Sat, 10am-2pm Sun)

Libraries

Kenya National Library (Map pp282-3; ☎ 020-2725550; www.knls.or.ke; Ngong Rd; ☼ 8am-6.30pm Mon-Thu, 8am-4pm Fri, 9am-5pm Sat)
McMillan Memorial Library (Map pp284-5; ☎ 020-221844; Banda St; ☼ 9am-6pm Mon-Fri, 9.30am-4pm Sat)

Medical Services

Avoid the Kenyatta National Hospital if you can – although it's free, its resources are stretched.

AAR Health Services Nairobi (Map pp282-3; ☎ 020-715319; Williamson House, Fourth Ngong Ave); Westlands (Map p289; ☎ 020-446201; Sarit Centre, Parklands Rd, Westlands)

Acacia Medical Centre (Map pp284-5; ☎ 020-212200; info@acaciamed.co.ke; ICEA Bldg, Kenyatta Ave; ⏱ 7am-7pm Mon-Fri, 7am-2pm Sat)

Aga Khan Hospital (Map pp282-3; ☎ 020-740000; Third Parklands Ave; ⏱ 24hr)

KAM Pharmacy (Map pp284-5; ☎ 020-251700; Executive Tower, IPS Bldg, Kimathi St) Pharmacy, doctors' surgery and laboratory.

Medical Services Surgery (Map pp284-5; ☎ 020-317625; Bruce House, Standard St; ⏱ 8.30am-4.30pm Mon-Fri)

Nairobi Hospital (Map pp282-3; ☎ 020-722160; off Argwings Kodhek Rd; ⏱ 24hr)

Money

In the centre of Nairobi, Barclays branches with guarded ATMs include those located on Muindi Mbingu St (Map pp284–5), Mama Ngina St (Map pp284–5), and on the corner of Kenyatta and Moi Aves (Map pp284–5). You will also find multiple branches in Westlands and Hurlingham. The other big bank in town is the Standard Chartered, which has numerous central branches.

Post

Post office (Map pp284-5; ☎ 020-243434; Kenyatta Ave; ⏱ 8am-6pm Mon-Fri, 9am-noon Sat)

Telephone

Telkom Kenya Haile Selaissie Ave (Map pp284-5; ☎ 020-232000; ⏱ 8am-6pm Mon-Fri, 9am-noon Sat); Kenyatta Ave (Map pp284-5; ☎ 020-243434; ⏱ 8am-6pm Mon-Fri, 9am-noon Sat)

Tourist Information

Despite the many safari companies with signs saying 'Tourist Information', there is still no official tourist office in Nairobi.

Travel Agencies

Bunson Travel (Map pp284-5; ☎ 020-248371; www.bunsonkenya.com; Pan-African Insurance Bldg, Standard St)

Flight Centre (Map pp284-5; ☎ 020-210024; Lakhamshi House, Biashara St)

Let's Go Travel (www.lets-go-travel.net); Central Nairobi (Map pp284-5; ☎ 020-340331; Caxton House, Standard

St); Karen (Map p292; ☎ 020-882505; Karen shopping centre); Westlands (off Map p289; ☎ 447151; ABC Pl, Waiyaki Way, Westlands)

Tropical Winds (Map pp284-5; ☎ 020-341939; www.tropical-winds.com; Barclays Plaza, Loita St) Nairobi's STA Travel representative.

DANGERS & ANNOYANCES

Prospective visitors to Nairobi are usually understandably daunted by the city's unenviable reputation. Carjacking, robbery and violence are daily occurrences, and the underlying social ills behind them are unlikely to disappear in the near future.

However, the majority of problems happen in the slums, far from the main tourist zones. The central Nairobi area bound by Kenyatta Ave, Moi Ave, Haile Selassie Ave and Uhuru Hwy is comparatively trouble-free as long as you use a bit of common sense, and there are plenty of askaris (security guards) around at night. Stay alert and you should encounter nothing worse than a few persistent safari touts and the odd con artist.

Even around the city centre, though, there are places to watch out for: danger zones include the area around Latema and River Rds, a hotspot for petty theft, and Uhuru Park, which tends to attract all kinds of dodgy characters.

Once the shops have shut, the streets empty rapidly and the whole city takes on a slightly sinister air – mugging is a risk anywhere after dark. Take a taxi, even if you're only going a few blocks. This will also keep you safe from the attentions of Nairobi's street prostitutes, who flood into town in force after sunset.

SIGHTS
City Centre
NATIONAL MUSEUM

A grand alternative to the dozens of poky little local museums around the country, Kenya's **National Museum** (Map pp282-3; ☎ 020-742131; www.museums.or.ke; Museum Hill Rd; adult/child KSh800/400; ⏱ 9.30am-6pm) is housed in an imposing building amid lush leafy grounds just outside the city centre, and has a good range of cultural, geological and natural-history exhibits. Volunteer guides offer tours in English, Dutch and French; it's worth booking them in advance. There's no charge for their services, but a donation is appropriate.

NATIONAL ARCHIVES

Right in the bustling heart of Nairobi is the distinctive **National Archives** (Map pp284-5; ☎ 020-749341;

KENYA

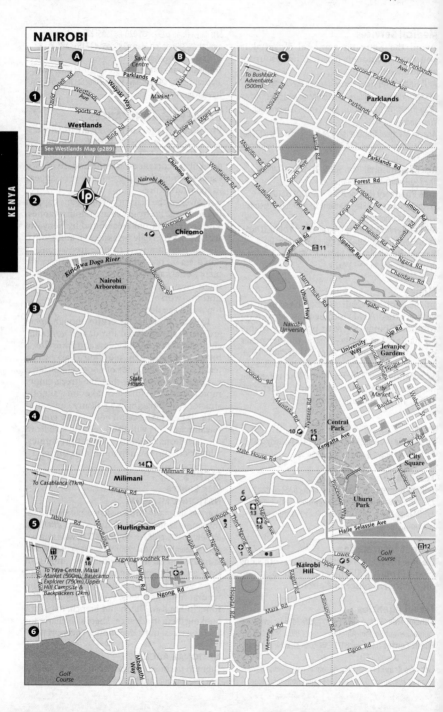

NAIROBI

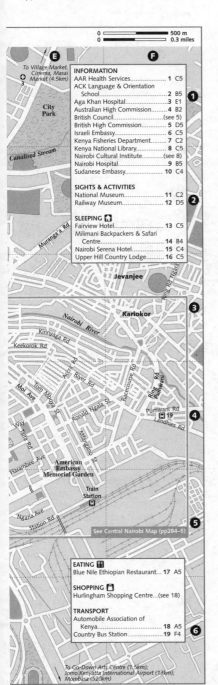

Moi Ave; admission free; 8.30am-5pm Mon-Fri, 8.30am-1pm Sat), an enormous collection of documents and reference material housed in the impressive former Bank of India building. The ground-floor atrium and gallery display an eclectic selection of contemporary art, historical photos of Nairobi, cultural artefacts, furniture and tribal objects, giving casual visitors a somewhat scatter-gun glimpse of East African heritage.

RAILWAY MUSEUM
This interesting little **museum** (Map pp282-3; Station Rd; adult/child/student KSh200/20/100; 8.15am-4.45pm) displays relics from the East African Railway. There are train and ship models, photographs, tableware and oddities from the history of the railway, such as the Engine Seat that allowed visiting dignitaries like Theodore Roosevelt to take pot shots at unsuspecting wildlife from the front of the train. In the grounds are dozens of fading locomotives in various states of disrepair, dating from the steam days to independence, including the steam train used in the movie *Out of Africa*.

PARLIAMENT HOUSE
If you fancy a look at how democracy works in Kenya, it's possible to obtain a permit for a seat in the public gallery at **parliament house** (Map pp284-5; 020-221291; Parliament Rd) – just remember, applause is strictly forbidden! If parliament is out of session, you can tour the buildings by arrangement with the sergeant at arms.

KENYATTA CONFERENCE CENTRE
Towering over City Sq, **Kenyatta Conference Centre** (Map pp284-5; City Hall Way), Nairobi's signature building, was designed as a fusion of modern and traditional African styles, though the distinctive saucer tower looks a little dated now. Staff will accompany you up to the rooftop **viewing platform** (adult/child KSh400/200; 9.30am-6pm) for wonderful views over Nairobi. The sight line goes all the way to the suburbs, and on clear days you can see aircraft coming in to land over the Nairobi National Park. You can take photographs from the viewing level but not elsewhere. Access may be restricted during events and conferences.

ARTS CENTRES
The **Go-Down Arts Centre** (off Map pp282-3; 020-5552227; Dunga Rd; admission free), a converted

CENTRAL NAIROBI

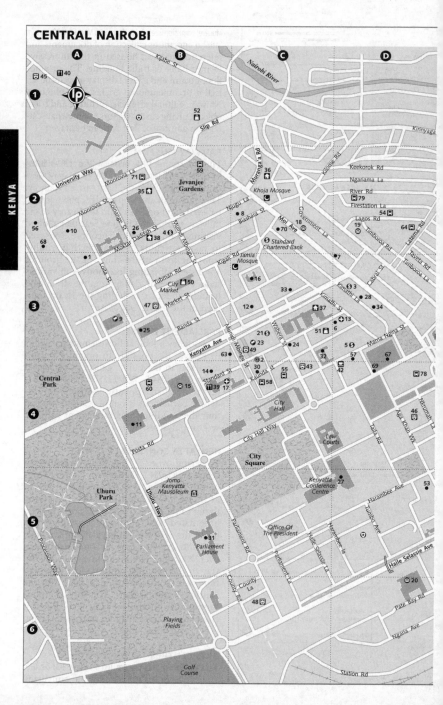

0 — 200 m
0 — 0.1 miles

INFORMATION
AGX....................................(see 9)
Acacia Medical Centre............(see 12)
Alliance Française.........................1 A3
Avant Garde e-centre....................2 C3
Barclays Bank...............................3 D3
Barclays Bank...............................4 B2
Barclays Bank...............................5 D3
Book Villa....................................6 D3
Bookpoint....................................7 D3
Flight Centre................................8 C2
French Embassy............................9 A3
Goethe Institut............................10 A2
Immigration Office.......................11 B4
Italian Embassy........................(see 57)
Japan Information & Culture
  Centre....................................12 A3
Japanese Embassy.....................(see 12)
KAM Pharmacy............................13 D3

Let's Go Travel............................14 B4
Main Post Office..........................15 B4
McMillan Memorial Library..........16 C3
Medical Services Surgery..............17 B4
Post Office..................................18 C2
Post Office..................................19 D2
Post Office..................................20 D5
Postbank....................................21 C3
Spanish Embassy.....................(see 57)
Telkom Kenya..............................22 E5
Telkom Kenya...........................(see 9)
Tropical Winds........................(see 15)
Ugandan High Commission (Consular
  Section).................................23 C3

SIGHTS & ACTIVITIES
Bunson Travel.............................24 C3
Eastern & Southern Safaris...........25 B3
Gametrackers Ltd........................26 B2

Kenyatta Conference Centre.........27 D5
Mzizi Arts Centre.........................28 D3
National Archives.........................29 E3
Origins Safaris.............................30 C4
Parliament House.........................31 B5
Safari Seekers.............................32 C3
Safe Ride Towns and Safaris.........33 C3
Sana Highlands Trekking
  Expeditions.............................34 D3

SLEEPING
Kenya Comfort Hotel...................35 B2
Meridian Court Hotel...................36 C2
New Stanley Hotel.......................37 C3
Terminal Hotel............................38 B2

EATING
Beneve Coffee House...................39 B4
Lord Delamere Terrace & Bar........40 A1
Tamarind Restaurant....................41 E5
Thorn Tree Café.......................(see 37)

DRINKING
Nairobi Java House......................42 D4

ENTERTAINMENT
20th Century Cinema...................43 C4
Kenya Cinema..............................44 E4
Kenya National Theatre................45 A1
Nairobi Cinema...........................46 D4
New Florida.................................47 B3
Professional Centre.....................48 C6
Simmers.....................................49 C3

SHOPPING
City Market.................................50 B3
Gallery Watatu............................51 C3
Maasai Market.............................52 B1

TRANSPORT
Air India.....................................53 D5
Airport Bus Departure Point.....(see 78)
Akamba......................................54 D2
Akamba Booking Office................55 C4
Avis..56 A2
British Airways............................57 D3
Budget.......................................58 C4
Bus & Matatu Stop......................59 B2
Bus & Matatu Stop (for Hurlingham &
  Milimani)................................60 B4
Bus Stop (for Langata, Karen &
  Airport)..................................61 E4
Buses to Kisii & Migori.................62 F3
Central Rent-a-Car......................63 B3
Coastline Safaris Office................64 D2
Crossland Services.......................65 F3
Easy Coach Office........................66 F5
Egypt Air....................................67 D3
Emirates.....................................68 A2
Ethiopian Airlines....................(see 17)
Glory Car Hire.............................69 D4
Glory Car Hire.............................70 C2
KBS Booking Office......................71 B2
KBS Bus Station..........................72 F4
KLM..(see 9)
Kenya Airways.........................(see 9)
Main Bus & Matatu Area..............73 E2
Matatus to Mtito Andei................74 G3
Matatus to Naivasha &
  Namanga..............................(see 75)
Matatus to Nyahururu & Nyeri...75 F3
Matatus to Thika.........................76 G2
Matatus to Wilson Airport, Nairobi
  National Park, Langata &
  Karen.....................................77 E5
Metro Shuttle Bus Stand..............78 D4
Scandinavia Express....................79 D2

KENYA

warehouse in the Industrial Area in Nairobi's southeast, contains 10 separate art studios and is rapidly becoming a hub for Nairobi's burgeoning arts scene.

The **Mzizi Arts Centre** (Map pp284-5; ☎ 020-574372; Sonalux House, Moi Ave; admission free) is a good place to view contemporary Kenyan art, craft, dance, literature and performance art.

Karen & Langata

NAIROBI NATIONAL PARK

Founded in 1946, this national park's incongruous suburban location makes it unique in Africa, and adds an intriguing twist to the usual safari experience. Indeed, abundant wildlife plays out the drama of Mother Nature against a backdrop of looming skyscrapers, speeding *matatus* and jets coming into land at the nearby airport.

The **national park** (Map p287; nonresident adult/ student/child US$40/10/20, smartcard required) is easily the most accessible of all Kenya's wildlife park. The headquarters of the **Kenya Wildlife Service** (KWS; ☎ 020-600800; www.kws.org) are also located at the park entrance.

The main entrance to the park is on Langata Rd – the roads in the park are passable for 2WDs, but travelling in a 4WD is never a bad idea, especially if the rains have been heavy. *Matatus* 125 and 126 pass right by the park entrance (KSh40) – departing from the railway station, the ride should take you about 30 to 45 minutes depending on traffic. A taxi should cost between KSh800 and KSh1000 from the city centre.

DAVID SHELDRICK WILDLIFE TRUST

Occupying a plot within Nairobi National Park, this nonprofit **trust** (Map p287; ☎ 020-891996; www.sheldrickwildlifetrust.org) was established shortly after the death of David Sheldrick in 1977, who served as the antipoaching warden of Tsavo National Park. Together with his wife Daphne, David pioneered techniques of raising orphaned black rhinos and elephants and reintroducing them back into the wild, and the Trust retains close links with Tsavo for these and other projects. Rhinos and elephants are still reared on-site, and can be viewed daily between 11am and noon. There's no official charge for visiting, but a donation of KSh300 per person is appropriate.

By bus or *matatu*, take 125 or 126 from Moi Ave and ask to be dropped off at the KWS central workshop on Magadi Rd (KSh40, 50 minutes). It's about 1km from the workshop gate to the Sheldrick centre – it's signposted and KWS staff can give you directions. Be advised that at this point you are walking in the national park, which does contain lions, so you're advised to stick to the paths and not stray into the bush. A taxi should cost between KSh800 and KSh1000 from the city centre.

GIRAFFE CENTRE

This vitally important **breeding centre** (Map p292; ☎ 020-891568; www.giraffecenter.org; Koitobos Rd; nonresident adult/child KSh500/250, resident KSh100/20; ☺ 9am-5.30pm), run by the African Fund for Endangered Wildlife (AFEW), was started in 1979 by Jock Leslie-Melville, the Kenyan grandson of a Scottish earl. Things started when Jock and his wife Betty started raising a baby giraffe in their Langata home, though the couple (now deceased) had been successful in introducing several breeding pairs of Rothschild giraffes into Kenyan national parks.

To get here from central Nairobi by public transport, take *matatu* 24 via Kenyatta Ave to the Hardy shops in Langata, and walk from there. Alternatively, take *matatu* 26 to Magadi Rd, and walk through from Mukoma Rd. A taxi should cost between KSh800 and KSh1000 from the city centre.

UTAMADUNI

A charitable organisation set in a large colonial house near the Giraffe Centre, **Utamaduni** (Map p292; ☎ 020-890464; Bogani East Rd; ☺ 9.30am-6pm) is essentially a large crafts emporium, with more than a dozen separate rooms selling all kinds of excellent artworks and souvenirs from around Africa.

KAREN BLIXEN MUSEUM

This **museum** (Map p292; ☎ 020-882779; karenblixen@ bidii.com; Karen Rd; adult/child nonresident KSh200/100, resident KSh50/20; ☺ 9.30am-6pm) is the farmhouse where Karen Blixen, author of *Out of Africa*, lived between 1914 and 1931. She left after a series of personal tragedies, but the lovely colonial house has been preserved as a museum. It was presented to the Kenyan government at independence by the Danish government along with the adjacent agricultural college.

The museum is about 2km from Langata Rd. The easiest way to get here is by *matatu* 24 via Kenyatta Ave, which passes right by the entrance. A taxi should cost between KSh800 and KSh1000.

KENYA

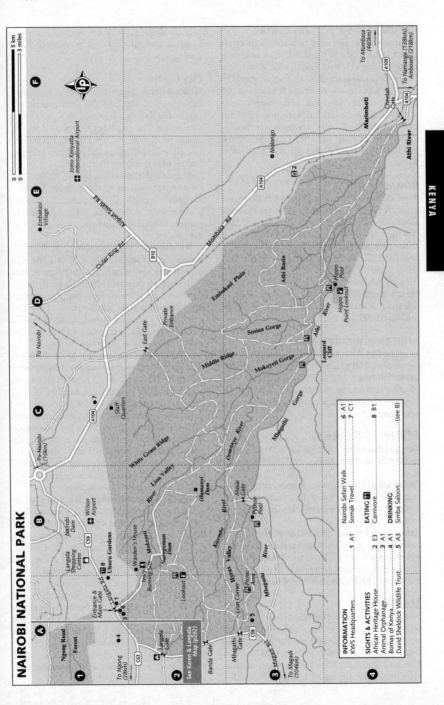

NAIROBI NATIONAL PARK

Ngong Road Forest

To Ngong (28km)

See Karen & Langata Map (p292)

To Nairobi (10km)

To Nairobi

Jomo Kenyatta International Airport

To Mombasa (460km)

To Namanga (138km); Amboseli (218km)

Marimboti

Athi River

Cheetah Gate

Malongo

Embakasi Village

Outer Ring Rd

Airport South Rd

Mombasa Rd

Athi Basin

Embakasi Plain

East Gate

Private Entrance

Sosian Gorge

Hippo Pool

Hippo Point Lookout

Athi River

Leopard Cliff

Middle Ridge

Mokoyeti Gorge

Gorge

Mbagathi

Ormanyie River

White Grass Ridge

Staff Quarters

Lion Valley

Mokoyeti River

Olomanyi Dam

Masai Gate

Kisembe River

Python Pool

Wilson Airport

Nairobi Dam

Langata Shopping Centre

Uhuru Gardens

Warden's House

Nagogman Dam

Ivory Burning Site

Lookout

Loa Corner Hyrax Valley

Picnic Area

Mbagathi River

Langata Rd

Entrance & Main Gate

Langata Gate

Banda Gate

Mbagathi Gate

To Magadi (104km)

INFORMATION
KWS Headquarters............................1 A1

SIGHTS & ACTIVITIES
African Heritage House......................2 E3
Animal Orphanage.............................3 A1
Bomas of Kenya................................4 A1
David Sheldrick Wildlife Trust............5 A3
Nairobi Safari Walk...........................6 A1
Somak Travel....................................7 C1

EATING
Carnivore...8 B1

DRINKING
Simba Saloon..................................(see 8)

0   5 km
0   3 miles

KAZURI BEADS & POTTERY CENTRE

An interesting diversion in Karen is this **craft centre** (Map p292; ☎ 020-883500; www.kazuri.com; Mbagathi Ridge; ⏰ 8am-4.30pm Mon-Sat, 11am-4.30pm Sun), which was started by an English expat in 1975 as a place where single mothers could learn a marketable skill and achieve self-sufficiency. A tasteful gift shop is right on the premises, and the prices are considerably cheaper than at other retail locations. It's located just off Karen Rd near the Karen Blixen Museum.

BOMAS OF KENYA

This **cultural centre** (Map p287; www.bomasofkenya.co.ke; ☎ 020-891801; Langata Rd; nonresident adult/child KSh600/300, resident KSh100/25; ⏰ performances 2.30pm Mon-Fri, 3.30pm Sat & Sun) at Langata, is near the main gate to Nairobi National Park. Bus or *matatu* 125 or 126 runs here from Nairobi train station (KSh30, 30 minutes). Get off at Magadi Rd, from where it's about a 1km walk, clearly signposted on the right-hand side of the road. A taxi should cost between KSh800 and KSh1000.

AFRICAN HERITAGE HOUSE

Designed by Alan Donovan, an African heritage expert and gallery owner, this stunning **exhibition house** (Map p287; ☎ 0721-518389; www.africanheritagebook.com; off Mombasa Rd) overlooking Nairobi National Park can be visited by prior arrangement only.

FESTIVALS & EVENTS

Kenya Fashion Week (☎ 0733-636300; Sarit Centre, Parklands Rd, Westlands) An expo-style fashion event held in June.

Tusker Safari Sevens (www.safarisevens.com; Impala Club, Ngong Rd, Karen) A high-profile international seven-a-side rugby tournament held every June. The Kenyan team has a strong record.

Kenya Music Festival (☎ 020-2712964; Kenyatta Conference Centre) Held over 10 days in August, the country's longest-running music festival was established almost 80 years ago by the colonial regime. African music now predominates, but Western musicians still take part.

SLEEPING

The heart and soul of Nairobi is the city centre, so if you want to go to bed and wake up in the centre of it all, then look no further. Of the outlying areas, the eastern districts of Nairobi Hill and Milimani have the most promising selection, catering for all budgets. For a decidedly different take on Nairobi, consider heading out into the 'burbs, namely Karen and Langata.

City Centre

Terminal Hotel (Map pp284-5; ☎ 020-228817; Moktar Daddah St; s/d KSh 2000/2500) The Terminal Hotel is preferable to other budget crash pads in the city centre. The emphasis here is on doing the basics well, with no overblown attempts at tourist frills, and clean and perfectly adequate rooms that speak for themselves.

Kenya Comfort Hotel (Map pp284-5; ☎ 020-317606; www.kenyacomfort.com; cnr Muindi Mbingu & Monrovia Sts; s/d from US$38/56; 🖳) This cheerily painted place is kept in top nick, offering a fine selection of modern tiled rooms and a lift for easy access.

Meridian Court Hotel (Map pp284-5; ☎ 020-313991; Muranga'a Rd; s/d from KSh5250/6750; 🖳 🏊) The elaborate lobby here is rather more prepossessing than the grey concrete blocks above it, but it's hardly worth complaining when you're essentially getting a suite for the price of a standard room. There's no great luxury involved, but the pool, bar and restaurants make good value, especially at this price range.

New Stanley Hotel (Map pp284-5; ☎ 020-316377; www.sarovahotels.com/stanley; cnr Kimathi St & Kenyatta Ave; s/d from US$225/250; ✂ 🖳 🏊) A Nairobi classic: the original Stanley Hotel was established in 1902, though the latest version is a very smart and modern construction run by the sophisticated Sarova Hotels. Colonial décor prevails inside, with lashings of green leather, opulent chandeliers and old-fashioned fans, though the real highlight (at least from our perspective!) is the Thorn Tree Café, which inspired Lonely Planet's own online community.

ourpick Nairobi Serena Hotel (Map pp282-3; ☎ 020-2822000; www.serenahotels.com/kenya/nairobi/home.asp; Central Park, Procession Way; r/ste from US$400/500; ✂ 🖳 🏊) Consolidating its reputation as one of the best top-flight chains in East Africa, this entry in the Serena canon has a fine sense of individuality, with its international-class facilities displaying a touch of safari style. A member of the prestigious 'Leading Hotels of the World' group, the Nairobi Serena is considered by many to be the capital's most elegant accommodation. Of particular note is the on-site Maisha health spa, which offers a wide range of holistic cures aimed at soothing your travel-worn bones and balancing your wanderlust-ridden mind.

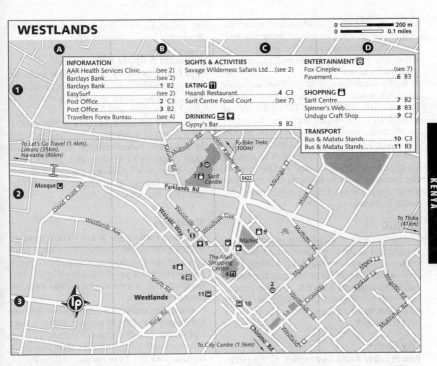

WESTLANDS

INFORMATION
AAR Health Services Clinic........(see 2)
Barclays Bank..............................(see 2)
Barclays Bank.............................1 B2
EasySurf....................................(see 2)
Post Office..................................2 C3
Post Office..................................3 B2
Travellers Forex Bureau...............(see 4)

SIGHTS & ACTIVITIES
Savage Wilderness Safaris Ltd....(see 2)

EATING
Haandi Restaurant......................4 C3
Sarit Centre Food Court.............(see 7)

DRINKING
Gypsy's Bar................................5 B2

ENTERTAINMENT
Fox Cineplex..............................(see 7)
Pavement...................................6 B3

SHOPPING
Sarit Centre................................7 B2
Spinner's Web.............................8 B3
Undugu Craft Shop......................9 C2

TRANSPORT
Bus & Matatu Stands..................10 C3
Bus & Matatu Stands..................11 B3

KENYA

Milimani & Nairobi Hill

our pick **Upper Hill Campsite & Backpackers** (off Map pp282-3; ☎ 721-517869; www.upperhillcampsite.com; Othaya Rd, Kileleshwa; camping KSh350, dm KSh500, banda 1200, d without bathroom 2000/15000; 🖳) An attractive and secure compound that is an oasis from the mean city streets, Upper Hill offers a range of accommodation that attracts a loyal following of overland trucks as well as an international mix of backpackers and budget travellers. Take the 46 *matatu* or bus along Othaya Rd until you pass the Egyptian embassy on the left-hand side; the entrance to the property is just past on the right-hand side.

Milimani Backpackers & Safari Centre (Map pp282-3; ☎ 202-724827; www.milimanibackpackers.com; Milimani Rd, Milimani; camping KSh350, dm KSh600, permanent tent KSh 450, s/d cabin KSh1300/1500; 🖳) Formerly known as Nairobi Backpackers, this up-and-coming spot has tremendous potential, and we're confident that the new owners are going to do a great job with the place. Whether you camp out back, cosy up in the dorms or splurge on your own cabin, you'll end up huddled around the fire at night, swapping travel stories and dining on home-cooked meals with fellow travellers.

Upper Hill Country Lodge (Map pp282-3; ☎ 020-2881600; www.countrylodge.co.ke; 2nd Ngong Ave, Milimani; s/d from KSh5100/7800; 🖳) This brand-spanking new property was constructed by the owners of the adjacent Fairview Hotel, though rather than striving for over-the-top opulence, the focus here is solely on affordable luxury for business travellers. The Country Lodge is one of the best-priced midrange options in Nairobi, though its minimalist yet stylish living quarters can compete with the best of them.

Fairview Hotel (Map pp282-3; ☎ 020-2711321; www.fairviewkenya.com; Bishops Rd, Milimani; s/d from KSh7500/11,000; 🗙 🖳 🖭 🖳) An excellent top-end choice that is nicely removed from the central hubbub, the Fairview is defined by its winding paths and green-filled grounds, which creates a refined atmosphere, especially around the charming courtyard restaurant.

Karen & Langata

Karen Camp (Map p292; ☎ 020-883475; www.karencamp.com; Marula La; camping US$4, dm US$6, r US$20) You wouldn't expect to find a backpacker-friendly option out here in affluent Karen, which is why we like this friendly little spot so much. The quiet location and smart facilities are reason enough to make the trek out to the suburbs as are the shady campsites, spic-and-span dorms and permanent safari-style tents.

Giraffe Manor (Map p292; ☎ 020-891078; www.giraffe manor.com; Mukoma Rd; full board s/d US$425/625, half board s/d US$375/580) Built in 1932 in the typical English style, this elegant manor is situated on 56 hectares, much of which is given over to the adjacent Giraffe Centre (p286). As a result, you may have a Rothschild's giraffe peering through your bedroom window first thing in the morning, which, needless to say, is just about one of the most surreal experiences you could imagine!

EATING

Nairobi is well stocked with places to eat, particularly in the city centre, where you can choose anything from the cheap workers' canteens around River Rd to Chinese feasts and full-on splurges off Kenyatta Ave. For dinner it's worth heading out to the suburbs, which offer dozens of choices of cuisine from all over the world.

City Centre

Beneve Coffee House (Map pp284-5; ☎ 020-217959; cnr Standard & Koinange Sts; dishes KSh50-150; ☯ Mon-Fri) A small self-service café that has locals queuing outside in the mornings waiting for it to open.

Lord Delamere Terrace & Bar (Map pp284-5; ☎ 020-216940; www.fairmont.com/NorfolkHotel; Harry Thuku Rd; light meals KSh300-600) Since 1904, this popular rendezvous spot at the Norfolk Hotel has existed as the unofficial starting and ending spot for East African safaris.

Thorn Tree Café (Map pp284-5; ☎ 020-228030; New Stanley Hotel, Kimathi St; mains KSh500-850) The Stanley's legendary café still serves as a popular meeting place for travellers of all persuasions, and caters to most tastes with a good mix of food. The original thorn-tree noticeboard in the courtyard gave rise to the general expression, and inspired Lonely Planet's own online Thorn Tree community.

Tamarind Restaurant (Map pp284-5; ☎ 020-251811; www.tamarind.co.ke; Aga Khan Walk; mains KSh1000-2000; ☯ 2.30-4.30pm & 8.30pm-midnight) Kenya's most prestigious restaurant chain runs Nairobi's best seafood restaurant – you can dine on all manner of exotic flavours, and the lav-

ish dining room is laid out in a sumptuous modern Arabic Moorish style.

Milimani & Upper Hill

Yaya Centre (off Map pp282-3; Argwings Khodek Rd, Hurlingham) This expat favourite is home to a speciality food court as well as a reasonable selection of cafés and kiosks.

Blue Nile Ethiopian Restaurant (Map pp282-3; ☎ 0722-898138; bluenile@yahoo.com; Argwings Kodhek Rd, Hurlingham; mains KSh500-700) One of those rare places with a character all its own, Blue Nile's quirky lounge, painted with stories from Ethiopian mythology, couldn't be mistaken for anywhere else.

Westlands

Sarit Centre (Map p289; ☎ 020-3747408; www.sarit centre.com; Parklands Rd, Westlands) This huge food court on the 2nd floor of this popular shopping mall has a great variety of small restaurants and fast-food places that cater to discerning pallets.

Haandi Restaurant (Map p289; ☎ 020-4448294; The Mall Shopping Centre, Ring Rd Westlands, Westlands; mains KSh750-1250; ☯ noon-2.30pm & 7-10.30pm; ⊠) An international award-winner that is widely regarded as the best Indian restaurant in Kenya, Haandi has sister restaurants in Kampala, London and Middlesex.

Karen & Langata

Talisman (Map p292; ☎ 020-883213; 320 Ngong Rd; mains KSh800-1400; ☯ from 9am Tue-Sun) This classy café-bar-restaurant is incredibly fashionable with the Karen in-crowd, and rivals any of Kenya's top eateries for imaginative international food.

ourpick Carnivore (Map p287; ☎ 020-605933; www .carnivore.co.ke; off Langata Rd; veg/meat buffet KSh1200/1550) Love it or hate it, Carnivore is hands-down the most famous *nyama choma* restaurant in Kenya, beloved of tourists, expats and wealthier locals alike for the last 25 years. It is also something of an institution for overlanders on the Cape to Cairo circuit, who make the obligatory pilgrimage here for the purpose of consuming copious amounts of chargrilled meat.

Self-Catering

There are very few places to stay with self-catering facilities, but you can buy supplies for snack lunches, safaris etc as well as cook-

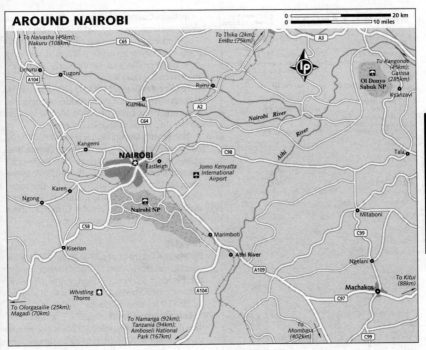

AROUND NAIROBI

KENYA

ing ingredients from the many supermarkets downtown and in the suburbs.

DRINKING

There are plenty of cheap but very rough-and-ready bars in Nairobi, though these places aren't recommended for female travellers, and even male drinkers should probably watch themselves. Even in the 'burbs however, foreign women without a man in tow will draw attention virtually everywhere.

Casablanca (off Map pp282-3; ☎ 020-2723173; Lenana Rd, Hurlingham; ☼ from 6pm) This Moroccan-style lounge-bar has been an instant hit with Nairobi's fastidious expat community, and you don't have to spend much time here to become a convert.

Gypsy's Bar (Map p289; ☎ 020-4440836; Woodvale Grove) This is probably the most popular bar in Westlands, pulling in a healthy and mixed crowd of Kenyans, expats and prostitutes. This is also as close as you'll get to a gay-friendly venue in Kenya, though it's still best to use discretion.

Nairobi Java House (Map pp284-5; ☎ 020-313565; www .nairobijava.com; Mama Ngina St; ☼ 7am-8.30pm Mon-Sat)

This fantastic coffeehouse is rapidly turning itself into a major brand, and aficionados say the coffee's some of the best in Kenya.

Outside Inn (Map p292; ☎ 020-882110; Plains House, Karen Rd) Perfect for a bit of rowdy drinkage, this semiopen barn of a bar is a firm favourite with residents for its relaxed, boozy atmosphere.

ENTERTAINMENT

For information on all entertainment in Nairobi and for big music venues in the rest of the country, get hold of the *Saturday Nation*, which lists everything from cinema releases to live-music venues. There will also be plenty of suggestions run by the magazine *Going Out*.

Nightclubs

New Florida (Map pp284-5; ☎ 020-215014; Koinange St; men/women KSh200/100; ☼ to 6am, later Sat & Sun) The 'Mad House' is a big, rowdy club housed in a bizarre blacked-out saucer building above a petrol station.

Pavement (Map p289; ☎ 020-4441711; Waiyaki Way, Westlands; admission KSh500) Split between a relaxed ground-level bar and the big, modern basement club where the action happens, Pavement is the

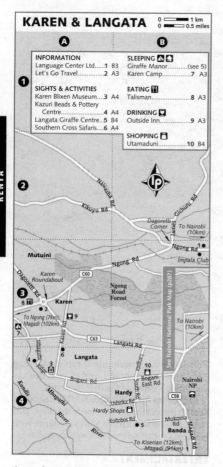

KAREN & LANGATA

INFORMATION	
Language Center Ltd......**1** B3	
Let's Go Travel..............**2** A3	

SIGHTS & ACTIVITIES	
Karen Blixen Museum....**3** A4	
Kazuri Beads & Pottery	
Centre......................**4** A4	
Langata Giraffe Centre...**5** B4	
Southern Cross Safaris....**6** A4	

SLEEPING	
Giraffe Manor.............(see 5)	
Karen Camp.................**7** A3	

EATING	
Talisman....................**8** A3	

DRINKING	
Outside Inn.................**9** A3	

SHOPPING	
Utamaduni.................**10** B4	

dance floor of choice for most resident expats, and isn't as messy as its counterparts in town.

Simba Saloon (Map p287; ☎ 020-501706; off Langata Rd; admission KSh200-300; ☺ Wed-Sun) This huge, partly open-air bar and nightclub pulls in a huge crowd, and pumps out unashamedly Western music on the dance floor.

Simmers (Map pp284-5; ☎ 020-217659; cnr Kenyatta Ave & Muindi Mbingu St; admission free) The atmosphere at this open-air nightclub is invariably amazing, with the ever-enthusiastic crowds turning out to wind and grind the night away.

Cinemas

Nairobi is a good place to take in a few films at a substantially lower price than back home. The best deals are available on Tuesday.

Nu Metro Cinema (off Map pp282-3; ☎ 020-522128; nu metro@swiftkenya.com; Village Market, Gigiri; tickets KSh350) The first entry in a chain of modern multiplexes springing up around Nairobi, showing new Western films fairly promptly after their international release.

Fox Cineplex (Map p289; ☎ 020-227959; Sarit Centre, Parklands Rd, Westlands) A good modern cinema in the same price bracket as Nu Metro, located on the 2nd floor of the Sarit Centre.

20th Century Cinema (Map pp284-5; ☎ 020-210606; 20th Century Plaza, Mama Ngina St), **Kenya Cinema** (Map pp284-5; ☎ 020-227822; Kenya Cinema Plaza, Moi Ave) and **Nairobi Cinema** (Map pp284-5; ☎ 020-338058; Uchumi House, Aga Khan Walk) are all owned by the same chain. The first two show mainly Western movies, while the Nairobi Cinema often screens Christian 'message' films.

Theatre

Professional Centre (Map pp284-5; ☎ 020-225506; www .phoenixplayers.net; Parliament Rd) Local theatre troupe the Phoenix Players perform regularly here. Tickets cost KSh650, though strictly it should be US$20 for nonresidents.

Kenya National Theatre (Map pp284-5; ☎ 020-225174; Harry Thuku Rd; tickets from KSh200) This is the major theatre venue in Nairobi, staging contemporary and classic plays and special events.

For African theatre, the foreign cultural centres (p280) are often the places to head for.

SHOPPING

City Market (Map pp284-5; Muindi Mbingu St) The city's souvenir business is concentrated in this covered market, which has dozens of stalls selling wood carvings, drums, spears, shields, soapstone, Maasai jewellery and clothing.

Gallery Watatu (Map pp284-5; ☎ 228737; Lonhro House, Standard St) If you want fine Kenyan art and/or potential museum pieces, this is a reliable place to make a big purchase.

Maasai Market Central Nairobi (off Map pp284-5; off Slip Rd; ☺ Tue); Gigiri (Village Market, Limuru Rd; ☺ Fri); Yaya Centre (Argwings Kodhek; ☺ Sun) These busy curio markets are held every Tuesday on the waste ground near Slip Rd in town, and Thursday in the rooftop car park at the Village Market shopping complex and Sunday next to the Yaya Centre. The markets are open from early morning to late afternoon – check with your accommodation however as locations and schedules do change.

Spinners Web (Map p289; ☎ 020-4440882; Viking House, Waiyaki Way, Westlands) Works with workshops and self-help groups around the country – it's a bit like a handicrafts version of Ikea, with goods displayed the way they might look in Western living rooms.

Undugu Craft Shop (Map p289; ☎ 020-4443525; Woodvale Grove, Westlands) Another good charitable venture, this nonprofit organisation supports community projects in Nairobi and has very good-quality crafts.

You can also find good quality items from Kazuri Beads & Pottery Centre (p288) and Utamaduni (p286).

GETTING THERE & AWAY
Air
Kenya Airways (Map pp284-5; ☎ 32074100; www.kenya -airways.com; Barclays Plaza, Loita St), the country's principle international and domestic carrier, has a booking office in the city centre, though its website is efficient and reliable.

Airkenya (Map p287; ☎ 020-501601; www.airkenya .com; Wilson Airport, Langata Rd) services domestic airports throughout the country. Like Kenya Airways, it's best to book online, though you can always visit its office at Wilson Airport.

Safarilink (Map p287; ☎ 020-600777; www.safarilink -kenya.com; Wilson Airport, Langata Rd) offers similar services as Airkenya, though it's a much smaller player on the domestic air scene.

Note that fares and frequency of flights vary considerably depending on availability and the season, so it's best to check the internet for current information.

Bus
Most long-distance bus-company offices in Nairobi are in the River Rd area. Numerous companies do the run to Mombasa, leaving in the early morning or late in the evening; the trip takes eight to 10 hours. Buses leave from outside each company's office, and fares cost from KSh400 to KSh700. **Coastline Safaris** (Map pp284-5; ☎ 020-217592; cnr Latema & Lagos Rds) buses are the most comfortable.

Akamba (Map pp284-5; ☎ 020-340430; akamba_prs@ skyweb.co.ke; Lagos Rd) is the biggest private bus company in the country, with an extensive, reliable network. Buses serve Eldoret, Kakamega, Kericho, Kisii, Kisumu, Kitale, Mombasa, Uganda and Tanzania, leaving from Lagos Rd; there's a **booking office** (Map pp284-5; ☎ 020-222027; Wabera St) near City Hall.

The government-owned **Kenya Bus Service** (KBS; ☎ 020-229707) is another large operator. It's cheaper than Akamba, but the buses are much slower. The main depot is on Uyoma St, and there's a **booking office** (Map pp284-5; ☎ 020-341250; cnr Muindi Mbingu & Monrovia Sts) in the city centre.

Easy Coach (Map pp284-5; ☎ 020-210711; easycoach@ wananchi.com; Haile Selassie Ave) is a reliable company serving western Kenyan destinations on the Kisumu/Kakamega route.

The **Country Bus Station** (Map pp284-5; Landhies Rd) is a disorganised place with buses running to Busia, Eldoret, Kakamega, Kisumu, Malaba, Meru, Nakuru, Nanyuki and Nyeri.

Typical fares and durations:

Destination	Fare (KSh)	Duration (hr)
Eldoret	700	6
Kakamega	1250	8
Kisii	800	8
Kisumu	1350	7
Kitale	700	6
Malindi	1100	12
Meru	500	5
Mombasa	800-1300	6-10
Naivasha	150	1 ½
Nakuru	250	3
Nanyuki	400	3
Nyeri	300	2 ½

Matatu
Most *matatus* leave from Latema, Accra, River and Cross Rds, and fares are similar to the buses. The biggest operator here is **Crossland Services** (Map pp284-5; ☎ 020-245377; Cross Rd), which serves destinations including Eldoret, Kisii, Kisumu, Naivasha, Nakuru, Nanyuki and others.

Head to the main bus and *matatu* station on Accra Rd (Map pp284–5) for *matatus* to Chogoria (KSh350, four hours), Embu (KSh300, three hours) and others. *Matatus* leave from Latema Rd for Nyahururu (KSh300, three hours).

There are loads of *matatus* to Naivasha (KSh150, 1½ hours) and the Tanzanian border at Namanga (KSh250, three hours) from the corner of Ronald Ngala St and River Rd (Map pp284–5). For Thika (KSh100, one hour), go to the Total petrol station on Racecourse Rd (Map pp284–5).

Train
Nairobi train station has a small **booking office** (Map pp284-5; Station Rd; ☽ 9am-noon & 2-6.30pm), though don't bother trying to get in touch with them – you need to stop in person to book tickets a few days in advance of your

intended departure. For Mombasa (1st/2nd class US$65/43, 14 to 16 hours), trains leave Nairobi at 7pm on Monday, Wednesday and Friday; arrive early.

GETTING AROUND
To/From Jomo Kenyatta International Airport

Kenya's main **international airport** (Map p287; ☎ 020-827638) is 15km out of town, off the road to Mombasa. There's now a dedicated airport bus run by Metro Shuttle (part of KBS), which can drop you off at hotels in the city centre. Going the other way, the main departure point is across from the Hilton Hotel. The journey takes about 40 minutes and costs US$5 per person. Buses run every half-hour from 8am to 8.30pm daily and stop at both air terminals.

A cheaper way to get into town is city bus 34 (KSh30), but a lot of travellers get ripped off on the bus or when they get off. Always hold onto valuables and have small change ready for the fare. Buses run from 5.45am to 9.30pm weekdays, 6.20am to 9.30pm Saturday and 7.15am to 9.30pm Sunday, though the last few evening services may not operate. Heading to the airport, buses travel west along Kenyatta Ave.

A much safer method (and also your only option at night) is to take a taxi. The asking price is usually about KSh1500 in either direction, but you should be able to bargain down to KSh1000 from town. If you book at one of the 'information' desks at the airport, you'll still end up in a public taxi, but it isn't any more expensive.

To/From Wilson Airport

To get to **Wilson Airport** (Map p287; ☎ 020-501941), for Airkenya services or charter flights, the cheapest option is to take bus or *matatu* 15, 31, 34, 125 or 126 from Moi Ave (KSh20). A taxi from the centre of town will cost you KSh600 to KSh800 depending on the driver. In the other direction, you'll have to bargain the driver down from KSh1000. The entrance to the airport is easy to miss – it's just before the large BP petrol station.

Bus

The ordinary city buses are run by **KBS** (☎ 020-229707) but hopefully you won't need to use them much as they tend to be over-crowded. Forget about them if you're carrying luggage – you'll never get on, and even if you do, you'll never get off! Most buses pass through downtown, but the main KBS terminus is on Uyoma St, east of the centre.

Useful buses include the 46 from Kenyatta Ave for the Yaya Centre in Hurlingham (KSh20), and 23 from Jevanjee Gardens for Westlands (KSh20). There are services about every 20 minutes from 6am to 8pm Monday to Saturday.

Car

If you are driving, beware of wheel-clampers: parking in the centre is by permit only, available from the parking attendants who roam the streets in bright yellow or red jackets. If you park overnight in the street in front of your hotel, the guard will often keep an eye on your vehicle for a small consideration.

Matatu

Nairobi's horde of *matatus* follow the same routes as buses and display the same route numbers. For Westlands, you can pick up the 23 on Moi Ave or Latema Rd. *Matatu* 46 to the Yaya Centre stops in front of the main post office, and the 125 or 126 to Langata leave from in front of the train station. As usual, you should keep an eye on your valuables on all *matatus*.

Taxi

Taxis here are overpriced and undermaintained, but you've little choice, particularly at night. Taxis don't cruise for passengers, but you can find them parked on every other street corner in the city centre – at night they're outside restaurants, bars and nightclubs.

Fares around town are negotiable but end up pretty standard. Any journey within the downtown area costs KSh300, from downtown to Milimani Rd costs KSh400, and for longer journeys such as Westlands or the Yaya Centre fares range from KSh500 to KS650. From the city centre to Karen and Langata is around KSh850 one way.

NAIROBI TO THE COAST

Although this tiny region is straddled by Nairobi and Mombasa, southern Kenya is quite simply safari country par excellence. With the sole exceptions of Masai Mara

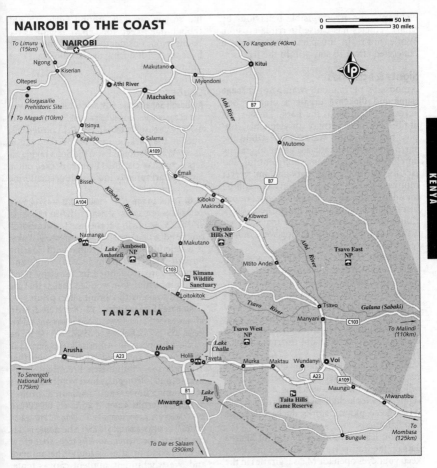

NAIROBI TO THE COAST

KENYA

and Lake Nakuru National Parks, Amboseli and Tsavo rank at the top of Kenya's national park offerings. Along the border with Tanzania, where the slopes of Mt Kilimanjaro meet the Amboseli plains, enormous herds of elephants roam the imperial court of Africa's highest peak. At Tsavo, a national park so massive it's divided into east and west sectors, you can bush camp in some of Kenya's wildest environs.

AMBOSELI NATIONAL PARK

While it may lack the profusion of wildlife found at Masai Mara and Lake Nakuru National Parks, Kenya's third most popular park boasts one of the country's most spectacular backdrops, namely Mt Kilimanjaro.

Africa's highest peak broods over the southern boundary of the park, and while cloud cover can render the mountain's massive bulk invisible for much of the day, you'll be rewarded with some stunning vistas when the weather clears. Amboseli is also prime elephant country; so add this park to your safari itinerary if you want to shoot some pics of these monolithic beasts.

Orientation & Information

At 392 sq km, Amboseli is a small **national park** (☎ 045-622251; www.kws.org/amboseli.html; nonresident adult/child US$40/20, smartcard required), though the landscape provides limited cover for wildlife. The vegetation here used to be much denser, but rising salinity, damage by elephants and irresponsible behaviour by safari vehicles has caused terrible erosion. While you're in the park, please make a concerted effort to stay within the tracks.

Sights & Activities

Amboseli's permanent swamps of **Enkongo Narok** and **Olokenya** create a marshy belt across the middle of the park. These spots are the centre of activity for elephants, hippos, buffaloes and water birds, while the surrounding grasslands are home to grazing antelopes. Spotted hyenas are plentiful, and jackals, warthogs, olive baboons and vervet monkeys can all be seen. Lions can still be found in Amboseli, although the once famous black-maned lions are no longer here. Black rhinos are also absent – the few that survived a sustained period of poaching were moved to Tsavo West in 1995.

Normatior (Observation Hill) provides an ideal lookout from which to orientate yourself to the plains, swamps and roads below. From the top, you can spot hundreds of dots on the plains, typically zebras, gazelles and wildebeests. Amboseli is also well known for its elephant herds, which can be seen raising dust as they cross the plains to drink and feed at the swamps.

From Observation Hill, the northern route runs across the **Sinet Delta**, which is an excellent place for bird-watching. Commonly sighted species include jacanas, herons, egrets, ibises, geese, plovers, storks, ducks, fish eagles and flamingos.

If you leave Amboseli by way of **Kimana Gate** on the way to Tsavo West National Park, keep your eyes open for Maasai giraffes in the acacia woodlands. This is also where you'll find gerenuks, an unusual breed of gazelle that browses by standing on their hind legs and stretching their necks.

Sleeping & Eating

All lodge prices given here are for full board. For nonguests, a buffet lunch at any of the upmarket lodges will cost around US$20 to US$25.

CAMPING

KWS campsite (camping per adult/child US$10/2) Just inside the southern boundary of the park, with toilets, an unreliable water supply (bring your own) and a small bar selling warm beer and soft drinks. It's fenced off from the wildlife, so you can walk around safely at night, though *don't* keep food in your tent as baboons (who consider themselves unrestricted by fences) visit during the day looking for an uninvited feed.

LODGES

Amboseli Sopa Lodge (☎ Nairobi 020-3750460; www .sopalodges.com/amboseli/home.html; s/d low season US$71/142, high season US$142/198; ⚑) Located just outside the park boundaries on the road to Tsavo West National Park, the Sopa Lodge offers a clutch of clay huts that are decked out in lavish safari spreads and a healthy smattering of Kenyan curios.

Ol Tukai Lodge (☎ Nairobi 020-4445514; www .oltukailodge.com; s/d low season US$150/180, high season US$210/255; ⚑) Lying at the heart of Amboseli on the edge of a dense acacia forest, Ol Tukai is a splendidly refined lodge with soaring *makuti* (thatched palm-leaved) roofs and tranquil gardens defined by towering trees. Accommodation is in wooden chalets that are brought to life with vibrant safari prints.

Amboseli Serena Lodge (☎ Nairobi 020-2710511; www.serenahotels.com/kenya/amboseli/home.asp; s/d low season US$155/255, high season US$285/385; ⚑) The poshest property in Amboseli, the Serena is comprised of fiery-red adobe cottages that overlook the wildlife-rich Enkongo Narok swamp, and is fringed by lush tropical gardens of blooming flowers and manicured shrubs.

our pick **Tortilis Camp** (☎ Nairobi 020-604053; www.chelipeacock.com/camps/tortilis.htm; s/d low season US$468/740, high season US$516/858) The name is derived from the *Acacia tortilis* trees that grow in thick concentrations around the intimate and overwhelmingly opulent canvas tents. Lavish meals, which are based on North Italian traditional recipes from the owner's family cookbook, feature herbs and veg from the huge on-site organic garden. And, just so you don't feel guilty about leaving behind an ecological footprint, take comfort in the fact that everything is cooked without firewood, and solar power is used exclusively to heat the water.

Getting There & Away

AIR

Airkenya (www.airkenya.com) has daily flights (around US$175) between Wilson Airport in Nairobi and Amboseli. You'll need to arrange with one of the lodges or a safari company for a vehicle to meet you at the airstrip.

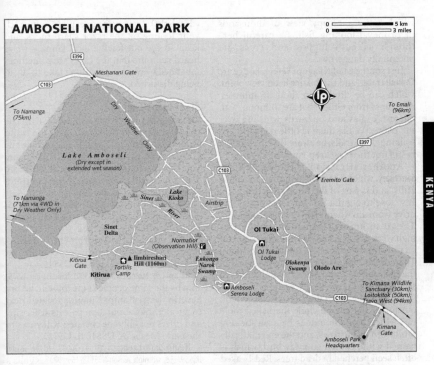

AMBOSELI NATIONAL PARK

CAR & 4WD

The usual approach to Amboseli is via Namanga. The road is sealed and in surprisingly good condition from Nairobi to Namanga – the 75km dirt road to the Meshanani Gate is pretty rough but passable (allow around four hours from Nairobi). In the dry season it's also possible to enter through Kitirua Gate, but this is a bumpy old road and it's hard to follow. The track branches right off the main Amboseli road after about 15km. Some people also enter from the east via the Amboseli–Tsavo West road, although this track is in bad shape, and shouldn't be considered in a conventional vehicle.

During the 1990s there were bandit attacks in this area, so vehicles have to travel together, accompanied by armed guards. Convoys leave from the Tsavo turnoff near the Sopa Lodge at scheduled times – inquire at your lodge as times change frequently. Allow approximately 2½ hours to cover the 94km from Amboseli to the Chyulu Gate at Tsavo West.

Self-drivers will need a 4WD to make the most of the park. Petrol is available at the Serena and Sopa Lodges.

TSAVO WEST NATIONAL PARK

Tsavo West covers a huge variety of landscapes, from swamps, natural springs and rocky peaks to extinct volcanic cones, rolling plains and sharp outcrops dusted with greenery. But for all of its diversity, Tsavo West is not a park where you will see animals constantly. Indeed, much of its appeal lies in its dramatic scenery and sense of space. If possible, come here with some time to spare, rather than a need to dash about and tick off animals.

Orientation & Information

For the complete rundown on useful information about Tsavo West, see the boxed text, p299.

Sights & Activities

The focus of Tsavo West is undoubtedly **Mzima Springs**, which produces an incredible 350 million litres of fresh water a day. The springs are the source of the bulk of Mombasa's fresh water, and you can walk down to a large pool that is a favourite haunt of hippos and crocodiles. There's an underwater viewing chamber, which gives a creepy view of thousands of primeval-looking fish. Be careful here though as both hippos and crocs are potentially dangerous.

Just southeast of Kilaguni Serena Lodge are **Chaimu Crater**, and the **Roaring Rocks** viewpoint, which can be climbed in about 15 minutes. The views from either spot are stunning, with falcons, eagles and buzzards whirling over the plains. While there is little danger when walking these trails, be aware that the wildlife is still out there, so keep your eyes open.

Another attraction is the **Ngulia Rhino Sanctuary**, which is located at the base of Ngulia Hills, and is part of the Rhino Ark program. It's close to Ngulia Safari Lodge, but a long drive from anywhere else – with good reason. The 70-sq-km area is surrounded by a 1m-high electric fence, and provides a measure of security for the park's last 50-odd black rhinos. There are driving tracks and waterholes within the enclosed area, and there's a good chance of seeing one of these elusive creatures.

Some of the more unusual species to look out for in the park include the naked mole rat, which can sometimes be seen kicking sand from its burrows, and the enigmatically named white-bellied go-away bird, which is often seen perched in dead trees. Red-beaked hornbills and bateleur eagles are also common. Look out for dung beetles rolling huge balls of elephant poo along the tracks.

It's possible to go **rock climbing** at Tembo Peak and the Ngulia Hills, but you'll need to arrange this in advance with the **park warden** (☎ 043-622483). This area is also fantastic for birdlife, and there's a very reliable hippo pool on the Mukui River, near the Ngulia Safari Lodge.

Lake Jipe (ji-*pay*), at the southwest end of the park, is reached by a desperately dusty track from near Taveta. You can hire boats at the campsite to take you hippo- and crocodile-spotting on the lake (US$5). Huge herds of elephants come to the lake to drink, and large flocks of migratory birds stop here from February to May.

About 4km west of the Chyulu Gate of Tsavo West National Park, on the road to Amboseli, is the spectacular **Shetani lava flow**. This vast expanse of folded black lava spreads for 50 sq km across the savannah at the foot of the Chyulu Hills, looking strangely as if Vesuvius dropped its comfort blanket here.

Nearby are the **Shetani Caves**, which are also a result of volcanic activity. You'll need a torch

(flashlight) if you want to explore, but watch your footing on the razor-sharp rocks, and keep an eye out for the local fauna – we've heard rumours that the caves are sometimes inhabited by hyenas, who don't take kindly to being disturbed.

Sleeping & Eating

KWS campsites (camping per adult/child US$10/5) The public sites are at Komboyo, near the Mtito Andei Gate, and at Chyulu, just outside the Chyulu Gate. Facilities are basic, so make sure you're prepared to be self-sufficient. There are also some small independently run campsites along the shores of Lake Jipa.

Ngulia (☎ Voi 043-30050; bandas from US$55) This hillside camp is Tsavo's best luxury bargain, offering thatched stone cottages on the edge of the escarpment overlooking a stream where leopards are known to hide out. Meals are US$10 to US$15.

Kitani (☎ Mombasa 041-5485001; bandas from US$75) Run by the same people as the top-end luxury Severin Safari Camp, Kitani is located next to a waterhole, about 2km past its sister site, and offers possibly the cheapest Kili views in the park. Meals are US$10 to US$15.

Ngulia Safari Lodge (☎ 043-30000; s/d low season US$59/118, s/d high season US$118/165; ☒) Ngulia's more upmarket offering is a curiously unattractive block in a spectacular location. The surrounding Ngulia Hills attract loads of birds, and there's a waterhole right by the restaurant with sweeping views over the Ngulia Rhino Sanctuary on the other side.

Severin Safari Camp (☎ Mombasa 041-5485001; www.severin-kenya.com; s/d low season US$78/156, high season US$159/224) This is a fantastic complex of thatched luxury tents with affable staff, Kilimanjaro views from the communal lounge area and nightly hippo visitations. Room facilities are surprisingly luxurious (you even get a bidet!) given that it's much cheaper than some of Tsavo's more opulent spots.

Kilaguni Serena Lodge (☎ 045-340000; www.serena hotels.com; s/d/ste low season US$115/225/575, high season US$320/435/700; ☐ ☒) The centrepiece here is a splendid bar and restaurant overlooking a busy illuminated waterhole – the vista stretches all the way from Mt Kilimanjaro to the Chyulu Hills. The extravagant suites are practically cottages in their own right, boasting chintzy living rooms and epic balconies.

Finch Hatton's Safari Camp (☎ Nairobi 020-553237; www.finchhattons.com; s/d/tr low season US$315/415, high

EXPLORING TSAVO NATIONAL PARK

At nearly 21,000 sq km, **Tsavo National Park** is by far the largest national park in Kenya. For administrative and practical purposes, it has been split into **Tsavo West National Park** (9000 sq km) and **Tsavo East National Park** (11,747 sq km), divided by the Nairobi–Mombasa road (A109).

Both parks feature some excellent scenery, but the undergrowth here is considerably higher than in Amboseli or Masai Mara National Parks, so it takes a little more effort to spot the wildlife, particularly the big predators. The compensation for this is that the landscapes are some of the most dramatic in Kenya, the animals are that little bit wilder, and the parks receive comparatively few visitors comparedwith the hordes who descend on Amboseli and the Mara.

The northern half of Tsavo West is the most developed, with a number of excellent lodges, as well as several places where you can get out of your vehicle and walk. The landscape is also striking, and is largely comprised of volcanic hills and sweeping expanses of savannah. The southern part of the park, on the far side of the dirt road between Voi and Taveta on the Tanzanian border, is rarely visited.

Tsavo East is more remote, though most of the action here is concentrated along the Galana River – the north part of the park isn't truly secure due to the threat of banditry. The landscape here is drier, with rolling plains hugging the edge of the Yatta Escarpment, a vast prehistoric lava flow.

Entry is US$40/20 per adult/child per day, and camping is US$10 per adult; as the two parks are administered separately you have to pay separate entrance fees for each. Both use the smartcard system – you'll need enough credit for your entry fee and any camping charges for as long as you're staying. Smartcards can be bought and recharged at the Voi Gate to Tsavo East.

There's a small **visitor centre** (admission free; 8am-5pm) near the Mtito Andei Gate to Tsavo West, with interesting displays on conservation issues and some of the animals and birds in the park.

All the track junctions in Tsavo East and Tsavo West have numbered and signposted cairns, which in theory makes navigation fairly simple. In practice, some signposts are missing, and the numbering system is often confusing, so a map is helpful.

---

season US$355/585;) This upmarket tented camp, which is distinguished by its signature bone china and gold shower taps (guests are requested to dress for dinner), was named after Denys Finch Hatton, the playboy hunter and lover of Karen Blixen, who died at Tsavo, and was known for his obsession with maintaining civility in the middle of the bush.

Getting There & Away

The main access to Tsavo West is through the Mtito Andei Gate on the Mombasa–Nairobi road in the north of the park, where you'll find the park headquarters and visitor centre. The main track cuts straight across to Kilaguni Serena Lodge and Chyulu Gate. Security is a problem here, so vehicles for Amboseli travel in armed convoys, leaving Kilaguni Serena Lodge at 8am and 10am.

Another 48km southeast along the main road is the Tsavo Gate – it is handy for the Ngulia Hills lodges and the rhino sanctuary. Few people use the Maktau Gate on the Voi–Taveta road in the south of the park.

The tracks here are only really suitable for 4WDs, and the roads in the south of the park are particularly challenging.

TSAVO EAST NATIONAL PARK

Despite the fact that one of Kenya's largest rivers flows through the middle of the park, the landscape in Tsavo East is markedly flatter and predominantly drier than in Tsavo West. However, the contrast between the permanent greenery of the river and the endless grasses and thorn trees that characterize much of the park is visually arresting. In comparison with its more developed brother, Tsavo East doesn't see as many visitors, though it has an undeniable wild and primordial charm. The park is also home to some enormous elephant herds, particularly near the Voi Gate, as well as the rare but striking melanistic (black) servals.

Orientation & Information

For the complete rundown on exploring Tsavo East, see the boxed text, above.

lonelyplanet.com

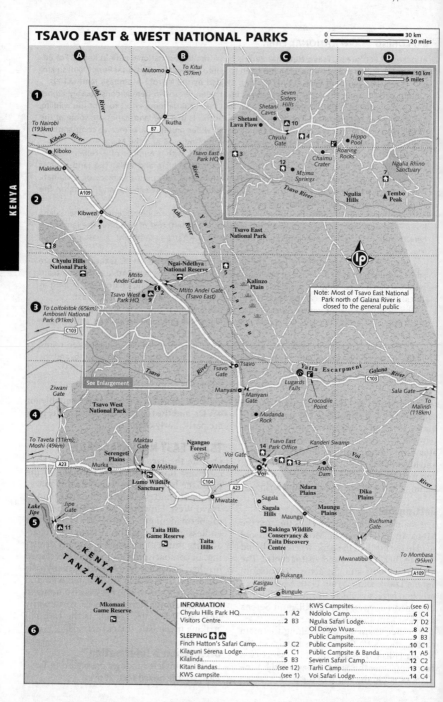

TSAVO EAST & WEST NATIONAL PARKS

Note: Most of Tsavo East National Park north of Galana River is closed to the general public

Sights & Activities

Much of the wildlife is concentrated on the **Galana River**, which cuts a green gash across the dusty plains of the park, and supports plentiful numbers of crocs, hippos, kudus, waterbucks and dik-diks. There are several places along the flat-topped escarpments lining the river where you can get out of your vehicle (with due caution of course). Most scenic are **Lugards Falls**, a wonderful landscape of water-sculpted channels, and **Crocodile Point**, where you may see abundant numbers of crocs and hippos.

Towering over a natural dam near the Manyani Gate is **Mudanda Rock**, which attracts elephants in the dry season, and is somewhat reminiscent of Uluru (Ayers Rock) in Australia.

The rolling hills in the south of the park are also home to large herds of elephants, usually covered in thick coats of orange dust (to keep their skin cool and prevent insect bites). The action is concentrated around the waterhole at Voi Safari Lodge, **Kanderi Swamp** and the public campsite.

Further into the park, about 30km east of Voi Gate, is the **Aruba Dam**, which spans the Voi River and attracts heavy concentrations of diverse wildlife.

The area north of the Galana River is dominated by the **Yatta Escarpment**, a vast prehistoric lava flow. However, much of this area is off limits because of the ongoing campaign against poachers.

Until their partial translocation to Tsavo East, the sole surviving population of **hirola antelopes** was found near the Kenya–Somalia border in the south Tana River and Garissa districts. Intense poaching (for meat) and habitat destruction have reduced their numbers from an estimated 14,000 in 1976 to a pitiful 450 today. At the time of writing, there were approximately 100 left within the park confines.

Sleeping & Eating

Ndololo Camp (camping US$10) There's a single public camping area with basic facilities near Kanderi Swamp. Note that elephants wander through here frequently, so be extremely aware of your surroundings.

Tarhi Camp (☎ Mombasa 041-5486378; www .camp-tarhi.de in German; s/d half board US$65/120) This German-run campsite, located on the edge of the Voi River about 14km east of Voi Gate,

is a good compromise between bare-bones camping and over-the-top luxury. It's a lovely, peaceful spot, and the rates include proper Deutschland-inspired meals and wildlife walks with a Maasai guide.

Voi Safari Lodge (☎ Mombasa 041-471861; s/d low season US$88/115, high season US$118/165; ▣) Just 4km from Voi Gate, Voi is a long, low complex perched on the edge of an escarpment overlooking an incredible sweep of savannah. There is an attractive rock-cut swimming pool, as well as a natural waterhole that attracts elephants, buffaloes and the occasional predator.

Kilalinda (☎ Nairobi 020-882598; www.privatewilderness .com; s/d low season US$350/550, high season US$400/650; ▣) Proof that even top-end resorts can take environmental issues seriously – this very fine ecolodge was built without felling a single tree, and the owners are spearheading a campaign to reintroduce wildlife to areas that were depleted by poachers in previous decades.

Getting There & Away

The main track through the park follows the Galana River from the Tsavo Gate to the Sala Gate. Most tourist safaris enter Tsavo East via the Sala Gate, where a good dirt road runs east for 110km to the coast. If you're coming from Nairobi, the Voi Gate (near the town of the same name) and the Manyani Gate (on the Nairobi–Mombasa road) are just as accessible.

Roads within the park are decidedly rough, and a 4WD with decent ground clearance is recommended. Expect longish journey times however you're travelling.

CHYULU HILLS NATIONAL PARK

Just northwest of Tsavo West National Park are the dramatic **Chyulu Hills** (adult/child US$15/5), a collection of ancient volcanic cinder cones and eloboarate underground caverns. The hills were gazetted as a national park in 1983, and have splendid views of Mt Kilimanjaro, as well as thriving populations of elands, giraffes, zebras and wildebeests, plus a small number of elephants, lions and buffaloes.

Within the Chyulu Hills is the aptly named **Leviathan**, believed to be the longest lava tube in the world, which was formed by hot lava flowing beneath a cooled crust. You'll need full caving equipment to explore it, and perhaps a bit of prior experience spelunking in claustrophobic conditions – caving and trekking trips in the hills are possible with

KENYA

MAN-EATERS OF TSAVO

Wild felines the world over are rightfully feared and respected, though the famed 'man-eaters of Tsavo' were probably the most dangerous lions to have ever roamed the planet. During the building of the Kenya–Uganda Railway in 1898, Engineer Lieutenant Colonel John Henry Patterson led the construction of a railway bridge over the Tsavo River in Kenya. However, efforts soon came to a halt when railway workers started being dragged from their tents at night, and devoured by two maneless male lions.

The surviving workers soon decided that the lions had to be ghosts or devils, which put the future of the railway in jeopardy. This drove Patterson to create a series of ever more ingenious traps, though each time the lions evaded them, striking unerringly at weak points in the camp defences. Patterson was finally able to bag the first man-eater by hiding on a flimsy wooden scaffold baited with the corpse of a donkey. The second one was dispatched a short time later, although it took six bullets to bring the massive beast down.

According to Patterson's calculations, the two lions killed and ate around 135 workers in less than one year. He detailed his experiences in the best-selling book, *The Man-Eaters of Tsavo* (1907), which was later rather freely filmed as *Bwana Devil* (1952) and *The Ghost and the Darkness* (1996).

In an ironic display of revenge, Patterson turned the two man-eaters into floor rugs, which he kept for more than a quarter of a century. In 1924 however, he finally rid himself of the lions by selling their skins to the Chicago Field Museum for the sum of US$5000. The man-eaters of Tsavo were then stuffed and placed on permanent display, where they remain to this very day.

To date, scientists have offered up a number of hypotheses to explain the ferocious behaviour of the man-eaters. Research has shown that Tsavo lions have noticeably elevated levels of the male sex hormone testosterone, which could have been responsible for their hair loss and increased territorial behaviour. The pair themselves had badly damaged teeth, which may have driven them to abandon their normal prey and become man-eaters.

It has also been suggested by historians that an outbreak of rinderpest might have decimated the lions' usual prey, forcing them to find alternative food sources. Alternatively, the man-eaters may have developed their taste for human flesh after growing accustomed to finding corpses buried in shallow graves at the Tsavo River crossing, where slave caravans often crossed en route to Zanzibar and the Middle East.

While the descendants of Tsavo's man-eaters aren't quite the indiscriminate killing machines that their forbearers were, they still do have a reputation for ferocity, and are much more wild than the lazy kitty-cats you come across in the Mara. On that note, be aware of your surroundings, sleep in closed campsites, and give Mother Nature's predators a healthy amount of respect and distance.

Savage Wilderness Safaris Ltd (Map p289; ☎ Nairobi 020-2521590; www.whitewaterkenya.com; Sarit Centre, Parklands Rd, Westlands).

The park headquarters are 1.3km inside the northwest gate, not far from Kibwezi on the Nairobi–Mombasa road. For the time being, the best access is on the west side of the park, from the track between Amboseli and Tsavo West. Note that the track into the hills from the headquarters is extremely tough going, so you're going to need a durable 4WD vehicle to attempt this route.

If you're completely self-sufficient, you can spend the night at the extremely basic but perfectly functional **KWS campsite** (camping per adult/child US$10/2), located near the park headquarters.

If you're travelling with a decidedly larger budget, **Ol Donyo Wuas** (Map p300; ☎ Nairobi 020-600457; www.richardbonhamsafaris.com; s/d from US$590/970; 🖃) is a well-established ecolodge that was constructed entirely of local materials, and employs advanced water-recycling and solar-power systems. While guests are treated to paramount luxury, the real highlights of this property are the wildlife drives and horse-riding excursions in the national park.

Until the road from Kibwezi is brought up to standard, your best bet to get here is the dirt track that branches off the Amboseli–Tsavo West road about 10km west of Chyulu Gate. Ol Donyo Wuas can be reached via this track, although most guests fly in on air charters from Nairobi. The park headquarters is signposted just outside Kibwezi, about 41km northwest of Mtito Andei on the main Nairobi–Mombasa road.

VOI
☎ 043

Voi is a key service town at the intersection of the Nairobi–Mombasa road, the road to Moshi in Tanzania and the access road to the Voi Gate of Tsavo East National Park. While there is little reason to spend any more time here than is needed to get directions, fill up on petrol and buy some snacks for the road, you'll inevitably pass through here at some point.

If you need to bed down for the night, and don't want to spend another night in Tsavo East, the centrally located **Tsavo Park Hotel** (☎ 043-30050; s/d from US$35/45) is probably the best option in town. However it's very much a spartan affair that isn't very inspiring, though it is a good place to stop for a hot meal if you want to break up the driving.

From Voi, frequent buses and *matatus* run to Mombasa (KSh400, three hours), and buses to Nairobi (KSh500 to KSh800, six hours) pass through town, usually in the morning and in the late evening. There are daily *matatus* to Wundanyi (KSh150, one hour) and Taveta (KSh300, two hours), on the Tanzanian border.

THE COAST

There's something in the air here.

It's not just the salt that fades the streets and sidings of the buildings of Mombasa, *Kisiwa Cha Mvita,* The Island of War. Or the smell of sweat, spice and petrol leaking from a Zanzibar-bound cargo ship. Or the sun's glint off coral castles, ribbons of white sand and the teal break of a vanishing wave.

It enriches the shade cast by thick copses of coconut and banana plantations, their dark recesses concealing the sacred forests of the Nine Homesteads. It amplifies the power of muttered chants echoing over the flagstones of a Jain temple, and the ecstatic passion of the Call to Prayer pushing a full moon behind the Indian Ocean.

This is the romance of Kenya's coast: one of the great entrepôts of Africa, a land as notable for its history as its pure salt breezes. As different as it may feel from the interior, this region is still Kenyan; the word Swahili comes from the Arab *Sawahil* (coast). Yet the sea is also, undeniably, separated from the centre. The interplay of Africa, India and Arabia impacted this region hundreds of years before European colonization and Bantu migration. A distinctive Indian Ocean society evolved here, built on trade, notably of slaves, intermarriage, Arabian poetry, Gujarati sweet stalls, Portuguese castles and Mijikenda tree-tending.

This interlaying and interlacing of cultures is exemplified by the Swahili themselves, one of the most distinctively 'blended' ethnicities in Africa. The coast is their beautiful homeland, a land of sugar-powder beaches and a city the poets have embraced for as long as ivory has been traded for iron. When you arrive, know that you won't be the first visitor in these parts, and be warned: that first trip here is never the last.

HISTORY
The Swahili culture of the coast was a product of trade, initiated by Persian and Arab merchants, who used the monsoon winds to reach African shores and quickly established trading posts. By the 9th century a series of fully fledged city-states had spread out along the coast from Somalia to Mozambique, and the first African slaves began to appear in Arabia.

Intermarriage between Arabs and Africans gradually created the Swahili race, language and culture, and established some powerful dynasties. In the early 16th century the Portuguese swanned over the horizon, attracted by the wealth and determined to end the Arab trade monopoly.

It's fashionable to portray the Portuguese as the bad guys, but the sultans of Oman, who defeated them in 1698, were no more popular with the locals. Despite their shared faith, the Swahilis staged countless rebellions, even passing Mombasa into British hands from 1824 to 1826 to keep it from the sultans. Things only really quietened down after Sultan Seyyid Said moved his capital to Zanzibar in 1832.

Said's huge coastal clove plantations created a massive need for labour, and the slave caravans of the 19th century marked the peak of the trade in human cargo. News of massacres and human rights abuses soon reached Europe, galvanising the British public to demand an end to slavery. Through a mixture of political savvy and implied force, the British

KENYA

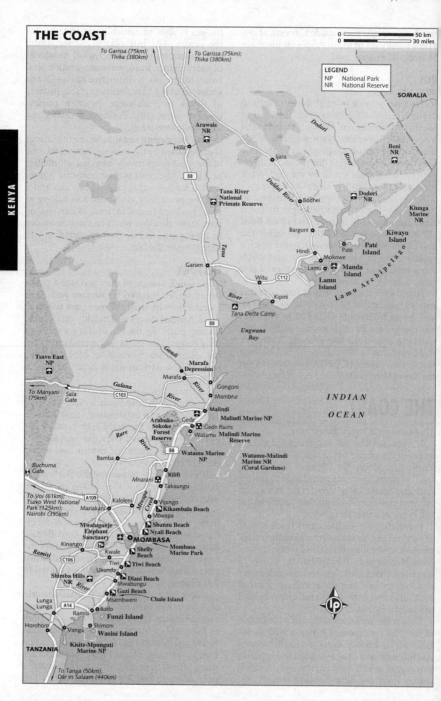

THE COAST

| 0 | 50 km |
| 0 | 30 miles |

LEGEND
NP   National Park
NR   National Reserve

KENYA

SOMALIA

To Garissa (75km);
Thika (380km)

To Garissa (75km);
Thika (380km)

Arawale NR

Hola

Ijara

Dodori River

Boni NR

B8

Tana River National Primate Reserve

Bodhei

Dodori NR

Duddul River

Kiunga Marine NR

Bargoni

Kiwayu Island

Tana River

Hindi

Paté

Paté Island

Lamu Archipelago

Garsen

Witu

C112

Mokowe

Lamu

Manda Island

Lamu Island

Kipini

River

Tana Delta Camp

Ungwana Bay

Tsavo East NP

Gandi

Marafa Depression

INDIAN

To Manyani (75km)

Galana

C103

Sala Gate

River

Marafa

Gongoni

Mambrui

OCEAN

Rare

River

Arabuko Sokoke Forest Reserve

Gede

Malindi

Malindi Marine NP

Gede Ruins

Watamu   Malindi Marine Reserve

Bamba

B8

Watamu Marine NP

Watamu-Malindi Marine NR (Coral Gardens)

Buchuma Gate

Mnarani

Kilifi

Takaungu

To Voi (61km);
Tsavo West National Park (125km);
Nairobi (395km)

A109

Kaloleni

Vipingo

Kikambala Beach

Mariakani

Mtwapa

Shanzu Beach

Mwaluganje Elephant Sanctuary

Nyali Beach

Kinango

MOMBASA

Ramisi

C106

Kwale

Shelly Beach

Mombasa Marine Park

Tiwi

Tiwi Beach

Shimba Hills NR

Ukunda

Diani Beach

River

Mwabungu

Gazi Beach

Lunga Lunga

A14

Msambweni

Chale Island

Ramisi

Bodo

Horohoro

Shimoni

Funzi Island

Vanga

Wasini Island

TANZANIA

Kisite-Mpunguti Marine NP

To Tanga (50km);
Dar es Salaam (440km)

government was eventually able to pressure Said's son Barghash to ban the slave trade.

Of course, this 'reform' didn't hurt British interests: as part of the treaty, the British East Africa Company took over administration of the Kenyan interior. A 16km-wide coastal strip was recognised as the territory of the sultan and was leased by the British from 1887. Upon independence in 1963, the last sultan of Zanzibar gifted the land to the new Kenyan government.

Today the coast province remains culturally and socially distinct from the rest of the country, still heavily influenced by its Swahili past. Indians are the largest minority, descendants of railway labourers and engineers brought here by the British, and the population as a whole is predominantly Muslim.

MOMBASA
☎ 041 / pop 880,000

Mombasa, like the coast it dominates, is both quintessentially African and somehow…not.

If your idea of Africa is roast meat, toasted maize, beer and cattle and farms and friendliness, those things are here (well, maybe not the cows). But it's all interwoven into the humid peel of plaster from Hindu warehouses, filigreed porches that lost their way from a Moroccan *riyad,* spice markets that escaped India's Keralan coast, sailors chewing *miraa* (twigs and shoots that are chewed as a stimulant) next to boats bound for the Yemeni Hadramat and a giant coral castle built by invading Portuguese sailors. Thus, while this city sits perfectly at home in Africa, it could be plopped anywhere on the coast of the Indian Ocean without too many moving pains.

Therein lies Mombasa's considerable charm. But said seduction doesn't hide this town's warts, which includes a sleazy underbelly, bad traffic and ethnic tension; the latter ebbs and flows and is smoothed by the unifying faith of Islam, but it's not entirely sublimated. Overlaying everything is the sweating, tropical lunacy you tend to get in the world's hot zones (and it gets *hot* here). But what would you expect from East Africa's largest port? Cities by the docks always attract mad characters, and Mombasa's come from all over the world.

History

Mombasa has always been at the centre of the coast's key events, a crucial stronghold for local and invading powers ever since the Arab-Swahili Mazrui clan emerged as one of the most powerful families in 9th-century East Africa.

The first Portuguese forays into Arab territory took place here in 1505, when Dom Francisco de Almeida arrived with a huge armada and levelled the city in just 1½ days. The plundered remains were soon rebuilt, but in 1528 Lisbon struck again as Nuña da Cunha captured the city, first by diplomacy (offering to act as an ally in Mombasa's disputes with Malindi, Pemba and Zanzibar) and then by force. Once again Mombasa was burned to the ground while the invaders sailed on to India.

The Portuguese made a bid for permanency in 1593 with the construction of Fort Jesus, but the hefty structure quickly became a symbolic target for rebel leaders and was besieged incessantly. During the 17th and 18th centuries Mombasa changed hands dozens of times before the Portuguese finally gave up their claim to the coast in 1729.

Waiting to step into the power vacuum were the sultans of Oman, who had defeated the Europeans and occupied Fort Jesus after an incredible 33-month siege in 1698. The city remained in their control up until the 1870s, when British intervention ended the slave trade and gained for the Empire a foothold in East Africa.

Mombasa subsequently became the railhead for the Uganda Railway and the most important city in British East Africa. In 1920, when Kenya became a fully fledged British colony, Mombasa was made capital of the separate British Coast Protectorate.

Today the cut and thrust of politics and power play largely passes Mombasa by, but it's still Kenya's second city and a crucial social barometer for the coast province as a whole.

Orientation

The main thoroughfare in Mombasa is Digo Rd and its southern extension Nyerere Ave, which run north–south through the city. The ferry to Likoni and the south coast leaves from the southern end of Nyerere Ave.

Running west from the junction between Nyerere Ave and Digo Rd is Moi Ave, where you'll find the tourist office and the famous sculpted 'tusks', two huge pairs of aluminium elephant tusks forming an M over the road, which were erected to mark a visit by British

KENYA

royal Princess Margaret in 1956. Heading east from the junction, Nkrumah Rd has the easiest access to the Old Town and Fort Jesus.

North of the city centre, Digo Rd becomes Abdel Nasser Rd, where you'll find many of the bus stands for Nairobi and destinations north along the coast. There's another big group of bus offices west of here at the intersection of Jomo Kenyatta Ave and Mwembe Tayari Rd. The train station is at the intersection of Mwembe Tayari and Haile Selassie Rds.

Information

BOOKSHOPS
Bahati Book Centre (Map p308; ☎ 041-225010; Moi Ave)
Books First (Map p307; ☎ 041-313482; Nakumatt, Nyerere Ave; 🖳)

EMERGENCY
AAR Health Services (☎ 041-312409; 🕑 24hr)
Police (☎ 041-222121, 999)

INTERNET ACCESS
Blue Room (Map p308; ☎ 041-224021; www .blueroomonline.com; Haile Selassie Rd; per min KSh2; 🕑 9am-10pm)

KENYA WILDLIFE SERVICE
KWS office (Map p307; ☎ 041-312744/5; Nguua Court, Mama Ngina Dr; 🕑 6am-6pm) Sells and charges smartcards.

MEDICAL SERVICES
All services and medication must be paid for up-front, so have travel insurance details handy.
Aga Khan Hospital (Map p307; ☎ 041-312953; akhm@mba.akhmkenya.org; Vanga Rd; 🕑 24hr)
Pandya Memorial Hospital (Map p307; ☎ 041-229252; Kimathi Ave; 🕑 24hr)

MONEY
Barclays Bank Digo Rd (Map p308; ☎ 041-311660); Nkrumah Rd (Map p308; ☎ 041-224573)
Fort Jesus Forex Bureau (Map p307; ☎ 041-316717; Ndia Kuu Rd)
Kenya Commercial Bank Moi Ave (Map p308; ☎ 041-220978); Nkrumah Rd (Map p307; ☎ 041-312523)
Pwani Forex Bureau (Map p308; ☎ 041-221727; Digo Rd)
Standard Chartered Bank (Map p307; ☎ 041-224614; Treasury Sq, Nkrumah Rd)

POST
Post office (Map p308; ☎ 041-227705; Digo Rd)

TELEPHONE
Post Global Services (Map p308; ☎ 041-230581; inglobal@africaonline.co.ke; Maungano Rd; 🕑 7.30am-8pm; 🖳)
Telkom Kenya (Map p308; ☎ 041-312811)

TOURIST INFORMATION
Mombasa & Coast Tourist Office (Map p308; ☎ 041-225428; mcta@ikenya.com; Moi Ave; 🕑 8am-4.30pm)

TRAVEL AGENCIES
Dial-A-Tour (Map p307; ☎ 041-221411; dialatour@ ikenya.com; Oriental Bldg, Nkrumah Rd)
Fourways Travel (Map p308; ☎ 041-223344; Moi Ave)

VISA EXTENSIONS
Immigration office (Map p307; ☎ 041-311745; Uhuru ni Kari Bldg, Mama Ngina Dr)

Dangers & Annoyances

Mombasa is relatively safe compared with Nairobi, but the streets still clear pretty rapidly after dark so it's a good idea to take taxis rather than walk around alone at night. You need to be more careful on the beaches north and south of town. The Likoni ferry is a bag-snatching hot spot.

Visitors should also be aware of anti-Western sentiment among some Kenyan Muslims: hostile graffiti and Osama Bin Laden T-shirts abound, and demonstrations against Israel and America are increasingly common. Keep a low profile during any escalation of violence in the Middle East or terrorist activity in the West.

Malaria is a big risk on the coast, so remember to take your antimalarial drugs (see p630).

Sights & Activities
FORT JESUS

Mombasa's biggest tourist attraction dominates the harbour entrance at the end of Nkrumah Rd. The metre-thick coral walls make it an imposing edifice, despite being partially ruined. The fort was built by the Portuguese in 1593 to enforce their rule over the coastal Swahilis, but they rarely managed to hold onto it for long. It changed hands at least nine times in bloody sieges between 1631 and 1875, finally falling under British control.

The fort was the final project completed by Italian architect Joao Batista Cairato in his long career as Chief Architect for Portugal's eastern colonies. There are some ingenious elements in

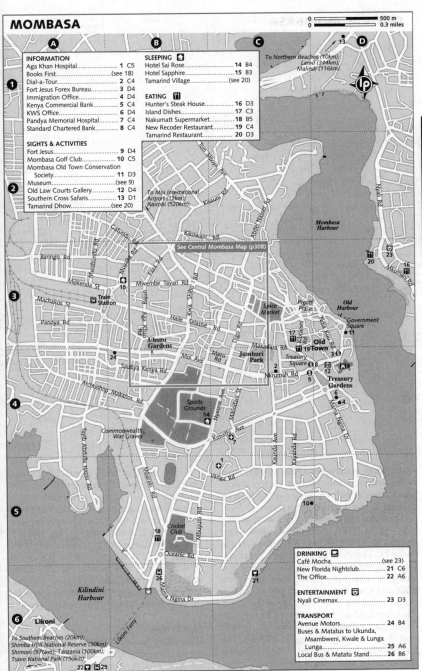

MOMBASA

0 — 500 m
0 — 0.3 miles

INFORMATION
Aga Khan Hospital...................... 1 C5
Books First............................(see 18)
Dial-a-Tour.............................. 2 C4
Fort Jesus Forex Bureau............... 3 D4
Immigration Office..................... 4 D4
Kenya Commercial Bank................ 5 C4
KWS Office.............................. 6 D4
Pandya Memorial Hospital............. 7 C4
Standard Chartered Bank.............. 8 C4

SIGHTS & ACTIVITIES
Fort Jesus............................... 9 D4
Mombasa Golf Club.................... 10 C5
Mombasa Old Town Conservation
  Society............................... 11 D3
Museum...............................(see 9)
Old Law Courts Gallery................ 12 D4
Southern Cross Safaris................ 13 D1
Tamarind Dhow......................(see 20)

SLEEPING
Hotel Sai Rose......................... 14 B4
Hotel Sapphire......................... 15 B3
Tamarind Village....................(see 20)

EATING
Hunter's Steak House.................. 16 D3
Island Dishes........................... 17 C3
Nakumatt Supermarket................ 18 B5
New Recoder Restaurant.............. 19 C4
Tamarind Restaurant.................. 20 D3

DRINKING
Café Mocha..........................(see 23)
New Florida Nightclub................ 21 C6
The Office.............................. 22 A6

ENTERTAINMENT
Nyali Cinemax......................... 23 D3

TRANSPORT
Avenue Motors......................... 24 B4
Buses & Matatus to Ukunda,
  Msambweni, Kwale & Lunga
  Lunga................................. 25 A6
Local Bus & Matatu Stand........... 26 B6

To Northern Beaches (10km);
Lamu (344km);
Malindi (116km)

To Moi International
Airport (12km);
Nairobi (520km)

See Central Mombasa Map (p308)

Mombasa Harbour

Old Harbour

Government Square

Spice Market

Pigott Place

Treasury Square

Treasury Gardens

Old Town

Uhuru Gardens

Jumhuri Park

Sports Grounds

Commonwealth War Graves

Cricket Club

Kilindini Harbour

Likoni

To Southern Beaches (20km);
Shimba Hills National Reserve (30km);
Shimoni (976km); Tanzania (100km);
Tsavo National Park (150km)

KENYA

KENYA

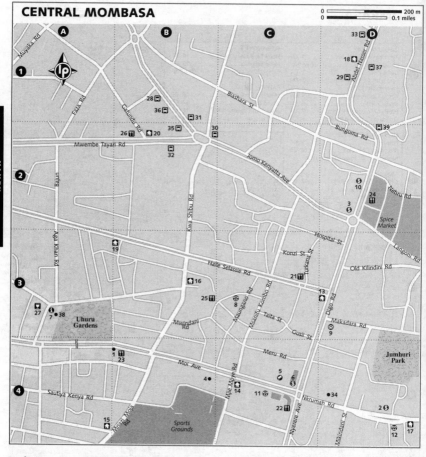

its design, especially the angular configuration of the west walls, which makes it impossible to attack one wall without being a sitting duck for soldiers on the opposite battlements.

These days the fort houses a **museum** (Map p307; ☎ 041-222425; nmkfortj@swiftmombasa.com; adult/child KSh800/400; ☯ 8am-6pm), built over the barracks. The exhibits are mostly ceramics, reflecting the variety of cultures that traded along the coast, but include other interesting odds and ends donated from private collections or dug up from sites along the coast. Also displayed are finds from the Portuguese frigate *Santo António de Tanná*, which sank near the fort during the siege in 1698, and the far end of the hall is devoted to the fascinating culture of the nine coastal Mijikenda tribes.

Exploring the battlements and ruined buildings within the compound is just as interesting, though the fort feels much smaller than it looks from the outside. The **Omani house** in the San Felipe bastion in the northwestern corner of the fort was built in the late 18th century, and houses a small exhibition of Omani jewellery and artefacts. Nearby is a ruined church, a huge well and cistern. The **eastern wall** of the fort includes an Omani audience hall and the **Passage of the Arches**, a passage cut through the coral to give access to the sea.

OLD TOWN

While Mombasa's Old Town doesn't quite have the medieval charm of Lamu or Zanzibar, it's still an interesting area to wander around. The houses here are characteristic of coastal East African architecture, with ornately carved doors and window frames and fretwork balconies, designed to protect the modesty of the female inhabitants. Sadly, many of these have been destroyed; there is now a preservation order on the remaining doors and balconies, so further losses should hopefully be prevented. The **Mombasa Old Town Conservation Society** (Map p307; ☎ 041-312246; Sir Mbarak Hinawy Rd) is encouraging the renovation of many dilapidated buildings.

From the outside there's little evidence of what any of these buildings were once used for. To flesh out their history, it's worth picking up a copy of the booklet *The Old Town Mombasa: A Historical Guide* (KSh200) from the tourist office or the Fort Jesus ticket office. This guide features old photos, a good map and building-by-building descriptions.

OLD LAW COURTS

The old law courts on Nkrumah Rd have been converted into an informal **gallery** (Map p307; Nkrumah Rd; admission free; ⏰ 8am-6pm), with regularly changing displays of local art, Kenyan crafts, school competition pieces and votive objects from various tribal groups.

HARBOUR CRUISES

Luxury dhow cruises around the harbour are popular in Mombasa and, notwithstanding the price, they are an excellent way to see the harbour, the Old Town and Fort Jesus and get a slap-up meal at the end of it.

Topping the billing is the **Tamarind Dhow** (Map p307; ☎ 041-475074; www.tamarinddhow.com), run by the posh Tamarind restaurant chain. The cruise embarks from the jetty below Tamarind

restaurant in Nyali, and includes a harbour tour and fantastic meal. The lunch cruises leave at 1pm and cost US$40/20 per adult/child, or US$80/40 when combined with a city tour. Longer and more splendid evening cruises leave at 6.30pm and cost US$70/35; vegetarians are catered for. Prices include a complimentary cocktail and transport to and from your hotel, and the dhow itself is a beautiful piece of work (you can hire it out exclusively for the day for US$650).

Festivals & Events

The **Mombasa Carnival** is the major annual event, held every November. The festival sees Moi Ave come alive for the day with street parades, floats and lots of music from tribes of the coastal region and the rest of Kenya.

For sporty types or keen spectators, the **Mombasa Triathlon** (www.kenyatriathlon.com) is an open competition with men's, women's and children's races.

Sleeping

BUDGET

Most of the really cheap choices are in the busy, noisy area close to the bus stations on Abdel Nasser Rd and Jomo Kenyatta Ave. Women travelling alone might want to opt for something a little further up the price scale.

Tana Guest House (Map p308; ☎ 041-490550; cnr Mwembe Tayari & Gatundu Rds; s/d/tr KSh400/500/600) A simple but friendly place, with rooms that are small, tidy and pretty much what you'd expect for the price.

New People's Hotel (Map p308; Abdel Nasser Rd; s/d KSh600/700, with shared bathroom KSh600/700) Near the 'Ideal Chicks' poultry building ('Because Chicks

KENYA

is the Boss'), you'll get loads of noise from traffic and the Noor Mosque next door, but rooms are clean and security is good. There's a nice, cheap restaurant downstairs and it's convenient for buses to Lamu and Malindi.

Evening Guest House (Map p308; ☎ 041-221380; Mnazi Moja Rd; s KSh800, d KSh1200, with shared bathroom s/d KSh800/1000) If you need a budget doss set away from the bus-stand chaos, this is a good option. The doubles are good value (the singles a bit less so), service is friendly and you'll get a good night's sleep.

Beracha Guest House (p308; ☎ 0725-006228; Haile Selassie Rd; s/d KSh800/1300) This popular central choice is located in the heart of one of Mombasa's best eating streets and has variable but clean rooms in a range of unusual shapes. It's on the 2nd floor of the building it occupies – on the stair landing, turn right into the hotel, and not left into the evangelical church.

New Palm Tree Hotel (Map p308; ☎ 041-311758; Nkrumah Rd; s/d KSh1600/2200) This sociable option has rooms set around a terraced roof, and while the amenities (such as hot water) aren't always reliable, service is fine and there's a good vibe about the place.

Hotel Dorse (Map p308; ☎ 041-222252, 31856; hotel dorse@africaonline.co.ke; Kwa Shibu Rd, off Moi Ave; s/d KSh2500/3000) Marketed at a conference clientele, this low-lying building with balconies, big beds and showers designed for very tall people is a good option. Knock about KSh500 off the price in low season.

MIDRANGE
Hotel Sapphire (Map p307; ☎ 041-2494841, 041-2492257; hotel sapphire@africaonline.co.ke; Mwembe Tayari Rd; s/d/tr KSh2550/3980/4795; ❄ ☎) Come for the saggy beds, stay for the neon palm trees! The Sapphire is a good option, especially if you want to stay close to the train station. Some of the rooms could do with better lighting, but they're all nicely fitted out with TVs and, yes, squishy beds.

Hotel Sai Rose (p307; ☎ 222897; hotelsairose@ iconnect.co.ke; Nyerere Ave; s/d/tr KSh3500/4500/6500; ❄) This outrageous hotel is a good example of what happens when Chinese money and design aesthetic meets the Kenyan penchant for going over the top (answer: bling-blingy-bling). Rooms resemble the velvet set of a Prince video crossed with a Vietnamese opium den, and the hotel itself is one long, narrow corridor set between two patches of wasteland.

our pick Castle Royal Hotel (Map p308; ☎ 041-220373, 041-2222682; www.castlemsa.com; Moi Ave; s/d/tr KSh3500/4500/6000; ❄ ☐) In the West this would be the sort of big boxy but slightly boutique place you stop in at after a long drive and wake up to feeling absolutely refreshed. In Mombasa, all of the above equals the best hotel deal in town. Electronic door locks, TVs, air-con, balconies and rooms that actually have a decent design aesthetic all equal joy.

TOP END
Royal Court Hotel (Map p308; ☎ 041-223379; royal court@ swiftmombasa; Haile Selassie Rd; s US$75-100, d US$85-120, ste US$180; ❄ ☎) The swish lobby is the highlight of this stylish business hotel – executive rooms are reasonably plush, but the standard rooms are beaten by those at the Castle Royal. Still, service and facilities are good, disabled access is a breeze and you get great views and food at the Tawa Terrace restaurant on the roof, which also has a pool.

Tamarind Village (Map p307; ☎ 041-474600; www.tamarind.co.ke; Silos Rd, Nyali; apt KSh9500-20,000; ❄ ☐ ☎) This is bar none the best hotel in town, especially if you're going upscale. Located in a modern (and quite elegantly executed) take on a Swahili castle overlooking the blue waters of the harbour, the Tamarind offers crisp, fully serviced apartments with satellite TV, palm-lined balconies and a general sense of white-washed, sun-lathered luxury.

Eating
BUDGET
New Recoder Restaurant (Map p307; Kibokoni Rd; mains KSh50-180) A local favourite, slightly tattier than Island Dishes but with much the same coastal cuisine.

Island Dishes (Map p307; ☎ 0720-887311; Kibokoni Rd; mains KSh80-220) Once your eyes have adjusted to the dazzling strip lights, feast them on the tasty menu at this whiter-than-white Lamu-themed canteen. *Mishkaki* (kebabs), chicken tikka, fish, fresh juices and all the usual favourites are on offer to eat in or take away, though the biriani (curry and rice) is only available at lunchtime.

Little Chef Dinners Pub (Map p308; ☎ 041-222740; Moi Ave; mains KSh120-300) Thankfully this funky green-hued pub-restaurant has nothing to do with the British motorway diners of the same name, and dishes up big, tasty portions of Kenyan and international food.It has a pool table.

MIDRANGE
Blue Room Restaurant (Map p308; ☎ 041-224021; www.blueroomonline.com; Haile Selassie Rd; mains KSh200-

450; ⌨) Between the steaks, pizzas, curries and…internet access (really!), the Blue Room has basically been constructed to serve the needs of every traveller anywhere.

Singh Restaurant (Map p308; ☎ 041-493283; Mwembe Tayari Rd; mains KSh250-320) This used to be a very simple cafeteria, but its gotten an extensive makeover during the years and now looks like your standard, dark-wood and Mughal painting–bedecked classy Indian restaurant. With that said the food is excellent, and this spot also caters to vegetarians.

Shehnai Restaurant (Map p308; ☎ 041-222847; Fatemi House, off Maungano Rd; mains from KSh300; noon-2pm & 7.30-10.30pm Tue-Sun) Mombasa's classiest curry house specialises in tandoori and rich *mughlai* (North Indian) cuisine complemented by nice décor that's been pulled out in Indian restaurants from the world over (pumped-in sitar music thrown in for free).

China Town Restaurant (Map p308; ☎ 041-315098; Nyerere Ave; mains KSh400-600) More incredibly chintzy décor, plus good Korean and Chinese food. This spot is attracting more and more well-heeled Chinese businessmen who like to snack here before heading to gamble in the casinos.

TOP END

Hunter's Steak House (Map p307; Königsallee, Mkomani Rd, Nyali; mains KSh450-2000; Wed-Mon) Where's '*die*' beef? Here, *meine freunde*, at this German-run steakhouse, generally regarded as the best purveyors of cooked cow in town. Aimed mainly at visitors, it's often closed for a month or so in June.

ourpick **Tamarind Restaurant** (Map p307; ☎ 041-474600; Silos Rd, Nyali; mains KSh1100-1800) If you're entertaining the good old 'I'm a Swahili sultan overlooking my coastal kingdom with a giant plate of chili crab' fantasy, can we recommend the Tamarind? Big Moorish palace exterior, big jewellery box–dining room, big keyboard music (ugh) and a big menu that concentrates on seafood (but does everything well) equals big satisfaction (and yeah, a big bill).

SELF-CATERING

Nakumatt supermarket (Map p307; ☎ 041-228945; Nyerere Ave) Close to the Likoni ferry, with a good selection of provisions, drinks and hardware items – just in case you need a TV, bicycle or lawnmower to go with your groceries.

Main market (Map p308; Digo Rd) Mombasa's dilapidated 'covered' market is packed with stalls selling fresh fruit and vegetables. Roaming produce carts also congregate in the surrounding streets, and dozens of *miraa* sellers join the fray when the regular deliveries come in, adding some amphetamine energy to the mix.

Drinking

Café Mocha (Map p307; Nyali Centre) Mocha is usually brimming with well-heeled Mombasan teeny- and tweeny-boppers and their parents enjoying the good coffee, air-conditioning and lovely cakes and pastries.

New Florida Nightclub (Map p307; ☎ 313127; Mama Ngina Dr; 24hr;) This vast seafront complex houses Mombasa's liveliest nightclub, which boasts its own open-air swimming pool. It's owned by the same people as the lively and rowdy Florida clubs in Nairobi and offers the same atmosphere, clientele and Las Vegas–style floorshows.

The Office (Map p307; ☎ 041-451700; Shelly Beach Rd, Likoni) Perched above the Likoni ferry jetty and *matatu* stand, the entirely unaptly named Office is a real locals' hangout with regular massive reggae and dub nights shaking the thatched rafters. Any business that goes on here is definitely not the executive kind.

Bella Vista (p308; Aga Khan Rd) This two-storey beer-o-fest is plenty of fun for those who feel the need to kick back with a cold one, some sports on the tube, a few rounds of pool and a great view of Mombasa's nightlife action unfolding in all its storied, slightly sleazy glory.

Entertainment

Nyali Cinemax (Map p307; ☎ 041-470000; info@nyali cinemax.com; Nyali Centre, Nyali Rd, Nyali; tickets KSh250-350) A multiscreen, modern cineplex that's a great air-conditioned escape from the oppressive humidity. It shows a lot of Holly- and Bollywood, although the DVD copyright line in the bottom corner of the show we saw didn't inspire a lot of confidence in ethical royalty practices.

Getting There & Away

AIR

Daily flights to Mombasa are available with **Kenya Airways** (Map p308; ☎ 041-221251; www .kenya-airways.com; TSS Towers, Nkrumah Rd) between Nairobi and Mombasa's **Moi International Airport** (☎ 041-433211).

Airkenya (☎ Nairobi 020-605745; www.airkenya .com) doesn't have a ticket office in Mombasa

KENYA

(you can book online), but it flies between Nairobi and Mombasa once a day.

Mombasa Air Safari (☎ 041-433061; www.mombasaair safari.com; Moi International Airport) flies to Amboseli, Tsavo and Masai Mara National Parks; it can also arrange complete safari packages.

Note that fares and frequency of flights vary considerably depending on availability and the season, so it's best to check the internet for current information.

BUS & MATATU

Most bus offices are either on Jomo Kenyatta Ave or Abdel Nasser Rd. Services to Malindi and Lamu leave from Abdel Nasser Rd, while buses to Tanzania leave from the junction of Jomo Kenyatta Ave and Mwembe Tayari Rd.

For buses and *matatus* to the beaches south of Mombasa, you first need to get off the island via the Likoni ferry. Frequent *matatus* run from Nyerere Ave to the transport stand by the ferry terminal.

Nairobi

There are dozens of daily departures in either direction (mostly in the early morning and late evening). Companies include the following:

Akamba (Map p308; ☎ 041-490269; Jomo Kenyatta Ave)
Busscar (Map p308; ☎ 041-222854; Abdel Nasser Rd)
Coastline Safaris (Map p308; ☎ 041-220158; Mwembe Tayari St)
Falcon (Map p308; ☎ Nairobi 020-229662; Abdel Nasser Rd) Offices in Abdel Nasser Rd and Jomo Kenyatta Ave.
Mombasa Raha (Map p307; ☎ 041-225716) Offices in Abdel Nasser Rd and Jomo Kenyatta Ave.
Msafiri (Map p307; ☎ 041-314691; Aga Khan Rd)

Daytime services take at least six hours, and overnight trips eight to 10 hours and include a meal/smoke break about halfway. The trip isn't particularly comfortable, although it's not bad for an African bus ride (which isn't saying much). Fares vary from KSh800 to KSh1300. Most companies have at least four departures daily.

All buses travel via Voi (KSh500), which is also served by frequent *matatus* from the Kobil petrol station on Jomo Kenyatta Ave (KSh200). Several companies go to Kisumu and Lake Victoria, but all go via Nairobi.

Heading North

There are numerous daily *matatus* and small lorry-buses up the coast to Malindi, leaving from in front of the Noor Mosque on Abdel Nasser Rd. Buses take up to 2½ hours (KSh100), *matatus* about two hours (KSh120). You can also catch an 'express' *matatu* to Malindi (KSh150), which takes longer to fill up but is then supposedly nonstop all the way.

Tawakal, Falcon, Mombasa Raha and TSS Express have buses to Lamu, most leaving at around 7am (report 30 minutes early) from their offices on Abdel Nasser Rd. Buses take around seven hours to reach the Lamu ferry at Mokoke (KSh650 to KSh800), stopping in Malindi (KSh200 to KSh300).

Heading South

Regular buses and *matatus* leave from the Likoni ferry terminal and travel along the southern coast.

For Tanzania, Falcon and a handful of other companies have daily departures to Tanga (KSh600, two hours) and Dar es Salaam (KSh1000 to KSh1300, eight hours) from their offices on Jomo Kenyatta Ave, near the junction with Mwembe Tayari Rd. Dubious-looking buses to Moshi and Arusha leave from in front of the Mwembe Tayari Health Centre in the morning or evening.

TRAIN

Few subjects divided our readers' letters more fiercely than the train from Nairobi to Mombasa. Once one of the most famous rail lines in Africa, today the train is, depending on who you speak to, either: a) a sociable way of avoiding the rutted highway and spotting wildlife from the clackety comfort of a sleeping car; or b) a ratty, tatty overrated waste of time. The truth lays somewhere in the middle. The train's state could be described as 'faded glory' that occasionally bumps up to 'romantically dishevelled' or slips into 'frustrating mediocrity'. The latter isn't helped by spotty scheduling and lax timetable enforcement. The 'iron snake' departs Mombasa at 7pm on Tuesday, Thursday and Sunday, arriving the next day somewhere between 8.30am and 11am. Fares are US$65/54 in 1st/2nd class including bed and breakfast (you get dinner with 1st class) – reserve as far in advance as possible. The **booking office** (Map p307; ☎ 041-312220; ⏰ 8am-5pm) is at the station in Mombasa.

Getting Around

TO/FROM THE AIRPORT

There is currently no public transport to or from the airport, so you're best taking a taxi –

the fare to central Mombasa is around KSh800 to KSh1000. Coming from town, the usual fare is KSh1000, but you have to bargain.

If you don't have much luggage, you can take a Kwa Hola/Magongo *matatu* from the Kobil petrol station on Jomo Kenyatta Ave to just beyond the Akamba Handicrafts Cooperative on Airport Rd for KSh40 and walk the last few kilometres.

BOAT

The two Likoni ferries connect Mombasa Island with the southern mainland. There's a crossing roughly every 20 minutes between 5am and 12.30am, less frequently outside these times. It's free for pedestrians and KSh50 per car. To get to the jetty from the centre of town, take a Likoni *matatu* from Digo Rd.

CAR & MOTORCYCLE

There's not much difference between the car-hire companies in town apart from the possible insurance excesses (see p414). Rates are the same as in Nairobi – about KSh7000 per day for a small jeep and KSh6000 per day for a saloon car. Companies with offices in central Mombasa include the following:

Avenue Motors (Map p307; ☎ 041-225126; Moi Ave)

Budget (☎ 221281; budgetmba@budget-kenya.com; Moi International Airport)

Glory Car Hire (Map p308; ☎ 041-228063; Moi Ave)

Hertz (☎ 3432405; mombasa@hertz.co.ke; Moi International Airport)

MATATU, TAXI & TUK-TUK

Matatus charge between KSh10 and KSh20 for short trips. Mombasa taxis are as expensive as those in Nairobi, and harder to find; a good place to look is in front of Express Travel on Nkrumah Rd. Assume it'll cost KSh250 to KSh400 from the train station to the city centre. There are also plenty of three-wheeled tuk-tuks about, which run about KSh70 to KSh150 for a bit of open-air transit.

SHIMBA HILLS NATIONAL RESERVE

If you're in n7ed of traditional African landscapes of the rolling hills variety, this 320-sq-km **reserve** (adult/child US$20/10; ☺ 6am-6pm) is just 30km from Mombasa, directly inland from Diani Beach. Actually, it's a bit more than rolling hills (the Marare and Pengo, to be exact); throw in an escarpment of Triassic rock, riverine valleys dotted with clumps of tropical rainforest and leopards, sable antelopes and elephants and you've got a national park that holds it own against anything in the hinterland.

There are more than 150km of 4WD tracks that crisscross the reserve; Marere Dam and the forest of Mwele Mdogo Hill are good spots for birdlife. Highly recommended guided forest walks are run by the **Kenya Wildlife Service** (KWS; ☎ 025-404159; PO Box 30, Kwale) from the Sheldrick Falls ranger post. Walks are free but a tip would be appropriate.

Shimba Rainforest Lodge (☎ 025-4414077; Kinango Rd; full board with shared bathroom per person US$170) is a great lodge of the Treetops genre, the sort of place where you feel like you're Tarzan getting spoiled with a menu of plush amenities.

Mukurumuji Tented Camp (☎ 025-402412; www .campkenya.com; full board per person US$94) is a series of luxury tents which does the whole posh African bush thing quite well, but it also runs development projects in the local community including managing wildlife-human interactions, landscaping and classroom refurbishment.

The **public campsite** (per person US$8) and **bandas** (per person US$35) are superbly located on the edge of an escarpment close to the main gate, with stunning views down to Diani Beach.

You'll need a 4WD to enter the reserve, but hitching may be possible at the main gate (see p624 for risks associated with hitching). From Likoni, small lorry-buses to Kwale pass the main gate (KSh50). Mukurumuji Tented Camp can organise transfers from Diani.

MWALUGANJE ELEPHANT SANCTUARY

This **sanctuary** (☎ 040-41121; nonresident adult/child US$15/2, vehicles KSh150-500; ☺ 6am-6pm) is a good example of community-based conservation and most local people are stakeholders in the project. It was opened in October 1995 to create a corridor along an ancient elephant migration route between the Shimba Hills National Reserve and the Mwaluganje Forest Reserve, and comprises 2400 hectares of rugged, beautiful country along the valley of the Cha Shimba River.

More than 150 elephants live in the sanctuary and you're likely to see a large variety of other fauna and flora, including rare cycad forest. (This primitive, palmlike plant species is over 300 million years old.) There's a good information centre close to the main gate and a second ticket office on the outskirts of Kwale. Don't miss the chance to buy the unique postcards and paper goods as souvenirs for the folks back home – they're all made from recycled elephant dung!

Mwaluganje Elephant Camp (☎ Mombasa 041-5485121; www.travellersbeach.com; per person US$110) is a rather fine place to stay. There's a waterhole used by the elephants that provides a good vantage point, and accommodation is in permanent tents. Most travellers come here on day or overnight packages (US$115/213 per person), which include transfers from the south coast and wildlife drives.

Campsites (per person KSh300) are located near the main gate and southern end of the park.

The main entrance to the sanctuary is about 13km northeast of Shimba Hills National Reserve on the road to Kinango. A shorter route runs from Kwale to the Golini Gate, passing the Mwaluganje ticket office. It's only 5km, but the track is 4WD only.

TIWI BEACH
☎ 040

The sleepy sister to manic Diani is a string of blissed-out resorts, accessible by dirt tracks, about 20km south of Likoni. It's good for a quiet, cottage-y escape by the sand. One of the best features of Tiwi is Diani reef (which, funnily enough, isn't as evident in Diani), which creates a stable, pool-like area between the shore and the coral that's great for swimming. The main drawbacks are the occasional beach boys, who tend to cluster towards the southern end of the beach. Tiwi is a lot less visited than Diani, but you'll still need to book ahead during high season.

A bunch of dumb, friendly dogs greet you as you enter **Sand Island Beach Cottages** (☎ 040-3300043; www.sandislandtiwi.com; cottages low season KSh3500-6500, high season KSh4000-7500), a garden-like strip of lovely cottages fronting an even better beach. Run by a British expat, there's all kinds of peaceful serenity awaiting, either here or on pretty Sand Island itself, which lays just off shore.

our pick **Coral Cove Cottages** (☎ 040-3300010; www.coralcove.tiwibeach.com/cottages KSh5000-8000) is where Doctor Doolittle would happily vacation. There are dogs, roosters, monkeys, geese, ducks and other fluffy denizens scattered throughout, and they're all tame. We were greeted by a manager cradling a baby thumb-sucking monkey, and if that doesn't melt your heart, well, you're pretty hard to please. The cottages, by the way, are as lovely

and paradise-evocative as you'd hope for. Buses and *matatus* on the Likoni–Ukunda road can drop you at the start of either track down to Tiwi (KSh30).

Although it's only 3.5km to the beach, both access roads are notorious for muggings so take a taxi or hang around for a lift. If you're heading back to the highway, you'll need to call ahead for a cab.

DIANI BEACH
☎ 040

Diani, the biggest resort town on the Kenyan coast, is a mixed bag. It's got undeniably stunning swathes of white-sand perfection, and if you're looking to party, you're in the right spot. On the other hand it's rife with the sort of uniform uber-resorts that could be plopped anywhere the world over. With this in mind, we've tried to include those places that offer a bit of distinctive fun in our reviews. Just remember: there's a lot beyond the stale blocks of hotel overdevelopment. Visiting coral mosques with archways that overlook the open ocean and sky, sacred forests where guides hug trees that speak in their ancestors' voices and (well, why not?) a monkey reserve are all good ways of experiencing more of the coast then the considerable charms of sun and sand.

Orientation
The town of Ukunda, which is basically a traffic junction on the main Mombasa–Tanzania road, is the turn-off point for Diani Beach. There's all sorts of essentials here – post office, banks, etc. From here a tarmac road runs about 2.5km to a T-junction with the beach road, where you'll find everything Diani has to offer.

Information
EMERGENCY
Diani Beach Hospital (☎ 040-3202435; www .dianibeachhospital.com; ☼ 24hr)
Police (☎ 040-3202121, 040-3202229; Ukunda)

INTERNET ACCESS
CMS Cybercafé (Palm Ave, Ukunda; per min KSh1.50; ☼ 8am-8pm Mon-Sat, 10.30am-7pm Sun)
Hot Gossip (☎ 040-3203307; wellconnectednet@ hotgossip.co.ke; Legend Casino Complex; per min KSh5; ☼ 9am-6pm Mon-Fri, 9am-2pm Sat)

MONEY
Barclays Bank (☎ 040-3202448; Barclays Centre)
Diani Forex Bureau (☎ 040-3203595)

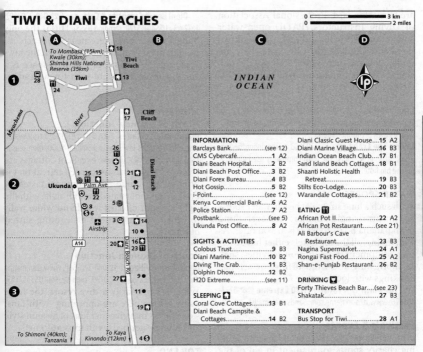

TIWI & DIANI BEACHES

INFORMATION
Barclays Bank.................(see 12)
CMS Cybercafé....................1 A2
Diani Beach Hospital...........2 B2
Diani Beach Post Office.......3 B2
Diani Forex Bureau...............4 B3
Hot Gossip........................5 B2
i-Point...........................(see 12)
Kenya Commercial Bank.......6 A2
Police Station...................7 A2
Postbank........................(see 5)
Ukunda Post Office............8 A2

SIGHTS & ACTIVITIES
Colobus Trust.....................9 B3
Diani Marine.....................10 B2
Diving The Crab.................11 B3
Dolphin Dhow...................12 B2
H20 Extreme..................(see 11)

SLEEPING
Coral Cove Cottages.........13 B1
Diani Beach Campsite &
Cottages.....................14 B2

Diani Classic Guest House...15 A2
Diani Marine Village...........16 B3
Indian Ocean Beach Club...17 B1
Sand Island Beach Cottages..18 B1
Shaanti Holistic Health
Retreat.........................19 B3
Stilts Eco-Lodge...............20 B3
Warandale Cottages...........21 B2

EATING
African Pot II.....................22 A2
African Pot Restaurant.......(see 21)
Ali Barbour's Cave
Restaurant...................23 B3
Nagina Supermarket.........24 A1
Rongai Fast Food...............25 A2
Shan-e-Punjab Restaurant.. 26 B2

DRINKING
Forty Thieves Beach Bar....(see 23)
Shakatak.........................27 B3

TRANSPORT
Bus Stop for Tiwi...............28 A1

KENYA

Kenya Commercial Bank (☎ 040-3202197; Ukunda)
Postbank (Diani shopping centre) Western Union money
transfers.

POST
Diani Beach post office (Diani Beach Rd)
Ukunda post office (Ukunda)

TOURIST INFORMATION
i-Point (☎ 040-3202234; Barclays Centre; ⏰ 8.30am-
6pm Mon-Fri, 9am-4pm Sat) Private information office
with plenty of brochures.

Dangers & Annoyances
Take taxis at night and try not to be on the beach
by yourself after dark. Souvenir sellers are an
everyday nuisance, sex tourism is pretty evident
and beach boys are a hassle; you hear a lot of
'Hey, one love one love' rasta-speak spouted by
guys trying to sell you drugs or scam you into
supporting fake charities for 'local schools'.

Sights
Package holiday tat seems ubiquitous in Diani,
but there's far more waiting to be discovered
by independent travellers.

Kaya Kinondo (☎ 0722-344426; www.kaya-kinondo
-kenya.com, admission KSh500) is probably the easiest
accessible *kaya* (sacred forest) on the Kenyan
coast. For more on this incredible ecotourism
site, see p318.

Notice the monkeys clambering over rope
ladders over the road? That's the work of the
Colobus Trust (☎ 040-3203519; www.colobustrust.org;
Diani Beach Rd; tours KSh500; ⏰ 8am-5pm Mon-Sat), which
works to protect the Angolan black-and-white
colobus monkey *(Colobus angolensis palliatus)*,
a once-common species now restricted to a few
isolated pockets of forest south of Mombasa.
Besides being vulnerable to traffic, the monkeys
only eat the leaves of certain coastal trees and
are particularly vulnerable to habitat destruction, another big problem in this area. The Trust
works to insulate power lines (another serious
threat to the monkeys), reduce poaching, provides veterinary services and gives excellent
tours of its facilities.

Activities
DIVING
All the big resorts either have their own dive
schools or work with a local operator. Rates

are fairly standard: Professional Association of Diving Instructors (PADI) open-water courses cost US$630, and reef trips with two dives cost US$115. Most dive sites here are under 29m and there's even a purposely sunk shipwreck, the 15m former fishing boat MFV *Alpha Funguo*, at 28m.

Main operators:

Diani Marine (☎ 040-3203450; www.dianimarine.com; Diani Marine Village) Very professional German-run centre with its own accommodation.

Diving The Crab (☎ 040-3202003; www.divingthecrab .com; Sands at Nomads) The most commonly used outfit for the big hotels.

WATER SPORTS

With such a long stretch of beach, water sports are unsurprisingly popular, and everything from banana boats to jet skis are on offer. As with diving, all the big hotels either have their own equipment (for common activities, such as snorkelling and windsurfing) or arrange bookings with local firms.

The main operator is **H20 Extreme** (☎ 0721-495876; www.h2o-extreme.com; Sands at Nomads).

Festivals & Events

Diani Rules (www.dianirules.com) is an entertaining charity sports tournament in aid of the Kwale District Eye Centre, held at Diani Sea Lodge around the first weekend of June. It's more of an expat event than a tourist attraction, but if you're staying locally there's every chance you'll be invited to watch or asked to join a team.

Sleeping

BUDGET

Diani Classic Guest House (☎ 040-3203305, 0710-267920; Ukunda; s/d KSh700/800) The cheapest option in town is, thankfully, excellent: sparkling clean and quite sizable rooms, en suite toilets with seats (we can't stress how rare this is for the price!), even balconies. Which, OK, look out onto Ukunda Junction, but whatever.

Stilts Ecolodge (☎ 0722-52378; s/d KSh1500/2400) The only dedicated backpacker lodgings as of our research, Stilts offers just that: seven charming stilted tree houses set back in a sandy swathe of coastal forest, located across the street from 40 Thieves. It attracts a young, fun-seeking crowd, has its own thatched lounge-bar area and is basically all-around enjoyable.

Diani Beach Campsite & Cottages (☎ 040-3203192; 1 r/2 r/3 r US$40/55/70, camping US$5) This is the only budget choice anywhere near the beach, although unless you're camping, even the low-season prices are steep. The tent space is a small, simple lawn site with toilets and an eating area.

MIDRANGE

North of Ukunda Junction

Warandale Cottages (☎ 040-3202186; http://waran dale.com; cottages low season KSh4000-9000, high season KSh5000-13,000; ⊠) These excellent cottages are strung along a pleasant garden retreat that is utterly Eden-esque. The rooms are tastefully done in an understated Swahili style, with the right amount of dark wood and white walls to evoke Africa without a steaming surfeit of safari tat.

South of Ukunda Junction

Diani Marine Village (☎ 040-3202367; www.dianimarine .com; s/d low season US$60/90, high season US$65/115) While it's primarily a dive resort, the huge guest rooms here are appealing, with fans, stone floors that give that hint of Swahili style and four-poster beds with mosquito nets.

TOP END

North of Ukunda Junction

Indian Ocean Beach Club (☎ 040-3203730; www.jacaranda hotels.com; full board s/d low season from US$98/135, high season from US$105/192; ⊠ ⌨ ⊠) Probably our favourite designer top-end option in Diani, the Beach Club consists of a series of pearl-bright Moorish-stye houses strung out along a long, low lawn that slopes into the lovely ocean.

South of Ukunda Junction

Shaanti Holistic Health Retreat (☎ 040-3202064; www.shaantihhr.com; s/d US$300/500; ⊠ ⊠) If you don't have any hippy in you, get some, fast. Actually, let's be fair: while this place offers all sorts of yoga relaxation, Ayurvedic activities and spa bliss, it's also a flat-out beautiful resort. The interiors look like Swahili rooms run through a modern art museum, with sculpted curves, airy portholes and beds sunk into the yielding stone.

Eating

African Pot Restaurant (☎ 040-3203890; Coral Beach Cottages; mains KSh150-230) This place and its culinary siblings (there are two branches: one about halfway down Ukunda road and another at Ukunda Junction) does an excellent stock in trade of traditional African and Swahili dishes.

Rongai Fast Food (Palm Ave, Ukunda; mains KSh200) This rowdy joint is a pretty popular place for *nyama choma*; if you've been missing your roast meat and boiled maize, Rongai's here for you.

Shan-e-Punjab Restaurant (☎ 040-3202116; Diani Complex; mains KSh350-800) One of the only dedicated Indian options in town could easily hold its own against any high-class curry house in the world. The food is well-spiced, rich and delicious, but this place is often closed in the low-season.

Ali Barbour's Cave Restaurant (☎ 040-3202033; mains KSh550-1200; ☽ from 7pm) Well, they've got coral mosques and palaces on the coast – why not a restaurant set in a coral cave? The focus here is seafood, done up posh and generally quite tasty, served under stars, jagged rocks and fairy lights.

Self-caterers can stock up at the supermarkets in Diani's shopping centres, or Ukunda.

Drinking & Entertainment
Forty Thieves Beach Bar (☎ 040-3203419) Part of the Ali Barbour empire, this is easily the best bar on the strip, frequented on a daily basis by a crowd of expats and regulars known affectionately as the Reprobates. Food is served during the day, and it's open until the last guest leaves, ie pretty damn late.

Shakatak (☎ 040-3203124) Essentially the only full-on nightclub in Diani not attached to a hotel, Shakatak is quite hilariously seedy, but can be fun once you know what to expect. Like most big Kenyan clubs, food is served at all hours.

Getting There & Around
BUS & MATATU
Numerous *matatus* run south from the Likoni ferry directly to Ukunda (KSh60, 30 minutes) and onwards to Msambweni and Lunga Lunga. From the Diani junction in Ukunda, *matatus* run down to the beach all day for KSh30; check before boarding to see if it's a Reef service (heading north along the strip, then south) or a Neptune one (south beach only).

TAXI
Taxis hang around Ukunda Junction and all the main shopping centres; most hotels and restaurants will also have a couple waiting at night. Fares should be between KSh150 and KSh800, depending on distance.

SHIMONI & WASINI ISLAND
☎ 040
Shimoni village is on the tip of a peninsula, 76km south of Likoni. Dhow tours to Wasini Island and the coral reefs of Kisite Marine National Park have become a big industry here. They're well run, but you can easily organise your own trip directly with the boatmen.

Sights & Activities
Villagers have opened up the old **slave caves** (adult/child KSh100/25; ☽ 8.30-10.30am & 1.30-6pm) as a tourist attraction, with a custodian who'll take you around the dank caverns to illustrate this little-discussed part of East African history.

Wasini Island is at its most appealing in the peace of the evening. There are several worthwhile things to see, including some ancient **Swahili ruins** and the **coral gardens** (adult/child KSh100/20), a bizarre landscape of exposed coral reefs with a boardwalk for viewing.

KISITE MARINE NATIONAL PARK
Just off the south coast of Wasini Island, this **marine park** (adult/child US$5/2) is one of the best in Kenya, also incorporating the **Mpunguti Marine National Reserve**. The park covers 28 sq km of pristine coral reefs, and offers excellent diving and snorkelling. You have a reasonable chance of seeing dolphins in the Shimoni Channel, and humpback whales are sometimes spotted between August and October.

It's easy to organise your own boat trip with a local captain; the going rate is KSh1500 per person or KSh6000 per boat, including lunch and a walk in the coral gardens on Wasini Island. Masks and snorkels can be hired for KSh200. A good place to start looking for a boatman is the office of **KWS** (☎ 040-52027; ☽ 6am-6pm), about 200m south of the main pier.

The best time to **dive** and **snorkel** is between October and March. Avoid June, July and August because of rough seas, silt and poor visibility.

Tours
Various companies offer organised dhow tours for snorkelling, all leaving Shimoni by 9am. Transfers from north- and south-coast hotels are available (US$10 to US$20), and longer trips with overnight stays can also be arranged. Certified divers can take one/two

KENYA

ENTERING THE SACRED FOREST *Matthew D Firestone*

Entering the sacred forests, or *kaya,* of the Mijikenda, can be one of the crowning experiences of a visit to Kenya. Visiting these groves takes on elements of wildlife safari, nature walk, historical journey and all-around awe-inspiring experience. Hopefully, more *kaya* will become the focus of responsible tourism initiatives by the time you read this: 11 of the forests were inscribed together as Kenya's fourth World Heritage Site in July of 2008.

Currently, the most visited and easiest-accessible *kaya* is Kaya Kinondo, near Diani Beach. The irony is extreme: one of the best ecotourism sites in Kenya mere minutes from some of its gaudiest resorts.

Entering *kaya* always requires a certain amount of ritual, but this is toned down at Kinondo. You have to remove headwear, promise not to kiss anyone inside the grove, wrap a black *kaniki* (sarong) around your waist and go with a guide; ours was Juma Harry, a local *askari* (soldier, but in this case, security guard) and member of the Digo tribe.

The Mijikenda, or Nine Homesteads, are actually nine subtribes united, to a degree, by culture, history and language. Yet each of the tribes – Chonyi, Digo, Duruma, Giriama, Jibana, Kambe, Kauma, Kambe, Rabai and Ribe – remains distinct and speaks its own dialect of the Mijikenda language. Still, there is a binding similarity between the Nine Homesteads, and between the modern Mijikenda and their ancestors: their shared veneration of the *kaya.*

This historical connection becomes concrete when you enter the woods and realise – and there's no other word that fits here – they simply feel *old,* in the dark-scented, green-shaded, crackle of twigs and creak of leaves sense of the word. Many trees are 600 years old, which corresponds to the arrival of the first Mijikenda from Singwaya, their semilegendary homeland in southern Somalia. Cutting vegetation within the *kaya* is strictly prohibited, to the degree that visitors may not even take a stray twig or leaf from the forest. Why, we asked, was this the case?

Harry explained: 'When we are near the trees, we feel close to our ancestors. I know my father, and my grandfather, and his grandfather and so on all cared for this tree.' Here Harry, who is a tough-looking character (and decidedly not a hippie) literally hugged a tree so large his arms could not begin to encircle it.

'We feel if the tree is old, it is talking. If you hold it and hear the wind,' and there was a pause for breezy effect, 'you can hear it talking.'

The preserved forests do not just facilitate dialogue to the ancestors; they provide a direct link to ecosystems that have been clearcut out of existence elsewhere. A single *kaya* such as Kinondo contains five possible endemic species within its 30 hectares (74 acres). *Five* endemic species – ie trees that only grow here – and 140 tree species classified as 'rare' within the space of a suburban residential block.

The main purpose of the *kaya* was to house the villages of the Mijikenda which were located in a large central clearing. Entering the centre of a *kaya* required ritual knowledge to proceed through concentric circles of sacredness that surrounded the node of the village; sacred talismans and spells were supposed to cause hallucinations that disoriented enemies who attacked the forest.

The *kaya* were largely abandoned in the 1940s, and conservative strains of Islam and Christianity have denigrated their value to the Mijikenda, but the recent World Heritage status and a resurgence of interest in the forests will hopefully preserve them for future visitors and tourists. The *kaya* have lasted 600 years; with luck, the wind will speak through their branches for much long longer.

scuba dives for an extra US$30/50 with any of these companies.

Main operators:

Dolphin Dhow (Map p315; ☎ 040-52255, office 3202144; office Barclays Centre, Diani Beach; tours US$75)

Kisite Dhow Tours (☎ 040-3202331; www.wasini-island.com; office Jadini Beach Hotel, Diani Beach; tours US$55-75) Popular ecotourist trips.

Pilli-Pipa (☎ 040-3202401; www.pillipipa.com; office Colliers Centre, Diani Beach; tours US$80) Diving trips from US$130.

Sleeping & Eating

Mpunguti Lodge (☎ 040-52288; Wasini Island; camping KSh300, half board s/d per person KSh1500/3500) This funny place is run by local character

Masood Abdullah and his many nephews. The rooms are uncomplicated, with mosquito nets and small verandas; running water is collected in rain barrels and doesn't always look pleasant!

Camp Eden (☎ 040-52027; KWS, Shimoni; camping per adult/child US$8/5, bandas per person US$10) Behind KWS headquarters, this camping ground offers accommodation with 'birdsong and insect noise' in the tropical forest south of the main jetty. There's a campsite, a covered cooking area, pit toilets and showers.

Pemba Channel Fishing Club (☎ 0722-205020; www .pembachannel.com; Shimoni; full board per person low season US$85, high season US$150; 🏊) A proper slice of elegant colonial style, with a handful of airy cottages set around a swimming pool and three big daft dogs to make you feel welcome.

Getting There & Around
There are *matatus* every hour or so between Likoni and Shimoni (KSh100, one hour) until about 6pm. It's best to be at Likoni by 6.30am if you want to get to Shimoni in time to catch one of the dhow sailings.

The price of getting across the channel to Wasini Island depends to a degree on who you meet on arrival, how many are in your group and how affluent you look. Crossings should cost KSh300 to KSh500 each way, less if you negotiate return journeys.

JUMBA LA MTWANA
These **Swahili ruins** (nonresident adult/child KSh500/100; 🕐 8am-6pm), just north of Mtwapa Creek, are easily comparable in terms of archaeological grandeur to the more famous Gede. The remains of buildings, with their exposed foundations for mangrove beam poles, ablution tanks, floors caked with millipedes, swarms of safari ants and the twisting arms of 600-year-old trees leftover from what may have been a nearby *kaya*, are quite magical. Jumba la Mtwana means 'Big House of Slaves,' and while there is no hard historical evidence to back the theory, locals believe the town was once an important slaveport.

The **House of Many Doors**, is believed to have been a guesthouse (no breakfast included) and includes dried out, 40m deep wells. You'd be remiss to miss the **Mosque by the Sea**, which overlooks a crystal-sharp vista of the Indian Ocean. Notice the Arabic inception on the stellae adjacent to the nearby graveyard: 'Every Soul Shall Taste Death'. Underneath is a small hole representing the opening all humans must pass through on the way to paradise. There are three other mosques on the site, and evidence of extensive sanitation facilities in all the main buildings.

Regular *matatus* and buses run from Mtwapa to Mombasa (KSh50) and Malindi (KSh80).

KILIFI
☎ 041

Kilifi is a gorgeous river estuary with effortlessly picture-perfect views from its massive road bridge. Many white Kenyans have yachts moored in the creek and there are numerous beach houses belonging to artists, writers and adventurers from around the globe. The main reasons that most travellers come here are to stay at one of the pleasant beach resorts at the mouth of the creek or to visit the ruins of Mnarani, high on a bluff on the south bank of the creek.

The **Mnarani ruins** (nonresident adult/child KSh100/50; 🕐 7am-6pm) are high on a bluff just west of the old ferry landing stage on the southern bank of Kilifi Creek. Only partly excavated, the site was occupied from the end of the 14th century to around the first half of the 17th century, when it was abandoned following sieges by Galla tribespeople from Somalia and the failure of the water supply.

The best preserved ruin is the **Great Mosque** with its finely carved inscription around the mihrab (the niche showing the direction of Mecca). A group of **carved tombs** (including a restored pillar tomb), a small mosque dating back to the 16th century and parts of the town wall are also preserved.

The Kausa Mijikenda are considering opening their main *kaya* – **Kaya Kausa** – to the public, although their visitor policy remained under discussion as of our visit. If the forest does open up, don't miss the chance to go, as this is one of the best-preserved *kaya* in Kenya. We had to pay KSh1000 to tribal elders to enter the site – the money bought a goat that was sacrificed to purify the area following our visit, proving the Kausa still take the sacred status of these woods very seriously. The forest is about 15km south of Kilifi; if you'd like to visit, contact the **Coastal Forest Conservation Unit** (☎ 041-522140; cfcukilifi@yahoo.com), which manages relations with Kausa elders.

The **Dhows Inn** (☎ 041-522028; dhowsinn_kilifi@ yahoo.com; Malindi Rd; s/d KSh650/900), on the main road south of Kilifi Creek, is a small, well-maintained hostelry with simple but decent thatched blocks set around a garden.

If you need a little more comfort, **Kilifi Bay Beach Resort** (☎ 041-522511; www.madahotels.com; full board s/d US$120/160, high season US$172/230; 🟩 🛒 🛁) is about 5km north of Kilifi on the coast road. It's a pleasant, small resort with a nice beach and plenty of facilities, although the rooms don't quite match the grandeur of the Swahili palace design.

The **Kilifi Members Club** (☎ 041-525258; mains KSh150-400) is a fantastic spot for sunset, perched on the northern cliff edge with a clear sightline to the creek bridge. There's a good menu with lots of *nyama choma*, and despite the name you don't have to be a member.

All buses and *matatus* travelling between Mombasa (up to 1½ hours) and Malindi (1¼ hours) stop at Kilifi; the fare to either destination is KSh70. Buses to Mombasa and on to Nairobi leave at around 7.45am and 7.45pm (KSh600).

WATAMU
☎ 042

This small fishing village has evolved into a small expat colony, a string of high-end resorts and it makes a good base for exploring a glut of ruins, national parks and eco-sites that are within an easily accessible radius. The main attraction is 7km of pristine beach and a cosy scene that caters to peace, quiet and/or big-game fishing (although there's still some bad behaviour and beach boys). Watamu is a real village as well; on the road you'll see mud-and-thatch houses overlooking family-sized *shambas* (farm plots). If you wade out into the water, wear beach shoes or sandals; there's a lot of sharp coral out there.

Information

There are now no banks in Watamu, so your only options are the foreign exchange bureaus at the big hotels and Tunda Tours. If you need to use an ATM, your nearest choices are Kilifi and Malindi. Online information can be found at www.wat amu.net.

Corner Connections (Watamu Supermarket) Internet access.

Post office (Gede Rd)

Telkom Kenya office (Beach Way Rd)

Tunda Tours (☎ 042-32079; Beach Way Rd; per min KSh5) Heavily touted internet access.

Sights

BIO KEN SNAKE FARM & LABORATORY

This excellent **snake farm** (☎ 042-32303; snakes@africaonline.co.ke; adult/child KSh500/free; 🕙 10am-noon & 2-5pm) is by far the best of the snake parks along the coast. It was established by the late James Ashe, a reptile expert and former curator from the National Museums of Kenya. As well as touring the facilities, staff can take you on a day safari to look for snakes in their natural habitat (KSh4500).

The centre is just north of Watamu village on the main beach road.

WATAMU MARINE NATIONAL PARK

The southern part of Malindi Marine Reserve, this **marine park** (adult/child US$5/2) includes some magnificent coral reefs and abundant fishlife. It is situated around 2km offshore from Watamu. To get to the park you'll need to hire a glass-bottomed boat, which is easy enough at the **KWS office** (☎ 042-32393), at the end of the coast road, where you pay the park fees. For marine-park trips, boat operators ask anything from KSh1800 to KSh3500 per person, excluding park fees; it's all negotiable. All the big hotels offer 'goggling' (snorkelling) trips to nonguests for around KSh1500.

TURTLES

All credit to the good guys: **Watamu Turtle Watch** (www.watamuturtles.com) provides a service, and that is protecting the marine turtles that come here to lay eggs on the beach. Contact the trust's **Marine Information Centre** (☎ 042-32118; paradise@swiftmalindi.com; 🕙 9.30am-12.30pm & 2-5pm Mon-Sat) if you're interested in seeing this spectacle, volunteering, 'adopting' a turtle or buying medicine for sick turtles; programs run from KSh500 to KSh5000 (see www.adoptaseaturtle.com).

Activities

Aqua Ventures (☎ 042-32420; www.diveinkenya.com), at Ocean Sports Hotel, offers guided dives in the marine park for US$35 and a PADI course for US$335; it's also good for diving expeditions around Malindi. The best time to be underwater is between October and March. Avoid diving from June to August because of rough seas and poor visibility. Dive trips to the Tewa Caves at the mouth of Mida Creek are popular, where a group of giant rock cod loiter menacingly at the bottom.

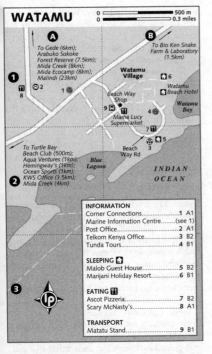

Tunda Tours (☎ 0733-952383; www.tundatourssafaris .com; Beach Way Rd) runs fishing safaris (half/full day US$355/500).

A lot of anglers head to **Hemingway's** (☎ 32624; www.hemingways.co.ke), where rates run around US$785 per boat (high season, up to four anglers). Hemingway's is also a luxury lodge, but was under renovation when we visited – it's open now during the high season (mid-July to April). People are a little more environmentally sensitive now than in old Ernie's day – tag and release is standard procedure.

Sleeping & Eating

Malob Guest House (☎ 042-32260; Beach Way Rd; s KSh800) This is a good option: a series of simple rooms set around an open court-yard, comfy and friendly and, for this area, incredibly cheap.

Marijani Holiday Resort (☎ 042-32448; www.mari jani-holiday-resort.com; KSh1950/2500, cottages €38.50-52) Best described as a coral villa, Marijani is a friendly, German-owned place that's probably the best sleep in Watamu village. Rooms are airy and elegant, and the grounds are home

of several parrots, curious housecats and chillin' tortoises.

Turtle Bay Beach Club (☎ 042-32003; www.turtlebay .co.ke; s/d/tr KSh5500/6400/7000; 🅿 💻 🛒 🏊) This is easily our favourite resort in Watamu, if not the coast: an ecominded hotel that uses managed tree cover to hide its environmental imprint, runs enough ecotourism ventures to fill a book (including bird-watching safaris and turtle-protection programmes), contrib-utes to local charities and all sorts of other do-gooder stuff.

Ocean Sports (☎ 042-32624; www.oceansports.net; s/d low season US$135/166, high season US$165/200; 🛒 🏊) Some of the rooms are a bit mildew-y (ask to have a sniff), but this is a fine and friendly eccentric fishing lodge. The layout is quite smart, with most rooms commanding a teal vista all the way down to the beach.

Ascot Pizzeria (Ascot Hotel; mains KSh250-750) Many places on the coast hide a distinctly good Italian place, and the Ascot, located in the hotel of the same name, is Watamu's note-worthy contribution to the cause.

Scary McNasty's (☎ 042-32500; KSh350-700) With a name like that, how could we not include this place? For the record it's owned by an expat Brit, serves genuine black pudding (not McNasty, if scary) and does a very good line in all the other UK pub greats you may be missing.

Getting There & Around

There are *matatus* between Malindi and Watamu throughout the day (KSh50, one hour). All *matatus* pass the turn-off to the Gede ruins (KSh10). For Mombasa, the easi-est option is to take a *matatu* to the highway (KSh10) and flag down a bus or *matatu*. A handful of motorised rickshaws ply the vil-lage and beach road; a ride to the KWS office should cost around KSh250.

MIDA CREEK

Mida Creek is hugged by a gentle, silver-tinged mudflats flowing with ghost crabs and long tides; the dark, creeping marriage of land and water epitomized by a mangrove forest and the salt-and-fresh sweet scent of wind over an estuary.

Visiting here helps the local Giriama community, which works with A Rocha and Arabuko-Sokoke Schools & Eco-Tourism Scheme (Assets, which also works in Arabuko-Sokoke National Forest) to create one of our

KENYA

favourite ecotourism projects in Africa: **Mida Ecocamp** (☎ 0729-213042; www.midaecocamp.com; cottage KSh850-1100, camping KSh200) located just off the coast highway (B8) about 8km south of Watamu.

Excellent Giriama **guides** (tickets adult/child KSh 150/100, guides KSh200) will take you through the water-laced landscape of the creek to the nearby mangrove forest. A bird blind looks out over the surrounding wetlands, while a rope bridge leads back into the mangroves, where giant crabs cling to tree trunks and oysters can be plucked and eaten off the ground.

At the ecocamp itself is a lovely restaurant (mains KSh250 to KSh650), wind-conditioned *makuti*-topped bar, the opportunity to venture into nearby villages on culture tours (your money goes to local schools) and three huts – Giriama, Swahili and Zanzibari – for sleeping. They're all lovely.

Mida Creek saves its real appeal for evening, when bonfires are lit and the stars, and we're not exaggerating, simply rain down on you.

ARABUKO SOKOKE FOREST RESERVE

Elephants are such an indelibly African image, but what about the elephant shrew? Specifically, the golden-rumped elephant shrew, which is about the size of a rabbit and cute as a playground full of kittens?

They're only found here, in **Arabuko Sokoke Forest Reserve** (adult/child US$20/10), the largest tract of indigenous coastal forest remaining in East Africa. But there's way more than yellow-butted *macroscelidea* – try 240 bird species, including the also completely endemic Clarke's Weaver. Throw in a herd of forest elephants, the scops owl (only 15cm tall) and 260 species of butterfly and you start to understand why this habitat is so vital for wildlife conservation (see p318).

The **Arabuko Sokoke Visitor Centre** (☎ 042-32462; Malindi Rd; ⏰ 8am-4pm) is very helpful; it's at Gede Forest Station, with displays on the various species found here. The noticeboard in the centre shows the sites of recent wildlife sightings.

From the visitor centre, a series of nature trails, running tracks and 4WD paths cuts through the forest. There are more bird trails at **Whistling Duck Pools**, **Kararacha Pools** and **Spinetail Way**, located 16km further south. Near Kararacha is **Singwaya Cultural Centre**, where traditional dances can be arranged.

There are basic **campsites** (camping per person US$8) close to the visitor centre and further

south near Spinetail Way. With permission, camping is also allowed deeper within the forest or at the treehouse by Sand Quarry. (Acrobatic nymphomaniacs take note: a painted warning prohibits sex here!)

The forest is just off the main Malindi–Mombasa road. The main gate to the forest and visitor centre is about 1.5km west of the turn-off to Gede and Watamu, while the Mida entrance is about 3km further south. All buses and *matatus* between Mombasa and Malindi can drop you at either entrance. From Watamu, *matatus* to Malindi can drop you at the main junction.

GEDE RUINS

Some 4km from Watamu, just off the main Malindi–Mombasa road, are the famous **Gede ruins** (adult/child KSh500/250; ⏰ 7am-6pm), one of the principal historical monuments on the coast. Hidden away in the forest is a vast complex of derelict houses, palaces and mosques, made all the more mysterious by the fact that there seem to be no records of Gede's existence in any historical texts.

Gede (or Gedi) was established and actively trading by at least the 13th century. Excavations have uncovered porcelain, glass and glazed earthenware, indicating not only trade links, but a taste for luxury among Gede's Swahili elite. Within the compound are ruins of ornate tombs and mosques, and the regal ruins of a Swahili palace, further evidence of Gede's prosperity.

When the city was abandoned in the 17th or 18th century, the forest took over and the site was lost to the world until the 1920s. Since then, there have been extensive excavations, revealing the remains of substantial Swahili houses and complex sanitation facilities, including toilets and cisterns for ritual washing. Most of the excavated buildings are concentrated in a dense cluster near the entrance gate, but there are dozens of other ruins scattered through the forest.

Walking Tour

The tree-shrouded ruins are very atmospheric and you'll often have the site to yourself if you visit early in the morning. Guides are available at the gate for KSh300; they definitely help bring the site to life, pointing out the various trees and plants as well as interesting features of the buildings, but will generally stick to a standard circuit of the most important ruins.

Gedi – Historical Monument (KSh50), a guidebook to the ruins containing a map and descriptions of many buildings, should be available at the ticket office or the museum shop.

On your right as you enter the compound is the **Dated Tomb (1)**, so called because of the inscription on the wall, featuring the Muslim date corresponding to 1399. This tomb has provided a reference point for dating other buildings within the complex. Near it, inside the wall, is the **Tomb of the Fluted Pillar (2)**, which is characteristic of such pillar designs found along the East African coast.

Past the tomb, next to the **House of the Long Court (3)**, the **Great Mosque (4)** is one of Gede's most significant buildings. It originally dates from the mid-15th century, but was rebuilt a century later, possibly after damage sustained at the time of Gede's first abandonment. The mosque is of typical East African design with a mihrab or echo chamber facing Mecca.

Behind the mosque are the ruins of an extensive **palace (5)** spread out over 100 sq metres and thought to have been owned by the former ruler of Gede. This regal structure is entered through a complete arched doorway and many interesting features have been preserved, including the great audience hall and a strongroom with no doors or windows. The palace also has a particularly fine **pillar tomb (6)**; the hexagonal shape is unique in East Africa.

Follow the path past the tomb, around old **Swahili houses (7)** that have been excavated

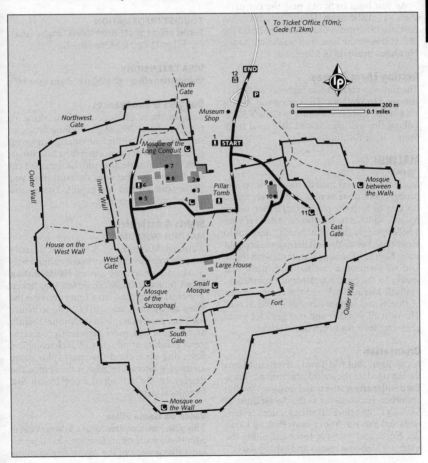

here, in a compact group beside the Great Mosque and the palace. They're each named after particular features of their design or after objects found in them by archaeologists. The **House of the Cistern (8)** is particularly interesting, with ancient illustrations incised into the plaster walls.

The other excavations on the site are more spread out, with numerous paths running through the woods from the main complex. The most interesting structures are east of the Great Mosque, including the **House of the Dhow (9)**, the **House of the Double Court (10)** and the nearby **Mosque of the Three Aisles (11)**, which has the largest well at Gede. There are a handful of other structures in the forest if you wish to explore further.

As you head back out past the car park, there's a small **museum (12)** and 'interpretation centre' with displays of artefacts found on the site, although the best stuff was taken to the Fort Jesus museum in Mombasa.

Getting There & Away
The ruins lay off the main highway on the access road to Watamu. The easiest way here is via a Watamu-bound *matatu* to Gede Village. Follow the well-signposted dirt road from there – it's a 10-minute walk.

MALINDI
☎ 042

Malindi is lot nicer than its haters realise, and probably not quite as nice as its lovers insist. It's easy to bash the place as an Italian beach resort – which it is. But you can't deny it's got a *bella spiaggia* (beautiful beach), and not to stereotype, but all those Italians have brought some high gastronomic standards with them. Did we mention a fascinating history that speaks to the great narrative of exploration, Malindi Marine Park and the twisty warren of thatch and whitewash that is Old Town? Throw it all together and you get a lot more character than the beach bums let on.

Orientation
It's no Lamu, but Old Town, which runs from the bus stands to the oceanfront curio market, is filled with narrow streets and medieval Swahili ambience. It also serves as the closest thing to Malindi's 'city centre'. Tourist services, restaurants and bars run from Uhuru Park up Lamu Rd. North and south of town and along the water are high-end resorts and expat palaces.

Information
EMERGENCY
Ambulance (☎ 042-30575)
Fire (☎ 042-31001, 0733-550990)
Police (☎ 042-31555; Kenyatta Rd)

INTERNET ACCESS
Bling Net (☎ 042-30041; Lamu Rd; per min KSh2)

MONEY
Barclays Bank (☎ 042-20036; Lamu Rd)
Dollar Forex Bureau (☎ 042-30602; Lamu Rd)
Standard Chartered Bank (☎ 042-20130; Stanchart Arcade, Lamu Rd)

POST
Post office (Kenyatta Rd)

TOURIST INFORMATION
Tourist office (☎ 042-20689; Malindi Complex, Lamu Rd; ☯ 8am-12.30pm & 2-4.30pm Mon-Fri)

VISA EXTENSIONS
Immigration office (☎ 042-20149; Mama Ngina Rd)

Dangers & Annoyances
Being on the beach alone at night is asking for trouble. There's lots of guys selling drugs, so remember: everything from marijuana on up is illegal. Sales of drugs often turn into stings, with the confidante drug supplier getting a cut of whatever fee that cops demand from you (if they don't throw you in jail). There's also a lot of prostitution here.

Sights & Activities
MALINDI MUSEUM
National Museums of Kenya has smartly brought together the three major cultural sites of Malindi under one general **Malindi Historic Circuit** (adult/child KSh500/250; ☯ 8am-6pm) ticket. The most compelling attraction covered is the **House of Columns** (Mama Ngina Rd). The structure itself is a good example of traditional Swahili architecture and, more pertinently, contains great exhibits of all sorts of archaeological finds dug up around the coast (plus some amusingly interactive areas – don't miss the display on the netting of a coelacanth fish from local waters).

Vasco da Gama Pillar
This **pillar** (turn-off on Mama Ngina Rd, by Scorpio Villas) is admittedly more impressive for what it represents (the genesis of the Age of Exploration)

than the edifice itself. Erected by Vasco da Gama as a navigational aid in 1498, the coral column is topped by a cross made of Lisbon stone, which almost certainly dates from the explorer's time. There are good views from here down the coast and out, thousands of kilometres east, to India, where Portugal and eventually Europe would extend its political control. If you can (the guards didn't mind when we visited) come at night; the rock pools glow with phosphorescence and firefly larvae, all quite magical under an Indian Ocean star-studded sky.

Portuguese Church

This tiny thatched **Portuguese church** (Mama Ngina Rd) is so called because Vasco da Gama is reputed to have erected it, and two of his crew are supposedly buried here. While the veracity of this claim is somewhat dubious, it's certainly true that St Francis Xavier visited on his way to India. The rest of the compound is taken up by the graves of Catholic missionaries.

JUMAA MOSQUE

Behind the main Malindi mosque are the ruins of **Jumaa Mosque and Palace** (Mama Ngina Rd), but if you're not a Muslim, you can't get inside. The main appeal is a large pillar tomb, which stands incongruously in the centre of Old Town.

MALINDI MARINE NATIONAL PARK

The oldest **marine park** (adult/child US$10/5; ⌚ 7am-7pm) in Kenya covers 213 sq km of rainbow clouds of powder blue fish, organ pipe coral, green sea turtles and beds of Thalassian sea grass. If you're extremely lucky, you may spot mako and whale sharks. Unfortunately, these reefs have suffered (and continue to suffer) extensive damage, evidenced by the piles of seashells on sale in Malindi. Note that silt from the Galana River reduces underwater visibility between March and June.

You'll likely come here on a snorkelling or glass-bottom-boat tour, which can be arranged at the **KWS office** (☎ 042-20845; malindimnp@kws.org, malindimnp@swiftmalindi.com) on the coast road south of town. Boats only go out at low tide, so it's a good idea to call in advance to check times (your hotel can help). The going rate is around KSh4000 per boat (five to 10 people) for a two-hour trip.

DIVING

Most hotels offer diving excursions. Or try the following:

Aqua Ventures (☎ 042-32420; www.diveinkenya.com; Driftwood Beach Club)

Blue Fin (☎ 0722-261242; www.bluefindiving.com) Operates out of several Malindi resorts.

Sleeping

Tana Guest House (☎ 042-30940; Jamhuri St; s/d/tr KSh550/550/650, s/d with shared bathroom KSh350/450) If you're scraping the budget barrel, you probably can't come up with a better price and location than this place, by one of the town's bus stops. Rooms are clean, with mozzie nets, squat toilets and other joys of budget travel life.

Gossip Hotel (☎ 0723-516602; Mama Ngina Rd; s/d KSh800/1400) This quirky little place has piles of amusing junk/antiques downstairs along with a TV. The rooms themselves are decent, if a little dusty, and views from upper-floor balconies onto the water are lovely.

Ozi's Guest House (☎ 042-20218; ozi@swiftmalindi .com; Mama Ngina Rd; r KSh1500) Ozi's has long been popular with backpackers, likely because it perches on the attractive edge of Old Town (and next to a mosque). It runs good tours and has friendly service that knows the needs of independent travellers.

Jardin Lorna (☎ 042-30658; harry@swiftmalindi .com; Ngowe Rd; r KSh2500-3500; ✕ ❑) Lorna is very unpretentious, providing accommodation mainly for students of the Hospitality Training & Management Institute. Rooms are endearingly quirky, zebra rugs and local art punctuate the interior.

Kilili Baharini Resort (☎ 042-20169; www.kililibaharini .com; Casuarina Rd; half board s/d from US$153/182; ✕ ❑) Italian-run and gorgeous, Kilili's options run between breeze-catching Swahili-inspired suites and a new wing inspired by a lush (but elegantly executed) *Arabian Nights* theme. The beach is particularly fine, as are the restaurants.

Driftwood Beach Club (☎ 042-20155; www.driftwood club.com; Mama Ngina Rd; s/d/tr KSh8750/12,500/18,7500, cottages KSh35,600; ✕ ❑ ♿) One of the best-known resorts in Malindi, Driftwood prides itself on an informal atmosphere and attracts a more independent clientele than many of its peers. The ambience is closer to palm-breezed serenity than the party atmosphere at similar hotels.

Eating

Jardin Lorna Restaurant (☎ 042-30658; Mtangani Rd; mains KSh250-550) Who likes creatively concocted

KENYA

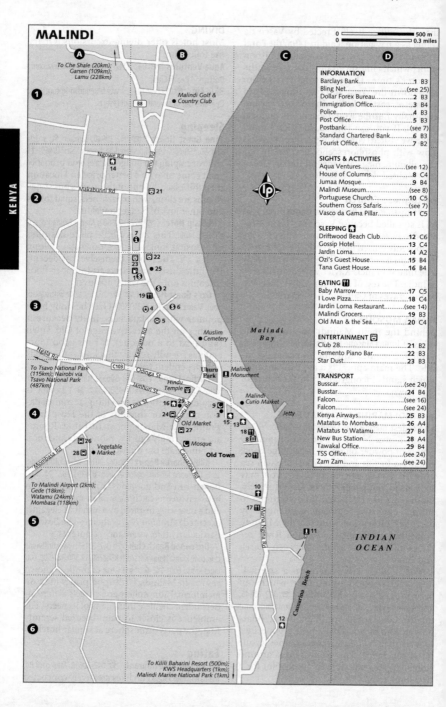

MALINDI

0	500 m
0	0.3 miles

INFORMATION

Barclays Bank	1 B3
Bling Net	(see 25)
Dollar Forex Bureau	2 B3
Immigration Office	3 B4
Police	4 B3
Post Office	5 B3
Postbank	(see 7)
Standard Chartered Bank	6 B3
Tourist Office	7 B2

SIGHTS & ACTIVITIES

Aqua Ventures	(see 12)
House of Columns	8 C4
Jumaa Mosque	9 B4
Malindi Museum	(see 8)
Portuguese Church	10 C5
Southern Cross Safaris	(see 7)
Vasco da Gama Pillar	11 C5

SLEEPING 🏠

Driftwood Beach Club	12 C6
Gossip Hotel	13 C4
Jardin Lorna	14 A2
Ozi's Guest House	15 B4
Tana Guest House	16 B4

EATING 🍴

Baby Marrow	17 C5
I Love Pizza	18 C4
Jardin Lorna Restaurant	(see 14)
Malindi Grocers	19 B3
Old Man & the Sea	20 C4

ENTERTAINMENT 🎭

Club 28	21 B2
Fermento Piano Bar	22 B3
Star Dust	23 B3

TRANSPORT

Busscar	(see 24)
Busstar	24 B4
Falcon	(see 16)
Falcon	(see 24)
Kenya Airways	25 B3
Matatus to Mombasa	26 A4
Matatus to Watamu	27 B4
New Bus Station	28 A4
Tawakal Office	29 B4
TSS Office	(see 24)
Zam Zam	(see 24)

To Che Shale (20km);
Garsen (109km);
Lamu (228km)

Malindi Golf &
Country Club

Ngowe Rd

Makaburini Rd

Muslim
Cemetery

*Malindi
Bay*

To Tsavo National Park
(115km); Nairobi via
Tsavo National Park
(487km)

Odinga St

Jamhuri St

Tana St

Uhuru
Park

Malindi
Monument

Hindu
Temple

Malindi
Curio Market

Jetty

Old Market

Malindi
Curio Market

Mosque

Old Town

Vegetable
Market

To Malindi Airport (2km);
Gede (18km);
Watamu (24km);
Mombasa (118km)

*INDIAN
OCEAN*

Casuarina Beach

To Kilili Baharini Resort (500m);
KWS Headquarters (1km);
Malindi Marine National Park (1km)

French food served in a green garden? The endearingly enthusiastic service from the staff (students at the local Hospitality Training & Management Institute) is the best feature.

I Love Pizza (☎ 042-20672; Mama Ngina Rd; nwright@africaonline.co.ke; pizzas KSh250-750, mains from KSh600) We do too, and the pizza is done really, really well here. Waaay better than you might expect this far from New York or Naples. The porch-front and Mediterranean atmosphere puts the olive on this excellent pizza pie.

Old Man and the Sea (☎ 042-31106; Mama Ngina Rd; mains KSh400-750, seafood KSh550-1100) The Godfather of Malindi's dining mafia, this Old Man's been serving elegant, excellent cuisine using a combination of local ingredients and fresh recipes for years. The classy waitstaff and wicker-chic ambience all combine for some nice colonial-style, candelit meals under the stars.

Baby Marrow (☎ 0733-542584; Mama Ngina Rd; mains KSh500-2000) Everything about this place is quirkily stylish, from the thatched veranda and plant-horse to the Italian-based menu and tasty seafood (KSh1400 to KSh1800). We're hoping the 'titramisu' is a misprint though.

Drinking & Entertainment

Fermento Piano Bar (☎ 042-31780; Galana Centre, Lamu Rd; admission KSh200; ☽ from 10pm Wed, Fri & Sat; ☢) 'For those of the night' – Fermento has the town's hippest dance floor, apparently once frequented by Naomi Campbell. It's young, trendy and Italian, so try to look as such yourself if you show up here.

The main nightclubs outside the resorts are **Star Dust** (Lamu Rd) and **Club 28** (Lamu Rd), which open erratically in the low season but are generally crammed when they do. Expect lots of working-girl/beach boy attention.

Getting There & Away

AIR

There are daily flights with **Airkenya** (☎ 042-30646; Malindi Airport) to Nairobi. **Kenya Airways** (☎ 042-20237; Lamu Rd) flies the same route at least once a day. **Mombasa Air Safari** (☎ 041-433061) has daily flights to Mombasa and Lamu (US$62, 30 minutes) in the high season.

BUS & MATATU

There are numerous daily buses to Mombasa (KSh150, two hours). Companies such as Busstar, Busscar, TSS and Falcon have offices opposite the old market in the centre of Malindi. All have daily departures to Nairobi at around 7am and/or 7pm (KSh850 to KSh1100, 10 to 12 hours), via Mombasa. *Matatus* to Watamu (KSh50, one hour) leave from the old market in town.

There are usually at least six buses a day to Lamu. Tawakal buses leave at 8.30am, Falcon at 8.45am and Zam Zam at 10.30am; the fare runs from KSh400 to KSh600. The journey takes at least four hours between Malindi and the jetty at Mokowe. The ferry to Lamu from the mainland costs KSh50 (20 minutes) or KSh100 for a speedboat.

Getting Around

You can rent bicycles from most hotels or the KWS for KSh200 to KSh500 per day. This is the best way to get around town unless you prefer to walk, which is a great way of exploring the Old Town area (conversely, cycling can be tough in Old Town's narrow streets). Cycling at night is not permitted. Tuk-tuks are ubiquitous – a trip from town to the KWS office should cost KSh150 to KSh200.

MARAFA

The Marafa Depression, also known as Hell's Kitchen or Nyari (the Place Broken by Itself) is the most underrated site on the coast (if not Kenya). It's a real Natural Wonder, an eroded sandstone gorge where jungle, red rock and cliffs upheave themselves into a single stunning Marscape. We're not exaggerating when we say going to Malindi and missing the Depression – like many do – is like visiting Arizona and giving the Grand Canyon a pass.

About 30km northeast of Malindi, the Depression is currently managed as a local tourism concern by Marafa village. It costs KSh250 (which goes into village programs) to walk around the lip of the gorge, and a bit more (depending on your generosity; we'd recommend at least KSh200) for a guide who can walk you into the sandstone heart of the ridges.

Most people visit here on organised tours, with a self-drive car or by taxi (KSh7000). Alternatively, there are one or two morning *matatus* from Mombasa Rd in Malindi to Marafa village (KSh140, three hours), and from there it's a 30-minute walk to Hell's Kitchen. You may have to spend the night in one of the basic lodges, as all *matatus* travel in the morning.

KENYA

LET'S GO SURF A KITE

There are plenty of beach resorts offering kite-surfing classes, which are very popular on the Kenyan coast. Our favourite place to pick up this pastime and experience utter tropical escapism is **Che Shale** (☎ 0722-230931; www.cheshale.com; s/d US$65/115), one of the best-executed sandy retreats we've stumbled across. Located at the end of a long dirt track (you'll need a 4WD, or arrange pick up with the hotel) about 30 minutes north of Malindi is this village that manages to blend Swahili aesthetic with contemporary flash in a way that's luxurious and tasteful. There's a huge thatched bar and playfully irreverent riffs on the 'coconut-chic' thing. To top it off, Che Shale's isolated location and instructors make for some of the best kite-surfing instruction on the coast; a full course for beginners is US$300

LAMU
☎ 042

Lamu town has that excellent destination quality of immediately standing out as you approach it from the water (and let's face it – everything is cooler when approached from water). The shopfronts and mosques, faded under the relentless kiss of the salt wind, creep out from behind a forest of dhow masts. Then you take to the streets, or more accurately, the labyrinth: donkey-wide alleyways; robed children grinning from the alleys; women whispering by in full length *bui-bui*; cats casually ruling the rooftops; blue smoke from meat grilling over open fires; and the organic, biting scent of cured wood affixed into a townhouse made of stone and coral. Many visitors call this town, the oldest living one in East Africa, the highlight of their trip to Kenya. Residents call it *Kiwa Ndeo* – The Vain Island – and to be fair, there's plenty for them to be vain about.

History

In pre-Arab times the islands were home to the Bajun, but their traditions vanished almost entirely with the arrival of the Arabs. A distinctly nautical culture emerged; as A H J Prins describes it in *Sailing From Lamu* '…one can fairly say that the coast is characterised by this [Lamu's] very culture: at same time Islamic, African and Maritime.'

Lamu was also, as islands are wont to be, extremely insular. Breaking into the aristocracy, even with polished Arab credentials, was difficult for outsiders. When Ali Habib Saleh, founder of Lamu's mosque college (one of the most respected Islamic institutions in East Africa), arrived here, he initially was not allowed to live in a stone house and was lodged on the outskirts of town.

In the 19th century, the soldiers of Lamu caught the warriors of Paté on open mud at low tide and slaughtered them; this victory, plus the resultant cash cows of ivory and slavery as Lamu gained control of both trades, made Lamu a splendidly wealthy place, and most of the fine Swahili houses that survive today were built during this period.

It all came to an end in 1873, when the British forced Sultan Barghash of Zanzibar to close down the slave markets. With the abolition of slavery, the economy went into rapid decline. The city-state was incorporated into the British Protectorate from 1890, and became part of Kenya with independence in 1963.

Until it was 'rediscovered' by travellers in the 1970s, Lamu existed in a state of humble obscurity. Today, only Zanzibar can offer such a feast of Swahili culture and uncorrupted traditional architecture. In 2001 Lamu town was added to Unesco's list of World Heritage Sites.

Orientation

Although there are several restaurants and places to stay along the waterfront (Harambee Ave), most of the guesthouses are tucked away in the maze of alleys behind. Lamu's main thoroughfare is Kenyatta Rd, a long winding alley known popularly as 'Main St', which runs from the northern end of town, past the fort, and then south to the Muslim cemetery and the inland track to Shela. If you walk west the town peters out in a series of row houses, then fields, then nothing.

Information

INTERNET ACCESS
Lynx Infosystems (per min KSh2; ⊙ 8am-10pm)

MEDICAL SERVICES
King Fadh Lamu District Hospital (☎ 042-633012; Kenyatta Rd) One of the most modern and well-equipped hospitals on the coast. It's south of the town centre.

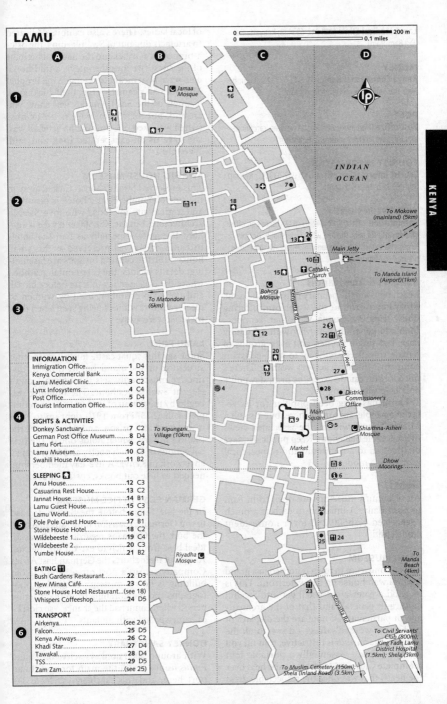

LAMU

KENYA

INDIAN OCEAN

To Mokowe (mainland) (5km)

Main Jetty

To Manda Island (Airport)(1km)

To Matondoni (6km)

To Kipungani Village (10km)

Main Square

Market

Dhow Moorings

To Manda Beach (4km)

Riyadha Mosque

To Civil Servants' Club (800m); King Fadh Lamu District Hospital (1.5km); Shela (3km)

To Muslim Cemetery (150m); Shela (Inland Road) (3.5km)

Kenyatta Rd

Harambee Ave

Kenyatta Rd

0 — 200 m
0 — 0.1 miles

Jamaa Mosque

Catholic Church

Bohora Mosque

Shiaithna-Asheri Mosque

District Commissioner's Office

INFORMATION
Immigration Office	**1**	D4
Kenya Commercial Bank	**2**	D3
Lamu Medical Clinic	**3**	C2
Lynx Infosystems	**4**	C4
Post Office	**5**	D4
Tourist Information Office	**6**	D5

SIGHTS & ACTIVITIES
Donkey Sanctuary	**7**	C2
German Post Office Museum	**8**	D4
Lamu Fort	**9**	C4
Lamu Museum	**10**	C3
Swahili House Museum	**11**	B2

SLEEPING ⌂
Amu House	**12**	C3
Casuarina Rest House	**13**	C2
Jannat House	**14**	B1
Lamu Guest House	**15**	C3
Lamu World	**16**	C1
Pole Pole Guest House	**17**	B1
Stone House Hotel	**18**	C2
Wildebeeste 1	**19**	C4
Wildebeeste 2	**20**	C3
Yumbe House	**21**	B2

EATING 🍴
Bush Gardens Restaurant	**22**	D3
New Minaa Café	**23**	C6
Stone House Hotel Restaurant	(see 18)	
Whispers Coffeeshop	**24**	D5

TRANSPORT
Airkenya	(see 24)	
Falcon	**25**	D5
Kenya Airways	**26**	C2
Khadi Star	**27**	D4
Tawakal	**28**	D4
TSS	**29**	D5
Zam Zam	(see 25)	

Lamu Medical Clinic (☎ 042-633438; Kenyatta Rd; ☯ 8am-9pm)

MONEY
Kenya Commercial Bank (☎ 042-633327; Harambee Ave) The only bank on Lamu has an ATM.

POST
Post office (Harambee Ave) Postal services, cardphones and the best internet connections in town.

TOURIST INFORMATION
Tourist information office (☎ 042-633132; Kenyatta Rd; ☯ 9am-1pm & 2-4pm)

VISA EXTENSIONS
Immigration office (☎ 042-633032) There's an office off Kenyatta Rd near the fort where you should be able to get visa extensions, although travellers are sometimes referred to Mombasa.

Dangers & Annoyances
Beach boys are the primary nuisance in Lamu. Most loiter around the waterfront offering dhow trips, marijuana and other 'services'. Men can generally get away with a friendly chat, but single women and even groups of female travellers are likely to have constant company, which can get *very* wearing. There's not a lot you can do except be firm, stay polite and keep on walking.

Lamu has long been popular for its relaxed and tolerant atmosphere, but it's still a Muslim island, with all the associated views of acceptable behaviour. Keep public displays of affection to a minimum and respect local attitudes to modesty.

Sights
All of Lamu's museums are open from 8am to 6pm daily. Admission to each is a much overpriced KSh500/250 for a nonresident adult/child

LAMU MUSEUM
The best museum in town is housed in a grand Swahili warehouse on the waterfront. This is as good a gateway as you'll get into Swahili culture in general, and that of the archipelago in particular. Of note are the displays of traditional women's dress – if you think the head-to-toe *bui-bui* is restrictive, wait till you see the *shiraa* – essentially a portable tent (complete with wooden frame to be held over the head) that was once the respectable dress of local ladies. There's also exhibits dedicated to artefacts dug out of Swahili ruins, the bric-a-brac of local tribes and the nautical heritage of the coast (we love the *mtepe*, a traditional coir-sewn boat meant to resemble the Prophet Muhammad's camel – ergo, their nickname: 'Camels of the Sea'). Guides will show you around, but their knowledge is hit-or-miss (when we asked one how old an artefact was, she gave us an exasperated look and said, 'Very old').

SWAHILI HOUSE MUSEUM
This preserved Swahili house, tucked away to the side of Yumbe House hotel, is beautiful, and a great site for those who love Swahili architecture. But the KSh500 entry fee is very hard to justify, especially as half the hotels in Lamu are as well preserved as this small house. Still, the cultural insights are fascinating; details include the ceremonial deathbed where the deceased lay in state before burial, and the echo chamber, used by women to receive visitors without being seen when their menfolk were away.

LAMU FORT
Some say this squat castle lords it over other structures on the island, but we think its distinctive muscularity sets it off from Lamu's elegant Swahili aesthetic. The building was begun by the Sultan of Paté in 1810 and completed in 1823. From 1910 right up to 1984 it was used as a prison, and now houses the island's library, which holds one of the best collections of Swahili poetry and Lamu reference work in Kenya. A five-day membership, needed to take out books, costs KSh200.

GERMAN POST OFFICE MUSEUM
In the late 1800s, before the British decided to nip German expansion into Tanganyika in the bud, the Germans regarded Lamu as an ideal base from which to exploit the interior. As part of their efforts the German East Africa Company set up a post office, and the old building is now a museum exhibiting photographs and memorabilia from that fleeting period when Lamu had the chance – so close! – of being spelled with umlauts.

DONKEY SANCTUARY
With around 3000 donkeys active on Lamu, *Equus asinus* is still the main form of transport here, and this **sanctuary** (☎ 042-633303;

Harambee Ave; admission free; 🕑 9am-1pm Mon-Fri) was established by the International Donkey Protection Trust of Sidmouth, UK, to improve the lot of the island's hard-working beasts of burden. The project provides free veterinary services to donkey owners and tends to injured, sick or worn-out animals.

Activities

Taking a **dhow trip** is almost obligatory and drifting through the mangroves is a wonderful way to experience the islands. Prices vary depending on where you want to go and how long you go for; with a bit of bargaining you should pay around KSh500 per person. Groups of more than five aren't recommended as the boats aren't very big.

Whatever you arrange, make sure you know exactly how much you'll be paying and what that will include, to avoid misunderstandings and overcharging. Don't hand over any money until the day of departure, except perhaps a small advance for food. On long trips, it's best to organise your own drinks. Make sure you take a hat and some sunscreen, as there is rarely any shade on the dhows.

Most day trips meander around the channel between Lamu and Manda Islands, and the price includes fishing and snorkelling. Lunch is usually served on a beach on Manda Island. Longer trips head for Manda Toto Island, which has better snorkelling. Multiday trips head out to the remote island of Kiwayu (p334).

Dhows without an outboard motor are entirely dependent on wind and tides, so it's probably unwise to go on a long trip if you have a flight or other appointment to meet.

Walking Tour

The best, indeed only, way to see Lamu town is on foot. This tour will take you past some of the more noteworthy buildings in under an hour, but don't feel bound to follow it too rigidly. In fact, getting slightly lost is a vital part of the process!

Most of Lamu's buildings date back to the 18th century and are constructed out of local materials, with cut coral-rag blocks for the walls, wooden floors supported by mangrove poles and intricately carved shutters for windows. Lavish decorations were created using carved plaster, and carpenters were employed to produce ornately carved window and door frames as a sign of the financial status of the

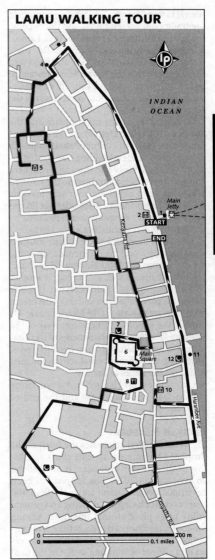

LAMU WALKING TOUR

owners. There are so many wonderful Swahili houses that it's pointless to specify examples – keep your eyes open and don't forget to look up.

Starting at the **main jetty (1)**, head north past the **Lamu Museum (2**; opposite) and along the waterfront until you reach the **door carving workshops (3)**. In recent years there has been a real revival in woodcarving, and you can once again see traditional carved lintels and doors being made in workshops like these all over Lamu.

From here head onto Kenyatta Rd, passing an original Swahili **well (4)**, and head into the alleys towards the **Swahili House Museum (5**; p330). When you've had your fill of domestic insights, take any route back towards the Kenyatta Rd.

Once you've hit the main square and the **fort (6**; p330), take a right to see the crumbled remains of the 14th-century **Pwani Mosque (7)**, one of Lamu's oldest buildings; an Arabic inscription is still visible on the wall. From here you can head round and browse the covered **market (8)**, then negotiate your way towards the bright Saudi-funded **Riyadha Mosque (9)**, the centre of Lamu's religious scene, founded by the great scholar Habib Swaleh in 1891.

From here head back to the waterfront, then stroll back up along the promenade, diverting for the **German Post Office Museum (10**; p330) if you haven't already seen it – the door is another amazing example of Swahili carving. If you're feeling the pace, take a rest and shoot the breeze on the **baraza ya wazee** (Old Men's Bench; **11)** outside the appealing stucco minarets of the **Shiaithna-Asheri Mosque (12)**. Benches of this kind were a crucial feature of any Swahili home, providing an informal social setting for men to discuss the issues of the day.

Carrying on up Harambee Ave will bring you back to the main jetty and the end of our tour.

Festivals & Events

The **Maulid Festival** celebrates the birth of the Prophet Mohammed. Its date shifts according to the Muslim calendar; it will fall on 26 February in 2010. The festival has been celebrated on the island for more than 100 years and much singing, dancing and general jollity takes place around this time. Among the cooler traditional dances is the quivering-sword dance, where sword-wielding dancers set up a chorus of vibrating steel. On the final day a procession heads down to the tomb of the man who started it all, Ali Habib Swaleh. The **Lamu Cultural Festival** is another colourful carnival, held in the last week of August.

Sleeping

BUDGET

There's always scope for price negotiation here, especially if you plan to stay for more than a day or two. Touts will invariably try and accompany you to get commission; the best way to avoid this is to book at least one night in advance, so you know ahead of time what you'll be paying.

If you plan on staying for a while it's worth making inquiries about renting a house, so long as there's a group of you to share the cost. Note that most streets in Lamu do not have street names.

Casuarina Rest House (☎ 042-633123; s/d KSh400/800, s/d/tr with shared bathroom KSh300/500/700) Some of the rooms (notably the triples) do seem a bit worse for wear, but this is still a budget bargain: an Escher-esque tilted palace with a social lounge rooftop, fun staff and a general sense of that feelgood backpacker-y camaraderie you'd have to be an ogre not to love.

Lamu Guest House (☎ 042-633338; Kenyatta Rd; s/d KSh500/1000, s/d/tr with shared bathroom KSh400/800/900) The basic rooms here are very plain, but the upper-floor ones are better and catch the sea breeze. The 'official' rates posted in reception are a good KSh500 more than quoted here and not worth paying.

Pole Pole Guest House (☎ 0722-652477; s/d KSh500/1000) Pole Pole is north of the centre of town and back from the waterfront. One of the tallest buildings in Lamu, it has bright doubles with fans and nets. There's a spacious *makuti*-roofed terrace area with great views and its own mini 'tower'.

MIDRANGE

Low-season deals here equal some of the best-value lodging rates in Kenya. Most of these places are located in well-appointed Swahili houses, and are frankly as beautiful as any high-end option. Prices, again, are usually negotiable.

ourpick Yumbe House (☎ 042-633101; lamuold town@africaonline.co.ke; s/d/tr low season KSh1000/2100/2900, high season KSh1290/2700/3860) As coral castles go, Yumbe's pretty good…wait a minute, did we just write, 'As coral castles go?' It's a freaking coral castle! With spacious rooms decorated with pleasant Swahili accents, open-air verandas that are open to the stars and the breeze and a ridiculously romantic top-floor suite that's perfect for couples needing a palace tower retreat, Yumbe's a winner in a field of standouts.

ourpick Wildebeeste 1&2 (☎ 042-32261, 0723-6874008; www.wildebeeste.com; apts KSh1500-6000) Locals often call it the 'Wild Beast'; we prefer 'coolest hotel in Lamu'. A combination art gallery/ hotel, the Wildebeeste buildings are stuffed with all manner of generally eccentric stuff (including, but not limited to, an iron crown, a 19th-century surgeon's handbook and a coconut bong). The Swahili aesthetic is realised in a classy but playful manner while the staff is fantastically friendly and in touch with many local artists. The compound is divided into apartments that sleep between two and six people. If you can score the upstairs rooms, do so: they're often either open-air towers (with thatch roofs that protect from the elements) or 'three-walled' niches that provide a breezy look onto the rooftops as you fall asleep.

Amu House (☎ 042-633420; www.amuhouse.com; s/d/tr KSh2200/2800/3500) This restored 16th-century Swahili 'house' feels more like an urban medieval Sultan's retreat, set with fine wooden doors, a spacious, red-tiled courtyard and wonderfully carved out rows of *vidakah* (wall niches). Did we mention the rooms are plush?

Jannat House (☎ 042-633414; www.jannathouse.com; s/d KSh3400/5950; ☒) The architects clearly had a field day designing Jannat; it's essentially two houses spliced together around a courtyard, with several levels and multiple terraces. Lower rooms are a little disappointing, but the upper levels are as nice as you'd hope for and the pool is a rare refresher in these parts.

TOP END

Lamu World (☎ 042-633491; www.lamuworld.com; Harambee Ave; s/d US$225/290; ☐ ☒) In a city where every building wants to top the preservation stakes, what are the modern hotels like? In the case of Lamu World: absolutely luxurious. It looks like an old Swahili villa, but it feels like a contemporarily decked out four-star resort where they've blended the pale, breezy romance of the Greek islands into an African palace, with predictably awesome results.

Stone House Hotel (☎ 042-633544; half board s/d US$55-70/90-110) This Swahili mansion is set into a Fezlike alleyway and is notable for its fine, white-washed walls and fantastic rooftop, which includes a superb restaurant (no alcohol) with excellent views over the town and waterfront.

Eating

New Minaa Café (meals KSh120-200; ☒ 6.30am-midnight) This is the place to eat Swahili food with Swahilis. Its version of fish (grilled or fried) and chips is pretty decent, as is the atmosphere of rowdy locals yelling at the nightly news.

Bush Gardens Restaurant (☎ 042-633285; Harambee Ave; mains KSh180-800) Bush Gardens is the template for a whole set of restaurants along the waterfront, offering breakfasts, seafood – excellent fish, top-value 'monster crab' and the inevitable lobster in Swahili sauce.

Whispers Coffeeshop (Kenyatta Rd; mains KSh240-750; ☒ 9am-9pm) For a fresh pizza, real cup of cappuccino or the best desserts in town, we highly recommend this garden café.

Stone House Hotel (☎ 042-633544; mains KSh250-750; ☒ noon-2pm & 7-9pm) A fine rooftop restaurant that really catches the breeze. The wonderful panorama of the town and seafront is matched by the quality of the food. There are usually several choices for lunch or dinner, and menus often feature crab and grilled barracuda.

Drinking & Entertainment

As a Muslim town, Lamu caters very poorly for drinkers.

Along the waterfront towards Shela village, the Civil Servants' Club is virtually the only reliable spot for a drink and a dance at weekends. It's small, loud, rowdy and great fun, though women travelling alone should run for cover.

Getting There & Away

AIR

Airkenya (☎ 042-633445; Baraka House, Kenyatta Rd) offers daily afternoon flights between Lamu and Wilson Airport in Nairobi. The inbound flights also continue on to Kiwayu Island. **Kenya Airways** (☎ 042-633155; Casuarina House, Harambee Ave) has daily afternoon flights between Lamu and the domestic terminal at Nairobi's Kenyatta International Airport. Note that fares vary considerably based on season and availability.

The airport at Lamu is on Manda Island and the ferry across the channel to Lamu costs KSh100. You will be met by 'guides' at the airport who will offer to carry your bags to the hotel of your choice for a small consideration (about KSh200). Many double as touts, so be cautious about accepting the first price you are quoted when you get to your hotel.

BUS

There are booking offices for several bus companies on Kenyatta Rd. The going rate for a trip to Mombasa is KSh600 to KSh700;

most buses leave between 7am and 8am, so you'll need to be at the jetty at 6.30am to catch the boat to the mainland. Tawakal also has 10am and 1pm bus services. It takes at least four hours to get from Lamu to Malindi, plus another two hours to Mombasa. Book early.

Getting Around

There are ferries (KSh50) between Lamu and the bus station on the mainland (near Mokowe). Boats leave when the buses arrive at Mokowe; in the reverse direction, they leave at around 6.30am to meet the departing buses. Ferries between the airstrip on Manda Island and Lamu cost KSh100 and leave about half an hour before the flights leave. Expect to pay KSh200 for a custom trip if you miss either of these boats.

Between Lamu village and Shela there are plenty of motorised dhows in either direction throughout the day until around sunset; these cost about KSh150 per person and leave when full.

SHELA

Shela is sort of like Lamu put through a high-end wringer. It's cleaner and more medievally 'authentic' in spots, mainly because a lot of the houses have been lovingly done up by expats, who make up a sizable chunk of the population. There's a long, lovely stretch of beach and a link to a specific slice of coast culture – the locals speak a distinct dialect of Swahili that they're quite proud of. Thanks to the expat presence Shela feels somewhere between the East African coast and a swish Greek island, which you'll either find off-putting or appealing based on your travelling tastes.

Most people are here for the **beach** – a 12km-long sweep of sand where you're guaranteed an isolated spot to pitch your kit and catch some rays. But as locals say, *'Yana vuta kwa kasi'* – 'There is a violent current there.' And no lifeguards. Tourists drown every year, so don't swim out too far. Some backpackers camp in the long dunes behind the beach, but you risk a mugging if you do so.

Dodo Villas/Talking Trees Campsite (☎ 042-633500; camping per tent KSh400, r KSh600-1200, apt per person KSh200) is Lamu's main budget beach option. Its nominal identity crisis reflects the varied nature of the accommodation: the main building has large, unfussy rooms and several concrete blocks hold apartments for up to 10 people, with more being built.

Shella Pwani Guest House (☎ 042-633540; d KSh3000-3500) is all decked out with carved plasterwork and pastel accents. Some rooms have fine sea views, as does the airy roof terrace, and the bathrooms are the best in Shela – they're modelled to look like kiblahs (mosque niches).

If there were a capital of Shela it would be located here at **Peponi Hotel** (☎ 042-633421; www .peponi-lamu.com; s/d high season from US$230; ⊗ closed May & Jun; ⚲) This top-end resort has a grip on everything in this village, from tours to watersports to whatever the hell else you can imagine.

There's waterfront restaurants all over, but the **Stopover Restaurant** (☎ 042-633459; mains KSh250-800) has friendly staff and excellent grub (of the spicy Swahili seafood sort) that make it the clear cut above the competition.

To get to Shela, you can take a motorised dhow from the moorings in Lamu for KSh150 per person (or KSh250 to KSh300 for a solo ride). Alternatively, you can walk it in about 40 minutes.

ISLANDS AROUND LAMU

The Lamu archipelago has plenty to offer outside Lamu itself. The easiest to get to is **Manda Island**, just across the channel, where most visitors go on dhow trips for snorkelling and to visit the Takwa ruins. The tiny **Manda Toto Island**, on the other side of Manda, has perhaps the best reefs on the coast.

Further northeast, **Paté Island** was the main power centre in the region before Lamu came to prominence, but is rarely visited now, preserving an uncomplicated traditional lifestyle as much by necessity as by choice. A regular motor launch shuttles between the towns of Mtangawanda, Siyu, Faza and Kizingitini.

Even further out, remote **Kiwayu Island** is part of the Kiunga Marine National Reserve, and gets most of its scant tourist traffic from extended dhow trips and visitors to the exclusive luxury resort on the mainland. Snorkelling here is highly recommended.

THE RIFT VALLEY

Coming from Nairobi the first glimpses of the spectacular Rift Valley are breathtaking. The escarpment on which the city rests crashes sheer to the floor of a volcano-studded valley hundreds of metres below, across which

RIFT VALLEY

0 ——— 20 km
0 ——— 12 miles

To Lodwar (339km);
Lake Turkana (406km)
To Maralal (25km);
Lake Turkana (235km)

Loruk

To Eldoret
(73km)
Lake
Baringo

Kabarnet
C51 Marigat
C77 Distances are
Approximate

Lake
Bogoria
Rumuruti

Lake Bogoria
NR

LEGEND
GS Game Sanctuary
NP National Park
NR National Reserve

B4
Nyahururu
C76

Nanyuki

Menengai
Crater
A104
Nakuru Hyrax Hill
C56 Prehistoric Site
Ol Donyo
Lesatima
(4001m)

To Kericho
(107km);
Eldoret
(107km);
Kisumu
(192km)
Njoro
Lake
Nakuru
Lake Elmenteita
Gilgil Kariandusi
Site
Kigio Wildlife
Conservancy
Kiganjo

Nyeri
Aberdare
NP

Lake
Nakuru
NP

Lake Naivasha Naivasha

Crater Lake
GS Mt Longonot
(2777m)
Old Naivasha Rd

Hell's Gate
NP
A104

To Masai Mara
National Reserve
(70km)
Longonot NP
Thika

Narok
B3
Limuru

Ewaso Ngiro
Mt Susua
(2357m)
NAIROBI

Ngong

KENYA

A western branch forms a string of lakes in the centre of the continent, including Albert and Edward on the Uganda–DR Congo border, Kivu on the DR Congo–Rwanda border, and Tanganyika on the Tanzania–DR Congo border, which joins the main system at the northern tip of Lake Malawi.

In Kenya the Rift Valley can be traced through Lake Turkana; the Cherangani Hills; and Lakes Baringo, Bogoria, Nakuru, Elmenteita, Naivasha and Magadi. A string of volcanic peaks and craters also lines the valley. While most are now extinct, 30 remain active, and according to local legend, Mt Longonot erupted as recently as 1860. This continuing activity supports a considerable number of hot springs and provides ideal conditions for geothermal power plants, which are increasingly important in Kenya's energy supply.

Besides providing fertile soil, the volcanic deposits have created alkaline waters in most Rift Valley lakes. These shallow soda lakes, formed by the valley's lack of decent drainage, experience high evaporation rates, which further concentrates the alkalinity. The strangely soapy and smelly waters are, however, the perfect environment for the growth of microscopic blue-green algae, which in turn feed lesser flamingos, tiny crustaceans (food for greater flamingos) and insect larvae (food for soda-resistant fish).

LONGONOT NATIONAL PARK

Few places offer better Rift Valley views than the serrated crater rim of Mt Longonot, rising 1000m above the baking valley floor. In dog years this dormant volcano is ancient, while in geological terms it's just a wee pup at 400,000 years of age. It's a good idea to take a KWS ranger – this would be a lonely old walk on your own. Guides, who are available at the gate, cost KSh1500 to the summit or KSh2000 for the full Monty around the rim.

The basic **Oloongonot Campsite** (camping per person US$5) sits just beyond the gate and has basic facilities (no water or firewood), though a toilet and shower block was under construction at the time of research. You will need to bring all your own food and cooking supplies.

If you're driving, the national park is 75km northwest of Nairobi on the Old Naivasha Rd. If you're without a vehicle, take a *matatu* from Naivasha to Longonot village, from where there's a path to the park's access road (ask locals how to find it).

savannah grasslands reach out beyond the horizons. If the view could speak it would surely say, 'Welcome to Africa', and what a welcome the Rift Valley provides.

In places these giants continue to roam; towering giraffes peer over the heads of a million pink flamingos and rhinos look like something from the age of the dinosaurs in Lake Nakuru National Park. Not far away you can cycle right up to the gates of Hell where legends tell of a Maasai girl turning to stone and you'll see buffalo getting hot under the collar. It's not all monsters and violent eruptions though; the calming panoramas over the freshwater lakes of Naivasha and Boringo, full of diva-voiced song birds and floppy-winged butterflies, are perfect places to while away the days and be thankful to Mother Earth for trying to break Africa in two.

Geography

Kenya's Rift Valley is part of the Afro-Arabian rift system, which stretches 6000km from the Dead Sea in the Middle East to Mozambique in southern Africa, passing through the Red Sea then Ethiopia, Kenya, Tanzania and Malawi.

NAIVASHA
☎ 050

Accessed by the new A104 Hwy to Nairobi, Naivasha has become an agricultural backwater that now exists primarily to service the area's blossoming flower industry. Although a convenient base for visits to Longonot National Park it's hard to see why you would choose to stay the night here rather than at the lake shore (below). It is, however, a good place to stock up on supplies for your lakeside adventure.

Naivasha's oldest hotel, **La Belle Inn** (☎ 020-3510404; Moi Ave; s/d KSh2500/2900) is a classic colonial-style option, with rooms of various sizes sporting dark wooden floors, local artwork and a refined atmosphere of times long past. Prices quoted include breakfast. It's also a top place for drinks with the Happy Valley bar worth propping up in the evenings.

Getting There & Away
The main bus and *matatu* station is off Mbaria Kaniu Rd, close to the municipal market. Frequent buses and *matatus* leave for Nakuru (KSh150, 1¼ hours), Nairobi (KSh150, 1½ hours), Nyahururu (KSh250, 1¾ hours) and places west. Frequent *matatus* plough down to the lake, with Kongoni costing KSh 100, and Fisherman's Camp area (KSh70, 45 minutes). As well as from the bus station you can also catch these from Kenyatta Ave.

LAKE NAIVASHA
☎ 0311

The area around Naivasha was one of the first settled by *wazungu* (whites) and was a favourite haunt of the decadent Happy Valley set in the 1930s. Along with Karen, near Nairobi, it is now probably the largest remaining settler and expat community in Kenya.

The lake level has ebbed and flowed over the years, as half-submerged fencing posts indicate. Early in the 1890s it dried up almost completely, but over the next 20 years it rose a phenomenal 15m and inundated a far larger area than it presently occupies. It currently covers about 170 sq km and is home to an incredible variety of bird species, including the fish eagle. Water levels remain low and are a source of concern.

As a freshwater lake, Naivasha's ecology is quite different from that of the Rift Valley's soda lakes. Since the water can be used for irrigation, the surrounding countryside is a major agricultural production area; the flower market has become a major industry here.

Naivasha has been a focus of conservation efforts in Kenya, and in 1995 the Lake Naivasha Riparian Association was formed to educate the estimated 300,000 people dependent on the lake about the environmental issues involved. The results are promising, but so far improvement has been slow, and further drops in the water level are predicted for the next 15 to 20 years.

Sights & Activities
On the western side of Lake Naivasha, north of the village of Kongoni, is the **Crater Lake Game Sanctuary** (admission KSh700), a small park set around a beautiful volcanic crater. On the eastern side of the lake is **Crescent Island Wildlife Sanctuary** (adult/child nonresident US$20/10), a protruding rim of a collapsed volcanic crater that can be explored by boat.

Elsamere Conservation Centre (☎ 0311-2021055; www.elsamere.com; admission KSh600; ◷ 8am-6.30pm) is the former home of the late Joy Adamson of *Born Free* fame. Now a conservation centre focused on lake ecology and environmental awareness programs, the site is open to the public and entry includes afternoon tea complete with a mountain of biscuits on the hippo manicured lawns.

Sleeping & Eating
Fisherman's Camp (☎ 00311-5050462/0726-870590; fishermanscampkenya@msn.com; camping KSh300, tent hire from KSh400, bandas per person Sun-Thu KSh1000, Fri & Sat KSh4000 per banda) Spread along the grassy tree-laden southern shore and full of hungry hippos, this is a perennial favourite of campers, overland companies and backpackers. The site is huge, but at weekends is very busy and has a beer-swilling, noisy, party atmosphere more akin to Glastonbury than Africa

Top Camp (☎ 0720-550409; camping KSh300, s/tw bandas from KSh700/1400, cottages KSh200-4000) It lacks Fisherman's lakeside location, but Top Camp boasts crazy lake views from its hill-top perch. It's a quiet place with various tin-roofed, bamboo-walled *bandas* huts – almost all have bathrooms.

Crayfish Camp (☎ 0311-2020239; www.crayfishcamp .com; camping KSh500, s with shared bathroom KSh1000, s/d with breakfast KSh2500/3200; ▢) Following Fisherman's lead, the Crayfish Camp can seem more like a beer garden than a camp-

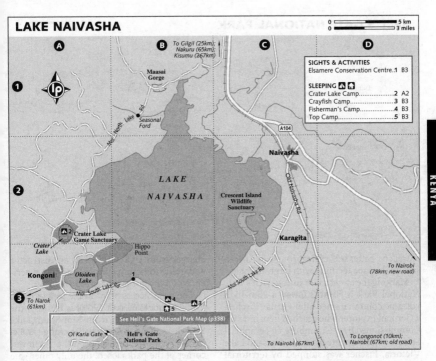

LAKE NAIVASHA

0 _____ 5 km
0 _____ 3 miles

To Gilgil (25km); Nakuru (65km); Kisumu (267km)

Maasai Gorge

Moi North Lake Rd

Seasonal Ford

A104

Naivasha

LAKE NAIVASHA

Crescent Island Wildlife Sanctuary

Old Naivasha Rd

Crater Lake Game Sanctuary

Crater Lake

Hippo Point

Karagita

Kongoni

Oloiden Lake

Moi South Lake Rd

To Narok (61km)

Moi South Lake Rd

To Nairobi (78km; new road)

See Hell's Gate National Park Map (p338)

Ol Karia Gate

Hell's Gate National Park

To Nairobi (67km)

To Longonot (10km); Nairobi (67km; old road)

SIGHTS & ACTIVITIES
Elsamere Conservation Centre..1 B3

SLEEPING
Crater Lake Camp.................2 A2
Crayfish Camp.....................3 B3
Fisherman's Camp................4 B3
Top Camp..........................5 B3

KENYA

site, but it's not a bad option. The pricey new rooms are a bit minimalist, but have some charm, while the petite rooms with shared facilities are very plain Jane.

Crater Lake Camp (☎ 0311-2020613; crater@africa online.co.ke; camping KSh500, full board s/d US$187/280) A luxury tented camp nestled among trees and overlooking the tiny jade-green crater lake dotted with blushing pink flamingos. This is one of those ever-so-exclusive and romantic hideaways that Kenya so excels at, and as is if to reinforce that point the Honeymoon tent contains a whirlpool bath and other romantic essentials.

Getting There & Away
Matatus (KSh80, one hour) run along Moi South Lake Rd between Naivasha town and Kongoni on the lake's western side, passing the turn-offs to Hell's Gate National Park and Fisherman's Camp.

It's a 5km walk from Kongoni to Crater Lake, but don't do this alone due to recent muggings. There's one daily *matatu* along Moi North Lake Rd, leaving from the Total petrol station in Naivasha around 3pm.

Returning to town, you'll need to be on the road by about 7am, otherwise it's a long, dusty walk.

Getting Around
Most budget and midrange accommodation options hire reasonable boats for lake trips (KSh2500 per hour). Top-end lodges charge KSh3000 to KSh4000 per hour for similar rides. If you'd rather row row row yourself, Fisherman's Camp can help you out (KSh300 per hour).

Most sites also hire mountain bikes; Fisherman's Camp and Fish Eagle Inn both charge KSh500 per day. You'll find cheaper rides at various places signposted off Moi South Lake Rd, but check the contraptions carefully before paying.

HELL'S GATE NATIONAL PARK
Looking at animals from the safety of your car seat is all well and good, but, let's be honest, after a while who doesn't get the urge to get out of the vehicle and re-enter the food chain? Well at Hell's Gate you really can do that, because this unique park actively encourages you

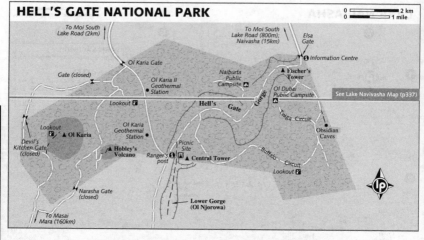

HELL'S GATE NATIONAL PARK

to walk or, better still, cycle through an African savannah scape teeming with large animals.

Marking the eastern entrance to Hell's Gate National Park is **Fischer's Tower**, a 25m-high volcanic column named after Gustav Fischer, a German explorer who reached here in 1882. Commissioned by the Hamburg Geographical Society to find a route from Mombasa to Lake Victoria, Fischer was stopped by territorial Maasai, who comprehensively and most efficiently kyboshed his campaign by slaughtering almost his entire party.

Rising from the gorge's southern end is the large **Central Tower**. A picnic site and ranger's post are close by, from where an excellent walk descends into the **Lower Gorge** (Ol Njorowo; which is outside of the park). This narrow sandstone ravine has been stunningly sculpted by water, and the incoming light casts marvellous shadows. You'd do well to spend a couple of hours exploring here. It's a steep and very slippery descent, but some steps have been cut into the rock and whole school parties manage it on a regular basis.

The park's western half is much less scenic and hosts the **Ol Karia Geothermal Station**, a power project utilising one of the world's hottest sources of natural steam. The plumes of rising steam can be seen from many of the park's viewpoints. It's usually possible to have a look around the site – ask the guards at Ol Karia II.

If walking with mega fauna doesn't light your fire then get the adrenaline flowing with some technical rock climbing. The park's resident climber, **Simon Kiane** (☎ 0720-9090718),

charges from US$10 to act as an instructor and guide to both beginners and the experienced on the gorges sheer red walls.

The usual access point to the **park** (adult/child US$20/10, bicycle KSh50, guide KSh500) is through the main Elsa Gate, 2km from Moi South Lake Rd, where there's an **information centre** (☎ 050-2020284). With the two gates on the northwest corner of the park closed, the only other gate is Ol Karia.

Although it's convenient to sleep at Lake Naivasha's many lodges and camps, the park's two gorgeous **public campsites** (camping per adult/child US$8/5) can't be recommended enough.

The round trip from the park's turn-off on Moi South Lake Rd to the shore of Lake Naivasha via Elsa Gate and Ol Karia Gate is 22km; the distance between the two gates via Moi South Lake Rd is 9km. If you intend to walk through the park, allow a full day, and take plenty of supplies.

LAKE ELMENTEITA

Lake Elmenteita's beautiful soda shoreline is often fringed in rainbow shades, thanks to hundreds of brilliant flamingos and other birds. It's not a national park, so there are no entry fees, and you can walk around parts of the shoreline that aren't privately owned.

Sitting around a mazelike bougainvillea garden, the slightly dated **Lake Elmenteita Lodge** (☎ 050-50648; full board s/d US$138/176; 🏊) represents good value for money. The bar's terrace, with stunning lake views, is crying out for the company of you and a G&T.

The frequent *matatus* plying the route between Naivasha and Nakuru will happily drop you anywhere you like.

NAKURU
☎ 051 / pop 300,000

Kenya's fourth-largest centre doesn't feel like anything more than an overgrown country town; it has a relaxed atmosphere and makes a pleasant base for a few days. It's on the doorstep of the delightful Lake Nakuru National Park and is only a few kilometres from the deep, dramatic Menengai Crater.

Information

Changing cash and travellers cheques in Nakuru is easy, with numerous banks and foreign exchange bureaus. Barclays Bank's ATMs are the most reliable.

Aga Khan Satellite Laboratory (off Court Rd) Various lab services including malaria tests.

Crater Travel (☎ 051-2215019; off Kenyatta Ave) One of the few reputable travel agencies in town.

Post office (Kenyatta Ave)

Sleeping & Eating

Carnation Hotel (☎ 051-2215360; Mosque Rd; s/tw KSh750/1300) The plastic flower-filled Carnation Hotel is the town's prettiest budget rose. Rooms, with their multicoloured tiled floors and kitsch bed sheets, have plenty of character as well as hot showers.

Merica Hotel (☎ 051-2216013; merica@kenyaweb .com; Kenyatta Ave; half board s/d US$65/110; ☒ ☒) This

KENYA

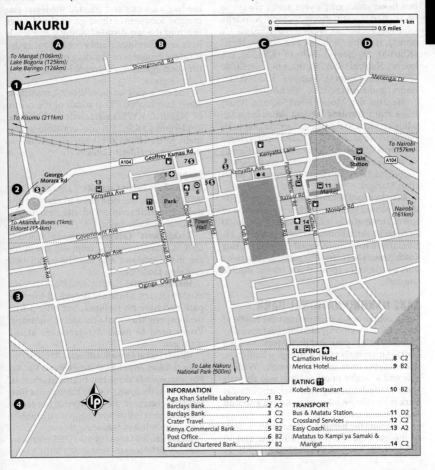

NAKURU

0 — 1 km
0 — 0.5 miles

To Marigat (106km);
Lake Bogoria (125km);
Lake Baringo (126km)

Showground Rd

Menengai Dr

To Kisumu (211km)

Kenyatta Lane

To Nairobi (157km)

Geoffrey Kamau Rd

Train Station

A104

George Morara Rd

Kenyatta Ave

Kenyatta Ave

To Nairobi (161km)

Park

Market

Mosque Rd

To Akamba Buses (1km);
Eldoret (154km)

Government Ave

Town Hall

Kipchoge Ave

Oginga Odinga Ave

To Lake Nakuru
National Park (500m)

INFORMATION
Aga Khan Satellite Laboratory.........1 B2
Barclays Bank..................................2 A2
Barclays Bank..................................3 C2
Crater Travel..................................4 C2
Kenya Commercial Bank...................5 B2
Post Office.....................................6 B2
Standard Chartered Bank.................7 B2

SLEEPING 🏠
Carnation Hotel..............................8 C2
Merica Hotel..................................9 B2

EATING 🍴
Kobeb Restaurant..........................10 B2

TRANSPORT
Bus & Matatu Station......................11 D2
Crossland Services.........................12 C2
Easy Coach...................................13 A2
Matatus to Kampi ya Samaki &
Marigat.....................................14 C2

contemporary tower hosts Nakuru's only top-end rooms. Ride the glass elevators up the sunlit atrium to well-appointed rooms large enough to host a wildebeest migration in.

Kokeb Restaurant (Moses Mudavadi Rd; meals KSh200-300) A relaxed garden restaurant serving an unlikely mixture of Ethiopian and Italian fare. If you're not making the big adventure north to the real deal then try some *injera* (flat bread) and *wat* (stew) here.

Getting There & Away

Regular buses, *matatus* and the odd Peugeot (shared taxi) leave the chaotic stands off Mburu Gichua Rd. Check the prices with several different people before handing over your cash as the ticket touts and even the bus ticket office employees aren't always to be trusted. Destinations include Naivasha (KSh150, 1¼ hours), Nyahururu (KSh140, 1¼ hours), Kericho (KSh300, two hours), Nyeri (KSh300, 2½ hours), Eldoret (KSh300, 2¾ hours), Nairobi (KSh250, three hours), Kitale (KSh500, 3½ hours), Kisumu (KSh500, 3½ hours) and Kisii (KSh500, 4½ hours).

Matatus for Molo (KSh150, one hour) leave from **Crossland Services** (Mburu Gichua Rd), while services to Kampi ya Samaki (for Lake Baringo) via Marigat (for Lake Bogoria) leave further south on Mburu Gichua Rd. Kampi ya Samaki (KSh250, 2½ hours) costs slightly more and takes 30 minutes longer to reach than Marigat.

Akamba (George Morara Rd) buses leave from its depot behind the Kenol petrol station west of town. Destinations include Nairobi (KSh400 to KSh650, three hours), Eldoret (KSh250, 2¾ hours) and Kisumu (KSh800, 3½ hours). **Easy Coach** (Kenyatta Ave) offers the same destinations and a little extra comfort for almost double the cost.

LAKE NAKURU NATIONAL PARK

Just a couple of kilometres from the hustle of central Nakuru an army of flamingos turn a sky-blue lake bright pink and prehistoric-looking horned mammals crash through a landscape of euphorbia trees and acacia forests. With all this and a wealth of other birds and animals there's little doubt why Lake Nakuru National Park is rivalling Amboseli as Kenya's second most-visited-park.

Alongside the flamingos the star attractions of this park are the rhinos (80 white and 56 black at the time of writing) and sightings of white rhinos, rumbling like steamrollers through the bushes, are now almost a given at the lake's southern end. Since this species was re-introduced some years ago Lake Nakuru has become far and away the best place in the country to see these animals. By contrast the shy black rhinos, browsers by nature and much more aggressive, are more difficult to spot.

Information

Since the 180-sq-km park's creation in 1961, the population of lesser and greater flamingos has risen and fallen with the soda lake's erratic water levels. When the lake dried up in 1962, the population plummeted, as it later did in the 1970s when heavy rainfall diluted the lake's salinity and affected the lesser flamingos' food source (blue-green algae). Over much of the last decade healthy water levels have seen flamingo numbers blossom again. If future droughts or flooding make them fly the coop again, you'll probably find them at Lake Bogoria.

The main **park** (adult/child US$40/20, smartcard required) gate is about 2km south of the centre of Nakuru. KWS smartcards and official guidebooks (KSh750) are available at the main gate's **office** (☎ 051-2217151), but not at the Lanet or Nderit Gates.

Sleeping

Makalia Falls Public Campsite (camping adult/child US$10/5) This is the best place to camp in the park. It's picturesque and sits next to the seasonal Makalia Falls.

Backpackers' Campsite (camping adult/child US$10/5) This large public campsite sits inside the main gate and also has the park's best camping facilities.

Special campsites (camping adult/child US$25/5, plus set-up fee KSh7500) These are dotted all over the park and have no facilities, but offer a true bush experience – just you and the animals. You'll need to make a reservation at the main gate.

Wildlife Club of Kenya Guesthouse (☎ 051-851559; PO Box 33, Nakuru; per person with shared bathroom KSh1000) For atmosphere alone this beats anywhere in Nakuru hands down. It's like having your own secluded cottage in the countryside but rather than a garden full of bouncing bunny rabbits it's a garden full of bouncing rhinos!

Sarova Lion Hill Lodge (☎ 051-850235; www.sarova hotels.com; s/d full board US$310/410; 🏊) Sitting high

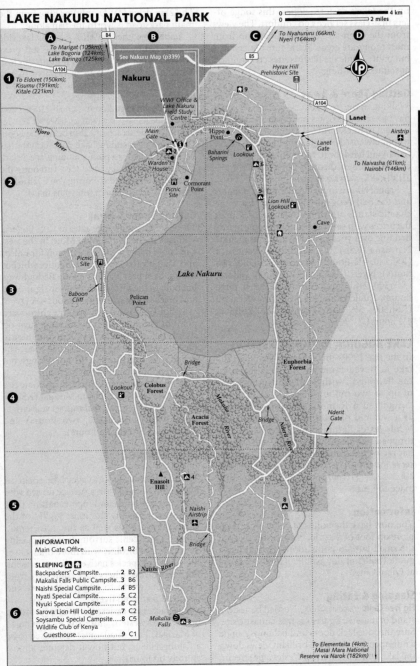

LAKE NAKURU NATIONAL PARK

| 0 | 4 km |
| 0 | 2 miles |

To Marigat (105km);
Lake Bogoria (124km);
Lake Baringo (125km)

To Eldoret (150km);
Kisumu (191km);
Kitale (221km)

To Nyahururu (66km);
Nyeri (164km)

Nakuru

See Nakuru Map (p339)

Hyrax Hill
Prehistoric Site

WWF Office &
Lake Nakuru
Field Study
Centre

Lanet

Airstrip

Njoro River

Main
Gate

Hippo
Point

Baharini
Springs

Lookout

Lanet
Gate

To Naivasha (61km);
Nairobi (146km)

Warden's
House

Picnic
Site

Cormorant
Point

Lion Hill
Lookout

Cave

Lake Nakuru

Picnic
Site

Baboon
Cliff

Pelican
Point

Bridge

Euphorbia
Forest

Lookout

Colobus
Forest

Acacia
Forest

Makalia River

Bridge

Nderit River

Nderit
Gate

Enasoit
Hill

Naishi
Airstrip

Bridge

Naishi River

Makalia
Falls

To Elementeita (4km);
Masai Mara National
Reserve via Narok (182km)

INFORMATION
Main Gate Office..................1 B2

SLEEPING
Backpackers' Campsite............2 B2
Makalia Falls Public Campsite..3 B6
Naishi Special Campsite..........4 B5
Nyati Special Campsite............5 C2
Nyuki Special Campsite...........6 C2
Sarova Lion Hill Lodge 7 C2
Soysambu Special Campsite....8 C5
Wildlife Club of Kenya
Guesthouse......................9 C1

KENYA

up the lake's eastern slopes, this lodge offers first-class service and comfort. The views from the open-air restaurant-bar and from most rooms are great. Rooms are understated but pretty, while the flashy suites are large and absolutely stunning.

Getting There & Away

Walking in the park isn't permitted, so you'll have to rent a taxi, go on a tour or be lucky enough to hitch a ride. A taxi for a few hours will likely cost KSh2500, though you'll have to bargain hard for it. More enjoyable options can be arranged through **Crater Travel** (☎ 051-2215019; off Kenyatta Ave, Nakuru).

From Nakuru town, regular buses, *matatus* and the odd Peugeot (shared taxi) leave the chaotic stands off Mburu Gichua Rd. Check the prices with several different people before handing over your cash. Destinations include Naivasha (KSh150, 1¼ hours), Nyahururu (KSh140, 1¼ hours), Kericho (KSh300, two hours), Nyeri (KSh300, 2½ hours), Eldoret (KSh300, 2¾ hours), Nairobi (KSh250, three hours), Kitale (KSh500, 3½ hours), Kisumu (KSh500, 3½ hours) and Kisii (KSh500, 4½ hours).

LAKE BOGORIA NATIONAL RESERVE

In the late 1990s this reserve's shallow soda lake achieved fame as 'the new home of the flamingo', with a migrant population of up to two million birds. In 2000 it was designated a Ramsar site, establishing it as a wetland of international importance. While lesser flamingo numbers have since dropped significantly, now that Lake Nakuru has recovered from earlier droughts, this **reserve** (☎ 051-2211987; PO Box 64, Marigat; adult/child KSh2000/200; ☺ 6am-7pm) is still a fascinating place to visit.

Information

You now have the bonus of being able to explore on foot or bicycle, though stay clear of the small buffalo population. If you'd like a guide (half/full day KSh500/1000), enquire at Loboi Gate.

Sleeping & Eating

Fig Tree Camp (camping KSh500) Nestled beneath a stand of massive fig trees is this fantastic site. Sure the loos lack doors and baboons can be a nuisance, but there are brilliant views down the lake and a permanent freshwater stream.

The 2km drive (4WD only) or hike from the main park road is worth the trip alone.

Acacia Camp (camping KSh500) A pretty lakeside site shaded by acacias, with some soft grass on which your tent and your bottom can rest. You'll have to bring your own water. Acacia and Fig Tree blow the socks off the dismal Hot Springs and VIPS campsites.

Lake Bogoria Spa Resort (☎ 051-2216867; www .lbogoriasparesort.com; s/d incl breakfast US$70/90; ☒) Set in lovely grounds around 2km before the Loboi Gate, the long-standing Lake Bogoria Hotel has been relaunched as a posh-sounding 'spa' resort. However, the money must have run out – the rooms are bland and so boring you'll fall asleep as soon as you see them (one plus then).

Getting There & Away

There are three entrance gates to Lake Bogoria – Emsos in the south, Maji Moto in the west and Loboi in the north. The turnoff for Emsos and Maji Moto Gates is at Mogotio, which is about 38km past Nakuru on the B4 highway, but both of these routes are poorly signposted and inaccessible without a serious 4WD.

Loboi Gate is a far more straightforward point of entry, reached by taking a turn-off shortly before Marigat. It's 20km from here to the actual gate along a good sealed road. The sealed road continues to the hot springs, but is horrendous shape in this section.

Without your own vehicle, Loboi Gate can be accessed by *matatu* from Marigat (KSh70, 30 minutes). Regular *matatus* serve Marigat from Nakuru (KSh200, two hours) and Kabarnet (KSh140, 1¼ hours).

LAKE BARINGO
☎ 051

This rare freshwater Rift Valley lake, encircled by mountains and with a surface dotted with picturesque islands and hippos batting their eyelids, is probably the most idyllic of the Rift Valley lakes as well as the most remot. Topping the scenic surrounds is an amazing abundance of birdlife, with more than 450 of the 1200 bird species native to Kenya present. For years birdwatchers have come here from all over the world to glimpse the rare and beautiful feathered flyers.

Lake access is easiest from **Kampi ya Samaki** on the lake's western shore, some 15km north of Marigat. This small, quiet town used to be a fishing village, but now it depends almost entirely on tourism.

The 'authorities' at Kampi ya Samaki charge a toll (KSh200 per person, KSh100 per car) to enter the town; get a receipt to avoid being asked to pay again. The nearest banking facilities are in Kabarnet about 40km west.

The most popular activities around Lake Baringo are **boat rides**. There are boat offices all over town, and literally everyone you talk to will claim to have access to a boat and be able to undercut anyone else's price.

As one reader said about **Roberts' Camp** (☎ 0727-06895, Nairobi 020 2057718; www.robertscamp .com; camping KSh350, bandas per person with shared bathroom KSh1500, 4-person cottages KSh7500), 'This place 'keeps getting better and better' and we couldn't agree more. Right on the lake shore and full of chirping birds, wallowing hippos and toothy-grinned crocodiles, it doesn't matter whether you opt for camping in your own tent, a beautifully furnished *banda*, or an extravagant cottage – what you get for your money here is quite simply superb.

ourpick Samatian Island (☎ bookings 0727-06895, Nairobi 020 2057718; www.samatianislandlodge.com; full board s/d US$570/960) is run by the same delightful couple as Roberts' Camp and it's a slice of Heaven that proves they can do top end just as well. Located on a tiny, private island in the middle of the lake this place, with an infinity pool perched above the hippos and five open-plan cottages, stuffed full of antique Zanzibar chests, book cases and other treasures, is the stuff princesses dream of and just screams honeymoon.

The **Thirsty Goat** (Roberts' Camp; meals KSh300-450) is a lovely open-air restaurant and bar which serves a welcome variety of foreign fare. It might seem pricey, but when your nose gets a whiff of the Moroccan meatballs, your taste buds will step on your whingeing wallet's tongue.

Getting There & Away

A 25-seater bus leaves for Nakuru each morning (KSh250) between 6.30am and 9.30am (it departs when it's full). Bar that, hop onto one of the regular pick-up trucks heading to Marigat (KSh70, 30 minutes) and catch more frequent *matatus* from there on to Nakuru (KSh200, two hours) or Kabarnet (KSh150, 1¼ hours).

A gravel track connects Loruk at the top end of the lake with the Nyahururu – Maralal road. If you have your own transport, it's a rough but bearable road; there's no public transport along it and hitching is extremely difficult. You can usually buy petrol at Lake Baringo Club; if you're heading northeast, it's worth noting that after Marigat, there's no reliable supply until Maralal.

CENTRAL HIGHLANDS

Cut Kenya and she bleeds soil. It is the land the Mau Mau fought for that lies at the heart of lingering communal tensions, and captures the dreams of both Nairobi-bound businessmen and farmers scratching the earth.

And if the land is this nation's blood, that essence runs deepest in this place of wet air and long shadows. The Central Highlands are the fertile, mist-and rain-fattened breadbasket of a nation, and the green-girt, red-dirt

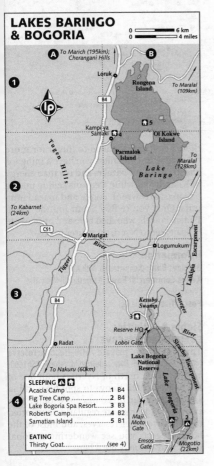

LAKES BARINGO & BOGORIA

0 _____ 6 km
0 _____ 4 miles

To Marich (195km); Cherangani Hills

Loruk

Rongena Island

To Maralal (109km)

B4

Kampi ya Samaki

Ol Kokwe Island

Parmalok Island

To Maralal (128km)

Lake Baringo

Tugen Hills

To Kabarnet (24km)

C51

Marigat

Logumukum

River

Laikipia Escarpment

Tigeri

B4

Kesubo Swamp

Waseges

River

Reserve HQ

Siracho Escarpment

Radat

Loboi Gate

To Nakuru (60km)

Lake Bogoria National Reserve

Lake Bogoria

Maji Moto Gate

Emsos Gate

To Mogotio (22km)

SLEEPING 🛏️ 🏠	
Acacia Camp	1 B4
Fig Tree Camp	2 B4
Lake Bogoria Spa Resort	3 B3
Roberts' Camp	4 B4
Samatian Island	5 B1

EATING 🍴	
Thirsty Goat	(see 4)

KENYA

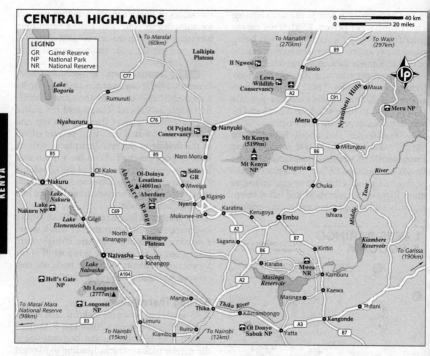

CENTRAL HIGHLANDS

LEGEND
GR Game Reserve
NP National Park
NR National Reserve

spiritual heartland of that country's largest tribe, the Kikuyu.

In these valleys lay the blessed, best fields of people still tied to agriculture, where the cyclical patterns of nature mirror slow rhythms of movement. The latter is etched into the steps of the Highlands' easily identifiable residents: the wobbly lope of twisty-horned cattle over sweet grass, the weary squelch of rubberboots in mud as labourers head into the fields and the gossipy bounce of a matron decked in her Sunday best coming home from church.

The prime attraction here is Kirinyaga, the Mountain of Mysteries (or Ostriches, depending on who's translating). Better known as Mt Kenya, this icy mastiff dominates the small towns and *shambas* (farm plots) scattered in its shadow, which also creeps over some of the nation's most stunning, and least visited, national parks.

NYERI & AROUND
☎ 061

Nyeri is sort of the epitome of a busy Kikuyu market town, and is as welcoming and bustling as the Central Highlands gets. With that said,

there's not much reason to linger for more than a day or two unless you have a thing for chaotic open-air bazaars and the mad energy of Kikuyu and white Kenyans selling maize, bananas, arrowroot, coffee and macadamia nuts. Or if you're Boy Scout founder Lord Baden-Powell, who died here and once wrote 'The nearer to Nyeri, the nearer to bliss.'

Information
Barclays Bank (Kenyatta Rd) With ATM.
Kenya Commercial Bank (Kenyatta Rd) With ATM (Visa only).
Post office (Sulukia Rd).

Sights & Activities
SOLIO GAME RESERVE
This family-run, private 7100-hectare **reserve** (☎ 061-55271; B5 Hwy; adult/child/vehicle KSh1600/free/500), 22km north of Nyeri, is both one of the best places in Kenya to spot black rhino and an important breeding centre for the species besides. Rhinos are regularly transported from here to other reserves, and most of the horned beasts you see wandering national parks were actually born here.

BADEN-POWELL MUSEUM

Lord Baden-Powell, the founder of the International Scout Association, spent his last three years at Paxtu Cottage in the Outspan Hotel. The ultimate scoutmaster's retirement was kind of poetic; to 'outspan' is to unhook your oxen at the end of a long journey, and, as Baden-Powell's former home was named 'Pax' (peace) in honour of Armistice Day after WWI, it made sense to dub his second digs 'Paxtu.' Famed tiger-hunter Jim Corbett later occupied the grounds. Baden-Powell's grave, tucked behind **St Peter's Church** (B5 Hwy) faces Mt Kenya and is marked with the Scouts trail sign for 'I have gone home'. Paxtu is now a **museum** (admission KSh300; ☽ 8am-6pm) filled with scouting paraphernalia and great mid-20th-century photos.

Sleeping

Paresia Hotel (☎ 0720-986142; off Gakere Rd; s/tw KSh400/700) With its red cement floors and blue linoleum showers, Paresia is as colourful as it is cheap, and a good option if you're willing to go a little cheaper for a little more Developing World discomfiture. It's located right behind the main market.

Green Hills Hotel (☎ 2030604; Bishop Gatimu Rd; s/tw from KSh1900/3300; ☒) The best deal in town is actually a little way out of Nyeri. The small drive is worth it for the palm-lined, pool-side ambience and general sense of serenity located a few minutes, and several levels of peace from Nyeri's crazy core.

Aberdare Country Club (Map p347; ☎ 061-2055620, Nairobi 020-3742744; www.choiceswild.com; low season full board s/tw US$87/172, high season US$162/230; ☒) Surrounded by its own 500-hectare sanctuary east of Mweiga, the stately club sits atop a hill and proffers glorious views. It's one of the more luxurious options in this corner of Kenya.

Outspan Hotel (Map p347; ☎ 061-2032424, 0722-207762; www.aberdaresafarihotels.com; r $180-225) This rather gorgeous lodge tries to impart the character of an old-school highland colonial retreat, and does a pretty good job of it, too. Nineteen of the 34 standard rooms have cosy fireplaces, and all have a whiff of historical class. The on-site Kirinyaga club gets pretty crazy on weekends.

Eating

Town View Cafe (Kimathi Way; meals KSh80-200; ☽ 6am-11pm) There's a heavy Mama Africa vibe going

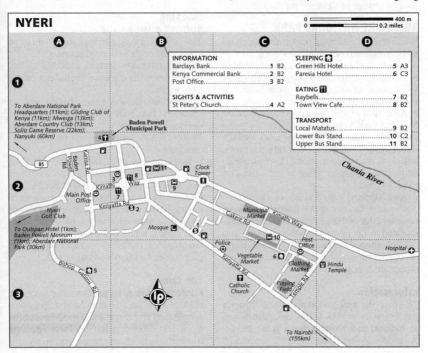

NYERI

INFORMATION		
Barclays Bank	1	B2
Kenya Commercial Bank	2	B2
Post Office	3	B2

SIGHTS & ACTIVITIES		
St Peter's Church	4	A2

SLEEPING ⌂		
Green Hills Hotel	5	A3
Paresia Hotel	6	C3

EATING ⊞		
Raybells	7	B2
Town View Cafe	8	B2

TRANSPORT		
Local Matatus	9	B2
Lower Bus Stand	10	C2
Upper Bus Stand	11	B2

To Aberdare National Park Headquarters (11km); Gliding Club of Kenya (11km); Mweiga (13km); Aberdare Country Club (13km); Solio Game Reserve (22km); Nanyuki (60km)

Baden Powell Municipal Park

B5

Baden Powell Rd

Kanisa Rd

Kimathi Way

Main Post Office

Kenyatta Rd

Nyeri Golf Club

To Outspan Hotel (1km); Baden Powell Museum (1km); Aberdare National Park (30km)

Bishop Gatimu Rd

Clock Tower

Chania River

Mosque

Gakere Rd

Municipal Market

Kimathi Way

Police

Vegetable Market

Kenyatta Rd

Post Office

Clothing Market

Temple Rd

Hindu Temple

Hospital

Catholic Church

Playing Field

To Nairobi (155km)

0   400 m
0   0.2 miles

on here, both with the menu (*nyama choma* galore) and the colourful décor. The dining room ain't 'open air,' but it does, as the café's name promises, look out onto a breezy view of 'downtown' Nyeri.

Raybells (Kimathi Way; meals KSh120-380) Pretty much anything you want to eat (well, anything Kenyan or Western), from pizza to *choma,* is available and cooked passably well here. The presence of fresh juice (surprisingly rare in this agricultural town) is very welcome.

Green Hills Hotel (Bishop Gatimu Rd; buffets KSh650) As with accommodation, so with food: Green Hills dominates again. The full buffet is an impressive piece of work, with some tasty mixed-grill options done up in a satisfyingly fancy fashion.

Getting There & Away

Matatus run to Nanyuki (KSh150, one hour), Nyahururu (KSh230, 1¼ hours), Thika (KSh200, two hours), Nakuru (KSh300, 2½ hours), Nairobi (KSh300, 2½ hours) and Eldoret (KSh700, eight hours). Buses duplicate most of these lines; you may occasionally have to change at Karatina for Nairobi.

ABERDARE NATIONAL PARK

While there's plenty of reason to wax rhapsodic over herds of game thundering over an open African horizon, there's also something to be said for the soil-your-pants shock of seeing an elephant thunder out of bush that was, minutes before, just plants.

And that's why people love Aberdare National Park. Your camera reflexes are tested as the abundant wildlife pops unexpectedly out of bushes, including elephants, warthogs, buffaloes, black rhinos, spotted hyenas, bongo antelopes, bush pigs, black servals and rare black leopards.

And baboons. Lots and lots of baboons.

The park has two major environments: an eastern hedge of thick rainforest and waterfall-studded hills known as the Salient, and the Kinangop Plateau, an open tableland of coarse moors that huddles under cold mountain breezes.

Information

To enter the **park** (adult/child US$40/20) through the Treetops or Ark Gates, ask permission at **national park headquarters** (☎ 061-2055465, 061-2055024; Mweiga, PO Box 753, Nyeri). Smartcard

is supposedly required, but enforcement was lax as of our visit. Excellent 1:25,000 maps (KSh450), which are essential if you are on a self-drive safari, are available at the gates. Note that during the rains roads get rough, and the numbered navigation posts in the Salient are often difficult to follow.

Activities
TREKKING

The high moorland and four main peaks (all 3500m to 4000m) are excellent trekking spots; the tallest mountain in the park is Ol Donyo Lesatima, which is a popular bag for those on the East African mountain circuit. Between Honi Campsite and Elephant Ridge is the site of the hideout of Mau Mau leader Dedan Kimathi, who used these mountains as a guerrilla base; many of his companions learned the ropes of jungle warfare fighting with the British in Burma in WWII.

To trek the Salient you'll need advance permission from the warden at park headquarters, who'll provide an armed ranger (KSh1500/2500 half/full day) to guide and protect you against inquisitive wildlife.

Sleeping
BUDGET & MIDRANGE

The following accommodation must be booked through park headquarters.

Public campsites (camping adult/child US$10/5) Basic sites with minimal facilities – some have water.

Sapper Hut (US$50) A simple *banda*, with an open fire, two beds and a hot-water boiler, overlooks a lovely waterfall on the Upper Magura River. Again, it's best to bring your own gear.

Tusk Camp (Jan-Jun US$100, Jul-Dec US$120) Four dark and cosy alpine cottages located near Ruhuruini Gate sleep eight to 10 people. The lounge area is comfy, there are great views (if the fog hasn't rolled in), and plenty of rhinos around to boot. Hot water, blankets, kerosene lamps, a gas cooker, and some utensils are provided, but bring your own equipment (plus water and firewood) to be safe.

TOP END

Kiandongoro Fishing Lodge (7-person cottages Jan-Jun US$200, Jul-Dec US$230) Two stone houses sleep seven people each and command a good view of the moors that sweep into the Gura River. There are two bathrooms in each house, and all utensils

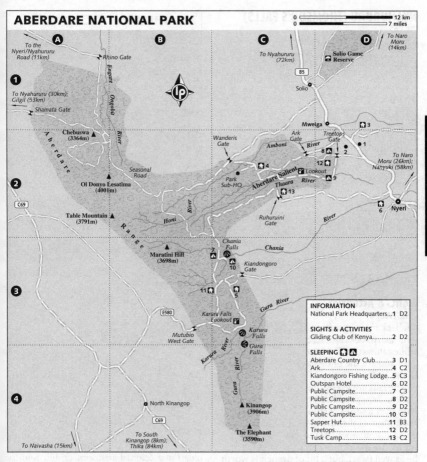

ABERDARE NATIONAL PARK

INFORMATION	
National Park Headquarters...1	D2

SIGHTS & ACTIVITIES	
Gliding Club of Kenya............2	D2

SLEEPING	
Aberdare Country Club.........3	D1
Ark...4	C2
Kiandongoro Fishing Lodge...5	C3
Outspan Hotel........................6	D2
Public Campsite.....................7	C3
Public Campsite.....................8	D2
Public Campsite.....................9	D2
Public Campsite...................10	C3
Sapper Hut...........................11	B3
Treetops..............................12	D2
Tusk Camp...........................13	C2

KENYA

and linens are provided, along with gas-powered kitchens, paraffin cookers and fireplaces.

Ark (☎ Nairobi 020-216940, 0724478058; www.choices wild.com; low season full board s/tw US$150/210, high season US$180/250) The Ark is more modern (1960s as opposed to 1950s chic) and roomier than Treetops, and has a lounge that overlooks a water hole. Watch buffalo as you sip wine in a moulded chair lifted from 'Austin Powers'. An excellent walkway leads over a particularly dense stretch of the Salient, and from here and the water hole lounge you can spot elephants, rhinos, buffaloes and hyenas.

Treetops (☎ 020-3242425; www.aberdaresafarihotels .com; mid-Apr–mid-Jun full board s/tw with shared bathroom US$168/225, mid-Jun–Nov & late Dec–early Jan US$277/348, all other times US$247/312) 'Every time like the first time'

goes the Treetops slogan, and we agree: sleeping here feels like travelling back to the day the place re-opened in the late 1950s. Rooms are small and decorated in that special kind of mid-20th-century wood panelling/floral linens chic, but there is excellent wildlife viewing and a sense of rusticity (and a little neglect) pervades.

Getting There & Away

Access roads from the B5 Hwy to the Wanderis, Ark, Treetops and Ruhuruini Gates are in decent shape. Keep in mind that it takes a few hours to get from the Salient to the moorlands and vice versa. Regular Nyeri–Mweiga *matatus* (KSh70, 35 minutes) pass KWS headquarters and the main park gates.

NYAHURURU (THOMSON'S FALLS)
☎ 065

This unexpectedly attractive town leaps out of the northwest corner of the highlands and makes a decent base for exploring the western edge of the Aberdares. But Nyahururu has its own charms. Its former namesake, Thomson's Falls, are beautiful in their own right and offer an excellent day's worth of trekking options. And at 2360m, this is Kenya's highest major town, with a cool and invigorating climate that lends itself to thorough exploration of the small forested tracks that surround the falls and lead into friendly nearby farming villages.

Information
Barclays Bank (cnr Sulukia & Sharpe Rds) With ATM.
Clicks Cyber Cafe (Mimi Centre, Kenyatta Rd; per hr KSh180) Best internet in town, which isn't saying much.
Kenya Commercial Bank (Sulukia Rd) With ATM (Visa only).
Post office (Sulukia Rd).

Sights & Activities
THE FALLS
Set back in an evergreen river valley studded with sharp rocks and screaming baboons, the white cataracts of **Thomson's Falls** plummet over 72m and are the undeniable main attraction in the area.

The falls are fed by the Ewaso Narok River and can be approached by a fairly straight shot path over a series of stone steps that leads to the bottom of the ravine. Don't attempt to go down any other way, as the rocks on the side of the ravine are often very loose and wet. You'll be as well (wet), but a bit of drench is worth the dramatic site of looking up at the falls as baboons pad over the surrounding cliffs. It's 45 minutes there and back, and there's a sign charging KSh100 to take the path, but no one was collecting this fee during our visit.

There are some fantastic **walks** downstream through the forested valley of the Ewaso Narok River and upstream a couple of kilometres to one of the highest hippo pools in Kenya. Guides are fairly easy to find, especially around the souvenir shacks overlooking the falls, but you'll have to bargain hard.

Sleeping & Eating
Safari Lodge (☎ 065-22334, 0724-485182; Go Down Rd; s/d KSh500/700) Well: clean toilets with *seats*; big, soft beds with couches in the rooms; a

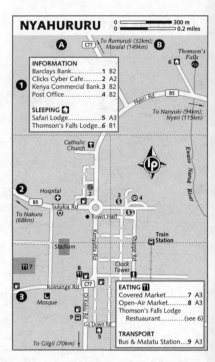

nice balcony; TV; and a place to charge your phone. What did we do to deserve this luxury? Especially at this price, which makes Safari one of the best budget deals around.

Thomson's Falls Lodge (☎ 065-22006; www.tfalls.co.ke; off B5 Hwy; s/d incl breakfast KSh2500/3200) The undisputed nicest spot in the area sits right above the falls and does a great job of instilling that good old, 'I'm a colonial aristocrat on hill country holiday' vibe. Rooms are spacious but cosy, thanks in no small part to the log fireplaces.

Thomson's Falls Lodge Restaurant (off B5 Hwy; breakfast/lunch/dinner KSh455/850/900) This is the best (and only) place in town to go for a fancy feast. There's a set buffet for each of the day's three meals, and while they're pricey for this area, you'll walk away well-stuffed and satisfied.

Getting There & Away
Numerous *matatus* run to Nakuru (KSh120, 1¼ hours) and Nyeri (KSh200, two hours) until late afternoon. Less plentiful are services to Naivasha (KSh250, 1½ hours), Nanyuki (KSh300, three hours) and Nairobi (KSh300, three hours). The odd morning *matatu* reaches Maralal (KSh500, three hours).

Several early morning buses also serve Nairobi (KSh250 to KSh350, three hours).

MT KENYA NATIONAL PARK

Africa's second-highest mountain attracts spry trekkers, long, dramatic cloud cover and all the eccentricities of its mother continent in equal measure. Here, mere minutes from the equator, glaciers carve out the throne of Ngai, the old high God of the Kikuyu. To this day the tribe keeps its doors open to the face of the sacred mountain, and some still come to its lower slopes to offer the prayers of their villages and the foreskins of their young men – this was the traditional place for holding boy-to-man circumcision ceremonies. Besides being venerated by the Kikuyu, Mt Kenya has the rare honour of being both a Unesco World Heritage Site and a Unesco Biosphere Reserve.

In the past, 12 glaciers wore Mt Kenya down to 5199m worth of dramatic remnants, but today it is the ice itself that is under threat, disappearing under increased temperatures and taking with it crystalline caves and snowy crevasses. That means the climb up the mountain is easier than it has ever been – but by no means does it mean the ascent is easy.

The highest peaks of Batian (5199m) and Nelion (5188m), can only be reached by mountaineers with technical skills, but Point Lenana (4985m), the third-highest peak, can be reached by trekkers and is the usual goal for most mortals. The views are awe-inspiring – when they're not hemmed in by opaque mist.

Information

The daily fees for the **national park** (☎ 061-55645; PO Box 753, Nyeri; adult/child US$20/8) are charged upon entry, so you must estimate the length of your stay. If you overstay, you pay the difference when leaving. You'll have to pay an additional KSh200 per day for each guide and porter you take with you. Always ask for a receipt.

Lonely Planet's *Trekking in East Africa* has more information, details on wilder routes and some of the more esoteric variations that are possible on Mt Kenya.

Technical climbers and mountaineers should get a copy of **Mountain Club of Kenya's** (MCK; ☎ Nairobi 020-602330; www.mountkenya.org/mck .htm) *Guide to Mt Kenya & Kilimanjaro*.

SAFETY

Many people ascend the mountain too quickly and suffer from headaches, nausea and other (sometimes more serious) effects of altitude sickness. By spending at least three nights on the ascent, you'll enjoy yourself much more; responsible guides will require you take an acclimation day on the way up the mountain. Be wary of hypothermia and dehydration; fluids and warm clothing go a long way towards preventing both.

Unpredictable weather is another problem. The trek to Point Lenana isn't an easy hike and people die on the mountain every year. Bring proper clothes and equipment; the best time to go is from mid-January to late February or from late August to September.

Unless you're a seasoned trekker with high-altitude experience and a good knowledge of reading maps and using a compass, you'd be flirting with death by not taking a guide or hiking with someone who isn't qualified. Even those with ample experience should take a guide on the Summit Circuit.

CLOTHING & EQUIPMENT

Nightly temperatures near the summit often drop to below -10°C, so bring a good sleeping bag and a closed-cell foam mat or thermarest if you're camping. A good set of warm clothes (wool or synthetics – never cotton, as it traps moisture) is equally important. As it can rain heavily any time of year, you'll need waterproof clothing (breathable fabric such as Gore-Tex is best). A decent pair of boots and sandals or light shoes (for the evening when your boots get wet) is a great idea. At this altitude the sun can do some serious damage to your skin and eyes, so sunblock and sunglasses are also crucial items.

If a porter is carrying your backpack, always keep essential clothing (warm and wet-weather gear) in your day-pack because you may become separated from it for hours at a time.

It's not a good idea to sleep in clothes you've worn during the day because the sweat your clothes absorbed keeps them moist at night, reducing their heat-retention.

If you don't intend to stay in the huts along the way, you'll need a tent, stove, basic cooking equipment, utensils, a 3L water container (per person) and water-purifying tablets. Stove fuel in the form of petrol and kerosene (paraffin) is fairly easily found in towns, and methylated spirits is available in Nairobi, as are gas

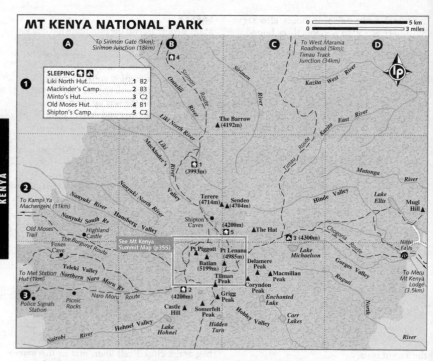

MT KENYA NATIONAL PARK

SLEEPING 🏠 🏕️
Liki North Hut...................1	B2
Mackinder's Camp.............2	B3
Minto's Hut.....................3	C2
Old Moses Hut.................4	B1
Shipton's Camp................5	C2

cartridges. Fires are prohibited in the open except in an emergency; in any case, there's no wood once you get beyond 3300m.

If you have a mobile phone, take it along; reception on the mountain's higher reaches is actually very good, and a link to the outside world is invaluable during emergencies.

GUIDES, COOKS & PORTERS

Having a porter for your gear is like travelling in a chauffeured Mercedes instead of a *matatu*. A good guide will help set a sustainable pace and hopefully dispense interesting information about Mt Kenya and its flora and fauna. With both on your team, your appreciation of this mountain will be enhanced a hundred-fold. If you hire a guide or porter who can also cook, you won't regret it.

Considerable effort has been made in recent years to regulate guides and porters operating on the mountain. The KWS now issues vouchers to all registered guides and porters, who should also hold identity cards; they won't be allowed into the park without them.

Female guides are becoming more common. Often, you'll be asked to hire a trekking guide for the first leg of the journey and a more expensive technical guide for the summit.

COSTS

The cost of guides varies depending on their qualifications, whatever the last party paid and your own negotiating skills. You should expect to pay a minimum of US$20 per day for a basic guide, while technical climbing guides can cost as much as US$50 per day. Cooks and porters cost US$15 to US$20 per day. Agree on all costs before you depart.

These fees don't include park entry fees and tips, the latter should only be made for good service.

Sleeping

You can **camp** (adult/child US$10/5) anywhere on the mountain – the nightly fee is payable to KWS at any gate. Most people camp near the huts or bunkhouses, as there are often toilets and water nearby. KWS operates two more upscale lodges on the mountain: **Batian Guest House** (Map p353; US$180), a plush, four-bedroom cottage located a kilometre from Naro Moru Gate, and the surprisingly comfy stone **Sirimon**

Bandas (Map p353; US$80), which are located 9km from the Sirimon Gates. Reservations for both lodgings must be made through the KWS at ☎ 020-600800 or reservations@kws.org. You can also contact the warden of the national park at ☎ 061-55645/55201.

Accommodation along the major trekking routes, whether in huts or larger bunkhouses, is described in detail in each route's accommodation section.

Eating

In an attempt to reduce luggage, many trekkers exist entirely on canned and dried foods. You can do this by keeping up your fluid intake, but it's not a good idea. Keep in mind that your appetite for 'heavy' meals (ie lots of big solids) drops considerably at high altitudes.

Increased altitude creates unique cooking conditions. The major consideration is that the boiling point of water is considerably reduced. At 4500m, for example, water boils at 85°C; this is too low to sufficiently cook rice or lentils (pasta is better) and you won't be able to brew a good cup of tea (instant coffee is the answer). Cooking times and fuel usage are considerably increased as a result, so plan accordingly.

When you're buying dehydrated foods, get the precooked variety to cut down on cooking time – two-minute noodles are a solution. It's a good idea to bring these from home. Take plenty of citrus fruits and/or citrus drinks as well as chocolate, sweets or dried fruit to keep your blood-sugar level high.

To avoid severe headaches caused by dehydration or altitude sickness, drink at least 3L of fluid per day and bring rehydration sachets. Water purification tablets, available at most chemists, aren't a bad idea either.

Environment

There are flora, fauna and ecosystems on the slopes of Mt Kenya that cannot be found anywhere else in the country.

This extinct volcano hosts, at various elevations, upland forest, bamboo forest (2500m), high-altitude equatorial heath (3000m to 3500m) and lower alpine moorland (3400m to 3800m), which includes several species of bright everlasting flowers. Some truly surreal plantlife grows in the Afro-Alpine zone (above 3500m) and the upper alpine zone (3800m to 4500m), including hairy carpets of tussock grass, the brushlike giant lobelias, or rosette plants, and the sci-fi worthy *Senecio Brassica*, or giant groundsel, which looks like a cross between an aloe, a cactus and a dwarf. At the summit it's all rock and ice, a landscape that possess its own stark beauty, especially this close to the equator.

Unfortunately, there's more rock than ice these days. 'In 15 years I've seen all the glaciers move. I don't need crampons any more,' one guide told us. Warmer weather has led to disappearing glaciers, and ice climbing in Mt Kenya is largely finished. We've heard the above conditions have led to drier rivers in the region, which makes sense as Mt Kenya is the country's most important permanent watershed.

In lower elevations large game are around; you may need to clap and hoot as you trudge to stave off elephants and buffaloes. Rock hyraxes are common, as are, rather annoyingly, bees. There are also Sykes monkeys, Mackinders eagle owls, waterbucks, and (very rarely spotted) leopards, hyenas and cervals about, but these animals tend to stay hidden in the thick brush of the lower forests.

Give extra supplies to your guides, rather than leave them out for wildlife, whose feeding patterns are disrupted by foreign food. Carry all your litter (including used toilet paper) off the mountain; animals will dig up buried refuse. Bury faeces below 3500m, but above this altitude, leave on the surface of the ground (and scatter them about or scrape them with a stick to speed up decomposition). Hundreds of kilos of waste are removed from the mountain each year via locally run cleanup operations; try not to add to the mess.

Organised Treks

If you negotiate aggressively, a package trek may end up costing only a little more than organising each logistical element of the trip separately. As always, you need to watch out for sharks; picking the right company is even more important here than on regular safari, as an unqualified or inexperienced guide could put you in real danger.

Mountain Rock Safaris Resorts & Trekking Services (Map pp284-5; ☎ 020-242133, 0722-511752; www.mountain rockkenya.com; PO Box 15796-00100, Nairobi) is based in Jubilee Insurance House in Nairobi. A four day Naro Moru–Sirimon crossover trek, its most popular option, runs US$960 for a single person, but runs US$560 for groups of three and as low as US$450 for groups of nine or more.

KENYA

Naro Moru River Lodge (Map p353; ☎ 062-31047, Nairobi 020-4443357, 0724082754; www.alliancehotels.com, alliance@africaonline.co.ke; PO Box 18, Naro Moru) also runs a range of all-inclusive trips. Its prices are more expensive than most, but it's the only company that can guarantee you beds in the Met Station Hut and Mackinder's Camp on the Naro Moru route (because it owns said lodges!).

IntoAfrica (☎ UK 0114-255 5610, Nairobi 0722-511752; www.intoafrica.co.uk; 40 Huntingdon Crescent, Sheffield, UK, S11 8AX) is an environmentally and culturally sensitive company which places an emphasis on fair trade and offers both scheduled and exclusive seven-day trips (six days of trekking) ascending Sirimon route and descending Chogoria. Joining scheduled one-week trips costs US$192 per day (minimum two people), while private treks range from US$77 to US$355 per person per day, depending on group size.

KG Mountain Expeditions (☎ 062-62403; www.kenyaexpeditions.com; PO Box 199, Naro Moru) run by a highly experienced mountaineer, offers all-inclusive four-day treks for US$710 for single climbers, which goes down to US$460 for groups of five or more.

Montana Trek & Information Centre (Map p357; ☎ 062-32731; Jambo House Hotel, Lumumba St, Nanyuki) has staff who are are pretty friendly and as knowledgeable as hell about the mountain. A four-day trip will run around US$420 per person for a group of two or more. It's particularly useful for Sirimon trekkers.

EWP (Executive Wilderness Programmes) (☎ UK +44(0)1550-721319, USA/Canada +1800-514-6143; www.ewpnet.com/kenya; Haulfryn, Cilycwm SA20 0SP, UK). is a UK-based outfit employs some knowledgeable local guides; three-day trips cost US$800 per person for a single trekker, down to US$490 per person for groups of three and lower for larger parties.

Sana Highlands Trekking Expeditions (Map pp284-5; ☎ 020-227820; www.sanatrekkingkenya.com; Contrust House, Moi Ave, PO Box 5400-00100, Nairobi) operates five-day all-inclusive treks on the Sirimon and Chogoria routes that start at US$325 per person (based on a group of five).

The Routes

There are at least seven different routes up Mt Kenya. Of those, we cover Naro Moru, the easiest and most popular, as well as Sirimon and Chogoria, which are excellent alternatives. The Burguret and Timau routes are less well-known and are described in Lonely Planet's *Trekking in East Africa*.

We also delve into the exciting but demanding Summit Circuit, which circles Batian and Nelion, thus enabling you to mix and match ascending and descending routes.

NARO MORU ROUTE

Although the least scenic, this is the most straightforward and popular route and is still spectacular. Begin in Naro Moru and allow a minimum of four days for the trek. While possible in three, you risk serious altitude sickness.

Sleeping

There are three good bunk houses along this route: **Met Station Hut** (Map p353; dm US$12) is at 3000m, **Mackinder's Camp** (Map p350; dm US$15) is at 4160m and **Austrian Hut** (Map p355; dm KSh1000) is at 4790m. Beds in Met Station and Mackinder's are harder to find, as they're booked through **Naro Moru River Lodge** (Map p353; ☎ 062-31047, Nairobi 020-4443357, 0724-082754; www.alliancehotels.com; PO Box 18, Naro Moru). If you're denied beds, you can still climb this route if you're willing to camp and carry all the appropriate equipment. Those needing more luxury can doss in lovely **Batian Guest House** (Map p353 US$180), a kilometre from Naro Moru gate.

The Trek

Starting in Naro Moru town, the first part of the route takes you along a gravel road through farmlands for some 13km (all the junctions are signposted) to the start of the forest. Another 5km brings you to the park entry gate (2400m), from where its 8km to the road head and the Met Station Hut (3000m), where you stay for the night and acclimatize.

On the second day, set off through the forest (at about 3200m) and Teleki Valley to the moorland around so-called **Vertical Bog**; expect the going here to be, well, boggy. At a ridge the route divides into two. You can either take the higher path, which gives better views but is often wet, or the lower, which crosses the Naro Moru River and continues gently up to Mackinder's Camp (4160m). This part of the trek should take about 4½ hours. Here you can stay in the dormitories or camp.

On the third day you can either rest at Mackinder's Camp to acclimatise or aim for **Point Lenana** (4895m). This stretch takes

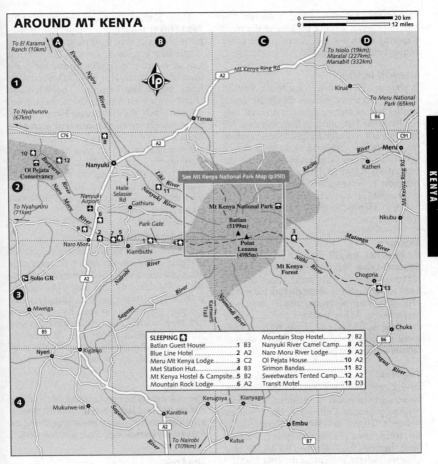

AROUND MT KENYA

SLEEPING 🏠		
Batian Guest House	1	B3
Blue Line Hotel	2	A2
Meru Mt Kenya Lodge	3	C2
Met Station Hut	4	B3
Mt Kenya Hostel & Campsite	5	B2
Mountain Rock Lodge	6	A2
Mountain Stop Hostel	7	B2
Nanyuki River Camel Camp	8	A2
Naro Moru River Lodge	9	A2
Ol Pejata House	10	A2
Sirimon Bandas	11	B2
Sweetwaters Tented Camp	12	A2
Transit Motel	13	D3

three to six hours, so it is common to leave around 2am to reach the summit in time for sunrise. From the bunk house, continue past the ranger station to a fork. Keep right, and go across a swampy area, followed by a moraine, and then up a long scree slope – this is a long, hard slog. KWS' Austrian Hut (4790m) is three to four hours from Mackinder's and about one hour below the summit of Lenana, so it's a good place to rest before the final push.

The section of the trek from Austrian Hut up to Point Lenana takes you up a narrow rocky path that traverses the southwest ridge parallel to the Lewis Glacier, which has shrunk more than 100m since the 1960s. Be careful, as the glacier's shrinkage has created

serious danger of slippage along the path. A final climb or scramble brings you up onto the peak. In good weather it's fairly straightforward, but in bad weather you shouldn't attempt to reach the summit unless you're experienced in mountain conditions or have a guide. Plenty of inexperienced trekkers have come to grief on this section, falling off icy cliffs or even disappearing into crevasses. With all that said the disappearing glacier phenomenon (Gregory Glacier has practically vanished) has made the climb generally easier, although it makes the lives of those who rely on those glaciers for meltwater a hell of a lot more difficult.

From Point Lenana most people return along the same route. Alternatively, you can return to Austrian Hut, then take the Summit Circuit around the base of the main peaks to reach the top of one of the other routes before you descend.

SIRIMON ROUTE

A popular alternative to Naro Moru, Sirimon has better scenery, greater flexibility and a gentler rate of ascent, although it is still easy to climb too fast; allow at least five days for the trek. It's well worth considering combining it with the Chogoria route for a six- to seven-day traverse that really brings out the best of Mt Kenya. Although Naro Moru is the most popular route, Sirimon is probably the easiest for inexperienced trekkers.

Nanyuki (p357) is the best launching point for this route.

Sleeping

Old Moses Hut (Map p350; dm US$10) at 3300m and **Shipton's Camp** (Map p350; dm US$14) at 4200m serve trekkers on this route. They're both booked through the **Mountain Rock Lodge** (Map p353; ☎ 062-62625; info@mountainrockkenya.com), near Naro Moru. Many trekkers acclimatize by camping at Liki North. If you'd like a little more comfort, book into the KWS' excellent **Sirimon Bandas** (Map p353; US$80).

The Trek

It is 23km from Nanyuki to the Sirimon Gate, and transport is included with pre-booked packages. Otherwise take a *matatu* towards Timau or Meru, or arrange a lift from town. From the gate it's about 9km through the forest to Old Moses Hut (3300m), where you spend the first night.

On the second day you could head straight through the moorland for Shipton's Camp, but it is worth taking an extra acclimatisation day via **Liki North Hut** (Map p350; 3993m) a tiny place on the floor of a classic glacial valley. The actual hut is a complete wreck and meant for porters, but it's a good campsite with a toilet and stream nearby.

On the third day, head up the western side of Liki North Valley and over the ridge into Mackinder's Valley, joining the direct route about 1½ hours in. After crossing the Liki River, follow the path for another 30 minutes until you reach the bunkhouse at Shipton's Camp (4200m), which is set in a fantastic location right below Batian and Nelion.

From Shipton's you can push straight for **Point Lenana** (4895m), a tough 3½- to five-hour slog via Harris Tarn and the tricky north-face approach, or take the Summit Circuit in either direction around the peaks to reach Austrian Hut (4790m), about one hour below the summit. The left-hand (east) route past Simba Col is shorter but steeper, while the right-hand (west) option takes you on the Harris Tarn trail nearer the main peaks.

From Austrian Hut take the standard southwest traverse up to Point Lenana – see p352. If you're spending the night here, it's worth having a wander around to catch the views up to Batian and down the Lewis Glacier into Teleki Valley.

CHOGORIA ROUTE

This route crosses some of the most spectacular and varied scenery on Mt Kenya, and is often combined with the Sirimon route (usually as the descent). The only disadvantage is the long distance between Chogoria and the park gate. Allow at least five days for a trek here; many guides will recommend you spend a full week on the trip. As befits its length and difficulty, this is usually the most expensive route up the mountain.

Sleeping

The only option besides camping on this route is **Meru Mt Kenya Lodge** (Map p353; s/tw US$22/44), a group of comfortable cabins administered by **Meru County Council** (Map p359; Kenyatta Hwy, Meru).

The Trek

The main reason this route is more popular as a descent is the 29km bottom stage. While not overly steep, climbing up that distance is much harder than descending it. Either way, it's a beautiful walk through farmland, rainforest and bamboo. You can camp near the Forest Station 6km out of town, but you'll still have 23km to walk the next day. Transport is available from the village, but it'll cost you.

Camping is possible at the gate, or you can stay nearby in Meru Mt Kenya Lodge (3000m), with transport to town available and a small shop selling beer, which is also popular with people coming down.

On the second day, head up through the forest to the trailhead (camping is possible

KENYA

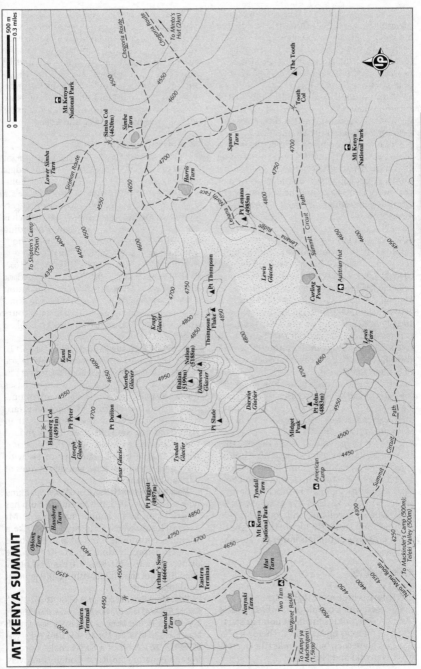

MT KENYA SUMMIT

here). From here it's another 7km over rolling foothills to the Hall Tarns area and **Minto's Hut** (Map p350; 4300m). Like Liki North, this place is only intended for porters, but makes for a decent campsite. Don't use the tarns here to wash anything, as they have already been polluted by careless trekkers.

From here follow the trail alongside the stunning **Gorges Valley** (another possible descent for the adventurous) and scramble up steep ridges to meet the Summit Circuit. It is possible to go straight for the north face or southwest ridge of Point Lenana, but stopping at Austrian Hut or detouring to Shipton's Camp is probably a better idea and gives you more time to enjoy the scenery – see Sirimon (p354) and Naro Moru routes (p352) for details.

SUMMIT CIRCUIT

While everyone who summits Point Lenana gets a small taste of the spectacular Summit Circuit, few trekkers ever grab the beautiful beast by the horns and hike its entire length. The trail encircles the main peaks of Mt Kenya between the 4300m and 4800m contour lines and offers challenging terrain, fabulous views and a splendid opportunity to familiarise yourself with this complex mountain. It is also a fantastic way to acclimatise before bagging Point Lenana.

One of the many highlights along the route is a peek at Mt Kenya's southwest face, with the long, thin Diamond Couloir leading up the Gates of the Mists between the summits of Batian and Nelion.

Depending on your level of fitness, this route can take between four and nine hours. Some fit souls can bag Point Lenana (from Austrian Hut or Shipton's Camp) and complete the Summit Circuit in the same day.

The trail can be deceptive at times, especially when fog rolls in, and some trekkers have become seriously lost between Tooth Col and Austrian Hut. It is imperative to take a guide.

NARO MORU
☎ 062

Naro Moru is little more than a string of shops and houses, with a couple of very basic hotels and a market, but it's the most popular starting point for treks up Mt Kenya. There's a post office with internet, but no banks (the nearest are at Nanyuki and Nyeri).

Apart from gawking at Mt Kenya and starting the Naro Moru route up to its summit (p352), there are some fine things to do here. Mt Kenya Hostel & Campsite organises a number of excursions, including **nature walks** and hikes to the **Mau Mau caves**, which are impressive from both a physical and historical perspective. Mountain Rock Lodge and Naro Moru River Lodge also run similar trips, as well as offering **horse riding** and **fishing**.

Sleeping & Eating

Blue Line Hotel (Map p353; ☎ 062-62217; camping KSh150, s/d KSh400/800) This is an excellent budget option; rooms don't get much cleaner or comfortable for such a bargain price. There's a restaurant and bar on the premises that gets pretty busy with locals on weekends, which is either a good thing or a drawback depending on what you're in the mood for. You're about 13km from the park entrance here.

Mt Kenya Hostel & Campsite (Map p353; ☎ 062-62412, 0722-598974; wanjaujoseph2000@yahoo.com; camping KSh250, dm KSh500) The closest accommodation to the park is friendly in a youth hostel kind of way, and frequently hosts group tours and treks (and therefore should be booked in advance).

Mountain Rock Lodge (Map p353; ☎ 062-62625, 020-242133, 0722-511752; www.mountainrockkenya.com; camping US$5, standard s/tw KSh3000/4000, superior s/tw KSh3500/5200) This is one of the major bases for Mt Kenya climbers and all sorts of outdoor activities. It's located 6km north of Naro Moru, tucked away in the woods less than 1km from the Nanyuki road. The standard rooms are decent value, while the 'superior' rooms have a bit of character to go with their fireplaces (and eerie wooden statues of African tribesmen).

Mountain Stop Hotel (Map p353; s KSh500) Spanking new when we visited, the Mountain Stop has cheerful staff and a similar ambience to Mt Kenya Hostel, which is to say it feels like a friendly, communal kind of place to base yourself before heading up Mt Kenya. The owners organise Mt Kenya treks and other encounters of the hiking, fishing and general outdoorsy kind.

Naro Moru River Lodge (Map p353; ☎ 062-31047, Nairobi 020-4443357, 0724-082754; www.alliancehotels.com; PO Box 18, Naro Moru; camping US$10, May-Jun half board from s/tw US$61/90, Mar-Apr US$73/106, rest of year US$99/132; ☒) A bit of a Swiss chalet bordering the equator, the River Lodge is a lovely collection of dark, cosy cottages and rooms embedded into a sloping hillside that overlooks a rushing river.

Getting There & Away
There are plenty of buses and *matatus* heading to Nanyuki (KSh80, 30 minutes), Nyeri (KSh100, 45 minutes) and Nairobi (KSh350, three hours).

Naro Moru River Lodge operates transfers between the lodge and Nairobi (US$120) or Nanyuki airstrip (US$25), but you must book 24 hours in advance.

NANYUKI
☎ 062
This small but bustling mountain town makes a living from sales, be it of treks to climbers, curios to soldiers of the British Army (which has a training facility nearby) or drinks to pilots of the Kenyan Air Force (this is the site of their main air base). For all that mercantilism, it's laidback for a market town. And entrepreneurship and conservation have combined in a particularly attractive fashion: the town sits on the edge of the Laikipia

Plateau, one of Africa's most important wildlife conservation sites.

Information
Barclays Bank (Kenyatta Ave) With ATM.
Kenya Commercial Bank (Kenyatta Ave) With ATM (Visa only).
Mt Kenya Cyberworld (Kenyatta Ave; per hr KSh60) Internet and international calls.
Post office (Kenyatta Ave)
Standard Chartered Bank (Kenyatta Ave) With ATM.

Sights & Activities
Besides tackling Mt Kenya's Sirimon (p352) route, you should stroll 3km south to the **Equator** (there's a sign) and get a lesson on the Coriolis force from the Mid-World Curio Shop (see p360). 'Graduates' of the course can buy a 'diploma' for KSh300.

About 3km east of town is a **Commonwealth War Cemetery**, a meditative spot which is kept in immaculate shape. If you ask politely, the stewards of the local **Hindu Temple** (they live behind the building) may let you have a peek inside. There are shrines to Shiva, Rama, Sita and Hanuman and not much else, but you are being

KENYA

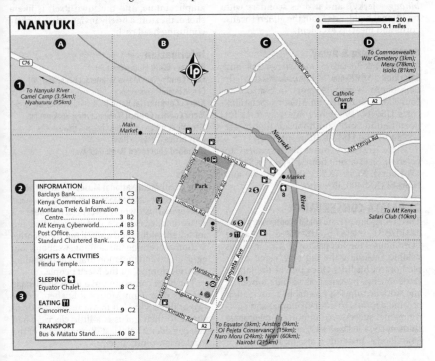

NANYUKI

0 — 200 m
0 — 0.1 miles

To Nanyuki River
Camel Camp (3.5km);
Nyahururu (95km)

To Commonwealth
War Cemetery (3km);
Meru (78km);
Isiolo (81km)

Main Market

Catholic Church

Park

Market

To Mt Kenya
Safari Club (10km)

To Equator (3km); Airstrip (9km);
Ol Pejeta Conservancy (15km);
Naro Moru (24km); Nyeri (60km);
Nairobi (215km)

INFORMATION	
Barclays Bank	1 C3
Kenya Commercial Bank	2 C2
Montana Trek & Information Centre	3 B2
Mt Kenya Cyberworld	4 B3
Post Office	5 B3
Standard Chartered Bank	6 C2

SIGHTS & ACTIVITIES	
Hindu Temple	7 B2

SLEEPING	
Equator Chalet	8 C2

EATING	
Camcorner	9 C2

TRANSPORT	
Bus & Matatu Stand	10 B2

afforded a nice peak into the lives of what's left of Nanyuki's South Asian community (there's about 29 Indian families left in town).

Sleeping & Eating

Nanyuki River Camel Camp (Map p353; ☎ 0722-361642; camellot@wananchi.com; off C76 Hwy; camping US$6, half board huts with shared bathroom low/high season KSh1500/2500) The most innovative sleep in town (well, 4km outside of it) is this eco-camp, set off in a dry swab of scrub. Inhabited by 200 camels (available for hire) and a pack of friendly dogs, the camp offers lodging in genuine Somali grass huts imported from Mandera.

Equator Chalet (☎ 062-31480; Kenyatta Ave; theequatorchalet@yahoo.com; s/tw/d incl breakfast KSh1300/1700/2000) This is as plush as it gets if you opt to stay inside the Nanyuki town limits, and while it's no four-star hotel, the Equator is welcoming and comfortable. The very fine rooms surround a breezy internal courtyard that opens onto two balcony areas and a roof terrace.

Camcorner (Kenyatta Ave; meals KSh60-260) If you're in 'downtown' Nanyuki, this is your best option. It serves up the usual stews and steaks, as well as camel products (including camel *biltong* – jerky), and it does wonders with traditional highlands food; the *githeri* (beans, corns and meat) is excellent.

Getting There & Away

Airkenya (☎ 020-605745; www.airkenya.com) and **Safarilink** (☎ 020-600777; www.safarilink.co.ke) fly daily from Wilson Airport in Nairobi to Nanyuki. A return trip on Airkenya/Safarilink costs US$160/195, while one-way fares for northbound and southbound flights are US$80/91 and US$80/117 respectively.

There are daily buses and *matatus* to Nyeri (KSh150, one hour), Isiolo (KSh200, 1½ hours), Meru (KSh150, 1½ hours) and Nairobi (KSh400, three hours).

OL PEJATA CONSERVANCY

This 364-sq-km private **wildlife conservancy** (adult/child US$25/13), owned by UK-based Fauna and Flora, houses the full palette of African plains wildlife, including the Big Five, eland and a plethora of birdlife. Once one of the largest cattle ranches in Kenya, as wildlife moved in and stock became less profitable, conservation became a means to both economic and environmental success. An important **chimpanzee sanctuary** (☻ 9-10.30am & 3-4.30pm), operated by the Jane Goodall Institute, is also located here.

Sleeping

Sweetwaters Tented Camp (Map p353; ☎ 062-31970, 0734-699852, Nairobi 020-2842333; sweetwaters@serena .co.ke; low season full board s/d US$180/295, high season US$295/360, peak season US$445/575) Recently purchased by Serena Hotels, this camp sits beside a floodlit waterhole (tent numbers one and two have the best view).

Ol Pejata House (Map p353; ☎ 062-32400, Nairobi 020-2710511; swtc@kenyaweb.com; high season s/d US$545/695, low season US$400/495) On the grounds of Sweetwaters Tented Camp is this massive bush villa that was once home to Lord Delamere.

Getting There & Away

You can visit the reserve independently if you have your own vehicle. Access is off the A2 Hwy south out of Nanyuki.

MERU
☎ 064

The pick-up trucks race down the highway, screaming their ancient gears while weighed down with enormous loads of twigs, the basis of this town's economy: *miraa*. Meru is the epicentre of Kenyan production of this amphetamine, and the town itself is like a shot of the stuff: a briefly invigorating, slightly confusing head rush.

Information

Barclays Bank (Tom Mboya St)
Cafe Candy (Tom Mboya St; internet per hr KSh180) Decent internet connections.
Kenya Commercial Bank (KCB; Njiru Ncheke St)
Meru County Council (Kenyatta Hwy) Bookings for Meru Mt Kenya Lodge on the Chogoria route.
Post office (Kenyatta Hwy)
Standard Chartered Bank (Moi Ave)

Sights

The small **Meru National Museum** (☎ 064-20482; off Kenyatta Hwy; admission KSh500; ☻ 9.30am-6pm, 1-6pm public holidays) is awfully overpriced. There's a series of faded exhibits, desultory stuffed and mounted wildlife and a small but informative section concerning the clothing, weapons, and agricultural and initiation practices (including clitoridectomies) of the Meru people.

The large compound of a local **Sikh Temple** perches over Tom Mboya Rd. There's only two or three Sikhs left in Meru, and the small shrine to their gurus is a little elegiac when you consider it's the last physical trace of the local Asian community.

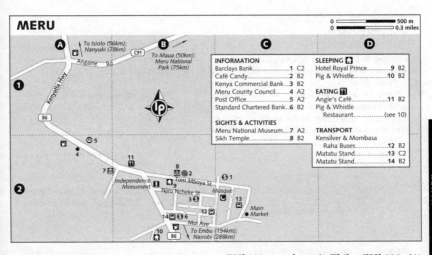

MERU

INFORMATION	
Barclays Bank	1 C2
Café Candy	2 B2
Kenya Commercial Bank	3 B2
Meru County Council	4 A2
Post Office	5 A2
Standard Chartered Bank	6 B2

SIGHTS & ACTIVITIES	
Meru National Museum	7 A2
Sikh Temple	8 B2

SLEEPING	
Hotel Royal Prince	9 B2
Pig & Whistle	10 B2

EATING	
Angie's Café	11 B2
Pig & Whistle Restaurant	(see 10)

TRANSPORT	
Kensilver & Mombasa Raha Buses	12 B2
Matatu Stand	13 C2
Matatu Stand	14 B2

Sleeping & Eating

Hotel Royal Prince (☎ 064-30567; Tom Mboya St; s/d KSh600/1000) A great budget option, the Royal Prince is well-lit and clean and the on-site restaurant and bar keep the atmosphere lively (but not sleazy). Some rooms are smallish, but all of them serve their simple purpose admirably.

Pig & Whistle (☎ 064-31411; off Kenyatta Hwy; s/tw incl breakfast KSh1100/1500) There's a rambling sense of alpine chaos here, offset by friendly staff and truly comfortable cottages set around a sprawling rustic compound. The concrete huts don't look like much from the outside, but they are actually nicely self-contained slices of good-value sleeping pleasure. More memorable stays are to be had in the old (1934) wooden cabins.

Meru County Hotel (☎ 064-32432; Kenyatta Hwy; s/tw incl breakfast from KSh1200/1700) This hotel doesn't have the character of the Pig & Whistle, but it does have amiable staff and spic-and-span rooms that are, for Meru, the height of luxury and service.

Angie's Café (Kenyatta Hwy; meals KSh50-150) Sedated goldfish patrol the aquarium and watch over simple menus. Locals recommend the biriani.

Pig & Whistle Restaurant (off Kenyatta Hwy; meals KSh150-270) The food (of the Kenyan and Western staples sort) is pretty good and the settings is even better: a lush, lovely garden interspersed with cute, lawn-jockey furniture. It's also great for an afternoon beer.

Getting There & Away

Kensilver (Mosque Hill Rd) has 13 daily departures from 6.45am onwards, covering Embu (KSh250, two hours), Thika (KSh300, 3½ hours) and Nairobi (KSh500, 4½ hours). **Mombasa Raha** (Mosque Hill Rd) has daily 5pm services to Mombasa (KSh1000, 10 hours).

Regular *matatus* serve the same destinations for similar cost. *Matatus* also serve Nanyuki (KSh200, 1½ hours) and Isiolo (KSh180, 1½ hours).

MERU NATIONAL PARK

One of Kenya's best-kept secrets, Meru combines the sun-kissed open savannah of East African dreams with a dark, intensely alive jungle that sprouts along the banks of the *mamba* (crocodile) rich Tana River. Driving into the park, which sits at the end of a long and uninspiring road, you suddenly shift into yellow, sharp-grassed plains pulsing with zebra, waterbuck, buffalo and elephants, while Hemingway-esque green hills loom like dark, dramatic sentinels in the deep blue distance. It's a pleasantly overwhelming shock to the senses, to say the least.

The park is well worth a few days of your time, not least because it is a fairly sizable place to explore. Morning, when the dawn breaks over yet another textbook-picture of African bush, is the best time to drive, and you'll often feel as if you have the park to yourself; there's no Samburu-style game drive congestion in Meru – yet.

There's an excellent rhino sanctuary on-site and a bridge across the Tana River at **Adamson's Falls** accessing Kora National Park, and if you're very lucky, you may spot a leopard in the

KENYA

GICHIMU JOSEPH

At the signpost for the equator is the Mid-World Curio Shop and a pitcher of water. As we took a picture in front of the equator, Gichimu Joseph approached us:

'Hello sirs. Welcome to the equator! Would you like a demonstration of the Coriolis Force?'

'Hello. Sure.'

'Now we are at the centre. On either side is the Northern [gestures north] and Southern [gestures south] hemisphere. If I pour water from this pitcher into this bowl with a hole inside it [holds up bowl] 15m to the north, it will drain clockwise. Observe!' (He does so, dropping a stick in the water to demonstrate its draining direction.)

'Wow.'

'Now, if we go 15m to the south, it will go out in an anticlockwise direction.' (He repeats the procedure.)

'OK.'

'This whole effect is known as the Coriolis force. It was described by Gaspard-Gustave Coriolis in 1835 and is based off Newton's 2nd Law of Motion. Now, here at 0 degrees, when I pour out the water, it will drain out in a straight line. Watch!' (the water drains out in a straight line.)

'Wow! That's pretty damn impressive, Gichimu.'

'Thank you. I am the professor of the Coriolis force. I am also a carver. Would you like to see my art?'

Author's note: While the demonstration seems to work, scientists say the Coriolis force doesn't actually cause water to drain in the manner Gichimu depicted.

jungle. Elephant and giraffe herds lope over the marshy Bisandi Plains on the north end of the park, while lions wait under the tall grass, surrounded by oryxes, eland and kudu. Guinea fowl and gazelle hop through the savannah, and every now and then a streaking cheetah leaves ghost tracks across the edge of eyesight.

The park is the cornerstone of the Meru Conservation Area, a 4000-sq-km expanse that also includes the adjacent Kora National Park, and Bisanadi, Mwingi and North Kitui National Reserves (which are closed), covering the lowland plains east of Meru town.

Information

Entrance to **Meru National Park** (☎ 064-20613, 0733-662439; adult/child US$40/20) doesn't entitle you to enter the adjacent **Kora National Park** (adult/child US$40/20). Visits into Kora must be prearranged with Meru's warden.

At present you need a 4WD or to be on a tour to visit; the 4WD runs an extra KSh800. KWS' *Meru National Park* map (KSh450), sold at the gate, is essential if you want to find your way around. Even so you may want to hire a guide (4-hr/full-day tour KSh1500/2500).

Sleeping

Special campsites (adult/child US$15/5, plus set-up fee KSh5000) There are about a dozen of these bush campsites (no facilities) located throughout

the park. The staff at the gate will let you know which are currently open.

Leopard Rock Lodge (☎ 020-600031, 0733-333100; www.leopardmico.com; mid-Dec–Mar & Jul-Nov s/d US$480/570, Apr-Jul & Nov–mid-Dec s/d US$450/490; ☑) This beautiful unfenced lodge lets the wildlife right in; little crocodiles wander out of the Murera River to lounge by the pool (don't worry, security is good). The above, plus a thatched restaurant and plush rooms, equals top-class.

our pick **Elsa's Kopje** (☎ 020-604053; www.cheli peacock.com/camps/elsas.htm, high season full board s/d US$740-1190, low season full board US$820-2000; ☑) Plenty of hotels claim to blend into their environment, but Elsa's did so in such a seamless manner that the bar on chic ecosuites was permanently raised. Carved into Mughwango Hill, these highly individualized 'three-walled' rooms open out onto views that Disney animators at the time of *The Lion King* would have killed for. Stone-hewn infinity pools plunge over the clifftops, while rock hyraxes play tag in your private garden.

Getting There & Away

There's no point reaching the park without a vehicle. If you don't want to join a tour, your cheapest option is to acquire a 4WD (and driver) from a local in Meru or the village of Maua, which is 31km from the gate.

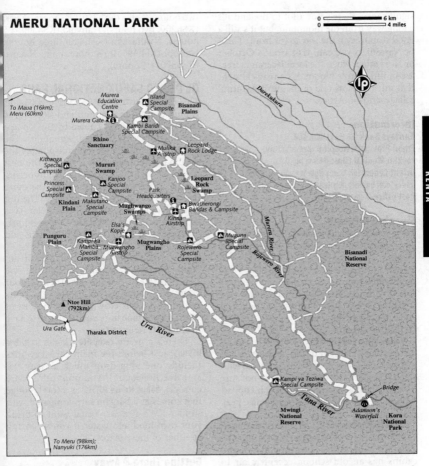

MERU NATIONAL PARK

0 ___ 6 km
0 ___ 4 miles

To Maua (16km);
Meru (60km)

Murera
Education
Centre

Murera Gate

Island
Special
Campsite

Bisanadi
Plains

Darekutura

Rhino
Sanctuary

Kambi Baridi
Special Campsite

Mulika
Airstrip

Leopard
Rock Lodge

Kithanga
Special
Campsite

Mururi
Swamp

Kanjoo
Special
Campsite

Leopard
Rock
Swamp

Princess
Special
Campsite

Park
Headquarters

Kindani
Plain

Makutano
Special
Campsite

Mughwango
Swamps

Bwatherongi
Bandas & Campsite

Elsa's
Kopje

Kinna
Airstrip

Punguru
Plain

Kampi ka
Mamba
Special
Campsite

Mugwangho
Airstrip

Mugwangho
Plains

Rojewero
Special
Campsite

Muguna
Special
Campsite

Murera River

Rojewero River

Bisanadi
National
Reserve

Ntoe Hill
(792km)

Ura River

Ura Gate

Tharaka District

To Meru (98km);
Nanyuki (176km)

Kampi ya Teziwa
Special Campsite

Tana River

Mwingi
National
Reserve

Adamson's
Waterfall

Bridge

Kora
National
Park

KENYA

Regular *matatus* service Maua from Meru town (KSh150, one hour).

Airkenya (☎ 020-605745; www.airkenya.com) has daily flights connecting Meru to Nairobi (one way/round-trip US$158/335).

CHOGORIA
☎ 064

This town shares its name with the most difficult, rewarding route up Mt Kenya (p354). It's a friendly enough place, albeit with little to do besides get coiffed in a wooden shack dubbed the Los Angeles Hair Salon.

You can probably arrange local accommodation with one of the many touts offering Mt Kenya climbs; otherwise, head to **Transit Motel** (Map p353; ☎ 064-22096; PO Box 190, Chogoria; camping per tent KSh500, s/tw incl breakfast KSh1000/1600) 2km south of town. This is a large, friendly lodge with nice rooms and a decent restaurant (meals KSh300 to KSh600) that makes a good base for organising Mt Kenya treks, and a relaxing spot to unwind once the slog is over. Don't believe touts claiming the motel has burnt down – it's a cement structure!

Regular buses and *matatus* ply the road heading north to Meru (KSh90, 30 minutes) and south to Embu (KSh170, 1½ hours) and Nairobi (KSh350, four hours).

EMBU
☎ 068

This sleepy town is the unlikely capital of Eastern Province, but despite its local significance, there's not a lot to do, and it's a long way from the mountain, but it's still a good stopover on the way to (or from) Thika or Nairobi. If you can, visit around October or November, when the local Jacaranda trees are in full, purple bloom; it's a magical sight that must rank as one of the most beautiful foliage shifts in Africa.

Information

Barclays Bank (B6 Hwy) With ATM.
Embu Provincial Hospital (Kenyatta Hwy)
Joykim Medical Clinic (Mama Ngina St)
Orient Cybers (off Mama Ngia St Hwy; per hr KSh120) As fast as local internet gets (which is slow).
Post office (Kenyatta Hwy)

Sleeping & Eating

Kenya Scouts Training Centre (☎ 068-30459; Kenyatta Hwy; camping KSh100, dm KSh250, s KSh650) It is what the title says: a training facility for the Kenyan Scouts that happens to rent spotless, well-maintained rooms. It's a real bargain, embellished with shy, friendly service and a *very* strict no drugs, alcohol or tobacco policy. If you can give the above up for a night, this may be the best sleep in town.

Valley View Lodge (☎ 068-31714; off B6 Hwy; s/d from KSh650/800) Painted in pea soup shades of institutional green, this is a decent sleep with clean if slightly faded rooms. We're not sure how much of a valley view you can cop, although the top floors may afford a nice peek down the B6.

Izaak Walton Inn (☎ 068-20128; izaakwalton@winnet .co.ke; Kenyatta Hwy; s/d incl breakfast from KSh2500/3500) This rambling series of warm cottages and cabins has an old-school, eccentric air to it, like a hill station operated by a slightly off colonial bureaucrat. You can opt between older, rustic wood lodges or more contemporary cottages.

Getting There & Away

Regular Kensilver buses heading to Meru (KSh300, two hours) and Nairobi (KSh300, three hours) pick up passengers at the BP petrol station in the centre of town. There are also express buses to Nairobi (KSh500, 1½ to two hours).

Mombasa Liners leave the BP station for Mombasa (KSh900, 10 hours) each morning at 7.30am.

There are numerous *matatus* serving Chogoria (KSh170, 1½ hours), Meru (KSh320,

two hours), Thika (KSh250, two hours), Nyeri (KSh200, two hours), Nanyuki (KSh300, 2½ hours), Nyahururu (KSh400, three hours), Nairobi (KSh300, three hours) and Nakuru (KSh500, 4½ hours).

OL DONYO SABUK NATIONAL PARK

This tiny **park** (☎ 067-4355257; adult/child US$20/10) is built around the summit and slopes of **Ol Donyo Sabuk** (2146m), known by the Kikuyu as Kilimambongo (Buffalo Mountain). The name fits, as buffaloes are indisputably the dominant animals; this is one of the best places in Kenya to spot these lumbering beasts, which are actually one of the more dangerous members of the Big Five. The rest of the mountain is surrounded by an oasis of dense primeval forest that supports primates such as black-and-white colobus and blue monkeys.

It's possible to explore on foot if accompanied by a ranger (per half/full day KSh2500/1500). It's a 9km hike (three or four hours) to an amazing 360-degree view at the summit, which is crowned with the sort of weird Afro-alpine flora you'd otherwise have to climb Mt Kenya to see.

There's a pretty **campsite** (camping adult/child US$10/5) just before the main gate. Facilities include one long-drop toilet, a rusty tap and free firewood. If you want a bit more comfort, **Sabuk House** (US$30) is a lovely lodge that comes at a bargain rate compared with similar KWS *bandas*. You'll want to bring your own food and water if you're staying at either of these places.

Getting There & Away

From Thika, take a *matatu* to the village of Ol Donyo Sabuk (KSh90, 50 minutes), from where it's a 2km walk along a straight dirt road to the gate. You could also take a *matatu* heading to Kitui and hop off at Kilimambongo (KSh70, 45 minutes), which is 6km from Ol Donyo Sabuk village.

THIKA
☎ 067

Those famous flame trees aren't around anymore, replaced with the bustle of a highway service town and red earth-caked pineapple plantations (Del Monte is a big player in these parts). The only true 'attractions' are **Chania Falls** and **Thika Falls**, about 1km north of town on the busy Nairobi–Nyeri road;

primarily, Thika is a base for a visit to Ol Donyo Sabuk National Park. You can also visit **Jomo Kenyatta's house** about 40km north of here; you'll need your own transport and it's a 100KSh admission to see…well, just a house, but if you're a Kenyan history buff, you might not want to pass it up.

WESTERN KENYA

For most people the magic of western Kenya is summed up in two poetic words: Masai Mara. This is understandable. After all, the Mara has fuelled African fantasies for years and, without a shadow of doubt, its wildebeest-spotted savannahs are the star attraction of what is a star-studded region. But there is much more to western Kenya than these plains of herbivores and carnivores.

Just like the incredible chameleons inhabiting the dense forests of this region, western Kenya can change its colours from shades of savannah brown to luminous teagarden green in the rain-soaked hills, or it can fade into deep, Lake Victoria blues speckled with red, yellow and orange fishing boats. And, just as the chameleon's eyes bulge from its body, so too does the land of western Kenya, in a series of mountain peaks that reach far above the clouds, and provide a home to elephants searching for salt 100m underground. This region also has humid jungles buzzing with weird and wonderful creatures generally more at home in the forests of the Congo, and tribal groups that are as varied and fascinating as the landscape. Yes, western Kenya is a perfect place for those who like surprises, contrasts and an ever-changing kaleidoscope of experiences and colours. And the best news of all is that, away from those Masai Mara wildebeest, most of it is virtually untouched by foreign tourists.

NAROK
☎ 050

Three hours west of Nairobi, this ramshackle provincial town is the Masai Mara National Reserve's main access point and the regions largest, no, only, town. It's a friendly and surprisingly hassle-free place.

Information
Kenya Commercial Bank is the town's only bank and it has an unreliable ATM (Visa only). Internet is available at Sky Apple Computer Training for KSh2 per minute.

Sleeping & Eating
Kim's Dishes Hotel (☎ 050-22001; s/tw KSh650/1300) Porn star beds straight out of the disco days of '77 make this a highly memorable place for a night's kip, but alas it's overpriced. The restaurant (meals KSh80 to KSh200) downstairs serves tasty Kenyan dishes.

Chambai Hotel (☎ 050-22591; s/d from KSh800/950) The standard rooms out the back are simple, spotless and sport mosquito nets. The new, super rooms in the main building have inviting beds, balconies, large TVs and huge bathrooms – sit on your throne and rule your porcelain kingdom. The bar and restaurant (mains KSh250) are civilised and worth trying.

Fast Food Cafe (mains from KSh100) This is a magic little place with a '50's feel where everyone sits around sipping milky tea and gorging on egg and chips.

Self-catering animal hunters should stock up on supplies from the Jalumat Supermarket on the road into town from the north.

Getting There & Away
Frequent *matatus* run between Narok and Nairobi (KSh400, tjree hours) and less-frequent departures serve Naivasha (KSh350, 2½ hours) and Kisii (KSh400, three hours). There is also usually daily transport to Sekenani and Talek gates for between KSh300 to KSh400 depending on the condition of the road at the time.

Several petrol stations pump the elixir of vehicular life – fill up, it's much cheaper than in the reserve.

MASAI MARA NATIONAL RESERVE
Backed by the spectacular Esoit Oloololo (Siria) Escarpment, watered by the Mara River National Reserve and littered with an astonishing amount of wildlife is the world-renowned Masai Mara. Its 1510 sq km of open rolling grasslands, the northern extension of the equally famous Serengeti Plains, form just a fraction of the immense Narok (managed by Narok County Council) and Transmara National Reserves (managed by Mara Conservancy), all of which is equally wildlife stuffed.

Although concentrations of wildlife are typically highest in the swampy area around the escarpment on the reserve's western edge, superior roads draw most visitors to

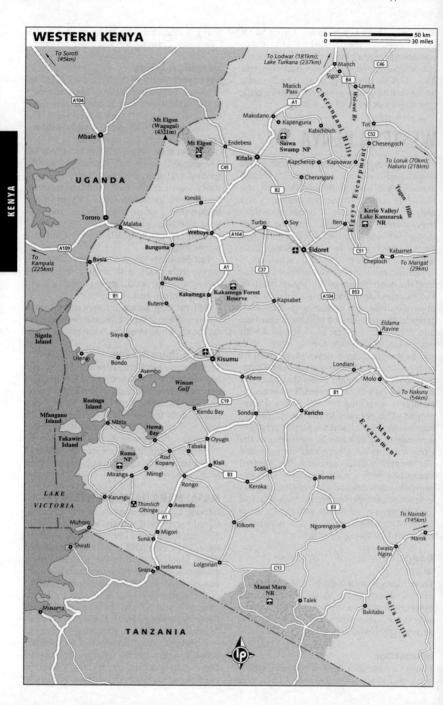

the eastern side. Of the big cats, sandy-eyed lions are found in large prides everywhere, and it is not uncommon to see them hunting. Cheetahs and leopards are less visible, but still fairly common and elephants, buffaloes, zebras and numerous other grazers occur in quantities that boggle the mind.

Breathtaking at any time of year the Mara reaches its pinnacle during the annual wildebeest migration in July and August, when literally millions of these ungainly beasts move north from the Serengeti seeking lusher grass before turning south again around October.

The reserve's fame means that it can get very busy and during the migration there seem to be as many minibuses as animals, and many tend to take off, making new tracks wherever they feel fit. This shouldn't be encouraged. In addition the Mara is also very expensive (and prices are continuing to rise out of all proportion to inflation).

Information

Because most of the gates are located inside the **reserve** (adult/child US$40/20) boundary it is easy to enter the Mara unknowingly. Most confusion arises when people camping outside the gates are requested to pay park fees – cue confrontation. For the record, campsites outside Oloolaimutiek Gate are inside the reserve, while Talek Gate's campsites north of the Talek River are outside it.

Wherever you enter, make sure you ask for a receipt: it is crucial for passage between the reserve's Narok and Transmara sections and your eventual exit. It also ensures your money ends up in the reserve's hands, not elsewhere. Gates also seem to charge KSh800 for all vehicles instead of KSh300 for ones with less than six seats – be insistent but polite and all will be well.

Sights & Activities
WILDLIFE DRIVES & WALKS

Whether you're bouncing over the plains in pursuit of elusive elephant silhouettes or parked next to a pride of lions and listening to their bellowed breaths, wildlife drives are *the* highlight of a trip to the Mara.

All top-end places offer wildlife drives, which can be negotiated into the rate while booking – it's usually cheaper than arranging them on arrival. However, guided walks and activities such **bush dinners** are booked during your stay.

If you've arrived by *matatu*, you can organise drives with most lodges, as they're fairly friendly towards independent travellers. Most of the cheaper camps charge around KSh12,000 for a full day's vehicle and driver hire which can be split between however many of you there are in a group. If you're arriving solo and are worried about the cost of doing this alone then you can often jump in another group's jeep. Alternatively, walk with a Maasai *moran* (warrior) outside the park (KSh1000 per person), where there is still a large amount of wildlife. Many old Africa hands swear that the best way of experiencing the African bush is on foot and doing this is a wonderful experience; you'll learn all about the medicinal properties of various plants, see the tell-tale signs of passing animals and have some heart-in-the-mouth close encounters with the local wildlife. If you do go on a walk be aware that some local Maasai groups may charge you for crossing their land.

If the idea of trotting around lion-infested countryside on the back of a creature that looks remarkably like a zebra sounds appealing then a number of lodges and camps outside the park gates also organise **horse-riding safaris**.

BALLOONING
If you can afford US$530 (and yes, that is per person), then balloon safaris are superb and worlds away from the minibus circuit. Trips can be arranged through top-end lodges.

MAASAI VILLAGE
The Maasai village between Oloolaimutiek and Sekenani Gates welcomes tourists, though negotiating admission can be fraught – prices start as high as KSh1500 per person, but you should be able to wrangle it down to KSh1000 or even a little less. If you're willing to drop this kind of cash for free rein with the camera, go ahead, but don't expect a genuine cultural experience.

Sleeping
In general accommodation in the Masai Mara National Reserve is insanely overpriced. Don't be at all surprised if you end up paying more for a lacklustre room or tent here than you would for a decent hotel room in a major West European city. For budget and midrange travellers the situation is especially dire with only a handful of campsites and a couple of exceedingly overpriced 'lodges'.

KENYA

MASAI MARA NATIONAL RESERVE

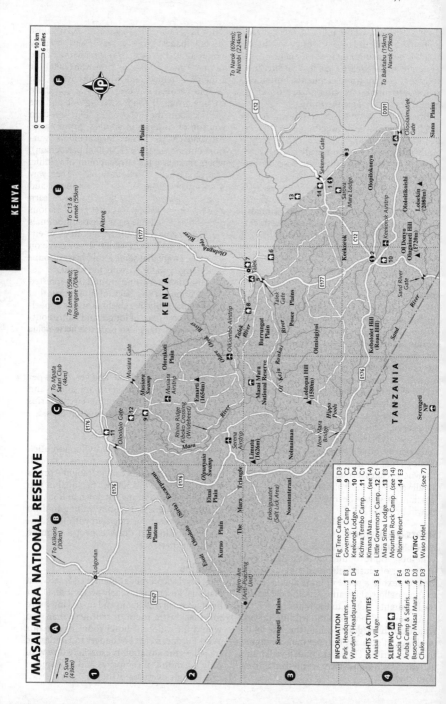

INFORMATION	
Park Headquarters......................**1** E3	
Warden's Headquarters..............**2** D4	

SIGHTS & ACTIVITIES	
Maasai Village............................**3** E4	

SLEEPING	
Acacia Camp................................**4** E4	
Aruba Camp & Safaris.................**5** D3	
Basecamp Masai Mara................**6** D3	
Chake...**7** D3	
Fig Tree Camp.............................**8** D3
Governors' Camp........................**9** C2
Keekorok Lodge.........................**10** D4
Kichwa Tembo Camp..................**11** C1
Kimana Mara........................(see 14)
Little Governors' Camp..............**12** C1
Mara Simba Lodge......................**13** E3
Mountain Rock Camp...........(see 14)
Oltome Resort............................**14** E3

EATING	
Waso Hotel.........................(see 7)

OLOOLAIMUTIEK & SEKANANI GATES
Budget & Midrange
While outside the Oloolaimutiek Gate, these camps are within the reserve and sleeping here will incur park fees (even if the camps state otherwise).

Acacia Camp (☎ 020-210024; camping US$8, s/tw US$27/47) Thatched roofs shelter closely spaced, spartan semipermanent tents in this quaint camp. They're slightly cheaper (single/twin US$20/40) without bedding. There are numerous cooking areas, a bar and a campfire pit, but no restaurant. Bathrooms are clean and hot water flows in the evening. The only downside for campers is the lack of shade.

Mountain Rock Camp (☎ 0736-149041, 0722-511252; www.mountainrockkenya.com; camping per tent KSh500, safari tent per person KSh1500, s/d full board US$95/165) Also known as the Mara Springs Safari Camp the simple self-contained safari tents here have cloth wardrobes and firm beds and sit in pretty, individual gardens. The camping area is pleasant and you can use the kitchen to prepare your own food or pay for full board.

our pick Kimana Mara (☎ 020-217335,0723-052867; www.kimanamara.com; camping KSh500, safari tent per person half/full board KSh3500/5000) Entirely owned, managed and run by the local community with profits returning to the community as a whole, this camp has several large, clean self-contained tents under the trees. It's a no-fuss kind of place, the staff are very cool and the food excellent. There's a cosy bar and kitchen facilities for campers.

Oltome Resort (☎ 020-3529640; www.oltomeresorts .com; s/tw full board US$165/250) Beautifully furnished, brand spanking new, luxury camp with below average prices and above average standards. There are only 10 spacious tents with plenty of privacy. It was only just opening for business at research so remains untested but it looks very promising.

Top End
Keekorok Lodge (bookings ☎ 020-532329; s/d full board US$350/440; ⧉) The oldest lodge in the Mara has more than 100 rooms and chalets kitted out in a modern tribal style and despite its size it still manages to retain a personal service. The crowning glories are the manicured gardens and the hippo pool.

TALEK GATE
Budget & Midrange
Chake (r per person KSh300) On the edge of Talek village and very different to all the other accommodation in and around the reserve. Chake is a local hotel with tin-roofed cubicles, comfy beds, clean sheets and friendly management. Foreign guests are rare but quite welcome and it offers not just better value than many of the standard camps but it also immerses you in day-to-day Maasai village life.

our pick Aruba Camp & Safaris (☎ 0723-997524; info@aruba-safaris.com; camping KSh450, safari tents per person full board/accommodation only KSh6000/4200) With only five safari tents available you'll have to fight tooth and nail to get one in high season but it's a battle well worth fighting because this is one of the few lodges in Kenya where you actually feel as if you're getting value for money. The tents are luxuriously appointed, but not overpowering, have lots of privacy as well as memorable views over the Talek River. The restaurant is an intimate candle-lit affair and the food excellent. The nearby campsite is also decent.

Top End
our pick Basecamp Masai Mara (☎ 020-577490; www .basecampexplorer.com; s/d full board US$155/310) 'Eco' is a much abused word in the tourism industry and sadly so-called 'eco-friendly' establishments are often nothing of the sort. To see what an eco-friendly hotel really looks like come to this superb lodge. Everything has been thought through in the finest detail in order to reduce its impact. If all this green scheming makes you worry that the accommodation might be rustic fear not. The safari tents here fall squarely into the divine luxury bracket and just wait till you get a load of the bathrooms. Basecamp runs the Bushbuck Reforestation project and has already planted thousands of trees in the hope of regenerating native woodland (which has been so successful that animals that haven't occurred here for years are reappearing) – a US$20 donation enables you to plant five trees.

Fig Tree Camp (☎ 020-605328; www.madahotels .com; s/d full board US$300/400; ⧉) Vegetate on your tent's verandah, watching the Talek's waters gently flow by in this sumptuous camp with its colonial feel. The gardens are about the most luxuriant you'll ever see and the bathrooms about the biggest and most inviting you'll find under canvas. To round things off, there is a small but scenic pool and a trendy treetop bar. One big drawback is that breakfast is only served between 7am and 9am meaning you can't go on a morning safari and get a feed.

KENYA

MUSIARA & OLOOLOLO GATES

Sadly, there are no secure budget or midrange options here.

Kichwa Tembo Camp (☎ 020-3740920; www.kich watembo.com, full board per person US$475; ⚲) Just outside the northern boundary, Kichwa has permanent tents with grass-mat floors, stone bathrooms and tasteful furnishings. Hop in a hammock and take in spectacular savannah views. The food has an excellent reputation.

Governors' Camp (☎ 020-2734000; www.governors camp.com; s/d full board US$596/890; ⚲) This camp, and Little Governors' Camp (single/double full board US$652/972, with a swimming pool) are widely regarded as the most magisterial camps in the Mara and offer great service, riverside locations and activities a-plenty. The extraordinary rates include three wildlife drives and someone keen to wash your dirty underwear.

Eating & Drinking

If you can't afford the lodges' accommodation, drop in for drinks or a meal. Lovely lunches/dinners will set you back US$20/30, but the views and ambience are free.

The Waso Hotel in Talek village has cheap meals that have kept the Maasai filled for around KSh70. There's also a lively Maasai market.

Getting There & Away

AIR

Airkenya (☎ 020-605745; www.airkenya.com) and **Safarilink** (☎ 020-600777; www.safarilink-kenya .com) each have daily flights to Masai Mara from Nairobi. Return flights on Airkenya are US$237, while Safarilink will get you there and back for US$279.

MATATU, CAR & 4WD

Although it's possible to arrange wildlife drives independently, keep in mind that there are few savings in coming here without transport. That said, it is possible to access Talek and Sekenani Gates from Narok by *matatu*. From Kisii a *matatu* will get you as far as Kilkoris or Suna on the main A1 Hwy, but you will have problems after this.

For those who drive, the first 52km west of Narok on the B3 and C12 are smooth enough, but after the bitumen runs out you'll find that it gets pretty bumpy. The C13, which connects Oloololo Gate with Lolgorian out in the west, is very rough and rocky, and it's poorly signposted – a highway it's not.

Petrol is available (although expensive) at Mara Sarova, Mara Serena and Keekorok Lodges as well as in Talek village.

LAKE VICTORIA

Spread across 70,000 sq km and gracing the shores of Kenya, Tanzania and Uganda, Lake Victoria is East Africa's most important geographical feature. Amazingly, despite its massive girth, the lake is never more than 80m deep, compared to 1500m in smaller Rift Valley lakes.

The lake's 'evolving' ecosystem has proved to be both a boon and a bane for those living along its shores. For starters, its waters are a haven for mosquitos and snails, making malaria and bilharzia too common here. Then there are Nile perch (introduced 50 years ago to combat mosquitos), which eventually thrived, growing to over 200kg in size and becoming every small fishing boat's dream. Sadly, now it's only large commercial fishing vessels thriving. Horrifyingly, the ravenous perch have wiped out more than 300 species of smaller tropical fish unique to the lake.

Last and not least is the ornamental water hyacinth. First reported in 1986, this 'exotic' pond plant had no natural predators here and quickly reached plague proportions, covering 17,230 hectares and confining many large ships to port. Millions of dollars have been spent solving the problem; the investment seems to be paying off and the most recent satellite photos show hyacinth covering just under 400 hectares.

Despite the ecological and economic turmoil, the lives of Kenyans living along the shore go on, and a peek into their world is as fascinating as ever.

KISUMU

☎ 057

Set on the shore of Lake Victoria's Winam Gulf, the town of Kisumu is the third-largest in Kenya. Declared a city during its centenary celebrations in 2001, it still doesn't feel like one; its relaxed atmosphere is a world away from that of places such as Nairobi and Mombasa. Amazingly, like much of western Kenya, Kisumu receives relatively few travellers.

Despite the lake being its lifeblood from inception, geographically Kisumu has always had its back to the water, something that now echoes the sentiment and economy of the city today. Until 1977 the port was one of the busiest in Kenya, but decline set in with the demise of the East African Community (Kenya, Tanzania and Uganda), and it sat virtually idle for two decades.

Although increasing cooperation between these countries (now known collectively as Comesa) has established Kisumu as an international shipment point for petroleum products, surprisingly the lake plays no part – raw fuel for processing is piped in from Mombasa and the end products are driven out by truck. With Kisumu's fortunes again rising, and the water hyacinth's impact reduced, it is hoped Lake Victoria will once more start contributing to the local economy.

Orientation
Kisumu is a fairly sprawling town, but everything you will need is within walking distance. Most shops, banks, cheap hotels and other facilities can be found around Oginga Odinga Rd, while the train station and ferry jetty are short walks from the end of New Station Rd.

Jomo Kenyatta Hwy is the major thoroughfare, connecting the town with the main market and the noisy bus and *matatu* station, both a 10-minute walk northeast from Oginga Odinga Rd.

The most pleasant access to the lake itself is at Dunga, a small village about 3km south of town along Nzola Rd.

Information
INTERNET ACCESS
Abacus Cyber Cafe (Al-Imran Plaza, Oginga Odinga Rd; per hr KSh60; ☽ 8am-8pm)
Crystal Communications (Mega Plaza, Oginga Odinga Rd; per hr KSh60; ☽ 8am-6pm) Internet access.
Sanhedrin Cyber Joint (Swan Centre, Accra St; per hr KSh60; ☽ 8am-10pm)

MEDICAL SERVICES
Aga Khan Hospital (☎ 057-2020005; Otiena Oyoo St; ☽ 24hr) A large hospital with modern facilities and 24-hour emergency room.

MONEY
Barclays Bank (Kampala St)
Kenya Commercial Bank (Jomo Kenyatta Hwy)
Standard Chartered Bank (Oginga Odinga Rd)

POLICE
Police station (Uhuru Rd)

POST
Post office (Oginga Odinga Rd)

TOUR GUIDES
Ibrahim (☎ 0723-083045) A well-known tour guide to the sights and sounds of the Kisumu region. He can arrange boat trips, bird-watching tours, nature walks and excursions to Ndere Island National Park. Contact him through the New Victoria Hotel (p372).

TRAVEL AGENCIES
Pel Travels (☎ 057-2022780; travels@pel.co.ke; Oginga Odinga Rd) The main agent for Kenya Airlines.

VISA EXTENSIONS
Immigration office (1st fl, Reinsurance Plaza, cnr Oginga Odinga Rd & Jomo Kenyatta Hwy) Visa extensions are available at this office, behind the Format Supermarket.

Sights & Activities
KISUMU MUSEUM
Unlike many local museums, **Kisumu Museum** (Nairobi Rd; admission KSh500; ☽ 6am-6pm) is an interesting delve through the historical and natural delights of the Lake Victoria region.

The displays are wide ranging and most are well presented with a good collection of traditional everyday items that are used by the region's various peoples, including bird and insect traps, weapons and musical instruments.

The main highlights though are the new aquarium which displays the nearby lake's aquatic assets and a large snake pit and tortoise pen as well as separate vivariums displaying all the local snakes you don't want to meet on a dark night (or even in daylight!).

HIPPO POINT & BOAT TRIPS
Everyone seems to make the pilgrimage out to Hippo Point, sticking into Lake Victoria at Dunga, about 3km south of town, and though it's pleasant enough there is actually nothing at all to see or do here – except sigh over the sunsets – and you're certainly not guaranteed to see any hippos.

If you want virtually guaranteed hippo sightings, you will have to venture onto the lake. As you might imagine, plenty of people offer just such a boat trip. Prices start at KSh2500 but quickly drop to a more sensible KSh1000 to Ksh1500. A *matatu* from Kisumu to Hippo Point is KSh50.

MARKETS
Kisumu's **main market** (off Jomo Kenyatta Hwy) is one of Kenya's most animated, and certainly one of its largest, now spilling out onto the surrounding roads. If you're curious or just

KENYA

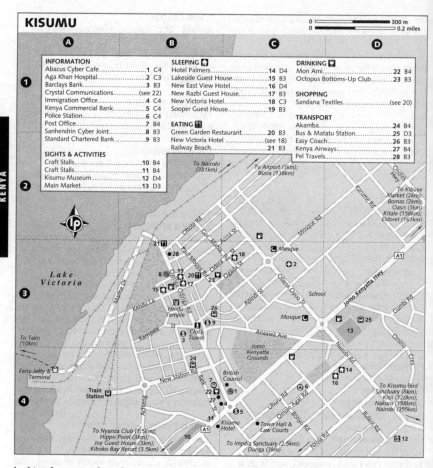

KISUMU

INFORMATION		
Abacus Cyber Cafe	1	C4
Aga Khan Hospital	2	C3
Barclays Bank	3	B3
Crystal Communications	(see 22)	
Immigration Office	4	C4
Kenya Commercial Bank	5	C4
Police Station	6	C4
Post Office	7	B4
Sanhendrin Cyber Joint	8	B3
Standard Chartered Bank	9	B3

SIGHTS & ACTIVITIES		
Craft Stalls	10	B4
Craft Stalls	11	B4
Kisumu Museum	12	D4
Main Market	13	D3

SLEEPING 🛏		
Hotel Palmers	14	D4
Lakeside Guest House	15	B3
New East View Hotel	16	D4
New Razbi Guest House	17	B3
New Victoria Hotel	18	C3
Sooper Guest House	19	B3

EATING 🍴		
Green Garden Restaurant	20	B3
New Victoria Hotel	(see 18)	
Railway Beach	21	B3

DRINKING 🍷		
Mon Ami	22	B4
Octopus Bottoms-Up Club	23	B3

SHOPPING		
Sandana Textiles	(see 20)	

TRANSPORT		
Akamba	24	B4
Bus & Matatu Station	25	D3
Easy Coach	26	B3
Kenya Airways	27	B4
Pel Travels	28	B3

looking for essentials such as suits or wigs, it's worth a stroll around.

Come past the huge **Kibuye Market** (Jomo Kenyatta Hwy) on any quiet weekday and you'll find it as empty as a winter's landscape, but visit on a Sunday and it's transformed into a blossoming spring flower of colour and scents.

The various **craft stalls** near Kisumu Hotel are some of the best places in Kenya for soapstone carvings.

IMPALA SANCTUARY

On the road to Dunga is Kenya Wildlife Service's 1-sq-km **Impala Sanctuary** (adult/child US$10/5; ☯ 6am-6pm). Besides being home to a small impala herd, it also provides important grazing grounds for local hippos.

KISUMU BIRD SANCTUARY

This **sanctuary** (off A1 Hwy; ☯ 6am-6pm), 8km southeast of town, has suffered from human interference and, with many of the birds flapping off to less disturbed sites, local guides in Kisumu now recommend a new 'sanctuary' called **Tako**, 10km south of Kisumu and only accessed by boat. Around 150 bird species have been recorded here and it's an important breeding ground for herons, storks, cormorants and egrets. The best time to visit is April or May. Boats can be organised in Kisumu for around KSh2000 per hour; plan three hours for the round trip.

NDERE ISLAND NATIONAL PARK

Gazetted as a **national park** (adult/child US$20/10) back in 1986, tourism to this 4.2-sq-km island

---

OBAMA & THE KENYA CONNECTION *Matthew D Firestone*

Regardless of your individual politics, it's hard to deny the rock-star qualities of US President Barack Obama.

Following Obama's convincing win in the 2008 election, many around the world erupted in fanfare as the first-ever African American presidential candidate succeeded in his bid for the White House. Indeed, there were perhaps no greater festivities than in Kenya, which saw its own 'native son' ascend to one of the world's highest seats of power.

So what exactly is Obama's Kenya connection?

President Obama is the son of Barack Obama Sr, a Luo from the town of Nyang'oma Kogelo in Nyanza Province. Barack Sr met the president's mother while attending the University of Hawai'i at Mānoa, though the couple separated when young Obama was just two years old. Tragically, Barack Sr only saw his son once more before dying in an automobile accident in 1982.

In 1988, Obama travelled to Kenya for the first time, and spent five weeks in the company of his paternal relatives. He later returned to Africa as a member of the US Senate Foreign Relations Committee, and gave a keynote address at the University of Nairobi, condemning corruption in the Kenyan government.

However, his most high-profile visit came in 2006, when tens of thousands of Kenyans lined the streets of Kisumu and greeted Obama with a hero's welcome. Always the crowd pleaser, the then Senator Obama shouted 'I greet you all!' in the local Luo language.

The 2006 visit was intended to encourage Kenyans to get tested for HIV/AIDS, an action that still carries a deep social stigma in much of Africa. In the spotlight of ordinary Kenyans, Obama and his wife Michelle both had their blood drawn and tested for the virus.

At the time, Obama boldly declared: 'I and my wife are personally taking HIV tests. And if someone all the way from America can come and do that, then you have no excuse.'

Considering the fact that an estimated 20% of people in Kisumu are infected, the Obamas' bold act did not go unnoticed. In fact, a local secondary school was later renamed in Barack Obama's honour, as well as a number of newborn babies – this trend has picked up momentum since the outcome of the presidential elections.

At the time of publication, the future of Obama and his Kenya connection was still open to speculation. Given that he has always displayed pride at having African roots, it's likely that President Obama's influence across the continent will be significant.

---

has never taken off. It is forested and very beautiful, housing a variety of bird species, plus hippos, impalas (introduced) and spotted crocodiles, a lesser-known cousin of the larger Nile crocodile.

Unfortunately there is nowhere to stay and chartered boats are your only option to get there for which you'll pay around KSh2000 per hour, with typical return trips taking five hours (including three hours on shore) – keep an eye out for hippos en route.

Sleeping
BUDGET
New Razbi Guest House (☎ 0721-824349; Kendu Lane; s with/without bathroom KSh700/400, d with shared bathroom KSh600) A secure place with small, mosquito net–clad rooms, some decidedly brighter than others. The shared toilets pass the nostril test and there is a private TV lounge-restaurant upstairs. Unusually, the double rooms are pretty messy in comparison with the singles.

Lakeside Guest House (☎ 057-2023523/0722-723591; Kendu Lane; r KSh800) With a new extension in progress the former Western Inn has more than just a name change underway. Fortunately not everything's changed; the high standards of this lime-green hotel remain undiminished, the balcony as nice to sit on and the views of the lake just the same – in other words partial! Hot water is available in the mornings and evenings (note that at the time of research it was still known by the old name).

Sooper Guest House (☎ 0725-281733; kayamchatur@yahoo.com; Oginga Odinga Rd; s/d/tr KSh800/1000/1500) This spotless ice-cube white hotel boasts 18 highly sought after rooms that really are 'sooper'. We've received mountains of positive feedback about this place and the gleaming, spacious rooms with hot showers, informative staff and a low-key traveller vibe are certain to ensure that we receive mountains more.

MIDRANGE

Joy Guest House (☎ 0725-074837; Dunga; tw with/without bathroom KSh1000/800) Think of a small-town Portuguese pension with a tropical African soundtrack and that's exactly what you get at this charmer located 3km south of town near Hippo Point's turnoff. It's a great place to escape the city and get a peep into village life.

New Victoria Hotel (☎ 057-2021067; newvictoriahotel @africaonline.co.ke; Gor Mahia Rd; s with shared bathroom KSh800, s/tw/tr KSh1300/1650/2300) This bouncy and fun Yemeni-run hotel has character in abundance and is something of a focal point for the town's small Arab population. Rooms have fans, mozzie nets and comfy foam mattresses. The next-door mosque, which will rouse you at 5am, adds to the shades of Arabia.

New East View Hotel (☎ 0722-556721; Omolo Agar Rd; s/tw KSh1200/1600) A converted family home on a peaceful street, the New East View has just enough furniture and decoration to give the rooms a homely feel.

Hotel Palmers (☎ 057-2024867; Omolo Agar Rd; s/tw KSh1400/1700) Poky, but fresh and comfortable rooms with enormous double beds. The hotel also has a comfortable lounge, an outdoor restaurant, secure parking and a nasty pink paint job.

Nyanza Club (☎ 057-2022433; off Jomo Kenyatta Hwy; s/tw incl breakfast KSh4000/4500; 🏊 🍴) This recently renovated hotel might feel a little like a western chain hotel, but after a while in the Kenyan back blocks that might be no bad thing. It offers great-value, well-appointed rooms; some have balconies and lake views. There is a plethora of activities available but since they're strictly for members, you will have to become a temporary member (per day KSh100).

Kiboko Bay Resort (☎ 057-2025510; www.kibokobay .com; Dunga; s/d US$90/120; 🏊 🍴) If you couldn't afford the high prices of the Masai Mara National Reserve's luxury tents then these tightly packed safari tents, huddling under the trees on the banks of the lake, could be a good way of experiencing the African safari dream on a cut price level.

Eating

The fact that Kisumu sits on Lake Victoria isn't lost on restaurants here and fish is abundant.

If you want an authentic local fish fry, there is no better place than the dozens of smoky tin-shack restaurants siting on the lake's shore at **Railway Beach** at the end of Oginga Odinga Rd. Open flames, a whole lot of mud and dirt and boisterous locals all add to the ultimate Kisumu eating experience. Dive in between 7am and 6pm; a midsized fish served with *ugali*)a staple made from maize or cassava flour) or rice is sufficient for two people and will set you back KSh400.

New Victoria Hotel (Gor Mahia Rd; meals KSh200) Descend into the subdued interior of this brightly coloured hotel for a filling Arabian and Indian tasting feed. In the mornings you can grab a few cakes from the next-door pastry shop, under the same management, and come here for coffee.

Green Garden Restaurant (☎ 0727-738000; Odera St, off Oginga Odinga Rd; meals KSh300-400; ⏰ 11am-11pm) Tuck into homemade pasta and lasagne surrounded by colourful elephants and baboons at this German-run, Italian-flavoured courtyard restaurant that sits squarely on the top of the town's list of current expat hotspots.

Drinking & Entertainment

Kisumu's nightlife has a reputation for being even livelier than Nairobi's, but thanks to many of the best parties, live Congolese bands and KisSwahili hip hop cropping up at various venues such as **Bomas** (Jomo Kenyatta Hwy) and **Oasis** (Jomo Kenyatta Hwy) , it's harder to find. Check flyers and ask locals who are plugged into the scene. Oasis tends to have live music most nights while Bomas is more of a weekend affair. Entry to both depends on the performer but averages KSh200 for all but the biggest names.

Mon Ami (Mega Plaza, Oginga Odinga Rd) Easy to find and always good for having a drink, this is a lively bar with a pool table, welcoming expat crowd and satellite TV, which blasts European footy in the evenings. Friday evenings might see the odd live act.

Octopus Bottoms-Up Club (Ogada St; club admission KSh200, bar is free) A short stroll from Oginga Odinga Rd, this heavy weight bar and club rages all night but be warned that it isn't too pretty. Be careful on leaving as muggings and worse are not unheard of on the surrounding streets.

Shopping

Sadana Textiles (☎ 0733-87434; Odera St off Oginga Odinga Rd; ⏰ 8am-6pm Mon-Sat) Got a big soirée coming up? Then choose from a huge range of material on offer here and the folks here will whip up a dapper West African–style outfit in a few hours. KSh600 to KSh900 should see you looking good.

Getting There & Away

AIR

Kenya Airways (☎ 057-2020081; Alpha House, Oginga Odinga Rd) has twice-daily flights to Nairobi (KSh9000, 50 minutes, 9.20am and 6.40pm). Newer, though not necessarily better, airlines serving this route include Fly540.com, East African and Jet Link. Prices start as low as KSh4250 and seats can be booked through **Pel Travels** (☎ 057-2022780; travels@pel.co.ke; Oginga Odinga Rd).

BOAT

Despite the reduced hyacinth in the Winam Gulf, ferry services to Tanzania and Uganda haven't restarted. If you're heading to the wilderness islands of Rusinga and Mfangano then by far the fastest and most comfortable way of getting there is by the regular ferry from Luanda Kotieno, a small village two hours, and a KSh300 *matatu* ride west of Kisumu. Ferries from Luanda Kotieno to Mbita depart (roughly!) at 8am, 11am, 3pm and 6pm. Foot passengers cost KSh100 and a car between KSh800 to KSh1000 depending on the size. The journey takes around an hour, Note that there is no accommodation in Luanda Kotieno.

BUS & MATATU

Most buses, *matatus* and Peugeots to destinations within Kenya leave from the large bus and *matatu* station just north of the main market.

Matatus offer the only direct services to Kakamega (KSh200, 1½ hours) and Eldoret (KSh300, 2½ hours). Plenty of other *matatus* serve Busia (KSh300, two hours), Kericho (KSh300, two hours); Kisii (KSh300, two hours); Homa Bay (KSh300, three hours); Nakuru (KSh500 to KSh600, 3½ hours); Nairobi (KSh800 to KSh900, 5½ hours) and Isebania (KSh400, four hours), on the Tanzanian border. Peugeots do still serve some destinations, but they cost about 25% more than *matatus*.

There are very few direct services to Kitale (KSh350, four hours); it is best to take a vehicle to Kakamega or Eldoret and change there.

Akamba (off New Station Rd) has its own depot in the town's centre. Besides four daily buses to Nairobi (KSh1100 to KSh1350, seven hours) via Nakuru (KSh800, 4½ hours), Akamba also has daily services to Busia (KSh400, three hours) and Kampala (KSh1350, seven hours). **Easy Coach** (off Mosque Rd) serves similar destinations, as well as Kakamega (KSh250, one hour), with some added comfort and cost.

TRAIN

At the time of research no trains were running between Kisumu and Nairobi. The latest information is that passenger trains are definitely, maybe, possibly, doubtfully restarting sometime in 2009.

Getting Around

BODA-BODA

Bicycle-taxis have proliferated and they are a great way to get around Kisumu. No journey should be more than 20 bob.

MATATU

The 7 and 9 *matatus* (KSh25), which run north along Oginga Odinga Rd before turning up Anaawa Ave and continuing east down Jomo Kenyatta Hwy, are handy to reach the main *matatu* station, main market and Kibuye Market – just wave an arm and hop on anywhere you see one.

TAXI

A taxi around town costs between KSh100 and KSh200, while trips to Dunga range from KSh200 to KSh350 with heavy bargaining.

HOMA BAY
☎ 059

Homa Bay has a slow, tropical, almost Central African vibe to it and the near total absence of other tourists means it's extraordinarily, and genuinely, friendly. There is little to do other than trudge up and down the dusty, music-filled streets, enjoy the seductive lake views, pass the time of day with the locals in one of the rainbow-coloured cafes and climb some of the cartoonlike hills that surround the town. The easiest summit to bag is the unmistakable conical mound of **Asego Hill**, which is just beyond the town and takes about an hour to clamber up.

Bay Lodge (r with/without bathroom KSh350/300) is a small and maniacally clean little aquamarine lodgings. It has basic cube rooms and lots of friendly banter. The staff are also embarrassingly polite and greet you with phrases such as 'I'm afraid we have not yet had the opportunity to polish up this room. I hope this does not delay or frustrate you'. No it won't!

Lurking behind a messy entrance, **Ruma Tourist Lodge** (☎ 0727-460492; s/d KSh600/900) offers stuffy, but otherwise comfy rooms. Unfortunately the town's best bar – which has cold beers, decent tunes, a pool table and a restaurant (meals KSh80 to KSh160) – also lives here, so noise can be problematic.

Akamba's office is just down the hill from the bus station and its buses serve Nairobi (KSh900, nine hours, 7.30pm) via Kericho (KSh450, four hours) and Nakuru (KSh700, six hours). Several other companies and *matatus* (operating from the bus station) also ply these routes, as well as Mbita (KSh200, 1½ hours) and Kisumu (KSh300, three hours).

RUMA NATIONAL PARK

Bordered by the dramatic **Kanyamaa Escarpment**, and home to Kenya's only population of roans (one of Africa's rarest and largest antelopes), is the surprisingly seldom-visited **Ruma National Park** (adult/child US$20/10). While hot and often wet, it is beautiful and comprises 120 sq km of verdant riverine woodland and savannah grassland within the Lambwe Valley.

Besides roan, other rarities such as Bohor's reedbucks, Rothschild's giraffes, Jackson's hartebeests and tiny oribi antelopes can be seen. Birdlife is prolific, with 145 different bird species present.

The best thing about this park is its utter seclusion and the fact that you and you alone will have this slab of truly wild Africa all to yourself.

The park is set up for those with vehicles, but contact the **warden** (☎ 020-3529119, Homa Bay 059-22544) and you may be able to organise a hike.

There are two simple **campsites** (US$15) near the main gate and a new **guesthouse** (US$100) which is extortionate if there are only two of you but quite good value for groups.

Head a couple of kilometres south from Homa Bay and turn right onto the Mbita road. About 12km west is the main access road, and from there it's another 11km. The park's roads are in decent shape, but require a mega 4WD in the rainy season.

KISII
☎ 058

Let's cut straight to the chase. Kisii is a noisy, polluted congested mess, and most people, quite sensibly, roll right on through without even stopping.

While the fêted Kisii soapstone obviously comes from this area, it's not on sale here. Quarrying and carving go on in the village of **Tabaka**, 23km northwest of Kisii, where you can usually visit the workshops.

Information
Barclays Bank (Moi Hwy) With ATM.
National Bank of Kenya (cnr Hospital & Sansora Rds) With ATM (Cirrus and Plus cards only).
Pemo Cyber Cafe (Hospital Rd; per hr KSh60) Reasonable internet connections.
Post office (Moi Hwy) With card phones.

Sleeping & Eating
Sabrina Lodge (s/tw with shared bathroom KSh350/600) Just up from Postbank, you'll find real Africa at this friendly hotel. By that we mean basic cubicles, common bathrooms with bucket showers and toilets that leave you exposed for everyone to see. The staff think foreigners are hilarious – they're probably right.

Kisii Hotel (☎ 058-30134; off Moi Hwy; s/tw/tw incl breakfast KSh750/950/1400) Double the price, but triple the pleasure. This is a relaxed place in what feels like an old school building. It boasts large gardens and sizeable rooms, each with decent bathrooms. The restaurant (meals KSh150 to KSh300) is deservedly popular.

St Vincent Guesthouse (☎ 0733-650702; off Moi Hwy; s/d/tw with breakfast KSh1300/1650/2200) This Catholic-run guesthouse may not be the place for a party but it's perfect for a quiet night's sleep. Rooms are very clean and cosy. Couples travelling together pay a lot less than just friends so, if you're 'just friends', we'd recommend pushing the beds together and saving 500 bob. You never know, you might even enjoy the experience!

Victoria Cafe (Moi Hwy; meals KSh60-160) A deep green locals' café with fried food on the inside and a music stall adding beats on the outside.

Nile Restaurant & Fast Food (Hospital Rd; meals KSh150-250) Chicken and chips will set you back KSh250 at this cheeky little restaurant right in the town centre.

Getting There & Away

Matatus line the length of Moi Hwy – look for the destination placards on their roofs. Regular departures serve Homa Bay (KSh150, one hour), Kisumu (KSh300, two hours), Kericho (KSh300, two hours) and Isebania (KSh250, 1¾ hours) on the Tanzanian border.

Tabaka *matatus* leave from the Victoria Cafe, while local *matatus* (and additional Kericho services) leave from the stand at the end of Sansora Rd.

Akamba (Moi Hwy) has a daily bus to Nairobi (KSh800, eight hours) via Nakuru (KSh600, 5½ hours) departing at 9pm; book a day in advance. International bus departures for Mwanza (KSh1700) in Tanzania also leave from here.

KERICHO
☎ 052

The polar opposite of Kisii, Kericho is a haven of tranquillity. Its surrounds are blanketed by a thick patchwork of manicured tea plantations, each seemingly hemmed in by distant stands of evergreens. With a pleasant climate and a number of things to see and do Kericho makes for a very calming couple of days' rest.

Information

Aga Khan Satellite Laboratory (Moi Hwy)
Barclays Bank (Moi Hwy) With ATM.
Kenya Commercial Bank (Moi Hwy) With ATM (Visa only).
Post office (Moi Hwy)
Standard Chartered Bank (Moi Hwy) With ATM (Visa only).
Telecare Centre (Temple Rd) Calling cards and card phones.

Sights & Activities

Tea is the reason the English colonialists came to Kericho and tea is probably the reason you've come too. As the centre of the most important tea gardens in all of Africa you might expect **tea plantation tours** to be touted left, right and centre. Surprisingly though, they are fairly few and far between. However, the Tea Hotel does have excellent guides (KSh200 per person) to the estates that begin immediately beyond the hotel gardens. Most tours involve walking around the fields and watching the picking in process (note that the pickers don't work on Sunday). If you want to actually see the process through to the end and visit a factory you should book at least a week in advance through the Tea Hotel.

KENYA

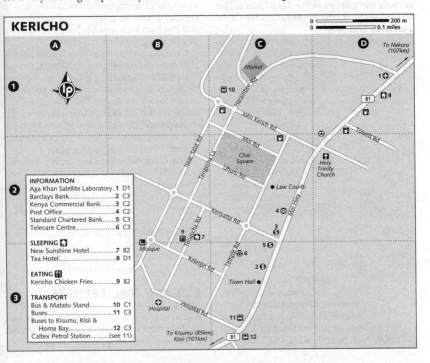

KERICHO

0 — 200 m
0 — 0.1 miles

To Nakuru (107km)

Market

Harambee Rd

Isaac Salat Rd

John Kerich Rd

Moi Rd

Chai Square

Uhuru Rd

Towett Rd

Tengecha La

Tengecha Rd

Holy Trinity Church

Law Courts

Kenyatta Rd

Mosque

Temple Rd

Ketenjin Rd

Town Hall

Hospital

Hospital Rd

To Kisumu (85km); Kisii (101km)

To Kisumu, Kisii & Homa Bay

INFORMATION
Aga Khan Satellite Laboratory..1 D1
Barclays Bank......................2 C3
Kenya Commercial Bank.......3 C2
Post Office..........................4 C2
Standard Chartered Bank......5 C3
Telecare Centre...................6 C3

SLEEPING
New Sunshine Hotel..............7 B2
Tea Hotel............................8 D1

EATING
Kericho Chicken Fries...........9 B2

TRANSPORT
Bus & Matatu Stand............10 C1
Buses.................................11 C3
Buses to Kisumu, Kisii & Homa Bay.....................12 C3
Caltex Petrol Station..........(see 11)

HARMAN KIRUI

Harman, how did the recent election violence affect Kericho?

There wasn't much fighting in Kericho itself compared with elsewhere. I think this is because all the workers on the tea estates are of mixed tribes and have lived together in these mixed communities like brothers and sisters for years.

It hit tourism here badly though. At the time we had some tourists who arrived from Kisumu under a police escort and then they had to be airlifted out of town by helicopter from the hotel grounds. From the end of December until the end of February not a single tourist came to Kericho and all the bookings we had were cancelled. It wasn't until May that things started to pick up again and now they are OK.

For now the coalition seems stable and things are returning to normal, but it was a scary time and we did not know what would happen. I think the violence was just a mad wave that swept over the country, but now I hope it's over for good and that the people are more united than they were before.

Harman Kirui works as a tea estate guide and waiter for the Tea Hotel in Kericho.

Sleeping & Eating

Tea Hotel (☎ Nairobi 020-2050790; teahotel@africa online.co.ke; Moi Hwy; camping KSh300, s/d US$65/90; ☒) The rooms are fading fast, but this grand property, built in the 1950s by the Brooke Bond company, is still a fantastic choice full of period charm, vast hallways and dining rooms stuffed full of the mounted heads of animals you just saw in the Masai Mara. The real highlight are the beautiful gardens with a tea bush backdrop.

New Sunshine Hotel (☎ 0725-146601, 0723-455516; Tengecha Rd; s/tw KSh1000/1400) The best budget hotel in town, the New Sunshine will put a little sunshine into your life with its well-cared-for rooms, hot showers and management who'll bend over backwards to help. It's NGO-friendly and will often offer groups of NGO workers discounts. There's good security and an equally good attached restaurant (meals KSh100 to KSh200), which serves Western snacks, sandwiches and burgers.

Kericho Chicken Fries (Tengecha Rd; chicken & chips KSh210) Grab a stall on one of the communal tables and tuck into some excellent chicken and chips. It does a roaring lunchtime trade.

Getting there & Away

While most buses and *matatus* stop at the main stand in the town's northwest corner, many also pick up passengers on the Moi Hwy near the Caltex petrol station. If you simply state your destination to anyone in town, they'll be happy to point you in the right direction.

Buses to Nairobi (KSh600, 4½ hours) are quite frequent, as are *matatus* to Kisumu (KSh300, two hours), Kisii (KSh300, two hours), Eldoret (KSh400 to KSh500, 3½ hours) and Nakuru (KSh300, two hours). The odd Peugeot also serves these destinations, but costs about 25% more.

KAKAMEGA
☎ 056

There is no real reason to stay in this small agricultural town, but if you arrive late in the day it can be convenient to sleep over and stock up with supplies before heading to nearby Kakamega Forest Reserve.

Comfortable rooms at **Friends Hotel** (☎ 056-31716; Mumias Rd; s normal/deluxe KSh1000/1300, d normal/deluxe KSh1300/1600) are pleasing to the eye. There's 24-hour hot water, but it's a little overpriced for what you get. The downstairs restaurant is the swankiest place in town to eat.

Snack Stop Cafe (Cannon Awori Rd; meals KSh70-150) The restaurant of choice for locals. Simple Kenyan standards, including *ugali*.

Easy Coach (off Kenyatta Ave) serves Kisumu (KSh400, 1½ hours) at 7.30am and 8pm, and Nairobi (KSh1250, 7½ hours) at 8am and 8pm via Nakuru (KSh750, five hours). Nearby, **Akamba** (off Kenyatta Ave) has 7.30am and 8pm buses to Nairobi (KSh1050).

Behind the Total station on the northern edge of the town, *matatus* leave for Kisumu (KSh200, one hour), Kitale (KSh250, 2½ hours) and Eldoret (KSh250, 2½ hours).

KAKAMEGA FOREST RESERVE
☎ 056

Not so long ago much of western Kenya was hidden under a dark veil of jungle and formed a part of the mighty Guineo-Congolian forest ecosystem – even gorillas are rumoured to have played in the mists here. However, the British soon did their best to turn all that lovely virgin forest into tea estates and now all that's left is the superb slab of tropical rainforest surrounding Kakamega. Though seriously degraded this forest is unique in Kenya and contains plants, animals and birds that occur nowhere else in the country (disappointingly the gorillas died out long, long ago). It's so wild here trees actually kill each other – really! Parasitic fig trees grow on top of unsuspecting trees and strangle their hosts to death.

Less murderous is the forest's array of wildlife. An astounding 330 species of bird, including casqued hornbill, Ross' turaco and great blue turaco, have been spotted here. During darkness, hammer-headed fruit bats and flying squirrels take to the air. The best viewing months are June, August and October, when many migrant species arrive. The wildflowers are also wonderful in October, supporting around 400 species of butterfly.

Dancing in the canopy are no less than seven different primate species, one being the exceedingly rare De Brazza's monkey.

The northern section of the forest around Buyangu is both more accessible and more pristine. This makes up the **Kakamega Forest National Reserve**. Maintained by the KWS, this area has a variety of habitats but is generally very dense, with considerable areas of primary forest and regenerating secondary forest; there is a total ban on grazing, wood collection and cultivation in this zone.

The southern section, centred on Isecheno, forms the **Kakamega Forest Reserve** and is looked after by the Forest Department. Predominantly forested, this region supports several communities and is under considerable pressure from both farming and illegal logging. Despite being more degraded it's to this part of the park that most visitors head – thanks no doubt to better accommodation and no entry fees.

Tribal practices in the forest persist: *mugumu* trees are considered sacred, circumcisions are sometimes performed in the forest and bullfights, between bulls not between man and animal, are still held on Sunday mornings in Khayega and Shinyalu. Intervillage wrestling also used to be common, but was eventually banned, as the prize (the victor's pick of the young women present) tended to provoke more fights than the match itself.

Information
KWS currently only charges admission to the **Kakamega Forest National Reserve** (adult/child US$20/10).

Sights & Activities
WALKING TRAILS
The best, indeed the only real-way to appreciate the forest is to walk, and trails radiate from Buyangu and Isecheno areas.

Official **guides** (per person for short/long walk KSh300/600), trained by the Kakamega Biodiversity Conservation & Tour Operators Association, are well worth the money. Not only do they prevent you from getting lost, but most are walking encyclopaedias and will reel off both the Latin and common name of almost any plant or insect you care to point out. They are also able to recognise and imitate any bird call so effectively that you wouldn't be surprised if they suddenly sprouted wings and flew off. The guides are also highly knowledgeable in the medicinal properties of many of the plants around you, so many of which have some sort of medical

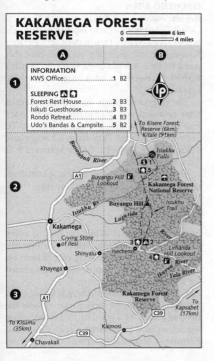

KAKAMEGA FOREST RESERVE

0 — 6 km
0 — 4 miles

INFORMATION
KWS Office.....................................1 B2

SLEEPING
Forest Rest House............................2 B3
Isikuti Guesthouse...........................3 B3
Rondo Retreat.................................4 B3
Udo's Bandas & Campsite.................5 B2

To Kisere Forest; Reserve (6km); Kitale (91km)

Buyangu River
Isiukhu Falls
A1
Buyangu Hill Lookout
Buyangu Hill
Kakamega Forest National Reserve
Isiukhu Rv
Isiukhu Trail
Lugusida
Kakamega
Crying Stone of Ilesi
Shinyalu
Isecheno
Lirhanda Hill Lookout
Ikuywa River
Khayega
Yala River
Kakamega Forest Reserve
A1
To Kapsabet (17km)
To Kisumu (35km)
C39
Kaimosi
Chavakali
C39

value that you can't help but wonder what potential medicines man may already have destroyed through deforestation.

Rangers state that trails vary in length from 1km to 7km; of the longer walks **Isiukhu Trail**, which connects Isecheno to **Isiukhu Falls**, is the most rewarding and takes a minimum of half a day. Short walks to **Buyangu Hill** in the north or **Lirhanda Hill** in the south for sunrise or sunset are highly recommended. As ever, the early morning and late afternoon are the best times to view birds, but night walks can also be a fantastic experience. Though the forest is crawling with life this isn't the Masai Mara National Reserve and sightings of animals are fleeting at best (except for the primates, which are normally easy to find) and so, rather than expecting to see leopards, forest hogs and the like it's better to think little. Concentrate on the birds and the bees – the insect life here is phenomenal (it's said that if you spend one hour rummaging through the leaf litter of a tropical rainforest then you will discover a new species of insect!). However, it's the birds that really steal the show and Kakamega, with its unique collection of species more common to the forests of the Congo, is easily one of the top birding destinations in Kenya.

Sleeping & Eating

BUYANGU AREA

If staying at either of the following you will have to pay park entry fees for each night you're there.

Udo's Bandas & Campsite (☎ 056-30603/0727-415828; PO Box 879, Kakamega; camping US$5, bandas per person US$10) Named after Udo Savalli, a well-known ornithologist, this lovely site is tidy, well-maintained and has seven simple thatched *bandas*; nets are provided, but you will need your own sleeping bag and other supplies.

Isikuti Guesthouse (☎ 056-30603/0727-415828; per cottage US$50) Hidden in a pretty forest glade are four massive cottages (sleeping up to four), with equipped kitchens and bathrooms. For either the *bandas* or the cottage it's best to book ahead.

ISECHENO AREA

Forest Rest House (☎ 0720-700949; camping KSh225, r per person KSh225) The four rooms of this wooden tree house, perched on stilts 2m above the ground and offering views straight onto a mass of impenetrable Tarzan jungle, might be

as basic as basic gets (no electricity, no bedding and cold water baths that look like they'd crash through the floor boards if you tried to fill one), but it has to be one of the most atmospheric places to stay in all of Kenya.

ourpick **Rondo Retreat** (☎ 0331-30268; www.rondo retreat.com; full board adult/child KSh7400/5400) Arrive at the Rondo Retreat, a couple of kilometres on from the Forest Rest House, and you'll be greeted by some dark-green gates. These may look like any old gates but they are in fact a magical time portal that whisks you back to 1922 and the height of the British Empire. A series of wooden bungalows filled with families clutter this gorgeous and eccentric place that is a wonderful retreat from modern Kenya.

Getting There & Away

BUYANGU AREA

Matatus heading north towards Kitale can drop you at the access road about 18km north of Kakamega town (KSh70). It is a well signposted 2km walk from there to the park office and Udo's.

ISECHENO AREA

Regular *matatus* link Kakamega with Shinyalu (KSh70), but few go on to Isecheno. Shinyalu is also accessed by a rare *matatu* service from Khayega. From Shinyalu you will probably need to take a *boda-boda* (bicycle taxi)for KSh50 to Isecheno or a rarer motorbike taxi (KSh100).

The improved roads are still treacherous after rain and you may prefer to walk once you've seen the trouble vehicles have. To Shinyalu it's about 7km from Khayega and 10km from Kakamega. From Shinyalu it is 5km to Isecheno.

The dirt road from the rest house continues east to Kapsabet, but transport is rare.

ELDORET

☎ 053

Mmmmm…cheese! While the pull of a fine Gouda, Gruyere, Stilton, Brie or Cheddar can vary depending on how long you've been on your African safari, a stop in Eldoret is a must for all cheese lovers.

For you cheese haters, there is little else to draw you to this large service town besides the need of a bank or a good night's sleep before venturing into the nearby Kerio Valley and Kamnarok National Reserves.

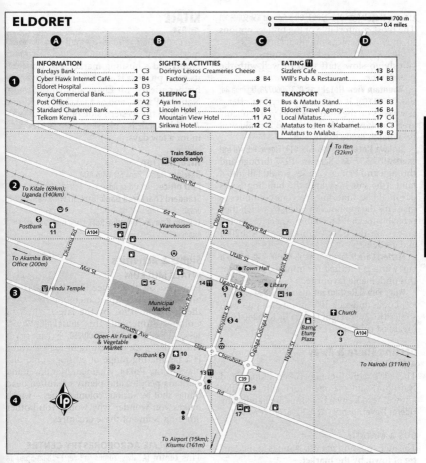

ELDORET

INFORMATION	**SIGHTS & ACTIVITIES**	**EATING**
Barclays Bank 1 C3	Dorinyo Lessos Creameries Cheese	Sizzlers Cafe 13 B4
Cyber Hawk Internet Café..........2 B4	Factory............................8 B4	Will's Pub & Restaurant..............14 B3
Eldoret Hospital 3 D3		
Kenya Commercial Bank............4 C3	**SLEEPING**	**TRANSPORT**
Post Office 5 A2	Aya Inn 9 C4	Bus & Matatu Stand....................15 B3
Standard Chartered Bank 6 C3	Lincoln Hotel 10 B4	Eldoret Travel Agency 16 B4
Telkom Kenya 7 C3	Mountain View Hotel 11 A2	Local Matatus...................17 C4
	Sirikwa Hotel........................12 C2	Matatus to Iten & Kabarnet........18 C3
		Matatus to Malaba....................19 B2

Information

Barclays Bank (Uganda Rd) With ATM.

Cyber Hawk Internet Café (Nandi Arcade, Nandi Rd; per hr KSh60) Fast connections.

Eldoret Hospital (off Uganda Rd) One of Kenya's best hospitals. With 24-hour emergency.

Kenya Commercial Bank (Kenyatta St) With ATM (Visa only).

Post office (Uganda Rd)

Standard Chartered Bank (Uganda Rd) With ATM (Visa only).

Telkom Kenya (cnr Kenyatta & Elijaa Cheruhota Sts) Calling cards and card phones.

Sights & Activities

The only real attraction is an odd but tasty one, the **Doinyo Lessos Creameries Cheese Factory** (Kenyatta St; 8am-6pm) produces more than 30 different types of cheese. You can taste most for free and the average price is KSh500 per kilogram, with a minimum purchase of 250g. The company also makes yummy ice cream (KSh23 for 100mL).

Sleeping & Eating

Aya Inn (053-2062259; Oginga Odinga St; r with/without bathroom KSh650/550) The staff will think you're off your head wanting to look at the rooms before handing over your cash – as if you can't trust them when they say it's like the Hilton! Alas, it's not, but it's also a lot cheaper and for the money it's probably better value. Opt for one of the quieter and secluded self-contained rooms with hot water.

Lincoln Hotel (☎ 053-22093; Oloo Rd; s/d KSh500/800) The most comfortable of the budget options in town, this pleasant place offers decent rooms spread around its courtyard and seriously go-slow staff who fit well with the overall vibe.

Mountain View Hotel (☎ 053-2060728; Uganda Rd; s/tw KSh600/800) It ain't too pretty but after a few weeks on the road in Kenya you probably aren't looking too hot either, so it could well be a match made in Heaven.

Sirikwa Hotel (☎ 053-2063614; Elgeyo Rd; s/d incl breakfast US$66/77; 🏊) Screams 1977 through and through and Prince Charles would fall into a faint if he saw how ugly the building is. Its day might be done, but everyone continues to insist it's the top hotel in town; by which they probably mean it's the most expensive. Saving graces are the pool (nonresidents KSh200) and gardens.

Sizzlers Cafe (Kenyatta St; meals KSh100-250) Grab a curry and get stuffed for minimal coinage at this undeniable favourite.

Will's Pub & Restaurant (Uganda Rd; meals KSh200-450) Looks and feels like an English pub with similarly heavyweight food. The KSh250 fried breakfast rules.

Getting There & Away

AIR

There are daily flights between Eldoret and Nairobi (KSh6300, one hour) with the little-known Aero Kenya. Bookings are handled by **Eldoret Travel Agency** (☎ 053-2062707; Kenyatta St).

BUS & MATATU

The main bus and *matatu* stand is in the centre of town, by the market.

Regular *matatus*/Peugeots serve Kitale (KSh150/200, 1¼ hours), Kisumu (KSh250/300, 2½ hours), Kericho (KSh250/300, 3½ hours), Nakuru (KSh300/400, 2¾ hours) and Nairobi (KSh600/700, six hours). Buses duplicate these routes.

Local *matatus* and more Kericho services leave from Nandi Rd. Irregular *matatus* to Iten and Kabarnet leave opposite Paradise Bar on Uganda Rd. Further west on Uganda Rd, *matatus* leave for Malaba (KSh400, 2½ hours) on the Uganda border.

Akamba (Moi St) buses to Nairobi (KSh500, 10.30am and 9pm) via Nakuru (KSh250) leave from their depot. There is also a 9am and noon service to Kampala (KSh1000, six hours).

KITALE

☎ 054

Agricultural Kitale is a small and friendly market town with a couple of interesting museums and a bustling market. For travellers its main purpose is as a base for explorations further afield – Mt Elgon and Saiwa Swamp National Parks – and as a take-off point for a trip up to the western side of Lake Turkana. As such, Kitale is a pleasant town to kick back in for a few days.

Information

Barclays Bank (Bank St) With ATM.
Post office (Post Office Rd)
Standard Chartered Bank (Bank St) With ATM (Visa only).
Telkom Kenya (Post Office Rd) Calling cards and card phones.

Sights & Activities

KITALE MUSEUM

Founded on the collection of butterflies, birds and ethnographic memorabilia left to the nation in 1967 by the late Lieutenant Colonel Stoneham, this **museum** (☎ 054-30996; A1 Hwy; adult/child KSh500/250; 🕙 8am-6pm) is one of the more interesting in Kenya. There is a fascinating range of ethnographic displays of the Pokot, Akamba, Marakwet and Turkana peoples and plenty of stuffed dead things shot by various colonial types – which makes you wonder why would you bother 'hunting' some of these creatures.

OLAF PALME AGROFORESTRY CENTRE

This **centre** (A1 Hwy; admission free; 🕙 8am-5pm) is home to a Swedish-funded program aimed at educating local people about protection and rehabilitation of the environment by integrating trees into farming systems. The project includes a small demonstration farm and agroforestry plot, an information centre and an arboretum containing 46 rare species of indigenous trees; it's well worth a visit.

TREASURES OF AFRICA MUSEUM

This private **museum** (☎ 054-30867; toam@multitechweb.com; A1 Hwy; admission KSh250; 🕙 9am-noon & 2-5.30pm Mon-Sat) is the personnel collection of old Africa hand Mr Wilson, a former colonial officer in Uganda. Based mainly on the Karamojong of northern Uganda, it illustrates his theory that a universal worldwide agricultural culture existed as far back as the last Ice Age – far older than was currently thought. Guided tours can be arranged with advance notice.

Sleeping & Eating

Bongo Lodge (☎ 054-30972; Moi Ave; s/d/tw KSh600/600/800) Stop wasting time and come straight here if you want to get your hands on the best budget beds in town. All rooms are self-contained and kept scrupulously clean.

Alakara Hotel (☎ 054-31554; Kenyatta St; s with/ without bathroom KSh1000/700, d with/without bathroom KSh1300/1000) We came, we saw, we liked. The comfortable rooms have phones, staff are friendly and prices include breakfast. It has a good bar, restaurant, TV room and parking facilities.

Pinewood (☎ 054-30011; A1 Hwy; s/d/tw KSh1500/2000/2500) The best place to rest weary eyes is in one of the wooden huts on offer here. The quality of the very comfortable rooms actually isn't that far off some of the national park lodges, but though, unlike in those, you won't see any lions from your terrace you might see some domestic cats, which if viewed through binoculars look kind of similar.

Iroko Boulevard Restaurant (Moi Ave; meals KSh120-200) It's got style, it's got glamour, it's got big-city aspirations and it's totally unexpected in Kitale. With cheap dishes that include a different African special everyday and an old Morris car hanging from the ceiling this is easily the best, and most popular, place to eat in town.

Getting There & Away

Matatus, buses and Peugeots are grouped by destination, and spread in and around the main bus and *matatu* park.

Regular *matatus* run to Endebess (KSh100 to KSh150, 45 minutes), Kapenguria (KSh100, 45 minutes), Eldoret (KSh150 to KSh200, 1¼ hours) and Kakamega (KSh250, two hours). Less regular services reach Mt Elgon National Park (KSh100, one hour), Nakuru (KSh450, 3½ hours) and Kisumu (KSh450, four hours).

Most bus companies have offices around the bus station and serve Eldoret (KSh150, one hour), Nakuru (KSh400, 3½ hours) and Nairobi (KSh700, six hours).

Several buses now run up to Lodwar (KSh1200, 8½ hours) each day.

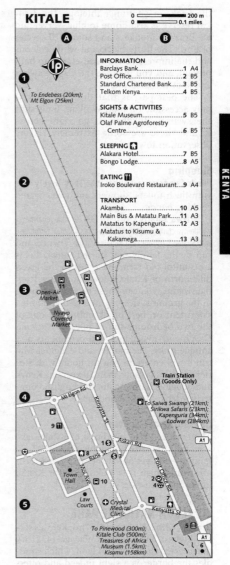

KITALE

INFORMATION
Barclays Bank..................................1 A4
Post Office......................................2 B5
Standard Chartered Bank...........3 B5
Telkom Kenya................................4 B5

SIGHTS & ACTIVITIES
Kitale Museum...............................5 B5
Olaf Palme Agroforestry
    Centre.......................................6 B5

SLEEPING
Alakara Hotel................................7 B5
Bongo Lodge.................................8 A5

EATING
Iroko Boulevard Restaurant........9 A4

TRANSPORT
Akamba..10 A5
Main Bus & Matatu Park............11 A3
Matatus to Kapenguria...............12 A3
Matatus to Kisumu &
    Kakamega..............................13 A3

Akamba (Moi Ave) runs buses from outside its office to Nairobi at 8.30am (KSh1000; nine hours).

SAIWA SWAMP NATIONAL PARK

This small and rarely visited **park** (adult/child US$20/10) north of Kitale is a real treat. Originally set up to preserve the habitat of the *nzohe* or sitatunga antelope, the 3-sq-km reserve is also home to blue, vervet and De Brazza's monkeys and some 370 species of bird. The fluffy black-and-white colobus and the impressive crowned crane are both present, and you may see the Cape clawless and spot-throated otters.

The best part is that this tiny park is only accessible on foot. Walking trails skirt the swamp, duckboards go right across it, and there are some extremely rickety observation towers.

Sleeping

Public Campsite (adult/child US$8/5) A lovely site with flush toilets, showers and two covered cooking *bandas*.

Sirikwa Safaris (☎ 0737-133170; sirikwabarnley@ swiftkenya.com; camping KSh450, tents KSh900, farmhouse with shared bathroom s/d KSh3000/4000) Owned and run by the family that started Saiwa, this is a beautiful old farmhouse lost in the green hills north of Kitale, a few kilometres from the swamp. You can chose between camping in the grounds, sleeping in a well-appointed safari tent or, best of all, opting for one of the two bedrooms full of piles of *National Geographic* magazines, old ornaments and antique sinks. The mother and daughter who run it will entertain you for hours with stories from their more than 70 years in Kenya and equally charming are the English country gardens – just sit and smile.

Getting There & Away

The park is 18km northeast of Kitale; take a *matatu* towards Kapenguria (KSh100, 30 minutes) and get out at the signposted turn-off, from which it is a 5km walk or KSh50 motorbike-taxi ride.

MT ELGON NATIONAL PARK

Peaking with Koitoboss (4187m), Kenya's second highest, and Uganda's Wagagai (4321m), the forested slopes of Mt Elgon, which straddles the border is a sight indeed and offers superb trekking.

Despite its lower altitude making conditions less extreme than Mt Kenya, Elgon sees a fraction of its bigger cousin's visitors. Not least because of its wetter weather and, recently, a dicey security situation, which in the latter half of 2007 even led to the park being closed. Fortunately, the situation has improved considerably and the mountain is once again back open for business.

While rarely seen, the mountain's most famous attractions are the elephants known for their predilection for digging salt out of the lower eastern slopes' caves. Sadly, the number of these saline-loving creatures has declined over the years, mainly due to incursions by Ugandan poachers.

Four main lava tubes (caves) are open to visitors: **Kitum**, **Chepnyalil**, **Mackingeny** and **Rongai**. Kitum holds your best hope for glimpsing elephants (especially before dawn), while Mackingeny, with a waterfall cascading across the entrance, is the most spectacular.

The mountain's fauna and flora are also great attractions. With rainforest at the base, the vegetation changes as you ascend, to bamboo jungle and finally alpine moorland featuring the giant groundsel and giant lobelia plants. Common animals include buffaloes, bushbucks, olive baboons, giant forest hogs and duikers, while Defassa waterbucks are also present. The lower forests are the habitat of the black-and-white colobus, and the blue and De Brazza's monkeys.

There are more than 240 species of bird here, including red-fronted parrots, Ross' turacos and casqued hornbills. On the peaks you may even see a lammergeyer raptor gliding through the thin air.

Information

The **park** (adult/child US$20/10) is wet much of the year, but driest between December and February. As well as bringing waterproof gear, you will need warm clothes, as it gets cold up here at night. Altitude may also be a problem for some people.

Access to the 169-sq-km national park is permitted without a vehicle. Indeed walking is the best way to get around as the roads are treacherous.

Due to the odd elephant, a **ranger** (per half/full day KSh500/1000) must escort you on walks on the lower slopes, such as to the caves.

For trekking the higher slopes you will need a tent and all your own camping gear. A **guide** (per day KSh1000) is also essential (see p605 for general advice).

Lonely Planet's *Trekking in East Africa* has more juicy details on the various trekking and walking routes.

MT ELGON NATIONAL PARK

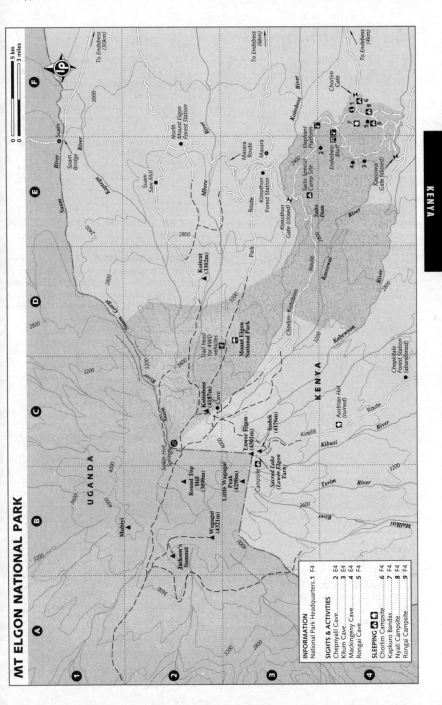

KENYA

0   5 km
0   3 miles

MT ELGON VIOLENCE

Since 2005 the area around Mt Elgon has seen a violent uprising that has left around 600 people dead and thousands displaced. The Sabot Land Defence Force (SLDF) was formed in 2005 to resist government attempts to evict squatters in the Chebyuk area of Mt Elgon. It quickly resorted to intimidation and widespread violence against those who opposed them. This included murder, rape, theft and torture – a favourite tactic was cutting the ear off a victim and forcing them to eat it. There have also been many reported incidents of gang rape as well as the use of child soldiers. In March 2008 the Kenyan military launched a major operation to bring a halt to the insurgency; though initially welcomed by the general populace they themselves now face widespread accusations of human rights abuses including unlawful murder, rape and torture.

With the killing of the SLDF leader in May 2008 things began to calm down and at the time of research major operations appeared to be over, but check the security situation very carefully if travelling to the Mt Elgon area.

Trekking

Check out the security situation with **KWS headquarters** (☎ 020-600800; kws@kws.org; PO Box 40241, Nairobi) in Nairobi or **Mt Elgon National Park** (☎ 054-31456; PO Box 753, Kitale) before you plan anything. Crossing into Uganda isn't currently permitted, but ask for the latest at the gate.

Allow at least four days for any round trip and two or three days for any direct ascent of **Koitoboss** if you're walking from the Chorlim Gate.

The **Park Route** offers some interesting possibilities and there is a well-worn route from Chorlim Gate up to Koitoboss Peak that requires one or two overnight camps.

Descending, you have a number of options. You can descend northwest into the crater to **Suam Hot Springs**. Alternatively you could go east around the crater rim and descend the **Masara Route**, which leads to the small village of Masara on the eastern slopes of the mountain (about 25km) and then returns to Endebess. Or you can head southwest around the rim of the crater (some very hard walking) to **Lower Elgon Tarn**, where you can camp before ascending **Lower Elgon Peak** (4301m).

Sleeping

If you're trekking your only option is to camp (adult/child US$8/5). This fee is the same whether you drop tent in the official campsites or on any old flat spot during your trek.

Chorlim Campsite (next to Chorlim Gate; adult/child US$8/5) This campsite has the park's best facilities but is less scenic than the other two public sites, Nyati and Rongai.

Kapkuro Bandas (US$30) These excellent stone *bandas* can sleep three people in two beds and have simple bathrooms and small kitchen areas.

Getting There & Away

Sporadic *matatus* and Peugeots now reach the Chorlim Gate from Kitale (KSh100, one hour). More regular services reach Endebess (KSh100 to KSh150, 45 minutes), a 9km walk from the gate. Locals will happily point you in the right direction.

NORTHERN KENYA

Situation Vacant: Adventurers required to boldly go where few have gone before.

We are searching for daring explorers to challenge themselves against one of the most exciting wildernesses in Africa. This role will most suit somebody able to withstand appalling roads that would shake a lesser mortal into submission, searing heat, clouds of dust and sand torn up by relentless winds, primitive food and accommodation, vast distances and more than a hint of danger (see p386).

The generous compensation package we're offering the successful applicant will include memories of vast shattered lava deserts, camel herders walking their animals to lost oases, fog-shrouded mountains full of mysterious creatures, prehistoric islands crawling with massive reptiles, jokes shared with traditionally dressed warriors and nights spent in smoky village huts. Additional perks will include camel trekking through piles of peachy dunes, elephant encounters in scrubby acacia woodlands, nights spent out in the open wishing upon shooting stars and, of course, the chance to walk barefoot along the fabled shores of a sea of jade.

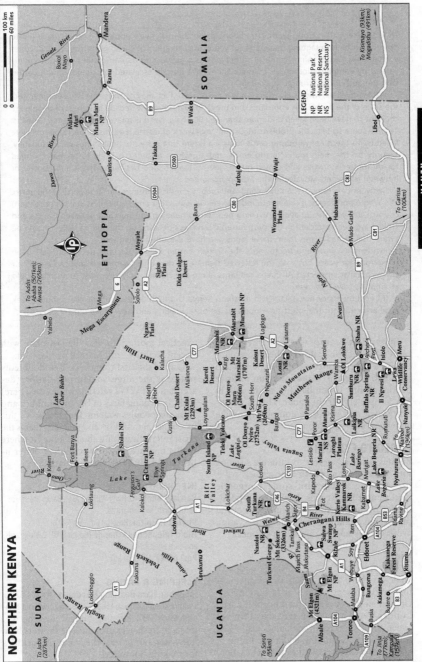

NORTHERN KENYA

LEGEND
NP National Park
NR National Reserve
NS National Sanctuary

0 ─── 100 km
0 ─── 60 miles

WARNING

Unfortunately, the strong warrior traditions of northern Kenya's nomadic peoples have led to security problems plaguing the region for years. With an influx of cheap guns from conflict zones surrounding Kenya, minor conflicts stemming from grazing rights and cattle rustling (formerly settled by compensation rather than violence) have quickly escalated into ongoing gun battles that the authorities struggle to contain.

While travellers, who rarely witness any intertribal conflict, may consider the issue exaggerated, the scale of the problem is enormous and growing. Over the past decade hundreds of people are thought to have been killed and more than 160,000 have been displaced by intertribal conflicts. To give some scale to the problem, in just the final week of research of this guide 15 people were killed in northern Kenya during cattle raids – a figure that is by no means unusual. Fortunately, security on the main routes in the north, and anywhere a tourist is likely to be, has changed for the better. Convoys and armed guards are no longer used between Marich and Lodwar or between Isiolo and Moyale, on the Ethiopian border.

Sadly, not everything is on the mend, and bloody conflict continues in large parts of the north. The whole northeastern region around Garsen, Garissa, Wajir and Mandera is still *shifta* (bandit) country and you should avoid travelling here. Buses heading to Lamu and between Garissa and Thika have been attacked in the past. Intrepid travellers heading up the Suguta Valley should be aware that armed gangs roam these lands and have assaulted foreigners.

Incidentally, travelling up towards the Somali border (which is currently closed) has been dangerous for years, but with the renewed fighting in that blood-saturated country and US air strikes against suspected Al-Qaeda militants along the border, only the most foolhardy would attempt to travel up here.

Improvements or not, security in northern Kenya is a fluid entity, and travellers should seek local advice about the latest developments before travelling and never take unnecessary risks.

In our 21st-century world of wireless internet connections and dumbed-down TV this is a rare opportunity to experience a land and a lifestyle that allows you to leave behind all that is familiar and secure and to fall completely off the radar. This is northern Kenya and it will be completely unlike anywhere else you know.

ISIOLO TO ETHIOPIA

Besides being a gateway to Ethiopia's riches, this route offers northern Kenya's best wildlife viewing along with some incredible culture and landscapes. New hiking possibilities in the Ndoto Mountains and several pioneering community wildlife-conservation projects only add to the region's appeal.

Isiolo

☎ 064

Isiolo is where anticipation and excitement first starts to send your heart a flutter. This vital pit stop on the long road north is a true frontier town, a place on the edge, torn between the cool, verdant highlands just to the south and the scorching badlands, home of nomads and explorers, to the north. On a more practical footing it's also the last place with decent facilities until Maralal or Marsabit.

One of the first things you'll undoubtedly notice is the large Somali population (descendants of WWI veterans who settled here) and the striking faces of Boran, Samburu and Turkana peoples walking the streets; it's this mix of people, cultures and religions that is the most interesting thing about Isiolo. Nowhere is this mixture of worlds colliding better illustrated than in the hectic market.

INFORMATION

Barclays Bank (A2 Hwy) With an ATM. Banks are scarce in the north, so plan ahead.

District Hospital (Hospital Rd; 24hr).

Isiolo Telephone Exchange (Hospital Rd) Calling cards and card phones.

Post office (Hospital Rd)

SLEEPING & EATING

Jabal-Nur Plaza Boarding & Lodging (☎ 064-52460; s with/without bathroom KSh400/300, d with/without bathroom KSh500/400) Pleasing budget digs that get frequent fresh licks of paint. The showers have hot water – or at least they have the facilities for making hot water!

Bomen Hotel (☎ 064-52389; s/tw/ste KSh900/1500/2500) A favourite home for NGOs away from home, the Bomen Hotel has the town's brightest (ask for one facing outward) and most comfortable rooms. Room prices are steep and you can get much the same at the Isiolo Transit Hotel for less, but bonus options include TVs and shared terraces with views.

Gaddisa Lodge (☎ 724-201115; www.gaddisa.com; s/tw KSh3000/4000) Around 3km northeast of town is this lonely Dutch-run lodge where peaceful cottages overlook the fringes of the northern savannah country. There's a pool, though you won't need to pack your bathers as it's normally empty. It's overpriced for what you get.

Silver Bells Hotel (meals KSh80-200) Decent Kenyan favourites will be brought to your blue- and white-checked table. It's a good spot for grabbing a cheap predeparture breakfast.

GETTING THERE & AWAY
Although convoys are no longer being used north to Marsabit, check the security situation thoroughly before leaving. This is especially critical if heading towards Garissa, Wajir or Mandera, which are currently considered unsafe for travellers.

Car
Isiolo marks the tarmac's northern terminus and the start of the corrugated dirt and gravel, which will shake the guts out of you and your vehicle. There are several petrol stations, so top up as prices climb and supplies diminish northward. If you're heading south, Central Highlands petrol is cheaper.

Bus & Matatu
Lots of bus companies serve Nairobi (KSh500, 4½ hours) with most buses leaving between 6am and 6.30am from the main road through town and also stopping at the *matatu* and bus stand just south of the market. **Nairobi Express** (A2 Hwy), is one of the more reliable operators. Nightly buses creep north to Marsabit (KSh800, nine hours) and Moyale (KSh1500, 20 hours) and with a bit of luck you'll get the bus operated by the brilliantly named **Sir Alex Ferguson Bus Company**. Buses pick up passengers from outside the Nairobi Express office sometime between 11pm and midnight. Tickets cannot be bought in advance so get there early and shout, push and shove with the best of them.

For Maralal take an early-morning *matatu* to Wamba (KSh300, 2½ hours), and then a Maralal-bound *matatu* (KSh400, 2½ hours) from there. Regular *matatu* leave from a chaotic stand around the market and also serve Archer's Post (KSh120, 45 minutes) and Meru (KSh150, 1½ hours). Peugeots also service Nanyuki (KSh200, 1¾ hours).

Lewa Wildlife Conservancy
While the massive 263-sq-km **Lewa Wildlife Conservancy** (LWC; ☎ 064-31405; www.lewa.org; admission incl in accommodation rates), just south of Isiolo, could boast about its luxury lodges, stunning scenery, astounding wildlife activities and having hosted Prince William, it would rather talk about its community and conservation projects. Founded in 1995, LWC is a

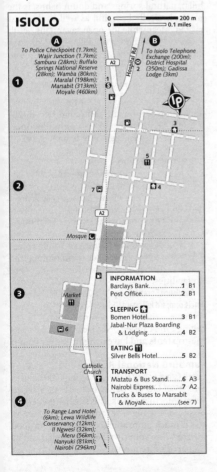

ISIOLO

0 _____ 200 m
0 _____ 0.1 miles

To Police Checkpoint (1.7km);
Wajir Junction (1.7km);
Samburu (28km); Buffalo
Springs National Reserve
(28km); Wamba (80km);
Maralal (198km);
Marsabit (313km);
Moyale (460km)

To Isiolo Telephone
Exchange (200m);
District Hospital
(350m); Gadisa
Lodge (3km)

Mosque

Market

Catholic
Church

To Range Land Hotel
(6km); Lewa Wildlife
Conservancy (12km);
Il Ngwesi (32km);
Meru (56km);
Nanyuki (81km);
Nairobi (296km)

INFORMATION	
Barclays Bank	1 B1
Post Office	2 B1

SLEEPING 🏠	
Bomen Hotel	3 B1
Jabal-Nur Plaza Boarding	
& Lodging	4 B2

EATING 🍴	
Silver Bells Hotel	5 B2

TRANSPORT	
Matatu & Bus Stand	6 A3
Nairobi Express	7 A2
Trucks & Buses to Marsabit	
& Moyale	(see 7)

KENYA

nonprofit organisation that invests around 70% of its annual US$2-million-plus budget into healthcare, education and various community projects for surrounding villages while the rest funds further conservation and security projects.

Wildlife drives in private vehicles aren't permitted and only guests of the LWC's lodges are allowed into the conservancy. A plethora of activities, ranging from drives (day and night) and walks to horse riding and camel rides, are available at most lodges. Guests are encouraged to take part in conservation activities, such as tracking and tagging animals.

There are a number of very exclusive, expensive places to stay inside the wildlife conservancy. These include the beautiful Lewa House, with its three sublime thatched cottages and even more sublime main building and Lewa Safari Camp, which isn't really like camping at all. For all these you must book through **Bush and Beyond** (☎ 020-600457; www.bush-and-beyond.com) in Nairobi and reckon on a minimum of US$600 per person, per day for full-board lodging.

GETTING THERE & AWAY
LWC is only 12km south of Isiolo and is well signposted on A2 Hwy. **Airkenya** (☎ 020-605745; www.airkenya.com) and **Safarilink** (☎ 020-600777; www.safarilink-kenya.com) have daily flights to LWC from Nairobi. Return fares on Airkenya/Safarilink are US$234/282 excluding taxes.

Il Ngwesi
Il Ngwesi is a project linking wildlife conservation and community development. The Maasai of Il Ngwesi, with help from their neighbour LWC, have transformed this undeveloped land, previously used for subsidence pastoralism, into a prime wildlife conservation area hosting white and black rhinos, water bucks, giraffes and other plains animals. It's truly fitting that Il Ngwesi translates to 'people of wildlife'.

The community now supplements their herding income with tourist dollars gained from their award-winning ecolodge, **Il Ngwesi Group Ranch** (☎ 020-340331; info@letsgosafari.com; s/d incl all meals US$209/418; ☒). Six open-fronted thatched cottages boast views over the dramatic escarpment. The best part is that profits go straight to the Maasai community.

Samburu, Buffalo Springs & Shaba National Reserves
Blistered with termite skyscrapers, shot through with the muddy **Ewaso Ngiro River** and heaving with heavy-weight animals the three contagious parks of Samburu, Buffalo Springs and Shaba are not as famous as some reserves, but they have a beauty that is unsurpassed as well as a population of creatures that occur in no other major Kenyan park. These include the blue-legged Somali ostrich, super-stripy Grevy's zebra, unicorn-like Beisa oryxes, ravishing reticulated giraffes and the gerenuk – a gazelle that dearly wishes to be a giraffe. Despite comprising of just 300 sq km the breadth of vegetation and landscapes here is amazing; Shaba, with its great rocky *kopjes* (isolated hills), natural springs and doum palms, is the most physically beautiful as well as the least visited. Meanwhile the open savannahs, scrub desert and verdant river foliage in Samburu and Buffalo Springs virtually guarantee close encounters with elephants and all the others.

INFORMATION
Conveniently, admission for Buffalo Springs, Shaba and Samburu (adult/child US$40/20) are interchangeable, so you only pay once, even if you're visiting all three in one day.

SLEEPING & EATING
Buffalo Springs National Reserve
Public campsites (camping US$10) The five public sites close to Gare Mara Gate are overgrown, hard to find and have absolutely no facilities or water. For toilets, showers and less solitude, camp in Samburu.

Special campsites (camping US$15) While scenically located by freshwater springs along the Isiolo and Maji ya Chumvi Rivers, there are no facilities.

Samburu Serena Lodge (☎ 020-2842333; www.serenahotels.com; s/d full board US$285/385; ☒) The comfy cottages, with breezy verandahs, reed-lined ceilings and canopy beds, feel a little like over-the-top tents and have delightful river views.

Samburu National Reserve
Beach Camp (☎ 0721-252737; camping KSh500, tents for hire KSh500) On the banks of the Ewaso Ngiro River's northern bank, this site has the setting of any of the big-boy lodges but let's face it, this is much more authentic Africa. It's a good idea to bring your own bedding. Meals can be prepared on request.

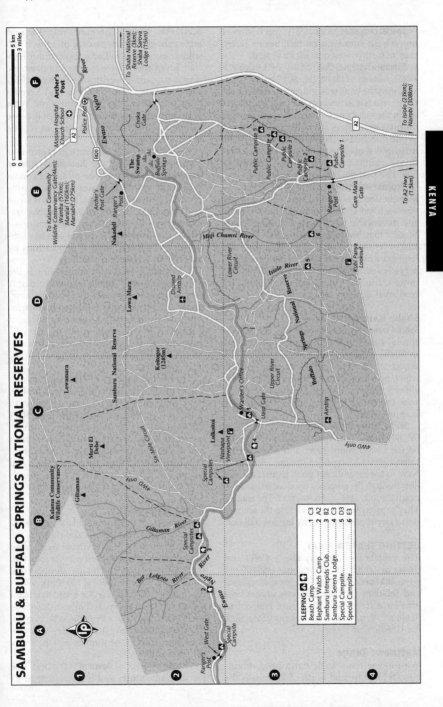

SAMBURU & BUFFALO SPRINGS NATIONAL RESERVES

KENYA

To Shaba National Reserve (3km); Shaba Sarova Lodge (15km)

Archer's Post

Mission Hospital; Church School

Police Post

To Kalama Community Wildlife Conservancy Gate(4km); Wamba (57km); Marabit (275km)

Choka Gate

Ewaso Ngiro River

The Swamp

Buffalo Springs

Archer's Post Gate

Ranger's Post

Nakadeli

Gare Mara Gate

To Isiolo (23km); Nairobi (308km)

To A2 Hwy (1.5km)

Ranger's Post

Public Campsite 5

Public Campsite 4

Public Campsite 3

Public Campsite 2

Public Campsite 1

Maji Chumvi River

Lowa Mara

Lower River Circuit

Disused Airstrip

Isiolo River

Kubi Panya Lookout

Samburu National Reserve

Buffalo Springs National Reserve

Lowamara

Koitogor (1245m)

Warder's Office

Uaso Gate

Upper River Circuit

Buffalo Airstrip

4WD only

Merti El Debe

Six-Mile Circuit

Loikatioi

Nashapa Viewpoint

Special Campsites

Giltaman

Kalama Community Wildlife Conservancy

4WD only

Giltaman River

Special Campsites

Bur Loigoto River

Ewaso Ngiro River

West Gate

Special Campsite

Ranger's Post

5 km / 3 miles

Special campsites (camping US$15) Special they're not – bush sites with no facilities or water, they're further west and tricky to find.

Samburu Intrepids Club (☎ 064-30453, Nairobi 020-446651; full board s/d US$195/225; 🏊) Grab a G&T, sink into the bar's teak lounges and gaze over the Ewaso Ngiro towards the poor people living in the village just outside the reserve – the ultimate example of the haves and have nots! While thatched roofs and canopy beds in the luxurious tents scream safari Africa, the refined furniture unfortunately shrieks Fortune 500. The friendly service is unmatched.

Elephant Watch Camp (☎ 020-891112; www.elephant watchsafaris.com; s/d full board incl guided walks US$550/1000; closed Apr & Nov) Undoubtedly the most unique and memorable place to stay in the reserves. Massive thatched roofs cling to acacia branches and tower over palatial, eight-sided tents and large grass mat-clad terraces. Natural materials pervade and the bathrooms are stunning. The owners, Iain and Oria Douglas-Hamilton, are renowned elephant experts.

Shaba National Reserve

Special campsites (camping US$15) Of the several special sites (no facilities) here, Funan, set in Shaba's core, takes the cake. Shaded by acacias, it's next to a semipermanent spring, which provides water for visitors and wildlife alike. A ranger must accompany you to these sites; the cost is included in the fee but a tip is appropriate.

Shaba Sarova Lodge (☎ 020-713333; s/d full board US$270/320; 🏊) This spectacular place nestles on the Ewaso Ngiro River and it's pathways intertwine with frog-filled streams and ponds. Next to the magnificent pool, natural springs flow through the gorgeous open-air bar and beneath the lofty 200-seat restaurant. The rooms? They're pretty lavish too! Staff turn the animals into a circus performance by leaving bait out.

GETTING THERE & AWAY

The vehicle-less can wrangle a 4WD and driver in Archer's Post for about US$100 per day. **Airkenya** (☎ 020-605745; www.airkenya.com) and **Safarilink** (☎ 020-600777; www.safarilink-kenya.com) have frequent flights from Nairobi to Samburu. Return fares on Airkenya/Safarilink are US$253/296.

Matthews Range

West of the remarkable flat-topped mountain Ol Lolokwe and north of Wamba is the Matthews Range. The name might sound tame enough, but rest assured that this is real wilderness Africa full of a thousand forest-clad adventures. These forests and dramatic slopes support a wealth of wildlife including elephants, lions, buffaloes and Kenya's most important wild dog population. With few roads and almost no facilities, only those willing to go the extra mile on foot will be rewarded with the spoils.

In 1995 the local Samburu communities collectively formed the **Namunyak Wildlife Conservation Trust**, now one of Kenya's most successful community conservation programs. The trust is unique because it's run by a democratically elected board, each community having one trustee. Now endorsed by KWS, it oversees 750 sq km and has substantially increased animal populations by successfully combating poaching.

The main base for the mountains is the one-street town of **Wamba**, remarkable only for the amount of drunks that roam around. If you intend to explore the mountains independently and on foot then you will need a guide. Unfortunately, most of the self-appointed guide, are in fact the aforementioned drunks and none of them can really be recommended.

The basic **El-Moran** (s KSh250, with shared bathroom KSh150) in Wamba is the only option besides bush camping. It's very basic indeed, but if it's Africa you want then it's Africa you'll get! If it's full you could try the local mission (which incidentally has northern Kenya's best hospital, a fact worth remembering while in the bush).

While *matatus* from Isiolo (KSh300) and Maralal (KSh350) do reach Wamba, there's little point in coming without a vehicle.

Ndoto Mountains

Climbing from the Korante Plain's sands are the magnificent rusty bluffs and ridges of the Ndoto Mountains. Kept a virtual secret from the travelling world by their remote location, the Ndotos abound with hiking, climbing and bouldering potential. **Mt Poi** (2050m), which resembles the world's largest bread loaf from some angles, is a technical climber's dream, its sheer 800m north face begging to be bagged. If you're fit and have a whole day to spare, it's a great hike to the summit and the views are extraordinary.

The tiny village of **Ngurunit** is the best base for your adventures and is interesting in its own right, with captivating, traditionally dressed Samburu people living in simple, yet elegantly woven grass huts.

Ngurunit is best accessed from Loglogo, 47km south of Marsabit and 233km north of Archer's Post. From Loglogo it's a tricky 79km (1¾-hour) drive, with many forks, through the Kaisut Desert. Offer a lift to someone in Loglogo looking for a ride to Ngurunit – they are cheap (free!) and helpful guides.

To access Ngurunit from Baragoi, head about 40km north towards South Horr and, after descending the first steep paved section and crossing the following *lugga* (dry river bed), look out for Lmerim Nursery School. Found it? The Ngurunit turn-off is 200m behind you!

Marsabit
☎ 069

Marsabit is a long way from anywhere. The road from Isiolo will rattle your fillings and shatter your vehicle and for hour after scorching hour you'll bounce past an almost unchanging monoscape of scrubby bush where encounters with wildlife are common and elegant Samburu walk their herds of camels and goats with pride. As the afternoon heats up, and your brain starts to cook, you'll find the world around you sliding in and out of focus as strange mirages flicker on the horizon. Then, as evening comes on, one final mirage appears. A massive wall of forested mountains complete with trickling waters and cool nightly fogs providing an unlikely home to mammoth tusked elephants. But this is no mirage, this is Marsabit.

INFORMATION
Cyber Wireless Internet World (off A2 Hwy; per hr KSh120; ☼ 8am-7pm Mon-Sat)
Kenya Commercial Bank (off Post Office Rd) No ATM.
Medical clinic (Post Office Rd; ☼ 8am-7pm Mon-Sat, noon-7pm Sun)
Post office (Post Office Rd)

SLEEPING & EATING
JeyJey Centre (☎ 069-2296; A2 Hwy; s KSh400, s KSh400, s/tw/tr with shared bathroom KSh250/400/600) Owned by government MP JJ Falana, this mud-brick castle bedecked in flowers is something of a travellers centre and always bursting with road-hardened souls. Basic rooms with mozzie nets surround a courtyard, and bathrooms (even shared ones) sport on-demand hot water.

Nomads Trail Resthouse (☎ 069-2287; A2 Hwy; r incl breakfast from KSh600) The best accommodation in town are the prim and proper rooms in this new guesthouse opposite JeyJey. All rooms have attached bathrooms that come with, wait for it, real hot water from a real shower!

Al-Subra Modern Hotel (off A2 Hwy; meals KSh70-150) You'll probably need someone to point this place out to you as it's tricky to find, but the hunt is worthwhile because as well as Kenyan staples it also presents the first flavours of Ethiopia with its *injera* (Ethiopian breadlike staple) and *wat* (stew; an acquired taste).

GETTING THERE & AWAY
Although improved security meant convoys and armed guards weren't being used to Moyale or Isiolo during our research, it's still wise to get the latest security and Ethiopian border information from locals and the police station before leaving town.

Bus
A bus now connects Marsabit to Moyale (KSh600, 8½ hours). There's no designated stop – simply flag it down on the A2 Hwy as it comes through town around 5pm each day (en route from Nairobi!). The same service heads south to Isiolo (KSh800, 8½ hours) at 9am.

Car
The Moyale road is less corrugated than the one to Isiolo, but its sharp stones will devour your tyres and the deep ruts will scrub your undercarriage. The only fuel north is in Moyale, so stock up here. As a rule, if buses and trucks travel in a convoy or take armed soldiers on board, you should too! For advice on travel to Loyangalani, see p395.

Marsabit National Park
This small **park** (adult/child US$20/10), on Mt Marsabit's upper slopes and watered by frequent rains and morning fogs, is coated in thick forests and contains a wide variety of wildlife, including lions, leopards, elephants and buffaloes. However, the dense forest makes spotting wildlife very hard, but fortunately help is at hand in the form of a couple of natural clearings (which occasionally become lakes) and where animal sightings are almost guaranteed.

You can drive in the park, but the roads are appalling and you won't see much. A better idea is to hire a KWS guide (KSh1200 for half a day) and explore on foot. You'll see thousands

KENYA

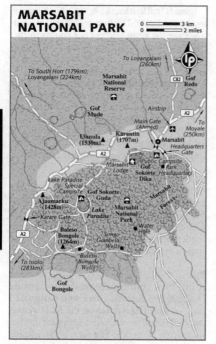

MARSABIT NATIONAL PARK

of butterflies, birds and other little creatures and almost certainly have some heart-stopping elephant and buffalo encounters.

SLEEPING & EATING

Public Campsite (adult/child US$8/5) This site, which is next to the main gate, has water and firewood, but the facilities, especially the showers, really are in severe need of an overhaul.

Lake Paradise Special Campsite (adult/child US$15/5, plus set-up fee KSh5000) Although there's nothing except lake water and firewood, this picturesque site is easily the best place to stay in the park. Thanks to roaming buffaloes and elephants, a ranger must be present when you camp here.

Marsabit Lodge (s/tw incl breakfast KSh5500/5900) This lodge is in a dreadful state and tremendously overpriced. The whole place is literally falling to bits; however, renovations are starting so maybe things will have improved. The location, on the edge of the lake occupying Gof Sokorte Dika, is spectacular.

MOYALE

Let's be honest, nobody comes to Moyale to see Moyale; people come because it's the gateway to one of the world's most fascinating countries, Ethiopia. The drive from Marsabit is long and hard (on you and your 4WD), with the Dida Galgalu Desert's seemingly endless black shattered lava fields stretching out before you, and the Mega Escarpment seemingly climbing ever higher as you approach near Sololo.

In stark contrast to the solitary journey here, Moyale's small, sandy streets burst with activity. The town's Ethiopian half is more developed, complete with sealed roads, and there's a palpable difference in its atmosphere.

It's possible to enter Ethiopia for the day without a visa, but Ethiopian officials will hold your passport until you return. The border closes at 6pm – don't be late! The Commercial Bank of Ethiopia, 2km from the border, changes travellers cheques (0.5% commission), as well as US dollars and euros. While it doesn't exchange Kenyan Shillings, the Tourist Hotel will swap them for Ethiopian Birr (10KSh to Birr1).

There are a few simple places to stay and eat on both sides of the border: **Sherif Guest House** (s/tw with shared bathroom KSh150/200) and **Baghdad Hotel II** (meals KSh80-150) fly the Kenyan flag, while the **Tourist Hotel** (s with shared toilet Birr15) and **Ethio-Kenya** (breakfast Birr3-6) keep up the Ethiopian end.

Buses leave town daily at 9am for Marsabit (KSh600, 8½ hours) and Isiolo (KSh1500, 17 hours). Trucks servicing the same destinations on a daily basis pick up passengers near the main intersection in town (Marsabit/Isiolo KSh500/1000).

On the Ethiopian side, a bus leaves for Addis Ababa (Birr95) each morning at around 5am. The two-day journey is broken with a night's sleep at either Awasa or Shashemene.

MARALAL TO TURKANA'S EASTERN SHORE

Journeying to a sea of jade shouldn't be something that is easy to do and this route, the ultimate Kenyan adventure, is certainly not easy. But for the battering you'll take you'll be rewarded a thousand times over with memories of vibrant tribes, camel caravans running into a rouge sunset, mesmerising volcanic landscapes and, of course, the north's greatest jewel, the Jade Sea, Lake Turkana.

Maralal
☎ 065

Walking down Maralal's dusty streets it wouldn't come as much of a surprise to see

Clint Eastwood stride slowly from a bar and proclaim the town not big enough for the two of you. With its swinging cowboy doors and camels tied up outside colourful wooden shop fronts it's impossible not to think that you've somehow been transported to the Wild West of old.

Maralal has gained an international reputation for its fantastically frenetic **International Camel Derby** (see the boxed text, p394) and a visit over its duration is truly unforgettable. Less crazy but almost as memorable are the year-round camel safaris and treks that are offered here.

INFORMATION
Kenya Commercial Bank (behind market) With ATM (the last one going north).
Maralal Medical Clinic (Mon-Sat)
Post office Next to the market.

SIGHTS & ACTIVITIES
Trekking the Loroghi Hills Circuit, which takes in one of Kenya's most astounding vistas, Lesiolo, is a rewarding five days and 78km.

Yare Camel Club & Camp (065-62295) organises guides and camels for independent camel safaris in the region. Self-catered day/overnight trips cost US$20/35 per person.

Surrounding the town is the **Maralal National Sanctuary**, home to zebras, impalas, hyenas, elephants and all the rest. There is no entry fee and you may have the place much to yourself.

SLEEPING & EATING
Yare Camel Club & Camp (065-62295, (Nairobi) 020-2163758; www.yaresafaris.co.ke; camping KSh200, s/tw/tr US$23/28/35;) Superbly well-run campsite, 3km south of town, that's justifiably popular with overlanders. You can camp on the bouncy grass or stay in one of the cosy, but dated, wooden *bandas*, which boast bathrooms, towels and hot water.

Maralal Safari Lodge (065-62220, Nairobi 020-211124; www.angelfire.com/jazz/maralal/; camping KSh500, s/d full board US$165/230;) The wooden cottages are starting to show their age, but the low lighting helps hide the worst of it and as discounts are as common as impala at the waterhole right outside your window you can't really moan. Talking of moaning the open fireplaces in each

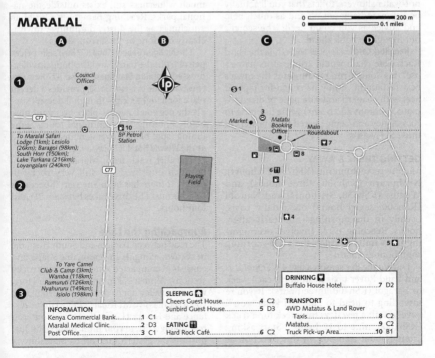

MARALAL

0 — 200 m
0 — 0.1 miles

Council Offices

Market

Matatu Booking Office

Main Roundabout

BP Petrol Station

To Maralal Safari Lodge (1km); Lesiolo (26km); Baragoi (98km); South Horr (150km); Lake Turkana (216km); Loyangalani (240km)

Playing Field

To Yare Camel Club & Camp (3km); Wamba (118km); Rumuruti (126km); Nyahururu (149km); Isiolo (198km)

INFORMATION
Kenya Commercial Bank.............1 C1
Maralal Medical Clinic................2 D3
Post Office...................................3 C1

SLEEPING
Cheers Guest House....................4 C2
Sunbird Guest House..................5 D3

EATING
Hard Rock Café...........................6 C2

DRINKING
Buffalo House Hotel....................7 D2

TRANSPORT
4WD Matatus & Land Rover
Taxis...8 C2
Matatus.......................................9 C2
Truck Pick-up Area....................10 B1

MARALAL INTERNATIONAL CAMEL DERBY

Inaugurated by Yare Safaris in 1990, the annual Maralal International Camel Derby held in early August is one of the biggest events in Kenya, attracting riders and spectators from the world's four distant corners. The races are open to anyone and the extended after-parties at Yare Camel Club & Camp are notorious – you're likely to bump into some genuine characters here.

Not interested in parties and just want some fast-moving camel action? Then the derby's first race has your name written all over it – it's for amateur camel riders. Ante up KSh1000 for your entry and another KSh3000 for your slobbering steed and get racing! It's a butt-jarring 11km journey. Don't even start feeling sorry for your arse – the professional riders cover 42km.

For further information contact **Yare Safaris** (☎ Maralal 065-62295, Nairobi 020 2163758; www .yaresafaris.co.ke) or Yare Camel Club & Camp in Maralal.

room and the views over animal-filled plains should be romantic enough to get you both in the mood for making some moaning noises!

Sunbird Guest House (☎ 065-62015; PO Box 74, Maralal; s/d KSh500/700) This shiny and friendly place has quiet, clean and comfortable rooms with nice linen, mosquito nets, sparkling bathrooms, 24-hour hot water and sockets to charge your mobile phone.

Cheers Guest House (☎ 065-62204; s/tw KSh600/900) An excellent option in the town centre this slickly run joint has immaculate rooms with hot-water showers, toilets that you'll actually be happy to hang out on and as much help and advice as you could need. The secret's out though so book ahead.

Hard Rock Café (meals KSh60-170) While the Hard Rock Café chain would cringe at its name's use, this Somali-run restaurant is the town's best restaurant. Enjoy its *chapo*-fry (spiced beef with chapatti and side plate of diced tomatoes, onions and beans) while listening to Rick Astley and being peered at by posters of those Spicy girls.

GETTING THERE & AWAY

Matatus serve Rumuruti (KSh250, 2½ hours), Nyahururu (KSh300, three hours) and Wamba (KSh350, 3½ hours) and Nairobi (KSh600, seven hours) on a daily basis, usually in the mornings and early afternoons. Reaching Isiolo involves overnighting in Wamba to catch the early-morning southbound *matatu*.

During the dry season a few 4WD *matatus* and Land Rover taxis head north each week to Baragoi (KSh400, three hours). If you're intending to head to Lake Turkana, you'll have to wait a few days to a week for a truck (KSh1000, nine to 12 hours). Start asking around about transport in this direction as

soon as you arrive in town. While breaking the truck journey in Baragoi or South Horr may seem like a good idea, remember that you may have to wait there for week before another truck trundles through.

Baragoi

The long descent off the Loroghi Plateau towards Baragoi serves up some sweet vistas and for mile after gorgeous mile you'll literally see nothing but tree-studded grasslands alive with wildlife. It's encouraging to see that so much wilderness still exists outside the national parks. Reaching Baragoi is a bit of an anticlimax as the dusty, diminutive town is clearly outdone by its surroundings.

The **Mt Ngiro General Shop** (C77 Hwy) sells pricey petrol from the barrel and the bougainvillea-dressed **Morning Star Guest House** (C77 Hwy; r per person with shared bathroom KSh250) provides a decent place for a night's kip – though it doesn't supply the peg you'll need to place over your nose before entering the communal toilets. Fine dining (spot blatant overstatement) is found at the **Widwid Hotel** (C77 Hwy; meals KSh60).

The dirt track from Maralal to Baragoi is much improved but still very rocky in places. If there has been any rain it becomes treacherous. The drive takes between 2½ and four hours.

Approaching the Lake

The road between Baragoi and South Horr, the next town along, is in reasonable shape and consists of compacted sand and bumpy rocky sections. Almost 23km north of South Horr, when the valley opens to the northern plains, you'll see massive Mt Kulal (2293m) in the distance and Devil's Hand, a large rock outcrop resembling a fist, to your immediate right. Just north is the eastern turn-off to Marsabit via

Kargi, so if you're heading for Turkana keep left. If you get mixed up, just remember that Mt Kulal on your right is good and that Mt Kulal on your left is very, very bad (unless, of course, you're heading to Marsabit!).

Further north, the scrub desert suddenly scatters and you'll be greeted by vast volcanic armies of shimmering bowling ball–size boulders, cinder cones and reddish-purple hues – if they could talk they'd welcome you to Mt Kulal's shattered lava fields. If this arresting and barren Martian landscape doesn't take your breath away, the first sight of the sparkling Jade Sea a few kilometres north certainly will.

As you descend to the lake, South Island stands proudly before you, while Teleki Volcano's geometrically perfect cone lurks on Turkana's southern shore. Before you jump in the water, remember that Turkana has a large crocodile population.

Loyangalani

Standing in utter contrast to the dour desert shades surrounding it, tiny Loyangalani assaults all your senses in one crazy explosion of spears, clashing colours, feather headdresses and bloody red robes. Overlooking Lake Turkana and surrounded by small ridges of pillow lava (evidence that this area used to be underwater), the sandy streets of this one-camel town are a meeting point of the great northern tribes, Turkana and Samburu, Gabbra and El-Molo. It's easily the most exotic corner of Kenya and a fitting reward after the hard journey here.

The El-Molo tribe, which is one of Africa's smallest, lives on the lakeshore just north of here in the villages of **Layeni** and **Komote**. Although outwardly similar to the Turkana, the El-Molo are linguistically linked to the Somali and Rendille people. Unfortunately the last speaker of their traditional language died before the turn of the millennium.

INFORMATION

Other than the post office and the Catholic mission occasionally selling petrol out of the barrel at exorbitant prices, there's little in the way of services.

SIGHTS & ACTIVITIES
South Island National Park

Opened as a public reserve in 1983 and made a World Heritage Site by Unesco in 1997, this tiny 39-sq-km purplish volcanic island and **park** (adult/child US$20/10) is completely barren and uninhabited apart from large populations of crocodiles, poisonous snakes and feral goats. Spending the night at a **special campsite** (adult/child US$8/5) makes for an even more eerie trip. All the sites lack water, firewood (there are no trees on the island) and toilets. The southern site is the most sheltered from the wind, so your tent is less likely to take flight here.

In calm weather a speedboat can reach the island in 30 minutes and circumnavigate it in another hour. If winds crop up, trip times can easily double. As speed boats are limited in number you will probably end up in something much more sedate: reckon on a six-hour return trip for which you will pay about KSh3000 per hour. Ask at either the KWS office in town or the Palm Shade Camp about hiring boats.

Mt Kulal

Mt Kulal dominates Lake Turkana's eastern horizon, and its forested volcanic flanks offer up some serious hiking possibilities. This fertile lost world in the middle of the desert is home to some unique creatures including the Mt Kulal Chameleon, a beautiful lizard first recorded in only 2003. No matter what the local guides tell you, trekking up to the summit (2293m) from Loyangalani in a day isn't feasible. Plan on several days for a return trip; guides (KSh1000 per day) and donkeys (KSH500 per day) to carry your gear can be hired in Loyangalani or part with substantial sums of cash (KSh8000 to KSh12,000) for a lift up Mt Kulal to the villages of Arapal or Gatab. From there you can head for the summit and spend a long day (eight to 10 hours) hiking back down to Loyangalani. If you pass by Arapal be sure to whistle a tune at the singing wells from where the Samburu gather water (and sing while doing so – hence the name).

Loyangalani Desert Museum

Worth a quick look this new **museum** (adult/child KSh500/250; ☉ 9am-6pm), standing on a bluff above the lake several kilometres north of town, contains lots of photo heavy displays; but its real use is as an information centre about the surrounding area. You will probably have to track down the man with the key in town.

SLEEPING & EATING

Let's face it; you came north for adventure, not comfort. If you're camping remember to tie down your tent as early evening winds pick up tremendously and can be blowing at 60km/h by 8pm.

our pick Palm Shade Camp (☎ 0726-714768; camping KSh450, s/tw rondavel with shared bathroom KSh750/1500) Drop your tent on some grass beneath acacias and doum palms or crash in the tidy domed rondavels (round huts). The huts have simple wood beds with foam mattresses and unique walls with meshed cut-outs that let light and heavenly evening breezes in. Throw in the town's best toilets and showers, a cooking shelter and electricity until 10pm, and your decision is an easy one.

Oasis Lodge (☎ 0729-954672; s/tw KSh3000/4000; ⛱) The German owner doesn't extend the warmest of welcomes and neither do his dated rooms. The best asset is the enticing pool, which nonguests might, if they ask politely and pay KSh500, be allowed to wallow in.

Cold Drink Hotel (meals KSh50-110) Not just cold drinks but also, according to locals, the finest eating experience in all of Turkana country. The mama who runs it whips up a mean bowl of rice, potatoes and meat for KSh100.

If you ask around, you may find a villager who'll cook up a meal of Nile perch for you in their home.

GETTING THERE & AWAY
Trucks, loaded with fish and soon-to-be smelly passengers, leave Loyangalani for Maralal (KSh1000 to KSh1500, 10 to 12 hours) around once or twice a week at best. Trucks heading in any other direction are even rarer.

If you're travelling in your own vehicle, you have two options to reach Marsabit: continue northeast from Loyangalani across the dark stones of the Chalbi Desert towards North Horr, or head 67km south towards South Horr and take the eastern turn-off near Devil's Hand. The 270km Chalbi route (10 to 12 hours) is hard in the dry season and impossible after rain. It's also wise to ask for directions every chance you get, otherwise it's easy to take the wrong track and not realise until hours later. The 241km southern route (six to seven hours) via Devil's Hand, the Karoli Desert and Kargi is composed of compacted sands and is marginally less difficult in the rainy season.

Sibiloi National Park
A Unesco World Heritage Site and probably Kenya's most remote **national park** (www.kws .org/sibiloi.html; adult/child US$20/10), Sibiloi is lo-

cated up the eastern shore of Lake Turkana and covers 1570 sq km. It was here that Dr Richard Leakey discovered the skull of a *Homo habilis* believed to be 2½ million years old, and where others have unearthed evidence of *Homo erectus*. Despite the area's fascinating prehistory, fossil sites and wonderful arid ecosystem, the difficulties involved in getting this far north tend to discourage visitors, which is a real shame. It seems slightly ironic that the so-called 'Cradle of Mankind' is now almost entirely unpopulated.

The National Museums of Kenya maintain a small museum and **Koobi Fora** (www.kfrp.com), a research base that is often home to permanent researchers, visiting scientists and students. It's usually possible to sleep in one of the base's **bandas** (per person KSh1000) or to pitch a tent in one of the **campsites** (KSh200).

It's best to come in July and August, when the ferocious temperatures break slightly and when activity increases at Koobi Fora. Contact the staff of the Loyangalani Desert Museum, the **KWS** (kws@ kws.org) and **NMK** (☎ 020-3742131; www.museums. or.ke; PO Box 40658, Nairobi) before venturing in this direction.

In the dry season it's a tricky seven-hour drive north from Loyangalani to Sibiloi. You will need a guide from either KWS or the Loyangalani Desert Museum; Alex Lenapir (☎ 0726-470002), who works at the museum, is a good bet).

MARICH TO TURKANA'S WESTERN SHORE
Despite boasting some of northern Kenya's greatest attributes, such as copious kilometres of Jade Sea shoreline, striking volcanic landscapes and vivid Turkana tribes, this remote corner of the country has seen relatively few visitors. With security on the mend there's now a unique opportunity for independent travellers to explore here, thanks to regular public transport currently covering the breadth of the region. The only downside is that you can't get your vehicle across the lake or into Sudan, which makes for a lot of backtracking.

Marich
The spectacular descent from Marich Pass through the lush, cultivated Cherangani Hills leads to arid surroundings, with saisol

---

DID YOU KNOW?

- Lake Turkana's shoreline is longer than Kenya's entire Indian Ocean coast.

- The lake's water level was over 100m higher some 10,000 years ago and used to feed the mighty Nile.

- The first Europeans to reach the lake were Austrian explorers Teleki and von Höhnel in 1888. They proudly named it Lake Rudolf, after the Austrian Crown Prince at the time. It wasn't until the 1970s that the Swahili name Turkana was adopted.

---

plants, cactus trees and acacias lining both the road and the chocolate-brown Kerio River. Just north, the minuscule village of Marich, near the A1's junction with the B4 Kerio Valley road, marks your entrance into northern Kenya.

SIGHTS & ACTIVITIES
Although the northern plains may beckon, it's worth leashing the 4WD and heading into the hills for some eye-popping and leg-loving trekking action. **Mt Sekerr** (3326m) is a few kilometres northwest of Marich and can be climbed comfortably in a three-day round trip via the agricultural plots of the Pokot tribe, passing through forest and open moors. The views from the top are magnificent in clear weather.

The **Marich Pass Field Studies Centre** offers English-speaking Pokot and Turkana guides for half-day (KSh550), full-day (KSh750) and overnight (KSh1000) treks. The guides can also help you explore the numerous small **caves** dotted around the hills, most of which have special significance for the local Pokot.

If you'd rather explore with your vehicle, you can head southeast from Marich past Sigor and check out the **Elgeyo Escarpment**, which rises above the Kerio Valley to more than 1830m in places, and offers spectacular views and waterfalls. At the foot of the escarpment (and accessible by *matatu*) is **Lomut** and its fascinating Saturday market, which brings together the pastoral Pokot from the northern plains and the farming Pokot from the southern hills.

About 15km north of Marich along the A1 Hwy to Lokichar is the turn-off for **Nasolot** National Reserve (admission adult/child US$15/5) and **Turkwel Gorge** (admission incl with Nasolot NR). Although the reserve is home to elephants, lesser kudus, lions and leopards, you'll likely only spot the diminutive dik-diks bounding by the roadside. The main attraction is the gorge itself, with towering rock walls and plenty of pretty precipices. The imposing hydroelectric dam sits about 23km from the reserve gate, which is 6km off the A1. Those without vehicles are allowed to hike in the park with an escort (free with reserve admission). With security back under control, the KWS is hoping to soon reopen the campsites.

SLEEPING & EATING
The only reasonable accommodation between Marich and Lokichar is at **Marich Pass Field Studies Centre** (www.gg.rhul.ac.uk/MarichPass; PO Box 564, Kapenguria; camping KSh360, dm KSh420, s/tw KSh1450/1950, with shared bathroom KSh900/1240), which is well signposted just north of Marich and the A1's junction with the B4. Essentially a residential facility for visiting student groups, it's also a great place for independent travellers to base their adventures. The centre occupies a beautiful site alongside the misty Morun River and is surrounded by dense bush and woodland. The birdlife is prolific, monkeys and baboons have the run of the place, and warthogs, buffaloes, antelopes and elephants are occasional visitors. Facilities include a secure campsite with drinking water, toilets, showers and firewood, as well as a tatty dorm and simple, comfortable *bandas*.

GETTING THERE & AWAY
The road from Kitale via Makutano is the oh-so-scenic A1 Hwy, which is often described as 'Kenya's most spectacular tarmac road'. The buses plying the A1 between Kitale and Lodwar can drop you anywhere along the route, whether at Marich, the field studies centre or at the turn-off to Nasolot National Reserve. You may be asked to pay the full fare to Lodwar (KSh600), but a smile and some patient negotiating should reduce the cost.

Between Marich and Lokichar the A1 is a bumpy mess of corrugated dirt and lonely islands of tarmac. The first 40km north of Lokichar is better but you'll still spend more time on the shoulder than on the road. The opposite is true for the remaining 60km to Lodwar, where patches outnumber potholes and driving is straightforward.

KENYA

The security situation is in a constant state of flux in this area. At the time of research convoys were not required and the situation was considered stable even though guns were far more visible in civilian hands on this side of the lake than the east side (we even saw a 12 year old trotting around with his camels and a Kalashnikov!).

Lodwar
☎ 054

Besides Lokichoggio near the Sudan border, Lodwar is the only town of any size in the northwest. Barren volcanic hills skirted by traditional Turkana dwellings sit north of town and make for impressive early morning sunrise spots. Lodwar has outgrown its days as just an isolated administrative outpost of the Northern Frontier District, and has now become the major service centre for the region. If you're visiting Lake Turkana, you'll find it convenient to stay here for at least one night.

The Kenya Commercial Bank (no ATM) changes cash and travellers cheques. For internet surf on over to **Turkana Cyber Café** (per hr KSh180; ⏱ 7.30am-7pm Mon-Sat).

There's little to do in the town itself, but the atmosphere is not altogether unpleasant if you can stand the heat, and just listening to the garrulous locals is entertainment in itself. The small market is a good place to watch women weaving baskets, and there's an endless stream of Turkana hawkers who wander around town selling the usual souvenirs.

SLEEPING & EATING

Nawoitorong Guest House (☎ 054-21208; camping KSh200, s/tw/tr with shared bathroom KSh500/800/900, s/tw cottages from KSh800/1600) Built entirely out of local materials and run by a local women's group, Nawoitorong is an excellent option, and the only one for campers. Thatched roofs alleviate the need for fans and all rooms have mozzie nets. There's a pleasant restaurant that needs plenty of notice. Ask here about organising onward transport.

Hotel Splash (☎ 020-8017922; PO Box 297, Lodwar; s/tw KSh500/700) Each room at this immaculate hotel has double swinging cowboy doors and is named after a less than pleasant African country – choose from Nigeria, Cameroon, Libya or Rumtek – wherever that might be.

Turkwel Lodge (☎ 0735-459530; s/tw KSh500/700, cottages s/d KSh950/1350) Turkwel offers spacious rooms containing fans and nets, but lacks the crisp, clean feel of its neighbour, Hotel Splash. Some beds are a bit of an Ikea slat experiment gone horribly wrong. There's secure parking and roomy cottages at the rear, but it's overpriced and the attached bar is noisy.

Turkwel Hotel (meals KSh60-210) The green lentil curry is particularly good, but you have to get your order in about three hours prior! Oh, and don't forget to order the chapattis at the same time. Local dishes require less waiting and are some of the best in town.

GETTING THERE & AWAY

Several companies have daily buses to Kitale (KSh600, 8½ hours) which depart nightly between 5pm and 7pm (most services pick up passengers near the New Salama Hotel), while *matatus* serve Kalokol (KSh150, one hour) and Lokichoggio (KSh400, three hours).

Eliye Springs

Spring water percolates out of crumbling bluffs and oodles of palms bring a taste of the tropics to the remote sandy shores of Lake Turkana. Down on the slippery shore children play in the lake's warm waters while Central Island lurks magically on the distant horizon.

Beneath the bluff, the skeleton of an old beach resort (day visitors KSh200) sits half eaten by its surroundings and makes for an interesting place to drop your tent. Locals now manage the leftovers and charge KSh500 for camping in your own tent or you can hire one of theirs for an additional KSh400. Besides the spring water there are no facilities, so you'll have to be entirely self-sufficient.

GETTING THERE & AWAY

The turn-off for Eliye Springs is signposted a short way along the Lodwar–Kalokol road. The gravels are easy to follow until they suddenly peter out and you're faced with a fork in the road – stay left. The rest of the way is a mix of gravel, deep sand and even deeper sand, which can turn into a muddy nightmare in the wet season. Over the really bad sections locals have constructed a 'road' out of palm fronds which means that on a good day normal saloon cars can even make it here (though expect to do a bit of pushing and shoving).

If you don't have your own vehicle, you can usually arrange a car and driver in Lodwar for about KSh5000 including waiting time. Very occasionally you might find a truck travelling there for which a seat on top of the load will set you back about KSh150, but be prepared for a long wait back out again!

Ferguson's Gulf

Ferguson's Gulf, while more accessible than Eliye Springs has none of its southern neighbour's tropical charm. Fishing boats in various states of disrepair litter its grubby western beach and a definite feeling of bleakness pervades.

Birdlife is prolific, particularly in March and April, when thousands of European migratory birds stop here on their way north. There are also hippos and crocodiles so seek local advice before diving in.

If you're planning on visiting Central Island National Park or Sibiloi National Park, this is the best place to arrange a boat.

Set on the eastern shore, Lake Turkana Lodge has long since gone to lodge Heaven but the remnants are now managed by the local community who charge KSh500 for camping and an insane KSh1500 to sleep in the shell of the building. There are no facilities whatsoever.

Otherwise you should be able to find some very primitive, but cheaper, accommodation in the nearby village of **Kalokol**.

GETTING THERE & AWAY

Few people in Lodwar have heard of Ferguson's Gulf so you need to ask around for transport to nearby Kalokol, which is 75km along a good stretch of tarmac. Ferguson's Gulf is only a few kilometres from there. *Matatus* to Kalokol cost KSh150 or a taxi direct to Ferguson's Gulf will be around KSh4000 with waiting time.

Central Island National Park

Bursting from the depths of Lake Turkana and home to thousands of living dinosaurs is the Jurassic world of Central Island Volcano. Last seen belching molten sulphur and steam just over three decades ago, it is one of the most otherworldly places in Kenya. Quiet today, its stormy volcanic history is told by the numerous craters scarring its weathered facade. Several craters have coalesced to form two sizeable lakes; one of which is home to thousands of fish that occur nowhere else.

Both a **national park** (adult/child US$20/10) and Unesco World Heritage Site, Central Island is an intriguing place to visit and budding Crocodile Dundees will love the 14,000 or so Nile crocodiles, some of which are massive.

Camping (adult/child US$15/5) is possible and, unlike on South Island National Park, there are trees to tie your tent to. However, there's no water or any other facilities, so come prepared.

Hiring a boat from Ferguson's Gulf is the only real option to get here. Depending on what you drive up in, locals can ask anywhere from KSh6000 to KSh20,000 for the trip. A fair price is KSh6500 for a motorboat – don't ever think about being cheap and taking a sailboat. The 10km trip and sudden squalls that terrorise the lake's waters aren't to be taken lightly. Once you've found a boat (not as easy as it sounds) you have the additional problem of finding some fuel. You should also visit the KWS office, a couple of kilometres out of Kalokol towards Ferguson's Gulf, to pick up a guide and get the latest low-down on the island.

LOKICHOGGIO

Although the A1 Hwy from Lodwar to Lokichoggio via the UN refugee camps at Kakuma has been off limits to everyone but armed aid convoys for the last several years, improved security has meant that the odd intrepid traveller is now able to taste this remote northwest corner of Kenya. Remember that it's imperative to check with locals, NGOs and police in Lodwar before heading off.

The perfect tarmac between Lodwar and Lokichoggio is almost a sight in itself – simply transcendent! As you head northwest from Lodwar, you'll wind through some rocky bluffs before dropping into a vast valley resembling a lush lawn in wet season and a white sea during drier periods. After passing through the Pelekech Range's stratified slopes that mark the valley's western side, you'll see a dramatic and seemingly fictitious horizon of sharp mountainous peaks beyond the numerous refugee camps at Kakuma. In reality your eyes are making mountains out of mole hills, as the seemingly large peaks are only 100m- to 200m-high volcanic cinder cones.

Along the entire route you'll encounter rather marvellous Turkana people in striking tribal attire, either walking the roadside, selling sacks of charcoal or resting in the shade of lonely trees. Your steady gaze at these colourful souls will only be broken by the odd termite mound mystifyingly giving you the middle finger.

KENYA

Despite being backed by the impressive Mogila Range, Lokichoggio itself is rather unattractive. However, what it lacks in looks it makes up for in aid activity, with the World Food Program (WFP), UN and other NGOs basing their Sudanese operations here.

Lokichoggio has a post office, but no banks. The need to house NGO workers has resulted in some pretty plush accommodation options being added to the mix; **Trackmark Camp** (☎ 054-32245; lokicamp@yahoo .com; full board tents s US$50, bandas s/d US$55/80; ✉ ▯ ▣) is an absolute haven despite the junkie name, while **Makuti Bar** (☎ 0722-257262; A1 Hwy; d with shared bathroom KSh400-500) is the only reasonable budget option in town.

Petrol is readily available and costs KSh10 less per litre than in Lodwar. The border with Sudan was closed at the time of writing – check for updates at Lodwar's military post.

KENYA DIRECTORY

ACCOMMODATION

Kenya has a good range of accommodation options, from basic cubicle hotels overlooking city bus stands to luxury tented camps hidden away in the national parks. There are also all kinds of campsites, budget tented camps, simple *bandas* (often wooden huts) and cottages scattered around the parks and rural areas.

Where appropriate accommodation options are split into budget, midrange and top-end categories for ease of reference. In general, a budget double room is anything under KSh1000. You can pay as little as KSh150 for four walls and a bed, with foam mattress and shared squat toilet; for KSh400 and up you'd usually get a private bathroom, and at the upper end of the scale shower heaters and breakfast may be on offer. Surprisingly, bedding, towels and soap are almost always provided however much you pay, though cleanliness varies widely and toilet seats can be rare luxuries.

In most of the country, midrange accommodation falls between KSh1000 and KSh3500 for a double room – the major exception to this is Nairobi, where you can pay anything up to KSh6000 for the same standards. In this bracket you'd usually expect breakfast, private bathroom, telephone and good-size double beds with proper mattresses; the more you pay the more facilities you get, from restaurants and bars to TVs, hot showers and the odd swimming pool.

Everything over KSh3500 (or US$80 in Nairobi) counts as top end, and what you get for your money varies enormously. Once you hit US$100 you should count on breakfast, TV, phone, air-con (on the coast), room service and toiletries as standard, and in the upper realms of the price range the extras can include anything from complimentary minibars to casinos, jacuzzis and free activities. The most expensive places are the exclusive getaways tucked away in national parks and other remote corners of the country, which can exceed US$600 for a double but don't necessarily include all the trappings you'd expect elsewhere.

Bandas

Bandas are basic huts and cottages, usually with some kind of kitchen and bathroom, that offer excellent value for budget travellers. Some are wooden huts, some are thatched stone huts and some are small brick bungalows with solar-powered lights; facilities range from basic dorms and squat toilets to kitchens and hot water provided by wood-burning stoves. The cost varies from US$10 to US$20 per person. You'll need to bring all your own food, drinking water, bedding and firewood.

Camping

There are many opportunities for camping in Kenya and it is worth considering bringing a tent with you, although gear can also be hired in Nairobi and around Mt Kenya. There are KWS campsites in just about every national park or reserve, though these are usually very basic. There will be a toilet block with a couple of pit toilets, and usually a water tap, but very little else.

Hostels

The only youth hostel affiliated with Hostelling International (HI) is in Nairobi. It has good basic facilities and is a pleasant enough place

---

LEGAL AGE

- Age of majority: 18 years
- Voting age: 18 years
- Age of consent (heterosexual): 16 years
- Age of criminal responsibility: 8 years
- Drinking age: 18 years

PRACTICALITIES

■ Major newspapers and magazines in Kenya include the *Daily Nation*, the *East African Standard*, the *East African*, the *Weekly Review* and the *New African*.

■ KBC Radio broadcasts across the country on various FM frequencies. Most major towns also have their own local music and talkback stations, and the BBC World Service is easily accessible.

■ KBC and NTV are the main national TV stations; the CNN, Sky and BBC networks are also widely available on satellite or cable (DSTV).

■ Kenyan televisual equipment uses the standard European PAL video system.

■ Kenya uses the 240V system, with square three-pin sockets as used in the UK. Bring a universal adaptor if you need to charge your phone or run other appliances.

■ Kenya uses the metric system; distances are in kilometres and most weights are in kilograms.

---

to stay, but there are plenty of other cheaper choices that are just as good. Other places that call themselves 'youth hostels' are not members of HI and standards are very variable.

Hotels & Guesthouses

Real budget hotels (often known as 'board and lodgings' to distinguish them from 'hotelis', which are often only restaurants) are widely used as brothels and tend to be very rundown. Security at these places is virtually nonexistent; the better ones are set around courtyards and are clean if not exactly comfortable.

Safari Lodges & Tented Camps

Hidden away inside or on the edges of national parks are some fantastic safari lodges. These are usually visited as part of organised safaris, and you'll pay much more if you just turn up and ask for a room. Some of the older places trade heavily on their more glorious past, but the best places feature five-star rooms, soaring *makuti*-roofed bars and restaurants overlooking waterholes full of wildlife.

ACTIVITIES
Ballooning

Balloon trips in the wildlife parks are an absolutely superb way of seeing the savannah plains and, of course, the animals. The almost ghostly experience of floating silently above the plains with a 360-degree view of everything beneath you is incomparable, and it's definitely worth saving up your shillings. The flights typically set off at dawn and go for about 1½ hours, after which you put down for a champagne breakfast. You'll then

be taken on a wildlife drive in a support vehicle and returned to your lodge. Ask at your lodge for information about balloon trips.

Flights are currently available in the Masai Mara National Reserve for around US$500. Check out the following companies:

Governors' Balloon Safaris (☎ 020-2734000; www .governorscamp.com) This company operates out of Little Governors' Camp in the Mara.

Transworld Balloon Safaris (☎ 020-2713333; www .transworldsafaris.com/ballooning.php) Based at the Sarova Mara Lodge in the Mara.

Cycling

An increasing number of companies offer cycling and mountain-biking trips in Kenya. Popular locations include the edge of the Masai Mara National Reserve, Hell's Gate National Park, the Central Highlands and the Kerio Valley.

The best operator is **Bike Treks** (☎ 020-446371; www.biketreks.co.ke), which offers specialised trips for around US$120 per day.

Diving & Snorkelling

There is a string of marine national parks spread out along the coast with plenty of opportunities for snorkelling and scuba diving. There are distinct seasons for diving in Kenya. October to March is the best time, but during June, July and August it's often impossible to dive due to the poor visibility caused by heavy silt flow from some of the rivers on the coast.

If you aren't certified to dive, almost every hotel and resort on the coast can arrange an open-water diving course. By international standards, they aren't cheap – a five-day PADI certification course will cost between US$350 and US$500. Trips for certified divers including two dives go for around US$100.

Fishing

The **Kenya Fisheries Department** (Map pp282-3; ☎ 020-3742320; Museum Hill Rd, Nairobi), opposite National Museums of Kenya, operates a number of fishing camps in various parts of the country. However, they're difficult to reach without your own vehicle and directions from the Fisheries Department, from which you'll also need to get a fishing licence.

The deep-sea fishing on the coast is some of the best in the world, and various private companies and resorts in Shimoni, Diani Beach, Watamu and Malindi can arrange fishing trips. For freshwater fishing, there are huge Nile perch as big as a person in Lakes Victoria and Turkana, and some of the trout fishing around the Aberdares and Mt Kenya is quite exceptional.

Gliding & Flying

The **Gliding Club of Kenya** (Map p347; ☎ 0733-760331; gliding@africaonline.co.ke; PO Box 926, Nyeri), near Nyeri in the Central Highlands, offers silent glides over the Aberdares.

Flying lessons are easily arranged in Nairobi, and are much cheaper than in Europe, the USA and Australasia. Contact the **Aero Club of East Africa** (☎ 020-608990) and **Ninety-Nines Flying Club** (☎ 020-500277), both at Wilson Airport.

Sailing

Kilifi, Mtwapa and Mombasa all have sailing clubs, and smaller freshwater clubs can also be found at Lake Naivasha and Lake Victoria, which both have excellent windsurfing and sailing. If you're experienced, you may pick up some crewing at the various yacht clubs, although you'll need to become a temporary member. While it isn't hands-on, a traditional dhow trip out of Lamu is an unforgettable experience.

Trekking & Climbing

For proper mountain trekking, Mt Kenya (p352) is the obvious choice, but other promising and relatively unexplored walking territory includes Mt Elgon (p384) on the Ugandan border and the upper reaches of the Aberdares (p346).

Get hold of a copy of Lonely Planet's *Trekking in East Africa*. Also be sure to contact the **Mountain Club of Kenya** (MCK; ☎ 020-602330; www.mck.or.ke) in Nairobi.

Savage Wilderness Safaris (☎ 020-521590; www.whitewaterkenya.com; Sarit Centre, PO Box 1000, Westlands, Nairobi) offers mountaineering trips to Mt Kenya and rock climbing at sites around the country, as well as some more unusual options such as caving.

Water Sports

Conditions on Kenya's coast are ideal for windsurfing – the country's offshore reefs protect the waters, and the winds are usually reasonably strong and constant. Some of the larger resorts have water-sports centres giving visitors the opportunity to try out absolutely everything from jet skis and banana boats to bodyboarding and traditional surfing.

White-Water Rafting

The Athi/Galana River has substantial rapids, chutes and waterfalls and there are also possibilities on the Tana River and Ewaso Ngiro River near Isiolo. The most exciting times for a white-water rafting trip are from late October to mid-January and from early April to late July, when water levels are highest.

The people to talk to are **Savage Wilderness Safaris** (☎ 020-521590; www.whitewaterkenya.com; Sarit Centre, PO Box 1000, Westlands, Nairobi), run by the charismatic Mark Savage. Depending on water levels, rafting trips of up to 450km and three weeks' duration can be arranged, although most trips last one to four days and cover up to 80km.

BUSINESS HOURS

Most government offices are open Monday to Friday from 8.30am to 1pm and from 2pm to 5pm. Post offices, shops and services open roughly from 8am to 5pm Monday to Friday and 9am to noon on Saturday. Banking hours are 9am to 3pm Monday to Friday and 9am to 11am Saturday; some smaller branches may only open on the first and last Saturday of the month.

Restaurant opening hours vary according to the type of establishment: as a rule cafés and cheap Kenyan canteens will open at around 6am or 7am and close in the early evening, while more expensive ethnic restaurants will be open from 11am to 10pm daily, sometimes with a break between lunch and dinner. Lunch and dinner hours are roughly 11am to 2pm and 5pm to 9pm, respectively.

THANK YOU FOR NOT SMOKING

Following the passage of the Tobacco Control Act in 2008, smoking is no longer allowed in restaurants, bars and public areas. While enforcement varies across the country, note that police are particularly vigilant in Nairobi, and will hand out large fines without a second thought. Be sure to take stock of your surroundings before lighting up as it could be the most expensive cigarette of your life.

Bars that don't serve food are open from around 6pm until late, while nightclubs open their doors around 9pm and can keep going until 6am or later on weekends.

CHILDREN

The coast is the best region to aim for, with most resorts offering European-standard kids' facilities and dedicated staff to take them off your hands once in a while.

Local attitudes towards children vary in Kenya just as they do in the West: screaming babies on *matatus* elicit all the usual sighs and tuttings, but usually kids will be welcomed anywhere that's not an exclusively male preserve, especially by women with families of their own.

CLIMATE

Kenya's diverse geography means that temperature, rainfall and humidity vary widely, but there are effectively four distinct zones.

The hot, rainy plateau of western Kenya has rainfall throughout the year, the heaviest usually during April when as much as 200mm may be recorded, and the lowest in January with an average of 40mm. Temperatures range from a minimum of 14°C to 18°C to a maximum of 30°C to 36°C throughout the year.

In the temperate Rift Valley and Central Highlands, average temperatures vary from a minimum of 10°C to 14°C to a maximum of 22°C to 28°C. Rainfall varies from a minimum of 20mm in July to 200mm in April, falling in essentially two seasons – March to the beginning of June (the 'long rains') and October to the end of November (the 'short rains'). Mt Kenya and the Aberdare mountains are the country's main water catchments, with falls of up to 3000mm per year.

In the semiarid bushlands of northern and eastern Kenya, temperatures vary from highs of up to 40°C during the day to less than 20°C at night. July is usually the driest month, and November the wettest. The average annual rainfall varies between 250mm and 500mm.

The consistently humid coast region has rainfall averages from 20mm in February to around 300mm in May. The average annual rainfall is between 1000mm and 1250mm (less in drought years). Average temperatures vary little during the year, ranging from 22°C to 30°C.

COURSES

If you intend to spend considerable time in Kenya, learning Swahili is an excellent idea. The best language school is run by the Anglican Church of Kenya (ACK). Taking a language course (or any course) also entitles you to a 'Pupils' Pass', an immigration permit allowing continuous stays of up to 12 months. The following language schools offer courses:

ACK Language & Orientation School (Map pp282-3; ☎ 020-2721893; www.ackenya.org/ack_language_school.htm; Bishops Rd, Upper Hill, PO Box 47429, Nairobi) Full-time courses of varying levels last 14 weeks and take up five hours a day. More flexible is private tuition, which is available on a part-time schedule.

Language Center Ltd (Map p292; ☎ 020-3870610; www.language-cntr.com/welcome.shtml; Ndemi Close, off Ngong Rd, PO Box 40661, Nairobi) Another good option, the language centre offers a variety of study options ranging from private hourly lessons to daily group courses.

CUSTOMS

There are strict laws about taking wildlife products out of Kenya. The export of products made from elephants, rhinos and sea turtles are prohibited. The collection of coral is also not allowed. Ostrich eggs will also be confiscated unless you can prove you bought them from a certified ostrich farm. Always check to see what permits are required, especially for the export of any plants, insects and shells.

The usual regulations apply to items you can bring into the country: 50 cigars, 200 cigarettes, 250g of pipe tobacco, 1L of alcohol, 250mL of perfume and other personal items, such as cameras, laptop computers and binoculars. Obscene publications are banned, which may extend to some lads' magazines.

DANGERS & ANNOYANCES

While Kenya is generally a safe destination, there are still plenty of pitfalls for the unwary or inexperienced traveller, from everyday irritations to more serious threats. A little street sense goes a long way here, and getting the latest local information is essential wherever you intend to travel.

Banditry

Wars in Somalia, Sudan and Ethiopia have all had their effect on the stability and safety of northern and northeastern Kenya. AK-47s have been flowing into the country for many years, and the newspapers are filled with stories of hold-ups, shoot-outs, cattle rustling and general lawlessness. Bandits and poachers infiltrating from Somalia have made the northeast of the country particularly dangerous, and it has gotten worse in recent years due to a number of complicated factors.

In the northwest, the main problem is armed tribal wars and cattle rustling across the Sudanese border. There are Kenyan *shifta* (bandits) too, of course, but cross-border problems seem to account for most of the trouble in the north of the country.

Despite all the headlines, tourists are rarely targeted, as much of the violence and robberies take place far from the main tourist routes. Security has also improved considerably in previously high-risk areas, such as the Isiolo–Marsabit, Marsabit–Moyale and Malindi–Lamu routes. However, you should check the situation locally before taking these roads, or travelling between Garsen and Garissa or Thika.

The areas along the Sudanese and Ethiopian borders are very risky, although most visitors are very unlikely to have any reason to go there in the first place.

Crime

Even the staunchest Kenyan patriot will readily admit that the country's biggest problem is crime. It ranges from petty snatch theft and mugging to violent armed robbery, carjacking and, of course, white-collar crime and corruption. As a visitor you needn't feel paranoid, but you should always keep your wits about you, particularly at night.

The best advice for when you're walking around cities and towns is don't carry anything valuable with you. Most hotels provide a safe or secure place for valuables, although you should be cautious of the security at some budget places.

Cheap digital watches and plastic sunglasses can be bought in Kenya for under KSh100 and you won't miss them if they get taken.

While pickpocketing and bag-snatching are the most common crimes, armed muggings do occur in Nairobi and on the coast. However, they usually happen at night or in remote areas, so always take taxis after dark or along lonely dirt roads. Conversely, snatch-and-run crimes happen more in crowds. If you suddenly feel there are too many people around you, or think you are being followed, dive straight into a shop and ask for help.

In the event of a crime, you should report it to the police, but this can be a real procedure. You'll need to get a police report if you intend to make an insurance claim. In the event of a snatch theft, think twice before yelling 'Thief!'. It's not unknown for people to administer summary justice on the spot, often with fatal results for the criminal.

Although crime is a fact of life in Kenya, it needn't spoil your trip. Above all, don't make the mistake of distrusting every Kenyan just because of a few bad apples – the honest souls you meet will far outweigh any crooks who cross your path.

Scams

At some point in Kenya you'll almost certainly come across people who play on the emotions and gullibility of foreigners. Nairobi is a particular hot spot, with 'friendly' approaches a daily if not hourly occurrence. It's OK to talk to these people if they're not actively hassling you, but you should always ignore any requests for money.

Be sceptical of strangers who claim to recognise you in the street, especially if they're vague about exactly where they know you from – it's unlikely that any ordinary person is going to be *that* excited by seeing you twice. Anyone who makes a big show of inviting you into the hospitality of their home also probably has ulterior motives. The usual trick is to bestow some kind of gift upon the delighted traveller, who is then emotionally blackmailed into reciprocating to the order of several hundred shillings.

Tourists with cars also face a whole set of potential rip-offs. Don't trust people who gesticulate wildly to you as you are driving along, indicating your front wheels are wobbling; if you stop, chances are you'll be relieved of your valuables. Another trick is to splash oil on your wheels, then tell you the wheel bearings, differential or something else has failed, and direct you to a nearby garage where their friends will 'fix' the problem – for a substantial fee, of course.

Terrorism

Kenya has twice been subject to terrorist attacks: in August 1998 the US embassy in Nairobi was bombed, and in November 2002 the Paradise Hotel, north of Mombasa, was car-bombed at the same time as a rocket attack on an Israeli jet. While these events caused a brief panic in the tourist industry, it now seems they were isolated incidents and that Western travellers to Kenya can expect to have a trouble-free time in the country. Visitors to the predominantly Muslim coast region should be aware that anti-American sentiment can run high here, but actual violence against foreigners is highly unlikely.

EMBASSIES & CONSULATES
Kenyan Embassies & Consulates

Australia (☎ 02-62474788; www.kenya.asn.au; Manpower Bldg, 33-35 Ainslie Ave, Canberra, ACT 2601)

Austria (☎ 01-7123919; www.kenyamission-vienna .com; Neulinggasse 29/8, 1030 Vienna)

Canada (☎ 613-5631773; www.kenyahighcommission .ca; 415 Laurier Ave, East Ottawa, Ontario, KIN 6R4)

Ethiopia (☎ 01-610033; kengad@telecom.net.et; Fikre Miriam Rd, PO Box 3301, Addis Ababa)

France (☎ 01-56622525; www.kenyaembassyparis.org; 3 Rue Freycinet, 75116 Paris)

Germany (☎ 030-25922660; embassy-kenya.bn@ wwmail.de; Markgrafenstr 63, 10969 Berlin)

India (☎ 011-26146537; www.kenyamission-delhi.com; 34 Paschimi Marg, Vasant Vihar, 10057 New Delhi)

Israel (☎ 03-57546333; kenya04@ibm.net; 15 Rehov Abba Hillel Silver, Ramat Gan 52522, PO Box 52136, Tel Aviv)

Italy (☎ 396-8082714; www.embassyofkenya.it; Via Archmede 165, 00197, Rome)

Japan (☎ 03-37234006; www.kenyarep-jp.com; 3-24-3 Yakumo, Meguro-Ku, Tokyo 152)

Netherlands (☎ 070-3504215; Niewe Parklaan 21, 2597, The Hague)

South Africa (☎ 012-3622249; 302 Brooks St, Menlo Park, 0081, Pretoria)

Sudan (☎ 0155-772801; www.kenembsud.org; Block 1, 516, West Giraif, Street 60, Khartoum)

Tanzania (☎ 022-266 8285; www.kenyahighcomtz.org; 127 Mafinga St, Kinondoni, PO Box 5231, Dar es Salaam)

Uganda (☎ 041-258235; Plot No 41, Nakasero Rd, PO Box 5220, Kampala)

UK (☎ 020-76362371; www.kenyahighcommission.net; 45 Portland Pl, London W1B 1AS)

USA (☎ 202-3876101; www.kenyaembassy.com; 2249 R St NW, Washington DC 20008)

Embassies & Consulates in Kenya

A selection of countries that maintain diplomatic missions in Kenya are listed below. Missions are located in Nairobi unless otherwise stated.

Australia High Commission (Map pp282-3; ☎ 020-445034; www.kenya.embassy.gov.au; ICIPE House, Riverside Dr, off Chiromo Rd)

Austria (Map pp284-5; ☎ 020-319076; City House, Wabera St)

Canada High Commission (☎ 020-3663000; www .nairobi.gc.ca; Limuru Rd, Gigiri)

Ethiopia (Map pp282-3; ☎ 020-2732050; State House Rd)

France (Map pp284-5; ☎ 020-316363; www.amba france-ke.org; Barclays Plaza, Loita St)

Germany (☎ 020-4262100; www.nairobi.diplo.de; 113 Riverside Dr)

India High Commission (Map pp284-5; ☎ 020-222566; www.hcinairobi.co.ke; Jeevan Bharati Bldg, Harambee Ave)

Ireland Honorary Consulate (Map pp282-3; ☎ 020-556647; www.dfa.ie; ICDL Rd, off Mombasa Rd)

Israel (Map pp282-3; ☎ 020-2722182; http://nairobi .mfa.gov.il; Bishops Rd)

Italy Embassy (Map pp284-5; ☎ 020-2247750; www .ambnairobi.esteri.it; International House, Mama Ngina St); Honorary Consulate (Map p308; ☎ 041-314705; Moi Ave, Mombasa)

Japan (Map pp284-5; ☎ 020-2898000; www.ke.emb -japan.go.jp; Mara Rd, Upper Hill)

Netherlands (☎ 020-4288000; http://kenia.nlembassy .org; Riverside Lane)

South Africa High Commission (☎ 020-2827100; Roshanmaer Pl, Lenana Rd)

Spain (Map pp284-5; ☎ 020-26568; embespke@mail .mae.es; International House, Mama Ngina St)

Sudan (Map pp282-3; ☎ 020-575159; www.sudan embassynrb.org; Kabernet Rd, off Ngong Rd))

Switzerland (Map pp284-5; ☎ 020-2228735; International House, Mama Ngina St)

Tanzania High Commission (Map pp284-5; ☎ 020-331056; Reinsurance Plaza, Aga Khan Walk)

Uganda Consular section (Map pp284-5; ☎ 020-311814; Uganda House, Kenyatta Ave); High Commission (☎ 020-4445420; Riverside Paddocks)

UK High Commission (Map pp282-3; ☎ 020-2844000; www.britishhighcommission.gov.uk/kenya; Upper Hill Rd)

USA (☎ 020-3636000; http://nairobi.usembassy.gov; United Nations Ave)

FESTIVALS & EVENTS

Major events happening around Kenya include the following:

Maulid Festival Falling in March or April for the next few years, this annual celebration of the prophet Mohammed's birthday is a huge event in Lamu town, drawing hundreds of visitors.

Rhino Charge (www.rhinoark.org) Charity cross-country rally in aid of Rhino Ark, pitting mad motorists against crazy obstacles. Held in June.

Tusker Safari Sevens (www.safarisevens.com) International rugby tournament held every June near Nairobi.

Kenya Music Festival (☎ 020-2712964) The country's longest-running music festival, held in Nairobi over 10 days in August.

Mombasa Carnival November street festival, with music, dance and other events.

East Africa Safari Rally (www.eastafricansafarirally .com) Classic car rally now in its 50th year, covering Kenya, Tanzania and Uganda using only pre-1971 vehicles. Held at the end of November.

GAY & LESBIAN TRAVELLERS

Even today there is still a widespread perception across much of Africa that homosexuality is somehow an un-African phenomenon, and negativity towards homosexuality is widespread. It goes on covertly, of course, but under Kenyan law homosexuality is still punishable by up to 14 years in prison. There are very few prosecutions under this law, but it's certainly better to be discreet; some local conmen do a good line in blackmail, picking up foreigners then threatening to expose them to the police! Although there are probably more gays and lesbians in Nairobi, the coast is more tolerant of gay relationships, at least privately.

The **Purple Roofs travel directory** (www.purpleroofs .com/africa/kenyata.html) lists a number of gay or gay-friendly tour companies in Kenya and around the world who may be able to help you plan your trip. For luxury all-inclusive packages, the travel agents **Atlantis Events** (www .atlantisevents.com) and **David Tours** (www.davidtours .com) can arrange anything from balloon safaris to luxurious coastal hideaways, all with a gay focus. For information, **Behind the Mask** (www .mask.org.za) is an excellent website covering gay issues and news from across Africa.

HOLIDAYS

All government offices and banks close on public holidays, and most shops and businesses will either close or run according to their usual Sunday opening hours. Popular events can cause a run on accommodation at the lower end of the budget scale, and transport may run less frequently or be more crowded than usual.

Muslim festivals are significant events along the coast. Many places to eat in the region close until after sundown during the Muslim fasting month of Ramadan, which runs for 30 days frk 21 August 2009, 11 August 2010 and 1 August 2011. The Maulid Festival (p332), marking the birth of the Prophet Mohammed, is also widely celebrated, especially on Lamu. This runs for five days from 9 March 2009, 26 February 2010 and 15 February 2011

Public Holidays
New Year's Day 1 January
Easter (Good Friday and Easter Monday) March/April
Labour Day 1 May
Madaraka (Self-Rule) Day 1 June
Moi Day 10 October
Kenyatta Day 20 October
Independence Day 12 December
Christmas Day 25 December
Boxing Day 26 December

INTERNET ACCESS

Email is firmly established in Kenya, although connection speeds fluctuate wildly, even in Nairobi. Most towns have at least one internet café where you can surf freely and access webmail accounts or instant messenger programs. In Nairobi or Mombasa you can pay as little as KSh1 per minute for access, but in rural areas and top-end hotels the rate can be as high as KSh20 per minute.

LEGAL MATTERS

All drugs except *miraa* are illegal in Kenya. Marijuana (commonly known as *bhang*) is widely available but highly illegal, and possession carries a penalty of up to 10 years in prison. Dealers are common on the beaches north and south of Mombasa, and frequently set up travellers for real or phoney cops to extort money. African prisons are unbelievably harsh places; don't take the risk.

Note that *miraa* is illegal in Tanzania, so if you do develop a taste for the stuff in Kenya you should leave it behind when heading south.

MAPS

Bookshops, especially the larger ones in Nairobi, are the best places to look for maps in Kenya. The *Tourist Map of Kenya* gives good detail, as does the *Kenya Route Map*; both cost around KSh250. Marco Polo's 1:1,000,000 *Shell Euro Karte Kenya* and Geocenter's

Kenya (1:1,000,000) are useful overview maps that are widely available in Europe. For those planning a longer trip in southern and East Africa, Michelin's 1:4,000,000 map 955 (Africa Central and South) is very useful.

MONEY

The unit of currency is the Kenyan shilling (KSh), which is made up of 100 cents. Notes in circulation are KSh1000, KSh500, KSh200, 100, KSh50 and KSh20, and there are also new coins of KSh40, KSh20, KSh10, KSh5 and KSh1 in circulation. Old coins are much bigger and heavier, and come in denominations of KSh5 (seven-sided) and KSh1. The old 50¢, 10¢ and 5¢ coins are now pretty rare, as most prices are whole-shilling amounts. Note that most public telephones accept only new coins. Locally the shilling is commonly known as a 'bob', after the old English term for a 1-shilling coin.

The shilling has been relatively stable over the last few years, maintaining fairly constant rates against a falling US dollar and a strong British pound. Both these currencies are easy to change throughout the country, as is the euro, which is rapidly replacing the US dollar as the standard currency quoted for hotel prices on the coast. Cash is easy and quick to exchange at banks and foreign exchange bureaus, but carries a higher risk of theft, while travellers cheques are replaceable, but not as widely accepted and often carry high commission charges. Carrying a combination of these and a Visa ATM card will ensure you're never stuck for cash.

ATMs

Virtually all banks in Kenya now have ATMs at most branches, but their usefulness to travellers varies widely. Barclays Bank has easily the most reliable ATMs for international withdrawals, with a large network of ATMs covering most major Kenyan towns. It supports MasterCard, Visa, Plus and Cirrus international networks.

Cash

While most major currencies are accepted in Nairobi and Mombasa, once away from these two centres you'll run into problems with currencies other than US dollars, British pounds or euros. Away from the coast, you may even struggle to change euros. Play it safe and carry US dollars – it makes life much simpler.

Credit Cards

Credit cards are becoming increasingly popular, with old fraud-friendly, fully manual swipe machines slowly being replaced by electronic systems that dial up for every transaction. While there's less chance of someone making extra copies of chits this way, the connections fail with tedious regularity. Visa and MasterCard are now widely accepted, but it would be prudent to stick to upmarket hotels, restaurants and shopping centres to use them.

Moneychangers

The best places to change money are foreign exchange or 'forex' bureaus, which can be found everywhere and usually don't charge commission. Watch out for differing small bill (US$10) and large bill (US$100) rates; the larger bills usually get the better rates.

Banks also change money, but they charge large commissions and there's a fee per travellers cheque, so you're better off carrying larger denominations. Travellers cheque rates may be better than at the bureaus, and you'll have the added bonus of being able to put your money away in the secure setting of the bank foyer. Amex has offices in Mombasa and Nairobi, where you can buy and sell Amex travellers cheques.

Tipping

Tipping is not common practice among Kenyans, but there's no harm in rounding up the bill by a few shillings if you're pleased with the service in a cheap restaurant. In tourist-oriented businesses a service charge of 10% is often added to the bill, along with the 16% VAT and 2% catering levy. Most tourist guides and all safari drivers and cooks will expect some kind of gratuity at the end of your tour or trip. As fares are negotiated in advance, taxi drivers do not need to be tipped unless they provide exceptional service.

PHOTOGRAPHY & VIDEO

Photographing people remains a sensitive issue in Kenya as some ethnic groups including the Maasai request money for you to take their photo. You should never get your camera out at border crossings or near government or army buildings – even bridges can sometimes

KENYA

be classed as sensitive areas. You may also be able to find memory cards and other accessories for digital and DV cameras in cities and large towns, but prices are high and quality is not guaranteed.

POST

The Kenyan postal system is run by the government Postal Corporation of Kenya, now rebranded as the dynamic-sounding **Posta** (www.posta.co.ke). Letters sent from Kenya rarely go astray but can take up to two weeks to reach Australia or the USA. Incoming letters to Kenya take anywhere from four days to a week to reach the poste-restante service in Nairobi.

If sent by surface mail, parcels take three to six months to reach Europe, while airmail parcels take around a week. Most things arrive eventually. Curios, clothes and textiles will be OK, but if your parcel contains anything of obvious value, send it by courier. Posta has its own courier service, EMS, which is considerably cheaper than the big international courier companies. The best place to send parcels from is the main post office in Nairobi.

TELEPHONE

The Kenyan fixed-line phone system, run by **Telkom Kenya** (www.telkom.co.ke), is more or less functional. International call rates from Kenya are relatively expensive, though you can save serious cash by using voiceover IP programs such as Skype. Operator-assisted calls are charged at the standard peak rate, but are subject to a three-minute minimum. You can always dial direct using a phone card. All phones should be able to receive incoming calls (the number is usually scrawled in the booth somewhere). The international dialling code for Kenya is ☎ 254.

More than two-thirds of all calls in Kenya are now made on mobile phones, and coverage is good in all but the furthest rural areas. Kenya uses the GSM 900 system, which is compatible with Europe and Australia but not with the North American GSM 1900 system. If you have a GSM phone, check with your service provider about using it in Kenya, and beware of high roaming charges. Remember that you will generally be charged for receiving calls abroad as well as for making them.

Alternatively, if your phone isn't locked into a network, you can pick up a prepaid starter pack from one of the Kenyan mobile-phone companies – the main players are **Safaricom** (www.safaricom.co.ke) and **Celtel** (www.ke.celtel.com). A SIM card costs about KSh100, and you can then buy top-up 'scratchcards' from shops and booths across the country. Cards come in denominations of KSh100 to KSh2000; an international SMS costs around KSh10, and voice charges vary according to tariff, time and destination of call.

Telkom Kenya phone cards can be used for prepaid calls – you dial the **access number** (☎ 0844) and enter in the number and passcode on the card. There are booths selling the cards all over the country. Cards come in the following denominations of KSh200, KSh500, KSh1000 and KSh2000, and call charges are slightly more expensive than for standard lines.

TIME

Time in Kenya is GMT/UTC plus three hours year-round. For further information, including Swahili time, see p613.

TOURIST INFORMATION
Local Tourist Offices

Considering the extent to which the country relies on tourism, it's incredible to think that, at the time of writing, there was still no tourist office in Nairobi. There are a handful of information offices elsewhere in the country, ranging from helpful private concerns to underfunded government offices; most can at least provide basic maps of the town and brochures on local businesses and attractions.

Diani Beach (Map p315; ☎ 040-3202234; Barclays Centre)

Lamu (Map p329; ☎ 042-633449; off Kenyatta Rd)

Malindi (Map p326; ☎ 042-20689; Malindi Centre, Lamu Rd)

Mombasa (Map p307; ☎ 041-225428; Moi Ave)

Tourist Offices Abroad

The Ministry of Tourism maintains a number of overseas offices. Most only provide information by telephone, post or email.

TRAVELLERS WITH DISABILITIES

Very few tourist companies and facilities are geared for disabled travellers, and those that are tend to be restricted to the expensive hotels and lodges. However, Kenyans are generally very accommodating, and willing to offer whatever assistance they can. Visually or hearing-impaired travellers, however, will find it very hard to get by without an able-bodied companion. There are no facilities that we are aware of catering specifically for visually or hearing-impaired travellers.

In Nairobi, only the ex-London taxis are spacious enough to accommodate a wheelchair, but many safari companies do regularly take disabled people out on safari. The travel agency **Travel Scene Services** (☎ 020-3871530; travelscene@insightkenya.com) has lots of experience with disabled travellers.

Many of the top-end beach resorts located on the coast have facilities for the disabled, whether it's a few token ramps or fully equipped rooms with handrails and bathtubs. Mount Kenya Safari Club has its own wheelchair for guests' use and in Amboseli National Park, **Ol Tukai Lodge** (☎ Nairobi 020-4445514; oltukai@mitsuminet.com) has two disabled-friendly cottages.

VISAS

Visas are now required by almost all visitors to Kenya, including Europeans, Australians, New Zealanders, Americans and Canadians, although citizens from a few smaller Commonwealth countries are exempt. Visas (US$50/€40/£30/Swiss Fr79) are valid for three months from the date of entry and can be obtained on arrival at Jomo Kenyatta International Airport in Nairobi. Tourist visas can be extended for a further three-month period – see right.

It's also possible to get visas from Kenyan diplomatic missions overseas, but you should apply well in advance, especially if you're doing it by mail. Visas are usually valid for entry within three months of the date of issue. Applications for Kenyan visas are simple and straightforward in Tanzania and Uganda, and payment is accepted in local currency. Visas can also be issued on arrival at the land borders with Uganda and Tanzania.

Under the East African partnership system, visiting Tanzania or Uganda and returning to Kenya does not invalidate a single-entry Kenyan visa, so there's no need to get a multiple-entry visa unless you plan to go further afield. The same applies to single-entry Tanzanian and Ugandan visas, though you do still need a separate visa for each country you plan to visit. Always check the latest entry requirements with embassies before travel.

Visa Extensions

Visas can be renewed at immigration offices during normal office hours, and extensions are usually issued on a same-day basis. Staff at the immigration offices are generally friendly and helpful, but the process takes a while. You'll need two passport photos and KSh2200 for a three-month extension. You also need to fill out a form registering as an alien if you're going to be staying more than 90 days. Immigration offices are only open Monday to Friday; note that the smaller offices may sometimes refer travellers back to Nairobi or Mombasa for visa extensions.

Local immigration offices:

Kisumu (Map p370; 1st fl, Reinsurance Plaza, cnr Jomo Kenyatta Hwy & Oginga Odinga Rd)

Lamu (Map p329; ☎ 042-633032) Off Kenyatta Rd.

Malindi (Map p326; ☎ 042-30876; Mama Ngina Rd)

Mombasa (Map p307; ☎ 041-311745; Uhuru ni Kari Bldg, Mama Ngina Dr)

Nairobi (Map pp284–5; ☎ 020-222022; Nyayo House, cnr Kenyatta Ave & Uhuru Hwy)

WOMEN TRAVELLERS

Within Kenyan society, women are poorly represented in positions of power, and the few high-profile women in politics run the same risks of violence as their male counterparts. However, in their day-to-day lives, Kenyans are generally respectful towards women, although solo women in bars will attract a lot of interest from would-be suitors. Most are just having a go and will give up if you tell them you aren't interested. The only place you are likely to have problems is at the beach resorts on the coast, where women may be approached by male prostitutes as well as local romeos. It's always best to cover your legs and shoulders when away from the beach so as not to offend local sensibilities.

With the upsurge in crime in Nairobi and along the coast, women should avoid walking around at night. The ugly fact is that while men are likely just to be robbed without violence, rape is a real risk for women. Lone night walks along the beach or through quiet city streets are a recipe for disaster, and criminals usually work in gangs, so take a taxi, even if you're in a group.

Regrettably, black women in the company of white men are often assumed to be prostitutes, and can face all kinds of discrimination from hotels and security guards, as well as approaches from Kenyan hustlers offering to

STREET KIDS

Nairobi in particular has huge problems with street children, many of whom are AIDS orphans, who trail foreigners around asking for food or change. It's up to you whether you give, but if you do, the word will go around and you won't get a moment's peace. It's also debatable how much your donations will help as the older boys operate like a mini-mafia, extorting money from the younger kids. If you want to help out, money might be better donated to a charity, such as the **Consortium for Street Children** (www.streetchildren.org.uk), which works to improve conditions for these children.

help rip off the white 'customer'. Again, the worst of this can be avoided by taking taxis between hotels and restaurants etc.

WORK

It's difficult, although by no means impossible, for foreigners to find jobs. Apart from voluntary and conservation work, which you usually pay to participate in, the most likely areas for gainful employment are the safari business, teaching, advertising and journalism. As in most countries, the rule is that if an African can be found to do the job, there's no need to hire a foreigner.

Work permits and resident visas are not easy to arrange. A prospective employer may be able to sort out the necessary paperwork for you, but otherwise you'll find yourself spending a lot of time and money at the **immigration office** (Map pp284–5; ☎ 020-222022; Nyayo House, cnr Kenyatta Ave & Uhuru Hwy) in Nairobi.

TRANSPORT IN KENYA

GETTING THERE & AWAY

Unless you are travelling overland from southern Africa or Egypt, flying is by far the most convenient way to get to Kenya. Nairobi is a major African hub, and flights between Kenya and the rest of Africa are easy to come by and relatively cheap. Most overland routes pass through several war zones and should only be considered after some serious planning and preparation.

For information on getting to Kenya from outside East Africa, see the Transport in East Africa chapter (p616).

Entering Kenya

Entering Kenya is generally straightforward, particularly at the international airports, which are no different from most Western terminals. Visas are typically available on arrival for most nationalities, but you should contact your nearest Kenyan diplomatic office to get the most up-to-date information.

Air

Most international flights to and from Nairobi are handled by **Jomo Kenyatta International Airport** (NBO; ☎ 020-825400; www.kenyaairports.co.ke), 15km southeast of the city. Some flights between Nairobi and Kilimanjaro International Airport or Mwanza in Tanzania, as well as many domestic flights, use **Wilson Airport** (WIL; ☎ 020-501941), which is 6km south of the city on Langata Rd. The other arrival point in the country is **Moi International Airport** (MBA; ☎ 041-433211) in Mombasa, 9km west of the city centre, but apart from flights to Zanzibar this is mainly used by charter airlines and domestic flights.

Kenya Airways is the main national carrier, and has a generally good safety record, with just one fatal incident since 1977.

The following are airlines flying to and from Kenya, with offices in Nairobi except where otherwise indicated:

African Express Airways (3P; ☎ 020-824333; hub Wilson Airport, Nairobi)

Air India (AI; Map pp284–5; ☎ 020-340925; www .airindia.com; hub Mumbai)

Air Kenya (QP; ☎ 020-605745; www.airkenya.com; hub Wilson Airport, Nairobi)

Air Madagascar (MD; ☎ 020-225286; www.airmada gascar.mg; hub Antananarivo)

Air Malawi (QM; ☎ 020-240965; www.airmalawi.com; hub Lilongwe)

Air Mauritius (MK; ☎ 020-229166; www.airmauritius .com; hub Mauritius)

Air Zimbabwe (UM; ☎ 020-339522; www.airzimbabwe .com; hub Harare)

British Airways (BA; Map pp284–5; ☎ 020-244430; www.british-airways.com; hub Heathrow Airport, London)

Daallo Airlines (D3; ☎ 020-317318; www.daallo.com; hub Hargeisa)

Egypt Air (MS; Map pp284–5; ☎ 020-226821; www .egyptair.com.eg; hub Cairo)

Emirates (EK; Map pp284–5; ☎ 020-211187; www
.emirates.com; hub Dubai)
Ethiopian Airlines (ET; Map pp284–5; ☎ 020-330837;
www.ethiopianairlines.com; hub Addis Ababa)
Gulf Air (GF; ☎ 020-241123; www.gulfairco.com; hub
Abu Dhabi)
Jetlink Express (J0; ☎ 020-244285; www.jetlink.co.ke;
hub Jomo Kenyatta International Airport, Nairobi)
Kenya Airways (KQ; Map pp284–5; ☎ 020-3274100;
www.kenya-airways.com; hub Jomo Kenyatta Interna-
tional Airport, Nairobi)
KLM (KL; Map pp284–5; ☎ 020-3274747; www.klm.com;
hub Amsterdam)
Oman Air (WY; Map p308; ☎ 041-221444; www.oman
-air.com; hub Muscat)
Precision Air (PW; ☎ 020-602561; www.precisionairtz
.com; hub Dar es Salaam)
Qatar Airways (QR; www.qatarairways.com; hub Doha)
Rwandair (WB; ☎ 0733-740703; www.rwandair.com;
hub Kigali)
Safarilink Aviation (☎ 020-600777; www.safarilink
.co.ke; hub Wilson Airport, Nairobi) Kilimanjaro only.
SN Brussels Airlines (SN; ☎ 020-4443070; www.flysn
.com; hub Brussels)
South African Airways (SA; ☎ 020-229663; www
.flysaa.com; hub Johannesburg)
Swiss International Airlines (SR; ☎ 020-3744045;
www.swiss.com; hub Zurich)

Land
BUS
Entering Kenya by bus is possible on several major routes, and it's generally a breeze:
while you need to get off the bus to sort out
any necessary visa formalities, you'll rarely
be held up for too long at the border. That
said, arranging your visa in advance can save
you time and a few angry glares from your
fellow passengers.

CAR & MOTORCYCLE
Crossing land borders with your own vehicle
is straightforward as long as you have your
papers in order. Petrol, spare parts and repair shops are readily available at all border
towns, though if you're coming from Ethiopia
you should plan your supplies carefully, as
stops are few and far between on the rough
northern roads.

BORDER CROSSINGS TO/FROM ETHIOPIA
With the ongoing problems in Sudan and
Somalia, Ethiopia offers the only viable overland route into Kenya from the north. The
security situation around the main entry point
at Moyale is changeable, and although the
border is usually open, security problems have
forced its closure several times. Cattle- and
goat-rustling are rife in the area, triggering
frequent cross-border tribal wars, so check the
security situation carefully before attempting
this crossing.

BORDER CROSSINGS TO/FROM SUDAN
Recent progress in the Sudanese peace process has raised many people's hopes for the
future, but Kenya's neighbour to the north is
still far from untroubled. If things continue
to improve, the Kenya–Sudan border may
reopen, but at time of writing it was still only
possible to travel between the two countries
by air or via Ethiopia.

BORDER CROSSINGS TO/FROM TANZANIA
The main land borders between Kenya and
Tanzania are at Namanga, Taveta, Isebania
and Lunga Lunga, and can be reached by public transport. There is also a crossing from the
Serengeti to the Masai Mara National Reserve,
which can only be undertaken with your own
vehicle, and one at Loitokitok, which is closed
to tourists. See also p262.

Arusha & Moshi
From Nairobi, there are frequent services
to Moshi, travelling via Arusha in Tanzania.
Most leave from the hectic River Rd area in
Nairobi; thefts are common here so watch
your baggage. The average cost of these services is KSh1000 to KSh1500 to Arusha and
KSh1700 to KSh2000 to Moshi, more for the
real luxury liners.

It's also easy, though less convenient, to
do this journey in stages, since the Kenyan
and Tanzanian border posts at Namanga are
right next to each other and regularly served
by public transport.

If you're coming from Mombasa, there are
a number of rickety local buses to Arusha and
Moshi that leave every evening from in front
of the Mwembe Tayari Health Centre on Jomo
Kenyatta Ave.

Between Arusha and Nairobi, there are
several buses daily (KSh1000 to KSh1500, six
hours) in each direction departing between
6.30am and 8am. Departures in Arusha are
from the bus station; in Nairobi most leave
from Accra Rd. It's more comfortable to
take one of the daily shuttle buses, departing

daily at 8am and 2pm in each direction (five hours). Following are the main bus companies – both of which also have one bus daily to/from Moshi:

Impala Arusha (☎ 027-250 7197, 027-250 8448/51; Impala Hotel, cnr Moshi & Old Moshi Rds); Nairobi (☎ 020-273 0953; Silver Springs Hotel)

Riverside Arusha (☎ 027-250 2639, 027-250 3916; riverside_shuttle@hotmail.com; Booking office Sokoine Rd, departure point Bella Luna, Moshi Rd); Nairobi (☎ 020-229618, 020-241032; Pan African Insurance House, 3rd fl, Room 1, Kenyatta Ave, departure point Parkside Hotel, Monrovia St)

Both charge about US$25 one way between Nairobi and Arusha. In Arusha, departure and drop-off points are at Bella Luna. In Nairobi, the departure point is Parkside Hotel – from where several other Arusha-bound shuttles also depart – and from Jomo Kenyatta International Airport, if you've made an advance booking (they'll meet your flight). Drop offs are at centrally located hotels and at Jomo Kenyatta International Airport. Confirm the drop-off point when booking, and insist on being dropped off as agreed.

Mwanza
A sealed road runs all the way from Kisumu to Mwanza in Tanzania, offering a convenient route to the Tanzanian shore of Lake Victoria. From Nairobi, prices cost around KSh1000 to KSh2000, and the journey should take roughly 12 hours.

From Kisumu, regular *matatus* serve the Tanzanian border at Isebania/Sirari; local services head to Mwanza from the Tanzanian side. Buses going direct to Mwanza leave frequently from Kisii.

Tanga & Dar es Salaam
Several Kenyan companies have buses from Nairobi to Dar es Salaam. Scandinavia Express and Akamba both have reliable daily services from their offices in the River Rd area, with prices ranging from KSh2000 to real luxury coaches at KSh4000. Journey time is around 16 to 18 hours with stops.

Numerous buses run along the coast road from Mombasa to Tanga and Dar, crossing the border at Lunga Lunga/Horohoro. Most people travel on through buses from Mombasa, but it's easy enough to do the journey in stages by local bus or *matatu* if you'd rather make a few stops along the way.

In Mombasa, buses to Dar es Salaam leave from around Jomo Kenyatta Ave, near the junction with Mwembe Tayari Rd. The average cost is around KSh1500 to Dar (eight hours) and KSh750 to Tanga (two hours), depending on the company you travel with and the standard of the buses.

BORDER CROSSINGS TO/FROM UGANDA
The main border post for overland travellers is Malaba, with Busia an alternative if you are travelling via Kisumu. Numerous bus companies run between Nairobi and Kampala, or you can do the journey in stages via either of the border towns. See also p529.

Kampala
Various companies cover the Nairobi to Kampala route, and depart from the Accra Rd area in Nairobi. Ordinary buses cost around KSh1500, while full-blown luxury services with drinks and movies hover around the KSh2500 mark. All buses take about 10 to 12 hours and prices include a meal at the halfway point.

The Ugandan and Kenyan border posts at Malaba are about 1km apart, so you can walk or take a *boda-boda*. Once you get across the border, there are frequent *matatus* until the late afternoon to Kampala, Jinja and Tororo.

Buses and *matatus* also run from Nairobi or Kisumu to Busia, from where there are regular connections to Kampala and Jinga.

Tours
It's possible to get to Kenya as part of an overland truck tour originating in Europe or other parts of Africa (many also start in Nairobi bound for other places in Africa). See p60 for more details on tours and safaris.

GETTING AROUND
Air
Four domestic operators of varying sizes, including the national carrier Kenya Airways, now run scheduled flights within Kenya. All appear to have a clean slate safetywise. Destinations served are predominantly around the coast and the popular southern national parks, where the highest density of tourist activity takes place.

Airlines flying domestically:

Airkenya (☎ 020-605745; www.airkenya .com) Amboseli, Kiwayu, Lamu, Lewa Downs, Masai Mara, Malindi, Meru, Nanyuki, Samburu.

Kenya Airways (Map pp282-3; ☎ 020-3274100; www.kenya-airways.com) Kisumu, Lamu, Malindi, Mombasa.

Mombasa Air Safari (☎ 041-433061; www.mombasa airsafari.com)Amboseli, Lamu, Masai Mara, Malindi, Mombasa, Tsavo, Ukunda.

Safarilink (☎ 020-600777; www.safarilink-kenya.com) Amboseli, Chyulu Hills, Kiwayu, Lamu, Lewa Downs, Masai Mara, Naivasha, Nanyuki, Samburu, Tsavo West.

Bicycle

Cycling is easier in rural areas, and you'll usually receive a warm welcome in any villages you pass through. Many local people operate *boda-bodas*, so repair shops are becoming increasingly common along the roadside. Be wary of cycling on dirt roads as punctures from thorn trees are a major problem.

The hills of Kenya are not particularly steep but can be long and hard. You can expect to cover around 80km per day in the hills of the western highlands, somewhat more where the country is flatter. Hell's Gate National Park, near Naivasha, is particularly popular for mountain biking.

It's possible to hire road and mountain bikes in an increasing number of places, usually for less than KSh500 per day. Few places require a deposit, unless their machines are particularly new or sophisticated.

Boat
DHOW

Sailing on a traditional Swahili dhow along the East African coast is one of Kenya's most memorable experiences, and unlike Lake Victoria certain traditional routes are very much still in use.

Dhows are commonly used to get around the islands in the Lamu archipelago and the mangrove islands south of Mombasa. For the most part, these operate more like dhow safaris than public transport. Although some trips are luxurious, the trips out of Lamu are more basic.

LAKE VICTORIA

There has been speculation for years that ferry transport will start again on Lake Victoria, but for the foreseeable future the only regular services operating are motorised canoes going to Mfangano Island from Mbita Point, near Homa Bay. An occasional ferry service runs between Kisumu and Homa Bay.

Bus

Kenya has an extensive network of long- and short-haul bus routes, with particularly good coverage of the areas around Nairobi, the coast and the western regions. Services thin out the further away from the capital you get, particularly in the north, and there are still plenty of places where you'll be reliant on *matatus*.

Buses are operated by a variety of private and state-owned companies that offer varying levels of comfort, convenience and roadworthiness. They're considerably cheaper than taking the train or flying, and as a rule services are frequent, fast and often quite comfortable. However, many travellers are put off taking buses altogether by the diabolical state of Kenyan roads.

Main bus companies operating in Kenya:

Akamba (Map pp284-5; ☎ 020-340430) Eldoret, Kakamega, Kericho, Kisii, Kisumu, Kitale, Machakos, Mombasa, Nairobi, Namanga.

Busways (☎ 020-227650) Kilifi, Kisumu, Malindi, Mombasa, Nairobi.

Coastline Safaris (Map pp284-5; ☎ 020-217592) Kakamega, Kisumu, Mombasa, Nairobi, Nakuru, Voi.

Easy Coach (Map pp284-5; ☎ 020-210711) Eldoret, Kakamega, Kisumu, Kitale, Nairobi.

Eldoret Express (☎ 020-6766886) Busia, Eldoret, Kakamega, Kisii, Kisumu, Kitale, Malaba, Nairobi.

Falcon (Map pp284-5; ☎ 020-229662) Kilifi, Lamu, Malindi, Mombasa, Nairobi.

Kenya Bus Services (KBS; Map pp284-5; ☎ 020-229707) Busia, Eldoret, Kakamega, Kisii, Kisumu, Kitale, Malaba, Mombasa, Nairobi.

Mombasa Metropolitan Bus Services (Metro Mombasa; ☎ 041-2496008) Kilifi, Kwale, Malindi, Mombasa, Mtwapa.

Car & Motorcycle

Many travellers bring their own vehicles into Kenya as part of overland trips and, expense notwithstanding, it's a great way to see the country at your own pace. Otherwise, there are numerous car-hire companies which can hire you anything from a small hatchback to Toyota Land Cruiser 4WDs.

Hiring a vehicle to tour Kenya (or at least the national parks) is an expensive way of seeing the country, but it does give you freedom of movement and is sometimes the only way of getting to the more remote parts of the country. Note that an International Driving Permit (IDP) is not necessary in Kenya, but can be useful. Also, unless you're just

KENYA

planning on travelling on the main routes between towns, you'll need a 4WD vehicle.

HIRE
Costs
Starting rates for rental almost always sound very reasonable, but once you factor in mileage and the various types of insurance you'll be lucky to pay less than KSh7500 per day for a saloon car, or KSh10,000 per day for a small 4WD. As elsewhere in the world, rates come down rapidly if you take the car for more than a few days.

Vehicles are usually rented with either an allowance of 100km to 200km per day (in which case you'll pay an extra fee for every kilometre over), or with unlimited kilometres, which is often the best way to go. Rates are usually quoted without insurance, and you'll be given the option of paying around KSh1000 to KSh2000 per day for insurance against collision damage and theft. It would be financial suicide to hire a car in Kenya without both kinds of insurance. Otherwise, you'll be responsible for the full value of the vehicle if it's stolen or damaged.

Even if you have collision and theft insurance, you'll still be liable for an excess of KSh2500 to KSh150,000 (depending on the company) if something happens to the vehicle; always check this before signing. You can usually reduce the excess to zero by paying another KSh1000 to KSh2000 per day for an Excess Loss Waiver. Note that tyres, damaged windscreens and loss of the tool kit are always the hirer's responsibility.

As a final sting, you'll be charged 16% value added tax (VAT) on top of the total cost of hiring the vehicle. Any repairs that you end up paying for will also have VAT on top. And a final warning: always return the vehicle with a full tank of petrol; if you don't, the company will charge you twice the going rate to fill up.

Agencies
At the top end of the market are some international companies. All have airport and town offices in Nairobi and Mombasa.

Central Rent-a-Car, which comes highly recommended by readers, is probably the best of the local firms, with a well-maintained fleet of fairly new vehicles and a good back-up service. Adventure Upgrade Safaris also has a good fleet of lean and mean 4WD for tackling the worst of Kenya's roads.

The following are local and international hire companies:

Adventure Upgrade Safaris (☎ 020-228725; www .adventureupgradesafaris.co.ke)

Avis (Map pp284-5; ☎ 020-316061; www.avis.com)

Budget (Map pp284-5; ☎ 020-223581; www.budget.com)

Central Rent-a-Car (☎ 020-222888; www.carhirekenya .com)

Hertz (☎ 020-248777; www.hertz.com)

ROAD CONDITIONS
Road conditions vary widely in Kenya, from flat smooth highways to dirt tracks and steep rocky pathways. Many roads are severely eroded at the edges, reducing the carriageway to a single lane, which is usually occupied by whichever vehicle is bigger in any given situation. The roads in the north and east of the country are particularly poor. The main Mombasa-Nairobi-Malaba road (A104) is badly worn due to the constant flow of traffic.

Roads in national parks are all *murram* (dirt) and have been eroded into bone-shaking corrugations through overuse by safari vehicles. Keep your speed down, slowly increasing until you find a suitable speed (when the rattling stops), and be careful when driving after rain. Although some dirt roads can be negotiated in a 2WD vehicle, you'll be much safer in a 4WD.

ROAD HAZARDS
The biggest hazard on Kenyan roads is quite simply the other vehicles on them, and driving defensively is essential. Ironically, the most dangerous roads in Kenya are probably the well-maintained ones, which allow drivers to pick up enough speed to do really serious damage in a crash. On the worse roads, potholes are a dual problem: driving into them can damage your vehicle or cause you to lose control, and sudden erratic avoidance manoeuvres from other vehicles are a constant threat.

Certain routes have a reputation for banditry, particularly the Garsen–Garissa–Thika road, which is still essentially off limits to travellers, and the dirt track from Amboseli National Park to Tsavo West National Park, where you're usually required to join a convoy. The roads from Isiolo to Marsabit and Moyale and from Malindi to Lamu have improved considerably securitywise in the last few years, but you're still advised to seek local advice before using any of these routes.

ROAD RULES

You'll need your wits about you if you're going to tackle driving in Kenya. Driving practices here are some of the worst in the world and all are carried out at breakneck speed. Indicators, lights, horns and hand signals can mean absolutely anything, and should never be taken at face value.

Kenyans habitually drive on the wrong side of the road whenever they see a pothole, an animal or simply a break in the traffic – flashing your lights at the vehicle hurtling towards you should be enough to persuade the driver to get back into their own lane. Never drive at night unless you absolutely have to, as few cars have adequate headlights and the roads are full of pedestrians and cyclists. Drunk driving is also very common.

Hitching

Hitchhiking is never entirely safe in any country in the world, and we don't recommend it. Travellers who decide to hitch should understand that they are taking a small but potentially serious risk; it's safer to travel in pairs and let someone know where you are planning to go. Also, beware of drunken drivers.

On the other side of the wheel, foreign drivers will be approached all the time by Kenyan hitchers demanding free rides, and giving a lift to a carload of Maasai is certainly a memorable cultural experience.

Local Transport

BOAT

The only local boat service in regular use is the Likoni ferry between the mainland and Mombasa island, which runs throughout the day and night, and is free for foot passengers (vehicles pay a small toll).

BODA-BODA

Boda-bodas are common in areas where standard taxis are harder to find, and also operate in smaller towns and cities, such as Kisumu. There is a particular proliferation on the coast, where the bicycle boys also double as touts, guides and drug dealers in tourist areas. A short ride should never cost more than KSh20.

BUS

Nairobi is the only city with an effective municipal bus service, run by KBS. Routes cover all the suburbs and outlying areas during daylight hours, and generally cost no more than KSh40.

MATATU

Local matatus are the main means of getting around for local people, and any reasonably sized city or town will have plenty of services covering every major road and suburb. Fares start at KSh10 and may reach KSh50 for longer routes in Nairobi.

Minibus transport is not unique to Kenya, but the matatu has raised it into a cultural phenomenon, and most Kenyans use them regularly for both local and intercity journeys. The vehicles themselves can be anything from dilapidated Peugeot 504 pick-ups with a taxi on the back to big 20-seater minibuses. The most common are white Nissan minibuses (many local people prefer the name 'Nissans' to matatus).

Apart from in the remote northern areas, where you'll rely on occasional buses or paid lifts on trucks, you can almost always find a matatu going to the next town or further afield, so long as it's not too late in the day. Simply ask around among the drivers at the local matatu stand or 'stage'. Matatus leave when full and the fares are fixed.

Wherever you're going, remember that most matatu crashes are head-on collisions – under no circumstances should you sit in the 'death seat' next to the matatu driver. Play it safe and sit in the middle seats away from the window.

SHARED TAXI (PEUGEOT)

Shared Peugeot taxis are less common but make a good alternative to matatus, though they're not subject to the same regulations. The vehicles are usually Peugeot 505 station wagons (hence the local name) that take seven to nine passengers and leave when full.

Peugeots take less time to reach their destinations than matatus as they fill quicker and go from point to point without stopping, and so are slightly more expensive. Many companies have offices around the Accra, Cross and River Rds area in Nairobi, and serve destinations mostly in the north and west of the country.

TAXI

Even the smallest Kenyan towns generally have at least one banged-up old taxi for easy access to outlying areas or even remoter

KENYA

villages, and you'll find taxis on virtually every corner in the larger cities, especially in Nairobi and Mombasa, where taking a taxi at night is virtually mandatory. Fares are invariably negotiable and start at around KSh200 for short journeys.

Train

The Uganda Railway was once the main trade artery in East Africa, but these days the network has dwindled to two main routes, Nairobi–Kisumu and Nairobi–Mombasa. At the time of research however, only the Nairobi–Mombasa train was running, and there remain a few question marks over the comfort and reliability of this route. Indeed, with a night service of around 13 hours, the Nairobi–Mombasa train is much slower and less frequent than going by air or road.

There are three classes on Kenyan trains, but only 1st and 2nd class can be recommended. Fares are US$65/54 in 1st/2nd class including bed and breakfast. Note that passengers are divided up by gender.

First class consists of two-berth compartments with a washbasin, wardrobe, drinking water and a drinks service. Second class consists of plainer, four-berth compartments with a washbasin and drinking water. No compartment can be locked from the outside, so remember not to leave any valuables lying around if you leave it for any reason. You might want to padlock your rucksack to something during dinner and breakfast. Always lock your compartment from the inside before you go to sleep. Third class is seats only and security can be a real problem.

Passengers in 1st class on the Mombasa line are treated to a meal typically consisting of stews, curries or roast chicken served with rice and vegetables. Tea and coffee is included; sodas (soft drinks), bottled water and alcoholic drinks are not, so ask the price before accepting that KSh1500 bottle of wine. Cold beer is available at all times in the dining car and can be delivered to your compartment.

There are booking offices in Nairobi and Mombasa, and it's recommended that you show up in person rather than trying to call. You must book in advance for 1st and 2nd class, otherwise there'll probably be no berths available. Two to three days is usually sufficient, but remember that these services run just three times weekly in either direction. Note that compartment and berth numbers are posted up about 30 minutes prior to departure.

Uganda

Uganda is Africa condensed, with the best of everything the continent has to offer packed into one small but stunning destination. It's home to the tallest mountain range in Africa, the glacier-capped Rwenzoris. The mighty Nile River, the world's longest river, surges out of Lake Victoria, the continent's largest lake. One of the highest concentrations of primates in the world, including more than half of all remaining mountain gorillas, roams its forests. And the merging of habitats from eastern, western and northern Africa produces arguably the world's best bird-watching. On top of all this a growing variety of activities has made Uganda the adrenaline centre of East Africa, there's no such thing as a crowd in even the most popular national parks and the capital Kampala is safer and friendlier than most in Africa. Winston Churchill called it the 'Pearl of Africa'. He was right.

Despite this scrumptious blend, Uganda just can't catch a break in the image department. Idi Amin's evil antics and Uganda's long string of subsequent tragedies are etched into the Western consciousness to such an extent that some people, wrongfully, still regard the country as dangerously unstable. The reality is vastly different. It's been over two decades since Yoweri Museveni took the reins and steered the country back on the straight and narrow, and visitors have no more to worry about here than they do in most other countries.

Uganda is a captivating country with a great deal to offer, and now is an ideal time to go because the country sits on the cusp of discovery. It's already popular enough that the facilities are well developed in the places where most visitors go, but there's a genuine sense of discovery for those who get off the tiny tourist trail.

UGANDA

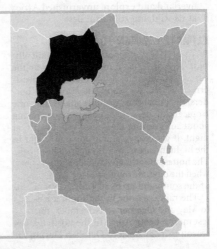

FAST FACTS

- **Area** 241,038 sq km
- **Capital** Kampala
- **Birthplace of** John 'The Beast' Mugabi, professional boxer
- **Country code** ☎ 256
- **Famous for** Idi Amin; source of the Nile River; white-water rafting
- **Languages** English, Luganda
- **Money** Ugandan Shilling (USh); US$1 = USh1660; €1 = USh2225
- **Population** 31.4 million

HOW MUCH?

- **Tracking mountain gorillas** US$500
- **Meal at decent restaurant** US$5 to US$15
- **National park entry** US$25 to US$30
- **Daily Monitor newspaper** US$0.60
- **White-water rafting** US$125

LONELY PLANET INDEX

- **Litre of petrol** US$1.65
- **1.5-litre bottled water** US$1
- **Bell beer** US$1.10
- **Souvenir T-shirt** US$7
- **Plate of matoke (mashed plantains) and beans** US$0.90

HIGHLIGHTS

- **Bwindi Impenetrable National Park** (p488) Jaunt through the jungle to marvel at mountain gorillas
- **Nile River** (p454) Take on the wild waters of the Nile River, some of the best white-water in the world
- **Murchison Falls** (p511) Check out the world's most powerful waterfall on a wildlife-watching bonanza of a boatride up the Victoria Nile
- **Lake Bunyonyi** (p494) Chill out at the most beautiful lake in Uganda
- **Kidepo Valley National Park** (p469) Travel overland and explore unvarnished Africa at its wild and colourful best

CLIMATE & WHEN TO GO

As most of Uganda is at a fairly constant altitude, with significant mountains only on the eastern (most notably Mt Elgon) and western (the Rwenzoris and the Virungas) borders, the bulk of the country enjoys the same tropical climate, with temperatures averaging about 26°C during the day and about 15°C at night. It gets considerably cooler at night in the highland areas, including around Kabale. The hottest months are January and February, when the daytime range is 27° to 29°C in most of the south and up to 32°C in the north.

The rainy seasons in the south are March to May and October to November, the wettest month being April. In the north the wet season is from April to October. During the wet seasons the average rainfall is 175mm per month and the humidity is higher but never oppressive. For more details, see p606.

The best times for a visit to Uganda are the dryer months of January and February and June to September. Travel to most destinations during the wet seasons is possible, just a bit slower; and you probably won't enjoy your time in the great outdoors as much.

HISTORY

For the story on Uganda's history in the years before independence, see p25.

Independence

Unlike Kenya and, to a lesser extent, Tanzania, Uganda never experienced a large influx of European colonisers and the associated expropriation of land. Instead, farmers were encouraged to grow cash crops for export through their own cooperative groups. Consequently, Ugandan nationalist organisations sprouted much later than those in neighbouring countries, and when they did, it happened along tribal lines. So exclusive were some of these that when Ugandan independence was discussed, the Baganda people (p45) considered secession.

By the mid-1950s, however, a Lango schoolteacher Dr Milton Obote managed to put together a loose coalition headed by the Uganda People's Congress (UPC), which led Uganda to independence in 1962 on the promise that the Buganda kingdom would have autonomy. The *kabaka* (king), Edward Mutesa II, became the president of the new nation, and Milton Obote became Uganda's first prime minister.

It wasn't a particularly favourable time for Uganda to come to grips with independence. Civil wars were raging in neighbouring Sudan, Democratic Republic of the Congo (DRC; formerly Zaire) and Rwanda, and refugees streamed into Uganda, adding to its problems. Also, it soon became obvious that Obote had no intention of sharing power with the *kabaka*. A confrontation loomed.

Obote moved in 1966, arresting several cabinet ministers and ordering his army chief of staff, Idi Amin, to storm the *kabaka*'s palace. The raid resulted in the flight of the *kabaka* and his exile in London, where he died in 1969. Following this coup, Obote proclaimed himself president, and the Bugandan monarchy was abolished, along with those of the Bunyoro, Ankole, Toro and Busoga kingdoms. Meanwhile, Idi Amin's star was on the rise.

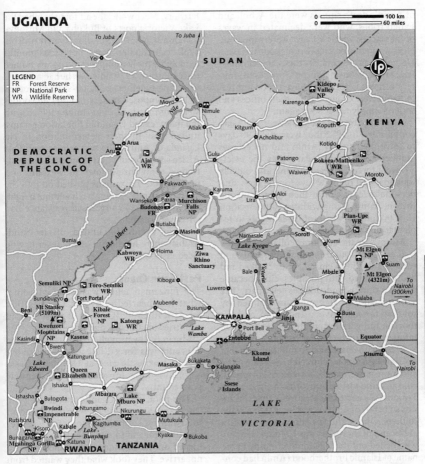

UGANDA

LEGEND
FR   Forest Reserve
NP   National Park
WR   Wildlife Reserve

SUDAN

DEMOCRATIC
REPUBLIC OF
THE CONGO

KENYA

The Amin Years

Under Obote's watch, events began to spiral out of control. Obote ordered his attorney general, Godfrey Binaisa, to rewrite the constitution to consolidate virtually all powers in the presidency and then moved to nationalise foreign assets.

In 1969 a scandal broke out over US$5 million in funds and weapons allocated to the Ministry of Defence that couldn't be accounted for. An explanation was demanded of Amin. When it wasn't forthcoming, his deputy, Colonel Okoya, and some junior officers demanded his resignation. Shortly afterwards Okoya and his wife were shot dead in their Gulu home, and rumours began to circulate about Amin's imminent arrest. It never

came. Instead, when Obote left for Singapore in January 1971 to attend the Commonwealth Heads of Government Meeting (CHOGM), Amin staged a coup. Uganda's former colonial masters, the British, who had probably suffered most from Obote's nationalisation program, were among the first to recognise the new regime. Obote went into exile in Tanzania.

So began Uganda's first reign of terror. All political activities were quickly suspended and the army was empowered to shoot on sight anyone suspected of opposition to the regime. Over the next eight years an estimated 300,000 Ugandans lost their lives, often in horrific ways such as being bludgeoned to death with sledgehammers and iron bars. Prime targets of Amin's death squads were the Acholi and Lango tribes, who were decimated in waves of massacres; whole villages were wiped out. Next Amin turned on the professional classes. University professors, doctors, cabinet ministers, lawyers, businesspeople and even military officers who might have posed a threat to Amin were dragged from their offices and shot or simply never seen again.

Also targeted was the 70,000-strong Asian community. In 1972 they were given 90 days to leave the country. Amin and his cronies grabbed the billion dollar booty the evictees were forced to leave behind and quickly squandered it on 'new toys for the boys' and personal excess. Amin then turned on the British, nationalising without compensation US$500 million worth of investments in tea plantations and other industries.

Meanwhile the economy collapsed, industrial activity ground to a halt, hospitals and rural health clinics closed, roads cracked and became riddled with potholes, cities became garbage dumps and utilities fell apart. The prolific wildlife was machine-gunned by soldiers for meat, ivory and skins, and the tourism industry evaporated. The stream of refugees across the border became a flood.

Faced with chaos and an inflation rate that hit 1000%, Amin was forced to delegate more and more powers to the provincial governors, who became virtual warlords in their areas. Towards the end of the Amin era, the treasury was so bereft of funds it was unable to pay the soldiers. One of the few supporters of Amin at the end of the 1970s was Colonel Gaddafi, who bailed out the Ugandan economy in the name of Islamic brotherhood (Amin had conveniently become a Muslim by this stage) and began an intensive drive to equip the Ugandan forces with sophisticated weapons.

The rot had spread too far, however, and was beyond the point where a few million dollars in Libyan largesse could help. Faced with a restless army beset with intertribal fighting, Amin looked for a diversion. He chose a war with Tanzania, ostensibly to teach that country a lesson for supporting anti-Amin dissidents. It was his last major act of madness, and in it lay his downfall.

War with Tanzania

On 30 October 1978 the Ugandan army rolled across northwestern Tanzania virtually unopposed and annexed more than 1200 sq km of territory. Meanwhile, the air force bombed the Lake Victoria ports of Bukoba and Musoma.

Tanzanian President Julius Nyerere ordered a full-scale counter-attack, but it took months to mobilise his ill-equipped and poorly trained forces. By early 1979, however, he had managed to scrape together a 50,000-strong people's militia composed mainly of illiterate youngsters from the bush. This militia joined with the many exiled Ugandan liberation groups; united only in their determination to rid Uganda of Amin. The two armies met. East Africa's supposedly best-equipped and best-trained army threw down its weapons and fled, and the Tanzanians pushed on into the heart of Uganda. Kampala fell without a fight, and by April 1979 organised resistance had effectively ceased.

Amin eventually ended up in Saudi Arabia where he died in 2003, never having faced justice.

Post-Amin Chaos

The Tanzanian action was criticised, somewhat half-heartedly, by the Organisation for African Unity (OAU), but most African countries breathed a sigh of relief to see the madman finally brought to heel. All the same Tanzania was forced to foot the entire bill for the war, estimated at US$500 million, a crushing blow for an already desperately poor country.

The rejoicing in Uganda was short-lived. The Tanzanian soldiers, who remained in the country, supposedly to assist with reconstruction and to maintain law and order, turned on the Ugandans when their pay did not arrive. They took what they wanted from shops at gunpoint, hijacked trucks arriving from Kenya with international relief aid and slaughtered more wildlife.

Once again, the country slid into chaos and gangs of armed bandits roamed the cities, killing and looting. Food supplies ran out and hospitals could no longer function. Nevertheless, thousands of exiled Ugandans began to answer the call to return home and help with reconstruction.

Yusuf Lule, a modest and unambitious man, was installed as president with Nyerere's blessing. But when he began speaking out against Nyerere, he was replaced by Godfrey Binaisa, sparking riots supporting Lule in Kampala. Meanwhile, Obote bided his time in Dar es Salaam.

Binaisa quickly came under pressure to set a date for a general election and a return to civilian rule. Obote eventually returned from exile to an enthusiastic welcome in many parts of the country and swept to power in what is widely regarded as a rigged vote.

It was 1981 and the honeymoon with Obote proved short. Like Amin, Obote favoured certain tribes. Large numbers of civil servants and army and police commanders belonging to the tribes of the south were replaced with Obote supporters belonging to the tribes of the north. The State Research Bureau, a euphemism for the secret police, was re-established and the prisons began to fill once more. Obote was on course to complete the destruction that Amin had begun. More and more reports of atrocities and killings leaked out of the country. Mass graves unrelated to the Amin era were unearthed. The press was muzzled and Western journalists were expelled. It was obvious that Obote was once again attempting to achieve absolute power. Intertribal tension was on the rise, and in mid-1985 Obote was overthrown in a coup staged by the army under the command of Tito Okello.

The NRA Takeover

Okello was not the only opponent of Obote. Shortly after Obote became president for the second time, a guerrilla army opposed to his tribally biased government was formed in western Uganda under the leadership of Yoweri Museveni.

A group of 27 soon swelled to a guerrilla force of about 20,000, many of them orphaned teenagers. In the early days few gave the guerrillas, known as the National Resistance Army (NRA), much of a chance, but the NRA wasn't a bunch of unruly thugs like the armies of Amin and Obote had been. New recruits were indoctrinated in the bush by political commissars and taught they had to be servants of the people, not oppressors. Discipline was tough. Anyone who got badly out of line was executed. Museveni was determined that the army would never again disgrace Uganda. A central thrust of the NRA was to win the hearts and minds of the people, who learnt to identify with the persecuted Bagandans in the infamous Luwero Triangle, where people suffered more than most under Obote's iron fist.

By the time Obote was ousted and Okello had taken over, the NRA controlled a large slice of western Uganda and was a power to be reckoned with. Museveni wanted a clean sweep of the administration, the army and the police. He wanted corruption stamped out and those who had been involved in atrocities during the Amin and Obote regimes brought to trial. These demands were, of course, anathema to Okello, who was up to his neck in corruption and responsible for many atrocities.

The fighting continued in earnest, and by January 1986 it was obvious that Okello's days were numbered. The surrender of 1600 government soldiers holed up in their barracks in the southern town of Mbarara brought the NRA to the outskirts of Kampala itself. With the morale of the government troops low, the NRA launched an all-out offensive to take the capital. Okello's troops fled, almost without a fight, though not before looting whatever remained and carting it away in commandeered buses. It was a typical parting gesture, as was the gratuitous shooting-up of many Kampala high-rise offices.

During the following weeks, Okello's rabble were pursued and finally pushed north over the border into Sudan. The long nightmare was finally over.

Rebuilding

Despite Museveni's Marxist leanings, he proved to be a pragmatist after taking control. He appointed several arch-conservatives to his cabinet and made an effort to reassure the country's large Catholic community.

In the late 1980s, peace agreements were negotiated with most of the guerrilla factions who had fought for Okello or Obote and were still active in the north and northeast. Under an amnesty offered to the rebels, as many as 40,000 had surrendered by 1988, and many were given jobs in the NRA. In the northwest of the country, almost 300,000 Ugandans returned home from Sudan.

With peace came optimism: services were restored, factories that had lain idle for years were again productive, agriculture was back online, the main roads were resurfaced, and the national parks' infrastructure was restored and revitalised.

The 1990s

The stability and rebuilding that came with President Museveni's coming to power in 1986 were followed in the 1990s with economic prosperity and unprecedented growth.

UGANDA

For much of the decade Uganda was the fastest-growing economy in Africa, becoming a favourite among investors. One of the keys to the success was the bold decision to invite back the Asians who, as in Kenya, had held a virtual monopoly on business and commerce. Not surprisingly, they were very hesitant about returning, but assurances were given and kept, and property was returned.

The darkness didn't end for northern Uganda, however, due to the Lord's Resistance Army (LRA), the last remaining rebel group founded during the time of the NRA rebellion. Its leader, Joseph Kony, grew increasingly delusional and paranoid and shifted his focus from attacking soldiers to attacking civilians in his bizarre attempt to found a government based on the Biblical Ten Commandments.

His vicious tactics included torture, mutilation (slicing off lips, noses and ears), rape and abducting children to use as soldiers and sex slaves. Eventually over one million northerners fled their homes to Internally Displaced Persons (IDP) camps and tens of thousands of children became 'night commuters', walking from their villages each evening to sleep in schools and churches or on the streets of large and (sometimes) safer towns. In their half-hearted fight against the LRA, government forces reportedly committed their own atrocities too.

In 1993, a new draft constitution was adopted by the National Resistance Council (NRC). One surprising recommendation in the draft was that the country should adopt a system of 'no-party' politics. Given the potential for intertribal rivalry within a pluralist system it was a sensible policy. Under the draft constitution, a Constituent Assembly was formed, and in 1994 elections for the assembly showed overwhelming support for the government. Also in 1993 the monarchies were restored, but with no actual political power.

Democratic 'no-party' elections were called for May 1996. The main candidates were President Museveni and Paul Ssemogerere, who had resigned as foreign minister in order to campaign. Museveni won a resounding victory, capturing almost 75% of the vote. The only area where Ssemogerere had any real support was in the anti-NRM north.

Museveni's election carried with it great hope for the future, as many believed Uganda's success story could only continue with a genuine endorsement at the ballot box. However,

Museveni's period as a democratically elected leader has been far less comfortable than his leadership period prior to the elections. At home, one corruption scandal after another has blighted the administration, though Museveni has so far stayed clean. Museveni can't seem to keep his focus on the homefront and has played a heavy hand with events in DRC and Rwanda. Despite this, Museveni remained popular for the stability he brought to the lives of average Ugandans and he was re-elected in 2001.

Uganda Today

Eventually Museveni shifted his position on political parties, and in July 2005 a referendum was held that overwhelmingly endorsed the change. This political shift was of much less concern to the average Ugandan than the other that occurred the same month; parliament approving a constitutional amendment scrapping presidential term limits. Museveni himself had put the two-term limit in place, but had regrets as the end of his tenure drew closer. It was alleged that MPs were bullied and bribed into voting for the change. International criticism was strong and even many Ugandans who back Museveni remain angry at his move. The 'Big Man' school of African politics is better known to Ugandans than most, and plenty of people are worried he is setting himself to be president for life. Some even draw unflattering comparisons with Robert Mugabe.

Despite all this, Museveni won his third election in 2006 with 59% of the vote, albeit not without some shenanigans along the way – such as imprisoning the main opposition leader, Kizza Besigye of the Forum for Democratic Change (FDC), for three months. Besigye had also been the runner up in 2001 and spent most of the subsequent years in self-imposed exile due to previous harassment by the government. There's little doubt Museveni will run again in 2011, and though he continues to lose popularity, no credible opposition has arisen.

By early in the 2000's the LRA's campaign of terror had ebbed, though certainly not ceased. In 2002 the LRA lost its Sudanese support and the Ugandan military launched Operation Iron Fist, attacking the LRA's bases across the northern border. The mission failed and an angered Kony not only increased attacks in Uganda but expanded his targets to areas like Soroti that had not previously been affected.

In the years that followed there were various ceasefires and nominal peace talks, but little progress until 2005 when the LRA fled to Garamba National Park in DRC. The following year the Juba Peace Talks commenced, and though things progressed slowly they showed genuine promise. Museveni guaranteed Kony amnesty (a move supported in Uganda as practical) and a legitimate ceasefire began in September. After on-again, off-again talks a peace deal was reached in February 2008, though Kony then broke his promise to sign it and the LRA began abducting more child soldiers and even attacked a Sudanese army base. Although they haven't threatened Uganda for several years, most northern Ugandans remain too terrified to return to their homes.

Although Uganda is only ranked 154 out of 177 on the UN's Human Development Index, it is a country with much promise. But, there are two main hurdles for it to overcome before it can fulfil its potential. Firstly it needs to address the rampant corruption that continues to plague government, rattling confidence among donors and the electorate. As you spend a little time in Uganda you'll be impressed by the number of headlines about the government investigating corruption. But this is a result of a vibrant free press, not of a will by the government to reform. Ask yourself: how many stories do you see about corruption convictions? Secondly, as pluralism returns to Uganda, it's to be hoped that a new generation of politicians brought up on the no-party system will form their parties based on policy not pedigree; although the sad truth is that this does not appear to be happening.

THE CULTURE
The National Psyche

Despite the years of terror and bloodshed, Ugandans are a remarkably positive and spirited people, and no one comes away from the country without a measure of admiration and affection. Most Ugandans are keen debaters, discussing politics and personality in equal measure. They are opinionated and eloquent during disagreements, yet unfailingly polite and engagingly warm.

They are also worried. Many Ugandans fear a fractured future. The country has had a remarkable run since 1986 when Museveni saved the nation, but nationalism has never taken hold. Tribe comes first. In fact, many Baganda still desire independence. This tribal divide has always manifested itself in politics, but the re-emergence of political parties is exacerbating the problem. Recently, even opposition to a vital land reform bill fell largely along tribal not economic lines.

There is also a serious north–south divide, and it doesn't appear to be closing with the advent of peace. Without Joseph Kony around to blame any more, northerners seem to be turning their resentment for the lack of prosperity and education opportunities towards the south; and not without some justification. During the war, many military officers used their power to swipe land, and today many of the new businesses are owned and new jobs taken by carpetbaggers. Even most of the students in the vast new Gulu University, opened in 2002, come from the south.

Societal leaders in Uganda need to decide if they are going to make pains to bridge these growing rifts or ride them for personal gain. As the rhetoric rises, you can't help but worry that people's fears are justified.

Daily Life

Ugandans are a very polite and friendly people, and will often greet strangers on public transport or while walking in rural areas. The greeting comes not just with a simple 'hello' but also with an inquiry into how they and their family is doing; and the interest is genuine. In fact, though people likely would never show it, you genuinely risk offending someone if you don't at least ask 'How are you?' before asking a question or beginning a conversation. In fact, if you just say 'Hello', you'll often get a response of 'I'm fine' simply because they were expecting a more personal greeting.

Life in Uganda has been one long series of upheavals for the older generations, while the younger generations have benefited from the newfound stability. Society has changed completely in urban areas in the past couple of decades, but in the countryside it's often business as usual.

Uganda has been heavily affected by HIV/AIDS. One of the first countries to be struck by an outbreak of epidemic proportions, Uganda acted swiftly in promoting AIDS awareness and safe sex. This was very effective in radically reducing infection rates throughout the country, and Uganda went from experiencing an infection rate of around 25% in the late 1980s to one that dropped as low as 4% in 2003.

UGANDA

But things have changed. Due in large part to pressure from the country's growing evangelical Christian population, led on this issue by Museveni's outspoken wife (though the president himself has taken her lead), Uganda has reversed its policy on promoting condoms and made abstinence the focus of fighting the disease. The result is no surprise. The infection rate has since risen to 6.7%.

Education has been a real priority in Uganda and President Museveni has been keen to promote free primary education for all. It's a noble goal, but Uganda lacks the resources to realise it, and one-third of the population is illiterate. Sure, more pupils are attending class, but often the classes are hopelessly overcrowded and many teachers lack experience.

Agriculture remains the single most important component of the Ugandan economy, and it employs 75% of the workforce. The main export crops include coffee, sugar, cotton, tea and fish. Crops grown for local consumption include maize, millet, rice, cassava, potatoes and beans.

Population

Uganda's population is estimated at 31.4 million, and its annual growth rate of 3.6% is one of the world's highest, leading to some serious deforestation, erosion and other environmental problems, which will only get worse with time. The median age is 15.

Uganda is made up of a complex and diverse range of tribes. Lake Kyoga forms the northern boundary for the Bantu-speaking peoples, who dominate much of east, central and southern Africa and, in Uganda, include the Baganda (17%) and several other tribes, such as the Banyankole (9.5%), Basoga (8.5%) and Bagisu (4.6%). In the north are the Lango (6%) near Lake Kyoga and the Acholi (4.7%) towards the Sudanese border, who speak Nilotic languages. To the east are the Iteso (6.4%) and Karamojong (2%), who are related to the Maasai, and also speak Nilotic languages. Small numbers of Batwa pygmies live in the forests of the southwest. Non-Africans, including a sizeable community of Asians, compose about 1% of the population.

SPORT

The most popular sport in Uganda, as in most of Africa, is football (soccer) and it's possible to watch occasional international games at the Nelson Mandela Stadium on the outskirts of Kampala. There's also a domestic league (October to July), but few people follow it.

Rugby is quickly gaining popularity, at least among well-to-do Ugandans. The Rugby Cranes were Confederation of African Rugby Champions in 2007 and you can watch them try for a 2011 World Cup berth at the Kampala Rugby Club in the Lugogo neighbourhood.

Cricket is also growing in popularity (tests are held at Lugogo Cricket Ground), while boxing has lost much of its popularity in recent years, though past world champions include John 'The Beast' Mugabi and Kassim 'The Dream' Ouma, a former child soldier.

RELIGION

Eighty-five percent of the population is Christian, split evenly between Catholics and Protestants, including a growing number of born-agains. Muslims, mostly northerners, compose about 12% of the population. The Abayudaya are a small but devout group of native Ugandans living around Mbale who practice Judaism.

ARTS
Cinema

Hollywood recently put Uganda on the movie map with a big screen version of *The Last King of Scotland* (2006; see Literature below) starring Forrest Whitaker as the 'Big Daddy'.

The conflict in the north has spawned many harrowing documentaries including *Invisible Children* (2006), *The Other Side Of The Country* (2007), and *Uganda Rising* (2006). In a different vein is the Oscar-nominated *War/Dance* (2006), an inspiring tale of northern refugee schoolchildren competing in Uganda's National Primary and Secondary School Music and Dance Competition.

The local film industry, known as Kina-Uganda or Ugawood, is in its infancy but growing. Most movies go straight to DVD, but you can sometimes catch one at the National Theatre (p441) in Kampala and you'll surely have a chance during the Amakula Kampala International Film Festival (p434), held in May.

Literature

Most of the interesting reading coming out of Uganda revolves around the country's darkest hours. Aristoc (p429) in Kampala stocks a good selection of local writers.

Giles Foden's *The Last King of Scotland* (1998) chronicles the experience of Idi Amin's personal doctor as he slowly finds himself becoming confidant to the dictator. This best-selling novel weaves gruesome historical fact into its Heart of Darkness-esque tale.

The highly regarded and somewhat auto-biographical *Abyssinian Chronicles* (2001) is the best known work by Moses Isegawa. It tells the story of a young Ugandan coming of age during the turbulent years of Idi Amin and offers some fascinating insights into life in Uganda.

Waiting (2007), the fourth novel by Goretti Kyomuhendo, one of Uganda's pioneering female writers (and founder of Femrite: the Ugandan Women Writers' Association and publishing house), was published in the United States. It looks in on a rural family's daily life (and daily fear) as they await the expected arrival of marauding soldiers during the fall of Idi Amin. Femwrite titles include *A Woman's Voice* (1998) and *Words From a Granary* (2001), two collections of short stories.

Song of Lawino (1989) is a highly-regarded poem (originally written in Acholi) by Okot p'Bitek about how colonialism led to a loss of culture.

Fong & the Indians (1968) by Paul Theroux is set in a fictional East African country that bears a remarkable likeness to Uganda, where he taught English for four years in the 1960s. It's set in pre-civil war days, and is at times both funny and bizarre as it details the life of a Chinese immigrant and his dealings with the Asians who control commerce in the country.

Music & Dance

You won't be in Uganda long before you discover that Dolly Parton and Kenny Rogers (yes, really!) are the most popular singers here; but there's plenty of home-grown talent too.

Afrigo Band are one of the longest-running groups in Uganda and their classic Congolese rumba sound, which they haven't changed in over three decades, is popular with people in all generations. Chameleone, who combines rap and traditional chanting in a cutting-edge combination, and dance hall stars Bebe Cool and Bobi Wine are three other long-time favourites. Maurice Kirya offers a poetic, soulful take on R&B. Suzan Kerunen, who, unlike most of Uganda's current crop of young singers, insists on singing live, is one up-and-comer to watch out for.

Kampala is the best place to experience live music and several local bands play at nightclubs each weekend. Try to catch the aforementioned Afrigo Band at Club Obbligato (p441) and Maurice Kirya at Rouge (p441) every last Tuesday of the month, plus the weekly events at the National Theatre (p442).

To listen to Ugandan music, from hip-hop to northern-style thumb piano playing, log on to www.musicuganda.com. To learn traditional African instruments, see Courses on p523.

The most famous dancers in the country are the Ndere Troupe (p441). Made up from a kaleidoscope of Ugandan tribes in, they perform traditional dances from all regions of the country.

Handicrafts

Uganda's most distinctive craft is bark-cloth, made by pounding the bark of a fig tree. Originally used for clothing and in burial and other ceremonies, these days it's turned into a multitude of items for sale to tourists including hats, bags, wall hangings, pillows and picture frames.

Ugandans also produce some really good raffia and banana stem basketry, particularly the Toro of the west who have the most intricate designs and still use natural dyes. Traditional products are easy to find, but the old methods have been also adopted to make new items such as table mats and handbags for sale to tourists.

Bugandan drum-makers are well known: the best place to buy is at Mpambire, (p448). Uganda also has interesting pottery, though all the soapstone carving comes from Kenya and almost all the interesting woodwork is Congolese.

ENVIRONMENT

Uganda suffers the same environmental problems as the rest of the region: poaching, deforestation and overpopulation See p54 for more details.

Currently the biggest threat to Uganda's national parks and other protected areas comes from the oil industry. Significant oil finds in the Kabwoya Wildlife Reserve on Lake Albert have spurred invasive searches for more black gold in the Ishasha sector of Queen Elisabeth National Park and the delta area at Murchison

Falls National Park. Providing the drilling companies explore and extract responsibly, then there may be hope for a sustainable marriage of interests; but conservationists are justifiably skeptical.

The Land

Uganda has an area of 236,040 sq km, small by African standards, but a similar area in size to Britain. Lake Victoria and the Victoria Nile River, which cuts through the heart of the country, combine to create one of the most fecund areas in Africa. Most of Uganda is a blizzard of greens, a lush landscape of rolling hills blanketed with fertile fields where almost anything will grow if you stick it in the soil. The climate is drier in the north and some of the lands of the far northeast are semi-desert.

The tropical heat is tempered by the altitude, which averages more than 1000m in much of the country and is even higher in the cooler southwest. The highest peak is Mt Stanley (5109m) in the Rwenzori Mountains on the border with DRC.

Wildlife

Uganda can't compete with Kenya or Tanzania for sheer density of wildlife, but with 500 species of mammal it has amazing diversity; and with the opening of the Ziwa Rhino Sanctuary (p507), the Big Five are all here again. Uganda is also home to more than half the world's mountain gorillas, and viewing them in their natural environment is one of the main attractions for visitors. On top of this, Uganda has a good number of chimpanzees and there are several places where you can track them. With well over 1000 species recorded inside its small borders, Uganda is one of the best bird-watching destinations in the world. See p521 for more information.

National Parks & Reserves

Uganda has an excellent collection of national parks and reserves. While they may not be bursting with wildlife on the level of the best in Kenya or Tanzania, they're also not bursting with visitors, which make them altogether more enjoyable places to be. Twenty percent of your admission fees benefit local communities for things like construction of schools and health clinics, so you earn a warm fuzzy for every park you visit.

While the low number of visitors is a great bonus, it's also a disadvantage in that the infrastructure of the parks is less developed than elsewhere in the region, though there's lodging at all the parks and new luxury lodges keep opening. Also, for budget travellers organised safari options are much more limited and it's not as easy to put a group together to cut costs. Despite this many of the parks are relatively easy to visit by public transport, and the rewards are ample for those who make the effort.

The **Uganda Wildlife Authority** (UWA; Map pp428-9; ☎ 0414-355000; www.uwa.or.ug; 7 Kira Rd, Kampala; ☽ 8am-5pm Mon-Fri, 9am-1pm Sat) administers all Uganda's protected areas. This is the place to make bookings to see the gorillas in Bwindi Impenetrable National Park (p488) and to reserve *banda* accommodation in the parks that offer it. Some other activities, such as the launch trips in Murchison Falls (p511) and Queen Elizabeth National Parks (p484) can also be reserved here, though things like nature walks are arranged at the parks. Payments are accepted in shillings, dollars, euros and pounds and in cash or travellers cheques (1% commission). Staff are well versed on activities within the parks, but less so on getting to them for those without transport. Their free brochures about each of the parks are very informative: if there are none on the shelf, ask.

Most national parks charge US$30 (US$15 for children ages five to 15) per 24 hours. There is, however, a 25% discount for students with valid ID (preferrably an ISIC, but your home student card should also suffice). Other charges, which can add up quite fast, include vehicle entry (motorcycles/saloon cars and Land Cruisers US$30/US$50) in a few of the big parks, nature walks (US$10 per person) and rangers for game drivers (US$20). Most prices are lower for Ugandan residents and much lower again for Ugandan citizens.

FOOD & DRINK

Local food is much the same as elsewhere in the region, except in Uganda *ugali* (food staple usually made from maize flour, or rarely cassava) is called *posho*, and is far less popular than *matoke* (cooked plantains). Rice, cassava and potatoes are also common starches and vegetarians travelling beyond the main tourist destinations will end up eating any of these with beans quite often, although Indian food is available in the larger cities. Kampala, Jinja and Entebbe (plus the top hotels in many provincial towns) offer other international flavours such as Italian, Thai, Japanese and Mexican; don't get too excited by the menus though as there are far more misses than hits when it comes to authenticity. One uniquely Ugandan food is the *rolex*, a chapatti rolled around an omelette. Grasshoppers are very popular during April and November and are sold by many street vendors. For more info on local cuisine, see p40.

Soft drinks (sodas) are everywhere, the most popular being the international giants plus regional favourites Krest (bitter lemon) and Stoney (ginger beer). Red Bull is gaining popularity, but the government has suggested it might be banned as a health hazard. Like all East Africans, Ugandans love their beer and, mercifully, they don't have a fetish for drinking the stuff warm. If a town has electricity you can be sure it will have a fridge, and this will have beer in it! However, to be safe, be sure to request a cold one before the cap is popped; and tell them to keep the straw.

Uganda Breweries and Nile Breweries (p453) are the two main local brewers, and they produce some drinkable lagers. Bell is a light beer produced from waters of Lake Victoria while Club (another light beer) and Nile Special are proudly brewed from the source of the Nile River. Nile Special, with an alcohol content of 5.6%, is substantially stronger and is a firm favourite of new arrivals in Uganda. For the brave (or impatient), there's also Chairman's ESB, a potent brew with an alcohol content of 7.2%. Moonberg is a new brewery that follows German purity laws of 1516, though it doesn't seem to have caught on yet. You'll also find locally brewed South African Castle and Tusker Malt. Guinness is available, but it's not the real thing. Bottled beer costs USh1500 to USh2500 a bottle, depending on where you're drinking.

Waragi is the local millet-based alcohol and is relatively safe, although it can knock you around and give you a horrible hangover. It's a little like gin and goes down well with a splash of tonic. In its undistilled form it's known as *kasezi bong* and would probably send you blind if you drank enough of it.

Imported wines are quite expensive and not common beyond the tourist trail. Imported spirits are relatively cheaper, although, like wine, availability is somewhat restricted.

KAMPALA

☎ 041 / pop 1.5 million

Unlike what Nairobi does for Kenya, Kampala makes a good introduction to Uganda. It's a dynamic and engaging city, with few of the hassles of its eastern neighbour and several worthy attractions to keep you occupied for a couple of days. Best of all, it's safe to walk around virtually everywhere in the daytime and downtown doesn't shut down until well into the evening.

Today's forward-looking capital is vastly different from the battered city to which it was reduced in the 1980s. In the period since Museveni's victory, Kampala has been transformed from a looted shell to a thriving, modern place befitting the capital of the pearl of Africa. Modern buildings have transforming the skyline and invigorated the economy, and the building boom continues today with new properties springing up everywhere you look.

Mix in the excellent international restaurants and a nightlife that's something to savour, and you'll see why you won't want to just touch down and rush off.

ORIENTATION

Like Rome, Kampala is known as the city of seven hills, although it has since engulfed many, many more; and that rolling topography is where the comparisons begin and end.

The city centre is on Nakasero Hill, and it's almost a tale of two cities. Towards the bottom of the valley are heaps of shops and small businesses, budget hotels, markets, Hindu temples, the bus station and two of the most mind-boggling taxi parks you're ever likely to see. The streets are thronging with shoppers, hawkers and hustlers; battered old delivery trucks; and impromptu pavement stalls. Even *boda-bodas* get trapped in traffic here. The upper end, on the other hand, has lots of office blocks and good restaurants and is far more orderly; even cars get around mostly unobstructed. The dividing line, for the most part, is Kampala Rd (which turns into Jinja Rd to the east and Bombo Rd to the west). This artery stays busy (and safe) well into the night.

Heading up Nakasero Hill you quickly hit Kampala's most expensive hotels as the urban core fades into something of a garden city with wide, quiet avenues lined with flowering trees and large detached houses behind

UGANDA

KAMPALA

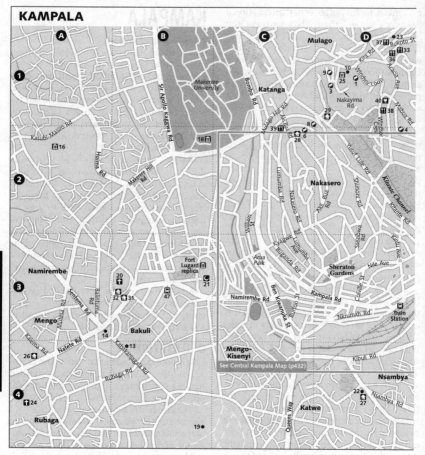

imposing fences. Here you'll find many of the embassies, international aid organisations, and government buildings.

Old Kampala lies just west of the centre, around the namesake Kampala Hill, formerly home of Fort Lugard and now topped by the immense National Mosque. Further out are Namirembe and Rubaga hills, topped by the Protestant and Catholic cathedrals respectively; Mengo Hill, heart of the Buganda nation; and Kasubi Hill, topped by the can't-miss Kasubi Tombs. Directly north of Old Kampala is Makerere Hill, home to the well-regarded Makerere University.

To the east, across the golf course, is Kololo, a fairly exclusive residential zone, home to the popular Cooper Rd area (called Kisimenti)

with its restaurants and bars, and the side-by-side Uganda Wildlife Authority and Uganda Museum; all best reached from the centre along Acacia Ave, which has several good restaurants of its own.

South of the city centre lie Kabalagala and Tank Hill, where there are more hotels and good restaurants. Kabalagala, home to some of the city's wildest bars, is bustling with life day and night and is a fun place to spend some time.

An irritating orientation obstacle is that street names can change depending on which sign you're looking at.

Maps

The best available map of the city of Kampala is the *Kampala A-Z* street atlas,

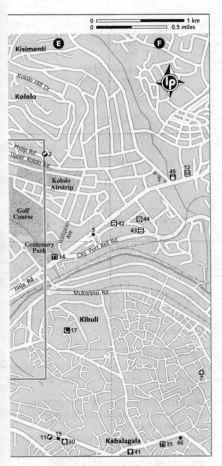

but Macmillan's *Kampala Traveller's Map* (1:8500) is good enough for most visitors. Both are available in bookshops and hotels around Kampala.

INFORMATION
Bookshops

For English-language publications **Aristoc** (Map p432; Kampala Rd; 8.30am-5.30pm Mon-Fri, 9am-4.30pm Sat) is the best place in Kampala. It has a great selection of books on Uganda, East Africa and beyond, plus novels and educational texts. Prices are very reasonable for imported books, so stock up here for reading material before a long road trip. There's a second branch in Garden City that also opens 10am to 2pm on Sunday.

For used books, first stop is **Bookend** (Map p432; Acacia Ave; 11am-4pm Mon-Fri, 10am-1pm Sat) on the grounds of Surgery (below). It has a good selection of literature. All books are sold for USh6000 and bought for USh3000. **Rent-A-Book Centre** (Map p432; 2nd fl, Colline House, Pilkington Rd; 8am-6pm Mon-Fri, 8am-5.30pm Sat) lacks Bookend's quality selection, but it's conveniently located downtown.

Cultural Centres

Alliance Française (Map p432; 0414-344490; 6 Mackinnon Rd; 8.30am-6pm Tue-Sat) Shares a space with the Ugandan German Cultural Society. There are French language movies Fridays at 7pm.

British Council (Map p432; 0414-560800; www.britishcouncil.org; Rwenzori Courts, 2-4 Lumumba Ave; 8.30am-5pm Mon-Fri) Sponsors monthly Words and Pictures events, which highlight locals artists, poets and musicians.

Ugandan German Cultural Society (Map p432; 0414-533410; www.ugcs-kampala.de; 6 Mackinnon Rd; 8.30am-5pm Mon-Fri) Sponsors art and cultural exhibits and events. Movies at 6pm on second Tuesday of the month.

Emergency

Police or ambulance (999) You can also dial 112 from mobile phones.

Internet Access

You can't walk far in Kampala without passing an internet café. Prices usually cost USh2000 to USh3000 per hour. The following are pretty reliably fast, though even they get bogged down at times.

MBL (Map p432; Garden City; per hr USh3000; 8am-8.30pm Mon-Fri, 8.30am-8pm Sat & Sun)

MF Internet (Map p432; Hotel City Square, Kampala Ave; per hr USh3000; 8am-9pm Mon-Sat, 8am-4pm Sun)

Web City Café (Map p432; Kimathi Ave; per hr USh3000; 8am-10pm Mon-Sat, 9am-8pm Sun)

Wi-fi hotspots are becoming more common these days. Look for 'Infocom Hotspot' signs at various places around town: a passcode costs USh3000 per hour. Bubbles O'Learys (p440) is more of an internet café than pub during the day thanks to its free connections. Access is also free at Panorama Coffee Shop (p438).

Medical Services

International Hospital Kampala (Map pp428-9; 0772-200400 emergency; St Barnabus Rd; 24hr) This should be your destination if you suffer serious trauma.

Surgery (Map p432; 0414-256003, emergency 0752-756003; www.thesurgeryuganda.org; 2 Acacia Ave;

8am-6pm Mon-Sat, emergency 24hr) A highly-respected clinic run by Dr Dick Stockley, an expat British GP. Stocks self-test malaria kits.

Money

Most main bank branches and foreign exchange bureaus are along or near Kampala Rd. The Speke Hotel (p437) changes money 24 hours a day at competitive rates. There are ATMs all over the city.

Barclays Bank (Kampala Rd & Lugogo Mall) is the most useful bank in Kampala. It converts American Express, Thomas Cook and Visa travellers cheques and give cash advances on Visa, MasterCard and JCB credit cards. Amex cheques can also be changed at **Crane Bank** (Map p432; Kampala Rd) and **Orient Bank** (Map p432; Kampala Rd), while the later also gives cash advances (shillings only) on Visa credit cards, and at a much lower commission than Barclays.

See p525 for more information about money matters.

Post

Main post office (Map p432; Kampala Rd; 8am-6pm Mon-Fri, 9am-2pm Sat) Offers postal and telecom services. The reliable poste restante service is at counter 14.

Tourist Information

The free, bi-monthly listings magazine *The Eye* is available from selected hotels and restaurants.

Tourism Uganda (Map p432; ☎ 0414-342196; www .visituganda.com; 15 Kimathi Ave; 8.30am-5pm Mon-Fri, 9am-1pm Sat) Staff will try to answer your questions, but are frequently unable to.

Travel Agencies

The following are reliable places to buy plane tickets. For information on tours and safari companies in Uganda, see p73.

Global Interlink (Map p432; ☎ 0414-235233; www .global-interlink.org; Grand Imperial Hotel) Hidden away in the mall behind the hotel.

Let's Go Travel (Map pp428-9; ☎ 0414-346667; www .ugandaletsgotravel.com; Garden City) Part of the Uniglobe empire and also a representative for STA Travel.

Swanair (Map p432; ☎ 0414-250966; www.swanair travel.biz; 4 Kimathi Ave) A franchise of Carlson Wagonlit.

DANGERS & ANNOYANCES

Other than the traffic and the horrendous pollution it creates (with all the belching fumes of the minibuses, sometimes you can chew the air), Kampala is a very hassle-free city. The occasional scammer may try to chat you up, but the biggest annoyances you're likely to face are the aggressive menu boys at the Garden City food court.

Kampala is also very safe as far as Africa's capitals go. Take care in and around the taxi parks, bus parks and market, as pickpockets operate there. Bigger incidents can and sometimes do happen, like anywhere else in the world, so follow the ordinary big-city precautions. Although it's nothing on the scale of Nairobi, car break-ins have increased lately, so never leave your vehicle unattended if there are valuables in it; even if they're in the boot. Like elsewhere in Africa, thieves who are caught red-handed will often face a mob-justice beating, but the Kampala twist is that they'll also be stripped down to their 'Adam suits' before being sent off.

Uganda doesn't have much of a social-security system, so begging is quite common on some streets in the centre. Some of these are genuine hard luck cases, but others are exploited children so it's best not to give. Choose a recognised charity instead.

SIGHTS & ACTIVITIES

Low key is the phrase to remember here. What's on offer in Kampala is fairly limited when compared with the amazing attractions elsewhere in the country. Quite a few activities beyond the city can be easily done as day-trips, including everything in the Around Kampala (p444) section as well as all the activities in and around Jinja (p451).

Buganda Historic Sites

A visit to the **Kasubi Tombs** (Map pp428-9; adult/child incl guideUSh10,000/5000; 8am-6pm) offers a strong dose of traditional culture; at the centre is a ginormous thatched-roof building lined with bark-cloth. Built in 1882 as the palace of Muteesa I, it was converted into his tomb following his death two years later. Subsequently, the next three *kabaka* – Mwanga; Daudi Chwa II; and Edward Muteesa II, father of the current *kabaka*, Ronald Mutebi II (known also by his Bugandan name, Muwenda) – broke with tradition and chose to be buried here instead of in their own palaces. It's now a Unesco World Heritage site. Outside, forming a ring around the main section of the compound are homes of the families of the widows of former *kabaka*. Royal family members are buried amid the trees out the back. Minibuses don't come here directly, so you'll need to alight at Kasubi Trading Centre. From there it's 500m uphill.

If you found the Kasubi Tombs too crowded, then the even older **Wamala Tombs** (Map p444; adult/child USh3000/500 incl guide; 8am-5pm), burial place of the despotic Kabaka Sunna II, father of Muteesa I, might be worth your while, even

though the roof is collapsing. The caretaker here is a bundle of energy and is grateful for every visitor she gets. The tombs are 11km north of Kasubi Tombs along Hoima Rd. From the new taxi park head to Wakiso and get out at '8 Mile' stage after Nansana. From here, a *boda-boda* should cost USh1500 for the final 2.7km.

Across a small valley from Wamala, under the mobile phone towers, is the **Tomb of Nnamasole Kanyange** (Map p444; adult/child incl guide USh2000/500; 10am-6pm), Sunna II's mother. It looks just like an ordinary village house from the outside, but has the same setup inside. Frankly, it's not very interesting, but you have the option of taking a guided 45-minute walk through the villages from Wamala, which is worthwhile. It can be reached by car (4.3km) direct from Wamala, but not without some very careful manoeuvring over the worst stretches of road. It's better to go around to Kagoma on Bombo Rd; it's 400m from there.

Buildings of the Modern Buganda Kingdom

Kampala remains the heartland of the Buganda kingdom, and within the capital are a number of administrative centres and royal buildings. Most of these are located on and around Mengo Hill, including **Mengo Palace** (Twekobe; Map pp428–9) inside a vast walled enclosure. The *kabaka* has other palaces, but may live in this one again when renovations are finished. Though it's an attractive building, the main reason to come here isn't for the palace itself (which can't be entered), but rather the muddy ruins of an underground prison and torture-execution chamber built by Idi Amin in the 1970s and later used by President Obote for the same sinister purposes. Charcoal messages written by former prisoners are still readable on the walls: one asks 'Obote, you have killed me, but what about my children!'. Entry is negotiable with the caretaker. Try to pay no more than USh5000 (and don't pay extra for your camera).

At the other end of a ceremonial drive leading from the palace is the **Buganda Parliament** (Map pp428-9; 0414-274926; Kabakanjagala Rd; admission USh5000; 8am-6pm Mon-Fri). Buy your ticket at the adjacent Buganda Tourism Centre (they may take over tours at the palace, in which case the disagreeable visitation situation currently there should change) out front and you'll get a quick tour of the

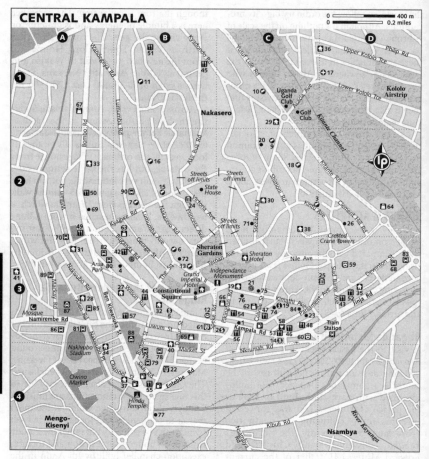

CENTRAL KAMPALA

building and brief history of the Buganda Kingdom. There are some enormous **tortoises** in the nearby grassy yard.

Between parliament and the palace is situated the former **Buganda Court of Justice** (Map pp428–9), now home to Uganda's Supreme Court.

Uganda Museum

With its burnt-out lights and broken display cases, the **Uganda Museum** (Map pp428–9; Kira Rd; adult/child USh3000/1500, camera/video camera USh5000/20,000; ⏰ 10am-6pm Mon-Sat, noon-6pm Sun) is crying out for some TLC. Despite the neglect, there's plenty to catch your interest here. The halls hold many good ethnographical exhibits covering hunting, agriculture, war,

religion and recreation (get the lowdown on banana beer here), as well as archaeological and natural history displays. Perhaps its most interesting feature is a collection of traditional musical instruments, some of which you can play. Out back are replicas of the traditional homes of the various tribes of Uganda.

Religious Buildings

The prominent **National Mosque** (Map pp428–9; Old Kampala Rd) was begun by Idi Amin in 1972 and finished in 2007 by Colonel Gadaffi. For a small donation (USh1000 should suffice) someone will show you around the simple but striking interior. Less impressive in terms of size but more attractive, the gleaming white

UGANDA

Kibuli Mosque (Map pp428–9), dominating Kibuli Hill south of the centre, was the previous principal mosque in Kampala. For another donation someone will take you up the minaret for superb city views.

The huge domed Anglican **Namirembe Cathedral** (Map pp428–9), finished in 1919, has a distinct Mediterranean feel. In years past the congregation was called to worship by the beating of enormous drums which can still be seen in a little hut located alongside the church. The twin-towered Roman Catholic **Rubaga Cathedral** (Map pp428–9) is just as large as Namirembe, but not nearly as impressive. In the transept is a memorial to the Uganda Martyrs (dozens of Ugandan Christians burnt or hacked to death by Kabaka Mwanga II during the course of 1885 and 1886 for refusing to renounce the white man's religion); 22 Catholic victims, later declared saints, are enshrined in the stained-glass windows.

The main execution site, now known as the **Uganda Martyr's Shrine**, is in Namugongo and has two churches. The Catholic one, built where the leader, Charles Lwanga, was burnt alive (on or around 3 June, which is now celebrated at Martyrs' Day), represents an African hut but looks more like something built by NASA than the

Catholic church. The water in the little lake out back is supposedly holy and people take it home to try to heal the sick. One and a half kilometres up the road, where 25 of Lwanga's followers met a similar fate that same day, has an older Anglican church; this site costs USh2000 and someone will show you around and tell you the whole story of the Martyrs. Both sites have statues of the gruesome events. The shrine is just outside Kampala off Jinja Rd. To get here, you'll need to take a minibus from the old taxi park.

Right in the city centre is **Kampala Hindu Temple** (Map p432; Snay Bin Amir Rise; ☿ 4-7.30pm) with its elaborate towers and swastika-emblazed gate. Peek inside to see the unexpected dome.

Way north of the city on Kikaaya Hill is the beautiful nine-sided **Baha'í Temple**, (Map p444), the first in Africa. Its manicured gardens are full of birdsong. A *boda-boda* costs USh1000 from where the minibus (ask for Kanyanya at the old taxi park) will drop you.

Art Galleries

A contemporary arts scene is emerging in Kampala, and until the proposed modern art museum crosses the threshold from dream to brick and mortar the best place to try and uncover it is **Tulifanya Gallery** (Map p432; ☎ 0782-327131; 28 Hannington Rd; ☿ 9.30am-5pm Tue-Fri, 9.30am-4pm Sat). The knowledgeable owners can inform you about artists who matter, such as Henry Mzili Mujunga (prints and paintings) and Maria Naita (paintings and sculpture). Another good gallery with work by serious artists is **Afriart** (Map pp428-9; ☎ 0414-375455; Jinja Rd; ☿ 9am-6pm) in the UMA Showgrounds just past the Lugogo Mall. Plus you can buy works at both these galleries.

The **Makerere University Art Gallery** (Map pp428-9; ☎ 0782-026812; admission free; ☿ 9am-4.30pm Tue-Fri, 9am-noon Sat, 2-5pm Sun) is small but has worthwhile and fascinating monthly exhibitions. There's also some cool sculpture on the grounds.

Usually less relevant are the **Nommo Gallery** (Map p432; ☎ 0414-234475; Princess Ave; admission free; ☿ 8am-6pm Mon-Fri & 10am-4pm Sat & Sun) and the **National Theatre** (Map p432; ☎ 0414-254567; Siad Barre Ave; admission free; ☿ hours vary), which sometimes has art on display upstairs.

Parliament House

The big, white **Parliament House** (Map pp428-9; Parliament Ave; ☿ 8.30am-4.30pm Mon-Fri) downtown is open to visitors. If you want to see government in action you need to make a written request to the public relations department (Room 114) which should decide by the next business day if you're worthy. You can see the cool cultural map of Uganda in the main lobby just by showing photo ID to the guard.

Volunteering

One of the best known charities in Uganda, **Sanyu Babies Home** (Map pp428-9; ☎ 0414-274032; www .sanyubabies.com; Natete Rd) receives and raises abandoned babies, many who have been left to die in ditches or latrines. To raise money, they have a craft shop and hostel (opposite). The website has a list of needed items if you have extra room in your luggage.

East Africa's only **skate park** (Map p444; ☎ 0752-397100), in Kitintale, a poor neighbourhood near Red Chilli Hideaway, sometimes has volunteer opportunities; and they always need old boards, pads and shoes. Money for cement would help too. Jack, the local director, can tell you how to get there from wherever you are. Kids skate all weekend and after 4pm weekdays.

See p527 for more on volunteering.

TOURS

You can trace back your coffee from the cup to the farm with the **Coffee Safari** (☎ 0772-505619; per person US$85; ☿ 7.30am Fri) run by 1000 Cups Coffee House (p438). Book before noon on Thursday.

Kampala Sightseeing Tours (☎ 0702-124124; www.sightseeing.co.ug; per person USh120,000; ☿ 9am Tue, Thu & Sun) offers a convenient way to see the city's top sights including Owino Market (p442) and Kasubi Tombs (p431). Tours depart from the Grand Imperial Hotel.

FESTIVALS & EVENTS

The **Amakula Kampala International Film Festival** takes place at the National Theatre and smaller halls around town roughly over the first 10 days of May.

The recently inaugurated **Kampala Street Art Festival** has the twin aims of raising the profile of art in Uganda and money for a modern art museum. Artists sell their works and there are plenty of music and dance performances. Sponsored in part by the Ugandan German Cultural Society (p429), it takes place in late May or early June.

Dates vary, but the finals of the **National Primary & Secondary School Music & Dance Competition**, featured in the movie *War/Dance* (p424) are held at the National Theatre. It was most recently in September.

The biggest event on the *muzungu* social calendar is the **Royal Ascot Goat Races** (www.thegoat races.com), a charity event at the enormous and gorgeous Speke Resort and Conference Centre (Map p444) on Lake Victoria. Goats really do race, but that's largely beside the point. People come here to eat, drink and wear funny hats.

SLEEPING

Kampala has good accommodation in all price brackets. But few places, especially at the top end where many rates are utterly ridiculous (always ask for discounts, you'll often get them), offer good value for your money. We predict that many of these prices will prove unsustainable, so if a place out of your price range appeals to you, it's worth checking if rates have dropped.

Budget

Most budget travellers choose to stay at Backpackers Hostel or Red Chilli Hideaway (both excellent places if that's your sort of vibe), but for those who don't want such an isolated experience, there are good choices in the heart of the city. There are also many flea pits, so always ask to see a room first.

HOSTELS & CAMPGROUNDS

These places are all located outside the city centre, but are easy to reach by minibus. The two backpacker places, which have more similarities than differences, both fill up fast during peak season, so be sure to book ahead.

Tuhende Safari Lodge (Map p432; ☎ 0772-468360; www.tuhendesafarilodge.com; 8 Martin Rd, Old Kampala; dm USh11,000, r USh60,000) Not many travellers stay in Old Kampala, but this place on the east side of Kampala Hill has become a favourite with Peace Corps volunteers and other aid workers due to its large comfortable rooms (no bunks here) and good food.

Backpackers Hostel (Map pp428-9; ☎ 0772-430587; www.backpackers.co.ug; Natete Rd, Lunguja; camping USh6000, dm USh8000-15,000 s/d without bathroom USh20,000/40,000,

bandas USh40,000, d USh50,000; 🖳) The first budget hostel to open its doors in Kampala and still going strong. Set in lush gardens with lots of shade, it's an escape from the bustle of the city. The facilities are quite good and become almost sophisticated at the top of the price range. Cooking facilities are available, but so are tasty, inexpensive meals. The bar draws a mix of travellers and expats, includes a pool table and stays open late. It's a 10-minute minibus ride out of the city centre, not far from Namirembe Cathedral. Take a Natete/Wakaliga minibus from the new taxi park (USh1000 uphill, but only USh500 return!). The team leads tours to Uganda's top national parks, with the budget trips to Murchison Falls (p511) being the most popular. This is also the best place for reliable information on visiting DRC, as they have, in the past, arranged gorilla permits.

Red Chilli Hideaway (Map p444; ☎ 0414-223903; www.redchillihideaway.com; camping USh7000, dm USh12,000-14,000, s/d/tr without bathroom from USh18,000/35,000-40,000/50,000, safari tent d USh30,000-50,000, cottage USh100,000; 🖳 🖳) Red Chilli is very popular with long-term and return guests, and it gets most of the overland truck business. The sweet cottages with lounge, bathroom and kitchen facilities are in the former managers' quarters of an old soap factory. Recreation options include playing badminton or billiards, cooling off in the world's smallest pool or watching the resident goats. There's food available throughout the day and a lively bar. Equally popular is the free internet access. Check out the reliable travel information here before moving on and take a look at its bargain three-day Murchison Falls (p511) trips. This great spot is off the road to Port Bell, about 6km out of the city centre. Take a minibus from the eastern end of Kampala Rd to Bugolobi for USh800, get off at the Shell station and take the road up the hill, following signs from there.

Sanyu Babies Home (Map pp428-9; ☎ 0414-274032; www.sanyubabies.com; Natete Rd; dm incl half board & laundry USh30,000; 🖳) These simple but cosy two-bed dorm rooms (self-contained rooms are planned) with nets and fans are used to raise money for this excellent charity (opposite). There are great views of the city.

HOTELS

our pick **New City Annex Hotel** (Map p432; ☎ 0414-254132; 7 Dewinton Rd; s USh12,000-15,000, d USh20,000-30,000 without bathroom, r USh30,000-45,000) A great

UGANDA

city centre location across from the National Theatre. Rooms range from simple shared-bath ones to larger self-contained units with TVs; all are clean. Walls in the cheapest rooms are thin, but the tiled floors give the place a hint of distinction and the restaurant downstairs is excellent.

China Palace 888 Hotel (Map p432; ☎ 0414-234888; Nabugabo Rd; s without bathroom USh18,000-22,000, d without bathroom USh25,000-30,000, s USh22,000-25,000, d USh30,000-40,000) This labyrinthine, Chinese-owned place by the new taxi park has small but good-value rooms and a great location if you have an early departure or late arrival, or just like staying in this part of town. The self-contained rooms have hand-held hookups from the sink rather than real showers.

L'Hotel Fiancé (Map p432; ☎ 0414-236144; Channel St; s/d/tr USh22,000/25,000/36,000) Promising a 'concentration of elegancy', this is the smartest place in this not-so-smart part of the city and better value than the nearby Samalien since rooms are ensuite. Get inside and it's a cheery place with bright and clean rooms.

Hotel City Square (Map p432; ☎ 0414-256257; hotelcitysquare@yahoo.com; 42 Kampala Rd; s/d USh35,000/45,000) Sitting in a strategic position on Kampala Rd, the hotel looks pretty drab from the exterior, but the rooms, with a TV and new paint, aren't bad. There's a popular terrace restaurant and fast connections in the adjacent internet café.

Embassy Hotel (Map pp428-9; ☎ 0414-267672; Muyenga Rd; r USh35,000-60,000) If you're looking for a different experience from most other visitors to Kampala, consider staying up in the city's fun Kabalagala district. This clean, respectable place is right in the thick of the action and has satellite TV in the rooms.

ourpick Aponye Hotel (Map p432; ☎ 0414-349239; www.aponyehotel.com; 17 William St; s USh45,000-70,000, d USh55,000-85,000; ▢ &) An astonishing find in this chaotic corner of the city, Aponye's shiny glass tower opened in 2007. The comfy rooms have satellite TV and wi-fi and those at the front have balconies. There's also secure parking and even white linen in the restaurant. Its 70 rooms are often empty so they'll usually bump you up a class (or knock off some money) if you think it will make the sale. Even at full price, Aponye is unbeatable value. Airport transfers are just US$15.

Also recommended:

Samalien Guesthouse (Map p432; ☎ 0414-533489; Nakivubo Green; s/d/tr without bathroom USh18,500/20,000/28,000, r USh28,000) A friendly, social place between the old taxi park and Owino Market.

Hotel Bonita (Map p432; ☎ 0414-236900; 66 William St; s USh35,000, d USh40,000-50,000) About the same standards as Hotel City Square with added satellite TV but minus hot water in the singles.

Midrange

There are some superb, beautiful hotels at the upper end of the midrange, though most are well outside the centre. All of these places include breakfast in the price.

Jeliza Hotel (Map p432; ☎ 0414-232249; 7 Bombo Rd; s USh65,000, d USh75,000-90,000; ▨) Nothing fancy (unless you count the lustrous blankets and tiny sitting areas) just good value. It's near the action of Kampala's chaotic core, but far enough away to offer slight respite.

Tourist Hotel (Map p432; ☎ 0414-251471; www.touristhotel.net; Dastur St; s USh63,000-74,000, d USh92,000-102,000) This large, older hotel overlooking Nakasero Market does a good job on the high standards-to-low prices ratio. Rooms are fitted with key card entry, satellite TV and telephones. The restaurant serves local, Indian and Chinese food.

Namirembe Guesthouse (Map pp428-9; ☎ 0414-273778; www.namirembe-guesthouse.com; Willis Rd; s without bathroom USh45,000, s USh70,000, d USh80,000-90,000; ▢) This church-run place promises 'a million dollar view', and does indeed offer some great cityscapes. Set in spacious grounds below Namirembe Cathedral, there are several buildings housing a variety of old but meticulously clean rooms. There's an onsite restaurant and juice bar.

Fang Fang Hotel (Map p432; ☎ 0414-235828; www.fangfang.co.ug; 9 Ssezibwa Rd; s US$60-100, d US$88-118; ▨ ▢) Just beyond the city centre, this old-timer warrants consideration less on its own merits than the outlandish prices of most of its neighbours. Although Fang Fang could use a renovation, rooms are perfectly adequate and there are a few cheaper (US$40) ones at the back. The attached Chinese restaurant is quite good.

Fairway Hotel (Map p432; ☎ 0414-257171; www.fairwayhotel.co.ug; 1 Kafu Rd; s/d/tr US$76/96/130; ▨ ▢ ▨) Overlooking the golf course, this older property has a few quirks and is fast approaching the classic category, but for central Kampala it offers good value; especially considering the free airport transfers. The rooms, set around a garden area, have carpet and refrigerators and most have balconies. There's a Chinese-Indian restaurant out front.

Le Bougainviller (Map p444; ☎ 0414-220966; www
.bougainviller.com; Port Bell Rd, Bugolobi; r US$90-120;
🅿 🖳 🐾) A little slice of the Mediterranean in
Africa, Le Bougainviller is arguably the loveliest hotel around town. The 13 rooms have
covered porches facing a flower-filled garden,
and the largest feature lofts and kitchens. A
French restaurant rounds out the experience.
Traffic noise is a bit of a nuisance.

Cassia Lodge (Map p444; ☎ 0755-777002; www.cassia
lodge.com; Buziga Hill; s/d US$95/120; 🅿 🖳 🐾) This
quiet spot boasts the best view in Kampala.
The sweeping vistas of Lake Victoria and the
hills backing it seem to never end. The rooms,
all facing the lake with balconies and patios
for taking it all in, are simple but tasteful and
feature minibars and wi-fi. The building has a
few gratuitous 'safari-style' touches like stone
walls and a mock-thatch roof. It's a long way
from the centre, signposted 2.3km off Gaba
Rd. Perfect for if you have to be in Kampala,
but don't want to be.

Speke Hotel (Map p432; ☎ 0414-259221; www
.spekehotel.com; Nile Ave; r US$137; 🅿 🖳) One of
Kampala's oldest hotels, this characterful,
refurbished address adds creature comforts
to age and grace. All rooms are rather simple, but have wooden floors and many have
balconies. It's a great central location (hence
the high price) and the terrace bar is a popular meeting place. There's also a good Italian
restaurant (Mammamia; see p439) but the
heaving Rock Garden (p440) bar is right
next door so take a room in the back.

Also recommended:

Capitol Palace (Map p444; ☎ 0414-289344; 26-32
Katalima Cres, Naguru; r US$50-130; 🅿 🖳) Quiet, out
of the way place (clearly signposted off Old Kira Rd) with a
lush garden setting. The cheapest rooms are great value.

Humura (Map pp428-9; ☎ 0414-700400; www.humura
.org; Yusuf Lule Rd, Kololo; s/d from US$135/155;
🅿 🖳 🐾) A funky mix of olde English furniture, tiled
floors and a blue wave wall in a quiet garden setting just
north of downtown. The pool is tiny.

Top End

It's hard to justify the prices, but other than
that, the following are excellent properties.
All have wi-fi, and all but Le Petit Village
have business centres.

Le Petit Village (Map pp428-9; ☎ 0312-265530;
www.lepetitvillage.net; Gaba Rd; r US$177, ste US$195-
218; 🅿 🖳 🐾) These big rooms are under
huge thatched roofs, which, along with
the extensive use of stone, creates a safari-

chic ambiance, even though the facilities
are ultra-modern. Le Chateau (p439) and
Quality Hill (p440) are right out front, so
you'll be able to eat as well as you sleep.

Serena Hotel (Map p432; ☎ 0414-309000; www.serena
hotels.com; Kintu Rd; r from US$307; 🅿 🖳 🐾 🅿 🅱)
Setting the standard in large, luxurious hotels,
the stunning Serena is the result of an 18-
month, US$1.5 million renovation of the
former Nile Hotel. The classiest address in
Kampala is set in 17-acre grounds full of
streams and ponds while the building itself
is full of flair like mosaic pillars and wrought
iron fixtures. Both the public areas and the
152 fully fitted rooms, each with a large balcony, feature art from across the continent,
and fresh flowers greet you in the hallways.
Facilities include a top-notch spa, enormous
pool and great dining.

Emin Pasha Hotel (Map pp428-9; ☎ 0414-236977;
www.eminpasha.com; 27 Akii Bua Rd; s/d from US$307/342;
🅿 🖳 🐾) Kampala's first boutique hotel is
beautifully housed in an elegant old colonial
property. The 20 rooms are the best in the
city, blending atmosphere and luxury, and
more expensive suites feature such touches
as claw-foot bathtubs. All have classic writing desks. Respected Fez Brasserie (p439)
restaurant shares the grounds.

Also recommended:

Protea Hotel (Map p432; ☎ 0414-550000; www
.proteahotels.com; Acacia Ave; r from US$174;
🅿 🖳 🅱) A new property delivering style rather
than flash, it has large rooms and is convenient to both
downtown and some of Kampala's best dining.

EATING

Kampala is packed with quality restaurants,
and the international population brings considerable variety to the dining scene. And,
unlike getting a good hotel in Kampala,
dining out can be very reasonable. Buffets
are very popular and usually great value at
USh5000 to USh10,000.

African

The best advice for eating good local food is
to find a place that's busy and join the crowd.
Failing that, these are some reliable options.

Tasty Bites (Map p432; Luwum St; snacks USh500-3500)
Recommended not for the food, which is just
ordinary take-away, but for the views over the
old taxi park. From here you can almost make
out the order in the apparent chaos. It's on

UGANDA

level five of the mall between Luwum St and the pedestrian walkway.

Amani (Map p432; ☎ 0752-488-726; Dewinton Rd; lunch USh3000-5000, dinner USh5000-16,000; ⏰ noon-10pm) Since northern Uganda features on few travel itineraries, this may be your best chance to try *olel*-style northern Ugandan food (served until 4pm; they switch to Indian at night), which puts sesame in everything.

New City Annex Hotel (Map p432; 7 Dewinton Rd; mains USh3500-12,000) The menu has all the expected meat and fish dishes, but also features more vegie choices than usual, including *firinda*, a simple but tasty bean sauce. Many locals eat here.

Ethiopian Village (Map pp428-9; ☎ 0414-510378; Muyenga Rd, Kabalagala; mains USh5000-9000, traditional coffee ceremony USh10,000; ⏰ 9am-10pm) There are many Ethiopian eateries in the fun Kabalagala part of town, but this long-timer has the most pleasant setting with thatched-roof huts and a little garden. If you're new to Ethiopian food, you eat with your hands by scooping up the meats, sauces and vegies with *injera* (spongy, unleavened flat bread).

Tuhende Safari Lodge (Map p432; ☎ 0772-468360; 8 Martin Rd, Old Kampala; mains USh7500-9900; ⏰ 10am-midnight) Besides a mix of simple snacks and professionally prepared meals, this little café serves up an old European feel. The char-grilled steaks and fish are the speciality, but vegetable stew is pretty good too.

Also recommended:

Mama Ashanti (Map p432; ☎ 0774-997123; 3 Bombo Rd; mains USh4500-11,500) Real-deal Ghanaian dishes such as pepper soup and fried rice. It even imports its yams from across the continent.

Hotel Equatoria (Map p432; ☎ 0414-250780; Kyagwe Rd; buffet USh15,000; ⏰ 12.30-3.15pm) The Sunday lunch buffet features Ugandan food, salad and dessert; and the price includes use of the hotel's pool until 5pm.

Cafés

Kampala has an emerging café culture and there are many places to kick back.

1000 Cups Coffee House (Map p432; ☎ 0772-505619; 18 Buganda Rd; spiced coffee USh3000; ⏰ 8am-8pm Mon-Sat, 9am-6pm Sun) For a coffee kick from Kentucky to Vietnam to Uganda and everything in between, caffeine cravers should head here. There's also a menu of light bites and ice cream. It's a good place to hang out and catch up with the rest of the world, as there's a large selection of international newspapers and magazines.

Vasili's Bakery (Map p432; ☎ 0414-340842; Kampala Rd; espresso USh3000, chocolate croissant USh1300; ⏰ 6.30am-midnight Sun-Thu, to 2am Fri & Sat; 💻) A top spot for breakfast or afternoon tea, this is a bakery to remember. It serves perhaps the best range of pies and cakes in the city plus baguettes, apple crumble and other old-world favourites are plentiful here. The outdoor patio is always bustling.

our pick Café Pap (Map p432; ☎ 0414-254570; 13 Parliament Ave; mains USh10,000-20,000; ⏰ 7.30am-11pm Mon-Sat, 9.30am-11pm Sun) This stylish café might be the place to meet some movers and shakers. The house coffee comes from the slopes of Mt Elgon, and many will tell you it's the best in town. There's also a full menu with breakfasts, sandwiches, salads, fajitas and pastas.

Also recommended:

Tulifanya Gallery (Map p432; 28 Hannington Rd; mains USh4500-12,000; ⏰ 9.30am-5.30pm Mon-Fri, 9.30am-4pm Sat) This little outdoor café fronting the great art gallery (p434) is a popular lunchspot for sandwiches, salads and more.

Panorama Coffee Shop (Map p432; 9th fl Worker's House, Portal Ave; sandwiches USh6500-8000; ⏰ 8.45am-10.15pm; 💻 💻) This little art-rimmed spot delivers big views and free wi-fi along with sandwiches and snacks.

European

Efendy's (Map pp428-9; ☎ 0414-374507; off Jinja Rd; mains USh7000-20,0000; ⏰ 8am-late) One of a string of garden restaurants in Centenary Park, this happening place (football on TV, movies or DJs on most nights) has authentic Turkish cuisine such as spiced mutton chops (*pirzola kebap*), fish cubes in tomato sauce (*firinda balik sote*) and barbeque chicken (*tavok sis*). The meze plate is so good you may just want to make it your meal, along with something off the wine list.

Crocodile (Map pp428-9; ☎ 0414-254593; Cooper Rd; sandwiches & salads USh6000-14,000, mains USh10,000-17,000; ⏰ 11am-11pm Mon-Sat) Now a Kisimenti classic, this popular café-bar manages to pull off something of an old Parisian vibe. The menu is a tempting mix of salads, sandwiches, pastas and heartier meat dishes. Try the stuffed tilapia (Nile perch) with creamy saffron sauce.

Iguana (Map pp428-9; ☎ 0777-020658; 8 Bukoto St; lunch USh9000-11,000, dinner USh15,000-17,000; ⏰ 12.30-3pm & 6pm-late Tue-Sun) Don't judge this popular place by the pedestrian dining room in the front, head upstairs and let the comfy couches and jazz music pull you in. The food, mostly French, is simple fare done well. There's a

Ugandan buffet at lunch and DJs on Friday and Saturday nights.

Le Chateau (Map pp428-9; Gaba Rd; lunch USh10,000-17,500, dinner USh20,500-37,000; ☼ 7am-11pm Mon-Sat, 7am-10pm Sun; 🖳) Popular for serious steaks, Le Chateau shares a home with the Quality Cuts Butchery, guaranteeing top meat. The extensive Belgian menu, served under an enormous thatched roof, includes steak tartar and frogs' legs, so if you're looking to indulge, this is a good place to do it. The simpler lunch menu features salads, burgers and croquettes. You can link up to the wi-fi network while relaxing here.

Mamba Point Pizzeria (Map pp428-9; ☎ 0772-743227; 62 Lumumba Ave; large pizza USh16,000-23,000; ☼ noon-2.30pm & 6-10pm Tue-Sat, noon-10pm Sun); Restaurant (Map p432; ☎ 0772-243225; 22 Akii Bua Rd; mains USh17,900-76,000; ☼ noon-2.30pm & 7-10.30pm Mon-Fri, 7-10.30pm Sat) Mamba Point is the first and last word in genuine Italian dining in Kampala. The pasta is home-made and many other ingredients imported, making the menu as close to the homeland as you might hope to find in Africa. Save space for the exquisite desserts, which include lime syllabub and chocolate truffle torte. The restaurant has no pizzas, but you can get some wood-fired beauties just a few minutes away.

Fez Brasserie (Map pp428-9; ☎ 0414-236977; 27 Akii Bua Rd; mains USh30,000-38,000; ☼ 12.30-3pm & 7-10pm; 🖳) One of Kampala's most renowned restaurants, this gorgeous spot looking out over the leafy grounds of the Emin Pasha Hotel (p437) does not coast by on its reputation. The ever-evolving fusion menu, which respects vegetarians, unites flavours from five continents. Typical options include cashew and coriander chicken, grilled vegetable tartlet and the ever-popular char-grilled beef fillet. And, how about homemade ice cream or baked mango cardamom cheesecake for dessert? Or, just come for the comfy couches in the wine bar.

Also recommended:

Rocks & Roses (Map p432; Surgery, 2 Acacia Ave; sandwiches USh6500-8000; ☼ 9.30am-5pm Mon-Fri) Despite the traffic noise, NGO workers and expats love this place for afternoon tea.

Mammamia (Map p432; ☎ 0414-346340; Speke Hotel, Nile Ave; pizza from USh15,000; ☼ 24hr; 🖳) The wood-fired pizzas (available in animal shapes for kids) at this outdoor café aren't quite straight out of Italy, but are good all the same. There's also genuine gelato.

East Asian

Great Wall (Map p432; ☎ 0712-937148; 21 Kampala Rd; mains USh4000-18,000) Your ordinary Chinese take-away from back home wrapped in a half-hearted attempt at elegance.

Fang Fang (Map p432; ☎ 0414-344806; Colville St; mains USh6000-28,000; ☼ 11am-midnight; 🍴) Although there's much more competition these days, and there's no question the service has slipped, the consensus in the city remains that this is one of Kampala's best Chinese restaurants. At first glance the anonymous office block it's located in (on the 2nd floor) might make you hesitate, but the interior is lovely, typical of a pricey Chinese restaurant anywhere, and there's a large, quiet outdoor terrace. There's a full selection of Chinese classics, and specialities include fried crispy prawns with ginger and garlic.

Arirang (Map p432; ☎ 0414-346777; Kyadondo Rd; mains USh7000-37,000; ☼ 10am-10pm) The huge menu at Kampala's only Korean restaurant covers all the bases, from seafood to hot pot to pork ear salad. There are karaoke rooms and, for large groups, VIP rooms that look traditional, but have a hole cut in the floor so you don't need to sit cross-legged.

Krua Thai (Map pp428-9; ☎ 0414-234852; 34 Windsor Cres, Kololo; mains USh10,000-41,000; ☼ noon-3pm & 6.30-10.30pm Mon-Sat) If you're after the taste of Thailand, Krua Thai is your best bet. The reasonably authentic menu includes all the familiar greatest hits, including *pad Thai, tôm yam kung,* and a very tasty *gaang pet* (red curry). Those used to dining in Thailand might want to ask staff to up the chilli count, as they tone down the spices on most dishes.

Fast Food

Some of the cheapest places to eat in Kampala are the ubiquitous take-aways. It's pointless to recommend any in particular as they're fairly standard outfits offering greasy quick-serve dishes such as chicken, meat, sausages, fish and chips, pilau rice and samosas. Prices are the same whether you eat in or take-away, and a meal costs about USh1500 to USh3500.

At the other end of the spectrum, the **Garden City Food Court** (Map p432; Yusuf Lule Rd; ☼ 10am-10pm) has several appealing international options including Cuban, Thai, Indian and Italian.

There's also a little fast-food complex on Kampala Rd at Parliament Ave with **Nando's** (Map p432; Kampala Rd) for chicken among some local outlets. It stays open very late. A bit further west is a similar spot with a **Steers** (Map p432; Kampala Rd) burger joint and a **Debonairs** (Map p432; Kampala Rd) for pizza.

UGANDA

Also recommended:

Antonio's (Map p432; Kampala Rd; mains USh3500-7500; 6.30am-4.30pm) A pretty good greasy spoon serving Uganda, Kenyan and western favourites. The menu claims burritos, but you won't recognise them as such.

New York Kitchen (Map p432; Garden City, lower lever car park; slice USh4000) New York–style pizza (well, almost) and Kampala's only bagels.

Indian

Masala Chaat House (Map p432; ☎ 0414-236487; 3 Dewinton Rd; mains USh4000-12,000; 9.30am-10pm) A winning combination of authentic flavours and affordable prices have kept this local institution going strong over the years. Located opposite the National Theatre, it offers plenty to keep both vegetarians and carnivores smiling for the night.

Pavement Tandoori (Map pp428-9; ☎ 0414-344994; Cooper Rd; mains USh8300-56,600; 10.30am-3pm & 5.30-10.30pm) This superb subcontinental spot right in the middle of the action on the popular Cooper Rd strip is as good for the food as the setting, a plant-shielded patio and a stylish dining room with an open kitchen in-between. It gives Haandi a run for their money.

our pick **Haandi** (Map p432; ☎ 0414-346283; 7 Kampala Rd; mains USh9700-41,700; noon-2.30pm & 7-10.30pm;) The gold standard in subcontinental cuisine, Haandi is worth a splurge even if you're travelling on a budget. This is a great place to experiment a little: try the tilapia tikka or *bharva simla mirch* (BBQ stuffed peppers). They have a fast-food outlet at Garden City.

Self-Catering

Quality Hill (Map pp428-9; Gaba Rd) To pack a four-star picnic, visit this fashionable foodie enclave, home to Quality Cuts Butchery for meat and cheese, the superb La Patisserie bakery and The Cellar wine shop.

Ranchers (Map p432; Garden City) This delicatessen has a good range of cheeses and meats plus some little luxuries such as maple syrup. There's a small deli-café and they'll even cook up what you've just bought if you can't wait to taste your fresh red snapper.

Shoprite Clock Tower Roundabout (Map p432; Ben Kiwanuka St); Lugogo Mall (Map pp428-9; Jinja Rd) and **Uchumi** (Map p432; Garden City) are large supermarkets ideal for stocking up before heading upcountry. **Checkers** (Map pp428–9) and **Millennium** (Map pp428–9) on Cooper Rd are smaller, but also stock plenty of imports.

Tex-Mex

Fat Boyz (Map pp428-9; ☎ 0782-416900; 7 Cooper Rd; mains USh12,000-25,000; 11am-late Mon-Sat) The closest thing Uganda has to a *cantina*, this fun, low-brow place in Kisimenti does vaguely Tex-Mex standards such as nachos and chilli-marinated prawns, has a well-worn pool table and at night sells far more beer than burritos. This is the bar that closes down Cooper Rd.

DRINKING

Nightlife in Kampala is something to relish these days, with a host of decent bars and clubs throughout the city. There's generally something happening in the city on most nights, although Friday is the biggest bash. There's a tail-off on Saturday since many of the previous night's clubbers will be going to church early on Sunday. Many places host Fresh Wednesdays, with reduced beer prices.

Most places are open at least from 7pm until midnight and many of the popular places are open much later. Fat Boyz (above) and Iguana (p438) are as much about libation as the food and Red Chilli (p435) and Backpackers (p435) can also get pretty busy.

CITY CENTRE

Mateo's (Map p432; Parliament Ave) This pub-like place is a relaxing spot for an evening tipple, unless a big football match is on or the DJ is spinning on Friday nights. It has a good lunch buffet (USh7000) too.

Rock Garden (Map p432; Nile Ave) One of the definitive stops on the Kampala nightshift, this cool place has a covered bar and a huge outdoor area, often heaving with people as early as 9pm. The complex includes a couple of small dance floors and drinks are a fair deal. Prostitutes hang out here in droves and pick-pocketing is often part of the experience.

The Pub (Map p432; Dewinton Rd) A local, low-key place facing the National Theatre. This one 'never dies' one fan told us.

Mist (Map p432) The Serena Hotel's (p437) watering hole walks a fine line between lovely and theme-park, but most people, including us, think it falls on the correct side. Of course, it's a moot point if you don't want to pay USh6000 for a Nile Special.

OUTSKIRTS

Bubbles O'Learys (Map pp428-9; ☎ 0312-263815; 9 Acacia Ave) Kampala's contribution to the growing legion of Irish pubs, the bar and furnishings were shipped in from an old Irish pub back on the Emerald Isle. The food's not so great and the 'Guinness' isn't the real thing, but it draws a fun crowd. There are movies on Tuesday, live music on Wednesday, quiz night on Thursday, and DJs at weekends; mind the cheeky USh5000 cover charge on big nights.

Al's Bar (Map p444; Gaba Rd) A legend in Kampala, this is the most famous bar in Uganda, although notorious might be a better word! This is the one place in Kampala that never sleeps. It gets very busy at weekends, and attracts a regular crowd of expats, Ugandans and a fair number of prostitutes; meaning half the customers or more. Drinks are reasonable.

Capital Pub (Map pp428–9; Muyenga Rd) Another infamous imbibing institution in Kabalagala, cut from the same cloth as Al's, but with many more pool tables; it gets going earlier in the evening.

Café Cheri (Map pp428–9; Muyenga Rd) This is a smaller, less raucous spot than Capital and Al's. The prostitutes are a lot less pushy here, and sometimes even a bit of dancing breaks out. Check out both of the buildings.

ENTERTAINMENT

Nightlife in Uganda may be fairly low-key, but Kampala, the rocking capital, is thankfully the exception to the rule. Here there are nightclubs and discos that rage on well into the night.

Nightclubs

Several of the bars have a nightclub feel to them in the early hours of the morning, and at weekends there's pretty much guaranteed to be dancing at Rock Garden (opposite) and Bubbles O'Learys (opposite).

The leading discos are out in the industrial area of the city, just off Jinja Rd. Charges rise as the weekend comes around and both places have more-expensive VIP areas upstairs.

Ange Noir (Map pp428–9; 1st St; admission USh2000-10,000; 9pm-5am Thu-Sun) The 'black angel' is pronounced locally as 'Angenoa', a pretty fair rendition of the French. Despite the dour exterior, it has long held Kampala's most popular dance floor. When you're this cool you don't have to flaunt it

Club Silk (Map pp428–9; 1st St; admission USh3000-10,000; 9pm-5am Thu-Sat) On the same street as Ange Noir, this is an identikit club that's usually full of university students. Most people will tell you that Silk Royale has the best music of all the rooms.

There are also two more intimate places where nights start out with drinking but eventually turn to dancing.

Rouge (Map p432; Kampala Rd; admission USh10,000 Fri & Sat; 9pm-5am Tue-Sun) Kampala's first lounge club, the über-hip Rouge wouldn't be out of place in a Euro-capital. Wednesday is rock night and local pop starts make appearances on Friday. For something genuinely musical, try to catch the Maurice Kirya Experience on the last Tuesday of the month.

Sway (Map p432; Kampala Rd; admission USh10,000 Wed, Fri, & Sat; 9pm-5am Mon-Sat) This newer place is trying, unsuccessfully so far, to steal some of Rouge's thunder. It's a little blander, but has an excellent sound system.

Live Music

It's sad to say, but lip-synching or singing to canned music is the main musical entertainment these days. To see who's on stage on any given weekend, check out Friday's listings page in the *New Vision* newspaper or look for banners along Kampala Av.

Club Obbligato (Map pp428–9; Old Port Bell Rd) Once a top joint for Ugandan musicians, Obbligato is still home to the popular Afrigo Band, which plays here every weekend (10.30pm, USh10,000), but the stage is empty the rest of the week.

Traditional Dance

If you're interested in traditional dance and music, try to catch a dinner-theatre performance of the Ndere Troupe. It showcases dances from many of Uganda's ethnic groups. The troupe has a lovely base way out in Ntinda, the **Ndere Centre** (Map p444; ☎ 0414-288123; www.ndere .com; Kisaasi Rd), which includes a 700-seat amphitheatre, a restaurant-bar and a guesthouse. The high-energy shows take place every Sunday from 6pm to 9pm and cost USh10,000/5000 per adult/child. A new Wednesday 7pm to 10pm show mixes in the standard performances with some afro-jazz music and storytelling.

The **Grand Imperial Hotel** (Map p432; ☎ 0414-250681; 6 Nile Ave) hosts the Crane Performers down by the pool on Sunday nights from 6pm to 8pm. Buy a meal or some drinks and the show is free.

Cinemas

The only remaining movie house in Kampala is **Cineplex** (Map p432; ☎ 0312-261415; Garden City; USh11,000) in the Garden City mall. It screens a mix of Hollywood and Bollywood fare.

UGANDA

A NIGHT OUT AT THE NATIONAL THEATRE

The **National Theatre** (Map p432; ☎ 0414-254567; Siad Barre Ave) is one of the most happening places in Kampala. Besides one-off music, film, dance and drama performances, it hosts a trio of weekly events that you really ought to attend if you're in town at the right time. Usually they take place outdoors and have a festival atmosphere.

The **Musicians Club** (⌚ 8pm-midnight) kicks things off on Monday with an informal open-stage jam. Musicians jump in and out after a few songs and *muzungu* are welcome to take a turn.

The infectious grooves of **Percussion Discussion Africa** (USh3000; ⌚ 8-9.30pm), an African fusion band playing every Tuesday, attract far fewer locals, but are probably more rewarding for visitors.

The biggest crowds come for Thursday's **Comedy Night** (USh5000; ⌚ 8.30-10pm), where the merriment comes in a mix of English and Luganda.

To see some Ugandan-born movies try **Film Chat** (⌚ discussion 2-6.30pm, film 7pm) on the last Tuesday of the month at the National Theatre.

SHOPPING

Kampala is a good place to do your craft shopping since items from all regions of the country are available, though much of the merchandise comes from neighbouring Kenya, despite what the sellers claim. For fine arts, see Art Galleries p434.

Banana Boat (Map p428-9; ☎ 0414-232885; Cooper Rd) This sophisticated craft shop has three branches. The original has smart local items including some excellent batiks plus stuff from all over Africa, including Congolese carvings. There's a similar branch at Garden City (Map p432), plus an outlet with an emphasis on homes and interiors in Lugogo Mall (Map pp428–9).

Buganda Tourism Centre (Map pp428-9; ☎ 0414-274926; Kabakanjagala Rd) The craft shop here is tiny, but it's the only one selling bark-cloth clothing. Dresses and vests are in stock and they'll take custom orders.

Quality Hill (Map pp428-9; Gaba Rd) A guy with a great selection of Congolese carvings lays out his wares near the pharmacy at this small shopping mall.

Uganda Crafts 2000 (Map p432; ☎ 0414-250077; Bombo Rd) A small nonprofit, fair trade shop selling the usual crafts and trinkets; these made mostly by widows and the disabled. There are some interesting sustainable paper products.

Roberto Andreetta Antiques (Map p432; Pilkington Rd) Has stamps and money from the past and present, plus tribal artefacts that may or may not be old.

The city's craft 'villages' are top attractions with visitors. All stock the same woodcarvings, drums, sandals, batiks, basketry, beaded jewellery and '*muzungo*' t-shirts. Some items have price tags, but everything is negotiable. Visit several stalls before buying, and bring your bargaining hat. With over 50 venders, **Exposure Africa** (Map p432; 13 Buganda Rd) is the largest and **Craft Africa** (Map p432; Buganda Rd) sits right next door. Craft Africa has one standout stall with some great Congolese and Sudanese carvings. The same vender also has a stall at the **National Arts & Crafts Village** (Map p432; Dewinton Rd) behind the National Theatre, which has the best overall selection of all these markets. Finally, the **African Crafts Market** (Map p432; Portal Rd) is a fourth choice.

At the other end of the spectrum, the best place for shopping is **Garden City** (Map p432; Yusuf Lule Rd) which has several floors of shops and banks plus a cinema, bowling alley, casino and food court.

Markets

If Kampala's taxi parks make you agoraphobic then you'll definitely want to stay out of the markets.

The partially covered **Nakasero Market**, (Map p432) near the junction of Kampala and Entebbe Rds, is all about food, plus the attractive building at the lower half has an outer ring of hardware and housewares stores.

The incredible **Owino Market** (aka St Balikuddembe Market; Map p432), which sprawls around Nakivubo Stadium, has everything else; from traditional medicines to televisions. It's most famous for its second-hand clothing, but you can also buy some material and let one of the army of tailors sew you something new. You're bound to spend a lot of time here: not only because it's so much fun, but also because once you're inside it's really difficult to find your way out.

GETTING THERE & AWAY

Air
See p531 for domestic and international flight details.

Boat
It's possible to book passage on cargo ships sailing between Kampala's Port Bell and Mwanza, Tanzania. See p262 for details.

Bus
Most bus companies use the **main bus park** (Map p432), aka old bus park, but there are also many departures from the more pleasant **new bus park** (Map p432), both just off Namirembe Rd near Nakivubo Stadium. For Arua, head to the nearby Arua Park (Map p432) area along Wilson Rd.

Destinations are posted in the front windows and buses generally follow the times they tell you, though the later it is in the day, the more likely there are to be delays. Buses leave early if they're full. See the appropriate town listing for prices and travel times.

POST BUS
These mail-delivery buses depart at 8am Monday to Saturday from the **main post office** (Map p432; Kampala Rd) for Kabale (USh16,000) via Mbarara (USh10,000); Fort Portal (USh10,000); Hoima (USh12,000) via Masindi (USh10,000); and Gulu (USh16,000). The Soroti (USh12,000) service, via Tororo (USh9000) and Mbale (USh10,000), has infrequent departures.

These buses take a little longer than a normal bus, but are much safer. You can get information and make day-before reservations at counter 11 in the post office, or you can just rock along Speke Rd around 7am. From originating provincial towns to Kampala, they depart from the post offices earlier in the morning, often at 6am.

INTERNATIONAL BUSES
Numerous bus companies offer direct daily links from Kampala to Kenya, Tanzania, Rwanda, Sudan, and even Burundi. See p528 for details and prices.

Minibus
Kampala has two main taxi parks for minibuses, and both serve destinations around the country as well as within Kampala itself. Although packed beyond belief there's a significant degree of organisation. The old taxi park (Map p432) is the busier of the two and serves towns in eastern Uganda; the nearby new taxi park (Map p432) services western and northern destinations. Buses to Entebbe leave from both.

GETTING AROUND
Traffic jams are a major headache in Kampala, so no matter where you're going in the city, plan ahead if you need to get there at an appointed time. Rush hour is particularly bad, usually from 7.30am to 9.30am, 1pm to 2.30pm and 4.30pm to 7.30pm; on Friday it seems to last all day.

To/From the Airport
The international airport is at Entebbe (p444), 40km from Kampala. A special-hire from Kampala to the airport costs about USh50,000. Ask at the tourist office in the airport to see if this has changed before bargaining with the drivers. The cheapest option is to take a minibus between Kampala (from either taxi park) and Entebbe (USh2500, 45 minutes), and then catch a saloon car shared taxi (USh1500 per person) to the airport, if you can find one. But, since these are rare you'll probably end up needing a special-hire. The correct price for this, from Entebbe's taxi park, is USh6000, but you'll probably end up paying USh10,000.

Most of the upmarket hotels and some midrange ones offer airport pick-up services, but it usually costs more than getting your own special-hire.

Boda-bodas
Motorbike taxis are the fastest way to get around Kampala since they can weave in and out of the traffic jams. It's not necessarily the safest way to travel since some of the drivers are quite reckless: the *New Vision* newspaper has reported that on average there are five deaths daily as a result of *boda-boda* accidents. A new law requires drivers to provide helmets for passengers, but they rarely have one of their own. *Boda-bodas* are best avoided at night.

Drivers have imposed an unofficial minimum fare of USh1000 around the city centre and are pretty good about sticking to it. The fare from the centre out to the UWA office or museum is likely to be USh2000. *Boda-bodas* can also be hired by the hour or day, but prices will depend on how big a swath of the city you plan to tackle. If you go this route, give them USh1000 at the start to buy a newspaper and you'll have a new best friend.

Minibus

The ubiquitous white and blue minibus taxis fan out from the city centre to virtually every point in Kampala. Many start in the taxi parks (for most destinations you can use either park), however it's quicker to flag one down on Kampala Rd as they don't need to navigate the nightmare tailbacks around the taxi parks.

Special-Hire Taxi

In Kampala there are plenty of 'special-hire' taxis. Most are unmarked to avoid licensing and taxes, but if you see a car with its door open or with the driver sitting behind the wheel while parked, it's probably a special-hire. They're always found outside hotels (except for the cheapest), near busy shopping areas and at the taxi and bus parks. At night they wait in great numbers outside popular bars and clubs.

A standard short-distance fare is around USh3000 to USh5000. You'll be looking at

USh6000 from the city centre to the UWA office or Kisimenti, and USh10,000 to the Kabalagala/Gaba Rd area. If you hire by the hour, and aren't moving much beyond the city centre, you should be able to pay USh10,000. Prices will be higher at night and during rush hour.

City Cab (☎ 0414-233330) has expensive (USh500 flagfall and USh1500 per kilometre) 24-hour dispatch and metres.

AROUND KAMPALA

There are some pretty nice places to visit around Kampala; and if you have the time, most can be reached by public transport.

ENTEBBE

Located on the shores of Lake Victoria, Entebbe is an attractive, verdant town that served duty as the capital city during the early years of the British protectorate; though it's the relaxed pace of life and natural attractions rather than any notable colonial relics that give the city its charm.

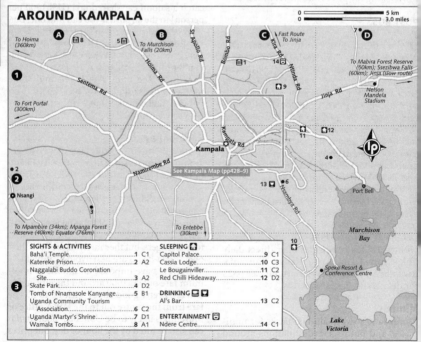

AROUND KAMPALA

SIGHTS & ACTIVITIES		
Baha'i Temple	1	C1
Katereke Prison	2	A2
Naggalabi Buddo Coronation		
Site	3	A2
Skate Park	4	D2
Tomb of Nnamasole Kanyange	5	B1
Uganda Community Tourism		
Association	6	C2
Uganda Martyr's Shrine	7	D1
Wamala Tombs	8	A1

SLEEPING 🏠		
Capitol Palace	9	C1
Cassia Lodge	10	C3
Le Bougainviller	11	C2
Red Chilli Hideaway	12	D2

DRINKING 🍸 🍷		
Al's Bar	13	C2

ENTERTAINMENT 🎭		
Ndere Centre	14	C1

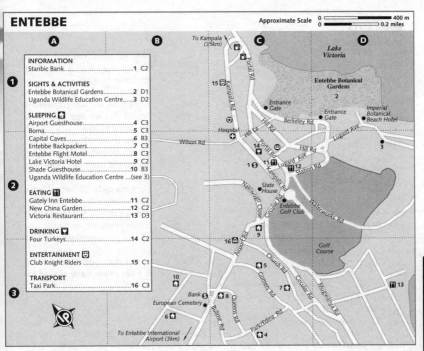

ENTEBBE

Approximate Scale

INFORMATION
Stanbic Bank.............................1 C2

SIGHTS & ACTIVITIES
Entebbe Botanical Gardens............2 D1
Uganda Wildlife Education Centre.....3 D2

SLEEPING
Airport Guesthouse......................4 C3
Boma.......................................5 C3
Capital Caves.............................6 B3
Entebbe Backpackers....................7 C3
Entebbe Flight Motel....................8 C3
Lake Victoria Hotel......................9 C2
Shade Guesthouse......................10 B3
Uganda Wildlife Education Centre ...(see 3)

EATING
Gately Inn Entebbe......................11 C2
New China Garden.......................12 C2
Victoria Restaurant......................13 D3

DRINKING
Four Turkeys..............................14 C2

ENTERTAINMENT
Club Knight Riders.......................15 C1

TRANSPORT
Taxi Park..................................16 C3

Unless you have reason to rush into Kampala, Entebbe makes a nice, relaxing introduction to Uganda. It's also the ideal place to end your trip if you're stuck with one of the many early morning flights out of Uganda's only international airport.

Information

There are payphones and a couple of internet cafés along Kampala Rd in the centre of town, plus more internet access out at the Wildlife Education Centre and the airport.

Exchange rates at the banks in town are better than those at the airport, but lower than Kampala. **Stanbic Bank** (Kampala Rd) changes travellers cheques as well as cash.

Sights & Activities

The **Uganda Wildlife Education Centre** (☎ 0414-320520; www.ugandawildlifecentre.com; Lugard Ave; adult/child USh15,000/10,000, per camera/video camera USh1000/5000; ☽ 9am-6.30pm) functions as a zoo, but is actually a world-class animal refuge that has benefited from international assistance in recent years. Most of the animals on display were once injured or were recovered from poachers and

traffickers. Star attractions include white rhinos, lions, chimpanzees and shoebill storks, plus lots of freerange monkeys including black-and-white colobus. If you want to get closer to the animals, i-to-i (www.i-to-i.com) offers volunteer programs. There's a restaurant by the lake, an internet café and lodging.

A short walk from the Wildlife Education Centre, the **Entebbe Botanical Gardens** (adult/child USh2000/1000, per car/camera/video camera USh2000/2000/5000; ☽ 9am-7pm) was laid out in 1898. Most of the trees' labels are missing and there's too much trash strewn about, but there are some interesting, unusual trees and shrubs making it worth a wander. And, if you're a bird-watcher, then it's a must for the often unobstructed viewing. The trail through the garden's thick rainforest centre (where locals claim some of the Johnny Weissmuller *Tarzan* films were made) is known as the 'spider walk', and if you look carefully you might see some rather large examples. There's a little restaurant and picnic area down by the lake.

There are several **beaches** around town, which get very crowded at weekends, but are nearly empty on weekdays.

BODA BOYS

Makaidu Michael, Kampala, age 30

The good thing about this job is that you never fail to get money for food. You may not save anything some days, but at least you get food. I bought a small plot and I built a small house. Now I am saving for my children's school fees. I am blessed with three daughters.

I started driving in 2001. I was at secondary school, doing HEAD (History, Economics And Divinity), but I dropped out because I failed to raise the fees. I didn't have any luck finding a job. There is a factory where I went and looked for anything they could give me and they wanted to know about experience. I had never done anything, so they refused to give me a job. After that I had a neighbour who hired his motorcycle to me. I gave him USh6500 per day. I didn't like it at first. I used to get scared of all the other vehicles. I wanted to quit, but I saw if I quit I wouldn't get another job. So I continued. It took me three years to get used to it. Ever since I started I never crashed. God blessed me with that.

I kept on changing motorcycles until God blessed me and I got my own. It's uncomfortable driving someone else's motorcycle because you always have stress. There is a lady who gave me a loan for USh1.6 million. I paid her USh10,000 a day. I can make USh20,000 to USh25,000 most days. Sometimes you fail to make that and only get USh15,000. There are even days where you make USh10,000. But there are days when you are blessed and you can make USh30,000 or more.

I start at 7am because I drop my children at school and then I start taking others. Some people pay me weekly and monthly to take their kids to school. I get to my stage around 8am. Sometimes I go back home at 8.30pm; sometimes nine.

I like the freedom of being my own boss, but there are many bad things about the work. Sometimes you can take people and they reach their destination and they run away without paying. And there are thieves who kill drivers and take the motorcycles. Somebody tried to rob me once, but when he looked at my motorcycle he didn't like it, so he told me to go away. I'm having a problem now because the dust is finishing up my eyes.

Nsubuga Patrick, Kalangala, age 25

I like this job because I'm earning something. I used to do fishing, but I don't want to go back on the water. I'd rather stay on land. I started in January of this year [2008] when I finished school. I went to Makerere University in Kampala and studied environmental science. I tried to apply for jobs but I didn't have the chance to get one so I drive my *boda-boda* instead of waiting for those good jobs. I am still looking now; however I want to make my own business, but now I don't have the capital. It takes a lot of money to buy trees and things.

I start early in the morning at six and then at ten at night I go home to sleep. I work daily, even on Sundays. In the morning I bring passengers to the ship at the pier. That's the busiest time; and also picking passengers up at five in the evening. However, between those times there are some people to take around the island, but we are always busy at those two hours.

I got a loan from Stanbic Bank to buy my *boda-boda,* so I have to pay them little by little. It cost USh2,250,000. I've paid USh1,800,000, so I'm about to clear the debt. Every day I always make something like USh15,000. On good days I can make something like USh30,000. Bad days are there too, like when it rains or I wake up late; then I can make something like USh6000. When I clear that debt I might hire the *boda-boda* out to another driver. Then I hope I will get another job, but if I don't find one I will buy another motorcycle and keep on driving.

Sleeping

Entebbe has a very good selection of accommodation options. Most places, except the cheapest, offer free airport transfers.

Entebbe Backpackers (☎ 0414-320432; www.entebbe backpackers.com; 33-35 Church Rd; camping USh6000, dm USh10,000, s/d without bathroom USh15,000/20,000, s/d USh25,000/35,000-45,000) This colourful, spic-and-span place is much cosier than the similar spots in Kampala and Jinja. Rooms are spacious, shared facilities are kept clean and the helpful owners can suggest things to do around town and beyond. They're often full, so book ahead.

Shade Guesthouse (☎ 0414-321715; Kiwafu Close; s/d USh18,000/20,000) The pick of the bottom-end places around the taxi park. Rooms are clean and not cramped. Bathrooms are shared.

Entebbe Flight Motel (☎ 0414-320812; entebbe flightmotel@yahoo.com; Airport Rd; s/d/tr/q USh50,000/60,000/80,000/100,000) Rooms are rather dated, but still comfortable and fair for the price. A massive expansion is adding 100 more rooms, and if, as the manager predicted, prices remain the same, then this will be an even better choice since they're also adding a gym and sauna.

Uganda Wildlife Education Centre (☎ 0414-322169; www.ugandawildlifecentre.com; Lugard Ave; camping US$5, dm US$10, rooms s/d US$20/30, bandas s/d US$30/50) The choices here are very smart for the price, especially the *bandas*, but the top highlight is the nightly lions' roars and hyenas' howls. Plus, your money helps fund the centre's rescue activities.

Airport Guesthouse (☎ 0414-370932; www.gorilla tours.com; 17 Mugulu Rd; s/d US$40/50; 🖳) Owned by Gorilla Tours (p74), this small, friendly spot is the best value in town. The rooms are centred on a big, leafy garden, and you can use free wi-fi from your little porch. Four-course dinners cost USh17,000.

Boma (☎ 0772-467929; www.thebomaentebbe.com; Gomers Rd; s/d US$75/100; 🖳) Entebbe's answer to the upmarket B&B, this little luxurious guesthouse has grown to 12 rooms, but hasn't lost its intimate atmosphere thanks to lovely décor and a flower-filled yard. The food gets rave reviews.

Bulago Island (☎ 0772-709970; www.bulagoisland.com; per person weekday/weekend US$99/109 with half board; 🏊) It's not too hard to reach this 509-acre island in Lake Victoria – it's just a 45-minute boat ride from Garuga Landing (adult/child US$50/35), itself just 20 minutes from Entebbe – but once you land you feel world's away. The lodge has six rooms on a beachfront just made for relaxing, whether it's in a hammock or on the croquet field. Trails criss-cross the island offering peaceful walks (or horse rides) while two hills offer stunning 360-degree vistas. The rooms aren't as luxurious as you'd expect but still large, comfortable and tasteful. Much of the food (sandwiches and snacks for lunch and a set menu four-course dinner) is grown out back. They offer waterskiing on Lake Victoria and can take you over to nearby Ngamba Island Chimpanzee Sanctuary (p448). Future plans include a golf course and the introduction of animals such as zebras.

Also recommended:

Capital Caves (☎ 0772-869774; Moroto Rd; s/d USh40,000/50,000) This grotto-themed place has small rooms, but by Entebbe standards it's good value.

Lake Victoria Hotel (☎ 0414-351600; www.lvhotel .co.ug; Circular Rd; s/d from US$150/190; 🖳 🖳 🖳) This hotel has finally got the renovation it needed, but it wiped out nearly all the colonial character from the interior. Rooms are well-appointed, though.

Eating & Drinking

When it comes to food in Entebbe, most people end up eating at their hotel, but there are some good choices if you want to go out.

New China Garden (☎ 0782-180088; 6 Lugard Ave; mains USh3000-29,000; ⏰ 8am-11pm) Pleasant, though a little plain, this centrally located restaurant delivers where it matters: good food at fair prices. Most people dine in the garden.

Victoria Restaurant (☎ 0414-303000; Imperial Resort Beach Hotel, Mpigi Rd; mains USh5000-25,000; ⏰ 24hr) Those with jetlag can hit this 24-hour spot inside the big blue 'wave' that's the Imperial Resort Beach Hotel. The menu isn't large, but it spans Indian, Italian and African, and there are themed buffets (ie Asian and Mediterranean) nightly from 6pm to 10pm.

Gately Inn Entebbe (☎ 0414-321313; Portal Rd; mains USh8000-15,000) A sister spot to Jinja's Gately on Nile (p455), this version serves the exact same menu. There are rooms too, but the traffic noise is way too loud for us to recommend them.

The standard night out in Entebbe involves meeting for some good pub grub and beers at friendly **Four Turkeys** (Kampala Rd) and then heading up the road to dance at **Club Knight Riders** (Kampala Rd; ⏰ 9pm-late Wed & Fri-Sun).

Getting There & Away

Minibuses run between Entebbe and either taxi park in Kampala (USh2000, 45 minutes) throughout the day.

For details on the Ssese Island ferry, which leaves from near Entebbe, see p506.

Getting Around

Saloon car shared taxis run very infrequently to the airport (USh1500) from the taxi park, so most people use a special-hire. This should cost USh6000 from the taxi park and USh10,000 from elsewhere in town. To town, the taxi desk at the airport quotes USh15,000, but just walk out to the parking area and negotiate something cheaper.

UGANDA

Ngamba Island Chimpanzee Sanctuary

'Chimp Island', 23km from Entebbe, is home to over 40 orphaned or confiscated chimpanzees who are unable to return to the wild. Humans are confined to about one of the 40 hectares while the chimps wander freely through the rest. **Day trips** cost US$60 per person (depending on group size) and must be booked in advance with tour companies in Kampala (see p430), who can also arrange transport to Entebbe. Feedings can be watched from a raised platform and staff give informative talks on chimp life.

There's also the **overnight experience** (singles/doubles including full board US$405/670) where you spend two days on the island and one night in a self-contained, solar-powered safari tent. Recommended add-ons (for those aged 18 to 65) include a one-hour **forest-walk** (US$350) with the chimps, who'll climb all over you, and the **caregiver experience** (US$150) where you spend a day behind the scenes. Both of these require passing a long health checklist (www.wildfrontiers.co.ug/pdf/Ngamba_Heath_Check_List.pdf).

ALONG MASAKA ROAD
Buganda Historical Sites

Shortly after departing Kampala you'll pass **Katereke Prison** (Map pp428-9; adult/child USh3000/1000 incl guide; 🕑 8am-5pm), a prison ditch where royal prisoners were starved during the upheavals of 1888–89. Kabaka Kalema killed 30 of his brothers and sisters here in 1889 in his quest to keep control of his throne. It's not much more than just a deep, circular trench, but it's a very evocative site and worth the trip if you have time. The unmarked turnoff is opposite the police post in Nsangi and the prison is 1.7km north. A *boda-boda* from Kampala should cost USh1000.

Five and a half kilometres before Nsangi is the turnoff for the **Naggalabi Buddo Coronation Site**, a concrete platform where Buganda kings are crowned. It's the most important but least interesting of the Buganda historical sites around Kampala. A short walk behind it is the sheet metal shell of a neglected tomb. If you really want to visit, head south at the big red-and-white King's College sign and go uphill to the college, then turn right. It's a 4km drive. Minibuses from the new taxi park (ask for Naggalabi Buddo stage) will drop you at the entrance to the college, just a 10-minute walk away.

Mpanga Forest Reserve

About 35km out of Kampala, the 453-hectare **Mpanga Forest** (☎ 0782-493958; admission USh5000) hasn't nearly the diversity or density of fauna as Uganda's larger, more famous reserves but it's one of the most accessible. It's best known for its 181 species of butterfly, which are best seen along the wide, sometimes sunny Baseline Trail; smaller trails branch off the Baseline Trail, snaking through thicker forest. Red-tailed monkeys can be seen during the day and bushbabies during guided **night walks** (USh10,000 per person).

Recently, nearby communities have begun organising various **cultural tours** (from USh5000 to USh10,000 per person) including visits to bee keepers, drum-makers, and bark-cloth makers. You can do all of these things and more for USh100,000, including food and lodging.

Sleeping options have recently been upgraded, and though not fancy are quite good. Top choice is a romantic stilted cottage (USh40,000) made of elephant grass, but there are also regular rooms (USh30,000 to USh50,000), dorm beds (USh10,000) and camping (USh5000 per person, tent hire USh5000). Food can be prepared if you ask ahead.

Take a minibus from the new taxi park in Kampala to Mpigi (USh2500, 45 minutes) and then a *boda-boda* on to Mpanga for USh1500. Alternatively, take a Masaka (USh4000) minibus and get off at Mpanga, walking the last 800m.

Mpambire

This little highway-side village is where Buganda royal drums are made. Small workshops-cum-showrooms line the road turning out a variety of drums topped with the hides of cows, goats and (illegally) snakes. It's 1.5km past the turnoff to Mpanga or a 20-minute walk through the forest.

The Equator

The equator crosses the Kampala–Masaka road at a point 65km southwest of the capital, and here you'll find the expected monument of the sort that spring up in equator-hopping destinations from Ecuador to Indonesia. Two cement circles mark the spot, though if you have a GPS you could get your photo taken on the real equator, about 30m to the south; but it's not nearly as photogenic.

Some guys hang around hoping to snag a few shillings by performing the sham water drain demonstration. (The coriolis force isn't strong enough to affect a bowl of water here or anywhere else in the world.) There are tons of craft shops too, and several are actually worth a look. The one place nearly everybody hits is the excellent **Equation Café** (www.aidchild.org) where all profits fund activities to assist HIV/AIDS orphans. They have a smaller, pricier shop in the Sheraton in Kampala. **Papula Paper** makes all sorts of sustainable paper products and Kampala's **Tulifanya Gallery** (p434) has an outlet here too.

To get here from Kampala, jump on a Masaka bus or minibus and hope to pay USh3000, although you'll probably be charged the full Masaka fare. All in all, it's hard to justify a stop if you're using public transport.

ALONG JINJA ROAD
Ssezibwa Falls

Buganda legend says a spirit laid down the Ssezibwa River and then made his home in the small cave above **Ssezibwa Falls** (Map p450; ☎ 0414-230168; www.ssezibwafallsresort.com; adult/student USh3000/1000; ☺ 8am-6pm). People still leave offerings here, but for most people this site, halfway between Kampala and Jinja, is just a popular spot for picnics and sightseeing. A guide (included in admission) will lead you over a rock outcropping to a view of the falls and share the cultural history as well. There were no facilities during our last visit, but the community group that manages the site was in the process of adding a restaurant, camping ground, and boat trips. Future plans call for a lodge.

Take a Lugazi-bound minibus from either taxi park in Kampala as far as Kayanja (USh3000, 45 minutes) and then a *boda-boda* (USh1000) to the falls. For drivers, there's a sign along the highway, but it's hard to see.

Mabira Forest Reserve

This 306-sq-km **forest reserve** (admission 1/2 days USh6000/10,000) recently survived an attempt by the Sugar Corporation of Uganda and President Museveni to replace one-third of the forest with sugarcane. There's a well-established trail system, and though no guide is needed, they don't charge much (prices are negotiable) so consider bringing one along to tell you about the surprisingly diverse forest life: 218 species of butterfly, 312 species of tree and 315 species of bird. The trails are open to bikes and these can be rented here for USh20,000.

The **Mabira Forest Ecotourism Centre** (☎ 0712-487173; camping USh3000, dm USh5000) is a decent place to stay, but it does suffer highway noise. It's best to bring your own food. A new place, **Griffin Falls Community Campsite** (☎ 0752-634926) was set to open at the time of research 10km from Lugazi at Wasswa. There's also the luxurious **Rainforest Lodge** (☎ 0414-4258273; www.geolodgesafrica.com; s/d incl full board US175/300; ☻) with very private cabins 2½km south of the highway.

To get here, jump on a minibus travelling between Kampala and Jinja and get off at Najjembe (from Jinja, USh2000), 20km west of Jinja. The visitor centre is a short walk to the north.

EASTERN UGANDA

Eastern Uganda, where the mighty Nile begins its epic journey north, is becoming a must on any East African sojourn thanks to an intoxicating blend of adrenaline adventures and superb scenery. Bujagali Falls is the region's answer to Victoria Falls, though for now it's a much friendlier and more relaxing place. White-water rafting on the Nile River leads the way, but besides the many other daring diversions there are also more sedate activities, such as exploring islands on Lake Victoria or helping renovate local schools.

Jinja, sitting right atop the source of the Nile, is the largest and most enjoyable town in the east, and the roster of dining and lodging options here is second only to Kampala. Other towns in the region pale in comparison, but Mbale and Soroti have a certain time-worn charm.

Up on the Kenyan border is the massif of Mt Elgon, an extinct volcano offering superb trekking at some of the most affordable prices in the region, while nearby Sipi Falls is stunning; a beautiful spot to soak up the scenery and a great place to recover from the rigours of a trek.

If you're the adventurous sort, consider the overland assault on seldom-seen Kidepo Valley National Park, a textbook rough journey passing right through the heartland of the Karamojong people, a tough tribe of

UGANDA

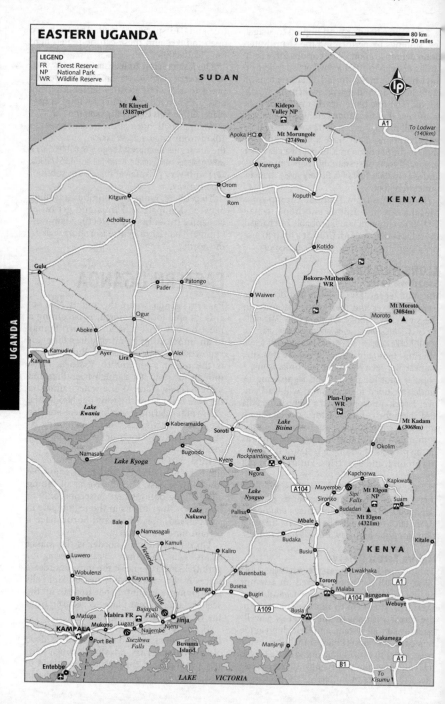

EASTERN UGANDA

0 ___ 80 km
0 ___ 50 miles

LEGEND
FR Forest Reserve
NP National Park
WR Wildlife Reserve

S U D A N

▲ Mt Kinyeti (3187m)

Kidepo Valley NP

Apoka HQ

▲ Mt Morungole (2749m)

Karenga

Kaabong

Orom

Rom

Koputh

K E N Y A

Kitgum

Acholibur

Kotido

Gulu

Patongo

Bokora-Matheniko WR

Pader

Waiwer

Mt Moroto (3084m) ▲

Ogur

Moroto

Aboke

Kamudini

Ayer

Aloi

Karuma

Lira

Pian-Upe WR

Lake Kwania

Mt Kadam ▲ (3068m)

Lake Bisina

Kaberamaido

Soroti

Namasale

Okolim

Bugondo

Nyero Rockpaintings

Kumi

Lake Kyoga

Kyere

Ngora

Kapchorwa

Kapkwata

Muyembe

Mt Elgon NP

A104

Sipi Falls

Sironko

Suam

Lake Nyaguo

Budadiri

Pallisa

Mbale

Mt Elgon (4321m) ▲

Lake Nakuwa

Bale

Budaka

Namasagali

Kamuli

Busiu

K E N Y A

Victoria

Kaliro

Kitale

Luwero

Wobulenzi

Kayunga

Busenbatia

Tororo

Lwakhaka

A1

Bombo

Iganga

Busesa

Bugiri

Malaba

A104

Bungoma

Matuga

Bujagali Falls

Njeru

A109

Busia

Webuye

Mabira FR

Jinja

Mukono

Lugazi

Najjembe

Nile

Kampala

Port Bell

Ssezibwa Falls

Buvuma Island

Manjanji

Kakamega

Entebbe

A1

B1

To Kisumu

LAKE VICTORIA

To Lodwar (140km)

A1

cattle herders who have managed to resist control from outsiders, black and white, for centuries now.

With the exception of what lies beyond Soroti, the major roads in eastern Uganda are generally good and transport is frequent, so there's no excuse for not exploring beyond the usual short stopover in the Jinja and Sipi areas.

JINJA

Jinja is famous as the source of the Nile River, known locally as Omugga Kiyara, though this is hardly the only reason to come here. This area has become something of a retirement community for overland truck drivers and guides, plus many expats, aid workers and missionaries use it as a weekend retreat, resulting in some unexpected pockets of sophistication. For short-term visitors the principal attractions are much less urbane. Jinja has emerged as the adrenaline capital of East Africa and you can get your fix white-water rafting, kayaking, quad biking, mountain biking, horseback riding and bungee jumping.

The town has a lush location on the shores of Lake Victoria and is the major market centre for eastern Uganda. It's a buzzing little place with much Indian-influenced architecture. Check out the spacious mansions overlooking the lake along Nile Cres, opposite the town's golf course, for an insight into how wealthy this town once was.

Coming from Kampala, the Owen Falls Dam forms a spectacular gateway to the town: as you coast across the top you can look right down on the mighty Nile. Don't take pictures though, people have been arrested for doing so even though there are no signs informing people of this law.

Orientation

The centre of town is built on a simple grid, with Main St at its heart. This wide avenue has tons of craft shops, internet cafés, takeaways, banks, and just about any other service you would want. All roads that cross Main St have an east and west side, like in New York, indicated in this section as 'E' and 'W'. Most hotels in Jinja, and all of the pricey ones, are in quiet residential neighbourhoods a short way from the centre.

Overall Jinja is safe place, but it is a city, so don't carry valuables or walk around isolated areas at night.

Information

INTERNET ACCESS

You can get online at tons of places along Main St including the following:

Giga Trends (Main St; per hr USh1200; 6am-midnight) Appears to be the fastest connection in town. Also a good choice for cheap international calls.

Source Café (Main St; per hr USh2000; 8am-8pm Mon-Sat)

MONEY

Main St has many banks that change cash while **Crane Bank** (Lubas Rd) and **Stanbic Bank** (Busoga Rd) also take American Express travellers cheques. **Trend Forex** (Iganga Rd; 8.30am-5pm Mon-Fri & 8.30am-1pm Sat) is Jinja's only foreign exchange bureau, though its rates aren't better than all the banks.

Note that the white-water rafting companies accept credit cards, but charge a commission of 5% to 8%.

POST

Main post office (cnr Main St & Bell Ave)

TOURIST INFORMATION

There's no government-run tourist office in Jinja. The best place to snag the local lowdown is at Explorers Backpackers (p453) or at the places out at Bujagali Falls (p457). Their handy noticeboards are packed with flyers and information covering Jinja and beyond.

Tourist Centre (0712-463474; Main St) handles car rental, plane tickets and Nairobi bus bookings.

Sights & Activities

SOURCE OF THE NILE RIVER

The source of the Nile is one of Jinja's premier drawcards and hoards of people, many bussed in from Kampala, come here expecting to marvel at the birthplace of the mighty river. It's a rare individual indeed who isn't ultimately disappointed because there really isn't much to see.

The water spills out of Lake Victoria on its journey to the Mediterranean near two small islands, flowing fast from the get-go. All the signs directing you to the source actually take you a little downstream to where Ripon Falls now lie under the river, buried behind the Owen Falls Dam. This is now the **Ripon Falls Leisure Centre** (0782-026060; admission per person/car/motorcycle USh10,000/2000/500; admission charged 7am-7pm, open 24hr) with craft vendors, a

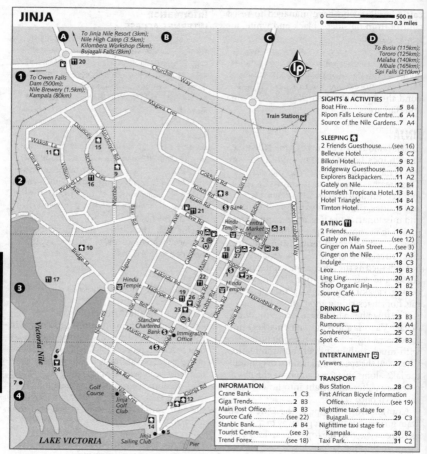

JINJA

0 — 500 m
0 — 0.3 miles

To Jinja Nile Resort (3km);
Nile High Camp (3.5km);
Kilombera Workshop (5km);
Bujagali Falls (8km)

To Busia (115km);
Tororo (125km);
Malaba (140km);
Mbale (165km);
Sipi Falls (210km)

To Owen Falls
Dam (500m);
Nile Brewery (1.5km);
Kampala (80km)

Churchill Way

Magwa Cres

Train Station

Victoria Nile

LAKE VICTORIA

Golf
Course

Jinja
Golf
Club

Jinja
Sailing Club

Pier

SIGHTS & ACTIVITIES	
Boat Hire	5 B4
Ripon Falls Leisure Centre	6 A4
Source of the Nile Gardens	7 A4

SLEEPING	
2 Friends Guesthouse	(see 16)
Bellevue Hotel	8 C2
Bilkon Hotel	9 B2
Bridgeway Guesthouse	10 A3
Explorers Backpackers	11 A2
Gately on Nile	12 B4
Hornsleth Tropicana Hotel	13 B4
Hotel Triangle	14 B4
Timton Hotel	15 A2

EATING	
2 Friends	16 A2
Gately on Nile	(see 12)
Ginger on Main Street	(see 3)
Ginger on the Nile	17 A3
Indulge	18 C3
Leoz	19 B3
Ling Ling	20 A1
Shop Organic Jinja	21 B2
Source Café	22 B3

DRINKING	
Babez	23 A4
Rumours	24 A4
Sombreros	25 C3
Spot 6	26 B3

ENTERTAINMENT	
Viewers	27 C3

TRANSPORT	
Bus Station	28 C3
First African Bicycle Information	
Office	(see 19)
Nighttime taxi stage for	
Bujagali	29 C3
Nighttime taxi stage for	
Kampala	30 B2
Taxi Park	31 C2

INFORMATION	
Crane Bank	1 C3
Giga Trends	2 B3
Main Post Office	3 B3
Source Café	(see 22)
Stanbic Bank	4 B4
Tourist Centre	(see 3)
Trend Forex	(see 18)

small restaurant and, at weekends, an orphans group performing music and dance. Bell Breweries sponsors the area, so everything has been painted yellow and red in keeping with the corporate image. It's pretty garish, but at least you can get a cold drink.

It's much more rewarding to take in the view from the seldom visited **Source of the Nile Gardens** (now a spot for weddings and other events) on the west bank. This is where, on 28 July 1862, John Hanning Speke identified this spot as the source, although his proclamation was purely conjecture: it wasn't definitively proven correct for many more years. There's a modest memorial here and steps lead down to the river. You can take a boat across or drive, turning south off Kampala Rd at the Nile Brewery. Officially there's a small admission fee, but it's unlikely anyone will ask for it.

The best way to see the source is by boat. Several guys hang about the leisure centre offering rides, but it's better to arrange things out at Ripon Landing, next to the defunct Jinja Sailing Club, since you'll avoid the entry fee and probably get a better price. From here, a half-hour ride to the source and back costs USh20,000 while longer trips, which could include visiting a fishing village or seeing hippos and crocodiles, are also available. Other options are a **sunset canoe cruise** (US$50) with Kayak the Nile (p454), a hom-hum **booze cruise** (☎ 0752-545561; per person incl snacks

& drinks USh25,000; 5.30-7pm Thu-Tue) from Ginger on the Nile restaurant (p455) and two-three-hour **family floats** (adult/child US$30/20) in rafts from the source to Bujagali Falls that can be arranged at Explorers Backpackers (below).

NILE BREWERY

For those consuming copious amounts of Nile Special, this alternative 'source of the Nile', just over the bridge, makes a worthy trip. Free, hour-long guided tours are available by appointment on Tuesday and Thursday by calling ☎ 0751-503521. After the tour there's a small souvenir shop where you can buy T-shirts, bottle openers and the like.

KILOMBERA WORKSHOP

The colourful cotton textiles (place mats, table runners, bedspreads) for sale in spots around Jinja are made on hand-operated looms at the Nile-side workshop of **Kilombera** (☎ 0772-824206; 9am-5pm Mon-Fri, 9am-noon Sat), and visitors are welcome to stop by to watch the process. It's signposted 200m off the road, halfway between Jinja and the falls.

Sleeping

Bujagali Falls (p456), which has some appealing options, is just a short way from the city and also worth considering for the night.

BUDGET

Explorers Backpackers (☎ 0434-120236; www.raftafrica.com; 41 Wilson Ave; camping US$5, dm US$7, d US$25;) Jinja's original budget crash pad is still going strong. The most popular place in town, it has a buzzing bar plus free internet, free pool table and satellite TV. Dorms are decent and there's one double room available. Overland trucks pop in now and then, but this is a much quieter spot than Bujagali.

Bellevue Hotel (☎ 0434-120328; 4 Kutch Rd W; s/d USh15,000/20,000 without bathroom, s/d USh30,000/40,000;) Long popular with NGO workers for its combination of cleanliness and good value, new paint (still sticky when we checked in) has brightened up the rooms in this towering place. It's located just off Main St making it convenient but quiet. It's the pick of the litter in the budget category.

Bridgeway Guesthouse (☎ 0772-480142; bridgewayguesthouse@yahoo.com; 34 Bridge St; s/d USh26,000/36,000)

Boasting rates that are 'not just affordable, but also adorable', this simple, quiet place is good for those who want a little extra comfort, but don't want to break the bank. And how's this for a guarantee? 'You won't leave empty handed, but with 1000kgs of satisfaction!'

Timton Hotel (☎ 0434-120278; 15 Jackson Cres; camping USh5000, s USh35,000, d USh40,000-60,000;) The long-running Timton is a friendly, well-kept place with a very homey feel. It also has a pleasant garden where tents can be pitched for a cheaper and quieter night than at the backpacker places. At the other end, the top-priced rooms include satellite TV.

Hornsleth Tropicana Hotel (☎ 0434-122975; 47 Nile Cres; s/d USh35,000/50,000) The former Commonwealth Beach Hotel was undergoing an extensive restoration and transformation into a hotel/art gallery when we last dropped by. Work hadn't hit the six guestrooms yet, but the inviting common areas are now full of tiles and murals, and plans are afoot for an open-kitchen restaurant and more greenery in the garden. If prices stay the same, this will be the best bargain in Jinja.

Bilkon Hotel (☎ 0434-123944; www.bilkonhotel.com; Nalufenya Rd; s/d USh40,000/50,000;) Filling a funky white building that has a few art deco touches, this hotel takes cleaning and maintenance so seriously it looks nearly new. Rooms are good value with satellite TV and refrigerators in all. It's right on the road into town so there's some highway noise, but rooms out the back are actually pretty quiet.

Nile High Camp (☎ 0772-286433; www.adrift.ug; Kimaka Rd; camping US$5, dm US$10, safari tent US$40, chalet US$50) Located a short way off the road to Bujagali Falls, 4km north of Jinja, Adrift's base for rafting and bungee jumping offers fine views of the Nile but its accommodation is poor value. The cramped dorm beds are stacked

---

GANDHI IN UGANDA?

A surprising find at the Ripon Falls Leisure Centre is a shrine to Mahatma Gandhi. As per his wishes, on his death in 1948 his ashes were divided up to be scattered in several of the world's great rivers, including the Nile in Uganda. This bronze bust, donated by the Indian government, commemorates the act. So, Gandhi was rafting the Nile long before the Adrift team came to town.

RUNNING THE NILE RIVER

The upper stretch of the Nile, a long, rollicking string of Class IV and V rapids, is one of the world's most spectacular white-water rafting destinations, and for many people a river trip is the highlight of their visit to Uganda. The new Bujagali Dam is definitely going to change things on the river, but despite the rumours floating around, there will still be adrenaline and adventure in large doses: the dam isn't wiping out *all* the rapids. Trips now start above Bujagali Falls, but at some point in the life of this book the put-in points will just move a bit downstream.

The two main companies are **Nile River Explorers** (NRE; ☎ 0434-120236; www.raftafrica.com), with offices at Explorers Backpackers (p453) in Jinja and Explorers Campsite (p457) at Bujagali, and the pioneers **Adrift** (☎ 0312-237438; www.adrift.ug), based in Kampala (in the Uganda Wildlife Authority compound) and at Nile High Camp (p453) between Jinja and Bujagali. **Nalubale Rafting** (☎ 0782-638938; www.nalubalerafting.com) is under the same ownership as NRE but doesn't run rapids rougher than class 3. Trips are still fun though; and US$30 cheaper. These are the only three companies operating at the time of research that we feel have a serious attitude about safety, and thus the only ones we are confident about recommending. But things do change, so ask around before you pick any company. Also, make sure that there is a first aid kit and that the person piloting your boat speaks good English and has a mobile phone.

Both NRE and Adrift charge US$115/125/250 for a half-/full-/two-day trips and offer a second day of rafting at half-price for repeat offenders. Both will shuttle you out from Kampala for free, picking up punters from popular hostels and hotels in Kampala, and back again in the evening if you just want to make it a day-trip, and they'll give you a free night's accommodation if you want to stick around. NRE uses smaller boats for a bigger rush, but Adrift will, if the river is high enough, let you substitute a boogie board for the raft to confront the surging Nile head on. Besides the standard big water runs, there are also family float trips which bypass the big waves and are guaranteed to garner squeals of delight from young kids. A full-day family float with NRE costs US$120/105 adult/child while Adrift's overnighters (staying at Hairy Lemon, p458) are US$170/80.

It used to be all about rafting, and this is still the most popular way to run the river, but **Kayak the Nile** (☎ 0772-880322; www.kayakthenile.com), based at Explorers Campsite (p457) at Bujagali, lets you steer yourself through the raging river with a variety of paddling courses, starting with a one-day intro at US$115. Tandem trips (US$145) give you all the fun without the effort. Several locals they've trained as staff have gone on to compete on the world stage. Kayak the Nile also offer some quieter trips in sit-on-top kayaks, including the recommended Lake Victoria Discovery (US$125 per person, minimum three people) trip where a motorboat shuttles you out to explore some islands in the lake's serene interior. In an attempt to cut their carbon footprint, clients can plant trees during their paddle.

four-high, and while the wooden cottages are very nice and have big river views, they don't have their own bathrooms. It's a good stop for a meal though. The restaurant and bar is perched on a riverside cliff and offers wood-fired pizzas, steak and chicken dishes. For a *boda-boda* out here, USh2000 is a fair price.

MIDRANGE

Hotel Triangle (☎ 0434-122099; Nile Cres; s USh60,000, d USh70,000-80,000, ste 130,000; 🖳 🛎) Occupying a commanding ridge above Lake Victoria, the Triangle has a great location and every room looks out over the lake and the fishermen working it. Ask to be upstairs to get the best views. The building itself has a slightly

institutional feel, but even without the views, the large rooms are right for the price. There's a pool area and a gym.

2 Friends Guesthouse (☎ 0772-984821; www.2friends .info; 5 Jackson Cres; s/d USh80,000/100,000; 🖳) Jinja's popular pizzeria (see opposite) has added 11 rooms in an adjoining house. The rooms boast stone and tile floors and some plush décor with more of a log cabin than an African village feel. Very nice and relaxing all around.

ourpick Gately on Nile (☎ 0434-122400; www .gately-on-nile.com; 34 Kisinja Rd; annex s/d US$50/70, house s/d US$75/100, cottages s/d US$90/120; 🖳) Set in a grand old colonial house with sumptuous grounds, this is the leading choice in Jinja if you want a little pampering. It offers a selection of thoughtfully decorated rooms, some with fine views, and boasts communal areas that have a great atmosphere for relaxing. Bungalows in the garden include Balinese-style open bathrooms and even the no-frills annex is homey. The restaurant (right) is one of the best in town.

Jinja Nile Resort (☎ 0434-122190; www.madahotels .com; Kimaka Rd; s/d/tr from US$140/180/205; ❊ 🖳 🏊) Next-door neighbour to Nile High Camp, this popular conference venue is the biggest resort in the Jinja area. It's rather expensive, but tastefully done and there's a swimming pool, gym, and tennis and squash courts. In most cases, a Nile-view cottage costs an extra US$20. If there's no conference business in town, you might get a discount.

Although it has been closed for renovation for years, it's worth inquiring whether the **Samuka Island Retreat** (☎ 0772-401508) on Lake Victoria has reopened. It's reportedly a good bird-watching spot.

Eating

The cuisine scene in Jinja has really emerged, with some fine restaurants in town and other great options north along the Nile.

Source Café (☎ 0434-120911; 20 Main St; mains USh3000-7000; ❊ 7.30am-6.30pm Mon-Fri & 8am-6pm Sat; 🖳) The superb bakery and coffee at this church-affiliated place makes 'The Source' a *muzungu* magnet. More substantial meals, such as lemon-pepper grilled fish and pita pizzas, are priced right.

Indulge (☎ 0782-648544; cnr Iganga & Ripon Rd W; smoothies USh4000-5000, sandwiches USh5500; ❊ 10am-5pm Mon & Wed-Sat, 11am-4pm Sun) This small, but thriving upscale deli stocks little delights you just won't find elsewhere in town, such as olives and brie. You can also dine in with sandwiches, salads and juices.

Leoz (☎ 0434-120298; 11 Main St; mains USh5000-10,000; ❊ 9am-10.20pm Wed-Mon) This is the kind of unassuming place you'd normally just walk right on by, but it's the first place locals will recommend for Indian food. And, if that isn't your companion's preference, the menu also has Chinese, Ugandan and pizza. We especially like it because when you order spicy they really turn up the heat.

Ginger on the Nile (☎ 0774-765365; Bridge Close; mains USh5000-16,500; ❊ 8am-midnight Thu-Tue) This new spot doesn't look like much at first glance, but follow the path downhill, past the tiki bar, and you've got the best

river views in town. The menu has a global, eclectic touch with choices such as cous-cous, chicken *satay*, jacket potatoes and all-day breakfast, plus a two-page drinks list spanning cinnamon lattes to piña co-ladas. Several items, like the Mexican rolex (made with tomato salsa, guacamole and beef chilli) offer soya meat substitutes. The only knock is the slow service. They have a second, daylight hours-only outlet on Main St with a similar menu.

Ling Ling (☎ 0772-489616; Kampala Roundabout; mains USh5000-42,500) Attached to a petrol station, Ling Ling has a none-too-promising location, but great service and even better food (our favourite Chinese in Uganda) more than compensate. And even with the traffic noise, a sizzling vegie platter or chicken curry in the back garden can make for a pleasant dining experience.

Gately on Nile (☎ 0434-122400; 34 Kisinja Rd; mains USh8000-15,000; ❊ 7am-9.30pm) The restaurant on the back porch of Jinja's popular boutique hotel (opposite) is a must for lovers of fine food. The fusion menu blends the best of local produce and international flair, and includes memorable moments such as grilled tilapia with pesto. One page of the menu is Thai, though the recipes certainly aren't straight out of Siam.

2 Friends (☎ 0772-984821; 6 Jackson Cres; mains USh10,500-16,500) Tucked away in a front-yard garden on a quiet crescent near Explorers Backpackers, this is the number one name for Italian food in Jinja, but the menu also mixes in Indian and even a few local dishes. The wood-fired pizza oven isn't lit until 6pm. There's a guesthouse (opposite) in an adjoining house.

There are several supermarkets on Main St and many more around the junction of Lubas Rd and Clive Rd E. **Shop Organic Jinja** (Clive Rd W; ❊ 8am-8pm Mon-Sat, 1-8pm Sun) is tiny, but worth supporting.

Drinking & Entertainment

There's not much entertainment in Jinja, though Main St offers a suitable strip for a bar crawl. **Spot 6** (Main St) and **Babez** (Main St), a few doors down from each other at the junction of Nadiope, are two happening places with lots of working girls. **Sombreros** (Spire Rd) is a little more hassle-free than these two, plus it doesn't allow smoking, and so attracts many more *muzungus*. **Viewers** (54 Lubas Rd), attached to the Nile View Casino, has the only proper dance floor in town, though it doesn't seem to have stolen any thunder from Sombreros. **Rumours** (off Bridge St) is right near the source of the Nile and used to be a happening place for a beer or three, but it's pretty run down these days.

The Hotel Triangle (p454) has pretty, watery views and the bar at the Bellevue Hotel (p453) is popular, though the revelry is low-key and unlikely to keep you awake if you're sleeping there. Explorers Backpackers (p453) is always a popular drinking hole with budget travellers and local volunteers, although it's tame compared to the real action out at Bujagali Falls.

Getting There & Away

The road between Jinja and Kampala (USh4000) takes anything from one to two hours by minibus (from the old taxi park), depending on the traffic. At about 7pm minibuses move out to Clive Rd. If you're driving yourself, the best route is the longer but faster and almost completely truck-free road north through Kayunga.

There are also frequent minibuses from Jinja to Tororo (USh8000, 2½ hours), Mbale (USh8000, two hours) and Busia (USh8000, 1½ hours) on the Kenyan border. There's no need to travel to Nairobi in stages since you can book tickets on the big buses coming from Kampala.

Getting Around

The centre of Jinja is compact enough to wander about on foot; elsewhere you'll probably want a *boda-boda*. A few longish trips in town will cost USh1000, but most, including between Explorers Backpackers and Main St, will be half that.

Jinja is a good place to explore by bike, and the **First African Bicycle Information Office** (☎ 0434-121255; 9 Main St; ☾ 9am-5pm Mon-Fri), with the unfortunate acronym FABIO, rents simple, but well-maintained bikes for USh10,000 per day. Explorers Backpackers (p453) has high-end rides for US$25 per day including helmet and map if you want to explore further.

AROUND JINJA
Bujagali Falls

Not an actual waterfall, but rather a widespread series of large rapids, **Bujagali Falls** (admission/car USh3000/1000; ☾ 24hr) is one of Uganda's outstanding natural beauty spots (admission is charged between 9am and 7pm). A thriving backpacker community has grown up near the falls and many travellers end up chilling here for a few days after their rafting trip.

A few local men, calling themselves the **Bujagali Swimmers**, have created a cottage industry by throwing themselves into the falls with one arm wrapped tight around a jerry can and the other paddling them through the safe route; all for a USh5000 fee. They make it look easy, but every once in a while a 'swimmer' loses his grip and goes missing.

The controversial and long-delayed Bujagali Dam is finally under construction, and it's sure to affect the falls, though exactly how much of the roar will end up under water is still unclear. Also likely to change things, a posh resort has been discussed for this site for many years. Regardless of these developments, most of the facilities are clustered atop the hill and the Nile views will still be beautiful no matter what happens down below.

Activities
QUAD BIKING

Quad biking along the beautiful banks of the Victoria Nile is a real blast thanks to **All Terrain Adventures** (☎ 0772-377185; www.atadventures .com). After a little spin on the practice circuit, it's time to explore the paths and trails criss-crossing the nearby countryside; kid-sized rides are available. There are several possible circuits including a one-hour short-haul safari (USh70,000) and the 3½-hour twilight safari (USh120,000) that includes dinner in a village. They also offer overnight trips. Contributions are made to local communities in the area, ensuring a warm welcome on the way.

MOUNTAIN BIKING

The four-hour ride through the villages between Bujagali Falls and Jinja offered by **Explorers Mountain Biking** (☎ 0772-422373; www .raftafrica.com; US$45 incl lunch), is good fun. The trip finishes off with a boat ride to the source of the Nile River. There are also four-hour rides through the Mabira Forest (p449) and they'll tailor-make other trips.

HORSEBACK RIDING

Nile Horseback Safaris (☎ 0774-101196; www.nile horsebacksafaris.com) offers a new way to explore the area; and no experience is necessary.

A two-hour ride along the hills above the Nile River and through local villages costs USh80,000 and there are longer rides for experienced riders including an overnighter sleeping downstream at Haven (p458).

The stables are on the west side of Bujagali Falls, directly opposite the built-up Bujagali area, although unless you can kayak over, you'll need to go by road. It's just five kilometres from Jinja. Reservations are a good idea because they're often booked days in advance.

BUNGEE JUMPING

Nearer to Jinja, but more in tune with Bujagali's vibe, Uganda's only **bungee jump** (☎ 0772-286433; US$65) is a 44m plunge to the Nile River from the Adrift rafting company's Nile High Camp (p453).

COMMUNITY PROJECTS

When you bear in mind that the cost of rafting is equivalent to many months' salary for the average Ugandan, you may feel some motivation to get involved in the community. There are many ways to do so.

One of Uganda's most popular volunteer programs, **Soft Power Education** (☎ 0774-162541; www.softpowereducation.com) has a number of projects to upgrade schools and improve education in the area, and also around Murchison Falls National Park (p511). The results are evident for all to see, with school buildings in better shape and education standards improving. They offer two options. Most people do the one-day program (only half-days available at weekends) which begins with a visit to the village and then it's out to a school for some painting, building or repair work. Among the many volunteering possibilities for those who want to stick around longer are teaching or building fuel-efficient stoves.

A sister project, **Soft Power Health** (☎ 0782-690127; www.softpowerhealth.com) runs similar one-day programs selling mosquito nets at subsidised prices while educating locals about malaria or doing family planning work. No medical training is necessary, but if you have it you'll be most welcome as a long-term volunteer at the health clinic or other projects.

You can sign up for either Soft Powers' outings at Explorers Campsite (right). Lunch and transport are provided with both, though you're expected to make a small donation to cover costs. Long-term volunteers pay small weekly fees and are responsible for room and board.

Explorers also offers **community walks** (US$5 per person) that help fund projects in area villages. You'll visit farms and a health clinic, eat local food and sample village beers on the three-hour tour. Eden Rock Resort (below) has a similar program on offer.

Sleeping

When the rafting launch site moves upstream, it's likely some of the lodging will too, so put your ear to the ground in Kampala before booking a room to see what else is out there.

Speke Camp (☎ 0752-711725; camping USh3500, tent hire USh10,000) Sitting right next to the falls themselves, Speke can boast the best location of any camping ground in Uganda, but facilities are being left to rot as the site awaits construction of a mega-resort. It's a good spot for a sundowner, although the beers aren't always cold.

Eden Rock Resort (☎ 0772-501222; www.edenrocknile.com; camping USh5500, dm USh11,000, bandas USh36,000-80,000; 🖳) Usually a quieter option than Explorers, even though overland trucks stop here sometimes. It offers a variety of *bandas* with bathrooms set amid good gardens; and moving up in price really does bring a jump in quality. The loft *bandas* (which they call 'staired *bandas*') can sleep six. There's a nice central bar and restaurant, with a satellite TV link plus a weird right-angle pool table to confuse the hustlers.

Explorers Campsite (☎ 0782-320552; www.raftafrica.com; camping US$5, dm US$7, r US$25, bandas US$25; 🖳) Nile River Explorers (p454) runs the most popular place to stay in the Jinja area, always full with overland trucks and backpackers. Thoughtful terracing means some brilliant views for those in *bandas* (which are due for a much needed renovation) and tents, while the showers look out over the river, which can make a scrub a whole lot more interesting than usual. The restaurant and bar are packed to the rafters come evening, so pitch your tent far enough away if you plan a quiet one. If not, just join the party.

Nile Porch (☎ 0782-321541; www.nileporch.com; safari tent s/d/tr/f US$75/95/120/120; 🖳 🍴) Sitting tight against Explorers Campsite, but a world away in style and standards, the Nile Porch brings the lodge experience to Bujagali; and the roar of the river drowns out all sounds from the campsite. The eight luxurious tents are

---

ACCOMMODATION DOWNRIVER FROM JINJA

These two incredible places sit on the west side of the Nile, deliberately way outside Jinja, pretty much in the middle of nowhere, and are each something special in their own way. If things finally work out for the Adrift rafting company (p454), there will be a third option opening in the near future.

First up, 15 kilometres along the road from Jinja and then three more down to the riverbank, is **our pick** **Haven** (☎ 0702-905959; www.thehaven-uganda.com; camping US$35, non–self-contained bandas s/d US$75/110, self-contained bandas s/d US$100/160), a small lodge powered by solar panels and utilising rainwater through a clever catchment system. Kudos for the ecofriendly design, of course, but the prime selling point here are the wide waterfall views, far more beautiful than Bujagali Falls, and that's some tough competition. The four-star food (prices include full board) is another draw. There's a swimming spot in the river and boat trips are available, but the main leisure activity is time in the strategically placed hammocks. You can come out just for a meal (set-menu breakfast/lunch/dinner US$15/20/25), but as with lodging, you must make a reservation. By public transport, take a minibus to Kirugu stage (USh2000) and then a *boda-boda* (USh2000) to the lodge.

Another 15km downstream on a small island, the **our pick** **Hairy Lemon** (☎ 0772-828338; www.hairylemonuganda.com; camping USh30,000, 10-bed dm USh40,000, bandas s/d/q USh70,000/110,000/180,000) is a unique place: a getaway, a retreat and an isolated escape for relaxation and reflection. Grab a rock on a riverbank and you can have a little world all to yourself. Three hearty meals are served a day (prices include full board), including vegie options if requested in advance. Volleyball, swimming and bird-watching are all possible, and a short paddle away is Nile Special, a world-class hole for those with their own kayak and plenty of experience. As space is limited, it's essential to book ahead. To get here, take a minibus from Jinja to Nazigo (USh3000, one hour) and then a *boda-boda* (USh2000) for the last 9km to the Hairy Lemon. A special-hire should be USh40,000. Bang on the wheel hub and a boat will come across to welcome you. You need to arrive here before 6pm.

---

superbly set on a cliff above the river, and include elegant furnishings and hammocks on the porches. There's a swimming pool for guests and some family units (minus the views) available for those travelling in numbers.

Eating

All of the lodging options, except Speke Camp, have restaurants with the usual Western dishes you've come to expect in Uganda. If you'd prefer to eat local, there are busy chapatti stands and the very basic **Green Light** (☎ 7am-11pm) restaurant across the road from Nile River Explorers.

DeNile Café (☎ 0772-377185; mains USh3000-6000; ☎ 8am-5.30pm) Drop in on this friendly little café, part of the quad-bike set up, for good views and cheap eats. From the second-storey porch you'll have big river views as you chow down on the best-value all-day breakfast in Uganda.

Black Lantern (☎ 0782-321541; mains USh10,000-22,000) Bujagali's premier dining destination, this is the restaurant at the Nile Porch (p457). Set under a traditional thatched roof looking through trees at the river, the extensive menu offers several stops around the world, including Mexican, Spanish, Indian and Chinese. Spare ribs are a speciality and the portions are enormous. Vegetarians, quiver not at the mention of ribs; there are several non-meat options as well.

Getting There & Away

Bujagali Falls is about 10km from central Jinja. To get here, head northwest out of town and go straight ahead at the Kampala roundabout. Follow this sometimes smooth, sometimes busy road and turn left at the large signpost pointing to the falls. Minibuses to Budondo pass this junction (USh500, 30 minutes) but can take a while to fill up. A *boda-boda* ride to/from Jinja should cost about USh3000 and a special-hire USh10,000; prices go up late at night. Because the road is really rough it's best not to use *boda-bodas* at night.

Most of the adventure companies featured above offer free transport to and from Kampala if you book with them.

TORORO

There's not much reason for travellers to come to Tororo, and now that most transport between Jinja and Mbale bypasses the town, few do. If you think you've heard the name Tororo before, you probably have: its celebrated cement factory is helping drive Uganda's building boom and Tororo Cement signs are found around the country. Though we aren't sure who's keeping count, Tororo is often identified as the most thundery place on earth, and, wouldn't you know it, a loud storm blew through the last time we stayed there.

Information
There are branches of Barclays and Stanbic banks plus several internet cafés right around the clocktower in the centre of town.

Sights
Tororo's main redeeming feature is **Tororo Rock**, an intriguing, forest-covered volcanic plug that rises up abruptly behind the town. The views from the top are impressive; you can see Lake Victoria on a clear day. On the south side is a cable car used for maintenance work on the mobile phone tower, and locals tell us the guards will often take people up for a small consideration, though we had no luck in this regard. If you'd rather ascend by foot, take it on from the northeast side. It can be climbed in about an hour.

Sleeping & Eating
Blue Mountain Inn (☎ 0702-668136; 35 Bazaar St; s/d USh20,000/25,000) Nothing fancy, just simple, clean rooms; and much better than the cheapies by the market for only a little more money. The music in the bar can get a little loud; which wouldn't be so bad if the CDs didn't skip so damn often.

Motel Dot Com (☎ 0772-652832; cnr Bazaar St & Mbale Rd; s/d USh41,000/51,000) Ignore the stupid name (they don't even have a website) but don't overlook Tororo's best value hotel. This shiny surprise just north of the clocktower opened in 2007 and has comfy rooms with wrought-iron four-poster beds.

TLT Hotel (☎ 0774-268686; 9 Bazaar St; s USh60,000, d USh70,000-80,000; ☒) Another newly built hotel, the higher price at the Town Lodge Tororo is more a matter of bigger rather than better rooms compared to its neighbour, Dot Com; though the views of Tororo Rock are another bonus. Its restaurant (mains USh7000 to USh20,000) is surprisingly sophisticated for this part of Uganda with choices such as tila-

pia amandine, pork chops with red wine sauce and, according to every shopkeeper we spoke with, the best Indian food in town (although there's not much competition).

Rock Classic Hotel (☎ 0772-468535; www.rockclassichotel.com; Malaba Rd; camping 10,000, r USh80,000-160,000; ☒ ☐ ☒) A venerable hangover from the British era, this hotel, 5km out of town on the Malaba Rd, was recently given a facelift. Still, except for the fridge, the regular rooms are no better than the best found in the town centre. Use of the pool is free for guests (including campers), but the gym, sauna, Jacuzzi, and steam bath all cost USh5000 extra.

Jubilee Spring (☎ 0772-664761; 10 Mbale Rd; mains USh1500-3000) Recommended for local food.

Getting There & Away
Minibuses run to Mbale (USh3000, one hour), Jinja (USh8000, 2½ hours), and the old taxi park in Kampala (USh13,000, four hours). Gateway has a daily bus at 6am to Kampala.

There's onward transport to Nairobi via both of the nearby border towns, Malaba (USh1500, 15 minutes) and Busia (USh2500, one hour), but it's more frequent at the latter.

MBALE
(is a bustling provincial city, and if you're charitable in your evaluation you might even say it has some charm. In the background is Wanale Ridge, a foothill of Mt Elgon; you'll probably pass through the city if planning an assault on the mountain or some time around Sipi Falls. There's an abundance of good accommodation in all price ranges, which almost makes you wish there was a reason to stay here longer than it takes to get on a minibus to your actual destination.

Mbale is a very diverse city. It has the usual medley of churches plus the main campus of the Islamic University in Uganda is here and the Abayudaya, native Bagandan Jews, live in and around town.

Sights & Activities
Probably the most fun you can have in Mbale without a beer or a pool cue is to watch the **Mbale Youth Brass Band** practice. They meet weekdays from 5.30pm to 6.30pm across the street from the Mbale Municipal Council. This band, as well as several others, is sponsored by the **Foundation for Development of Needy**

UGANDA

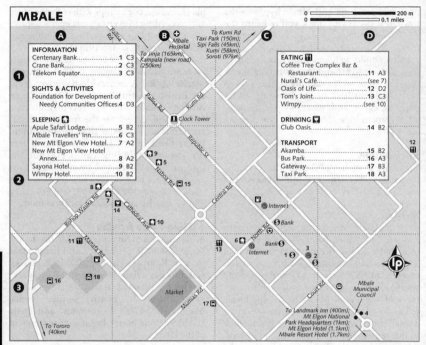

Communities (FDNC; ☎ 0772-494285; www.fdncuganda
.org; Republic St), which runs a host of community development programs in the area and
is always happy to receive volunteers.

Information

All the big banks, including **Centenary Bank**
(Republic St) and **Crane Bank** (Republic St), which are
the best bet for foreign exchange, are concentrated on the southwest end of Republic St,
a few hundred metres from the clocktower.
None of them take travellers cheques. Internet
cafés are spread throughout the centre.

Telekom Equator (Republic St; per hr USh2000;
🕑 8am-8pm Mon-Sat, 11am-7pm Sun) Reliable internet
connections.

Mt Elgon National Park Headquarters (☎ 0454-
433170; 19 Masaba Rd; 🕑 8am-5pm Mon-Fri, 8am-3pm
Sat & Sun) Organise your Mt Elgon visit here; about 1km
from town.

Sleeping

Apule Safari Lodge (☎ 0454-433323; 5 Naboa Rd; s
USh10,000 without bathroom, s/d USh12,000/16,000) Apule
has simple but passable rooms and is looked
after by a friendly manager.

New Mt Elgon View Hotel (☎ 0772-445562; 5
Cathedral Ave; s/d USh13,000/16,000-26,000 without bathroom, annex d USh36,000-41,000, annex f USh81,000) The
only thing new about this hotel, long the most
popular budget place in town, is this particular word was recently added to its name.
Double rooms are better value than the cubicles that pass as singles, but all are well looked
after. Best of the bunch are the spacious self-
contained rooms in the annex across the street.
The main building has a pool table on the first
floor, while downstairs is the excellent Nurali's
Café (opposite). Note the 9am checkout time.

Mbale Travellers' Inn (☎ 0782-257999; Mumias Rd;
s/d USh20,000/30,000) Following a recent renovation, these fantastic-value rooms (they have
fans, satellite TV and large bathrooms) are so
clean you could eat off the tiled floors.

Landmark Inn (☎ 0777-283352; Wanale Rd; r
USh40,000) Set in a grand old house that's slightly
run-down, but in a very charismatic way, this
is Mbale's answer to the budget boutique hotel.
The three huge rooms have high ceilings and
bathrooms so large they would pass as a single
room in other budget crash pads. There's an
excellent Indian restaurant (opposite) down-

stairs. The wonderful new owners are giving it a slow-paced renovation, so rates may rise.

Mbale Resort Hotel (☎ 0782-787333; www.mbale resorthotel.com; 50 Bungokho Rd; r USh50,000-85,000; 🖳 🗐) Rooms here are no match for the Mt Elgon Hotel, especially the very cramped standard-class ones, but the range of facilities, including a pool with swim-up bar, a gym and a sauna (all available for USh5000 to non-guests), makes this place a good choice. A new building under construction out the back will soon make this top bill in Mbale. It's about a kilometre outside of town.

Mt Elgon Hotel (☎ 0454-433454; www.mountelgon hotel.com; s USh60,000-95,000, d USh65,000-105,000; 🔀 🖳) After a major makeover that tacked on some modern flair like grooved doors, you wouldn't ever guess this is a co-lonial-era stalwart. Rooms are spacious and quite plush at the top of the price range. It's in a quiet part outside the city, surrounded by its own verdant grounds, and has a little crazy golf course (3pm to 11pm Monday to Friday and 9am to 11pm at weekends; USh1000) out front. The restaurant is good and the bar is a lively gathering place for guests, aid workers and government officials. A pool is planned.

Also recommended:

Sayona Hotel (Bishop Wasika Rd; s without bathroom USh8,000-10,000, d without bathroom USh12,000) The shared bathrooms here are cell-like, but as clean as you could expect at this price.

Wimpy Hotel (☎ 0454-431208; Cathedral Ave; r USh36,000-51,000) Nobody could tell us what the real prices will be after these promotional rates end, but this 2008-built beauty is still likely to be worth considering.

Eating & Drinking

Tom's Joint (Naboa Rd; mains USh2000-3000) The beer is cold, the food is cheap, the staff is cheerful and the big chairs invite you to stick around for a while, which is what most of the local crowd does.

Coffee Tree Complex Bar & Restaurant (Manafa Rd; mains USh3000-8000) This local canteen is a busy spot for breakfast, lunch and beers in the evening. The open-air terrace overlooking the street is a prime people-watching spot, if you can snag a seat.

Landmark Inn (☎ 0777-283352; Wanale Rd; mains USh3000-7200) Nurali's is often mentioned as the best Indian dining in Mbale, but for our money this less-convenient place in the hotel (opposite) of the same name is the current curry champ. The delightful owners and shady backyard, full of the sounds of nature, just make the experience that much better. It's also got local and Chinese food.

Nurali's Café (☎ 0772-445562; 5 Cathedral Ave; mains USh4500-10,000) Nurali's, located beneath the Mt Elgon View Hotel (opposite), is a fine Indian restaurant that dishes out delicious flavours from the tandoori grill, plus some less reli-able Chinese, a few Ugandan greatest hits and creative Italian. (How about steak and kidney or sausage and apple pizzas?). Its bar is the closest thing to a proper pub in Mbale and screens football matches.

Club Oasis (Cathedral Ave) Next to Nurali's, the top club in town has karaoke on Saturday and DJs other nights, plus the occasional live band.

Also recommended:

Wimpy (☎ 0454-431208; Cathedral Ave; mains USh3000-6000; ⏰ 9am-midnight) Far more Ugandan than a real Wimpy, it's still got the same greasy burgers you love to hate.

Oasis of Life (☎ 0352-275113; Aryada St; mains USh7000-20,000) Features essentially the same menu as Tororo's TLT Hotel (p459), although we've heard with less consistent results.

UNDER THE KNIFE

The local Bagisu people, whose homeland includes Mbale and the surrounding villages, perform very public circumcision ceremonies in August (and occasionally other months) of even years. Before meeting the knife, the boy, wildly bedecked in goat skins, beads and often a giant hat and arm bands, is paraded around town by throngs of people waving branches and wearing grass skirts. There's dancing and drinking, and everyone, *muzungu* (white people) included, is welcome to join the throng, and then bear witness to the act!

The Sabiny (pronounced Sabine), who live on the north side of Mt Elgon, undertake a similar rite of passage in December (also even years) for both men and women. Women can choose to have their initiation at any time of the year, but most follow the same schedule as the men. The Sabiny are the only people in Uganda who practice female genital mutilation, aka female circumcision, and there's fierce resistance to ending the practice.

Getting There & Away

There are frequent minibuses to Tororo (USh3000, one hour), Kampala (USh12,000, three hours), Jinja (USh8000, two hours), Kumi (USh3000, one hour) and Soroti (USh5000, two hours) from the main taxi park off Manafa Rd. Behind it is the bus stand, with less-frequent transport to Jinja, Kampala, and Soroti. Prices are similar to minibus prices.

For Sipi Falls (USh5000, one hour), Kapchorwa (USh6000, 1½ hours) and Budadari (USh3000, 45 minutes), head to the Kumi Rd taxi park northeast of town. Services are infrequent to these smaller places so it's best to travel in the morning.

Both **Akamba** (☎ 0454-434106; Naboa Rd; ☒ 4.30pm) and **Gateway** (☎ 0752-954046; Cathedral Rd; ☒ 5pm) have once-a-day services from Mbale to Nairobi departing from their own offices rather than the bus station. Both charge USh25,000. There's also an occasional Post Bus (see p443).

MT ELGON NATIONAL PARK

Mt Elgon is a good alternative to climbing Uganda's Rwenzori Mountains or Mt Kilimanjaro in Tanzania since it offers a milder climate, lower elevation and much more reasonable prices. Also, it's arguably a more scenic climb than the latter. The park encompasses the upper regions of Mt Elgon to the Kenyan border and this is said to be one of the largest surface areas of any extinct volcano in the world.

Elgon, whose name is derived from the Maasai name, Ol Doinyo Ilgoon ('Breast Mountain'), has five major peaks with the highest, Wagagai (4321m), rising on the Ugandan side. It's the second tallest mountain in Uganda (after Mt Stanley) and the eighth in Africa, though millions of years ago it was the continent's tallest. The mountain is peppered with cliffs, caves, gorges and waterfalls, and the views from the higher reaches stretch way across eastern Uganda's wide plains.

The lower slopes are clothed in tropical montane forest with extensive stands of bamboo. Above 3000m the forest fades into montane heath and then afro-alpine moorland which blankets the caldera, a collapsed crater covering some 40 sq km. The moorland is studded with giant groundsel and endemic *Lobelia elgonensis*, and you'll often see duikers bounding through the long grass and endangered lammergeier vultures overhead. In September it's decorated with wildflowers. You'll probably see a few primates and lots of birds, including the rare Jackson's francolin, alpine chat and white-starred forest robin, but you'll be lucky to spot one of the leopard, hyena, buffalo, elephant or other big mammals.

See p382 for information on Kenya's smaller Mt Elgon National Park.

Trekking on Mt Elgon

Even as the number of visitors on Mt Elgon increases, tourism remains relatively underdeveloped and no more than 250 people reach the caldera in the busiest months. It's possible to hike for days without seeing another climber; an impossible dream on Kilimanjaro. The climb is non-technical and relatively easy, as far as 4000-plus metre ascents go.

The best time to climb is from June to August or December to March, but the seasons are unpredictable and it can rain at any time. You can get information and organise your trek at the **Mt Elgon National Park Headquarters** (☎ 0454-433170; www.uwa.or.ug; 19 Masaba Rd; ☒ 8am-5pm Mon-Fri, 8am-3pm Sat & Sun) in Mbale or at the visitor centres at each of the trailheads, all open in theory the same hours as the HQ.

Trekking on Mt Elgon costs US$50 per person per day, which covers park entry fees and a ranger-guide. Guides are mandatory whether heading to the summit or just doing a day-trip. Camping fees are USh15,000 more per night and porters, who are highly recommended, charge USh8000 per day for carrying 18kg. Tents and sleeping bags can be hired at Budadari (not at HQ in Mbale) for USh10,000 and USh2500 per night respectively. Also, factor in tips, which are highly appreciated, to your grand total.

Mbale supermarkets (there are several in town) don't have nearly the selection of those in Kampala or Jinja, but you can pick up some indulgences such as biscuits or pasta. For simple staples it's best to buy from locals at the trailheads with assistance from the guides. Porters can make campfires for cooking, but for environmental reasons the park requests that you bring a campstove if you have one.

TRAILS

There are currently three routes up the mountain; and two more expected to be ready sometimes in 2009. Many people combine different routes going up and down for maxi-

---

WARNING: TREKKING MT ELGON

Mt Elgon may be a relatively easy climb, but this is still a big, wild mountain. Rain, hail and thick mists aren't uncommon, even in the dry season, and night-time temperatures frequently drop below freezing. Pack adequate clothing and at least one day's extra food, just in case. Altitude sickness is rarely a problem, but heed the warning signs (p633).

You should also check on the security situation before coming here. A Belgian climber was shot dead in February 2008. It's not known who fired shots into the camp, and it's unlikely she was the intended target, but it highlights the fact that there are armed smugglers and cattle rustlers in the area. Additionally the Sabaot Land Defence Force militia operates on Kenyan soil and likely tries to evade the Kenyan military by crossing to the Ugandan side of the border at times, though there have been no incidents between them and park visitors. Uganda has responded to both situations by increasing patrols and an armed escort now joins all climbs.

---

mum variety. We've given the normal travel times for the various routes, but if you're up to the challenge these can all be shortened by a day or two. On the other hand, you may want to add an extra day to further explore the caldera or visit the Suam Gorge, or let the guides take you to waterfalls and caves. If summiting at Wagagai, it only takes an extra hour to hit Jackson's Summit (4165m) via Jackson's Pool, a little crater lake. You must use designated camp sites, all of which have tent pads, latrines, rubbish pits and nearby water sources. Bunkhouses are being added, but it's probably going to be some time before you can trek without a tent.

The **Sasa Trail** is the original route to Wagagai, and still the busiest since it can be easily be reached by public transport from Mbale. It's a four-day roundtrip to the summit with a 1650m ascent on first day. From Budadari, which is considered the trailhead, a road leads 5km to Bumasola, and you can take a car up this leg if you want, then it's a short walk to the forest. Almost as soon as you enter the forest, you reach Mudangi Cliffs, which are scaled via ladders and then it's 2½ hours of pure bamboo forest. The second day is an easier walk. On summit day, it's four hours from your campsite to Wagagai.

The **Sipi Trail**, which begins at the Forest Exploration Centre in Kapkwai, has become a popular return route since it lets you chill out at Sipi Falls following your trip to the top. It's a longer trip, taking five days roundtrip. Also, note that it's an easier hike if you choose to descend via the Sasa Trail because the Sipi Trail starts at a higher elevation. On the first day you can camp inside the huge Tutum Cave, which has a small waterfall over its entrance and once attracted elephants to dig salt out of

the rock like some more famous caves on the Kenyan side still do.

Also starting high, the **Piswa Trail** has an even gentler ascent than the Sipi Trail. It's the best wildlife watching route since it doesn't pass through bamboo stands, and it also offers the longest pass through the other-worldly moorland in the caldera. It's a six-day journey when returning by the Sasa Trail and seven day when coming back via the Sipi Trail. Piswa is the least-used trail because it begins in the difficult to reach village of Kapkwata.

The two new routes will be the **Suam Trail**, another five-day route starting at a higher elevation than the Sasa Trail and climbing through the Suam Gorge right along the Kenyan border, and the short **Bushiri Trail** that will allow a three-day hit on Wagagai.

Climbers have the option of continuing their trek into Kenya, or starting there and ending up in Uganda. Park staff at the headquarters will take you to the immigration office in Mbale for the requisite paperwork and then hand you off to the Kenya Wildlife Service at the hot springs in the caldera. It's a two day hike down the Kenyan side.

DAY TRIPS

Although more are planned, there are currently two day-hike destinations. The main one is a trio of short loops around the Forest Exploration Centre at the start of the Sipi Trail. Truth be told, the scenery is more striking around Sipi Falls, but these trails offer insight into Mt Elgon's forests, and there are no longer many trees around the falls. The **Mountain Bamboo Trail** takes in some huge bamboo and passes some petrified wood, as well as offering a view of Elgon's summits on a clear day; few and far between, unfortunately. The **Chebonet Falls Trail** passes a modest waterfall, while the **Ridge Trail** offers some good views above and below. Most people can complete these in far less than the times posted on the signs. Perhaps a more rewarding choice here is the 11km walk to the huge **Tutum Cave** along the Sipi Trail.

The other day-trail is an easy four-hour walk along the **Wanale Ridge**, visible from Mbale, where you can see red-tailed monkeys and petrified wood at **Khauka Cave**.

Although it's probably a long-term proposition, the **Atari River** near Kapchorwa passes through a cave and the park would like to develop this into a float-trip of some sort.

Sleeping & Eating

Rose's Last Chance (☎ 0772-623206; camping USh10,000, dm USh15,000, r USh22,000) Those climbing the Sasa Trail can sleep in Mbale before the trek, but for many people a night with Rose is part of the Mt Elgon experience. Located near the trailhead in Budadari, this is a basic but fun and friendly place that brings guests closer to the local scene. Testing local brews is a favourite activity and Rose sometimes brings in musicians and dancers at night. She began with one bed and her hospitality has led to plans for a second little lodge down the road. It's worth staying here even if you aren't trekking, and Rose can direct you to caves and waterfalls in the area. Prices include a local dinner and breakfast; vegie dishes available. Camping gear can be hired for the same price as the park office and there's a car if you want to explore the area.

Forest Exploration Centre (camping USh15,000, dm USh10,000, s USh20,000, d USh30,000-50,000) This lovely, spread-out setup is right at the Sipi trailhead. The self-contained cottages here are really tasteful. There are also safari tents for the same price as the cottages, but you have to walk to the toilets. The little restaurant (with satellite TV) has meals for USh7000 and the park staff will cook any food you bring.

Kapkwata Guesthouse (per tent or bed USh15,000) This simple (cold-water only) UWA-run place is right at the trailhead and if you bring food, staff can cook it for you. You currently don't need to pay park fees to sleep here, but this may change.

The **Wirr Community Campsite** is just outside the park gate next to the Forest Education Centre, but the community seem to have given up on it. Sipi Falls is a better bet if you'd rather not pay the park fee the first night.

Getting There & Away

There are regular, if infrequent, mini-buses from Mbale to Budadari (USh3000, 45 minutes).

There's no regular transport to the Forest Exploration Centre, but minibuses between Mbale and Kapchorwa (USh6000; 1½ hours) pass the signposted turn-off to Kapkwai, 6km up from Sipi, from where it's a 6km walk to the centre; there's little chance of catching a ride. A *boda-boda* from Sipi should cost USh10,000 to USh15,000 depending on how dry the road is; fair special-hire prices range from USh30,000 to USh50,000. A more interesting way to get to the centre is to hire a guide at Sipi to walk you through the villages, about a 90-minute trip.

Getting to the Piswa trailhead in Kapkwata takes a little more effort. The excellent paved road ends at Kapchorwa, and so do all the minibuses. From here you'll have to ride in one of the infrequent trucks (USh5000, 2½ hours) for the often rough 33km trip. They run until around 3pm, so it's possible to make it from Mbale in a day.

From Kapkwata there are infrequent trucks to the border at Suam (USh5000) via a terrible road. In the best of conditions it will take at least two hours. Trucks from Kapchorwa go to Suam (USh10,000, three hours) via a lower route with a better road. If you reach the border by early afternoon, you should have little problem moving straight on to Kitale by *matatu*. There's basic lodging if you can't.

SIPI FALLS

Sipi Falls, in the foothills of Mt Elgon, is a stunner; arguably the most beautiful waterfall in all of Uganda. There are three levels, and though the upper two are beautiful, it's the 95m main drop that attracts the crowds, and most of Sipi's lodging looks out over it. Not only are the falls spectacular, so too are the views of the wide plains disappearing into the distance below. It's well worth spending a night or two in this peaceful and pretty place.

Sights & Activities

There are some excellent walks on a network of well-maintained (though often muddy) local trails and beautiful scenery in every direction. It's easy enough to just ramble off on your own, but a guide is highly recommended since you'll cross much private property (without a guide you'll need to pay at several points) and also will be pestered by children asking for money (either to be your guide or just because). All the lodges can arrange guides and prices are pretty similar. Figure on about USh5000 to get to the bottom of the main drop and USh10,000 to USh12,000 per person for the four-hour, 8km walk to all three. There's a cave behind the easy to reach second falls, and though most people end up deleting the top falls from their itinerary due to exhaustion, it's really worth the climb since if you have a clear day (which happens a couple of times each week) you can literally see halfway across Uganda from the ridge at the top. There are also village walks and the forest walking trails at Mt Elgon National Park's Forest Exploration Centre (p463) nearby, though you have to pay the national park fees to hike there.

Rob's Rolling Rock (☎ 0752-369536) is a reliable local outfit offering climbing and abseiling around Sipi Falls. Their mainstay is a 100m abseil alongside the main falls for USh50,000 per person.

If the guys at Sipi River Lodge (right) have their way, there will soon be tandem paragliding, canyoning and many more activities available. They would also like to offer overnight trips to the nearby **Pian-Upe Wildlife Reserve**, which has little development but lots of potential.

There's not much to see in **Mise Cave** (admission USh1000), next to the little waterfall at the bend in the road just above the village, but the caretaker will tell you a few tales about how the Sabiny people used to live.

There's a **craft shop** open irregular hours in the village. Unless they've finally added a sign, you'll need to ask directions.

Sleeping & Eating

Sipi has a good range of tasteful lodges; all good in their own way. At the first three, you'll be lucky if your food (mostly Western favourites with a few local choices, all very reasonably priced) takes a long time to arrive: it will probably take a very long time. The others do set menus.

Moses' Campsite (☎ 0752-208302; camping USh5000, bandas per person USh10,000) Sipi's original backpacker destination, this small, laid-back oper-

ation is arguably the best, situated with a good look at the falls (available from hammocks on the terrace) and unhindered views of the Karamojaland plains below. The *bandas* are decent, the staff friendly and colobus monkeys often hang around here.

Crow's Nest (☎ 0752-286225; thecrowsnets@yahoo.com; camping USh6000, dm USh12,000, cabins USh30,000) Crow's Nest was set up by Peace Corps volunteers and the cabins are Scandinavian-style with private baths and expansive waterfall views from their terraces. Overland trucks occasionally stop here and the well-stocked bar can get a little happening on some nights. Yes, someone really did make a mess of the email address: crowsnets, not nest!

Twalight Campsite (☎ 0772-625199; www.twalightsipicampsite.com; camping USh4000, dm USh8000, bandas s/d USh20,000/40,000 without bathroom, banda USh60,000) Right next door to Crow's Nest, this is a smaller, quieter option and, in our opinion the views are just a tad better, though you can't get them direct from your room. The *bandas* are comfy, the dorm less crammed and the large terrace is a great place to watch the stars. Though prices are higher than Crow's Nest, they'll quickly match their neighbour's rates.

Lacam Lodge (☎ 0752-292554; www.lacamlodge.co.uk; camping USh35,000, dm 50,000, room without bathroom s/d USh60,000-100,000, bandas s/d/tr USh110,000/180,000/210,000) This attractive lodge is the closest to the big waterfall, and from the viewing area you can see the water crash land. Accommodation here, from the three-bed dorms to the large self-contained *bandas*, is very comfy and the service is good. Accommodation is full board; except during the July to August and Christmas-time high season (when all prices rise 10,000 to USh20,000 per night), when half-board rates are available.

Sipi Falls Resort (☎ 0753-153000; sipiresort@yahoo.com; camping USh10,000, s/d/tr USh104,000/117,000/140,000) This small place, set very close to the main falls, is no longer up to the standard of when it was run by Volcanoes Safaris, though it also no longer costs in excess of US$200. The *bandas* are well-appointed and have private bathrooms, although the resort's small size is its only selling point over Lacam. The old house here was used as a residence by the last British governor of Uganda; today it's available for groups.

Sipi River Lodge (☎ 0751-796109; www.sipiriver.com; dm US$40, banda s/d US$75/95, cottage d/q US$155/295, all prices full board, half-board available; 🖵) Still under construction when we popped in, but already a stunner, this colourful place was founded by three river guides from Jinja. Its namesake rushes through the front yard and the second waterfall drops right in the back. A nightly set menu (USh25,000 for drop-in diners), with many of the ingredients coming from their vegetable garden, is served around a fireplace.

Getting There & Away

Minibuses run between Mbale and Sipi Falls (USh5000, one hour), but can take a long time to fill up. Drivers will drop you right at your lodge. Those travelling in a group should consider a special-hire if it's late in the day. If you're lucky this could be as low as USh30,000, but probably higher.

For the return trip, most minibuses start at Kawpchorwa and are often full when they pass through Sipi, so you may end up waiting a while. Ask at your lodge if they know when any minibuses will start the trip in Sipi.

NYERO ROCKPAINTINGS

Of the many ancient rock art sites scattered around eastern Uganda, this is one of the easiest to reach; and one of the few worth the effort to do so. The main site, known as Nyero 2, is a big white wall covered in groups of red circles, boats and some vaguely human and animal forms. Archaeologists have yet to unravel the significance of the designs, who painted them and even when they did so. If the caretaker is around, he'll charge USh5000 for an informative tour, otherwise any child can fill in a few details. Nyero 1, with a few more circles, lies just below the main site while Nyero 3, where you probably won't notice the modest painting unless someone shows you, is a few hundred metres north. The surrounding countryside is littered with similar bouldery peaks, and it would be fun to spend a day exploring. Locals insist there are no snakes in the area; just 'small monkeys'.

Nyero is an easy day-trip from Mbale, Sipi, Soroti or even Jinja, but Kumi has you covered if you need to say the night. The spotless self-contained rooms at **Axsa Inn** (☎ 0702-658080; 29 Ngora Rd, Kumi; r USh21,000) makes a big leap over the nearby cheapies. There's an internet café and a Stanbic Bank with an ATM on this same block. You could also arrange with the caretaker to camp by the site, but you'll need to bring your own food.

Getting There & Away

The Nyero rockpaintings are 9km west of Kumi, just past Nyero village. Look for the small, white signpost. Saloon-car shared taxis (from the taxi park just north of the Kumi city centre) to Ngora can drop you at the site (USh2000, 20 minutes), but departures are infrequent in the morning and rare in the afternoon. A roundtrip by *boda-boda*, with some time to explore, will cost USh4000.

Minibuses between Mbale (USh3000, one hour) and Soroti (USh3000, one hour) are frequent and stop along the highway.

SOROTI

Few travellers make it to Soroti, unless they're attempting the overland route to Kidepo Valley National Park. Like Tororo to the southeast, it has a curious volcanic plug, called **Opiyai Rock**, poking skywards on the edge of town, this one naked rock. From the top you can look out over nearby Lake Kyoga and spy Mt Elgon in the distance. Get permission from the assistant town clerk at the Soroti Municipal Council-Eastern Division Offices, right at the base of the hill, before climbing it or you'll be in for a massive hassle when you meet the guards at the top.

Information

The main road through town, Gweri Rd, has the post office and several banks which will change cash, but not travellers cheques. Solot Ave, one block over, has several hotels and restaurants. There are a few internet cafés on both streets.

Sleeping & Eating

Several good cheapies line Solot Ave in the centre of town. The best of the bunch is currently **Silent Night Inn** (☎ 0454-661239; Solot Ave; s USh10,000-15,000, d USh20,000), with clean enough rooms, all with private bathroom. The **Garden Guesthouse** (☎ 0772-454471; 11 Engwau Rd; r USh25,000, banda USh30,000), down a quiet lane 200m from the centre of town, has good rooms and cute little *bandas*, while the **Golden Ark Hotel** (☎ 0772-350038; 74 Gweri Rd; r USh35,000-60,000; 🖳), in the centre right as you roll into town from the south, has so much tile you might think you're in the Middle East. It also has a sauna. The plain **Landmark Hotel** (☎ 0782-515959; Solot Ave; r USh52,000-82,000) in the centre and the garden-set **Soroti Hotel**

(☎ 0772-301154; s USh50,000-60,000, d USh60,000-80,000) behind the rock also have modern and comfortable rooms.

When it comes to eating, Soroti doesn't inspire, but there are a few cheap local joints on Solot Ave, while the better hotels offer more choice. Rumour has it an Indian restaurant is in the works. For a night out, Solot Ave has several beer halls, while **Trends** (Moroto Rd; ☿ Wed-Sat), a few kilometres out of town, is an actual nightclub.

Getting There & Away

Minibuses and buses all stop at various points along Station Rd on the west edge of downtown. Minibuses run between Soroti and Kampala (USh15,000, five hours) via Mbale (USh5000, two hours) on a good sealed road and to Gulu (USh12,000, seven hours) on a rough dirt road.

Gateway has the most buses to/from town with roughly an hourly departure for Kampala during the day plus a few middle-of-the-night rides. They also have a daily departure to Gulu (USh20,000, six hours). Teso Coach goes to Kampala about every two hours. The Post Bus (see p443) only heads to Kampala occasionally, and it makes many stops along the way.

OVERLAND TO KIDEPO VALLEY NATIONAL PARK

For those hardy souls heading to Kidepo Valley National Park without using an airport, there are two possible routes. Both are long and at times difficult journeys, but this is one place where travel is its own reward. Unless the security situation precludes it (read the boxed texts on p468 and p508 carefully before travelling), the ideal plan is to head in on one route and out on the other.

All roads past the gateway towns of Mbale, Soroti and Gulu are dirt, and you'll need four-wheel-drive if driving yourself. Except for staple foods like rice and beans, buy anything you want or need before departing as store shelves are very limited along the way. Also bring enough cash: Stanbic Bank has ATMs in Kotido and Kitgum, but they're often offline.

Eastern Route

Once the only way to cross to Kidepo, due to the Lord's Resistance Army (LRA) campaign of terror across northern Uganda (see p421), this two- or three-day journey takes you though the wilds of Karamojaland where many of the Karamojong people still wear traditional dress (similar to the Maasai) and AK-47s are as common as walking sticks. You'll cross great plains peppered with tall peaks, and good wildlife watching begins before you even reach the park gate. This is the more difficult of the two routes, but the up-close look at this distinct culture makes it the most rewarding.

Begin by heading to **Kotido**, a small but fast-growing town three hours north of Moroto that's actually more prosperous than it looks. The Wednesday **cattle market** is a good opportunity to meet Karamojong from the countryside. Be sure to stop by the friendly **Uganda Wildlife Authority Information Office** (☎ 0774-209002; ☿ 7am-8pm Mon-Fri & most weekends), next to the central roundabout, where Omara Faustine can give you onward travel advice and help you buy the food you'll need in the park.

There are a handful of hotels in town. **Skyline Hotel** (☎ 0774-802159; Kotido; r without bathroom USh10,000, r USh15,000), just down the road past the UWA office, has small but clean rooms and friendly staff, while the bed-and-breakfast-style **La Maison Hotel** (☎ 0782-875725; s USh36,000, d USh40,000-60,000), a kilometre out of town, is as good as you're gonna get. Bear in mind there's no municipal electricity supply here (or in any of the towns further north); and water shortages are common; both of these hotels run generators from 7pm to 11pm. Gateway has daily buses to Kotido (USh30,000, 15 hours), departing Kampala's new bus park at 5.30am and passing through Mbale (USh20,000) at about 9am.

From Kotido there are frequent trucks and pick-ups to **Kaabong** (USh5000, two to three hours), a rough 'wild east' town; there are rumours Gateway will add a bus service with the previous day's coach from Kampala continuing on early in the morning. From there, jump on the less frequent trucks to **Karenga** (USh7000, two to three hours) and get off at what locals call 'Tsetse Control', just 2km from the park's Nataba Gate. If you visited Omara back in Kotido just before leaving on this final stage, a truck or motorcycle will be waiting to ferry you the final 14km to the park headquarters. You only pay for the kilometres when you're actually travelling in the park's truck, though it would be wise to double-check this. If things have changed and you

---

WARNING: SECURITY IN KARAMOJALAND

Despite a heavy military presence, Karamojaland in the northeast has a deserved reputation as a dangerous destination. Groups of local cattle herders, the Karamojong, have been known to ambush highway travellers: sometimes to steal food or money, sometimes for vengeance and sometimes just for fun. There's also occasional fighting between the Karamojong and the army and among the Karamojong themselves. And, to make matters more complicated, large numbers of armed Turkana tribesmen from Kenya often cross the border looking to steal cattle.

Aid workers and government officials travel with a military escort, and for the time being, driving your own vehicle would be foolish. It has long been considered safe to travel on the Gateway bus, but you'll want to check on this following two bus shootings with one death and a dozen injuries in August 2008. These appear to have been for revenge after a child was struck and killed by a bus, so they will probably prove nothing more than isolated incidents. The trucks that carry goods and locals between towns are *almost* never attacked.

We don't have statistics to back this up, and it flies in the face of conventional wisdom, but we feel that if you travel by public means, coming here is pretty safe; probably safer than riding a *boda-boda* in Kampala. Still, it's of paramount importance to check on security before setting out (national park staff will have the latest details) and again at every step of the way. Things can change very fast out here. One final note: when inquiring about the current situation, don't just ask locals 'is it safe?'. Invariably the answer will be yes: ask specifics about when the last ambushes happened so you can make an informed decision about whether you want to take the risk.

---

now have to pay for a round trip from the park visitor centre it will be cheaper to continue to Karenga (an extra USh3000 and 30 minutes) and get a special-hire (USh40,000) there.

If you catch the first truck of the morning out of Kaabong you'll likely make it to the park that same day. However, should you get stuck in Kaabong there's simple accommodation. We love the sign for the Rock Hotel, but **Memoma House** (☎ 0752-352188; Kaabong; r USh12,000) has a higher standard.

Northern Route

Most people heading to Kidepo travel through Gulu, which is both the shortest and easiest route; and currently the only one to consider if you're driving. Depending on where you begin, the road north from Lira to Kitgum may be a shortcut, but it sees far less traffic so you'll have much bigger hassles if you breakdown.

Using public transport, you'll be able to make it from Gulu to the park in one day if you get an early start. The first leg of the journey is by one of the frequent buses running to **Kitgum** (USh10,000, three hours), a surprisingly bustling little town. UWA is planning to open an office here. Many coach lines have buses straight from Kampala (USh25,000, seven hours) to Kitgum so you could skip Gulu, though the choice of lodging is much better there. In Kitgum, the **Bomah**

Hotel (☎ 0471-439388; Uhuru Dr, Kitgum; s USh62,000, d USh72,000-82,000; ⌘), where UN personnel stay, has a sauna, steam bath, pool and satellite TV, though spotty upkeep make these prices higher than they should be. **Maicamo Bar & Lodging** (Kitgum; r USh7500) is a friendly little flophouse right by the bus park.

The second half of the journey sees you bidding goodbye to civilisation, although some would suggest that happened upon leaving Kampala. Up until around midday, trucks head east past scattered villages and former IDP camps. Just about when you feel you must be hopelessly lost and heading toward Sudan, you'll hit the petite town of **Karenga** (USh20,000, five to seven hours), 24km from the park's headquarters and lodging area. There's rumour of a future bus service direct to Karenga from Kampala. We think it's unlikely, but it's worth asking about it.

In Karenga you might get lucky and be able to hitch a ride (this is far more likely heading out of the park in the morning), but you'll probably need a special-hire (USh40,000). You could also call the park's office in Kotido (p467) (or, the park once they get a telephone – ask at the UWA office in Kampala) to have them pick you up at a cost of USh3000 per kilometre. (You should only have to pay for 24km, not 48km, but ask first.) Either way, let the driver know you want to take your time travelling since there's plenty of wildlife along this road and the scenery is gorgeous.

KIDEPO VALLEY NATIONAL PARK

This lost valley in the extreme northeast, along the Sudanese border, has the most stunning scenery of any protected area in Uganda. The rolling, short-grass savannah of the 1442-sq-km **Kidepo Valley National Park** (admission US$30) is ringed by mountains and cut by rocky ridges.

Kidepo is most notable for harbouring a number of animals found nowhere else in Uganda, including cheetah, bat-eared foxes, aardwolf, caracal, greater and lesser kudu, and Rothschild's giraffe. There are also large concentrations of elephant, zebra (curiously, these lack manes), buffalo, bushbuck, lion, jackal and Nile crocodile.

Amazingly, most of these animals, including even the occasional lion, are content to graze and lounge right near the park's accommodation, so you can see a whole lot without going very far: it's a safari from a lounge chair. One particular elephant, named Bull-bull by park staff, has taken a liking to the local brew and is sure to be seen up close and personal. But don't get foolishly close; he seems tame, but we've seen him charge people.

The bird checklist is fast approaching 500 species (second among the national parks only to the larger Queen Elizabeth National Park; p484) and there are many 'Kidepo specials', birds such as ostrich, kori bustard, pygmy falcon, secretary bird, Karamoja apalis and Abyssinian ground hornbill that are found in no other Ugandan national park.

The dry months of November to January, when you might see some of the biggest buffalo herds in Africa, are the best months to visit but you're sure to see lots of animals at any time.

Activities

Game drives are available here using a park vehicle, but cost a hefty USh3000 to USh4000 per kilometre plus the US$20 guide fee. Mighty expensive if you have come overland on a budget, but there's a whole lot to see so it's worth it if you can divvy up the costs. A top target is the Narus Valley where the lions began climbing trees around 2005. Also popular are the borassus palm forest and Kanangorok hot springs by the usually dry Kidepo River.

Another great option is a **nature walk** (US$10 per person) with armed rangers. Both the park and the Apoka Lodge staff can arrange **traditional dance performances** with a little notice. A future option planned by the park staff will be **trekking** in the Morungole Mountains with visits to Karamojong and Ik villages.

Sleeping & Eating

UWA's **Apoka Hostel** (s/d USh30,000/50,000 full board) offers good *bandas* with private bathrooms and dorms will probably be added in the future. The park also maintains two isolated **camp sites** (camping USh15,000) with latrines and water. If you don't have a vehicle to reach them you can just pitch your tent around the *bandas*.

If you want something really special, you want **our pick Apoka Safari Lodge** (☎ 0414-251182; www.wildplacesafrica.com; s/d US$430/760; ☻). Its 10 large and very private thatched-roof cottages, each featuring porches, outdoor tubs (watch buffalo during a bubblebath) and, as more than one person has told us, the best showers in Uganda, are built across a rocky ridge. They look out over watering holes always full of wildlife. The dining area has the same great views and there's a tower where you can arrange for a romantic, private dinner. The price includes game drives, walking safaris and airport transfers. Everything is flown in, so you must book in advance.

There are absolutely no walk-ins for meals or drinks at Apoka Lodge, though if you make arrangements in Kampala first, you may be able to have dinner there. Those staying at the hostel should come with their own food; cold drinks are available.

Some investors have recently inquired about rebuilding the Grand Katurum Lodge, built into a huge rock bluff during Idi Amin's regime.

Getting There & Away

Although an increasing number of visitors are travelling to Kidepo Valley National Park by land (see p467), most still fly. **Eagle Air** (☎ 0414-344292; www.flyeagleuganda.com) currently comes here on diversion status, arriving on Friday and returning on Monday (US$1025 one-way diversion fee plus the price of the ticket, US$135/235 one-way/return). If the park's popularity continues to grow, it may become a regular, and thus cheaper, stop. You can also come by charter (p531).

UGANDA

SOUTHWESTERN UGANDA

If Uganda is the 'pearl of Africa', then southwestern Uganda is the mother of pearl. Easily the most beautiful part of the country, it's a lush region of lakes, islands and mountains. And whether you're here for adventure or respite, the southwest's got you covered in spades.

There are top-notch treks all along the western Rift Valley, whether it be taking in the three-nation vistas from atop the Virunga volcanoes or making a weeklong slog though the otherworldly moorlands on the snow-

capped Rwenzoris. After the mountains, head to the water for an all out R&R assault on Lake Bunyonyi or the Ssese Islands.

With most of the nation's national parks, the southwest is Uganda's top wildlife watching region too; and one of the world's best for primates. There are, of course, the mountain gorillas, living *la vida* languorous on the steep slopes of Bwindi Impenetrable Forest and Mgahinga Gorilla National Parks. Kibale Forest National Park has what's often described as the greatest variety of primates on the planet, and this is just one of the places where you can track a habituated troop of chimpanzees as they groove through the treetops. The famous tree-climbing lions steal the show at Queen Elizabeth National Park, but

SOUTHWESTERN UGANDA

0 _____ 60 km
0 _____ 40 miles

LEGEND
FR   Forest Reserve
NP   National Park
WR   Wildlife Reserve

the area's largest and most diverse park is full of big game and is one place certain to satisfy your safari urge.

As in the rest of the country, it can take a long time to get from place to place. And it's tough to properly explore most of the national parks without your own set of wheels, but as this is the most popular part of Uganda it's usually not too tough to team up with other travellers to share the costs.

FORT PORTAL

The fort may be gone, but this far western city near the north end of the Rwenzori Mountains is definitely a portal to places that offer sublime scenery, abundant nature and genuine adventure. Explore the beautiful crater lakes, track the chimps in Kibale Forest National Park or Toro-Semliki Wildlife Reserve, and drop into Semuliki National Park with its hot springs and Central African wildlife.

Fort Portal is the heartland of a verdant tea-growing area and an important commercial centre, but not a particularly appealing place. Still, its central location makes it a very convenient base to explore the area from, so many people end up staying here a few days.

Information

Lugard Rd, Fort's main drag, has just about everything travellers may need including crafts shops, internet cafés, the post office and **Stanbic Bank** (Lugard Rd), which changes cash and American Express travellers cheques. **Centenary Bank** (Rukidi III St) and **Barclays Bank** (Babitha Rd) only handle cash.

Sights & Activities

Fort Portal's attractions are pretty minor; even more so considering what's on offer outside the town.

Looking down on the town from its highest hill, **Tooro Palace** is the someday-to-be home of King Oyo, who ascended the throne in 1995 at age three. The circular structure was built in 1963, fell into ruins after the abolition of the royal kingdoms, and was restored in 2001 after Colonel Gadaffi met the king and donated the money for repairs. There's usually someone around who, for USh5000, will give you a quick history of the kingdom and explain the ceremonies that take place on the hill, but you can't go inside.

Eventually King Oyo will join the previous three kings at the **Karambi Royal Tombs** (Kasese Rd; admission USh5000; 8am-6pm) further south out of town. The three run-down brick buildings are of no interest at all, but you get to look inside and see some drums, spears and other personal effects.

An altogether more enjoyable place to visit is the out-of-town **Tooro Botanical Garden** (0752-500630; Km 2 Kampala Rd; admission USh5000; 8am-5pm), an organic farming project growing herbs, flowers, trees, natural dyes, vegetables and medicinal plants. Admission includes a tour through the extensive grounds where you can ask about the various plants.

The best way to enjoy Fort Portal is to stop by **Kabarole Tours** (0483-422183; www .kabaroletours.com; Moledina St; 8am-6pm Mon-Sat, 10am-4pm Sun) who can take you anywhere in Uganda but focus on its little corner of the country. The staff is keen to answer questions about the area and lead a variety of tours, including two into the foothills of the Rwenzoris; see the Short Circuit box on p484. The company hires cars and mountain bikes (USh15,000 per day) and can give you some rough maps of the area, or send a guide with you.

The Wednesday **Mugusu Market** (Kasese Rd); 11km south of Fort Portal, is the largest market in the west and attracts traders from all over, including many from DRC.

If you'd like to do some voluntary work with children in the area, see Y.E.S. Hostel (p472) and Mpora Rural Family (p472).

Sleeping
TOWN CENTRE
Exotic Lodge (0774-771829; Moledina St; s/d USh5500/7500 without bathroom) Fort Portal is flush with flophouses, but this one is cleaner and, dare we say it, cosier than the competition. There are several similarly priced places further south along Balya Rd that will also do for a night.

Continental Hotel (0752-514696; Lugard Rd; s/d USh13,000/16,000 without bathroom, r USh26,000) Far from the friendliest place in town this centrally located next-level spot is also not the scruffiest. And, since the self-contained rooms have TV and hot water showers, it's the pick of the pack.

Palace Motel (0772-837226; 33 Muzosi Rd; s USh25,000, d USh30,000-40,000) Newer, cleaner, quieter, more comfortable and just plain better

UGANDA

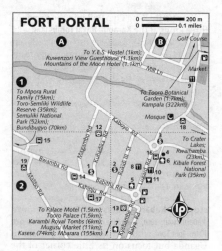

than most of its competition at this price. It's a little hard to find; turn right off Kasese Rd just before then entrance to the king's palace. The USh40,000 rooms are full of furniture and they all have satellite TV.

Rwenzori Travellers Inn (☎ 0482-422075; www .rwenzoritravellersinn.com; 16 Kyebambe Rd; r USh36,000-87,000; 🖳) This modern hotel with a range of rooms has been popular ever since it opened, though it seems to be coasting on its reputation these days. Prices are high and they've fallen behind in minor maintenance: look at a couple of rooms before taking the keys. Still, you could do much worse and, with a good restaurant (best Indian food in town after the only proper Indian restaurant shut its doors), two bars, an internet café, and craft shop on site, it's certainly the most convenient stop.

BOMA

This leafy, peaceful suburb just north of town has good mountain views and Fort Portal's best lodging. It's made even more appealing by the fact that downtown Fort Portal is one of Uganda's noisiest places.

Y.E.S. Hostel (☎ 0772-780350; yesuganda@gmail.com; Lower Kakiiza Rd; camping USh4000, dm USh7000, s USh10,000) The hostel at this Christian charity, which supports orphans, is simple but remarkably tidy and offers a nice pastoral setting. There's a large kitchen, solar hot-water showers and internet access is supposedly coming; plus with 50 beds (four to six per room) but relatively few guests (unless a large group is there), you usually get a room to yourself. It's 3km from the centre; a

boda-boda costs USh1000. There are some long-term volunteer opportunities available, and the staff can also connect people to schools and hospitals in the area for those with less time.

our pick Ruwenzori View Guesthouse (☎ 0483-422102; ruwview@africaonline.co.ug; Lower Kakiiza Rd; s/d 40,000/55,000 without bathroom, s/d USh65,000/85,000; 🖳) A blissful little guesthouse run by an Anglo-Dutch couple, it feels refreshingly rural and is the most atmospheric place in town. The self-contained rooms have their own patios overlooking the lovely garden. Rates include a hearty breakfast, and dinners are served around the family table. As homey as it gets!

Mountains of the Moon Hotel (☎ 0483-423200; www.mountainsofthemoon.co.ug; Nyaika Ave; s USh160,000; d USh210,000-240,000; 🖳 🐾) This colonial-era gem reopened in 2007 following an extensive makeover that added lots of eclectic little touches. All rooms have terraces and guests have use of a gym, sauna and business centre. Prices are high, but so are the standards.

OUTSIDE TOWN

Mpora Rural Family (☎ 0752-555732; mmorence@ yahoo.com; banda per person incl full board USh40,000)

Morence Mpora has long been offering accommodation at his orphanage in an effort to help finance it, as well as the two schools he runs. Visitors are welcome to volunteer or just enjoy the friendly, rural setting. Either way, it's a rewarding experience. Many people end up sticking around for a long time. Minibus drivers can drop you off at Kihondo (USh1500, 45 minutes) on the road to Bundibugyo, 15km from Fort Portal. Then it's a little over 1km to walk: turn left at the Kisanga Valley School and start asking directions soon after.

Eating & Drinking

The best dining options are the home-cooked meals at **Ruwenzori View Guesthouse** (dinner USh18,000; ☺ 8pm) and small but wide-ranging international menu at the **Mountains of the Moon Hotel** (USh8,000-20,000; ☺ 12.30-3pm & 7-10.30pm). Rwenzori Travellers Inn (USh5000 to USh9000) in the town centre is also popular and not too bad.

A solid choice to try some Uganda staples is **Exotic Lodge** (☎ 0774-771829; Moledina St; mains USh1500-3000). Many locals lunch here.

Pulling in much of the safari traffic passing through Fort Portal, **Gardens** (☎ 0772-694482; Lugard Rd; mains USh2700-8800) is a busy spot on the way into town. It has a lively menu of foreign and local dishes including vegetable curry, fish stew, pizza, *firinda* (mashed skinless beans) and lots of *mochomo* (barbecued meat). There's also a good liquor list and a large African lunch buffet (USh5500); a great chance to sample some new foods. Live bands sometimes play on weekend nights.

For those needing to buy their own provisions, **Andrew & Brothers** (Lugard Rd) is the best of several supermarkets in town. **Shop Organic** (10 Lugard Rd) across the street is also worth a peek. Both stay open late.

Don's Plaza (8 Lugard Rd), and its next-door neighbour **Sunset Bar** (8 Lugard Rd), are Fort Portal's most-pub like joints; good places for drinks, snacks and premiership games on TV. The Parrot Bar upstairs at the Rwenzori Travellers Inn is a quieter place for a drink. If quiet is not what you're after, try **Club Heartbeat** (Kuhadika Rd; entry USh5000; ☺ Saturday) dance club in the basement of the Hotel Cornerstone or, for a more earthy experience, join the jam-packed crowd in the disco at the **Wooden Hotel** (Lugard Rd).

Getting There & Away

Kalita Transport has the most daily buses to Kampala (USh10,000, four hours) but you can also get there with Link Coaches, whose buses tend to be more comfortable. There's also a Post Bus (see p443).

Both bus companies also journey to Kasese (USh4000, one hour); catch the Kalita bus at their office in town, not at their bus park as you would for Kampala. There are also two early morning buses that make the journey all the way to Kabale (USh20,000, eight hours), via Katunguru (USh8000, 1½ hours) for Queen Elizabeth National Park, from the Kalita bus park.

The easiest way to Hoima (USh25,000, six hours) is the coaster that goes at 7am every other day from in front of the Bata shoe store, but you can also do the trip by minibus (USh20,000, seven hours) in two stages: first to Kagadi and then to Hoima. There are also regular-ish departures from the **taxi park** (Malibo Rd) to Mbarara (USh20,000, four hours), Ntoroko (USh5000, three hours) and Bundibugyo (USh7000, three hours); often in the backs of pick-up trucks for the latter two.

Minibuses and saloon car shared taxis to Kamwenge (for Kibale Forest National Park; USh5000, 45 minutes) and Rwaihamba (for Lake Nkuruba; USh4000, 45 minutes) leave from the intersection near where the main road crosses the river.

Special-hire drivers hang around the vacant lot by the Continental Hotel and charge as little as USh50,000 per day if you aren't travelling too far. Kabarole Tours (p471) has 4WDs for USh180,000 per day.

AROUND FORT PORTAL
The Crater Lakes

The landscape south of Fort Portal is dotted with picturesque crater lakes (some over 400m deep), all of which are ringed with improbably steep hills. It's a great spot to settle in for a few days to explore the footpaths or cycle the seldom-used roads. Much of the land is cultivated, but there are still plenty of primates and birds at the lake shores. Accommodation caters for all budgets and it's increasingly popular for visitors to stay at the lakes before continuing on to Kibale Forest National Park (p475).

Most lodges and guesthouses organise walks through the local villages or to other area attractions (which have entrance fees if you go without a guide) such as **Top of the World** (admission USh5000) viewpoint on the highest hill behind Lake Nyamirima where you can see up to five lakes (depending on the air clarity) and **Mahoma Waterfall** (admission USh5000); small but attractive and a great spot for a natural power-shower.

The common wisdom is that the lakes are bilharzia-free, but we can't guarantee it. The manager of Ndali Lodge (right) told us his lake, Nyinambuga, does have it; but not the section in front of the lodge. If this lake is infested, perhaps others might be too. Also be aware that a lone hippo roams between Nyamirima, Nyinabulitwa, Nyamikere and, according to some, Nkuruba, so check with locals before plunging into the waters.

LAKE NKURUBA

Probably the winner among the contenders for title of most beautiful crater lake, Nkuruba is one of the few still surrounded by forest. Many monkeys, including black-and-white and red colobus, frolic here. Limited supplies are available in the village of Rwaihamba, 2km away.

There are two competing places here: we can only recommend one; for further information about the other, ask locals from around the backpacker hostels in Kampala or people involved in the tourism industry in the Fort Portal area. As the blue and yellow sign at the entrance gate says, our pick **Lake Nkuruba Nature Reserve Community Campsite** (☎ 0773-266067; www .lakenkuruba.com; camping USh5000, tent hire USh5000, dm USh16,000, banda USh51,000, lakeside cottage USh36,000) is the original. It's owned by the Catholic Church and the funds go towards health and education programs. The camp is set on a hill with some nice views and there's easy access to the lake. The *bandas* are clean and comfortable: some are self-contained and others function as dorms (two to four beds). The cottage is down on the lakeshore for more privacy. Meals will set you back USh4000 to USh8000. Guides lead walks all around the area. It's USh5000 per person for a quick village tour, and you can add Top of the World to this for another USh10,000. Bicycles (USh5000 to USh10,000 per day) and motorcycles (USh20,000) are available for exploring the area on your own.

Minibuses and saloon car shared taxis from Fort Portal to Rwaihamba pass Lake Nkuruba (USh4000, 45 minutes), as do the trucks going to Kasenda, but they're not frequent, even on market days (Monday and Thursday). A special-hire will set you back about USh20,000.

LAKE NYINABULITWA

Yet another beautiful and tranquil spot, the mid-sized 'Mother of Lakes', set back a bit off the road to Kibale Forest National Park, is home to the expensive (ask about discounts) but attractive **Nyinabulitwa Country Resort** (☎ 0712-984929; www.nyinabulitwaresort.com; camping US$15, s US$100-130, d US$160-200, tr US$210-270), an intimate little place on the lake's south shore with three thatched-roof bandas and an excellent camping ground. They do boat trips (US$10 per person) around the lake and can deliver you to a treehouse for bird- and primate-watching. It's 20km from Fort Portal, 1.5km off the main road just before Rweetera Trading Centre.

LAKE NYABIKERE

The 'Lake of Frogs' (you'll hear how it got its name at night!) lies just off the road to Kibale Forest National Park, 12km northwest of Kanyanchu visitor centre or 21km from Fort Portal. A recommended footpath circles the lake.

Facilities at the longest running Crater Lakes accommodation, **CVK Resort** (☎ 0772-906549; camping per tent USh10,000, s bandas USh12,000-15,000,d bandas 24,000-30,000, room s/d USh25,000/50,000-60.000) are fairly basic, but the prices are right. The further you go from restaurant-bar (mains USh4000 to USh15,000) the better the lake views and the quieter your night will be if an overland truck rolls in. Village walks cost US$4 and a guided stroll around the lake cost US$3. They'll rustle up a boat if you'd rather paddle your way around. It's just past Rweetera Trading Centre. Any minibus (USh3000) heading south from Fort Portal can drop you right at the entrance.

Not actually on the lake, but near enough to snatch some views of it, **Chimpanzee Forest Guesthouse** (☎ 0772-486415; www.chimpanzeeforest guesthouse.com; camping USh6000, s/d/tr USh60,000/80,000 /100,000, s/d bandas USh80,000/120,000) is ambitiously priced based on the quality of the accommodation (two of the rooms even share a shower) but people love the gardens, the warm welcome and the hillside location. Meals, mostly local with some international touches cost USh15,000. The entrance is 300m south of the Kibale Forest National Park office on the Fort Portal Rd.

LAKE NYINAMBUGA

This lake, ringed by more farm fields than forest, is located south of Lake Nkuruba. It's home to the luxurious **Ndali Lodge** (☎ 0772-221309; www .ndalilodge.com; s/d incl full board US$245/330; 💻 🏊), used mostly by tour operators. It's stunningly situated on a ridge above the lake and the restaurant looks out this way, while the elegant cottages face west towards Mwamba and Rukwanzi lakes with the Rwenzori Mountains looming on the horizon.

LAKE KIFURUKA & LAKE LYANTONDE

The former owners of the attractive and now closed Lake Lyantonde Campsite have moved one lake west to open the **Lake Kifuruka Eco-Camp** (☎ 0772-562513), 2km southwest of Rwaihamba. Work had just started when we stopped by, but a campsite and bandas were planned. With the lack of trees at the new site, we aren't sure they can replicate the appeal, but the high hillside location means both sunrise and sunset views will be on offer.

It will also be interesting to see what arises on Lake Lyantonde as the forested lakeside location is excellent. Inquire in Fort Portal about developments; Kabarole Tours (p471) should know what's up.

LAKE KASENDA

Little Lake Kasenda isn't at the end of the road, but it sure feels like it. **Ruigo Beach Lodge** (☎ 0752-391826; camping USh8000, s/d/tr USh20,000/30,000/45,000) sits right down on its shore looking up at the steep hills on the other side. Considering how few people come here (the visitor's log is almost comical) it's rather surprising how well maintained the three self-contained *bandas* are. The beer is cold, but they sometimes run out: a good reason to call ahead. Despite the name, there's no actual beach, but you can swim or paddle the boat around; plus there's plenty of thick forest for walking and you can easily wander over to nearby lakes Mulusi and Murigamire. Day entry for nonguests is USh2000 and meals cost USh5000 to USh15,000.

Ruigo Beach is 35km south of Fort Portal and 11km south of Rwaihamba. There are no minibuses to Kesenda Trading Centre, 2km before the resort, but overloaded trucks make the trip from Fort Portal. If you're lucky you'll find one parked by the Continental Hotel, otherwise ask around at the Kalita bus park. The bumpy trip costs USh4000 and will take at least a couple of hours. A *boda-boda* will probably want USh1000 for the final leg

to the lodge. You can drive here in about one hour: call to ask if the road is still in good enough shape for a saloon car to make it (it was when we went). A special-hire from Fort Portal should cost around USh30,000 to USh40,000, but drivers are unlikely to know where it is. The owners may pick you up for this price if you call ahead.

Kibale Forest National Park

Kibale is a lush tropical rainforest, believed to have the highest density of primates in Africa. This 795-sq-km **national park** (☎ 0483-422202; admission US$30; 🕐 8am-5pm) is home to 13 primate species, including the rare red colobus and L'Hoest's monkey. The stars of the show are the chimpanzees, three groups of which have been habituated to human contact.

Larger but rarely seen residents include bushbucks, sitatungas, buffaloes, leopards and quite a few forest elephants, while on the smaller side Kibale also has a great birdlist (over 375 species), but keen birdwatchers may want to bypass it and concentrate their time in Bigodi Wetland Sanctuary (p476) and Kihingami Wetland (p476) where open-canopy and wetland species can be seen alongside most of the same forest species living in the national park.

The park visitor centre is at Kanyanchu, 35km southeast of Fort Portal.

ACTIVITIES

Despite this being the most expensive place in Uganda to do **chimp tracking** (US$90 per person; 🕐 8am & 2pm), it's also the most popular, so reservations are a good idea. You stand a 90% chance of finding them on any particular day; and even if you don't, you'll see other primates and the incredible number of butterflies (250 species) that live here. There are plenty of hills along the trails, but the walking isn't difficult if you're in shape. Children 12 and under aren't permitted. Regular trackers get just one hour with the playful primates, but those on the **Chimpanzee Habituation Experience** (CHEX; 1-/2-/3-days US$220/400/550; 🕐 Feb-Jun & Sep-Nov) can spend the whole day with them. If you want to join the experience, you must the spend night before at Kanyanchu since you head out to the nests around 5.30am.

You probably won't see any chimps on the ordinary **nature walks** (US$10), but since nearly 1500 dwell here there's a good chance you'll

UGANDA

hear some scamper off through the treetops. Nature walks are also offered at the seldom-visited Sebitoli sector, 12km east of Fort Portal. This is the place to come if you want to see blue monkeys; some chimpanzees are in the process of habituation here. With frequent sightings of owls, civets and the 12cm-long Demidoff's dwarf galago, **night walks** (US$25 per person; ☽ 7.30pm) can be very rewarding.

SLEEPING & EATING

Besides the following places, listed by distance from Kanyanchu, you can easily visit Kibale while spending the night in Fort Portal, at the Crater Lakes (p473) or with Tinka John Homestay (right).

Primate Lodge (☎ 0414-267153; www.ugandalodges .com; camping USh15,000, treehouse USh50,000, cottages s/d US$50/70, safari tents s/d incl full board US$170/290) Right in the thick of the forest at Kanyanchu (meaning you have to pay the park entrance to sleep here), this renovated lodge operated by Great Lakes Safaris has a good choice of accommodation. The lovely cottages, with stone floors and verandas, are a better bet than the nice but overpriced safari tents, but, if you don't mind roughing it a little, take the treehouse (800m from the lodge) which overlooks an elephant wallow. The lounge area surrounds two fire pits and has a well-regarded restaurant (set menu breakfast/lunch/dinner US$12/18/20). They also manage the camping ground and serve an à la carte menu (mains USh15,000 to USh20,000) next to the visitor centre.

Safari Hotel (☎ 0772-468113; camping USh5000, r & bandas per person USh10,000) This popular budget digs is located in Nkingo village, 3km from Kanyanchu towards Bigodi. Facilities are basic, but the welcome is warm. Food (USh5000 per meal), including a popular pineapple pie, is available with advance notice.

Our pick **Chimps' Nest** (☎ 0774-669107; www .chimpsnest.com; camping USh10,000, dm USh10,000, cottages s/d USh90,000/120,000, treehouse s/d USh160,000/200,000) This brand-new stunner of a lodge borders Kibale Forest and Magombe Swamp, and there's lots of wildlife around including a profusion of birds, and sometimes elephants and chimps. The camping ground is peaceful and the cottages are lovely, but take the treehouse if you can. It's perched up in the canopy and has great views right from the bed. The sun powers them all, so there's no generator rattle to ruin the mood. Add USh25,000 per day if

you want full board. Chimps' Nest is 4km down a rough road from Nkingo. A *boda-boda* from Bigodi costs USh3000, or, with advance notice, they might pick you up.

Sebitoli Forest Camp (camping USh15,000, s/d bandas USh20,000/30,000) Up in the northern end of the park, it's decent, but seldom-used. There may be a budget or midrange lodge opening here in the lifetime of this book.

GETTING THERE & AWAY

Minibuses to Kamwenge from Fort Portal pass the park visitor centre (USh5000, 45 minutes). For Sebitoli, take any minibus (USh1500, 30 minutes) heading east from Fort Portal.

Bigodi Wetland Sanctuary

The **Bigodi Wetland Sanctuary** (☎ 0772-886865; comm-tour@infocom.co.ug; ☽ 8am-5pm), established by the local development organisation Kibale Association for Rural and Environment Development (KAFRED) to protect the 4-sq-km **Magombe Swamp**, is a haven for birds (around 200 species) plus butterflies and a number of primates including black-and-white colobus and grey-cheeked mangabey. Three-hour guided walks (USh30,000 per person, including binoculars and gumboots) depart from the visitor centre on demand and some of the guides are birding specialists who can help you find papyrus gonolek, white-winged warbler and great blue turaco.

Other activities available from the visitor centre include **village walks** (USh20,000 per person), Saturday-afternoon **basket-weaving** demonstrations, **dance** and **drama performances**, and fun **interpretive meals** (USh7000 per person; book in advance) where your hosts share the stories behind the local food they serve you. Volunteer opportunities are also available.

There's no lodging at the swamp itself, but **Tinka's Homestay** (☎ 0772-468113; per person incl full board USh30,000) is by the visitor centre. Rooms are basic, but the experience is genuine Uganda.

Bigodi is 6km south of the Kibale Forest National Park visitor centre at Kanyanchu. Any minibus (USh5000, 45 minutes) between Fort Portal and Kamwenge can drop you there.

Kihingami Wetland

This **eco-tourism site** (☎ 0752-323699; ☽ 8am-6pm), set up with the help of Fort Portal's Kabarole Tours, preserves an attractive 15-sq-km valley that otherwise would have been gobbled up by the surrounding tea plantations. Despite its small size, a remarkable 236 bird species have been spotted here and there are easy sightings of white-spotted flufftail and Jameson's wattle eye. There's also a good chance of seeing red colobus monkey and spotted-necked otter. Local guides lead forest walks (USh20,000 per person) and bird-watching walks (USh35,000 per person), and for an extra USh5000 you can plant a tree. You can also tour a fair trade tea factory (USh30,000 per person) at 9am and 2pm.

Kihingami is 15km east of Fort Portal, just before the Sebitoli section of Kibale Forest National Park. Take any minibus (USh1500, 30 minutes) heading east.

Semuliki National Park

The Semliki Valley is a little corner of Congo poking into Uganda. The only tropical lowland rainforest in East Africa is a continuation of the huge Ituri Forest in DRC and forms a link between the heights of East Africa and the vast steaming jungles of central Africa. The views on the descent into the valley from Fort Portal are breathtaking. The **national park** (☎ 0382-276424; admission US$25) covers 220 sq km of the valley floor and harbours some intriguing wildlife, though sightings are difficult due to the thick vegetation.

Bird-watchers come for the central African species residing at their eastern limits, such as the Congo serpent eagle. At least 133 of the 144 Guinea-Congo forest species have been recorded in the forest and nearly 50 species are found nowhere else in East Africa. There are nine primate species, including De Brazza's monkey, and many mammals not found elsewhere in Uganda, such as Zenker's flying mice. Both the resident elephant and buffalo are the forest variety, smaller than their savannah brethren.

Most people are here to see the **hot springs**, although this is worlds away from the geysers of Rotorua (New Zealand) and Iceland. The 'female' hot spring, just behind the Sempaya entrance, has a petite geyser while the 'male' spring, a roughly half-hour walk away, fills a 12m pool. You pay US$10 per person for the guided walk whether you visit one or both. Bring an egg and the rangers will boil it for you. Two other hiking options are the 11km **Kirimia Trail**, a full-day romp through the heart of the forest and the favoured destination of bird-watchers, and the shorter but hillier **Red**

Monkey Trail. Both end at the Semliki River, which forms the border between Uganda and DRC.

Outside the park is the **Batwa pygmy village** of Bundimusoli. They were relocated here when the park was established and, with no other choice, have since adopted agriculture, but they're keeping hold of their traditions as best as possible. The park allows them to collect rattan, leaves, mushrooms, medicines and other forest products and even practice limited hunting. Village visits (USh15,000 per person), which include singing dancing, should be arranged at the **Office of the King of Batwa** (☎ 0382-277215) in Ntandi, 5km past the Sempaya Gate. The village, which they call a camp, is another 2km away. They're talking of opening a museum and leading cultural tours, though we have no idea how likely this is to actually happen. See p498 for more information about visiting the Batwa.

SLEEPING & EATING

The simple **Bumaga Campsite** (camping USh15,000, r USh20,000), 2km past the Sempaya Gate, has showers and latrines. There's a lovely elevated dining area, but you should bring your own food.

Another camping ground is planned down the Kirimia Trail, which will allow bird-watchers to start scoping at the break of dawn.

The owner of the J&J Tourist Centre across from the Sempaya Gate has given up on his project due to a lack of business, but perhaps it will be renovated. You can still pitch a tent here for very cheap, if you want.

GETTING THERE & AWAY

The park is just 52km from Fort Portal, but plan on two hours to reach it by car in the dry season. There are regular minibuses and pick-ups between Fort Portal and Bundibugyo that pass the park (USh6000, 2½ hours). The last one heads to Fort Portal around 4pm, so if you leave early and hustle on the trails, you can see the hot springs and hike the Red Monkey Trail as a daytrip. You can also catch Kalita's Kampala–Bundibugyo bus in Fort Portal around 2pm for USh6000; it returns to Fort Portal around 5am.

Toro-Semliki Wildlife Reserve

The **Toro-Semliki Wildlife Reserve** (☎ 0382-276424; admission US$25, saloon cars local/foreign-registered USh20,000/US$50, trucks & 4WDs local/foreign-registered

UGANDA

UGANDA

COMMUNITY PROJECTS

A visit to Uganda proves definitively that travel can make a positive impact. Near all the national parks and in many towns where tourists tend to go, there are a variety of community-run programs where all profits go towards schools, health clinics and other projects that benefit local residents. The community-run Bigodi Wetland Sanctuary (p476), for example, is the main reason Bigodi is one of the few villages in Uganda where nearly everyone lives above the poverty line.

Besides small ecotourism projects like Bigodi there are a variety of other initiatives, from the nearly ubiquitous village walks to dance groups to the creative cooking tours offered by the wonderful Boomu Women's Group community-run Bigodi Wetland Sanctuary (p476) on the edge of Murchison Falls National Park. There are also some superb places to sleep such as Ruboni Community Campsite (p483). Many of these projects were set up and supported by the **Uganda Community Tourism Association** (Ucota; Map pp428–9; ☎ 0414-501866; www.ucota.or.ug; Church Rd, Kansanga, Kampala).

Not all are small-scale. The residents of Nkuringo village are part owners of Clouds Lodge (p491) at Bwindi Impenetrable National Park, which charges US$900 per night.

On a different note, you should keep in mind that poverty is profitable, and there are many corrupt aid organisations in Uganda, particularly those arranging sponsorships for orphans. Very often the money never goes any further than the directors' bank accounts, or at best the children only receive a small portion of what the donors send. We're not suggesting you don't give money; to the contrary, please do! But try to check out a few different projects a little before you open your wallet.

USh30,000/US$50) is the oldest protected natural area in Uganda, having first been set aside in 1926. Once one of the best-stocked and most popular wildlife parks in East Africa, it suffered significantly during the civil war years, and after the war with Tanzania, the Tanzanian soldiers went home with truckloads of dead bush-meat.

Wildlife is recovering and you may encounter waterbucks, reedbucks, bushbucks, buffaloes, elephants and hyenas. A number of lions have also recently returned to the reserve, most likely refugees from the conflict in DRC, and leopards are sighted quite regularly. With a line of mountains behind it, the savannah scenery from the main road is often superb, but the **wildlife viewing** along it aren't: Ugandan kob and baboons are the only sure things. Best to get a ranger (US$20) from the park headquarters to lead you down other tracks. You don't need to be a guest of Semliki Safari Lodge (opposite) to join their spotlit night drives (US$30 per person).

Likely the best wildlife experience in the park is the morning **chimp tracking** (US$30 per person) which the park prefers to call a primate walk. The hiking is more difficult than in Kibale and you're a little less likely to encounter them, but when you do, the thinner forest means your views are superior. These are rare 'dry-habitat chimps'

that spend considerable time in the savannah and so walk upright more often than the others.

Rangers also lead **nature walks** (US$10 per person) in various places around the park, including **Nyaburogo Gorge** behind the headquarters, which has lots of primates, butterflies and snakes; along the shore of **Lake Albert**; and the steep climb to great views atop the mountains on the southeastern edge of the park. Some people arrange for a driver to take them to the top of the mountain (via Fort Portal) and then walk down to the lodge.

A **Lake Albert boat trip** will likely reveal hippo and crocodiles, but it's mostly undertaken by bird-watchers for the near-guaranteed shoebill stork sightings. Semliki Safari Lodge charges US$180 for a half-day on the water. You could also arrange the trip with fishermen in Ntoroko village for about half the price: in a boat about half the size.

SLEEPING & EATING

UWA Campsites (camping USh15,000, bandas s/d USh10,000/15,000) The small UWA camp site at Ntoroko is on the shores of Lake Albert, meaning you often have hippos joining you in the evening. There are three non–self-contained *bandas* here and you can either cook your own food or head into the village for meals. There's a brand new camp site (no *bandas* yet, but they're planned) at the headquarters, a more convenient but less attractive location; bring your own food.

Ntoroko has some basic guesthouses, but several locals have told us they attract some shady characters; so if you try them, don't leave any valuables behind in your room.

Semliki Safari Lodge (☎ 0414-251182; www.wild placesafrica.com; s/d incl full board US$370/640; ☒) One of the first, but still one of the best luxury lodges in Uganda. Eight luxury tents are set under thatched *bandas,* and all have Persian carpets and four-poster beds. You have to make the difficult decision of a sunrise or sunset view. The lounge and dining room feature a huge eaved thatch roof, with plush furnishings, Congolese crafts and plenty of room to relax. Wildlife viewing is included in the price, and bush breakfasts and dinners are available.

GETTING THERE & AWAY

Some visitors arrive at Semliki Safari Lodge by light aircraft from Kampala. By road, head west toward Bundibugyo and then fork right at Karugutu, 27km from Fort Portal; the headquarters is 3km further on. A saloon car can handle travel inside the reserve, but ask about conditions between Fort Portal and Karugutu as the road can be quite poor.

Minibuses and trucks connect Fort Portal to Ntoroko (USh5000, three hours) and these can drop you at the park headquarters. You could also get one of the more frequent Bundibugyo-bound vehicles and get off at Karugutu (USh25,000, 1½ hours) to continue on from there.

Amabeere Cave

The water dripping from the roof of this small **cave** (☎ 0752-975720; admission USh5000; ⏱ 8am-6pm) is milky white, hence the name Amabeere ('Breasts'). Most of the rock formations are broken, but it's fun to walk behind the waterfall covering it and past the wall of vines along the adjacent ridge. For an extra USh5000 the guides also walk you out to a crater lake.

There's a basic camp site (USh5000 per person, tent hire USh20,000) and a comfortable lodge (s/d USh40,000/50,000) at the site. Campers can use the lodge's kitchen.

It's 8km northwest of Fort Portal, signposted 1.5km off the Bundibugyo road. It's a nice walking destination; Kabarole Tours (p471) in Fort Portal can set you off in the right direction, though it's probably easier to minibus (USh2500, 30 minutes) there and walk back.

Katonga Wildlife Reserve

This small, seldom-visited **wildlife reserve** (☎ 0772-590018; admission US$20) is one of the best places to spy the elusive sitatunga antelope, known for its curious webbed feet. If you start your guided nature walk (US$10 per person) at 6am or 7pm you have an excellent chance of an encounter. Black-and-white colobus, red and blue duiker, reedbuck, a few elephant and loads of waterbuck can also be seen in the savannah. The southern side of the reserve is papyrus swamp and while you won't see much wildlife here (though you may meet a hippo), a one-hour canoe trip (US$5 per person) through it offers a primordial-like experience.

There's a decent **dormitory** (per person USh10,000) with showers and electricity and a very basic **camp site** (per person USh15,000). Both sit on a hill way back from the road, but the park staff will drive you there from the headquarters at the reserve entrance; and if you didn't bring your own food to have cooked by the ranger, they may go into the nearby village of Kabagore (2km from the headquarters) and bring back dinner (USh2000 to USh3000) for you. **Bush camping** (per person USh30,000) is also possible if you have your own gear. Another overnight option is the **Katonga View Tourist Lodge** (☎ 0751-003083; r USh8000), in Kabagore. It's very basic, but Joyce and her family will make you feel at home.

The reserve is 40km south of Kyegegwa on the road between Fort Portal and Kampala. A minibus to Kabagore (USh17,000, five hours) leaves Kampala's new taxi park around midday (it goes when it's full) and returns early the next day sometime between 3am and 5am. Another minibus connects Kabagore to Kyegegwa (USh5000, one hour) at 10am the next day, returning in the afternoon. If coming from Fort Portal, you'll have to change vehicles at Kyegegwa (USh5000, two hours). You can also get from Kabagore to Mbarara (USh10,000, three hours) on a 7am coaster, which turns around and comes back right away. Hitching from the reserve in either direction is pretty easy.

KASESE

The long-closed Kilembe Copper Mines once brought great prosperity to this drab

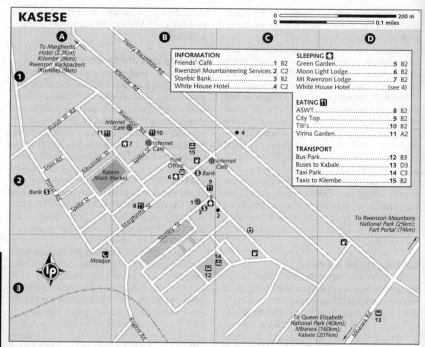

KASESE

INFORMATION	
Friends' Café...................................1 B2	
Rwenzori Mountaineering Services..2 C2	
Stanbic Bank..................................3 B2	
White House Hotel.........................4 C2	

SLEEPING	
Green Garden................................5 B2	
Moon Light Lodge..........................6 B2	
Mt Rwenzori Lodge........................7 B2	
White House Hotel....................(see 4)	

EATING	
ASWT..8 B2	
City Top...9 B2	
Titi's...10 B2	
Virina Garden...............................11 A2	

TRANSPORT	
Bus Park......................................12 B3	
Buses to Kabale...........................13 D3	
Taxi Park.....................................14 C3	
Taxis to Kilembe..........................15 B2	

and dusty town, and the also-defunct train line from Kampala used to deposit a steady stream of visitors here. But now Kasese seems to have passed its use-by-date and the main (if not only) reason travellers come here is to organise an assault on the Rwenzori Mountains (opposite).

If you have to spend some time here, nearby Kilembe, in the foothills of the Rwenzoris, is an interesting town to walk through with all the old mining equipment and company housing.

Information

Stanbic Bank (Stanley St) changes both cash and American Express travellers cheques. For some reason, Kasese has very fast internet connections (or we were just very lucky every time we checked email). **Friends' Café** (Stanley St; per hr USh3000r; 8am-9pm Mon-Sat, 10am-8pm Sun) and **White House Hotel** (Henry Bwambale Rd; per hr USh3000; 7.30am-10pm Mon-Sat, 11am-10pm Sun) are two good places to test the high speeds.

Organise your trek in the national park at **Rwenzori Mountaineering Services** (0483-444235; Rwenzori Rd; 8am-7pm).

Sleeping & Eating

Stanley St, not far from the taxi park, hosts almost nothing but cheap hotels and no-nonsense bars. Great if you want to celebrate, not so great if you want a good night's sleep. For low-end lodging it's best to move further into town to a place such as **Mt Rwenzori Lodge** (0772-930265; Alexander St; r USh5000-10,000) or **Moon Light Lodge** (0483-444347; Margarita St; s/d USh5000/7000), both of which have acceptable rooms with shared baths.

Better still, move up a class and a half to the **White House Hotel** (0782-536263; whitehse_hotel@ yahoo.co.uk; Henry Bwambale Rd; s/d USh13,000/20,000 without bathroom, r USh27,000;) far and away the pick of the pack at this level. A mix of cleanliness and good prices makes it one of the city's most popular hotels. The restaurant is pretty good too.

Filling restored miners' housing up in Kilembe, **Rwenzori Backpackers** (0774-199022; camping USh8000, dm USh10,000, s/d 20,000/30,000) is more scenic and peaceful (since you'll probably have the place to yourself) place to stay. The restaurant does meals, even pizza, for USh5000 to USh15,000, and they lead some hikes (p484) in the surrounding hills.

The fanciest hotel in town, **Hotel Margherita** (☎ 0483-444015; www.hotel-margherita.com; camping per tent USh18,000, s/d/ste from US$70/95/140; ☐) is really 3km out of town on the road up to Kilembe. The hotel has a delightful setting looking out towards the Rwenzoris, but prices are high for a room that, while comfortable, feels like Grandma's spare bedroom.

When we were last in town the former Saad Hotel was being reborn as **Green Garden** (Rwenzori Rd). There was nobody around to give us any solid information, but it looks like it will be pretty nice.

With the broadest menu for miles (even though they can't actually make about half of it anymore) **Virina Garden** (☎ 0782-082861; Square II Rd; mains USh5000-8000) is the only place right in town to get pizza and Indian food. The Hotel Margherita (USh8000 to USh12,000) has a bigger menu and probably has the best food available, but that's due to the lack of competition more than culinary skill.

Titi's (Rwenzori Rd), **ASWT** (Margarita St) and **City Top** (Rwenzori Rd) are all fairly well-stocked supermarkets for the provinces; useful ports of call if you're heading up to the Rwenzori Mountains or down to Queen Elizabeth National Park.

Getting There & Away

The quickest connection to Kampala (USh15,000, five hours) is via Fort Portal (USh4000, one hour). Buses and minibuses also run to Mbarara (USh10,000, three hours). For the long ride to Kabale (USh18,000, seven hours) two buses come through town from the north, stopping to get passengers at the roundabout on the highway around 8am.

For Kilembe (USh2000, 20 minutes), take one of the frequent saloon car shared taxis from near the Shell petrol station on Kilembe Rd or, less frequently, the taxi park.

Getting to Queen Elizabeth National Park is straightforward. Catch any Mbarara vehicle and ask for the national park entrance (USh3000, one hour), which is signposted on the left just before the village of Katunguru. See p488 for transport options from here.

RWENZORI MOUNTAINS NATIONAL PARK

The legendary, mist-covered Rwenzori Mountains on Uganda's western border with DRC are presumed to be the Mountains of the Moon, described in AD 350 by Ptolemy, who proclaimed them the source of the Nile River. This is the tallest mountain range in Africa and several of the peaks are permanently (at least until global warming finishes the job – it has already started up here) covered by ice and glaciers. The three highest peaks in the range are Margherita (5109m), Alexandria (5083m) and Albert (5087m), all on Mt Stanley, the third highest mountain in Africa.

The mountain range, which isn't volcanic, stretches for about 110km by 50km wide and is a haven for an extraordinary number of rare plants and animals, and new examples of both are still being discovered. Two mammals are endemic to the range, the Rwenzori climbing mouse and the Rwenzori red duiker, as are 19 of the 241 known bird species. There's thick tropical rainforest on the lower slopes transitioning to the bizarre afro-alpine moorland on higher reaches. Because of both its beauty and biodiversity, Unesco named this a World Heritage site.

Information

Back in Uganda's heyday, the Rwenzoris were as popular with travellers as Mt Kilimanjaro and Mt Kenya, but this is definitely a more demanding expedition. They have a well-deserved reputation for being very wet and the trails are often slippery and steep. Six days is the standard for a trek through the range, but climbers need to add a day for each of the peaks they want to bag. The best times to trek are from late December to mid-March and from mid-June to mid-August, when there's less rain. Even at these times, the higher reaches are often enveloped in mist, though this generally clears for a short time each day. April and October are the wettest months.

All Central Circuit treks must be arranged through the community-based **Rwenzori Mountaineering Services** who have offices in Kasese (☎ 0483-444936; Rwenzori Rd, Kasese; ☽ 8am-7pm), at the trailhead in Nyakalengija (☎ 0782-586304; ☽ 8.30am-5pm) and at the UWA compound in Kampala (☎ 0414-237497; ☽ 8am-5pm Mon-Fri & 9am-noon Sat). Guides, who are compulsory, even if you've conquered the seven summits, are on perpetual standby so you can book in the morning and leave the same day.

Walking trails and huts are in pretty good shape thanks to significant USAID help in the 1990s. The huts have kitchens and some have

RWENZORI MOUNTAINS NATIONAL PARK

ecosan toilets, and there are wooden pathways over the bogs and bridges over the larger rivers. All this lessens the impact of walkers on the fragile environment.

The routes to the peaks on Mts Stanley require the use of ice-axes, ropes and crampons (depending on conditions you may have to rope in for Baker and Speke), but you don't need mountaineering experience to reach the summits if your guide is experienced – the catch is that not all of them are. You can request specific guides from RMS if you get a reliable recommendation or let the experienced and wilderness first aid-certified guides at **Adrift** (☎ 0414-252720; www.adrift.ug) accompany you up the peaks, just to be sure. You'll eat far better with this last option too.

Do beware of the dangers of Acute Mountain Sickness (AMS, altitude sickness). In extreme cases it can be fatal. See p633 for more information.

BOOKS & MAPS
Before attempting a trek in the Rwenzoris get a copy of the *Guide to the Rwenzori* (2006) by Henry Osmaston which covers routes, natural history and all other aspects of the mountains. A good companion to Osmaston's opus is *Rwenzori Map & Guide*, an excellent large-scale contour map by Andrew Wielochowski.

FOOD & EQUIPMENT
No special equipment is required for a trek if you don't go onto the ice or snow (and if you do, this gear can be hired at the trailhead), but bring clothing that's warm (temperatures often drop below zero) and waterproof. You'll also want a good sleeping bag, and a sleeping mat since some of the huts don't have mattresses. The most important item is a good, broken-in pair of trekking boots to get you over the slippery rock slabs, which can be quite treacherous at times. Gaiters are also highly recommended for the bogs. A small day pack is useful since your porters will travel at their own pace.

Rwenzori Mountaineering Services (RMS) has the following equipment for hire in Nyakalengija at USh20,000 a pop: climbing boots, crampons, harnesses, ice-axes, ropes, rubber boots, and sleeping bags. Sleeping mats cost USh10,000.

As far as food supplies are concerned, be warned that the variety available in Kasese is limited. If there's anything you particularly want to eat on the trek, bring it with you. RMS will cook for you, but it's recommended you supply some of your own food.

GUIDES, PORTERS & FEES
The standard Central Circuit trek costs USh1,170,000 including park entrance, rescue fees, guides, porters, accommodation, heating fuel and VAT. It's USh1,530,000 if you want to add a Margherita peak summit. Extra days cost USh150,000 and extra peaks are USh180,000. The fee includes two porters per person, who can carry a total of 22kg; additional porters cost US$64. A cook can be hired for US$10.

Central Circuit
The Central Circuit starts at Nyakalengija village and loops back between the peaks of Mts Baker and Stanley. It takes six days, but if you just can't get enough of the scenery, there are other minor trails to lakes, glaciers and caves branching off the main route, but few people follow them.

NEW ROUTES

The Rwenzori Mountaineering Services (RMS) monopoly on the mountains is due to be broken during the course of 2009, which will be a good thing for trekkers and climbers. The new company, **Rwenzori Trekking Services** (www.rwenzoritrekking.com), run by John Hunwick of Backpackers Hostel (p435) in Kampala and operating out of Kilembe, will offer a variety of routes and climbs and has already started building huts and trails. If all goes to plan, standards will be excellent.

DAY 1

Nyakalengija (1646m) to Nyabitaba Hut (2650m) is a fairly easy walk taking about five hours. There are many primates and some forest elephant around.

DAY 2

The trail drops to cross the Bujuku River and then begins a long ascent on a rough, muddy path that eventually enters the amazing afro-alpine zone just before arriving at John Mate Hut (3505m). This is the longest day's walk, taking at least seven hours, and, for most people, the most difficult.

DAY 3

You slog, often knee-deep, through Lower and Upper Bigo Bogs (there's a boardwalk on part of this path) before things dry out and you reach lovely Lake Bujuku, plopped between Mts Baker, Stanley and Speke. After some more thick mud you reach Bujuku Hut (3962m), the base for those climbing Mt Speke. This is a three- to five-hour day depending on how wet things are, so there's usually time to check out the Irene Lakes or, if you want a more alpine experience you can choose to continue three more difficult hours and sleep at Elena Hut (4430), the primary starting point for ascending Mt Stanley.

DAY 4

Another short day, typically four hours, so take time to enjoy the most interesting section of the trek. The trail cuts through a profusion of giant groundsel before crossing Scott Elliot Pass (4372m), the highest point on the Central Circuit. There are great views of Margherita peak and Elena and Savoia Glaciers. It then weaves though boulders at the foot of Mt Baker and passes the twin Kitandara Lakes before dropping in on the lakeside Kitandara Hut (4023m).

DAY 5

Day five begins with a long climb to Freshfield Pass (4282m) and then it's all downhill to the scenically set Guy Yeoman Hut (3505m). On the descent you pass through a bog to the attractive Kabamba rock shelter and waterfall. Count on at least five hours, but as this is another muddy, slippery stage, it often takes longer.

DAY 6

The start of the trail descends very steeply (which is why almost everyone travels the circuit anti-clockwise) and follows the Mubuku River down for five hours to Nyabitaba Hut, where it's possible to sleep a second time. But by this point almost everyone is ready for a warm shower and a cold beer and continues the last two to three hours back to the bottom. Keep in mind that an hour from Guy Yeoman Hut there's an unbridged river crossing, and when the river is high, it can be dangerous. Your guides will surely want to get over it as fast as possible, but if you have any reservations about this, wait for the river level to fall.

Sleeping & Eating

our pick **Ruboni Community Campsite** (☎ 0414-501866; www.rcdctourism.org/ruboni; camping USh3000, safari tents per person USh10,000, bandas per person USh25,000) This community-run place 2km down the road from Nyakalengija just outside the park boundary has an attractive setting and comfortable lodging: and all profits go towards a health centre; tree planting projects and more. The restaurant (mains USh3500 to 10,000) here (and another in Nyakalengija village) serves local food and international snacks, and guides lead walks into the hills outside the park. It's a great place to stay before or after your trek, but the pastoral setting makes it a great place to visit even if you won't be heading to the park.

Halfway between Nyakalengija and Ruboni, **Rwenzori Turaco View Campsite** (☎ 0774-365296; camping USh5000, bandas USh10,000) isn't bad, but it lacks the vibe and views of Ruboni.

Getting There & Away

Nyakalengija is 25km from Kasese, though minibuses only run as far as Ibanda (USh2000,

---

SHORT CIRCUIT

If the thought of an entire week of rain and strain sounds like too much, there are several less demanding options for experiencing a bit of the Rwenzoris. One possibility is to head into the park along the Central Circuit, but turn back before completing the whole trek. An overnight at Nyabitaba Hut is popular for bird-watchers, but if you really want to see the mountains it's best to add a second night at John Matte Hut. All overnight trips are organised by Rwenzori Mountaineering Services (RMS) who charge a daily fee of USh180,000, but for day hikes get a ranger-guide (US$15 per person) from the **Rwenzori Mountains National Park Office** (☎ 0392-841133; ☼ 8am-5pm) just off the Fort Portal highway on the road to the trailhead.

Rwenzori Backpackers (p480) offers two hikes out its backdoor in Kilembe that provide a small taste of the terrain: a short overnighter (USh50,000 per person, tents provided) that climbs up to 2150m for some fantastic mountain views and a daytrip (USh15,000 per person) to Rucoochi Falls.

Kabarole Tours (p471) in Fort Portal leads two treks across the far northern end of the range that get rave reviews from travellers. Their Rwenzori Mini-Trek (USh850,000 for two people) is a two-day trip walking over the range to Bundibugyo and then exploring Semuliki National Park the next day. There's also a one-day Karangora Peak Climb (USh320,000 for two people), a steep ascent to the summit of the tallest mountain in the area (3014m).

---

one hour). From here you can take a *boda-boda* to Nyakalengija (USh2000) or Ruboni Community Camp (USh3000). Chartering a special-hire taxi from Kasese will set you back USh25,000 to USh30,000.

QUEEN ELIZABETH NATIONAL PARK

Covering 1978 sq km, and bordered to the north by the Rwenzori Mountains and to the west by Lake Edward, this **national park** (☎ 0483-444266; admission US$30, saloon cars local/foreign-registered USh20,000/US$50, trucks & 4WDs local/foreign-registered USh30,000/US$50; ☼ booking office 6.30am-7pm, park gates 7am-7pm) is one of the most popular in Uganda.

Back in the 1970s, with its great herds of elephants, buffaloes, kobs, waterbucks, hippos and topis, Queen Elizabeth was one of the premier safari parks in Africa. However, during the troubled 1980s, Ugandan and Tanzanian troops (which occupied the country after Amin's demise) did their ivory-grabbing, trophy-hunting best. Thankfully, animal populations are recovering. And though the numbers remain lower than the top Tanzanian and Kenyan parks, few reserves in the world can boast such a high biodiversity rating. Nothing exemplifies this better than the amazing 610 bird species here; more than found in all of Great Britain.

Besides the usual wildlife drives, the park is well worth a visit for a boat trip on the Kazinga Channel and a walk through beautiful Kyambura Gorge, a little Eden brimming with chimpanzees and other primates. The remote Ishasha sector, in the far south of the park, is famous for its tree-climbing lions.

Information

The main entrance is Katunguru Gate on the Mbarara–Kasese highway, very near the small village of Katunguru, where the road crosses the Kazinga Channel. From here it's 21km along a track that follows the channel to the Mweya Peninsula, where the visitor centre and a variety of lodging is found. Despite its name, Main Gate, on the road to Katwe sees far less traffic, though it is a scenic approach.

The famous Ishasha sector is 100km from Mweya down a pretty good road (due to oil exploration in the area) in the far south of the park. It hasn't had problems before, but it would still be wise to inquire about security before visiting due to its proximity to an unstable region of DRC.

Activities
KAZINGA CHANNEL LAUNCH TRIP

Almost every visitor takes a launch trip up the Kazinga Channel to see the thousands of hippos and pink-backed pelicans, plus plenty of crocodiles, buffaloes and fish eagles. With a little luck, it's also possible to catch sight of one of the elephant herds and very occasionally see a lion or a leopard. The two-hour trip costs US$15 per person, but if numbers are low you may have to chip in to cover the boat's minimum USh300,000 charge.

There are departures at 9am, 11am, 3pm and 5pm. The boat docks below Mweya Safari Lodge (a five to 10 minute walk), but you buy tickets at the visitor centre. The lodge does their own channel trips at 11.30am and 4pm. The price is the same, but the minimum charge is only US$90.

KYAMBURA GORGE
In the eastern region of the park, the 100m-deep Kyambura (Chambura) Gorge is a beautiful scar of green cutting through the savannah. It's full of primates, including many chimpanzees, and from the viewing platform, you can sometimes watch them frolic in the treetops below. **Chimpanzee tracking** (US$50 per person; 8am & 2pm) walks last from two to four hours, and you stand the best chance of finding the habituated troop on the morning walk. Bookings can be made at the visitor centre, or you can just show up and hope there are spots available. Children under 15 years aren't permitted.

WILDLIFE DRIVES
There's a small network of trails between Mweya Peninsula and Katunguru gate that usually reveal waterbucks and kobs, sometimes elephants and occasionally leopards, but you need to go elsewhere for the best wildlife spotting.

Kasenyi, in the northeast of the park, gets most of the wildlife viewing traffic, and visits are usually fruitful. Kasenyi offers the best chance to see lions, though the tree-climbers only live in Ishasha; also the best place to for elephants and the only place to see topis and sitatungas. Three salt lakes in the Kyambura Wildlife Reserve, behind Kyambura Gorge, sometimes attract huge numbers of flamingos, but they only nest at Lake Maseche north of Mweya on the road to Katwe. The 'explosion craters' in this area make for a beautiful drive, but there's not much wildlife. Baboon Cliffs gives excellent views over the surrounding area.

You can get just about everywhere by saloon car if it isn't raining, though having a 4WD is a good idea in Ishasha year-round. If you don't have your own vehicle you can get special-hires from Katunguru. Count on paying USh100,000/150,000 for a half-/full day, including fuel and drivers' admission. If you're in Mweya, the visitor centre will call a driver for you. Mweya Safari Lodge

(p487) has an open-topped 4WD for US$240 for half a day. Taking a UWA ranger-guide (US$20) along for your drive is always a good idea, but more so in Ishasha than anywhere else because they know every fig tree in the area, and these are the lion's preferred perches.

NATURE WALKS
Guided nature walks (US$10 per person) are available, but aren't very popular. There used to be cave trips (to see the hordes of Egyptian fruit bats and the rock pythons who eat them) in the **Maramagambo Forest**, below the Kichwamba Escarpment near Kyambura Gorge, but they were suspended in July 2008 after a Dutch tourist who visited the cave died of Marburg Fever. Trips on the forest trails here are taken mostly by bird-watchers, though there are nine species of primate.

Down at Ishasha, hippo encounters are pretty likely on short walks along the river and if done early in the morning, probably giant forest hog. You won't see much on a walk at Mweya that you can't see just hanging around on your own.

Walks (USh30,000 per person) can also be arranged in the 147-sq-km **Kalinzu Forest Reserve** (0751-360073; 7am-5pm), which is a cheaper option, as it lies outside the national park boundary, and is easy to reach since the visitor centre, known as the Kalinzu Ecotourism Site, is right on the Kasese–Mbarara highway. The trailhead, however, is 3km away down a rough road. You can try to track chimps (USh68,000) here in the morning, but they're not fully habituated and so only found about half the time. No children under 15 are allowed on the chimp walks. Follow-up your forest walk with a community tour (USh25,000) that can include a turn in the kitchen making your own local meal.

KATWE
This interesting village on the north shore of Lake Edward, 4km west of Main Gate, is famous for its salt industry. Sir Henry Morton Stanley visited in 1875, but salt mining on the crater lake behind the village goes back to at least the 15th century. Today some 3000 people still use the same traditional methods. Women pull salt from evaporation ponds when it's dry enough (generally December to March and July to September) while men dig rock salt year-round.

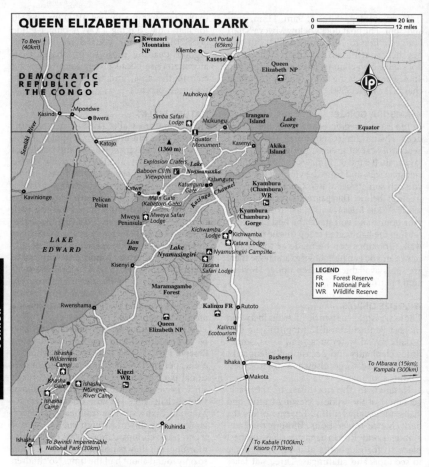

You can get a tour (US$20 per group) of the salt works from the **Katwe Tourism Information Centre** (☎ 0752-618265; nkagongo@yahoo.com; ⏱ 8am-5pm) on the west side of the village, across from a defunct salt factory. Guides here will also take you bird-watching, give you a **fishing industry tour** (US$20; ⏱ 8am-11pm) and accompany you to the Kasindi Market (Tuesday and Friday) in DRC. Katwe is enveloped by the park, but technically outside it, so no park fees apply.

Sleeping & Eating

Queen Elizabeth has a good variety of lodging available, and if some of the planned places come to fruition, it's bound to get better. Great Lakes Safaris (www.safari-uganda.com) is due to open Simba Safari Lodge, which will have camping, a dormitory, and mid-priced rooms, less than a kilometre from the equator along the Kasese–Mbarara highway. There are also rumours that camping will return to Kyambura Gorge and that Adrift (www.adrift.ug) will open a midrange tented camp.

MWEYA PENINSULA

The best variety of places to stay is on the Mweya Peninsula. A lot of wildlife roams through here, so you genuinely need to be careful at night; especially if you're walking to/from the Mweya Campsite. You can also spot lots of wildlife along the river down below, so it's a great place to hang out during the day.

Campgrounds (camping USh15,000) Although the facilities are rustic, the settings are superb, making

Mweya a great place to pitch a tent. The main Mweya Campsite has little shade but is set off from the other development on the peninsula and looks out over the channel. Much more isolated are Campsites 1 and 2, 3.5km and 4.5km east of the visitor centre respectively. They have nothing but pit toilets and good channel views, especially Campsite 2. Expect a lot of animal sightings and sounds. Book all camping at the visitor centre before setting up your tent.

Wildlife Education Centre (dm USh10,000) Known to everyone as the Students' Camp, the park's cheapest beds are here, but it's very basic and chances are that it will be full of Ugandan schoolchildren on educational visits. Book your stay at the park visitor centre, where you'll need to show student ID.

Mweya Hostel (☎ 0414-373050; dm USh30,000, s USh45,000) Still basic, but not with a capital B like the Students' Camp, this is the more reliable option for finding a cheap (well, relatively speaking) bed. It's frequently full in the July to August and December to January high seasons, so book ahead. All rooms are twins.

Mweya Safari Lodge (☎ 0312-260260; www.mweya lodge.com; s US$115, d US$ 210-250, ste US$275, cottages US$500-750; 🍴 🖥 🍸) This large, sophisticated outfit has excellent views over Lake Edward and the Kazinga Channel and way out to the Rwenzori Mountains. The rooms have nice furniture and all have views of water. It's good value by national park lodge standards. Sitting on the terrace with a cold drink at sunset is perfect and the swimming pool has an enviable setting. À la carte lunches (meals USh6000 to USh10,000) and set-menu or buffet dinners (USh30,000 to USh35,000) are available at the classy restaurant (open 7am to 11am, 1pm to 3pm and 7pm to 10pm). Book ahead during peak season as the lodge gets very busy.

Tembo Canteen (meals USh4000-8000; 🕑 7.30am-10.30pm) Overlooking the channel near the Students' Camp, this is where the safari drivers hang out during the day and park staff kicks back at night. There's a pool table and satellite TV.

Simba Canteen (meals USh4000-8000; 🕑 8am-noon & 5pm-8pm Tue-Sun) Not far from Tembo, this is a small grocery store. There are also a few smaller shops just to the south inside the workers' village.

KATUNGURU

If you get stuck in Katunguru, **Rwenzori Salaama Hotel & Lodging** (☎ 0782-156015; s/d USh5000/7000) has both the cheapest and cleanest rooms.

MARAMAGAMBO FOREST

Nyamusingiri Campsite (camping USh15,000) A very basic and rarely used camping ground with pit toilets but no showers. Bring your own food.

Jacana Safari Lodge (☎ 0414-4258273; www .geolodgesafrica.com; s/d incl full board US$150/260; 🍸) Jacana's 11 large and luxurious cottages sit widely spaced in the forest and all look out over Lake Nyamusingiri. Relax at the pool, in the sauna or on the lake with a kayak, and then dine lakeside or on a pontoon boat. It's competitively priced compared to most other safari camps in Uganda, but it sits a long way from the best game drive locales.

KICHWAMBA ESCARPMENT

This ridgetop spot along the Kasese–Mbarara highway, outside the park's eastern boundary, has some of the best views in Uganda. It looks over the Maramagambo Forest and a wide sweep of savannah out to Lake Edward and the Rwenzori Mountains. It's a 15 minutes drive to chimp tracking at Kyambura Gorge and 45 minutes to game drives at Kasenyi.

OUR PICK **Kichwamba Lodge** (☎ 0774-159579; www .kingfishersafaris.net; camping US$9, s/d/tr US$65/135/160; 🖥 🍸) This lovely little compound of whitewashed and thatched-roof towers is as lovely as it is unique. Rooms are a bit small but still good and come with their own little covered porches. Even the pool has amazing views; the best to be had on the escarpment.

Katara Lodge (☎ 0773-011648; www.kataralodge.com; per person incl full board US$150) Katara suffered some hiccups during its mid-2008 opening, but, assuming things get rectified, this will be a nice addition to the park's lodging scene. The five wood, thatch and canvas cottages were made for the views. The sides roll up, the bed rolls out to the deck and even the clawfoot tubs looks out over the valley

KALINZU FOREST

Kalinzu Ecotourism Site (camping USh8000) Facilities are basic, but camping is possible at the Kalinzu Forest's visitor centre. Bring your own food, or let them cook a local meal for you. They plan to add showers.

ISHASHA

Ishasha Camp (☎ 0782-308808; camping USh15,000, dm USh10,000, banda s/d USh15,000/20,000) This basic and blissfully remote setup has two rooms (with two beds each) and two *bandas* plus you can pitch a tent. (The lovely camp site on the Ishasha River, which forms the border with DRC, is currently closed over concern about rebels.) Local meals are available for USh7000 to USh10,000. If you aren't pitching a tent, call ahead because the beds are often full.

Ishasha Ntungwe River Camp (☎ 0772-602205; www.treelionsafarilodge.com; s/d incl full board US$170/210) This new place outside the park, 3km from Ishasha Gate, had just unzipped its tent flaps when we swung by, but work was still continuing so it was too early to give it a final grade. From what we saw, they're going to have to drop their prices if they want to succeed. There's no shade, no river view and no panache.

Ishasha Wilderness Camp (☎ 0414-321479; www .wildfrontiers.com; s/d incl full board US$260/380) Another tented camp that's not as luxurious as it should be at these prices. This one, however, is much better than Ishasha Ntungwe River Camp, and, more importantly, it's perfectly positioned for wildlife watching. The 10 tents look out over the forest-lined Ntungwe River, which elephants wander down to like clockwork at lunch time.

Getting There & Away

The regular minibuses between Kasese (USh3000, one hour) and Mbarara (USh9000, three hours) stop at Katunguru. Hitching out of the park from Mweya is easy; just stand by the barrier at Mweya Safari Lodge. Hitching into the park is tougher, although weekends aren't too bad. If traffic is thin, it may be necessary to charter a vehicle from Katunguru for USh25,000 to USh30,000. There's petrol available at Mweya, but it's pricier than in towns.

Kyambura Gorge is 8km south of Katunguru on the highway and then 2km west down a dirt road, so it's worth heading there even if you don't have your own wheels, but Maramagambo Forest is 12km off the highway, and you're likely looking at a *very* long wait if you want to hitch down here.

The Kalinzu Forest Reserve is half-way between Kasese and Mbarara and any minibus between the two (or, from Kasese, a minibus to Bushenyi) can drop you here; count on USh7000 and about 1½ hours from either. If the driver doesn't know about Kalinzu, tell him Kayanga, the name of the nearest village.

Just a few minibuses a day go from Kasese to Katwe (USh5000, 1½ hours), and a few more can get you to or from Katunguru. These can also drop you at Main Gate, which is just 7km from Mweya. Little traffic passes here, but the guards will call for a ride to the peninsula, which may cost as little as USh10,000.

The road from Katunguru to the village of Ishasha cuts through the park and passes Ishasha Gate. Although no park entry fees are needed to travel this road, you'll be fined US$150 if you're caught venturing off it and into the park. From Ishasha, you can head south for Butogota and Bwindi Impenetrable National Park in about two hours in the dry season.

All tour operators can put together a short safari to Queen Elizabeth. On the budget end, Kampala-based Great Lakes Safaris (p73) has fantastically priced three-day trips (from US$210 per person with six people) departing every Wednesday and Friday and the Home of Edirisa (p492) has a three-day (US$300 per person for four people) trip out of Kabale with the nights spent in tents rather than rooms.

BWINDI IMPENETRABLE NATIONAL PARK

Bwindi (☎ 0486-424121; admission US$30; ☼ park office 7.45am-5pm) is one of Africa's most famous national parks. Its 331 sq km of improbably steep mountain rainforest is home to almost half of the world's surviving mountain gorillas; an estimated 340 individuals. The Impenetrable Forest, as it's also known, is one of Africa's most ancient habitats since it thrived right through the last Ice Age (12,000 to 18,000 years ago) when most of Africa's other forests disappeared. Along with the altitude span (1160–2607m) this antiquity has resulted in an incredible diversity of flora and fauna, even by normal rainforest standards. And we do mean rainforest; up to 2.5 metres of rain falls here annually.

Its 120 species of mammal is more than any of Uganda's other national parks, though sightings are less common because of the dense forest. Lucky visitors might see forest elephants, 11 species of primate (including chimpanzees and l'Hoest's monkeys), duikers, bushbucks, African golden cats and the rare giant forest hog, as well as a host of bird and insect species. For bird-watchers it's one of the most exciting destinations in the country, with almost 360 species, including 23 of the 24 Albertine Rift endemics and several endangered species, including the African green broadbill. With a good guide, daily totals of over 150 species are possible. On the greener side of the aisle, Bwindi harbours eight endemic plants.

Information & Orientation

The park headquarters is at Buhoma on the northern edge of the park; most of the gorilla visits start from here and most of the accommodation is here too. If you're really desperate to check your email, you can use the **CTPH Telecentre** (per min USh200; ☺ 9am-7pm Mon-Sat, 3-7pm Sun) in Buhoma Trading Centre, 3km from the park gate. There are also newer sectors at Nkuringo in the south (a *very* long way by road from Buhoma) and Ruhija in the east.

The *Mgahinga Gorilla National Park & Bwindi Impenetrable National Park,* (1998) booklet available at the park or UWA headquarters in Kampala is dated, but still informative about the park's environment.

Activities

GORILLA TRACKING

There are now six habituated gorilla groups living in Bwindi Impenetrable National Park: three around Buhoma, two at Nkuringo while the newest, the Shongi group, lives near Ruhija.

Eight tourists per day can visit each family, but because this is the real world and not maths class that does not mean that there are always 48 permits. The Rushegura group near Buhoma has recently slipped over the border to Congo and so can't currently be tracked, and the Uganda Safari Company was granted a controversial monopoly on six of the Nkuringo permits.

Tracking permits cost US$500 (including park entry) and should be booked through the UWA office (p426) in Kampala. Demand exceeds supply for most of the year. During April to May and October to November (the rainiest months) you may be able to confirm a space a week or two in advance of your trip, but during the rest of the year permits are sometimes grabbed three months in advance. If nothing is available that fits your schedule, check at the backpacker places in

Kampala and Jinja, where the safari companies advertise excess permits they want to sell. It's no problem to buy these, even when someone else's name is on them. Cancellations and no-shows are rare, but you can get on the list at the park office: it's first-come, first-served.

When the Rushegura group crosses back into Uganda, UWA is considering instituting a new procedure similar to that used at Mgahinga Gorilla National Park (p499) whereby the permits would be booked not in Kampala but at the park office on short notice only.

The trips leave (from the park office nearest the group you'll be tracking) at 8.30am daily, but you should report to park headquarters by 7.45am. Note that it can take two hours to drive from Buhoma to Ruhija. Once you finally join a tracking group, the chances of finding the gorillas are almost guaranteed. But, since the terrain in Bwindi Impenetrable National Park is mountainous and heavily forested, if the gorillas are a fair distance away it can be quite a challenge reaching them. Nkuringo in particular is very tough going since you have to climb 600m down a valley before getting to the park. Make sure you're in good enough shape.

See p78 for additional rules regarding gorilla tracking as well as information on the mountain gorillas themselves.

FOREST WALKS

Even if you didn't score or can't afford gorilla tracking, Bwindi is a rewarding park to visit just for a chance to explore the lush virgin rainforest. Several three to four hour nature walks penetrate the Impenetrable Forest around Buhoma. The walks can begin at 9am and 2.15pm and cost US$10.

The **Waterfall Trail** includes, surprise, surprise, a 33m waterfall on the Munyaga River, but just as worthwhile is the magnificently rich forest it passes through. This is the best trail for spotting both orchids and primates. Weather permitting, the **Muzabijiro Loop Trail** and **Rushura Hill Trail** offer excellent views south to the Virunga volcanoes and the western Rift Valley in DRC. The latter, which is a more difficult climb, also serves up views of Lake Edward and, on an exceptionally clear day, the Rwenzoris.

A longer but much easier trek is along the **River Ivi Trail**, which follows the path of

UGANDA

a planned-but-never-built road between Buhoma and Nkuringo. It's 14km through the forest and then another 6km uphill along a road to Nkuringo village; you might be able to hitch this last part. If you're heading to or from Kisoro, this is the most rewarding way to go. It's also the best bird-watching destination in the Buhoma area.

COMMUNITY PROJECTS

There are several community projects in this region, some heavily promoted. These are the most worthwhile.

The **Buhoma Village Tourist Walk** (per person USh15,000; ☼ 9am & 2pm), offered by Buhoma Community Rest Camp (right), is very popular. Depending on who's home during your three- to four-hour walk through the surrounding countryside, you'll visit a local healer and a school, watch a Batwa pygmy song-and-dance show, and witness the none-too-appetising production of banana wine and gin (the bananas are mashed by foot).

Another group based at Buhoma, **Nyundo Community Eco-Trails** (☎ 0772-930304; per person USh15,000-30,000) offers a wide variety of village walks including several with farming focuses and others that go to caves and waterfalls. Traditional dances can also be arranged. They have an information office by Buhoma Gate, but the walks all begin an inconvenient 6km away.

Finally, the **Nkuringo Community Walk** (☎ 0754-825219; US$10; ☼ 8.30am-5pm) is a similar tour on the south side of the park. The walks start at the Nkuringo Community Development Foundation office across from the park office.

Proceeds from all of these walks are ploughed back into the community for projects such as supporting schools and teaching adult literacy. All three groups can arrange volunteer opportunities if you contact them in advance.

Another community project, of sorts, is the **Bwindi Orphans Development Centre** in Buhoma. Their nightly dance show seems to be a stop for tour groups in the area. If you do end up going, feel free to ignore the plea for funds. Ask locals for alternative ways to donate to ensure your money goes to those who need it.

Sleeping & Eating

BUHOMA

Given that there are only 24 gorilla permits per day available at Buhoma, there are a whole lot of lodges competing for your business. But, despite the competition, Buhoma offers the worst overall value in the country when it comes to sleeping and eating. On the plus side, you don't need to pay park entrance to stay in any of these places.

Jungle View Lodge (☎ 0782-494823; r USh20,000) A great option for those watching their wallets, Jungle View is where many safari drivers stay. Rooms are simple and bathrooms are shared, but cleanliness comes standard. There's a first floor bar with simple meals (USh4000 to USh5000) available. They've never got around to putting up a sign, but it's the place that looks like a hotel just past Gorilla Resort.

Bwindi View Bandas (☎ 0752-399224; camping USh8000, s/d USh35,000/45,000 without bathroom, s/d USh40,000/80,000) This older place is the next step up in price over Jungle View, but other than a private-bath option, it's not a whole lot better in quality. There's a choice of rooms and safari tents.

Buhoma Community Rest Camp (☎ 0772-384965; www.buhomacommunity.com; camping US$5, dm US$10, s/d US$17/33 without bathroom, r US$47) Enjoying a beautiful setting right near the park headquarters, this is one of the most popular places to stay, even though its prices have shot up in recent years. *Bandas* and safari tents are spaced out on a hill heading down the valley, and the best are at the bottom, which puts you right near the jungle; gorillas sometimes pass by the clearing here. Breakfast is US$5 and a set four-course dinner is US$10. All profits go towards funding community-development projects.

Engagi Lodge (☎ 0414-321552; www.kimbla-mantana .com; s/d incl full board US$175/270) Kimbla-Mantana Safaris recently moved their Bwindi base to this new lodge, building eight tasteful *bandas* with wooden furniture, big bathrooms and close-up views of the river and jungle. It's a nice place for a meal (set-menu lunch/dinner US$15/20).

Silverback Lodge (☎ 0414-258273; www.geolodges africa.com; s/d incl full board US$210/300) If you can walk up to this hilltop place you should be fine on your gorilla trek. The isolated location earns you the best Bwindi views, and they're especially evocative with clouds floating between the peaks: that whole gorillas in the mist thing. The seven rooms are small but stylish and have some swell decorative touches such as carved wooden headboards and artistic lampshades. Set-menu four-course meals cost USh30,000. Service here is superb.

Most visitors at Buhoma eat where they're staying. Most of the fancier places are include full board, so this is no surprise. At the budget end, there are a couple of local spots outside the park gate knocking together cheap food and pouring cold beer, but choices are limited.

BUTOGOTA & KIHIHI

Some travellers end up spending a night in Butogota on the way to the park or Kihihi on the way out.

Pineapple Lodge (Butogota; r USh3000) This simple place has tiny rooms by the Gateway bus stop. Some self-contained rooms were under construction on our last visit.

Green Tree Hotel (☎ 0772-830878; Butogota; s/d without bathroom USh20,000/30,000) Despite the much higher price, the rooms at this nearby place are only a little better than Pineapple Lodge and also share bathrooms.

Westland Inn (☎ 0772-673085; Nzabandora St, Butogota; s/d USh6000/10,000 without bathroom, r USh20,000) A spic-and-span choice near where the buses depart in the morning. The self-contained rooms are in an annex a few doors down.

Meeting Point (Butogota; mains USh2000-4000) Just down from the Westland, this is as sophisticated as it gets in these parts, and the food is quite good. This is where the area's oil workers gather in the evening.

NKURINGO

Nkuringo is spectacularly set on a ridge opposite the wall of green that is Bwindi. From various spots you can spy Lake Edward, the Rwenzoris, all of the Virungas and even the little red speck of Nyiragongo Volcano by Goma, DRC. Now that there are two habituated gorilla groups here, more places are coming.

ourpick Nkuringo Gorilla Campsite (☎ 0754-805580; camping USh8000, s/d without bathroom USh22,000/35,000) Facilities at the former Hammerkop Guesthouse are fairly basic, but the staff make you feel like guests instead of customers. There's a choice of hotel-style rooms and two traditionally built (thatch roof, wattle-and-daub walls) *bandas*, all of which share baths. The camp site has phenomenal views, but this may become the location of the restaurant (meals USh5000 to USh8000) in the future. Note: the welcome tea isn't free.

Clouds Lodge (☎ 0414-251182; www.wildplaces africa.com; s/d incl full board US$650/900; 🖳) No, those prices aren't a typo. This new lodge, built as a

project between the Uganda Safari Company, African Wildlife Foundation, International Gorilla Conservation Programme and the local community, offers a subtle sort of luxury, but if you can afford it you'll enjoy it. The large stone cottages have big windows, original art and double-sided fireplaces, plus you get a butler during your stay. Drop-in diners are welcome for the à la carte lunch (USh10,000 to USh20,000), and if you make reservations you can also prepare for tracking with a big breakfast (USh30,000) or recharge after the encounter with four-course set dinner (USh40,000).

RUHIJA

During research time, most people visiting the gorillas here stayed in Buhoma, but several new places, both luxury and community-camp style, were under construction, so there should no longer be the need for an early morning drive. The park office can fill you in on all the details.

Getting There & Away
BUHOMA

Whether you have your own vehicle or not, getting to Buhoma can be complicated. By public transport, the first step is getting to Butogota. There are trucks between Kabale and Butogota (USh20,000, four hours) on Tuesday, Friday and occasionally other days. These sometimes continue to Buhoma for USh5000 more. They start their journey in Butogota at 3am and head back from Kabale at 11am. The other option is to take a Kihihi vehicle as far as Kanyantorogo (USh15,000, three hours) and get another pickup to Butogota (USh3000, 30 minutes) or wait for the Gateway bus from Kampala to pass (as early as 3pm, but usually later). If all else fails, or you're in a group, charter a vehicle from Kabale to Buhoma for USh120,000 to USh140,000.

That aforementioned bus (USh20,000, 10 to 12 hours) runs daily in each direction, departing Kampala's new bus park at 7.30am and leaving Butogota at 5am. It's actually usually much faster from Kampala to take a bus (several companies make the trip in each direction early each morning, including Gateway and Perfect Coach) to Kihihi (USh16,000, eight hours) and change there for a pickup or saloon car shared taxi (USh4000, 1½ hours) to Buhoma.

For the last leg of the trip, pickups between Butogota and Buhoma (USh2000, one hour) are infrequent, except on market days (Thursday and Saturday). You can also hitch, but this usually involves a long wait too. If nothing else works out, a special-hire will be USh30,000 and a *boda-boda* half that.

If you're driving from Kabale to Buhoma, the best route is the long way through Kanungu (which can be done in a saloon car if you're an experienced driver) rather than the totally rough road through Ruhija. At research time there was a bridge out on the Kanungu road necessitating an awkward detour. Get details at the Gorilla Parks Information office (right) in Kabale before departing.

If you're in a rush, charter flights can get you to the Kanyonza Airstrip, 19km from Buhoma. If you're not in a rush, consider going by canoe and foot, a trip described under Nkuringo.

NKURINGO

On Monday and Thursdays there's a truck travelling between Kisoro and Nkuringo (USh4000, three to four hours). It leaves Nkuringo around 8am and returns about 3pm. In Kisoro it parks at 'Kanyaruju's House', about 50m north of junction on road to Nkuringo. Other times you can try to hitch, but there's not much traffic going all the way to Nkuringo, and the UWA trucks that sometimes come to town are usually too full to take passengers.

Because Nkuringo lodging falls squarely in the budget and luxury extremes, many visitors sleep in Kisoro and make the early morning drive for their gorilla trek; this usually takes 1½ hours. A special-hire costs USh60,000, or USh100,000 if you want the driver to wait and take you back in the afternoon. A *boda-boda* driver will charge you USh25,000, but it's a long, bottom-shaking ride.

The best way to travel from Nkuringo (you can also do it uphill from Kisoro) is to leave the road behind. **Nkuringo Walking Safaris** (☎ 0774-805580; www.nkuringowalkingsafaris.com; US$130 for two people) will lead you on an 18km trek to Lake Mutanda (this can be shortened to 10km with some driving) and then a 2½-hour paddle (lifejackets provided) in a dugout canoe. From here it's another 4km on foot to Kisoro, but you may want to just chill out at Mutanda Eco-Community Centre (p499) that night instead. There's also the option to divide this trip into two days.

You can also slip through the forest to/from Buhoma along the River Ivi Trail (p489). The Walking Safari team will accompany you on this walk too, if you want, but there's no need since a park ranger guide is required regardless of who else is with you.

RUHIJA

Ruhija is about 50km (up to two hours) from Buhoma Gate, and a special-hire will cost about USh100,000 there, and waiting to bring you back.

KABALE

While Kabale itself is nothing to write home about, it's a handy base from which to explore some superb hiking country, as the area is honeycombed with tracks and paths, trading centres and farms. It's also the gateway to Lake Bunyonyi, the number one spot for serious rest and relaxation in Uganda, and a good staging post for trips to see the gorillas at Bwindi Impenetrable National Park. Even if you're just planning on passing through, take an hour to visit the Home of Edirisa, Uganda's only proper museum outside Kampala.

Kabale is Uganda's highest town at about 2000m and can get pretty cool at night, so keep some warm clothes handy. But, despite what you may hear, there are still plenty of mosquitoes, so use your net at night.

Information

For some added flavour from Kabale, pick up a copy of the free *Lake Bunyonyi & Kabale In Your Pocket* guide available at the Home of Edirisa (below).

Both the Home of Edirisa and Amagara Guesthouse have internet access for USh30 per minute; the former also offers wi-fi, when it's functioning. There are several more internet cafés in town.

Exchange rates are very good by provincial standards. **Stanbic Bank** (Kisoro Rd) changes cash and American Express travellers cheques while **Centenary** (Kisoro Rd) and **Barclays** (Kisoro Rd) are both cash only.

You can't actually book gorilla permits at the UWA's **Gorilla Parks Information Office** (☎ 0486-424121; Kisoro Rd; ⊙ 8am-5pm) but the staff can help you with anything else relating to Bwindi Impenetrable (p488) or Mgahinga Gorilla National Parks (p499), including reserving seats for you on the trucks that go to Butogota.

Sights & Activities

Home of Edirisa (☎ 0752-558222; www.edirisa.org; Muhumuza Rd; admission USh4000; ⊙ 9am-11pm) This

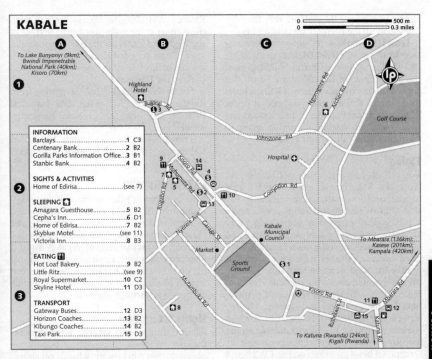

KABALE

0   500 m
0   0.3 miles

To Lake Bunyonyi (9km);
Bwindi Impenetrable
National Park (40km);
Kisoro (70km)

Highland Hotel

Golf Course

INFORMATION
Barclays................................1 C3
Centenary Bank.....................2 B2
Gorilla Parks Information Office..3 B1
Stanbic Bank.........................4 B2

SIGHTS & ACTIVITIES
Home of Edirisa.....................(see 7)

SLEEPING
Amagara Guesthouse.............5 B2
Cepha's Inn...........................6 D1
Home of Edirisa.....................7 B2
Skyblue Motel........................(see 11)
Victoria Inn............................8 B3

EATING
Hot Loaf Bakery.....................9 B2
Little Ritz..............................(see 9)
Royal Supermarket.................10 C2
Skyline Hotel.........................11 D3

TRANSPORT
Gateway Buses......................12 D3
Horizon Coaches....................13 B2
Kibungo Coaches...................14 B2
Taxi Park...............................15 D3

Hospital

Kabale Municipal Council

Market

Sports Ground

To Mbarara (136km);
Kasese (201km);
Kampala (420km)

To Katuna (Rwanda) (24km);
Kigali (Rwanda)

UGANDA

interesting little museum houses a replica traditional homestead, built of sticks and papyrus, showing how the local Bakiga people lived a century ago. Besides the museum, you'll find a little travellers' village tucked away inside the attention-grabbing polka-dotted building. There's accommodation, food, a good gift shop (local basketry and Congolese masks) and internet access.

Edirisa also leads canoe trekking trips on Lake Bunyonyi (see p494) and three-day tours to Queen Elizabeth National Park (p484; USh545,000 per person for a group of four). If you're interesting in volunteering in the area, apply on their website (click Smiles) before you arrive.

Sleeping

There's a row of cheap lodges down by the main junction, where many of the minibuses and buses drop people off, but they're not up to the standard of the places we've listed here; so, unless you plan an early departure, it's best to head into town. All of the following have hot water (as do all but the very roughest places in town), which is a real plus on those chilly mornings.

Home of Edirisa (☎ 0752-558222; www.edirisa.org; Muhumuza Rd; dm USh5000, s/d USh8000/15,000 without bathroom, d USh20,000; ☐) It's a hostel, it's a museum, it's a restaurant, it's a cultural centre, it's a fair trade craft shop: and it's a great place to hang out no matter which of these components tickles your fancy. The rooms are priced right and the staff are great. Internet is free for guests or those eating in the restaurant, and films are shown nightly. Book ahead to avoid disappointment.

Amagara Guesthouse (☎ 0772-959667; Muhumuza Rd; s USh17,000, d USh22,000-32,000; ☐) The people behind Byoona Amagara (p495) on Lake Bunyonyi also run this little spot in town. There's no island vibe here, just simple, meticulously clean rooms. Many locals drink here at night, so it's a good place to break out of that backpacker shell. All but two rooms are self-contained, but there's no discount if you end up sharing the bath with your neighbour. There's also one larger, snazzier room.

Victoria Inn (☎ 0486-423414; off Nyerere Ave; s/d USh21,000/26,000) This little place just past the bustle of downtown offers nothing fancy, but it's almost homey and the staff are very friendly. They load up the fireplace on cold nights.

Cepha's Inn (☎ 0486-422097; birungicephas@yahoo.com; Archer Rd; s USh40,000, d USh60,000-80,000, ste USh120,000; 🅿) Taking up two colourful buildings near the golf course on the hill above town, this isn't the most expensive place in Kabale, but it offers rooms that are nearly as good at prices that are far better. Facilities include a sauna and steam bath, plus satellite TV and intercom in the rooms. Book ahead as it's often full.

Eating

You can eat well at the Home of Edirisa and Amagara Guesthouse, which have a mix of local and international favourites in the USh3000 to USh10,000 range. Both make a pretty good pizza. For something more Ugandan, the side-by-side Skyline Hotel and Skyblue Motel, out at the main junction, have good lunch and dinner buffets for USh6000.

Little Ritz (Rugabo Rd; mains USh2000-6000; ⏰ 7.30am-midnight) Located above the popular Hot Loaf Bakery, this is the leading restaurant in town, both for the food and atmosphere. The eclectic menu of Western, Indian, Chinese and African dishes can be enjoyed outside on the balcony or inside by the fireplace and with international news programs on the TV. There's also a pool table for passing the night.

Royal Supermarket (Kisoro Rd) Anyone planning to do a bit of self-catering at Bwindi or Lake Bunyonyi should hit the Royal, the best-stocked supermarket in town.

Getting There & Away

There are numerous daily buses to Kampala (USh20,000, eight hours). Some of the companies have offices in town, and you can begin your journey there, but all buses (including those coming from Rwanda) also pick up passengers in front of the Skyblue Motel at the main junction. Minibuses to Mbarara (USh10,000, 3½ hours) also park near the Skyblue, but in the morning you're better off using the buses. The Post Bus (see p443) departs for Kampala via Mbarara around 7am.

For Fort Portal (USh20,000, eight hours), via Queen Elizabeth National Park and Kasese (USh18,000, seven hours), there are two daily departures available. Set your alarm clock: Horizon leaves at 2am and Gateway goes an hour later.

Many of the buses from Kampala, including Horizon and Gateway, continue on to Kisoro (USh10,000, two hours). You can catch these either at the main junction or in front of the Highland Hotel on the northwest side of town. There are a few Kisoro minibuses from the taxi park while saloon car shared taxis also park by the Highland.

For all the difficult details on getting from Kabale to Bwindi Impenetrable National Park, see p491. For travel to Lake Bunyonyi, see below.

Transport to the Rwandan border at Katuna and on to Kigali is frequent. See p529 for full details.

LAKE BUNYONYI

Lake Bunyonyi ('place of many little birds') is undoubtedly the loveliest lake in Uganda. Its contorted shore encircles 29 islands, and the steep surrounding hillsides are intensively terraced, almost like parts of Nepal. A magical place, especially with a morning mist rising off the placid waters, it has supplanted the Ssese Islands as *the* place for travellers to chill out on their way through Uganda.

Sights & Activities

All guesthouses can arrange boat trips on the lake, either in motorboats or dugout canoes, which is still how most locals get about. Charges are reasonable, but practice for a while before paddling off on an ambitious trip since many tourists end up going round in circles, doing what's known locally as the *muzungu* corkscrew.

One potential destination is tiny **Akampeine Island** (Punishment Island), so named because it was once the place where unmarried pregnant women were dumped to die. Their only rescue from drowning or starvation was if a man who was too poor to pay a bride price would come over to claim the banished woman as his wife. It's easy to spot; it has just one spindly tree in the centre. Many boat drivers will also take you to **Bwama** and **Njuyeera (Sharp's) Islands**, where Scottish missionary Dr Leonard Sharp founded a leper colony and settled in 1921, but the story is more interesting than the sights. The colony on Bwama shut down in the 1980s (there are two schools on the island now) and nearly all history was stripped from Sharp's home on Njuyeera when it was converted into a (not recommendable) hotel.

There are a few **Batwa pygmy villages** near the lake's south end around Kyevu, which has a mildly interesting (mostly because nearly everybody arrives by dugout canoe) Wednesday and Saturday market. **Rotobo village** is an hour by motorboat and then an hour on foot and boat owners at Rutinda will take you there for USh80,000, a quarter of which should go to the Batwa. See p498 for more information about visiting the Batwa.

The best way to get intimate with Bunyonyi is on the **canoe trekking** (USh250,000 per person for a group of four) trips offered on Tuesday and Saturday by Home of Edirisa (p492) in Kabale. The all-inclusive three-day tours (two on the water and one walking in the hills) hit the points detailed above and many more. You'll get a very up-close look at local life.

The Edirisa folk are also the people to talk to about volunteer opportunities in area schools or teaching swimming lessons. (When storms blow in people are sometimes knocked out of their boats, and many drown because they can't swim.) Either check the website (www.edirisa.org) or drop by the **Heart of Edirisa** commune out on a peninsula past all the lodging. Everyone is welcome for lunch or dinner (USh3000). On some Saturdays, local women sometimes do basket weaving here. Volunteers can stay here for US$5 per day.

The guesthouses will also set you up for **guided walks** to see, among other things, local blacksmiths (*abahesi*) who have replaced locally mined iron ore with scrap metal, but otherwise use traditional methods. However, if you just want an easygoing amble along the lakeshore, it's straightforward enough to find your own way around. If you want to venture further, Bunyonyi Overland Resort has **bikes** (per day USh12,000) for hire, although getting to Kabale would require a king of the mountains, Tour de France–style effort since these are local, one-speed behemoths.

Sleeping & Eating

The lake has a good choice of accommodation, both on the mainland and some islands; and more places were under construction when we last visited. All have restaurants and bars (and surely you know the drill by now; order well in advance) and swimming piers. Go ahead and jump in, Bunyonyi has no crocodiles, hippos or bilharzia.

MAINLAND

ourpick **Kalebas Camp** (☎ 0312-294894; camping USh7500, safari tent s/d USh25,000/25,000, room s/d USh30,000/40,000) The original lakeside lodging and its lovely garden have gone through several owners over the years, but its present incarnation is now one of Bunyonyi's best. The accommodation is great value by Bunyonyi standards and the restaurant makes a good wood-fired pizza (large pizza USh12,000 to USh14,000).

Bunyonyi Overland Resort (☎ 0486-426016; www.bunyonyioverland.com; camping USh10,000, furnished safari tent s/d USh30,000/40,000, room without bathroom s/d USh35,000/50,000, room s/d USh50,000/65,000, family cottage with kitchen USh160,000; 🖳) If you've seen Backpackers (p435) or Red Chilli (p435) in Kampala, then you already know the drill; only the sculpted gardens and lakeside setting make Bunyonyi Overland much more attractive. It's just as noisy though, since the wide range of accommodation, food (USh3000 to USh16,000) and leisure facilities (from badminton to satellite TV) ensure it's extremely popular with travellers and overland companies. They run a shuttle (USh5000) from the Highland Inn in Kabale at 9.30am and 4.30pm. You can also sometimes ride for free in the supply truck around midday.

Arcadia Cottages (☎ 0486-423400; arcadia cottages@yahoo.com; camping per tent USh20,000, bandas s/d USh80,000/120,000; 🖳) Wow! Built not on the lake but high on a hill, Arcadia has some intoxicating views over dozens of islands way down below and the Virunga volcanoes off in the distance. The *bandas* are plain (nicer inside than the ugly brick exterior suggests) and prices are a little high, but with these views you'll forget about these minor shortcomings mighty fast. Lower priced safari tents are coming, but they won't have views. Even if you won't be sleeping here, stop by for a meal or a drink in the restaurant (mains USh7000 to USh15,000). It sits 2km uphill off the main road to the lake.

ISLANDS

Secure parking is available by the Rutinda landing for those driving here.

ourpick **Byoona Amagara** (☎ 0752-652788; www.lakebunyonyi.net; Itambira Island; camping USh5000, dm USh10,000, tw dm USh12,500, geodome per person USh16,000-21,000, cabin per person USh24,000, cottage per person USh100,000; 🖳) Run by an American guy from New York who spends all proceeds on community projects, Byoona Amagara bills itself as a backpacker's paradise, and it's hard to disagree. There's a great choice of rooms,

UGANDA

lonelyplanet.com

most built of natural materials and all very reasonably priced. (Private rooms have a two person minimum June to September, December to January and Easter and a 50% single supplement other times, and they stick to this even if you're the only person on the island.) The stars of the show are the open-faced geodomes: birds and lizards can come in, but so do unencumbered views. And all power comes from the sun, so there's no irritating generator rumble at night. The originality doesn't take a break in the kitchen, which turns out some yummy, creative dishes (USh4000 to USh9000) such as crayfish avocado and *matoke* chips. A motorboat out here from Rutinda costs USh15,000; and while the dugout *to* the island is free, it costs USh3000 per person for the return.

Bushara Island Camp (☎ 0772-464585; www.bushara islandcamp.com; Bushara Island; camping US$9, safari tents s/d US$22/28, cottages US$22-50) This camp is run by the Church of Uganda to raise funds for community development projects. It offers a choice of cottages (one set on stilts) and safari tents (bathrooms out back), all widely spaced through the eucalyptus forest. All are pretty plain, but not bad for the price, and there are many return visitors. The well-regarded restaurant (USh2500 to 6500) serving pizza, crayfish dishes and tasty desserts, such as caramelised bananas and crepes. There's also an outdoor barbecue, volleyball court and sailboat and windsurfer rentals, so you'll never get bored. A motorboat transfer from Rutinda is free unless you're camping, in which case it costs USh10,000.

Nature's Prime Island (☎ 0772-423215; www.natures primeisland.com; Akarwa Island; safari tents/cabins per person incl full board US$45/50) Nature's Prime occupies a lovely little wooded island right near Rutinda. Scandinavian-style wooden cabins (probably a little too rustic for some people, but we like the summer-camp vibe) and safari tents set on raised platforms are spread out over the island so views vary, but all see at least some of the lake from the front porches. The boat transfer is free.

Heritage Lodge (☎ 0312-279552; www.tangaza tours.co.ug; Habuharo Island; s/d incl full board USh75,000/USh145,000) Lodging on this peaceful, wooded island consists of safari tents (with solid bathroom blocks) on raised platforms and attractive two-bedroom cottages built out over a hillside for lake views through the treetops. The menu is small but sophisticated (try the crayfish ma-

sala) and many ingredients come from their organic garden. Meals are served in a cosy lounge hung with art and filled with warmth from the fireplace. They recently added a tiny pitch and putt golf course. Habuharo Island ('The Island of Birdsong') is the furthest of the bunch from Rutinda landing; the free motorboat transfer takes 30 minutes.

Getting There & Away

There are many pickups (USh1500) and saloon car shared taxis (USh2000) travelling from Kabale's main market on Monday and Friday to Rutinda, where most of the lodging and the main jetty is. It's 9km from Kabale. On other days, you can check at the taxi park, but transport is rare so you'll probably have to choose between a special-hire (USh13,000) or a *boda-boda* (USh4000). A few people just choose to walk, though it's a long way with a backpack. Get directions for the scenic route through the hills from Home of Edirisa (p492).

KISORO

The far southwest corner of Uganda has been dubbed the 'Switzerland of Africa' by some, although there weren't many volcanoes in the Alps at last count. 'New Zealand of Africa' could be closer to the mark, but neither nation has such extensively terraces hillsides. Whatever the comparisons, this little part of Uganda is undeniably beautiful. On a clear day, the views of the Virunga chain of volcanoes from town are fantastic. They're even better on the approach from Kabale, which loops around the back side of Lake Bunyonyi and then crosses the forested Kanaba Gap before dropping into town.

Most travellers are here to visit the gorillas of Mgahinga Gorilla National Park (p499) to the south or Parc National des Virungas (p538) at Djomba, just over the border in DRC, but there are several other attractive activities in the area. First introductions are poor since you have to face Uganda's most obnoxious *boda-boda* drivers, but once you're in the groove, you may well find yourself hanging out here for a while.

Like Kabale, cold winds blow through town, so pack that jacket.

Information

Stanbic Bank (Bunagana Rd) Changes cash and has an ATM, but it goes offline fairly often, so to be on the safe side it's best to arrive in town with your gorilla tracking money.

IP Internet Café (Bunagana Rd; per min USh50; 8am-9pm Mon-Sat, 11am-9pm Sun) The best bet for getting online.

Mgahinga Gorilla National Park Office (0486-430098; Main St; 8am-5pm) The place to book your gorilla permits. Staff here are very friendly and have information about everything in and around Kisoro.

Sights & Activities

You won't be here long before would-be guides will approach you about a variety of trips they can lead you on. Not all of these guys are reliable, so get a recommendation from a fellow traveller or the UWA office. The guides at Countryside Guesthouse are great, and this is also a good place to arrange a special-hire since you won't likely beat their prices by negotiating with drivers in town.

The most popular trips are **snake safaris** on Lake Mutanda (p499) and visits to **Batwa pygmy villages**. The Batwa were forcibly removed from the forests of Mgahinga and Bwindi when these were turned into national parks. The price of these trips depends on which of the 21 villages you'll be visiting, but all guides will tell you they give USh30,000 to the village chairman; the good ones actually do it. You may want to drop into the **United Organisation for Batwa Development in Uganda** (0486-430140; Bunagana Rd; 8am-5.30pm) office before a village visit to ensure that your trip will be culturally sensitive, and thus, ultimately, rewarding. See p498 for more information about visiting the Batwa.

When the border with DRC is open, people often visit the Tuesday and Friday **markets** at Bunagana. For a small tip (ask the going rate in Kisoro before you go) the border guards on the Congolese side will conveniently forget to stamp your passport, which means you won't have to buy another Ugandan visa on your return. Kisoro's Monday and Thursday **markets** are also large, colourful affairs, well worth some of your time.

Sleeping

Rugigan Campsite (0772-647660; off Bunagana Rd; camping USh5,000) It's just on the western edge of town, but it feels like it's deep in the countryside, which makes this the best place to pitch a tent in Kisoro; although a new bathroom block would be nice. A few overland trucks stop here (most go to Hotel Virunga) but at other times it will likely just be you, the staff and their families. With notice, they can cook local meals (USh3000 to USh5000).

Shobore Rutare Site Lodge (0782-414000; Bunagana Rd; s/d without bathroom USh6,000/10,000) On the cheap, cheap front, there are many choices in Kisoro, but little quality. Shobore is above the norm in both the cleanliness and maintenance departments, so its basic shared-bath rooms get our nod.

Graceland Motel (0382-276964; Kabale Rd; s/d USh15,000/20,000) There's not much hip-shaking going on here; though what you do in the privacy of your room is your own business. What Graceland does have is quality self-contained rooms, good food and exemplary service.

Countryside Guesthouse (0782-412741; countrysideguesthouse@yahoo.com; Bunagana Rd; s/d without

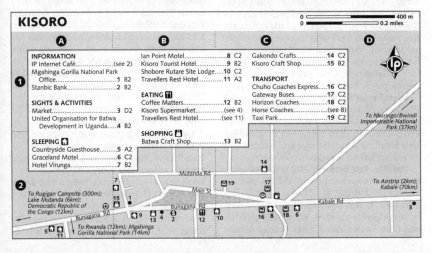

KISORO

0 — 400 m
0 — 0.2 miles

INFORMATION	
IP Internet Café	(see 2)
Mgahinga Gorilla National Park Office	1 B2
Stanbic Bank	2 B2

SIGHTS & ACTIVITIES	
Market	3 D2
United Organisation for Batwa Development in Uganda	4 B2

SLEEPING	
Countryside Guesthouse	5 A2
Graceland Motel	6 C2
Hotel Virunga	7 B2

Ian Point Motel	8 C2
Kisoro Tourist Hotel	9 B2
Shobore Rutare Site Lodge	10 C2
Travellers Rest Hotel	11 A2

EATING	
Coffee Matters	12 B2
Kisoro Supermarket	(see 4)
Travellers Rest Hotel	(see 11)

SHOPPING	
Batwa Craft Shop	13 B2

Gakondo Crafts	14 C2
Kisoro Craft Shop	15 B2

TRANSPORT	
Chuho Coaches Express	16 C2
Gateway Buses	17 C2
Horizon Coaches	18 C2
Horse Coaches	(see 8)
Taxi Park	19 C2

To Nkuringo/Bwindi Impenetrable National Park (37km)

To Rugigan Campsite (300m); Lake Mutanda (6km); Democratic Republic of the Congo (12km)

Mutanda Rd

Main St

Bunagana Rd

To Rwanda (12km); Mgahinga Gorilla National Park (14km)

Kabale Rd

To Airstrip (2km); Kabale (70km)

UGANDA

BATWA PYGMY TOURS: TO GO OR NOT TO GO...

The Batwa are Uganda's most marginalised people, and are viewed with disdain by most Ugandans. Almost all Batwa have been forced out of their ancestral forest homes, where they lived as nomadic hunters and gatherers, either because the forest has been cleared for agriculture by neighbouring tribes or it's now part of a national park.

Many Ugandans will tell you the Batwa are lazy. This is both unfair and wrong. What the Batwa are is uninterested in living in modern agro-industrial society. Life in the forest was anything but easy, but this is the only life the older generation know, and even those who are making an effort to adopt farming have found it very hard to adapt to modern life.

In many of the places where the Batwa now live, particularly near Lake Bunyonyi and Mgahinga, Bwindi and Semuliki National Parks, guides will offer to take you to visit one of their villages. The visits invariably involve a song and dance demonstration, and once the music begins you can't help but notice that they project a genuine pride.

Most Batwa today still rely on handouts, and so they're only too happy for a chance to cash in on their culture (your guide should be giving a good chuck of change to the village chairman for the performance, and basketry is usually offered for sale) but ironically in some ways it's only this commercialisation process that ensures the survival of the pygmies as a distinct ethnic group within Uganda.

Despite this, visits can still end up taking on a 'human safari' feel, which is pretty unfortunate for everyone involved.

---

bathroom USh12,000/15,000, r USh20,000) Another friendly place with rooms at about the same standard as Graceland. Good food too. This is the Kisoro contact for Nkuringo Walking Safaris (p492).

Ian Point Motel (☎ 0775-116343; Bunagana Rd; r without USh15,000, r USh35,000) A step up from the nearby Graceland, this centrally located place has bright and clean rooms. The self-contained ones have mini-fridge and satellite TV.

Hotel Virunga (☎ 0486-430109; camping USh8000, r without USh22,000, r Ush42,000) Despite being overpriced, this is the busiest backpacker place in Kisoro. Out front is a buzzing little restaurant that rocks on as a bar when the overland trucks are in town. The Golden Monkey Guesthouse nearly next door has similar rooms at similarly inflated prices, but since there are fewer guests, prices may be open to negotiation.

Kisoro Tourist Hotel (☎ 0712-540527; Buganana Rd; s/d US$50/65; 🖵) Lacking the charm and history of Travellers Rest, this modern hotel is more about function than form, but if Travellers Rest is full, or you want access to a sauna and steam bath, then it makes a good choice.

Travellers Rest Hotel (☎ 0772-533029; Mahuabura Rd; www.gorillatours.com; s/d/tr US$55/65/75, s/d/tr incl full board US$72/99/109; 🖵) This is a hotel with a history. It was once run by the so-called father of gorilla tourism, Walter Baumgärtel, and Dian Fossey called it her 'second home'.

Through various little touches, this otherwise simple place has become a lovely little oasis. The garden has lots of shade and the dining room/bar areas are full of Congolese crafts (all for sale).

For an alternative to a night in town, there are also a few good choices at Mgahinga Gorilla National Park (opposite) and on Lake Mutanda (opposite).

Eating & Drinking

There's not a great deal of choice in town, so most visitors usually end up eating at their hotel. The best menu is found at **Travellers Rest** (lunch USh5000-9000, dinner USh20,000; ☯ noon-5pm & 7.30pm), which also has a well-stocked bar and fireplace. Lunch is an à la carte menu while dinner (order before 3pm) is a buffet. A filling packed lunch for gorilla tracking costs USh9000. The Graceland Motel (mains USh2000 to USh5000) offers discount dining with some international touches, and the food here is excellent.

One non-lodge place worth popping into is **Coffee Matters** (Bunagana Rd; cappuccino USh2000, mains USh3000-5000) where you can get locally grown coffees and fruit smoothies plus a small selection of simple meals. The **Kisoro Supermarket** (Bunagana Rd) is the best stocked grocery in town.

Mutanda Rd is a bar-hopping friendly street with a few pool tables and lots of cheap beer. Or check out the aforementioned Hotel Virunga if you see some overland trucks in town.

Shopping

Kisoro has no shortage of craft shops. **Gakondo Crafts** (Mutanda Rd) stocks some traditional items that may make good decorations in your home, but a conversation with the gregarious owner Mugisha Jean alone is worth a stop. If the door is closed, read the directions on the wall about how to get in.

Others stand-out stores are **Kisoro Craft Shop** (Bunagana Rd) with Congolese carvings and **Batwa Craft Shop** (Bunagana Rd) with basketry unlike what's on sale elsewhere in Uganda.

Getting There & Away

Several bus companies, all departing from the east side of the city between 5am and 7am, make the long run to Kampala (USh20,000 to USh25,000). The best of them by far is Chuho Coaches Express which makes the trip nonstop. They depart at 7am and usually reach their own station (near the National Mosque) in Kampala by 3pm. Chuho departs Kampala at 7am too. The other companies take two or three hours more than Chuho.

Between Kisoro and Kabale (USh10,000, two hours) there are frequent daily minibuses, which wait outside the taxi park. On market days (Monday and Thursday) minibuses also run to Bunagana (USh3000, 45 minutes) on the DRC border from the same place.

For details on how to get to Mgahinga Gorilla National Park, see right.

The Rwandan border south of Kisoro at Cyanika is open and it's a pretty simple and quick trip to Musanze. See p529 for full details.

LAKE MUTANDA

This beautiful hippo, crocodile and bilharzia-free lake lies just north of Kisoro. The **snake safaris** (most guides charge US$20 plus transport) so heavily hyped in Kisoro take place here, and if it's a sunny day you have a good chance of meeting up with a two- to three-metre python.

One other good reason to come out to the lake is **Mutanda Eco-Community Centre** (☎ 0712-500562; camping per tent USh16,000, cottage USh30,000), a peaceful spot next to a papyrus swamp on the lake's south shore. There's currently only one simple log cabin (with excellent views across the lake from the porch) and a grassy camping ground, but construction was underway when we stopped by and they said a dorm, more cottages, safari tents and a hot-water shower block were coming. Deals can be made for volunteer swimming teachers to stay free. They'll cook local food for USh10,000 and rent you a dugout canoe for USh8000 a day.

You can walk to the lake from Kisoro in under an hour. The easiest, though not most direct, route, is to head west to the hospital and then ask someone to show you which gap in the hills to cross. A *boda-boda* or special-hire should cost USh3000/12,000 respectively

MGAHINGA GORILLA NATIONAL PARK

Although it's the smallest of Uganda's national parks at just 34 sq km, **Mgahinga Gorilla National Park** (☎ 0486-430098; admission US$30) punches above its weight. Tucked away in the far southwest corner of the country, the tropical rainforest cloaks three dramatic extinct volcanoes and, along with the contiguous Parc National des Volcans (p562) in Rwanda and Parc National des Virungas (p538) in DRC (which together with Mgahinga form the 434-sq-km Virunga Conservation Area), this is the home of half the world's mountain gorilla population. Elephants, buffaloes and servals are rarely seen, but they're also out there, and 115 species of bird flutter through the forests, including Rwenzori turaco and mountain black boo boo.

As in Bwindi Impenetrable National Park (p488), it's possible to track gorillas here, though not always since the one habituated family has a tendency to duck across the mountains into Rwanda or DRC. But, also like Bwindi, there's much more on offer here than just gorillas. Mgahinga also serves up some challenging but rewarding treks and an interesting cave, plus golden monkey tracking is almost as fun as hanging out with the big boys.

No matter what brings you here, take a few minutes to walk up to the viewing platform near the headquarters for some great photos of the looming volcanoes.

Activities

GORILLA TRACKING

When the gorillas are living on Ugandan soil, which is most of the time, eight people can visit per day. The cost is US$500, including the entrance fee, a ranger-guide and armed guards. Trips depart from park headquarters at 8.30am, but try to check in at the office in Kisoro the day before your trip to confirm your arrival.

Unlike Bwindi, bookings aren't taken at the UWA head office in Kampala. You must make your reservation by calling the park office in Kisoro (p496) no more than two weeks in advance. (The staff are very nice and will probably extend this to three if you ask.) You pay at the park on the day of your tracking. Because of this system, tour operators rarely come here, making it a good place to get permits last minute. All eight places are usually filled in the summer and Christmas high-seasons, but even in these months one or two people can often arrive and get a tracking spot in a day or two.

It usually takes longer to reach the gorillas here than at Bwindi, but the going is much easier than in the Impenetrable Forest. And photography is usually better because the gorillas are often found out in the open.

For more information on the mountain gorillas, including a list of tracking rules, see p75.

GOLDEN MONKEY TRACKING

When the gorillas are hanging out on the other sides of the mountains, golden monkeys, a very rare subspecies of the rare blue monkey, become the top lure to Mgahinga. These beautiful creatures live in large groups and are quite playful. It costs US$20 to spend an hour with them, but don't forget to throw in the US$30 park fee on top. Tracking starts at 8.30am, and the guides can find the habituated troop 85% of the time.

TREKKING

Any one of the park's volcanoes can be climbed for US$20 per person (plus the park entry fee), including a ranger-guide. The treks, which are strenuous (you just have to look at the mountains to know there's no point in trying if you aren't in good shape) but require no mountaineering experience, take you up for some stunning views and into the other-worldly afro-alpine moorland, home of bizarre plants such as giant groundsel and lobelias.

The crater lake at the summit of Mt Muhavura (4127m) is almost too perfect to be true, and the views up here reach all the way to the Rwenzori Mountains. It's a 12km (at least seven hours) return trip. The hook with

climbing Mt Sabyinyo (3669m), which involves some breathtaking walks along gorges and a few ladder ascents, is that when you get to the third and final peak you'll be standing in Uganda, Rwanda and DRC at once. This is the longest (many would say most fun) climb, at 14km (eight hours). It's only 8km (five hours) to the swamp that was once a lake at the top of Mt Gahinga (3474m).

Two less taxing treks (US$10 per person), both about 10km long and great for bird-watchers, are the Border Trail, which starts out up Sabyinyo but then cuts back south along the Congolese border, and the Gorge Trail, which heads to a small waterfall in a gorge halfway up Sabyinyo. You could combine these into one longer trek.

CAVING

Once a haven for Batwa pygmies, **Garama Cave** is an easy 2km walk from park headquarters. The three-hour visit (US$10 per person) to the 342m cave involves listening to Batwa history and legend, soon the stories will be told by the Batwa themselves. They're being trained as guides. Bring a torch (flashlight).

Sleeping & Eating

Most people sleep in Kisoro, but there are two choices just outside the park gate. Despite choice views of the Virunga volcanoes, they don't get many guests due to the out of the way location; but for some people the peace and quiet is a bonus. UWA is planning to add a camp site and some *bandas* at Muhavura Base for people climbing the park's highest peak.

Amajambere Iwacu Community Campground (☎ 0382-278464; www.amajamberecamp.org; camping USh5000, dm USh10,000, banda without bathroom USh30,000, banda USh45,000) A friendly place with a variety of rooms and a nice veranda for relaxing. Local meals (USh2500 to USh5000) are available, but only if you order early. They lead community walks in the area, and if you contact them in advance, they can hook you up with some volunteer opportunities. Proceeds fund school projects in the area.

Mt Gahinga Lodge (☎ 0414-346464; www.volcanoes safaris.com; s/d incl full board US$420/700) The facilities are lovely, but we've heard mixed reports, which just shouldn't happen at these prices.

Getting There & Away

There's no scheduled transport along the rough 14km track between Kisoro and park headquarters. You can try to hitch, although traffic is light so it's best to arrange a ride the night before.

The most straightforward way to get out to the park is to arrange a special-hire. This should cost USh25,000; probably more in the wet season. *Boda-boda* drivers will take you there too for USh10,000 to USh15,000, but be prepared for a very rough ride. You could also ask at the UWA office about free lifts with national park vehicles, although they're usually completely full when they leave town.

Kisoro has an airfield if you want to come by chartered flight.

MBARARA

Mbarara is a prosperous town, a fact that brings many Ugandan business travellers here. But there's no reason for others to stop unless you want a well-stocked place to break your journey between Kampala and the far southwest. In that case, you'll find a good range of hotels and eateries. Stanbic Bank exchanges American Express travellers cheques while several other banks also handle cash.

The only thing that qualifies as an attraction is **Nkokonjeru Tombs**, burial ground of the last two Anokole kings and other members of the royal family; but it's in sorry shape and uninteresting to boot. It's 2.5km northwest of town if you don't believe us.

Sleeping & Eating

Westland Hotel (☎ 0772-586769; Bananuka Dr; s/d USh8000/12,000 without bathroom, s USh16,000-21,000, d USh25,000-41,000) A construction project that just never ends, this labyrinth place is a little rough around the edges, but it has a big array of rooms with good value available throughout: the top tier has satellite TV. If only the staff could cheer up a tad.

Oxford Inn (☎ 0772-683097; Bananuka Dr; r USh62,000-87,000, ste USh122,000) This is a fairly sophisticated little hostelry, where all rooms have satellite TV and refrigerators. The regular rooms are good value, but forget about the suites (take a room at the Lake View instead). There are a couple of nightclubs on this stretch of the street, but they're not too loud, so if you take an interior room you'll probably sleep just fine. Other places with similar standards in this price range have their own traffic noise issues.

Lake View Resort Hotel (☎ 0485-433123; s/d USh60,000/75,000; ste USh130,000; 🖳 🐾) On the

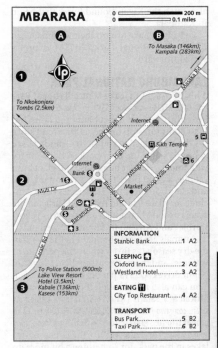

MBARARA

INFORMATION
Stanbic Bank................1 A2

SLEEPING 🏨
Oxford Inn................2 A2
Westland Hotel................3 A2

EATING 🍴
City Top Restaurant......4 A2

TRANSPORT
Bus Park.....................5 B2
Taxi Park.....................6 B2

outskirts of town off the road to Kasese, this modern hotel sits in front of a tiny lake and has long been the place to be in Mbarara. The 100 rooms (all with balconies) aren't as flash as the public areas, but are still easily the best in town. Facilities include a swimming pool (USh5000 for hotel guests, USh10,000 for non-guests), sauna, tennis courts and a garden restaurant.

City Top Restaurant (☎ 0485-420555; High St; mains USh4500-14,000; ⏰ 10am-9.30am Mon-Sat, 10am-3pm Sun) This first-floor spot claims it 'feeds like a mother'. If your mother cooked Indian and Ugandan food, prohibited all alcohol and kept telling you 'sorry we don't have that today' when you try to order, then it's true. But, most importantly, what's available is invariably excellent.

Getting There & Away

There are frequent buses and minibuses, departing from side-by-side parks, to Kampala (USh15,000, 4½ hours), Masaka (USh8,000, 2½ hours), Kabale (USh10,000, 3½ hours) and Kasese (USh10,000, three hours). The Post Bus (see p443) to Kabale stops in Mbarara, leaving for Kampala about 9.30am. You can

UGANDA

also catch the Kigali-bound buses that begin in Kampala.

Getting to Lake Mburo (below) and Queen Elizabeth National Parks (p484) is pretty straightforward.

LAKE MBURO NATIONAL PARK

The 370-sq-km **Lake Mburo National Park** (☎ 0392-711346; admission US$30; 🕑 7am-6.30pm) lacks heavy hitters such as elephants and lions, but it's a common stop on the safari circuit since it's the only place in southern Uganda to see zebra. It's also the only park in the country with impala, slender mongoose and giant bush rat plus a good place to look for leopard, topi and eland. Some of the 325 species of bird include martial eagle and red-faced barbet in the acacia-wooded savannah and papyrus yellow warbler and African finfoot in the wetlands.

Animals are most abundant in the south in the dry season (as this is where the permanent water is) and the northeast in the wet season. Night drives (US$15 per person) are allowed. You can also roll through the savannah with **African ATV Safaris** (☎ 0776-377187; www.africanatvsafaris.com; two-/four-hr USh100,000/USh180,000) or take a **boat trip** (US$10 per person; 🕑 8am, 10am, noon, 2pm, 4pm & 5.30pm) on Lake Mburo, the largest of five lakes in the park, for something a bit more up close and personal with the hippos, crocodiles and waterbirds. Reservations are advisable June through August and in December.

Lake Mburo has some good nature walks, particularly the early morning **hyena walk** at 6.30am. The other popular pedestrian destination is an observation blind overlooking a salt lick. Both walks take about 2½ hours and cost US$10 per person. Bird-watchers should inquire about the Rubanga forest, which has a closed canopy in some places and you may find birds not yet recorded on the park's official list.

Adjacent to the park are the ranches of people of the Bahima tribe, who herd the famed long-horned Ankole cattle that are a common sight here (all too often inside as well as outside the park). A new, still developing project just outside the Sanga Gate is the **Ankole Eco-Cultural Village** (☎ 0772-888394; 🕑 7.30am-6.30pm) where you can arrange farm tours (USh30,000). There's also a craft shop and a plan to add *bandas*.

Sleeping & Eating

The park has three **camp sites** (USh15,000), but most people stay at the attractive Lakeside Camp 2, 1¼km from the park headquarters. The **Lakeside Restaurant** (mains USh8000; 🕑 7am-9.30pm) here is pretty good if you can spare a long time to wait for your food. You can also pitch a tent at Rwonyo Campsite 1, right at the headquarters. Both of these camps have hot water. If you have your own vehicle, consider Kingfisher Campsite 3, which is more rustic, but the whole site is first-come, first-served.

Rwonyo Rest Camp (banda s/d USh10,000/15,000, safari tents s/d USh30,000/40,000) Located at park headquarters, the rest camp has simple *bandas* and safari tents on wooden platforms, all with shared bathroom facilities and kerosene lanterns for light. Overall, it's a nice setup, but you have to walk to the Lakeside Restaurant for food.

Arcadia Cottages (☎ 0392-833705; arcadiacottages l.mburo@yahoo.com; s/d incl full board US$180/280) Near but not right on the lake, this brand new camp features something of a playhouse style. The bright, attractive cottages are a melange of concrete, canvas, wood and thatch. Facilities are better than at Kimbla-Mantana, but Arcadia lacks the views. The small daily menu (USh15,000) always has something Italian on it; non-guests are welcome to dine here.

Kimbla-Mantana Lake Mburo Camp (☎ 0414-321552; www.kimbla-mantana.com; s/d incl full board US$180/300) This luxury tented camp sits on a hill with commanding views of Lake Mburo (and sunsets behind the hills) available right from the hammocks on the big porches.

Mihingo Lodge (☎ 0752-410509; www.mihingolodge.com; s/d incl full board US$300/420; 🏊) The most sumptuous and stylish lodging lies just outside the park's eastern border. The long, winding uphill drive fills you with anticipation and the facilities do no disappoint. The tent-cottage combos are spread out along the ridge (if you have a tough time walking, be sure to tell them when you book a room) and a busy watering hole is visible from the pool and some of the rooms. The best views are not of the park, but behind, looking out over Lake Kacheer where you can take a horseback ride (one hour per person USh70,000, four hours per person USh200,000).

Getting There & Away

There are two possible ways into the park from the main Masaka–Mbarara road. If you're driving your own vehicle, it's better to use the Nshara Gate, 13km after Lyantonde because you'll see much more wildlife on

UGANDA

the drive in. But, if you're hoping to hitch in or arrange a special-hire (USh20,000 to USh30,000) or *boda-boda* (USh7000) it's best to use the route from the Sanga Gate, 27km after Lyantonde and 40km from Mbarara. Minibuses to Sanga cost USh4000 from Mbarara (45 minutes) and USh7000 from Masaka (two hours). It's about a 25km drive to Rwonyo from either gate.

If you're really rushed for time, Lake Mburo can be done as a day-trip from Kampala. It's about a 3½-hour drive each way.

MASAKA

In 1979 Masaka was trashed by the Tanzanian army during the war that ousted Idi Amin, and, unlike Mbarara, which suffered a similar fate, the scars remain very visible. There's a lot of construction going on these days, so perhaps Masaka has finally turned the corner. Regardless, it's going to be a long time before anyone wants to spend more time here than is absolutely necessary. For most, it's just a quick vehicle-swapping stop en route to the Ssese Islands or Tanzania.

There are many banks in town. **Stanbic Bank** (Birch Ave) exchanges cash and American Express travellers cheques, while the other usual suspects do cash only. For internet, try **Masaka Internet Services** (Kampala Rd; per min USh45, wi-fi per 30 min USh1000; ⏰ 8am-8.30pm Mon-Fri, 8am-7pm Sat) where all proceeds support children's education.

Sights & Activities

Despite being crossed by a busy highway and sharing space with a water treatment plant, the **Nabajjuzzi swamp**, just out of Masaka on the way to Mbarara, offers excellent opportunities to spy two of Uganda's most elusive animals: the shoebill stork and the sitatunga, an aquatic antelope. You can get a good look at them from Nature Uganda's **Sitatunga Corner Observatory** (☎ 0414-540719; eanhs@imul.com; admission USh2000; ⏰ 8am-5.30pm Mon-Sat), which has a spotting scope available: just be careful on the rickety stairs. The shoebill is best seen in the morning, while the sitatunga may show up any time if the sun is shining.

Sleeping & Eating

Masaka Tourist Cottage & Campsite (☎ 0752-619389; masakabackpackers@yahoo.com; camping USh6000, dm USh7000; d USh20,000, bandas USh22,000) Formerly

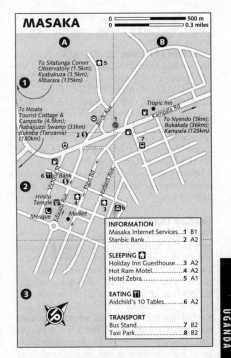

INFORMATION
Masaka Internet Services....1 B1
Stanbic Bank......................2 A2

SLEEPING 🛏
Holiday Inn Guesthouse......3 A2
Hot Ram Motel.....................4 A2
Hotel Zebra.........................5 A1

EATING 🍴
Aidchild's 10 Tables...........6 A2

TRANSPORT
Bus Stand.........................7 B2
Taxi Park...........................8 B2

Masaka Backpackers, this fun, friendly place 4.5km south of town has a nice rural feel and a helpful owner. Meals (USh6000 to USh8000) are available. To get here from Masaka, take a Kirimya minibus for USh700, get off at Kasanvu and follow the signs for 700m. A *boda-boda* will cost USh1000 coming here, but only USh500 going back.

Holiday Inn Guesthouse (☎ 0481-420395; Horbert St; r USh13,000-26,000) This spic-and-span place opened in 2007, and while they still haven't finished the restaurant, everything else is fully in order. Rooms are a mix of self-contained and not-self-contained.

Hot Ram Motel (☎ 0481-420906; Elgin Rd; s/d USh25,000-30,000/40,000-50,000) No, it's not a dodgy brothel, though with a name like this it probably should be. It does give you good rooms (with carpeting and TVs) in a central location.

Hotel Zebra (☎ 0782-863725; www.hotelzebra.net; s USh35,000, d USh60,000-65,000, tr USh80,000; 🖥) All in all, when you combine price, facilities and location (not to mention the snazzy striped uniforms) we think this is the top place to stay in town. All rooms have satellite TV and

UGANDA

balconies with surprisingly nice views over town, plus there's a little garden for dining under the stars.

Aidchild's 10 Tables (☎ 0772-982509; Victoria St; lunch USh5000, dinner USh12,500; ☺ 9.30am-11pm) One of Uganda's most surprising finds, this little pocket of sophistication (white linens and candlelight) puts all proceeds towards supporting AIDS orphans. Lunch is snacks and local food while the three-course set dinners feature mains such as fajitas or garlic-marinated tilapia. The titular 10 tables are downstairs while up above is a comfy lounge and a balcony with some sunset views. They also screen movies (USh5000) nightly at 6pm and 8.30pm.

Getting There & Away

Most minibuses pickup and drop-off passengers at the Shell petrol stations on Kampala Rd. Most buses, on the other hand, use the bypass rather than coming into town, so it's usually quickest to take a *boda-boda* (USh500 to USh1000) out to the nearby villages of Nyendo for eastbound services and Kyabakuza for westbound services. Service is frequent to Kampala (USh6000, two hours) and Mbarara (USh8000, 2½ hours), and less so to Kabale (USh15,000, five hours). The Kabale Post Bus (see p443) arrives around midday on its way to Kampala; it heads west to Mbarara around 10am.

If you're crossing into Tanzania and onto Bukoba, either take a morning minibus to Kyotera (USh4000, one hour) and then another to the border at Mutukula (USh5000, one hour) where you can catch a third ride to Bukoba (Tsh2000, 1½ hours); or hop on the direct buses from Kampala out at the junction. See p530 for further information.

For Ssese Island transport information see p506.

SSESE ISLANDS

While not exactly the Bahamas of Lake Victoria, this lush group of 84 islands along the lake's northwestern shore does boast the best beaches in Uganda. The early 1990s saw their popularity peak, but the suspension of the ferry service largely took them off the *muzungu* map until 2006 when a new ferry began running from Entebbe. The number of visitors is growing again, though Lake Bunyonyi (p494) remains the top spot in Uganda for serious R&R.

History

Life in the islands has had its own ups and downs. The original inhabitants were the Bassese, a tribe closely related to the Buganda. Many important Buganda spirits lived on the islands, including Mukasa, the spirit of the lake, who had a shrine on Bubembe Island, and kings regularly came to pay tribute.

Early in the 20th century, sleeping sickness hit the islands (Ssese = Tsetse) and most residents fled. People slowly drifted back beginning about a decade and a half later, but it wasn't until the troubles of the 1980s that serious settlement took place again when Ugandans found safety in the islands' remoteness. There are very few Bassese anymore and their Lussese language has all but died. Most residents are new arrivals from across East Africa, and this gives the islands real Wild West character. Many wanted criminals and former rebels hide out here, and the AIDS rate is alarmingly high.

The lack of settlement left the islands largely unspoiled, though things have changed dramatically in the recent past. Massive scars of deforestation are visible on many of the islands, especially Buggala (the road from Luku to Kalangala was a nearly solid tunnel of shade just a few years ago), and overfishing has gone largely unchecked since the mid 1990s: it's entirely possible that by the next edition of this book the industry will have wiped itself out.

Few people venture far beyond Buggala Island's Lutoboka Bay, where the ferry lands and almost all accommodation sits, but if you make a little effort there are some good exploration opportunities. The biggest islands, including Buggala, Bufumira and Bukasa, are hilly and many spots afford beautiful views across to other islands, most of which are still ringed by virgin rainforest. You'll have no problems persuading fishermen to take you out on their boats, but try to get a group together first, as prices are very high. Most of the accommodation at Lutoboka Bay sit on white sand beaches; swimming is also possible off most of the other islands, but ask locals first as many spots do harbour bilharzia, as well as an occasional hippo and crocodile.

Information

The only full-on town is Kalangala on Buggala Island. There's a post office and a Stanbic Bank, which changes cash, but currently has

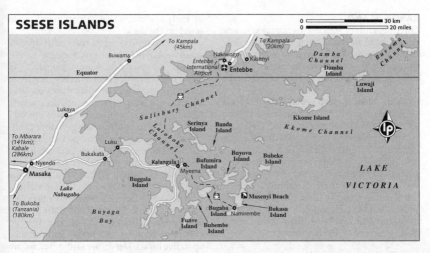

SSESE ISLANDS

0 ——— 30 km
0 ——— 20 miles

To Kampala (45km)
To Kampala (20km)

Buwama
Nakiwogo
Kasenyi

Damba Channel
Buvuma Channel

Equator
Entebbe International Airport
Entebbe
Damba Island

Luwaji Island

Lukaya
Salisbury Channel

Lutoboka Channel

Kkome Island
Kkome Channel

To Mbarara (141km); Kabale (286km)
Luku
Serinya Island
Banda Island

Bukakata

Nyendo
Masaka

Kalangala
Bufumira Island
Myeena

Buyovu Island
Bubeke Island

LAKE VICTORIA

Lake Nabugabo
Buggala Island

Musenyi Beach

To Bukoba (Tanzania) (180km)
Buyaga Bay

Bugaba Island
Namirembe
Bukasa Island

Funve Island
Bubembe Island

---

no ATM. You can surf the Web at **KIC** (Kalangala, Buggala Island; per min USh60; ⏱ 8am-10pm).

There are two petrol stations in Kalangala, but they sometimes run dry, so play it safe and come with a full tank. The electricity supply on the island is also erratic, though most lodges have generators.

Sleeping & Eating

Almost all visitors limit themselves to Buggala Island, though the two other islands with accommodation are much more rewarding.

BUGGALA ISLAND

Most of the lodging is centred on attractive Lutoboka Bay, right where the ferry drops you off. Generally speaking, the further you walk from the jetty, the better the rooms and facilities get. Always ask for a discount if things look slow; you'll often get one.

The once great Hornbill Camp still operates, but can't be recommended until it's rescued from its current owners.

Panorama Cottages (☎ 0772-406371; camping USh5000, tent hire USh10,000, bandas s USh30,000-50,000, bandas d USh35,000-55,000) It's a curious name since there are no views on offer, but the large, clean *bandas*, surrounded by plenty of trees and flowers, are worth a look. Hot water hadn't been hooked up to all the *bandas* when we stayed, but should be by the time you read this. It's a five minute walk to the beach.

Mirembe Resort (☎ 0392-772703; www.mirembe resort.com; camping per tent USh15,000, safari tent per person USh35,000, rooms s/d/tr USh60,000/90,000/110,000; 🖳) In Luganda, 'mirembe' means peace, and by walking (about 1½km following the road) out to the last resort on this stretch of beach you'll see more of it than at any of the other lodges on this side of the bay. There's a variety of rooms available, but the exterior ones, which have their own porches with lake views, are the best bet. The food (USh7000 to USh10,000) is good and, there's a surprising number of vegie options.

Ssese Palm Beach (☎ 0772-503315; www.islandssese .com; bandas s/d/tr incl breakfast from USh47,000/102,000/122,000, bandas s/d/tr incl full board from USh62,000/142,000/182,000) Boasting the best location of any of the resorts here, it's on a headland with its own private beach. There are three types of *banda* available; some are paired up in a single unit, but all include a private bathroom. Moving up in price here brings you an appropriate rise in quality.

Ssese Habitat Resort (☎ 0712-354494; www.ssese habitat.com; camping USh10,000 per person, tents USh20,000; s/d breakfast only USh55,000/110,000, s/d incl full board USh80,000/150,000) Boasting the best views and the best value on Buggala, this well-managed spot sits outside Kalangala, 5km from the jetty. Rooms are in three modern buildings and have flat-screen TVs and patios with lake views. It's a steep 15-minute walk to their private beach (where the camping ground is located), but they'll drive you down. The restaurant has a big international menu (mains USh10,000) and many locals come out to the bar to shoot pool. A new beach-side restaurant was under construction when we stopped by.

BANDA ISLAND

Once legendary among backpackers, few people head to Banda Island anymore now that it's so much easier to get to Buggala. But the place is as good as ever and now it's much more peaceful, which is what an island escape should be.

Banda Island Resort (☎ 0772-222777; banda _island@yahoo.com; dm USh30,000, d without/with bathroom USh70,000/100,000) This ever-evolving Gilligan's Island–like place sits on a big beach and a little peninsula. The accommodation is comfortable (all prices include 'very full board' and you can pay for five days, stay for seven), the food is good and the entertaining owner is full of stories (most of them true). Guests can walk around island, paddle around Lake Vic in canoes and kayaks or just perform some quality control on the hammocks.

BUKASA ISLANDS

Bukasa Island, out at the far end of the archipelago, is the second largest of the Sseses and has several spots worth exploring including lovely little Musenyi Beach, a small waterfall and a shrine to Wammena (a spirit associated with physical handicaps), all less than an hour's walk from Bukasa's only proper lodging, which sits above the jetty.

Bukasa Island Guesthouse (☎ 0752-643746; camping USh5000, dm USh20,000) Formerly known as Agnes's, this simple hilltop spot, just above the jetty, has superb sunset views from the front porch; and you'll almost certainly be the only guests. To avoid disappointment, be sure to call before heading out here as it wasn't officially open when we stayed. The owner is planning to turn it upmarket, and there was no food or drink available.

Father Christopher's (☎ 0782-006577; camping USh5000) There used to be rooms at this Russian Orthodox Church and farmstead, but these days all you can do is pitch a tent. It's about a 30-minute walk from the jetty.

Getting There & Away

Most island visitors get to Buggala Island on the MV *Kalangala* ferry from Nakiwogo near Entebbe (p444). It departs the mainland at 2pm daily and leaves the island at 8am. The trip usually takes 3½ hours. First-class seating costs USh14,000 and second-class USh10,000, but there's little difference between the two. Vehicles cost USh50,000. At weekends and holidays the boat can be crowded, so show up early to claim a seat or you may have to stand on the deck.

Another option from the north are the small wooden boats from Kasenyi (a 30-minute minibus ride from Kampala's old taxi park; USh3000) near Entebbe, but these aren't the safest way to go as winds on Lake Victoria can whip up some really big waves. Also note that schedules and prices are very fickle, so try to confirm things before heading out to the landing. Boats to Banda Island (USh10,000) leave at noon on Tuesday, Friday and Saturday and arrive three to four hours later, which is when you need to board the boat to get back to Kasenyi. There's also a 5pm departure from Kasenyi every other day. Boats to Bukasa Island (USh6000) land at Chuwungu, right by the guesthouse. They go at 6pm on Monday and Friday and can take up to five hours. Departures from Bukasa are always very early the same day. Grace, friendly owner of Kasenyi Takeaway, has been helping travellers catch these boats for years, so stop at her shop before even talking to anyone else.

From the west, a free (though when running low on fuel they often request money from drivers) ferry links Bukakata (36km east of Masaka) on the mainland with Luku on Buggala Island. The ship sails to Luku at 8am, 11am, 1pm and 4pm and to Bukakata at 9am, noon, 3pm and 6pm Monday to Saturday. There are no morning trips on Sunday. The schedule changes often, so call one of the resorts on Buggala Island to get the current times: people in Masaka are unlikely to know. There's usually at least one minibus (USh9000) or coaster connecting Nyendo (3km east of Masaka) to Kalangala for every ferry departure, except the last one of the day. If you're in a hurry, a special-hire to the pier will cost USh30,000; there are always lots of trucks on the ferry so it's easy to catch a ride to Kalangala.

Getting to Bukakata with your own transport can be an exercise in frustration, as there are few signposts. Basically, in Nyendo turn south at the 'Good Foundation' sign, then head left at the T-junction by the petrol station. Continue on this road for about 30km and take the left fork at the major junction by the mobile phone towers and then the right fork at the next junction.

Getting Around

On Buggala Island, Kalangala trading centre is 2km uphill from the pier; a *boda-boda* costs

USh1500. Several of the resorts on Lutoboka Bay hire bicycles.

A special-hire boat from Buggala Island to Banda Island is USh100,000, but if all goes to plan, Dom, owner of Banda Island Resort, will be picking guests up in his rebuilt dhow by the time this book hits shelves.

The best bet for getting to Bukasa Island from Buggala Island is to hire a boat at Myeena (expect to pay around USh150,000 return; the driver will stay on the island and bring you back the next day). The public boats from Myeena aren't as favourable because they land at Namirembe village after dark and then it's a long walk to the lodge. These depart at around 6pm, take about two hours and cost USh5000. Bukasa also has an airstrip if you want to charter a plane.

NORTHWESTERN UGANDA

For decades, the Lord's Resistance Army's war put most of northwestern Uganda effectively off limits. But now that the LRA has fled Uganda, this vast region is once again on the traveller map. It isn't, however, on the traveller radar and visitors are rare. In fact, Uganda north of the Nile also remains politically isolated from the more prosperous south, a great source of frustration and resentment for those living here.

As before, Murchison Falls National Park remains the region's saving grace. The best all-round protected area in the country for wildlife and attractions, Murchison has large populations of lions, leopards, buffaloes, elephants, giraffes, hippos and chimpanzees, plus its namesake waterfall is world-class. Here the broad Nile River thrashes through a narrow gorge in a fit of white-water fury, and the boat trip up the river brings you up close to both the animals and the cascade. Also popular, Ziwa Rhino Sanctuary, halfway between Kampala and Murchison, is the only place to see these big beasts in the wild.

Other attractions are much more mundane. Hoima, hub of the Bunyoro Kingdom, has more to see than most Ugandan towns, but it's hardly going to become the next Jinja. Gulu has an undeniable energy, but it's unlikely to be anything other than a destination for volunteers and an overnight stop for

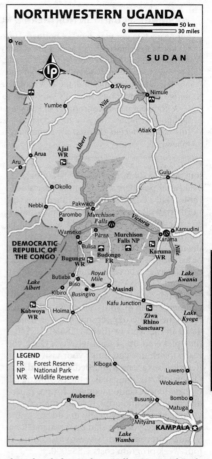

those headed to Kidepo Valley National Park. Intrepid travellers looking for something well removed from the same-old, same-old will find it on the shores of Lake Albert, but even with your own wheels, it takes quite a bit of time to travel out here.

Most of the main roads are in pretty good shape and public transport is frequent to the big towns, available to most of the villages, but nonexistent to Murchison Falls National Park.

ZIWA RHINO SANCTUARY

The Big Five is back. In 2005, Rhino Fund Uganda opened this private 70-sq-km **reserve** (☎ 0772-713410; www.rhinofund.org; admission adult/child US$20/10, guide fee US$15; ⏱ 8am-5pm; last tracking

---

WARNING: SECURITY IN NORTHERN & NORTHWESTERN UGANDA

For nearly two decades, most of northern Uganda was a virtual no-go area, but Joseph Kony and his Lord's Resistance Army has fled the country and, while still not signed, a peace deal was tantalisingly close. Though there remains sporadic banditry in the border regions, particularly the far northwest, where aid workers rather than travellers are likely to go, Gulu, Arua and the rest of the north is safe again. Still, until the LRA completely disappears it would be wise to follow the news before boarding a bus, since it's impossible to say they won't begin their marauding again.

A potential newer concern is oil. Pumping is expected to begin on Lake Albert in 2009 and firefights by rebels there in 2007 claimed lives, including that of a British geologist. Although this hasn't affected tourists, it's something to keep an eye on since, in Africa, trouble often follows oil.

---

starts at 3pm), 170km northwest of Kampala, 23 years after poachers shot the nation's last wild rhino. Half a dozen southern white rhinos (the northern white rhino once found in Uganda is so close to extinction there's little hope of its survival) roam the savannah and wetland and the much more dangerous black rhino should be arriving soon. Eventually these magnificent beasts may also be reintroduced to Murchison Falls and Kidepo Valley National Parks.

A guide will lead you on an up-close encounter, either in your vehicle (a saloon car is alright in the dry season, but you'll need 4WD in the wet) or theirs (US$30, US$40 if they pick you up at the highway). Once you reach the rhinos you finish your visit on foot. Reservations are rarely needed, but a good idea. Other animals living inside the two-metre tall electric fence include leopard, hippo, crocodile, bushbuck and oribi. If you're interested in volunteering here, typically in education and maintenance, you can sign up through Global Vision International (www.gviusa.com). A four-week program costs US$2000.

Accommodation, set out in the centre of the reserve, is nice. Prices are per bed (adult US$12 to US$15, child US$6 to US$8), but it's all one- and two-bed rooms rather than crowded dormitories. You can also camp for US$10 per person. A big thatched-roof restaurant (meals adult/child US$8/5) and swimming pool are coming soon. Book a day in advance.

All buses from Kampala heading to Gulu or Masindi pass nearby. Get off at little Nakitoma (USh9000, three hours) and take a *boda-boda* to the sanctuary gate for USh1500.

MASINDI

Masindi is a quiet provincial headquarters, the last town of any substance on the road to Murchison Falls National Park. It's a good place to stock up on provisions, but there's little of intrinsic interest in the town itself. This fact hasn't stopped a group of VSO volunteers from producing a Walking Trail of Masindi Town brochure pointing out various historical sites. The stories are better than the sights, but it can still make for a few fun hours. Pick up a copy at the New Court View Hotel or Travellers' Corner.

Information

There are a few internet cafés on Masindi Port Rd. **Stanbic Bank** (Kijunjubwa Rd) exchanges cash and American Express travellers cheques. Not a proper forex bureau, but **James Stores** (Tongue St) will beat bank rates.

The **UWA Masindi Information Office** (☎ 0465-420428; ☉ 7am-6.30pm), down a dirt road north of the post office, has national park information.

Sights & Activities

Kigaju Forest (☎ 0772-551484), about 5km out of town, is a genuine eco-tourism project whose success or failure may determine the future of this small forest, and the chimpanzees who live in it. The owners had intended to clear the forest because of crop damage caused by baboons that live here, but were convinced to save it, at least for now. The chimps aren't yet habituated, and the forest is far from pristine, but sightings are quite common, especially around 6.30am and 5pm. There are also black-and-white colobus and lots of butterflies. A guided walk is US$20, and they'll pick you up in town. There's a small camp site and they hope to add a restaurant and *bandas*. Note that you can't visit by yourself. You make reservations and meet the guides in town.

Eye-opening two-hour tours showcasing the work of **AIDS Support Organization** (TASO;

www.tasouganda.org; by donation) offers they're doing in the area. Book through the New Court View Hotel. Also, **Soft Power Education** (p457) has begun doing some volunteer work in the area. Contact them in Jinja if interested.

Sleeping & Eating

Masindi has lots of good lodging, including some of the best bottom-budget rooms in Uganda. Hoteliers here apparently understand the value of a new coat of paint.

Naju Guesthouse (☎ 0772-517955; Stone Ln; r USh5000-7000) The sign claims 'for best accommodation'. Apparently truth-in-advertising laws are pretty weak in Uganda. Rooms are very basic (double check that they have finally hooked up the showers) but bright, and its hidden location on Stone Lane gives it an almost exotic feel.

Karibuni Guesthouse (☎ 0772-923477; Market St; s/d USh16,000/22,000) Hidden behind an unlikely shopfront are comfy, newly renovated rooms (all have private bath) with lots of greenery in between. Excellent value. There's even a little gym.

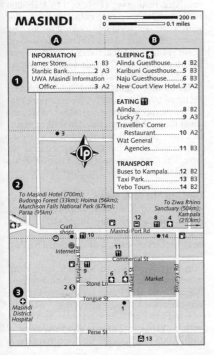

MASINDI

INFORMATION	
James Stores.................1	B3
Stanbic Bank...............2	A3
UWA Masindi Information	
Office....................3	A2

SLEEPING	
Alinda Guesthouse.......4	B2
Karibuni Guesthouse....5	B3
Naju Guesthouse........6	B3
New Court View Hotel.7	A2

EATING	
Alinda....................8	B2
Lucky 7...................9	A3
Travellers' Corner	
Restaurant..........10	A2
Wat General	
Agencies.............11	B3

TRANSPORT	
Buses to Kampala......12	B2
Taxi Park...............13	B3
Yebo Tours.............14	B2

Alinda Guesthouse (☎ 0772-520382; alindamasindi@ yahoo.co.uk; 86 Masindi Port Rd; s/d without bathroom USh15,000/18,000, s USh20,000, d USh30,000-40,000) You can't help notice that the ever popular Alinda, with big clean rooms and right on the main road from Kampala, is a bit tattered these days, but the mix of dead plants and plastic flowers almost gives it an unintended shabby chic feel. Rooms in the nearby annex lack hot water. The restaurant under the tent is popular and features a USh4000 all-you-can-eat dinner buffet.

New Court View Hotel (☎ 0465-420461; Hoima Rd; camping USh5000, s/d USh46,000/57,000) This great little hotel has large, comfy *bandas* and smiling staff. There's even a book exchange. The food in the restaurant (mains USh4000 to USh10,000) is really good and served promptly, which helps you overlook the high prices. The only significant strike is the traffic noise, but it's really not that bad.

Masindi Hotel (☎ 0465-420023; www.masindihotel .com; Hoima Rd; camping USh10,000, s/d USh100,000/120,000; 💻 🚫) Up the road from New Court View, this lovely lodge, built in 1923 by East Africa Railways, is reportedly Uganda's oldest hotel and has hosted Ernest Hemingway, Katherine Hepburn and the Queen of England. A 2005 renovation brought out the historic character, though the rooms themselves only have a light dusting of it. The restaurant (mains USh12,000 to USh15,000) and bar are popular, but prices are even higher than New Court View.

Travellers' Corner Restaurant (☎ 0465-520461; Masindi Port Rd; mains USh4000-6000; 💻) With the same owners as New Court View Hotel, this is a popular gathering spot for locals and tourists alike. The food is cheaper than at the hotel, though the menu is much more limited: no Indian or Chinese choices here, but there are petite pizzas. It's more of a bar than restaurant at night and the pool table is always in use.

If you forget to pack anything in Kampala, there are three small supermarkets with some imported goods: **Alinda** (Masindi Port Rd) and **Lucky 7** (Commercial St) and **Wat General Agencies** (Commercial St).

Getting There & Away

Minibuses from Masindi to Kampala (USh13,000, four hours) and Hoima (USh5000, two hours) travel throughout the day. Buses to Kampala (USh12,000, 3½ hours) leave from Masindi Port Rd between 4.30am and 10am. The Post Bus (see p443) stops here on its way to and from Hoima.

UGANDA

Minibuses to Gulu (USh15,000, four hours) are infrequent, so it's usually quicker to go to Kafu Junction on the main highway and catch a northbound bus there. There are also departures to Butiaba (USh7000, two hours), Bulisa (USh10,000, 2½ hours) and Wanseko (USh10,000, 2¾ hours).

For details of getting to Murchison Falls National Park, see p514.

HOIMA

Hoima is the hub of the Bunyoro Kingdom, the oldest in East Africa. But, despite having more attractions than most Ugandan towns, the city sees few visitors. It's a useful starting point for a back route into Murchison Falls National Park via Lake Albert (see p514), so if you're headed up that way you don't need to go to Masindi first.

Information

Barclays Bank (Main St), west of the centre, is the most useful bank in town as it has an ATM and exchanges cash. You can get online at **Net** (per hr USh3000; 8am-8pm Mon-Sat, noon-8pm Sun), down a dirt road by the mobile phone tower in the centre of town.

Sights

If you call in advance you can visit **Karuziika Palace** (Main St), part-time home of the Bunyoro king, to see the throne room, which is draped with leopard and lion skins and filled with drums, spears, crowns and other traditional items. The king often makes time to meet his subjects, so you could ask to visit at one of those times and say hello. Out front are thatch buildings used during the June 11 Coronation Day Anniversary celebration. To schedule a visit call either the Bunyoro Prime Minister Dr Kiiza Aliba Emmanuel (☎ 0772-625162) or the king's private secretary Yolamu Nsamba (☎ 0752-580946).

On the other side of town, 2km down the Masindi Rd (4km out of Hoima), the **Mparo Tombs** (8am-5pm) is the final resting place of the renowned Bunyoro king Omukama ('King') Chwa II Kabalega and his son. Kabalega was a thorn in the side of the British for much of his reign until he was exiled to the Seychelles in 1899. The tomb is similar in style to Kampala's Kasubi Tombs (p431) on the outside, but quite different inside with his spears, bowls, throne and other personal effects on display above the actual resting place.

For a small tip the caretaker will open the gate and show you inside. A wedding cake-shaped monument in the front memorialises the 1877 meeting of Kabalega and Emin Pasha.

The African Village Guest Farm has a funky little **art museum** (admission USh1000) with traditional and contemporary art plus other odd curiousity from Uganda. And a camel.

Sleeping & Eating

Classic Inn (☎ 0754-285565; s/d USh8000/10,000) A good budget choice in the centre of town, just off Fort Portal Rd by the side-by-side petrol stations. It has pretty clean rooms with shared facilities.

Nsamo Hotel (☎ 0754-134557; s USh12,000, r USh20,000) Once a great place to stay, the aging Nsamo, right near the Classic, is still pretty good.

African Village Guest Farm (☎ 0772-335115; camping USh8000, bandas s/d/f USh30,000/45,000/75,000, deluxe banda USh100,000) One of Uganda's more interesting places to sleep has great *bandas* with balconies on a small dairy farm. Betty and her daughters are great hosts, and there's a well-regarded restaurant (USh5000 to USh7000 for a Ugandan meal with chips) that's popular with locals on weekends looking for an easy escape from town. To get there, head west on Main St and turn left at the sign; continue past St Peter's Anglican Cathedral and the bridge. A *boda-boda* will cost USh1000.

Eco Gardens (☎ 0332-967592; Butiaba Rd; camping US$10, s/d USh40,000/60,000) Offering monkeys rather than cows, these attractive *bandas* are set at the back (bring a torch to walk at night) of a lush garden 2km out of town. There's a little traffic noise, but it's pretty peaceful out here. The restaurant-bar (mains USh6000) has a pool table under the huge thatch roof.

Getting There & Away

Minibuses to Kampala (USh12,000, three hours) run all day while buses (USh10,000, 2½ hours), departing from their own spot next to the taxi park, stop at 2pm. The Post Bus (see p443) goes via Masindi.

A few minibuses to Masindi (USh5000, two hours) use the main taxi park, but most depart from the Petro Uganda station on Kampala Rd.

For Fort Portal it takes two minibuses with a change in Kagadi. The total price is USh20,000 and it usually takes seven hours.

There's also one coaster (USh25,000, six hours) leaving each town on alternate days that make the run directly.

Minibuses also run to Butiaba (USh6000, two hours) in the morning plus Bulisa (USh10,000, three hours) and Wanseko (USh10,000, 3¼ hours) all day long.

MURCHISON FALLS NATIONAL PARK

Uganda's largest **national park** (☎ 0772-746287; admission US$30, saloon cars local/foreign-registered USh20,000/US$50, trucks & 4WDs local/foreign-registered USh30,000/US$50; ☺ booking office 7am-7pm, park gates 7am-6pm) is the best all-rounder in Uganda, with animals in plentiful supply and the raging Murchison Falls a sight to behold. Sir Samuel Baker named Murchison Falls in honour of a president of the Royal Geographical Society, and the park was subsequently named after the falls. The Victoria Nile River flows through the park on its way to Lake Albert.

During the 1960s, Uganda's biggest national park (3893 sq km; 5081 sq km with the adjoining Bugungu and Karuma reserves) was one of Africa's best and as many as 12 launches filled with eager tourists would buzz up the river to the falls each day. The park also used to contain some of the largest concentrations of wildlife in Africa, including as many as 15,000 elephants. Unfortunately, poachers and troops wiped out practically all wildlife, except the more numerous (or less sought-after) herd species (see the boxed text, p513). There are now no rhinos and only a few prides of lions, but other wildlife is recovering fast and you can find good numbers of elephants, giraffes, Ugandan kobs (antelopes), waterbuck, buffaloes, hippos and crocodiles these days. Sitatungas, leopards and spotted hyenas might also be seen and there are rumours that cheetah have returned. Birdlife consists of some 460 species, including quite a few shoebill storks.

Despite this new beginning, the concentrations of game are relatively low, so don't come to Murchison expecting a scene from the Serengeti. Still, we've never heard of anybody going away disappointed in their visit. And, even if there were no animals, the awesome power of Murchison Falls would make this park worth visiting. Once described as the most spectacular thing to happen to the Nile along its 6700km length, the 50m river is squeezed through a 6m gap in the rock and crashes through this narrow gorge with un-

believable power. The 45m waterfall featured in the Katherine Hepburn and Humphrey Bogart film *The African Queen*. Murchison was even stronger back then, but in 1962 massive floods cut a second channel creating the smaller Uhuru Falls 200m to the north.

For more information on the park, pick up a copy of *Murchison Falls Conservation Area Guidebook* (2002) by Shaun Mann at the park office.

Activities

LAUNCH TRIP TO THE FALLS

The three-hour launch trip from Paraa up to the base of the falls is the highlight of the park for most visitors. It sails daily at 9am and 2pm if there's enough demand and costs US$15 per person if there are 10 or more people. You may have to cough up extra if there are fewer, though if tour company clients are on board, the boat will go regardless of the numbers. Paraa Safari Lodge (p513) has its own launch trips at 8.30am and 2.30pm for the same price, but if their boat isn't full, they put passengers onto the park's boat.

There are abundant hippos, crocodiles and buffaloes; thousands of birds, including many fish eagles; and usually elephants along this 17km stretch of the Nile. In the rainy season even shoebills might make an appearance. The animals are there all day long, but the best photos of the falls come on the afternoon trip.

TOP OF THE FALLS

The boat can't get too close to the base of the falls, but there are viewpoints right above it that give you the complete Murchison experience. The concrete pillars are from a short-lived footbridge that was wiped out by the 1962 flood.

An unsigned track leads off from the main road just west of Sambiya River Lodge, and from here it's about a 30-minute drive. The park is planning to add a snack and souvenir shop, plus a US$10 admission fee at this spot.

There's a beautiful **walking trail** from the top down to the river, and the upper stretch of this path offers views of Uhuru Falls. A ranger (US$10 per person) is required on this walk. If you take the morning launch trip, the captain will let you off at the trailhead and a ranger will meet you there. (You won't have to pay the admission fee at the top.) The boat can then pick you up later *if* there's an afternoon

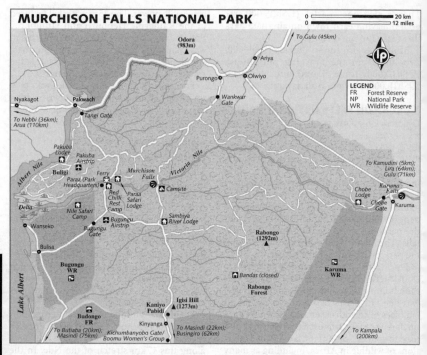

MURCHISON FALLS NATIONAL PARK

LEGEND
FR   Forest Reserve
NP   National Park
WR   Wildlife Reserve

launch. This is also a good way for backpackers to get to the camp site at the top of the falls before returning to Paraa the next morning. The hike takes about 45 minutes from the bottom, and some people find it difficult as there's no shade on the steepest parts.

OTHER BOAT TRIPS

The park offers a daily five-hour **Delta Cruise** (US$150; ☼ departs 7am) downstream to the papyrus-filled delta where the Nile empties into Lake Albert; and, just like the trip upstream to the falls, the wildlife watching is fantastic. You may see leopards lounging in trees and shoebill sightings are very common. Tour companies often book the boat so you should be able to join for a fraction of the whole cost.

Nile Navigation (☎ 0782-169474; www.nilenavigation .com) runs a variety of day- and overnight trips from Pakuba up the rarely explored Albert Nile (they can even take you as far as Sudan) in the *Mardi Gras,* a traditionally built 16-metre flat-bottomed boat. Overnight trips involve camping.

If you'd like to do your own river exploration, the park has a boat for hire at US$50

per hour or USh20,000 per person per hour, whichever is higher. You can also ask around at the hotels or down by the ferry about other boats, but these cost more.

WILDLIFE DRIVES

Pretty much all wildlife watching on land happens in the Buligi area, on the point between the Albert and Victoria Niles. Just about all the park's resident species might be seen in the savannah on the Albert, Queen's and Victoria tracks, and the chances of spotting lions and leopards are quite good. There's very little wildlife south of the river, and driving in from Masindi you'll probably only see baboons and warthogs, though various antelope sometimes come out to play.

Drives can't begin before 7am and you'll want to budget a minimum of four hours to get out there and back. Paraa Safari Lodge (opposite) offers game drives for US$160 while Sambiya River Lodge (p514) charges just US$130. Budget travellers sometimes have luck hanging out at the ferry and finding space in someone's vehicle. Those with their own vehicle should definitely take a UWA ranger-guide (US$20) to boost their chances of close encounters.

CHIMPANZEE TRACKING
The chimp visits are at Kaniyo Pabidi, officially part of the park but operated separately. See p515 for all the details.

NATURE WALKS
The 1½km guided **nature walk** (US$10 per person) along the north bank of the Nile by Paraa Safari Lodge (right) is pretty much only done by bird-watchers as you're not likely to see many other animals.

SPORT FISHING
Murchison is a popular place to fish for the gargantuan Nile perch, and there's now an annual fishing competition here if you fancy yourself as a serious angler. The normal catch ranges 20 to 60kg, but the record haul is 108kg. A permit costs US$70/120/150 for one/two/three days. You can fish from the shore (many people walk down from the top of the falls) or get a boat. Red Chilli Rest Camp (right) has small fishing boats for US$150/300 per half-/full-day. Red Chilli and Parra Safari Lodge (right) have gear for hire, as do (completely unofficially) some of the rangers.

Other fish lurking below the surface include electric catfish and tiger fish. For more information, check out **Fishing Murchison** (www.fishingmu rchison.com).

Sleeping & Eating
New accommodation is planned both in and outside the park, including a new place built by Backpackers Hostel (p435) from Kampala and renovations of the old Chobe Lodge in the far east of the park and Pakuba Lodge in the northwest. Both have great river-view settings.

There's also talk of something new happening to the disued *bandas* in the Rabongo Forest in the park's remote southeast sector, an area with many chimps.

PARAA
Red Chilli Rest Camp (☎ 0772-509150; www.red chillihideaway.com; camping USh10,000, safari tent d USh25,000, banda without bathroom tw USh40,000, banda tw/q USh50,000/100,000) The popular Red Chilli team from Kampala (see p435) brings a budget option to Murchison. The *bandas* are very nice, and the restaurant-bar is set under a huge thatched roof. There are sandwiches (USh3500 to USh6000) for lunch and set dinners (USh6500 to USh8500) at night plus the signature hippo breakfast so popular in Kampala.

Paraa Safari Lodge (☎ 0312-260260; www.paraa lodge.com; s/d/ste incl full board US$133/210/270; 🖳 🐾) On the northern bank of the river, this hotel-style lodge has a great location and excellent facilities, including a swim-up bar. From across the river it looks rather like a POW camp, but up close it's lovely and the rooms are pretty much four-star standard. The business centre has the only internet access (USh3000 per 15 minutes) in the park.

ELSEWHERE IN THE PARK
For information on accommodation at Kaniyo Pabidi, near Kichumbanyobo Gate, see p515.

Top of the Falls Campsite (camping USh15,000) This simple spot has a very nice position right on the river, though no waterfall views. You'll need to be self-sufficient, as, for the time being, the only facilities are a pit toilet. At dusk you can watch a mass exodus of bats from a nearby cave. See Top Of The Falls p511 for directions on how to get here without your own vehicle.

UGANDA

'ALWAYS LOOK ON THE BRIGHT SIDE...'

Although it seems like sacrilege to say it, the mass slaughter of wildlife that took place in Murchison Falls National Park may have been a good thing from an ecological viewpoint. Before Idi Amin's regime the park was carrying many more animals (particularly elephants, with herds of more than 500 commonly seen) than it could sustain. The elephants alone, which numbered more than 15,000, chomped their way through 1.4 million tonnes of vegetation each year! Add to this the 26,000 buffaloes, plus herds of hartebeest, kobs and hippos, and the scale of the ecological problem can be appreciated.

The wiping out of most of the large animals has given the environment here a breather, and while it was obviously a major disaster from a wildlife point of view, it means that the park's ecology is now in excellent condition.

Bush Camping (camping USh20,000) For a fantastic night in the wild (and an early start on your morning game drive), sleep with the wildlife out at Delta Point overlooking Lake Albert in the Buligi section of the park. The park has no tents, so the armed guard (compulsory) who accompanies you will probably want to sleep in your vehicle. Book the trip at the park office.

Sambiya River Lodge (☎ 0465-423174; www .afritourstravel.com; bandas without bathroom s/d USh60,000/100,000, bandas s/d USh150,000/85,000, cottages s/d US$85/140; ☒) Sambiya Stream is more like it. Located just off the main track from Masindi, beside the turn-off to the falls, this is a modern, comfortable lodge in a secluded spot with a very attractive restaurant-bar area. Their cottages are very nicely appointed while the self-contained *bandas* are okay. The smallest *bandas* aren't worth considering at this price.

OUTSIDE THE PARK

Wanseko has a few not-so-nice lodges to choose from should you get stuck out there.

Boomu Women's Group (☎ 0772-448950; www.boomuwomensgroup.org; camping USh4000, s/d USh10,000/20,000) Just before the Kichumbanyobo Gate, this small set-up offers a chance to learn how rural Ugandans live, and your money funds a pre-school. The five thatched-roof shared-bathroom *bandas*, a mix of concrete and traditional (ie mud), are great for the price. Even if you don't plan to sleep here, you should make some time for a visit. Local meals cost USh4500 to USh6000, and if you call before leaving Masindi, they'll have breakfast waiting for you. If you have more time, their fascinating cooking tour (USh8000) lets you follow the preparation of your meal starting in the farm field. Call from Masindi and they'll send a *boda-boda* to pick you up for USh5000. For another USh4000 they'll deliver you to Kaniyo Pabidi.

Nile Safari Camp (☎ 0414-258273; www.geolodges africa.com; camping USh10,000, s/d incl full board US$150/260; ☒) This fantastic lodge has an unrivalled position, high up on the south bank of the Victoria Nile River, with sweeping views over the water and tons of monkeys and birds in the trees below. Accommodation is in comfortable permanent tents and wooden cottages, each with a river-view balcony. There's also an atmospheric bar and dining area (set-menu three-course lunch and dinner USh25,000), as well as a swimming pool with a view. Ask for directions to get here because the unmarked shortcut from Paraa is more convenient than the main entrance, which is 15km from Bulisa then a further 11.5km north. Both roads are very rough. They can pick you up in Paraa by boat.

Getting There & Away

AIR

Several of the top-notch safari companies include charter flights to Murchison, which has two airstrips (Pakuba and Bungungu).

ROAD

The park headquarters at Paraa is on the southern bank of the Victoria Nile. From Masindi there's the choice of the direct route through the Kichumbanyobo Gate or the longer but more scenic route, which heads west to Lake Albert (p516) and then enters the park via the western Bugungu Gate. A round trip might be best for those with a vehicle, entering via one route and leaving by the other. Both routes go through Budongo Forest Reserve (opposite), a recommended stopover. Don't be lulled into inattentive driving on the almost relentlessly straight road north from Masindi. There are many rollovers and the very subtle corners.

With security now restored to northern Uganda, the northern gates, Tangi (reached from Pakwach) and Wankwar (from Purongo), are now viable options again; and are perhaps the best options because your wildlife watching will begin the moment you enter the park. The Chobe Gate near Karuma Falls on the Gulu Rd is scheduled to be ready by 2010, though you'll want to inquire about the condition of the road.

Getting from Masindi directly to Paraa by public transport isn't possible. With a bit of bargaining you can charter a special-hire taxi for around USh120,000 including fuel and the driver's park fees. The UWA office (p508) and all the hotels can help you find a driver. Rounding out the day with a wildlife viewing drive will bump the price up to at least USh180,000. **Yebo Tours** (Map p509; ☎ 0772-637493; Masindi Port Rd) in Masindi hires 4WDs for US$80 per day while the New Court View Hotel (p509) charges USh150,000; these prices include a driver, but not fuel.

Park vehicles come to Masindi a few times a week and they'll take you to Paraa if they have room, but it's a matter of luck as they're often full. The park office in Masindi (p508) will know if something is available. You could also try chatting to other tourists. Hang out at Travellers' Corner Restaurant during lunch and at the New Court View or Masindi hotels at night, as these are popular rest stops. If this doesn't work, you could hitch along the road next to the Masindi Hotel, but you'll likely have more success if you take a *boda-boda* (USh8000 to USh10,000) 21km to the Kichumbanyobo Gate where the guards will help you get a ride. Getting out of the park is much easier as you can find out where vehicles are heading to and arrange a ride in advance.

Besides hitching, the cheapest way into the park is to get to Bulisa or Wanseko, an interesting fishing village where the Nile empties into Lake Albert. Minibuses run to these neighbouring towns daily from Hoima and Masindi for USh10,000. Either go as far as Bulisa, from where you can negotiate for a *boda-boda* to take you to Paraa for around USh35,000 (*Boda-boda* drivers are required to pay park admission of USh15,000 but often don't, so negotiate a fee without the admission costs and you might get lucky.) or continue the 6km to Wanseko and then negotiate with the minibus drivers to continue to Paraa as a special-hire.

The special-hire cost should be much cheaper (perhaps as low as USh60,000) from Wanseko than Masindi, but you have two strikes against you. First, the drivers hold all the cards in negotiating, and they know it. (Are you really prepared to go back to Masindi and pay the same price from there?) Second, it's very rare for people to travel to the park this way so most drivers haven't done the trip before and aren't likely to take a chance on offering you a price they're not positive is worth if for them.

TOURS

There's also, of course, the option of joining an organised safari from Kampala. Most safari companies have Murchison-specific packages, plus Paraa Safari Lodge (p513) and Sambiya River Lodge (opposite) have their own all-inclusive multi-day trips.

The three-day budget trips offered by Red Chilli Hideaway (see p435) in Kampala leave at least thrice weekly in the high season, and include transport, park entrance fees, a launch trip, a wildlife drive and accommodation for US$210 per person, making them one of the best deals in East Africa. Backpackers Hostel (p435) has similar but slightly broader Murchison trips that include chimp tracking and all meals for around US$300, another great deal.

Getting Around
BOAT

A vehicle ferry crosses the river at Paraa. The crossings take just a few minutes and are scheduled at least every two hours between 7am and 7pm. The ferry holds just eight vehicles, but will make as many crossings as necessary to get everyone over. The one-day fare is USh2000 for passengers and USh20,000 for cars and light trucks. Unscheduled crossings cost USh100,000. Ferry fees are payable at a small booth near the landing.

CAR

Tracks within the park are generally well maintained, and though 4WD is highly recommended, saloon cars should have little trouble getting to the main places (except Nile Safari Lodge); at least with a good local driver at the wheel. However, some tracks, especially in the Buligi area, where most wildlife drives are done, can be treacherous in the wet season.

Fuel is available on the northern side of the Victoria Nile River at Paraa, but it costs about 10% more than in Masindi.

BUDONGO FOREST RESERVE

The Budongo Forest Reserve is a large (825 sq km) tract of virgin tropical forest on the southern fringes of Murchison Falls National Park. Its main attractions are chimps and birds (366 species), but the huge mahogany trees are also worth a look. It's a great add-on to your Murchison Falls National Park visit.

The **Budongo Ecotourism Development Programme** (☎ 0465-424348; www.budongo.org), operated in part by the Jane Goodall Institute, runs two tourism sites, Kaniyo Pabidi Tourist Site and Busingiro Tourist Site. It's best to book trips and rooms in advance, but you can just show up and hope space is available.

Kaniyo Pabidi

Kaniyo Pabidi Tourist Site is on the main park road, 29km north of Masindi and inside the southern boundary of Murchison Falls National Park. You have to pay the park entry fee on top of the site fees. This was the first place in Uganda to employ a female ranger, and Sauda still works here.

Chimpanzee tracking ($40 per person) takes place daily and there's a limit of 24 people. Trekkers must be over 15 years old. Visibility is good and walking is easy as the terrain is level. Walks last two to four hours and once you find the chimps, you get to spend an hour with them. Two lucky visitors (October through June only) are allowed to spend a whole day for US$100 per person.

Also worthwhile are the **forest walks** (US$10/15 for 1½-/four-hours) which pass through East Africa's last remaining mahogany forest. The largest specimens are 60m tall and 300-years old. Black-and-white colobus and duiker are commonly seen. The four-hour walks climb Pabidi Hill from which you can see most of the park and Lake Albert.

Those on **bird-watching walks** (US$10/15 for half-/full-day) usually seek Puvel's Illadopsis, which isn't known anywhere else in East Africa. Other highly sought species are the rufous-sided broadbill and white-naped pigeon.

Lodging options consist of very nice cabins (singles/doubles/tr US$50/85/100) and dorms (US$15) with hot water and solar electric. For dinner you have the choice of Italian (US$10 per person) or local meals (USh3000).

Kaniyo Pabidi isn't served by public transport, but it's possible to arrange a charter from Masindi for about USh50,000 or take a *boda-boda* for about USh10,000 (more if the guards make the driver pay admission fees).

Busingiro

Busingiro Tourist Site, 40km west of Masindi on the Bulisa Rd, is for the birds. Or rather bird-watchers. It's a great place to add yellow-footed flycatcher and African pitta to your life list. There used to be chimp tracking here too, but when the chimps lost their fear of humans they started raiding local farms, forcing an end to the program. The chimps are still here though, so you may get lucky and meet them.

Fifteen kilometres away is the **Royal Mile**, regarded by many to offer the best bird-watching in the whole country, both because there are some rare species but mostly because sightings are so easy. The bird-list exceeds 350 species including several types of flycatchers, sunbirds, kingfishers, hornbills and eagles. At dusk it's possible to view bat hawks. Vincent

Odama has been enthusiastically recommended as a birding guide.

Guided walks cost the same as at Kaniyo Pabidi, but Busingiro and the Royal Mile lie outside the national park so there are no additional fees.

Lodging options here are poor. Busingiro Tourism Site has an overpriced but peaceful campsite (US$10 per person; bring your own food) and **Nyabyeya Forestry College** (☎ 0772-536108; r without bathroom USh18,000, s/d USh20,000/23,000) has a basic guesthouse. Breakfast costs another USh2500 while local lunches and dinners are USh4000.

Busingiro is on the route used by minibuses heading for Bulisa (see p514). The trip costs USh5000 and can take about an hour. You'll need your own vehicle to get to the Royal Mile. The first turn-off is 25km from Masindi, marked by the Nyabyeya Forestry College signpost, and there's another, also with a college sign, closer to Busingiro. Locals don't seem to know the name Royal Mile, but if you ask for the place where *muzungu* go to look at birds, someone should be able to direct you. It's about three kilometres from the forestry college.

LAKE ALBERT

Lake Albert, part of the Rift Valley system extending from the Middle East to Mozambique, runs for 160km (by 35km wide) along the border between Uganda and DRC. The first European to spot the lake was the British explorer Sir Samuel Baker in 1864, who named it after Albert, prince consort of Queen Victoria. Oil has been found below its surface and pumping should begin soon.

Butiaba

Most of the people who live by the lake make their living by fishing its waters, and a visit to this large, busy fishing village makes an interesting diversion. The approach is wonderful as you wind down the Albertine Escarpment, with sweeping views of the lake and the Blue Mountains of DRC running along the far shore. The village itself is poor, but the few old buildings from the colonial era still standing (just barely) are a fading reminder that it was once a prosperous port. At the end of a palm and flower covered peninsula is the rusting **wreck** of the 207-foot SS *Robert Coryndon*, once part of the East African Railways transport network. Locals call it 'The Ship'.

The best time to visit Butiaba is early morning when the catch is brought ashore in small fishing boats. Nile perch weighing in excess of 20kg are quite common and a massive 50-kilogrammer comes up about once a week. The Butiaba Landing Site, where most of the fishermen unload their catch and repair their nets, is at the far end of town.

Spending the night here would definitely not be your ordinary vacation. There are several rough guesthouses, the best of which is the **Lunar Bar** (☎ 0392-945339; s/d USh5,000-7,000/ USh10,000), but best is a relative term. A better bet is **Neul Tourist Camp** (☎ 0782-958788; www.neul .co.ug; camping per tent USh15,000, r & bandas USh30,000) with lots of palm trees and a small beach for the Costa del Congo experience.

Minibuses come here from Masindi (USh7000, two hours) and Hoima (USh6000, two hours) The road to the village, which branches off the Masindi–Wanseko road, is in excellent shape, courtesy of the oil workers' camp along it.

Kibiro

South of Butiaba, Kibiro is a remote village surrounded by hot springs that has been nominated as a Unesco World Heritage Site. These days most resident fish and/or raise cattle, but women from about 30 families still extract salt from the soil in much the same way their ancestors did for perhaps a thousand years, only today they use metal instead of pottery. When you arrive, introduce yourself to the chairman and then (for a small tip, of course) someone will show you the salt mining process, which involves repeatedly piling and spreading the salty soil for a week and then boiling out the accumulated salt.

There's no road to Kibiro, but you can drive a saloon car to within 3km before hiking down the rocky escarpment. Park at the home of the friendly Kabiribwa family for USh1000. The road towards Kibiro begins 21km north of Hoima at Kigorobya and it's a 7km drive to the end. There's no accommodation here, but if you really want to spend the night you can sleep at the health centre.

Kabwoya Wildlife Reserve

This beautiful reserve offers an entirely different Lake Albert experience. It protects a large chunk of the Rift Valley's last ecologically intact savannah between Murchison Falls National Park (p511) and Toro-Semliki Wildlife Reserve (p477). While the tide has been turned against poachers and cattle grazers, truth be told, this isn't a top wildlife watching destination since populations are mostly low. Still, buffaloes, Jackson's hartebeests, waterbuck, chimpanzees and leopards all roam field and forest, and the birdlist stands at 460 species. Cheetah and giraffe could be coming soon and this is likely to be the first place in Uganda where rhino are reintroduced in a truly wild setting.

Kabwoya probably wouldn't be worth a detour right now if it weren't for the superb **Lake Albert Safari Lodge** (☎ 0772-221003; www.lakeal bertlodge.com; camping US$15, safari tents incl full board s/d US$95/150, cottages incl full board s/d US$125/190; ☒), whose owner, Bruce Martin (with funding from USAID) is almost singlehandedly reviving the reserve (entrance fee US$10). The lodge makes the most of the sunset views and the spacious stone and thatch cottages offer good value (unlike the non-self-contained tents) compared to similar places in national parks. Excellent locally grown food is served *alfresco* in the dining room or, if you wish, all-*fresco* out in the bush. Many expats head out here for a quick dose of repose, but there's plenty to do, from horseback rides to walking trails to boat cruises to fishing village visits, for those who don't like sitting still.

The lodge is nearly due west of Hoima, near Kaiso. There's no public transport, but if you're driving between Murchison Falls and Fort Portal, it's an ideal journey-break. Because of oil exploration in the lake area, the road should be paved sometime in 2009.

GULU

Gulu is a city in transition. Though the north's largest town hosted the biggest military base in the government's war against the LRA, it still suffered many attacks. But in a sure sign of optimism, seemingly half the city is now under construction. Store shelves are full and people are arriving from elsewhere in the country hoping to cash in on the coming boom. But not everybody is feeling the glow. Even as the IDP camps around town are closing, there are still many people too frightened to return to their land; and many orphans never got an education and lack any skills needed to land a job. Despite the best efforts of an alphabet soup of NGOs, for many people the despair is growing rather than shrinking. It's perhaps not surprising that crime is a growing concern

UGANDA

in Gulu, so be cautious at night; especially on the outskirts of town.

Information

All the major banks have branches here. **Crane Bank** (Nehru Rd) will change cash and American Express travellers cheques. Internet cafés are common, especially in the lower half of downtown near Hotel Kakanyero.

Street names aren't very helpful for finding your way around since every block has its own.

Sights & Activities

Gulu's only real attraction is the little **Luo Talent Centre** (☎ 0777-074458; Kampala Rd; ☼ Tue-Sun), 2km from the centre. It hosts a variety of events, from theatre to movies to philosophy discussions. There's traditional Acholi music every Saturday night at 5pm.

Also of interest is large-and-lively **Gulu Main Market** where you'll find traditional Acholi cloth on sale.

VOLUNTEERING

A city that has suffered as much as Gulu, can always use a helping hand.

HEALS (☎ 0774-099919) Founded by a local dynamo, HEALS (Health, Education And Literacy/Sports) offers affected children 'play therapy' through dance, music, arts and sports. Volunteers can teach kids to draw, polka, play the guitar or anything else. They can also use help in the office on the outskirts of town.

St Jude Children's Home (☎ 0782-896897) People are always welcome to stop by this orphanage to teach or play with the children even if only for a day. It's 3km west of town.

Founded by the makers of the documentary of the same name, **Invisible Children** (☎ 0471-432583; www.invisiblechildren.com; 101 Acholi Rd) lends a helping hand to area students and schools. It offers three-month internships and can recommend other volunteer opportunities in the area. With a little advanced notice, they'll take you to visit the schools they work with.

Sleeping

Gulu has a good number of good hotels, but because of all the aid workers passing through, prices are usually higher than they should be. According to locals, the cheap hotels inside the bus park cannot be considered secure.

HEALS (☎ 0774-099919; dm USh10,000) This charity has two simple dorm rooms, and the kids

will be a great welcoming committee when you arrive. The only knock is its tough-to-find location hidden in a village-like setting on the outskirts of town.

Hotel Binen (☎ 0772-405038; Coronation Rd; s/d without bathroom USh11,000/17,000) Far less tatty than most of the competition in this price range, though try to look at several rooms as not all mattresses are equal. Bathrooms are shared. It's a few blocks west of the bus station.

JoJo's Palace (☎ 0471-435770; 5 Market St; s without bathroom USh20,000; s/d USh30,000/45,000) Easily the best value in town, it's bright, spotless, friendly and priced-right. What more do you need? It's below the bus station and then a short jaunt to the right.

Acholi Hotel (☎ 0471-432880; Elizabeth Rd; s/d/ste USh60,000/120,000/150,000; ⌘ ⌘ ⌘) This large compound in the northern section of the city is currently the smartest option in town, but staying here at these prices isn't so smart. Its saving grace is the range of extras including a pool (USh7000 for non-guests), sauna and in-room fridges.

Eating & Drinking

Hotel Binen (☎ 0772-405038; Coronation Rd; mains USh1500-3500) A good place to try northern Ugandan food such as *malakwang* (a sour, leafy green vegetable) and *lapena* (pigeon peas).

Kope Café (☎ 0777-649558; Olya Rd; mains USh4000-6000; ☼ 7.30am-late) This colourful Western-style coffeehouse south of the market has a small menu with Indian, pizzas and salads, plus good coffees and breakfasts. Although it's a *muzungu* magnet, prices are kept low enough that many locals eat here too. Sunday is movie night. All proceeds go to HEALS.

KSP (15 Queen's Ave; mains USh5000-8500) This oddly attractive place with rather average service is currently the only Indian restaurant in town. And for many travellers, therein lies the attraction as it offers a break from Ugandan food.

Havana Pub (Aliker Rd) Gulu's most popular club is a rollicking place where people drink as much whisky and wine as beer and live bands take the stage at weekends. It's in the heart of downtown, below the bus station; and if it doesn't suit your fancy there are many more watering holes nearby.

Da Pub (Nehru Rd; ☼ Tue-Sun) A little more low-key than the nearby Havana, and thus a little more popular with *muzungu*.

Italian Wine (Gulu Senior Rd) A little concrete box next to Crane Bank selling imported spirits from far more nations than the sign signifies, plus bags of penne pasta.

Getting There & Away

Gulu has a busy taxi/bus park right in the centre of town. Buses and minibuses go between Kampala and Gulu (USh20,000, five hours) all day long. Much of this road is new and in excellent shape, and soon the rest of it, between Kampala and the Masindi Rd junction will be resurfaced: drivers expect to 'fly' to Kampala in as little as three hours. There's also a Gulu–Kampala Post Bus: see p443 for details.

Minibuses to Masindi (USh15,000, four hours) are also infrequent, so it may be quicker to go to Kafu Junction on the main highway and catch a connection there. There's one bus a day to Soroti (USh20,000, six hours).

For Arua, you'll need to head south to the ramshackle truck-stop town of Karuma (USh8000, one hour) and hop on an Arua-bound bus (USh12,000, four hours) there. Just north of Karuma town, the road crosses the Nile River at beautiful Karuma Falls (sit on the right-hand side when coming from Kampala for views), formerly a notorious ambush site for the LRA. Don't let the military see you taking any photographs here without getting their permission or you'll be looking at heaps of hassle. There are lots of begging baboons around here.

All buses to Juba, Sudan originate in Kampala, but they stop in Gulu between 4am and 8am to pick up passengers by the UTL tower along the Kampala Rd. The price is USh70,000 and the journey will take about 10 hours if the road remains dry. For a masochistic adventure, you could also hop one of the trucks leaving from the bus park every morning. The price is a little less, but it may take two or three days to get there.

Eagle Air (☎ 0414-344292; www.flyeagleuganda.com) flies here on Monday, Wednesday and Friday afternoons, charging US$125/225 one-way/return from Kampala.

ARUA

Arua is the West Nile region's largest town and the distribution centre for relief efforts in southern Sudan and northeastern DRC, the latter just 10km away. Idi Amin grew up in Arua, and still has many family members living here. Near the end of his life Amin rebuilt one of his homes here with the desire to return, though he never did.

Arua isn't an unpleasant place, and the roads leading to it feature several scenic spots, but, unless you're an aid worker, it's hard to think of a reason to venture out here. If you do make it, however, you'll want to budget some trawling time in the markets. The **Arua Market** is for foods while the next-door **Gaga Market**, one of Uganda's largest, sells just about everything else. One section stocks nothing but West African wax-print fabrics smuggled (along with cigarettes and petrol) in from Congo. There are plenty of tailors around if you can't wait for a new dress. You could also make a few divots in one of the world's more unlikely locations for a proper golf course.

Information

Arua's hectic centre holds several internet cafés, well-stocked supermarkets and banks with internationally-linked ATMs. For changing cash, **Shumuk Forex Bureau** (5 Avenue St) next to Centenary Bank has slightly better rates and slightly longer hours than the banks.

Sleeping & Eating

Twin Lodge (Adumi Rd; r USh8,000) As you walk into this rather rough place, hidden in the back of the building along Arua's noisy main drag, you sure won't be expecting much, so when you see the rooms you won't be disappointed. You will, however, find them pretty clean.

Dolphin Guesthouse (☎ 0712-190206; 30 Afra Rd; s/d 15,000/20,000 without bathroom, r USh25,000) Simple but clean, and in a whole other league than Twin Lodge, this new hotel also has a good little restaurant with a big menu of Indian and Chinese food. (If you take a *boda-boda* here, make sure the driver doesn't mistakenly deliver you to Ediofe, the village by the large Protestant cathedral.)

Hotel Delambiance (☎ 0772-464311; 15 Afra Rd; r USh20,000-40,000) Arua's former top lodge, across the road from Dolphin, has gotten a tad tatty these days, but it still offers comfy rooms, increasing more in size than quality until you hit the USh40,000 mark, in which case you get satellite TV and decorative furniture.

White Castle (☎ 0772-880830; www.whitecastlehotel.com; Km 4 Nebbi Rd; s USh52,000, d USh72,000-92,000, ste USh202,000; 🖳 🐒) The best hotel in town is quite a way out of town, which is a shame for those without their own transport because Arua's best restaurant (mains USh8000 to USh16,000) is also here serving the usual international roster plus wood-fired pizzas. There are carpeted rooms and cottages in attractive gardens with flowers and fountains. Besides the pool (USh5000 for non-guests), there's a big playground for the kids.

Several of the hotels along Weatherhead Park Ln, in the leafy suburb of Anyafio, just 2km from the centre, have garden restaurants that make pleasant destinations for dinner. At some, such as **Oasis Inn** (☎ 0392-948125), the action turns to drinking and even a bit of dancing on Friday nights.

Getting There & Away

If you're leaving Arua, get up early since most transport has already departed by 7.30am. Several bus companies run between Kampala and Arua (USh23,000; seven to eight hours). They all arrive/depart from their own offices on Transport Rd near Barclays Bank and downhill from here on Rhino Camp Rd. See p519 for all the details on travel to Gulu.

If you're headed to Sudan, the best way to go is in the Land Cruisers bought in Kampala and driven to Juba where they are sold. They park at Metino Stage along Rhino Camp Rd (below Barclays Bank) looking for passengers just about every morning. The going rate is USh60,000 (USH30,000 to Yei) and they can make it to Juba in as little as eight hours, much faster than the few minibuses and buses that charge USh50,000.

Eagle Air (☎ 0414-344292; www.flyeagleuganda.com) flies here daily, charging US$135/235 one-way/return to/from Kampala.

UGANDA DIRECTORY

This section covers information specific to Uganda. For general information applicable to the region, see p602.

ACCOMMODATION
Camping

Almost every popular destination in Uganda offers some sort of camping, so it's worth carrying a tent if you're on a budget, although the cheapest hotel rooms often cost less than camping. In provincial towns, many fancy hotels allow camping on their grounds. While this won't be the cheapest place to pitch a tent, prices are usually reasonable since they include the use of swimming pools and other facilities.

See National Parks & Reserves (opposite) for more information.

Hotels

Hotels range from fleapit to five-star, and even in many smaller towns there's plenty of choice. You can even count on very small towns having at least one basic (and perhaps clean) lodge. There are few genuine upmarket hotels outside Kampala, Entebbe and some national parks, but all sizeable cities have something at about three-star quality. Keep in mind that in most of Uganda if you ask for a hotel you'll be directed to a restaurant, so if you want a place to sleep inquire about accommodation or lodging. Also, be sure to always read the facility's list of rules: not because you're likely to flaunt them, but for some unintended comic relief.

In Uganda, the term *banda* means any detached sleeping quarters, as does cottage or bungalow; the later two usually signifying something of better quality. Checkout time is usually 10am, but we've seen it as early as 8.30am.

Uganda does not offer exceptional value accommodation when compared with some other parts of Africa, and in Kampala there's currently a lot of price gouging going on, but a surfeit of empty rooms should bring prices down. Outside the capital, single/double rooms are available from around USh5000/9000, rooms with bathroom usually start at USh12,000/16,000 and for another USh5000 to USh10,000 breakfast will be included. Modern, comfortable rooms with satellite TV (although

---

PRACTICALITIES

- Uganda uses the metric system.

- Electricity in Uganda is 240V, 50 cycles, and British three-pin plugs are used.

- Local newspapers include the government-owned daily the *New Vision* and the more independent *Daily Monitor*. International magazines, such as *Time* and *The Economist*, are readily available in Kampala.

- The state-run UBC and the private WBS are the main stations available on broadcast TV, but most hotels and bars have satellite TV for international news and sport.

- BBC World Service broadcasts on 101.3MHz and the phenomenally popular Capital FM can be found at 91.3MHz.

often only the same channel that's turned on in the restaurant/bar) can be found from single/double USh40,000/50,000. Even most budget places, except at the very bottom of the price range, have hot water and attached restaurants. In Kampala a few hotels offer in-room wireless, but this is still uncommon. Top-end hotels and lodges start at around US$150 and can go much higher. Out in remote places, like national parks or Lake Bunyonyi, hot-water showers may be of the bucket kind, no matter what price you're paying. Same sex couples, regardless of whether or not they're a 'couple', will usually have to pay a premium for twin rooms, which have two beds, over the standard double.

The most expensive places almost always exclude the 18% value-added tax (VAT) and often a deceptive 5% to 10% 'service charge' from their quoted prices. We do what they should (and what all other hotels do) and include it. All lodging is also subject to a Local Hotel Tax of up to US$2 and another 'tourism tax' is in the works.

National Parks & Reserves

The main national parks have a wide range of accommodation available, including luxury lodges and tented camps with outlandish prices. Always ask for discounts at these top-end places. The less-popular parks have simple camp sites and basic *bandas*.

Camping in national parks costs USh15,000 per person per night, and tents are sometimes available for hire (the quality is usually low) for an additional USh10,000. Inexplicably, *bandas* are usually cheaper: USh10,000/15,000 for singles/doubles with shared facilities. Few national park camp sites have canteens so it's best to bring food (which someone will cook for you for a small fee); in most cases you can buy beans, rice and maybe chicken or fish from park staff. A few parks also have 'student centres', with dormitory accommodation that can be used by travellers if no school group is there.

Accommodation charges don't include park entry fees, so many independent travellers opt to stay just outside the national parks where the choice of accommodation usually mirrors the quality of what's available inside.

ACTIVITIES
Bird-Watching

Uganda is one of the world's best bird-watching destinations, a twitcher's fantasy offering 1041 species; that's almost half the total found in all of Africa. Even non–bird-watchers will be enthralled by the diversity of beauty among Uganda's birdlife.

The country's unique geographical position, where eastern, western, northern and southern ranges merge, allows visitors to view the 24 Albertine rift endemics (such as African green broadbill and handsome francolin) in Semuliki National Park (p477) on the same trip as dry-season eastern specials (karamoja apalis and red-billed oxpecker) in Kidepo Valley National Park (p469).

The country's top guides are members of the **Uganda Bird Guides Club** (www.ugandabirdguides .org). **Bird Uganda** (www.birduganda.com) has detailed site reports for all national parks and many other hot-spots.

Visiting bird-watchers may wish to contact the **Young Birders Club** (☎ 0777-912938; youngbirders @birduganda.com) to see about joining the kids (most aged seven to 12), on one of their outings in the Kampala area.

Caving

Uganda's principal underground attraction is Garama Cave (p500) in Mgahinga Gorilla National Park. Spelunkers may want to inquire with park staff at Mt Elgon National Park (p462) since there are a number of unexplored caves on the mountain, including one that locals insist links Uganda to Kenya.

Chimpanzee Tracking

Chimpanzee tracking is a very popular activity in Uganda and there are several places where it's possible. The main ones are Kyambura Gorge (p485) in Queen Elizabeth National Park; Kibale Forest National Park (p475); and Budongo Forest Reserve (p515), part of Murchison Falls National Park. Another good option is the little-known Toro-Semliki Wildlife Reserve (p477). It has a thinner forest and so often offers the best viewing, and, because there's plenty of savannah around, the little guys are a little more likely to be seen walking upright. Although the troop at the private Kigaju Forest (p508) has yet to be habituated, it's found quite often; and this is by far the cheapest place to seek out chimps. The half-habituated troop in the Kalinzu Forest Reserve (p485) near Queen Elizabeth National Park is only found about half the time.

As with tracking the gorillas, you get to spend one hour with humans' closest living

UGANDA

relatives; although they move much further and faster, so the chance of actually finding them is a little less certain. Still, the likelihood is quite high (80% to 90%); and unlike the gorillas who sometimes just laze around doing next to nothing, chimpanzees put on a show, swinging through the trees, fighting, mating and generally whooping it up. All this makes the day-long encounters that are also available at Kibale and Budongo very appealing.

Although golden monkeys lack the cache of chimpanzees, tracking this very rare primate in Mgahinga Gorilla National Park (p500) is also rewarding.

Fishing

The Victoria Nile River in Murchison Falls National Park is a favoured habitat of the massive Nile perch, some weighing more than 100kg. See p513 for details. Some companies also offer fishing trips on Lake Victoria, though overfishing has really taken its toll here.

If mountain streams are more your style, call **Mt Elgon Fly Fishing** (☎ 0772-900451).

Gorilla Tracking

Gorilla tracking is one of the major draws for travellers in Uganda. These gentle giants live in two national parks: Bwindi Impenetrable (p488) and Mgahinga Gorilla (p499). For more information on gorilla tracking see p75.

Hiking & Trekking

Uganda has always had a strong attraction among the dedicated trekking fraternity, mainly for the opportunities presented by the Rwenzori Mountains (p481) and Mt Elgon (p462), which are both gorgeous, but attract far fewer climbers than Mt Kilimanjaro and Mt Kenya. The Rwenzoris or 'Mountains of the Moon' present one of the most challenging mountain experiences in Africa and offer the chance for genuine climbing if you attempt one of the peaks. However, Mt Elgon is a more affordable option.

It's also possible to walk up the three volcanoes at Mgahinga Gorilla National Park (p499).

White-Water Rafting & Kayaking

The Nile River offers world-class white-water with some Grade Five rapids waiting for brave boaters. The companies are all based near Jinja (p451), but doing it as a day-trip out of Kampala doesn't cost any extra since transport is included in the price. For details, see the boxed text, p454.

Wildlife Watching

There are four national parks in Uganda that offer the opportunity for wildlife drives: Murchison Falls (p512), Queen Elizabeth (p484), Kidepo Valley (p469) and Lake Mburo (p502). With more mammal and bird species than any park in Uganda, Queen Elizabeth offers the greatest variety; however, Murchison Falls offers the larger mammals in greater concentration and also giraffes, which aren't found at Queen Elizabeth. At both parks you're very likely to elephants, buffaloes, hippos, bushbucks and kobs; and, although it's not so easy to spot predators, with a bit of luck you'll also see lions and leopards.

Wildlife drives at Lake Mburo are very popular because it's the only place in the south with zebras and eland. These beauties can also be found in seldom-visited Kidepo Valley, which offers the chance to see cheetahs, ostriches, kudus, bat-eared foxes and many other animals found in no other part of Uganda. Game drives are available in Toro-Semliki Wildlife Reserve (p477) too, although most people come here for chimpanzees.

Regardless of where you drive and what you're seeking, taking a UWA ranger-guide will almost guarantee more and better encounters. It must be stated again that Uganda doesn't have the mammalian bounty of Kenya and Tanzania, but, it also doesn't have the masses. In Uganda, two trucks watching the same scene is a crowd.

Advantages to driving include covering more ground and getting closer to the animals, but nothing beats stalking animals on foot, and you can do this in the company of an armed ranger-guide in all parks mentioned above except Murchison Falls. Of course, bird-watching and gorilla and chimp tracking take place on foot too.

BOOKS

See the Arts section p424 for information about notable literature that has come out of Uganda.

Guidebooks

Keen bird-watchers will be best served by *The Birds of East Africa* (2006) by Terry Stevenson and John Fanshawe, with *The Bird Atlas of Uganda* (2005) making a good secondary source. Also available is *Butterflies of Uganda* (2004) by Nancy Carder et al.

The Uganda Wildlife Authority has published informative books on the natural history of some of the most popular national parks. They can be bought at the UWA office (p426) in Kampala, although you may have to request them. Andrew Roberts' *Uganda's Great Rift Valley* (2006) is an entertaining study of the natural and human history of western Uganda.

For information on books about East African wildlife see p105.

History & Politics
Uganda: From the Pages of Drum (1994) is a lively compilation of articles that originally appeared in the now-defunct *Drum* magazine. These chronicle the rise of Idi Amin and the atrocities he committed, as well as President Museveni's bush war and his coming to power. It forms a powerful record of what the country experienced.

Ugandan Society Observed (2008) is another recommended collection of essays, these by expat Kevin O'Connor that originally appeared in the *Daily Monitor* newspaper.

The Man with the Key has Gone! (1993) by Dr Ian Clarke is an autobiographical account of the time spent in Uganda's Luwero Triangle district by a British doctor and his family. It's a lively read and the title refers to a problem travellers may encounter in provincial Uganda.

Widely available in Uganda, Henry Kyemba's *State of Blood* (1977) is an inside story of the horrors committed by Idi Amin, with insight only one of his former ministers could provide.

BUSINESS HOURS
Government offices and businesses in Uganda are generally open between 8.30am and 5pm, often with a short break for lunch sometime between noon and 2pm. Most shops and banks don't break for lunch, but most banks close at 3pm. Few banks are open on Saturday, but more and more shops are adding weekend hours, usually closing about 1pm.

Local restaurant hours are 7am to 9pm or 10pm, while international-type restaurants are likely to be open 11.30am to 2.30pm and 5.30pm to 10.30pm.

CHILDREN
Although there are some special risks and challenges to travelling the region with kids (see p605), with some great national parks and lots of water-based activities, Uganda can be a lot of fun for children. On the city side of things, Kampala (p427) isn't exactly bursting with activities for young people, but Entebbe (p444) and Jinja (p451) have plenty on offer.

COURSES
The **Ndere Centre** (p441) offers traditional dance and cooking classes from USh20,000 per hour.

There are free modern African dance classes Monday to Saturday at 3pm at the **National Theatre** (Map p432; ☎ 0414-254567; Siad Barre Ave).

The **Kampala Language Centre** (Map p432; ☎ 0392-837558; National Theatre, Siad Barre Ave) offers private lessons in Luganda, Luo and Swahili for USh25,000 per hour. Much better value are the three-month Luganda classes for USh210,000.

Chillum Woods Sound (☎ 0782-952229; www.chillum woodssound.com) is a Masindi-based world music label run by British expat Gareth Woods. He can arrange lessons in traditional African instruments, or volunteer opportunities teaching Western music.

DANGERS & ANNOYANCES
Three decades on from the Idi Amin era, Uganda has not fully shaken its image as a dangerous and unstable country to visit. This is a great shame, as it's actually a very safe and stable country. Even more so now that the Lord's Resistance Army's hold across the north appears to be over. Mugging and petty theft are still relatively rare, even in Kampala.

That said, there are some places where you'll want to check on the latest situation before travelling. Despite a disarmament program, banditry remains rife in the far northeast (though not within Kidepo Valley National Park), and the border areas in the far northwest have their own problems. Various rebel groups hang out in far eastern DRC and they occasionally slip across the porous border to make havoc and, even with additional Ugandan troops in the area, the chances of this happening again can not be completely discounted. Finally, there are smugglers and Kenyan rebels on and around Mt Elgon, though the risk to visitors is small. For more information on these particular dangers, see the Warning boxes in the appropriate chapters.

Power cuts are nowhere near as common as they once were, but you should still expect them in the north and the east, and less frequently in the west. Even Kampala has occasional rolling blackouts.

DISCOUNT CARDS

It's worth carrying a student identity card when travelling to Uganda, as they get you a 25% discount for entry into national parks. ISIC is preferred, but your regular old school ID will work most of the time.

EMBASSIES & CONSULATES

For Ugandan embassies in Kenya, Rwanda and Tanzania, see the relevant section in those chapters.

Embassies & Consulates in Uganda
Belgium (Map p432; ☎ 0414-349559; www.diplomatie.be/kampala; Rwenzori House, Lumumba Ave, Kampala)
Burundi (Map p432; ☎ 0414-235850; Kintu Ave, Kampala; ☉ 8am-1pm & 3-5pm Mon-Fri) A one-month single-entry visa costs US$40, requires two passport photos and will be ready the next day. They're also issued at land borders and the airport.
Canada (Map p432; ☎ 0414-258141; kampala@canadaconsulate.ca; Parliament Ave, Kampala)
Denmark (Map p432; ☎ 0312-263211; 3 Lumumba Ave, Kampala)
DRC (Map pp428-9; ☎ 0414-250099; 20 Philip Rd, Kololo, Kampala; ☉ 9am-3pm Mon-Fri) One-month s-entry visas, costing US$55 and requiring two passport photos, are processed in 24hrs. You can also get a seven-day visa at the border for US$35.
Ethiopia (Map pp428-9; ☎ 0414-348340; Nakayima Rd, Kampala; ☉ 8.30am-12.30pm & 2-5pm Mon-Fri)
France (Map p432; ☎ 0414-304500; 16 Lumumba Ave, Kampala)
Germany (Map pp428-9; ☎ 0414-501111; www.kampala.diplo.de; 15 Philip Rd, Kololo, Kampala)
India (Map pp428-9; ☎ 0414-342994; 11 Kyadondo Rd, Nakasero, Kampala)
Ireland (Map p432; ☎ 0414-344344; 25 Yusuf Lule Rd, Nakasero, Kampala)
Italy (Map pp428-9; ☎ 0414-250450; 11 Lourdel Rd, Nakasero, Kampala)
Kenya (Map p432; ☎ 0414-258235; 41 Nakasero Rd, Kampala; ☉ 9am-12.30pm Mon-Fri) A single-entry visa costs US$50 and one passport photo is required. It will be ready the next day between 11am and 12.30pm. It's easier to get it on arrival.

Netherlands (Map p432; ☎ 0414-346000; Rwenzori Courts, Lumumba Ave, Kampala)
Rwanda (Map pp428-9; ☎ 0414-344045; 2 Nakayima Rd, Kampala; ☉ 9.30am-noon Mon-Fri) Visas cost USh110,000 (for those who need them: see p591 for details) require two passport photos and can be picked up between 10am-noon the next day. They're also available on arrival at the airport and borders.
South Africa (Map p432; ☎ 0414-343543; 15A Nakasero Rd, Kampala)
Southern Sudan (Map p432; ☎ 0414-271625; 2 Ssezibwa Rd; ☉ 9am-1pm & 2-5pm) The Government of Southern Sudan (GOSS) issues their own travel permits for people only visiting in the bottom half of the country, and they're much easier to come by than a proper Sudanese visa. Bring in US$35 and one passport photo in the morning and pick up a one-month s-entry visa in the afternoon; or get it at the border.
Sudan (Map p432; ☎ 0414-230001; 21 Nakasero Rd, Kampala; ☉ 9am-2pm Mon-Thu) A single-entry visa costs USh55,000 (USh270,000 for Americans) and you need two passport photos. Applicants require a sponsor in Sudan. Search Lonely Planet's Thorn Tree discussion forum (lonelyplanet.com/thorntree) for the current details on the often arduous process.
Tanzania (Map p432; ☎ 0414-256272; 6 Kagera Rd, Kampala; ☉ 9am-11.30pm Mon-Fri) Visas are valid for three months, require two passport photos and take 24 hours to issue. Costs vary according to your country of origin. Single-entry visas are also available on entry.
UK (Map pp428-9; ☎ 0312-312000; Windsor Loop, Kampala)
USA (Map pp428-9; ☎ 0414-259791; http://kampala.usembassy.gov; Gaba Rd, Kampala)

HOLIDAYS
New Year's Day 1 January
Liberation Day 26 January
International Women's Day 8 March
Easter (Good Friday, Holy Saturday and Easter Monday) March/April
Labour Day 1 May
Martyrs' Day 3 June
Heroes' Day 9 June
Independence Day 9 October
Christmas Day 25 December
Boxing Day 26 December

Banks and government offices also close on the major Muslim holidays. See p609 for the list.

INTERNET ACCESS
Internet cafés, charging around USh3000 per hour, are ubiquitous in Kampala, and wi-fi hotspots are getting more common. Elsewhere

in the country, even most small towns have access for about the same price, albeit usually pretty slow.

INTERNET RESOURCES

Both the **Uganda Travel Guide** (www.aboutuganda.com) and the **Uganda Travel Planner** (www.traveluganda.co.ug) are comprehensive online resources. **Tourism Uganda**'s website (www.visituganda.com) is more inspirational than helpful.

For all the latest national news, check the websites of Uganda's leading newspapers: **Daily Monitor** (www.monitor.co.ug) and the **New Vision** (www.newvision.co.ug). **Uganda-CAN** (www.ugandacan.org) has near-daily updates on the conflict and peace process in the north.

The **Buganda Home Page** (www.buganda.com) contains sections on the kingdom's history, culture and language.

MAPS

The Uganda maps by ITMB (1:800,000) and Nelles (1:700,000) will get you where you need to go. Only the latter is available in Uganda.

Being both beautiful and useful, Uganda Maps national park maps, available at Aristoc bookstore, UWA, safari lodges and tour companies, are a great buy if you're headed to Queen Elizabeth or any of the other popular parks.

MONEY

The Ugandan shilling (USh) is a relatively stable currency that floats freely on international markets. Most tour operators and upscale hotels quote in US dollars (a few in euros) but you can always pay with shillings.

Notes in circulation are USh1000, USh5000, USh10,000, USh20,000 and USh50,000, and commonly used coins are USh50, USh100, USh200 and USh500. Uchumi and Shoprite supermarkets give change in USh1, USh5, USh10, USh20 coins, but these are useless anywhere else.

ATMs

Making life far easier for travellers in Uganda these days, the biggest banks (Barclays, Centenary, Crane, Orient, Stanbic and Standard Chartered) finally have ATMs that accept international cards. Even many remote small towns will have at least one of these banks, though try not to let your cash run out

in the assumption that you can easily get more, since the system sometimes goes down and machines sometimes run out of cash. You'll also notice tents and benches outside ATMs, which tells you how long the lines can get.

Cash

The Ugandan shilling trades at whatever it's worth against other major currencies and there's usually little fluctuation from day to day. US dollars are the most useful hard currency, especially in small towns, though euros and pound sterling are also widely accepted. Several forex bureaus in the capital change less common currencies such as Australian, Canadian, Danish, Swedish, Indian and Japanese, but these will be useless elsewhere in Uganda.

For dollars, bills printed before 2000 attract a lower (often dramatically so) rate of exchange than newer bills, but most of the big banks in Kampala don't play this game. Small denominations, however, *always* get a much lower rate than US$50 and US$100 notes.

The best exchange rates by far are offered in Kampala. Forex bureaus offer slightly better rates than banks plus much faster service and longer hours; however they're rare outside Kampala. There's no black market, but if you really need to change cash after hours, you can try Indian-owned supermarkets, you won't get a very good rate though.

Note that UWA offers fair exchange rates for park fees and accepts dollars, pounds and euros and either cash or travellers cheques.

Credit Cards

For credit-card cash advances, the only realistic options are Orient Bank and Barclays Bank main branches in Kampala (see p430), although upmarket hotels will probably give you a small cash advance against your card if you're staying there. Barclays offers advances (up to US$700) in US dollars, British pounds, euros or Ugandan shillings from your Visa, MasterCard and JCB credit cards, but charges a hefty US$25 commission above and beyond what your bank at home may take. Orient Bank only gives shillings from Visa cards, but the commission is just USh3500 and they told us there's no maximum limit; however we aren't rich enough to test that claim. Very few places other than top-end hotels and tour companies accept cards for payment; and there's usually a surcharge of 5% to 8%.

UGANDA

Tipping & Bargaining

Tipping isn't expected in Uganda, but as wages are very low by Western standards, it will always be appreciated. The size of a given tip is up to the individual, but as a guideline USh500 to USh1000 is enough in ordinary restaurants, while USh5000 to USh10,000 is reasonable for ranger-guides in national parks.

You'll usually need to bargain with *boda-bodas* and special-hires, though there are still many honest drivers out there. Hotel prices are also sometimes negotiable, especially for multi-day stays and in Kampala, where vacancy rates are high. You can also usually shave some shillings by skipping breakfast. For bargaining tips while shopping, see p611.

Travellers Cheques

Try not to rely on travellers cheques as anything other than emergency backup. Few banks or foreign exchange bureaus outside Kampala handle them, and they get lower rates than cash; often dramatically so. American Express is the only type accepted outside Kampala, but Barclays Bank in the capital also handles Thomas Cook and Visa cheques. Cheques issued in dollars are preferred, but pound sterling and euro cheques are fine in Kampala. See p611 for more traveller cheque information.

PHOTOGRAPHY & VIDEO

Memory cards and colour print film are widely available in Ugandan cities, though the latter can be very old, even in Kampala. There's also no shortage of places that can print photos, but they usually just use ordinary computer printers. Try internet cafés or look for secretarial services shops if the memory card is filling up fast and you want to burn your photos to CD or DVD.

The best camera shop in Uganda is **Colour Chrome** (Map p432; ☎ 0441-230556; www.colour-chrome.com; 54 Kampala Rd; ☒ 8am-7pm Mon-Sat). They stock an impressive selection of film, including black and white and 400-speed slide film (for gorilla photos) and also clean cameras. This is the only place to reliably develop film (except for a few other places that send their film here); if you want a washed-out look for artistic purposes, then you can go anywhere.

POST

Sending a postcard costs USh1100 to Europe and USh1200 to the US or Australia.

Kampala's post office (p430) is slow but reliable while there's a chance things will go missing at provincial branches.

TELEPHONE

Telephone connections, both domestic and international, are pretty good, although not always so reliable in the provincial areas. The cheapest and easiest way to make a local call is from a payphone, which in Uganda is a person with a phone sitting in a kiosk or at a little table along the street. Prices are almost always USh200 per unit, but these can range from 30 to 59 seconds, so always ask.

Cardphones, which you would call a payphone back home, have all but disappeared outside Kampala: pretty much the only people who use them are *muzungu* who don't realise the payphones are cheaper. Their only redeeming quality is they come in handy in the mornings and evenings when payphones can be hard to find.

For international calls, many internet cafés in Kampala, Jinja and a few other towns offer rates ranging from USh200 to USh450 per minute depending on the country and whether you're calling a landline or mobile number. Otherwise mobile phones are your best as they're far cheaper than payphones.

The country code for Uganda is ☎ 256. To make an international call from Uganda, dial ☎ 000 or, on a mobile, the + button. If you're calling Uganda from outside the country, drop the ☎ 0 at the start of the phone number.

Mobile Phones

Mobile (cell) phones are very popular as the service is better than landlines, though it's not one hundred percent reliable. All mobile numbers start with ☎ 07.

Mobile-phone companies sell SIM cards for USh2000 and then you buy airtime vouchers for topping up credit from street vendors. Simple phones are available for USh45,000 in all sizeable towns and also at the airport. MTN currently has the best coverage across the country, though the quality of Warid's connection is superior. Other not-so-popular operators include Zain (formerly CelTel) and UTL/Mango. Calls are cheaper when calling someone on the same network as you.

TOURIST INFORMATION

Tourism Uganda (Map p432; ☎ 0414-342196; www.visituganda.com; 15 Kimathi Ave, Kampala) Uganda's official tourism bureau. They also have a booth at the airport.

Uganda Wildlife Authority (Map pp428-9; ☎ 0414-355000; www.uwa.or.ug; 7 Kira Rd, Kampala; ⏰ 8am-5pm Mon-Fri, 9am-1pm Sat) Promotes the country's national parks and protected areas.

VISAS

Most non-African passport holders visiting Uganda require visas, including Americans, Australians, Canadians and almost all Europeans. Single-entry tourist visas valid for up to 90 days (but unless you ask for 90, you'll probably be given 30 or 60) cost US$50. It's easiest just to rock up at the airport or border and arrange one there; no photos needed. A yellow fever certificate is required if arriving from an affected area, but is rarely requested. For those who like to organise things in advance, two passport photos are required and the embassy will issue the visa within 24 hours to two weeks. Officially the issuance of multiple-entry visas (6-month/one-year US$100/$200) has been temporarily suspended, though at press time we found that some embassies continued to sell them.

For visas requirements to neighbouring countries, see p524. Kampala is a good place for picking up visas to other countries, as there are rarely queues at the various embassies.

VISA EXTENSIONS

In Kampala, the **immigration office** (Map pp428-9; ☎ 0414-595945; Jinja Rd; ⏰ 8am-1pm & 2.30-5pm) is just west of the centre. Regardless of how many days you were given on your original tourist visa, you can apply for a free two-month extension. Submit a letter explaining the reason for your request, stating where you're staying and detailing when and how you'll be leaving the country. Attach a copy of your passport and plane ticket, if you have one. Extensions are much quicker at immigration offices outside the capital, and these exist in most large towns, including Jinja and Fort Portal.

VOLUNTEERING

Uganda has more volunteer opportunities than many African countries thanks to a number of good grassroots organisations. We've listed many specific opportunities in individual regions, plus the following organisations can provide placements in multiple regions.

The newly founded **Volunteer Support Network** (☎ 0782-610657; www.volunteersupport network.org) aims to match you with an organisation that can benefit from your skills. Volunteers pay for food, lodging and administration fees.

People With Disabilities Uganda (Map pp428-9; ☎ 0312-262134; www.pwd-u.org; 18-20 Bukoto St, Kampala) helps to integrate disabled children into their schools and communities, and can use volunteers in most parts of the country. Placements require a minimum commitment of one week, and food and lodging are usually provided. Shorter opportunities are available for office work: perhaps you could begin by making a sign for the office.

The **Uganda Community Tourism Association** (opposite) is in touch with many communities around the country and can connect you to a variety of projects including tree-planting and teaching.

For details on volunteer opportunities teaching music, see Courses on p523.

Also see the volunteering (p614) section in the regional directory.

TRANSPORT IN UGANDA

GETTING THERE & AWAY

For information on getting to Uganda from outside East Africa, see p616.

Air

Located about 40km south of the capital, **Entebbe International Airport** (EBB) is the only aerial gateway to Uganda. Few budget travellers enter Uganda by air because most of the discounted airfares available in Europe and North America use Nairobi (Kenya) as the gateway to East Africa. However, for tourists on a short trip, it doesn't usually cost much extra to continue to Entebbe after changing planes in Nairobi.

AIRLINES IN UGANDA

Air Tanzania (airline code TC; ☎ 0414-236944; www.airtanzania.com; hub Dar es Salaam)

DEPARTURE TAX

The US$40 departure tax on international flights from Entebbe is always included in the ticket price.

CASH AT THE AIRPORT

There are no banks, ATMs or forex bureaus before immigration, but if you're in a pinch an officer will hold your passport while you go get money for your visa.

Air Uganda (airline code U7; ☎ 0414-258262; www.air-uganda.com; hub Entebbe)
British Airways (airline code BA; ☎ 0414-257414; www.britishairways.com; hub London)
Brussels Airlines (airline code SN; ☎ 0414-234201; www.brusselsairlines.com; hub Brussels)
Eagle Air (airline code H7; ☎ 0414-344292; www.flyeagleuganda.com; hub Entebbe)
EgyptAir (airline code MS; ☎ 0414-341276; www.egyptair.com.eg; hub Cairo)
Emirates (airline code EK; ☎ 0414-770444; www.emirates.com; hub Dubai)
Ethiopian Airlines (airline code ET; ☎ 0414-345577; www.flyethiopian.com; hub Addis Ababa)
Fly540 (airline code 5H; ☎ 0414-346915; www.fly540.com; hub Nairobi)
Kenya Airways (airline code KQ; ☎ 0312-360121; www.kenya-airways.com; hub Nairobi)
KLM (airline code KL; ☎ 0414-338000; www.klm.com; hub Amsterdam)
Precision Air (airline code PW; ☎ 0772-792311; www.precisionairtz.com; hub Dar es Salaam)
Royal Daisy (airline code 6D; ☎ 0414-256213; www.royaldaisy.com; hub Entebbe)
Rwandair Express (airline code WB; ☎ 0414-344851; www.rwandair.com; hub Kigali)
South African Airways (airline code SA; ☎ 0414-345772; www.flysaa.com; hub Johannesburg)

BURUNDI
The best way to get to Bujumbura is with Rwandair Express via Kigali. The price is around US$265/480 one-way/return.

KENYA
Somehow or other Kenya Airways continues to keep its stranglehold on the Entebbe–Nairobi route. Other carriers keep coming, but they always end up going soon after. Currently Air Uganda is taking them on at the same price (US$225/339 one-way/return) while Fly540 charges US$144/268 one-way/return.

There are no direct flights to Mombasa: Kenya Airways (US$355/485 one-way/return) and Fly540 (US$189/378 one-way/return) go via Nairobi.

RWANDA
Rwandair Express offers reliable flight connections between Entebbe and Kigali up to twice a day for about US$200/300 one-way/return.

SUDAN
Between Air Uganda, Eagle Air and Royal Daisy, each charging about US$220/430 one-way/return, there are a couple flights most days to Juba.

At the time of research there were no direct flights to Khartoum; go via Nairobi or Addis Ababa at a rough cost of US$460/745 one-way/return.

TANZANIA
Air Tanzania and Air Uganda fly non-stop to Dar es Salaam for about US$285/370 one-way/return. Air Uganda goes to Kilimanjaro Airport (US$260/420; Monday only) near Arusha non-stop while Precision Air touches down in Mwanza (US$270/370 one-way/return; Monday, Thursday and Saturday) first. Kenya Airways goes to all three cities via Nairobi: they charge about the same to Dar es Salaam and much more for the others.

Land
Uganda shares popular land border crossings with Kenya, Rwanda and Tanzania. Direct bus services connect the major cities in each country, and local transport from towns nearer the border is available for those wanting to break their journey along the way. There are also seldom used (by travellers) border crossings with Sudan and DRC, though check very carefully on the security situation locally before using them as the peace process is very fluid in both places.

DRC
As things stand at press time, it would be very unwise to visit DRC and not possible from Uganda anyway since Uganda has closed most of their border crossings. Assuming the fighting stops again, with the exception of the Bunagana border post (west of Kisoro) for mountain gorilla visits in Parc National des Virungas (p538), it will surely still be inadvisable to visit DRC due to civil instability. Check, check and check again in Kampala and Kisoro about the current security situation before risking a crossing. See the Kisoro (p496) text for information on transport.

KENYA

There continues to be talk of reviving the train line between Kampala and Nairobi, but we'll believe it when we see it. For now you've got to go by road.

The busiest border crossing is at Busia on the direct route to Nairobi through Kisumu. Frequent minibuses link Jinja to Busia (USh7000, 2½ hours), and then again between Busia and Kisumu or Nairobi (KSh1000 to KSh2500; 10 to 12 hours). The border crossing is straight-forward, though there are a number of shady money-changers: check everything twice.

The other busy border crossing to Kenya is through Malaba, a bit north of Busia and just east of Tororo. Though finding onward transport from here to Nairobi and Kisumu isn't difficult, it's less frequent than at Busia, so even if you're already in Tororo, the local advice these days is to go to Busia (USh2500, one hour) and continue into Kenya from there.

Taking a vehicle through these border crossings is slow but fairly straightforward and shouldn't take more than an hour or two of paperwork.

For people visiting Mt Elgon National Park or Sipi Falls, the seldom-used Suam border crossing, beyond which lies the Kenyan city of Kitale, may be convenient, but this is a pretty rough route. Trekkers in either the Ugandan or Kenyan national parks on Mt Elgon also have the option of walking over the border. See the Mt Elgon National Park section, p462 for information on both of these crossings.

Most travellers avoid local transport altogether and opt for the direct buses running between Kampala and Nairobi, which range from luxurious to basic. You can also pick up these buses (or get dropped off on your way into Uganda) in Jinja. The journey takes about 12 hours. See p623 for information on bus safety. All prices listed below are one-way.

Akamba (Map p432; ☎ 0414-250412; www.akamba bus.com; 28 Dewinton Rd, Kampala) Operates two classes daily and is the company of choice these days. The 'executive' class buses cost USh43,000, and depart at 7am, 2pm and 3pm. The 7am daily 'royal' service is more comfortable, with huge, comfy seats, only three per row! Tickets cost USh58,000. Akamba also has service from Mbale.

Kampala Coach (Map p432; ☎ 0711-553377; Jinja Rd, Kampala) Uses spiffy new air-con buses showing movies. It has departures for Kenya at 6.30am and 3pm from its Jinja Rd office. The price is USh45,000.

Scandinavian Express (Map p432; ☎ 0772-377174; www.scandinaviagroup.com; Lumumba Ave, Kampala) Another reliable operator with good quality buses, these costing USh50,000. They leave four times a week: at 1pm on Tuesday and Sunday, and noon on Thursday and Saturday.

The following run old, crowded coaches and you may want to take a look inside before buying a ticket.

Busscar (Map p432; ☎ 0414-233030; Burton St) Operates twice-daily services, departing at 7am and 3pm, for USh40,000.

Falcon (Map p432; ☎ 0772-576196; Market St) Its daily Nairobi departure is at 3pm and costs USh40,000.

Gateway (Map p432; ☎ 0392-967481; Wilson Rd, Kampala) Has two rattle-trap buses a day at 3pm, one going via Malaba and the other via Busia. Gateway charges USh35,000. Gateway also has services from Mbale.

Kalita (Map p432; ☎ 0312-286137; Namirembe Rd, Kampala) Departs at 6am and 3pm from just outside the bus park and charges USh35,000.

RWANDA

There are two main border crossing points: between Kabale and Kigali via Katuna (Gatuna on the Rwandan side), and between Kisoro and Musanze (Ruhengeri) via Cyanika. The Kagitumba border isn't very practical for most people, but there is public transport on both sides. Remember than many nationalities need visas for Rwanda (see p591) so bring enough cash: many disappointed day-trippers get turned back. Also remember that you'll have to buy a new Ugandan visa when you return.

The busiest crossing by far is at Katuna/Gatuna, and it can take over an hour to get through both immigration stations on both sides. From Kabale there are lots of saloon car shared taxis (USh3000, 30 minutes) to the border, and a few minibuses each morning (except Sunday) direct to Kigali. You can also wait at the main junction in the morning for the Kigali-bound buses from Kampala to pass through and hope they have free seats. On the Rwandan side there are minibuses travelling to Kigali (RFr1300, two hours) throughout the day. There are still several police checkpoints between the border and Kigali, though full baggage searches are no longer very common.

From Kisoro to Cyanika the road is very rough and there's no public transport, so you'll need to get a special-hire (USh20,000) or a *boda-boda* (USh5000). Transport on the Rwandan side to Musanze (Ruhengeri)

UGANDA

is frequent and the road in excellent condition. Very few people cross here so you can fly through immigration; altogether it only takes about 1½ hours to travel between Kisoro and Musanze (Ruhengeri).

There's also the option of taking a direct bus between Kampala and Kigali, a seven- to eight-hour journey including a slow border crossing.

Amhoro (Map p432; ☎ 0414-592869; William St, Kampala) Also leaves at 1am (Tuesday to Sunday only) to Kigali (USh25,000) and continues to Bujumbura (USh40,000) in Burundi.

Gaso Bus (Map p432; ☎ 0414-572917; Shoppers Stop Plaza, Sikh Rd, Kampala) Has one bus per day to Kigali (USh25,000) leaving at 1am. This service continues right on to Bujumbura (USh40,000) in Burundi, usually arriving at 5pm local time. Gaso previously had direct buses to Goma, DRC, and may again if the security situation improves.

Jaguar Executive Coaches (Map p432; ☎ 0414-251855; Namirembe Rd, Kampala) Offers three classes of service: VIP (USh30,000, departing at 1am), standard (USh25,000, 9am) and economy (USh20,000, 3am, 6am and 7am). The VIP bus is worth the extra cost and includes movies. Jaguar has its own terminal just west of the centre.

Kampala Coach (Map p432; ☎ 0711-553377; Wilson St, Kampala) Also has good, modern buses, but Jaguar is a better choice because Kampala Coach's Kigali (USh25,000) bus begins its journey in Nairobi, and if it's late arriving in Kampala (around 3am at Arua Park) to pick up passengers, you may end up sitting around a while.

Onatracom (☎ 0782-867991; Mackay Rd, Kampala) Like Gaso and Amhoro, this company uses older buses, but it has convenient departure times: 6am, 7.30am and 8.30am.

SUDAN

With the advent of peace in northern Uganda and southern Sudan, tenuous as it may be, travel has picked up dramatically. The principal, and shortest, route from Kampala to Juba is the 15-hour (much longer if it rains) trip via Gulu, crossing at Nimule. At research time the road was so horrible that some companies were shifting to the longer Arua route, which passes though Yei and takes at least 20 hours from Kampala, but the Gulu road was due for improvement. There are no buses originating in Gulu, but it's easy to catch one of the Kampala buses there for the final 10 hours. In Arua, you have the quicker and more comfortable option of hopping in a Land Cruiser, which might make it to Juba in as little as eight hours.

Although the southern border is open again and Government of Southern Sudan travel permits are available at the border, arranging permission to travel by land between northern and southern Sudan is nearly impossible, so Juba is effectively a dead-end. And, because of the surfeit of aid workers and business people there, it's a very expensive one.

Kampala Coach (☎ 0711-553377; USh100,000 one-way; ☽ depart 2.30am) and **National Coaches** (☎ 0775-368913; USh80,000 one-way; ☽ depart 2am) are two new companies with big, modern air-conditioned buses that are definitely worth the extra cash. There are many other companies making the run in old, crowded buses for USh70,000 to USh75,000. All leave in the early morning hours. During our time in Kampala one company failed and two new ones started operations, so the best advice is just to go to Arua Park (the name of the spot along Wilson Rd where all Juba buses depart from) and ask around.

TANZANIA

The most commonly used direct route between Uganda and Tanzania is on the west side of Lake Victoria between Bukoba and Masaka, and goes via the border crossing at Mutukula. Road conditions are good and the journey takes about six hours by bus from Kampala. Companies making this run are Ariazi Tours (USh17,000, 10.30am daily), Falcon (USh20,000, 6.30am Thursday) from the main bus park and Gateway (USh12,000, 11am daily) from the new bus park. You can also catch these buses in Masaka or travel from Masaka in stages; see (p503) for details.

There's another border crossing located at Nkurungu, west of Mutukula, but the road is bad and little transport passes this way.

For the marathon journey to Dar es Salaam taking a day and a half via Nairobi there are Akamba (executive/royal USh116,000/131,000), Scandinavian Express (USh120,000), and Kampala Coach (USh120,000). Falcon also connects Kampala to Dar es Salaam (USh100,000; departures 6am Sunday and Thursday), but on less comfortable buses. All of these companies also stop in Arusha for two-thirds the price of the trip to 'Dar'.

Akamba also links Kampala direct to Mwanza (USh43,000, 20 hours) with departures on Monday, Thursday and Saturday at 3pm.

See the Kenya section (p529) for all of these coach companies' contact information and departure times.

Lake

There's no longer proper passenger service on Lake Victoria to Mwanza, but intrepid travellers can book passage on the MV *Umoja* cargo ferry that goes from Kampala's Port Bell. Typically these sail two or three days a week, but departures depend on demand. It usually leaves around 6pm to 7pm, but show up before 5pm to allow enough time to get through immigration and make all arrangements. Pay your USh5000 port fee in the office in the green shipping container and then USh30,000 direct to the captain. The trip takes 16 to 17 hours and it's usually possible to make a deal with one of the crew for their bunk.

You can check the schedule at the Marine Services offices on the second floor of the train station in downtown Kampala. Enter through the eastern gate.

Tours

For all the juicy details on safaris and tours in Uganda, see the comprehensive Safaris section (p73). For more on international operators organising tours to Uganda and elsewhere in East Africa, see p624.

GETTING AROUND
Air

Few travellers fly within Uganda. **Eagle Air** (Map p432; ☎ 0414-344292; www.flyeagleuganda.com; 11 Portal Ave, Kampala), with regular flights to Arua, Gulu and several smaller towns, all in the north, is currently the only carrier.

Kampala Aeroclub (☎ 077-706107; www.flyuganda .com) and **Eagle Air** (☎ 0772-777338; www.flyeagle uganda.com) operate charter flights, which let you get to the national parks in comfort.

Boat

Boat travel in Uganda is limited to reaching the Ssese Islands (p504), either by ferry from Nakiwogo (right by Entebbe) or Bukakata (east of Masaka) or with the less safe small boats operating from Kasenyi (also near Entebbe).

Bus

Standard buses and sometimes half-sized 'coasters' connect major towns on a daily basis and the longer your journey is the more likely it will be on a bus rather than a minibus. Fares are usually a little less than minibuses and buses stop far less frequently, which saves time. Buses generally leave Kampala at fixed departure times; however, returning from provincial destinations, they usually wait until full. The first bus of the day usually departs at a ridiculously early time, so inquire the day before. Conductors on buses sometimes try to cheat you on the fare, but since the real price is written on the ticket, you shouldn't fall for this. There are many reckless drivers, but buses are safer than minibuses.

In addition to the normal private buses, there are also Post Buses (see p443).

MINIBUS

Uganda is the land of shared minibuses (called taxis or occasionally *matatus*), and there's never any shortage of them. Except for long distances, these are the most common vehicles between towns. There are official fares (you can check at the taxi park offices if you want) but in reality the conductor charges whatever they think they can get, and not just for a *muzungu* but for locals as well. Ask fellow passengers the right price.

Minibuses leave when full; and 'full' means exactly that! As soon as you're a fair distance away from towns, where police spot-checks are less likely, more passengers will be crammed in. As is clearly painted on their doors, minibuses are licensed to carry 14 passengers, but travelling with less than 18 is rare, and the number often well exceeds 20. For all but the shortest journeys, you're better off taking a bus since they stop less frequently and are safer due to their size. Many minibus and bus drivers are maniacs who go much too fast to leave any leeway for emergencies. Crash stories are regular features in the newspapers. Most crashes are head on, so sit at the back for maximum safety.

Way out of the way places use saloon car shared taxis rather than minibuses. If the roads are exceptionally bad, then the only choice is to sit with bags of maize and charcoal, empty jerry cans and other cargo in the backs of trucks.

Car & Motorcycle

There's a pretty good system of sealed roads between most major population centres. It's somewhat pointless to talk of which particular roads are good and which are bad, as this changes rapidly; often in a matter of weeks. Uganda has two wet seasons, which means the roads take a serious pounding from the elements, and surfaces can deteriorate rapidly. Keep your wits about you when driving; cyclists, cows and large potholes often appear from nowhere.

The quality of dirt roads varies widely depending on whether it's the wet or dry season. In the dry, dirt roads are very dusty and you'll end up choking behind trucks and minibuses while everything alongside the road gets covered in a fine layer of orange-brown dust. In the wet season, a number of the dirt roads become muddy mires, almost carrot soup, and may be passable only in a 4WD vehicle. If you're travelling around Uganda in the wet seasons, always ask about the latest road conditions before setting off on a journey.

Road signs are rare in Uganda so it's possible to get hopelessly lost. Don't hesitate to ask directions frequently along the way.

DRIVING LICENCE
If you have an International Driving Permit, you should bring it, although you really only need your local driving licence from home.

FUEL & SPARE PARTS
In Kampala petrol costs about USh2700 per litre while diesel is about USh2640 per litre. Prices rise as you move out into provincial areas.

Filling and repair stations are found even in some small towns, but don't let the tank run too low or you may end up paying around USh5000 per litre to fuel up from a jerry can in some really remote place.

HIRE
Due to high taxes and bad roads, car hire prices tend to be high compared to other parts of the world. Add fuel costs and there will be some real shock at the total price if you're considering driving around the country. Also remember that if you're going to national parks, you'll have to pay the driver's fees as well as your own.

The big international operators are **Budget** (Map p432; ☎ 0414-234915; www.budget.com; 9 Portal Ave, Kampala), **Europcar** (Map p432; ☎ 0414-237211; www.europcar.com; Nsambya Rd, Kampala), and **Hertz** (Map p432; ☎ 0772-450460; www.hertz.com; Colville

St, Kampala), each with offices in downtown Kampala and at the airport in Entebbe. Daily rates are nearly US$100 for a small car with insurance and US$175 and up for 4WDs. This doesn't include excess kilometres above the paltry 100km allowance, which are charged at US$0.30.

In virtually all instances it's better to deal with one of the local companies, though you need to shop around. Quoted prices for a small car with driver can range from US$35 to US$150. The highest prices are just rip-offs by companies who hope *muzungu* don't know any better, but with the others, the difference is in the details. Always ask about the number of free kilometres (and the price for exceeding them) and driver costs for food and lodging. You can also try negotiating with special-hire drivers, but generally speaking these guys aren't as reliable.

One of the best small operators we know is **Alpha Car Rentals** (Map p432; ☎ 0772-411232; www.alpharentals.co.ug; 3/5 Bombo Rd, EMKA House, Kampala). A saloon car with driver costs USh60,000 for the day around Kampala while a small 4WD with driver is just USh150,000 (his food and lodging inclusive if you head upcountry); both with unlimited mileage.

Wemtec (☎ 0772-221113; wemtec@source.co.ug), based in Jinja but delivering everywhere in the country, is a well-known company hiring a variety of Land Rovers with driver from USh180,000 to USh220,000. These prices are all-inclusive (minus fuel, of course), with no limits on mileage.

City Cars (Map pp428-9; ☎ 0772-412001; www.drive uganda.com; Tank Hill Rd, Kampala) is expensive but reliable. It charges US$71 per day including insurance for a self-drive small car, while beefy Land Rovers begin at US$165. They give 150 free kilometres per day and charge US$0.30 for each extra kilometre. Drivers cost an extra US$28 per day and are mandatory with the big vehicles. They also have camping gear available for US$10 per day.

Hitching
Without your own transport, hitching is virtually obligatory in some situations, such as getting into national parks. Most of the lifts will be on delivery trucks, usually on top of the load at the back, which can be a very pleasant way to travel, though sun protection is a must. There's virtually always a charge for these rides.

See p624 for more on hitching in the region, including safety.

Local Transport

Kampala has a local minibus network, as well as 'special-hire' taxis for private trips. Elsewhere you'll have to rely solely on two-wheel taxis, known as *boda-bodas* as they orig-inally shuttled people between border posts: from 'boda to boda'. Most are still bicycles though motorcycles are now very common. Never hesitate to tell a driver to slow down if you feel uncomfortable with his driving skills, or lack thereof. Outside Kampala, there are few trips within any town that should cost more than USh500.

Detour: Democratic Republic of the Congo

The haunting yet unforgettable setting of Joseph Conrad's classic *Heart of Darkness*, the Democratic Republic of the Congo (DRC; formerly Zaire) occupies a vast swathe of land in the centre of the African continent. The same size as Western Europe, the country is home to the mighty Congo River, some of the last remaining unexplored wildernesses on the planet, and a whole slew of primates from chimpanzees and bonobos to lowland and mountain gorillas. Of course, the DRC isn't exactly an up-and-coming ecotourism destination, especially since it's only just now emerging from a decade of civil war.

So just how safe is DRC? Optimists compare the country's present situation to Uganda in the late 1980s or Rwanda in the mid-1990s, though the unfortunate reality is that nobody really knows. DRC's greatest blessing – and its inescapable curse – has always been its abundance of natural resources. As a direct consequence, the country is still something of a volatile powder keg, and armed struggles to control these riches could ignite the fuse at a moment's notice.

While most of DRC falls outside of East Africa, the city of Goma near the Rwandese and Ugandan borders is starting to attract a small trickle of hard-core travellers. The capital of Kivu province, Goma serves as a good jumping-off point for Parc National des Virungas, home to the critically endangered eastern mountain gorilla, and the towering volcano of Nyiragongo, one of the most active on the continent.

With that said, the peace in DRC is young and fragile, security is tenuous at best, and can change very fast in this part of the world. Before you even consider stepping foot in DRC, make sure that you're well informed about the latest situation on the ground.

FAST FACTS

- **Area** 2.35 million sq km
- **Birthplace of** Mobutu Sese Seko, Claude Makalele (Real Madrid, Chelsea, now Paris St, Germain)
- **Capital** Kinshasa
- **Country Code** ☎ 243
- **Famous for** Congo River, *Heart of Darkness*, gorillas
- **Languages** French and Kingwana
- **Money** Congo francs (CFr); US$1 = CFr653; €1 = CFr875
- **Population** 66 million

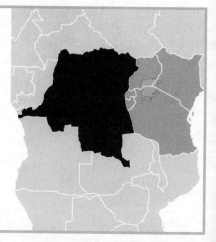

A WORD OF WARNING ABOUT THE DEMOCRATIC REPUBLIC OF THE CONGO

While we were able to safely visit Goma and the surrounding area in mid-2008, the information in this chapter is best viewed as a reference material as opposed to up-to-date coverage. The security in the Democratic Republic of the Congo (DRC) at the time of research was – in a single word – uncertain. Furthermore, the outbreak of violence throughout Eastern Congo in late 2008 continues to call into question the future stability of the region. This means that the situation on the ground will inevitably change and change again during the shelf life of this edition. Quite simply, if you are contemplating a detour to DRC, there is absolutely no substitute for your own careful research. Perhaps the most reliable source of information is the UN Mission in Congo – you can visit its website at www.monuc.org. It is also recommended that you inquire locally in Kampala or Kisoro (Uganda), or in Kigali or Gisenyi (Rwanda).

At the time of research, it was generally considered safe to stay in Goma, and to climb Nyiragongo Volcano. While tourists are once again heading to Parc National des Virungas, the high-profile killings of seven gorillas in the summer of 2007 sadly calls into question the security of the park. Travel to and from the Ugandan border at Bunagana is also not advisable due to ongoing instability.

While the vast remainder of DRC is outside the extents of this book, it's worth mentioning that heading overland through the bush is definitely a big no-no, but continuing to Kinshasa by plane is easy, if somewhat expensive. Ituri province and the area around Bunia was considered to be the most dangerous area in all of DRC, though the tribal conflict between the Hema and Lendu is finally ending. (The 'Ituri Conflict' is used to refer to the longstanding grievances between the agriculturalist Lendu and pastoralist Hema ethnic groups in the Ituri region of northeastern DRC. While it's difficult to trace the full historical extent of this conflict, the most recent clashes were from 1999 to 2007, and were prompted by the increasing number of armed groups in the region that fought in the Second Congo War. As with the vast majority of DRC's civil strife, the primary issue at stake was control over the area's abundant reserve of natural resources.)

To the south of Goma, Bukavu is on the rise as a functioning urban centre, though there are still scars from the thrashing it took in summer 2004 at the hands of a dissident pro-Rwandan faction. Nearby Parc National Kahuzi-Biéga is once again open for lowland gorilla viewing, though be sure you get the latest reports before visiting. During the civil war much of the park was occupied by rebel forces, who strip-mined it for coltan and lived off bush meat. As you might imagine, there are still security risks in the area, so check and check again.

Step by step, things can and do improve, and before you know it, tourism is a viable industry once more. If the recent peace accords hold, then there is reason to believe that the security in DRC will improve over the next few years. So, keep your fingers crossed and stay up to date. More and more places are opening up to foreign tourists, and the Congolese certainly deserve all the support they can get in rebuilding their lives after the long years of war.

History

While colonialism in any capacity is fundamentally an exploitative force, there are few examples as harsh and severe as that of the Congo Free State (1877–1908). King Leopold of Belgium, who essentially ran the country like his own private colony for nearly three decades, raped and pillaged the Congo by subjecting the population to forced labour on his massive rubber plantations. Leopold eventually transferred power to his own parliament, though the colony was run under equally undemocratic means until 1960.

Parliamentary elections in the newly dubbed 'Democratic Republic of the Congo' did initially have a measure of democracy, producing nationalist Patrice Lumumba as prime minister and pro-Western Joseph Kasavubu as president. However, it wasn't long before power struggles in DRC launched a proxy war between the United States and the Soviet Union. As in other corners of the globe that played host to the Cold War, the struggle between capitalism and communism severely limited the growth and development of young countries. With the aid of the American government and the CIA, and the Belgian government, Kasavubu and his 'loyal' colonel Joseph Mobutu assassinated Lumumba, ushering in five years of political infighting and civil unrest.

In 1965, Mobutu seized control in a bloodless coup, declaring himself President Mobutu Sese Seko Kuku Ngbendu Waza Banga, or 'the fearless warrior who will go from strength to strength leaving fire in his wake'. Despite the lofty title, President Mobutu is best remembered for using state coffers to fund Concorde charters to Paris for extravagant shopping trips. He took plunder to a new level, creating a new form of government along the way: kleptocracy, or governance by theft.

The country was officially known as the 'Republic of Zaire' from October of 1971 to May of 1997, which coincided with much of the reign of President Mobutu Sese Seko. The name change was in line with the absoulte ruler's strict policy of promoting nationalism while condemning regionalism and tribalism. When Mobutu fled the country in 1997, Kabila seized Kinshasa without a fight, consolidated power and changed the country's name back to the Democratic Republic of the Congo.

Mobutu was eventually deposed in 1997, though the massive black hole that followed resulted in the Great War of Africa. At its height, the war sucked in as many as nine countries, and led to the deaths of an estimated three to five million people, largely from disease and starvation. Add to the mess the Interahamwe (Those Who Kill Together), responsible for the Rwandan genocide, and the Mai Mai, who wear sink plugs around their necks, and believe that holy water protects them from bullets. The Mai Mai were community-based militia groups that banded together to defend their territory against other armed groups including Rwandan forces and Rwandan-affiliated Congolese rebel groups. After the genocide in Rwanda, they repeated the famous words from after the Jewish Holocaust: 'never again', though in Congo that turned out to mean 'à la prochaine' or 'till the next time'.

Formal peace treaties were signed in 2002, though it will take time to overcome the trauma of the last several decades. The Transitional Government saw DRC through its first multiparty elections since independence. On 30 July 2006, Joseph Kabila took 45% of the votes, while his opponent Jean-Pierre Bemba took 20%. Fighting broke out on the streets following allegations of fraud, though it was eventually quelled by UN peacekeepers. A new election was held on 29 October 2006, and this time Kabila took 70% of the vote. On 6 December 2006 the Transitional Government came to an end as Joseph Kabila was sworn in as President. Of course, it remains to seen whether or not Kabila can bring stability to an enormous landmass that has been plagued by ill governance since its original demarcation.

It's not that democratic, it's barely a republic, but it is Congo.

Information

Eight-day Congolese visas are available at the Goma border for US$35. Visas for longer stays of 30 days are also available in advance through a Congolese embassy for up to US$80. The local currency is Congo francs, though the US dollar is king in DRC. Note that only bills issued from 2000 onwards are accepted.

GOMA

Goma is something of a modern-day Pompeii. On 17 January 2002, Nyiragongo Volcano blew its top, blanketing the city in ash and lava. While the flow moved slow enough to give residents time to evacuate, Goma was buried under 2m of molten mess. Today, parts of the city centre are moonscape, though it's largely business as usual in this bustling commercial centre on the shores of Lake Kivu.

For foreign tourists up for the challenges of DRC, Goma serves as a base for trekking up Nyiragongo Volcano, or for tracking the mountain gorillas in Parc National des Virungas (see below). However, be advised that there is still a considerable amount of instability in the Kivu region, so be absolutely sure that you're up to date on the latest security situation before travelling here. For more on safe travel in DRC, see p535.

Sights

NYIRAGONGO VOLCANO

Beautiful and brooding, locals in Goma fear and respect the power of Nyiragongo Volcano. Having destroyed half the city in 2002, the volcano certainly deserves its reputation, though this isn't to say that you shouldn't climb it if you're feeling fit and you've checked the safety situation. There is quite literally a lava lake at the top – please, please watch your footing, there have been deaths here up here in the recent past.

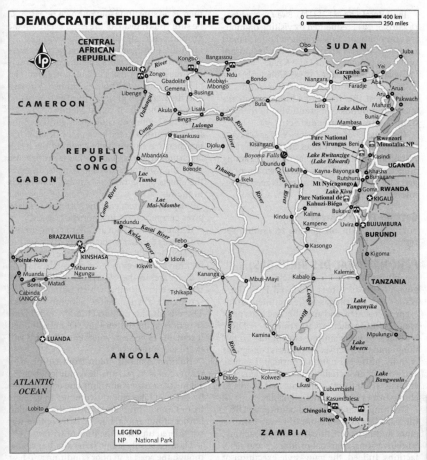

DEMOCRATIC REPUBLIC OF THE CONGO

It takes about five hours to climb and about half that to descend, but it is more atmospheric to spend the night here – bring a tent, a sleeping bag and plenty of warm clothes. Please inquire about safety before camping out in the open. There is a small ranger post at the start of the climb, about 15km from Goma in Kibati on the road north to Bunagana and Uganda, though you should stock up on provisions in Goma as nothing is available here.

Before starting the climb, you must buy a permit from the rangers, which costs US$100. While this is a hefty price, bear in mind that this money directly contributes to the preservation of Parc National des Virungas (see p538). Note that it is mandatory that you take a guide along with you,

and you will be expected to pay a negotiable price for their services. Porters are also available if you need some help carrying your gear to the top.

A taxi to the ranger station from Goma shouldn't cost more than US$5, though it can be difficult to get a ride back to town. However, you can always arrange a pick-up time if you plan ahead, or try to flag down any of the buses heading south to Goma.

Sleeping & Eating

Hotel des Grands Lacs (☎ 9889 9943; Blvd Kanyamuhanga; s/d from US$20/30) Once Goma's grandest hotel, this colonial relic would struggle to earn just one star these days, though it's atmospheric enough for a cheapie.

Ihusi Hotel (☎ 081-3532300; Blvd Kanyamuhanga; r from US$75; ❄) Frequented by visiting dignitaries and politicos, this large hotel offers smart rooms as well as an open-air bar-restaurant with sweeping views of Lake Kivu.

Stella Matutina Lodge (☎ 085-87616; Himbi; r from US$85; ❄) The most comfortable rooms in town are at this luxurious lodge, set in the spacious grounds of a grand villa to the west of the centre in Himbi district.

Chez Doga (Blvd Kanyamuhanga; ☽ 11am-late) One of the most popular places in town, this bar-restaurant really picks up at night, attracting an eclectic mix of UN workers, smart locals and a few unsavoury characters to keep things interesting.

Getting There & Away

For information on getting to Goma, see right.

PARC NATIONAL DES VIRUNGAS

Established in 1925 by the Belgian colonial government as Albert National Park, Parc National des Virungas is the continent's oldest protected area, and arguably one of its most vital. Befitting such a vast country as DRC, Virungas is, quite simply, enormous. To put things into perspective, Virungas is contiguous with five different national parks in Uganda, and protects an incredible range of endangered animals, from forest elephants and okapis to chimpanzees and mountain gorillas.

Befitting such a tortured country as DRC, the park lies at the centre of a war-torn region, and has been threatened by poaching, land invasions, charcoal producers and rebel factions. Indeed, the gang-style execution of seven mountain gorillas in July 2007 made the international headlines, as did the personal stories of the devoted park rangers, who have been virtually fighting a war to protect our primate relatives. Sadly, it was difficult to say at the time of writing which side was winning the fight, which certainly calls into question the future of tourism in Virungas.

Tracking the rare and wonderful mountain gorilla is one of the most magical experiences to be had in Africa, though it is advisable that you do this in either Uganda (p417) or Rwanda (opposite). While the information presented in this section does provide a general overview of the national park, it is contingent on whether or not the security situation improves during the shelf life of this guidebook. Once again,

there is no substitute for your own research, so be sure you're aware of the latest events on the ground before stepping foot in Virungas.

In the past, gorilla-tracking permits were issued for two sectors of the park, namely Bukima and Djomba. The four gorilla families at Bukima include Kabirizi, Humba, Munaga and the Rugendo group, while the habituated family at Djomba is called Mapuwa.

In 2007, gunmen shot seven gorillas in the Rugendo group in the back of the head. While poachers have historically removed the heads and hands of gorillas, these killings were believed to be the work of factions looking to discredit the efforts of the rangers. An excellent article in the July 2008 issue of *National Geographic* entitled 'Who Murdered the Virunga Gorillas?' gives perspective on this horrific tragedy.

There is a small hut at Bukima ranger post, which was derelict at the time of our visit, but the UN Development Programme (UNDP) is looking to redevelop it for overnight stays.

Beds are, in theory, available at the small resthouse in Djomba, which has a stunning setting on a ridge below Sabyino volcano. There is also an upmarket lodge under construction on the hilltop above Djomba, though it remains to be seen whether or not this will ever be completed.

Bukima is about 40km from Goma. The main road is in reasonable condition, but the 15km access road is appalling and only passable by 4WD. It takes about two hours to get here from Goma, three hours from the Ugandan border at Bunagana, but the latter option was considered unsafe at the time of writing.

Djomba is only about 7km from Bunagana, though the road is in poor condition and best undertaken by 4WD.

TRANSPORT

For the full lowdown on crossing into DRC from Uganda, Rwanda or Burundi, see the Transport sections of these individual chapters. The most commonly used crossings to enter or exit DRC are the Bunagana border with Uganda near Kisoro (p496) and the Goma border with Rwanda at Gisenyi (p572). Visitors wanting to carry on to Kinshasa are advised to fly. Flights are expensive, but it saves more than a month of dangerous overland travel by road and river, and, quite possibly, your life.

Rwanda

Mention Rwanda to anyone with a small measure of geopolitical conscious, and they'll no doubt recall images of the horrific genocide that brutalised this tiny country in 1994. In the span of 100 days, an estimated one million Tutsis and moderate Hutus were systematically butchered by the Interahamwe in one of the most savage genocides in the history of mankind.

While the scars still run deep, Rwanda has done a remarkable job of healing its wounds and turning towards the future with a surprising measure of optimism. The government has taken measures to eliminate tribal identities, and successfully rallied the country under the unifying Rwandan banner. And, in the hopes of stimulating its developing economy through ecotourism, the country is protecting its most vital natural resource – the mountain gorilla.

Forming a natural frontier with the Democratic Republic of the Congo (DRC; formerly Zaire) and Uganda, the Virunga volcanoes are home to some of the world's last remaining mountain gorillas. Tracking these primate relatives through bamboo forests and equatorial jungles is for many the highlight of their African travels.

Of course, 'Le Pays des Mille Collines' or the Land of a Thousand Hills as it is frequently known, isn't all monkey business. On the contrary, Rwanda is a lush country of endless mountains and stunning scenery. The shores of Lake Kivu conceal some of the best inland beaches on the continent, while Parc National Nyungwe Forest protects extensive tracts of montane rainforest.

Given its dark history, travellers in East Africa are often unsure about crossing the border into Rwanda. However, the country remains stable and peaceful, and its attempts to build a sustainable ecotourism industry are certainly worth your support.

FAST FACTS

- **Area** 26,338 sq km
- **Birthplace of** Paul Kagame
- **Capital** Kigali
- **Country Code** ☎ 250
- **Famous for** Dian Fossey, mountain gorillas, *Hotel Rwanda*
- **Languages** Kinyarwanda, French and English
- **Money** Rwandan franc (RFr); US$1 = RFr552; €1 = RFr710
- **Population** 10.2 million

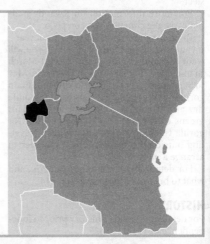

RWANDA

HIGHLIGHTS

- **Parc National des Volcans** (p562) Hike along the forested slopes of the Virungas in search of silverback gorillas and golden monkeys

- **Parc National de Nyungwe** (p579) Trek through steamy rainforests in search of colobus monkeys and chimpanzees

- **Parc National de L'Akagera** (p585) Have a Rwandan-style safari experience in this up-and-coming game park

- **Gisenyi** (p572) Kick back with a passionfruit cocktail on the sandy shores of Lake Kivu

- **Kigali Memorial Centre** (p553) Confront the horrors of the genocide at this haunting memorial on the outskirts of the capital

CLIMATE & WHEN TO GO

The average daytime temperature in Rwanda is around a pleasant 24°C with a possible maximum of 30°C. In the higher mountainous regions, which take up a lot of the country's space, the daytime range is as low as 10° to 15°C. There are four discernible seasons: the long rains from mid-March to mid-May, the long dry from mid-May to September, the short rains from October to mid-December and the short dry from mid-December to mid-March. It rains more frequently and heavily in the northeast, where volcanoes are covered by verdant rainforest. The summit of Karisimbi (4507m), the highest of these volcanoes and the highest peak in Rwanda, is often covered with snow and is prone to sleet.

For more information on Rwanda's climate, see the climate charts on p606.

Rwanda can be visited at any time of year – if you don't like getting wet however, you will want to avoid the long rains of mid-March to mid-May. The dry season from mid-May to September is easier for tracking mountain gorillas, but the endless hills can look quite dry and barren, a contrast to the verdant greens of the wet season. Peak season for gorilla tracking is July and August; travelling outside this time means it is easier to arrange a permit.

For details about planning your trip, and what to bring, see the boxed text, p14.

HISTORY

For detail on Rwanda's history prior to independence in 1962, see p25.

Decolonisation & Independence

Rwanda and neighbouring Burundi were colonised by Germany and later Belgium, both of whom played on ethnic differences to divide and conquer the population. Power was concentrated in the hands of the minority Tutsi, with the Tutsi *mwami* (king) playing the central role in political and legislative decision-making.

In 1956, Mwami Rudahigwa called for independence from Belgium, which influenced Rwanda's colonial occupiers to switch allegiance to the Hutu majority. The Tutsi favoured fast-track independence, while the Hutu wanted the introduction of democracy followed later by independence.

After the death of Rudahigwa in 1959, tribal tensions flared as the 'Hutu Revolution' resulted in the deaths of an estimated 20,000 to 100,000 Tutsis. Another 150,000 Tutsis were driven from the country, and forced to resettle as refugees in Uganda, Kenya and Tanzania.

Following independence in 1962, the Hutu majority came to power under Prime Minister Gregoire Kayibanda, who introduced quotas for Tutsis that limited their opportunities for education and work. In the fresh round of bloodshed that followed, thousands more Tutsis were killed, and tens of thousands fled across the borders.

Intertribal tensions erupted once again in 1972 when tens of thousands of Hutu were massacred in Burundi by the Tutsi-dominated government in reprisal for a coup attempt. The

HOW MUCH?

- **Tracking the mountain gorillas** US$500

- **Fresh fish at a decent restaurant** US$5 to US$10

- **Internet access per hour** US$1 to US$2

- **New Times newspaper** US$0.50

- **100km bus ride** US$2

LONELY PLANET INDEX

- **Litre of petrol** US$1 to US$2

- **Litre of bottled water** US$0.75

- **Primus Beer 720ml** US$2

- **Souvenir T-shirt** US$10

- **Street snack (beef brochettes)** US$1

RWANDA

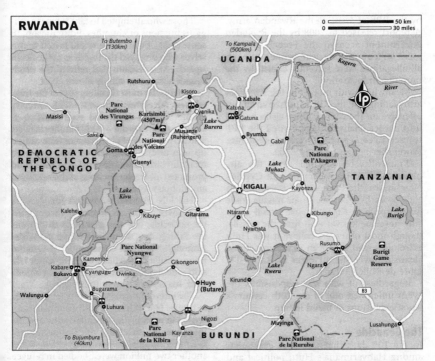

slaughter reignited old hatreds in Rwanda, which prompted Major General Juvenal Habyarimana to oust Kayibanda in 1973.

During the early years of his regime, Habyarimana made progress towards healing tribal divisions, and the country enjoyed relative economic prosperity. However, events unfolding in Uganda in the 1980s were to have a profound impact on the future of Rwanda.

In 1986, Yoweri Museveni became president of Uganda after his National Resistance Army (NRA) fought a brutal bush war to remove General Tito Okello from power. One of Museveni's key lieutenants was the current Rwandan President Paul Kagame, who capitalised on the victory by joining together with other exiled Tutsis to form the Rwandan Patriotic Front (RPF).

The Civil War Erupts

On 1 October 1990, 5000 well-armed soldiers of the RPF invaded Rwanda. All hell broke loose. Two days later at Habyarimana's request, France, Belgium and DRC flew in troops to help the Rwandan army repel the invasion.

With foreign support assured, the Rwandan army went on a rampage against the Tutsis, as well as any Hutu suspected of having collaborated with the RPF. Thousands of people were shot or hacked to death, and countless others indiscriminately arrested, herded into football stadiums or police stations and left there without food or water for days.

Many died. Congolese Hutu troops joined in the carnage. Once again thousands of Tutsi refugees fled to Uganda. However, the initial setback for the RPF was only temporary as President Museveni was keen to see the repatriation of the now 250,000 Tutsi refugees living in western Uganda.

While he fervently denied such allegations, Museveni allegedly helped to re-organise and re-equip the RPF. In 1991, Kagame's forces invaded Rwanda for a second time, and by 1993 was garrisoned only 25km outside of Kigali.

With Habyarimana backed into a corner, the warring parties were brought to the negotiating table in Arusha, Tanzania. Negotiations stalled, hostilities were renewed, and French troops were flown in to protect foreign nationals in Kigali, though they were accused by the RPF of assisting the Rwandan army. A report released in 2008 by the Rwandan government accused the French government of committing war crimes, though all allegations were fervently denied by the present administration.

Meanwhile, with morale in the Rwandan army fading fast, the RPF launched an all-out offensive on the capital. Once again backed into corner, Habyarimana invited the RPF to attend a conference of regional presidents. Power sharing was on the agenda.

Tragically, on 6 April 1994, the airplane carrying Habyarimana and Cyprien Ntaryamira, the President of Burundi, was shot down by a surface-to-air missile while on approach to Kigali airport. It will probably never be known who fired the missile, though most observers believe it was Hutu extremists who had been espousing ethnic cleansing over the airwaves of Radio TV Libre de Mille Collines.

Regardless of who was responsible, the event unleashed one of the 20th century's worst explosions of blood letting.

The Genocide

In the 100 days that followed, extremists among Habyarimana's Hutu political and military supporters embarked on a well-planned 'final solution' to the Tutsi 'problem'. One of the principle architects of the genocide was the cabinet chief of the Ministry of Defence, Colonel Theoneste Bagosora, who had been in charge of training the Interahamwe ("those who stand together") militia for more than a year.

One of Bagosora's first acts was to direct the army to kill the 'moderate' Hutu prime minister, Agathe Uwilingiyimana, as well as 10 Belgian UN peacekeepers. The killing of the UN peacekeepers prompted Belgium to withdraw all of its troops – precisely what Bagosora had calculated – which paved the way for the genocide to begin in earnest.

Rwandan army and Interahamwe death squads ranged at will over the countryside, killing, looting and burning, and roadblocks were set up in every town and city to prevent Tutsis from escaping. Every day, thousands of Tutsi and any Hutu suspected of sympathising with them or their plight were butchered on the spot. The streets of Kigali were littered with dismembered corpses, and the stench of rotting flesh was everywhere.

Those who attempted to take refuge in religious missions or churches did so in vain. In some cases, it was the nuns and priests themselves who betrayed the fugitives to the death squads. Any mission that refused the death squads access was simply blown apart.

Perhaps the most shocking part of the tragedy was the enthusiasm with which ordinary Hutu – men, women and even children as young as 10 years old – joined in the carnage. The perpetrators of the massacre were caught up in a tide of blind hatred, fear and mob mentality, which was inspired, controlled and promoted under the direction of their political and military leaders.

The UN Assistance Mission for Rwanda (UNAMIR) was in Rwanda throughout the genocide, but was powerless to prevent the killing due to an ineffective mandate. Although UN Force Commander Lt General Romeo Dallaire had been warning senior UN staff and diplomats about the coming bloodshed, his warnings went unheeded.

The international community left Rwanda to face its fate. While the RPF eventually succeeded in pushing the Rwandan army and the Interahamwe into DRC and Burundi, more than one million people were killed, while another two million were huddled in refugee camps across the border.

UNAMIR was finally reinforced and giving a more open mandate in July, but it was in the words of Dallaire, 'too much, too late'. The genocide was already over – the RPF had taken control of Kigali.

The Aftermath

Of course, that is far from the end of the story. Within a year of the RPF victory, a legal commission was set up in Arusha (Tanzania) to try those accused of involvement in the genocide. However, many of the main perpetrators – the Interahamwe and former senior army officers – fled into exile out of the reach of the RPF.

Some went to Kenya, where they enjoyed the protection of President Moi, who long refused to hand them over. Others – including Colonel Theoneste Bagosora, the principle architect of the genocide, and Ferdinand Nahimana, the director of the notorious Radio TV Libre de Mille Collines, which actively encouraged Hutus to butcher Tutsis – fled to Cameroon where they enjoyed the protection of that country's security boss, John Fochive. However, when Fochive was sacked by the newly elected president of Cameroon, Paul Biya, the Rwandan exiles were arrested.

Of greater importance were the activities of the Interahamwe and former army personnel in the refugee camps of DRC and Tanzania. Determined to continue their fight against the RPF, they spread fear among the refugees that if they returned to Rwanda, they would be killed. When Rwanda began to demand the repatriation of the refugees, the grip of the Interahamwe on the camps was so complete that few dared move.

What was of most concern to the RPF was that the Interahamwe was using the refugee camps as staging posts for raids into Rwanda, with the complicity of the Congolese army. By 1996, Rwanda was openly warning DRC that if these raids did not stop, the consequences would be dire.

The raids continued, and the RPF held true to its threat by mounting a lightning strike two-day campaign into DRC, targeting one of the main refugee camps north of Goma. The Interahamwe fled deep into the jungles of Congo, which allowed hundreds of thousands of refugees to return home to Rwanda.

Events changed in October of 1996 when a new guerrilla movement known as the Alliance of Democratic Forces for the Liberation of Congo/Zaïre, led by Laurent Kabila, emerged with the secret support of Rwanda and Uganda. The rebels, ably supported by Rwandan and Ugandan regulars, swept through eastern DRC, and by December were in control of every town and city in the region.

The Congolese army, alongside the Interahamwe and former Rwandan army personnel, retreated west in disarray towards Kisangani, looting and pillaging as they went. However, the grip the Interahamwe had on the refugee camps was finally broken, which allowed the remaining refugees to stream back into Rwanda, not only from DRC, but also from Tanzania.

Faced with a huge refugee resettlement task, the government began to build new villages throughout the country. Huge tracts of Parc National de l'Akagera (p585) were degazetted as a national park, and given over to this 'villagisation' program, along with much of the northwest region, which had previously hosted some of the most intense battles of the civil war.

The Healing Begins

Rwanda has done a remarkable job healing its wounds, and has achieved an astonishing level of safety and security in a remarkably short space of time – albeit with considerable help from a guilty international community that ignored the country in its darkest hour. Visiting Kigali today, it is hard to believe the horror that swept across this land in 1994, though the scars are much more visible in the countryside.

On the international front however, things have been rather less remarkable. In 1998, Rwanda and Uganda joined forces to oust their former ally Laurent Kabila. What ensued was Africa's first great war, sucking in as many as nine neighbours at its height, and costing an estimated 3 to 5 million deaths, mostly from disease and starvation.

Rwanda and Uganda soon fell out, squabbling over the rich resources that were there for the plunder in DRC. Rwanda backed the Rally for Congolese Democracy, Uganda the Movement for the Liberation of Congo, and the two countries fought out a brutal and prolonged proxy war.

Peace treaties were signed in 2002, and foreign forces were withdrawn from DRC, though if and when an international inquiry is launched, Rwanda may find itself facing accusations of war crimes. Rwanda's motives for entering the fray were to wipe out remnants of the Interahamwe militia and former soldiers responsible for the genocide, but somewhere along the line, elements in the army may have lost sight of the mission.

Back on the domestic front, Paul Kagame assumed the presidency in 2000, and was overwhelmingly endorsed at the ballot box in presidential elections in 2003 that saw him take 94% of the vote. Meanwhile, the search for justice continues at home and abroad – for more information, see the boxed text, p546.

An Optimistic Future

Looking at the bigger picture, Rwanda remains the home to two tribes, the Hutu and the Tutsi. The Hutu presently outnumber the Tutsi by more than four to one, and while the RPF government is one of national unity with a number of Hutu representatives, it's viewed in some quarters as a Tutsi government ruling over a predominantly Hutu population.

However, the RPF government has done an impressive job of promoting reconciliation, and restoring trust between the two

RWANDA

VOICES AGAINST GENOCIDE

While it's difficult to convey the enormity of the Rwandan genocide, the following quotes describe the horrors that unleashed themselves on this tiny country during a brief period of madness in 1994.

■ 'Genocide is any of the following acts committed with intent to destroy, in whole or in part, a national, ethnical, racial or religious group, as such: killing members of the group; causing serious bodily or mental harm to members of the group; deliberately inflicting on the group conditions of life, calculated to bring about its physical destruction in whole or in part; imposing measures intended to prevent births within the group; [and] forcibly transferring children of the group to another group.' – genocide as defined by the UN Convention of 1948

■ 'The dead of Rwanda accumulated at nearly three times the rate of Jewish dead during the Holocaust. It was the most efficient mass killings since the atomic bombings of Hiroshima and Nagasaki.' – US journalist Philip Gourevitch, author of *We Wish to Inform You That Tomorrow We Will Be Killed With Our Families: Stories from Rwanda*

■ 'I lay down again among the dead bodies. It was three days after the killings, so the bodies stank. The Interahamwe would pass by without entering the room, and dogs would come to eat the bodies. I lived there for 43 days.' – Rwandan Valentine Iribagiza, who survived the genocide

■ 'The horror of Rwanda is too high a price to pay for a very vaporous and whimsical notion of what constitutes inviolable territorial boundaries.' – Nigerian author Wole Soyinka, the first African to win the Nobel Prize in Literature.

■ 'During the 1994 Rwandan genocide against the Tutsis, the OAU (Organisation of African Unity) was furiously doing the watutsi.' – Ghanaian economist George Ayittey, president of the Free Africa Foundation

■ 'What I have come to realise as the root of it all, however, is the fundamental indifference of the world community to the plight of seven to eight million black Africans in a tiny country that had no strategic or resource value to any world power. An overpopulated little country

communities. This is no small achievement after the horrors that were inflicted on the Tutsi community during the genocide of 1994, especially since it would have been all too easy for the RPF to embark on a campaign of revenge and reprisal.

On the contrary, Kagame and his government are attempting to build a society with a place for everyone, regardless of tribe. There are no more Tutsis, no more Hutus, only Rwandans. Idealistic perhaps, but it is also realistically the only hope for the future.

THE CULTURE
The National Psyche
Tribal conflict has torn Rwanda apart during much of the independence period, culminating in the horrific genocide that unfolded in 1994. With that said, there are basically two schools of thought when it comes to looking at Rwandan identity.

The colonial approach of the Belgians was to divide and rule, issuing ID cards that divvied up the population along strict tribal lines. They tapped the Tutsis as leaders to help control the Hutu majority, building on the foundations of pre-colonial society in which the Tutsi were considered more dominant. Later, as independence approached, they switched sides, pitting Hutu against Tutsi in a new conflict, which simmered on and off until the 1990s when it exploded onto the world stage.

In the new Rwanda, the opposite is true. Tribal identities have been systematically eliminated, and everyone is now treated as a Rwandan. The new government is at pains to present a singular identity, and blames the Belgians for categorising the country along tribal lines that set the stage for the savagery that followed. Rwanda was a peaceful place beforehand: Hutu and Tutsi lived side by side for generations, and intermarriage was common – or so the story goes.

The truth, as always, is probably somewhere in between. Rwanda was no oasis before

that turned in on itself and destroyed its own people, as the world watched and yet could not manage to find the political will to intervene.' – Lieutenant-General Roméo Alain Dallaire, who served as force commander of UNAMIR during the Rwandan genocide

- 'If the pictures of tens of thousands of human bodies being gnawed on by dogs do not wake us out of our apathy, I do not know what will.' – Former Secretary General of the UN Kofi Annan, who served as Under-Secretary of Peace Keeping Operations during the Rwandan genocide

- 'There was a glaring and tragic lack of political will to intervene to stop the genocide, especially on the part of the most powerful members of the UN organisation.' – Former Under-Secretary General of the UN Ibrahim Gambari

- 'It didn't happen under my administration. It happened under me.' – Former United States President Bill Clinton

- 'You kept quiet… When these victims wanted your help to survive, you kept quiet.' – Rwandan President Paul Kagame

- 'We all knew we would die, no question. The only question was how. Would they chop us in pieces? With their machetes they would cut your left hand off. Then they would disappear and reappear a few hours later to cut off your right hand. A little later they would return for your left leg etc. They went on till you died. They wanted to make you suffer as long as possible. There was one alternative: you could pay soldiers so they would just shoot you.' – Manager of the Hotel des Mille Collines, Paul Rusesabagina, whose heroic acts during the genocide were portrayed in the movie *Hotel Rwanda*

- 'If there is one thing sure in this world, it is certainly this: that it will not happen to us a second time.' – Jewish-Italian chemist and holocaust survivor Primo Levi, author of *Survival in Auschwitz*

- 'When they said 'never again' after the holocaust, was it meant for some people and not for others.' – Rwandan Apollon Katahizi, who survived the genocide

the colonial powers arrived, but it was a sophisticated state compared to many others in Africa at this time. However, Tutsis probably had a better time of it than Hutus, something that the Belgians were able to exploit as they sought control.

But, it is true to say that there was no history of major bloodshed between the two peoples before 1959, and the foundations of this violence were laid by the Belgian insistence on ethnic identity and their cynical political manipulation. The leaders of the genocide merely took this policy to its extreme, first promoting tribal differences, and then playing on them to manipulate a malleable population.

Paul Kagame is trying to put the past behind, and create a new Rwanda for Rwandans. Forget the past? No. But do learn from it, and move on to create a new spirit of national unity.

All this of course will take time, maybe a generation or more, but what has been achieved in just over a decade is astonishing. Rwandans are taking pride in their country once more, investment is on the boil, and people are once again optimistic about their future. The real challenge, however, is to make sure that the countryside comes along for the ride.

At present, many of the investors in Kigali are overseas Tutsi finally returning home, and many of the poorest farmers in the countryside are Hutus who have always tilled the land. To avoid the divisions of the past once again surfacing in the new Rwanda, democratic development that favours all – urban and rural, rich and poor – and is blind to tribal ethnicity is required.

As East Africa moves towards greater economic and political integration once more, it is to be hoped that Rwanda will be invited along for the ride. In an ideal world, the ethnic divide between Hutu and Tutsi may become submerged in a wider mosaic of regional peoples.

RWANDA

THE SLOW HAND OF JUSTICE

Following a slow and shaky start, the **International Criminal Tribunal for Rwanda** (www.ictr.org) has managed to net most of the major suspects wanted for involvement in the 1994 genocide.

The tribunal was established in Arusha, Tanzania in 1995, but was initially impeded in its quest for justice by the willingness of several African countries to protect suspects. Countries such as Cameroon and Kenya long harboured Kigali's most wanted, frustrating the Rwandan authorities in their attempts to seek justice. However, due to changes in attitude or government, some big fish have been netted in the last decade.

Most important was former Rwandan Prime Minister Jean Kambanda, one of the first to be tried in 1998, who filed a guilty plea and provided the trial with much inside information on other architects of the genocide. His was the first-ever conviction of a head of state for the crime of genocide.

Many of the former ministers of the interim cabinet that presided over the country during the genocide have also been located. Since the 1996 change of government in Cameroon, the authorities there have arrested many suspects including the most senior military figures who oversaw the killing. One such individual is Colonel Theoneste Bagosora, who presided as commander of the Rwandan army during the genocide. Other suspects were tracked down all over Africa and beyond, in Belgium and the UK.

In April 2002, former chief of staff General Augustin Bizimungu was handed over by the Angolan authorities. Even more encouraging was the arrest of Colonel Tharcisse Renzaho, prefect of Kigali-ville during the genocide, the first time DRC had actually cooperated with the tribunal. Many of the Interahamwe militia leaders involved in the genocide had managed to evade justice by fighting with the Kinshasa government against forces from Rwanda and Uganda. However, with the Congolese on board in the quest for justice, there are now very few places left for the genocidaires to hide.

It is not just Congolese cooperation that is important, but also the US 'Rewards for Justice Program', which offers significant cash for information leading to the arrest of key suspects. This may have played its part in the Angolan arrest, as well as the arrests of literally dozens of other suspected criminals.

However, the prisons in Rwanda are still overflowing with genocide suspects. Prison numbers are thought to be around 120,000, and many of these prisoners are seen all over the country in their pink uniforms, helping on civil works programs.

There are three categories of prisoner: category-one suspects are those who planned and orchestrated the genocide; category-two prisoners are those who oversaw massacres and failed to prevent them when in a position to do so; and category three are those who killed or looted during the genocide. Most prisoners are category three, but evidence against them is mainly hearsay – hence the government has revived the *gacaca*, a traditional tribunal headed by village elders, to speed up the process.

However, the quest for justice in Rwanda looks set to be a long one – justice is a necessary part of reconciliation, but remains a principle rather than priority. Rwanda simply has too many cases to deal with, and too many other problems to worry about.

Daily Life

Urban Rwanda is a very sophisticated place – people follow a Mediterranean pattern of starting early before breaking off for a siesta or a long and boozy lunch. Late dinners inevitably lead into drinking and socialising that sometimes doesn't wind down until the early morning.

The rhythm of rural life is very different and follows the sun. People work long hours from dawn until dusk, but also take a break during the hottest part of the day. However, it is a hard life for women in the countryside, who seem burdened with the lion's share of the work, while many menfolk sit around drinking and discussing.

Faith is an important rock in the lives of many Rwandan people, with Christianity firmly rooted as the dominant religion. Churches from different denominations in Rwanda were tainted by their association with the genocide in 1994, though that doesn't seem to have dampened people's devotion to the faith.

Rwanda's economy was decimated during the genocide – production ground to a halt, and foreign investors pulled out all together. However, the current government has done a commendable job of stimulating the economy, which is now fairly stable, and boasts steady growth and low inflation. Foreign investors are once again doing business in Kigali, and there are building projects springing up all over the capital.

The agriculture sector is the principle employer and export earner, contributing about half of Rwanda's GDP. Coffee is by far the largest export, accounting for about 75% of export income, while tea and pyrethrum (a natural insecticide) are also important crops. However, the vast majority of farmers live subsistence lives, growing plantain, sweet potato, beans, cassava, sorghum and maize.

Like many countries in Africa, Rwanda actively promotes universal primary education, though the education system suffered terribly during the genocide. Teachers and professors were targeted, and a large number of schools and colleges were destroyed.

Today, only about half of the current teachers hold proper credentials, though a number of international organisations are involved in programs to train teachers. Furthermore, schools are overcrowded and illiteracy runs as high as 50%.

Population

The population is moving towards 11 million, which gives Rwanda one of the highest population densities of any country in Africa. While tribal identities are very much a taboo subject in Rwanda, the population is believed to be about 85% Hutu, 15% Tutsi and 1% Twa (pygmy). The Twa are a Central Africa indigenous group that has suffered from discrimination over the generations, though is slowly gaining a political and cultural foothold.

One of Rwanda's largest 'exports' during the long years of conflict and instability was refugees, though most of these returned home in the second half of the 1990s.

SPORT

Football is Rwanda's national obsession and the Wasps, as the national team are known, are a growing force in the sport. In 2004 they qualified for the African Nations Cup for the first time.

RELIGION

About 65% of the population are Christians of various sects (Catholicism is predominant), a further 25% follow tribal religions, often with a dash of Christianity, and the remaining 10% are Muslim.

ARTS
Dance

Rwanda's most famous dancers are the *Intore* troupe – their warrior-like displays are accompanied by a trance-like drumbeat similar to that of the famous Tambourinaires (see p597) in Burundi.

Cinema

Hotel Rwanda put Rwanda on the map for movie-goers the world over. Although it was shot in South Africa, it tells the story of Hotel des Mille Collines (see p555) manager Paul Rusesabagina, played by Don Cheadle, turning this luxury hotel into a temporary haven for thousands fleeing the erupting genocide. *100 Days* and the HBO miniseries *Sometimes in April* also convey the story of the Rwandan genocide through stark yet powerful narratives.

Gorillas in the Mist is based on the autobiography of Dian Fossey (see boxed text p564), who worked with the rare mountain gorillas in Parc National des Volcans. This is essential viewing for anyone visiting the gorillas.

ENVIRONMENT
The Land

Known as the 'Land of a Thousand Hills', it is hardly surprising to find that Rwanda's endless mountains stretch into the infinite horizon. Rwanda's 26,338 sq km of land is one of the most densely populated places on earth, and almost every available piece of land is under cultivation (except the national parks). Since most of the country is mountainous, this involves a good deal of terracing, and the banded hillsides are similar to those seen in Nepal or the High Atlas of Morocco. Coffee and tea plantations take up considerable areas of land.

Wildlife

Rwanda is home to the vast spectrum of East African wildlife, as well as both classic safariscapes and verdant equatorial rainforest. For more information on the rare mountain gorillas of Parc National des Volcans, see p79.

RWANDA

LEAVE YOUR PLASTIC BAGS AT HOME

In an effort to preserve the natural beauty of Rwanda, the government enforces a strict ban on plastic bags throughout the country. Police are particularly vigilant at border crossings, and you will be searched and possibly fined if contraband is found. So please, help support this worthwhile initiative and leave your plastic bags at home.

National Parks & Reserves

Due to its small size and high demand for cultivatable land, Rwanda only has a small network of national parks. The most popular protected area (and the focus of most visits to Rwanda) is Parc National des Volcans (p562), a string of brooding volcanoes that provides a home for the rare mountain gorilla. Parc National de Nyungwe (p579), Rwanda's newest national park, is a tropical montane forest that is one of the richest primate destinations in the region. Parc National de l'Akagera (p585) is the third of Rwanda's parks, but is sadly a shadow of its former self due to habitat destruction during the civil war as well as post-war 'villagisation.' With that said, Akagera has staged an impressive comeback in recent years, and wildlife populations are stabilising and flourishing again

Environmental Issues

Soil erosion, resulting from overuse of the land, is the most serious problem confronting Rwanda today. The terracing system in the country is fairly anarchic, and unlike much of Southeast Asia, the lack of coordinated water management has wiped out much of the topsoil on the slopes. This is potentially catastrophic for a country with too many people in too small a space as it points to a food-scarcity problem in the future.

Population density has also had a detrimental effect on the country's national park system, reducing Parc National des Volcans by half in 1969, and Parc National de l'Akagera by two-thirds in 1998.

When travelling through the countryside by bus, you will see children chasing the vehicle shouting 'agachupa', which means 'little bottle'. They want your water bottle to carry water to school or to sell to recyclers – either way, this is an easy way to get involved in helping the environment.

FOOD & DRINK

In the rural areas of Rwanda, food is very similar to that in other East African countries. Popular meats include *tilapia* (Nile perch), goat, chicken and beef brochettes (kebabs), though the bulk of most meals are centred on *ugali* (maize meal), *matoke* (cooked plantains) and so-called 'Irish' potatoes (the name. In the cities however, Rwanda's francophone roots are evident in the *plat du jour* (plate of the day), which is usually excellently prepared and presented Continental-inspired cuisine.

It is not recommended that you drink the tap water in Rwanda, though bottled water is cheap and widely available. Soft drinks (sodas) and the local beers, Primus (720ml) and Mulzig (330ml and 660ml), are available everywhere, as is the local firewater, *konyagi*. Wines (both South African and European) are generally only available in upmarket restaurants and hotels, though they can be quite expensive. A pleasant, non-alcoholic alternative is the purplish juice from the tree tomato or tamarillo, which is a sweet and tasty concoction that somewhat defies explanation – give it a try!

KIGALI

pop 850,000

Spanning several ridges and valleys, the Rwandan capital of Kigali is an attractive city of lush hillsides, flowering trees, winding boulevards and bustling streets. Compared to the choking congestion of Kampala, and the sinister edge of Nairobi, Kigali is more akin to a tranquil mountain hamlet, perched on the edge of an intensively cultivated and terraced countryside.

It wasn't always like this. Kigali exists as a testament to the peace and order that has defined Rwanda's trajectory for more than a decade, though it bore the brunt of the genocide in 1994. When the Rwandan Patriotic Front (RPF) finally captured Kigali after 100 days of systematic slaughter, dead and decaying bodies littered the streets. Dogs were shot en masse as they had developed a taste for human flesh.

In recent years, a massive amount of rehabilitation work has restored the city to its former graces, while increasing waves of foreign investment have sparked a number of ambitious building projects. As new shopping centres and high rises slowly define the new face of Kigali, residents are looking ahead to development rather than looking back at its destruction.

While simply being in Kigali is a powerful experience for anyone who has read its name in newspapers or heard it spoken on news programs, there aren't many sights in the traditional tourist sense. However, a visit to the Kigali Memorial Centre, which documents the genocide, is simply a must for all visitors to Rwanda.

Kigali is also home to a burgeoning restaurant and café scene, which is partly being fuelled by the large number of international aid workers that have taken up residence in the city. Indeed, the rebirth of the capital has seen a surprising measure of cosmopolitanism take hold, and today Kigali is arguably one of the most pleasant cities in the whole of East Africa.

HISTORY

Kigali was founded in 1907 by German colonisers, though it did not become the capital until Rwandan independence in 1962. Although Rwandan power was traditionally centred in Huye (Butare), Kigali was chosen because of its central location. Walking the streets of Kigali today, it is hard to imagine the horrors that unfolded here during those 100 days of madness in 1994. Roadblocks, manned by Interahamwe militia, were set up at strategic points throughout the city and thousands upon thousands of Rwandans were bludgeoned or hacked to death. People swarmed to the churches in search of sanctuary, but the killers followed them there, and showed a complete lack of mercy or compassion.

While all of this horror took place for days and nights on end, the UN Assistance Mission for Rwanda (UNAMIR) stood by and watched, held back by the bureaucrats and politicians who failed to grasp the magnitude of what was unfolding. In their defence, UNAMIR was bound by a restrictive mandate that prevented them from taking preliminary action, though it has been argued that the tragedy is that more deliberate action could have saved untold lives.

After 10 Belgian peacekeepers were murdered at the start of the genocide, the Belgian government withdrew its contingent, leaving UNAMIR to fend for itself with a minimal mandate and no muscle. There was little the 250 troops that remained could do but watch, and rescue or protect the few that they could.

Even more unbelievable is the fact that a contingent of the RPF was holed up in the parliamentary compound throughout this period, a legacy of the Arusha 'peace' process. Like the UNAMIR troops, there was little they could do to stop such widespread killing, though they did mount some spectacular rescue missions from churches and civic buildings around the city.

Throughout the massacre, the Hotel des Mille Collines (p552) became a refuge for those fleeing the violence, and thousands of people were holed up there, living in the direst of conditions. The Academy Award–winning film *Hotel Rwanda* tells the story of manager Paul Rusesabagina, who risked his life and the life of his family to selflessly help so many others.

When the RPF finally swept the genocidaires from power in early July 1994, Kigali was wrecked, much of the city's buildings were destroyed, and what little of the population remained alive were traumatised. As the Kigali Memorial Centre so aptly puts it, Rwanda was dead.

Remarkably, there are few visible signs of this carnage today. Kigali is now a dynamic and forward-looking city, the local economy is booming, investment is a buzzword, and buildings are springing up like mushrooms.

The inner damage? That's impossible to fully comprehend, though Kigali and Rwanda have recrossed the Rubicon, and deserve all of the support that they can get.

ORIENTATION

It is not that easy to come to grips with Kigali when you first arrive as it is spread across several hills and valleys. The centre fans out above Place de l'Unité Nationale, the busy commercial heartland along Ave de la Paix and the side streets heading west. Heading north down the valley from the centre of town is Blvd de Nyabugogo, which leads to the Nyabugogo bus terminal and all roads upcountry.

South of the centre along Blvd de la Revolution and surrounding streets is where many of the embassies are found, and to the southwest is the plush suburb of Kiyovu, with

RWANDA

KIGALI

0 ————— 500 m
0 ————— 0.3 miles

INFORMATION
Banque de Kigali	1	A4
BCDI	2	B4
BCR	3	B4
Belgian Embassy	4	B5
Bizidanny Tours & Safaris	(see 16)	
Bourbon Coffee Shop	(see 36)	
Canadian Embassy	5	D5
Centre D'Echanges Culturels Franco-Rwandais	(see 31)	
French Embassy	6	C6
Iposita Cybercafé	7	A4
Kiboko Tours & Travel	(see 38)	
Librairie Caritas	8	A4
Librairie Ikirezi	9	B5
Main Post Office	10	A4
ORTPN Tourist Office	11	B4
Tanzanian Embassy	12	B4
Thousand Hills	(see 15)	
Ugandan Embassy	13	B5
Volcanoes Safaris	(see 15)	

SLEEPING
Auberge La Caverne	14	B3
Hotel des Mille Collines	15	B4
Hôtel Gloria	16	A4
Hotel Gorillas	17	D4
Hôtel Isimbi	18	A4
Kigali Serena Hotel	19	B6
Motel Le Garni du Centre	20	B4
Okapi Hotel	21	B3
Sky Hotel	22	A6

EATING
Athenée	23	A4
Bourbon Coffee Shop	(see 36)	
Centre du Frais Alimentation Generale	24	A5
Chez John	25	D6
Chez Robert	26	B4
Heaven Restaurant & Bar	27	C4
Indian Khazana	28	C4
Le Dos Argente	(see 17)	
Le Panorama	(see 15)	
Le Poseidon Bar & Restaurant	29	B4
Nakumatt	(see 36)	
New Cactus	30	C6

DRINKING
Centre D'Echanges Culturels Franco-Rwandais	31	B3
Republika Lounge	32	D5

ENTERTAINMENT
Nyira Rock	33	B3

SHOPPING
Caplaki	34	D6
Dancing Pots	35	C4
Union Trade Centre	36	B3

TRANSPORT
Atraco Express	37	B3
Kenya Airways	38	B4
Okapi Car	39	A3
Rwandair Express	40	B4
SN Brussels Airline	(see 15)	
South African Airways	41	B4
Trans Express 2000	42	A3
Virunga Ponctuel	43	A3
Yahoo Car	44	B3

To Nyabugogo
Bus Station (1.5km);
Onatracom Express (1.5km);
Katuna (82km);
Musanze (Rugengeri) (93km);
Huye (Butare) (135km);
Kibuye (138km);
Gisenyi (155km)

To Kigali Hotel (500m);
Hotel Baobab (3km);
Nyamirambo (3km)

To Kigali Memorial Centre (2km);
Solace Ministries Guest House (3km);
Adventist Dental Clinic (3.5km);
British Embassy (3.5km);
Burundian Embassy (3.5km);
Flamingo (3.5km);
Hôtel Novotel Kigali (3.5km);
Kacyiru (3.5km); Kenyan Embassy (3.5km);
Netcare King Faycal Hospital (3.5km);
Planet Club (3.5km); South African
Embassy (3.5km); US Embassy (3.5km);
Chez Rose Guesthouse (7.5km);
Hôtel Chez Lando (7.5km); Sol u Luna (7.5km);
Gregoire Kayibanda International Airport (10.5km)

Rue du Lac Nasho
Ave de la Justice
Rue de Nyabugogo
Place de l'Unité Nationale
Blvd de l'OUA
Rue de la Concorde
Rue de l'Akagera

To New Cadillac (500m);
One Love Club (600m);
Lalibela Restaurant (600m)

Market
Place de l'Indépendance
Rue du Travail
Ave du Commerce
Rue de la République
Rue de Ntarwa
Rue Paul VI
Rue Député VI
Ave de Rusumo
Mont Juru
Rue Député Kayihura
Rue des Parcs

Kiyovu

Ave des Milles Collines
Ave des Grands Lacs
Blvd de la Revolution
Ave de l'Aimée
Ave de la Paix
Rue de Nyarugunga
Ave Paul VI
Rue de la Jeunesse
Rue de Bigogwe
Rue Député Kayihura
Ave de l'Akanyaru
Ave de Kiyovu
Ave de Masaka
Ave de l'Akagera

Rue de l'Hôpital
Military Camp
Rue de la Culture

To Nyatama (30km);
Ntarama (25km)

To Nyabugogo

Rivière Mrazi

several popular restaurants and upmarket hotels. Located a few kilometres across the valley east of the city centre is Kacyiru, a sophisticated suburb home to government buildings and embassies. Further out, the airport is located in the quiet district of Remera, located 10km north of the city centre and home to a number of hotels and restaurants.

It can be hard to get hold of good maps of Kigali, though ORTPN (see right) sells a number of decent foldout maps and basic city guides.

INFORMATION
Bookshops

There are a few bookshops in Kigali, selling mainly French-language publications.

Librairie Caritas (Ave du Commerce) A central bookshop for French and some English titles.

Librairie Ikirezi (☎ 571314; Ave de la Paix; ☼ 9am-12.30pm & 2-6pm Mon-Fri, 9am-12.30pm Sat & Sun) Stocks a wide range of French- and English-language books and magazines.

Cultural Centres

Centre D'Echanges Culturels Franco-Rwandais (Ave de la République) Overlooking Place de l'Unité Nationale, this place has live music at the weekend (see p557).

Emergency

Police (☎ 083-11170) A 24-hour emergency number.

Internet Access

Internet access is widespread and very cheap in Kigali. There are plenty more places throughout the centre than those listed here, meaning no online junkie need go without their fix.

Iposita Cybercafé (per hr RFr500) Part of the post office complex.

Bourbon Coffee Shop (Union Trade Centre; free with purchase of item) The most popular café in town has a great wi-fi spot if you're travelling with your laptop (see p556).

Medical Services

Some embassies also have medical attachés who offer services through private practices.

Adventist Dental Clinic (☎ 582431) Located near the Novotel about 3.5km from the centre of town in Kacyiru district, this place is run by an international dentist based in Kigali.

Netcare King Faycal Hospital (☎ 582421) Also near the Novotel, this South African–operated hospital is the best in Kigali. Prices are high but so are standards.

Money

Before heading out into the countryside, you're going to want to stock up on cold, hard cash. At the time of writing, ATMs throughout Rwanda were not yet accepting international cards, and credit cards were only being accepted at upmarket hotels and restaurants. As a result, you're going to need to either change money, or rely on cash advances, which sadly can be a pricey affair.

For exchanges, banks are best avoided as the bureaucracy and paperwork is a pain. Street rates are generally better, but it may be safer to use one of the many foreign exchange (forex) bureaus in Kigali, mainly located around the post office.

For cash advances on your credit or ATM card, any of the following banks can sort you out, though be prepared for long lines, lots of forms and a hefty charge.

BCR (Banque Commerciale de Rwanda; Blvd de la Revolution)

Banque de Kigali (Ave du Commerce)

BCDI (Banque de Commerce, de Developement et de l'Industriel; Ave de la Paix)

Post

Main post office (Ave de la Paix; ☼ 8am-5pm Mon-Fri, to noon Sat) Poste restante services available.

Telephone

There are quite a few telecommunications kiosks opposite the post office that are open throughout the day and into the night. There are also MTN kiosks and public payphones throughout the city.

Tourist Information

ORTPN (Office Rwandais du Tourisme et des Parcs Nationaux; ☎ 576514; ☎ /fax 576515; www.rwandatourism.com, info@rwandatourism.com, reservation@rwandatourism.com; 1 Blvd de la Revolution, BP 905; ☼ 7am-5pm Mon-Fri, 7am-12pm Sat & Sun) Known locally as 'Or-ti-pen,' Rwanda's national tourism office is located right in the centre of town behind the Hotel des Mille Collines. The office stocks a number of brochures, maps and leaflets (in French and English) that detail all of Rwanda's tourist attractions. The friendly staff here is keen on answering your questions (in French and English), and promoting Rwandan tourism to the increasing streams of foreign visitors.

ORTPN is also where independent travellers can make reservations to track the mountain gorillas in Parc National des Volcans,

RWANDA

though it's recommended that you contact them several months in advance as permits are extremely difficult to come by during the high season. If you've arrived in Kigali without a permit, and are hoping that one will materialise in light of a last minute cancellation, the staff at ORTPN can phone around to different operators for you. While there are certainly no guarantees, you might get lucky if you're flexible and prepared to wait a few days. For more details on gorilla tracking, see p566.

This office is also a good spot to inquire about golden monkey tracking in Parc National des Volcans – for more information, see p568.

Travel Agencies

If you want some help in securing a gorilla permit, or in arranging transportation to/from any of the national parks, the following travel agencies/tour operators are a recommended first port of call. Any of the following can also help you book onward flight tickets to other countries in East Africa and beyond.

Note that there are also a couple of recommended operators in the town of Musanze (Ruhengeri) who can also help you arrange gorilla tracking permits – see p559.

Bizidanny Tours & Safaris (☎ 55102004; www .bizidanny.com; Ave du Commerce) This small start-up operator runs individually customised tours throughout the country, and can help you organise tracking permits.

International Tours & Travels (☎ 574057; Rue de la Paix) This is a reliable place for air tickets that represents a number of East African airlines, including Kenya Airways and Rwandair Express.

Kiboko Tours & Travel (☎ 501741; www.kiboko travels.org.rw; Rue de la Paix) Another small operator that is a good starting point for securing permits and organising trips and treks throughout the country.

Thousand Hills (☎ 501151; www.thousandhills.rw; Hotel des Mille Colines, Ave de la République) One of the more well-established tour operators, Thousand Hills is an excellent choice if you want to increase your likelihood of getting your hands on a gorilla permit.

Volcanoes Safaris (☎ 502452; www.volcanoessafaris .com; Hotel des Mille Colines, Ave de la République) Probably the most professional operator in Rwanda, Volcanoes Safaris runs customised trips ranging from budget-friendly transfers to exclusive fly-ins. It owns the exclusive Virunga Lodge (p562) in Parc National Des Volcans.

FESTIVALS & EVENTS

For information on Kwita Izina, the gorilla naming ceremony, see the box text on p570.

SIGHTS
Kigali Memorial Centre

Don't leave Kigali without a visit to this sombre memorial to the 1994 Rwandan genocide – for more information, see the boxed text, opposite.

Hotel des Mille Collines

The inspiration for the film *Hotel Rwanda*, this **luxury hotel** (☎ 576530; www.millecollines.net; Ave de la République) in the centre of Kigali was owned by the Belgian airline Sabena in 1994. At the time of the genocide, the hotel's European managers were evacuated, and control of the Mille Collines was given to Paul Rusesabagina, manager of the smaller Hotel des Diplomates.

As the situation in Kigali reached its boiling point, Paul opened the floodgates, and allowed fleeing Tutsis and moderate Hutu to take refuge in the hotel. His heroic story is one of self-sacrifice in the most dire of situations – he managed to bribe the Interahamwe with money and alcohol, which allowed him to provide food and water for the refugees.

Paul, his family and a few lucky survivors were eventually evacuated in a UN convoy as the Interahamwe seized the hotel. Eventually, he arrived safely behind RPF lines, and fled to Belgium with his wife, children and two adopted nieces. Today, Paul still lives in Brussels with his family, owns a small trucking company, and is an outspoken humanitarian and public hero.

A visit to the Hotel des Mille Collines is something of a must while you're in Kigali. However, it can be incredibly surreal to sip cocktails by the poolside knowing full well the tragic events that played out here just over a decade ago.

It is just business as usual here, especially given the new found international fame of the Hotel des Mille Collines. So, do your best to take a few moments to pause and reflect on the gravity of your surroundings, even if it is over a chilled lager or two.

TOURS

ORTPN (p551) offers a Kigali city tour (US$20, three hours) departing at 8am or 2pm daily. The tour includes the Kigali Memorial Centre, as well as a few other prominent buildings around town. It's not amazing value given the memorial currently has

KIGALI MEMORIAL CENTRE

More than a memorial for Kigali, more than a memorial for Rwanda and its tragedy, this is a memorial for all of us, marking the Rwandan genocide and many more around the world that never should have come to pass. The **Kigali Memorial Centre** (www.kigalimemorialcentre.org; admission free, donations welcome, ☺ 10am-5pm, closed public holidays) is a must for all visitors to Rwanda wanting to learn more about how it was that the world watched as a genocide unfolded in this tiny, landlocked country.

Downstairs is dedicated to the Rwandan genocide; the informative tour includes background on the divisive colonial experience in Rwanda and the steady build-up to the genocide. Exhibits are professionally presented and include short video clips in French and English. As the visit progresses, it becomes steadily more powerful, as you are confronted with the crimes that took place here.

The sections on the cold and calculated planning of the genocide and its bloody execution are particularly disturbing, and include moving video testimony from survivors. The story continues with sections on the refugee crisis in the aftermath of the genocide and the search for justice through the international tribunal in Arusha as well as the local *gacaca* courts (traditional tribunals headed by village elders).

Finally, you are confronted with a room full of photographs of Rwandan victims of the genocide. The effect is very similar to Tuol Sleng, the Khmer Rouge prison in Phnom Penh, Cambodia. You feel yourself suffocating under the weight of sadness and despair, the wasted lives and loves of the nameless people surrounding you.

Upstairs is a moving section dedicated to informing visitors about other genocides that have taken place around the world to set Rwanda's nightmare in a historical context. Armenians, Jews, Cambodians, all have been victims of the mass slaughter we now know as genocide.

There is also a section on Rwandan children who fell victim to the killers' machetes. Young and innocent, if you have remained impassionate until this point, the horror of it all catches up with you here. Life-size photos are accompanied by intimate details about their favourite toys, their last words and the manner in which they were killed.

Why did Rwanda descend into 100 days of madness? The Kigali Memorial Centre explains it as best it can, but no one can answer the fundamental question of what it takes to turn man into beast. However, the centre is a fitting memorial to the 1994 genocide, especially since the memorial gardens here hold the remains of more than 250,000 victims.

The Kigali Memorial Centre was set up with assistance from the **Aegis Trust** (www.aegistrust .org), which was established in 2000 at the Holocaust Centre in the UK. The organisation, which is dedicated to understanding and preventing genocide, is involved in a number of activities including academic research, policy advocacy, education, public awareness and humanitarian support for victims of genocide.

The Kigali Memorial Centre is located in the northern Kisozi district of the capital, which is a short taxi ride from the centre (2000 RFr). You can also come here as part of an organised tour, which can be arranged through ORTPN (see Tours opposite).

no entry charge, but the guides are very knowledgeable, and can give you a local's perspective on the capital.

KIGALI FOR CHILDREN

This definitely isn't the world's most exciting city for children. The best bet if you're travelling with the little ones is to check into a hotel with a swimming pool and take it from there. Otherwise, head out to one of the national parks or to Gisenyi (p572) for some 'beach' time on Lake Kivu.

SLEEPING

In the years since the genocide, Kigali has played host to legions of international aid workers, diplomats, bureaucrats, investors etc, all of whom have played their own small part in driving up the city's hotel prices. While there is a wide range of accommodation spread out across the town, the vast majority is decidedly upmarket. Of course, there are a few good spots at the budget end of the spectrum, though this is one city where it might be worth splashing out with a bit of extra cash.

RWANDA

Finding a hotel is not a great problem, but advance reservations at more expensive places are recommended. Accommodation is spread across town, but those without their own transport should head for the city centre. Note that prices are quoted in US dollars, although hotels will accept just about any form of hard cash that you have on you.

Budget

Hôtel Gloria (☎ 571957; cnr Rue du Travail & Ave du Commerce; s/d from US$10/15) Possibly the longest running budget digs in town, Hôtel Gloria's location is right in the heart of Kigali, though it doesn't appear to have benefited from any of the renovation plans that are transforming the city centre. Still, if you can deal with the dingy rooms and the cold-water showers, it's definitely cheap.

Kigali Hotel (☎ 571384; s/d from US$10/15) Another good hotel on the bang-for-your-buck basis, the Kigali has large rooms that are thoroughly sanitised with en suite bathrooms and the occasional blast of hot water. However, the big drawback is that it is quite a long way from the action, tucked away behind the mosque on the road to Nyamirambo. Oh, and that mosque – don't forget the early morning wake-up calls.

Auberge La Caverne (☎ 574549; Blvd de Nyabugogo; s/d from US$10/20) A significant cut above the rough and ready cheapies at this end of the scale, this little auberge is home to just 15 rooms of varying sizes and shapes. You can keep things simple by shoestringing it in the smaller rooms, or paying a bit extra for larger suites with satellite TV and raised bathtubs (yes, there's hot water).

our pick One Love Club (☎ 575412; www.onelove project.org; Ave des Poids Lourds; camping US$10, r US$20-30; 🖳) 'Let's get together and feel alright, altogether now…' If it's the spirit of peace and harmony you are after, then this little retreat is the place for you. Since 1997, profits from this small guesthouse have been ploughed back into a local nongovernmental organisation (NGO) to help the disabled community in Rwanda. You can support this noble cause, which has so far supplied artificial limbs to more than 5000 Rwandans at no cost, by either pitching a tent in their shady campsite or bedding down in their simple but cosy en suite rooms. Even if you're not staying here, make a point of stopping by for dinner as the lush gardens

of the One Love Club are also home to the Lalibela Restaurant (p556), the best spot in the city for spongy *injera* (sourdough bread) and hearty *wats* (stews).

Solace Ministries Guest House (☎ 588005; www .solacem.org/solace_guest_house.htm; Kacyiru; r per person with meals US$25) Located in the suburb of Kacyiru, Solace Ministries is dedicated to providing antiretroviral drugs to women who were raped by the Interahamwe during the 1994 genocide. Funding for this vitally important project is partially obtained by opening up the doors of the church to foreign tourists. En suite rooms are bright, airy and have proper bathtubs, though the highlight is the traditional Rwandan cooking provided with gusto to hungry guests. Even if you're not a religious person, the mission of Solace Ministries is certainly worth supporting.

Midrange

Chez Rose Guesthouse (☎ 085-05545; s/d US$30/34) Located in the suburb of Remera, which is convenient to the airport if you have an early morning flight, this bucolic little guesthouse offers a nice respite from the city centre. The management is friendly, the rooms are more than adequate and the price is right, although it is a bit far out if you don't have your own car.

Hôtel Isimbi (☎ 575109; www.hotelisimbi.co.rw; Rue de Kalisimbi; s/d from US$30/36) The most central of all the midrange hotels, Isimbi is a good option for those who don't fancy walking up and down Kigali's endless hills. While the functional rooms here are somewhat lacking in atmosphere, it's a comfortable enough place that attracts a lot of local business travellers.

Sky Hotel (☎ 516693; Ave de la Justice; s/d from US$30/36) Perched on the edge of the road to Nyamirambo, the inspiration for this hotel's name probably comes from the first-class views of the valley below. Rooms are smart and well equipped, and there is a great little terrace bar below the hotel with big breezes blowing down from the hills.

Okapi Hotel (☎ 576765; www.okapi.co.rw; Blvd de Nyabugogo; s/d from US$35/46; 🖳) A well established midrange hotel that attracts a loyal following, the Okapi benefits from a decent location that's within easy walking distance of the city centre. The rooms themselves benefit from modern amenities, so you can watch satellite TV and take a steaming hot bath, or just relax on the balcony and watch the city go by. There

RWANDA

is also a reliable on-site internet café as well as an excellent restaurant that serves a variety of African and international cuisine.

Hôtel Chez Lando (☎ 584328; www.hotelchezlando .com; s/d from US$60/70) A long-standing Kigali institution located out in the suburb of Remera, the rooms at Chez Lando are single-storey units set around a lush garden. While it's a long way out of town, the peace and quiet on offer here are big draws, assuming you either have your own wheels or don't mind relying on taxis.

our pick **Hotel Gorillas** (☎ 501717; www.hotel gorillas.com; Rue des Parcs; standard s/d US$85/105, deluxe s/d US$95/115; ⌨) It's a bit more expensive than other midrange hotels, but the Hotel Gorillas is arguably one of the best options in town. A slick little hotel in the upmarket Kiyovu area of the city, this place is winning over a lot of customers thanks to its spacious rooms with a touch of decorative flair. The highlight of the property is Le Dos Argente (p556) or the Silverback Restaurant, which is an open-air bistro in the French tradition that has an eclectic offering of Rwandan and Continental classics. If you're travelling with your laptop, there is also a strong wireless signal here, and plenty of al fresco seating where you can surf the web while sipping an ice cold Primus.

Top End

Motel Le Garni du Centre (☎ 572654; garni@rwanda1 .com; Ave de la République; s/d incl breakfast US$125/140; ⌨) Kigali's first and only boutique hotel, this intimate and atmospheric little auberge is tucked away on a side road below Hotel des Mille Collines. By far the smallest upmarket property in town, Le Garni du Centre boasts individually decorated rooms that are built around an inviting swimming pool – if you've been traipsing up and down Kigali's hills, be kind to your feet and reward them with a relaxing soak.

our pick **Hotel des Mille Collines** (☎ 576530; www .millecollines.net; Ave de la République; s/d US$135/155; ⌨ ⌨) Welcome to the *Hotel Rwanda*. With the international success of the movie, the 'Hotel of a Thousand Hills' looks set to see a surge in bookings, which is probably why it was in the midst of a major renovation at the time of research. The hotel used in the movie was actually down in South Africa, though the original hotel where horror and hope collided was right here. Of course, the actual property is a bit more of a cement and glass construction than the colonial compound that appeared in the film, though the exceedingly elegant and spacious rooms are four-star quality all the way. Even if you're not staying here, stop by for a poolside drink – for more information, see p552.

Hôtel Novotel Kigali (☎ 585816; www.accorhotels .com/accorhotels/fichehotel/gb/nov/3410/fiche_hotel.shtml; s/ d US$135/185; ⌨ ⌨ ⌨) Long considered the best in town, the Novotel has now lost that title to the Kigali Serena, though this popular French-owned hotel is still a refined and sophisticated spot. It's a long way out in the suburb of Kacyiru, but francophones will still appreciate this luxurious offering from the Accor family, with both premium business amenities and resort-quality bars and restaurants.

Kigali Serena Hotel (☎ 597100; www.serenahotels .com/rwanda/kigali/home.asp; Blvd de la Revolution; s/d from US$275/300; ⌨ ⌨ ⌨) The capital's first and currently only five-star hotel, the Kigali Serena is certainly the smartest address in town. Formerly the Diplomates, and later the Intercontinental, the Kigali Serena was born after the Aga Khan Foundation pumped some serious style (and money) into this property in a bid to reel in Kigali's high-flying diplomats and businessmen. The result is the swishest spot in all of Rwanda, although you're going to need to peel some serious bills out of your bank roll if you want to bed down with the country's top movers and shakers.

EATING

The dining scene in Kigali is getting increasingly more sophisticated with each passing year, especially since the city's resident expats have been known to spend serious sums of cash in search of gourmet cuisine. While Rwanda's cosmopolitan capital has always been the country's best spot for innovative African dishes alongside European-inspired creations, Kigali now boasts a broad palette of international offerings.

Much like its inflated hotel scene, eating out in Kigali is not a cheap experience, though you can generally expect a higher standard here than in other East African capitals. Furthermore, the country's francophone roots shine through in its rich cuisine, which means that meals in Rwanda are best enjoyed at a leisurely pace in the company of good friends with lots and lots of wine to go around. Bon appétit!

RWANDA

Budget

Le Poseidon Bar & Restaurant (Ave de la République; mains RFr1500-3000) This is Kigali's very own fast food spot, with a lively bar and local restaurant offering sandwiches, burgers, pizzas and pastas. It draws a healthy work crowd at lunchtime, and can fill up with stragglers leaving the office on Fridays.

our pick **Bourbon Coffee Shop** (☎ 505307; Union Trade Centre; coffee & pastry RFr1500-3000; 🖳) While Rwanda produces some of the finest coffee beans in the world, the vast majority are marked for export, leaving behind only instant coffee. However, if you don't like your morning blend served in a packet, head to this popular spot where locals and expats alike queue up for the real stuff. Frothy cappuccinos and potent espressos are made all the better by the varied selection of continental pastries. And here's the best part – you get an hour of free wi-fi access with your purchase, so bring along your laptop if you need a quick internet fix.

Sol e Luna (☎ 583062; near Kisementi crossroads; pizzas RFr2000-3500) Out in the 'burbs near Hotel Chez Lando, locals swear that this Italian pizzeria is the best around. Rwanda may be a long way from the boot shaped peninsula, but we agree – fresh ingredients inevitably create awesome pizza.

Chez John (Rue de Masaka; meals RFr2000-4000) A popular local haunt with more than its fair share of foreign patrons, Chez John serves up true Rwandan standards, namely meat and maize. The surroundings may have gone upmarket in light of its recent success, but this is still authentic country-style cooking at its finest.

Midrange

Lalibela Restaurant (☎ 575412; Ave des Poids Lourds; mains RFr3000-4000) Kigali's premiere Ethiopian restaurant is set in the grounds of the One Love Club (p554), so you can dine comfortably knowing that part of the proceeds of your meal are going to charity. It has a laid-back atmosphere in keeping with the Rasta owner, and serves big portions of spicy chicken and the like on *injera*. It also rocks on as a bar later in the evening.

Hotel Baobab (☎ 575633; dishes RFr3000-5000) It is worth venturing into the wilds of Nyamirambo to this al fresco restaurant, which offers diners a welcome measure of intimacy by serving meals in private pavilions set in a lush garden.

The menu is an extensive list of African and continental favourites, ranging from grilled tilapia straight from the Great Lakes or an aged cut of beef in a French-reduction sauce.

New Cactus (☎ 572572; Rue Député Kayuku; mains RFr3000-5000) Outrageously popular with expats and well-to-do Rwandans alike, the New Cactus is set on a commanding ridge up in Kiyovu where you can soak up the sparkling lights of Kigali by night. Boasting a broad menu of French favourites, gourmet pizzas, rich fondues and a well-rounded wine list, you should spend a bit liberally here if you really want to live well.

Indian Khazana (Rue Député Kajangwe; plates RFr3500-5000) Kampala's most celebrated Indian restaurant has come south to Kigali; Khana Khazana has been spicing up people's lives for years in the Ugandan capital and now Rwanda can enjoy the subtle flavours of the subcontinent. One of the hottest places in town, Khazana is the perfect antidote to too many days on the road with nothing more than *ugali* and *nyama choma* (barbecued meat) to choose from.

Flamingo (☎ 586589; 6th fl, Telecom House, Blvd de l'Umuganda; mains RFr3500-5000) Something of a Kigali institution, the Flamingo has moved into an anonymous office block in Kacyiru, though it's still hands down the best Chinese in the country. The sizzling platters are quite a sight, and there is a serious selection for vegetarians, though most diners are content to tuck into hearty portions of stir-fried noodles.

Heaven Restaurant & Bar (☎ 500234; Rue Du Mont Juru; mains RFr3500-5000) A relative newcomer on the burgeoning Kigali restaurant scene, Heaven is highlighted by the handcrafted wooden tables and chairs produced by local artisans. The menu itself is akin to a relaxed bistro offering fine dining, as evident by the eclectic menu drawing from a variety of international influences.

Top End

Chez Robert (☎ 501305; Ave de la République; meals RFr5000-7000) Formerly home to the extravagant Aux Caprices du Palais, Chez Robert now plays host to a Brussels exile, and offers a sophisticated menu of French and Belgian classics. Many of the dishes feature luxury ingredients such as fine European cheeses and wines; but it's the quality of the local produce that makes the dishes here truly shine.

Le Dos Argente (☎ 501717; Hotel Gorillas, Rue des Parcs; mains RFr5000-10,000) Also known as the Silverback

Restaurant, this is one of the best restaurants in Kigali, set in an open-air garden at the Hotel Gorillas and staffed by an extremely attentive wait staff. The accent here is most definitely French – *foie gras*, *duck à l'orange* and even rabbit and frogs legs are available for the discerning diner, as is an impressive wine list (with equally impressive prices!).

Le Panorama (☎ 576530; www.millecollines.net; Hotel des Mille Collines, Ave de la République; mains RFr5000-10,000) Proudly perched at the top floor of the Hotel des Mille Collines, Kigali's most famous restaurant attracts its fair share of international scenesters, who flock here for formal banquets with panoramic views. Although dining here can be a decidedly stuffy experience, the food is of very high quality, and the views really do make it worth your while.

Self-Catering

Athenée (Rue de Kalisimbi) Travellers who want to do a spot of self-catering or who are planning some time in Parc National Nyungwe or Parc National de l'Akagera will find a small selection of things here.

Centre du Frais Alimentation Generale (Ave des Mille Collines) This is the spot for far-flung imports, although you'll do just as well checking out the bakery on the premises.

Nakumatt (Union Trade Centre, Place de l'Unite Nationale) By far the best option for self-caterers, this huge supermarket in the Union Trade Centre pretty much has everything you'll need.

DRINKING & ENTERTAINMENT

The good folk of Kigali take their drinking and partying pretty seriously, and there are a number of good bars around town, some of which turn into clubs as the night wears on. While you certainly don't need to dress to impress, Rwandans are mindful of appearances, especially in increasingly cosmopolitan Kigali. Besides, there's certainly no harm in donning some nice threads from time to time.

The swimming pool at the Hotel des Mille Collines (see p552) serves as the city's most popular daytime bar at weekends with expats coming here to relax by the water. There is a happy hour from 5pm to 7pm every day. Hotel Chez Lando (p555) is another popular hotel bar that draws a local crowd almost every night, whether for drinking, dining or dancing – it also has DJs on the weekends.

Centre D'Echanges Culturels Franco-Rwandais (Ave de la République; admission from RFr2000, drinks RFr500-1000) On Friday and Saturday, the Centre D'Echanges Culturels Franco-Rwandais plays host to leading local bands. The music is an eclectic mix of Rwandan, reggae and international covers, and after a few beers everyone finds their rhythm.

our pick **New Cadillac** (admission from RFr2500, drinks from RFr1500; Wed-Sun) This long-running club is just holding off all-comers to remain the most popular place in town. Located in the Kimikurure district not far from the centre of Kigali, this is a large, partly open-air venue that plays a mixture of East African pop, Congolese *soukous* (dance music) and Western hits most nights. It doesn't really pick up until after midnight, but once it does, it really rocks, and usually well into the early morning.

Nyira Rock (Ave du Commerce; admission from RFr1000, drinks from RFr500) This local nightclub in the city centre boasts DJs, cheap beers and plenty of action towards the weekend. It is one place in Kigali where you can expect to find something of a small gay and lesbian scene, though, as always in East Africa, use discretion.

Planet Club (Kigali Business Centre, Ave du Lac Muhazi; admission from RFr3500, drinks from RFr2000) This trendy nightclub is often called KBC by locals due to its location in the Kigali Business Centre, well out of the city centre. This is one weekend spot where you really need to pay to play, though you'll certainly be glad you did.

Republika Lounge (Rue de l'Akanyaru; drinks RFr1000-2500) Located in the fancy Kiyovu area of town, Republika is definitely the place to be in Kigali. Lush furnishings, a well-stocked bar and a small menu for the midnight munchies keep the crowds happy.

SHOPPING

Rwanda produces some attractive handicrafts, but the lack of tourists in the country has kept development of souvenir shops to a minimum. Look for basketry, batik, drums, woodcarvings and the famous cow-dung art of symmetrical symbols. There are also a lot of Congolese handicrafts, including the ever-popular wooden masks.

Kigali isn't exactly the shopping capital of Africa, but there are a few good places to have a sniff around. There are some good craft shops selling locally produced carvings, cards and paintings, mostly located near the main post office in the centre of town.

Caplaki (Ave de Kiyovu) Sellers are organised in fixed stalls and popular items include a range of carvings and masks from across the border in DRC. Sellers claim many items are 'antiques' and price their goods accordingly; the reality is most are modern replicas and you should bargain prices down to something more sensible.

Dancing Pots (Rue Député Kamuzinzi) This is an admirable fair trade project established to assist the Batwa pygmies. The Forest Peoples' Project has been training potters to produce terracotta pieces, which can be bought here at prices that are fair to both the artisan and the customer.

Union Trade Centre (Place de l'Unite Nationale) A sparkling new shopping centre at the heart of Kigali, the Union Centre is home to a large Nakumatt shopping centre as well as a few small shops, eateries and travel agents.

GETTING THERE & AWAY
Air
For contact details of the international airlines flying in and out of Gregoire Kayibanda International Airport, see p592. **Rwandair Express** (☎ 503687; www.rwandair.com; Ave de la Paix) is the national airline and is planning domestic flights to Gisenyi.

Bus & Minibus
Several bus companies operate services to major towns, which are less crowded and safer than local minibuses. Okapi Car runs to Huye (Butare), Gisenyi, Kibuye and Musanze (Ruhengeri); Atraco Express to Huye (Butare), Musanze (Ruhengeri) and Gisenyi, including a through service to Goma; Trans Express 2000 to Huye (Butare); and Virunga Ponctuel to Musanze (Ruhengeri). See the individual town entries for more details on journey times and road conditions.

All buses depart from company bus offices in the city centre. Onatracom Express have larger 45-seat buses, which could be considered safer, and these run to Musanze (Ruhengeri) and Gisenyi, plus Huye (Butare) and Cyangugu. These services depart from the Nyabugogo bus station.

Local minibuses depart from the Nyabugogo bus terminal for towns all around Rwanda, including Huye (Butare; RFr1400, two hours), Katuna (RFr1700, 1½ hours), Kibuye (RFr1500), Musanze (Ruhengeri; RFr1300, two hours) and Gisenyi (RFr1800,

four hours). These minibuses leave when full throughout the day, except at weekends when they tend to dry up after 3pm. Just turn up and tell someone where you're going. See the respective town entries for further details.

Nyabugogo is about 2km north of the city centre in the valley and minibuses (RFr300) are available from the city centre, although there is no longer a local bus station in the centre.

GETTING AROUND
To/From the Airport
Gregoire Kayibanda International Airport is at Kanombe, 10km east of the city centre. A taxi costs about RFr7500, but a direct minibus from the city centre is cheaper (RFr400).

Minibus
There is no longer a local bus station in the city centre, so minibuses cruise the streets looking for passengers. All advertise their destination in the front window and run to districts throughout the city. Costs are very cheap, from RFr100 to RFr300.

Taxi
There are no metered taxis, but a fare within the city centre costs, on average, RFr1500 to RFr2000, double that out to the suburbs or later at night.

Taxi-Motor
These small Japanese trail bikes can be a swift way to get around Kigali, although it can be quite scary travelling out to the suburbs as the drivers really hit the throttle. Short hops are just RFr200 to RFr500, while trips out to the suburbs cost RFr700 to RFr1000.

AROUND KIGALI

NYAMATA & NTARAMA GENOCIDE MEMORIALS
During the genocide, victims fled to churches seeking refuge, only to find that some of the clergy was providing information to the Interahamwe. As a result of their lack of compassion, some of the most horrific massacres took place inside the holy sanctums of churches throughout Rwanda.

Two of the most powerful genocide memorials are churches located on the outskirts of Kigali. **Nyatama**, about 30km south of Kigali, is a deeply disturbing memorial where skulls and bones of the many victims are on display. While the visual remains of the deceased are a visceral sight, their inclusion here is to provide firm evidence to would-be genocide deniers.

The church at **Ntarama,** about 25km south of Kigali, is more understated but no less powerful. The church has not been touched since the bodies were removed more than a decade ago, and there are many bits of clothing scraps still on the floor. Both of these memorials can be visited on a day trip, although you will need to either have your own transport or arrange for a taxi to bring you there and back.

NORTHWESTERN RWANDA

A formidable natural border between Rwanda, Uganda and DRC, the Virunga volcanoes are where Rwanda really earns its nickname as the Land of a Thousand Hills. Home to their share of the last mountain gorillas on the planet, the Rwandan Virungas are protected by Parc National de Volcans, the undisputed highlight of the country. The region is also home to the tranquil town of Gisenyi on the sandy shores of Lake Kivu, which is Rwanda's top spot for a 'beach' holiday.

MUSANZE (RUHENGERI)

For most travellers, Musanze (Ruhengeri) is the preferred staging post on their way to the magnificent Parc National des Volcans (p562), one of the best places in East Africa to track the rare mountain gorilla. Since permit holders are required to check in at the park headquarters in nearby Kinigi at 7am on the day of tracking, staying in Musanze is a much safer option than leaving from Kigali at the crack of dawn.

While you certainly need to check out of your hotel early enough to reach the national park, consider coming back to town for another night after tracking the gorillas. Musanze is a pleasant enough town to explore on foot, it's also situated near a number of interesting natural sights. Musanze Cave, just 2km outside the town centre, is presently being developed as a tourist attraction, while the nearby lakes of Ruhondo and Burera are ripe for independent exploration.

What's in a name? Good question. In 2006, the name of the town was changed from Ruhengeri to Musanze following an administrative reorganisation of Rwanda's 12 former provinces. Since prior boundaries were drawn along tribal divisions, the country was reorganised into more neutral divisions: North, South, East, West and Kigali. At the time of research, both names were still being used, though most Rwandans were promoting the new name of Musanze.

Orientation

Musanze is a somewhat small and relatively insignificant town, although the impressive views make up for it, with the mighty Virunga volcanoes – Karisimbi, Bisoke (Visoke), Sabinyo, Gahinga (Mgahinga) and Muhabura (Muhavura) – looming to the north and west.

Forget any ideas about climbing the hill (Nyamagumba) near the post office – it's a military area and access is prohibited.

Information

INTERNET
Karibu Internet & Giftshop (behind Rue Commerce; per hr RFr500)

MONEY
Banks in Musanze aren't that useful as they can only change cash and cannot be relied upon to deal with travellers cheques or credit cards. With that said, be sure to stock up on plenty of cash before departing from Kigali.
Banque de Kigali (Ave de 5 Juillet)
BCDI (Ave de la Nutrition) Represents Moneygram.
BCR (Rue Muhabura) Represents Western Union.

POST
Post office (⊙ 8am-noon & 2-4pm Mon-Fri) Offers basic telephone and postal services.

TOURIST INFORMATION
Located in the prefecture headquarters, the **Office Rwandais du Tourisme et des Parcs Nationaux (Rwandan Tourism Board)** (ORTPN; www.rwandatourism .com, info@rwandatourism.com, reservation@rwandatour ism.com; Ave du 5 Juillet) is the smaller sister of the main 'Or-ti-pen' office in Kigali. If you already have a gorilla permit, there is little to no reason to stop by here as permit holders are required to check in at 7am on the scheduled day of their tracking at the nearby park headquarters in Kinigi.

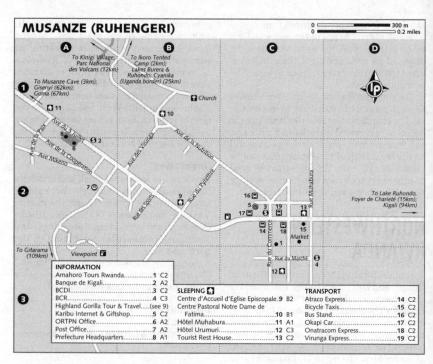

MUSANZE (RUHENGERI)

0 ———— 300 m
0 ———— 0.2 miles

If you don't have a gorilla permit, in theory you can stop by here a few days before you want to go tracking in the hopes of trying to snatch up an available permit. However, this is becoming less and less likely due to the soaring popularity of gorilla tracking in Rwanda. With that said, it is also much easier to deal with the ORTPN office (p551) in Kigali, or with any of the travel agencies listed in the Kigali section (see p552) or below.

For further details on gorilla tracking, see p566.

If you're planning on exploring the nearby Musanze Cave (see right), this office is the best place to arrange for the necessary permits and guides. It's also a good spot to inquire about golden monkey tracking in Parc National des Volcans – for more information, see p566.

TRAVEL AGENCIES

If you want some help in securing a gorilla permit, or in arranging transportation to/from any of the national parks, the following travel agencies/tour operators are recommended. Note that there are also quite a number

of recommended operators in Kigali – for more information, see p552.

Amahoro Tours Rwanda (☎ 8687448; www .amahoro-tours.com; Rue de Commerce) A small, locally run operator that gets rave reviews from readers, Amahoro can help you arrange permits as well as cultural activities and homestays in the surrounding area.

Highland Gorilla Tour & Travel (☎ 8414488; www .shyirsdiocese.or.rw; Ave du 5 Juillet) Another small but reliable operator, this agency is run by the local diocese.

Festivals & Events

For information on Kwita Izina, the gorilla naming ceremony, see the boxed text, p570.

Sights & Activities
MUSANZE CAVE

Following several internationally funded speleological projects, this massive **cave complex** (permit US$30) is now open to visitors for the first time in its history. Located just 2km from the town centre, the Musanze Cave lies in a volcanic region where different lava flows joined to create the Albertine Rift Valley.

The cave itself has no less than 31 entrances, and is comprised largely of lava basaltic layers from the Bisoke and Sabyinyo volcanoes. Bat roosts are a significant feature of Musanze Cave, as are huge roof collapses that create vast arrays of coloured light shafts.

During the 1994 Rwandan genocide, Musanze Cave was the sight of a bloody massacre, and today local people often view the complex as a tomb. Please keep this issue in mind when you're exploring the area and do not engage in any behaviour that might be deemed disrespectful.

As **spelunking** can be a high-risk activity, you need to get permission from ORTPN in Musanze before exploring the cave. You're also going to want to hire a local guide as the complex is massive, and there is potential for plenty to go wrong if you don't know where you're going.

Tourism at the site is still in its infancy, so there is potential here to chart some new territory. The complex is rumoured to be more than 2km long, and the cathedral-like main entrance and adjacent lava bridge near the town centre certainly provide evidence to the wonders that lie within.

To reach the main entrance, follow Ave du 5 Juillet for 2km from the centre of town towards Gisenyi. Look for a small sign that marks the access road, which winds past a school and a football field to the main entrance.

LAKES RUHONDO & BURERA

The outskirts of Musanze are home to two large lakes, which are dotted with small villages and accessed via a network of undeveloped dirt roads. While Ruhondo and Burera are not officially set up for tourism, you can easily have a do-it-yourself adventure here, especially if you can arrange boat transport with the local fishermen.

The scenery here is breathtaking as the shores of the lakes are heavily terraced and cultivated with crops, and the Virunga volcanoes loom ominously in the distance. Even if you don't take a boat trip on the lakes, self-drivers will enjoy exploring the area, stopping to take advantage of potential photo ops.

The shores of Lake Ruhondo are also home to two accommodation options, either of which provide a good alternative to staying in Musanze. Note that public transportation in this area is very limited, so it's best to have your own wheels.

Sleeping

As the main jumping off point for Parc National des Volcans (p562), there are quite a number of accommodation options in the centre of Musanze. If you want more natural surroundings however, you can also check out the couple of spots on the nearby shores of Lakes Ruhondo and Burera.

There are further options in and around the village of Kinigi, which is located on the edge of Parc National des Volcans – see p571 for more details.

TOWN CENTRE

Hotel Urumuri (☎ 546820; r RFr3500) For those wanting a bathroom on tap, this local hotel is the cheapest deal in town. Tucked away on a side street off Rue du Marché, it is a friendly enough spot assuming you're not too fussy about the lack of hot water and the somewhat dilapidated rooms.

Tourist Rest House (☎ 546635; Rue Muhabura; s/tw RFr4000/6000) Part of the same group as the popular Skyblue hotels in Uganda, this is a well-run little establishment for budget travellers. Rooms are on the smallish side, but they're good value considering their relative cleanliness and the somewhat reliable hot water.

Centre d'Accueil d'Eglise Episcopale (☎ 546857; cnr Rue du Pyrethre & Ave du 5 Juillet; r RFr5000-40,000) This church-run establishment has moved into the hotel stakes in recent years, and now offers the widest range of rooms in town. Cheap rooms are in a small block with shared bathrooms, but as you start spending more, facilities improve, including, at the top of the scale, satellite TV and palatial bathtubs.

Centre Pastoral Notre Dame de Fatima (☎ 546780; Ave des Virungas; s/d from RFr10,000/20,000, apt RFr30,000; 🖳) An excellent midrange option, this small guesthouse is also affiliated with a local Christian church. Modern rooms as well as one family-sized apartment are simple yet functional, and there is an on site bar-restaurant as well as a small internet café for guests.

Hotel Muhabura (☎ 546296; Ave du 5 Juillet; r/apt RFr15000/20,000; 🖳) The town's leading hotel, the Muhabura offers spacious rooms that catch plenty a mountain breeze, which is fine as you can always warm up with a steamy shower in the en suite bathrooms. There are also several apartments here that are verging on mini-suites, and definitely worth the extra cash. Even if you're not staying here, stop by for dinner as the hotel arguably has the best restaurant in town.

RWANDA

Ikoro Tented Camp (☎ 671572; www.elegantafrica .com; Cyanika Rd; luxury tent US$150, personal tent US$7 per person) This ecologically-sensitive tented camp was still a work in progress at the time of research, though there is a good chance it will be open for business during the life of this book. Owned by a British pair that fell in love with this corner of Rwanda, Ikoro is being constructed entirely of local materials, and is employing a large number of workers from the surroundings towns. Stop by, and send us an update to let us know how things are progressing!

Amahoro Tours can arrange homestays in the local community – for more information, see p560.

LAKES RUHONDO & BURERA

Foyer de Charieté (☎ 547024; s/d from RFr7000/10,000) Established as a Christian retreat in the 1960s, this secluded guesthouse is scenically located on the shores of Lake Ruhondo, just outside the village of Kadahero. While you will most likely need your own wheels to get out here, this is a good option if you want a quiet base near the lakes. Note that it's probably best to phone ahead as the Foyer is closed occasionally for religious events.

Virunga Lodge (☎ 502452; www.volcanoessafaris .com; s/d from US$465/700) One of the most stunningly situated camps in the region, the Virunga Lodge is nestled on a ridge above Lake Burera, offers incredible views across to the Virunga volcanoes, and is widely regarded as the finest lodge in all of Rwanda; rates include all meals and activities. Accommodation is in individual stone chalets that are decorated with local crafts and hardwood furnishings, though this place is definitely more about eco-atmosphere than opulent luxury. There is a striking bar and restaurant that specialises in organic foods, and is highlighted by a 360-degree view of the lakes and volcanoes beyond.

Eating & Drinking

Dining and drinking options are pretty limited in town given the number of foreigners passing through these days, though there are a handful of small local spots scattered around town.

The best restaurant in Musanze is at the Hotel Muhabura (p561), which has a continental menu of brochettes, steaks, tilapia and some well-dressed salads. Meals run from

RFr2500 to RFr5000, and the restaurant is usually buzzing with travellers heading to/ from the gorillas.

Hotel Urumuri has an outdoor courtyard restaurant with a good value menu, including brochettes, pastas and salads. Most meals run in the RFr1500 to RFr2500 and the place draws in a lot of locals in search of a hot dinner and a cold beer.

Although Musanze is generally a very quiet place in the evenings, the hotel bars are decent places to interact with other travellers. Big European football games are also screened here on weekends, which predictably draw a big crowd.

Getting There & Away

Numerous bus companies offer scheduled hourly services between Musanze and Kigali, including **Okapi Car** (Ave du 5 Juillet), **Virunga Express** (Ave du 5 Juillet) and **Atraco Express** (Ave du 5 Juillet), all charging around RFr1500. These buses are less crowded than minibuses. **Onatracom Express** (Ave du 5 Juillet) has three large buses per day passing through, connecting Kigali and Gisenyi – tickets are available at the petrol station.

There are normal minibuses from Musanze to Kigali (RFr1300, two hours), on a breathtaking mountain road, as well as to Cyanika (RFr500, 45 minutes), on the Rwanda–Uganda border, and to Gisenyi (RFr1000, 1½ hours).

Note that there is no public transportation between Musanze and Kinigi, where the park headquarters for Parc National des Volcans are located. For more information on accessing the national park, see p571.

Getting Around

There are few taxis in Musanze, but plenty of boda-bodas (bicycle taxis) for those needing a rest. A typical fare from the centre to the Hotel Muhabura is around RFr200. Taxi-motors are also available, but they can be pretty optimistic with their price offers (around RFr500 to RFr1000).

PARC NATIONAL DES VOLCANS

Volcanoes National Park, which runs along the border with DRC and Uganda, is home to the Rwandan section of the Virungas. Comprised of five volcanoes – the highest, Karisimbi, is more than 4500m – the Virungas are one of the most beautiful sights in both Rwanda and the whole of Africa. As if this wasn't enough of a drawcard, the bamboo- and rainforest-covered

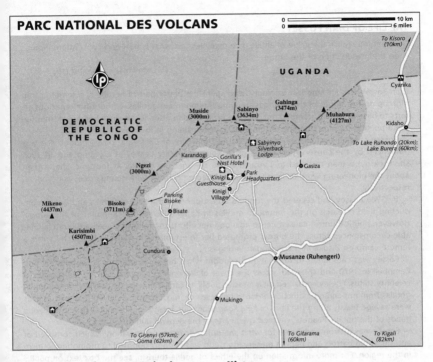

PARC NATIONAL DES VOLCANS

0   10 km
0   6 miles

To Kisoro
(10km)

UGANDA

Cyanika

DEMOCRATIC
REPUBLIC OF
THE CONGO

Muside
(3000m)

Sabinyo
(3634m)

Gahinga
(3474m)

Muhabura
(4127m)

Kidaho

Sabyinyo
Silverback
Lodge

To Lake Ruhondo (20km);
Lake Burera (60km);

Karandogi

Gorilla's
Nest Hotel

Ngezi
(3000m)

Kinigi
Guesthouse

Park
Headquarters

Gasiza

Parking
Bisoke

Kinigi
Village

Mikeno
(4437m)

Bisoke
(3711m)

Bisate

Karisimbi
(4507m)

Cundura

Musanze (Ruhengeri)

Mukingo

To Gisenyi (57km);
Goma (62km)

To Gitarama
(60km)

To Kigali
(82km)

slopes of these volcanoes are also home to some of the last remaining sanctuaries of the endangered eastern mountain gorilla (*Gorilla beringei beringei*).

The gorillas of Parc National des Volcans were first studied in depth by primatologist George Schaller, though they were thrust into the international spotlight during the life of Dian Fossey. Prior to 1999, the entire national park was out of bounds to tourists due to heavy poaching, armed conflict, the genocide and its aftermath. Since then, however, the park has emerged as the definitive location to track the captivating mountain gorilla.

While most tourists to the park are understandably driven by the desire to have a face-to-face encounter with real gorillas in the mist, there is good reason to stay in the area once you've finished tracking. In fact, the gorillas share the park with a troop of rare golden monkeys, which are slowly being habituated to human contact. The Virungas, which tower over Rwanda, Uganda and DRC, also present a variety of rewarding climbing and trekking options.

History

Belgian colonists, who intended to protect the mountain gorillas on Karisimbi, Visoke and Mikeno in Rwanda and Belgian Congo from poachers, first gazetted the Virungas as a national park in 1925. At the time, this small conservation triangle was the very first protected area to be created on the continent of Africa. Four years later, the borders were extended further to form Parc National Albert (Albert National Park), a massive area that encompassed more than 8000 sq km.

Following the independence of Congo in 1960 and Rwanda in 1962, Albert National Park was split into two entities. A few years prior, George Schaller had conducted a survey indicating that there were only about 450 mountain gorillas left in the range. As a result, the Rwandese government stated its intention to protect the Virungas as a conservation and a tourist area, despite mounting tensions across the country.

During the early years of Rwanda's fragile independence, it wasn't poaching or fighting that harmed the gorillas most, but rather a small daisy-like flower known as

RWANDA

THE LIFE OF DIAN FOSSEY

When you realise the value of all life, you dwell less on what is past and concentrate more on the preservation of the future.

Dr Dian Fossey, zoologist (1932–85)

Dian Fossey was an American zoologist who spent the better part of her life at a remote camp high up on the slopes of the Virungas studying the mountain gorillas. Without her tenacious efforts to have poaching stamped out, and the work of committed locals since her violent murder, there possibly wouldn't be any of the great apes remaining in Rwanda.

Fossey studied occupational therapy at the University of California, Davis, though she was influenced by the conservation efforts of Dr Louis and Mary Leakey at a young age. In 1963 she took out a loan to travel to Tanzania where she met the couple. At the time, she learned about the pioneering work of Jane Goodall and George Schaller with chimpanzees and gorillas, respectively.

By 1966 Fossey had secured the funding and support of the Leakey family, and began conducting field research on the mountain gorillas in Kabara, Democratic Republic of the Congo. However, political unrest caused her to abandon her efforts the following year, although favourable circumstances across the border prompted her to establish the Karisoke Research Centre, a remote camp on Bisoke in the Rwandan Virungas.

Fossey was catapulted to international stardom when her photograph was snapped by Bob Campbell in 1970 and splashed across the cover of *National Geographic*. Seizing her newfound celebrity status, Fossey embarked on a massive publicity campaign aimed at saving the mountain gorillas from impending extinction. Prior to her research, most people believed that wild gorillas were savage beasts along the lines of *King Kong*. However, images of Fossey touching the gentle hands of the gorilla 'Peanuts' warmed the hearts of the general public.

Fossey was a strong advocate for what she dubbed 'active conservation', which consisted of anti-poaching patrols and habitat preservation, and was strongly opposed to promoting tourism in the region. For more information on the ethics of gorilla tourism, see the box text on p568.

a pyrethrum. Due to a large grant by the European Community (EC), the 1960s saw the conversion of half Parc National des Volcans into commercial farms for pyrethrum, which can be processed into a natural insecticide.

By the early 1970s, census reports estimated that the mountain gorilla population in the Virungas had nearly halved. At the same time, poachers were making inroads on both sides of the Rwandese–Congo border as the demand for stuffed gorilla heads and hands (which were depressingly used as ashtrays) began to burgeon. Thankfully, the plight of the mountain gorilla became an international issue following the work of the late Dian Fossey – for more information, see the boxed text above.

Gorilla tracking in Rwanda was first launched in 1979 by Amy Vedder and Bill Webber, who marketed the charismatic creatures to tourists on overland trips. By the late 1980s, the sale of gorilla permits was the country's third largest revenue earner, which was enough to convince ordinary Rwandans that these great apes were indeed a valuable natural resource worth protecting.

In 1991, Rwanda was plunged into civil war, and Parc National des Volcans became a battlefield, a fact highlighted by an attack on the park headquarters in 1992. By the time the perpetrators of the genocide swept across Rwanda in 1994, the park had long been heavily land-mined and then abandoned as refugees fled into neighbouring DRC.

Across the border, however, the mountain gorillas were having an equally tough time surviving due to DRC's own brand of civil war and infighting. Additionally, the Congolese government showed little interest in promoting conservation, which prompted officials working in and around Parc National des Virunga to turn to corruption and illegal dealings in order to secure a living. While the national park did reopen to tourists in 2005, the situation remains tenuous at best (for more information, see the DRC chapter on p534).

In 1999, Parc National des Volcans was once again opened to tourist activities, and

Tragically, Fossey was brutally murdered on 26 December, 1985. Her skull was split open by a *panga*, a type of machete that was used by local poachers to cut the head and hands off gorillas. This bloody crime scene caused the media to speculate that poachers, who were angered by her conservationist stance, murdered her in a fit of rage.

However, a good measure of mystery surrounds Fossey's murder as she was carrying a gun at the time (although it did not have any bullets in it). This bizarre occurrence has lead many to believe that someone close to her was the murderer, perhaps even a team member or a supposed friend. Following her death, Fossey was buried in the Virungas next to her favourite gorilla, Digit, who had previously been killed by poachers.

From 1985 until the Rwandan genocide in 1994, the former students of Fossey (many of whom opposed her research) directed the Karisoke Research Centre. In 1986, one of these students was captured and convicted for the murder of Fossey, although many people believe that the evidence against him was contrived, and that he was simply chosen as a convenient scapegoat.

Without Fossey, poaching in the Virungas accelerated, and duiker and leopards were quickly extinguished from the region. Following the genocide, the area also filled with refugees, who logged the forests of the Virungas to construct temporary dwellings. During this time, Karisoke was looted and eventually destroyed.

Today, Fossey is best known for her book *Gorillas in the Mist*, which is both a description of her scientific research and an insightful memoir detailing her time in Rwanda. Her book remains the best-selling book about gorillas of all time, and is something of an obligatory read before tracking mountain gorillas.

Parts of her life story were later adapted in the film *Gorillas in the Mist: The Story of Dian Fossey*, starring Sigourney Weaver. The movie was criticised for several fictitious scenes in which Fossey aggressively harasses local poachers, as well as its stylised portrayal of her affair with photographer Bob Campbell. It does, however, serve as a good introduction to the ongoing plight of the endangered eastern mountain gorilla.

although there have been occasional infiltrations from rebel groups in DRC, they have all been stopped quickly by the Rwandan army. As a result, gorilla tracking in Rwanda is today largely considered to be a risk-free pursuit, and to date there have been no tourist-directed incidents in the Rwandan Virungas. At present, there are an estimated 400 mountain gorillas occupying the Virungas range.

Orientation

Parc National des Volcans protects 160 sq km of the Rwandan Virungas. The park is also part of a 430 sq km international conservation area that includes Parc National des Virunga (p538) in DRC and Mgahinga National Park (see p499) in Uganda.

The volcanoes range in altitude from 2400 to 4500 metres, and are linked by solidified lava flows that yield incredibly fertile soil. From west to east, the volcanoes are Karisimbi, Bisoke (Visoke), Ngezi, Muside, Sabinyo, Gahinga (Mgahinga) and Muhabura (Muhavura).

The closest population centre to the national park is the small village of Kinigi, which is also conveniently the home of the park headquarters.

Information

PARK HEADQUARTERS

The park headquarters for Parc National Volcans is located in the village of Kinigi, approximately 12km north of Musanze along rough dirt roads. Assuming the rains haven't been too heavy, and the road is in decent shape, you can make the trip from Musanze in about 30 to 45 minutes.

Note that you are absolutely required to register here at 7am on the day of your scheduled tracking. If you are late, your designated slot will be forfeited and your money will not be refunded. For an overview of gorilla tracking, see p566.

The park headquarters is also where you can arrange permits for golden monkey tracking (p568), as well as climbs and treks in the Virunga volcanos (p569).

RWANDA

WILDLIFE CONSERVATION

There are number of high profile international non-profit (NPO) organisations that are involved in wildlife conservation in the Virungas.

The Dian Fossey Gorilla Fund International
(www.gorillafund.org) Founded by the late Dian Fossey in 1978, this fund is dedicated to the protection of gorillas and their habitats through active conservation measures.

International Gorilla Conservation Programme
(www.igcp.org) Formed in 1991 through the joint efforts of the African Wildlife Foundation (AWF), Fauna & Flora International (FFI) and the World Wide Fund (WWF).

Mountain Gorilla Veterinary Project (http://mgvp.32ad.com) Since 1986, this organisation has provided free-ranging veterinary care to mountain gorillas.

Sights & Activities

GORILLA TRACKING

An encounter with these charismatic creatures is the highlight of a trip to Africa for many visitors. An encounter with a silverback male gorilla at close quarters can be a hair-raising experience, especially if you've only ever seen large wild animals behind the bars of a cage or from the safety of a car. Yet despite their intimidating size, gorillas are remarkably non-aggressive animals, entirely vegetarian, and are usually quite safe to be around. For most people, it's a magical encounter that is worth every single dollar spent.

Make no mistake about it – gorilla tracking is no joy ride. The guides can generally find the gorillas within one to four hours of starting out, but this often involves a lot of strenuous effort scrambling through dense vegetation up steep, muddy hillsides, sometimes to altitudes of more than 3000m. At higher altitudes, you'll also have to contend with the thick overgrowth of stinging nettles, which can easily penetrate light clothing. As if fiery skin rashes weren't enough of a deterrent, it also rains a lot in this area, so the going can certainly get tough (and muddy) in parts. At this altitude the air can thin out quickly, so descend to lower altitudes if you develop an intense headache.

There are seven habituated gorilla groups in Parc National des Volcans, including the **Susa group**, which has 35-plus members. Although nearly everyone who shows up at the park headquarters is most likely gunning to track the Susa group, the rangers usually select the most able-bodied and all-around fit individuals. Even though it's the largest group in the park, it's also the hardest to reach – you need to trek for three to four hours the up the slopes of Karisimbi at an altitude of more than 3000m.

Not everyone will get the chance to visit Susa (in fact most won't), but there were six other groups open to visitors at the time of research. The **Sabinyo group** is a good choice for anyone who doesn't want a strenuous tracking experience as they can usually be found in less than 30 minutes. **Group 13** and **Amahura** are also popular with visitors, although no matter which group you end up tracking, you're most likely going to have a memorable experience.

Visits to the gorillas are restricted to one hour and flash photography is banned. While you are visiting the gorillas, do not eat, drink, smoke or go to the bathroom in their presence. If you have any potential airborne illness, do not go tracking as gorillas are extremely susceptible to human diseases. If you must cough or sneeze in the presence of the gorillas, turn your head away and cover your face.

In theory, visitors are requested to remain more than 5m of the gorillas at all times, though in practice the guides (and the gorillas) tend to flaunt this rule. Although no tourists have ever been harmed by the gorillas, you should give them the respect and wide berth you would any wild animal.

Upon sighting the gorillas, the guides will make their presence known through a series of loud calls and grunts. This is an important part of the habituation process, and also helps to alert the gorillas to the presence and whereabouts of their visitors. Again, gorillas are surprisingly tolerant of humans, but don't be too surprised if a hormonal teen or a hulking silverback gives you a mock charge or even a playful swat!

The important thing to remember is that you should always stand your ground, and never, ever panic. Granted, it's very hard to not be scared when the largest primate on the planet is staring you down, but remember that animals have an uncanny ability to sense fear and respect authority. And, of course, it's worth pointing out that humans have caused gorillas a much, much greater degree of harm over the generations, than vice-versa.

For a compare and contrast look at the competing mountain gorilla experiences in Rwanda, Uganda and DRC, see p75.

RWANDA

Reservations

Fees are now a hefty US$500 per person for a gorilla visit, which includes park entry, compulsory guides and guards. Numbers of people allowed to visit each of the groups are limited to a maximum of eight people per day, limiting the total number of daily permits to an absolute maximum of 56. Children under 15 are not allowed to visit the gorillas.

Bookings for gorilla permits can be made through the ORTPN tourist office (p551) in Kigali or a Rwandan tour company (p552 and p560). Those visiting on a tour package will have everything arranged for them, while independent travellers can secure permits if they make reservations early on. Frustratingly enough, it is not always that easy to deal with ORTPN by phone or email from overseas, so it is sometimes easier to book a permit through a Rwandan tour operator to be twice as sure the booking is confirmed.

With tourism in Rwanda now on the up and up, it is getting more difficult to secure permits during the peak seasons of December/January and July/August, so book well in advance if you want to be assured of a spot. Bookings are secured with a US$100 deposit, and full payment must be paid upon your arrival in Kigali. However, given the uncertain nature of the banking system in Rwanda, it is much safer and wiser to transfer the full amount before arriving in country.

Independent travellers who have only decided to visit the gorillas in Rwanda once in the East Africa region can turn up at the ORTPN office in Kigali, and try to secure a booking at the earliest available date. During the high season, waits of several days to a week are not uncommon, but you might get lucky and snatch up a permit quickly as cancellations do occur.

If bookings are really solid, consider tracking the mountain gorillas in Bwindi Impenetrable Forest (p488) in Uganda.

Having made a booking and paid the fees, head to the park headquarters of Parc National des Volcans in Kinigi, and get ready for the experience of a lifetime. Ideally, you should spend the night before your track in either Kinigi or Musanze as you need to check in at 7am on the day that your permit is valid. Again, it's worth emphasising that if you are late, your designated slot will be forfeited, and your money will not be refunded.

At 7.30am, gorilla groups are assigned, and a small briefing is held over a cup of hot tea or coffee – it's colder in these parts than you might imagine. Around 8am, trackers are requested to start making their way to their respective trailheads, and by 8.30am the tracking has already commenced. For information on getting to the park headquarters in Kinigi, as well as the various trailheads for the track itself, see the Getting There & Away section on p571.

What to Bring

As we've previously mentioned, you need to be prepared for a potentially long, wet and cold trek through equatorial rainforest. A strong and sturdy pair of hiking shoes is a must, as is plenty of warm and waterproof clothing. The stinging nettles at higher elevations can really put a damper on your experience, so consider wearing pants and long sleeve shirts with a bit of thickness – if you have them, gloves can really make a difference.

Despite the potential for high altitudes and cold temperatures, you also need to be prepared for the strong sun. Floppy hats, bandanas, sunglasses and lots of sunscreen are a good idea, as are plenty of cold and hydrating fluids. Sugary snacks are also good for a quick energy boost, especially if you're tracking the Susa group for hours and hours on end. Before arriving at the park headquarters, it's probably a good idea to stock up on supplies in Musanze.

If your daypack isn't completely waterproof, be sure to wrap your camera in a waterproof bag – this is not the time for an equipment malfunction! While binoculars are certainly not necessary to spot the gorillas, they are useful for scoping birds or other distant animals.

When you check in at the park headquarters, you may be asked for identification by the park rangers. To avoid any potential hassles, carry your passport with you at all times in addition to your gorilla tracking permit.

Porters are available for the trek, though they're not absolutely necessary, and you are requested to pay a few dollars for this service. The guides, guards, drivers and any porters will expect a tip – the amount is entirely up to you, and ultimately depends on the quality of the service. However, keep in mind that

RWANDA

THE FUTURE OF THE EASTERN MOUNTAIN GORILLA

No, I won't let them turn this mountain into a goddamn zoo.

Sigourney Weaver as Dr Dian Fossey in the movie
'Gorillas in the Mist: The Life of Dian Fossey'

Teetering on the brink

Although a 2008 scientific study revealed that the total population of western gorillas in Africa is well above 125,000, these individuals are largely confined to the Congo Basin. Genetically speaking, western gorillas diverged from eastern gorillas about two million years ago, and are thus a very, very different species of primate.

In the mid-1990s, the total population of eastern gorillas was estimated to be around 17,000, though it is important to realise that there are two (and possibly even three) distinct subspecies: the eastern lowland gorilla and the eastern mountain gorilla (which may soon be further subdivided).

Here is where the numbers get a bit depressing: a 2004 article in *National Geographic* estimated that ongoing conflict in DRC had reduced the population of eastern lowland gorillas from 16,000 in the mid-1990s to no more than 5000. At present, mountain gorillas number no more than about 700 individuals, and are divided roughly in half between the Virunga range and Bwindi Impenetrable Forest (p488) in Uganda.

However, scientists now believe that the mountain gorillas in Bwindi and the Virungas are most likely different subspecies, and may in fact be different species all together. If this hypothesis were correct, it would be mean that the entire species of eastern mountain gorillas in the Virunga range number no more than 350 individuals. Regardless, eastern mountain gorillas are a critically endangered species that are teetering on the brink of extinction. Fortunately, both international and domestic conservation efforts in Rwanda have helped bolster the future chances of our closely related primate relatives.

Fossey's legacy

Throughout her life, Dian Fossey was a proponent of 'active conservation', or the belief that endangered species are best protected through rigorous anti-poaching measures and habitat

---

the locals know you're paying US$500 for the privilege of gorilla tracking, so try not to be too stingy.

GOLDEN MONKEY TRACKING

Golden monkey (*Cercopithecus kandti*) tracking is a relative newcomer on the wildlife scene of East Africa, but is rapidly rising in popularity both in Parc National des Volcans and across the border at Mgahinga National Park (p499) in Uganda. More like chimp viewing than a gorilla encounter, these beautiful and active monkeys bound about the branches of bigger trees. If you're looking for a reason to spend an extra day in the park, don't miss the chance to track these rare animals.

Golden monkeys, which are a subspecies of the wider spread blue monkey, are endemic to the Albertine Rift Valley, and are distinguished by their gold body colouration, which contrasts sharply to black patches on their extremities. Classified as an endangered species, golden monkeys can only be seen in the Virungas, as deforestation and population growth in the Great Lakes region has greatly affected their home range. While their exact number in Parc National des Volcans is unknown, a 2003 survey in neighbouring Uganda counted approximately 4000 individuals.

The idea to track golden monkeys first arose in 2002 as a joint effort between ORTPN and the Dian Fossey Gorilla Fund International. A couple of groups in accessible areas of the park were selected for habituation, and researchers set about studying the movements and habits of these little understand creatures. The work was extremely slow and frustrating as golden monkeys are shier than gorillas by nature, though significant progress was made.

In 2003, the first golden monkey tracking permits were issued to tourists, and in recent years the animals have become much more accustomed to human visitors. Since

protection. As a result, she strongly opposed the promotion of tourism in the Virunga range, though the Dian Fossey Gorilla Fund International has changed their position on the issue since her untimely death.

Fossey spent much of her life habituating mountain gorillas to human contact in an effort to expose the world to their tenuous plight for survival. As a result, she, perhaps more than anyone else in the world, was fully aware of the dangers of increased human traffic in the Virungas. Sadly, habituated gorillas are significantly more vulnerable to poachers, as evidenced by the 1995 murders of seven gorillas in Bwindi, the 2002 murders of two gorillas in Parc National des Volcans, and the 2007 debacle in DRC (see p538).

Humans and gorillas are also genetically similar enough to share many of the same diseases. Since the very first days of gorilla tourism, there has always been the fear that tourists could transmit a virulent strain of the measles or influenza to the habituated gorillas, which would have disastrous effects on such as small population group.

Conservation through tourism

The main argument against the conservation philosophy promoted by Fossey is that species cannot be preserved in a vacuum. On the contrary, eastern mountain gorillas exist alongside human communities, which means that a careful balance between man and animal must be reached.

Today, a policy of community-based conservation is being promoted in Rwanda, which seeks to encourage growth in tourism through environmental education and improved infrastructure. By encouraging a sense of local ownership, and funnelling part of the revenues from gorilla tracking permits back into the community, the government has been successful in convincing ordinary Rwandans that gorillas are a vital natural resource worth protecting.

If you're not convinced, just look at the numbers – gorilla tracking permits have the potential to generate as much as US$28,000 per day. Increased foot traffic in the Virunga range is also stimulating the local economy through job creation and tourist revenue (see the Sabyinyo Community Lodge on p572). While tourism is certainly not without its faults, eventually it might end up saving the eastern mountain gorilla from extinction.

golden monkeys are relatively unknown outside of Rwanda, the tracking initiative is certainly worth your support as it generates valuable income used to protect the species from extinction.

Permits to track the golden monkeys cost US$100 (this includes the US$25 park fee entry), and are easy to get a hold of – simply inquire at the ORTPN office (p551) in Kigali or Musanze (p559), or possibly even at the park headquarters (p565) in Kigini. Maximum group size is six individuals and, like the gorillas, you're only permitted to spend one hour with the golden monkeys. While it's certainly not a substitute for gorilla tracking, it is a good complement nevertheless.

CLIMBING & TREKKING THE VOLCANOES

Dian Fossey once famously declared: 'In the heart of Central Africa, so high up that you shiver more than you sweat, are great, old volcanoes towering up almost 15,000 feet, and nearly covered with rich, green rainforest – the Virungas'.

Indeed, these stunning volcanoes serve as an evocative backdrop for a guided climb or trek. The ascents pass through some remarkable changes of vegetation, ranging from thick forests of bamboo, giant lobelia or hagenia on to alpine meadows. If the weather is favourable, the reward is some spectacular views over the mountain chain.

There are several possibilities for climbing up to the summits of one or more of the volcanoes in the park, with treks ranging in length from several hours to two days. A guide is compulsory and is included in your US$25 per day park fee; additional porters are optional. Note that it is forbidden to cut down trees or otherwise damage vegetation in the park, and you are only allowed to make fires in the designated camping areas.

RWANDA

KWITA IZINA: THE GORILLA NAMING CEREMONY

In traditional Rwandan culture, the birth of a child is a momentous event that is celebrated with a tremendous amount of fanfare. The birth is marked by the presentation of the new infant to the general public, who then proceed to suggest round after round of possible names. After careful consideration, the proud parents select one for their newborn, and celebrate the naming with copious amounts of dining, drinking and dancing.

Gorillas in Rwanda are often awarded the same level of respect and admiration as humans, which is why it is only fitting that they should be named in a similar manner. Since June 2005, the annual Kwita Izina (Gorilla Naming Ceremony) has been a countrywide event that is increasingly drawing a larger share of the spotlight. From local community events in Musanze to gala balls in Kigali and Gisenyi, Kwita Izina is well on its way to becoming a global brand.

To date, more than 65 furry little baby gorillas have been named at Kwita Izina, which has subsequently generated a respectable amount of revenue through fundraising efforts. Following the 2007 celebration, enough funds were raised to help launch the Sabyinyo Silverback Lodge (p572), an upmarket community-run lodge that employs more than 600 locals, 80% of which are women.

The event has even attracted a number of celebrities and conservationists including Natalie Portman and Jack Hanna, testament to the growing appeal of the event and the future potential for Rwandan tourism. For more information on Kwita Izina, check out the official website at www.kwitizina.org.

One of the best parts of climbing and trekking the volcanoes is that you will be awarded ample opportunities to view wildlife (sans gorillas and golden monkeys of course). The most common herbivores in the park are bushbucks and black-fronted duikers; buffaloes, bushpigs and giant forest hogs are infrequently spotted. Also, be sure to inspect the hollows of trees for hyraxes, genets, dormice, squirrels and forest pouched rates.

There is also incredibly varied birdlife in the national park, so don't forget to bring along a good pair of binoculars and a field guide if you have one. The richest bird-watching zone is in the hagenia forests, where you can expect to see turaco, francolins, sunbrids, waxbills, crimsonwings and various hawks and buzzards.

Karisimbi

Climbing Karisimbi (4507m), the highest summit in the Virungas, takes two long and taxing days. The track follows the saddle between Bisoke and Karisimbi, and then ascends the northwestern flank of the latter. Some five hours after beginning the trek, there is a metal hut in which to spend the night (the hut keys are available at Parking Bisoke). The rocky and sometimes snow-covered summit is a further two to four hours walk through alpine vegetation.

To do this trek, take plenty of warm clothing and a very good sleeping bag. It gets very cold, especially at the metal hut, which is on a bleak shoulder of the mountain at 3660m. The wind whips through here, frequently with fog, so there is little warmth from the sun.

The two-day climb up Karisimbi costs US$150, including park fees and a guide, and can easily be arranged at either the ORTPN office (p559) in Musanze or the park headquarters (p565) in Kigini.

Bisoke

The return trip to Bisoke (3711m) takes six to seven hours from Parking Bisoke. The ascent takes you up the steep southwestern flanks of the volcano to the summit, where you can see the crater lake. The descent follows a track on the northwestern side, from where there are magnificent views over the Parc National des Virungas. This climb costs US$50, including park fees and a guide.

Dian Fossey's Grave

A popular trek is to the site of the former Karisoke Research Camp, where Dian Fossey (p564) is buried alongside many of her primate subjects, including the famous Digit. From the park headquarters, it's about a 30-minute drive to the trailhead, followed by two to three hour hike to the ruins of the camp. This excursion costs US$50, including park fees and a guide; though you are responsible for your own transportation to/from the trailhead.

Other Treks

Before the 1994 genocide, there were several other treks available that have not yet fully been reinstated by the park service; they may be reintroduced during the shelf life of this book.

- The return walk to Ngezi (about 3000m) takes three to four hours from Parking Bisoke. This is one of the easiest of the treks, and at the right time of the day it is possible to see a variety of animals coming down from the hills to drink at streams and springs.
- Climbing Sabinyo (3634m) takes five to six hours from the park headquarters near Kinigi. The track ascends the southeastern face of the volcano, ending up with a rough scramble over steep lava beds along a very narrow path.
- Climbing Gahinga (3474m; in Uganda) and Muhabura (4127m) is a two-day trip from Gasiza. The summit of the first volcano is reached after a climb of about four hours along a track that passes through a swampy saddle between the two mountains. The trip to the summit of Muhabura takes about four hours from the saddle.

Sleeping & Eating

Note that all of the lodges below include breakfast in the price. Lunch, dinner and drinks are also available for both non-guests and guests for a small fee.

our pick Kinigi Guesthouse (☎ 546984; s/d from US$40/50) This locally-run guesthouse gets our pick for being the best-value option in the vicinity of the national park, as well as an added distinction for its sustainable merits. Located very close to park headquarters in Kinigi village, all profits from this local lodge are ploughed back into the Association de Solidarité des Femmes Rwandaises, which assists vulnerable Rwandan women of all backgrounds and ages. Accommodation is in a small clutch of wooden bungalows that are set in lush gardens with views of the towering Virungas. The staff is extremely friendly and helpful, and they'll whip you up a hot breakfast before you dash off to track the gorillas.

Gorilla's Nest Camp (☎ 546331; s/d from US$80/120) Although it's more expensive than Kinigi Guesthouse, this upmarket option is one of the best accommodation choices in the vicinity of Parc National des Volcans. Situated near the park headquarters, you don't have to worry about getting up early and making the drive from Musanze to arrive before registration. The rooms themselves are very smart, with swish new amenities that complement the verdant views of the neighbouring forested slopes.

Getting There & Away

The main access point for Parc National des Volcans is the nearby town of Musanze (Ruhengeri). For information on getting here from other points in Rwanda, see p562.

The park headquarters, where you are required to check in at 7am on the day of your scheduled gorilla tracking, is located in the village of Kinigi, approximately 12km north of Musanze along dirt roads. The condition of these roads varies considerably based on the extent of recent rainfall, though you can expect to make the trip from Musanze in about 30 to 45 minutes.

Note that there is no public transportation from Musanze to Kinigi, although you can arrange to rent a vehicle and driver for the day (around US$100) through the ORTPN office or any of the travel agencies in Musanze (p560). However, considering that most people in Musanze need to be in Kinigi the next morning at 7am, it really isn't too hard to hitch a ride with fellow trackers, especially during the high season and at weekends.

It is also necessary to arrange transport from the park headquarters to the point where you start climbing up to where the gorillas are situated. Again, you can rent a vehicle and driver in Musanze if you want the assurance of your own wheels. In practice, however, it should be possible to hitch a ride with other tourists or expats who have their own vehicles.

One option worth considering if you have a few friends is to hire a car and a driver in Kigali. Prices are around US$150 per day, and will give you reliable transport to/from Musanze, the park headquarters in Kinigi and the trailhead for the gorilla tracking. Any of the travel agencies in Kigali (p552) can make all of the necessary arrangements.

RWANDA

COMMUNITY-BASED TOURISM

While it's certainly an expensive proposition to spend a night or two here, the **Sabyinyo Silverback Lodge** (☎ 254-202734000; www.governorscamp.com/property_descriptions_sabyinyo_silverback_lodge.php; r person low/high season US$371/644; 🖳) is a perfect example of how sustainable tourism can empower a local community to protect their natural environment.

Boasting a hefty price tag of US$1.2 million, the Sabyino Silverback Lodge was a joint partnership between the Sabyinyo Community Lodge Association (SACOLA) and the highly exclusive Governors' Camp Collection of tented camps and lodges. Part of the money used for construction was also derived from fundraising efforts associated with the Kwita Izina gorilla naming ceremony (see the box text on p570).

While the ecolodge certainly required a heavy investment by the local community, it has thus far benefited from the impeccable management of the Governors' Camp Collection. With only 18 beds on the property, hotel guests are treated as personal friends of the management, which results in a highly personalised level of service. Accommodation is in Venetian plaster cottages with Rwandese-style terracotta tile roofs, spacious sitting areas, individual fireplaces, stylish en suite bathrooms and sheltered verandas.

You really do need to dig deep into your pockets for the privilege of staying here (rates do include full board and activities), though you can take comfort in the fact that SACOLA gets US$50 per bed per night in addition to 7.5% of all quarterly profits. To date, these revenues have been used to implement several community projects, including a 74km buffalo wall to protect local crops as well as a public water facility.

More importantly, the Sabyinyo Silverback Lodge is an example of community-based conservation, which is absolutely pivotal to the future survival of the eastern mountain gorillas.

GISENYI

Land-locked Rwanda may be a long way from the ocean, but that doesn't mean that you can't have a beach holiday here. On the contrary, if you take another look at the map, you'll quickly realise that Rwanda's eastern border with DRC runs along the entire length of Lake Kivu. One of the Great Lakes in the Albertine Rift Valley, Lake Kivu has a maximum depth of nearly 500 metres, and is one of the 20 deepest and most voluminous lakes in the world.

Of course, most travellers in Gisenyi are perfectly content to stick to the shores, especially since they're surprisingly sandy, and fringed with all manners of tropical vegetation. While much of the Lake Kivu frontage is lined with landscaped villas, plush hotels and private clubs, the town itself projects a languid air of some forgotten upcountry backwater. But this is the precisely the low-key charm that lures an eclectic mix of rich Rwandans, expat escapees and independent travellers.

In fact, the biggest obstacle in the way of Gisenyi assuming a full-on resort status is simply its ongoing image problem. The town is unfortunately remembered as the location of a major flashpoint during the Rwandan

Civil War, the 1994 genocide and the First and Second Congo Wars. Indeed, sharing a border with DRC hasn't done wonders for the town's reputation, even though Gisenyi is today a safe haven of peace and tranquillity.

Even if you're not a devoted sun worshipper, Gisenyi is still an incredibly scenic and picturesque spot to relax after a few days of rough tracking and trekking in Parc National des Volcans. Gisenyi also serves as a base for day-trips to Goma (p536) in neighbouring DRC. From here, you can check out the lava flows from Nyiragongo (3470m), which blew its top in 2002 and swallowed much of the town. Deeper excursions into the Congo are ill advised, though the border crossing was stable and secure at the time of research. Check the situation carefully before making any decisions.

History

The first European to visit Lake Kivu was the German count Adolf von Götzen in 1894, although it was the early accounts of the Duke of Mecklenburg that are credited with fixing the lake in the European imagination. In 1907, the Duke declared that Kivu was 'the most beautiful of all the Central African lakes, framed in by banks which fall back steeply from the rugged masses of rock, at the rear the stately summits of eight Virunga volcanoes'.

Of courses, the lake's history stretches back eons and eons before the age of European colonisation. A shallow lake was most likely formed here approximately two million years ago by the very same tectonic activity that wrenched open the Rift Valley. However, the lake in its present shape formed about 20,000 years ago when lava flows from the Virungas created a natural dam, separating Kivu from Lake Edward, and substantially increasing its water levels.

Interestingly enough, Lake Kivu is one of only three known 'exploding lakes' (the other two are the Cameroonian Lakes Nyos and Monoun), which experience violent lake overturns dubbed limnic eruptions. This rare type of natural disaster results when carbon dioxide (CO_2) suddenly erupts from deep lake water, suffocating wildlife, livestock and humans, and causing violent tsunamis. For more information, see the box text p574.

Lake Kivu gained notoriety as a place where many of the victims of the Rwandan genocide were dumped. On the Congolese side of the border, the adjacent provinces of North and South Kivu remain major conflict areas that show little signs of abating despite a 2003 peace treaty ending the Second Congo War. Once again, however, Gisenyi was at the time of research a veritable oasis of sun and sand.

Orientation

Gisenyi is roughly divided into upper and lower towns, though most tourist services cluster around the lower end along the shores of Lake Kivu. The road into town from Musanze and Kigali deposits you at the eastern end of Gisenyi; you can continue west to the border post for DRC. The smoking massif that is Nyiragongo volcano marks the northern edge of town, and is clearly a force of nature that is not to be trifled with.

Information

BCR (Rue de Ruhengeri), representing Western Union, and **BCDI** (Rue des Poissons), representing Moneygram, both have branches near the market, while **Banque de Kigali** (Ave de Fleures) is near the lakefront in the lower part of town. Currently these banks can only deal with cash exchanges.

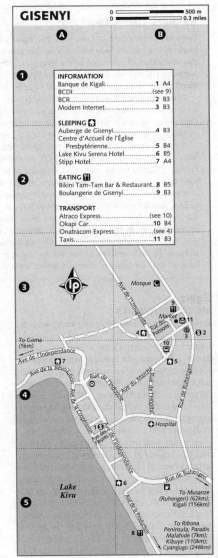

GISENYI

INFORMATION	
Banque de Kigali	1 A4
BCDI	(see 9)
BCR	2 B3
Modern Internet	3 B3

SLEEPING	
Auberge de Gisenyi	4 B3
Centre d'Accueil de l'Église Presbytérienne	5 B4
Lake Kivu Serena Hotel	6 B5
Stipp Hotel	7 A4

EATING	
Bikini Tam-Tam Bar & Restaurant	8 B5
Boulangerie de Gisenyi	9 B3

TRANSPORT	
Atraco Express	(see 10)
Okapi Car	10 B4
Onatracom Express	(see 4)
Taxis	11 B3

Modern Internet (Rue de Ruhengeri) offers the best internet connection in town, sometimes the only connection.

There is no DRC consulate here in Gisenyi, but visas (US$35) are available on the border if crossing to Goma or if you are going to visit the mountain gorillas in Parc National des Virungas (p538).

WARNING: LIMNIC ERUPTIONS

There are certain parts of Lake Kivu, particularly around Gisenyi, where it is very, very dangerous to swim. The culprits here are not hippos or crocs, but rather volcanic gases that are released from the lakebed. In the absence of a strong wind, these toxic gases can collect on the surface of the water, and quite a few people have been asphyxiated as a result of these so-called limnic eruptions. Moral of the story: watch where local people swim, and make sure you're doing the same.

To date, only two limnic eruptions have ever been observed; on both occasions the consequences were deadly. In 1984, 37 people were asphyxiated following a limnic eruption at Lake Monoun in Cameroon. Two years later, a second even deadlier eruption occurred at neighbouring Lake Nyos, releasing over 80 million cubic meters of CO_2, and killing between 1700 and 1800 people.

A major limnic eruption has never been recorded at Kivu, though the deepwater lake contains massive amounts of dissolved CO_2 as well as methane. In fact, sample sediments taken by Professor Robert Hecky from the University of Michigan indicate that living creatures in the lake tend to go extinct approximately every thousand years or so.

If an eruption does occur, the exploding underwater methane is likely to push a huge cloud of carbon dioxide above the surface of the lake, as well as triggering as a series of tsunamis along the shoreline. Since CO_2 is denser than air, it sinks quickly to the ground, pushing breathable air up into the sky. At this point, there is little you can really do to survive, and it's only a matter of time before you succumb to CO_2 poisoning, suffocation, drowning or a dastardly combination of all three. To make matters worse, the last thing you will probably smell will be the warm vapours from all the combusting methane, which are somewhat reminiscent of a giant, earthy fart.

Sights
RUBONA PENINSULA
Roughly 7km outside of town, along a lovely lakeshore road, is the Rubona peninsula, home to both Gisenyi's main harbour and the Bralirwa Brewery. The brewery, which produces the Primus lager you've no doubt been downing since your arrival in Rwanda, is not officially set up for tourism. However, the staff is usually keen on showing people around (they're expecting tips), though keep cameras well out of sight as they are very sensitive about photographs.

Actually, you may be surprised to discover that the boilers at the Bralirwa Brewery are largely powered by methane gas extracted from Lake Kivu. Seriously. The project is something of a litmus test to determine whether or not large-scale extraction of methane is possible, which in theory could increase Rwanda's energy generation capability by as much as 2000%, enabling the country to sell electricity to its neighbours. Degassing Lake Kivu also may help in preventing a Cameroonian-style limnic eruption from taking place in Rwanda and DRC.

Rubona is also home to some natural hot springs, which are reported by locals to cure a variety of ailments. While you're going to have to ask around if you want to find them, it's certainly worth the effort, especially if you're having second thoughts about swimming in Lake Kivu. Then again, you might change your mind when you see locals boiling their potatoes in the hot springs!

GOMA, DRC
A popular trip from Gisenyi involves crossing the border into the Democratic Republic of the Congo, from where you can visit the bustling market town of Goma, trek the slopes of Nyiragongo volcano or visit the gorillas in Parc National des Virungas. Keep in mind however that all of these activities are contingent on the security situation, which is extremely volatile given how undemocratic the Congo can be. For more information on the potential perils and pitfalls that await you in DRC, check out our detour chapter on p534.

Activities
For those with the money to burn, there are a variety of water sports available at the upmarket hotels. For those without the money, swimming and sunbathing on the sandy beaches are free. Generally speaking, far-reaching boat trips out on Lake Kivu are discouraged given the general climate of lawlessness in neighbouring DRC.

Sleeping
The cheaper places are all found around the upper part of town, but it is better to spend a little more and stay down near the shores

of Kivu where you can really soak up the lakeside atmosphere.

Centre d'Accueil de l'Église Presbytérienne (☎ 540397; Ave du Marché; dm/d from RFr1500/6000) This church-run hostel has the cheapest beds in town – dorms come with varying numbers of beds, while the double rooms are spic and span with en suite facilities Basic meals are served in a small restaurant, and there is a craft shop selling banana-leaf cards and stuffed toys to raise money for local women's groups.

Auberge de Gisenyi (☎ 540385; Ave de l'Umuganda; s/d RFr5000/6000) The pick of the pack among the cheaper guesthouses in the upper part of town, the rooms here face onto an attractive courtyard garden of tropical blooms. The doubles are almost suites, making them a good deal, and the restaurant is popular at night for hot food and cold beer.

Paradis Malahide (☎ 648650; Rubona Peninsula; d from US$30) Located along the shores of the Rubona Peninsula just south of Gisenyi, this brand new lodge gets wonderful reviews from loyal guests. Accommodation is in stone bungalows scattered around a small bar and restaurant, but the highlight of the property is clearly the stunning lakeside location. To get the most out of your stay, rent a motorboat and do some swimming and fishing, though please stay on this side of the border. To reach Paradis Malahide, follow the road towards Rubona, and turn right onto the lakeshore road just before you reach the brewery; the lodge will be on your left-hand side.

Stipp Hotel (☎ 540540; www.stippag.co.rw; Ave de la Révolution; s/d from US$125/150; 🍴 🖳 🌐) Gisenyi's first true boutique hotel rose from the ashes of a neglected colonial building and is now one of the classiest places to bed down along the shores of Lake Kivu. Preferring intimacy to opulence, the Stipp is only home to a small assortment of individually decorated rooms, which strike an ideal blend between colonial elegance and modern convenience. Whether you're soaking in the enormous bathtubs, strolling around the lush garden or dining in one of the town's best restaurants, you're sure to have a relaxing stay here.

Lake Kivu Serena Hotel (☎ 541111; www.serenahotels.com/rwanda/lake_kivu/home.asp; Ave de la Coopération; s/d from US$135/165; 🍴 🖳 🌐) This hotel has changed hands more times than can count though it's certainly in good hands now that the exalted Serena chain is running the show. The Lake Kivu Serena brims with refined luxury from the grand colonial dining rooms to the manicured grounds. While the Serena has a stunner of a swimming pool, and some prime beachfront of the lakeshore, the building itself has a dark past. During the genocide, it briefly served as the headquarters for the interim government, enabling them to flee into DRC when things got too hot.

Eating & Drinking

Most visitors end up eating at the bigger hotels as there isn't a great selection of restaurants in town. There are, however, several simple restaurants on the main road in the upper part of town serving cheap meals, though the standard isn't much.

Among the hotels, the Stipp Hotel probably has the best restaurant – the menu is predominantly French, and draws a large crowd most nights. The restaurant at the Lake Kivu Serena is also highly regarded, and serves a wide assortment of continental cuisine. Meals at both establishments run from about RFr3000 to RFr10,000 and service at either place is swift and professional.

In a great location on the beach in the south of town, the menu at **Bikini Tam-Tam Bar & Restaurant** (Ave de la Production; mains RFr1500-3000) is limited but the setting more than makes up for it. Who knows where they came up with the name, but it's easy to remember. It gets busier at the weekends when the drinking crowd rolls in.

For self-caterers, there's a wide variety of fruit and vegetables available at the main market. For cheese, meats, yoghurts and fresh bread try **Boulangerie de Gisenyi** (Rue des Poissons).

Getting There & Away

BOAT

All passenger ferries across Lake Kivu to other Rwandan ports were suspended at the time of writing. However, there are fast boats between Goma and Bukavu, though this would require a DRC visa, and there are potentially serious security question marks over this route.

BUS & MINIBUS

It is a beautiful journey from Musanze (Ruhengeri) through rural farms and villages and there are panoramic views of Lake Kivu as the road descends into Gisenyi. **Okapi Car** (Ave du Marché) and **Atraco Express** (Ave du Marché) operate minibuses between Gisenyi and Kigali (RFr2500, three hours); the advantage with these services is that it does not stop all the time for people getting on and off. There are also regular minibuses to Kigali (RFr1800, four hours) and Musanze (RFr1000, two hours).

Onatracom Express (Ave de l'Umuganda) runs big buses and has three services a day to Kigali (RFr2000), passing through Musanze (Ruhengeri) (RFr1200). All the buses terminate on Ave de l'Umuganda.

There are only infrequent minibuses running between Gisenyi and Kibuye (RFr1500, six hours) – inquire locally as schedules are highly variable.

It is easy enough to reach the border by taxi-motor for RFr250 or taxi for RFr1000. For the lowdown on crossing the border into DRC, see p593.

Getting Around

If you need wheels, taxi-motors do the run between the market and lakeside areas of town for around RFr250.

SOUTHWESTERN RWANDA

The endless mountains and valleys don't stop as you head south towards the border with Burundi. While the gorillas in Parc National des Volcans of Rwanda tend to garner almost everybody's attention, Southwestern Rwanda is home to East Africa's largest montane forest, namely Parc National de Nyungwe, one of the most primate-rich areas in the world. The region is also home to the historic colonial and intellectual centre Huye (Butare), which plays hosts to one of East Africa best ethnographic museums.

HUYE (BUTARE)

Huye (Butare) is one of the most distinguished towns in Rwanda, having served as the country's most prominent intellectual centre since the colonial era. Home to the National University of Rwanda, the National Institute of Scientific Research and the excellent National Museum of Rwanda, Huye may be a step down in size after the capital, but it is certainly no lightweight on the Rwandan stage.

Historically speaking, Huye has always played a prominent role in regional affairs. During the era of Belgian occupation, the town was the colonial administrative headquarters of the northern half of Ruanda-Urundi. While Huye may have lost a bit of ground to Kigali after independence, today it still manages to maintain its political relevance, especially since it's ruled by legions of Rwanda's academic elite.

While Huye isn't a tourist destination in the traditional sense, it is nevertheless an interesting stopover on your way out to Parc National de Nyungwe. The university is home to a couple of interesting sights, including the National Museum, which is widely regarded as one of the finest ethnographic museums in East Africa. The heavy concentration of liberal college students roaming the streets also makes for an interesting atmosphere.

Note that in 2006, the name of the town was changed from Butare to Huye following an administrative reorganisation of Rwanda's 12 former provinces. Since prior boundaries were drawn along tribal divisions, the country was reorganised into more neutral divisions: North, South, East, West and Kigali. At the time of research, both names were still being used, though most Rwandans were promoting the new name of Huye.

History

The tradition of Butare as an academic centre dates back to 1900 when it hosted the first catholic mission in present-day Rwanda. As prominent intellectuals and religious figures were drawn to the area, Butare grew in favour amongst the Belgian occupiers. Following the death of Queen Astrid, the Swedish wife of King Leopold III, the town was renamed Astrida in 1935.

After independence in 1962, the town's name was changed back to Butare as it launched a strong bid to serve as the capital of Rwanda. Although Kigali was eventually chosen due to its central location, Butare was selected to host the country's first university, which opened its doors to students in 1963.

In the early days of the 1994 genocide, Tutsis and moderate Hutus fled to Butare in the hopes that its intellectual tradition would reign over the ensuing madness. For a short while, the Tutsi prefect of Butare, Jean Baptiste-Habyarimana, managed to maintain peace and order in the town.

Sadly however, Habyarimana was quickly murdered by the Interahamwe, and replaced by Colonel Tharchisse Muvunyi. Under his

HUYE (BUTARE)

| 0 | 500 m |
| 0 | 0.3 miles |

INFORMATION
Banque de Kigali.................................1 D2
BCDI...2 D2
BCR..3 D1
Computer Link @ Butare.................4 D2
Librairie Caritas................................5 C2
Post Office...6 D1

SIGHTS & ACTIVITIES
Cathedral..7 D2
National Museum of Rwanda......8 D1

SLEEPING
Hôtel des Beaux-Arts.....................9 C2
Hôtel Faucon...................................10 D2
Hôtel Ibis...11 D2

EATING
Chez Venant....................................12 C2
Hôtel Ibis Restaurant...............(see 11)

SHOPPING
Expo Vente......................................13 D2

TRANSPORT
Atraco Express................................14 D2
Bus/Minibus Stand.......................15 D1
Okapi Car....................................(see 14)
Ontracom Express....................(see 14)
Trans Express 2000..................(see 11)
Volcano Express.............................16 D2
Yahoo Car...17 D2

To Gikongoro (28km); Cyangugu (155km)

To Gitarama (51km); Kigali (133km)

To Gitarama (51km); Kigali (133km)

Market

Ave du Commerce
Rue Rwamamba
Rue de la Prefecture
Ave de l'Université

To Hotel Credo (200m); National University of Rwanda (1km); Arboretum de Ruhande (1.2km); Gishamvu (12km)

Ave de la Cathédral

tenure, Butare was the site of horrific massacres that claimed the lives of nearly a quarter of a million people. Although Muvunyi fled to Britain after the genocide, he was eventually arrested and convicted.

Orientation

Despite its distinguished role as Rwanda's intellectual centre, Huye really isn't much more than a glorified town. Assuming the sun isn't beating down too hard, you shouldn't have any problem walking from the town centre out to either the National Museum or the university campus.

Information

There are branches of BCR, BCDI, and Banque de Kigali on the main Rue de Kigali, but they can only deal with cash.

Computer Link (Rue de Kigali; per hr RFr500) The place for Internet access in town.

Librairie Caritas (Rue de la Prefecture) A good bookshop frequented by students from the university.

Post office (Rue de Kigali)

Sights & Activities
NATIONAL MUSUEM OF RWANDA

This excellent **museum** (☎ 530586; Rue de Kigali; admission RFr1000; ⏰ 7-5pm) was given to the city as a gift from Belgium in 1989 to commemorate 25 years of independence. While the building itself is certainly one of the most beautiful structures in the city, this museum wins top marks from having one of the best ethnological and archaeological collections in the entire region.

While you certainly don't need more than hour to stroll though all of the exhibits, take your time as there are some very interesting items on display here. Some of the highlights include the costumes of Rwanda's famous Intore dancers (inquire at reception about performances; see Entertainment p578), traditional farming tools and household items, geological displays and life-size model villages.

The museum is about 1km north of the centre, past the minibus stand. You can either walk it, try for a short hitch or jump on a *bodaboda* for around RFr250.

NATIONAL UNIVERSITY OF RWANDA

Rwanda's finest institution of learning suffered terribly during the 1994 genocide, though today there are visible signs that it's turning towards the future with hope and optimism. Strolling through its campus is a pleasant diversion, especially if you find yourself at the **Arboretum de Ruhande**. Started by the Belgians in 1934, this attractive and peaceful arboretum is a great place to learn about African flora while indulging in a bit of leafy shade.

CATHEDRAL

Huye is also home to Rwanda's largest **cathedral**, which was constructed in the 1930s to commemorate the life of Princess Astrid. The redbrick building is still used for religious worship, so stop by if you happen to hear the sounds of gospel.

RWANDA

Sleeping

Hôtel des Beaux-Arts (☎ 530032; Ave du Commerce; r RFr4000-6000) Set a little way back from Ave du Commerce, this hotel has quite a bit of character for a cheapie. The hotel is attractively decorated with local products, and there's a handicraft shop selling a selection of what is displayed on the walls – all rooms include hot-water bathrooms, making them the real deal.

Hôtel Faucon (☎ 086-17657; Rue de Kigali; d/apt from RFr10,000/20,000) At one point in time, this place provided serious competition for the Ibis, though standards have slipped over the decades. However, this is great news for budget travellers as it offers huge rooms and apartments at rock-bottom prices.

Hotel Credo (☎ 530505; Ave de l'Université; s RFr10,000-25,000, d RFr15,000-30,000; 🖳 🕃) A modern hotel on the road to the university, this place draws well-to-do Rwandans visiting their kids at college, as well as business folk travelling between Rwanda and Burundi. Rooms are smart and thoroughly modern, and are priced according to their size and the degree of available amenities.

Hôtel Ibis (☎ 530335; Rue de Kigali; s RFr10,000-25,000, d RFr15,000-30,000; 🖳 🕃) Competing with the Credo for the title of the best accommodation in town, the Ibis is a classic hotel with a touch more class. While rooms and facilities aren't as slick as the Credo, the premises are positively brimming with personality.

Eating & Drinking

Like many towns in Rwanda, this is another place where most visitors tend to eat at the guesthouses and hotels. Budget hotels can turn out basic food such as brochettes and rice, while the fancier hotels have pretty impressive menus at attractive prices.

Chez Venant (☎ 085-04115; Rue Rwamamba; mains RFr1500-5000) One of the few recommended restaurants in town, this place brings the taste of China to Huye. All the usual suspects turn up on the menu, including spring rolls and beef in black bean sauce, but there are also a few local dishes for good measure.

Hôtel Ibis Restaurant (☎ 530335; Rue de Kigali; meals RFr2500-5000) This hotel restaurant serves delicious food including a selection of meats, fish and pastas, and a wholesome range of salads. The pleasantly faded dining room here also brings a good measure of atmosphere to your dinner.

Entertainment

There is a traditional Rwandan dance troupe based near Huye, and their show is simply spectacular. The Intore dance originated in Burundi and involves elaborate costumes and superb drumming routines. Performances can be organised through the National Museum, and start at around RFr10,000 for up to five people. This is pretty good value for a group considering that photography is allowed (although not video). Note that prices substantially increase on weekends and during the evening. Contact the **museum** (☎ 532136) to book and confirm the dancers are in town, as the troupe is sometimes on tour.

Shopping

Expo Vente (Rue de Kigali) is a large handicrafts shop exhibiting local products made by cooperatives in villages around Huye.

Getting There & Away

There are several bus companies operating between Huye and Kigali (two hours) found on Rue de Kigali: Atraco Express, Okapi Car, Trans Express 2000 and Volcano Express have almost hourly services in both directions, costing around RFr2000. Atraco Express and Onatracom Express have a few daily departures to Cyangugu for around RFr1700.

Yahoo Car and New Yahoo Coach operate minibuses between Kigali and Bujumbura (Burundi) that stop in Huye at 9.30am daily. Minibuses from Huye (Butare) to Bujumbura cost RFr3000 to RFr5000. However, check security conditions very carefully before crossing this way. There are also local minibuses to the Burundi border at Kayanza Haut.

The minibus stand is just a patch of dirt situated about 1km north of the town centre, by the stadium. Arriving minibuses often drop passengers in the centre of town, but when leaving, you must go to the bus stand. *Boda-bodas* abound around town, so this is no problem.

Minibuses run between Huye and Kigali (RFr1400, two hours) and Kamembe (for Cyangugu, RFr1800, three hours) on a spectacular road in places, passing through the Parc National de Nyungwe, which contains some amazing virgin rainforest between Uwinka and Kiutabe.

RWANDA

AROUND HUYE
Gikongoro Genocide Memorial

Gikongoro would be a fairly forgettable town if it were not for the unforgettable horrors that took place here during the genocide. The location of a well-known technical college before the war, refugees flocked here in the hopes of seeking protection from their killers. As in Huye, the Interahamwe could not be stopped, and in a matter of days, thousands of people were brutally murdered.

This is by far the most graphic of the many genocide memorials in Rwanda, as hundreds of bodies have been exhumed, preserved with powdered lime and appear exactly as they did when the killers struck. Wandering through the rooms at this former institute of learning, the scene becomes more and more macabre, beginning with the contorted corpses of adults, and finishing with a room full of toddlers and babies, slashes from the machetes still visible on the shrivelled bodies.

As you can imagine from this description, Gikongoro can be overwhelming, and not everyone can stomach it for more than a few minutes. It is, however, another poignant reminder to all of us of what came to pass here, and why it must never be allowed to happen again.

Gikongoro is 28km west of Huye, and there are regular minibuses running between the two, costing around RFr500. The memorial is 2km beyond the town, and taxi-motors can run you there for a few hundred francs.

PARC NATIONAL DE NYUNGWE

Quite simply, Nyungwe is Rwanda's most important area of biodiversity, and has been rated the highest priority for forest conservation in Africa. While Nyungwe is the newest of Rwanda's parks to receive national park status, its protected area covers one of the oldest rainforests in Africa. Within the national park, you'll find no less than 1000 plant species including rare endemic orchids, 13 species of primates including more than 500 chimpanzees, 75 species of mammals, at least 275 species of birds and an astounding 120 species of butterflies.

Despite rivalling Uganda's Kibale Forest National Park (p475) in virtually every comparison, Nyungwe is little known outside of East Africa, and is largely undeveloped for tourism. Given its recent successes in promoting gorilla tourism on the international market, the Rwandan government is presently mounting a strong campaign to swing the tourist circuit southwest to Nyungwe. While you're certainly going to need to make an effort to visit Nyungwe properly, you'll be rewarded tenfold for your efforts, and you may not see too many other tourists in the process.

Nyungwe's strongest drawcard is the chance to track chimpanzees, which have been habituated over the years to human visits. Hiking through equatorial rainforest in search of our closest living genetic ancestor is an unparalleled wildlife experience that is certainly on par with gorilla tracking. Little can prepare you for the experience of watching chimpanzees tumbling down from the canopy and racing along the forest floor, all the while being mesmerised by the sounds of their distinctive 'pant-hoot'.

While chimps tend to garner most of the spotlight in Nyungwe, the park's second billing is a habituated troop of around 400 Angolan colobus monkeys, the largest group of arboreal primates in all of Africa. The lush, green valleys of the rainforest also offer outstanding hiking across more than 20km of well-maintained trails, passing through enormous stands of hardwoods, under waterfalls and through large marshes.

History

Part of the Albertine Rift Valley, Nyungwe is virgin equatorial rainforest that survived the last Ice Age. As a result, it is one of the oldest green expanses on the African continent, and is something of a 'Lost World' for rare and endangered species. It also spans several altitudinal bands, which facilitates its largely unparalleled biodiversity of both flora and fauna.

As stunning as Nyungwe is in its present manifestation, it is sadly nothing but a poor shadow of its former grandeur. Today, the outskirts of Nyungwe are heavily cultivated with rolling tea plantations and lush banana plantations. Beautiful though they may be, agriculture to feed the burgeoning masses of the Great Lakes region is largely to blame for the past deforestation.

In the past 100 years, the rainforests of the Albertine Rift Valley were felled with little regard for the biodiversity that they harboured within. While Nyungwe received official protection under the Belgian colonial government

WATCHING WILDLIFE IN PARC NATIONAL DE NYUNGWE

Parc National de Nyungwe is an outstanding island of biodiversity, and a veritable monkey forest. At least 20% of the total primate species in Africa are found within the confines of Nyungwe, an impressive statistic that is only equalled by Kibale Forest National Park (p475) in Uganda.

While they're more difficult to track than slow-moving gorillas, communities of **chimpanzees** on the move will certainly make their presence known to you. Habituated troops of monkeys – **Angolan colobus** (troops of which number up to 400), **Dent's monkey** (a local race of blue monkey) and **grey-cheeked mangabeys** (the last two often seen together) – are virtually guaranteed on guided walks.

Other monkey possibilities include **l'Hoest's** and **diademed monkeys**, which sometimes associate with colobus and blue monkeys. **Olive baboons** and **vervet monkeys** loiter near the park's eastern edge, while **owl-faced monkeys** and possibly **golden monkeys** live in the extensive bamboo stands in the southeastern part of the reserve. Nocturnal prosimian attractions include **needle-clawed** and **greater galagos** as well as the **potto**.

In addition to primates, you also have a fairly good chance of spotting mammals, particularly in and around Kamiranzovu Marsh. **Marsh mongooses** and **Congo clawless otters** stick to the water's edge, while **giant forest hogs**, **bushpigs** and **duikers** are sometimes startled along the trails. Rainforest squirrels are also commonly spotted, and include **giant forest**, **montane sun** and **Boehm's bush squirrels**.

Hyraxes are easily heard after dark, though you're going to have to look inside the hollows of trees if you want to spot one. Nocturnal mammals are a bit tricky to spot, but you do have a chance of running across **jackals**, **civets** and **genets**.

Among bird-watchers in East Africa, Nyungwe has something of a legendary status, and is by far the country's top spot for bird watching. Even if you're not a hardcore birder, it's pretty easy to get excited by Nyungwe's 275-plus species, which include no less than 25 Albertine Rift Valley endemics.

The dirt road leading to Rangiro, and the Red, Blue and Kamiranzovu Trails are all highly recommended for bird-watching. The paved road through the park permits viewing at all levels of the forest: expect **mountain buzzards** and **cinnamon-chested bee-eaters** perched along here, plus numerous **sunbirds**, **wagtails** and flocks of **waxbills**. Other commonly sighted birds include **francolins**, **turacos**, **African crowned eagles**, **hornbills** and even **Congo bay owls**.

---

as early as 1933, it lost 15% of its original size in the 1960s and 1970s to encroaching farms.

Fortunately, the Peace Corps, the World Conservation Society and the Rwandan government targeted Nyungwe for increased conservation in the 1980s. The original project aims were to promote tourism in an ecologically sound way, while also studying the forest and educating local people about its value.

Although tourism in the region was brought to a standstill during the tragic events of the 1990s, Nyungwe Forest is once again firmly on the tourist map. Having received official national park status in 2004, Parc National de Nyungwe is now setting its sights on becoming one of East Africa's leading ecotourism destinations.

Orientation

One of the largest protected montane rainforests in Africa, Nyungwe covers 970 sq km, and extends across the border to Kibira National Park in Burundi. It also serves as a watershed for Africa's two largest rivers, the Nile and the Congo, and contains several springs that are believed to feed the headwaters of the Albertine Nile.

Parc National de Nyungwe is sliced in two by the Huye–Cyangugu road. Visitors can access the park through either the Uwinka Reception Centre or the ORTPN Resthouse, both of which lie along this road.

Uwinka serves as an access point for the Coloured Trails, while the ORTPN Resthouse is the jumping off point for Waterfall Trail and the Gisakura tea estate. Chimpanzees can cover great distances in a short period of time, so you need to inquire at either Uwinka or ORTPN about their whereabouts.

While public transportation does pass by the park, your ability to move around the park will be greatly restricted without access to a private vehicle. This is especially true if you want to see the chimps, as tracking can sometimes begin in the most seemingly random of locations.

Information

The park headquarters is at the Uwinka Reception Centre, where you must pay your visitor fees. It costs US$20 per day to enter Nyungwe, though you will need to pay additional fees depending on which activities you decide to engage in.

Chimpanzee tracking costs an additional US$50 per person, while all other guided walks cost an additional US$30 per person. It is also standard practice (and good manners) to tip your guides, especially if they do a good job tracking the primates. Note that unguided walks are not permitted in the park.

Sights & Activities

While it should go without saying, Nyungwe is equatorial rainforest, which means that it receives more than 2 metres of rainfall annually. This of course means that you need to dress appropriately – trails can get extremely wet and muddy, so make sure you have good hiking shoes, waterproof slacks, a solid raincoat and perhaps even a floppy hat or bandana.

CHIMPANZEE TRACKING

They may pale in size when compared to the hulking masses that are the eastern mountain gorillas, though there is no denying the incredible affinity that we humans have for chimpanzees. Sharing an estimated 94% of our genetic material, chimps display an incredible range of human-like behaviours ranging from tool use and waging war to face-to-face sex and possibly even rudimentary language.

Chimps are highly sociable creatures, and one of the few primates to form complex communities ranging upwards of 100 individuals. During the day, these communities break down into smaller units that forage for food, a behaviour that has been dubbed by anthropologists as 'fission-fusion'. Since they cover a greater daily distance than the relatively docile gorilla, chimpanzee tracking is a much more uncertain enterprise.

Chimpanzee habitation in Nyungwe is still very much a work in progress, and there are no guarantees that you'll come face-to-face with one in the wild. However, you'll certainly be aware of their presence – they're very

sensitive to territorial intrusions – especially since their distinctive 'pant-hoot' is one of the most distinctive sounds of the Central African rainforest.

If you are lucky, and happen to come across a group of chimps on the move, you need to be quick with the camera. Chimps do have a tendency to quickly disappear in the underbrush, or climb up into the canopy and out of sight. On the other hand, consider leaving the camera in your backpack for a few extra moments, and enjoying the privileged position you're in of being able to encounter mankind's closest living evolutionary link.

Much like gorilla tracking, you need to be prepared for lengthy and taxing hikes that can take up to several hours. Of course, it's certainly worth the effort – chimps are an endangered species that are becoming increasingly rare in the wild. Even if your efforts aren't successful, hiking through Nyungwe is still an amazing experience in and of itself.

As previously mentioned, chimpanzees have large day ranges, which means that you need to inquire with the rangers as to their general whereabouts. In the rainy season, you have a good chance of successfully tracking the chimps on the Coloured Trails (p582), though in the dry season they have a tendency to head for higher elevations. Given their mobility, having a car is something of a necessity for chimp tracking as you will need to arrange transportation for you and your guide to the trailhead.

If the chimps have moved deep into the forest, note that a second locale for tracking exists in nearby **Cyamudongo**, which is protected as an annexe of Parc National de Nyungwe. This tiny patch of forest, located approximately 45 minutes west of Gisakura on the road out to Cyangungu, covers no more than 6 sq km, though it is home to an estimated 20 chimps. Again, that you need to have your own vehicle in order to consider Cyamudongo a viable option.

COLOBUS MONKEY TRACKING

A subspecies of the widespread black-and-white colobus, the Angolan colobus is an arboreal Old World monkey that is distinguished by its black fur and long, silky white locks of hair. Weighing 10 to 20kg, and possessing a dextrous tail that can reach lengths of 75 centimetres, Angolan colobi are perfectly suited to a life up in the canopy.

RWANDA

Colobi are distributed throughout the rainforests of equatorial Africa, though they reach epic numbers in Parc National de Nyungwe. While they may not be as a charismatic as chimps, colobi are extremely social primates that form enormous troop group sizes – the semihabituated troop in Nyungwe numbers no less than 400 individuals, and is by far the largest primate aggregation on the continent.

As you might imagine, finding yourself in the presence of literally hundreds of primates bounding through the treetops can be a mesmerising experience. Curious animals by nature, colobi in Nyungwe seem to almost revel in their playful interactions with human visitors.

Troops of Angolan colobi maintain fairly regimented territories, which is good news for trackers as the semi-habituated group in Nyungwe tends to stick to the Coloured Trails (below). While watching wildlife is never a certainty, generally speaking, the rangers can find the colobus monkey troop in an hour or so.

COLOURED TRAILS

This system of marked trails was constructed in the late 1980s in an attempt to open up Nyungwe to tourists. While tourism in the national park remains relatively low-key, these seven trails are nevertheless reasonably well maintained. Hikers can choose from the 1km-long Grey Trail, a proverbial walk in the woods, up to the 10km-long Red Trail, which winds steeply up forested-slopes.

Although you need to specifically request to engage in either chimpanzee or colobus tracking, in theory you could run across either primate while hiking the coloured trails. Even if you don't come across these two star billings, you're likely to spot any of Nyungwe's other 11 primates, as well as a whole slew of birdlife, and possibly even the odd mammal or two.

The trails originate from the Uwinka Reception Centre.

WATERFALL TRAIL

While not as popular as the Coloured Trails, this stunner of a hike is one of the highlights of Nyungwe. Departing from the ORTPN Resthouse, the Waterfall Trail takes three to six hours to complete depending on your fitness level, and winds through a variety of landscapes from tea plantations to deep forest. The highlight of the trail is (quite obviously) a remote waterfall, where you can take a shallow dip and refresh your body after a potentially hot and humid hike.

GISAKURA TEA PLANTATION

Another interesting hike leads from the ORTPN Resthouse to this nearby tea plantation, which is home to a small group of semi-habituated Angolan colobus monkeys. The forest fringes around the tea plantation are also a particularly good area for bird watching, so bring your binoculars if you want to raise your bird count.

KAMIRANZOVU TRAIL

If you have your own wheels, this wilderness trail starts somewhere between Uwinka and Gisakura, and runs for about 4km to Kamiranzouv Swamp. Sadly, elephants haven't been seen in the area for decades, though the swamplands are your best bet for spotting other large mammals. Even if you don't come across any other fauna, this trail is particularly famous for its rare species of orchids.

BIGUGU TRAIL

While you need to be in good shape to attempt this trail, the route up to Mt Bigugu (2950m) puts you in the proximity of a freshwater spring that is reported to be the most remote source of the Nile River. The trailhead lies along the road between Uwinka and Huye.

RANGIRO ROAD

This dirt road starts 1.5km east of Uwinka, and is by far the best place in the park for bird watching. Since there are frequent changes in elevation along this route, you have increased chances of spotting a good number of Nyungwe's fine-feathered friends. There are more than 25 endemics in the park including Rwenzori turacos as well as other large forest specialties including African crowned eagles and various hornbills.

Sleeping & Eating

There is a camp site (per person US$20) at the Uwinka headquarters, occupying a ridge (2500m) overlooking the forest, that offers impressive views in all directions. Campers should bring pretty much everything they need – tent, sleeping bag, cooking equipment, food and warm clothes – as only drinks are available, and there is little here other than toilets, charcoal and wood. The nearest towns for

RWANDA

provisions are Cyangugu (below), Gikongoro (p579) and Huye (Butare; p576).

A more sophisticated option for those without a tent is the **ORTPN Resthouse** (r per person $15-20, meals US$5-10), which offers accommodation in simple but functional rooms that share communal showers and toilets. With advanced notice, you can also arrange for the staff to cook you hot meals. The big problem, however, is location, location, location – it is a long haul to Uwinka for those with no transport, though you are close to the Waterfall Trail and the Gisakura Tea Plantation. Note that advance bookings are recommended, and can be made through the ORTPN office in Kigali – see p551.

Getting There & Away
Parc National de Nyungwe lies between Huye and Cyangugu, and minibuses travel between Huye (90km, two hours. RFr1000) and Kamembe (for Cyangugu, 54km, one hour) throughout the day.

Hitching rides back and forth is certainly possible for the patient, though your ability to move around the park is severely limited if you don't have a car. This is especially true if you're planning on tracking chimpanzees since the hike usually begins in random locales. If you're sticking to the Coloured Trails, however, it is easy enough to base yourself at Uwinka.

The Uwinka headquarters is well marked with a picture of a colobus monkey. If you're coming in from Kigali, the trip takes between four and five hours depending on traffic.

CYANGUGU
Clinging to the southern tip of Lake Kivu, and looking across to Bukavu in DRC, Cyangugu is an attractively situated town on the shore. It is also the nearest major settlement to Parc National de Nyungwe, one of the richest primate destinations in Africa. Despite these two major drawcards, Cyangugu is a relatively low-key tourist destination; you'll certainly enjoy the peace and quiet if you happen to spend the night here.

Orientation & Information
Kamembe, a few kilometres above the lake, is the main town and transport centre and an important location for the processing of tea and cotton, while most of the better hotels are down below in Cyangugu proper, right next to the border.

There is a branch of BCR in Kamembe that changes cash, but for Congolese transactions, it is better to change near the border post in Cyangugu. Anyone planning to travel on to DRC can obtain an eight-day visa on the border for US$35, though Bukavu has experienced more unrest than most eastern towns – check carefully, and then check again before crossing.

Sights & Activities
Most visitors to Cyangugu are content with simply taking a dip in **Lake Kivu**, lounging on the shores or exploring the town on foot. If however you're feeling a bit more active, consider an excursion to nearby Parc National de Nyungwe (p579).

Sleeping & Eating
Peace Guesthouse (☎ 537799; www.aspk78.dsl.pipex .com; r RFr3000-6000, cabin/villa RFr20,000/30,000) It's situated kind of in the middle of nowhere, but that's the point. Run by the Anglican Church, the most popular option on this stretch of the lake is more or less equidistant from Kamembe and Cyangugu, though the view faces firmly towards Bukavu in DRC. The management is extremely keen on tending to the needs of their guests, and you won't find much to complain about as the rooms and private villas are all kept in immaculate order.

Hotel des Chutes (☎ 537405; r RFr8000-10,000) Situated back on the hill, this hotel offers well-equipped rooms with spacious balconies that boast fine views of the lake. There is also a great little restaurant here with a range of European cuisine available, as well as a bar and outdoor terrace that is popular with the locals.

Ten to Ten Paradise Hotel (☎ 537818; r RFr12,000-20,000; ⊠) Located up in more rough-and-ready Kamembe, this is the swishest hotel in town, boasting modern amenities such as air-con, satellite TV, steamy hot water showers. However, putting charm above comfort, you are better off down in Cyangugu.

Hotel du Lac (☎ 537172; r RFr12,000-20,000; ⊠) So close to the border it's almost in DRC, this local landmark has a good mix of rooms, even though some of them have aged gracefully over the years. The swimming pool is open to non-guests for a small fee, and the lively terrace bar and restaurant is the place to be at night.

The most popular eating spots in town are at the hotel restaurants – any of the listings above are certainly worth checking out, even if you're not staying there. Another good option is to check out the hole-in-the-wall local restaurants up in Kamembe close to the bus terminal, which can provide a quick snack before or after a bus journey.

Getting There & Away

Minibuses for the short hop between Cyangugu and Kamembe cost RFr200.

Atraco Express and Onatracom Express have several daily departures between them to Huye (Butare) for around RFr1700 (three hours). This road is incredibly spectacular in parts and passes through the superb Nyungwe rainforest, where it is possible to see troops of Angolan colobus playing by the roadside.

See opposite for details on the daily bus service connecting Cyangugu and Kibuye, and for information on boat transportation across Lake Kivu.

KIBUYE

Although it has a stunning location, spread across a series of tongues jutting into Lake Kivu, Kibuye is not quite able to rival Gisenyi for the title of Rwanda's leading destination for sun and sand. On this part of the lake, good beaches are a lot less common, and it doesn't help that Kibuye hosted the largest wholesale slaughter of Tutsis during the dark days of the genocide.

However, a new paved road from Kigali has made the town more accessible than ever before, and it may only be a matter of time before tourism development starts to pick up. In the meantime, Kibuye is certainly a pleasant enough place to relax for a few days. And, unlike Gisenyi, you can swim here without fear of drowning and asphyxiating in the event of an unforseen limnic eruption (see the boxed text p574).

History

During the 100 days of madness in 1994, Kibuye hosted some of the most horrific and despicable mass killings in all of Rwanda. Prior to the outbreak of the genocide, more than 20% of the local population was Tutsi; in 1994 the Interahamwe killed an estimated nine out of every 10 Tutsi. While these scars still run deep, today the residents of Kibuye are working together as a community to embrace the prospect of future tourism. A couple of memorials to the slain victims ensure that the past is not forgotten, while the frames of new buildings are sights of a brighter future.

Orientation & Information

Kibuye may not be as developed as Gisenyi (p572), but it is nevertheless an extremely pleasant place to explore. One of the best ways to get accustomed to the town is to follow the ring road around the shores of the lake. There are some amazing views to be had along the way, and you're likely to find a few sandy patches were you can pause to take a cooling dip.

There is a post office near Guest House Kibuye with international services, plus plenty of MTN phones in the centre of town. For internet access, try **Hotel Centre Béthanie** (☎ 568509; per hr RFr500).

Sights
GENOCIDE MEMORIALS

Kibuye was hardest hit of all prefectures during the killings, with about 90% of the Tutsi population murdered. To help ensure no one forgets the horrors that were perpetrated here in 1994, there is a genocide memorial in the **church** near Hôme St Jean. While a good number of memorials in Rwanda are stark reminders of the past atrocities, the church is a beautiful and evocative testament to the strength of the human spirit. The interior is adorned with colourful mosaics, vivid stained glass windows and flowing tapestries, each of which pays solemn tribute to the memory of lost loved ones.

The uphill road from Kibuye leads to the small village of **Bisesero**, which is home to an equally significant memorial. During the early days of the genocide, more than 50,000 Tutsis fled here in the hope of evading the Interahamwe. For more than a month, these brave individuals were able to fend off their aggressors with little more than basic farming implements.

On May 13, a reinforced regiment of soldiers and militia descended on Bisesero, slaughtering more than half of the refugees. By the time the French arrived on the scene in June, there were no more than 1300 Tutsis remaining. However, these individuals overcame insurmountable odds, and their stories of reflect humanity's incredible will to survive.

OTHER SIGHTS

There is a busy **market** on the lakeshore on Fridays which attracts traders from as far afield as DRC.

When returning on the road to Kigali, keep an eye out for the 100m-high waterfall **Les Chutes de Ndaba** after about 20km – buses usually slow down and helpful locals are quick to point it out.

Activities

Not surprisingly, most activities in Kibuye revolve around Lake Kivu. Most guests are content to simply sun themselves for days on end, occasionally taking breaks to go **swimming**. The other popular activity is **boating** to any of the small offshore islands, which can be arranged through any of the accommodation options listed below.

Sleeping & Eating

Hôme St Jean (☎ 568526; r RFr3500-6500) Sitting on an isolated hillside to the west of town, this church-run pad has great views and the rooms are some of the cheapest in town. For those without transport, it means a lot of walking, though you'll be rewarded for your efforts with a good measure of peace and tranquillity.

Hotel Centre Béthanie (☎ 568509; r RFr8000-12,000; 🖳) Another church-run spot, this popular guesthouse occupies a charming location on a wooded peninsula jutting into the lake. The small but cosy private rooms are kept spic and span, and there is also a basic restaurant on the premises, as well as internet access. It's wise to give a ring before stopping by as this is Kibuye's leading conference venue.

Hotel Golfe Eden Rock (☎ 568524; r from RFr14,000) This large and looming hotel is open to the public once more, having housed the Chinese road-construction crew working on the Kigali road for many years. The location is not as nice as Bethanie, but the rooms are far and above the smartest in town. The most expensive quarters come equipped with private balconies, which offer sweeping views over Lake Kivu.

Restaurant Nouveauté (meals RFr1000-4000) This place, in the centre of town near Okapi Car, has a basic menu of goat stew or brochettes, beans, rice, potatoes and so on. It also offers cold beers and soft drinks, and attracts a small but devoted crowd of locals in the evening hours.

Getting There & Away

The road linking Kibuye with Kigali is endlessly winding but in excellent shape, making it very accessible from the capital. Okapi Car runs a handful of daily buses between Kigali and Kibuye (2½ hours), costing around RFr1500. Local minibuses also run this way for a little less, but are much more crowded.

Getting between Kibuye and either Cyangugu or Gisenyi is more difficult without your own vehicle as shared taxis and buses are very infrequent. There is a daily morning bus in either direction between Kibuye and Cyangugu (RFr2500, six hours) which involves one of the most spectacular roads in the country, complete with hairpin bends and plunging drops. There are infrequent minibuses to Gisenyi charging RFr1500. Friday is generally the easiest day for heading north or south, due to the market.

At the time of writing, there were no regularly scheduled ferry services currently in operation on Lake Kivu. However, it is sometimes possible to arrange a boat trip to Gisenyi or Cyangugu if there is enough demand – inquire at your accommodation for more information. Note that due to the ongoing instability in DRC, international boat trips are of questionable safety.

EASTERN RWANDA

While much of Rwanda is characterised by equatorial rainforest and richly cultivated farmland, Eastern Rwanda is something else entirely. Contiguous with the dry and flat savannah lands of Tanzania, this region is more reminiscent of the classic images of East African landscapes. While sights are scarce in this part of the country, Parc National de l'Akagera is one of Rwanda's highlights, especially if you're looking to get your safari fix.

PARC NATIONAL DE L'AKAGERA

Created in 1934 to protect the lands surrounding the Kagera River, this national park once protected nearly 10% of Rwanda, and was considered to be one of the finest game reserves in the whole of Africa. However, due to the massive numbers of refugees who returned to Rwanda in the late 1990s, as much as two-thirds of the park was de-gazetted, and resettled with new villages. Increased human presence took an incredible toll on the national park. Human encroachment facilitated poaching and environmental degradation, and Akagera's wildlife was very nearly decimated.

For more than a decade, Akagera was something of a vegetarian safari, given that most animals on four legs were taking an extended holiday in neighbouring Tanzania. However, the Rwandan government has recently implemented strict conservation laws (which are certainly complementary to their increased push for tourism in Rwanda) aimed at protecting Akagera. Furthermore, the once decrepit Akagera Game Lodge has been rehabilitated by South African investors, and now stands as testament to the future potential of this once great safari park.

Truth be told, Akagera is still a shadow of its former self, and you will be extremely disappointed if you come here expecting concentrations of wildlife on par with Kenya and Tanzania. While the once grand herds that characterised Akagera are a mere fraction of their original numbers, populations are noticeably on the rise. And, even if you don't come across too many wild animals, it's very likely that you won't come across too many other wildlife-viewing drivers. Indeed, the tourist trail has yet to fully incorporate Akagera, which means that you can soak up the park's splendid nature in relative peace and isolation.

History

Akagera's strongest drawcard is its unique ecology, which is a mix of woodland habitats, swampy wetlands and jagged mountains. For much of its natural history, Akagera functioned as a self-sustaining ecological unit, which enabled a significant number of animals to survive year-round without the need to migrate out of the area. While the Belgians certainly didn't do Rwanda too many favours, they are credited with recognising the environmental significance of Akagera.

In 1934, the colonial government gazetted 2500 sq km as protected lands, including a buffer zone where human activities were strictly prohibited. Following independence in 1962, the Rwandan government largely upheld their commitment to protect the sanctity of the national park. In fact, prior to the start of the civil war, Akagera, together with the country's other national parks, was Rwanda's third largest revenue earner.

As history would have it, in 1997 Akagera was reduced to a mere 1085 sq km due to increased population pressures brought on by returning refugees. In an effort to resettle landless Rwandans, the government slashed the park's borders by two-thirds, devastating this once pristine ecosystem.

In response to substantial habitat loss, as well as depleted water supplies resulting from increased farming and ranching, Akagera's wildlife fled to Tanzania. Poachers, who carried out their illegal activities with virtual impunity, quickly decimated the animal herds that chose to stay put. In more recent years, the Rwandan government has changed its tune on Akagera, though it's going to take several more years before wildlife populations in the park can stabilise.

While human and wildlife conflicts are never a clear-cut issue, it's worth pointing out that Akagera is a vital part of Rwanda's push for a viable tourism industry. At present, the vast majority of tourists in Rwanda leave the country quickly after tracking gorillas, which is a trend the government would like to change. If people can be persuaded to spend a bit of extra time in Rwanda, then Akagera, along with Parc National de Nyungwe (p579), need to be preserved.

On that note, consider extending your stay in Rwanda, and be sure to visit Akagera – this up-and-coming national park could certainly use your support.

Orientation

There are three distinct environments in the park: standard savannah as seen in much of the region; an immense swampy area along the border with Tanzania that contains six lakes and numerous islands, some of which are covered with forest; and a chain of low mountains on the flanks of the park with variable vegetation, ranging from short grasses on the summits to wooded savannah and dense thickets of forest.

The best time to visit is during the dry season (mid-May to September). November and April are the wettest months. Tsetse flies and mosquitoes can be bad in the north and east, so bring a good insect repellent.

While in theory it is possible to reach the park by public transport, you really do need a private vehicle in order to move around the park.

Hiring a guide is a good idea, especially since the trails aren't that well marked. Plus it will help give the rangers some extra encouragement, which certainly goes a long way in helping to protect this vital national park.

Information

Parc Arc National de L'Akagera has a really, really confusing fee structure, so just bear with us for a few lines.

Admission for foreigners is US$10 – this is a one-off fee that covers your entire time in the park. There is also a one-off vehicle levy fee, which is US$4 to US$20 for locally registered vehicles, and US$10 to US$50 for foreigner registered vehicles; small 4WD vehicles incur a smaller charge than large trucks. On top of all of this, you need to pay a wildlife viewing fee – for non-resident foreigners, a one-/two-/three-day pass is US$20/30/50, while resident foreigners need only pay US$15/20/25.

Yes, this is annoying, and yes, it can add up to of money. However, keep in mind that the fees you pay to visit Akagera are essential to keeping the park operating at its top capacity.

Sights & Activities
WILDLIFE WATCHING

Akagera is home to the greatest diversity of large mammals in Rwanda, including recovering herds of buffalo, topi, plains zebras, impalas, elands, giraffes, reedbucks, waterbucks, elephants and sitatungas. The parks' vegetated waterways are inhabited by vast numbers of hippos and crocodiles – while you should never exit your car in a wildlife reserve, this adage holds doubly true near any source of water.

Carnivores in Akagera include lions, leopards, spotted hyenas, genets, cervals and jackals. There are even a few specialties, including the rare roan antelope and reintroduced black rhinos from Tanzania. The national park also lies on the great Nile Valley bird migration route, which means that you could potentially spot up to 525 species of birds including several endemics and more than 40 different kinds of raptors.

Again, it's worth pointing out that while Akagera supports a full compliment of East African wildlife, don't come here expecting your quintessential East Africa safari experience. Wildlife populations are only now starting to stabilise, but in time, Akagera has the potential to once again rank among the continent's great safari parks.

So how much wildlife is actually left in the park? That's the real question, though nobody truly knows the answer with any degree of certainty. There may only be one or two dozen lions left in the park, though hyenas, jackals and leopards are still active at night, and small cats such as the genet and serval are well represented. Since Akagera is contiguous with western Tanzania, there is hope that predatory cats will increase their ranges and move into Rwanda.

Akagera was once defined by its massive aggregates of herd animals and there is reason to believe that these densities will arise once more. There are no less than 11 different species of antelopes in the park, which includes the common safari staple that is the impala, as well as the majestic but rare roan antelope. Buffalo and zebra are also very well represented animals, while Maasai giraffes and elephants are making a slow but steady comeback.

The national park is also something of a hippo paradise, especially given that much of the environment is swampland. There are at least a thousand of the lumbering giants in and around the shores of the lake, as well as a large enough population of crocs to keep you from the temptation of taking a cooling dip.

In the 1950s, Akagera was the first national park in Africa to receive translocated black rhinos, which were flown in from neighbouring Tanzania. These animals thrived in the dense brush of the park, but poachers quickly decimated their numbers during the 1980s. At present, it is believed that there are still a few remaining individuals, and there are plans underway to translocate more of these highly endangered animals.

If you're a bird-watcher, you'll be happy to know that Akagera has Rwanda's greatest concentration of fine-feathered friends outside of Parc National de Nyungwe (p579). The many kilometres of waterside habitat support African eagles, kingfishers, herons, ibises, storks, egrets, crakes, rails, cormorants, darts and pelicans. Seasonal visitors include large flocks of ducks, bee-eaters and terns, and the woodlands areas are particularly good places for barbets, shrikes, orioles and weavers.

RWANDA

Sleeping

Akagera Game Lodge (☎ 567805; www.akageralodge
.co.rw; r from US$150; ☒) Great news for those on
an upmarket safari in the region, the Akagera
Lodge offers four-star comfort for park visitors. Fully renovated by a South African
group, this is really more of an upscale hotel
than a luxury wildlife lodge, though it's still an
excellent base for properly exploring Akagera.
Full-board deals are available, a wise choice
given there are no restaurants in the park; day-
trippers should head here for lunch.

Camping (adult/child US$10/5) is possible at
the park headquarters on the shores of
Lake Ihema, but more attractive is the second, basic camp site at Lake Shakani, a few
kilometres north. At either place facilities
are so minimal as to be verging on nonexistent, so be sure that you're prepared to be
virtually self-sufficient.

Getting There & Away

Akagera is only really accessible for those with
their own transport. Safari and tour companies in Kigali can arrange a vehicle (see
p552), or you can negotiate with private taxis
around Kigali.

RWANDA DIRECTORY

ACCOMMODATION
Camping

The only fully functioning camp sites in the
country are at Parc National de Nyungwe
(p579) and Parc National de l'Akagera (p585),
but it may be possible to camp at some of the
missions around the country on request. Note
that facilities are non-existent here, which
means that you will need to bring everything
with you and be entirely self-sufficient.

Hostels

Dorm accommodation at the mission hostels
costs a couple thousand francs per night without food, while a private double room can run
as high as RFr15,000 per night depending on
facilities. Bathrooms are generally shared.

Mission hostels are places run by churches
or missionaries. These differ from ordinary
places in that few foreigners stay at them, and
the hostels usually enforce a curfew – the door
is usually closed at 10pm (or earlier). They
seem to attract an exceptionally conscientious
type of manager who takes the old adage 'clean-

---

liness is next to godliness' fairly seriously –
there might not be hot water, but the bed and
room will be spotless. Note that couples may
be separated unless obviously married.

Hotels

Compared with mission hostels, hotels are
generally a bit more expensive, though you
can usually expect satellite TV, hot showers
and occasionally internet access.

Top-end hotels, mostly found in Kigali and
Gisenyi, adhere to international standards of
quality and service. Some of the newer, smaller
places offer better value for money, and more
character than the larger international chains.
There are also now a couple of upmarket camps
located near Musanze (Ruhengeri; p559) on
the edge of Parc National des Volcans.

ACTIVITIES
Bird-Watching

Bird-watching in Rwanda may not be in the
same league as the rest of East Africa, but
there are some good opportunities for ornithologists in Parc National de Nyungwe
(p579), where a host of Albertine Rift endemics can be seen. Another decent spot is Parc
National de l'Akagera (p585), in the east of the
country, which offers an alternative range of
savannah birds.

Hiking & Trekking

Trekking is beginning to take off again in
Rwanda. As the waiting list for gorilla permits
grows longer in peak season, more and more

travellers are taking the opportunity to climb and trek the volcanoes in Parc National des Volcans (p562). There is also an excellent network of walking trails at Parc National de Nyungwe (p579), the largest tropical montane forest in East Africa.

Primate Tracking

Without a doubt, this forms the number-one attraction for all visitors to Rwanda: an encounter with the enigmatic mountain gorillas is simply magical. It's possible to track the mountain gorillas in Parc National des Volcans (p562) throughout the year. Bookings should be made with the ORTPN office (p551)in Kigali . For more information on tracking the mountain gorillas in East Africa, see p75.

While not as popular as the gorillas, endangered golden monkeys can also be tracked in Parc National des Volcans – for more information, see p568.

Chimpanzee tracking is beginning to take off at Nyungwe (p579), though sightings are not as common as in Uganda as habituation is still ongoing. There are also huge troops of colobus monkeys in Nyungwe that are easy to spot from the well-marked walking trails that cut through the forest.

Wildlife Watching

The only opportunity for wildlife drives is in Parc National de l'Akagera (p585), though with wildlife numbers still recovering from years of conflict, it is not quite the Kenya or Tanzania experience yet.

BOOKS

Many of the most powerful books written about Rwanda cover the tragedy of the 1994 genocide. For an in-depth insight into the Rwandan genocide, read *The Rwanda Crisis – History of a Genocide* by French historian Gerard Prunier.

One of the most hard-hitting books on the genocide is *We Wish to Inform You That Tomorrow We Will Be Killed with Our Families* by Phillip Gourevitch.

Another journalist who bore witness to much of the killing was BBC correspondent Fergal Keane, who returned to write *Season of Blood*.

Shake Hands With the Devil by Lt Gen Romeo Dallaire tells the inside story of the UN mission in Rwanda.

Leave None to Tell the Story, published by African Rights Watch, is a meticulous record of the genocide through the eyes of victims who survived, and government records, which attest to the clinical planning of it all.

A Sunday by the Pool in Kigali by Gil Courtemanche is a fictional account of a relationship between a French reporter and a beautiful Tutsi woman during the genocide. No doubt based on very real events, this is an ill-fated love story that perfectly captures the horrors of the time.

Gorillas in the Mist by Dian Fossey is another classic – see p564 for more background.

BUSINESS HOURS

Government offices and businesses are generally open between 8.30am and 4.30pm or 5.30pm, with a short break for lunch sometime between noon and 2pm. Most shops and banks do not break for lunch, but some banks close early at 3.30pm.

Local restaurant hours are 7am to 9pm, and international-type restaurants are open 11.30am to 2.30pm and 5.30pm to 10.30pm Monday to Friday.

DANGERS & ANNOYANCES

Mention Rwanda to most people and they think of it as a highly dangerous place. However, the reality today is very different, and stability has returned to all parts of the country.

With that said, it is still worth checking security conditions before entering the country as it this is a very unstable region of the world. There is always the remote possibility of Interahamwe rebels re-entering the country, or problems spilling over from neighbouring DRC or Burundi.

The most important, and vital, thing to remember about security is that there is absolutely no substitute for researching current conditions in the country and surrounding neighbours before arrival and again once in the country. Read newspapers, ask other travellers and hostels for the latest and check again locally once in the provinces. Things can change very fast, for the better or worse, and it pays to be well informed.

Urban Rwanda is undoubtedly one of the safer places to be in this region, and Kigali is a genuine contender for the safest capital in Africa. However, like in any big city the world over, take care at night.

RWANDA

Out in the countryside, do not walk along anything other than a well-used track – there may still be land mines in some remote areas, though most have now been cleared by international organisations.

Never take photographs of anything connected with the government or the military (post offices, banks, bridges, border crossings, barracks, prisons and dams) – cameras can and will be confiscated. In fact, take care of where you point your camera anywhere in the country, as most Rwandans are very sensitive to who or what you are snapping.

The most common annoyance here are the roadblocks on all of the main roads, particularly close to the capital Kigali. Vehicles must stop at these, and passengers and their baggage may be searched. On roads near borders, soldiers will also want to check passports and travel documents.

EMBASSIES & CONSULATES
Rwandan Embassies

For Rwandan embassies in Burundi, Kenya, Tanzania or Uganda, see the relevant section in those chapters. Useful Rwandan embassies worldwide:

Belgium (☎ 02-771 2127; 1 Ave de Fleurs, Brussels)
South Africa (☎ 012-460 0709; 35 Marais St, Pretoria)
UK (☎ 020-7224 9832; 120-122 Seymour Place, London)
USA (☎ 202-232 2882; www.rwandaembassy.org; 1724 New Hampshire Ave, Washington DC)

Embassies in Rwanda

All embassies and consulates are in the capital, Kigali. Quite a number of embassies are now located on Blvd de l'Umuganda, across the valley in the Kacyiru suburb of Kigali.

Belgium (Map p550; ☎ 575551; www.diplomatie .be/kigali; Rue de Nyarugenge)
Burundi (off Map p550; ☎ 517529; Boulevard de l'Umuganda, Kacyiru)
Canada (Map p550; ☎ 571762; Rue de l'Akagera)
France (Map p550; ☎ 575206; 40 Ave Paul VI)
Kenya (off Map p550; ☎ 583332; Blvd de l'Umuganda, Kacyiru)
South Africa (off Map p550; ☎ 583185; Blvd de l'Umuganda, Kacyiru)
Tanzania (Map p550; ☎ 756567; tanzarep@rwandatell .rwandal.com; 15 Ave Paul VI, Kigali)
Uganda (Map p550; ☎ 503537; http://ugandaembassy .rw; Ave de la Paix)
UK (off Map p550; ☎ 585280; Blvd de l'Umuganda)
USA (Map p550; ☎ 596400; http://rwanda.usembassy .gov; 2657 Ave de la Gendarmerie, Kacyiru)

HOLIDAYS

New Year's Day 1 January
Democracy Day 8 January
Easter (Good Friday, Holy Saturday and Easter Monday) March/April
Labour Day 1 May
Ascension Thursday May
Whit Monday May
National Day 1 July
Peace & National Unity Day 5 July
Harvest Festival 1 August
Assumption 15 August
Culture Day 8 September
Kamarampaka Day 25 September
Armed Forces Day 26 October
All Saints' Day 1 November
Christmas Day 25 December

For information on Kwita Izina, the gorilla naming ceremony, see the box text on p570.

INTERNET ACCESS

Internet access in Rwanda is up to regional standards, and is now widely available in Kigali, as well as on a more limited basis in Gisenyi, Huye (Butare), Cyangugu, Kibuye and Musanze (Ruhengeri). It is cheap, generally between RFr500 and RFr1000 per hour.

INTERNET RESOURCES

Rwanda doesn't have a huge presence in cyberspace, but there are a few useful websites to keep an eye out for:

International Criminal Tribunal for Rwanda (www.ictr.org) The official website for the genocide trials taking place in Arusha.
New Times (www.newtimes.co.rw) For the latest news on Rwanda in English.
Tourism in Rwanda (www.rwandatourism.com) The official tourist website on Rwanda, with information on national parks and local culture.

MAPS

It's difficult to get hold of decent maps of Rwanda before getting to the country. The best map currently is *Rwanda Burundi – International Travel Map* by ITMB Publishing at a scale of 1:400,000. Once in Kigali, it may be possible to buy older maps of some of the national parks from the ORTPN office or from local bookshops. You may also find it useful to get hold of *Tanzania - Rwanda - Burundi Map* by Nelles.

MONEY

The unit of currency is the Rwandan franc (RFr). It is divided into 100 centimes, but these are no longer in circulation. Notes come in RFr100, RFr500, RFr1000, RFr5000 and RFr10,000 denominations. Coins come in RFr1, RFr5, RFr10, RFr20 and RFr50.

ATMs

Banks in Kigali have a network of ATMs, but they are not yet wired up for international transactions (despite the Visa signs at some.) Ask locals on arrival for the latest information, rather than wandering the city from ATM to ATM, experiencing disappointment and frustration.

There is still a bit of a black market in Rwanda, but there is not much difference in the rate offered on the street and in banks and forex places. Moneychangers gather around the main post office in Kigali, but count your cash very carefully if you change on the street.

Cash

You'll find it is definitely best to come to Rwanda with US dollars or euros as travellers cheques and credit-card withdrawals attract a hefty commission, and rates against other currencies are poor. There are a number of banks open in Kigali, but some can be very slow at dealing with currency exchange. There are also banks in Huye (Butare), Cyangugu, Gisenyi, Gitarama and Musanze (Ruhengeri). Another option is to change cash on the street or in shops, but note that this usually attracts a slightly higher rate than elsewhere, particularly for non-US currencies.

Credit Cards

Credit cards are generally only accepted in relatively expensive hotels and restaurants in Kigali, Gisenyi and Musanze (Ruhengeri). It is possible to make cash withdrawals against credit cards at banks in the capital, though you can expect to pay a hefty commission and lose a lot of time waiting for everything to clear.

Tipping

Tipping is common in the cities these days due to the large international presence. Rwandan salaries are low and a tip of about 10% will be appreciated.

Travellers Cheques

Travellers cheques draw commissions adding up to about US$15 per transaction, so it is well worth changing all the money you'll need in one go. Generally speaking however, your travellers cheques are useless beyond the capital.

PHOTOGRAPHY

Be extremely careful wherever you take photos in Rwanda; see p589.

You may also be able to find memory cards and other accessories for digital cameras in cities and large towns, but prices are high, and quality is not guaranteed.

POST

Postal rates for postcards going overseas are around RFr200 for Africa, RFr250 for Europe and North America and RFr300 elsewhere. There is a poste restante facility at the post office (p551) in Kigali.

TELEPHONE

There are two main operators in Rwanda, MTN and Rwandatel. International calls are relatively expensive at RFr500 to RFr1000 per minute to most countries including Europe, North America and Australia. There are currently no area codes in Rwanda. The international code for Rwanda is ☎ 250. Mobile telephone numbers start with the prefixes ☎ 083, ☎ 085 and ☎ 086.

TOURIST INFORMATION

The Office Rwandais du Tourisme et des Parcs Nationaux (Rwandan Tourism Board), otherwise known as ORTPN, is in Kigali; see p551 for more on contact details and its services. With no network of hostels or camps around the country, there is very little travel information available in Rwanda.

VISAS

Visas are required by everyone except nationals of Canada, Germany, South Africa, Sweden, the UK, the USA and other East African countries. For most other passport holders, visas cost US$60 and are issued instantly upon arrival at either the border or the airport.

Those driving their own vehicles are required to buy an entry permit at the border for RFr5000. Insurance is compulsory, and is available from **Sonarwa** (☎ Kigali 573350), starting at about RFr4000 per day.

RWANDA

VISA EXTENSIONS

Both tourist and transit visas can be extended in Kigali at **Ministère de l'Intérieur** (MININTER; ☎ 585856) in the Kacyiru district, about 7km northeast of the city centre. Extensions take a week or more to issue and cost RFr15,000 per month.

VISAS FOR ONWARD TRAVEL

Anyone wanting visas for neighbouring countries while in Rwanda should take note of the following (see p590 for the addresses):

Burundi Visas cost US$40 for one month single entry, although check on the security situation very carefully before visiting. Visas are also available at the border.

DRC At the time of research, visas were not being issued for travel to Kinshasa as the embassy had not yet reopened. However, for land crossings to eastern DRC eight-day visas are available at Bukavu or Goma for US$35.

Kenya Visas cost US$50 or the equivalent in local currency, require two photographs and are issued the same day if you apply before 11.30am. Visas are also available on arrival.

Tanzania Visas require two photos and generally take 24 hours to issue. The cost depends on nationality. Visas are also available on arrival.

Uganda Visas cost US$30, require two photos and are issued in 24 hours. Visas are available on the border.

WOMEN TRAVELLERS

Although Rwanda is a safe place for travelling, it is sensible not to venture too far off the beaten track alone and to avoid wandering down darks streets in larger towns. In general, women will find that they encounter far fewer hassles from men than elsewhere in the region.

WORK

With all the international money sloshing around Rwanda, one might be forgiven for thinking it would be easy to pick up some work here. However, most international organisations tend to recruit professionals from home and in the local community. Anyone considering looking for work must secure a work permit from a Rwandan embassy before entering the country.

TRANSPORT IN RWANDA

GETTING THERE & AWAY

For information on getting to Rwanda from outside East Africa, see p616.

If you're crossing borders, please be advised that Rwanda (and Burundi) is one hour behind the rest of East Africa.

Entering Rwanda

Yellow-fever vaccination certificates are in theory compulsory for entry or exit, but in reality are rarely requested.

Air

Gregoire Kayibanda International Airport (KGL) is located at Kanombe, 10km east of Kigali centre. Note that most of the discounted air fares available in Europe and North America use Nairobi as the gateway to East Africa. Most high-end tourists also enter by land as part of a two-country safari including Uganda. Air tickets bought in Rwanda for international flights are expensive, and compare poorly with what is on offer in Nairobi or Kampala.

AIRLINES IN RWANDA

Ethiopian Airlines (ET; ☎ 575045; www.flyethiopian .com; hub Addis Adaba)

Kenya Airways (KQ; Map p550; ☎ 577972; www .kenya-airways.com; Ave des Mille Collines; hub Nairobi)

Rwandan Express (WB; ☎ 503687; www.rwandair .com; hub Kigali)

SN Brussels Airline (SN; Map p550; ☎ 575290; www .brusselsairlines.com; Hotel des Mille Collines; hub Brussels)

South African Airways (SA; Map p550; ☎ 577777; www.flysaa.com; Blvd de la Revolution; hub Johannesburg)

TO/FROM BURUNDI

Rwandair Express and Kenya Airways connect Kigali and Bujumbura.

TO/FROM KENYA

Rwandair Express and Kenya Airways offer daily services between Kigali and Nairobi.

TO/FROM TANZANIA

Rwandair Express has direct flights between Kigali and Kilimanjaro.

TO/FROM UGANDA

Rwandair Express and Ethiopian Airlines connect Kigali with Entebbe International Airport for Kampala.

Land

Rwanda shares land borders with Burundi, DRC, Tanzania and Uganda. However, most travellers only tend to use the crossings with Uganda. The main crossing with Tanzania is considered safe, but passes through some pretty remote country. There are also land border crossings with DRC, but with the exception of the Gisenyi border post for visiting Goma and the mountain gorillas, it is currently not advisable to cross. Finally, the land border with Burundi has to be considered risky as long as rebels remain active there. We crossed here at the time of research, but check the security situation in Burundi before travelling this way.

TO/FROM BURUNDI

The main border crossing between Rwanda and Burundi is via Huye and Kayanza, on the Kigali to Bujumbura road, which is sealed pretty much all the way. The border post is called Kayanza Haut and Burundian visas are available on arrival for US$40. Bus companies Yahoo Car, New Yahoo Coach and Gaso Bus all run daily buses between Kigali and Bujumbura (RFr5000-6000, about six hours), departing at about 7am. There is also a direct road from Bujumbura to Cyangugu, but this is not in such good condition and should be considered comparatively unsafe.

TO/FROM DRC

There are two crossings between Rwanda and DRC, both on the shores of Lake Kivu. To the north is the crossing between Gisenyi and Goma; this was considered safe at the time of writing, though only for short trips to Goma, climbing Nyiragongo volcano or visiting the mountain gorillas. Longer trips into DRC or overland trips through the country are inadvisable at the time of writing. The southern border between Cyangugu and Bukavu is also open for crossing, but the security situation around Bukavu is more volatile than Goma. Check carefully in Cyangugu before venturing across, and be very wary of visiting Parc National Kahuzi-Biega as there have been security problems there.

TO/FROM TANZANIA

Daily minibuses go from Kigali to Rusumu (US$6, three hours), where you'll need to walk across the Kagera river bridge. Once across, there are pick-up taxis to the tiny town (and former refugee camp) of Benako (marked as Kasulo on some maps; Tsh2500, 25 minutes), about 20km southeast. For more detail on onward travel from Benako, see p261.

TO/FROM UGANDA

There are two main crossing points for foreigners: between Kigali and Kabale via Gatuna (Katuna), and between Musanze (Ruhengeri) and Kisoro via Cyanika.

The border is called Gatuna on the Rwandan side, Katuna on the Ugandan side. There are lots of minibuses between Kigali and the border at Gatuna (RFr2000, 1½ hours) throughout the day. There are also plenty of shared taxis (USh1000) and special hire taxis (USh15,000 for the whole car) travelling back and forth between Katuna and Kabale.

From Musanze (Ruhengeri) to Kisoro via Cyanika the road is in excellent shape on the Rwandan side and in poor condition on the Ugandan side. With Parc National des Volcans increasingly popular, the Rwandan military have prioritised security on this stretch. Minibuses link either side of the border with Musanze (RFr1000, 25km).

Those travelling direct between Kigali and Kampala can travel with **Jaguar Executive Coaches** (☎ 086-14838), which offers coaches (RFr5000 to RFr7000) departing in the morning from Nyabugogo Bus Station, and taking eight to nine hours, including a long border crossing. **Regional Coach** (☎ 575963) also offers morning buses to Kampala, which continue on to Nairobi (RFr16,000).

Tours

For more info on a few companies running organised tours, see p74.

CROSSING TO BURUNDI? DRC?

Don't cross into Burundi by land without carefully checking the current security situation in the north of the country. We were able to safely travel by bus from Bujumbura to Kigali, but there is no substitute for double-checking the latest story – ongoing conflict in Burundi means that ambushes are a distinct possibility.

And while we're on the subject, think twice, maybe twice again, before crossing into DRC. We were able to safely cross into Goma from Gisenyi, but things have been very volatile in DRC over the terrible years of civil war – it is extremely important to do your own homework before visiting. Should things stay stable, a DRC loop between Rwanda and Uganda is an enticing prospect, but check, check and check again before you sign up.

GETTING AROUND
Air
Rwandair Express (p592) recently introduced domestic flights between Kigali and Gisenyi.

Bus & Minibus
Rwanda has a reasonable road system, for the most part due to its small size and a large dose of foreign assistance. The only major unsealed roads are those running along the shore of Lake Kivu and some smaller stretches around the country.

The best buses are privately run, scheduled services operated by Okapi Car, Trans Express 2000, Atraco Express and Virunga Ponctuel. Destinations covered include Huye (Butare), Gisenyi, Kibuye and Musanze (Ruhengeri) and departures are guaranteed to leave, hourly in many cases. They are less crowded and drive more carefully than the normal minibuses, but cost a little more.

You will find there are plenty of well-maintained, modern minibuses serving all the main routes. Head to the bus stand in any town between dawn and about 3pm, and it is quite easy to find one heading to Kigali and nearby towns. Destinations are displayed in the front window and the fares are fixed (you can ask other passengers to be sure). However, anyone who gets stuck somewhere late in the afternoon is going to have to pay top price for the privilege of getting out.

Minibuses leave when full, and this means when all the seats are occupied (unlike in Kenya and Tanzania, where most of the time they won't leave until you can't breathe for the people sitting on your lap and jamming the aisle). They are, however, still quite cramped. There is no extra charge for baggage.

Whichever form of transport you end up taking, you should be prepared to be stopped at military checkpoints. These vary in number depending on the route, but at each it is necessary to get out and allow the soldiers to examine all luggage. Other than the time it takes, there's no hassle at all; and it pays to remember the checkpoints help ensure your security.

Car & Motorcycle
Cars are suitable for most of the country's main roads, but those planning to explore Parc National de l'Akagera or follow the shores of Lake Kivu might be better off with a 4WD.

Car hire isn't well established in Rwanda, but most travel agents and tour operators in Kigali can organise something for RFr25,000 to RFr50,000 per day for a small car and up.

Ferry
Before the latest civil war, there were ferries on Lake Kivu that connected the Rwandan ports of Cyangugu, Kibuye and Gisenyi, but these are suspended at present. Speedboat charters are currently the only option between these ports, but they are prohibitively expensive.

Hitching
Hitching around Rwanda can be relatively easy because of the prodigious number of NGO vehicles on the roads. Drivers will rarely ask for payment for a lift. Women who decide to hitch should realise that accepting a lift from long-distance truck drivers is unwise, but the NGOs should otherwise be OK. Travellers who decide to hitch should understand that they are taking a small but potentially serious risk.

Local Transport
TAXI
These are only really necessary in Kigali. See p558 for details. It is also possible to find the odd taxi in most other major towns.

TAXI-MOTOR
Most towns are compact enough to get around on foot, but where you need transport, the taxi-motor is a good bet. It's just a motorcycle, but the driver can usually sling a pack across the petrol tank. They generally drive safely, if a little fast, and there's usually a helmet for the passenger.

Burundi

A tiny little nation sandwiched between the Democratic Republic of the Congo (DRC; formerly Zaire) and Tanzania, Burundi is defined by an incongruous mix of soaring mountains, languid lakeside communities and ongoing ethnic conflict. Beautiful but tortured Burundi has been devastated by intertribal tensions since independence in 1962, and despite recent peace accords, violence could flare up at any time. Quite simply, Burundi remains a potentially unstable country in a potentially unstable region of Africa.

The tourist industry died a quick death with the outbreak of civil war in 1993. Since then, many of the upcountry attractions have been off limits for more than 15 years, including the southernmost source of the Nile, the ancient forest of Parc National de la Kibira, and the legendary spot where Stanley was reputed to have uttered those timeless words 'Dr Livingstone I presume?'.

However, the steamy capital Bujumbura has a lovely location on the shores of Lake Tanganyika, and just outside the city are some of the finest inland beaches on the continent. Burundians also have an irrepressible *joie de vivre*, which has largely carried them through the pain and suffering of the last few decades. At the time of research, travel to the capital Bujumbura was reasonably safe, as was the main road north to Rwanda, though greater caution needs to be exerted while travelling in the countryside. If the peace process holds and the situation stabilises, Burundi may once again find itself on the overland map of Africa. In the meantime, however, check, double check and triple check on the latest security situation before heading into the country or travelling anywhere beyond Bujumbura.

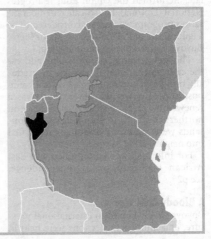

FAST FACTS

- **Area** 27,835 sq km
- **Birthplace of** The Nile River
- **Capital** Bujumbura
- **Country Code** ☎ 257
- **Famous for** Les Tambourinaires dancers
- **Languages** Kirundi, French and Swahili
- **Money** Burundi franc (BFr); US$1 = BFr1225; €1 = BFr1640
- **Population** 8.7 million

CLIMATE & WHEN TO GO

The rainy season in Burundi lasts from around October to May, with a brief dry spell in December and January. See Climate Charts, p606.

HISTORY
A Fragile Independence

Burundi, like Rwanda, was colonised first by Germany and later by Belgium, and like its northern neighbour, the Europeans played on ethnic differences to divide and conquer the population. Power was traditionally concentrated in the hands of the minority Tutsi, though Hutus began to challenge the concentration of power following independence in 1962.

However, in the 1964 elections, Tutsi leader Mwami Mwambutsa refused to appoint a Hutu prime minister, even though Hutu candidates attracted a majority of votes. Hutu frustration soon boiled over, and Hutu military officers and political figures staged an attempted coup. Although it failed, Mwambutsa was exiled to Switzerland, and replaced by a Tutsi military junta.

A wholesale purge of Hutu from the army and bureaucracy followed, and in 1972 another large-scale Hutu revolt resulted in more than 1000 Tutsi being killed. The Tutsi military junta responded with selective genocide of elite Hutu; after just three months, 200,000 Hutu had been killed and another 100,000 had fled into neighbouring countries.

In 1976, Jean-Baptiste Bagaza came to power in a bloodless coup, and three years later he formed the Union Pour le Progrès National (Uprona). His so-called democratisation program was largely considered to be a failure, and in 1987 his cousin Major Pierre Buyoya toppled him in another coup.

The new regime attempted to address the causes of intertribal tensions by gradually bringing Hutu representatives back into positions of power. However, there was a renewed outbreak of intertribal violence in northern Burundi in summer 1988; thousands were massacred and many more fled into neighbouring Rwanda.

For information on Burundian and East African history prior to independence, see p25.

A Bloody Civil War

Buyoya finally bowed to international pressure, and multiparty elections were held in

HOW MUCH?

- Cheapish hotel room with bathroom US$20 to US$40
- Plate of garnished brochettes US$2 to US$3
- Internet access per hour US$1 to US$2
- Local newspaper US$0.50
- 100km bus ride US$2

LONELY PLANET INDEX

- Litre of petrol US$1 to US$2
- Litre of bottled water US$0.50
- Primus beer US$1 to US$2
- Souvenir T-shirt There aren't any...
- Street snack (grilled goat) US$1

June 1993. These brought a Hutu-dominated government to power, led by Melchior Ndadaye, himself a Hutu. However, a dissident army faction, led by a Tutsi, Colonel Sylvestre Ningaba, staged yet another coup in late October the same year, and assassinated president Ndadaye. The coup eventually failed, though thousands were massacred in intertribal fighting, and almost half a million refugees fled across the border into Rwanda.

In April 1994 Cyprien Ntaryamira, the new Hutu president, was killed in the same plane crash that killed Rwanda's president Juvenal Habyarimana, and ignited the subsequent genocide over there. In Burundi, Sylvestre Ntibantunganya was immediately appointed interim president, though both Hutu militias and the Tutsi-dominated army went on the offensive. No war was actually declared, but at least 100,000 people were killed in clashes between mid-1994 and mid-1996.

In July 1996 former president Pierre Buyoya again carried out a successful coup, and took over as the country's president with the support of the army. However, intertribal fighting continued between Hutu rebels and the Tutsi-dominated government and Tutsi militia. Hundreds of thousands of civilian opponents, mostly Hutus, were herded into 'regroupment camps', and bombings, murders and other horrific activities continued throughout the country.

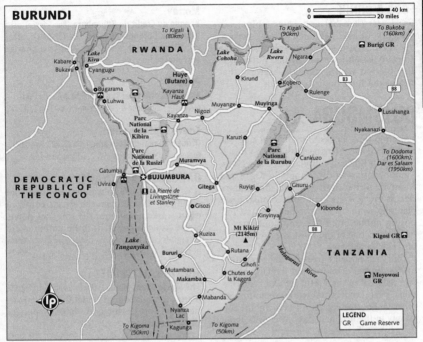

BURUNDI

A Fragile Peace

At the end of 2002, the Force for the Defence of Democracy (FDD), the largest rebel group, signed a peace deal. In April 2003, prominent Hutu Domitien Ndayizeye succeeded Pierre Buyoya as president, and a road map to elections was hammered out.

In 2004, the UN began operations in Burundi, sending more than 5000 troops to enforce the peace. Parliamentary elections were successfully held in June 2005, and the former rebels, the FDD, emerged victorious. Pierre Nkurunziza, leader of the FDD, was sworn in as president in August.

As of 2008, the Burundian government was in talks with the Hutu-led National Liberation Forces (NLF) to bring peace within the country. At long last, the country is on the road to stability, though both Hutu and Tutsi need to embrace the spirit of national unity to bring Burundi back from the brink.

THE CULTURE

Unlike Rwanda, Burundi debates its divisions. In Rwanda today, there are only Rwandans, and the history is being reinterpreted in the spirit of unity. In Burundi, there are Hutus and Tutsis and they work together in political parties, drink together in bars, and are happy to discuss their differences. Two very different approaches to the same problem of ethnic division, both countries could probably learn a little from each other. For now, Burundi and its people deserve all the support they can get as they try to forge a Burundian identity that transcends the tribalism of the past.

ARTS

Les Tambourinaires du Burundi is the country's most famous troupe; it has performed in cities such as Berlin and New York. Its performances are a high-adrenaline mix of drumming and dancing that drowns the audience in waves of sound and movement.

ENVIRONMENT

Taking up a mere 27,835 sq km, most of the country is made up of mountains that vanish into the horizon. Sadly however, Burundi's tourist infrastructure is in tatters after the long war, and most of the national parks have been closed for more than a decade.

FOOD & DRINK

Brochettes (kebabs) and *frites* (chips) are a legacy of the Belgian colonial period, but there is also succulent fish from Lake Tanganyika and serious steaks. Burundi is also blessed with a national brewery that churns out huge bottles of Primus.

BUJUMBURA

Frozen in time thanks to more than a decade of conflict, there has been almost no development in Burundi's capital since the 1980s, a stark contrast to the changes in Kigali and Kampala to the north. Indeed, Bujumbura retains much of its grandiose colonial town planning, with its wide boulevards and imposing public buildings, and continues to function as one of the most important ports on Lake Tanganyika.

'Buj' has earned a freewheelin' reputation for its dining, drinking and dancing scene, especially given the recent influx of international peacekeepers, aid workers and foreign officials. But, the capital isn't exactly the safest city in the region, so keep your wits about you, especially once the sun goes down.

ORIENTATION

Bujumbura has a striking location on the shores of Lake Tanganyika, and many of its suburbs sprawl up the looming mountains that ring the city to the north and east. However, most of the action takes place on Chaussée Prince Rwagasore and the streets nearby.

INFORMATION

Emergency

The official emergency number for police is ☎ 17, though it's best to make contact with your embassy in the event of an emergency. If your country doesn't have an embassy in Burundi, than either Kenya (p405) or Tanzania (p254) are your best bets.

Internet Access

There are various internet cafes throughout the city centre.

Medical Services

In the event of a medical emergency, it is best to get out of Burundi to somewhere with first-class medical facilities, such as Nairobi.

Money

Banque du Crédit de Bujumbura (Rue Science) and **Interbank Burundi** (Blvd de la Liberté) both offer credit-card cash advances and can change travellers cheques.

Post

Main post office (cnr Blvd Lumumba & Ave du Commerce; ☺ 8am-noon & 2-4pm Mon-Fri, 8-11am Sat)

Tourist Information

Office National du Tourisme (☎ 222202; Ave des Euphorbes; ☺ 7.30am-noon & 2-4.30pm Mon-Fri)

DANGERS & ANNOYANCES

It is generally safe to wander about on foot during the day, though the streets empty at night – take a taxi once the sun goes down. Street crime is prevalent in Bujumbura, and foreigners are especially vulnerable given their perceived wealth.

SIGHTS & ACTIVITIES

The **Musée Vivant** (Ave du 13 Octobre; admission BFr2000) is a reconstructed traditional Burundian village with some exhibits on baskets, pottery and drums.

Bujumbura's beaches are some of the best found in any landlocked country in Africa. The sand is white and powdery, and the waves should keep the bilharzia at bay. The stretch of beach that lies about 5km northwest of the capital is the most beautiful and used to be known as **Plage des Cocotiers** (Coconut Beach).

If you have your own transportation, and the security situation is stable, you might want to visit **La Pierre de Livingstone et Stanley**, a large rock that allegedly marks the spot where Livingstone met Stanley. The site is about 5km south of the city along the main road to Mutambara. You can also check out the small spring at Kasumo, southeast of Bujumbura, which may well be the southernmost **source of the Nile**.

SLEEPING

Saga Residence Hotel (☎ 242225; Chaussée Prince Rwagasore; r from US$45) One of the more atmospheric hotels in this price range, the Saga is safe, secure and affordable.

Hotel Botanika (☎ 226792; hotelbotanika@hotmail.com; Blvd de l'Uprona; r from US$85; ✷) Bujumbura's very own boutique hotel, the seven-room Botanika is a charming retreat from the rigours of life in Burundi.

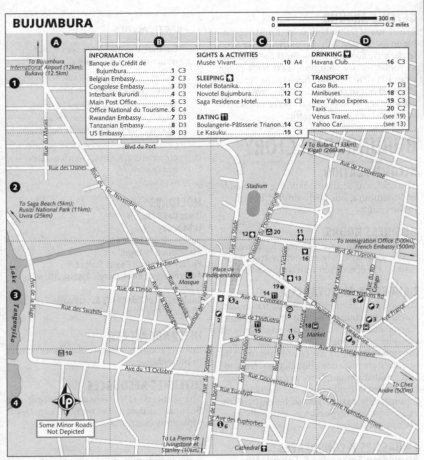

BUJUMBURA

0 300 m
0 0.2 miles

INFORMATION
Banque du Crédit de
  Bujumbura.....................................1 C3
Belgian Embassy..........................2 C3
Congolese Embassy......................3 D3
Interbank Burundi........................4 C3
Main Post Office..........................5 C3
Office National du Tourisme........6 C4
Rwandan Embassy.......................7 D3
Tanzanian Embassy.....................8 D3
US Embassy..................................9 D3

SIGHTS & ACTIVITIES
Musée Vivant............................10 A4

SLEEPING
Hotel Botanika..........................11 C2
Novotel Bujumbura...................12 C2
Saga Residence Hotel................13 C3

EATING
Boulangerie-Pâtisserie Trianon..14 C3
Le Kasuku.................................15 C3

DRINKING
Havana Club..............................16 C3

TRANSPORT
Gaso Bus...................................17 D3
Minibuses.................................18 C3
New Yahoo Express...................19 C3
Taxis..20 C2
Venus Travel.........................(see 19)
Yahoo Car.............................(see 13)

To Bujumbura
International Airport (12km);
Bukavu (12.5km)

Rue du Marais
Blvd du Port
Rue des Usines
Blvd du 1er Novembre

To Saga Beach (5km);
Rusizi National Park (11km);
Uvira (25km)

To Butare (133km);
Kigali (266km)

Ave de l'Université

Stadium

Chaussée du Peuple Burundi

To Immigration Office (500m);
French Embassy (500m)
Blvd de l'Uprona

Rue des Pêcheurs

Ave Victoire

Ave du Stade

Place de
l'Indépendance

Mosque

Rue de l'Imbo

Ave de la Nhanunga

Avenue des Paysans

Ave de la Tanzania

Rue de l'Industrie

Ave du Commerce

Chaussée Prince Rwagasore

Rue de l'Amitié

Ave du RD
Congo

United Nations Rd

Ave France

Lake Tanganyika

Ave de la Plage

Rue des Swahilis

Rue
Science

Blvd Lumumba

Blvd de la Révolution

Market

Ave de l'Enseignement

Ave du 13 Octobre

Ave du
Septembre

Blvd de la Liberté

Ave du

Rue de la Révolution

Rue Gouvernement

Rue Eucalypt

Ave Pierre Ngendandumwe

To Chez
Andre (500m)

Some Minor Roads
Not Depicted

To La Pierre de
Livingstone et
Stanley (10km)

Ave des Euphorbes

Cathedral

Novotel Bujumbura (☎ 222600; novobuja@cbinf.com;
Chaussée du Peuple Burundi; s/d US$120/135; 🅿 💻 🖥)
The preferred spot for visiting dignataries, the
Novotel is the only hotel in town that meets
international four-star standards.

EATING
Boulangerie-Pâtisserie Trianon (Ave du Commerce;
BFr1000-4000) This place is packed out for break-
fast thanks to a great combination of fresh
croissants, healthy omelettes and local coffee.
  Le Kasuku (☎ 243575; Rue de l'Industrie; mains
BFr5000-12,000) A little garden oasis in the heart
of the city, Kasuku has a hearty range of
European dishes.
  Chez André (Chaussée Prince Rwagasore; mains
BFr7500-20,000) Housed in a huge villa on

the eastern extreme of Chaussée Prince
Rwagasore, this French- and Belgian-
inspired institution is one of the best restaurants in the city.

DRINKING & ENTERTAINMENT
Havana Club (Blvd de l'Uprona) Havana Club is one
of the city's most popular nightspots, drawing a mixed crowd of locals and internation-
als most nights of the week.

GETTING THERE & AWAY
For more information on getting to and from
Burundi, see p601.
  Minibuses ply the major routes around
the country, and leave from the minibus
station near the market area.

BURUNDI

GETTING AROUND

The centre of Bujumbura is small and negotiable on foot by day. After 8pm, always take a taxi in the city, no matter how short the distance, as robberies are common. Taxi fares range from BFr1000 for short hops in the centre to BFr5000 out to the beaches. Motorbike taxis are another good option if you're not scared of Bujumbura's racing traffic.

BURUNDI DIRECTORY

ACCOMMODATION

The choice of accommodation is reasonable in Bujumbura, but fairly limited elsewhere in the country.

BUSINESS HOURS

Business tend to close for a couple of hours at lunch, approximately midday to 2pm. Most eateries are open from 7am to about 9pm.

DANGERS & ANNOYANCES

At long last, Burundi's civil war has ended, though the country is still far from stable. Travel overland as little as possible, and consider restricting your visit to the capital. Bujumbura is safe by day due to a massive UN and military presence, though the streets are best avoided at night. Once again, street crime is prevalent in Bujumbura, and foreigners are an especially easy target, so be particularly aware of your surroundings, especially once the sun goes down.

EMBASSIES & CONSULATES
Burundian Embassies & Consulates
Useful Burundian embassies worldwide:
Belgium (☎ 02-23 045 35; 46 Place Marie-Louise, Brussels)
France (☎ 1-4520-6061; 10-12, rue de L'Orme, Paris)
UK (☎ 020-8381 4092; 26 Armitage Rd, London)
USA (☎ 202-342 2574; 2233 Wisconsin Ave, Washington DC)

Embassies & Consulates in Burundi
Foreign embassies in Bujumbura include:
Belgium (☎ 233641; www.diplomatie.be/bujumbura; Blvd de la Liberté)
DRC (Ave du RD Congo)
France (☎ 251484; 60 Blvd de l'Uprona)
Rwanda (☎ 226865; Ave du RD Congo)
Tanzania (☎ 248636; 4 United Nations Rd)
USA (☎ 223454; Chaussée Prince Rwagasore)

HOLIDAYS
Unity Day 5 February
Labour Day 1 May
Independence Day 1 July
Assumption 15 August
Victory of Uprona Day 18 September
Anniversary of Rwagasore's Assassination 13 October
Anniversary of Ndadaye's Assassination 21 October
All Saints' Day 1 November

INTERNET ACCESS
Internet access is widespread and inexpensive in Bujumbura.

INTERNET RESOURCES
The official UN website covering the Burundi mission is www.un.org/Depts/dpko/missions/onub.

MAPS
Rwanda Burundi – International Travel Map published by ITMB Publishing at a scale of 1:400,000 is a good choice.

MONEY
The unit of currency is the Burundi franc (BFr). This is a cash economy and the US dollar is king. There were no ATMs on the international network in Burundi at the time of writing, though cash advances on credit cards are possible at major banks. There's an open black market in Bujumbura for changing money.

POST
The postal service is reasonably efficient and things take about one week to get to Europe or North America.

TELEPHONE

There are no telephone area codes within the country. The country code for Burundi is ☎ 257.

TIME

Burundi is one hour behind the rest of East Africa, so don't forget to wind your clock back.

VISAS

One-month tourist visas cost US$40, and are available on arrival at both the international airport and international land border crossings.

TRANSPORT IN BURUNDI

GETTING THERE & AWAY

Air

Bujumbura International Airport (BJM) is located about 12km north of the city centre. There are very few international airlines still serving Burundi as flights were severely disrupted during the long civil war.

Lake

TO/FROM TANZANIA

The regular passenger ferry service between Bujumbura and Kigoma is currently suspended.

Land

Burundi shares land borders with DRC, Rwanda and Tanzania. However, due to the long-running civil war, very few travellers have crossed this way in the last decade or more.

TO/FROM DRC

The main crossing between Burundi and DRC is at Gatumba on the road between Bujumbura and Uvira, about 15km west of the capital.

TO/FROM RWANDA

The main crossing point is between Kayanza (Burundi) and Butare (Rwanda) on the main road linking Bujumbura and Kigali. The safest and quickest option for travel between Bujumbura and Kigali is to use one of the scheduled bus services that depart daily. Yahoo Car, New Yahoo Express, Venus Travel and Gaso Bus all run buses in both directions (BFr9000 to BFr12,000, six hours). See also p593.

TO/FROM TANZANIA

For Kobero Bridge, the trip is done in stages via Nyakanazi and Lusahunga. There are several direct buses weekly between Mwanza and the border. Otherwise, take a Kigoma-bound bus, disembark at Lusahunga and get onward transport from there.

For the Manyovu crossing, *dalla-dallas* (pick-up trucks) leave Kigoma from behind Bero petrol station. Once through the Tanzanian side of the border, you'll need to take one of the many waiting vehicles on to Makamba, where the Burundian immigration post is located, and then from there get another vehicle on to Bujumbura. See also p258.

GETTING AROUND

Air

There are no internal domestic flights in Burundi.

Road

Travelling around the countryside is not as dangerous as it once was, though things change quickly (for better or for worse) in this part of the world. Ask around before heading out of Bujumbura, even to the second city of Gitega.

East Africa Directory

CONTENTS

This chapter contains general regional travel information. For country-specific details, see the country chapter Directory sections.

ACCOMMODATION

East Africa has a wide range of accommodation, ranging from humble cinderblock rooms with a communal bucket bath to some of Africa's most luxurious safari lodges.

Sleeping listings in this book are divided into three categories: budget (approximately US$50 and under per double room), midrange (US$50 to US$150) and top-end (US$150 and up). All prices listed in this book are high-season, except as noted. In much of the region it's often possible to negotiate significant discounts during the low-season travel months

PRACTICALITIES

- Use the metric system for weights and measures.
- Electricity is 220V to 250V AC, 50Hz. Most plugs are British-style three-square-pin or European-style two-round-pin.
- *The East African* is the main regional English-language weekly. For a pan-African focus check *New African;* BBC's *Focus on Africa; Business Africa;* and *Africa Today.* Try *Africa Geographic* for environmental issues, and *Africa – Birds & Birding* for ornithologists.
- Kenya, Uganda and Tanzania have government-run national broadcasters with radio and TV transmissions in English. BBC's World Service and Deutsche Welle transmit in English and Swahili.

from March through May. Also except as noted, hotel prices in this book include private bathroom and continental breakfast (coffee/tea, bread, jam and occasionally an egg).

Camping

There are established campsites in most national parks, as well as in or near many major towns, and in some rural tourist areas local villagers maintain camping grounds. Facilities range from none at all to well-established full-service places with hot showers and cooking areas. Prices average US$5 to US$10 per person per night away from the national parks – shoestring hotel rooms may be cheaper in many areas. Camping prices in this book are per person except as noted. Camping away from established sites is not advisable; in rural areas, ask permission from the village head or elders before pitching your tent. The exceptions to all this are Rwanda and Burundi, where camping possibilities range from limited to nonexistent.

In coastal areas, bungalows or *bandas* – simple wooden or thatched huts, often with only a mattress and mosquito net – offer an alternative to camping.

Hostels, Guesthouses & Budget Hotels

True hostels are rare, but mission hostels and guesthouses are scattered throughout the region. While intended primarily for missionaries and aid-organisation staff, they're generally happy to accommodate travellers if space is available. Most are clean, safe, spartan and good value.

In budget guesthouses and hotels, you generally get what you pay for, though there's the occasional good deal. The cheapest ones – and every town will have one – are poorly ventilated cement-block rooms with reasonably clean sheets, shared toilets, cold showers or a bucket bath, sometimes a fan and mosquito net and often only a token lock on the door. Rates for this type of place average from US$5 per room per night. A few dollars more will get you a somewhat more comfortable room, often with a bathroom (although not always with running or hot water).

Many budget places double as brothels, and at many of the cheapest ones, solo women travellers are likely to feel uncomfortable. For peace and quiet, guesthouses without bars are the best choice.

Backpackers and dormitory-style places aren't as common as in southern Africa, but there are a few, with prices similar to or slightly higher than you'd pay for a room in a basic guesthouse.

Hotels, Lodges & Luxury Safari Camps

Larger towns will have one or several midrange hotels, most with private bathroom, hot water and a fan or an air-conditioner. Facilities range from faded to good value, and prices range from US$25 to US$75 per person. Major tourist areas also have a good selection of top-end accommodation, with prices ranging from about US$100 to US$300 or more per person per night. On the safari circuits, top-end prices are generally all-inclusive.

National parks often also have 'permanent tented camps' or 'luxury tented camps'. These offer comfortable beds in canvas tents – usually en suite – with screened windows and most of the comforts of a hotel room, but they are less architecturally intrusive and with a wilderness feel. 'Mobile' or 'fly' camps are temporary camps set up for several nights, or for one season, and used for walking safaris or a more intimate bush experience away from the main tented camp.

ACTIVITIES

Each of the countries covered in this book has its own range of activities – everything from caving and white-water rafting in Uganda to chimpanzee tracking and mountain trekking in Tanzania. Following is a general overview of some of the more common activities in the region. See the country chapter Directories for much more.

Bird Watching

With well over 1000 species, East Africa is an excellent destination for ornithologists, with Uganda a particular highlight.

Boating

Local dhow trips can be arranged from various places along the coast, although this isn't always a good idea. Instead, contact a coastal or island hotel to help you charter a reliable dhow for a cruise. For more, see p622.

DIVE OPERATORS & SAFETY

When choosing a dive operator, quality rather than cost should be the priority. Consider the operator's experience and qualifications; knowledgeability and competence of staff; and the condition of equipment and frequency of maintenance. Assess whether the overall attitude is serious and professional, and ask about safety precautions: radios, oxygen, boat reliability and back-up engines, emergency evacuation procedures, first-aid kits, safety flares and life jackets. On longer dives, do you get an energising meal, or just tea and biscuits?

There are decompression chambers in Matemwe on Zanzibar's east coast, in Mombasa (although this latter one is an army facility, and not always available to the general public) and in Johannesburg. Also check the **Divers Alert Network Southern Africa** (DAN; www.dansa.org) website, which includes Tanzania and Kenya, and has a list of Zanzibar- and Pemba-based operators that are part of DAN. If you dive with an operator that isn't affiliated with DAN, it's highly recommended to take out insurance coverage with DAN.

RESPONSIBLE DIVING

Wherever you dive in East Africa, consider the following tips, and help preserve the ecology and beauty of the reefs:

■ Never use anchors on a reef, and take care not to ground boats on coral.

■ Avoid touching or standing on living marine organisms or dragging equipment across a reef. Polyps can be damaged by even the gentlest contact. If you must hold on to a reef, only touch exposed rock or dead coral.

■ Be conscious of your fins. Even without contact, the surge from fin strokes near a reef can damage delicate organisms. Take care not to kick up clouds of sand, which can smother organisms.

■ Practise and maintain proper buoyancy control. Major damage can be done by divers descending too fast and colliding with a reef.

■ Take great care in underwater caves. Spend as little time within them as possible, as your air bubbles may be caught within the roof and thereby leave organisms high and dry. Take turns inspecting the interior of a small cave.

■ Resist the temptation to collect or buy corals or shells – which you'll frequently be offered by vendors on the beaches – or to loot marine archaeological sites (mainly shipwrecks).

■ Ensure that you take home all your rubbish and any litter you may find as well. Plastics in particular are a serious threat to marine life.

■ Do not feed fish.

■ Minimise your disturbance of marine animals, and never ride on the backs of turtles or attempt to touch dolphins.

Cycling & Mountain Biking

For a brief overview of cycling in East Africa, see p621.

Diving & Snorkelling

If you're contemplating learning to dive, or want to brush up on your skills, East Africa is a rewarding if somewhat pricey place to do this. The main areas are the Zanzibar Archipelago in Tanzania and around Malindi in Kenya, both of which have an array of operators and courses. See the Activities in the country Directories for more.

Be sure to allow a sufficient surface interval between the conclusion of your final dive and any onward/homeward flights. The Professional Association of Dive Instructors (PADI) recommends at least 12 hours, or more if you have been doing daily multiple dives for several days. Another consideration is insurance, which you should arrange before coming to East Africa. Many policies exclude diving, so you'll likely need to pay a bit extra, but it's well worth it in comparison to the bills you will need to foot should something go wrong.

Gorilla & Chimpanzee Tracking

Most gorilla activity focuses on Uganda's Bwindi Impenetrable National Park and Rwanda's Parc National des Volcans. Also see p75.

For chimpanzee tracking, the main places are Mahale Mountains and Gombe Stream parks in Tanzania, Kibale Forest National Park and Budongo Forest Reserve in Uganda and Parc National de Nyungwe in Rwanda.

Hiking & Trekking

Most hikes and climbs in the East Africa region require local guides, and some require a full range of clothing, from lightweight for the semitropical conditions at lower altitudes to full winter gear for the high summits. Waterproof clothing and equipment is also important in much of the region at any altitude, no matter what the season.

Lonely Planet's *Trekking in East Africa* is a worthwhile investment if you're considering hiking in the region.

Wildlife Watching

East Africa is one of the best places on earth for observing large animals in their natural environment. For more see p60, p105, and the national park sections in the country chapters.

BUSINESS HOURS

Usual business hours are listed inside the front cover. Also see the boxed text, p613.

CHILDREN

Most East Africans are very friendly and helpful towards children, and travelling in the region with young ones is unlikely to present any major problems. The main concerns are likely to be the presence of malaria; the scarcity of decent medical facilities outside major towns; the length, discomfort and safety risks involved in many road journeys; and the difficulty of finding clean, decent bathrooms outside of midrange and top-end hotels.

Some wildlife lodges have restrictions on accommodating children under 12; otherwise, most hotels are family friendly. Many places – including most national parks – offer significant discounts for children on entry fees and accommodation or camping rates, although you'll generally need to specifically request these, especially if you're booking through a tour operator. In hotels, children

---

RESPONSIBLE TREKKING

The huge number of visitors in some of East Africa's wilderness and trekking areas are beginning to take their toll. Mt Kilimanjaro is a prime example, although there are many others. Following are some tips for helping to preserve the region's delicate ecosystems and beauty.

■ Carry out all your rubbish, and make an effort to carry out rubbish left by others. Sanitary napkins, tampons, condoms and toilet paper should be carried out despite the inconvenience. They burn and decompose poorly.

■ Minimise waste by taking minimal packaging and no more food than you will need. Take reusable containers or stuff sacks.

■ Contamination of water sources by human faeces can lead to the transmission of all sorts of nasties. Where there is a toilet, use it. Where there is none (as is the case in many of the region's trekking areas), bury your waste. Dig a small hole 15cm (6in) deep and at least 100m (320ft) from any watercourse. Cover the waste with soil and a rock. In snow, dig down to the soil. Also ensure that these guidelines are applied to a portable toilet tent if one is being used by a large trekking party.

■ Don't use detergents or toothpaste in or near watercourses, even if they are biodegradable. For personal washing, use biodegradable soap (best purchased at home) and a water container at least 50m (160ft) away from the watercourse. Disperse the waste water widely to allow the soil to filter it fully. Wash cooking utensils 50m (160ft) from watercourses using a scourer, sand or snow instead of detergent.

■ Hillsides and mountain slopes, especially at high altitudes, are prone to erosion. Stick to existing trails, and avoid short cuts. If a well-used trail passes through a mud patch, walk through the mud so as not to increase the size of the patch. Avoid removing the plant life that keeps topsoils in place.

■ Don't depend on open fires for cooking. The cutting of wood for fires in popular trekking areas such as Kilimanjaro can cause rapid deforestation. Cook on a light-weight kerosene, alcohol or Shellite (white gas) stove and avoid those powered by disposable butane gas canisters.

■ If you are trekking with a guide and porters, supply stoves for the whole team. In cold conditions, ensure that all members are outfitted with enough clothing so that fires are not a necessity for warmth. If you patronise local accommodation, try to select places that don't use wood fires to heat water or cook food.

■ Ensure that you fully extinguish a fire after use. Spread the embers and flood them with water.

under two or three years of age often stay free, and those up to 12 years old sharing their parents' room pay about 50% of the adult rate. In hotels without special rates, triple rooms are commonly available for not too much more than a double room. Many midrange and top-end places have pools or grassy areas where children can play.

It's a good idea to travel with a blanket to spread out and use as a makeshift nappy-changing area. Processed baby foods, powdered infant milk, disposable nappies and similar items are available in major towns, but otherwise carry your own wipes, as well as food (and avoid feeding your children street food). Informal childcare is easy to arrange; the best bet is to ask at your hotel. Child seats for hire cars and safari vehicles are generally not available unless arranged in advance.

For protection against malaria, it's essential to bring along mosquito nets for your children and ensure that they sleep under them, and to check with your doctor regarding the use of malarial prophylactics. Bring long-sleeved shirts, trousers and socks for dawn and dusk, and ensure that your children wear them, and use mosquito repellent.

In beach areas, keep in mind the risks of hookworm infestation in populated areas, and bilharzia infection in lakes. Other things to watch out for are sea urchins at the beach, and thorns and the like in the brush.

Wildlife watching is suitable for older children who have the patience to sit for long periods in a car, but less suitable for younger ones, unless it's kept to manageable doses. Coastal destinations are a good bet for all ages.

Lonely Planet's *Travel with Children* by Cathy Lanigan has more tips for keeping children and parents happy while on the road.

CLIMATE CHARTS

East Africa's climate varies tremendously, thanks to the region's diverse topography. Along the coast, the weather tends to be hot and humid, with temperatures averaging between 25°C and 29°C. Inland, altitude tempers the climate, with temperatures ranging from a minimum of about 14°C in highland areas to a maximum of about 34°C. One of the few places where you're likely to encounter extremely high temperatures is in the desert areas of northeastern Kenya, where the mercury can climb to 40°C. Throughout East Africa, the coolest months are from June to

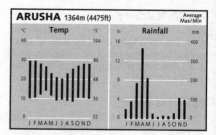

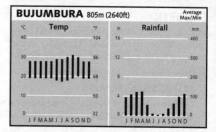

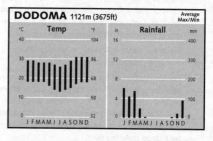

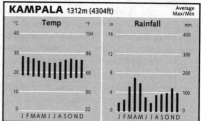

September, and the warmest from December to March.

In much of the region, there are two rainy seasons. The 'long' rains fall from mid-March through May, during which time it rains virtually every day, although seldom for the whole day. The 'short' rains fall for a couple of months between October and January, with the timing and conditions varying depending on where you are. Rainfall levels vary from less

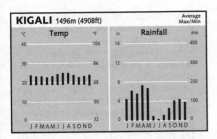

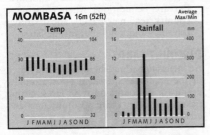

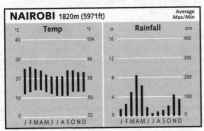

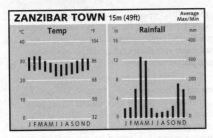

The main areas where political turmoil and banditry pose risks are in parts of Burundi, the Democratic Republic of the Congo (DRC) and Uganda and in northern and northeastern Kenya; see the country chapters, and check with your embassy and knowledgeable locals for security updates and advice if you're planning to head to any of these destinations.

Petty theft is a risk primarily in capital cities and tourist areas, particularly in a crowded setting, such as markets, public transport, and bus and train stations. Nairobi is notorious for muggings and more serious crimes. Throughout the region, however, most tourist-related crimes occur in isolated settings, in urban or tourist areas at night, or as part of confidence tricks or ruses playing on the emotions and gullibility of foreigners. By following a few simple precautions you'll minimise your risks and hopefully ensure that your journey will be trouble free.

- Avoid isolated areas – including beaches – at any time of day, whether you're alone or in a group. In cities, especially Nairobi, be alert for hustlers who will try any ploy to get you into a back alley and away from the watching eyes of onlookers so they can fleece you.
- Don't tempt people by flaunting your wealth. Avoid external money pouches, dangling backpacks and camera bags, and leave jewellery, fancy watches, portable stereos and the like at home. Daypacks instantly mark you as a tourist. Don't chat on your mobile phone on the street, or next to an open taxi window.
- Especially in crowded areas such as bus and train stations and markets, be wary of pick-pocketing. If you have doubts about the reliability of your hotel safe, carry your passport, money and other documents in an inside pocket or pouch. When out walking, keep a small amount of cash separate from your other money and handy, so that you don't pull out large wads of bills for paying taxi fares or making purchases. If you should happen to get robbed, this may also be useful as a decoy to give to your assailant, while the remainder of your valuables remain safely hidden.
- Try not to look lost, even if you are. Walk purposefully and confidently, and don't refer to this guidebook or a map on the street – duck into a shop if you need to get your bearings.

than 250mm per year in the semiarid areas of northeastern Kenya to about 1500mm along the coast and up to 3000mm in mountainous areas such as southwestern Uganda.

DANGERS & ANNOYANCES

It's difficult to generalise about personal safety in East Africa. While there are large risks in some areas, other places are as safe as you will find anywhere.

- Arriving for the first time at bus stations in places such as Nairobi and Arusha can be a fairly traumatic experience, as you're likely to be besieged by touts as you get off the bus, all reaching to help with your pack and trying to sell you a safari. Have your luggage as consolidated as possible, with your valuables well hidden under your clothes. Try to spot the taxi area before disembarking, and make a beeline for it. It's well worth a few extra dollars for the fare, rather than attempting to walk to your hotel with your luggage.
- Don't leave your possessions scattered around your hotel room. If you have valuables, store them in a hotel safe, if there's a reliable one, ideally inside a pouch with a lockable zip to prevent tampering.
- Keep the windows up in vehicles when stopped in traffic, and keep your bags out of sight, eg on the floor behind your legs.

- When bargaining or discussing prices, don't do so with your money or wallet in your hand.
- When arranging tour guides, do so through a reputable hotel or a travel agency.
- On buses and trains, never accept food or drink from fellow passengers, even if it's sealed. Also avoid travelling at night.
- Do your homework and stay informed. Research conditions when entering a country, read newspapers, and ask other travellers and hotel staff for the latest.

DISCOUNT CARDS

An International Student Identity Card (ISIC) or the graduate equivalent is occasionally useful for discounts on train fares, airline tickets and entry charges to museums and archaeological sites.

SCAMS

- Someone approaches you on the street saying 'Remember me?' or claiming to be an employee of the hotel where you're staying. Or perhaps collecting donations for school fees. Or perhaps claiming to be a refugee, showing you a list of all those who have already signed on to help them with donations. In general, be sceptical of anyone who approaches you familiarly on the street; decline any offers or invitations made on the street, and take requests for donations from 'refugees', 'students' or others with a grain of salt. Your money has a better chance of reaching those most in need when channelled through registered charities or churches, and dealings with supposed hotel employees and the like are best done at your hotel.

- You're walking along a busy city street, and suddenly find your way blocked – perhaps the man in front of you has just noticed something on his shoe that he needs to clean off. Before you know it, his buddy has come up behind you and relieved you of your wallet, and they both disappear into the crowds. Keep your wits about you, always be conscious of who is around you, and keep your valuables in an inner pocket where they would be hard to get at in such a situation.

- Your taxi driver passes a policeman, and is stopped for not wearing his seatbelt. The policeman takes his keys, and you need to pay the policeman to get the keys back to access your luggage in the trunk. The 'fine' is then divvied up among all the accomplices. To avoid this problem (or worse) in taxis, take taxis from hotels or established ranks, and always avoid freelancers cruising on the streets. If your luggage is relatively compact, keep it up front with you, on the floor under your feet.

- Someone tries to strike up a conversation and tries to sell you marijuana (*bangi* or *ganja*). Before you've had a chance to shake them loose, policemen (sometimes legitimate, sometimes not) suddenly appear and insist that you pay a huge fine for being involved in the purchase of illegal drugs. Once they've arrived, there's often little you can do, other than instantly hightailing it in the opposite direction if you smell this scam coming. If you're caught, insist on going to the nearest police station before paying anything, and whittle the bribe down as low as you can. Initial demands may be as high as US$300, but if you're savvy, you should be able to get away with under US$50.

GOVERNMENT TRAVEL ADVICE

The following government websites offer travel advisories and information on current hot spots.

Australian Department of Foreign Affairs & Trade (☎ 1300 139 281; www .smarttraveller.gov.au)

British Foreign & Commonwealth Office (☎ 0845-850-2829; www.fco.gov.uk/countryadvice)

Canadian Department of Foreign Affairs & International Trade (☎ 800-267 6788; www.dfait-maeci.gc.ca)

US State Department (☎ 888-407 4747; http://travel.state.gov)

EMBASSIES & CONSULATES

As a tourist, it's important to realise what your embassy – the embassy of the country of which you are a citizen – can and can't do.

Generally speaking, it won't be much help in emergencies if the trouble you're in is remotely your own fault, as you're bound by the laws of the country you are in. Your embassy will not be sympathetic if you end up in jail after committing a crime locally, even if such actions are legal in your own country.

In genuine emergencies you might get some assistance but only if other channels have been exhausted. For example, if you need to get home urgently, a free ticket is exceedingly unlikely – the embassy would expect you to have insurance. If you have all your money and documents stolen, it might assist with getting a new passport, but a loan for onward travel is out of the question.

For lists of diplomatic representations, see the country Directory sections.

GAY & LESBIAN TRAVELLERS

Officially, male homosexuality is illegal in Tanzania and Kenya. While prosecutions rarely occur, discretion is advised as gay sexual relationships are culturally taboo, and public displays of affection, whether between people of the same or opposite sex, are frowned upon. In Uganda, homophobics have become increasingly vocal in recent times.

All this said, it is unlikely that gay travellers will experience any particular difficulties. The coast – notably Lamu (Kenya) and Zanzibar (Tanzania) tends to be more tolerant of gay relationships, at least privately, than other areas in the region.

Good initial contacts include **Purple Roofs** (www.purpleroofs.com), which lists gay or gay-friendly tour companies in the region; **Gay2Afrika** (www.gay2afrika.com), with a range of regional tours; and – for more all-inclusive packages and general information, **David Travel** (www.davidtravel.com) and **Atlantis Events** (www.atlantis events.com). Also check the East Africa links on www.mask.org.za.

HOLIDAYS

For national holidays see the country chapter Directories.

Public Holidays

In Tanzania, in parts of Kenya and in Uganda, major Islamic holidays are also celebrated as public holidays. The dates depend on the moon and fall about 11 days earlier each year. The most important ones:

Eid al-Moulid (Maulid) The birthday of the Prophet Mohammed.

Ramadan The annual 30-day fast when adherents do not eat or drink from sunrise to sunset.

Eid al-Fitr The end of Ramadan, and East Africa's most important Islamic celebration; celebrated as a two-day holiday in many areas.

Eid al-Kebir (Eid al-Haji) Commemorates the moment when Abraham was about to sacrifice his son in obedience to God's command, only to have God intercede at the last moment and substitute a ram instead. It coincides with the end of the pilgrimage (haj) to Mecca.

Estimated dates for these events are shown following. Although Ramadan is not a public holiday, restaurants are often closed during this time in coastal areas.

Event	2009	2010	2011
Ramadan begins	22 Aug	11 Aug	1 Aug
Eid al-Fitr (end of Ramadan, 2-day holiday)	21 Sep	10 Sep	31 Aug
Eid al-Kebir (Eid al-Haji)	27 Nov	16 Nov	6 Nov
Eid al-Moulid	9 Mar	26 Feb	16 Feb

INSURANCE

Taking out travel insurance covering theft, loss and medical problems is highly recommended. Before choosing a policy spend time shopping around, as those designed for short package tours in Europe may not be suitable for East Africa. Be sure to read the fine print, as some policies specifically exclude 'dangerous activities', which can mean scuba diving, motorcycling and even trekking. A locally acquired motorcycle licence isn't valid under some policies. Some policies pay doctors or hospitals directly, while others require you to pay on the spot and claim later. If you have to claim later, keep all documentation. Most importantly, check that the policy covers an emergency flight home or at least medical evacuation to Western-standard health facilities, and understand in advance the procedures you need to follow in an emergency.

Before heading to East Africa, it's worth taking out a membership with the **African Medical & Research Foundation** (Amref; www.amref .org; Dar es Salaam branch office ☎ 022-211 6610, 022-211 3673; Nairobi emergency lines ☎ 254-20-315454, 254-20-600090, 254-733-628422, 254-722-314239, satellite tel 873 762 315580; Nairobi head office ☎ 254-20-699 3000). Membership entitles you to emergency regional evacuation by the Flying Doctors' Society of Africa, which operates 24-hour air-ambulance service based out of Nairobi's Wilson airport. A two-month membership costs US$25/50 for evacuations within a 500km/1000km radius of Nairobi. The 1000km membership covers the entire East African region, except for southernmost Tanzania around Songea, Tunduru and Mtwara.

Worldwide travel insurance is available at at www.lonelyplanet.com./travel_services. You can buy, extend and claim online anytime – even if you're already on the road. See also p626 and p623 for further details on insurance.

INTERNET ACCESS

Urban East Africa is online, with internet cafes in all capitals and major towns. In rural areas, connections remain spotty. Prices range from less than US$1 per hour up to US$7 per hour. Speed is not necessarily related to price, and varies greatly, though truly fast connections are rare. Reliable and reasonably priced internet cafes tend to fill up, and you'll often need to wait for a terminal. A small but increasing number of business-class hotels have wireless access points. Some upmarket safari camps have satellite connections, but it's generally not possible to connect while on safari.

LAUNDRY

Apart from top-end establishments, most hotels don't have laundry services as such. Sometimes it's possible to make arrangements with staff for your laundry to be washed and ironed, but it's well worth travelling with a small package of detergent (sold at roadside kiosks throughout the region for about US$0.20) and a drying line. Dry cleaning services are only found in major cities and at top-end hotels.

LEGAL MATTERS

Apart from traffic offences such as speeding and driving without a seatbelt (mandatory in many areas for driver and front-seat passengers), the main area to watch out for is drug use and possession. Marijuana (bangi or ganja) is widely available in places such as Nairobi, Dar es Salaam and Zanzibar, and is frequently offered to tourists – invariably part of a setup involving the police or fake police. If you're caught, expect to pay a large bribe to avoid arrest or imprisonment.

If you're arrested for whatever reason, you can request to call your embassy, but the help they can give you will be limited, see p609.

If you get robbed, most insurance companies require a police report before they'll reimburse you. You can get these at the nearest police station, though it's usually a time-consuming process.

MAPS

Regional maps include Nelles' *Tanzania, Rwanda, Burundi, Kenya* and *Uganda* maps, Bartholomew's *Kenya & Tanzania,* and Hallway's *Kenya & Tanzania,* which also includes Uganda, Rwanda and Burundi. Michelin's *Africa – Central & South* covers most of the region on a smaller scale.

MONEY

The best strategy with money is to bring a mix of dollars or euros cash (large and small denominations), a credit card (Visa is most widely accepted) for withdrawing money from ATMs and some travellers cheques as an emergency standby. (These are generally changeable in major cities only; ideally bring a mixture of American Express and Thomas Cook.)

ATMs

There are ATMs in capital cities and most major towns (except in Rwanda, where they are just in Kigali, and in Burundi, where there are none). They take either Visa or MasterCard, occasionally both. Some banks in Kenya, Tanzania and Uganda have machines linked to the Plus and Cirrus networks. However, despite their growing use, ATMs are out of order or out of cash with enough frequency that you should always have some sort of back-up funds. There are few ATMs away from major routes.

Black Market

Except for in Burundi, there is essentially no black market for foreign currency. Nevertheless, you'll still get shady characters sidling up beside you in Nairobi, Dar es Salaam and major tourist areas, trying to get you to change money and promising enticing rates. It's invariably a setup and changing on the street should be avoided.

Cash

US dollars, followed by euros, are the most convenient foreign currencies and get the best rates. Other major currencies are readily accepted in major cities, but often not elsewhere, or at less favourable rates. You'll get higher rates for larger denomination bills (US$50 and US$100 notes), but carry a supply of smaller denomination notes as well, as change can be difficult to find.

Credit Cards

Visa and MasterCard can be used for some top-end hotels and a few tour operators, especially in major towns and especially in Kenya. However, like ATMs, they're best viewed as a stand-by unless you've confirmed things in advance with the establishment. In Rwanda and Burundi, you'll need to rely on cash, although some banks in major cities give cash advances against a credit card. Many places, especially in Tanzania, attach a commission of about 5% to 10% to credit card payments.

Exchanging Money

You can change cash with a minimum of hassle at banks or foreign exchange (forex) bureaus in major towns and cities; rates and commissions vary, so it pays to shop around. In addition to regular banking hours, most forex bureaus are also open on Saturday mornings. If you get stuck for money outside banking hours and away from an ATM, ask shop owners if they can help you out, rather than changing with someone on the street (which should always be avoided). It's better to say something like 'The banks are closed; do you know someone who could help me out?' rather than directly asking if they will change money.

Tipping & Bargaining

Tipping generally isn't practised in small, local establishments. But in major towns, upmarket places and anywhere frequented by tourists, tips are expected. If a service charge hasn't been included, either round out the bill, or calculate about 10%.

Bargaining is expected by vendors in tourist areas, except in a limited number of fixed-price shops. However, away from tourist areas and for nontourist items, the price quoted will often be the 'real' price, so don't automatically assume that the quote you've been given is too high.

Where bargaining is appropriate, if you pay the first price asked – whether due to ignorance or guilt about how much you have compared with locals – you'll probably be considered naive. You'll also be doing fellow travellers a disservice by creating the impression that all foreigners are willing to pay any named price. Paying consistently above the curve can also contribute to goods being priced out of the reach of locals.

While there are no set rules for bargaining, it should be conducted in a friendly and spirited manner; losing your temper or becoming aggressive or frustrated will be counterproductive. In any transaction, the vendor's aim is to identify the highest price you will pay, while your aim is to find the lowest price at which the vendor will sell. Before starting, shop around to get a feel for the 'value' of the item you want, and ask others what they paid. Once you start negotiating, if things seem like a waste of time, politely take your leave. Sometimes sellers will call you back if they think their stubbornness is counterproductive. Few will pass up a sale, however thin the profit. If the vendor won't come down to a price you feel is fair, it means that they aren't making a profit, or that too many high-rolling foreigners have passed through already.

Travellers Cheques

Throughout the region, travellers cheques can only be changed in major cities, and with high commissions, and often with difficulty. Rates are lower (often considerably so) than for cash. American Express and Thomas Cook are the most widely recognised; it's best to get your cheques in US dollars or euros. Bring a range of denominations so you don't get stuck at the end of your trip changing large cheques for final expenses, and because some banks charge a per-cheque levy. Carry the *original* purchase receipt with you (and separately from the cheques), as many banks and forex bureaus ask to see it, and don't rely on travellers cheques as your main or only source of funds.

Direct payment with travellers cheques for accommodation and services is almost never accepted. If your cheques are stolen, getting replacements while still in the region ranges from extremely time-consuming to impossible.

PHOTOGRAPHY & VIDEO
Film & Equipment
Nairobi has the best selection of camera equipment, followed by Dar es Salaam and Kampala, though it's best to bring what you'll need, including extra memory cards, with you.

For film processing, most serious photographers get their film developed in Nairobi (where you can also get slides processed) or bring it home. An increasing number of internet cafes and speciality shops can help with transferring digital images to CDs or other storage. It's a good idea to carry a USB converter for memory cards if you may want to burn your photos onto CDs or DVDs, as many internet cafes and other shops don't have card reader slots.

If you're going to be in forested areas, keep in mind that flashes generally aren't permitted near the primates.

Whatever accessories you carry, be sure to keep them well wrapped in a good bag to protect them from the inevitable dust. Sunlight, humidity and heat can also spoil your camera and film, so take precautions. Lonely Planet's *Travel Photography: A Guide to Taking Better Pictures* by Richard I'Anson is full of helpful tips for taking photographs while on the road.

Photographing People
Always ask permission before photographing people, and always respect their wishes. In many tourist areas, locals will ask for a fee before allowing you to photograph them, which is fair enough, though rates can be high. If you promise to send someone a photo, get their address and follow through with it, as your promise will be taken seriously.

Restrictions
Avoid taking pictures of anything connected with the government or the military, including army barracks, land or people anywhere close to army barracks, government offices,

post offices, banks, ports, train stations, airports, bridges and dams.

Some locals may object if you take pictures of their place of worship – this includes natural features with traditional religious significance – so always ask first. It usually helps if you're appropriately dressed. In mosques, for instance, wearing a long skirt or trousers and removing your shoes may make it less likely that your hosts will object.

SHOPPING
Craft shopping is one of the many pleasures of travel in East Africa. You'll encounter a wide selection of crafts in the region, ranging from basketry and woodcarvings to textiles, paintings and jewellery. While there's plenty of cheap, low-quality work available, with a bit of looking and comparison shopping you should be able to find high-quality work at reasonable prices. When checking for quality, watch for attention given to detail and overall craftsmanship; with textiles, spread them out to check for flaws or uneven cuts. Always try to buy crafts and souvenirs directly from those who make them. Artists' cooperatives are always a good bet (check for listings in the country chapters).

SOLO TRAVELLERS
While you may be a minor curiosity in rural areas, especially solo women travellers, there are no particular problems with travelling solo in East Africa, whether you're male or female. Times when it is advantageous to join a group are for safaris and treks – when going in a group can be a significant cost saver – and when going out at night. If you go out alone at night, take taxis and use extra caution, especially in urban and tourist areas. Whatever the time of day, avoid isolating situations, including isolated stretches of beach. Also see Women Travellers, p614.

TELEPHONE
You can make domestic and international calls from telecom offices – either private, or run by the national telecom company – in many major towns, by using prepaid cards. Also common are local-style payphones – people sitting in a kiosk, in a small shop or at a table with a phone. The cheapest options are internet dialling where it's available, or dialling from mobile phones.

The mobile network covers major towns throughout the region, plus many rural areas.

ON TIME?

While the discussion of time makes everything sound quite official and precise, when all is said and done, time is a very different concept in East Africa than in many parts of the West. Buses that are going 'now' rarely leave until they're full, regardless of how much engine revving takes place in the meantime. Agreed-upon times for appointments are treated as very approximate concepts. A meeting set for 9am today could just as likely happen at 11am, or that afternoon, or even the next day. Getting upset when things don't go like clockwork is generally counterproductive. The best way to get things done efficiently is to stay relaxed, treat the person you're dealing with as a person, inquire how their family is going or how their children are doing at school, and take the time to listen to the answer. Then, sit back, wait and be patient – you'll usually get where you're going or what you're hoping for, but on East Africa's time rather than yours.

Most companies sell prepaid starter packages for about US$2, and top-up cards are on sale at shops throughout the country. With both Vodacom and Celtel, you can keep the same SIM card in Tanzania, Kenya and Uganda, and recharge with local currency, although it's cheaper just to buy a local SIM card.

If bringing your own phone to East Africa, check that it can operate on either 900MHz or 1800MHz band frequencies. This is usually no problem, unless you have a US phone, in which case be sure it's 'tri-band' or 'quad-band', and that it is unlocked.

Country codes are given inside the front cover. Throughout the region, except in Rwanda and Burundi, area codes must be used whenever you dial long-distance. In this book, codes are included in all listings.

TIME

Time in Kenya, Uganda and Tanzania is GMT/UTC plus three hours year-round; in Rwanda and Burundi it's GMT/UTC plus two hours.

In Swahili-speaking areas, locals use the Swahili system of telling time, in which the first hour is *saa moja (asubuhi)*, corresponding with 7am. Counting begins again with *saa moja (jioni)*, the first hour in the evening, corresponding with 7pm. Although most will switch to the international clock when speaking English with foreigners, confusion sometimes occurs, so ask people to confirm whether they are using *saa za kizungu* (international time) or *saa za kiswahili* (Swahili time). Signboards with opening hours are often posted in Swahili time.

TOILETS

Toilets vary from standard long drops to full-flush luxury conveniences that can spring up in the most unlikely places. Almost all mid-range and top-end hotels sport flushable sit-down types, although at the lower end of the price range, toilet seats are a rare commodity. Budget guesthouses often have squat toilets – sometimes equipped with a flush mechanism, otherwise with a bucket and scoop.

Cleanliness levels vary; if you go in expecting the worst, you'll often be surprised that they're not all that bad. Toilets with running water are a rarity outside major hotels. If you see a bucket with water nearby, use it for flushing. Paper (you'll invariably need to supply your own) should be deposited in the can that's usually in the corner.

Many of the upmarket bush camps have 'dry' toilets – just a fancy version of the long drop with a Western-style seat perched on the top – though it is all generally quite hygienic.

TOURIST INFORMATION

Kenya, Tanzania, Uganda and Rwanda all have tourist agency websites, and maintain tourist offices of varying degrees of helpfulness in major cities; see the country Directories for more. General background information is available from East African embassies.

TRAVELLERS WITH DISABILITIES

While there are few facilities specifically for the disabled, East Africans are generally quite accommodating, and willing to offer whatever assistance they can as long as they understand what you need. Disabled travel is becoming increasingly common on the Kenyan and Tanzanian safari circuits, and several tour operators listed in the Safaris chapter (p60) cater to disabled travellers. Some considerations are listed following:

▪ While the newer lodges have wheelchair-accessible rooms (noted in individual listings), few hotels have lifts, many have narrow stairwells and there are generally no grips or rails in bathrooms.

- Many park lodges and camps are built on ground level. However, access paths – in an attempt to maintain a natural environment – are sometimes rough or rocky, and rooms or tents raised, so it's best to inquire about access before booking.
- As far as we know, there are no Braille signboards at any parks or museums, nor any facilities for deaf travellers.
- In most places taxis are small sedans, with the exception of Nairobi where you'll find some old London cabs that are spacious enough to take a wheelchair. Minibuses are widely available in Kenya, Tanzania and Uganda, and can be chartered for transport and customised safaris. Large or wide-door vehicles can also be arranged through car-hire agencies in major cities, and often with safari operators as well.

In general, Kenya and northern Tanzania are probably the easiest destinations, and many safari companies in these areas have experience taking disabled people on safari. Organisations that disseminate information on travel for the mobility impaired include the following:

Access-Able Travel Source (www.access-able.com)
Accessible Journeys (www.disabilitytravel.com)
Holiday Care (www.holidaycare.org.uk)
Mobility International (www.miusa.org)
National Information Communication Awareness Network (www.nican.com.au)

VISAS

Your passport should have plenty of blank pages for entry and exit stamps, and be valid for at least six months after the conclusion of your planned travels.

It's best to arrange visas in advance, although currently all countries in the region are issuing visas at the airport and at most land borders. Regulations change frequently, so call the relevant embassy for an update. Many international airlines require you to have a visa before boarding the plane to East Africa.

Once in East Africa, a single-entry visa for Kenya, Tanzania or Uganda allows you to visit either of the other two countries (assuming you've met their visa requirements and have been issued a visa) and then return to the original country without having to apply for a second visa for the original country. Thus, if you're in Tanzania on a single-entry visa, you can go to Kenya (assuming you also have a Kenyan visa), and then return to Tanzania without needing a new Tanzanian visa. This doesn't apply to Rwanda and Burundi, so if you will be including visits to these or other African countries in your regional itinerary, it will save you money to get a multiple-entry visa at the outset. Note that visas issued at land borders are usually for single entry only. Also, at most borders (including the popular Namanga border crossing between Kenya and Tanzania) and at airport immigration, visa fees must be paid in US dollars cash. Carry extra passport-sized photos for visa applications.

Proof of an onward ticket or sufficient funds is rarely required if you apply for a visa at land borders. It's occasionally requested at airports in the region, but generally only if you give immigration officials reason to doubt that you'll leave.

VOLUNTEERING

There are various opportunities for volunteering, generally teaching, or in environmental or health work; these are almost always best arranged prior to arriving in East Africa.

Some places to start your search: **Voluntary Service Overseas** (VSO; www.vso.org.uk), which provides placements for young professionals, or the similar US-based **Peace Corps** (www.peacecorps .gov); **Volunteer Abroad** (www.volunteerabroad.com), with a good selection of volunteer listings for East Africa; and **Frontier** (www.frontier.ac.uk). There are also various volunteer holiday opportunities included in the East Africa listings of **ResponsibleTravel.com** (www.responsibletravel.com). Also check out **International Volunteer HQ** (www .volunteerhq.org), **Idealist.org** (www.idealist.org), **Travel Tree** (www.traveltree.co.uk), **i-to-i** (www.i-to-i.com) and **Earthwatch** (www.earthwatch.org).

WOMEN TRAVELLERS

East Africa (especially in Kenya, Tanzania and Uganda) is a relatively easy region to travel in, either solo or with other women, especially when compared with parts of North Africa, South America and certain Western countries. You're not likely to encounter any more specifically gender-related problems than you would elsewhere in the world and, more often than not, you'll meet only warmth, hospitality and sisterly regard, and find that you receive kindness and special treatment that you probably wouldn't be shown if you were a male traveller. That said, you'll inevitably attract some attention, especially if you're travelling alone, and there are some areas where caution is essential. Following are a few tips:

- Dressing modestly is the single most successful strategy for minimising unwanted attention. Wear trousers or a long skirt, and a conservative top with sleeves. Tucking your hair under a cap or scarf, or tying it back, also helps.

- Use common sense, trust your instincts and take the usual precautions when out and about. Try to avoid walking alone at night. Avoid isolated areas at all times, and be particularly cautious on beaches, many of which can become isolated very quickly. Hassling tends to be worse in tourist areas along the Kenyan coast than elsewhere in the region. While most of it is limited to verbal hassles, and many travellers – female and male – travel in this area without incident, take extra care here about where you go alone.

- If you find yourself with an unwanted suitor, creative approaches are usually fairly effective. For example, explain that your husband (whether real or fictitious) or a large group of friends will be arriving imminently at that very place. Creative approaches are also usually effective in dealing with the inevitable curiosity that you'll meet as to why you might not have children and a husband, or if you do have them, why they are not with you. The easiest response to the question of why you aren't married is to explain that you are still young (*bado kijana* in Swahili), which, whether you are or not, will at least have some humour value. Just saying '*bado*' ('not yet') to questions about marriage or children should also do the trick. As for why your family isn't with you, you can always explain that you will be meeting them later.

- Seek out local women, as this can enrich your trip tremendously. Good places to try include tourist offices, government departments or even your hotel, where at least some of the staff are likely to be formally educated young to middle-aged women. In rural areas, starting points include women teachers at a local school, or staff at a health centre.

- In mixed-race situations in some areas of the region – specifically if you're a black woman with a white male – some East Africans may assume that you're a prostitute. Taking taxis if you go out at night and ignoring any comments are among the tactics that may help minimise problems here.

- Arrange tour and trekking guides through a reputable hotel or travel agency. Avoid freelance guides who approach you on the street.

In Rwanda and Burundi, verbal hassles, hisses and the like tend to be more common than elsewhere in the region, although things rarely go further than this. The best strategy – in addition to following the preceding tips – is to ignore hissing and catcalls; don't worry about being rude, and don't feel the need to explain yourself. Due to the overall unstable security situation, especially in Burundi, you'll need to take particular care in more remote areas, but this applies to travellers of whatever gender.

A limited selection of tampons is available at pharmacies or large supermarkets in major towns throughout the region. Elsewhere, the choice is usually limited to pads.

WORK

The most likely areas for employment are the safari industry, tourism, scuba diving and teaching. For safari-, diving- and tourism-related positions, competition is stiff and the best way to land something is to get to know someone already working in the business. Also check safari operator and lodge websites, some of which advertise vacant positions.

Work and residency permits generally must be arranged through the employer or sponsoring organisation; residency permits normally should be applied for before arriving in the region. Be prepared for lots of bureaucracy.

Most teaching positions are voluntary, and best arranged through voluntary agencies (see opposite) or mission organisations at home. Also start your search from home for international staff positions with the many aid agencies operating in East Africa. There are numerous opportunities, especially in Kenya (dealing with the crises in Somalia and Sudan), Uganda and Burundi. However, most organisations require applicants to go through their head office.

Transport in East Africa

GETTING THERE & AWAY

This section covers reaching East Africa from elsewhere in the world. For travel between and around East African countries, and for border crossing information, see under Transport in the country chapters. Flights, tours and rail tickets can be booked online at www.lonelyplanet.com/travel_services.

AIR
Airports & Airlines

Nairobi (Kenya) is East Africa's major air hub, and the best destination for finding special airfares. Other major airports include Dar es Salaam and Kilimanjaro in Tanzania, and Entebbe in Uganda. There are also international airports in Kigali (Rwanda), Bujumbura (Burundi) and Zanzibar (Tanzania), and it's worth checking out cheap charter flights to Mombasa (Kenya) from Europe.

Tickets

Airfares from Europe and North America to East Africa are highest in December and January, and again from June through August. They're lowest from March through May, except around the Easter holidays. London is the main discount airfare hub, and

THINGS CHANGE

The information in this chapter is particularly vulnerable to change. Shop carefully, and check directly with the airline or travel agent to understand how a fare works. Details given in this chapter should be regarded as pointers and aren't a substitute for your own careful research.

a good place to look for special deals, especially into Nairobi. When planning your trip, consider buying an open-jaw ticket, which enables you to fly into one country and out of another. This often works out more cheaply and more environmentally friendly than booking a standard return in and out of one city, plus a connecting regional flight. Charter flights are generally cheaper than scheduled flights, and are also worth considering. Some come as part of a package that includes accommodation, but most charter companies sell 'flight only' tickets.

Online ticket sellers and search engines:
Cheap Tickets (www.cheaptickets.com)
Cheapflights (www.cheapflights.co.uk)
Expedia (www.expedia.com)
Flight Centre (www.flightcentre.com)
Kayak (www.kayak.com)
LowestFare.com (www.lowestfare.com)
OneTravel.com (www.onetravel.com)
Orbitz (www.orbitz.com)
STA Travel (www.statravel.com)
Travelocity (www.travelocity.com)

INTERCONTINENTAL (RTW) TICKETS

Intercontinental (round-the-world) tickets give you a limited period (usually a year) to circumnavigate the globe. You can go anywhere that the carrying airline and its partners go, as long as you stay within the set mileage or number of stops, and don't backtrack. As East African destinations generally aren't part of standard RTW packages, you'll need to pay extra – sometimes considerably – to include them. However, Johannesburg and Cairo often are included, both of which make interesting starting points for an overland foray into East Africa.

Travel agents can put together 'alternative' RTW tickets, which are more expensive, but more flexible, than standard RTW itineraries. For a multiple-stop itinerary without the cost of a RTW ticket, consider combining tickets from two low-cost airlines.

Online RTW ticket sellers:

Airbrokers (www.airbrokers.com) For travel originating in North America.

Airtreks (www.airtreks.com) For travel originating anywhere.

Oneworld (www.oneworld.com) An airline alliance offering RTW packages.

Roundtheworldflights.com (www.roundtheworld flights.com) For travel originating in the UK.

Star Alliance (www.staralliance.com) An airline alliance offering RTW packages.

Africa & the Middle East

Useful airlines and their connections:

Air Madagascar (www.airmadagascar.com) Antananarivo (Madagascar) to Johannesburg (South Africa), from where you can connect to Nairobi.

Air Tanzania (www.airtanzania.com) Moroni (Comoros), Johannesburg and Entebbe to Dar es Salaam.

Air Uganda (www.air-uganda.com) Juba (Sudan) to Entebbe

EgyptAir (www.egyptair.com.eg) Cairo to Nairobi via Entebbe.

Emirates (www.emirates.com) Cairo to Nairobi, Dar es Salaam or Entebbe via Dubai.

Ethiopian Airlines (www.ethiopianairlines.com) Abidjan, Lagos, Douala, Cairo and other cities to Addis Ababa, and then onward connections to all major East African airports.

Kenya Airways (www.kenya-airways.com) Abidjan, Cairo, Douala, Harare, Johannesburg, Khartoum, Lilongwe and other cities to Nairobi, with onward connections to all East African capitals and Zanzibar.

Linhas Aéreas de Moçambique (www.lam.co.mz) Maputo to Nairobi and Maputo to Dar es Salaam via Pemba (Mozambique).

Rwandair Express (www.rwandair.com) Kigali to Bujumbura, Nairobi, Kilimanjaro, Entebbe and Johannesburg.

South African Airways (www.flysaa.com) Johannesburg to Dar es Salaam, Nairobi and Entebbe.

SN Brussels Airline (www.flysn.com) Brussels to Entebbe, Nairobi and Kigali.

Always ask about return excursion fares (fares that have certain restrictions or prerequisites, such as advance purchase, limited lifespan or specified travel windows) for intra-African flights, as they are frequently significantly cheaper than standard return fares.

Ticket discounters include **Rennies Travel** (www.renniestravel.com) and **STA Travel** (www.statravel.co.za), with offices throughout southern Africa. **Flight Centre** (☎ 0860 400 727, 011-778 1720; www.flight centre.co.za) has offices in Johannesburg, Cape Town and several other cities. In the Middle East: **Al-Rais Travels** (www.alrais.com) in Dubai; **Egypt Panorama Tours** (☎ 2-359 0200; www.eptours .com) in Cairo; **Israel Student Travel Association** (ISTA; ☎ 02-625 7257) in Jerusalem; and **Orion-Tour** (www.oriontour.com) in Istanbul.

CLIMATE CHANGE & TRAVEL

Climate change threatens earth's ecosystems, and air travel is the fastest-growing contributor to the problem. Lonely Planet regards travel, overall, as a global benefit, but believes we all have a responsibility to limit our personal impact on global warming.

Flying & climate change

Most forms of motorised travel generate CO_2 (the main cause of human-induced climate change) but planes are the worst offenders because they release greenhouse gases high into the atmosphere. Two people taking a return flight between Europe and the US will contribute as much to climate change as an average household's annual gas and electricity consumption. This is then roughly doubled by continuing on to East Africa.

Carbon offset schemes

Climatecare.org and other websites use 'carbon calculators' that allow travellers to offset the level of greenhouse gases they generate with financial contributions to sustainable travel schemes that reduce global warming.

Lonely Planet, together with Rough Guides and other concerned partners in the travel industry, support the carbon offset scheme run by climatecare.org. Lonely Planet offsets all of its staff and author travel.

Asia

Popular connections from Asia are via Singapore and the United Arab Emirates, or via Mumbai (Bombay), from where there are connections to Dar es Salaam and Nairobi on Kenya Airways and **Air India** (www.airindia .com). Ethiopian Airlines (via Addis Ababa) also flies this route, and Kenya Airways flies from Hong Kong, Bangkok and Guangzhou to Nairobi. A longer but competitively-priced option is from Singapore or Hong Kong to Johannesburg, connecting to Dar es Salaam.

Discounters include **STA Travel** (www.statravel .com), with branches in **Bangkok** (☎ 02-236 0262; www.statravel.co.th), **Singapore** (☎ 6737 7188; www .statravel.com.sg), **Hong Kong** (☎ 2736 1618; www.sta travel.com.hk) and **Japan** (☎ 03 5391 2922; www.statravel .co.jp). In Japan, also try **No 1 Travel** (☎ 03-3205 6073; www.no1-travel.com); in Hong Kong try **Four Seas Tours** (☎ 2200 7760; www.fourseastravel.com/fs/en /index.jsp). **STIC Travels** (www.stictravel.com) has offices in many Indian cities, including **Delhi** (☎ 11- 233 57 468) and **Mumbai** (☎ 22-221 81 431).

Australia & New Zealand

There are no direct flights from Australia or New Zealand to anywhere in East Africa. However, from Australia, **Qantas** (www.qantas .com.au) from Sydney and Perth and South African Airways (from Perth) have several flights weekly to Johannesburg, with connections to Nairobi, Dar es Salaam and Entebbe. Other options include Emirates via Dubai to Dar es Salaam or Nairobi; Qantas or Air India via Mumbai to Dar es Salaam or Nairobi and **Air Mauritius** (www.airmauritius.com) to Nairobi via Mauritius. **STA Travel** (☎ 1300 733 035; statravel.com .au) and **Flight Centre** (☎ 133 133; www.flightcentre .com.au) have offices throughout Australia. For online bookings, try www.travel.com.au.

From New Zealand, try Emirates via Dubai to Dar es Salaam or Nairobi or Qantas and South African Airways via Sydney and Johannesburg. Both **Flight Centre** (☎ 0800 243 544; www.flightcentre .co.nz) and **STA Travel** (☎ 0508 782 872; www.statravel .co.nz) have branches throughout the country. Try www.travel.co.nz for online bookings.

UK & Continental Europe

There are flights from many European capitals directly to East Africa. The best deals, both on commercial and charter flights, are on the London–Nairobi route. Airlines to check include **Swiss** (www.swiss.com) to Nairobi and Dar es Salaam; **KLM Royal Dutch Airlines**

(www.klm.com) to Nairobi, Dar es Salaam, Kilimanjaro and Entebbe; **British Airways** (www .britishairways.com) to Nairobi, Dar es Salaam and Entebbe; and **SN Brussels Airline** (www.brus selsairlines.com) to Entebbe, Kigali and Nairobi. Non-European carriers – including Kenya Airways, Egypt Air via Cairo, Ethiopian Airlines via Addis Ababa, and Emirates via Dubai – service various European cities as well as East African destinations, and also offer good deals.

Whichever route you travel, flights from Europe tend to be heavily booked between late June and late August, so reserve well in advance. The lowest fares are usually for travel between January and May, apart from the Easter season.

In the UK, travel agency ads appear in the travel pages of the weekend broadsheet newspapers, in *Time Out*, the *Evening Standard* and in the free online magazine *TNT* (www.tntmagazine.com).

Discount ticket agencies in the UK:

Bridge the World (☎ 0870 444 7474)

Flight Centre (☎ 0870 890 8099; www.flightcentre .co.uk)

Flightbookers (☎ 0870 814 4001; www.ebookers.com)

North-South Travel (☎ 01245 608 291; www.northsouthtravel.co.uk)

Quest Travel (☎ 0870 442 3542; www.questtravel.com)

STA Travel (☎ 0870 160 0599; www.statravel.co.uk) For travellers under the age of 26.

Trailfinders (www.trailfinders.co.uk)

Travel Bag (☎ 0870 890 1456; www.travelbag.co.uk)

Options for discounted fares from continental Europe:

Airfair (☎ 020 620 5121; www.airfair.nl) Netherlands.

Barcelo Viajes (☎ 902 116 226; www.barceloviajes .com) Spain.

CTS Viaggi (☎ 06 462 0431; www.cts.it) Italy

Expedia (www.expedia.de) Germany.

Just Travel (☎ 089 747 3330; www.justtravel.de) Germany.

Lastminute (☎ 01805 284 366; www.lastminute.de) Germany.

Nouvelles Frontières (☎ 90 217 09 79; www.nouvelles-frontieres.es) Spain.

Nouvelles Frontières (☎ 0825 000 747; www.nouvelles-frontieres.fr) France.

OTU Voyages (www.otu.fr) France.

STA Travel (☎ 01805 456 422; www.statravel.de) Germany; for travellers under the age of 26.

Voyageurs du Monde (☎ 01 40 15 11 15; www.vdm.com) France.

USA & Canada

Most flights from North America are via Europe, and there are few bargain deals. Fares offered by Canadian discounters are generally about 10% higher than those sold in the USA.

Generally the cheapest way is to get to London on a discounted transatlantic ticket, then purchase a separate ticket on to Nairobi or elsewhere in East Africa. Most of the airlines mentioned under UK & Continental Europe (opposite) also offer through-fares from North America.

A roundabout – but sometimes cheaper – alternative is South African Airways from New York to Johannesburg, where you can connect easily to East Africa. Other options include Ethiopian Airways from New York to East Africa via Rome and Addis Ababa and Kenya Airways together with **Virgin Atlantic** (www.virgin-atlantic.com) from New York to Nairobi and Dar es Salaam via London. For online bookings, see the agencies listed under Tickets, earlier in this section (p616). In Canada, also try **Travel Cuts** (☎ 800-667-2887; www.travelcuts.com), Canada's national student travel agency.

LAKE

The main lake ferry connections to/from East Africa are between Malawi and Tanzania on Lake Nyasa (see p264), and between Zambia and Tanzania on Lake Tanganyika (see p262).

LAND

Several of the more popular possibilities for combining East Africa travels with overland travel elsewhere in Africa are outlined here. Detailing how to drive your own vehicle to the region is beyond the scope of this book, although information on the required *carnet de passage* is included (see p623). Other sources of information include the *Adventure Motorcycling Handbook,* by Chris Scott et al, with lots of useful information, especially if you're combining the Sahara and West Africa with your East Africa travels; and *Africa by Road* by Bob Swain and Paula Snyder – very useful if you're exploring Africa in your own vehicle, with details on everything from paperwork and logistics to driving techniques.

North & West Africa

For information on trans-Saharan routes, see Lonely Planet's *West Africa,* and check the website of **Chris Scott** (www.sahara-overland.com). Once through West Africa, most travellers fly from Douala (Cameroon) over the Central African Republic and Democratic Republic of the Congo (DRC; formerly Zaire) via Addis Ababa to any of the East African capitals, from where you can continue overland.

Northeast Africa

The Nile route through northeast Africa goes from Egypt into Sudan (via Lake Nasser, and then on to Khartoum). From Khartoum, it's fairly straightforward to make your way to Ethiopia, and then into Kenya. However, for all travel involving routings in Sudan, get an update on the security situation before setting your plans.

Southern Africa

If you have the time, a combined southern Africa–East Africa overland itinerary is an excellent way to experience the continent, and the most straightforward of the various overland approaches to the region.

The main gateways between southern and East Africa are Zambia and Malawi, both of which are readily reached from elsewhere in southern Africa. Once in Zambia, head to Kapiri Mposhi where you can get the Tanzania–Zambia Railway (Tazara) northeast to Mbeya (Tanzania). From Mbeya continue by road or rail towards Dar es Salaam, and then by road towards Mombasa and Nairobi. Another route from Zambia goes to Mpulungu on the Zambian shore of Lake Tanganyika, from where you can travel by steamer to Kigoma. From Kigoma head by rail east to Dodoma (continuing from here via road) or northeast towards Lake Victoria, Uganda and western Kenya.

From Malawi, after entering East Africa at Songwe River Bridge (at the Tanzanian border), head by bus to Mbeya and continue as outlined above.

For Burundi, options include following the route outlined earlier from Mpulungu to Kigoma, from where you can continue by boat or overland to Bujumbura, travel through Burundi, Rwanda and Uganda, and on into Kenya or Tanzania.

Overland travel into East Africa from Mozambique is detailed on p260.

SEA

To reach East Africa by sea, the main option is trying to hitch a lift on a private yacht sailing along the coast. Durban (South Africa) is one of the better places to start looking. Several cargo shipping companies sailing from Europe to East Africa also have passenger cabins. Contacts:

Cruise Lines International Association (www.cruis ing.org) For cruise ships stopping at Zanzibar.

Freighter World Cruises (www.freighterworld.com) Currently not servicing East African ports, though may resume in the future.

Strand Voyages (www.strandtravel.co.uk)

Given the rise in piracy off the northeast African coast in recent months, you'd be well advised to check well the routing of your ship and get an update on the current situation.

TOURS

Organised tours can be low-budget affairs, where you travel in an 'overland truck' with 15 to 30 other people and some drivers/leaders, carrying tents and other equipment, buying food along the way, and cooking and eating as a group. At the other end of the spectrum are individually tailored tours, ranging in price from reasonable to very expensive.

Following is a small sampling of tour companies operating in East Africa. For locally based companies, see p60.

Australia & New Zealand

African Wildlife Safaris (☎ 03-9249 3777, 1300 363302; www.africanwildlifesafaris.com.au) Customised safaris in East and southern Africa.

Classic Safari Company (☎ 1300 130 218, 02-9327 0666; www.classicsafaricompany.com.au) Upmarket customised itineraries in Kenya, Tanzania and Uganda.

Peregrine Travel (☎ 03-8601 4444, 1300 854 444; www.peregrine.net.au) Everything from overland truck tours to upscale wildlife safaris and chimpanzee tracking. Also family safaris.

South Africa

Wildlife Adventures (☎ 021-702 0643; www.wild lifeadventures.co.za) Overland tours combining East and southern Africa.

Wild Frontiers (☎ 011-702 2035; www.wildfrontiers .com) A range of itineraries in Kenya, Tanzania, Uganda, Rwanda and DRC, including gorilla tours.

UK

Abercrombie & Kent (☎ 0845-070 0611; www .abercrombiekent.co.uk) Customised tours & safaris, incl chimpanzee tracking.

African Initiatives (☎ 0117-915 0001; www.african -initiatives.org.uk) Fair-traded safaris in northern Tanzania.

Africa-in-Focus (☎ 01803-770956; www.africa-in -focus.com) East and southern Africa overland tours and Kenya safaris.

Baobab Travel (☎ 0870-382 5003; www.baobabtravel .com) A culturally responsible operator with itineraries in Kenya and Tanzania.

Dragoman (☎ 01728-861133; www.dragoman.com) East Africa overland tours.

Expert Africa (☎ 020-8232 9777; www.expertafrica .com) An experienced, quality operator with safari and primate itineraries in Tanzania and Rwanda.

Intrepid Guerba (☎ 0203-147 7777; www.guerba .com) Itineraries for a range of styles and budgets, including overland tours.

Responsible Travel.com (☎ 01273-600030; www .responsibletravel.com) Matches you up with ecologically and culturally responsible tour operators to plan an itinerary.

Safari Drive (☎ 01488-71140; www.safaridrive.com) Self-drive safaris, primarily in northern Tanzania and Kenya.

Tribes Travel (☎ 01728-685971; www.tribes.co.uk) Fair-traded safaris and treks in Tanzania, Kenya, Uganda and Rwanda, including gorilla trekking.

USA & Canada

Abercrombie & Kent (☎ 630-954 2944, 800-554 7016; www.abercrombiekent.com) Customised tours and safaris.

Africa Adventure Company (☎ 954-491 8877; www .africa-adventure.com) Upscale specialist safaris in Kenya, Tanzania, Uganda and Rwanda.

African Horizons (☎ 877-256 1074, 847-256 1075; www.africanhorizons.com) A small operator offering various packages throughout East Africa.

Big Five Tours & Expeditions (☎ 800-244 3483, 772-287 7995; www.bigfive.com) Upmarket.

Born Free Safaris (☎ 800-372 3274, 818-981 7185; www.bornfreesafaris.com) Itineraries in Kenya, Tanzania and Uganda, including a women's-only tour.

Deeper Africa (☎ 888-658 7102; www.deeperafrica .com) Socially responsible, upmarket safaris in Kenya and Tanzania, and gorilla trekking in Uganda and Rwanda.

Explorateur Voyages (☎ 514-847 1177; www .explorateur.qc.ca, in French) Itineraries in Kenya, Tanzania, Uganda and Rwanda.

Good Earth (☎ 813-929 7232; www.goodearthtours .com) Itineraries in Tanzania, Kenya and Uganda, with detours also to Rwanda.

International Expeditions (☎ 800-633 4734, 205-428 1700; www.ietravel.com) Naturalist-oriented safaris in Kenya, Tanzania and Uganda.

Mountain Madness (☎ 206-937 8389; www.mountainmadness.com) Upmarket treks on Mt Kilimanjaro and Mt Kenya.

Thomson Family Adventures (☎ 800-262 6255, 617-923 2004; www.familyadventures.com) Family-friendly northern Tanzania safaris and Kilimanjaro treks.

GETTING AROUND

Getting around East Africa is a big part of the fun of travelling there. For budget travellers, and for some midrange travellers, buses are likely to be the main form of transport. However, it's quite possible to break this up with a hired vehicle (arranged either through a safari operator or a lodge in safari areas) for visits to national parks or to reach places that might otherwise be inaccessible.

For specifics of getting around each country, see the country chapter Transport sections.

AIR

While air service within East Africa is relatively reliable, cancellations and delays should still be expected at any time of year. Always reconfirm your ticket, and allow cushion time between regional and intercontinental flights.

Airlines in East Africa

For airlines flying within East Africa, see the country chapter Transport sections.

BICYCLE

Cycling is an excellent way to explore East Africa if you have time and a sense of adventure. Main sealed roads are best avoided (as traffic moves dangerously fast) but secondary roads can be ideal. Because of the distances involved, you'll need to plan your food and water needs in advance, and to pay attention to choosing a route. Throughout much of the region, cycling is best well away from urban areas, in the early morning and late afternoon hours, and in the cooler, dry season between June and August. When calculating daily distances, plan on taking a break from the midday heat, and don't count on covering as much territory each day as you might in a northern European climate.

Mountain bikes are best for flexibility and local terrain, and should be brought from home. While single-speed bicycles (and occasionally mountain bikes) can be rented in many towns (ask hotel staff or inquire at the local bicycle repair stand), they're only suitable for short rides.

Other things to consider when planning are water (carry at least 4L), rampaging motorists (a small rear-view mirror is a worthwhile investment), sleeping (bring a tent) and punctures (thorn trees are a problem in some areas). Bring sufficient spares (including several spare inner tubes, a spare tyre and plenty of tube patches), and be proficient at repairs. Cycling isn't permitted in national parks or wildlife reserves.

Bicycles can be transported on minibuses and buses (though for express or luxury buses, you may need to make advance arrangements with the driver to stow your bike in the hold). There's also no problem and no additional cost to bring your bicycle on any of the region's lake or coastal ferries.

As elsewhere in the world, don't leave your bike unattended unless it's locked, and secure all removable pieces. Taking your bike into a hotel room is generally no problem (and is a good idea). A highly recommended contact is the US-based **International Bicycle Fund** (www.ibike.org/bikeafrica), a socially conscious, low-budget organisation that arranges tours in East Africa and provides information. Also see the country chapter Transport sections.

BOAT

On the Tanzanian section of Lake Victoria, there are passenger boats connecting Mwanza (Tanzania) with Bukoba, Ukerewe Island and various lakeside villages. In the Kenyan section of the lake, small boats connect the mainland around Mbita Point with Mfangano, Rusinga and the Takawiri Islands. In Uganda small boats connect mainland villages with the Ssese Islands; there are also regular cargo boats from Kampala to Mwanza that accept passengers.

On Lake Tanganyika, a passenger ferry connects Kigoma (Tanzania) with Mpulungu (Zambia). There are also cargo services that take passengers between Kigoma and Bujumbura, between Kagunga (north of Gombe Stream park) and Nyanza-Lac in Burundi, and Kigoma and Kalemie (DR C). On Lake Nyasa, the main route is between Mbamba Bay and Itungi (both in Tanzania),

---

DHOW TRAVEL

With their billowing sails and graceful forms, these ancient sailing vessels have become a symbol of East Africa for adventure travellers. Yet, despite their romantic reputation, the realities can be quite different.

If winds are favourable and the water calm, dhow travel can be enjoyable, and will give you a better sense of the centuries of trade that shaped East Africa's coastal communities. If you're becalmed miles from your destination, or in a leaky, overloaded boat on rough seas, if it's raining, or if the sun is very strong, the experience will be considerably less pleasant.

Before undertaking a longer journey, test things out with a short sunset or afternoon sail. Coastal hotels are generally good contacts for arranging reliable dhow travel. If you do decide to give a local dhow a try consider the following:

- Be prepared for rough conditions. There are no facilities on board, except possibly a toilet hanging off the stern. As sailings are wind and tide dependent, departures are often during predawn hours.

- Journeys can take much longer than anticipated; bring plenty of extra water and sufficient food.

- Sunblock, a hat and a covering are essential, as is waterproofing for your luggage, and a rain jacket.

- Boats capsize and people are killed each year. Avoid overloaded boats and don't set sail in bad weather.

- Travel with the winds, which blow from south to north from approximately July to September and north to south from approximately November to late February.

Note that what Westerners refer to as dhows are called either *jahazi* or *mashua* by most Swahili speakers. *Jahazi* are large, lateen-sailed boats. *Mashua* are smaller, and often with proportionately wider hulls and a motor. The *dau* has a sloped stem and stern. On lakes and inland waterways, the *mtumbwi* (dugout canoe) is in common use. Coastal areas, especially Zanzibar's east-coast beaches, are good places to see *ngalawa* (outrigger canoes).

---

via numerous lakeside villages. There's also a boat between Mbamba Bay and Nkhata Bay (Malawi).

The main coastal routes are between Dar es Salaam, Zanzibar and Pemba (covered in the Tanzania chapter), and the short run between the coast and the Lamu Archipelago (Kenya). There's also sporadic service between Tanga and Pemba in Tanzania.

BUS

Buses are the most useful type of public transport. They're usually faster than trains or trucks, and safer and more comfortable than minibuses. In Kenya and Tanzania you often have the choice of going by 'luxury' or 'ordinary' bus. Luxury buses are more comfortable and more expensive, though not always quicker than ordinary buses. Some also boast the dubious advantage of a video system, usually playing bad movies at full volume for the entire trip. Uganda has mostly ordinary buses, although there are luxury buses on some cross-border routes. There are a few full-size buses in Rwanda and Burundi, although, especially in Burundi, minibuses are the rule.

For details of major bus companies, routes and schedules, see the Transport sections in the country chapters.

CAR & MOTORCYCLE

It's quite feasible to make your way around much of East Africa by car or motorcycle, though it's generally only an option used by those already living in the region with local driving knowledge and access to their own vehicle (as rentals are expensive).

Throughout East Africa, main roads are sealed and in reasonable states of repair. In rural areas, however, they range from decent to terrible, especially in the wet season when many secondary routes become impassable. Many trips in more remote areas require 4WD; motorcycles generally aren't permitted in national parks.

Whether you drive your own or a rental vehicle, expect stops at checkpoints where police and border officials will ask to see your driving licence, insurance paperwork and vehicle papers.

Bring Your Own Vehicle

To bring your own vehicle into East Africa you'll need to arrange a *carnet de passage*. This document allows you to take a vehicle duty-free into a country where duties would normally be payable. It guarantees that if a vehicle is taken into a country but not exported, the organisation that issued the *carnet* will accept responsibility for payment of import duties (generally between 100% and 150% of the new value of the vehicle). The *carnet* should also specify any expensive spare parts that you'll be carrying.

To get a *carnet*, contact your national motoring organisation at home, which will give you an indemnity form for completion by either a bank or an insurance company. Once you have deposited a bond with a bank or paid an insurance premium, the motoring organisation will issue the *carnet*. The cost of the *carnet* itself is minimal; allow at least a week to complete the process.

For longer trips, in addition to a *carnet* and mechanical knowledge, bring along a good collection of spares.

Driving Licence

If you're taking your own vehicle or are considering hiring one in East Africa, arrange an International Driving Permit (IDP) before leaving home. They're available at minimal cost through your national motoring organisation.

Fuel & Spare Parts

Fuel costs in the region average US$1.40 per litre of petrol/diesel. Filling and repair stations are readily available in major towns, but scarce elsewhere. In many areas, diesel is often easier to find than petrol. Top your tank up whenever you get the opportunity and carry basic spares. For travel in remote areas and in national parks, also carry jerry cans with extra fuel. Petrol sold on the roadside is unreliable, as it's often diluted with water or kerosene.

Hire

Car, 4WD and motorcycle hire is expensive throughout the region, averaging US$100 to US$170 per day for a 4WD. Few agencies offer unlimited kilometres, and many require that you take a chauffeur (which is a good idea anyway). For self-drive rentals you'll need a driving licence and often an International Driving Permit as well. If you'll be crossing any borders, you'll need to arrange the necessary paperwork with the hire agency in advance.

Insurance

Throughout the region, liability insurance must generally be bought at the border upon entry. While cost and quality vary, in many cases you may find that you are effectively travelling uninsured, as there's often no way to collect on the insurance. With vehicle rentals – even if you're covered from other sources – it's a good idea to take the full coverage offered by hire companies.

Road Rules

Tanzania, Kenya and Uganda follow the British keep-left traffic system. In Rwanda and Burundi, driving is on the right-hand side. At roundabouts throughout the region, traffic already in the roundabout has the right of way.

Night-time road travel isn't recommended anywhere; if you must drive at night, be alert for stopped vehicles in the roadway without lights or hazard warnings. If you're not used to driving in Africa, watch out for pedestrians, children and animals, as well as for

---

BUS SAFETY

Public transport is a fine (and often the only) choice for getting around East Africa, but be savvy when using local buses and minibuses. Never accept food and drink from fellow passengers, even if it appears to be sealed. Avoid night travel, especially on long-distance routes such as Nairobi–Kampala. Be especially wary of pick-pockets on minibuses, and when boarding. At bus stations, keep your luggage compact and your valuables well-concealed. Road safety is a major issue. Get advice from the country chapters of this book, and locally, about the best (safest) bus lines, and stick to established lines.

oncoming vehicles on the wrong side of the road. Especially in rural areas, remember that many people have never driven themselves and are not aware of necessary braking distances and similar concepts; moderate your speed accordingly. Tree branches placed in the roadway are used to signal a stopped vehicle or other problem ahead, and indicate that speed should be reduced. Passing (including on curves or other areas with poor visibility) is common practice and a cause of frequent accidents.

HITCHING

Hitching may be your only option in remote areas, although it's rare that you'll get a free ride unless you're lucky enough to be offered a lift by resident expats, well-off locals or aid workers – even then, at least offer to make a contribution for petrol on longer journeys, or to pick up a meal tab. To flag down a vehicle, hold out your hand at about waist level and wave it up and down, with the palm to the ground; the common Western gesture of holding out your thumb isn't used.

A word of warning about taking lifts in private cars: smuggling across borders is common practice, and if whatever is being smuggled is found, you may be arrested even though you knew nothing about it. Most travellers manage to convince police that they were merely hitching a ride (passport stamps are a good indication of this), but the convincing can take a long time.

As in other parts of the world, hitching is never entirely safe, and we don't recommend it. Those travellers who decide to hitch should understand that they are taking a potentially serious risk. If you do hitch, you'll be safer doing so in pairs and letting someone know of your plans.

LOCAL TRANSPORT
Minibus

Most East Africans rely heavily on minibuses for transport. They're called *matatus* in Kenya, *dalla-dallas* in Tanzania, and taxis or *matatus* in Uganda. Except in Rwanda and Burundi, minibuses are invariably packed to bursting point, and this – combined with excessive speed, poor maintenance and driver recklessness – means that they're not the safest way of getting around. In fact, they can be downright dangerous, and newspaper reports of *matatu* and *dalla-dalla* crashes are a regular

feature. In Rwanda and Burundi travelling in minibuses is generally safer. If you have a large backpack, think twice about boarding, especially at rush hour, when it will make the already crowded conditions even more uncomfortable for others.

Taxi

In Kenya, northern Tanzania and Uganda shared taxis operate on some routes. These officially take between five and nine passengers, depending on size, leave when full and are usually faster, though more expensive, than bus travel. They're marginally more comfortable than minibuses, but have their share of accidents. Private taxis for hire are found in all major towns.

Truck

In remote areas trucks may be the only form of transport, and they're invariably the cheapest. For most regular runs there will be a 'fare', which is more or less fixed and is what the locals pay. It's usually equivalent to, or a bit less than, the bus fare for the same route. For a place in the cab, expect to pay about twice what it costs to travel on top of the load.

Many truck lifts are arranged the night before departure at the 'truck park' – a compound or dust patch that you'll find in most towns. Ask around for a truck that's going your way, and be prepared to wait, especially on remote routes where there may be trucks leaving only once or twice a week. For longer trips, ask what to do about food and drink, and bring plenty of extra drinking water – enough for yourself and to share.

TOURS

For safari and trekking operators, see p60. Many of the companies listed in this book can also organise local itineraries in addition to your safari or trek. For local tour operators, see listings in town sections of the country chapters.

TRAVEL TIP

Use only reliable hotel taxis, or those from established ranks, and avoid freelancers (known in Swahili-speaking areas as 'taxi bubu'). Also avoid taking *matatus*, *dalla-dallas*, *boda-bodas* and the like after dark.

TRAIN

The main passenger lines are the Nairobi–Mombasa route (Kenya), the Tazara 'express' line from Dar es Salaam to Mbeya (Tanzania), and the meandering Central line connecting Dar es Salaam with Mwanza and Kigoma (Tanzania), although the section between Dar es Salaam and Dodoma is currently closed.

First class costs about double what the bus would cost, but is well worth it for the additional comfort. Second class is reasonably comfortable, but the savings over 1st class are marginal. Economy-class travel is cheap, crowded and uncomfortable. There are no assigned seats, and for long trips you'll probably wind up sitting and sleeping on the floor.

Reservations for 1st class are best made as early as possible, although sometimes you'll get lucky and be able to book a cabin on the day of travel.

In all classes, keep an eye on your luggage, especially at stops. Particularly in 1st and 2nd class, make sure the window is jammed shut at night to avoid the possibility of someone entering when the train stops (there's usually a piece of wood provided for this), and keep your cabin door shut.

Food and drink (mainly soft drinks) are available on trains and from station vendors, although it's a good idea to bring sandwiches and extra water. Have plenty of small change handy.

TRANSPORT
IN EAST AFRICA

Health Dr Caroline Evans

CONTENTS

As long as you stay up to date with your vaccinations and take some basic preventive measures, you'd have to be pretty unlucky to succumb to most of the health hazards covered in this chapter. While East Africa has an impressive selection of tropical diseases on offer, you're much more likely to get a bout of diarrhoea, a cold or an infected mosquito bite than an exotic disease such as sleeping sickness. When it comes to injuries (as opposed to illness), the most likely reason for needing medical help in the region is as a result of road accidents – vehicles are rarely well maintained, the roads are potholed and poorly lit, and drink driving is common in the region.

BEFORE YOU GO

A little planning before departure, particularly for pre-existing illnesses, will save you a lot of trouble later. Before a long trip get a check-up from your dentist and from your doctor if you take any regular medication or have a chronic illness, such as high blood pressure or asthma. You should also organise spare contact lenses and glasses (and take your optical prescription with you), get a first aid and medical kit together and arrange necessary vaccinations.

It's tempting to leave it all to the last minute – don't! Many vaccines don't take effect until two weeks after you've been immunised, so visit a doctor four to eight weeks before departure. Ask your doctor for an International Certificate of Vaccination (otherwise known as the yellow booklet), which will list all the vaccinations you've received. This is mandatory for many African countries, including some in East Africa, that require proof of yellow fever vaccination upon entry, but it's a good idea to carry it anyway, wherever you travel.

Travellers can register with the **International Association for Medical Advice to Travellers** (IAMAT; www.iamat.org). Its website can help travellers to find a doctor who has recognised training. Those heading off to very remote areas might like to do a first aid course (contact the Red Cross or St John Ambulance) or attend a remote medicine first aid course, such as that offered by the **Royal Geographical Society** (www.wildernessmedicaltraining.co.uk; prices vary according to courses chosen).

If you are bringing medications with you, carry them in their original containers, clearly labelled. A signed and dated letter from your physician describing all medical conditions and medications, including generic names, is also a good idea. If carrying syringes or needles be sure to have a physician's letter documenting their medical necessity.

How do you go about getting the best possible medical help? It's difficult to say – it really depends on the severity of your illness or injury and the availability of local help. If malaria is suspected, seek medical help as soon as possible or begin self-medicating if you are off the beaten track (see p630).

INSURANCE

Find out in advance whether your insurance plan will make payments directly to providers or will reimburse you later for overseas health expenditures (throughout the region, most doctors will expect payment in cash). It's vital to ensure that your travel insurance will cover the emergency transport required to get you to a hospital in a major city, to better medical facilities elsewhere in the region, or all the way home, by air and with a medical attendant if necessary. Not all insurance covers this, so check the contract carefully. If you need medical help, your insurance company might be able to help locate the nearest hospital or clinic, or you can ask at your hotel. In an emergency, contact your embassy or consulate.

Membership of the **African Medical & Research Foundation** (Amref; www.amref.org) provides an air evacuation service in medical emergencies that covers most of East Africa, as well as air ambulance transfers between medical facilities. Money paid by members for this service goes into providing grass-roots medical assistance for local people (see p609 for more).

RECOMMENDED VACCINATIONS

The **World Health Organization** (www.who.int/en/) recommends that all travellers be covered for diphtheria, tetanus, measles, mumps, rubella and polio, as well as for hepatitis B, regardless of their destination. The planning stage before travel is a great time to ensure that all routine vaccination cover is complete. The consequences of these diseases can be severe, and outbreaks of them do occur.

According to the **Centers for Disease Control & Prevention** (www.cdc.gov), the following vaccinations are recommended for all parts of Africa, including East Africa: hepatitis A, hepatitis B, meningococcal meningitis, rabies and typhoid, and boosters for tetanus, diphtheria and measles. Yellow fever is required for Rwanda and recommended for elsewhere in the region, and the certificate is an entry requirement for many other countries (see p632).

MEDICAL CHECKLIST

It is a very good idea to carry a medical and first aid kit with you, to help yourself in the case of minor illness or injury. The following is a list of items you should consider packing.

- Acetaminophen (paracetamol) or aspirin
- Acetazolamide (Diamox) for altitude sickness (prescription only)
- Adhesive or paper tape
- Antibacterial ointment (eg Bactroban) for cuts and abrasions (prescription only)
- Antibiotics (prescription only), eg ciprofloxacin (Ciproxin) or norfloxacin (Utinor)
- Antidiarrhoeal drugs (eg loperamide)
- Antihistamines (for hayfever and allergic reactions)
- Anti-inflammatory drugs (eg ibuprofen)
- Antimalaria pills
- Bandages, gauze, gauze rolls
- DEET-containing insect repellent for the skin
- Permethrin-containing insect spray for clothing and tents, and bed nets
- Pocket knife
- Rehydration salts (oral)
- Scissors, safety pins, tweezers
- Sterile needles, syringes and fluids if travelling to remote areas
- Steroid cream or hydrocortisone cream (for allergic rashes)
- Sunblock
- Thermometer
- Water purification tablets (iodine)

If you are travelling through a malarial area, particularly an area where falciparum malaria predominates (see p630), consider taking a self-diagnostic kit that can identify malaria in the blood from a finger prick.

INTERNET RESOURCES

There is a wealth of travel health advice on the internet. For further information, the **Lonely Planet website** (www.lonelyplanet.com) is a good place to start. The World Health Organization publishes a superb book, also available online for free, called **International Travel & Health** (www.who.int/ith/), which is revised annually. Other websites of interest are **MD Travel Health** (www.mdtravelhealth.com), which provides complete travel health recommendations for every country, and is updated daily, also at no cost; the **Centers for Disease Control & Prevention** (www.cdc.gov); and **Fit for Travel** (www.fitfortravel.scot.nhs.uk), which has up-to-date information and is user-friendly.

It's also a good idea to consult your government's travel health website before departure, if one is available:

Australia (www.dfat.gov.au/travel)
Canada (www.phac-aspc.gc.ca/tmp-pmv/index.html)
UK (www.dh.gov.uk/en/Healthcare/Healthadvicefortravellers/index.htm)
USA (www.cdc.gov/travel)

FURTHER READING

- *A Comprehensive Guide to Wilderness and Travel Medicine* by Eric A Weiss (1998)
- *Healthy Travel* by Jane Wilson-Howarth (1999)
- *Healthy Travel Africa* by Isabelle Young (2000)
- *How to Stay Healthy Abroad* by Richard Dawood (2002)
- *Travel in Health* by Graham Fry (1994)
- *Travel with Children* by Cathy Lanigan (2004)

IN TRANSIT

DEEP VEIN THROMBOSIS (DVT)

Blood clots can form in the legs during flights, chiefly because of prolonged immobility. This formation of clots is known as deep vein thrombosis (DVT), and the longer the flight, the greater the risk to the passenger. Although most blood clots are reabsorbed uneventfully, some might break off and travel through the blood vessels to the lungs, where they could cause life-threatening complications.

The chief symptom of DVT is swelling or pain of the foot, ankle or calf, usually – but not always – on just one side. When a blood clot travels to the lungs, it can cause chest pain and breathing difficulty. Travellers with any of these symptoms should immediately seek medical attention.

To prevent the development of DVT on long flights you should walk around the cabin, perform isometric compressions of the leg muscles (ie contract the leg muscles while sitting), drink plenty of fluids and avoid alcohol.

JET LAG & MOTION SICKNESS

If you're crossing more than five time zones you could suffer jet lag, resulting in insomnia, fatigue, malaise or nausea. To avoid jet lag try drinking plenty of fluids (nonalcoholic) and eating light meals. Upon arrival, get exposure to natural sunlight and readjust your schedule (for meals, sleep, etc) as soon as possible.

Antihistamines such as dimenhydrinate (Dramamine) and meclizine (Antivert, Bonine) are usually the first port of call for treating motion sickness. The main side effect of these drugs is some drowsiness. A herbal alternative is ginger (in the form of ginger tea, biscuits or crystallized ginger), which works like a charm for some people.

IN EAST AFRICA

AVAILABILITY & COST OF HEALTH CARE

Good, Western-style medical care is available in Nairobi (which is the main medical hub for the region and the main regional destination for medical evacuations), and to a lesser extent in Dar es Salaam, Kampala and other major cities. Elsewhere, reasonable to good care is available in larger towns, and in some mission stations, though availability is extremely patchy once off the beaten track. In general, private or mission-run clinics and hospitals are better equipped than government ones. If you fall ill in an unfamiliar area, ask staff at a top-end hotel or resident expatriates where the best nearby medical facilities are, and in an emergency contact your embassy. Most towns in the region have at least one clinic where you can get an inexpensive malaria test and, if necessary, treatment. With dental treatment, be aware that there is often an increased risk of hepatitis B and HIV transmission via poorly sterilised equipment.

Most drugs can be purchased over the counter in East Africa, without a prescription. However, there are often problems with ineffectiveness, if the drugs are counterfeit, for example, or if they have not been stored under the right conditions. The most common examples of counterfeit drugs are malaria tablets and expensive antibiotics, such as ciprofloxacin. Most drugs are available in capital cities, but remote villages will be lucky to have a couple of paracetamol tablets. It is strongly recommended that all drugs for chronic diseases be brought from home.

There can be a high risk of contracting HIV from infected blood if receive a blood transfusion. To minimise this, seek out treatment in reputable clinics, such as those recommended in the country chapters of this book. If you have any doubts, the **BloodCare Foundation** (www.bloodcare.org.uk) is a useful source of safe, screened blood, which can be transported to any part of the world within 24 hours.

INFECTIOUS DISEASES

It's a long list, but a few precautions go a long way…

Bilharzia (Schistosomiasis)

This disease is spread by flukes (minute worms) that are carried by a species of freshwater snail. The flukes are carried inside the snail, which then sheds them into slow-moving or still water. The parasites penetrate human skin during swimming, and then migrate to the bladder or bowel. They are passed out via stool or urine and can contaminate fresh water, where the cycle starts again. Do not paddle or swim in any freshwater lakes or slow-running rivers anywhere in East Africa unless you have reliable confirmation that they are bilharzia-free. There might be no symptoms. There might be a transient fever and rash, and advanced cases might have blood in the stool or in the urine. A blood test can detect antibodies if you might have been exposed, and treatment is then possible in specialist travel or infectious disease clinics. If not treated the infection can cause kidney failure or permanent bowel damage. It is not possible for you to infect others.

Cholera

Cholera is usually only a problem during natural or artificial disasters – such as war, floods or earthquakes – although small outbreaks, including in East Africa, also occur at other times. Travellers are rarely affected. It is caused by a bacteria and spread via contaminated drinking water. The main symptom is profuse watery diarrhoea, which causes debilitation if fluids are not replaced quickly. An oral cholera vaccine is available in the USA, but it is not particularly effective. Most cases of cholera could be avoided by close attention to good drinking water and by avoiding potentially contaminated food. Treatment is by fluid replacement (orally or via a drip), but sometimes antibiotics are needed. Self-treatment is not advised.

Diphtheria

Found throughout East Africa, diphtheria is spread through close respiratory contact. It usually causes a temperature and a severe sore throat. Sometimes a membrane forms across the throat, and a tracheostomy is needed to prevent suffocation. Vaccination is recommended for those likely to be in close contact with the local population in infected areas and is more important for long stays than for short-term trips. The vaccine is given as an injection, alone or with tetanus, and lasts 10 years.

Filariasis

Tiny worms migrating in the lymphatic system cause filariasis. The bite from an infected mosquito spreads the infection. Symptoms include localised itching and swelling of the legs and/or genitalia. Treatment is available.

Hepatitis A

Hepatitis A is spread through contaminated food (particularly shellfish) and water. It causes jaundice and, although it is rarely fatal, it can cause prolonged lethargy and delayed recovery. If you've had hepatitis A, you shouldn't drink alcohol for up to six months afterwards, but once you've recovered, there won't be any long-term problems. The first symptoms include dark urine and a yellow colour to the whites of the eyes. Sometimes a fever and abdominal pain might be present. Hepatitis A vaccine (Avaxim, VAQTA, Havrix) is given as an injection: a single dose will give protection for up to a year, and a booster after a year gives 10-year protection. Hepatitis A and typhoid vaccines can also be given as a single dose vaccine (hepatyrix or viatim).

Hepatitis B

Hepatitis B is spread through infected blood, contaminated needles and sexual intercourse. It can also be spread from an infected mother to the baby during childbirth. It affects the liver, causing jaundice and occasionally liver failure. Most people recover completely, but some people might be chronic carriers of the virus, which could lead eventually to cirrhosis or liver cancer. Those visiting high-risk areas for long periods or those with increased social or occupational risk should be immunised. Many countries now routinely give hepatitis B as part of their routine childhood vaccination program. It is given singly or can be given at the same time as hepatitis A (hepatyrix).

A course will give protection for at least five years. It can be given over four weeks or six months.

HIV

Human immunodeficiency virus (HIV), the virus that causes acquired immune deficiency syndrome (AIDS), is an enormous problem throughout East Africa. The virus is spread through infected blood and blood products, by sexual intercourse with an infected partner and from an infected mother to her baby during childbirth and breastfeeding. It can

HEALTH

be spread through 'blood to blood' contacts, such as with contaminated instruments during medical, dental, acupuncture and other body-piercing procedures, and through sharing used intravenous needles. At present there is no cure; medication that might keep the disease under control is available, but these drugs are too expensive for the majority of East Africans, and are not readily available for travellers either. If you think you might have been infected with HIV, a blood test is necessary; a three-month gap after exposure and before testing is required to allow antibodies to appear in the blood.

Malaria

One million children die annually from malaria in Africa. It is endemic throughout East Africa (except at altitudes higher than 2000m, where risk of transmission is low). The disease is caused by a parasite in the bloodstream spread via the bite of the female Anopheles mosquito. There are several types of malaria, with falciparum malaria the most dangerous type and the predominant form in the region. Infection rates vary with climate and season. Rates are higher during the rainy season, but the risk exists year-round, and it is extremely important to take preventive measures, even if you will just be in East Africa for a short time.

Unlike most other diseases regularly encountered by travellers, there is no vaccination against malaria (yet). However, several different drugs are used to prevent malaria, and new ones are in the pipeline. Up-to-date advice from a travel health clinic is essential as some medication is more suitable for some travellers than others. The pattern of drug-resistant malaria is changing rapidly, so what was advised several years ago might no longer be the case.

Malaria can present in several ways. The early stages include headaches, fevers, generalised aches and pains, and malaise, which could be mistaken for flu. Other symptoms can include abdominal pain, diarrhoea and a cough. Anyone who develops a fever in a malarial area should assume malarial infection until a blood test proves negative, even if you have been taking antimalarial medication. If not treated, the next stage could develop within 24 hours, particularly if falciparum malaria is the parasite: jaundice, then reduced consciousness and coma (also known as cerebral malaria) followed by death. Treatment in hospital is essential, and the death rate might still be as high as 10% even in the best intensive-care facilities.

Many travellers are under the impression that malaria is a mild illness, that treatment is always easy and successful, and that taking antimalarial drugs causes more illness through side effects than actually getting malaria. This is unfortunately not true. Side effects of the medication depend on the drug being taken. Doxycycline can cause heartburn and indigestion; mefloquine (Larium) can cause anxiety attacks, insomnia and nightmares, and (rarely) severe psychiatric disorders; chloroquine can cause nausea and hair loss; and proguanil can cause mouth ulcers. These side effects are not universal, and can be minimized by taking medication correctly, eg with food. Also, some people should not take a particular antimalarial drug, eg people with epilepsy should avoid mefloquine, and doxycycline should not be taken by pregnant women or children younger than 12.

If you decide that you really do not wish to take antimalarial drugs, you must understand the risks, and be obsessive about avoiding mosquito bites. Use nets and insect repellent, and report any fever or flulike symptoms to a doctor as soon as possible. Some people advocate homeopathic preparations against malaria, such as Demal200, but as yet there is no conclusive evidence that this is effective, and many homeopaths do not recommend their use.

People of all ages can contract malaria, and falciparum causes the most severe illness. Repeated infections may result eventually in a less serious illness. Malaria in pregnancy frequently results in miscarriage or premature labour. Adults who have survived childhood malaria have developed immunity and usually only develop mild cases of malaria; most Western travellers have no immunity at all. Immunity wanes after 18 months of nonexposure, so even if you have had malaria in the past and used to live in a malaria-prone area, you might no longer be immune.

If you are planning a journey through a malarial area, and particularly where falciparum malaria predominates, such as much of East Africa, consider taking standby treatment. Emergency standby treatment should be seen as emergency treatment aimed at saving the patient's life, and not as routine self-medication. It should be used only if you will

---

ANTIMALARIAL A TO D

A Awareness of the risk – no medication is totally effective, but protection of up to 95% is achievable with most drugs, as long as other measures have been taken.

B Bites – avoid them at all costs. Sleep in a screened room, use a mosquito spray or coils, sleep under a permethrin-impregnated net at night. Cover up at night with long trousers and long sleeves, preferably with permethrin-treated clothing. Apply appropriate repellent to all areas of exposed skin in the evenings.

C Chemical prevention – antimalarial drugs are usually needed in malarial areas. Expert advice is required, as resistance patterns can change and new drugs are always in development. Not all antimalarial drugs are suitable for everyone. Most antimalarial drugs need to be started at least a week in advance and continued for four weeks after the last possible exposure to malaria.

D Diagnosis – if you have a fever or flulike illness within a year of travel to a malarial area, malaria is a possibility, and immediate medical attention is necessary.

---

be far from medical facilities (more than 24 hours away from medical help) and have been advised about the symptoms of malaria and how to use the medication. Medical advice should be sought as soon as possible to confirm whether the treatment has been successful. The type of standby treatment used will depend on local conditions, such as drug resistance, and on what antimalarial drugs were being used before standby treatment. The goal is to avoid contracting cerebral malaria, which affects the brain and central nervous system and can be fatal in 24 hours. As mentioned on p627, self-diagnostic kits, which can identify malaria in the blood from a finger prick, are also available in the West.

The risks from malaria to both mother and foetus during pregnancy are considerable. Unless good medical care can be guaranteed, travel throughout Africa when pregnant – particularly to malarial areas – should be discouraged unless essential.

Meningococcal Meningitis

Meningococcal infection is spread through close respiratory contact and is more likely in crowded situations, such as dormitories, buses and clubs. Infection is uncommon in travellers. Vaccination is particularly recommended for long stays and is especially important towards the end of the dry season. Symptoms include a fever, severe headache, neck stiffness and a red rash. Immediate medical treatment is necessary.

The ACWY vaccine is recommended for all travellers in sub-Saharan Africa. This vaccine is different from the meningococcal meningitis C vaccine given to children and adolescents in some countries; it is safe to be given both types of vaccine.

Onchocerciasis (River Blindness)

This is caused by the larvae of a tiny worm, which is spread by the bite of a small fly. The earliest sign of infection is intensely itchy, red, sore eyes. Travellers are rarely severely affected. Treatment in a specialised clinic is curative.

Poliomyelitis (Polio)

Generally spread through contaminated food and water. Vaccination is usually given in childhood and should be boosted every 10 years, either orally (a drop on the tongue) or as an injection. Polio can be carried asymptomatically (ie showing no symptoms) and can cause a transient fever. In rare cases it causes weakness or paralysis of one or more muscles, which may be permanent.

Rabies

Rabies is spread by receiving the bites or licks of an infected animal on broken skin. It is always fatal once the clinical symptoms start (which might be months after an infected bite), so postbite vaccination should be given as soon as possible. Postbite vaccination (whether or not you've been vaccinated before the bite) prevents the virus from spreading to the central nervous system. Animal handlers should be vaccinated, as should those travelling to remote areas where a reliable source of postbite vaccine is not available. Three preventive injections are needed over a month. If you haven't been vaccinated you will need a course of five injections starting 24 hours or as soon as possible after the injury. If you have been vaccinated, you will need fewer postbite injections, and have more time to seek medical help.

HEALTH

Rift Valley Fever

This fever is spread occasionally via mosquito bites. The symptoms are of a fever and flulike illness; and the good news is, it's rarely fatal.

Trypanosomiasis (Sleeping Sickness)

Spread via the bite of the tsetse fly. It causes a headache, fever and eventually coma. If you have these symptoms and have negative malaria tests, have yourself evaluated by a reputable clinic, where you should also be able to obtain treatment for trypanosomiasis.

Tuberculosis (TB)

TB is spread through close respiratory contact and occasionally through infected milk or milk products. BCG vaccination is recommended for those likely to be mixing closely with the local population, although it gives only moderate protection against TB. It is more important for long stays than for short-term visits. Inoculation with the BCG vaccine is not available in all countries, but it is given routinely to many children in developing nations. The vaccination causes a small permanent scar at the site of injection, and is usually given in a specialised chest clinic. It is a live vaccine and should not be given to pregnant women or immunocompromised individuals.

TB can be asymptomatic, only being picked up on a routine chest X-ray. Alternatively, it can cause a cough, weight loss or fever, months or even years after exposure.

Typhoid

This is spread through food or water contaminated by infected human faeces. The first symptom is usually a fever or a pink rash on the abdomen. Sometimes septicaemia (blood poisoning) can occur. A typhoid vaccine (typhim Vi, typherix) will give protection for three years. In some countries, the oral vaccine Vivotif is also available. Antibiotics are usually given as treatment, and death is rare unless septicaemia occurs.

Yellow Fever

Tanzania, Kenya, Uganda and Burundi no longer officially require you to carry a certificate of yellow fever vaccination unless you're arriving from an infected area (which includes from anywhere in East Africa). However, it's still sometimes asked for at some borders, and is a requirement in some neighbouring countries, including Rwanda. When trying to decide whether to get jabbed or not, it's also worth considering that the vaccine is recommended for most visitors to Africa by the **Centers for Disease Control & Prevention** (www.cdc .gov). Also, there is always the possibility that a traveller without a legally required, up-to-date certificate will be vaccinated and detained in isolation at the port of arrival for up to 10 days, or possibly even repatriated.

Yellow fever is spread by infected mosquitoes. Symptoms range from a flulike illness to severe hepatitis (liver inflammation) jaundice and death. The yellow fever vaccination must be given at a designated clinic and is valid for 10 years. It is a live vaccine and must not be given to immunocompromised or pregnant travellers.

TRAVELLER'S DIARRHOEA

Although it's not inevitable that you will get diarrhoea while travelling in East Africa, it's certainly very likely. Diarrhoea is the most common travel-related illness – figures suggest that at least half of all travellers to Africa will get diarrhoea at some stage. Sometimes dietary changes, such as increased spices or oils, are the cause. To help prevent diarrhoea, avoid tap water unless you're sure it's safe to drink (see p635). You should also only eat fresh fruits or vegetables if cooked or peeled, and be wary of dairy products that might contain unpasteurised milk. Although freshly cooked food can often be a safe option, plates or serving utensils might be dirty, so you should be highly selective when eating food from street vendors (make sure that cooked food is piping hot all the way through). If you develop diarrhoea, be sure to drink plenty of fluids – preferably lots of an oral rehydration solution containing water, and some salt and sugar. A few loose stools don't require treatment but, if you start having more than four or five stools a day, you should start taking an antibiotic (usually a quinoline drug, such as ciprofloxacin or norfloxacin) and an antidiarrhoeal agent (such as loperamide) if you are not within easy reach of a toilet. If diarrhoea is bloody, persists for more than 72 hours or is accompanied by fever, shaking chills or severe abdominal pain, you should seek medical attention.

Amoebic Dysentery

Contracted by consuming contaminated food and water, amoebic dysentery causes blood and mucus in the faeces. It can be relatively mild and tends to come on gradually, but seek medical advice if you think you have the illness, as it won't clear up without treatment (which is with specific antibiotics).

Giardiasis

This, like amoebic dysentery, is also caused by ingesting contaminated food or water. The illness usually appears a week or more after you have been exposed to the offending parasite. Giardiasis might cause only a short-lived bout of typical traveller's diarrhoea, but it can also cause persistent diarrhoea. Ideally, seek medical advice if you suspect you have giardiasis, but if you are in a remote area you could start a course of antibiotics, with medical follow-up when feasible.

ENVIRONMENTAL HAZARDS
Altitude Sickness

The lack of oxygen at high altitudes (over 2500m) affects most people to some extent. Symptoms of Acute Mountain Sickness (AMS) usually develop in the first 24 hours at altitude but may be delayed up to three weeks. Mild symptoms are headache, lethargy, dizziness, difficulty sleeping and loss of appetite. Severe symptoms are breathlessness, a dry, irritative cough (followed by the production of pink, frothy sputum), severe headache, lack of coordination, confusion, vomiting, irrational behaviour, drowsiness and unconsciousness. There's no rule as to what is too high: AMS can be fatal at 3000m, but 3500m to 4500m is the usual range. *Symptoms should never be ignored;* trekkers die every year on East Africa's mountains, notably Mt Kilimanjaro.

Treat mild symptoms by resting at the same altitude until you have recovered, usually a day or two. Paracetamol or aspirin can be taken for headaches. If symptoms persist or grow worse, however, immediate descent is necessary; even 500m can help. Drug treatments should never be used to avoid descent or to enable further ascent. Diamox (acetazolamide) reduces the headache of AMS and helps the body acclimatise to the lack of oxygen. It is only available on prescription.

Suggestions for preventing acute mountain sickness:

- *Ascend slowly* – have frequent rest days; spend two to three nights at each rise of 1000m. Acclimatisation occurs gradually.
- Sleep at a lower altitude than the greatest height reached during the day if possible. Also, once above 3000m, care should be taken not to increase the sleeping altitude by more than 300m per day.
- Drink extra fluids. Monitor hydration by ensuring that urine is clear and plentiful.
- Eat light, high-carbohydrate meals for more energy.
- Avoid alcohol, sedatives and tobacco.

Heat Exhaustion

This condition occurs following heavy sweating and excessive fluid loss with inadequate replacement of fluids and salt, and is particularly common in hot climates when taking unaccustomed exercise before full acclimatisation. Symptoms include headache, dizziness and tiredness. Dehydration is already happening by the time you feel thirsty – aim to drink sufficient water to produce pale, diluted urine. Self-treatment requires fluid replacement with water and/or fruit juice, and cooling by cold water and fans. Treatment of the salt-loss component consists of consuming salty fluids, as in soup, and adding a little more table salt to foods than usual.

Heatstroke

Heat exhaustion is a precursor to the much more serious condition of heatstroke. In this case there is damage to the sweating mechanism, with an excessive rise in body temperature; irrational and hyperactive behaviour; and eventually loss of consciousness and death. Rapid cooling by spraying the body with water and fanning is ideal. Emergency fluid and electrolyte replacement is usually also required by intravenous drip.

Hypothermia

Too much cold can be just as dangerous as too much heat. If you are trekking at high altitudes, such as on Mt Kilimanjaro or Mt Kenya, you'll need to have appropriate clothing and be prepared for cold, wet conditions. Even in lower areas, such as the Usambara Mountains, the rim of Ngorongoro Crater or the Ulugurus, conditions can be wet and quite chilly.

Hypothermia occurs when the body loses heat faster than it can produce it and the core temperature of the body falls. It is surprisingly easy to progress from being very cold

HEALTH

TRADITIONAL MEDICINE *Mary Fitzpatrick*

According to some estimates, over 70% of East Africans rely in part or in whole on traditional medicine, and close to two-thirds of the population have traditional healers as their first point of contact in the case of illness. The traditional healer holds a revered position in many communities throughout the region, and traditional medicinal products are widely available in local markets.

In part, the heavy reliance on traditional medicine is because of the high costs of conventional Western-style medicine, because of prevailing cultural attitudes and beliefs, or simply because it sometimes works. Often, though, it's because there is no other choice. In certain areas in Tanzania, for example, it is estimated that while there is only one medical doctor to 33,000 people, there is a traditional healer for approximately every 150 people. While the ratio is better in some parts of the region (and worse in others), hospitals and health clinics are concentrated in urban centres, and many are limited in their effectiveness by insufficient resources, and chronic shortages of equipment and medicine.

Although some traditional remedies seem to work on malaria, sickle cell anaemia, high blood pressure and some AIDS symptoms, most healers learn their art by apprenticeship, so education (and consequently application of knowledge) is inconsistent and unregulated.

Rather than attempting to stamp out traditional practices, or simply pretend they aren't happening, a positive first step taken by some East African countries is the regulation of traditional medicine by creating healers' associations and offering courses on such topics as sanitary practices. On a broader scale, the Organisation of African Unity declared 2001 to 2010 the 'Decade of Traditional Medicine' across the continent.

Under any scenario, it remains unlikely in the short term that even a basic level of conventional Western-style medicine will be made available to all the people of East Africa, even though the cost of doing so is less than the annual military budget of some Western countries. Traditional medicine, on the other hand, will almost certainly continue to be widely practised throughout the region.

---

to being dangerously cold due to a combination of wind, wet clothing, fatigue and hunger, even if the air temperature is above freezing. It is best to dress in layers; silk, wool and some of the new artificial fibres are all good insulating materials. A hat is important, as a lot of heat is lost through the head. A strong, waterproof outer layer (and a 'space' blanket for emergencies) is essential. Carry basic supplies, including food that contains simple sugars to generate heat quickly and fluid to drink.

Symptoms of hypothermia are exhaustion, numb skin (particularly of the toes and fingers), shivering, slurred speech, irrational or violent behaviour, lethargy, stumbling, dizzy spells, muscle cramps and violent bursts of energy. Irrationality may take the form of sufferers claiming they are warm and trying to take off their clothes.

To treat mild hypothermia, first get the person out of the wind and/or rain, remove their clothing if it's wet and replace it with dry, warm clothing. Give them hot liquids – not alcohol – and high-kilojoule, easily digest-ible food. Do not rub victims: allow them to slowly warm themselves instead. This should be enough to treat the early stages of hypothermia. The early recognition and treatment of mild hypothermia is the only way to prevent severe hypothermia, which is a critical condition.

Insect Bites & Stings

Mosquitoes might not always carry malaria or dengue fever, but they (and other insects) can cause irritation and infected bites. To avoid these, take the same precautions as you would for avoiding malaria (see p630). Use DEET-based insect repellents. Excellent clothing treatments are also available, and mosquitos that land on the treated clothing will die.

Bee and wasp stings cause real problems only to those who have a severe allergy to the stings (anaphylaxis.) If you are one of these people, carry an 'epipen' – an adrenaline (epinephrine) injection, which you can give yourself. This could save your life.

Scorpions are frequently found in arid or dry climates. They can cause a painful bite that is sometimes life-threatening. If bitten by a scorpion, seek immediate medical assistance.

Bed bugs are often found in hostels and cheap hotels. They lead to very itchy, lumpy bites. Spraying the mattress with crawling insect killer after changing bedding will get rid of them.

Scabies is also frequently found in cheap accommodation. These tiny mites live in the skin, particularly between the fingers. They cause an intensely itchy rash. The itch is easily treated with malathion and permethrin lotion from a pharmacy; other members of the household also need treatment to avoid spreading scabies, even if they do not show any symptoms.

Snake Bites

Avoid getting bitten! Do not walk barefoot, or stick your hand into holes or cracks. However, 50% of those bitten by venomous snakes are not actually injected with poison (envenomed). If you are bitten by a snake, do not panic. Immobilise the bitten limb with a splint (such as a stick) and apply a bandage over the site, with firm pressure – similar to bandaging a sprain. Do not apply a tourniquet, or cut or suck the bite. Get medical help as soon as possible so antivenom can be given if needed. Try to note the snake's appearance to help in treatment.

Water

Never drink tap water unless it has been boiled, filtered or chemically disinfected (such as with iodine tablets). Never drink from streams, rivers and lakes. It's also best to avoid drinking from pumps and wells – some do bring pure water to the surface, but the presence of animals can still contaminate supplies. When buying bottled water, check to be sure the bottles are properly sealed, and haven't just been refilled with ordinary tap water.

HEALTH

Language

CONTENTS

WHO SPEAKS WHAT WHERE?

In polyglot East Africa you'll find people speaking languages belonging to all four major African ethno-linguistic families. The largest of these is the Niger-Congo family, which encompasses Swahili and other Bantu languages. Others are the Nilo-Saharan family (which includes Nilotic and Nilo-Hamitic languages such as Maasai), and the Afro-Asiatic (or Hamito-Semitic) family, whose Cushitic branch includes Iraqw and Somali. The smallest family is Khoisan, which consists of only a few dozen languages, characterised by their distinctive 'clicks' (where clicking sounds are made by the tongue). The main click languages found in East Africa are Sandawe and, more distantly, Hadza (Hadzabe), both spoken by small, somewhat scattered populations in north-central Tanzania who still follow traditional hunter-gatherer lifestyles.

Throughout the region, attempting to speak even just a few words of Swahili – or whatever the local African language is – will enrich your travels and be greatly appreciated by the people you meet, no matter how rudimentary your attempts. Good luck and *Safari njema!* (happy travels).

Burundi

The official languages are Kirundi and French, although Swahili is also useful. Hardly anyone speaks English, except in Bujumbura.

Democratic Republic of Congo (DRC)

French is the official language and there are four local languages: Swahili, Kikongo, Tshiluba and Lingala. In the eastern part of the country covered in this book, Swahili predominates.

Kenya

English and Swahili are the official languages and are taught in schools throughout Kenya, but Hindi and Urdu are still spoken by south Asian residents.

Most urban Kenyans and even tribal people involved in the tourist industry speak English, and many speak some German or Italian, especially around the coast.

There are many other major tribal languages, including Kikuyu, Luo, Kikamba, Maasai and Samburu, as well as a plethora of minor tribal languages.

Rwanda

The official languages are Kinyarwanda (which also has the status of national language), French and English. Kinyarwanda is the medium of school instruction at primary level, and French is used at secondary level (only 10% of the population reach secondary level). Little English is spoken beyond Kigali, but Swahili can be useful in some areas.

A very useful Kinyarwanda mini-phrasebook is available as a free download from http://rwanda.harvestfields.net/downloads/KinyarwandaPhraseBook.pdf.

Tanzania

Swahili and English are the official languages. English is widely spoken in major towns, but in rural areas it helps to know at least a few Swahili phrases. Outside cities and towns, far fewer people speak English than in comparable areas of Kenya.

The main Swahili dialect on the Tanzanian mainland is Kiunguja (the Swahili of

Zanzibar Island), from which 'standard' Swahili has developed. Over 100 other African languages are spoken, including Sukuma, Makonde, Haya, Ha, Gogo and Yao, all of which belong to the Bantu group, and Maasai, which belongs to the Nilotic ethnolinguistic group.

Uganda

The official languages are English and Swahili, although the latter is not as widely spoken as it is in Tanzania and Kenya. The other major language is Luganda.

A quirk of pronunciation worth noting is that most people in Uganda pronounce the letter **k** as the 'ch' in 'chin' when it is followed by a vowel. For example, Kigali is pronounced 'Chigali' and Lake Kyoga is pronounced 'Lake Chyoga'.

SWAHILI

Standard Swahili is based on the variety of the language spoken in Zanzibar Town, although several other dialects can be found throughout East Africa. Written Swahili – the language of newspapers, textbooks and literature – usually conforms to the coastal standards. This language guide uses the standard variety, as it should be more universally understood.

Although Swahili may initially seem a bit daunting, its structure is fairly regular and pronunciation uncomplicated. You'll soon discover that just a handful of basic words will rapidly break down barriers between you and the many people you meet on your travels in East Africa.

If your time is limited, concentrate first on the greetings and then on numbers (very useful when negotiating with market vendors, taxi drivers etc). The words and phrases included in this chapter will help get you started. For a more comprehensive guide to the language, get hold of Lonely Planet's *Swahili Phrasebook*.

PRONUNCIATION

Perhaps the easiest part of learning Swahili is the pronunciation. Every letter is pronounced, unless it's part of the consonant combinations discussed in the 'Consonants' section below. If a letter is written twice, it is pronounced twice – *mzee* (respected elder)

has three syllables: *m-ZE-e*. Note that the 'm' is a separate syllable, and that the double 'e' indicates a lengthened vowel sound.

Word stress in Swahili almost always falls on the second-to-last syllable.

Vowels

Correct pronunciation of vowels is the key to making yourself understood in Swahili. There's a useful audio pronunciation guide available at www.kamusiproject.org.

If two vowels appear next to each other, each must be pronounced in turn, eg *kawaida* (usual) is pronounced *ka-wa-EE-da*.

a	as in 'calm'
e	as the 'ey' in 'they'
i	as the 'ee' in 'keep'
o	as in 'go'
u	as the 'oo' in 'moon'

Consonants

Most consonants in Swahili have equivalents in English. The sounds **th** and **dh** occur only in words borrowed from Arabic.

r	Swahili speakers make only a slight distinction between **r** and **l**; use a light 'd' for 'r' and you'll be pretty close.
dh	as 'th' in 'this'
th	as 'th' in 'thing'
ny	as the 'ni' in 'onion'
ng	as in 'singer'
gh	like the 'ch' in Scottish *loch*
g	as in 'get'
ch	as in 'church'

ACCOMMODATION

Where's a ...?	... iko wapi?
camping ground	Uwanja wa kambi
guesthouse	Gesti
hotel	Hoteli
youth hostel	Hosteli ya vijana

Can you recommend cheap lodging?
Unaweza kunipendekezea malazi rahisi?
What's the address?
Anwani ni nini?

Do you have a ... room?	Kuna chumba kwa ...?
single	mtu mmoja
double	watu wawili, kitanda kimoja
twin	watu wawili, vitanda viwili
triple	watu watatu

How much is it per day/person?
Ni bei gani kwa siku/mtu?
Can I see the room?
Naomba nione chumba?
Where's the bathroom?
Choo iko wapi?
Where are the toilets?
Vyoo viko wapi?
I'll take it.
Nataka.
I'm leaving now.
Naondoka sasa.

CONVERSATION & ESSENTIALS

Greetings are probably the most important vocabulary for a traveller to East Africa. It's worth taking the time to familiarise yourself with the few we include here.

Jambo is a pidgin Swahili word, used to greet tourists who are presumed not to understand the language. There are two possible responses: *Jambo* (meaning 'Hello, now please speak to me in English'), and *Sijambo* (or 'Things aren't bad with me, and I'm willing to try a little Swahili').

If people assume you can speak a little Swahili, greetings may involve one or a number of the following exchanges:

How are you?	*Hujambo?*
I'm fine.	*Sijambo.*
How are you all?	*Hamjambo?*
We're fine.	*Hatujambo.*

The word *habari* (meaning 'news') can also be used for general greetings. You may hear the word *salama* substituted for *habari*, or the *habari* may be dropped altogether.

How are you?	*Habari?*
How are you all?	*Habari zenu?*
What's the news?	*Habari gani?*
What's happening?	*Habari yako?*
Good morning.	*Habari za asubuhi?*
Good day.	*Habari za leo?*
Good afternoon.	*Habari za mchana?*
Good evening/night.	*Habari za jioni?*

By memorising these three simple words, you can reply to almost anything:

Good.	*Nzuri.*
Fine.	*Salama.*
Clean.	*Safi.*

There is also a respectful greeting for elders:

Greetings.	*Shikamoo.*
Greetings. (response)	*Marahaba.*

Once you've dealt with all the appropriate greetings, you can move onto other topics:

What's your name?	*Jina lako nani?*
My name is ...	*Jina langu ni ...*
Where are you from?	*Unatoka wapi?*
I'm from ...	*Natoka ...*
I like ...	*Ninapenda ...*
I don't like ...	*Sipendi ...*

Farewells are generally short and sweet:

Goodbye.	*Kwa heri.*
Until tomorrow.	*Kesho.*
Later on.	*Baadaye.*
Good night.	*Usiku mwema.*

And a few basics never hurt ...

Yes.	*Ndiyo.*
No.	*Hapana.*
Please.	*Tafadhali.*
Thank you (very much).	*Asante (sana).*
You're welcome.	*Karibu.*
Excuse me.	*Samahani.*
Sorry.	*Pole.*

DIRECTIONS

Where's ...?	*... iko wapi?*
It's straight ahead.	*Iko moja kwa moja.*
Turn ...	*Geuza ...*
at the corner	*kwenye kona*
at the traffic lights	*kwenye taa za barabarani*
left/right	*kushoto/kulia*

EMERGENCIES

Help!	Saidia!
There's been an accident!	Ajali imetokea!
Call the police!	Waite polisi!
Call a doctor!	Mwite daktari!
I'm lost.	Nimejipotea.
Leave me alone!	Niache!

behind	nyuma ya
in front of	mbele ya
near	karibu na
next to	jirani ya
opposite	ng'ambo ya

HEALTH

I'm sick.	Mimi ni mgonjwa.
It hurts here.	Inauma hapa.
I'm allergic to ...	Nina mzio wa ...
antibiotics	viuavijasumu
aspirin	aspirini
bees	nyuki
nuts	kokwa
peanuts	karanga

antiseptic	dawa ya kusafisha jeraha
condoms	kondom
contraceptives	kingamimba
insect repellent	dawa la kufukuza wadudu
iodine	iodini
painkillers	viondoa maumivu
thermometer	pimajoto
water purification tablets	vidonge vya kusafisha maji

LANGUAGE DIFFICULTIES

Do you speak (English)?
Unasema (Kiingereza)?
Does anyone speak (English)?
Kuna mtu yeyote kusema (Kiingereza)?
What does (asante) mean?
Neno (asante) lina maana gani?
Do you understand?
Unaelewa?
Yes, I understand.
Ndiyo, naelewa.
No, I don't understand.
Hapana, sielewi.
Could you please write ... down?
Tafadhali ... andika?
Can you show me (on the map)?
Unaweza kunionyesha (katika ramani)?

NUMBERS

0	sifuri
1	moja
2	mbili
3	tatu
4	nne
5	tano
6	sita
7	saba
8	nane
9	tisa
10	kumi
11	kumi na moja
12	kumi na mbili
13	kumi na tatu
14	kumi na nne
15	kumi na tano
16	kumi na sita
17	kumi na saba
18	kumi na nane
19	kumi na tisa
20	ishirini
21	ishirini na moja
22	ishirini na mbili
30	thelathini
40	arobaini
50	hamsini
60	sitini
70	sabini
80	themanini
90	tisini
100	mia moja
1000	elfu
100,000	laki

SHOPPING & SERVICES

Where's a ...?	... iko wapi?
department store	Duka lenye vitu vingi
general store	Duka lenye vitu mbalimbali

I'd like to buy ...	Nataka kununua ...
I'm just looking.	Naangalia tu.
How much is it?	Ni bei gani?
Can you write down the price?	Andika bei.
Can I look at it?	Naomba nione.
I don't like it.	Sipendi.
Do you have others?	Kuna nyingine?
That's too expensive.	Ni ghali mno.
Please lower the price.	Punguza bei, tafadhali.
I'll take it.	Nataka.
Enough.	Bas.
A bit more.	Ongeza kidogo.
Less.	Punguza.

Do you accept ...?	Mnakubali ...?
credit cards	kadi ya benki
travellers cheques	hundi ya msafiri

Where's (a/the) ...?	... iko wapi?
bank	Benki
market	Soko
tourist office	Maarifa kwa watalii
... embassy	Ubalozi ...
hospital	Hospitali
post office	Posta
public phone	Simu ya mtaani
public toilet	Choo cha hadhara
telecom centre	Telekom

TIME & DATES

What time is it?	Ni saa ngapi?
It's (ten) o'clock.	Ni saa (nne).
morning	asubuhi
afternoon	mchana
evening	jioni
today	leo
tomorrow	kesho

Monday	Jumatatu
Tuesday	Jumanne
Wednesday	Jumatano
Thursday	Alhamisi
Friday	Ijumaa
Saturday	Jumamosi
Sunday	Jumapili

January	mwezi wa kwanza
February	mwezi wa pili
March	mwezi wa tatu
April	mwezi wa nne
May	mwezi wa tano
June	mwezi wa sita
July	mwezi wa saba
August	mwezi wa nane
September	mwezi wa tisa
October	mwezi wa kumi
November	mwezi wa kumi na moja
December	mwezi wa kumi na mbili

TRANSPORT
Public Transport

What time is the ... leaving?
... inaondoka saa ngapi?
Which ... goes to (Mbeya)?
... ipi huenda (Mbeya)?

bus	Basi
minibus	Daladala
plane	Ndege
train	Treni

When's the ... (bus)?
(Basi) ... itaondoka lini?

first	ya kwanza
last	ya mwisho
next	ijayo

A ... ticket to (Iringa).
Tiketi moja ya ... kwenda (Iringa).

1st-class	daraja la kwanza
2nd-class	daraja la pili
one-way	kwenda tu
return	kwenda na kurudi
cancelled	imefutwa
delayed	imecheleweshwa
platform	stendi
ticket window	dirisha la tiketi
timetable	ratiba

Private Transport

I'd like to hire a/an ... Nataka kukodi ...

bicycle	baisikeli
car	gari
4WD	forbaifor
motorbike	pikipiki

Are you willing to hire out your car/motorbike?
Unaweza kunikodisha gari/pikipiki yako?
(How long) Can I park here?
Naweza kuegesha hapa (kwa muda gani)?
Is this the road to (Embu)?
Hii ni barabara kwenda (Embu)?
Where's a petrol station?
Kituo cha mafuta kiko wapi?
Please fill it up.
Jaza tangi/tanki.
I'd like ... litres.
Nataka lita ...

diesel	dizeli
leaded	risasi
unleaded	isiyo na risasi

I need a mechanic. Nahitaji fundi.
I've had an accident. Nimepata ajali.
I have a flat tyre. Nina pancha.
I've run out of petrol. Mafuta yamekwisha.

The car/motorbike has broken down (at Chalinze).
Gari/Pikipiki ime haribika (Chalinze).
The car/motorbike won't start.
Gari/Pikipiki haiwaki.
Could I pay for a ride in your truck?
Naweza kulipa kwa lifti katika lori lako?
Could I contribute to the petrol cost?
Naweza kuchangia sehemu ya bei ya mafuta?

Thanks for the ride.
Asante kwa lifti.

TRAVEL WITH CHILDREN

I need a/an ...	*Nahitaji ...*
Is there a/an ...?	*Kuna ...?*
baby seat	*kiti cha kitoto*
disposable nappies/ diapers	*nepi*
highchair	*kiti juu cha mtoto*

FRENCH

CONVERSATION & ESSENTIALS

Hello.	*Bonjour.*	bon·zhoor
Hi.	*Salut.* (inf)	sa·loo
Goodbye.	*Au revoir.*	o·rer·vwa
Yes.	*Oui.*	wee
No.	*Non.*	no
Please.	*S'il vous plaît.*	seel voo play
	S'il te plaît. (inf)	seel ter play
Thank you.	*Merci.*	mair·see
You're welcome.	*Je vous en prie.*	zher voo·zon pree
	De rien. (inf)	der ree·en
Excuse me.	*Excusez-moi.*	ek·skew·zay·mwa
Sorry. (forgive me)	*Pardon.*	par·don

What's your name?
Comment vous appelez-vous? ko·mon voo·za·pay·lay voo

My name is ...
Je m'appelle ... zher ma·pel ...

Where are you from?
De quel pays êtes-vous? der kel pay·ee et·voo

I'm from ...
Je viens de ... zher vyen der ...

I like ...
J'aime ... zhem ...

I don't like ...
Je n'aime pas ... zher nem pa ...

Where is ...?
Où est ...? oo e ...

Do you speak English?
Parlez-vous anglais? par·lay·voo zong·lay

I'd like to buy ...
Je voudrais acheter ... zher voo·dray ash·tay ...

How much is it?
C'est combien? say kom·byun

I want to go to ...
Je voudrais aller à ... zher voo·dray a·lay a ...

Which bus goes to ...?
Quel autobus/car part pour ...? kel o·to·boos/ka par poor ...

Is this the road to ...?
C'est la route pour ...? say la root poor ...

What time does ... leave/arrive?
À quelle heure part/arrive ...?
a kel er par/a·reev ...

boat	
le bateau	ler ba·to
bus	
le bus	ler bews
train	
le train	ler trun

0	*zero*	zay·ro
1	*un*	un
2	*deux*	der
3	*trois*	trwa
4	*quatre*	ka·trer
5	*cinq*	sungk
6	*six*	sees
7	*sept*	set
8	*huit*	weet
9	*neuf*	nerf
10	*dix*	dees
11	*onze*	onz
12	*douze*	dooz
13	*treize*	trez
14	*quatorze*	ka·torz
15	*quinze*	kunz
16	*seize*	sez
17	*dix-sept*	dee·set
18	*dix-huit*	dee·zweet
19	*dix-neuf*	deez·nerf
20	*vingt*	vung
21	*vingt et un*	vung tay un

LANGUAGE

phrasebooks

Swahili

with 2500-word two-way dictionary

Also available from Lonely Planet:
Swahili Phrasebook

Glossary

The following is a list of words and acronyms from Burundi (B), the Democratic Republic of the Congo (C), Kenya (K), Rwanda (R), Tanzania (T) and Uganda (U) that appear in this book. For a glossary of food and drink terms, see p42.

AMKO – Association of Mount Kenya Operators (tour guide association) (K)
askari – security guard, watchman
ASP – Afro-Shirazi Party on Zanzibar Archipelago (T)

banda – thatched-roof hut with wooden or earthen walls; simple wooden and stone-built accommodation
bangi – marijuana; also *ganja*
bao – a board game widely played in East Africa
baraza – the stone seats seen along the outside walls of houses in the Stone Towns of Zanzibar and Lamu, used for chatting and relaxing
benga – musical style originating among the Luo in western Kenya, and characterised by its electric guitar licks and bounding bass rhythms (K)
Big Five, the – the five archetypal large African mammals: lion, buffalo, elephant, leopard and rhino
boda-boda – bicycle taxi (U)
boma – a living compound; in colonial times, a government administrative office
bui-bui – black cover-all garment worn by some Islamic women outside the home

CCM – Chama Cha Mapinduzi (Party of the Revolution); Tanzania's governing political party (T)
chai – tea; bribe
chang'a – dangerous homemade alcoholic brew containing methyl alcohol
Cites – Convention on International Trade in Endangered Species
CUF – Civic United Front; Tanzania's main opposition party (T)

dalla-dalla – minibus (T)
dhow – traditional Arabic sailing vessel, common along the coast
duka – small shop or kiosk

fly camp – a camp away from the main tented camps or lodges, for the purpose of enjoying a more authentic bush experience
flycatcher – used mainly in Arusha and Moshi to mean a tout working to get you to go on safari with 'his' particular operator, from whom he knows he can get a commission. We assume the name comes from a comparison with the sticky-sweet paper used to lure flies to land (and then get irretrievably stuck) – similar to the plight of a hapless traveller who succumbs to a flycatcher's promises and then is 'stuck' (ie, with their money and time lost in a fraudulent safari deal (T)
forex – foreign exchange bureau
fundi – repairer of clothing, buildings, cars etc; expert

gacaca – traditional tribunal headed by village elders (R)
ganja – see *bangi*
gof – volcanic crater

hatari – danger
hoteli – small informal restaurant

injera – unleavened bread
Interahamwe – Hutu militia (R)

jamaa – clan, community
jua kali – literally 'hot sun'; usually an outdoor vehicle-repair shop or market (K)

kabaka – king (U)
kanga – printed cotton wraparound, incorporating a Swahili proverb, worn by Tanzanian women
karibu – Swahili for welcome
kikoi – printed cotton wraparound traditionally worn by men in coastal areas
kitenge – similar to a *kanga*, but usually a larger, heavier piece of cloth with no Swahili proverb
kitu kidogo – literally 'a little something'; bribe
KWS – Kenya Wildlife Service (K)

lingala – Congolese dance music; also *soukous*
lugga – dry river bed, mainly in northern Kenya (K)

makuti – palm thatching
malaya – prostitute
manamba – *matatu* tout, often a veritable style guru and all-round dude (K)
manyatta – Maasai or Samburu livestock camp often surrounded by a circle of thorn bushes (K)
marimba – musical instrument played with the thumb
masika – long rains
matatu – minibus (K)
Maulid – birth of the prophet Mohammed and Muslim feast day, celebrated in many areas of East Africa

mihrab – prayer niche in a mosque showing the direction of Mecca

miraa – bundles of leafy twigs and shoots that are chewed as a stimulant and appetite-suppressant

moran – Maasai or Samburu warrior (K)

mpingo – African blackwood

msenge – homosexual

murram – dirt or partly gravelled road

mvuli – short rains

Mwalimu – Swahili for teacher; used to refer to Julius Nyerere (T)

mwami – king (B, R)

mwizi – thief

mzee – elderly person; respected elder

mzungu – white person, foreigner (plural *wazungu*)

NCA – Ngorongoro Conservation Area (T)

Ngai – Kikuyu god

ngoma – dance and drumming

NRA – National Resistance Army (U)

NRM – National Resistance Movement (U)

nyatiti – traditional folk lyre

panga – machete, carried by many people in the east African countryside

papasi – literally 'tick'; used on the Zanzibar Archipelago to refer to street touts (T)

parking boys – unemployed youths who will help park a vehicle and guard it while the owner is absent

RMS – Rwenzori Mountaineering Services (U)

RPF – Rwandan Patriotic Front (R)

shamba – small farm or plot of land

shetani – literally, demon or something supernatural; in art, a style of carving embodying images from the spirit world

shifta – bandit

shilingi – shilling; money

shuka – tie-dyed sarong

soukous – see *lingala*

taarab – Zanzibari music combining African, Arabic and Indian influences (T)

taka-taka – rubbish

Tanapa – Tanzania National Parks Authority (T)

TANU – Tanganyika African National Union (T)

taxi-motor – motorcycle taxi

tilapia – Nile perch

TTB – Tanzania Tourist Board (T)

Ucota – Uganda Community Tourism Association

uhuru – freedom or independence

ujamaa – familyhood, togetherness (T)

Unguja – Swahili name for Zanzibar Island (T)

UWA – Uganda Wildlife Authority (U)

vibuyu – carved gourds

wazungu – see *mzungu*

ZIFF – Zanzibar International Film Festival (T)

ZNP – Zanzibar Nationalist Party

ZPPP – Zanzibar & Pemba People's Party

The Authors

MARY FITZPATRICK
Coordinating Author, Safaris, Tanzania

Mary is from the USA, where she spent her early years in Washington, DC – dreaming, more often than not, of how to get across an ocean or two to more exotic locales. After finishing graduate studies, she set off for several years in Europe. Her fascination with languages and cultures soon led her further south to Africa, where she has spent the past 15 years living and working all around the continent, including extended periods in Tanzania. She has authored and coauthored many guidebooks and articles on the continent, speaks Swahili and is convinced she holds an unofficial record for kilometres travelled in buses along Tanzania's roads. Mary also wrote the Destination East Africa, Getting Started, Itineraries, History, Culture, Environment, East Africa Directory and East Africa Transport chapters.

TIM BEWER
Mountain Gorillas, Uganda

While growing up, Tim didn't travel much except for the obligatory pilgrimage to Disney World and an annual summer week at the lake. He's spent most of his adult life making up for this, and has since visited more than 50 countries. After university he worked briefly as a legislative assistant before quitting capitol life in 1994 to backpack around West Africa. It was during this trip that the idea of becoming a freelance travel writer and photographer was hatched, and he's been at it ever since, returning to Africa several times for work and pleasure. He lives in Khon Kaen, Thailand.

LONELY PLANET AUTHORS

Why is our travel information the best in the world? It's simple: our authors are passionate, dedicated travellers. They don't take freebies in exchange for positive coverage so you can be sure the advice you're given is impartial. They travel widely to all the popular spots, and off the beaten track. They don't research using just the internet or phone. They discover new places not included in any other guidebook. They personally visit thousands of hotels, restaurants, palaces, trails, galleries, temples and more. They speak with dozens of locals every day to make sure you get the kind of insider knowledge only a local could tell you. They take pride in getting all the details right, and in telling it how it is. Think you can do it? Find out how at **lonelyplanet.com**.

MATTHEW D FIRESTONE

Kenya, Rwanda, Burundi, DR Congo

Matt is a trained anthropologist who is particularly interested in the health and nutrition of indigenous populations. His first visit to East Africa in 2001 brought him deep into the Tanzanian bush, where he performed a field study on the traditional diet of the Hadzabe hunter-gatherers. Unfortunately, Matt's promising academic career was postponed due to a severe case of wanderlust, though he has relentlessly traveled to more than 50 different countries in search of a cure. Matt is hoping that this book will help ease the pain of other individuals bitten by the travel bug, though he fears that there is a growing epidemic on the horizon.

CONTRIBUTING AUTHORS

Dr Caroline Evans wrote the Health chapter. Having studied medicine at the University of London, Caroline completed general practice training in Cambridge. She is the medical adviser to Nomad Travel Clinic, a private travel-health clinic in London, and is also a GP specialising in travel medicine. Caroline has acted as expedition doctor for Raleigh International and Coral Cay expeditions.

Dr David Lukas wrote the Wildlife & Habitat chapter. He is an avid student of natural history who has travelled widely to study tropical ecosystems in locations such as Borneo and the Amazon. He has also spent several years leading natural history tours to all corners of Costa Rica, Belize and Guatemala. He also wrote Wildlife chapters for the Lonely Planet guides to Kenya, Tanzania and South Africa.

Behind the Scenes

THIS BOOK

The 1st edition of *East Africa* was written by Geoff Crowther, who then teamed up with Hugh Finlay to write the next three editions. Hugh, Matt Fletcher, Mary Fitzpatrick and Nick Ray wrote the 5th edition. Mary coordinated the 6th and 7th editions with Tom Parkinson and Nick Ray. The 8th edition was also coordinated by Mary Fitzpatrick, with Tim Bewer and Matt Firestone rounding out the team. David Lukas wrote the Wildlife chapter.

This guidebook was commissioned in Lonely Planet's Melbourne office, and produced by the following:

Commissioning Editors Holly Alexander, Stefanie di Trocchio, Emma Gilmour, Lucy Monie
Coordinating Editor Jeanette Wall
Coordinating Cartographer Andrew Smith
Coordinating Layout Designer Frank Deim
Managing Editor Geoff Howard
Managing Cartographer Alison Lyall
Managing Layout Designer Laura Jane
Assisting Editors Kate Evans, Carly Hall, Margedd Heliosz, Kristin Odijk, Dianne Schallmeiner
Assisting Cartographers Andras Bogdanovits, Xavier di Toro, Khanh Luu, Marc Milinkovic, Brendan Streager, Bonnie Wintle

Assisting Layout Designers Nicholas Colicchia, Wibowo Rusli
Cover Designer Marika Mercer
Project Managers Craig Kilburn, Fabrice Rocher
Language Content Coordinator Quentin Frayne
Thanks to Sasha Baskett, Lucy Birchley, Daniel Corbett, Anna Demant, Diana Duggan, Bruce Evans, Laura Crawford, James Hardy, Trent Holden, Lisa Knights, Katie Lynch, John Mazzochi, Malisa Plesa, Amanda Sierp, Julie Sheridan, Lyahna Spencer, Jane Thompson, Glenn van der Knijff, Tashi Wheeler

THANKS
MARY FITZPATRICK

Many thanks to the countless people who helped me while researching this edition, especially Bernard Gikana; Peter Juma; Moses on Rubondo Island; Noah Amio in Mwanza; Chris and Louise on Lake Tanganyika; Tim and Matt, my co-authors; and – most of all – to Rick, Christopher and Dominic in Mtwara, Tabora, Arusha, Dar es Salaam and at so many other points along the way.

TIM BEWER

Too many cooks can spoil the soup, but when writing a guidebook you rely on a huge number of people. It isn't possible to thank everyone, but the following were especially helpful: John

---

THE LONELY PLANET STORY

Fresh from an epic journey across Europe, Asia and Australia in 1972, Tony and Maureen Wheeler sat at their kitchen table stapling together notes. The first Lonely Planet guidebook, *Across Asia on the Cheap*, was born.

Travellers snapped up the guides. Inspired by their success, the Wheelers began publishing books to Southeast Asia, India and beyond. Demand was prodigious, and the Wheelers expanded the business rapidly to keep up. Over the years, Lonely Planet extended its coverage to every country and into the virtual world via lonelyplanet.com and the Thorn Tree message board.

As Lonely Planet became a globally loved brand, Tony and Maureen received several offers for the company. But it wasn't until 2007 that they found a partner whom they trusted to remain true to the company's principles of travelling widely, treading lightly and giving sustainably. In October of that year, BBC Worldwide acquired a 75% share in the company, pledging to uphold Lonely Planet's commitment to independent travel, trustworthy advice and editorial independence.

Today, Lonely Planet has offices in Melbourne, London and Oakland, with over 500 staff members and 300 authors. Tony and Maureen are still actively involved with Lonely Planet. They're travelling more often than ever, and they're devoting their spare time to charitable projects. And the company is still driven by the philosophy of *Across Asia on the Cheap*: 'All you've got to do is decide to go and the hardest part is over. So go!'

Friday, Suni Magyar, Cam McLeay, Simon Musasizi, Dennis Ntege, Ralph Schenk, Richard Smith, Godfrey Pule Thomson, Richard Tooro, Anne-Marie Weeden and Debbie Willis. Apologies to anyone I forgot. Also, to Lucy, Holly, Mary, Matt, Nick and the rest of the LP crew, it was a pleasure; as always. Finally, thanks to all the people of Uganda who took the time to help me out; especially Uganda Wildlife Authority staff who probably never imagined one person could ask so many questions.

MATTHEW D FIRESTONE

First to my wonderful family, thank you all for your continued support, even though I've yet to hold down a 'real' job. Second, I'd like to give a big *asante sana* to my editor-extraordinaires: Lucy, for giving me the chance to contribute to such an important title, and Holly, for catching up on all-things Africa with incredible speed. And finally, to Adam and Stuart of Team Kenya for their wonderful work, and to Mary for coordinating the epic travel tome that is East Africa.

OUR READERS

Many thanks to the travellers who used the last edition and wrote to us with helpful hints, useful advice and interesting anecdotes:

A Sunita Abraham, Rob Armstrong **B** Claire Bankole, Sarah Bates, Zeev Bin, Melanie Blanchette, Nathalia Bolier, Jennifer Bouchet, Sylvia Braun, Helen Brittain, Marlene Buis **C** Margaret Caddell, David Carter, Paul Chamberlain, Alan Chambers, Rory Chapple, Dustin Choate, Erik Christensen, Crispin Cooper, Stefan Cotting, Leigh Cressin **D** Itamar Dar, Lauren David, John Deacon, Alejandro Del Peral, Amy Dibenedetto, Barbara Dibernard, Elise Dickerson, Melissa Dickey, Julie Dierstein, Mark Dubinsky **E** Trevor Espenant, Ben Everard **F** Richard Faulkner, Alexandre Ferrao **G** Uta Glaubitz, Brad Gledhill, Olivier Gros, Chris Guillebeau, Diego Manuel Gutierrez Garcia **H** Marian Hagler, Sylvia Holliman, James Howson, Peter Hyslop **I** Noah Impekoven, Mary Ingram **K** Alexandra Kennedy, Sam Kidder, Martin Kimani, Keisha Knight, Jan-Willem Knippels, Finn Koch, Rasmus Krath, Linda Kreitzer, Mateja Krivec **L** Georgina Langhans, Helen Le, Katherine Lowe, Fiona Lynas **M** Michael Machlis, Magnus Macnab, Anne-Marie Mascaro, Michael Mayall, Hannah Mckerchar, Beth Mckernan, Jon Mellor, Marie Mendes **N** Blair Nelson, Anders Neumuller, Katharina Nickoleit, Jaime Notman **O** Christin Oldebraaten, Irene Örander **P** Hellen Pam, Tom Phillips, Matt Poe, James Potter **R** Annelise Rasmussen, Madeline Ravesloot, Sonja Reifler, Jessica Remedios, Quik Riënne **S** Michael Schenk, Noam Schimmel, Gabi Schneeberger, Roi Shahar, Janet Simpson, Roswitha Smit, J Spain, Peter Sperling, James Spitz, Bea Staley, Ole Steinert, Samantha Sutherland **T** Tom Ternes, Julie Thompson, Mura Tierney, Rebecca

SEND US YOUR FEEDBACK

We love to hear from travellers – your comments keep us on our toes and help make our books better. Our well-travelled team reads every word on what you loved or loathed about this book. Although we cannot reply individually to postal submissions, we always guarantee that your feedback goes straight to the appropriate authors, in time for the next edition. Each person who sends us information is thanked in the next edition – and the most useful submissions are rewarded with a free book.

To send us your updates – and find out about Lonely Planet events, newsletters and travel news – visit our award-winning website: **lonelyplanet.com/contact**.

Note: we may edit, reproduce and incorporate your comments in Lonely Planet products such as guidebooks, websites and digital products, so let us know if you don't want your comments reproduced or your name acknowledged. For a copy of our privacy policy visit lonelyplanet.com/privacy.

Tinsley **V** Rineke Van Dam, Rob Van Den Hoven, Mirella Van Der Heide, Jacobus Van Der Merwe, Bram Loeffen Margriet Van Der Reis, Nettie Van Der Venne, Xavier Varela, Mark Vivian **W** Catharine Walls, Claire Whitley, Mark & Sarah Wilks, Adam Williams, Carole Wilson

ACKNOWLEDGMENTS

Many thanks to the following for the use of their content:

Globe on title page ©Mountain High Maps 1993 Digital Wisdom, Inc.

Internal photographs p4 (bottom left) by Stefano Olivi. All other photographs by Lonely Planet Images, and by Adrian Bailey p110 (#1, #4), p116 (#1), p119 (#2); Elliot Daniel p113 (#3); Alex Dissanayake p115 (#2), p118 (#4); Jason Edwards p105, p117 (#3); David Else p120 (#1); Dave Hamman p106 (#1), p107 (#3); Doug McKinlay p109 (#2); Mitch Reardon p106 (#4), p108 (#1), p111 (#3), p112 (#1, #4), p114 (#4), p115 (#3), p120 (#2); Ariadne Van Zandbergen p107 (#2), p108 (#4), p109 (#3), p111 (#2), p113 (#2), p114 (#1), p116 (#4), p117 (#2), p118 (#1), p119 (#3).

All images are the copyright of the photographers unless otherwise indicated. Many of the images in this guide are available for licensing from Lonely Planet Images: www.lonelyplanetimages.com.

Index

000 Map pages
000 Photograph pages